The Guide to the Major Trusts

2010/11 edition

Volume 2
A further 1,100 trusts

Alan French
Jessica Carver
John Smyth

DIRECTORY OF SOCIAL CHANGE

Published by
Directory of Social Change
24 Stephenson Way
London NW1 2DP
Tel: 08450 77 77 07; Fax: 020 7391 4804
Email: publications@dsc.org.uk
www.dsc.org.uk
from whom further copies and a full publications catalogue are available.

Directory of Social Change Northern Office
Federation House, Hope Street, Liverpool L1 9BW
Policy & Research 0151 708 0136; email: research@dsc.org.uk

Directory of Social Change is a Registered Charity no. 800517

First published 1993
Second edition 1995
Third edition 1997
Fourth edition 1999
Fifth edition 2001
Sixth edition 2003
Seventh edition 2005
Eighth edition 2007
Ninth edition 2010

ISBN 978 1 906294 42 7

British Library Cataloguing in Publication Data
A catalogue record for this book is available from the British
Library

Cover design by Kate Bass
Text designed by Lenn Darroux and Linda Parker
Typeset by Marlinzo Services, Frome
Printed and bound by Page Bros, Norwich

Contents

Introduction

Welcome to *The Guide to the Major Trusts Volume 2*. This edition contains over 1,100 UK trusts, following on from the 400 largest detailed in Volume 1. The trusts in this book give over £200 million a year collectively (trusts in Volume 1 gave a total of £2.53 billion).

The guide's main aim is to help people raise money from trusts. We aim to provide as much information as we can to enable fundraisers to locate relevant trusts and produce suitable applications. There is also a secondary aim: to be a survey of the work of grant-making trusts and to show where trust money is going and for what purposes.

Research for this guide took place during a period of global economic downturn. However, the majority of trust accounts available to us were for the period 2007/08. As such, these accounts would not be expected to show the full impact that this downturn may have been having on trusts' grant-making capacities. Although this generally proved to be the case, some early signs of its effect were evident.

For the 1,157 trusts included in the guide, grants for 2007/08 totalled £212 million with income standing at £419 million. Assets amounted to around £3.7 billion in total.

Comparing these figures to the previous year shows that although the value of trusts' assets remained fairly consistent, income fell by £31 million to £419 million. Despite this, total grants rose slightly from £209 million. In order to maintain this level of giving and honour previous grant commitments, it appears that trusts have delved into their reserves in some instances and/or increased fundraising efforts.

Nevertheless, although grantmaking for 2007/08 has remained relatively buoyant, we believe that a clearer and fuller picture regarding the effects of the economic downturn will only become apparent once we start to look at trust accounts for 2008/09.

A note on the impact of the global recession

Soon after the last edition of this guide was published at the end of 2007, we saw the beginnings of a global recession on a scale not seen for many generations. This undeniably had an impact on the voluntary sector during 2008 and 2009, with charities experiencing cuts in public spending, decreases in voluntary income and a drop in the value of their investments. At the beginning of 2010, the UK and the rest of the world were only just starting to show signs of moving out of the worst recession in living memory[1]. It could be argued that because of the current difficult economic climate the information contained in this publication has never been more useful.

The reduction in financial returns on investments mentioned in the previous paragraph has impacted greatly on many of the funders who feature in this guide and their ability to sustain their grant-making activities. During the course of researching this guide, evidence of the knock-on effect of the financial crisis has been noted in the annual reports of a number of funders. For example, the Hinrichsen Foundation told us that, in direct response to the recession, they made no donations during the autumn of 2008.

Many trusts that have tried to maintain levels of grantmaking have risked further eroding the value of their assets and endowments.

Many people we have spoken to in the sector have noted increased competition for funding. Ironically, alongside a fall in income, many voluntary groups have seen an increased demand for their services, particularly those working in the field of social welfare. The response has not been entirely predictable or negative, however. Some funders have noted that because fewer people are making applications there is more money available. Others have noticed a trend where charities are requesting smaller amounts of money and submitting more realistic and thoughtful applications.

What trusts do we include?

Our criteria are as follows: trusts must have the potential to give at least £30,000 a year in grants, and these grants should go to organisations in the UK. Many give far more than this: over 600 trusts have the potential to give £100,000 or more. There are actually over 150 trusts that have the potential to give £300,000 or more. These would appear to be large enough to be included in Volume 1. However, in a number of cases the income of the trust was lower than the total given in grants for the latest financial year – perhaps due to a substantial one-off donation from its capital – and therefore it is expected that the level of giving by such trusts will decrease in future. Other reasons for a trust to be included in Volume 2 are when the majority of the trust's grants are distributed overseas or in a particular part of the UK, or that its areas of work were too specific for Volume 1. For a full list of the trusts in size order see page xiii. Some trusts were included regardless of the fact that they gave less than £30,000 as they have the potential to increase this grant total in the future.

What is excluded?

Trusts which appear large enough to warrant inclusion in this guide may be excluded for the following reasons.

- Some or all of their money is given to individuals, meaning that £30,000 a year is not available for organisations. The following two guides provide information on trusts which support individuals: *A Guide to Grants for Individuals in Need* and *The Educational Grants Directory*, both published by DSC. Alternatively our subscription website, www.grantforindividuals.org.uk, contains the same information as these publications.
- They give exclusively to local causes in a restricted geographical area of England. There are many very large trusts which restrict their grantmaking in this way. So if a trust restricts its giving to a single county or city (or smaller geographical area) it is generally excluded. In this way we hope that Volume 2 remains a national directory and therefore relevant to more people.
- They only, or predominantly, support international charities. Such trusts were previously included in this guide, but information on these trusts can now be found in *The Directory of Grant Making Trusts*.
- They are company trusts, established as a vehicle for a company's charitable giving. These are detailed in *The Guide to UK Company Giving* or at www.companygiving.org.uk.

---

[1] Revised figures released at the end of February 2010 show that the UK technically came out of recession with a 0.3% growth in GDP (http://news.bbc.co.uk/1/hi/business/8538293.stm)

Top 25 trusts

Name	Grant Total
The R D Crusaders Foundation	£3,800,000
Dr Mortimer and Theresa Sackler Foundation	£1,700,000
Bourneheights Limited	£1,500,000
Kollel and Co. Limited	£1,500,000
The Francis Winham Foundation	£1,500,000
John Laing Charitable Trust	£1,400,000
Lewis Family Charitable Trust	£1,400,000
The Alan Sugar Foundation	£1,300,000
The Edith Winifred Hall Charitable Trust	£1,300,000
J P Moulton Charitable Foundation	£1,200,000
The Exilarch's Foundation	£1,100,000
The Martin Smith Foundation	£1,100,000
The Muriel Edith Rickman Trust	£1,100,000
TJH Foundation	£1,100,000
Truedene Co. Ltd	£1,100,000
Sir Siegmund Warburg's Voluntary Settlement	£1,000,000
The Geoff and Fiona Squire Foundation	£1,000,000
Vyoel Moshe Charitable Trust	£1,000,000
Help the Hospices	£996,000
The Park Charitable Trust	£991,000
Davidson Charitable Trust	£927,000
Royal Artillery Charitable Fund	£904,000
Keren Mitzvah Trust	£881,000
Coutts Charitable Trust	£870,000
Melow Charitable Trust	£870,000

DSC's subscription-based website www.trustfunding.org.uk contains details of over 4,400 trusts including those that give locally, UK-wide and internationally.

The layout of this book

The layout of the entries is similar to that established in the previous editions of Volumes 1 and 2, illustrated on page viii. Please also see page vii for other information on how to use this guide. We have used the word Chair in preference to Chairman unless specifically requested to do so by the trust. We have also rounded off the financial figures to allow for easier reading of the guide, which explains why in some places the totals do not add up exactly.

Indexes

The trusts are listed alphabetically in this guide. To help you locate the most relevant trusts there are two indexes. They are a useful starting point.

- Subject index – page 377. This can be useful for identifying trusts that have a particular preference for your cause. There are many trusts which have general charitable purposes (either exclusively or as well as other specific criteria). However, there we do not have general category in the indexes. This is because it would include so many trusts as to be useless. The subject index therefore should not be used as the definitive guide to finding the right trusts to apply to.
- Geographical index – page 399. Although trusts limiting their support to one particular area have been excluded, there are many which have some preference for one or more areas. These are listed in this index. Again, in a similar way to the subject index, care is needed. Many trusts state their beneficial area as the UK, so are not included in this index.

It is important to note that the trusts which appear under a particular index may have other criteria which exclude you. Always read the entry carefully so that you can be sure you fit in with all the trust's criteria. Do not just use the index as a mailing list.

How the guide was compiled

The following practical guidelines were followed to produce this guide.

- Concentrate on what the trust does in practice rather than the wider objectives permitted by its formal trust deed.
- Provide extensive information which will be of most use to readers; i.e. publish the trust's criteria and guidelines for applicants in full, where available.
- Include, where possible, details of the organisations which have received grants to give the reader an idea of what the trust supports and the amounts it usually gives.
- Provide the most up-to-date information available at the time of the research.
- Include all trusts which meet our criteria for inclusion.

Availability of information

DSC believes that charities should be publicly accountable and it supports the implementation of the Charity Commission regulations and the 2005 SORP (Statement of Recommended Practice). DSC's Chief Executive, Debra Allcock Tyler, is a SORP Committee Member.

Many trusts recognise the importance of providing good, clear information about the work they do. However, there are some that wish to believe they are private bodies and ignore their statutory obligation to provide information to the public. The information that is held on them at the Charity Commission is sometimes many years out of date.

Failing to supply accounts on request

Charities are required to send their annual report and accounts to the Charity Commission and also to any member of the public who requests them in writing. They are obliged to send the information, although they can make a 'reasonable charge' for this (i.e. the costs of photocopying and postage). Since the launch of the new format of the online Central Register of Charities on 1 October 2008, accounts that are overdue now have a red outline at the top of the page to show this, making it immediately apparent to the reader. When the overdue accounts are received the colour will revert to green. However, a record that a charity's accounts were late for a particular year will remain on the page for five years.

Failure to disclose grants

In SORP 2005, there is a clear emphasis on transparency. The report section is designed to help interested parties understand the work of charities and provide clarity and structure. It includes sections on charities':

- aims and objectives and the strategies and activities undertaken to achieve them
- achievements and performance
- plans for the future.

SORP 2005 also provides guidance on how grants payable during the year should be analysed. This should be sufficient to give an understanding of how its grant-making activity fits in with its particular charitable objectives.

As in SORP 2000, the 2005 update requires trusts to detail at least 50 grants (if these are of £1,000 or more). Of the trusts listed in this guide, over 100 trusts did not provide any details of the grants they made during the year. Where this is the case we have noted this in the 'information available' field.

Failing to provide a narrative report

All trusts should provide a narrative report describing its work. It is here that trusts should give accounts of their work during the year with an explanation and analysis of the grants they have made. Many trust reports are extremely brief and give very little away about their activities. However, following the introduction of the Charities Act 2006, a charity must now be able to demonstrate that, for each of its aims, there is a clear benefit for the public as a whole or a sufficient section of it. Charity trustees have a new duty to report on their charity's public benefit in their trustee annual reports and this will necessitate those trustees who have been less than open in the past to give a more detailed account of the trust's activities.

Good trust reports

On a positive note, there are some trusts which provide excellent reports that go beyond the basic 'The objective of this charity is to make grants to charitable institutions.' When they have been particularly interesting or informative for applicants we have reproduced them in the entries. A number of trusts stood out, including the Yapp Charitable Trust, which presented its activities in a clear and concise way.

What's new?

There are a number of trusts which are new to the series. There have also been trusts added that were in the previous edition of Volume 1 as they no longer give enough money to qualify for the top 400. Some trusts that were in the last edition of this guide have grown and now warrant entries in Volume 1. Others are newly established or newly discovered and include the Fuserna Foundation, the Hutton Foundation, Jusaca Charitable Trust and the Williams Charitable Trust.

Applying to trusts

There is a lot of competition for grants. Many trusts in this guide receive more applications than they can support. In 2007/08 the Casey Trust received 750 applications, of which 41 were successful; while in 2008/09 the Wilfrid and Constance Cave Foundation received 650 applications, of which 40 were successful.

It is important to do the research: read the trust's criteria carefully and target the right trusts. This can lead to a higher success rate and save you writing applications which are destined only for the bin. Applying to inappropriate trusts is bad practice and, as well as annoying trusts, can potentially cause problems for future applicants. Trusts tell us that around half the applications they receive are from organisations that work outside their stated areas of support.

Unsolicited applications

A number of trusts do not want to receive applications (and for this reason usually do not want to appear in the guide). There can be good reasons for this. For example, the trust may do its own research or support the same list of charities each year. There are some trusts, however, which believe that they are 'private' trusts. No registered charity is a private body. We believe that trusts should not resent applications but should be committed to finding those charities most eligible for assistance.

We include these trusts for two reasons. First, some trusts state 'no unsolicited applications' simply as a deterrent in an effort to reduce the number of applications they receive, but will still consider the applications they receive. The second reason relates to the secondary purpose of the guide: to act as a survey of grant-making trusts.

If you choose to write to one of these trusts, do so with caution. Only write to those where your organisation very clearly fits the trusts' criteria. We would advise you to include a stamped, addressed envelope and to state that you do not expect a response unless you are eligible. If they do not reply, do not chase them.

DSC policy and campaigning

Over the years, DSC has campaigned on a number of fronts for better grantmaking. We believe that funders have a responsibility that extends far beyond providing funding. The way funders operate and develop their programmes has a huge impact on the organisations, causes and beneficiaries which their funding supports, as well as on the wider voluntary sector. Transparency is a key principle for us: by providing information about funders in this book and in other DSC publications we have sought to open up their practices to greater scrutiny. Clearer and more accessible information enables fundraisers to focus their efforts effectively, and encourages open review and discussions of good practice. Our Great Giving campaign has grown out of these long-established beliefs.

We have identified some specific campaigning areas that we wish to focus on as part of an overall campaign for better grantmaking.

1) A clear picture of the funding environment
We think that more comprehensive information about where money is going and what is supported is needed to enable better planning and decision-making from funders and policy makers. Many of the funders in this book are leading the way, although some fall short in terms of the level of detail they provide about their activities and effectiveness.

2) Accessible funding for campaigning
Financial support for campaigning is vital to the role organisations play in achieving social change. Greater clarity from grant-making trusts is needed so that campaigning organisations can find the support they need more easily.

3) An end to hidden small print
DSC is asking all funders to provide the terms and conditions which govern the use of the funds at the outset when people apply and to be open to negotiating terms when applicants request it.

4) No ineligible applications
We know that most funders receive applications that do not fall within the funder's guidelines. Clearer guidelines can help, but applicants also need to take more heed of funder guidelines and target their applications appropriately.

DSC has always believed that clear and open application and monitoring processes are essential for both funders and fundraisers to produce more effective applications and better eventual outcomes. The availability of such information has come a long way since the first edition of this guide. However, an important element of the funding process often remains hidden from wider scrutiny.

The detailed terms and conditions which set out what the applicant is required to do to obtain and retain the grant are too often unavailable until the point at which a formal offer of a grant is made. For an applicant, seeing these terms and conditions for the first time only when there is an offer of money on the table is not helpful. Even if negotiating the conditions is an option, the balance of power is still squarely with the funder. If the funder is not willing to negotiate, the applicant is faced with a difficult decision: should any conditions conflict with their organisation's values or the wider needs of their beneficiaries, then they face a dubious choice between accepting conditions which may threaten their independence, and turning down much needed funding.

We surveyed the largest charitable, corporate and government funders to find out more about the availability and accessibility of their terms and conditions, which culminated in the research report, *Critical Conditions*[2]. This research found that many trusts and foundations were demonstrating what we consider to be good practice – 72% of those that responded said they made their terms and conditions publicly available, and there were a number of good examples. However, nearly half the trusts that responded stated that their terms were non-negotiable, a stance we consider to be not in the best interests of funders or applicants. Overall, these

---

[2] Critical Conditions, Directory of Social Change, 2009 (http://www.dsc.org.uk/NewsandInformation/PolicyandCampaigning#cmOW)

findings compared favourably to the central government funders that responded. By comparison these funders appeared to be less transparent and more averse to negotiating. They also tended to have more complicated and lengthy terms.

However, in late 2009 DSC asked similar questions of a much larger sample of trusts and foundations. The results paint a different picture. In this research, only half of respondents said their terms and conditions were publicly available, and a solid majority said they were non-negotiable. The rate of those which said their terms were not publicly available at all was three times greater than for the *Critical Conditions* survey. Some of the variation is accounted for by the fact that the larger sample contained a far greater number of smaller trusts and foundations that do not have any terms and conditions at all (49% of respondents to this survey said they had terms and conditions, compared to 86% in the *Critical Conditions* report). Nevertheless, this further research broadly suggests that there is room for improvement from trusts in the transparency of their funding terms and conditions.

Some may argue that providing more information at the beginning of the application process could make things more time consuming and costly, but we believe the benefits of greater transparency should take precedence. It is crucial that fundraisers have access to all the information that they need to make an informed decision about whether to apply. It is also vital that such information is publicly available so that funders and others can make comparisons and share good practice. Further, in this age of digital communication, there is an ever-increasing expectation that all the relevant information, guidance and application forms will be available online. A link to either a web page or a short document outlining the detailed terms and explaining their place in the application process is easy to provide and need not cost anything. Clear instructions should be provided for the fundraiser about the importance of the terms and conditions, why they are necessary and what they mean, as well as exhortations to read them thoroughly.

Again the onus is not entirely on the funder – fundraisers have a responsibility to inform themselves as fully as possible and to ask for relevant information if it isn't available or is not clearly presented by the funder. Reading and evaluating the criteria, guidance and detailed terms and conditions is part of making a well-targeted application which is more likely to be successful. More crucially, it is about protecting the organisation's independence and building funding relationships that will work well for both parties. The fundraiser, therefore, has an important role to play in scrutinising the conditions of the funding arrangement at the outset, and communicating their views to other decision-makers in the organisation (see www.dsc.org.uk for more advice on terms and conditions for fundraisers).

Finally . . .

The research for this book has been conducted as carefully as possible. Many thanks to those who have made this easier, especially the trusts themselves through their websites, their trust officers for providing additional information and the trustees and others who have helped us. Thanks also to the Charity Commission for making the annual reports and accounts available online.

We are aware that some of this information may be incomplete or will become out of date. We are equally sure we will have missed some relevant charities. We apologise for these imperfections. If you come across any omissions or mistakes, or if you have any suggestions for future editions of this book, do let us know. We can be contacted at the Liverpool Office Research Department at the Directory of Social Change either by phone on 0151 708 0136 or by email: research@dsc.org.uk

How to use this guide

The contents
The entries are in alphabetical order and describe the work of over 1,100 trusts. The entries are preceded by a listing of the trusts in order of size and are followed by a subject index and geographical index. There is also an alphabetical index at the back of this guide.

Finding the trusts you need
There are three basic ways of using this guide.

(a) You can simply read the entries through from A to Z (a rather time-consuming activity).

(b) You can look through the trust ranking table which starts on page xiii and use the boxes provided to tick the trusts which might be relevant to you (starting with the biggest).

(c) You can use the subject or geographical indexes starting on pages 377 and 399 respectively. Each has an introduction that explains how to use them.

If you use approaches (b) or (c), once you have chosen enough trusts to be getting on with, read each trust entry carefully before deciding to apply. Very often a trust's interest in your field will be limited and precise, and may demand an application specifically tailored to its requirements or often no application at all as they may not be currently accepting applications.

Sending off applications which show that the available information has not been read antagonises trusts and brings charities into disrepute within the grant-giving sector. Carefully targeted applications, on the other hand, are usually welcomed by most trusts.

A typical trust entry

The Fictitious Trust

Welfare
£180,000 (2009)
Beneficial area UK.

The Old Barn, Main Street, New Town ZC48 2QQ

Correspondent Ms A Grant, Appeals Secretary

Trustees *Lord Great; Lady Good; A T Home; T Rust; D Prest.*

CC Number 123456

Information available Accounts were on file at the Charity Commission.

The trust supports welfare charities in general, with an emphasis on disability, homelessness and ethnic minorities. The trustees will support both captial and revenue projects. 'Specific projects are preferred to general running costs.'

In 2009 the trust had assets of £2.3 million and an income of £187,000. Over 200 grants were given totalling £180,000. Grants ranged from £100 to £20,000, with about half given in New Town. The largest grants were to: New Town Disability Group (£20,000); Homelessness UK (£18,000); and Asian Family Support (£15,000). There were 10 grants of £2,000 to £10,000 including those to the Charity Workers Benevolent Society, Children without Families, New Town CAB and Refugee Support Group.

Smaller grants were given to a variety of local charities, local branches of national charities and a few UK welfare charities.

Exclusions No grants to non-registered charities, individuals or religious organisations.

Applications In writing to the correspondent. Trustees meet in March and September each year. Applications should be received by the end of January and the end of July respectively.

Applications should include a brief description of the project and audited accounts. Unsuccessful applicants will not be informed unless a stamped, addressed envelope is provided.

Name of the charity

Summary of main activities – what the trust will do in practice rather than what its trust deed allows it to do.

Grant total – total grants given (not income) for the most recent year available.

Geographical area of grantgiving – including where the trust can legally give and where it gives in practice.

Contact address – telephone and fax numbers; and email and website addresses, if available.

Contact person

Trustees

Sources of information – what we used and what is available to the applicant.

Background/summary of activities – a quick indicator of the trust's policies to show whether it is worth reading the rest of the entry.

Financial information – noting the assets, ordinary income and grant total, and comment on unusual figures.

Typical grants range – indicates what a successful applicant can expect to receive.

Large grants – indicates where the main money is going, often the clearest indication of trust priorities.

Other examples of grants – a list of typical beneficiaries and, where possible, the purpose of the grant. We also indicate whether the trust gives one-off or recurrent grants.

Exclusions – a list of any area, subjects or types of grant the trust will not consider.

Applications – this includes how to apply and when to submit an application.

Dates for your diary

X = the usual month of trustees' or grant allocation meetings, or the last month for the receipt of applications.

Please note that these dates are provisional, and that the fact of an application being received does not necessarily mean that it will be considered at the next meeting.

	Jan	Feb	Mar	Apr	May	Jun	Jul	Aug	Sep	Oct	Nov	Dec
The A B Charitable Trust	X			X			X			X		
The Adamson Trust		X			X			X			X	
The Alabaster Trust			X			X			X			X
All Saints Educational Trust				X								
The Anchor Foundation	X						X					
The Appletree Trust				X								
The Ove Arup Foundation			X			X			X			X
The Astor Foundation				X						X		
The Baker Charitable Trust	X			X			X			X		
Lord Barnby's Foundation		X				X					X	
The Misses Barrie Charitable Trust				X				X				X
The Bestway Foundation			X									
The Bisgood Charitable Trust		X							X			
Sir Alec Black's Charity			X						X			
The Charlotte Bonham-Carter Charitable Trust					X						X	
The Oliver Borthwick Memorial Trust				X								
The Bothwell Charitable Trust		X										
Burdens Charitable Foundation			X						X			X
Henry T and Lucy B Cadbury Charitable Trust		X										
The Joseph and Annie Cattle Trust	X	X	X	X	X	X	X	X	X	X	X	X
The Wilfrid and Constance Cave Foundation					X					X		
The Chapman Charitable Trust			X						X			
The Malcolm Chick Charity										X		
The Cotton Trust	X						X					
The Ronald Cruickshanks' Foundation									X			
The Daily Prayer Union Charitable Trust Ltd			X			X				X		
The Dickon Trust					X					X		
The DLM Charitable Trust		X					X				X	
The Dumbreck Charity				X	X							
The Edinburgh Trust, No. 2 Account				X								
Educational Foundation of Alderman John Norman		X			X					X		
The George Elias Charitable Trust	X	X	X	X	X	X	X	X	X	X	X	X
The Elmgrant Trust			X			X				X		
The Eventhall Family Charitable Trust	X	X	X	X	X	X	X	X	X	X	X	X
Elizabeth Ferguson Charitable Trust Fund	X						X					
Marc Fitch Fund				X					X			
The Fitton Trust				X				X				X
The Forbes Charitable Foundation						X					X	
Ford Britain Trust						X					X	
The Oliver Ford Charitable Trust					X					X		
The Gordon Fraser Charitable Trust	X			X			X			X		
The Frognal Trust		X			X			X			X	

	Jan	Feb	Mar	Apr	May	Jun	Jul	Aug	Sep	Oct	Nov	Dec
The Gale Family Charitable Trust							X					
The Golsoncott Foundation		X			X			X			X	
The Good Neighbours Trust			X			X			X			X
Grand Charitable Trust of the Order of Women Freemasons						X						
The Grand Order of Water Rats' Charities Fund	X	X	X	X	X	X	X	X	X	X	X	X
The GRP Charitable Trust			X									
The Harbour Foundation		X										
Hasluck Charitable Trust	X						X					
The Hawthorne Charitable Trust											X	
The Haymills Charitable Trust			X							X		
The Holly Hill Charitable Trust						X					X	
The Charles Littlewood Hill Trust			X				X				X	
Hockerill Educational Foundation						X						
The Dorothy Holmes Charitable Trust	X		X									
Mary Homfray Charitable Trust		X	X									
The Hope Trust						X						X
The Cuthbert Horn Trust												X
The Humanitarian Trust			X							X		
The Irish Youth Foundation (UK) Ltd (incorporating The Lawlor Foundation)		X										
The Ironmongers' Foundation	X		X					X		X		
The Ruth and Lionel Jacobson Trust (Second Fund) No. 2	X	X	X	X	X	X	X	X	X	X	X	X
The John Jarrold Trust	X					X						
Rees Jeffreys Road Fund	X			X			X		X		X	
The Jenour Foundation			X									
The Jephcott Charitable Trust				X						X		
The Johnson Foundation	X	X	X	X	X	X	X	X	X	X	X	X
The Nancy Kenyon Charitable Trust												X
The Peter Kershaw Trust					X					X		
The Kessler Foundation						X						X
The David Laing Foundation			X			X				X		X
The Lambert Charitable Trust								X				
Lancashire Environmental Fund	X			X			X			X		
LandAid Charitable Trust			X									
The Langdale Trust							X					
The R J Larg Family Charitable Trust		X						X				
Mrs F B Laurence Charitable Trust				X							X	
The Kathleen Laurence Trust	X					X						
The Law Society Charity				X			X		X			X
The Edgar E Lawley Foundation							X					
The Leche Trust		X				X				X		
The Leverhulme Trade Charities Trust		X										
The Linmardon Trust		X			X			X			X	
The Loseley and Guildway Charitable Trust		X			X				X			
The Charlotte Marshall Charitable Trust			X									
John Martin's Charity				X			X			X		X
The Millfield House Foundation			X						X			
The Peter Minet Trust		X				X				X		
Monmouthshire County Council Welsh Church Act Fund			X			X			X			X
The Morgan Charitable Foundation				X						X		
S C and M E Morland's Charitable Trust			X									X
The Morris Charitable Trust	X	X	X	X	X	X	X	X	X	X	X	X
Mountbatten Festival of Music	X						X					

	Jan	Feb	Mar	Apr	May	Jun	Jul	Aug	Sep	Oct	Nov	Dec
The Edwina Mountbatten Trust									X	X		
The F H Muirhead Charitable Trust			X							X		
Murphy-Neumann Charity Company Limited											X	X
The Music Sales Charitable Trust			X			X			X			X
The National Manuscripts Conservation Trust						X						X
The Norton Foundation							X					
The Oakdale Trust				X						X		
The Ogle Christian Trust					X						X	
The Oikonomia Trust		X										
The Ouseley Trust			X							X		
The Frank Parkinson Agricultural Trust				X								
Arthur James Paterson Charitable Trust			X						X			
The Constance Paterson Charitable Trust						X						X
Miss M E Swinton Paterson's Charitable Trust							X					
The David Pickford Charitable Foundation	X	X	X	X	X	X	X	X	X	X	X	X
The Bernard Piggott Trust					X	X					X	
The J S F Pollitzer Charitable Settlement				X							X	
The Porter Foundation			X				X				X	
The J E Posnansky Charitable Trust					X							
The Puebla Charitable Trust							X					
The R V W Trust				X				X				X
The Fanny Rapaport Charitable Settlement			X						X			
The John Rayner Charitable Trust	X											
The Albert Reckitt Charitable Trust			X									
The Clive Richards Charity	X	X	X	X	X	X	X	X	X	X	X	X
The Jean Sainsbury Animal Welfare Trust	X				X				X			
The Saintbury Trust				X						X		
The Sammermar Trust	X	X	X	X	X	X	X	X	X	X	X	X
SFIA Educational Trust Limited			X	X								
The Linley Shaw Foundation		X	X									
The Shipwrights' Company Charitable Fund		X				X				X		
The John Slater Foundation					X					X		
The SMB Charitable Trust			X			X			X			X
The N Smith Charitable Settlement					X							X
The South Square Trust			X			X				X		
The W F Southall Trust		X	X							X		
The Worshipful Company of Spectacle Makers' Charity				X								
The Jessie Spencer Trust			X			X			X			X
St Andrew Animal Fund				X								
St Gabriel's Trust	X		X						X			
The Late St Patrick White Charitable Trust		X			X			X			X	
St Teilo's Trust		X			X				X			
Miss Doreen Stanford Trust			X									
The Stoller Charitable Trust			X			X			X			X
The W O Street Charitable Foundation	X			X			X			X		
Swan Mountain Trust		X				X				X		
The Tabeel Trust					X						X	
C B and H H Taylor 1984 Trust					X						X	
The Thomas Wall Trust									X			
The R D Turner Charitable Trust	X			X			X				X	
The Ulverscroft Foundation		X				X			X			X
The Van Neste Foundation	X					X				X		
Mrs Maud Van Norden's Charitable Foundation					X							
The Scurrah Wainwright Charity		X				X			X			

	Jan	Feb	Mar	Apr	May	Jun	Jul	Aug	Sep	Oct	Nov	Dec
The F J Wallis Charitable Settlement			X						X			
The Weavers' Company Benevolent Fund		X				X				X		
The James Weir Foundation					X					X		
The Barbara Welby Trust			X							X		
The Wessex Youth Trust					X						X	
Dame Violet Wills Charitable Trust			X						X			
Women's World Day of Prayer											X	
Zephyr Charitable Trust							X					

The major trusts ranked by grant total

Trust	Grants	Main grant areas
☐ Royal Masonic Trust for Girls and Boys	£5.7 million	Children, young people
☐ The R D Crusaders Foundation	£3.8 million	General
☐ Dr Mortimer and Theresa Sackler Foundation	£1.7 million	Arts and culture, science, medical
☐ Bourneheights Limited	£1.5 million	Orthodox Jewish
☐ Kollel and Co. Limited	£1.5 million	Jewish, relief of poverty
☐ The Francis Winham Foundation	£1.5 million	Welfare of older people
☐ John Laing Charitable Trust	£1.4 million	Education, community regeneration, young people, homelessness, environment
☐ Lewis Family Charitable Trust	£1.4 million	Research into cancer, head injuries and birth defects; health; education; and Jewish charities
☐ The Alan Sugar Foundation	£1.3 million	Jewish charities, general
☐ The Edith Winifred Hall Charitable Trust	£1.3 million	General
☐ J P Moulton Charitable Foundation	£1.2 million	Medical, education, training and counselling
☐ The Exilarch's Foundation	£1.1 million	Jewish
☐ The Martin Smith Foundation	£1.1 million	Art, music, sports and education
☐ The Muriel Edith Rickman Trust	£1.1 million	Medical research, education
☐ TJH Foundation	£1.1 million	Social welfare, medical, racing welfare
☐ Truedene Co. Ltd	£1.1 million	Jewish
☐ Sir Siegmund Warburg's Voluntary Settlement	£1 million	Arts
☐ The Geoff and Fiona Squire Foundation	£1 million	General
☐ Vyoel Moshe Charitable Trust	£1 million	Education, relief of poverty
☐ Help the Hospices	£996,000	Hospices
☐ The Park Charitable Trust	£991,000	Jewish, patient care – cancer and heart conditions, hospitals
☐ Davidson Charitable Trust	£927,000	Jewish, general
☐ Royal Artillery Charitable Fund	£904,000	Service charities
☐ Keren Mitzvah Trust	£881,000	General, Jewish
☐ Coutts Charitable Trust	£870,000	General, social need
☐ Melow Charitable Trust	£870,000	Jewish
☐ Altamont Ltd	£850,000	Jewish causes
☐ Friends of Wiznitz Limited	£827,000	Jewish education
☐ Solev Co. Ltd	£827,000	Jewish charities
☐ The Kennel Club Charitable Trust	£824,000	Dogs
☐ The Pestalozzi Overseas Children's Trust	£804,000	Secondary education of deprived children
☐ Alvor Charitable Trust	£773,000	Christian, humanitarian, 'social change'
☐ The Ingram Trust	£766,000	General
☐ Bay Charitable Trust	£763,000	Jewish
☐ The Priory Foundation	£741,000	Health and social welfare, especially children
☐ The Catholic Trust for England and Wales	£737,000	Catholic
☐ E and E Kernkraut Charities Limited	£736,000	General, education, Jewish
☐ The Barcapel Foundation	£736,000	Health, heritage, young people
☐ The Clive Richards Charity	£730,000	Churches, schools, arts, disability and poverty
☐ Dezna Robins Jones Charitable Foundation	£720,000	Medical, general
☐ The Reta Lila Howard Foundation	£718,000	Children, arts, environment
☐ Foundation for Management Education	£706,000	Management studies
☐ Extonglen Limited	£673,000	Orthodox Jewish
☐ The Marjorie and Arnold Ziff Charitable Foundation	£664,000	General, education, Jewish, arts, young people, older people, medicine

☐ The Coltstaple Trust	£660,000	Medical, relief in need, education
☐ Premierquote Ltd	£650,000	Jewish, general
☐ George A Moore Foundation	£635,000	General
☐ The Persula Foundation	£622,000	Homeless, disablement, human rights, animal welfare
☐ The Kohn Foundation	£620,000	Scientific and medical projects, the arts – particularly music, education, Jewish charities
☐ Lancashire Environmental Fund	£613,000	Environment and community
☐ The Talbot Village Trust	£593,000	General
☐ The Costa Family Charitable Trust (formerly the Morgan Williams Charitable Trust)	£576,000	Christian
☐ Matliwala Family Charitable Trust	£567,000	Islam, general
☐ The Rayne Trust	£554,000	Jewish organisations; older and young people and people disadvantaged by poverty or socially isolation
☐ Mariapolis Limited	£544,000	Christian ecumenism
☐ The Nigel Moores Family Charitable Trust	£540,000	Arts
☐ Newpier Charity Ltd	£536,000	Jewish, general
☐ The Ruzin Sadagora Trust	£528,000	Jewish
☐ The Petplan Charitable Trust	£517,000	Welfare of dogs, cats, horses and rabbits
☐ John Coldman Charitable Trust	£516,000	General, Christian
☐ The Platinum Trust	£516,000	Disability
☐ The Bowerman Charitable Trust	£509,000	Church, the arts, medical, young people
☐ The Ruth Berkowitz Charitable Trust	£508,000	Jewish, medical research, young people, Jewish
☐ The Barbara Ward Children's Foundation	£506,000	Children
☐ The Robert McAlpine Foundation	£505,000	Children with disabilities, older people, medical research, welfare
☐ The Yapp Charitable Trust	£501,000	Social welfare
☐ Grand Charitable Trust of the Order of Women Freemasons	£500,000	General in the UK and overseas
☐ Rokach Family Charitable Trust	£500,000	Jewish, general
☐ The David Lean Foundation	£491,000	Film production
☐ The Ireland Fund of Great Britain	£489,000	Welfare, community, education, peace and reconciliation, the arts
☐ R S Charitable Trust	£485,000	Jewish, welfare
☐ The Bishop Radford Trust	£485,000	Church of England
☐ The Fowler, Smith and Jones Charitable Trust	£483,000	Social welfare
☐ The Fuserna Foundation	£478,000	Relief in need, children, older people, mental and physical illness
☐ The Locker Foundation	£477,000	Jewish
☐ The Swire Charitable Trust	£477,000	General
☐ The Rothermere Foundation	£476,000	Education, general
☐ The Leopold De Rothschild Charitable Trust	£475,000	Arts, Jewish, general
☐ The Esfandi Charitable Foundation	£468,000	Jewish
☐ The Laura Ashley Foundation	£464,000	Art and design, higher education, local projects in mid-rural Wales
☐ J I Charitable Trust	£457,000	General
☐ The Becker Family Charitable Trust	£444,000	General, orthodox Jewish
☐ The Matt 6.3 Charitable Trust	£441,000	Christian
☐ The Richard Wilcox Welfare Charity	£431,000	Health, medical research, welfare of patients, hospitals, animal welfare
☐ The Barbour Trust	£425,000	Health, welfare, conservation/restoration
☐ The John Swire (1989) Charitable Trust	£425,000	General
☐ The Fulmer Charitable Trust	£422,000	Developing world, general
☐ The Naggar Charitable Trust	£421,000	Jewish, the arts, general
☐ The Horne Trust	£416,000	Hospices
☐ The William Allen Young Charitable Trust	£416,000	General, health, social welfare
☐ Newby Trust Limited	£415,000	Welfare
☐ The Mactaggart Third Fund	£414,000	General
☐ Friends of Biala Ltd	£413,000	Jewish

☐ The W O Street Charitable Foundation	£410,000	Education, people with disabilities, young people, health, social welfare
☐ The Queen Anne's Gate Foundation	£398,000	Educational, medical and rehabilitative charities and those that work with underprivileged areas of society
☐ The Tisbury Telegraph Trust	£398,000	Christian, overseas aid, general
☐ The George Cadbury Trust	£393,000	General
☐ The John Beckwith Charitable Trust	£393,000	Young people, education, social welfare, medical research, arts
☐ The Emmandjay Charitable Trust	£389,000	Social welfare, medicine, young people
☐ Kirschel Foundation	£386,000	Jewish, medical

☐ Ambika Paul Foundation	£385,000	Education, young people
☐ The Essex Youth Trust	£385,000	Young people, education of people under 25
☐ The Sir John Ritblat Family Foundation	£384,000	Jewish, general
☐ The Stella and Alexander Margulies Charitable Trust	£384,000	Jewish, the arts, general
☐ Lloyd's Charities Trust	£383,000	General
☐ The Tanner Trust	£382,000	General
☐ Elshore Ltd	£379,000	Jewish
☐ The Schapira Charitable Trust	£379,000	Jewish
☐ The McKenna Charitable Trust	£378,000	Health, disability, education, children, general
☐ The Alborada Trust	£374,000	Veterinary causes, social welfare

☐ Tegham Limited	£372,000	Orthodox Jewish faith, welfare
☐ The Breast Cancer Research Trust	£368,000	Breast cancer research
☐ The Ward Blenkinsop Trust	£367,000	Medicine, social welfare, arts, education, general
☐ The De Laszlo Foundation	£366,000	The arts, general
☐ The Hutton Foundation	£366,000	Christian
☐ United Trusts	£365,000	General
☐ Spar Charitable Fund	£364,000	General, with a preference for children and young people
☐ The John Coates Charitable Trust	£363,000	General, arts, children, environment, medical
☐ The Rowlands Trust	£363,000	General, but mainly medical research, social welfare, music and the arts and the environment
☐ Talteg Ltd	£361,000	Jewish, welfare

☐ Viscount Amory's Charitable Trust	£360,000	Welfare, older people, education, Christian churches
☐ The Johnson Foundation	£359,000	Education, health, relief of poverty
☐ The Ellinson Foundation Ltd	£358,000	Jewish
☐ Wychville Ltd	£358,000	Jewish, education, general
☐ The Archbishop of Canterbury's Charitable Trust	£355,000	Christianity, welfare
☐ The Loftus Charitable Trust	£355,000	Jewish
☐ The Philip Green Memorial Trust	£355,000	Young and older people, people with disabilities, people in need
☐ The Kiawah Charitable Trust	£354,000	Young people whose lives are vulnerable due to health and/or education issues
☐ The Stoller Charitable Trust	£353,000	Medical, children, general
☐ Menuchar Ltd	£352,000	Jewish

☐ The H P Charitable Trust	£352,000	Orthodox Jewish
☐ The Bransford Trust	£351,000	General
☐ J A Clark Charitable Trust	£348,000	Health, education, peace, preservation of the earth, the arts
☐ The Norman Family Charitable Trust	£347,000	General
☐ The Batchworth Trust	£341,000	Medical, humanitarian aid, social welfare, general
☐ The Whitley Animal Protection Trust	£341,000	Protection and conservation of animals and their environments
☐ The Philips and Rubens Charitable Trust	£340,000	General, Jewish
☐ The Goodman Foundation	£336,000	General, social welfare, older people, health and disability
☐ The Norwood and Newton Settlement	£335,000	Christian
☐ Salo Bordon Charitable Trust	£334,000	Jewish

☐ The Tufton Charitable Trust	£334,000	Christian
☐ The Weavers' Company Benevolent Fund	£333,000	Helping disadvantaged young people; offenders and ex-offenders
☐ Marchig Animal Welfare Trust	£332,000	Animal welfare
☐ The P Y N and B Hyams Trust	£331,000	Jewish, general
☐ Meningitis Trust	£330,000	Meningitis in the UK
☐ The Bertie Black Foundation	£329,000	Jewish, general

☐ **The Cecil Rosen Foundation**	£327,000	Welfare, especially older people, infirm, people who are mentally or physically disabled
☐ **The Houghton Dunn Charitable Trust**	£326,000	Medical, health, welfare, environment, wildlife, churches, heritage
☐ **The W F Southall Trust**	£324,000	Quaker, general
☐ **Ian Mactaggart Trust**	£322,000	Education and training, culture, welfare and disability
☐ **The BACTA Charitable Trust**	£322,000	General
☐ **The Mole Charitable Trust**	£320,000	Jewish, general
☐ **The Law Society Charity**	£319,000	Law and justice, worldwide
☐ **The Dyers' Company Charitable Trust**	£318,000	General
☐ **The Jean Sainsbury Animal Welfare Trust**	£318,000	Animal welfare
☐ **Stervon Ltd**	£317,000	Jewish
☐ **The Joseph and Annie Cattle Trust**	£317,000	General
☐ **Trumros Limited**	£316,000	Jewish
☐ **The Woodcock Charitable Trust**	£315,000	General, children
☐ **The Austin and Hope Pilkington Trust**	£313,000	Categories of funding repeated in a three-year rotation
☐ **The English Schools' Football Association**	£313,000	Association football
☐ **The GNC Trust**	£312,000	General
☐ **The Leverhulme Trade Charities Trust**	£312,000	Charities benefiting commercial travellers, grocers or chemists
☐ **The Grahame Charitable Foundation Limited**	£311,000	Jewish
☐ **The Hospital Saturday Fund**	£307,000	Medical, health
☐ **The Hyde Charitable Trust – Youth Plus**	£307,000	Disadvantaged children and young people
☐ **The Jean Shanks Foundation**	£307,000	Medical research and education
☐ **The Toy Trust**	£306,000	Children
☐ **The Stewards' Charitable Trust**	£305,000	Rowing
☐ **The Grace Charitable Trust**	£303,000	Christian, general, education, medical and social welfare
☐ **Panahpur Charitable Trust**	£301,000	Missionaries, general
☐ **The M D and S Charitable Trust**	£301,000	Jewish
☐ **Elizabeth Ferguson Charitable Trust Fund**	£300,000	Children, medical research, health, hospices
☐ **The Sir Peter O'Sullevan Charitable Trust**	£300,000	Animal welfare
☐ **The Alchemy Foundation**	£299,000	Health and welfare, famine relief overseas
☐ **The Carole and Geoffrey Lawson Foundation**	£298,000	Child welfare, poverty, arts, education, research and Jewish organisations
☐ **The Doris Pacey Charitable Foundation**	£298,000	Jewish, medical, educational and social
☐ **The Constance Green Foundation**	£297,000	Social welfare, medicine, health, general
☐ **The Cayo Foundation**	£296,000	Medical research, crime, children and young people, general
☐ **The Millichope Foundation**	£295,000	General
☐ **The Cyril and Betty Stein Charitable Trust**	£294,000	Jewish causes
☐ **The Catherine Cookson Charitable Trust**	£292,000	General
☐ **The Fawcett Charitable Trust**	£292,000	Disability
☐ **The Simon Heller Charitable Settlement**	£292,000	Medical research, science and educational research
☐ **The Harbour Foundation**	£291,000	Jewish, general
☐ **The Vandervell Foundation**	£291,000	General
☐ **Saint Sarkis Charity Trust**	£289,000	Armenian churches and welfare, offenders
☐ **Tomchei Torah Charitable Trust**	£288,000	Jewish
☐ **Old Possum's Practical Trust**	£287,000	General
☐ **The Hon. M J Samuel Charitable Trust**	£287,000	General, Jewish
☐ **The Arnold Burton 1998 Charitable Trust**	£286,000	Jewish, medical research, education, social welfare, heritage
☐ **The Union of Orthodox Hebrew Congregation**	£285,000	Jewish
☐ **The Panacea Society**	£284,000	Christian religion, relief of sickness
☐ **The Truemark Trust**	£284,000	General
☐ **The Ajahma Charitable Trust**	£283,000	Development, poverty, human rights, health, disability, social welfare
☐ **The Lynn Foundation**	£283,000	General
☐ **The William Brake Charitable Trust**	£283,000	General
☐ **SFIA Educational Trust Limited**	£282,000	Education
☐ **The Radcliffe Trust**	£282,000	Music, crafts, conservation
☐ **The R V W Trust**	£281,000	Music education and appreciation

☐ The Chapman Charitable Trust	£280,000	Welfare, general
☐ Fordeve Ltd	£278,000	Jewish, general
☐ The Park House Charitable Trust	£278,000	Education, social welfare, ecclesiastical
☐ The Scotshill Trust	£277,000	General, particularly health, arts, conservation, education, social needs, animal welfare and conservation
☐ Sue Hammerson's Charitable Trust	£276,000	Health care, education, religion
☐ The Thornton Foundation	£275,000	General
☐ The Barnabas Trust	£273,000	Evangelical Christianity
☐ The Everard and Mina Goodman Charitable Foundation	£273,000	Jewish, general
☐ Ranworth Trust	£272,000	General
☐ The Christina Mary Hendrie Trust for Scottish and Canadian Charities	£272,000	Young people, older people, general
☐ The Violet and Milo Cripps Charitable Trust	£272,000	Prison and human rights
☐ The Melanie White Foundation Limited	£271,000	General
☐ The Homelands Charitable Trust	£270,000	The New Church, health, social welfare
☐ St Gabriel's Trust	£269,000	Higher and further religious education
☐ The Andrew Anderson Trust	£269,000	Christian, social welfare
☐ The Peter Kershaw Trust	£269,000	Medical research, education, social welfare
☐ The Saintbury Trust	£269,000	General
☐ The A B Charitable Trust	£268,000	Human rights
☐ Cuby Charitable Trust	£267,000	Jewish
☐ The Balint Family Charitable Trusts	£267,000	Jewish charities, general
☐ The Cobalt Trust	£267,000	General
☐ The Alan Evans Memorial Trust	£265,000	Preservation, conservation
☐ The Michael Bishop Foundation	£265,000	General
☐ The Van Neste Foundation	£265,000	Welfare, Christian, developing world
☐ Jacobs Charitable Trust	£264,000	Jewish charities, the arts
☐ The Rowland Family Foundation	£264,000	Relief in need, education, religion, community
☐ Sino-British Fellowship Trust	£263,000	Education
☐ The Misses Barrie Charitable Trust	£263,000	Medical, general
☐ The Inman Charity	£262,000	General
☐ C B and H H Taylor 1984 Trust	£261,000	Quaker, general
☐ The Anchor Foundation	£260,000	Christian
☐ The Thames Wharf Charity	£260,000	General
☐ The M J C Stone Charitable Trust	£259,000	General
☐ The Suva Foundation Limited	£258,000	General
☐ Lord Barnby's Foundation	£257,000	General
☐ The Avenue Charitable Trust	£257,000	General
☐ The Woodroffe Benton Foundation	£257,000	General
☐ The Second Joseph Aaron Littman Foundation	£256,000	General
☐ The William and Katherine Longman Trust	£255,000	General
☐ The Iliffe Family Charitable Trust	£254,000	Medical, disability, heritage, education
☐ The James Weir Foundation	£254,000	Welfare, education, general
☐ The Persson Charitable Trust	£254,000	Christian mission societies and agencies
☐ Seamen's Hospital Society	£253,000	Seafarers
☐ The Eleanor Rathbone Charitable Trust	£253,000	Merseyside, women, 'unpopular causes'
☐ The Irish Youth Foundation (UK) Ltd (incorporating The Lawlor Foundation)	£253,000	Irish young people
☐ The M A Hawe Settlement	£252,000	General
☐ The Sigmund Sternberg Charitable Foundation	£252,000	Jewish, inter-faith causes, general
☐ The George Elias Charitable Trust	£251,000	Jewish, general
☐ The Bestway Foundation	£250,000	Education, welfare, medical
☐ The Weinstock Fund	£250,000	General
☐ The G W Cadbury Charitable Trust	£248,000	Population control, conservation, general
☐ The Sammermar Trust	£248,000	General
☐ EAGA Partnership Charitable Trust	£246,000	Fuel poverty

☐ The Paul Bassham Charitable Trust	£246,000	General
☐ The Chevras Ezras Nitzrochim Trust	£245,000	Jewish
☐ The Eventhall Family Charitable Trust	£245,000	General
☐ Millennium Stadium Charitable Trust	£244,000	Sport, the arts, community, environment
☐ Mercury Phoenix Trust	£243,500	AIDS, HIV
☐ Oizer Dalim Trust	£243,000	Jewish
☐ The Joanna Herbert-Stepney Charitable Settlement	£243,000	General
☐ The Ulverscroft Foundation	£243,000	Visually impaired people (blind and partially sighted)
☐ The Doris Field Charitable Trust	£242,000	General
☐ The Kobler Trust	£242,000	Arts, Jewish, general
☐ The Lolev Charitable Trust	£241,000	Orthodox Jewish
☐ The Primrose Trust	£235,000	General
☐ Grimmitt Trust	£234,000	General
☐ Peltz Trust	£234,000	Arts and humanities, education and culture, health and welfare, Jewish
☐ Songdale Ltd	£234,000	Jewish, education
☐ GMC Trust	£232,000	Medical research, healthcare, general
☐ Peter Barker-Mill Memorial Charity	£232,000	General
☐ Schroder Charity Trust	£232,000	Medicine and health, older people, social welfare, education, humanities, arts, environment, international causes and general charitable purposes
☐ Country Houses Foundation	£231,000	Preservation of buildings of historic or architectural significance
☐ The Lind Trust	£231,000	Social action, community and Christian service
☐ Children's Liver Disease Foundation	£230,000	Diseases of the liver and biliary system in children
☐ The Altajir Trust	£229,000	Islam, education, science and research
☐ The British Council for Prevention of Blindness	£229,000	Prevention and treatment of blindness
☐ Garvan Limited	£228,000	Jewish
☐ The Cotton Trust	£227,000	Relief of suffering, elimination and control of disease, people who have disabilities and disadvantaged people
☐ The C A Redfern Charitable Foundation	£226,000	General
☐ The Roger Raymond Charitable Trust	£226,000	Older people, education, medical
☐ The Steinberg Family Charitable Trust	£226,000	Jewish, health
☐ The Armourers' and Brasiers' Gauntlet Trust	£225,000	Materials science, general
☐ The Nigel Vinson Charitable Trust	£225,000	Economic/community development and employment; general
☐ The Porter Foundation	£225,000	Jewish charities, environment, arts, general
☐ Mazars Charitable Trust	£224,000	General
☐ The Cooks Charity	£224,000	Catering, welfare
☐ The Lotus Foundation	£224,000	Children and families, women, community, animal protection, addiction recovery, education
☐ The Association of Colleges Charitable Trust	£223,000	Further education colleges
☐ Ner Foundation	£222,000	Orthodox Jewish
☐ The Tony Bramall Charitable Trust	£222,000	Medical research, ill health, social welfare
☐ Mahavir Trust (also known as the K S Mehta Charitable Trust)	£220,000	General, medical, welfare, relief of poverty, overseas aid, religion
☐ Tudor Rose Ltd	£219,000	Jewish
☐ The Hudson Foundation	£218,000	Older people, general
☐ The Ratcliff Foundation	£218,000	General
☐ The Thornton Trust	£218,000	Evangelical Christianity, education, relief of sickness and poverty
☐ The Sidney and Elizabeth Corob Charitable Trust	£216,000	General, Jewish
☐ The Tay Charitable Trust	£216,000	General
☐ Lifeline 4 Kids	£215,000	Equipment for children with disabilities
☐ The Leche Trust	£215,000	Preservation and restoration of Georgian art, music and architecture
☐ The Holden Charitable Trust	£213,000	Jewish
☐ The Holst Foundation	£213,000	Arts
☐ The David and Elaine Potter Foundation	£212,000	Advancement of education and scientific research
☐ The Scouloudi Foundation	£212,000	General
☐ Rees Jeffreys Road Fund	£211,000	Road and transport research and education

☐ The Mutual Trust Group	£211,000	Jewish, education, poverty
☐ The Thomas Sivewright Catto Charitable Settlement	£211,000	General
☐ Hockerill Educational Foundation	£210,000	Education, especially Christian education
☐ The Bisgood Charitable Trust (registered as Miss Jeanne Bisgood's Charitable Trust)	£210,000	Roman Catholic purposes, older people
☐ The Charlotte Heber-Percy Charitable Trust	£210,000	General
☐ The Sir Victor Blank Charitable Settlement	£209,000	Jewish, general

☐ The Doughty Charity Trust	£208,000	Orthodox Jewish, religious education, relief of poverty
☐ Toras Chesed (London) Trust	£208,000	Jewish, education
☐ Friends of Boyan Trust	£207,000	Orthodox Jewish
☐ The Ian Karten Charitable Trust	£207,000	Technology centres for people who are disabled
☐ C and F Charitable Trust	£205,000	Orthodox Jewish charities
☐ The Lillie Johnson Charitable Trust	£204,000	Children, young people who are blind or deaf, medical
☐ The Michael and Morven Heller Charitable Foundation	£204,000	University and medical research projects, the arts
☐ The Holly Hill Charitable Trust	£201,000	Environmental education, conservation and wildlife
☐ The SMB Charitable Trust	£201,000	Christian, general
☐ Beauland Ltd	£200,000	Jewish causes

☐ Gordon Cook Foundation	£200,000	Education and training
☐ Minton Charitable Trust	£200,000	General
☐ Roger Vere Foundation	£200,000	General
☐ The Bulldog Trust Limited	£200,000	General
☐ The D W T Cargill Fund	£200,000	General
☐ The Jephcott Charitable Trust	£200,000	Alleviation of poverty in developing countries, general
☐ The Russell Trust	£200,000	General
☐ The Sylvia Aitken Charitable Trust	£200,000	Medical research and welfare, general
☐ John Martin's Charity	£199,000	Religious activity, relief in need, education
☐ Mrs Pilkington's Charitable Trust	£199,000	Equine animals, aged, infirm and poor

☐ The Family Foundations Trust (also known as Mintz Family Foundation)	£199,000	General, Jewish
☐ The P and D Shepherd Charitable Trust	£199,000	General
☐ The Rowan Charitable Trust	£199,000	Overseas aid, social welfare, general
☐ The Stanley Kalms Foundation	£199,000	Jewish charities, general including arts, education and health
☐ EMI Music Sound Foundation	£197,000	Music education
☐ The Clover Trust	£197,000	Older people, young people, Catholic, health disability
☐ The Duke of Cornwall's Benevolent Fund	£196,000	General
☐ The Forest Hill Charitable Trust	£196,000	Mainly Christian causes and relief work
☐ The Hawthorne Charitable Trust	£196,000	General
☐ The Wilfrid and Constance Cave Foundation	£196,000	Conservation, animal welfare, health, social welfare, general

☐ R H Southern Trust	£195,000	Education, disability, relief of poverty, environment, conservation
☐ The Haymills Charitable Trust	£195,000	Education, medicine, welfare, young people
☐ The Roger Brooke Charitable Trust	£194,000	General
☐ Brian Mercer Charitable Trust	£193,000	Welfare, medical, visual arts in UK and overseas
☐ The Hilda and Samuel Marks Foundation	£193,000	Jewish, general
☐ Garrick Charitable Trust	£192,000	Theatre, music, literature, dance
☐ The Lauffer Family Charitable Foundation	£191,000	Jewish, general
☐ The Rainford Trust	£191,000	Social welfare, general
☐ The Sir Edward Lewis Foundation	£191,000	General
☐ Michael Marks Charitable Trust	£190,000	Culture, environment

☐ Barleycorn Trust	£188,000	Christian
☐ The Bay Tree Charitable Trust	£188,000	Development work, general
☐ The Shanti Charitable Trust	£185,000	General, Christian, international development
☐ The Sir James Roll Charitable Trust	£185,000	General
☐ The Ironmongers' Foundation	£184,000	General
☐ The Marchday Charitable Fund	£184,000	Education, health, social welfare, support groups, overseas aid
☐ The Migraine Trust	£184,000	Study of migraine
☐ Wallace and Gromit's Children's Foundation	£183,000	Improving the quality of life for sick children

☐ **The Peter Minet Trust**	£182,000	General, children and young people, health and disability and community
☐ **The Amalur Foundation Limited**	£181,000	General
☐ **The Henry C Hoare Charitable Trust**	£181,000	General
☐ **The Millward Charitable Trust**	£181,000	Social welfare, performing arts, medical research and animal welfare
☐ **Stevenson Family's Charitable Trust**	£179,000	Culture and arts, conservation and heritage, health, education and general charitable purposes
☐ **The David Laing Foundation**	£179,000	Young people, disability, the arts, general
☐ **Woodlands Green Ltd**	£179,000	Jewish
☐ **Brian and Jill Moss Charitable Trust**	£178,000	Jewish, healthcare
☐ **The Daniel Howard Trust**	£178,000	Jewish causes
☐ **The Laurence Misener Charitable Trust**	£178,000	Jewish, general
☐ **The Peter Stebbings Memorial Charity**	£178,000	General
☐ **The RRAF Charitable Trust**	£178,000	General, medical research, children who are disadvantaged, religious organisations, aid for the developing world and support for older people
☐ **The Williams Charitable Trust**	£178,000	Education, medicine, theatre, general
☐ **Child Growth Foundation**	£177,000	Institutions researching child/adult growth disorders, and people with such diseases
☐ **The Craps Charitable Trust**	£177,000	Jewish, general
☐ **The John Slater Foundation**	£177,000	Medical, animal welfare, general
☐ **The Sir Harry Pilkington Trust**	£177,000	General
☐ **The Burden Trust**	£175,000	Christian, welfare, medical research, education, general
☐ **The Normanby Charitable Trust**	£175,000	Social welfare, disability, general
☐ **The David Webster Charitable Trust**	£174,000	Ecological and broadly environmental projects
☐ **The Edgar E Lawley Foundation**	£174,000	Older people, disability, children, community, hospices and medical
☐ **The Marjorie Coote Animal Charity Trust**	£174,000	Wildlife and animal welfare
☐ **The Caron Keating Foundation**	£173,000	Support of cancer patients
☐ **The Helene Sebba Charitable Trust**	£173,000	Medical, disability and Jewish
☐ **The GRP Charitable Trust**	£172,000	Jewish, general
☐ **The Sheldon Trust**	£171,000	General
☐ **The Delves Charitable Trust**	£170,000	Environment, conservation, medical, general
☐ **Leslie Sell Charitable Trust**	£168,000	Scout and guide groups
☐ **The Charles Littlewood Hill Trust**	£167,000	Health, disability, service, children (including schools)
☐ **Golubovich Foundation**	£166,000	Arts
☐ **The Oakdale Trust**	£166,000	Social work, medical, general
☐ **The Weinberg Foundation**	£166,000	General
☐ **Joshua and Michelle Rowe Charitable Trust**	£165,000	Jewish
☐ **The Gale Family Charitable Trust**	£165,000	General
☐ **The Susanna Peake Charitable Trust**	£165,000	General
☐ **Criffel Charitable Trust**	£164,000	Christianity, welfare, health
☐ **T and J Meyer Family Foundation Limited**	£164,000	Education, healthcare, environment
☐ **The R D Turner Charitable Trust**	£164,000	General
☐ **Sueberry Ltd**	£163,000	Jewish, welfare
☐ **The Charles Shorto Charitable Trust**	£163,000	General
☐ **The Jewish Youth Fund**	£162,000	Jewish youth work
☐ **The Marsh Christian Trust**	£162,000	General
☐ **The N Smith Charitable Settlement**	£162,000	General including social work, medical research, education, environment/animals, arts and overseas aid
☐ **The Bernhard Heuberger Charitable Trust**	£161,000	Jewish
☐ **The Billmeir Charitable Trust**	£161,000	General, health and medical
☐ **The Dinwoodie Settlement**	£161,000	Postgraduate medical education and research
☐ **The Florence Turner Trust**	£161,000	General
☐ **The M and C Trust**	£161,000	Jewish, social welfare
☐ **The Christopher Laing Foundation**	£160,000	Social welfare, environment, culture, health and, children and young people

☐ The David Pearlman Charitable Foundation	£160,000	Jewish, general
☐ Yankov Charitable Trust	£160,000	Jewish
☐ Bill Brown's Charitable Settlement	£159,000	Health, social welfare
☐ Buckingham Trust	£159,000	Christian purposes, relief of poverty and sickness and support for older people
☐ The Bassil Shippam and Alsford Trust	£158,000	Young and older people, health, education, learning disabilities, Christian
☐ Calleva Foundation	£157,000	General
☐ Thackray Medical Research Trust	£157,000	History of medical products and of their supply trade
☐ The Odin Charitable Trust	£157,000	General
☐ All Saints Educational Trust	£156,000	Religious education, home economics
☐ Marc Fitch Fund	£156,000	Humanities
☐ Melodor Ltd	£156,000	Jewish, general
☐ The Millfield House Foundation	£156,000	Social disadvantage, social policy
☐ Golden Charitable Trust	£155,000	Preservation, conservation, medical research
☐ Scott (Eredine) Charitable Trust	£155,000	Service and ex-service charities, medical, welfare
☐ The Inverforth Charitable Trust	£155,000	General
☐ The Vivienne and Samuel Cohen Charitable Trust	£155,000	Jewish, education, health, medical, culture, general
☐ The A H and E Boulton Trust	£154,000	Evangelical Christian
☐ G M Morrison Charitable Trust	£153,000	Medical, education, welfare
☐ Nicholas and Judith Goodison's Charitable Settlement	£153,000	Arts, arts education
☐ The Tinsley Foundation	£153,000	Human rights, poverty and homelessness and health education in underdeveloped countries
☐ Dixie Rose Findlay Charitable Trust	£152,000	Children, seafarers, blindness, multiple sclerosis
☐ MYA Charitable Trust	£151,000	Jewish
☐ Miss A M Pilkington's Charitable Trust	£150,000	General
☐ The Bagri Foundation	£150,000	General
☐ The Hope Trust	£150,000	Temperance, Reformed Protestant churches
☐ The Miller Foundation	£150,000	General
☐ The Simon Whitbread Charitable Trust	£150,000	Education, family welfare, medicine, preservation
☐ The South Square Trust	£150,000	General
☐ Finnart House School Trust	£149,000	Jewish children and young people in need of care and/or education
☐ Prison Service Charity Fund	£149,000	General
☐ The Benham Charitable Settlement	£149,000	General
☐ The Three Oaks Trust	£149,000	Welfare
☐ Bear Mordechai Ltd	£148,000	Jewish
☐ David Solomons Charitable Trust	£148,000	Mental disability
☐ The Dorus Trust	£148,000	Health and welfare, disability, homelessness, addiction, children who are disadvantaged, environment
☐ The Inlight Trust	£148,000	Religion
☐ The Salters' Charities	£148,000	General
☐ Women's World Day of Prayer	£148,000	Promotion of the Christian faith through education and literature and audio-visual material
☐ The Epigoni Trust	£147,000	Health and welfare, disability, homelessness, addiction, children who are disadvantaged, environment
☐ The Ayrton Senna Foundation	£146,000	Children's health and education
☐ The J E Posnansky Charitable Trust	£145,000	Jewish charities, health, social welfare and humanitarian
☐ Wychdale Ltd	£145,000	Jewish
☐ Saint Luke's College Foundation	£144,000	Research or studies in theology
☐ The Leigh Trust	£144,000	Addiction, children and young people, criminal justice, asylum seekers, racial equality and education
☐ The Lawson Beckman Charitable Trust	£143,000	Jewish, welfare, education, arts
☐ Hinchley Charitable Trust	£142,000	Mainly evangelical Christian
☐ Marbeh Torah Trust	£142,000	Jewish education and religion, and the relief of poverty
☐ The Mitchell Charitable Trust	£141,000	Jewish, general

☐	**The Stanley Foundation Ltd**	**£141,000**	Older people, medical care and research, education, social welfare
☐	**Generations Charitable Trust**	**£140,000**	Children, overseas projects
☐	**Monmouthshire County Council Welsh Church Act Fund**	**£140,000**	General
☐	**The Follett Trust**	**£140,000**	Welfare, education, arts
☐	**The Langdale Trust**	**£140,000**	Social welfare, Christian, medical, general
☐	**The Norda Trust**	**£140,000**	Prisoners, asylum seekers, disadvantaged communities
☐	**The Richard and Christine Purchas Charitable Trust**	**£140,000**	Medical research, medical education and patient care
☐	**Farthing Trust**	**£139,000**	Christian, general
☐	**St Monica Trust Community Fund**	**£139,000**	Older people, disability
☐	**Coral Samuel Charitable Trust**	**£138,000**	General, with a preference for educational, cultural and socially supportive charities
☐	**Harold and Daphne Cooper Charitable Trust**	**£138,000**	Medical, health, Jewish
☐	**The Strawberry Charitable Trust**	**£138,000**	Jewish, young people
☐	**Ford Britain Trust**	**£137,000**	Community service, education, environment, disability, schools, special needs education, young people
☐	**The Nani Huyu Charitable Trust**	**£137,000**	Welfare
☐	**Henry Lumley Charitable Trust**	**£136,000**	General, medical, educational, relief of poverty/hardship
☐	**Riverside Charitable Trust Limited**	**£136,000**	Health, welfare, older people, education, general
☐	**Rosalyn and Nicholas Springer Charitable Trust**	**£136,000**	Welfare, Jewish, education, general
☐	**The Beryl Evetts and Robert Luff Animal Welfare Trust**	**£136,000**	Animal welfare
☐	**Dischma Charitable Trust**	**£135,000**	General, with a preference for Education, Arts and Culture, Conservation and Human and Animal Welfare
☐	**The Gordon Fraser Charitable Trust**	**£135,000**	Children, young people, environment, arts
☐	**The Isaac and Freda Frankel Memorial Charitable Trust**	**£134,000**	Jewish, general
☐	**The London Law Trust**	**£134,000**	Health and personal development of children and young people
☐	**The C S Kaufman Charitable Trust**	**£133,000**	Jewish
☐	**Jusaca Charitable Trust**	**£132,000**	Jewish, arts, research, religion, housing
☐	**The A M Fenton Trust**	**£132,000**	General
☐	**The DLA Piper Charitable Trust (previously known as the DLA Charitable Trust)**	**£132,000**	General
☐	**The Harris Family Charitable Trust**	**£132,000**	Health, sickness
☐	**The John Jarrold Trust**	**£132,000**	Social welfare, arts, education, environment/conservation, medical research, churches
☐	**The Cotton Industry War Memorial Trust**	**£131,000**	Textiles
☐	**The Geoffrey Woods Charitable Foundation**	**£131,000**	Young people, education, disability, health
☐	**The Gershon Coren Charitable Foundation**	**£131,000**	Jewish, welfare, general
☐	**Alexandra Rose Charities**	**£130,000**	Supporting charities helping people in need
☐	**P H Holt Foundation**	**£130,000**	General
☐	**Stuart Hine Trust**	**£130,000**	Evangelical Christianity
☐	**The Bernard Kahn Charitable Trust**	**£130,000**	Jewish
☐	**The Gibbs Charitable Trust**	**£130,000**	Methodism, international, arts
☐	**The Martin Laing Foundation**	**£130,000**	General, environment and conservation, disadvantaged young people and the elderly and infirm
☐	**Vision Charity**	**£130,000**	Children who are blind, visually impaired or dyslexic
☐	**The Boshier-Hinton Foundation**	**£129,000**	Children and adults with special educational or other needs
☐	**The Leslie Silver Charitable Trust**	**£129,000**	Jewish, general
☐	**The Manny Cussins Foundation**	**£129,000**	Older people, children, health, Jewish, general
☐	**Princess Anne's Charities**	**£128,000**	Children, medical, welfare, general
☐	**The Helen Roll Charitable Trust**	**£128,000**	General
☐	**Richard Rogers Charitable Settlement**	**£127,000**	General
☐	**The Ashworth Charitable Trust**	**£127,000**	Welfare
☐	**The Lord Faringdon Charitable Trust**	**£127,000**	Medical, general
☐	**Vivdale Ltd**	**£127,000**	Jewish
☐	**The John Oldacre Foundation**	**£126,000**	Research and education in agricultural sciences

☐	The Kyte Charitable Trust	£126,000	Medical, disadvantaged and socially isolated people
☐	The Michael Sacher Charitable Trust	£126,000	General, including arts, culture and heritage; medical and disability; community and welfare; education, science and technology; children and young people; and religion
☐	NJD Charitable Trust	£125,000	Jewish
☐	The Archie Sherman Cardiff Foundation	£125,000	Health, education, training, overseas aid, community and Jewish
☐	The Ogle Christian Trust	£125,000	Evangelical Christianity
☐	The Smith Charitable Trust	£124,000	General
☐	Adenfirst Ltd	£123,000	Jewish

☐	Mountbatten Festival of Music	£123,000	Royal Marines and Royal Navy charities
☐	The Idlewild Trust	£123,000	Performing arts, culture, restoration and conservation, occasional arts education
☐	The Ronald Cruickshanks' Foundation	£123,000	Welfare, education, general
☐	The J E Joseph Charitable Fund	£122,000	Jewish
☐	The Sir Jack Lyons Charitable Trust	£122,000	Jewish, arts, education
☐	The Whitaker Charitable Trust	£122,000	Music, environment, countryside conservation
☐	Annie Tranmer Charitable Trust	£121,000	General, young people
☐	Daisie Rich Trust	£120,000	General
☐	Help the Homeless	£120,000	Homelessness
☐	R G Hills Charitable Trust	£120,000	General

☐	The Children's Research Fund	£120,000	Child health research
☐	The Evan Cornish Foundation	£120,000	General, overseas aid
☐	The Forte Charitable Trust	£120,000	Roman Catholic, Alzheimer's disease, senile dementia
☐	The Starfish Trust	£120,000	Sickness, medical
☐	Diana and Allan Morgenthau Charitable Trust	£119,000	Jewish, general
☐	Disability Aid Fund (The Roger and Jean Jefcoate Trust)	£119,000	Disability
☐	Double 'O' Charity Ltd	£119,000	General
☐	Llysdinam Charitable Trust	£119,000	General
☐	The Dellal Foundation	£119,000	General, Jewish
☐	The Dumbreck Charity	£119,000	General

☐	The Jenour Foundation	£119,000	General
☐	The Jessie Spencer Trust	£119,000	General
☐	Cardy Beaver Foundation	£118,000	General
☐	Harbo Charities Limited	£118,000	General, education, and Jewish causes
☐	Localtrent Ltd	£118,000	Jewish, educational, religion
☐	The Harding Trust	£117,000	Arts, general charitable purposes
☐	The Noel Buxton Trust	£117,000	Child and family welfare, penal matters, Africa
☐	The Walter Guinness Charitable Trust	£117,000	General
☐	The Lady Eileen Joseph Foundation	£116,000	People who are disadvantaged by poverty or socially isolated and 'at-risk' groups; welfare, medical causes and general
☐	The Mayfield Valley Arts Trust	£116,000	Arts, especially chamber music

☐	The Samuel Storey Family Charitable Trust	£116,000	General
☐	The Willie and Mabel Morris Charitable Trust	£116,000	Medical, general
☐	Kupath Gemach Chaim Bechesed Viznitz Trust	£115,000	Jewish
☐	The Anson Charitable Trust	£115,000	General
☐	The Charlotte Marshall Charitable Trust	£115,000	Roman Catholic, general
☐	The P Leigh-Bramwell Trust 'E'	£115,000	Methodist, general
☐	The Charles Skey Charitable Trust	£114,000	General
☐	The H and M Charitable Trust	£114,000	Seafaring
☐	The Kathleen Laurence Trust	£114,000	Heart disease, arthritis, mental disabilities, medical research, older people, children's charities
☐	The Neville and Elaine Blond Charitable Trust	£114,000	Jewish, general

☐	The Oliver Morland Charitable Trust	£114,000	Quakers, general
☐	REMEDI	£113,000	Research into disability
☐	The Henry Angest Foundation	£113,000	General
☐	The Linden Charitable Trust	£113,000	Medical, healthcare, the arts
☐	The Tabeel Trust	£113,000	Evangelical Christian

☐ **Dromintee Trust**	**£112,000**	General
☐ **The Barbers' Company General Charities**	**£112,000**	Medical and nursing education
☐ **The Bedfordshire and Hertfordshire Historic Churches Trust**	**£112,000**	Churches
☐ **The Schmidt-Bodner Charitable Trust**	**£112,000**	Jewish, general
☐ **The Scott Bader Commonwealth Ltd**	**£112,000**	Young/disadvantaged people
☐ **Macdonald-Buchanan Charitable Trust**	**£111,000**	General
☐ **The Argentarius Foundation**	**£111,000**	General
☐ **The C L Loyd Charitable Trust**	**£111,000**	General
☐ **The King/Cullimore Charitable Trust**	**£111,000**	General
☐ **The Lister Charitable Trust**	**£111,000**	Outdoor activities for disadvantaged young people
☐ **Nesswall Ltd**	**£110,000**	Jewish
☐ **The Dugdale Charitable Trust**	**£110,000**	Christian education, the advancement of Methodist education and the Catholic religion
☐ **The George and Esme Pollitzer Charitable Settlement**	**£110,000**	Jewish, general
☐ **The Leslie Smith Foundation**	**£110,000**	General
☐ **Jack Livingstone Charitable Trust**	**£109,000**	Jewish, general
☐ **The Almond Trust**	**£109,000**	Christian
☐ **The Crescent Trust**	**£109,000**	Museums and the arts, ecology, health
☐ **The Michael and Ilse Katz Foundation**	**£109,000**	Jewish, music, medical, general
☐ **The Sir Jeremiah Colman Gift Trust**	**£109,000**	General
☐ **The Spear Charitable Trust**	**£109,000**	General, with some preference for animal welfare, the environment and health
☐ **Gilbert Edgar Trust**	**£108,000**	Welfare
☐ **Mickleham Charitable Trust**	**£108,000**	Relief-in-need
☐ **The Sydney Black Charitable Trust**	**£108,000**	Evangelical Christianity, social welfare, young people
☐ **The Treeside Trust**	**£108,000**	General
☐ **The Worshipful Company of Chartered Accountants General Charitable Trust (also known as CALC)**	**£108,000**	General, education
☐ **Sir Samuel Scott of Yews Trust**	**£107,000**	Medical research
☐ **The Astor Foundation**	**£107,000**	Medical research, general
☐ **The Fitton Trust**	**£107,000**	Social welfare, medical
☐ **Ulting Overseas Trust**	**£107,000**	Theological training
☐ **The CH (1980) Charitable Trust**	**£106,000**	Jewish
☐ **The DLM Charitable Trust**	**£106,000**	General charitable purposes
☐ **The Galanthus Trust**	**£106,000**	Medical, developing countries, environment, conservation
☐ **The Sue Thomson Foundation**	**£106,000**	Christ's Hospital School, education
☐ **The Cheruby Trust**	**£105,000**	Welfare, education, general
☐ **The Sutasoma Trust**	**£105,000**	Education, general
☐ **The Wyseliot Charitable Trust**	**£105,000**	Medical, welfare, arts
☐ **The Edward and Dorothy Cadbury Trust**	**£104,000**	Health, education, arts
☐ **The Hugh and Ruby Sykes Charitable Trust**	**£104,000**	General, medical, education, employment
☐ **The Jack Goldhill Charitable Trust**	**£104,000**	Jewish, general
☐ **The Norman Whiteley Trust**	**£104,000**	Evangelical Christianity, welfare, education
☐ **The David Uri Memorial Trust**	**£103,000**	Jewish, general
☐ **The Norton Foundation**	**£103,000**	Young people under 25 years of age (Currently restricted to the areas of Birmingham, Coventry and the County of Warwick)
☐ **The Stone-Mallabar Charitable Foundation**	**£103,000**	Medical, arts, religion, overseas appeals, welfare and education
☐ **Famos Foundation Trust**	**£102,000**	Jewish
☐ **Hasluck Charitable Trust**	**£102,000**	Health, welfare, disability, young people, overseas aid
☐ **The Duke of Devonshire's Charitable Trust**	**£102,000**	General
☐ **The National Manuscripts Conservation Trust**	**£102,000**	Conservation of manuscripts
☐ **The Ove Arup Foundation**	**£102,000**	Construction education and research
☐ **The Sydney and Phyllis Goldberg Memorial Charitable Trust**	**£102,000**	Medical research, welfare, disability
☐ **The W G Edwards Charitable Foundation**	**£102,000**	Care of older people
☐ **Marr-Munning Trust**	**£101,000**	Overseas aid

☐ The John Apthorp Charitable Trust	£101,000	General
☐ The Leslie Mary Carter Charitable Trust	£101,000	Conservation/environment, welfare
☐ The Michael Harry Sacher Trust	£101,000	General, with a preference for arts, education, animal welfare, Jewish, health and social welfare
☐ The Pyne Charitable Trust	£101,000	Christian, health
☐ AF Trust Company	£100,000	Higher education
☐ Anona Winn Charitable Trust	£100,000	Health, medical, welfare
☐ B E Perl Charitable Trust	£100,000	Jewish, general
☐ Briggs Animal Welfare Trust	£100,000	Animal welfare
☐ Maranatha Christian Trust	£100,000	Christian, relief of poverty and education of young people
☐ Quercus Trust	£100,000	Arts, general
☐ The Amelia Chadwick Trust	£100,000	General
☐ The Andrew Salvesen Charitable Trust	£100,000	General
☐ The Craignish Trust	£100,000	Arts, education, environment, general
☐ The Joseph and Lena Randall Charitable Trust	£100,000	General
☐ The R J Larg Family Charitable Trust	£100,000	Education, health, medical research, arts particularly music
☐ The Samuel and Freda Parkinson Charitable Trust	£100,000	General
☐ The Shipwrights' Company Charitable Fund	£100,000	Maritime or waterborne connected charities
☐ W W Spooner Charitable Trust	£100,000	General
☐ Florence's Charitable Trust	£99,000	Education, welfare, sick and infirm, general
☐ Premishlaner Charitable Trust	£99,000	Jewish
☐ The Daily Prayer Union Charitable Trust Ltd	£99,000	Evangelical Christian
☐ The Felicity Wilde Charitable Trust	£99,000	Children, medical research
☐ The Merchant Taylors' Company Charities Fund	£99,000	Education, training, church, medicine, general
☐ The Moshulu Charitable Trust	£99,000	Humanitarian', evangelical
☐ The Searchlight Electric Charitable Trust	£99,000	General
☐ Andor Charitable Trust	£98,000	Jewish, arts, health, general
☐ The Denise Cohen Charitable Trust	£98,000	Health, welfare, arts, humanities, education, culture, Jewish
☐ The Flow Foundation	£98,000	Welfare, education, environment, medical
☐ The Morris Charitable Trust	£98,000	Relief of need, education, community support and development
☐ The Old Broad Street Charity Trust	£98,000	General
☐ The Paragon Trust	£98,000	General
☐ Rix-Thompson-Rothenburg Foundation	£97,500	Learning disabilities
☐ The Edwina Mountbatten Trust	£97,000	Medical
☐ The G D Charitable Trust	£97,000	Animal welfare, the environment, disability, homelessness
☐ Gerald Micklem Charitable Trust	£96,000	General, health
☐ The Mishcon Family Charitable Trust	£96,000	Jewish, social welfare
☐ The Rock Foundation	£96,000	Christian ministries and charities
☐ Balmain Charitable Trust	£95,000	General in the UK
☐ Onaway Trust	£95,000	General
☐ The Albert Van Den Bergh Charitable Trust	£95,000	Medical research, disability, community, general
☐ The Ampelos Trust	£95,000	General
☐ The Jim Marshall Charitable Trust	£95,000	General
☐ The Kasner Charitable Trust	£95,000	Jewish
☐ The Lanvern Foundation	£95,000	Education and health, especially relating to children
☐ The Louis and Valerie Freedman Charitable Settlement	£95,000	General
☐ The Lyons Charitable Trust	£95,000	Health, animals, children
☐ The Peter Samuel Charitable Trust	£95,000	Health, welfare, conservation, Jewish care
☐ Michael Davies Charitable Settlement	£94,000	General
☐ The Company of Actuaries' Charitable Trust Fund	£94,000	Actuaries, medical research, young and older people, disability
☐ The Ouseley Trust	£94,000	Choral services of the Church of England, Church in Wales and Church of Ireland, choir schools
☐ The Phillips Family Charitable Trust	£94,000	Jewish charities, welfare, general
☐ AM Charitable Trust	£93,000	Jewish, general
☐ The Cecil Pilkington Charitable Trust	£93,000	Conservation, medical research, general
☐ The Elizabeth Frankland Moore and Star Foundation	£93,000	General in the UK

☐ The Stanley Smith UK Horticultural Trust	£93,000	Horticulture
☐ Mrs F B Laurence Charitable Trust	£92,000	Social welfare, medical, disability, environment
☐ T and S Trust Fund	£92,000	Orthodox Jewish
☐ The Ian Askew Charitable Trust	£92,000	General
☐ The Ruth and Stuart Lipton Charitable Trust	£92,000	Jewish, general
☐ The David Brooke Charity	£91,000	Young people, medical
☐ The Earl Fitzwilliam Charitable Trust	£91,000	General
☐ The Francis Coales Charitable Foundation	£91,000	Historical
☐ The Limbourne Trust	£91,000	Environment, welfare, arts
☐ The Baltic Charitable Fund	£90,000	Seafarers, fishermen, ex-service and service people
☐ The Diana Edgson Wright Charitable Trust	£90,000	Animal conservation, social welfare, general
☐ The Evangelical Covenants Trust	£90,000	Christian evangelism
☐ The Harold and Alice Bridges Charity	£90,000	General
☐ The John M Archer Charitable Trust	£90,000	General
☐ The Mason Porter Charitable Trust	£90,000	Christian
☐ The Raymond and Blanche Lawson Charitable Trust	£90,000	General
☐ The Arnold Lee Charitable Trust	£89,000	Jewish, educational, health
☐ The Charlotte Bonham-Carter Charitable Trust	£89,000	General
☐ The Westcroft Trust	£89,000	International understanding, overseas aid, Quaker, Shropshire
☐ The Leach Fourteenth Trust	£88,000	Medical, disability, environment, conservation, general
☐ The Matthews Wrightson Charity Trust	£88,000	General, smaller charities
☐ The Violet M Richards Charity	£88,000	Older people, ill health, medical research and education
☐ Leonard Gordon Charitable Trust	£87,000	Jewish religious, educational and welfare organisations
☐ The Fred and Della Worms Charitable Trust	£87,000	Jewish, social welfare, health, education, arts, young people
☐ The Peter Morrison Charitable Foundation	£87,000	Jewish, general
☐ Lindale Educational Foundation	£86,000	Roman Catholic; education
☐ MYR Charitable Trust	£86,000	Jewish
☐ The Anthony and Elizabeth Mellows Charitable Settlement	£86,000	National heritage, Church of England churches
☐ The Moss Charitable Trust	£86,000	Christian, education, poverty, health
☐ The Richard Kirkman Charitable Trust	£86,000	General
☐ The Scurrah Wainwright Charity	£86,000	Social reform
☐ Armenian General Benevolent Union London Trust	£85,000	Armenian education, culture and welfare
☐ Edith and Ferdinand Porjes Charitable Trust	£85,000	Jewish, general
☐ The Carron Charitable Trust	£85,000	Environment, education, medicine
☐ The Cyril Shack Trust	£85,000	Jewish, general
☐ Wakeham Trust	£85,000	Community development, education, community service by young people
☐ The Bintaub Charitable Trust	£84,000	Jewish
☐ The Dennis Curry Charitable Trust	£84,000	Conservation, general
☐ The Grand Order of Water Rats' Charities Fund	£83,000	Theatrical, medical equipment
☐ The Nadezhda Charitable Trust	£83,000	Christian
☐ The Spurrell Charitable Trust	£83,000	General
☐ The Thriplow Charitable Trust	£83,000	Higher and further education and research
☐ The Anna Rosa Forster Charitable Trust	£82,000	Medical research, animal welfare, famine relief
☐ The Gilbert and Eileen Edgar Foundation	£82,000	General
☐ The Huggard Charitable Trust	£82,000	General
☐ The James Trust	£82,000	Christianity
☐ The Kitty and Daniel Nabarro Charitable Trust	£82,000	Welfare, education, medicine, homeless, general
☐ The Seedfield Trust	£82,000	Christian, relief of poverty
☐ Gableholt Limited	£81,000	Jewish
☐ Houblon-Norman/George Fund	£81,000	Finance
☐ Philip Smith's Charitable Trust	£81,000	Welfare, older people, children
☐ Samuel William Farmer's Trust	£81,000	Education, health, social welfare
☐ St James' Trust Settlement	£81,000	General
☐ The Animal Defence Trust	£81,000	Animal welfare/protection
☐ The Aurelius Charitable Trust	£81,000	Conservation of culture and the humanities

☐ The Rose Flatau Charitable Trust	£81,000	Jewish, general
☐ The Salamander Charitable Trust	£81,000	Christian, general
☐ The Solo Charitable Settlement	£81,000	Jewish, general
☐ The TUUT Charitable Trust	£81,000	General, but with a bias towards trade-union-favoured causes
☐ East Kent Provincial Charities	£80,000	General, education, younger, older people
☐ The B G S Cayzer Charitable Trust	£80,000	General
☐ The Casey Trust	£80,000	Children and young people
☐ The Equity Trust Fund	£80,000	Theatre
☐ The Humanitarian Trust	£80,000	Education, health, social welfare, Jewish
☐ The Linley Shaw Foundation	£79,500	Conservation
☐ British Humane Association	£79,000	Welfare
☐ Redfern Charitable Trust	£79,000	General
☐ The Alfred And Peggy Harvey Charitable Trust	£79,000	Medical welfare
☐ The David and Ruth Behrend Fund	£79,000	General
☐ The John Spedan Lewis Foundation	£79,000	Natural sciences, particularly horticulture, environmental education, ornithology and conservation
☐ The Modiano Charitable Trust	£79,000	Arts, Jewish, general
☐ The Peter Beckwith Charitable Trust	£79,000	Medical, welfare, general
☐ The Sir William Coxen Trust Fund	£79,000	Orthopaedic hospitals or other hospitals or charities doing orthopaedic work
☐ The Vernon N Ely Charitable Trust	£79,000	Christian, welfare, disability, children and young people, overseas
☐ Malbin Trust	£78,000	Jewish, general
☐ The Acacia Charitable Trust	£78,000	Jewish, education, general
☐ The Hamamelis Trust	£78,000	Ecological conservation, medical research
☐ The Harry Bottom Charitable Trust	£78,000	Religion, education, medical
☐ The Heathcoat Trust	£78,000	Welfare, local causes to Tiverton, Devon
☐ The Lord Cozens-Hardy Trust	£78,000	Medical/health, education, general
☐ The River Trust	£78,000	Christian
☐ The Torah Temimah Trust	£78,000	Orthodox Jewish
☐ Jimmy Savile Charitable Trust	£77,000	General
☐ SEM Charitable Trust	£77,000	General, with a preference for educational special needs and Jewish organisations
☐ The Good Neighbours Trust	£77,000	People with mental or physical disabilities
☐ The Katzauer Charitable Settlement	£77,000	Jewish
☐ Ashburnham Thanksgiving Trust	£76,000	Christian
☐ Highcroft Charitable Trust	£76,000	Jewish, poverty
☐ Moshal Charitable Trust	£76,000	Jewish
☐ The Morgan Charitable Foundation	£76,000	Welfare, hospices, medical, Jewish, general
☐ The Wessex Youth Trust	£76,000	Young people, general
☐ The Witzenfeld Foundation	£76,000	General
☐ The Barbara Whatmore Charitable Trust	£75,000	Arts and music, relief of poverty
☐ The Blair Foundation	£75,000	Wildlife, access to countryside, general
☐ The Frognal Trust	£75,000	Older people, children, disability, blindness/ophthalmological research, environmental heritage
☐ The JMK Charitable Trust	£75,000	Art and Music, religions and their relations with other faiths – Worldwide
☐ The Richard Newitt Fund	£75,000	Education
☐ The Saints and Sinners Trust	£75,000	General but in practice mainly welfare and medical
☐ Coats Foundation Trust	£74,000	Textile and thread-related training courses and research
☐ The Albert Reckitt Charitable Trust	£74,000	General, Quaker
☐ The Ebenezer Trust	£74,000	Evangelical Christianity, welfare
☐ The Greys Charitable Trust	£74,000	General
☐ The Janet Nash Charitable Settlement	£74,000	Medical, hardship, general
☐ The Tory Family Foundation	£74,000	Education, Christian, medical
☐ The Viznitz Foundation	£74,000	Jewish
☐ Kinsurdy Charitable Trust	£73,000	General
☐ May Hearnshaw's Charity	£73,000	General

☐ Mrs H R Greene Charitable Settlement	£73,000	General, particularly at risk-groups, poverty, social isolation
☐ Sir John and Lady Amory's Charitable Trust	£73,000	General
☐ The Christopher Cadbury Charitable Trust	£73,000	Nature conservation, general
☐ The Hesed Trust	£73,000	Christian
☐ The International Bankers Charitable Trust (The Worshipful Compnay of Interntional Bankers)	£73,000	The recruitment and development of employees in the financial services
☐ The Mountbatten Memorial Trust	£73,000	Technological research in aid of disabilities
☐ The Sir Julian Hodge Charitable Trust	£73,000	General
☐ Blyth Watson Charitable Trust	£72,000	UK-based humanitarian organisations, hospices
☐ Burdens Charitable Foundation	£72,000	General
☐ Nathan Charitable Trust	£72,000	Evangelical Christian work and mission
☐ The Friarsgate Trust	£72,000	Health and welfare of young and older people
☐ The G D Herbert Charitable Trust	£72,000	Medicine, health, welfare, environmental resources
☐ The Hammonds Charitable Trust	£72,000	General
☐ Truemart Limited	£72,000	General, Judaism, welfare
☐ Alba Charitable Trust	£71,000	Jewish
☐ The Adrienne and Leslie Sussman Charitable Trust	£71,000	Jewish, general
☐ The Barnsbury Charitable Trust	£71,000	General
☐ The Joyce Fletcher Charitable Trust	£71,000	Music, children's welfare
☐ The Oliver Ford Charitable Trust	£71,000	Mental disability, housing
☐ The P and C Hickinbotham Charitable Trust	£71,000	Social welfare
☐ D D McPhail Charitable Settlement	£70,000	Medical research, disability, older people
☐ Dame Violet Wills Charitable Trust	£70,000	Evangelical Christianity
☐ Peter Storrs Trust	£70,000	Education
☐ Prairie Trust	£70,000	Third world development, the environment, conflict prevention
☐ The AS Charitable Trust	£70,000	Christian, development, social concern
☐ The Elaine and Angus Lloyd Charitable Trust	£70,000	General
☐ The John and Freda Coleman Charitable Trust	£70,000	Disadvantaged young people
☐ The Lambert Charitable Trust	£70,000	Health, welfare, education, disability, Jewish
☐ Webb Memorial Trust	£70,000	Education, politics, social policy
☐ The Annie Schiff Charitable Trust	£69,000	Orthodox Jewish education
☐ The Bernard Piggott Trust	£69,000	General
☐ The Bill Butlin Charity Trust	£69,000	General
☐ The Carpenter Charitable Trust	£69,000	Humanitarian and Christian outreach
☐ The Estelle Trust	£69,000	Overseas aid
☐ Rita and David Slowe Charitable Trust	£68,000	General
☐ The Adnams Charity	£68,000	General
☐ The E H Smith Charitable Trust	£68,000	General
☐ The Kreditor Charitable Trust	£68,000	Jewish, welfare, education
☐ The Laduma Dhamecha Charitable Trust	£68,000	General
☐ Blatchington Court Trust	£67,000	Supporting vision-impaired people under the age of 30
☐ The Colonel W H Whitbread Charitable Trust	£67,000	Education, preservation of places of historic interest and natural beauty
☐ The J R S S T Charitable Trust	£67,000	Democracy and social justice
☐ Michael and Leslie Bennett Charitable Trust	£66,000	Jewish
☐ P G and N J Boulton Trust	£66,000	Christian
☐ Sir Alec Black's Charity	£66,000	Relief in need
☐ Sir Clive Bourne Family Trust	£66,000	Jewish
☐ The Boris Karloff Charitable Foundation	£66,000	General
☐ The Edinburgh Trust, No. 2 Account	£66,000	Education, armed services
☐ The Jill Franklin Trust	£66,000	Overseas, welfare, prisons, church restoration
☐ The Kass Charitable Trust	£66,000	Welfare, education, Jewish
☐ The Lyndhurst Trust	£66,000	Christian
☐ The Millfield Trust	£66,000	Christian
☐ The Ripple Effect Foundation	£66,000	General, particularly disadvantaged young people, the environment and third world development
☐ Birthday House Trust	£65,000	General

☐ The B and P Glasser Charitable Trust	£65,000	Health, disability, Jewish, welfare
☐ The Dorothy Holmes Charitable Trust	£65,000	General
☐ The Dwek Family Charitable Trust	£65,000	General
☐ The Thistle Trust	£65,000	Arts
☐ The Violet Mauray Charitable Trust	£65,000	General, medical, Jewish
☐ The William and Ellen Vinten Trust	£65,000	Science and technology education
☐ J A R Charitable Trust	£64,000	Roman Catholic, education, welfare
☐ The Augustine Courtauld Trust	£64,000	General
☐ The Rayden Charitable Trust	£64,000	Jewish
☐ The Scarfe Charitable Trust	£64,000	Churches, arts, music, environment
☐ The Simpson Education and Conservation Trust	£64,000	Environmental conservation
☐ Elizabeth Cayzer Charitable Trust	£63,000	Arts
☐ The Balney Charitable Trust	£63,000	Preservation, conservation, welfare, service charities
☐ The Barry Green Memorial Fund	£63,000	Animal welfare
☐ The Loke Wan Tho Memorial Foundation	£63,000	Environment and conservation, medical causes, overseas aid
☐ The Mirianog Trust	£63,000	General
☐ The Moette Charitable Trust	£63,000	Education, Jewish
☐ The Wilkinson Charitable Foundation	£63,000	Scientific research
☐ C B Richard Ellis Charitable Trust	£62,000	General
☐ The Gould Charitable Trust	£62,000	General
☐ The Harbour Charitable Trust	£62,000	General
☐ The Noon Foundation	£62,000	General, education, relief of poverty, community relations, alleviation of racial discrimination
☐ The Ormsby Charitable Trust	£62,000	General
☐ Zephyr Charitable Trust	£62,000	Community, environment, social welfare
☐ Lord and Lady Lurgan Trust	£61,000	Medical charities, older people, children and the arts
☐ Philip and Judith Green Trust	£61,000	Christian and missions
☐ The Mizpah Trust	£61,000	General
☐ The W L Pratt Charitable Trust	£61,000	General
☐ Jacqueline and Michael Gee Charitable Trust	£60,000	Health, education (including Jewish)
☐ Lord Forte Foundation	£60,000	Hospitality
☐ The Adamson Trust	£60,000	Children, under 16, who are physically or mentally disabled
☐ The Bernard Morris Charitable Trust	£60,000	General
☐ The Chetwode Foundation	£60,000	Education, churches, general
☐ The Eleni Nakou Foundation	£60,000	Education, international understanding
☐ The Gamma Trust	£60,000	General
☐ The Gerald Fogel Charitable Trust	£60,000	Jewish, general
☐ The Goldmark Trust	£60,000	General
☐ The Harry Dunn Charitable Trust	£60,000	Medical, general, conservation
☐ The Merchants' House of Glasgow	£60,000	General
☐ The Monica Rabagliati Charitable Trust	£60,000	Children, Humanitarian, medical, general
☐ The Wilfrid Bruce Davis Charitable Trust	£60,000	Health
☐ The Artemis Charitable Trust	£59,000	Psychotherapy, parent education, and related activities
☐ The Chownes Foundation	£59,000	Religion, relief in need, social problems
☐ The Emmanuel Kaye Foundation	£59,000	Medical research, welfare and Jewish organisations
☐ The Owen Family Trust	£59,000	Christian, general
☐ Mandeville Trust	£58,000	Cancer, young people and children
☐ Mrs S K West's Charitable Trust	£58,000	General
☐ R S Brownless Charitable Trust	£58,000	Disability, relief in need, ill health, accommodation and housing, education, job creation, voluntary work
☐ The E M MacAndrew Trust	£58,000	Medical, children, general
☐ Weatherley Charitable Trust	£58,000	General
☐ A H and B C Whiteley Charitable Trust	£57,000	Art, environment, general
☐ Alan and Sheila Diamond Charitable Trust	£57,000	Jewish, general
☐ Audrey Earle Charitable Trust	£57,000	General, with some preference for animal welfare and conservation charities
☐ Blakes Benevolent Trust	£57,000	General
☐ The Alabaster Trust	£57,000	Christian Church and related activities

☐ **The Alex Roberts-Miller Foundation**	£57,000	Education, sport and social opportunities for disadvantaged young people
☐ **The Baker Charitable Trust**	£57,000	Mainly Jewish, older people, sickness and disability, medical research
☐ **The Demigryphon Trust**	£57,000	Medical, education, children, general
☐ **The Ellerdale Trust**	£57,000	Children
☐ **The J G Hogg Charitable Trust**	£57,000	Welfare, animal welfare, general
☐ **The Ruth and Jack Lunzer Charitable Trust**	£57,000	Jewish; children, young adults; education and the arts
☐ **The Soli and Leah Kelaty Trust Fund**	£57,000	General, education, overseas aid, religion
☐ **Thomas Betton's Charity for Pensions and Relief-in-Need**	£57,000	Children and young people
☐ **Limoges Charitable Trust**	£56,000	Animals, services, general
☐ **The Cumber Family Charitable Trust**	£56,000	General
☐ **The Edgar Milward Charity**	£56,000	Christian, humanitarian
☐ **The Harold Joels Charitable Trust**	£56,000	Jewish
☐ **The Michael and Anna Wix Charitable Trust**	£56,000	Older people, disability, education, medicine and health, poverty, welfare, Jewish
☐ **The Tresillian Trust**	£56,000	Overseas aid, welfare
☐ **The Benjamin Winegarten Charitable Trust**	£55,000	Jewish
☐ **The Cuthbert Horn Trust**	£55,000	Environment, people with disability/special needs, older people
☐ **The Shanley Charitable Trust**	£55,000	Relief of poverty
☐ **Cowley Charitable Foundation**	£54,000	Registered charities
☐ **Mary Homfray Charitable Trust**	£54,000	General
☐ **Peter Stormonth Darling Charitable Trust**	£54,000	Heritage, medical research, sport
☐ **Rosanna Taylor's 1987 Charity Trust**	£54,000	General
☐ **The A B Strom and R Strom Charitable Trust**	£54,000	Jewish, general
☐ **The Harebell Centenary Fund**	£54,000	General, education, medical research, animal welfare
☐ **The Homestead Charitable Trust**	£54,000	Medical, health and welfare, animal welfare, Christianity, arts
☐ **The Michael and Shirley Hunt Charitable Trust**	£54,000	Prisoners' families, animal welfare
☐ **The Pennycress Trust**	£54,000	General
☐ **The Searle Charitable Trust**	£54,000	Youth development with a nautical basis
☐ **The Seven Fifty Trust**	£54,000	Christian
☐ **A J H Ashby Will Trust**	£53,000	Wildlife, heritage, education and children
☐ **Anthony Travis Charitable Trust**	£53,000	General
☐ **Col-Reno Ltd**	£53,000	Jewish
☐ **Marmot Charitable Trust**	£53,000	Green' organisations, conflict resolution
☐ **Panton Trust**	£53,000	Animal wildlife worldwide; environment UK
☐ **The Blueberry Charitable Trust**	£53,000	Jewish, relief in need
☐ **The Catholic Charitable Trust**	£53,000	Catholic
☐ **The Eva Reckitt Trust Fund**	£53,000	Welfare, relief in need, extension and development of education, victims of war
☐ **The Golsoncott Foundation**	£53,000	The arts
☐ **The Lionel Wigram Memorial Trust**	£53,000	General
☐ **The Marina Kleinwort Charitable Trust**	£53,000	Arts
☐ **The Rest Harrow Trust**	£53,000	Jewish, general
☐ **The Worshipful Company of Spectacle Makers' Charity**	£53,000	Visual impairment, City of London, general
☐ **Archbishop of Wales' Fund for Children**	£52,000	Children
☐ **St Michael's and All Saints' Charities**	£52,000	Health, welfare
☐ **Stanley Spooner Deceased Charitable Trust**	£52,000	Children, general
☐ **Sumner Wilson Charitable Trust**	£52,000	General
☐ **The Derek Hill Foundation**	£52,000	Arts/culture
☐ **The Weinstein Foundation**	£52,000	Jewish, medical, welfare
☐ **CLA Charitable Trust**	£51,000	People who are disabled or disadvantaged
☐ **Malcolm Lyons Foundation**	£51,000	Jewish
☐ **The Olga Charitable Trust**	£51,000	Health, welfare, youth organisations, children's welfare, carers' organisations
☐ **The Cemlyn-Jones Trust**	£50,000	Small local projects in North Wales and Anglesey

☐ The Colin Montgomerie Charitable Foundation	£50,000	General
☐ The Hare of Steep Charitable Trust	£50,000	General
☐ The John Feeney Charitable Bequest	£50,000	Arts, heritage and open spaces
☐ The Burry Charitable Trust	£49,000	Medicine, health
☐ The Emerton-Christie Charity	£49,000	Health, welfare, disability, arts
☐ The Marjorie and Geoffrey Jones Charitable Trust	£49,000	General
☐ The Oakmoor Charitable Trust	£49,000	General
☐ The Oliver Borthwick Memorial Trust	£49,000	Homelessness
☐ The Whitecourt Charitable Trust	£49,000	Christian, general
☐ Minge's Gift and the Pooled Trusts	£48,000	Medical, education, disadvantage, disability
☐ The Bartlett Taylor Charitable Trust	£48,000	General
☐ The Ericson Trust	£48,000	Older people; community projects/local interest groups; prisons, prison reform, mentoring projects, as well as research in this area; refugees; mental health; environmental projects and research; aid to developing countries provided by a UK-registered charity
☐ The Ian Fleming Charitable Trust	£48,000	Disability, medical
☐ The Morel Charitable Trust	£48,000	Arts, particularly drama; organisations working for improved race relations; inner-city and developing-world projects
☐ The Oikonomia Trust	£48,000	Christian
☐ The Williams Family Charitable Trust	£48,000	Jewish
☐ William Dean Countryside and Educational Trust	£48,000	Education in natural history, ecology and conservation
☐ The Rock Solid Trust	£47,500	Christian causes
☐ Edwin George Robinson Charitable Trust	£47,000	Medical research
☐ The Carr-Gregory Trust	£47,000	Arts, social welfare, health, education
☐ The Cazenove Charitable Trust	£47,000	General
☐ The Drayson Foundation	£47,000	Relief of sickness, education
☐ The E L Rathbone Charitable Trust	£47,000	Social work charities
☐ The Montague Thompson Coon Charitable Trust	£47,000	Children with disabilities
☐ The Portrack Charitable Trust	£47,000	General
☐ The André Christian Trust	£46,000	Christian
☐ The Bothwell Charitable Trust	£46,000	Disability, health, older people, conservation
☐ The Elmgrant Trust	£46,000	General charitable purposes, education, arts, social sciences
☐ The Gur Trust	£46,000	Jewish causes
☐ The ISA Charity	£46,000	Arts, health and education
☐ The Kessler Foundation	£46,000	General, Jewish
☐ The Rofeh Trust	£46,000	General, religious activities
☐ Philip Henman Trust	£45,000	General
☐ The Annandale Charitable Trust	£45,000	Major UK charities
☐ The Barnett and Sylvia Shine No. 2 Charitable Trust	£45,000	General
☐ The Charter 600 Charity	£45,000	General
☐ The Nancy Kenyon Charitable Trust	£45,000	General
☐ The Norman Joels Charitable Trust	£45,000	Jewish causes, general
☐ The Red Rose Charitable Trust	£45,000	Older people and people with disabilities
☐ Thomas Roberts Trust	£45,000	Medical, disability, relief in need
☐ D G Albright Charitable Trust	£44,000	General
☐ The E Alec Colman Charitable Fund Ltd	£44,000	Religion, especially Jewish, children, social welfare
☐ The Magen Charitable Trust	£44,000	Education, Jewish
☐ The Rhododendron Trust	£44,000	Overseas aid and development, social welfare and culture
☐ The Robert Clutterbuck Charitable Trust	£44,000	Service, sport and recreation, natural history, animal welfare and protection
☐ Buckland Charitable Trust	£43,000	General, international development, welfare and health research
☐ Ellador Ltd	£43,000	Jewish
☐ Mrs Maud Van Norden's Charitable Foundation	£43,000	General
☐ The Hargrave Foundation	£43,000	General, medical, welfare
☐ The John Young Charitable Settlement	£43,000	General
☐ Bellasis Trust	£42,000	General
☐ The Barbara A Shuttleworth Memorial Trust	£42,000	People with disabilities

☐ The Corona Charitable Trust	**£42,000**	Jewish
☐ The Football Association National Sports Centre Trust	**£42,000**	Play areas, community sports facilities
☐ The Hinrichsen Foundation	**£42,000**	Music
☐ The Pallant Charitable Trust	**£42,000**	Church music
☐ The Victor Adda Foundation	**£42,000**	Fan Museum, welfare
☐ Vale of Glamorgan – Welsh Church Fund	**£42,000**	General
☐ West London Synagogue Charitable Fund	**£42,000**	Jewish, general
☐ The Birmingham Hospital Saturday Fund Medical Charity and Welfare Trust	**£41,000**	Medical
☐ The Carlton House Charitable Trust	**£41,000**	Jewish, education/bursaries, general
☐ The Col W W Pilkington Will Trusts The General Charity Fund	**£41,000**	Medical, arts, social welfare, international charities, drugs misuse, environment
☐ The E C Sosnow Charitable Trust	**£41,000**	Mainly education and arts
☐ The F J Wallis Charitable Settlement	**£41,000**	General
☐ The Forces Trust	**£41,000**	Military charities
☐ The Gay and Keith Talbot Trust	**£41,000**	Overseas aid, health, famine relief
☐ William Arthur Rudd Memorial Trust	**£41,000**	General in the UK, and selected Spanish charities
☐ LandAid Charitable Trust	**£40,000**	Homelessness, relief of need
☐ Mildred Duveen Charitable Trust	**£40,000**	General
☐ Miss M E Swinton Paterson's Charitable Trust	**£40,000**	Church of Scotland, young people, general
☐ Percy Hedley 1990 Charitable Trust	**£40,000**	General
☐ St Teilo's Trust	**£40,000**	Evangelistic work in the Church in Wales
☐ The Andy Stewart Charitable Foundation	**£40,000**	General
☐ The Appletree Trust	**£40,000**	Disability, sickness, poverty
☐ The Ardwick Trust	**£40,000**	Jewish, welfare, general
☐ The Barbara Welby Trust	**£40,000**	General
☐ The Helen Isabella McMorran Charitable Foundation	**£40,000**	General, Christian
☐ Paul Lunn-Rockliffe Charitable Trust	**£39,000**	Christianity, poverty, infirm people, young people
☐ The Ann and David Marks Foundation	**£39,000**	Jewish charities, general
☐ The Eagle Charity Trust	**£39,000**	General, international, welfare
☐ The Huntly and Margery Sinclair Charitable Trust	**£39,000**	General
☐ The Lili Tapper Charitable Foundation	**£39,000**	Jewish
☐ Brian Abrams Charitable Trust	**£38,000**	Jewish
☐ Eric Abrams Charitable Trust	**£38,000**	Jewish
☐ Forbesville Limited	**£38,000**	Jewish, education
☐ The A and R Woolf Charitable Trust	**£38,000**	General
☐ The A M McGreevy No. 5 Charitable Settlement	**£38,000**	General
☐ The Alexis Trust	**£38,000**	Christian
☐ The Beacon Trust	**£38,000**	Christian
☐ The Beaufort House Trust Limited	**£38,000**	Christian, education
☐ The D C Moncrieff Charitable Trust	**£38,000**	Social welfare, environment
☐ The Dickon Trust	**£38,000**	General
☐ The Forbes Charitable Foundation	**£38,000**	Adults with learning disabilities
☐ The Huxham Charitable Trust	**£38,000**	Christianity, churches and organisations, development work
☐ The Linmardon Trust	**£38,000**	General
☐ The Malcolm Chick Charity	**£38,000**	Youth character building, armed forces welfare, medical research and care
☐ The Ruth and Lionel Jacobson Trust (Second Fund) No. 2	**£38,000**	Jewish, medical, children, disability
☐ The Stephen R and Philippa H Southall Charitable Trust	**£38,000**	General
☐ Mr and Mrs F E F Newman Charitable Trust	**£37,000**	Christian, overseas aid and development
☐ T B H Brunner's Charitable Settlement	**£37,000**	Church of England, heritage, arts, general
☐ The Carvill Trust	**£37,000**	General
☐ The Judith Trust	**£37,000**	Mental health and learning disabilities with some preference for women and Jewish people

☐ **Arthur James Paterson Charitable Trust**	**£36,000**	Medical research, welfare of older people and children
☐ **Harry Bacon Foundation**	**£36,000**	Medical, animal welfare
☐ **Pearson's Holiday Fund**	**£36,000**	Young people who are disadvantaged
☐ **Sydney E Franklin Deceased's New Second Charity**	**£36,000**	Development
☐ **The Elephant Trust**	**£36,000**	Visual arts
☐ **The Emilienne Charitable Trust**	**£36,000**	Medical, education
☐ **The Music Sales Charitable Trust**	**£36,000**	Children and young people, musical education
☐ **William P Bancroft (No. 2) Charitable Trust and Jenepher Gillett Trust**	**£36,000**	Quaker
☐ **Ryklow Charitable Trust 1992 (also known as A B Williamson Charitable Trust)**	**£35,000**	Education, health, environment and welfare
☐ **Spears-Stutz Charitable Trust**	**£35,000**	Welfare causes
☐ **The Dorothy Hay-Bolton Charitable Trust**	**£35,000**	Deaf, blind
☐ **The Duncan Norman Trust Fund**	**£35,000**	General
☐ **The F H Muirhead Charitable Trust**	**£35,000**	Hospitals, medical research institutes
☐ **The Gretna Charitable Trust**	**£35,000**	General
☐ **The Kathleen Trust**	**£35,000**	Musicians
☐ **The Late St Patrick White Charitable Trust**	**£35,000**	General
☐ **The Loseley and Guildway Charitable Trust**	**£35,000**	General
☐ **The Minos Trust**	**£35,000**	Christian, general
☐ **The Mushroom Fund**	**£35,000**	General charitable purposes
☐ **Barchester Healthcare Foundation**	**£34,000**	Health and social care
☐ **S C and M E Morland's Charitable Trust**	**£34,000**	Quaker, sickness, welfare, peace and development overseas
☐ **The Angela Gallagher Memorial Fund**	**£34,000**	Children and young people, Christian, humanitarian, education
☐ **The Clifford Howarth Charity Settlement**	**£34,000**	General
☐ **The David Pickford Charitable Foundation**	**£34,000**	Christian, general
☐ **The Edith Maud Ellis 1985 Charitable Trust**	**£34,000**	Quaker, ecumenical, education, peace and international affairs, general
☐ **The Fairway Trust**	**£34,000**	General
☐ **The John Rayner Charitable Trust**	**£34,000**	General
☐ **The R M Douglas Charitable Trust**	**£34,000**	General
☐ **The Dorcas Trust**	**£33,500**	Christian, relief of poverty and advancement of education
☐ **H and L Cantor Trust**	**£33,000**	Jewish, general
☐ **Mejer and Gertrude Miriam Frydman Foundation**	**£33,000**	Jewish, Jewish education
☐ **The Dennis Alan Yardy Charitable Trust**	**£33,000**	General
☐ **The Geoffrey Burton Charitable Trust**	**£33,000**	General
☐ **The Haydan Charitable Trust**	**£33,000**	Jewish, general
☐ **The Leonard Trust**	**£33,000**	Christian, overseas aid
☐ **The Nicholas Joels Charitable Trust**	**£33,000**	Jewish, medical welfare, general
☐ **The Sylvanus Charitable Trust**	**£33,000**	Animal welfare, Roman Catholic
☐ **Miss V L Clore's 1967 Charitable Trust**	**£32,000**	General, arts, social welfare, health, Jewish
☐ **Swan Mountain Trust**	**£32,000**	Mental health, penal concerns
☐ **The Astor of Hever Trust**	**£32,000**	Young people, medical research, education
☐ **The Cyril Taylor Charitable Trust**	**£32,000**	Education
☐ **The Pat Allsop Charitable Trust**	**£32,000**	Education, medical research, children, relief of poverty
☐ **The R H Scholes Charitable Trust**	**£32,000**	General, including children and young people who are disabled or disadvantaged, hospices, preservation and churches
☐ **The Sandy Dewhirst Charitable Trust**	**£32,000**	General
☐ **The Thomas Wall Trust**	**£32,000**	Education, welfare
☐ **P H G Cadbury Charitable Trust**	**£31,000**	General, arts, conservation, cancer
☐ **The Earl of Northampton's Charity**	**£31,000**	Welfare
☐ **The Indigo Trust**	**£31,000**	Prisons and criminal justice
☐ **The Misselbrook Trust**	**£31,000**	General
☐ **The Helen and Geoffrey De Freitas Charitable Trust**	**£30,000**	Preservation of wildlife and rural England, conservation and environment, cultural heritage
☐ **The Swan Trust**	**£30,000**	General, arts, culture

☐ The Worshipful Company of Innholders General Charity Fund	£30,000	General
☐ Educational Foundation of Alderman John Norman	£29,000	Education
☐ The Frank Parkinson Agricultural Trust	£29,000	British agriculture
☐ The Hanley Trust	£29,000	Social welfare and people who are disadvantaged
☐ The Lady Tangye Charitable Trust	£29,000	Catholic, overseas aid, general
☐ The Maurice and Vivien Thompson Charitable Trust	£29,000	General
☐ The Metropolitan Drinking Fountain and Cattle Trough Association	£29,000	Provision of pure drinking water
☐ The Pamela Champion Foundation	£29,000	General, disability
☐ Murphy-Neumann Charity Company Limited	£28,500	Older and young people with disabilities
☐ Beatrice Hankey Foundation Ltd	£28,000	Christian
☐ Nazareth Trust Fund	£28,000	Christian, in the UK and developing countries
☐ The Calpe Trust	£28,000	Relief work
☐ The Dorema Charitable Trust	£28,000	Medicine, health, welfare, education, religion
☐ The Max Reinhardt Charitable Trust	£28,000	Deafness, fine arts promotion
☐ The Millhouses Charitable Trust	£28,000	Christian, overseas aid, general
☐ The Oak Trust	£28,000	General
☐ The Peggy Ramsay Foundation	£28,000	Writers and writing for the stage
☐ Morris Leigh Foundation	£27,000	Jewish, general
☐ R E Chadwick Charitable Trust	£27,000	General
☐ The Culra Charitable Trust	£27,000	General
☐ The Florian Charitable Trust	£27,000	General
☐ The Inland Waterways Association	£27,000	Inland waterways
☐ The John and Celia Bonham Christie Charitable Trust	£27,000	General
☐ Haskel Family Foundation	£26,000	Jewish, social-policy research, arts, education
☐ Henry T and Lucy B Cadbury Charitable Trust	£26,000	Quaker causes and institutions, health, homelessness, support groups, developing world
☐ Kermaville Ltd	£26,000	Jewish
☐ The Rowing Foundation	£26,000	Water sports
☐ Annette Duvollet Charitable Trust	£25,000	General
☐ Evelyn May Trust	£25,000	Currently children, older people, medical, natural disaster relief
☐ G S Plaut Charitable Trust Limited	£25,000	Sickness, disability, Jewish, older people, Christian, general
☐ St Andrew Animal Fund	£25,000	Animal welfare
☐ T F C Frost Charitable Trust	£25,000	Medical
☐ The Amanda Smith Charitable Trust	£25,000	General
☐ The Camilla Samuel Fund	£25,000	Medical research
☐ The Moss Spiro Will Charitable Foundation	£25,000	Jewish welfare
☐ The Sandhu Charitable Foundation	£25,000	General
☐ The Simpson Foundation	£25,000	Roman Catholic purposes
☐ The Late Sir Pierce Lacy Charity Trust	£24,000	Roman Catholics, general
☐ C J Cadbury Charitable Trust	£23,000	Environment, conservation
☐ Mageni Trust	£22,000	Arts
☐ Miss Doreen Stanford Trust	£22,000	General
☐ The Fanny Rapaport Charitable Settlement	£21,000	Jewish, general
☐ The J S F Pollitzer Charitable Settlement	£21,000	General
☐ Martin McLaren Memorial Trust	£20,000	General
☐ Maurice Fry Charitable Trust	£20,000	Medicine, health, welfare, humanities, environmental resources, international
☐ The British Dietetic Association General and Education Trust Fund	£20,000	Dietary and nutritional issues
☐ The Daniel Rivlin Charitable Trust	£20,000	Jewish, general
☐ The Star Charitable Trust	£20,000	General
☐ Mabel Cooper Charity	£19,000	General
☐ The Constance Paterson Charitable Trust	£19,000	Medical research, health, welfare of children, older people, service people

☐ **The Green and Lilian F M Ainsworth and Family Benevolent Fund**	£19,000	Young people, disability, health, medical research, disadvantage, older people, general
☐ **The Schreiber Charitable Trust**	£17,500	Jewish with a preference for education, social welfare and medical
☐ **Robyn Charitable Trust**	£17,000	General charitable purposes, particularly the support of young people
☐ **The Geoffrey John Kaye Charitable Foundation**	£17,000	Jewish, general
☐ **The Hellenic Foundation**	£17,000	Greek education in the UK
☐ **The Willie Nagel Charitable Trust**	£17,000	Jewish, general
☐ **The Geoffrey C Hughes Charitable Trust**	£16,000	Nature conservation, environment, performing arts
☐ **The River Farm Foundation**	£16,000	General, education, welfare, medical, disability, overseas aid
☐ **DG Charitable Settlement**	£15,000	General
☐ **The Boltons Trust**	£15,000	Social welfare, medicine, education
☐ **The Macfarlane Walker Trust**	£15,000	Education, the arts, social welfare, general
☐ **G R Waters Charitable Trust 2000**	£14,000	General
☐ **The Beaverbrook Foundation**	£14,000	General
☐ **Gerald Finzi Charitable Trust**	£13,000	Music
☐ **The Cleopatra Trust**	£13,000	Mental health, cancer welfare/education, diabetes, physical disability, homelessness, addiction, children
☐ **The Gunter Charitable Trust**	£13,000	General
☐ **Bud Flanagan Leukaemia Fund**	£11,000	Leukaemia research and treatment
☐ **The Gamlen Charitable Trust**	£11,000	Legal education, general
☐ **Laufer Charitable Trust**	£8,600	Jewish
☐ **The Bluff Field Charitable Trust**	£8,000	General
☐ **The Gough Charitable Trust**	£7,100	Young people, Episcopal and Church of England, preservation of the countryside, social welfare
☐ **Sellata Ltd**	£6,500	Jewish, welfare
☐ **The Langley Charitable Trust**	£4,000	Christian, general
☐ **The Roger and Sarah Bancroft Clark Charitable Trust**	£2,500	Quaker, general
☐ **The Charles Lloyd Foundation**	£2,000	Construction, repair and maintenance of Roman Catholic buildings; the advancement of Roman Catholic religion; and music
☐ **Tadlus Limited**	£0	Orthodox Jewish
☐ **The Puebla Charitable Trust**	£0	Community development work, relief of poverty

The A B Charitable Trust

Human rights

£268,000 (2007/08)
Beneficial area Mainly UK.

Monmouth House, 87–93 Westbourne Grove, London W2 4UL

Tel. 020 7313 8070 **Fax** 020 7313 9607

Email mail@abcharitabletrust.org.uk

Website www.abcharitabletrust.org.uk

Correspondent Mrs S Harrity, Director

Trustees Y J M Bonavero; Mrs A G M L Bonavero; Miss C Bonavero; O Bonavero; P Bonavero; P Day; A Harley; Mrs A Swan Parente.

CC Number 1000147

Information available Accounts were on file at the Charity Commission.

A B Charitable Trust supports charities working where human dignity is imperilled and where there are opportunities for human dignity to be affirmed.

Applications are particularly welcomed from charities working to support:

- refugees and victims of torture
- prisoners
- older people
- people with mental health problems.

In relation to the above, the following cross-cutting themes are of interest to the trustees:

- women
- homelessness
- therapeutic art.

Grants are awarded to charities registered in the UK; usually to those working in the UK, though a few are awarded to charities working internationally. It tends to support charities with annual income between £150,000 and £1.5 million which do not have substantial investments or surpluses.

The trust has a small grants programme (up to £5,000) which responds to appeals on a one-off basis. It seeks to identify charities working on its priorities for larger grants, which could be awarded on a regular basis subject to annual reports and an agreed exit strategy. It is happy to provide funding for core costs.

In 2007/08 the trust had assets of £557,000 and an income of £549,000, mostly from Gift Aid and other contributions. From 317 applications received, grants to 60 organisations were made totalling £268,000.

Beneficiaries included: Asylum Support Appeals Project, Redress and Women's Therapy Centre (£7,500 each); Asian Women's Organisation, C P Support, Citizenship Foundation, Contact the Elderly, Furniture Now, Harrogate Homeless, Praxis, Soundabout, Sudbury Neighbourhood Centre and Women's Link (£5,000 each); Soundabout and Tools for Self Reliance (£3,000 each); and Burnbake Trust and Headway (£2,500 each).

Exclusions Individuals are not eligible for support.

Applications Applications can be completed online at the trust's website.

As well as administrative and financial details, the online application form will ask you for a two page summary of your work, including:

- background
- aims and objectives
- activities
- achievements over the last year.

After filling in the online application form you will be sent a reference number. Please send the Director the following documents in hard copy quoting the reference number:

- a signed copy of your latest certified accounts/statements, published within six months of the end of the previous financial year
- publicity materials that illustrate the work of your charity, such as annual reviews or leaflets.

Send in your application six weeks ahead of the trustees' meeting at which you would like it to be considered. The trustees meet four times a year, in January, April, July and October. To get the exact dates, please contact us.

Eric Abrams Charitable Trust

Jewish

£38,000 (2007/08)
Beneficial area UK.

130–132 Nantwich Road, Crewe CW2 6AZ

Correspondent The Trustees

Trustees *Brian Abrams; Eric Abrams; Marcia Anne Jacobs; Susan Melanie Abrams.*

CC Number 275939

Information available Accounts were on file at the Charity Commission, without a list of grants.

In 2007/08 the trust had assets of £916,000 and an income of £51,000. Grants to 32 organisations totalled £38,000.

Previous beneficiaries have included: Friends of Ohr Akiva Institution; Centre for Torah Education Trust; Halacha Lemoshe Trust; Hale Adult Hebrew Education Trust; the Heathlands Village; Manchester Jewish Federation; Rabbi Nachman of Breslov Charitable Foundation; UK Friends of Magen David Adom; and United Jewish Israel Appeal.

Exclusions No grants to individuals.

Applications 'The trustees do not invite appeals, as the trust is fully committed until further notice.'

Brian Abrams Charitable Trust

Jewish

£38,000 (2007/08)
Beneficial area UK.

Alexander Layton, 130–132 Nantwich Road, Crewe CW2 6AZ

Correspondent Robert Taylor

Trustees *Betty Abrams; Brian Abrams; Eric Abrams; Gail Gabbie.*

CC Number 275941

Information available Accounts were on file at the Charity Commission, without a list of grants.

In 2007/08 this trust has assets of £808,000, an income of £51,000 and made 31 grants totalling £38,000.

Previous beneficiaries have included: Centre for Torah Education Trust; Friends of Ohr Akiva Institution; Halacha Lemoshe Trust; Hale Adult Hebrew Education Trust; the Heathlands Village; Manchester Jewish Federation; Rabbi Nachman of Breslov Charitable Foundation; Rainsough Charitable Trust; UK Friends of Magen David Adom; and United Jewish Israel Appeal.

Exclusions No grants to individuals.

Applications The trust has previously stated that its funds are fully committed and applications are not invited.

The Acacia Charitable Trust

Jewish, education and general

£78,000 (2007/08)

Beneficial area UK and Israel.

5 Clarke's Mews, London W1G 6QN

Tel. 020 7486 1884

Email acacia@dircon.co.uk

Correspondent The Secretary

Trustees *K D Rubens; Mrs A G Rubens; S A Rubens.*

CC Number 274275

Information available Full accounts were on file at the Charity Commission.

In 2007/08 the trust had assets of £1.8 million and an income of £84,000. Grants to 50 organisations totalled £78,000. Grants ranged from £15 to £11,000, although most were for under £1,000 each. About two-thirds of grants were recurrent. They were given in the following categories and are shown here with examples of beneficiaries in each category:

Arts and culture – 10 grants totalling £43,000
The Jewish Museum (£30,000); Jewish Historical Society of England (£3,000); the Hampstead Theatre (£2,500); Royal National Theatre (£1,000); Painters and Stainers Charity (£500); Beth Holim and RSA Trust (£100 each); and Royal Photographic Society (£24).

Community care and welfare – 13 grants totalling £13,000
Community Security Trust (£5,000); Spanish and Portuguese Jews' Congregation (£2,200); Institute for Jewish Policy Research and Jewish Care (£2,000 each); Norwood (£1,000); Bevis Marks Synagogue Trust (£500); Nighingale House (£250); Launderdale Road Synagogue Association (£200); Shelter (£100); the Royal Masonic Benevolent Institution (£50); and St John's Wood Society (£15).

Overseas – 1 grant totalling £10,500
World Jewish Relief was the sole beneficiary.

Education – 4 grants totalling £7,500
British Orgaisation for rehabilitation Through Training (£5,000); the Imperial War Musum and Wiener Library Institute of Contemporary History (£1,000 each); and Weizmann Institute of Science (£500).

Medical and disability – 10 grants totalling £2,800
Magen David Adom (£1,000); the Stroke Association (£600); the Speech, Language and Hearing Centre (£500); and Camphill Village Trust, Edinburgh House, Great Ormond Street Hospital for Children, Leukaemia Research, Marie Curie Hospice and Macmillan Cancer Support (£100 each).

General – 2 grants totalling £200
Jewish Women's Week and Wellbeing of Women (£100 each).

Exclusions No grants to individuals.

Applications In writing to the correspondent.

The Company of Actuaries Charitable Trust Fund

Actuaries, medical research, young and older people and people with disabilities

£94,000 (2007/08)

Beneficial area UK, with a preference for the City of London.

55 Station Road, Beaconsfield HP9 1QL

Email charity@companyofactuaries.co.uk

Website www.actuariescompany.co.uk

Correspondent Lyndon Jones, Honorary Almoner

Trustees *R Colbey, Chair; J A Jolliffe; Nick Dumbreck; Jeff Medlock; F J Morrison; Michael Turner.*

CC Number 280702

Information available Accounts were on file at the Charity Commission.

Objectives of the charity:

1) the relief of poverty of members of the profession of actuary
2) grants for the advancement of education of actuaries
3) grants for charitable research in the field of actuarial science and the award of bursaries
4) awards of educational exhibitions to persons intending the profession of actuary

5) awards of prizes in connection with the examinations for actuaries
6) assisting the general education of persons in need who are preparing to be actuaries
7) assisting and benefiting persons who are endeavouring to qualify as actuaries
8) making donations to any registered charity.

We are a small charity with limited funds. We therefore only donate to those charities where our donation will 'make a difference' and be used efficiently and effectively.

We normally only donate to the following types of registered charities:

1) those involved with supporting older or disabled people
2) charities helping children and young people
3) those involved in treating medical conditions or funding medical research
4) other worthy charities, such as those working with the needy or disadvantaged.

In 2007/08 it had assets of £270,000 and an income of £121,000. Grants to organisations totalled £94,000.

Awards were given ranging from £500 to £2,000, with larger amounts where liverymen had a significant connection.

Master's donations
Funds are given solely at the discretion of the Master of the Company each year. Grants totalling £11,000 were approved to 11 organisations. Beneficiaries included: the Sea Scouts (£2,000); British Red Cross (£1,300); St Peter and St James Trust and Reeds School Foundation Appeal (£1,000 each); RNLI (£750); and Central Foundation Girls School, Culham Institute and Treloar Trust (£500 each).

Donations from Master's events
Grants totalling £19,000 were approved to three organisations: Scouts Association (£8,000); Shelter (£7,000); and Children's Society (£4,500).

Education
Donations for educational purposes totalled £12,000, which was distributed in various bursaries and prizes.

City of London
Grants to eight organisations totalled £5,700. Aside from a grant of £3,250 to the Lord Mayor's Appeal, donations were in the range of £100 and £500. Beneficiaries included Mansion House Scholarship Appeal, Metropolitan Public Gardens Association, Musicians Benevolent Fund, Royal British Legion – City Poppy Appeal and Sheriffs' and Recorder's Fund.

Other donations

Grants were listed in the accounts under lists headed by the months in which they were awarded (October, January, April and July). Beneficiaries included: North London Hospice (£4,500); Children's Liver Foundation (£4,000); St Catherine's Hospice (£3,000); Edmonton Sea Cadets (£2,000); Chiltern MS (£1,500); Cerebral Palsy Sport (£1,400); British Stammering Association, Care for Carers, Changing Faces, Disabled Holiday Information, National Deaf Children's Society, Space, Trafford Multiple Sclerosis Therapy Centre and Volunteer Link Scheme (£1,000); Warwick and Northamptonshire Air Ambulance (£850); Guild of Disabled Homeworkers (£800); Express Link Up and Sick Children's Trust (£750 each); the Family Project – Coventry and Universal Beneficent Society (£600 each); and Hearing Concern, PSP Association and Working Families (£500 each).

Exclusions No grants for the propagation of religious or political beliefs, the maintenance of historic buildings or for conservation. The trustees do not usually support an organisation which has received a grant in the previous 24 months.

Applications On a form which can be downloaded from the fund's website. Further information about the trust can be obtained from the correspondent.

The Adamson Trust

Children, under 16, who are physically or mentally disabled

About £60,000 per year

Beneficial area UK, but preference will be given to requests on behalf of Scottish children.

PO Box 26334, Crieff PH7 9AB

Email edward@elworthy.net

Correspondent Edward Elworthy, Secretary

Trustees *R C Farrell; J W H Allen; Dr H Kirkwood; Dr M MacDonald Simpson; Mrs A Cowan.*

SC Number SC016517

Information available Limited information was provided by the trust.

Formerly known as Miss Agnes Gilchrist Adamson's Trust, grants are made to organisations providing holidays for children under 16 who are mentally or physically disabled. Donations are usually one-off.

About £60,000 is given in grants each year, mostly to organisations.

Previous beneficiaries have included Barnardo's Dundee Family Support Team, Children's Hospice Association Scotland, Lady Hoare Trust for Physically Disabled Children, Hopscotch Holidays, Over the Wall Gang Group, Peak Holidays, React, Scotland Yard Adventure Centre, Sense Scotland, Special Needs Adventure Play Ground and Scottish Spina Bifida Association.

Applications On a form available from the correspondent. A copy of the latest audited accounts should be included together with details of the organisation, the number of children who would benefit and the proposed holiday. Applications are considered in February, May, August and November.

The Victor Adda Foundation

Fan Museum and welfare

£42,000 (2007/08)

Beneficial area UK, but in practice Greenwich.

c/o Kleinwort Benson Trustees, PO Box 57005, 30 Gresham Street, London EC2V 7PG

Correspondent The Trustees

Trustees *Helene Alexander; Roy Gluckstein; Ann Mosseri.*

CC Number 291456

Information available Accounts were on file at the Charity Commission.

Virtually since it was set up in 1984, the foundation has been a stalwart supporter of the Fan Museum in Greenwich. Both the foundation and the museum share a majority of the same trustees; the foundation also owns the property in which the museum is sited and has granted it a 999-year lease.

In 2007/08 the trust had assets of £1.3 million and an income of £39,000. Grants were made totalling £42,000, all of which went to the Fan Museum.

Previous beneficiaries have included the Child Trust, Jewish Museum and St Christopher Hospice.

Applications In writing to the correspondent. Only successful applications are notified of a decision.

Adenfirst Ltd

Jewish

£123,000 (2007)

Beneficial area Worldwide.

479 Holloway Road, London N7 6LE

Correspondent I M Cymerman, Governor

Trustees *Mrs H F Bondi; I M Cymerman; Mrs R Cymerman.*

CC Number 291647

Information available Accounts were on file at the Charity Commission.

The trust supports mostly Jewish organisations, with a preference for education and social welfare. In 2007 it had an income of £192,000 and made grants totalling £123,000.

Beneficiaries included: Chevras Mo'os Ladol and Beis Aaron Trust (£20,000 each); Beis Rochel D'Satmar, Beis Yaakov Institutions, Friends of Harim Establishments, Telz Talmudical Academy Trust, Torah Vechesed Ezra L'Do, Gevuros Ari Torah Academy Trust and Yeshivat Kollel Breslov (£10,000 each); Yeshivah Lev Simcha (£5,000); Colel Polen Kupath Ramban (£4,300); Emunah Education Centre (£1,500); and Kollel Gur (£1,000).

Applications In writing to the correspondent.

The Adnams Charity

General

£68,000 (2007/08)

Beneficial area within a 25-mile radius of St Edmund's Church, Southwold.

Sole Bay Brewery, Southwold IP18 6JW

Tel. 01502 727200 **Fax** 01502 727267

Email charity@adnams.co.uk

Correspondent Rebecca Abrahall, The Charity Administrator

Trustees *Jonathan Adnams, Chair; Rob Chase; Guy Heald; Emma Hibbert; Melvyn Horn; Sadie Lofthouse; Simon Loftus; Andy Wood.*

CC Number 1000203

Information available Accounts were on file at the Charity Commission.

Set up in 1990 the charity gives support to a wide variety of organisations including those involved with social welfare, education, recreation, the arts and historic buildings. The trustees prefer applications for specific items. Grants are generally of a one-off nature. The trustees are reluctant to give grants to cover ongoing running costs, although in very exceptional circumstances they may do so. Grants are not made in successive years.

In 2007/08 the trust had an income of £92,000 and made grants totalling £68,000.

Beneficiaries included: NORCAS (£2,700); Waveney Crossroads Ltd (£2,300); Breakout (£2,200); Ipswich and East Suffolk Headway, More Fun and the Suffolk Foundation (£2,000 each); the Country Trust and TUTTI (£1,600 each); Cut Dance (£1,100); Bredfield Youth Club, Great Yarmouth Community Trust for Ageless Opportunities, Ilketshall St Andrew's Church and the Poetry Trust (£1,000 each); the Warden's Trust (£940); Wrentham Village Hall (£750); Lowestoft Shopmobility (£730); Greenfingers (£650); the May Centre (£500); and Waveney Sinfonia (£300).

Exclusions No grants are made to individuals, nor does it provide sponsorship of any kind. The charity does not normally make grants to religious organisations or private clubs unless these can demonstrate that the purpose of the grant is for something of clear public benefit, accessible to all. The charity does not provide raffle prizes.

Applications In writing to the correspondent. Applicants are asked to provide information on:

- the aims and objectives of the organisation requiring a grant
- what the grant is for
- who will benefit and how
- how much the item(s) will cost
- other fundraising activities being undertaken
- amount raised so far
- to whom cheques should be made payable in the event of a grant being made.

Where possible the most recent set of audited accounts should be enclosed with the application. If applying from a registered charity, a copy of the organisation's reserves policy should be included.

Trustees meet quarterly (usually January, April, July and October).

A F Trust Company

Higher education

£100,000 (2007/08)

Beneficial area England.

34 Chapel Street, Thatcham, Reading RG18 4QL

Correspondent P D Welch, Secretary

Trustees *Martin Wynne-Jones; David Charles Savage; Jeremy Lindley; Andrew Murphy; David Leah; Jean Strudley.*

CC Number 1060319

Information available Accounts were on file at the Charity Commission.

Support is given for charitable purposes connected with the provision of higher education in England. The company currently provides property services and leasing facilities to educational establishments on an 'at arms length' basis.

In 2007/08 the trust had assets of £228,000. The total income and expenditure for the year was £4.5 million. However, it is worth noting that this relates to the funds used to lease buildings from educational establishments and then enter into lease-back arrangements rather than describing the size of funds available. Grants were made totalling £100,000.

Beneficiaries included: University of Nottingham (£21,000); Imperial College (£17,000); University of Reading (£14,000); University of Southampton (£13,000); University of Canterbury Christ Church (£8,000); University of Surrey (£6,500); Royal Holloway (£3,500); University of Kent (£3,500); and University of Exeter Foundation (£2,000).

Exclusions No grants to individuals.

Applications In writing to the correspondent. However, unsolicited applications are only accepted from higher education institutions within England.

The Green and Lilian F M Ainsworth and Family Benevolent Fund

Young people, disability, health, medical research, disadvantage, older people and general

£19,000 (2007/08)

Beneficial area UK, with some preference for north-west England.

RBS Trust Services, Eden, Lakeside, Chester Business Park, Wrexham Road, Chester CH4 9QT

Correspondent The Trust Section Manager

Trustee *The Royal Bank of Scotland plc.*

CC Number 267577

Information available Full accounts were available at the Charity Commission.

The trust states that each year it supports UK charities covering a wide range of interests mainly involving people of all ages who are disadvantaged by either health or other circumstances.

In 2007/08 the trust had an income of £26,000 and grants totalled £19,000.

The largest grant of £1,000 was awarded to Dogs for the Disabled. Remaining grants were mostly for £500 or less each. Other beneficiaries included: the John Holt Cancer Foundation (£800); Edale Mountain Rescue (£750); Butterflies Children's Charity, Chopsticks, Community of the Holy Fire, Everyman Support Group, Groundwork Solent, Independent Age, the Joshua Foundation, the Macular Disease Society and Off the Fence (£500 each); Aid for Romanian Orphanages, Autism Bedfordshire, British Wireless for the Blind, Conwy Community Transport, Depaul Trust, Rutland House School and Sunny Days Children's Fund (£350 each); BIBIC, the Dystonia Society, Get Set Girls, Leukaemia Research, No Panic, Talking Newspaper Association and the Wood Street Mission (£250 each); Downside Fisher Youth Club (£200); and PDSA (£100).

Exclusions No grants to individuals or non-registered charities.

Applications In writing to the trustees, there is no application form.

The Sylvia Aitken Charitable Trust

Medical research and welfare and general

About £200,000 (2007/08)

Beneficial area UK, with a preference for Scotland.

Fergusons Chartered Accountants, 24 Woodside, Houston, Renfrewshire PA6 7DD

Correspondent The Administrator

Trustees *Mrs S M Aitken; Mrs M Harkis; J Ferguson.*

SC Number SC010556

Information available Despite making a written request for the accounts of this trust (including a stamped, addressed envelope) these were not provided. The following entry is based on information filed with the Office of the Scottish Charity Regulator.

Whilst this trust has a preference for medical projects, it has general charitable purposes, making small grants to a wide range of small local organisations throughout the UK, particularly those in Scotland. In 2007/08 the trust had an income of £284,000.

Previous beneficiaries have included Association for International Cancer Research, Barn Owl Trust, British Lung Foundation, British Stammering Association, the Roy Castle Lung Cancer Foundation, Disabled Living Foundation, Epilepsy Research Trust, Friends of the Lake District, Motor Neurone Disease Association, Network for Surviving Stalking, Royal Scots Dragoon Guards Museum Trust, Sense Scotland, Scottish Child Psychotherapy Trust, Tall Ships Youth Trust, Tenovus Scotland, Wood Green Animal Shelters and Young Minds.

Exclusions No grants to individuals; the trust can only support UK registered charities.

Applications In writing to the correspondent. Applicants should outline the charity's objectives and

current projects for which funding may be required. The trustees meet at least twice a year, usually in March/April and September/October.

The Ajahma Charitable Trust

Development, poverty, human rights, health, disability and social welfare

£283,000 (2007/08)

Beneficial area Unrestricted.

275 Dover House Road, London SW15 5BP

Correspondent Suzanne Hunt, Administrator

Trustees *Jennifer Sheridan; Elizabeth Simpson; James Sinclair Taylor.*

CC Number 273823

Information available Accounts were available at the Charity Commission.

This trust was established in 1977 for general charitable purposes. It aims to balance its donations between international and UK charities and focuses on the following areas of work:

- development
- health
- disability
- poverty
- women's issues
- family planning
- human rights
- social need.

Generally, established charities receive grants but new groups and those which may have difficulty finding funds from traditional sources are encouraged.

The 2007/08 trustees' report states that:

The trustees have adopted a policy of seeking and considering applications for charitable funding generally from established charities. They seek to maintain a reasonable balance between charitable activities overseas and in the United Kingdom. This is the first year of a new policy of making larger grants (currently of £50,000 per year) over a three year period from 2008 to 2011 to four specific charities working overseas.

In 2007/08 the trust had assets of almost £3 million and an income of £127,000. Grants were made totalling £283,000.

Headway groups continued to receive support totalling £42,000 (11 grants).

Other beneficiaries included: Action on Disability and Development (£40,000); Oxfam (£20,000); CAMFED, Project Hope; Refugee Council and World Development Trust (£15,000 each); Rainforest Foundation, Redress and Tropical Health and Education Trust (£10,000 each); and Africa Now, Brook and Speakability (£5,000 each).

Exclusions Large organisations with a turnover above £4 million will not normally be considered, nor will applications with any sort of religious bias or those which support animal rights/welfare, arts, medical research, buildings, equipment, local groups or overseas projects where the charity income is less than £500,000 a year. Applications for grants or sponsorship for individuals will not be supported.

Applications The trust have reviewed their grant-making criteria and will now proactively seek and select organisations to which they wish to award grants. They will no longer consider unsolicited applications.

The Alabaster Trust

Christian Church and related activities

£57,000 (2007/08)

Beneficial area UK and overseas.

1 The Avenue, Eastbourne BN21 3YA

Tel. 01323 644579

Email john@caladine.co.uk

Correspondent J R Caladine

Trustees *G A Kendrick; Mrs J Kendrick; Mrs A Sheldrake; Miss A Kendrick.*

CC Number 1050568

Information available Accounts were on file at the Charity Commission, without a list of grants.

This trust was set up to make grants to evangelical Christian organisations in the UK and abroad. In 2007/08 it had an income of £37,000, mostly derived from Gift Aid donations and grants totalled £57,000. Further information was not available.

Exclusions No grants to individuals.

Applications In writing to the correspondent. The trustees meet to consider grants quarterly, in March, June, September and December.

Alba Charitable Trust

Jewish

£71,000 (2006/07)

Beneficial area UK and overseas.

3 Goodyers Gardens, London NW4 2HD

Tel. 020 7434 3494

Correspondent Leslie Glatt, Trustee

Trustees *L Glatt, Chair; Mrs R Glatt; Mrs D Kestel.*

CC Number 276391

Information available Full accounts were on file at the Charity Commission.

This trust has stated that it mainly supports educational institutions in the UK and internationally, but also makes grants towards other causes.

In 2006/07 the trust's assets totalled £261,000. It had an income of £85,000 including £74,000 from voluntary income and made grants totalling £71,000.

Beneficiaries included: Lolev Charitable Trust (£33,000); Chasdey Kohn (£11,000); Inspirations (£6,000); Edu Poor and Friends of Yeshiva Was Sholem Shotz (£5,000 each); Hadras Kodesh Trust (£3,000); HAYC (£2,900); IJDS (£2,200); Ner Yisroel (£1,500); and Gateshead Beis Hatalmud Scholarship Fund (£1,000).

Applications In writing to the correspondent.

The Alborada Trust

Veterinary causes and social welfare

£374,000 (2007/08)

Beneficial area Worldwide.

Fladgate Fielder, 25 North Row, London W1K 6DJ

Correspondent The Trustees

Trustees *Miss K E Rausing; D J Way; R Lerner; Capt. J Nicholson.*

CC Number 1091660

Information available Accounts were on file at the Charity Commission.

This trust was established in October 2001 with an initial donation of £5 million being settled in April 2002.

Unsolicited applications are not requested as the trustees prefer to restrict the area of benefit to:

- Veterinary causes in the United Kingdom and Ireland with activities primarily devoted to the welfare of animals and/or in their associated research.
- Projects throughout the world associated with the relief of poverty, human suffering, sickness or ill health.

In 2007/08 the trust had an income of £5.2 million, including a further £5 million received from the settlor. Grants to 11 organisations totalled £374,000. Assets stood at £10.3 million.

Beneficiaries included: Animal Health Trust (£100,000); Médecins Sans Frontières (£70,000); Royal Veterinary College Animal Care Trust (£50,000); the Brooke Hospital (£30,000); Greenwich Hospital Foundation and Wildlife Vets International (£22,000); British Racing School, International League for Protection of Horses and Racing Welfare (£20,000 each); and Blue Cross and Injured Jockeys Fund (£10,000 each).

Applications Funds are fully committed. The trust does not accept unsolicited applications.

D G Albright Charitable Trust

General

£44,000 (2007/08)

Beneficial area UK, with a preference for Gloucestershire.

Old Church School, Hollow Street, Great Somerford, Chippenham SN15 5JD

Correspondent Richard G Wood, Trustee

Trustees *Hon. Dr G Greenall; R G Wood.*

CC Number 277367

Information available Accounts were on file at the Charity Commission.

In 2007/08 the trust had assets of £1.1 million and an income of £40,000. Grants were made to 28 organisations totalling £44,000.

Donations included those to: St Mary's School – Bromesberrow (£6,000); Maggie's Centres (£5,000); Bromesberrow Parochial Church Council (£2,500); British Empire and Commonwealth Museum, the Countryside Foundation for Education,

the Family Haven – Gloucester, Game Conservancy Trust, Gloucester Family Support, Gloucestershire Macmillan Cancer Service, SSAFA Gloucester Branch and St Luke's Hospital for the Clergy (£2,000 each); Butterfly Conservation, Dean and Chapter – Gloucester Cathedral, Gloucestershire Association for the Blind, Gloucestershire Life Education Centre, Swaziland Charitable Trust, Taste for Adventure Centre and the Three Choirs Festival 2008 (£1,000 each); Castle Gate Family Trust and Gloucestershire Historic Churches Trust (£500 each); Bibles for Children (£300); and Breakthrough Breast Cancer (£250).

Exclusions Grants are not usually made to individuals.

Applications In writing to the correspondent.

The Alchemy Foundation

Health, welfare and famine relief overseas

£299,000 (2007/08)

Beneficial area UK and overseas.

Trevereux Manor, Limpsfield Chart, Oxted RH8 0TL

Correspondent Annabel Stilgoe, Trustee

Trustees *Alex Armitage; Tony Elias; Andrew Murison; Esther Rantzen; Annabel Stilgoe; Holly Stilgoe; Jack E Z Stilgoe; Dr Jemima Stilgoe; Joseph Stilgoe; Richard Stilgoe; Rufus Stilgoe.*

CC Number 292500

Information available Accounts were on file at the Charity Commission, without a list of grants.

The charity was established, as The Starlight Foundation, by a charitable trust deed on 14 August 1985. The name was changed to The Alchemy Foundation on 2 June 1987. The charity's objects are particularly focused on the Orpheus Centre, water projects in the developing world, disability (particularly mobility, access, helplines and communications), social welfare (inner city community projects, disaffected young people, family mediation, homelessness), personal reform, penal reform (work with prisoners, especially young prisoners, and their families), medical research and aid (especially in areas of blindness and disfigurement), individual enterprise (by helping Raleigh International and similar organisations to give opportunities to young people according to need) and respite for carers.

In 2007/08 it had a total income of £330,000, of which £257,000 came from donations received and £48,000 was generated from assets, which totalled £2.6 million. There were 297 grants made totalling £299,000. Donations were broken down as follows:

Category	Value
Disability – mobility, helplines, access	£62,000
Orpheus Centre	£54,000
Developing world water projects	£54,000
Social Welfare – inner city community projects	£51,000
Respite for carers	£23,000
Penal reform and work with prisoners and their families	£16,000
Individuals on behalf of registered charities	£8,500
Medical Research, disability	£4,500
Other	£26,000

Applications In writing to the correspondent.

Alexandra Rose Charities

Supporting charities helping people in need

£130,000 (2008)

Beneficial area England and Wales.

5 Mead Lane, Farnham GU9 7DY

Tel. 01252 726171

Email enquiries@alexandrarose.org.uk

Website www.alexandrarosecharities.org.uk

Correspondent The National Director

Trustees Rt Hon. Lord Wakeham; Andrew Mitchell; March Hancock; Lady Grade; Rt Hon. the Lord Mayor of London (ex-officio); Ms Angela Anderson; Mrs Caroline Clark; March Hancock; Stephen King; Lady Falconer of Thoroton; Mrs Kathryn Langridge; Roger Lomax; Mike Morris; Sir Ian Rankin; Raymond Salisbury-Jones; Lord St John of Bletso; Dominic Tayler; Mrs Sophia Tayler.

CC Number 211535

Information available Accounts were on file at the Charity Commission.

Since being set up in 1912 by Queen Alexandra to sell pink roses on one day of the year to help the needy of London, Alexandra Rose Charities has moved with the times and now helps small charities and community organisations raise money throughout the year on a national basis. These charities look after the needs of children, people with disabilities, vulnerable adults, at risk people of all ages, ex-service personnel, the lonely, older people and the bereaved.

Charities taking part in Rose Days keep 90% of the money collected and those participating in the Rose Raffle keep 80% of ticket sales.

Charities who take over £100 in either activity are eligible to apply for a grant from our Special Appeal Fund each year. Applications are accepted for up to £1,000 for a special project that will benefit the charity or up to £500 for core costs.

To supplement the Special Appeal Fund, Alexandra Rose Charities organises events throughout the year from the annual Rose Golf Tournament to the spectacular Rose Opera Extravaganza.

In 2008 the charities had assets of £648,000 and an income of £262,000. Grants totalling £130,000 were approved.

Beneficiaries included: Manor Farm Boys Club – Bristol (£4,400); RAFA – Addlestone (£2,600); Dystonia Society – South East London (£2,500); Bradford Sea Cadets (£2,100); Disabled Sailing Association – Torquay (£2,000); Bishop's Stortford VIP Club and Harpenden Phoenix Holidays (£1,800 each); Trafford MS Therapy Centre (£1,600); and Bridport Older People's Forum and Enableability – Portsmouth (£1,400).

Applications Only charities participating in Rose Days or the Rose Raffle are eligible to apply.

The Alexis Trust

Christian

£38,000 (2007/08)

Beneficial area UK and overseas.

14 Broadfield Way, Buckhurst Hill IG9 5AG

Correspondent Prof. D W Vere, Trustee

Trustees Prof. D W Vere; C P Harwood; Mrs E M Harwood; Mrs V Vere.

CC Number 262861

Information available Accounts were on file at the Charity Commission.

Support is given to a variety of causes, principally Christian. In 2007/08 the trust had an income of £40,000 and made grants totalling £38,000.

The sum of £32,000 was distributed to various missionary societies with six organisations receiving £1,000 or more, including: County Workers Essex (£2,000); UCCF (£1,200); and Barnabas Fund, Epping Forest Youth for Christ and Tearfund (£1,000 each). A further 92 unlisted beneficiaries received a total of £23,000.

A further £6,500 was distributed to 91 short term missionary projects.

Exclusions No grants for building appeals, or to individuals for education.

Applications In writing to the correspondent, although the trust states that most of the funds are regularly committed.

All Saints Educational Trust

Religious education, home economics

£156,000 to organisations (2007/08)

Beneficial area UK and Commonwealth.

St Katharine Cree Church, 86 Leadenhall Street, London EC3A 3DH

Tel. 020 7283 4485 **Fax** 020 7621 9758

Email aset@aset.org.uk

Website www.aset.org.uk

Correspondent The Clerk

Trustees Revd Dr K G Riglin, Chair; D J Trillo; Mrs A E Cumbers; Dr R L Gwynne; Revd Canon P Hartley; Mrs B E Harvey; J K Hoskin; Dr A R Leeds; Ms D McCrea; Ms J R Moriarty; Dr C C A Pearce; Mrs F M Smith; Ms S J Valentine; Ven. S J Welch; C J Wright; M Behenna.

CC Number 312934

Information available Accounts were on file at the Charity Commission.

The All Saints Educational Trust makes awards annually to students and organisations.

Its main purposes is to:

- help increase the number of new teachers with Qualified Teacher Status
- improve the skills and qualifications of experienced teachers
- encourage research that can assist teachers in their work
- support specifically the teaching of Religious Studies and Home Economics and related areas – such as the promotion of public health and nutrition, both at home and in the Commonwealth.

The trust offers both 'Personal' and 'Corporate' awards.

Corporate awards
The trust wishes to stimulate and support imaginative new projects that will enhance the church's contribution to education.

The trustees are keen to identify and support proactive projects that promote the development of education, particularly in the areas of Religious Education, Home Economics and related areas or subjects, and multi-cultural/inter-faith education.

Priority is given to projects in our core disciplines – especially pump-priming projects – whereby teachers are helped directly or indirectly.

Projects most favoured are those that have the potential to result in lasting benefit, either through the intrinsic quality of the new ideas being put forward, or through the quantity of teachers and/or pupils who will share in the benefit.

Larger corporate applications will be scrutinised carefully to ensure that they are sustainable and give value for money.

Grants will not normally be made for a period in excess of five years.

Our most distinctive and long-term Corporate Award is the All Saints Saxton Fellowship, to which at least £100,000 is allocated every three years.

In 2007/08 the trust had assets totalling £9.4 million which generated an income of £617,000. Grants to organisations (Corporate Awards) totalled £156,000, with £423,000 going to individuals in scholarships and bursaries and £40,000 given for the All Saxton Fellowship.

Beneficiaries of corporate awards included: Sheffield Hallam University (£36,000); National Society (£25,000); British Nutrition Foundation (£20,000); and London Institute for Contemporary Christianity (£6,000).

Exclusions Please note that the trust will not support:

- general or core funds of any organisation
- public appeals
- school buildings, equipment or supplies (except library resources)
- the establishment of new departments in universities and colleges
- general bursary funds of other organisations.

Applications For applications from organisations (not individuals): applicants are invited to discuss their ideas informally with the clerk before requesting an application form. In some cases, a 'link trustee' is appointed to assist the organisation in preparing the application and who will act in a liaison role with the trust. Completed applications are put before the awards committee in April/May, with final decisions made in June.

In 2009 the trust stated: 'In the present financial climate, the trust is not, as far as possible, awarding multi-year grants. Existing grants with a duration of more that one year will be honoured.'

Application forms are available on the trust's website, either in interactive or printable form.

The Pat Allsop Charitable Trust

Education, medical research, children, relief of poverty
£32,000 (2006/07)
Beneficial area UK.

c/o Brown Cooper Monier-Williams, 71 Lincoln's Inn Fields, London WC2A 3JF
Correspondent J P G Randel, Trustee
Trustees *J P G Randel; P W E Kerr; W J K Taylor; N W M MacKilligin.*
CC Number 1030950
Information available Accounts were on file at the Charity Commission.

A number of educational grants are made each year, towards research and organising educational events. The founder of the trust was a partner in Allsop and Co. Chartered Surveyors, Auctioneers and Property Managers, therefore the trust favours supporting those educational projects and charities which have connections with surveying and property management professions. The trustees have a policy of making a small number of major donations (over £2,500) and a larger number of smaller donations.

In 2006/07 it had an income of £62,000 and made 30 grants totalling £32,000.

Beneficiaries included: Duke of Edinburgh's Award and Jewish Care – Minerva Business Lunch (£5,000 each); the Story of Christmas (£3,800); Cambridge International Land Institute, Geoff Marsh Scholarship Fund and Reading Real Estate Foundation (£2,500 each); Crisis, the Honeypot Charity and the Willow Foundation (£1,000 each); Cambridge Mencap, King Alfred School Trust, the Jumbalance Charity, MACS Charity, Maggie's Cancer Caring Centre and Scottish Community Charity (£500 each); Philip Green Memorial Trust (£400); Barnardo's, Get Kids Going, Muscular Dystrophy and Race for Life (£250 each); Cancer Research UK (£200); Children in Need (£150); and Variety Club Children's Charity (£100).

Exclusions No grants to individuals.
Applications The trust does not accept unsolicited applications.

The Almond Trust

Christian
£109,000 (2007/08)
Beneficial area UK and worldwide.

19 West Square, London SE11 4SN
Correspondent Sir Jeremy Cooke, Trustee
Trustees *Sir Jeremy Cooke; Jonathan Cooke; Lady Cooke.*
CC Number 328583
Information available Full accounts were on file at the Charity Commission.

The trust's aims are the support of evangelistic Christian projects, Christian evangelism and the translation, reading, study and teaching of the Bible. Donations are largely recurrent.

In 2007/08 it had an income of £61,000, including £51,000 from donations. Assets stood at £211,000. Grants totalled £109,000. The accounts listed 19 organisations receiving grants of £1,000 or more. All but four had received grants in the previous year.

Beneficiaries included: Lawyers' Christian Fellowship (£16,000 in two grants); London Institute for Contemporary Christianity (£10,000); Agape, Claypath Trust, Barnabas Fund, Daylight Christian Prison Trust, Friends International, Jesus Lane Trust, Latin Link, Overseas Missionary Fellowship, Prison Fellowship, St Mary's Warbleton, UCCF and Wycliffe Bible Translators (£5,000 each); and Baptist Missionary Society (£1,250).

One payment of £2,000 was made to an individual.

Applications In writing to the correspondent, but please note that the trust states it rarely responds to uninvited applications.

The Altajir Trust

Islam, education, science and research

£229,000 (2008)

Beneficial area UK and Arab or Islamic states.

11 Elvaston Place, London SW7 5QG

Tel. 020 7581 3522 **Fax** 020 7584 1977

Email awitrust@tiscali.co.uk

Website www.altajirtrust.org.uk

Correspondent The Trustees

Trustees *Prof. Alan Jones, Chair; Peter Tripp; Prof. Roger Williams; Prof. Charles Tripp.*

CC Number 284116

Information available Accounts were on file at the Charity Commission.

This trust makes grants for the advancement of science, education and research which is beneficial to the community in Britain or any Arab or Islamic state. Support is also given to students at universities in the UK and conferences and exhibitions are sponsored which promote understanding and the study of Islamic culture and arts throughout the world. Grants are made to both individuals and organisations.

In 2008 the trust had an income of £615,000 mostly from donations. Direct charitable expenditure totalled £594,000 of which £229,000 went on grants and £220,000 on student support.

Beneficiaries included: the Prince's School of Traditional Arts (£93,000); University of York – Lectureship (£44,000); the British Museum (£29,000); University of York – Scholarships (£17,000); the Women's Council (£14,000); St Ethelburga's Centre for Reconciliation and Peace (£12,000); Medical Aid for Palestinians (£10,000); Council for British Research in the Levant (£8,300); and Chatham House and University of Birmingham – Interfaith Conference (£1,000 each).

Applications On a form available from the trust's website.

Altamont Ltd

Jewish causes

£850,000 (2007/08)

Beneficial area Worldwide.

18 Green Walk, London NW4 2AJ

Correspondent David Last, Trustee

Trustees *D Last; H Last; Mrs H Kon; Mrs S Adler; Mrs G Wiesenfeld.*

CC Number 273971

Information available Accounts were on file at the Charity Commission, without a list of grants.

In 2007/08 the trust had an income of £73,000 and made grants totalling £850,000 (£170,000 in 2006/07). The sum of £790,000 was carried forward at year end.

Applications In writing to the correspondent.

Alvor Charitable Trust

Christian, humanitarian and social change

£773,000 (2007/08)

Beneficial area UK, with a preference for Sussex, Norfolk and north east Scotland.

Monks Wood, Tompsets Bank, Forest Row RH18 5LW

Correspondent I Wilkins, Chair

Trustees *C Wills; Mrs S Wills; M Atherton; Mrs F Atherton; I Wilkins; Mrs J Wilkins.*

CC Number 1093890

Information available Accounts were on file at the Charity Commission.

Established in August 2002, this Christian and humanitarian charity predominately supports Christian social change projects in the UK and overseas. A proportion of its target funding goes to local projects around Sussex, Norfolk and north-east Scotland where the trust has personal interests. The trust tends to support smaller projects where the grant will meet a specific need. It typically makes a few larger donations each year and a number of smaller grants.

In 2007/08 it had assets of £1.6 million and an income of £687,000, including £613,000 from donations (£325,000 in the previous year). Grants to 66 organisations totalled £773,000.

Beneficiaries included: Kenward Trust (£50,000 in two grants); Salt Sussex Trading Ltd (£40,000 in four grants); Anne Marie School, Ghana (£35,000); Urban Saints (£33,000); Hymns Ancient and Modern (£30,000 in two grants);

Care for the Family and Romance Academy (£25,000 each); Care, Hope UK, the Lighthouse Group, Message Trust, Mid Sussex Citizen Advice Bureau, Saltmine Trust and World In Need (£20,000 each); Carey Films Ltd, Christians in Sport, Positive Parenting, Scripture Union, Trussell Trust and Youth For Christ (£15,000 each); Church Army, First Base Agency, Proclaim Trust and Release International (£10,000 each); Opera Brava (£8,000); Brighton Fareshare, Furniture Now and n:Vision (£5,000 each); Caring 4 Life and Chestnut Tree House (£2,000 each); and Impact Initiatives (£500).

Exclusions The trust does not look to support animal charities or medical charities outside of the geographic areas mentioned above.

Applications In writing to the correspondent.

A M Charitable Trust

Jewish and general

£93,000 (2007/08)

Beneficial area UK and overseas.

Kleinwort Benson Trustees Ltd, 30 Gresham Street, London EC2V 7PG

Correspondent The Administrator

Trustee *Kleinwort Benson Trustees Ltd.*

CC Number 256283

Information available Accounts were on file at the Charity Commission.

This trust supports a range of causes, particularly Jewish organisations but also medical, welfare, arts and conservation charities. Certain charities are supported for more than one year, although no commitment is usually given to the recipient. Grants range between £50 and £5,000 each, but are mostly of £200 to £400.

In 2007/08 it had assets of £1.8 million and an income of £92,000. Grants were made to 45 organisations totalling £93,000 and were divided between 'Jewish' and 'General' donations.

Jewish – 13 grants totalling £81,000
Beneficiaries included: World Jewish Relief and Youth Aliyah – Child Rescue (£15,000 each); Weizmann Institute Foundation (£12,000); British Friends of the Hebrew University of Jerusalem, Jerusalem Foundation and Magen David Adom UK (£10,000 each); British

Friends of Israel Free Loan Association (£4,000); Norwood (£2,000); Yad Vashem Foundation (£200); and Jewish Care (£100).

General – 32 grants totalling £12,000
Beneficiaries included: Cancer Research UK (£2,500); British Heart Foundation (£2,000); Blond Mclndoe Research Foundation (£1,500); NSPCC (£500); Brain Research Trust (£400); Alzheimer's Research Trust and Royal College of Music (£300 each); Alder Hey Children's Hospital League of Friends, Cued Speech Association UK, Kent Air Ambulance Trust, National Osteoporosis Society, Samaritans and Sports Aid Trust (£200 each); Children's Country Holidays Fund (£150); Autism Speaks, Hardman Trust, Sandwich St Mary's Community Trust and Seeing Ear (£100 each); and Thrive (£50).

Exclusions No grants to individuals.

Applications 'Donations are decided periodically by the Trustee having regard to the wishes of the Settlor, and unsolicited appeals are considered as well as causes which have already been supported. Only successful applicants are notified of the trustee's decision.'

The Amalur Foundation Limited

General

£181,000 (2007/08)
Beneficial area Worldwide.

22 Cheyne Walk, London NW4 3QJ
Correspondent Kate Pink, Administrator
Trustees *Rodolfo Zurcher; David Way; Michael Giedroyc; Helen Mellor.*
CC Number 1090476
Information available Accounts were on file at the Charity Commission.

Registered in February 2002, in 2007/08 the charity had assets of £1.5 million, an income of £79,000 and made grants totalling £181,000.

Beneficiaries in the year were: Absolute Return for Kids (£110,000); St Patrick's Catholic Church (£50,000); Prostate Research Campaign UK (£10,000); Brain Tumour Research Campaign (£5,500); Breakthrough Breast Cancer (£3,000); and the Extra Care Charitable Trust (£2,000).

Applications In writing to the correspondent.

Ambika Paul Foundation

Education and young people

£385,000 (2007/08)
Beneficial area UK and India.

Caparo House, 103 Baker Street, London W1U 6LN
Correspondent Lord Paul, Trustee
Trustees *Lord Paul; Lady Paul; Hon. Angad Paul; Hon. Anjli Paul; Hon. Ambar Paul; Hon. Akash Paul.*
CC Number 276127
Information available Full accounts were on file at the Charity Commission.

The trust supports large organisations, registered charities, colleges and universities benefiting children, young adults and students in the UK and India. Main areas of interest are to do with young people and education. Grants usually range from £100 to £3,000.

In 2007/08 it had an income of £885,000, mostly from donations received. Assets stood at £6.7 million. Grants were made totalling £385,000 and were broken down as follows:

Category	Value
Educational projects	£348,000
Social projects	£18,000
Medical trust funds	£10,000
Other grants	£7,800

The beneficiary of the largest grant was University of Westminster (£300,000).

Other beneficiaries included: Bloomsbury Books (£25,000); Chance to Shine (£5,000); CAP Foundation (£11,000); Cultural Centre in Kolkata (£5,500); the Shela Dispensary and Victoria and Albert Museum (£5,000 each); St Mary's Paddington Charitable Trust (£4,000); Coran Family (£1,500); World Punjabi Organisation (£1,000); Earth Restoration Service (£200); Victoria and Albert Museum (£100); and Prostate Cancer (£25).

Exclusions Applications from individuals, including students, are mainly ineligible. Funding for scholarships is made directly to colleges or universities, not to individuals. No expeditions.

Applications In writing to the trustees at the address above. Acknowledgements are sent if a stamped, addressed envelope is enclosed. However, the trust has no paid employees and the enormous number of requests it receives creates administrative difficulties.

Sir John and Lady Amory's Charitable Trust

General

£73,000 (2007/08)
Beneficial area Devon, and elsewhere in the UK.

The Island, Lowman Green, Tiverton EX16 4LA
Tel. 01884 254899
Correspondent Lady Heathcoat Amory, Trustee
Trustees *Sir Ian Heathcoat Amory; Lady Heathcoat Amory; William Heathcoat Amory.*
CC Number 203970
Information available Accounts were on file at the Charity Commission.

The trust was set up in 1961 with a bequest from Sir John and Lady Amory. Its aim is to support charitable purposes principally by use of its annual income.

In 2005/06 the trust had assets of £2.1 million and an income of £440,000. The sale and purchase of investments during the year showed a significant increase in income (£363,000) and expenditure (£248,000). Grants totalled £73,000.

Donations to institutions exceeding £1,000 each went to: Knightshayes Garden Trust (£17,000); Relief for the Elderly and Infirm (£1,400); Tiverton Market Centre (£2,000); and Churches Housing Action Team, Dorchester Abbey Appeal, Queen Alexandra Hospital Home and Shelterbox (£1,000).

Applications In writing to the correspondent.

Viscount Amory's Charitable Trust

Welfare, older people, education and Christian churches

£360,000 to organisations (2007/08)

Beneficial area UK, primarily in Devon.

The Island, Lowman Green, Tiverton, Devon EX16 4LA

Tel. 01884 254899

Correspondent The Trust Secretary

Trustees *Sir Ian Heathcoat Amory; Mrs Catherine Cavender.*

CC Number 204958

Information available Accounts were on file at the Charity Commission.

The objectives of the trust are to donate the annual investment income to charitable institutions or other organisations primarily to benefit the inhabitants of the County of Devon; to assist young people, the poor and aged or in the advancement of education.

In 2007/08 the trust had assets of £12.4 million and an income of £510,000. Grants were made totalling £360,000, broken down into the following categories:

Education – 22 grants totalling £76,000
Beneficiaries included: Blundells Foundation (£20,000); Blundells School (£12,000); Exeter Cathedral School (£8,000); Grenville College (£2,900); King's College (£2,600); Vranch House School and Centre (£2,000); Shebbear College (£1,800); Rudolf Steiner School – South Devon (£1,200); and Bolham Primary School, Cheriton Out of School Group, Truro School and University of Liverpool (£1,000 each).

Religious – 21 grants totalling £61,000
Beneficiaries included: Exeter Cathedral Third Millennium Campaign, Templar Trust and Tiverton Methodist Church (£10,000 each); St Andrew's Church – Tiverton (£2,500); St John the Baptist's Church – Durston, St Mary's Church – Tedbury St Mary and St Rumon's Church – Romansleigh (£2,000 each); and St Andrew's Church – Feniton, St Petrock's Church – West Anstey and Tavistock United Reformed Church (£1,000 each).

General – 30 grants totalling £159,000
Beneficiaries included: London Sailing Project (£86,000); Tiverton Market Centre (£12,000); Devon Community Foundation (£10,000); National Trust (£8,000); Burlescombe and Westleigh Community Hall and Sunningmead Community Association (£5,000 each); Chevithorne Village Hall (£3,500); Tiverton Adventure Play Association (£3,000); Shaldon Regatta (£2,500); Langley House Trust (£2,000); Project Gem (£1,500); and Army Benevolent Fund, Exeter and District Mencap Society, Help for Heroes, Rainbow Living, SSAFA Forces Help and Uplowman Athletic Sports Club (£1,000 each).

Exclusions No grants to individuals from outside south-west England.

Applications In writing to the correspondent, giving general background information, total costs involved, amount raised so far and details of applications to other organisations.

The Ampelos Trust

General

£95,000 (2007/08)

Beneficial area UK.

9 Trinity Street, Colchester CO1 1JN

Correspondent G W N Stewart, Secretary

Trustees *G W N Stewart; Baroness Rendell of Babergh; A M Witt.*

CC Number 1048778

Information available Accounts were on file at the Charity Commission.

In 2007/08 the trust had an income of £254,000 and made grants to eight organisations totalling £95,000.

Beneficiaries included: Kids for Kids (£25,000); Handel House Trust (£20,000); Chester Zoo (£15,000); Medical Foundation for the Care of Victims of Torture, Shelter and Stroke Association (£10,000 each); Princess Royal Trust for Carers (£3,000); and the Seeing Ear (£1,000).

Applications In writing to the correspondent.

The Anchor Foundation

Christian

£260,000 (2007/08)

Beneficial area UK.

PO Box 21107, Alloa FK12 5WA

Email secretary@theanchorfoundation. org.uk

Website www.theanchorfoundation.org. uk

Correspondent The Secretary

Trustees *Mrs P M Thimbleby; Revd M S Mitton; Revd R B Anker-Petersen; Nina Anker-Petersen.*

CC Number 1082485

Information available Accounts were on file at the Charity Commission.

The foundation was registered with the Charity Commission in September 2000. It supports Christian charities concerned with social inclusion, particularly through ministries of healing and the arts.

The grant range for a project is between £500 and £10,000. It is not the normal practice of the charity to support the same project for more than three years (projects which have had three years funding may apply again two years from the payment of the last grant).

Applications for capital and revenue funding are considered. Only in very exceptional circumstances will grants be given for building work.

In 2007/08 it had assets of £5.5 million generating an income of £240,000. Grants totalled £260,000.

Beneficiaries included: Acorn Healing Trust and Good News Family Care (£10,000 each); St John's Church – Edinburgh (£7,500); Exousia (£7,000); London Jesus Centre (£6,100); Bournemouth Spirals Partnerships (£5,600); Sycamore Project (£5,500); and Dundas Foundation, Oasis Uganda, Liverpool YFC, Saltburn Christian Projects, SAT 7 Trust, Hospices of Hope (£5,000 each).

Exclusions No grants to individuals.

Applications Applications can be made online at the Anchor Foundation's website. Full details for applicants are also available online.

Applications are considered at twice yearly trustees meetings in April and November and need to be received by 31 January and 31 July each year.

The foundation regrets that applications cannot be acknowledged. Successful applicants will be notified as soon as possible after trustees' meetings.

Unsuccessful applicants may reapply after 12 months.

The Andrew Anderson Trust

Christian and social welfare

£269,000 to organisations and individuals (2007/08)

Beneficial area UK and overseas.

84 Uphill Road, Mill Hill, London NW7 4QE

Correspondent Miss M S Anderson, Trustee

Trustees *Revd A R Anderson, Chair; Miss A A Anderson; Miss M S Anderson; Mrs M L Anderson.*

CC Number 212170

Information available Accounts were on file at the Charity Commission.

The trust states in its trustees' report that it provides support to a wide range of charitable causes. Most of its money appears to go to evangelical organisations and churches, but it also makes a large number of small grants to health, disability and social welfare charities.

In 2007/08 it had assets of £9.8 million and an income of £278,000. Grants totalled £269,000.

Previous beneficiaries have included Aycliffe Evangelical Church, Christian Medical Fellowship, Concern Worldwide, Emmanuel Baptist Church – Sidmouth, Fellowship of Independent Evangelical Churches, Good Shepherd Mission, Kenward Trust, Latin Link, Proclamation Trust, Rehoboth Christian Centre – Blackpool, Scientific Exploration Society, St Ebbe's PCC – Oxford, St Helen's Church – Bishopsgate, TNT Ministries, Trinity Baptist Church – Gloucester, Whitefield Christian Trust, Weald Trust and Worldshare.

Exclusions Individuals should not apply for travel or education.

Applications The trust has previously stated that it prefers 'to honour existing commitments and initiate new ones through our own contacts rather than respond to applications'.

Andor Charitable Trust

Jewish, arts, health and general

£98,000 (2007/08)

Beneficial area UK and overseas.

c/o Blick Rothenberg, 12 York Gate, Regent's Park, London NW1 4QS

Correspondent The Trustees

Trustees *W D Rothenberg; N C Lederer; Dr D Dean; J Szego.*

CC Number 1083572

Information available Accounts were on file at the Charity Commission.

Registered with the Charity Commission in 2000, in 2007/08 the trust had assets of £3.4 million and an income of £151,000. Grants to 21 organisations totalled £98,000.

Beneficiaries included: Prostate Cancer Charitable Trust (£10,000); British Library – Turning the Pages, the Chicken Shed Theatre Trust and Multiple Sclerosis Trust (£7,500 each); National Autistic Society (£6,000); Battersea Arts Centre, Cove Park, Hampstead Theatre Limited, Pavilion Opera Educational Trust, the Slade School of Fine Art, the Wiener Library Institute of Contemporary History and the Willow Trust (£5,000 each); English National Ballet and National Youth Orchestra of Great Britain (£4,000 each); North London Piano School (£3,000); Young Music Makers (£1,500); and Cato Trust (£1,000).

Applications In writing to the correspondent.

The André Christian Trust

Christian

£46,000 (2008)

Beneficial area UK.

2 Clevedon Close, Exeter EX4 6HQ

Correspondent Andrew K Mowll, Trustee

Trustees *Andrew K Mowll; Stephen P Daykin.*

CC Number 248466

Information available Full accounts were on file at the Charity Commission.

The trust makes grants towards the advancement of Christianity, either through printing and distributing Bible scriptures or through evangelistic work. A number of charities are listed in the trust deed, and they are its principle beneficiaries. Grants appear to mainly be ongoing.

In 2008 the trust had assets of £1.1 million and an income of £47,000 and grants totalled £46,000.

Beneficiaries included: Care for the Family and Exeter Community Family Trust (£8,000 each); Open Air Campaigners – West Country, St Francis – Selsdon and SIFT (£5,000 each); Strangers' Rest Mission (£3,000); and Overseas Missionary Fellowship (£2,000).

Applications In writing to the correspondent. However, the trust states: 'Applications are discouraged since grants are principally made to those organisations which are listed in the trust deed.' Funds are therefore fully committed and unsolicited requests cannot be supported.

The Henry Angest Foundation

General

£113,000 (2008)

Beneficial area UK and overseas.

Arbuthnot House, 20 Ropemaker Street, London EC2Y 9AR

Correspondent The Trustees

Trustees *H Angest; D Angest.*

CC Number 1114761

Information available Accounts were on file at the Charity Commission.

Set up in 2006, in 2008 it had an income of £86,000, mostly from donations. Grants totalled £113,000. The sum of £35,000 was carried forward at year end.

Beneficiaries included: Perth College Development Trust (£80,000); World Pheasant Association (£6,000); Bowel and Cancer Research, British Olympic Association, the R D Crusaders

Foundation and East Midlands Zoological Society (£5,000 each); Cancer Research UK (£2,000); the Salvation Army (£1,000); and Botanic Foundation, PACT, Scottish Ballet and Wycombe Abbey School Foundation (£500).

Applications In writing to the correspondent.

The Animal Defence Trust

Welfare and protection of animals

£81,000 (2007/08)
Beneficial area UK.

Horsey Lightly Fynn, Devon House, 12–15 Dartmouth Street, Queen Anne's Gate, London SW1H 9BL
Website www.animaldefencetrust.org
Correspondent Roy Stokes, Grants Application Secretary
Trustees Marion Saunders; Carole Bowles; Richard J Vines; Jenny Wheadon.
CC Number 263095
Information available Accounts were on file at the Charity Commission.

The trust makes grants for capital projects purely to animal welfare charities. In 2007/08 it had assets totalling £1.2 million and an income of £63,000. Grants were made to 40 organisations, including 25 that had been supported in the previous year, totalling £81,000.

Beneficiaries included: Les Amis des Chats (£4,000); Ferne Animal Sanctuary, Safe Haven for Donkeys in Holy Land and Tree of Life for Animals (£3,000 each); Animals Asia, Blue Cross, Canterbury Horse Rescue, the Cat and Rabbit Centre, Great Dane Adoption Society, Greek Cat Welfare Society, Celia Hammond Animal Trust, Mayhew Animal Home, Saltburn Animal Rescue Association and Yorkshire Swan Rescue Hospital (£2,000 each); and Haworth Animal Rescue, Lagos Animal Protection and Worldwide Veterinary Service (£1,000 each).

Exclusions No grants to individuals.

Applications On a form which can be downloaded from the trust's website. Application must be returned by post to: PO Box 44, Plymouth PL7 5YW.

The Annandale Charitable Trust

Major UK charities

£45,000 (2007/08)
Beneficial area UK.

HSBC Trust Services, Norwich House, Nelson Gate, Commercial Road, Southampton SO15 1GX
Correspondent The Trust Manager
Trustees Mrs C J Duggan; HSBC Trust Company (UK) Ltd.
CC Number 1049193
Information available Accounts were on file at the Charity Commission.

The trust supports a range of major UK charities. In 2007/08 the trust had assets of £10 million, an income of £296,000 and made 15 grants totalling £45,000.

Beneficiaries included: Blue Cross, British Heart Foundation, Cystic Fibrosis Trust, Headway, Kidney Research UK, Make a Wish Foundation, National Stroke Association, NSPCC, RBIB, RNLI and Victim Support (£3,000 each).

Applications In writing to the correspondent. The trust stated that it has an ongoing programme of funding for specific charities and all its funds are fully committed.

The Anson Charitable Trust

General

£115,000 (2007/08)
Beneficial area UK.

Lilies, High Street, Weedon HP22 4NS
Correspondent George Anson, Trustee
Trustees G Anson; K Anson; P Nichols.
CC Number 1111010
Information available Accounts were on file at the Charity Commission.

The trust was set up in 2005 and in 2007/08 it had an income of £100,000 entirely from donations and made 131 grants totalling £115,000. Some organisations received more than one grant. Assets stood at £101,000.

Beneficiaries included: St John Ambulance (£10,000); Royal Opera House (£7,800); Oundle Society (£7,300); Army Benevolent Fund, British

Red Cross and the Pace Centre (£6,000 each); Children in Need (£5,000); Independent Age, Listening Books and National Autistic Society (£3,000 each); Child Bereavement, Give Youth a Break, Sense, Starlight Children's Foundation and UNICEF (£1,000 each); Water Aid (£600); Family Holiday Association, Help for Heroes (£500 each); and Alzheimer's Society (£250).

Grants can also be made to individuals.

Applications In writing to the correspondent.

The Appletree Trust

Disability, sickness and poverty

About £40,000 (2008/09)
Beneficial area UK and overseas, with a preference for Scotland and the north-east Fife district.

The Royal Bank of Scotland plc, Trust and Estate Services, Eden Lakeside, Chester Business Park, Wrexham Road, Chester CH4 9QT
Correspondent The Royal Bank of Scotland plc, Administrator
Trustees The Royal Bank of Scotland plc; Revd W McKane; Revd Dr J D Martin; Revd L R Brown.
SC Number SC004851
Information available Despite making a written request for the accounts of this trust (including a stamped, addressed envelope) these were not provided. The following entry is based on information filed with the Office of the Scottish Charity Regulator.

This trust was established in the will of the late William Brown Moncour in 1982 to relieve disability, sickness and poverty. The settlor recommended that Action Research for the Crippled Child, British Heart Foundation and National Society for Cancer Relief should receive funding from his trust, particularly for their work in the north-east Fife district.

In 2008/09 the trust had an income of £42,000.

Previous beneficiaries have included 1st St Andrews Boys Brigade, Alzheimer Scotland, Arthritis Care In Scotland, the Broomhouse Centre, Children's Hospice Association, Discovery Camps Trust, Home Start East Fife, Marie Curie

13

Cancer Care, PDSA, Prince and Princess of Wales Hospice, RNID, the Salvation Army, Scottish Motor Neurone Disease Association and Scottish Spina Bifida Association.

Exclusions No grants to individuals.

Applications In writing to the correspondent. Trustees meet to consider grants in April.

The John Apthorp Charitable Trust

General

£101,000 (2008)

Beneficial area UK, with a preference for Radlett.

Myers Clark, Iveco House, Station Road, Watford WD17 1DL

Correspondent Mrs L D Fenton

Trustees *John Dorrington Apthorp; Dr D Arnold; Justin Apthorpe.*

CC Number 289713

Information available Full accounts were available from the Charity Commission website.

The trust was established by its eponymous settlor in 1983 with general charitable purposes.

In 2008 it had assets of £100,000 and an income of £117,000, mostly from donations. Grants were made to 12 organisations totalling £101,000.

Recipients included: the Radlett Centre (£21,000); Radlett Lodge School – National Autistic Society (£11,000); All Saints Church, NACOA, London Academy, Radlett Music Club and Tay Ghillies Association (£10,000 each); RAFT (£6,000); Radlett Choral Society (£5,800); Radlett Art Society (£5,200); the Rotary Club of Radlett (£1,000); and Bronsdale Kids Club (£500).

Applications Unsolicited appeals are not welcome and will not be answered. The trustees carry out their own research into prospective grant areas.

The Archbishop of Canterbury's Charitable Trust

Christianity and welfare

£355,000 (2008)

Beneficial area Worldwide.

1 The Sanctuary, Westminster, London SW1P 3JT

Tel. 020 7222 5381

Correspondent Peter Beesley, Secretary

Trustees *Archbishop of Canterbury; Miss Sheila Cameron; Christopher Smith; Timothy Livesey.*

CC Number 287967

Information available Accounts were on file at the Charity Commission.

This trust was established in 1983 by the former Archbishop of Canterbury, Lord Runcie, to advance the Christian religion and Christian education, in particular the objects and principles of the Church of England, as well as supporting individuals working towards these goals. The trust deed states that trustees should hold particular interest towards:

- people training for the ministry and church work
- ministers, teachers and the church workers who are in need, and their dependants
- the extension of education in, and knowledge of, the faith and practice of the Church of England
- the development of work of any church, union of churches, denominations or sects which will further the Christian religion generally.

A proportion of the trust's funds are distributed through the Archbishop of Canterbury Trinity Church Fund, which can give support worldwide to Anglican projects at the discretion of the Archbishop of Canterbury. However, the correspondent states that there is much call on these funds and therefore the success rate of applications is very small.

There are also three smaller, restricted funds which are administered as part of this trust.

- The Michael Ramsey Chair Fund, which finances the Michael Ramsey Chair in Anglican and Ecumenical Theology at the University of Kent.
- The Dick and Sheila Stallard Fund, which supports church-related work in China and the Far East, rarely supporting work in the Middle East.

- The Living Memory Rogers Harrison Lozo Relief Fund, which supports British-born retired Anglican bishops and priests, and their wives and widows living in England, as well as supporting people who are poor, blind, older or disabled in Greater London.

In 2008 it had assets of £2.2 million. The total income was £202,000, including £95,000 in donations received. Grants were made totalling £355,000.

Beneficiaries included: the Lambeth Conference (£60,000); Common World Seminar (£10,000); Anglican Centre in Rome (£6,500); Windle Trust (£7,500); Diocese in Europe (£5,000); St Andrew's Ecumenical Trust (£2,000); and Action Around Bethlehem, Burning Bush Barn Project, the Cathedral Archer Project, Crisis, National Churches Trust, St John's College Durham and Terrence Higgins Trust (£1,000 each).

Applications The trust receives a number of enquiries for grants which are dealt with initially by the Bursar at Lambeth Palace. If the enquiry meets the grant criteria then the request is put to the trustees who will then consider and approve those grant requests which meet the objectives of the trust.

Archbishop of Wales' Fund for Children

Children

£52,000 (2007)

Beneficial area Wales.

Church in Wales, 37–39 Cathedral Road, Cardiff CF11 9XF

Email awfc@churchinwales.org.uk

Correspondent The Secretary

Trustees *Revd J Michael Williams, Chair; Cheryl Beach; Ruth Forrester; Caroline Owen; James Tovey.*

CC Number 1102236

Information available Accounts were on file at the Charity Commission.

This fund was established in 2004. Its purpose is to support children in need and their families and local communities, through the work of organisations in this order of priority:

- those in the Dioceses of the Church in Wales

- those associated with other Christian bodies which are members of Cytun (Churches Together in Wales)
- other organisations working with children in Wales.

The fund has received substantial donations from Church in Wales congregations, particularly from collections at the annual Christingle services. In 2007 it had an income of £63,000 and made grants totalling £39,000. Assets stood at £71,000.

Previous beneficiaries have included Aberdare Children's Contact Centre, Borth Out of School Club, Local Aid for Children, Maesgeirchen Healthy Living Centre, Penplas Family Centre Project, Salvation Army Risca Corps, Sennybridge Squirts and Youth Outreach Grosmont Group.

In 2008 total income was £65,000 and out of 52 applications, grants totalling £52,000 were distributed to 27 projects.

Beneficiaries included: the Bridge Mentoring Plus Scheme; Cardiff People First; Family Awareness Drug and Support; MENFA; Pontllanfraith, Brecon, Aberdare and Merthyr Tydfil Contact Centres; and Valley Kids. A number of church-based projects were also supported.

Applications Application forms are available from the correspondent.

The John M Archer Charitable Trust

General

About £90,000 (2008/09)
Beneficial area UK and overseas.

12 Broughton Place, Edinburgh EH1 3RX
Correspondent Mrs W Grant, Secretary
Trustees *Gilbert B Archer; Mrs A Morgan; Mrs W Grant; Mrs C Fraser; Mrs I C Smith.*
SC Number SC010583
Information available Despite making a written request for the accounts of this trust (including a stamped, addressed envelope) these were not provided. The following entry is based on information filed with the Office of the Scottish Charity Regulator.

The trust supports local, national and international organisations, in particular those concerned with:

- prevention or relief of individuals in need
- welfare of people who are sick, distressed or afflicted
- alleviation of need
- advancement of education
- advancement of religious or missionary work
- advancement of medical or scientific research and discovery
- preservation of Scottish heritage and the advancement of associated cultural activities.

In 2008/09 the trust had an income of £98,000.

Previous beneficiaries have included Cambodian Hospital Siem Reap for Children, the Canonmills Baptist Church, Castlebrae School Tutoring Programme, Erskine Stewarts Melville College – Arts Centre, Mercy Corps Scotland, the Bobby Moore Fund, Red Cross – Aberdeen Guest House and Royal Liverpool University Hospital – Macular Degeneration Research.

Applications In writing to the correspondent.

The Ardwick Trust

Jewish, welfare and general

£40,000 (2007/08)
Beneficial area UK, Israel and the developing world.

c/o Knox Cropper, 24 Petworth Road, Haslemere GU27 2HR
Correspondent Janet Bloch, Trustee
Trustees *Mrs J B Bloch; Dominic Flynn; Miss Judith Portrait.*
CC Number 266981
Information available Accounts were on file at the Charity Commission.

The trust supports Jewish welfare, along with a wide band of non-Jewish causes to include social welfare, health, education (especially special schools), older people, conservation and the environment, child welfare, disability and medical research. Although the largest grants made by the trust are to Jewish organisations, the majority of recipients are non-Jewish.

In 2007/08 it had assets of £1.1 million and an income of £190,000. Grants were made to 194 organisations totalling £40,000. The main beneficiary, as in previous years, was Nightingale House which received two grants totalling £5,000.

A further six organisations received grants of £1,000 each: British Friends of the Hebrew University – Jerusalem, British Technion Society, Jewish Care, UJIA, Weizmann UK and World Jewish Relief.

Remaining beneficiaries were all for £500, £200 or £100 each. Beneficiaries included: Book Aid International, Bowel Cancer UK, Cheltenham Ladies' College – bursaries fund, Combat Stress, Council of Christians and Jews, Dystonia Society, Elimination of Leukaemia Fund, Help the Aged, Holidays with Help, Jubilee Sailing Trust, Meningitis Trust, National Trust, North London Hospice, Princess Royal Trust for Carers, RNIB, Shaare Zedek UK, Talking Newspaper Association of the UK, Tree Aid, YWCA and Whizz-Kids.

Exclusions No grants to individuals.

Applications In writing to the correspondent.

The Argentarius Foundation

General

£111,000 (2007/08)
Beneficial area UK.

Goodman & Co, 14 Basing Hill, London NW11 8TH
Correspondent Philip Goodman
Trustees *E Marbach; J Jackson; A Josse.*
CC Number 1079980
Information available Accounts were on file at the Charity Commission, without a list of grants.

Set up in 2000 with general charitable purposes, in 2007/08 the trust had assets of £823,000 and an income of £50,000. Grants to 10 organisations totalled £111,000.

The Trustee's Report stated that: 'The trustees' intention is to continue to give away a substantial proportion of the foundation's assets each year for the foreseeable future'.

Applications In writing to the correspondent.

Armenian General Benevolent Union London Trust

Armenian education, culture and welfare

£85,000 to organisations and individuals (2008)

Beneficial area UK and overseas.

51c Parkside, Wimbledon Common, London SW19 5NE

Correspondent The Chair

Trustees *Dr Berge Azadian; Berge Setrakian; Hampar Chakardjian; Aris Atamian; Mrs Annie Kouyoumdjian; Mrs Noushig Yakoubian Setrakian; Assadour Guzelian; Mrs Anahid Manoukian; Mrs Arline Medazoumian; Haig Messerlian; Ms Armine Afrikian.*

CC Number 282070

Information available Accounts were on file at the Charity Commission.

The purpose of the trust is to advance education among Armenians, particularly those in the UK, and to promote the study of Armenian history, literature, language, culture and religion.

In 2008 it had assets of almost £3.1 million and an income of £165,000. Grants were made totalling £85,000 including £44,000 in 18 student loans and grants.

Grants categorised as 'Aid to Armenia, charitable and other grants' included those to: the Rural Development Project (£21,000); RP Musical Management (£3,000); and Spring Remembrance Concert (£2,500).

Exclusions No support for projects of a commercial nature or for education for individual students.

Applications In writing to the correspondent. Applications are considered all year around.

The Armourers' and Brasiers' Gauntlet Trust

Materials science and general

£225,000 (2007/08)

Beneficial area UK, with some preference for London.

Armourers' Hall, 81 Coleman Street, London EC2R 5BJ

Tel. 020 7374 4000 **Fax** 020 7606 7481

Email info@armourersandbrasiers.co.uk

Website www.armourersandbrasiers.co.uk

Correspondent The Secretary

Trustees *S G B Martin, Chair; J S Haw; D E H Chapman; Prof. C J Humphreys; Ven. C J H Wagstaff; Rr Adm. J P W Middleton.*

CC Number 279204

Information available Accounts were on file at the Charity Commission.

The trust, which provides the charitable outlet for the Worshipful Company of Armourers and Brasiers, was set up in 1979. The objectives of the trust are:

- support for education and research in materials science and technology and for basic science in schools
- encouragement of the understanding and preservation of historic armour
- encouragement of the armourers' trade in the armed services
- encouragement of professional excellence in the training of young officers in the Royal Armoured Corps
- to consider appeals in the following overall categories:
  – community, social care and armed forces
  – children, young people and general education; medical and health
  – art, arms and armour
  – Christian mission.

The trust funds are relatively modest; therefore applications for large sums should be avoided. Regular annual grants are not a policy of the trust at present, but charities can still apply for grants on an annual basis.

In 2007/08 the trust had assets of almost £6 million, an income of £399,000 and made grants totalling £225,000.

Exclusions In general grants are not made to:

- organisations or groups which are not registered charities

- individuals (including sponsorship)
- organisations or groups whose main object is to fund or support other charitable bodies
- organisations or groups which are in direct relief of any reduction of financial support from public funds
- charities with a turnover of over £1 million
- charities which spend over 10 per cent of their income on fundraising activities
- charities whose accounts disclose substantial financial reserves
- political or commercial appeals.

The trust does not make grants towards general maintenance, repair or restoration of buildings, including ecclesiastical buildings, unless there is a long standing connection with the Armourers' and Brasiers' Company or unless of outstanding importance to the national heritage.

Applications In writing to the correspondent, with a copy of the latest annual report and audited accounts. Applications are considered quarterly.

The Artemis Charitable Trust

Psychotherapy, parent education and related activities

£59,000 (2007)

Beneficial area UK.

Brook House, Quay Meadow, Bosham PO18 8LY

Correspondent Richard Evans, Trustee

Trustees *R W Evans; D S Bergin; W A Evans; D J Evans; M W Evans.*

CC Number 291328

Information available Accounts were on file at the Charity Commission.

The trust was set up in 1985, its 2005 trustees' report states: 'The policy of the trust has continued to be the making of grants to aid the provision of counselling, psychotherapy, parenting, human relationship training and related activities.'

In 2007 it had assets of £1.4 million and an income of £64,000. Grants totalled £59,000 and were categorised as follows, shown with examples of grants:

Research – £47,000
University of Leeds (£34,000); Durham University (£13,000); and Core System Trust (£270).

Social Welfare – £12,000
Primhe (£12,000).

Exclusions 'We cannot entertain applications either from individuals or from organisations which are not registered charities.'

Applications 'Applicants should [...] be aware that most of the trust's funds are committed to a number of major ongoing projects and that spare funds available to meet new applications are very limited.'

The Ove Arup Foundation

Construction: education and research

£102,000 (2007/08)
Beneficial area Unrestricted.

c/o 13 Fitzroy Street, London W1T 4BQ

Website www.theovearupfoundation. com

Correspondent The Secretary

Trustees R B Haryott, Chair; M Shears; D Michael; R F Emmerson; T M Hill; C Cole; R Hough; T O'Brien; R Yau.

CC Number 328138

Information available Accounts were on file at the Charity Commission.

The trust was established in 1989 with the principal objective of supporting education in matters associated with the built environment, including construction-related academic research. The trustees are appointed by the board of the Ove Arup Partnership. It gives grants for research and projects, including start-up and feasibility costs.

In 2007/08 the foundation had assets of £2.7 million and an income of £107,000. Grants were made to seven organisations totalling £102,000.

Beneficiaries were: University of Cape Town Trust (£50,000); John Doyle Construction Ltd – 'Constructionarium' (£15,000); the Industrial Trust (£14,000); Human Resources Theatre (£10,000); Midlands Architecture and Designed Environment (£7,000); Association of Teachers of Mathematics (£5,000); and Anglo-Danish Society (£1,500).

Exclusions No grants to individuals, including students.

Applications In writing to the correspondent, with brief supporting financial information. Trustees meet quarterly to consider applications (March, June, September and December).

The AS Charitable Trust

Christian, development and social concern

£70,000 (2007/08)
Beneficial area UK and developing countries.

Bix Bottom Farm, Henley-on-Thames RG9 6BH

Correspondent The Administrator

Trustees Roy Calvocoressi; Mrs Caroline Eady; George Calvocoressi; Simon Sampson.

CC Number 242190

Information available Accounts were on file at the Charity Commission.

This trust makes grants in particular to projects which combine the advancement of the Christian religion with Christian lay leadership, with developing world advancement, with peacemaking and reconciliation or with other areas of social concern.

In 2007/08 the trust had assets of £8.4 million, an income of £210,000 and made 29 grants to 17 different organisations totalling £70,000.

Beneficiaries included: Christian International Peace Service (£40,000 in nine grants); the De Laszlo Foundation (£10,000); GRACE (£9,000 in nine grants); Congo Church Association (£5,000); and Christian Healing Centre – the Well, Leamington Spa, Lambeth Partnership, the Message Trust and Toynbee Hall (£1,000 each).

Exclusions Grants to individuals or large charities are very rare. Such applications are discouraged.

Applications In writing to the correspondent.

Ashburnham Thanksgiving Trust

Christian

£76,000 to organisations
(2007/08)
Beneficial area UK and worldwide.

Agmerhurst House, Ashburnham, Battle TN33 9NB

Correspondent The Trustees

Trustees Mrs M Bickersteth; E R Bickersteth; R D Bickersteth; Mrs R F Dowdy.

CC Number 249109

Information available Full accounts were on file at the Charity Commission.

The trust supports a wide range of Christian mission organisations and other Christian organisations which are known to the trustees, in the UK and worldwide. Individuals are also supported.

In 2007/08 the trust's assets totalled £5.5 million and an income of £181,000. A total of £98,000 was distributed in 132 grants, of which £76,000 went to organisations. Further monies were distributed in restricted grants and grants to individuals.

There were 22 grants made of £1,000 or more. Beneficiaries included: New Destiny Trust (£4,800); Genesis Arts Trust (£3,900); St Stephen's Society – Hong Kong (£3,400); Open Doors (£3,000); Prison Fellowship (£2,700); Wycliffe Bible Translators (£2,500); Romance Academy (£2,100); Interserve (£2,000); Lawrence Barham Memorial Trust (£1,900); Ashburnham Christian Trust, London School of Theology and Overseas Missionary Fellowship (£1,800 each); Care Trust and Tear Fund (£1,400 each); Micah Trust and Universities and Colleges Christian Fellowship (£1,300 each); Latin American Missions (£1,200); and Lambeth Partnership and Wycliffe Hall Oxford (£1,000 each).

Other beneficiaries included: Advantage Africa (£700); Titus Trust (£600); Seed Savers Trust and Trinity Fellowship (£500 each); Edinburgh Medical Missionary Society (£400); SAT-7 Trust Ltd (£390); Slavic Gospel Association (£340); Hebron Trust (£330); United Mission to Nepal (£320); Ambassadors in Sport (£300); Operation Mobilisation (£250); Cancer Research UK (£200); Sussex Historic Churches Trust (£170);

Church Society (£120); and Latin Link and Media Watch UK (£100 each).

During the year the sum of £8,300 was distributed to nine individuals.

Exclusions No grants for buildings.

Applications The trust has stated that its funds are fully committed to current beneficiaries. Unfortunately, it receives far more applications than it is able to deal with.

A J H Ashby Will Trust

Wildlife, heritage, education and children

£53,000 (2007/08)

Beneficial area UK, especially Lea Valley area of Hertfordshire.

HSBC Trust Company (UK) Ltd, Trust Services, Norwich House, Nelson Gate, Commercial Road, Southampton SO15 1GX

Correspondent The Trust Manager

Trustee *HSBC Trust Company (UK) Ltd.*

CC Number 803291

Information available Accounts were on file at the Charity Commission.

The trust was established in 1990 to support wildlife throughout the UK, particularly birds, as well as heritage, education projects and young people specifically in the Lea Valley area of Hertfordshire.

In 2007/08 the trust had and an income of £243,000. There were 11 grants made totalling £53,000.

Beneficiaries included: RSPB (£25,000 in four grants); Downhills Primary School and St Joseph's R C Primary School (£5,000 each); the Hertford Museum Charity (£4,400); Cromwell Park Primary School and Greenhouse Schools Project Limited (£3,000 each); and Whizz Kidz (£500).

Exclusions No grants to individuals or students.

Applications In writing to the correspondent.

The Laura Ashley Foundation

Art and design, higher education and local projects in mid-rural Wales

£464,000 (2007/08)

Beneficial area Mostly Wales, other areas considered.

The Laura Ashley Foundation, Rhydoldog House, Cwmdauddwr, Rhayader, Powys LD6 5HB

Website www.lauraashleyfoundation.org.uk

Correspondent The Secretary

Trustees *Jane Ashley, Chair; Prof. Susan Golombok; Martyn C Gowar; Emma Shuckburgh; Helena Appio; David Goldstone.*

CC Number 288099

Information available Accounts were on file at the Charity Commission.

The foundation was set up in 1986 in memory of Laura Ashley by her family. It has a strong commitment to art and design and also to Wales, particularly Powys, where the Ashley business was first established.

The Laura Ashley Foundation is constantly reviewing funding policies. For this reason, we tend to be re-active grant givers, rather than proactive. Very few unsolicited applications receive funding. To avoid disappointment, we suggest checking before applying.

In 2007/08 the trust had assets of £10.4 million, an income of £342,000 and made grants totalling £464,000.

Exclusions The foundation does not fund individuals or business ventures.

Applications Potential applicants are encouraged to check the foundation's website before submitting an application.

The Ashworth Charitable Trust

Welfare

£123,000 to organisations (2007/08)

Beneficial area UK and worldwide, with some preference for certain specific needs in Honiton, Ottery St Mary, Sidmouth and Wonford Green surgery, Exeter.

Foot Anstey, Senate Court, Southernhay Gardens, Exeter EX1 1NT

Tel. 01392 411221 **Fax** 01392 685220

Email ashworthtrust@btinternet.com

Correspondent Mrs G Towner

Trustees *C F Bennett, Chair; Mrs S E Webberley; Mrs K A Gray; G D R Cockram.*

CC Number 1045492

Information available Accounts were on file at the Charity Commission.

The trust was founded by Mrs C E Crabtree in 1995. The trust currently considers applications for and makes grants as appropriate to:

- Ironbridge Gorge Museum Trust
- people living in the areas covered by the medical practices and social services in Honiton, Ottery St Mary, Sidmouth and Wonford Green surgery, Exeter. Such grants are to be paid for particularly acute needs
- humanitarian projects either to other charities or to individuals.

In 2007/08 the trust had assets of £3.9 million and an income of £146,000. Grants were made to 40 organisations totalling £123,000.

The largest grants went to: UNICEF UK (£11,000); Hospiscare and Ironbridge Gorge Museum Trust (£10,000 each). Other beneficiaries included: Find Your Feet (£5,000); Zero Centre (Merseyside) and Children's Overseas Relief Fund (£4,000 each); The John Fawcett Foundation and Cerebral Palsy Africa (£3,000 each); Hope Direct and The Woodford Foundation (£2,500 each); New Bridge (£2,000); Hope's Place (£1,500); Dream Holidays (£1,000); and Back to Work (£500).

A further £3,500 was given to 19 individuals from the Doctors' and Social Services Fund.

Please note: these grant examples are not necessarily indicative of future giving.

Exclusions No grants for:

- research-based charities
- animal charities
- heritage charities such as National Trust or other organisations whose aim is the preservation of a building, museum, library and so on (with the exception of the Ironbridge Gorge Museum)
- faith-based charities, unless the project is for primarily humanitarian purposes and is neither exclusive to those of that particular faith or evangelical in its purpose. Grants to individuals are strictly limited to the geographical area and purpose specified in the general section.

Applications In writing to the correspondent.

The Ian Askew Charitable Trust

General

£92,000 (2007/08)

Beneficial area UK, with a preference for Sussex.

c/o Baker Tilly, 18 Mount Ephraim Road, Tunbridge Wells TN1 1ED

Correspondent The Trustees

Trustees J R Hecks, Chair; Mrs C Pengelley; R A R Askew; J B Rank; R P G Lewis.

CC Number 264515

Information available Accounts were on file at the Charity Commission.

Grants are given to a wide variety of charitable bodies through the country with a preference for those connected with the county of Sussex.

In 2007/08 the trust had assets of £7.8 million and an income of £388,000. Grants to 192 charitable organisations totalled £92,000.

The majority of grants to organisations were for £500 or less, with 14 for £1,000 or more. Beneficiaries included: Sussex Heritage Trust (£2,500); Friends of Home Physiotherapy Service and Meningitis UK (£1,500 each); and Friends of Nakura, Kambia Hospital Appeal, Kids Kidney Research, the Landmark Trust, Laughton Community Primary School, the Salvation Army, Save the Children Fund, St Barnabas Hospice, St John Ambulance and Wells for India (£1,000 each).

In addition to the above mentioned donations the trust maintains the woodlands at Plashett Estate, East Sussex, the main part of which is designated as a site of special and scientific interest. The woodlands are used principally for educational purposes.

Applications In writing to the correspondent. Applications are considered every other month.

The Association of Colleges Charitable Trust

Further education colleges

£223,000 (2007/08)

Beneficial area UK.

2–5 Stedham Place, London WC1A 1HU

Website www.aoc.co.uk

Correspondent The Trust Manager

Trustees Alice Thiagaraj; Peter Brophy; M Doel; David Forrester; John Bingham; R Eve.

CC Number 1040631

Information available Accounts were on file at the Charity Commission.

The Association of Colleges was created in 1996 as the single voice to promote the interests of further education colleges in England and Wales. It is responsible for administering two programmes, the largest of these is the Beacon Awards, which provide monetary grants to specific initiatives within further education colleges. The other programme that operates within the trust is the AoC Gold Awards.

Established in 1994, the Beacon Awards recognise and promote the interdependence of further education colleges and business, professional and voluntary sector organisations to their mutual advantage. The aim of the programme is to highlight the breadth and quality of education in colleges throughout the UK and increase understanding of colleges' contribution to UK educational skills policy and economic and social development.

The awards:

- recognise imaginative and exemplary teaching and learning practice in colleges

- draw attention to provision which encourages and supports learners to approach challenges positively and creatively
- support learning and continuous improvement through the dissemination of award-bearing practice.

Applications may be for a programme, course, or project or for some other aspect of college provision – teaching, learning, guidance or support. To be eligible, initiatives should show evidence of imaginative yet sustainable teaching and learning practice or other relevant provision. It must also fulfil the following criteria.

- It must meet the specific requirements set out by the sponsors of the particular award (see relevant page in the awards section of the prospectus).
- It must be subject to evaluation/quality assurance to influence the continuing development of the initiative.
- It must have been running for at least one academic session before the deadline for applications.
- It must have features which actively promote exemplary teaching and learning.
- It must be of benefit to one or more groups of students or trainees who will be identified and described in the application.
- It must have wider relevance and applicability making it of value to other colleges as an example of good practice and innovation.

Each award has separate criteria in the interests of the area of work of the sponsor. They range from broad educational development to the promotion of particular courses or subjects, covering most aspects of further education.

The other scheme operated by the trust is the AoC Gold Awards for Further Education Alumni, which reward former members of further education colleges who have since excelled in their chosen field or profession.

In 2007/08 the trust had an income of £66,000. Total expenditure for the year was £223,000, mostly given in Beacon Awards.

Exclusions Grants are not made to individuals.

Applications See the trust's website for further information.

The Astor Foundation

Medical research and general

£107,000 (2007/08)

Beneficial area UK.

PO Box 3096, Marlborough SN8 3WP

Email astor.foundation@virgin.net

Correspondent Lisa Rothwell-Orr, Secretary

Trustees *R H Astor, Chair; Lord Astor of Hever; Lord Latymer; C Astor; Dr H Swanton; Prof J Cunningham.*

CC Number 225708

Information available Accounts were on file at the Charity Commission.

The following information is taken from the foundation's accounts.

The primary object of the charity is medical research in its widest sense, favouring research on a broad front rather than in specialised fields. For guidance, this might include general medical equipment or equipment for use in research, or grants to cover travelling and subsistence expenses for doctors and students studying abroad.

In general, the foundation gives preference to giving assistance with the launching and initial stages of new projects and filling in gaps or shortfalls.

In addition to its medical connection, historically the foundation has also supported initiatives for children and youth groups, the disabled, the countryside, the arts, sport, carers groups and animal welfare.

In 2007/08 the trust had assets of £3.5 million generating an income of £140,000. Grants to 60 organisations totalled £107,000.

Beneficiaries included: Special Boat Service (£7,000); League of Friends – University College London Hospitals (£5,000); Combat Stress and Help the Hospices (£4,000 each); Samaritans (£3,000); Alzheimer's Disease Society (£2,500); British Forces Foundation, RoSPA and Tank Museum (£2,000 each); Addaction, Barn Owl Trust, Meningitis Trust, Prostate Cancer Research Foundation and Winton's Wish (£1,500 each); and Aldeburgh Music, Bibles for Children and Broadway Trust (£1,000).

Exclusions No grants to individuals or towards salaries. Grants are given to registered charities only.

Applications There are no deadline dates or application forms. Applications should be in writing to the correspondent and must include accounts and an annual report if available.

The trustees meet twice yearly, usually in October and April. If the appeal arrives too late for one meeting it will automatically be carried over for consideration at the following meeting. An acknowledgement will be sent on receipt of an appeal. No further communication will be entered into unless the trustees raise any queries regarding the appeal, or unless the appeal is subsequently successful.

The Astor of Hever Trust

Young people, medical research and education

£32,000 (2007/08)

Beneficial area UK and worldwide, with a preference for Kent and the Grampian region of Scotland.

Frenchstreet House, Westerham TN16 1PW

Tel. 01959 565070

Correspondent The Trustees

Trustees *John Jacob, Third Baron Astor of Hever; Hon. Philip D P Astor; Hon Camilla Astor.*

CC Number 264134

Information available Accounts were on file at the Charity Commission.

The trust gives grants UK-wide and internationally. It states that there is a preference for Kent and the Grampian region of Scotland, although the preference for Kent is much stronger.

When Gavin Astor, second Baron Astor of Hever, founded the trust in 1955, its main areas of support were the arts, medicine, religion, education, conservation, young people and sport. Reflecting the settlor's wishes, the trust makes grants to local youth organisations, medical research and educational programmes. Most beneficiaries are UK-wide charities or a local branch.

In 2007/08 the trust had assets of £1.1 million and an income of £39,000. Grants to 83 organisations totalled £32,000.

In receipt of funding of £1,000 or more were: Royal British Legion (£2,100 in four grants); National Autistic Society (£1,800 in three grants); and Bryanston School, Game Conservancy Trust, Launde Abbey Trust and Leicester Samaritans, Logie Coldstone Trust, Mercy Ships, Luke Rees-Pulley Charitable Trust and Take Heart (£1,000 each).

Other beneficiaries included: Compaid Trust, Swinfen Charitable Trust and War Memorials Trust (£500 each); 3H Fund and NSPCC (£300 each); Asthma UK and Whizz Kidz (£250 each); Books Abroad and North East of Scotland Musical School (£150 each); Bone Cancer Research UK (£100); and Friends of Crockham Hill School, Kent Autistic Trust, Project Trust, Save the Children and St Christopher's Hospice (£50 each).

Exclusions No grants to individuals.

Applications In writing to the correspondent. Trustees meet twice each year. Unsuccessful applications are not acknowledged.

The Aurelius Charitable Trust

Conservation of culture and the humanities

£81,000 (2007/08)

Beneficial area UK.

Briarsmead, Old Road, Buckland, Betchworth RH3 7DU

Tel. 01737 842186

Email philip.haynes@tiscali.co.uk

Correspondent P E Haynes, Trustee

Trustees *W J Wallis; P E Haynes.*

CC Number 271333

Information available Accounts were on file at the Charity Commission.

During the settlor's lifetime, the income of the trust was distributed broadly to reflect his interests in the conservation of culture inherited from the past, and the dissemination of knowledge, particularly in the humanities field. Since the settlor's death in April 1994, the trustees have continued with this policy.

Donations are preferred to be for seed-corn or completion funding not otherwise available. They are usually one-off and range from £500 to £3,000.

In 2007/08 it has assets of £2.1 million, which generated an income of £96,000. Donations were made to 25 organisations totalling £81,000.

Beneficiaries included: the British Academy (£7,500); British School at Athens (£6,000); the Wallace Collection (£5,000); London International Film School (£4,000); University of Roehampton (£5,000); English National Opera (£3,400); National Museums Liverpool (£2,900); Courtauld Institute of Art (£2,800); Glasgow School of Art (£2,750); Royal Academy of Arts (£2,000); the Quaker Tapestry at Kendal Ltd and the Seeing Ear (£1,000 each); the Worcestershire Historical Society (£600); and the Dugdale Society (£200).

Exclusions No grants to individuals.

Applications In writing to the correspondent. Donations are generally made on the recommendation of the trust's board of advisors. Unsolicited applications will only be responded to if a stamped, addressed envelope is included. Trustees meet twice a year.

The Avenue Charitable Trust

General

£257,000 (2007/08)
Beneficial area Worldwide.

c/o Messrs Sayers Butterworth, 18 Bentinck Street, London W1U 2AR
Tel. 020 7935 8504
Correspondent Susan Simmons
Trustees R D L Astor; Hon. Mrs B A Astor; G W B Todd.
CC Number 264804
Information available Accounts were available from the Charity Commission.

In 2007/08 the trust an income of £378,000, mostly from donations and made grants totalling £257,000. Assets stood at £596,000.

There were 15 grants made in the year, by far the largest grant went to Delta Trust (£150,000).

Other beneficiaries included: Prison Video Trust and Tavistock and Portman Charitable Fund (£25,000 each); Living Landscape Project and Prisoners Abroad (£10,000 each); Adam von Trott Memorial Appeal (£5,000); Amnesty International (£2,000); Toynbee Hall (£1,000); and Polish Institute Sikowski Museum (£25).

A grant of £13,000 was made to an individual.

Applications The trust has previously stated that all available income is now committed to existing beneficiaries.

Harry Bacon Foundation

Medical and animal welfare

£36,000 (2007/08)
Beneficial area UK.

National Westminster Bank PLC, Trust and Estate Services, 5th Floor, Trinity Quay 2, Avon Street, Bristol BS2 0PT
Correspondent The Trust Manager
Trustee National Westminster Bank Plc.
CC Number 1056500
Information available Accounts were on file at the Charity Commission.

In 2007/08 the trust had an income of £73,000 and made grants totalling £36,000.

Grants were given to the following eight charities: Arthritis Research Campaign, British Heart Foundation, Cancer Research UK, the Donkey Sanctuary, International League for the Protection of Horses, Parkinson's Disease Society, PDSA and RNLI.

Applications In writing to the correspondent.

The BACTA Charitable Trust

General

£322,000 (2007/08)
Beneficial area UK.

Alders House, 133 Aldersgate Street, London EC1A 4JA
Website www.bacta.org.uk
Correspondent The Clerk to the Trustees
Trustees J Thomas, Chair; R Higgins; N Harding; M Horwood; S I Meaden; D Orton; J Stergides; M Gemson.
CC Number 328668
Information available Accounts were on file at the Charity Commission.

The trust only supports charities recommended by the British Amusement Catering Trade Association (BACTA) members.

In 2007/08 the trust had an income of £348,000, mostly from donations. Assets stood at £57,000. Grants for the year totalled £322,000. The main beneficiary was the Responsibility in Gambling Trust (£300,000).

Other grants went to: Association of Children's Hospices (£19,000); Sunfield School (£2,000); and BIBIC (£1,300).

Exclusions No grants for overseas charities or religious purposes.

Applications In writing to the correspondent via a BACTA member.

The Bagri Foundation

General

£170,000 to organisations and individuals (2007/08)
Beneficial area Worldwide.

80 Cannon Street, London EC4N 6EJ
Tel. 020 7280 0089
Correspondent The Hon. A Bagri, Secretary
Trustees Lord Bagri; Hon. A Bagri; Lady Bagri.
CC Number 1000219
Information available Accounts were on file at the Charity Commission, but without a list of grants.

This foundation was set up in 1990 with general charitable purposes. In 2007/08 it had assets of £2.2 million and an income of £118,000. During the year grants were made to organisations and individuals totalling £170,000. In previous years the majority of the foundation's charitable expenditure was given to organisations. No other information is provided by the foundation in its report and accounts.

Applications In writing to the correspondent.

The Baker Charitable Trust

Mainly Jewish, older people, sickness and disability and medical research

£57,000 (2007/08)

Beneficial area UK and overseas.

16 Sheldon Avenue, Highgate, London N6 4JT

Correspondent Dr Harvey Baker, Trustee

Trustees *Dr Harvey Baker; Dr Adrienne Baker.*

CC Number 273629

Information available Accounts were on file at the Charity Commission, without a list of grants.

The trust makes grants in the areas of older people, chronic sickness or disability and people who have had limited educational opportunity. The trust also supports medical research related to the above groups. There is a preference for Jewish organisations.

In 2007/08 it had assets of £1.2 million and an income of £76,000. Grants to 38 organisations totalled £57,000. A list of grants was not included in the accounts filed at the Charity Commission.

Previous beneficiaries have included British Council Shaare Zedek Medical Centre, Chai Cancer Care, Community Security Trust, Disabled Living Foundation, Friends of Magen David Adom in Great Britain, Hillel Foundation, Institute of Jewish Policy Research, Jewish Women's Aid, Marie Curie Cancer Care, National Society for Epilepsy, Norwood Ltd, United Jewish Israel Appeal, St John's Hospice, United Synagogue, Winged Fellowship and World Jewish Relief.

Exclusions No grants to individuals or non-registered charities.

Applications In writing to the correspondent. The trustees meet to consider applications in January, April, July and October.

The Balint Family Charitable Trusts

Jewish and general

£267,000 (2007/08)

Beneficial area UK and overseas, especially Israel.

c/o Carter Backer Winter, Enterprise House, 21 Buckle Street, London E1 8NN

Tel. 020 7309 3800 **Fax** 020 7309 3801

Email david.kramer@cbw.co.uk

Correspondent David Kramer

Trustees *Andrew Balint Charitable Trust: Dr Gabriel Balint-Kurti; Roy David Balint-Kurti; Agnes Balint.*
George Balint Charitable Trust: Dr Andrew Balint; George Rothschild; Marion Farkas-Balint.
Paul Balint Charitable Trust: Dr Andrew Balint; Dr Gabriel Balint-Kurti; Paul Balint; Marc Balint.

Information available Information had been filed at the Charity Commission.

The Balint Family Charitable Trusts are all closely associated with grants probably directed to similar beneficiaries. The trusts' grant-making capacity has reduced significantly in recent years, from a record high of £1.7 million in 1999/2000.

In 2007/08 the combined incomes of the three trusts was £136,000. Their total expenditures were as follows:

Trust	Value
Andrew Balint Charitable Trust (cc no. 273691)	£133,000
Paul Balint Charitable Trust (cc no. 273690)	£108,000
George Balint Charitable Trust (cc no. 267482)	£81,500

Grants were made by the three trusts totalling £267,000. The correspondent confirmed that grant expenditure would total around £100,000 in 2008/09 and 2009/10.

Applications In writing to the correspondent.

Balmain Charitable Trust

General in the UK

£95,000 (2007/08)

Beneficial area UK.

c/o Rutter and Allhusen, 2 Longmead, Shaftesbury SP7 8PL

Correspondent S Balmain, Trustee

Trustees *P G Eaton; A Tappin; D S Balmain; I D S Balmain; Mrs L Balmain; C A G Wells.*

CC Number 1079972

Information available Accounts were on file at the Charity Commission.

Registered with the Charity Commission in March 2000, in 2007/08 the trust had assets of £2.4 million, an income of £105,000 and made 42 grants totalling £95,000.

Beneficiaries included: British Red Cross and Oxfam (£8,000 each); the Light Dragoons Charitable Trust (£6,000); the Suzy Lamplugh Trust and Royal Opera House Foundation (£5,000 each); Crisis, Game and Wildlife Conservation Trust, Second Chance, Sydling St Nicholas Play Group and Zimbabwe Benefit Foundation (£3,000 each); Alzheimer's Society, Conservation Zambezi, Dorset and Somerset Air Ambulance Trust, Leukaemia Research Fund and the Wildfowl and Wetlands Trust (£2,000 each); and Age Concern, the British Museum Friends, Cancer Research UK, Foxglove Covert, Help for Heroes, Soil Association and the Zambezi Society (£1,000 each).

Applications In writing to the correspondent.

The Balney Charitable Trust

Preservation, conservation, welfare and service charities

£63,000 (2007/08)

Beneficial area UK, with a preference for north Buckinghamshire and north Bedfordshire.

The Chicheley Estate, Bartlemas Office, Paveham, Bedford MK43 7PF

Tel. 01234 823663

Correspondent G C W Beazley, Clerk

Trustees *Maj. J G B Chester; R Ruck-Keene.*

CC Number 288575

Information available Accounts were on file at the Charity Commission.

The following objectives of the trust are adapted from its accounts.

- the furtherance of any religious and charitable purposes in connection with the parishes of Chicheley, North Crawley and the SCAN Group i.e. Sherington, Astwood, Hardmead and churches with a Chester family connection.
- the provision of housing for persons in necessitous circumstances
- agriculture, forestry and armed service charities
- care of older people and the sick and disabled from the Chicheley area
- other charitable purposes.

In 2007/08 the trust had assets of £792,000 and an income of £74,000. Grants were made totalling £63,000.

The trust makes regular donations each year by standing order ranging from £25 to £1,000. In the year, 17 regular donations totalled £4,800. Beneficiaries included: Gurkha Welfare Trust (£1,000); St Lawrence Church – Chicheley (£500); Royal Agricultural Benevolent Institution (£350); Buckinghamshire Historic Churches Trust (£300); SSAFA (£250); Guards Museum Trust (£200); Country Landowners Association Charitable Trust (£100); and Friends of John Bunyan Museum – Bedford (£25).

Other donations totalled £38,000 and among the 16 organisations to benefit were: St Lawrence Church – Chicheley (£7,500); National Trust – Montecute House (£7,000 in two grants); Queen Alexandra Hospital Home (£5,000); CHIT, Combat Stress, Motor Neurone Disease Association and St Luke's Hospital for the Clergy (£2,000 each); Emmaus Village – Carlton, Help for Heroes, MS Therapy Centre and Tree Aid – Ghana Village Tree Enterprise (£1,000 each); and Fun 4 Young People (£500).

The sum of £1,100 also was donated to 'necessitous cases'.

Exclusions Local community organisations and individuals outside north Buckinghamshire and north Bedfordshire.

Applications In writing to the correspondent. Applications are acknowledged if a stamped, addressed envelope is enclosed, otherwise if the charity has not received a reply within six weeks the application has not been successful.

The Baltic Charitable Fund

Seafarers, fishermen, ex-service and service people

£90,000 (2007/08)

Beneficial area UK, with a preference for the City of London.

The Baltic Exchange, 38 St Mary Axe, London EC3A 8BH

Correspondent The Company Secretary

Trustee *The Directors of the Baltic Exchange Limted.*

CC Number 279194

Information available Accounts were on file at the Charity Commission.

The trust aims to support causes relating to the sea (including training for professionals and children), the City of London, Forces charities and for sponsorship for Baltic Exchange members. Support is given to registered charites only.

In 2007/08 the trust had assets of £1.6 million and an income of £70,000. Grants were made totalling £90,000 including £11,000 given from the Bonno Krull Fund.

Beneficiaries included: City of London School for Girls (£36,000); Lord Mayor's Appeal (£7,500); Marine Society and Sea Cadets, Sailors Society and UCL Development Fund (£5,000 each); the Mission to Seafarers (£3,600); Community Housing and Therapy (£3,000); Falkland Islands Chapel (£2,000); Jubilee Sailing Trust (£2,500); Medway Seamans Trust (£1,000); Annual National Service for Seafarers and Royal British Legion Poppy Appeal (£500 each); and Merchant Navy Medal Award (£300).

Exclusions No support for advertising or charity dinners, etc.

Applications Unsolicited applications are not considered.

William P Bancroft (No 2) Charitable Trust and Jenepher Gillett Trust

Quaker

£36,000 (2008)

Beneficial area UK and overseas.

Fernroyd, St Margaret's Road, Altrincham WA14 2AW

Correspondent Dr Roger Gillett, Trustee

Trustees *Dr Roger Gillett; Tony Yelloly; Dr Godfrey Gillett; Martin B Gillett; Dr D S Gillett; Mrs Jenepher Moseley.*

CC Number 288968

Information available Accounts were on file at the Charity Commission.

This trust is unusual as it consists of two separate trusts which are operated as one. For historical reasons there is a William P Bancroft trust giving in the UK and a Jenepher Gillet trust giving in Delaware, USA which shared a common settlor/joint-settlor; the two trusts are now being run jointly with the same trustees and joint finances.

It makes grants towards charitable purposes connected with the Religious Society of Friends, supporting Quaker conferences, colleges and Friends' homes for older people.

In 2008 it had an income of £36,000 and gave grants totalling £36,000. Assets stood at £597,000.

Previous beneficiaries have included Alternates to Violence, Bootham School, Cape Town – Quaker Peace Centre, Chaigley Educational Centre, FWCC, Mount School York Foundation, Oxford Homeless Medial Fund, Quaker Voluntary Action, QUIET – Ramallah Friends School, Sibford School – bursaries and Woodbrooke College.

Exclusions No appeals unconnected with Quakers. No support for individual or student grant applications.

Applications In writing to the correspondent. Trustees meet in May, applications must be received no later than April.

The Barbers' Company General Charities

Medical and nursing education

£112,000 (2006/07)

Beneficial area UK.

Barber-Surgeons' Hall, Monkwell Square, London EC2Y 5BL

Correspondent The Clerk

Trustee *The Barbers Company.*

CC Number 265579

Information available Accounts for year ending 2007/08 were overdue at the Charity Commission.

The charities were registered in May 1973; grants are made to organisations and individuals. It no longer has direct contact with the hairdressing fraternity. However, a small amount is given each year to satisfy its historical links. Causes supported include those related to medicine education and nursing.

In 2006/07 it had assets of £1.3 million and an income of £152,000 mostly from covenants and Gift Aid. Grants totalled £112,000.

There were 16 grants of £1,000 or more listed in the accounts. Beneficiaries included: Royal College of Surgeons (£40,000); Phyllis Tuckwell Hospice (£22,000); the corporation of London School for Girls and Reed's School (£5,000 each); the Guildhall School Trust (£2,500); the Lord Mayor's Appeal 2007 and Mercy Ships (£2,000 each); and City of London Freeman's School, Mansion House – Scholarship Scheme and St Giles Chipplegate (£1,000 each).

Applications The charities do not welcome unsolicited applications.

The Barbour Trust

Health, welfare, conservation and restoration

£425,000 (2007/08)

Beneficial area Mainly Tyne and Wear, Northumberland and South Tyneside.

J Barbour & Sons Ltd, Simonside, South Shields, Tyne and Wear NE34 9PD

Tel. 0191 455 4444

Website www.barbour.com

Correspondent The Secretary

Trustees *Dame Margaret Barbour, Chair; Henry Jacob Tavroges; Helen Barbour.*

CC Number 328081

Information available Accounts were on file at the Charity Commission.

The objects of the charity are to support any charitable institution (grants are not made directly to individuals) whose objects include:

- The relief of patients suffering from any form of illness or disease, the promotion of research into the causes and treatment of such illnesses or disease and the provision of medical equipment for such patients.
- The furtherance of education of children and young people by award of scholarship, exhibitions, bursaries or maintenance allowances tenable at any school, university or other educational establishment in England.
- The protection and preservation for the benefit of the public in England, of such features of cities, towns, villages and the countryside as are of special environmental, historical or architectural interest.
- The relief of persons, whether resident in England or otherwise who are in conditions of need, hardship or distress as a result of local, national or international disaster, or by reason of their social and economic circumstances.

In 2007/08 the trust had assets of £8.4 million and an income of £2.4 million. A total of 377 grants were made totalling £425,000 and were broken down by category as follows:

Category	Value
Community welfare	£120,000
Young people/children	£105,000
Medical care research and general health	£94,000
Housing/homeless	£38,000
Disabled people	£27,000
Older people	£13,000
Arts	£9,500
Maritime charities	£5,100
Conservation/horticultural	£4,100
Service charities	£3,700
Animal welfare	£3,600
Heritage/museums	£1,200
Education/expeditions	£540
Special appeals from overseas	£500

There were 152 grants of £1,000 or more listed in the accounts.

Beneficiaries included: Northumbria Youth Action Limited (£30,000); Alzheimer's Trust (£13,000); Action Medical Research and Northern Institute for Cancer Treatment (£10,000 each); Derwentside Domestic Abuse Centre, Genesis Appeal, Marie Curie Cancer Care, Newcastle Healthcare Charity, North of England Children's Cancer Research Fund and Shelter (£5,000 each); Fairbridge Tyne and Wear (£3,000); Project Northumberland and Wellbeing of Women (£2,000 each); Listening Books and Rainbow Trust (£1,500 each); and Butterwick Hospice Care, Combat Stress, National Farmers Network, Refuge, Ruskin Museum, Save the Children, Someone Cares, STOP, Sunderland North Family Zone, Textile Benevolent Association, Walk the Walk Worldwide and Whizz-Kids (£1,000 each).

Exclusions No support for:

- requests from outside the geographical area
- requests from educational establishments
- individual applications, unless backed by a particular charitable organisation
- capital grants for building projects.

Applications On an application form available from PO Box 21, Guisborough, Cleveland, TS14 8YH. The applications should include full back-up information, a statement of accounts and the official charity number of the applicant.

A main grants meeting is held every three to four months to consider grants of £500 and above. Applications are processed and researched by the administrator and secretary and further information may be requested.

A small grants meeting is held monthly to consider grants up to £500.

The trust always receives more applications than it can support. Even if a project fits its policy priority areas, it may not be possible to make a grant.

The Barcapel Foundation

Health, heritage and young people

£736,000 (2008)

Beneficial area Scotland and other parts of the UK.

The Mews, Skelmorlie Castle, Skelmorlie, Ayrshire PA17 5EY

Tel. 01475 521616

Email admin@barcapelfoundation.org

Website www.barcapelfoundation.org

Correspondent Moira Givens

Trustees *Robert Wilson, Chair; James Wilson; Andrew Wilson; Jed Wilson; Clement Wilson; Niall Scott.*

SC Number SC009211

Information available Information was available from the trust's website.

The foundation was established in 1964 after the sale of the family business, Scottish Animal Products.

The three priority areas of interest for funding are health, heritage and young people.

Health
The foundation supports all aspects of health, a wide ranging remit acknowledging that 'health is a state of complete physical, mental and social wellbeing and not merely the absence of disease or infirmity.

Heritage
The original financiers of the foundation had a keen interest in our heritage, specifying that one of the foundations aims was 'the preservation and beautification of historic properties'. The foundation continues to support the built environment and will support our literary and artistic heritage as well as architectural.

Young people
The development of people is one of the principal objectives of the foundation. Whilst charitable giving can be used to alleviate problems it can also be used to empower people and this is particularly true of young people.

In 2008 the foundation had an income of £2.1 million and made grants totalling £736,000.

Beneficiaries in 2008 included: the Princess Royal Trust for Carers and the Story Museum (£15,000 each); the Tunnell Trust (£12,000); and Scottish Civic Trust and the Scottish Lime Centre (£10,000).

Exclusions No support for:

- individual applications for travel or similar
- organisations or individuals engaged in promoting religious or political beliefs
- applications for funding costs of feasibility studies or similar.

Support is unlikely to be given for local charities whose work takes place outside the British Isles.

Applications A preliminary application form can be downloaded from the foundation's website. Please ensure that interests, aims and objectives are compatible with those of the foundation.

Applications are not accepted by email.

Barchester Healthcare Foundation

Health and social care

£34,000 to organisations (2008)

Beneficial area England, Scotland and Wales.

Suite 201, The Chambers, Chelsea Harbour, London SW10 0XF

Tel. 0800 328 3328

Email info@bhcfoundation.org.uk

Website www.bhcfoundation.org.uk

Correspondent The Administrator

Trustees *Prof Malcolm Johnson; Elizabeth Mills; Christopher P Vellenoweth; Christine Hodgson; Michael D Parsons; Janice Robinson; Nick Oulton.*

CC Number 1083272

Information available Accounts were on file at the Charity Commission. Information is available on the foundation's website.

The Barchester Healthcare Foundation was established in 2003 by Barchester Healthcare to reinvest into the communities it serves. It is a registered charity with independent trustees.

The following information is taken from the foundation's website.

We make grants available across England, Scotland and Wales to older people and other adults (18 plus) with a physical or mental disability whose health and/or social care needs cannot be met by the statutory public sector or by the individual. Our

mission is to make a difference to the lives of older people and other adults with a physical or mental disability, supporting practical solutions that lead to increased personal independence, self-sufficiency and dignity.

The foundation can provide grants of any amount, up to a maximum of £10,000.

In 2008 the foundation had an income of £324,000 and made grants totalling £306,000 of which £34,000 went to small charities or community groups and the remaining funds to individuals.

Exclusions The foundation's website states that funds will not normally be given to:

- provide services for which the health and social care authorities have a statutory responsibility
- services normally offered in a care home operated by Barchester Healthcare or by any other company
- indirect services such as helplines, newsletters, leaflets or research
- core/running costs or salaries or give financial support to general projects
- major building projects
- provide continuing year on year support for a project following an initial grant. Any further applications in respect of the same beneficiary will be considered after a period of three years from the initial grant.

The trustees reserve the right to put a cap on grants to a single charity (including all its branches) in any one year.

Applications Applications can be made via the foundation's website. A decision usually takes approximately ten weeks from the date of application.

All applications supported by Barchester Healthcare staff will be given priority.

Peter Barker-Mill Memorial Charity

General

£232,000 (2007/08)

Beneficial area UK, with a preference for Hampshire, including Southampton.

c/o Longdown Management Ltd, The Estate Office, Longdown, Marchwood, Southampton SO40 4UH

Correspondent Christopher Gwyn-Evans, Administrator

Trustees *C Gwyn-Evans; T Jobling; R M Moyse.*

CC Number 1045479

Information available Accounts were on file at the Charity Commission website.

In 2007/08 the trust had assets of £2.5 million and an income of £71,000. Grants were made to 43 organisations totalling £232,000.

Beneficiaries included: Colbury Scouts (£86,000); Colbury Parochial Church Council (£12,000); Nursling and Rownhams Village Hall (£10,000); the Pinder Centre (£8,000); the Rugby Portobello Trust (£6,000); Southampton Society for the Blind and Special Schools and Academy Trust (£5,000 each); Sussex House School (£4,000); Huntington's Disease Association, Tall Ships Youth Trust and Victim Support Hampshire and Isle of Wight (£3,000 each); Groundswell (£2,000); the Grasslands Trust, the Rose Road Association and Volunteer Reading Help (£1,000 each); and Planet Kids (£500).

Exclusions No grants to individuals.

Applications In writing to the correspondent.

Barleycorn Trust

Christian

£188,000 (2007)

Beneficial area Worldwide.

32 Arundel Road, Sutton SM2 6EU

Correspondent The Trustees

Trustees *Mrs H M Hazelwood; M R C Citroën; Mrs S A Beckwith.*

CC Number 296386

Information available Accounts were on file at the Charity Commission.

The trust's accounts state that:

The object of the charity is the advancement of the Christian faith, furtherance of religious or secular education, the encouragement of missionary activity, relief of the poor and needy and help and comfort of the sick and aged.

In 2007 its assets totalled £1.2 million, it had an income of £44,000 and made 38 grants totalling £188,000.

Beneficiaries included: Pathway Project (£70,000); Demand Design (£17,000); Off the Fence (£9,000); Bishop Hannington Church and Dorothy Kerin Trust (£5,000 each); Ethiopia School of

Nursing (£3,800); Moldova Ministries (£3,000); Adriatic Christian Trust and Hope HIV (£2,000 each); Keychange (£1,000); and Chalfont Heights Scouts (£500).

Applications In writing to the correspondent.

The Barnabas Trust

Evangelical Christianity

£273,000 (2008/09)

Beneficial area UK and overseas. Overseas projects are supported only if they are personally known by the trustees.

c/o 63 Wolsey Drive, Walton-on-Thames KT12 3BB

Correspondent Mrs Doris Edwards, Secretary

Trustees *Norman Brown; Kenneth C Griffiths; David S Helden.*

CC Number 284511

Information available Full accounts were on file at the Charity Commission.

In 2008/09 the trust had assets of £2.6 million generating an income of £135,000. Grants to organisations and individuals totalled £273,000. They were broken down as follows and are shown here with examples of beneficiaries in each category:

Christian mission overseas – £119,000
SGM Lifewords (£60,000); Naval, Military and Air Force Bible Society (£10,000 in 2 grants); Echoes of Service (£5,000); Medical Missionary News (£4,500); Bulgarian Support Fund and United Mission to Nepal (£3,500 each); Project Evangelism (£2,500); Far East Broadcasting Association (£2,000); Arab Vision Trust and OMF International (£1,500 each); and People International (£1,000).

Christian mission in the UK – £70,000
Green Hill Outreach (£8,000); Counties Evangelical Trust and WEC International (£5,000 each); Abernathy Trust, Latin Link and Open Air Mission (£2,500 each); Rural Ministries and Vision Ireland (£2,000 each); Bibles for Children (£1,500); Cutting Edge Ministries, Newland Christian Trust and Scottish Counties Evangelist Movement (£1,000 each); Stirling Baptist Church (£750); and Hope City Church (£500).

Community welfare – £37,000
Princess Alice Hospice (£7,000); Release International (£3,000); Torch Trust for the Blind (£2,500); Caring for Life (£2,000); Haven in Romania (£1,700); the Barnabas Fund (£1,500); and Trustees for Timothy House (£1,000).

Educational – £30,000
Redcliffe College (£5,000); Haggai Institute (£4,500); London School of Theology (£3,000); Nazareth Centre for Christian Studies (£2,500); Church Pastoral Aid Society (£2,000); Danoko Training College – Nairobi (£1,500); and National Bible Study Club and Tyndale House (£1,000 each).

Grants to individuals
Grants were made to individuals for: educational purposes (£16,000 in 18 grants); Christian mission overseas (£2,000 in 2 grants); and Christian Mission UK (£1,500 in 2 grants).

Exclusions 'The trust is no longer able to help with building, refurbishment or equipment for any church, since to be of any value grants need to be large.' Ongoing revenue costs such as salaries are not supported.

Applications In writing to the correspondent, giving as much detail as possible, and enclosing a copy of the latest audited accounts, if applicable. The trust states: 'Much of the available funds generated by this trust are allocated to existing donees. The trustees are willing to consider new applications, providing they refer to a project which is overtly evangelical in nature.' If in doubt about whether to submit an application, please telephone the secretary to the trust for guidance.

The trustees meet four times a year, or more often as required, and applications will be put before the next available meeting.

Please note: it is likely that the trust will cease to exist by 2012. Very little money is available for unsolicited applications.

Lord Barnby's Foundation

General

£257,000 (2007/08)

Beneficial area UK.

PO Box 71, Plymstock, Plymouth PL8 2YP

Correspondent Mrs J A Lethbridge, Secretary

Trustees *Hon. George Lopes; the Countess Peel; Sir Michael Farquhar; E J A Smith-Maxwell.*

CC Number 251016

Information available Accounts were on file at the Charity Commission.

The foundation has established a permanent list of charities that it supports each year, with the remaining funds then distributed to other charities.

Its priority areas include the following:

- heritage: the preservation of the environment, the countryside and ancient buildings, particularly the 'great Anglican cathedrals'
- charities benefiting people who are ex-service and service, Polish, disabled or refugees
- welfare of horses and people who look after them
- youth and other local organisations in Ashtead – Surrey, Blyth – Nottinghamshire and Bradford – Yorkshire
- technical education for the woollen industry.

In 2007/08 the trust had assets of £4.7 million and an income of £239,000. Grants totalled £257,000 and were divided between 'permanent' and 'discretionary' donations.

Examples of the 65 organisations receiving 'discretionary' donations included: European Squirrel Initiative (£50,000); Barnby Memorial Hall (£18,000); Help for Heroes (£12,000); Farms for City Children and St Luke's Hospital for the Clergy (£10,000 each); the Queen Alexandra Hospital Home (£7,000); Polish Veterans Association (£5,000); CLIC Sargent – Billy's Appeal, Listening Books, the Outward Bound Trust, Second Chance, Tall Ships Youth Trust and Wotton Under Edge Community Sports (£2,000 each); Dorothy House Hospice and the ISIS Project (£1,000 each); and Care International UK and the York Joint Scout Trust (£500 each).

Exclusions No grants to individuals.

Applications Applications will only be considered if received in writing accompanied by a set of the latest accounts. Applicants do not need to send a stamped, addressed envelope. Appeals are considered three times a year, in February, June and November.

The Barnsbury Charitable Trust

General

£71,000 (2007/08)

Beneficial area UK, but no local charities outside Oxfordshire.

26 Norham Road, Oxford OX2 6SF
Correspondent H L J Brunner, Trustee
Trustees *H L J Brunner; M R Brunner; T E Yates.*

CC Number 241383

Information available Accounts were on file at the Charity Commission website.

In 2007/08 the trust had assets of £2.8 million and an income of £74,000. Grants were made to 64 organisations totalling £71,000.

Beneficiaries included: Oxfordshire Chamber Music Festival (£10,000); the Oxfordshire Victoria County History Trust (£5,000); St Giles PCC (£3,000); Charlbury Community Centre and Oxfordshire Family Medication (£2,500 each); Blackfriars Priory, Hagbourne School, Merton College Charitable Trust, Oxford Christian Institute for Counselling, Oxford District Mencap, PCC of St Mary – Chalgrove and Trinity College – Oxford (£1,000 each); Oxfordshire Nature Conservation Forum (£500); Chipping Norton Town Charities, Oxford Oratory Trust and Royal British Legion Poppy Appeal (£100 each); the Royal Society of St George (£25); and Priory of England and the Islands (£15).

Exclusions No grants to individuals.

Applications In writing to the correspondent.

The Misses Barrie Charitable Trust

Medical and general

£263,000 (2007/08)

Beneficial area UK.

Messrs Raymond Carter and Co, 1b Haling Road, South Croydon CR2 6HS
Tel. 020 8686 1686

Correspondent Raymond Carter, Trustee

Trustees *R G Carter; R S Ogg; Mrs R Fraser.*

CC Number 279459

Information available Full accounts were on file at the Charity Commission.

In 2007/08 the trust had assets of £5.7 million and an income of £246,000. Grants to 115 organisations totalled £263,000.

Beneficiaries of larger grants of £5,000 or more were: Scottish Chamber Orchestra and University of Oxford (£10,000 each); and ARC Addington Fund, East Neuk Festival and Queen Victoria School Centenary Appeal (£5,000).

Other beneficiaries included: National Association of Youth Orchestras and Sutton Junior Tennis Centre (£4,000 each); Surrey Cricket Board (£3,300); Alcohol Focus Scotland, Brighton and Hove Parents & Children Group, Brittle Bone Society, Children's Hospice South West, Drake Music Scotland, Edinburgh Young Carers Project, Hearts and Minds, Maggie's Cancer Caring Centres, Perth Festival of the Arts, Scottish Opera, St Peter and St James Charitable Trust, West Lothian 50+ Network and Youth Link – Dundee (£3,000 each); Abbeyfield Sanderstead Society Ltd, Ardgowan Hospice, British Wireless for the Blind, Deafblind UK, Elimination of Leukaemia Fund, Gordon Russell Trust, HomeBase Community Housing, Interest Link Borders, New Jumbulance Travel Trust, Prostate Cancer Research Centre, Scottish Epilepsy Initiative, St Giles' Cathedral Renewal Appeal, Starlight Children's Foundation, Talking Newspaper Association, Wellbeing of Women and Worshipful Company of Hackney Carriage Drivers (£2,000 each); RNLI North Cotswold Branch (£1,500); and Cornerstone Community Care, the Eyeless Trust, Four Wheels Travel Fellowship, Home from Hospital Care, REHAB UK, Spadework, Sportability, Visibility and Wireless for the Bedridden (£1,000 each).

Exclusions No grants to individuals.

Applications In writing to the correspondent, accompanied, where appropriate, by up-to-date accounts or financial information. Trustees meet three times a year, in April, August and December.

'The trustees regret that due to the large number of unsolicited applications for grants received each week they are not able to notify those which are unsuccessful.'

The Bartlett Taylor Charitable Trust

General

£48,000 (2007/08)

Beneficial area Preference for Oxfordshire.

24 Church Green, Witney OX28 4AT

Tel. 01993 703941

Email krobertson@ johnwelchandstammers.co.uk

Correspondent Katherine Robertson

Trustees *Richard Bartlett; Gareth Alty; Katherine Bradley; Brenda Cook; James W Dingle; Rosemary Warner; Mrs S Boyd.*

CC Number 285249

Information available Accounts were on file at the Charity Commission.

In 2007/08 the trust had assets of £1.7 million and an income of £68,000. Grants were made totalling £48,000. There were 88 grants awarded to organisations during the year which were covered in the following categories:

International charities

- 13 grants were made ranging from £500 to £1,000 totalling £7,750.

UK national charities

- Medical – 23 grants were made ranging from £100 to £1,000 totalling £13,000.
- Educational – 5 grants ranging from £100 to £500 totalling £2,000.
- Other – 8 grants were made ranging from £250 to £500 totalling £3,000.

Local organisations

- Community projects – 23 grants were made ranging from £100 to £500 totalling £8,900.
- Medical – 8 grants were made ranging from £100 to £1,000 totalling £3,100.
- Educational – 7 grants were made ranging from £100 to £500 totalling £1,900.
- Other – 1 grant of £250 was made.

Grants were also made to individuals for educational, medical and relief in need purposes. There were 40 such donations made in the range of £100 and £600 totalling about £9,000.

Applications In writing to the correspondent. Trustees meet bi-monthly.

The Paul Bassham Charitable Trust

General

£246,000 (2007/08)

Beneficial area UK, mainly Norfolk.

c/o Howes Percival, The Guildyard, 51 Colegate, Norwich NR3 1DD

Correspondent R Lovett, Trustee

Trustees *C J Lingwood; R Lovett.*

CC Number 266842

Information available Accounts were on file at the Charity Commission.

This trust was established in the early 1970s and has general charitable purposes. 'The trustees will seek to identify those projects where the greatest and widest benefit can be attained.'

In 2007/08 it had assets of £10.5 million and an income of £403,000. During the year 125 donations were made totalling £246,000.

Beneficiaries of the three largest grants were: East Anglia Children's Hospice Quidenham and Norwich Theatre Royal Trust (£20,000 each); and Leonard Cheshire Disability (£11,000).

Other beneficiaries included: Norfolk Wildlife Trust (£7,500); Assist Trust, the Hawk and Owl Trust, Norfolk and Norwich Families' House and the Plantation Garden Preservation Trust (£5,000 each); City of Norwich School Association and Age Concern (£3,000 each); CLIC Sargent, Cruse Bereavement Care – Norwich, Norwich Door to Door, the Matthew Project, Sprowston Day Centre and Yare Hospice Care (£2,000 each); and Costessey Baptist Church, the Hamlet Centre Trust, London Road Methodist Church, the Methodist Church East Norfolk Circuit, Samaritans Great Yarmouth and Whizz-Kidz (£1,000 each).

Exclusions Grant are not made directly to individuals, nor to unregistered organisations.

Applications Only in writing to the correspondent, no formal application forms are issued. Telephone enquiries are not invited because of administrative costs. The trustees meet quarterly to consider general applications.

The Batchworth Trust

Medical, humanitarian aid, social welfare and general

£341,000 (2007/08)

Beneficial area Worldwide.

CLB Gatwick LLP, Imperial Buildings, 68 Victoria Road, Horley RH6 7PZ

Tel. 01293 776411

Email mrn@clbgatwick.co.uk

Correspondent M R Neve, Administrative Executive

Trustee *Lockwell Trustees Ltd.*

CC Number 245061

Information available Accounts were on file at the Charity Commission.

The trust mainly supports nationally recognised charities in a wide range of areas. In 2007/08 it had assets of £8.8 million, an income of £357,000 and made 34 grants totalling £341,000.

The trust's accounts state that:

The trustees have a policy of mainly distributing grants to nationally recognised charities but consider other charities where it felt a grant would be of significant benefit when matched with other funds to launch a new enterprise or initiative.

The beneficiaries of the 17 largest grants of £10,000 or more were: University of Bristol Research Post (£50,000); Cure Parkinsons (£30,000); Alzheimer's Society, Back Care, Brick by Brick, British Legion, Centre Point, CVT Appeals Fund, Farm Africa, Hertfordshire Air Ambulance, Lorica Trust, Macmillan Nurses, Manchester Royal Infirmary, the Mediae Trust, Merlin, MOSS and Oxford Radcliffe Hospital (£10,000 each).

Other beneficiaries included: Age Concern (£8,000); the Salvation Army (£7,000); Bathol Chapel Church, Friends United Network, the National Rheumatoid Arthritis Society, Prospect Burma, Royal Agricultural Benevolent Trust, Royal Botanic Gardens – Kew, Sandpiper Fund and the Waterside Trust (£5,000 each); and the Colston Society (£2,000).

Exclusions No applications from individuals can be considered.

Applications In writing to the correspondent. A stamped, addressed envelope should be included if a reply is required.

Bay Charitable Trust

Jewish

£763,000 (2008)

Beneficial area UK and overseas.

Hermolis House, Abbeydale Road, Wembley HA0 1AY

Correspondent I M Kreditor, Trustee

Trustees *I M Kreditor; M Lisser.*

CC Number 1060537

Information available Accounts were on file at the Charity Commission, without a list of grants.

Registered with the Charity Commission in February 2007, 'The objectives of the charity are to give charity for the relief of poverty and the advancement of traditions of the Orthodox Jewish Religion and the study of Torah.'

In 2008 it had an income of £881,000, mainly from donations. Grants totalled £763,000. The sum of £366,000 was carried forward at year end.

Applications In writing to the correspondent.

The Bay Tree Charitable Trust

Development work and general

£188,000 (2007)

Beneficial area UK and overseas.

PO Box 53983, London SW15 1VT

Correspondent The Trustees

Trustees *I M P Benton; Miss E L Benton; P H Benton.*

CC Number 1044091

Information available Accounts were on file at the Charity Commission.

In 2007 the trust had assets of £3.3 million, an income of £157,000 and made 13 grants totalling £188,000.

Beneficiaries were: Queen Alexander Hospital Home (£30,000); Médecins Sans Frontières – UK (£28,000); Disasters Emergency Committee Bangladesh Cyclone Appeal, NSPCC and UNICEF UK – South Asia Floods Children's Appeal (£20,000 each); Friends of the Earth and Help Tibet (£15,000 each); Friends of Home from

Home – UK and Save the Children (£10,000 each); and IFAW Charitable Trust and the Nelson Trust (£5,000 each).

The trustees aim to make grants totalling a minimum of £150,000 per annum in accordance with the guidelines set out in the grant-giving policy in the trust's accounts.

Exclusions No grants to individuals.

Applications The trust's accounts suggest that:

All appeals should be by letter containing the following:

- aims and objectives of the charity
- nature of appeal
- total target if for a specific project
- contributions received against target
- registered charity number
- any other relevant factors.

Letters should be accompanied by a set of the charitable organisation's latest report and full accounts.

The Beacon Trust

Christian

£38,000 (2007/08)

Beneficial area Mainly UK, but also some overseas (usually in the British Commonwealth) and Spain and Portugal.

Unit 3, Newhouse Farm, Old Crawley Road, Horsham RH12 4RU

Correspondent Grahame Scofield

Trustees *Miss J Benson; Miss J M Spink; M Spink.*

CC Number 230087

Information available Accounts were on file at the Charity Commission.

The trust's objects are 'to advance the Christian faith, relieve poverty and advance education'.

In 2007/08 the trust had assets of £1.5 million, an income of £350,000 and made grants totalling £38,000.

The emphasis of the trust's support is on Christian work overseas, particularly amongst students, although the trust does not support individuals. The trust has previously stated that it has a list of charities that it supports in most years. This leaves very little funds available for unsolicited applications.

Beneficiaries included: L'Abri Fellowship (£10,000); Arocha – Portugal (£4,000); Zambia Chicken Farm Project (£3,000); Cascadas (£2,000); Heythrop College (£1,700); and STREAT Trust (£1,500).

Exclusions Applications from individuals are not considered.

Applications The trust does not respond to unsolicited applications.

Bear Mordechai Ltd

Jewish

£148,000 (2007/08)

Beneficial area Worldwide.

40 Fountayne Road, London N16 7DT

Correspondent The Secretary

Trustees *Y Benedikt; E Benedikt.*

CC Number 286806

Information available Accounts were on file at the Charity Commission.

Grants are made to Jewish organisations. The trust states that religious, educational and other charitable institutions are supported.

In 2007/08 this trust had assets of £1 million, an income of £68,000 and made grants totalling £148,000.

Previous beneficiaries have included Agudat Yad Yemin Jerusalem, Almat, Chevras Mo'oz Ladol, Craven Walk Charities Trust, Havenpoint, Keren Tzedaka Vachesed, Lolev, UTA and Yetev Lev Yerusholaim.

Applications In writing to the correspondent.

The Beaufort House Trust Limited

Christian and education

£38,000 (2007)

Beneficial area UK.

Beaufort House, Brunswick Road, Gloucester GL1 1JZ

Correspondent Mrs R J Hall, Secretary

Trustees *M R Cornwall-Jones, Chair; W H Yates; N J E Sealy; H F Hart; M A Chamberlain; W N Stock; Ven A J Cooper.*

CC Number 286606

Information available Accounts were on file at the Charity Commission.

The company's accounts state that:

The object of the company is to promote all charitable objects and purposes including the advancement, promotion and furtherance of education and the Christian religion.

Primarily the trust awards grants in response to appeals received from schools, colleges, universities and other charitable bodies. Normally grants are made in the form of single payments but occasionally the trustees may support a special project over a longer period.

In 2007 the trust had assets of £97,000 and an income of £236,000, including a donation of £25,000 from Ecclesiastical Insurance Office plc and £180,000 in school fee annuities from Ecclesiastical Life Limited. Ecclesiastical Life Limited and Ecclesiastical Insurance Office plc are subsidiaries of Allchurches Trust Limited. Beaufort House Trust Limited and Allchurches Trust Limited are companies that are controlled by a common board of trustees. The sum of £38,000 was given in grants which were distributed accordingly: schools (80%); colleges (13%); other educational establishments (£7%).

Exclusions No grants are made to organisations with political associations, UK wide charities or individuals.

Applications On an application form. The following details will be required:

- the objectives of the charity
- the appeal target
- how the funds are to be utilised
- funds raised to date
- previous support received from the trust.

Beauland Ltd

Jewish causes

£200,000 (2007/08)

Beneficial area Worldwide, possibly with a preference for the Manchester area.

309 Bury New Road, Salford M7 2YN

Correspondent P Neumann, Trustee

Trustees *F Neumann; H Neumann; M Friedlander; H Rosemann; J Bleier; R Delange; M Neumann; P Neumann; E Neumann; E Henry.*

CC Number 511374

Information available Accounts were on file at the Charity Commission, without a list of grants.

The trust's objects are the advancement of the Jewish religion in accordance with the Orthodox Jewish faith and the relief of poverty. It gives grants to 'religious, educational and similar bodies'.

In 2007/08 the trust had assets of £7.2 million and an income of £449,000. Grants totalled £200,000.

Previous beneficiaries have included Asos Chesed, Cosmon Belz, Famos Charity Trust, Radford Education Trust, Sunderland Yeshiva and Yetev Lev.

Applications In writing to the correspondent.

The Beaverbrook Foundation

General

£14,000 (2006/07)

Beneficial area UK and Canada.

Cherkley Court, Reigate Road, Leatherhead KT22 8QX

Tel. 01372 380986

Email jane@beaverbrookfoundation.org

Website www.beaverbrookfoundation.org

Correspondent The Secretary

Trustees *Lord Beaverbrook, Chair; Lady Beaverbrook; Lady Aitken; T M Aitken; Hon. Laura Levi; J E A Kidd; Hon. M F Aitken.*

CC Number 310003

Information available Accounts for year ending 2007/08 were overdue at the Charity Commission. Those filed for 2006/07 contained an inadequate report and no list of grants.

As stated on its website, the object of this foundation include:

- the erection or improvement of the fabric of any church building
- the purchase of books, papers, manuscripts or works of art
- care of the aged or infirm in the UK.

The major project of the last decade has been the renovation of Beaverbrook's country house and gardens at Cherkley Court, near Leatherhead, Surrey.

In 2006/07 it had assets of £12.8 million and an income of £155,000. Out of a total expenditure of £3.3 million, grants to organisations totalled £14,000.

The following was taken from the foundation's website:

One of the areas that the foundation has concentrated on over the past twenty years has been supporting small charitable projects. We recognise that it is often more difficult to raise a few thousand to refurbish a church hall than it is to raise millions for a major public building. In the past twenty years, the foundation has donated to more than 400 charities.

Previous beneficiaries have included Aids Ark, Alzheimer's Society, Book Aid International, Bob Champion Trust, Down's Syndrome Organisation, London Lighthouse, NSPCC, Royal Academy of Dramatic Art, the Samaritans, St Teresa's Home for the Elderly, Surrey County Scouts Council, Victim Support, West of England School and College and Whizz Kids.

Exclusions Only registered charities are supported.

Applications There is an online application form on the foundation's website.

The Becker Family Charitable Trust

General and orthodox Jewish

£144,000 (2007/08)

Beneficial area UK and overseas.

5 North End Road, London NW11 7RJ

Correspondent L Becker, Trustee

Trustees *A Becker; L Becker; Mrs R Becker; Ms D Fried; C Guttentag.*

CC Number 1047968

Information available Accounts were on file at the Charity Commission.

The trust makes grants for general charitable purposes, particularly to orthodox Jewish organisations.

In 2007/08 it had assets of £232,000 and an income of £192,000, mainly from donations. Grants were made totalling £144,000.

Previous beneficiaries have included Keren Shabbas, Lolev CT, Menora Grammar School, Torah Temima and WST.

Applications In writing to the correspondent. However, please note that the trust has previously stated that its funds were fully committed.

The John Beckwith Charitable Trust

Young people, education, social welfare, medical research and the arts

£393,000 (2007/08)
Beneficial area UK and overseas.

124 Sloane Street, London SW1X 9BW
Correspondent Ms Sally Holder, Administrator
Trustees J L Beckwith; H M Beckwith; C M Meech.
CC Number 800276
Information available Accounts were on file at the Charity Commission.

In 2007/08 the trust had assets of £2.5 million and an income of £493,000. There were 56 grants made totalling £393,000, broken down as follows:

Category	Value	No.
Sport	£135,000	4
Social welfare	£130,000	32
Education	£95,000	5
Medical research	£25,000	14
Arts	£8,100	1

The accounts listed the 17 largest donations of £1,000 or more.

Beneficiaries included: Top Foundation (£100,000); Harrow Development Trust (£92,000); Unicorn theatre (£45,000); RNIB (£30,000); Caudwell Charitable Trust and Sense International (£10,000 each); Royal Opera House Trust (£8,100); Children's Hospice South West, Fairbridge, Tall Ships Youth Trust and Whizz Kids (£5,000 each); Wycombe Abbey School (£2,000); and KIDS (£1,000).

Smaller unlisted grants totalled £55,000.

Applications In writing to the correspondent.

The Peter Beckwith Charitable Trust

Medical, welfare and general

£79,000 (2007/08)
Beneficial area UK.

Hill Place House, 55a High Street, Wimbledon Village, London SW19 5BA
Tel. 020 8944 1288
Correspondent The Trustees
Trustees P M Beckwith; Mrs P G Beckwith; Mrs C T Van Dam; Mrs T J Veroni.
CC Number 802113
Information available Accounts were on file at the Charity Commission.

This trust was established in 1989. In 2007/08 it had an income from donations of £96,000 and made 42 grants totalling £79,000. Assets at the year end totalled £23,000.

Beneficiaries included: Great Ormond Street Hospital (£26,000); WCTT (£15,000); Polka Theatre (£4,200); Teenage Cancer Trust (£4,000); the Lucas Johnston Appeal (£2,000); Shelter (£1,100); and WWF – UK (£1,000).

One grant of £620 was paid to an individual.

Applications In writing to the correspondent.

The Bedfordshire and Hertfordshire Historic Churches Trust

Churches

£112,000 (2007/08)
Beneficial area Bedfordshire, Hertfordshire and that part of Barnet within the Diocese of St Albans.

Wychbrook, 31 Ivel Gardens, Biggleswade SG18 0AN
Tel. 01767 312966
Email wychbrook@yahoo.co.uk
Website www.bedshertshct.org.uk
Correspondent Archie Russell, Grants Secretary
Trustees C P Green, Chair; R C H Genochio; A A I Jenkins; P F D Lepper; P A Lomax; S A Russell; T Warburton; R W Wilson.
CC Number 1005697
Information available Accounts were on file at the Charity Commission.

The trust gives grants for the restoration, preservation, repair and maintenance of churches in Bedfordshire, Hertfordshire and that part of Barnet within the Diocese of St Albans. Annual income comes from member subscription and from the annual 'Bike 'n Hike' event. The trust also acts as a distributive agent for church grants made by the Wixamtree Trust and Waste Recycling Environmental Ltd (WREN).

In 2007/08 the trust had assets of £184,000 and an income of £353,000, including £200,000 from WREN. There were 25 grants made totalling £112,000 in the range of £1,000 and £7,500.

Exclusions No grants to individuals.

Applications Initial enquiries should be made to the Grants Secretary. Applications can only be made by members of the trust.

The David and Ruth Behrend Fund

General

£79,000 (2007/08)
Beneficial area UK, with a preference for Merseyside.

151 Dale Street, Liverpool L2 2AH
Correspondent The Secretary
Trustee Liverpool Charity and Voluntary Services.
CC Number 261567
Information available Accounts were obtained from the Charity Commission website.

'The trust was established to make grants for charitable purposes. Grants are only made to charities known to the settlors and unsolicited applications are therefore not considered.' Set up in

1969, it appears to give exclusively in Merseyside.

In 2007/08 the trust had assets of £1.4 million and an income of £86,000. Grants totalled £79,000. There were 32 listed beneficiaries in receipt of grants of £1,000 or more. Beneficiaries included: Merseyside Development Foundation and PSS (£6,000 each); Christian Aid and St John's Hospice in Wirral (£2,500 each); Ambergate Community Guide Hut, Dingle Multi Agency Centre Ltd, Liverpool Somali Youth Association, Norris Green Youth Centre, North West Disability Arts Forum, Shining Faces in India and Smart Charitable Trust (£2,000 each); Al Ghazali Multicultural Centre (£1,800); Home Farm Trust and the Missionary Training Service (£1,500 each); KIND (£1,300); and Merseyside Holiday Foundation, the National Trust, Oxfam and Shelter (£1,000 each).

Exclusions Anyone not known to the settlors.

Applications This trust states that it does not respond to unsolicited applications. 'The charity only makes grants to charities already known to the settlors as this is a personal charitable trust.'

Bellasis Trust

General

£42,000 (2007/08)
Beneficial area UK.

4th Floor, 65 Kingsway, London WC2B 6TD
Correspondent P C R Wates, Trustee
Trustees P C R Wates; Mrs A B Wates; Mrs A L M Elliott; J R F Lulham.
CC Number 1085972
Information available Accounts were on file at the Charity Commission.

Established in March 2001, it is the 'intention of the trustees to support local charities including those for the disadvantaged persons'. In 2007/08 the trust had assets of £921,000 and an income of £49,000. Grants totalled £42,000.

There were 14 beneficiaries of £1,000 or more listed in the accounts.

Beneficiaries included: Royal Horticultural Society, St Anne's School – Banstead, St Mary's School – Ascot and St Michael's PCC (£5,000 each); the David Lynne Charitable Trust (£3,500); Book Power (£3,000); the Laser Trust

Fund and St John Ambulance (£2,000 each); Macmillan Cancer Support (£1,500); the National Maritime Museum and St Catherine's Hospice (£1,000 each).

Applications 'The trustees research and consider applicants for grants.'

The Benham Charitable Settlement

General

£149,000 (2007/08)
Beneficial area UK, with very strong emphasis on Northamptonshire.

Hurstbourne, Portnall Drive, Virginia Water GU25 4NR
Correspondent The Secretary
Trustees Mrs M M Tittle; Lady Hutton; E N Langley; D A H Tittle; Revd. J A Nickols.
CC Number 239371
Information available Accounts were on file at the Charity Commission.

The charity was founded in 1964 by the late Cedric Benham and his wife Hilda, then resident in Northamptonshire, 'to benefit charities and other good causes and considerations'.

The object of the charity is the support of registered charities working in many different fields – including charities involved in medical research, disability, older people, children and young people, disadvantaged people, overseas aid, missions to seamen, the welfare of ex-servicemen, wildlife, the environment, and the arts. The trust also supports the Church of England, and the work of Christian mission throughout the world. Special emphasis is placed upon those churches and charitable organisations within the county of Northamptonshire [especially as far as new applicants are concerned].

In 2007/08 the charity had assets of £4.6 million and an income of £183,000. It made 174 donations totalling £149,000 with the majority of grants ranging from £100 to £600.

Grants of £1,000 or more were made to: Northamptonshire Association of Youth Clubs (£35,000 in two grants); All Saints Church – Peckham (£10,000); Progressive Supranuclear Palsy Association (£6,000); Holy Trinity

Church – Muheza Hospital, Tanzania (£5,000); and the Besom Foundation and Coworth Flexlands School (£5,000 each).

Beneficiaries of grants under £1,000 each included: Arthritis Care, British Heart Foundation, Camphill Village Trust, Cathedral Camps, the Children's Trust, Combat Stress, Deafbind UK, Diabetes UK, Huntingdon's Disease Association, Limbless Association, Meninigitis Trust, Muscular Dystrophy Campaign, RoRo Sailing Project and Victim Support – Northamptonshire (£600 each); Cued Speech Association, Farm Crisis Network, Living Paintings Trust, National Eye Research Centre, SENSE, Tall Ships Youth Trust and the Willow Trust (£500 each); and Peterborough Cathedral Trust and Whizz Kidz (£400 each).

Exclusions No grants to individuals.

Applications In recent years the trust has not been considering new applications.

Michael and Lesley Bennett Charitable Trust

Jewish

£66,000 (2007/08)
Beneficial area UK.

Bedegars Lea, Kenwood Close, London NW3 7JL
Correspondent Michael Bennett, Trustee
Trustees Michael Bennett; Lesley V Bennett.
CC Number 1047611
Information available Full accounts were on file at the Charity Commission.

The trust supports a range of causes, but the largest donations were to Jewish organisations. In 2007/08 the trust had assets of £395,000 and an income of £46,000 including £20,000 from donations. There were 37 grants made totalling £66,000.

Grants of £1,000 or more were made to nine organisations, including: Chai Cancer Care (£20,000); Jewish Care (£11,000); World Jewish Relief (£10,000); Magen David Adorn (£2,600); and Tel Aviv Foundation (£1,000).

Applications In writing to the correspondent.

The Ruth Berkowitz Charitable Trust

Jewish, medical research and young people

£508,000 (2007/08)

Beneficial area UK and overseas.

39 Farm Avenue, London NW2 2BJ

Correspondent The Trustees

Trustees *Philip Beckman; Brian Beckman.*

CC Number 1111673

Information available Accounts were on file at the Charity Commission.

Registered with the Charity Commission in October 2005, in 2007/08 the trust had assets of £4.4 million and an income of £493,000. Grants totalled £508,000 and were broken down as follows:

Category	Value	No.
Children/young people/education	£298,000	15
Community	£160,000	9
Medical	£30,000	4
Small Grants Fund	£20,000	1
Religion	Nil	0

Beneficiaries in each category included:

Medical
Cancer Research UK (£15,000); University College London (£7,500); Royal Free Hampstead Charitable Trust, – Paul Shrank Fund (£5,000); and Laniado Hospital UK (£2,500).

Children, young people and education
Wiener Library Institute of Contemporary History (£50,000); National Jewish Chaplaincy Board (£43,000); Kisharon (£30,000); Bnai Brith Hillel Foundation (£28,000); London School of Jewish Studies and Norwood (£25,000 each); London Jewish Cultural Centre and World ORT (£20,000 each); the National Yad Vashem Charitable Trust (£10,000); Union of Jewish Students (£15,000); Association of Jewish Sixth Formers (£7,500); and Camp Simcha, Hamayon and London Philharmonic Orchestra (£5,000 each).

Community
Community Security Trust (£35,000); Friends of Magen David Adorn and World Jewish Relief (£30,000 each); UK Friends of Meir Panim (£25,000); Nightingale House (£15,000); Northampton Door to Door Service (£10,000); and Langdon Foundation, Ohel Sarah and the ZSV Trust (£5,000 each).

Small Grants Fund
Lord Ashdown Charitable Settlement (£20,000).

Religion
In this category in the previous year, the sum of £11,000 was distributed in two grants.

Applications In writing to the correspondent.

The Bestway Foundation

Education, welfare and medical

£500,000 to organisations and individuals (2007/08)

Beneficial area UK and overseas.

Bestway Cash and Carry Ltd, Abbey Road, Park Royal, London NW10 7BW

Correspondent M Y Sheikh, Trustee

Trustees *A K Bhatti; A K Chaudhary; M Y Sheikh; Z M Choudrey; M A Pervez.*

CC Number 297178

Information available Accounts were on file at the Charity Commission.

The objects of this foundation are the 'advancement of education by grants to schoolchildren and students who are of Indian, Pakistani, Bangladeshi or Sri Lankan origin; and the relief of sickness, and preservation and protection of health in the UK and overseas, especially in India, Pakistan, Bangladesh and Sri Lanka'. Grants are made to individuals, UK registered charities, non-registered charities and overseas charities. All trustees are directors and shareholders of Bestway (Holdings) Limited, the parent company of Bestway Cash and Carry Limited.

In 2007/08 this trust had assets of £4.4 million, an income of £980,000 and made grants totalling £500,000.

Beneficiaries included: Bestway Foundation Pakistan (£200,000); Northern University (£50,000); British EduTrust Foundation (£36,000); Duke of Edinburgh Awards (£16,000); Silver Star Appeal (£15,000); Leonard Cheshire Disability (£10,000); SSAT – Southampton City Council for Bellemoor School (£5,500); Concern for Mental Health, GLMW Scout County Development Fund and National Grocers' Benevolent Fund (£2,000 each); Wines and Spirits Trades Benevolent

Society (£1,000); and Fleetwood Tigers (£500).

There were also 33 grants made to individuals during the year.

Exclusions No grants for trips or travel abroad.

Applications In writing to the correspondent, enclosing a stamped, addressed envelope. Applications are considered in March/April. Telephone calls are not welcome.

Thomas Betton's Charity for Pensions and Relief in Need

Children and young people

£57,000 (2007/08)

Beneficial area UK.

Ironmongers' Hall, Barbican, London EC2Y 8AA

Tel. 020 7776 2311

Website www.ironhall.co.uk

Correspondent The Charities Administrator

Trustee *The Worshipful Company of Ironmongers.*

CC Number 280143

Information available Accounts were on file at the Charity Commission.

This charity makes grants for educational activities for children and young people up to the age of 25 from disadvantaged backgrounds. It also gives to specific charitable organisations with which the trustee has an ongoing relationship (a block grant is made to Housing the Homeless which allocates grants to individuals).

In 2007/08 the trust had assets of £948,000 and an income of £35,000, including £34,000 from investments and £27,000 from Thomas Betton's Estate Charity. Grants totalled £57,000.

Beneficiaries included: Housing the Homeless Central Fund (£22,000); the Art Room and North East Community Forests (£5,000 each); Ivorian Advice and Support Group (£4,700); Living Paintings Trust (£2,500); John Boste

Youth Centre (£2,100); Rainy Day Trust and Sheriffs' and Recorder's Fund (£2,000 each); and Hope's Place (£1,200).

Exclusions Applications for grants to individuals are accepted only from registered social workers or other agencies, not directly from individuals.

Applications In writing to the correspondent.

The Billmeir Charitable Trust

General, health and medical

£161,000 (2007/08)

Beneficial area UK, with a preference for the Surrey area, specifically Elstead, Tilford, Farnham and Frensham.

Moore Stephens, St Paul's House, Warwick Lane, London EC4M 7BP

Tel. 020 7334 9191

Correspondent Keith Lawrence

Trustees B C Whitaker; M R Macfadyen; S Marriott; J Whitaker.

CC Number 208561

Information available Accounts were on file at the Charity Commission.

The trust states that it supports a wide variety of causes. About a quarter of the grants are given to health and medical charities and about a third of the grants are given to local organisations in Surrey, especially the Farnham, Frensham, Elstead and Tilford areas.

In 2007/08 the trust had assets of £4.4 million and an income of £161,000. Donations were made to 32 charities totalling £161,000. Of organisations supported during the year, 27 also received grants in 2006/07.

Beneficiaries included: Reed's School – Cobham and the Watts Gallery (£10,000 each); Arundel Castle Cricket Foundation, Lord Mayor Treloar School, Marlborough College, the Meath Home and the New Ashgate Gallery (£7,000 each); Army Benevolent Fund, Yvonne Arnaud Theatre, Disability Challengers – Farnham, Farnham Trust, RNIB, Woodlarks Workshop and Youth Sport Trust (£5,000 each); Fairbridge and Surrey Community Foundation (£3,000 each); and Checkendon Parochial

Church Council and Frensham Church (£2,000 each).

Applications The trust states that it does not request applications and that its funds are fully committed.

The Bintaub Charitable Trust

Jewish

£84,000 (2007/08)

Beneficial area Greater London, worldwide.

125 Wolmer Gardens, Edgware HA8 8QF

Correspondent Mrs Dahlia Rosenberg

Trustees James Frohwein; Tania Frohwein; Mrs Dahlia Rosenberg; Rabbi E Stefansky.

CC Number 1003915

Information available Accounts were on file at the Charity Commission.

This trust was set up in 1991 and provides grants to mainly London based organisations, towards 'the advancement of education in and the religion of the Orthodox Jewish faith'. Grants are also given for other charitable causes, mainly towards medical and children's work.

In 2007/08 it had an income from donations of £78,000 and made grants totalling £84,500.

The 13 beneficiaries of grants over £1,000 each included: Yeshiva Tiferes Yaacov (£12,000); Kupat Ha'ir (£7,700); EMF (£7,300); Gateshead Jewish Boys School (£6,500); Eitz Chaim Schools (£6,000); Va'ad Harabbanim L'inyanei Tzedaka (£5,700); Menorah Foundation School (£3,900); Jewish Day School (£3,000); LJGH. (£2,900); Well of Torah (£2,000); and Jewish Rescue and Relief (£1,500).

Unlisted grants under £1,000 each totalled £20,000.

Applications The trust has previously stated that new applications are not being accepted.

The Birmingham Hospital Saturday Fund Medical Charity and Welfare Trust

Medical

£41,000 (2007)

Beneficial area UK, but mostly centred around the West Midlands and Birmingham area.

Gamgee House, 2 Darnley Road, Birmingham B16 8TE

Tel. 0121 454 3601

Email charitabletrust@bhsf.co.uk

Correspondent The Secretary

Trustees Dr R P Kanas; S G Hall; E S Hickman; M Malone; D J Read; J Salmons.

CC Number 502428

Information available Accounts for year ending 2008 were overdue at the Charity Commission.

This trust supports the relief of sickness, with the trustees also holding an interest in medical research. The trustees continue to give priority to charities that benefit those living in the West Midlands area with some interest in the South West for historical reasons. The trust no longer receives an income from the parent company and so the trustees are now working purely with reserves and the interest from them. This has resulted in a more critical look at projects at each meeting and donations are now generally less than £2,000. Projects that are appropriate and well thought through, with realistic cost breakdowns, are given greater consideration.

In 2007 the trust had assets of £500,000 and an income of £27,000. Grants totalled £41,000. There were 34 grants of £300 or more listed in the accounts.

Beneficiaries included: Friends of Victoria School – Northfield (£3,800); NHS West Midlands (£3,400); Birmingham Centre for Arts Therapies and Starlight Children's Foundation (£2,500 each); Vascular Department, Selly Oak Hospital (£2,000); Dream Holidays – Isle of Wight (£1,900); the Mary Stevens Hospice – Stourbridge (£1,600); Institute of Ageing and Health – Birmingham (£1,500); Contact the

Elderly – Birmingham (£1,200); Christian Lewis Trust – Cardiff (£1,100); Action Medical Research – Horsham, Children's Heart Foundation and REACT Surrey (£1,000); Katherine House – Stafford (£900); St Martin's Centre for Health and Healing (£750); Deep Impact Theatre Company and Birmingham Heart Care – Walsall (£500 each); and Acorns Children's Hospice – Birmingham (£315).

Exclusions The trust will not generally fund:

- direct appeals from individuals or students
- administration expenditure including salaries
- bank loans/deficits/mortgages
- items or services which should normally be publicly funded
- large general appeals
- vehicle operating costs
- motor vehicles for infrequent use and where subsidised vehicle share schemes are available to charitable organisations.

Applications On a form available from the correspondent. The form requires basic information and should be submitted with financial details. Evidence should be provided that the project has been adequately considered through the provision of quotes or supporting documents, although the trust dislikes applications which provide too much general information or have long-winded descriptions of projects. Applicants should take great care to read the guidance notes on the application form. The trustees meet four times a year and deadlines are given when application forms are sent out.

Birthday House Trust

General

£65,000 to organisations (2007/08)

Beneficial area England and Wales.

Dickinson Trust Ltd, Pollen House, 10–12 Cork Street, London W1S 3LW

Correspondent Laura Gosling

Trustee *The Dickinson Trust Limited and Rathbone Trust Company Limited.*

CC Number 248028

Information available Accounts were on file at the Charity Commission.

Established in 1966, the main work of this trust is engaged with the running of a residential home for older people in Midhurst, West Sussex. In 2007/08 it had assets of £6 million and an income of £252,000. Grants to 16 organisations totalled £65,000. A further £72,000 was distributed to 14 pensioners.

Beneficiaries included: Drukpa Trust (£25,000); Soil Association Limited (£17,000); Merton Park Scouts and Sussex Community Foundation (£5,000 each); Mary Rose Appeal (£2,500); Royal Hospital Chelsea Appeal (£1,000); Fire Services National Benevolent Fund (£500); Bob Champion Cancer Trust, Mind in Brighton and Hove and National Memorial Aboretum (£250 each); Breakthrough Breast Cancer (£100); and the Murray Downland Trust (£50).

Exclusions No applications will be considered from individuals or non-charitable organisations.

Applications In writing to the correspondent, including a stamped, addressed envelope. No application forms are issued and there is no deadline. Only successful applicants are acknowledged.

The Bisgood Charitable Trust (registered as Miss Jeanne Bisgood's Charitable Trust)

Roman Catholic purposes and older people

£210,000 (2007/08)

Beneficial area UK, overseas and locally in Bournemouth and Dorset, especially Poole.

12 Waters Edge, Brudenell Road, Poole BH13 7NN

Correspondent Miss J M Bisgood, Trustee

Trustees *Miss J M Bisgood, Chair; Miss P Schulte; P J K Bisgood.*

CC Number 208714

Information available Accounts were on file at the Charity Commission, without a list of grants.

This trust has emerged following an amalgamation of the Bisgood Trust with Miss Jeanne Bisgood's Charitable Trust. Both trusts had the same objectives.

The General Fund has the following priorities:

1) Roman Catholic charities.
2) Charities benefiting people in Poole, Bournemouth and the county of Dorset.
3) National charities for the benefit of older people.

No grants are made to local charities which do not fall under categories 1 or 2. Many health and welfare charities are supported as well as charities working in relief and development overseas.

In 2007/08 the trust had assets of £5.6 million, an income of £217,000 and made grants totalling £210,000. Previous beneficiaries from the general fund have included Apex Trust, ITDG, Horder Centre for Arthritis , Impact, St Barnabas' Society, St Francis Leprosy Guild, Sight Savers International and YMCA.

In considering appeals the trustees will give preference to charities whose fundraising and administrative costs are proportionately low.

The trust was given 12 paintings to be held as part of the trust funds. Most of the paintings were sold and the proceeds were placed in a sub-fund, the Bertram Fund, established in 1998, the income of which is purely for Roman Catholic causes. It is intended that it will primarily support major capital projects. Most grants are made anonymously from this fund.

Exclusions Grants are not given to local charities which do not fit categories 1 or 2 above. Individuals and non-registered charities are not supported.

Applications In writing to the correspondent, quoting the UK registration number and registered title of the charity. A copy of the most recent accounts should also be enclosed. Applications should not be made directly to the Bertram Fund. Applications for capital projects 'should provide brief details of the main purposes, the total target and the current state of the appeal'. The trustees are unable to acknowledge appeals. The trustees normally meet in late February/early March and September.

The Michael Bishop Foundation

General

£265,000 (2007/08)

Beneficial area Worldwide with a preference for Birmingham and the Midlands.

Donington Hall, Castle Donington, Derby DE74 2SB

Correspondent The Trustees

Trustees *Sir Michael Bishop, Chair; Grahame N Elliott; John T Wolfe; John S Coulson.*

CC Number 297627

Information available Full accounts were on file at the Charity Commission.

Sir Michael Bishop of British Midland set up the foundation in 1987 by giving almost £1 million of shares in Airlines of Britain (Holdings) plc, the parent company of British Midland. A further sum was given in 1992.

In 2007/08 the trust had assets of £2.6 million, which generated an income of £106,000. Grants to 28 organisations totalled £265,000.

The beneficiaries of the largest grants were: the Royal Flying Doctor Service of Australia (£82,000); the D'Oyly Carte Opera Trust Ltd (£70,000); Alcohol and Drugs Abstinence Service (£30,000); Live Music Now! (£20,000); and the Terrence Higgins Trust and Policy Exchange (£15,000 each).

Other grants included those made to: Expat UK (£5,000); Nightingales Children's Project (£3,000); the Ivor Novello Statue Fund and Wellbeing (£2,500 each); the Morris Venables Charitable Trust (£2,000); Cancer Research (£1,250); and Birmingham Early Music Festival, Macmillian Cancer Support and the Star Appeal – National Star College (£1,000 each).

Applications In writing to the correspondent.

The Sydney Black Charitable Trust

Evangelical Christianity, social welfare and young people

£108,000 (2007/08)

Beneficial area UK.

30 Welford Place, London SW19 5AJ

Correspondent The Secretary

Trustees *Mrs J D Crabtree; Mrs H J Dickenson; S J Crabtree; P M Crabtree.*

CC Number 219855

Information available Accounts were filed at the Charity Commission, without a grants list.

In 2001 the Edna Black Charitable Trust and the Cyril Black Charitable Trust were incorporated into this trust.

In 2007/08 the trust had an income of £163,000 and total assets were £3.1 million. Grants totalled £108,000. A substantial donation was made to Endeavour (£20,000); others totalled £88,000 and were of between £125 and £250 each. About 700 institutions benefited.

Applications Applications, made in writing to the correspondent, will be considered by the appropriate trust.

The Bertie Black Foundation

Jewish and general

£329,000 (2007/08)

Beneficial area UK, Israel.

Abbots House, 198 Lower High Street, Watford WD17 2FG

Correspondent Harry Black, Trustee

Trustees *I B Black; D Black; H S Black; Mrs I R Seddon.*

CC Number 245207

Information available Information was on file at the Charity Commission.

The trust tends to support organisations which are known to the trustees or where long-term commitments have been entered into. Grants can be given over a three-year period towards major projects.

In 2007/08 it had assets of £2.8 million and an income of £143,000. There were 116 grants made totalling £329,000.

Beneficiaries included: I Rescue (£50,000); Magen David Adom (£47,000 in three grants); Alyn Hospital (£49,000 in two grants); Emunah (£38,000); Laniardo Hospital and Shaare Zedek (£25,000 each); Friends of Israel Sports Centre for Disabled (£20,000); Child Resettlement Trust (£10,000 in four grants); Norwood (£7,600 in four grants); and Hope (£5,200 in four grants).

Applications The trust states it 'supports causes known to the trustees' and that they 'do not respond to unsolicited requests'.

Sir Alec Black's Charity

Relief in need

£66,000 to organisations (2007/08)

Beneficial area UK, with a preference for Grimsby.

Wilson Sharpe and Co., 27 Osborne Street, Grimsby DN31 1NU

Correspondent Stewart Wilson, Trustee

Trustees *J N Harrison; P A Mounfield; Dr D F Wilson; S Wilson.*

CC Number 220295

Information available Accounts were on file at the Charity Commission.

The primary purposes of the trust are:

- the purchase and distribution of bed linen and down pillows to charitable organisations caring for people who are sick or infirm
- the provision of pensions and grants to people employed by Sir Alec Black during his lifetime
- the benefit of sick, poor fishermen and dockworkers from the borough of Grimsby.

In 2007/08 it had assets of £1.5 million and an income of £101,000. Grants to former employees of the settlor totalled £15,000. A further £66,000 went in grants to 41 organisations, with £300 given to fishermen and dockworkers.

Applications In writing to the correspondent. Trustees meet in May and November; applications need to be received in March or September.

The Blair Foundation

Wildlife, access to countryside and general

£75,000 (2007/08)

Beneficial area UK, particularly southern England and Scotland; overseas.

Smith and Williamson, 1 Bishops Wharf, Walnut Tree Close, Guildford, Surrey GU1 4RA

Tel. 01483 407100

Correspondent The Trustees

Trustees *Robert Thornton; Jennifer Thornton; Graham Healy; Alan Thornton; Philippa Thornton.*

CC Number 801755

Information available Full accounts were on file at the Charity Commission.

This foundation was originally established to create environmental conditions in which wildlife can prosper, as well as improving disability access to such areas. This work is focused on Scotland and southern England.

In 2007/08 the trust had assets of £1.5 million and an income of £98,000. Grants totalled £75,000.

There were 24 grants of £1,000 or more listed in the accounts with beneficiaries including: Ayrshire Wildlife Services (£20,000); Queen Elizabeth Foundation for the Disabled (£12,000); Scottish National Trust (£7,000); Home Farm Trust (£5,000); SENSE (£4,000); Music in Hospitals (£1,500); and Brainwave, British Youth Opera, Live Music Now! and RSPB (£1,000 each).

Donations of less than £1,000 each totalled just under £4,000.

Exclusions Charities that have objectives the trustees consider harmful to the environment are not supported.

Applications In writing to the correspondent, for consideration at trustees' meetings held at least once a year. A receipt for donations is requested from all donees.

Blakes Benevolent Trust

General

£57,000 to organisations (2007/08)

Beneficial area UK.

2 Yew Tree Road, Huyton-with-Roby, Liverpool L36 5UQ

Correspondent The Trustees

Trustees *N K Silk; B Ball; P M Davies.*

CC Number 225268

Information available Accounts are on file at the Charity Commission, but with only a brief narrative report and without a grants list.

In 2007/08 the trust had assets of £2.5 million and an income of £102,000. Grants were given to eight organisations totalling £57,000, with 25 individuals receiving £14,000.

Beneficiaries were: Motor Trade Benevolent Fund (£25,000); Crisis, Front Line, Liverpool City Mission and Salvation Army (£6,000 each); and Nugent Care Society, the Universal Beneficent Society and Wirral Churches (£3,000 each). All of the organisations received the same grants in the previous year.

Applications This trust has previously stated that it only gives to 'private beneficiaries'.

The Sir Victor Blank Charitable Settlement

Jewish and general

£209,000 (2007/08)

Beneficial area Worldwide.

c/o Wilkins Kennedy, Bridge House, London Bridge, London SE1 9QR

Correspondent R Gulliver, Trustee

Trustees *Sir M V Blank; Lady S H Blank; R Gulliver.*

CC Number 1084187

Information available Accounts were on file at the Charity Commission.

Registered with the Charity Commission in December 2000, in 2007/08 this charity had assets of £1.6 million generating an income of £150,000. Grants totalled £209,000.

There were 24 donations of £1,000 or more listed in the accounts. Beneficiaries included: United Jewish Israel Appeal (£52,000); Jewish Care and Oxford Centre for Hebrew and Jewish Studies (£25,000 each); One Voice Europe (£20,000); Oxford Philomusica (£15,000); Norwood Ltd (£11,000); the Lord Taverners (£5,000); Jewish Deaf Association (£3,000); London Jewish Forum and the St John of Jerusalem Eye Hospital (£2,500 each); Delamere Forest School (£2,000); and Deafblind UK, Edinburgh House, the Heathlands Village, Help the Hospices, Maccabi GB, University Jewish Chaplaincy Board and World Jewish Relief (£1,000 each).

Other grants of less than £1,000 each totalled £13,000.

Applications In writing to the correspondent.

Blatchington Court Trust

Supporting vision-impaired people under the age of 30

£67,000 to organisations (2007/08)

Beneficial area UK, preference for Sussex.

Ridgeland House, 165 Dyke Road, Hove BN3 1TL

Tel. 01273 727222

Website www.blatchington-court.co.uk

Correspondent The Executive Manager

Trustees *Richard Martin, Chair; Alison Acason; Daniel Ellmar-Brown; Georgina James; Roger Jones; Stephen Pavey; Robert Perkins; Jonathan Wilson; Anna Hunter.*

CC Number 306350

Information available Accounts were on file at the Charity Commission.

This trust's initial income arose from the sale of the former Blatchington Court School for people who are partially sighted at Seaford. Its aim is 'the promotion of education and employment (including social and physical training) of blind and partially sighted persons under the age of 30 years'. There is a preference for Sussex.

The Charity has two grant-making programmes; financial assistance and capital grants:

Financial Assistance

The primary and largest is the Sussex Programme, which provides services to individual clients including advocacy, counselling, education, training and assistance in finding employment and family support.

Capital Grants

The second programme is for capital grants which covers all the UK and through which the charity, usually in partnership with sister charities, will:

i) Award grants for the provision of recreational and leisure facilities (or contributions towards such facilities), which enable vision impaired people to develop their physical, mental and moral capacities.

ii) Make grants to any voluntary or charitable organisation approved by the trustees, the objects of which include the promotion of education, training and/or employment of vision impaired young people and their general wellbeing in pursuance of all the foregoing.

In 2007/08 the trust had assets of almost £11 million and an income, mainly from investments, of £581,000. Grants paid totalled £187,000, of which £67,000 went to organisations.

Applications In writing to the correspondent from whom individual or charity grant application forms can be obtained. Applications can be considered at any time. An application on behalf of a registered charity should include audited accounts and up-to-date information on the charity and its commitments.

The Neville and Elaine Blond Charitable Trust

Jewish and general

£114,000 (2007/08)
Beneficial area Worldwide.

c/o H W Fisher and Co, Chartered Accountants, Acre House, 11–15 William Road, London NW1 3ER

Tel. 020 7388 7000
Correspondent The Trustees
Trustees *Dame Simone Prendergast; P Blond; Mrs A E Susman; S N Susman; Mrs J Skidmore.*
CC Number 206319
Information available Full accounts were on file at the Charity Commission.

In 2007/08 the trust had assets of £1.3 million and an income of £65,000. Grants totalling £114,000 were made to 13 organisations, of which nine had been supported in the previous year. The main beneficiaries were: Beth Shalom Holocaust Memorial Centre (£50,000); United Jewish Israel Appeal (£30,000); and British WIZO (£10,000).

The remaining grants were in the range of £250 and £8,000 and included those to: Community Security Trust (£8,000); Holocaust Educational Trust (£5,000); Halle Orchestra (£4,000); Weizmann Institute Foundation (£2,000); British ORT, Chicken Shed Theatre and Institute of Child Health (£1,000 each); and Kids Company and Liver Research (£500 each).

Exclusions Only registered charities are supported.

Applications In writing to the correspondent. Applications should arrive by 31 January for consideration in late spring.

The Blueberry Charitable Trust

Jewish and relief in need

£53,000 (2007/08)
Beneficial area UK.

Number 14, The Embankment, Vale Road, Heaton Mersey, Stockport SK4 3GN
Correspondent I Aspinall, Trustee
Trustees *J H Lyons; I Aspinall; K Pinnell.*
CC Number 1080950
Information available Accounts were on file at Charity Commission

Registered with the Charity Commission in May 2000, 'the principal object of the charity is to use income for the relief of poverty and hardship amongst Jewish persons or the advancement of the Jewish religion, or for other charitable purposes'.

In 2007/08 it had an income of £418,000 mainly from donations of shares. It made grants totalling £53,000. Assets stood at £794,000.

There were nine grants made over £1,000 each. Beneficiaries were: United Jewish Israel Appeal (£13,000); Hale and District Hebrew Congregation (£8,700); Manchester Jewish Federation (£5,500); Outward Bound Trust (£4,500); Yeshwas Lubavitch (£3,750); King David School (£3,200); Lubavitch South Manchester (£3,000); North Cheshire Jewish Primary School (£1,400) and Community Security Trust (£1,250).

Applications In writing to the correspondent.

The Boltons Trust

Social welfare, medicine and education

£15,000 (2007/08)
Beneficial area Unrestricted.

12 York Gate, Regent's Park, London NW1 4QS
Correspondent The Trustees
Trustees *Mrs C Albuquerque; R M Baldock; S D Albuquerque.*
CC Number 257951
Information available Accounts were on file at the Charity Commission.

The main aims of the trust are:

- the pursuit of understanding and the reduction of innocent suffering
- support for education, research and welfare projects.

In 2007/08 the trust had assets of £1.2 million, an income of £44,000 and made grants totalling £15,000 (£180,000 in the previous year). The sole beneficiary during the year was Global Health Foundation (£15,000).

In the previous year, beneficiaries included Council for Christians and Jews, Dartington International Summer School, Jewish Association of Business Ethics, London Philharmonic Orchestra, Norwood, Trinity College of Music and World ORT.

Applications In writing to the correspondent. The trustees meet on a regular basis to consider applications.

The John and Celia Bonham Christie Charitable Trust

General

£27,000 (2007/08)

Beneficial area UK, with some preference for the former county of Avon.

PO Box 9081, Taynton, Gloucester GL19 3WX

Correspondent The Trustees

Trustees *Richard Bonham Christie; Robert Bonham Christie; Rosemary Ker.*

CC Number 326296

Information available Accounts were on file at the Charity Commission, without a list of grants.

In 2007/08 the trust had assets of £1.3 million and a total income of £50,000. Grants were made to 27 organisations totalling £27,000.

Previous beneficiaries have included BIBIC, Butterwick Hospice, Cancer Research Campaign, Derby TOC, Digestive Disorder Foundation, Dorothy House, Elizabeth Finn Trust, Foundation for the Study of Infant Cot Deaths, Frome Festival, Home Start South Wiltshire, Inspire Foundation, Kings Medical Trust, Royal Society for the Blind Winsley, Sea Cadet Association, St John Ambulance and Ten of Us.

Exclusions No grants to individuals.

Applications In writing to the correspondent. The trustees regret that the income is fully allocated for the foreseeable future. Only a small number of new applications are supported each year.

The Charlotte Bonham-Carter Charitable Trust

General

£89,000 (2007/08)

Beneficial area UK, with some emphasis on Hampshire.

66 Lincoln's Inn Fields, London WC2A 3LH

Correspondent Sir Matthew Farrer, Trustee

Trustees *Sir Matthew Farrer; Norman Bonham-Carter; David Bonham-Carter; Georgina Nayler; Eliza Bonham-Carter.*

CC Number 292839

Information available Accounts were on file at the Charity Commission.

The trust is principally concerned with supporting charitable bodies and purposes which were of particular concern to Lady Bonham-Carter during her lifetime or are within the county of Hampshire. 'The trustees continue to support a core number of charities to whom they have made grants in the past as well as reviewing all applications received and making grants to new charities within their grant-giving criteria.'

In 2007/08 the trust had assets of £3.9 million, which generated an income of £89,000. It gave £89,000 in 73 grants, ranging from £500 to £10,000.

Beneficiaries included: National Trust (£10,000); Hampshire Archives Trust (£5,000); Ashmolean Museum (£4,000); Clifton College, Handel House Museum, Holbourne Musum of Art, Pitt Rivers Museum, Rambert Dance Company and Wordsworth Trust (£2,000 each); and British Library, Charleston Trust, Deafway, Jubilee Sailing Trust, Listening Books, Oakhaven Hospice Trust, Royal Academy, Seeing Ear and St Paul's Cathedral Foundation (£1,000 each).

Grants of £1,000 or less included those to: Age Concern, Brighton and Hove Parent's and Children's' Group, Counsel and Care, Independent Age, Sailors' Families' Society, Society of St James and Whizz Kidz.

Exclusions No grants to individuals or non-registered charities.

Applications In writing to the correspondent. The application should include details of the funds required, funds raised so far and the timescale involved. The trust states that unsolicited general applications are unlikely to be successful and only increase the cost of administration. There are no application forms. Trustees meet in January and July; applications need to be received by May or November.

Salo Bordon Charitable Trust

Jewish

£334,000 (2007/08)

Beneficial area UK and worldwide.

78 Corringham Road, London NW11 7EB

Correspondent S Bordon, Trustee

Trustees *S Bordon; Mrs L Bordon; M Bordon.*

CC Number 266439

Information available Full accounts were on file at the Charity Commission.

This trust makes grants mainly to Jewish organisations, for social welfare and religious education. In 2007/08 it had assets amounting to £7.5 million and an income of £335,000. Grants were made totalling £334,000.

Previous beneficiaries have included Agudas Israel Housing Association Ltd, Baer Hatorah, Beth Jacob Grammar School, Brisk Yeshivas, Golders Green Beth Hamedrash Congregation Jaffa Institute, Jewish Learning Exchange, London Academy of Jewish Studies, Society of Friends of Torah and WST Charity.

Applications In writing to the correspondent.

The Oliver Borthwick Memorial Trust

Homelessness

£49,000 (2007/08)

Beneficial area UK.

c/o Donor Grants Department, Charities Aid Foundation, Kings Hill, West Malling ME19 4TA

Correspondent The Trustees

Trustees *M H R Brethedon; R A Graham; J Macdonald; J R Marriott; Mrs V Wrigley; Ms J S Mace; D Scott.*

CC Number 256206

Information available Accounts were on file at the Charity Commission.

The intention of the trust is to provide shelter and help the homeless. The trustees welcome applications from small but viable charities where the trust is able to make a significant contribution to the practical work of the charity, especially in disadvantaged inner-city areas.

In 2007/08 it had assets of £904,000, which generated an income of £48,000. Grants totalling £49,000 were made to 19 organisations.

Beneficiaries included: St Matthew Housing (£5,000); Manna Society, Mission in Hounslow Trust, Northampton Kitchen, Only Connect UK, Porch, Shrewsbury Homes for All, St George Dragon Trust and Streets Alive Theatre Company Ltd (£3,000 each); Scottish Churches Housing Action (£2,000); Derbyshire Housing Aid Ltd (£1,500); and Almshouse Association (£1,000).

Exclusions No grants to individuals, including people working temporarily overseas for a charity where the request is for living expenses, together with applications relating to health, disability and those from non-registered charitable organisations.

Applications Letters should be set out on a maximum of two sides of A4, giving full details of the project with costs, who the project will serve and the anticipated outcome of the project. Meetings take place once a year in May. Applications should be received no later than April.

The Boshier-Hinton Foundation

Children and adults with special educational or other needs

£129,000 (2007/08)
Beneficial area UK and overseas.

Yeomans, Aythorpe Roding, Great Dunmow CM6 1PD
Correspondent Peter Boshier, Trustee
Trustees *Thea Boshier, Chair; Peter Boshier; Peter Carr; Janet Beale.*
CC Number 1108886
Information available Accounts were on file at the Charity Commission.

Set up in 2005, the foundation's main area of interest is children and adults with special educational or other needs and their families.

In 2007/08 it had an income of £72,000 and made grants totalling £129,000. Assets at year end stood at £724,000.

The foundation considered 77 applications during the year, of which 54 were successful. Beneficiaries included: ACCURO (£11,000); Ability Sports, British Paralympic Association and Demand (£5,000 each); CHASE Children's Hospice (£3,000); Blind in Business (£2,500); Caring for Life and Royal London Society for the Blind (£2,000 each); Youth Create (£1,500); and Music Alive and Starlight Children's Foundation (£1,000 each).

Applications In writing to the correspondent.

The Bothwell Charitable Trust

Disability, health, older people and conservation

£46,000 (2007/08)
Beneficial area England, particularly the South East.

14 Kirkly Close, South Croydon CR2 0ET
Tel. 020 8657 3369
Correspondent Angela Bothwell, Chair of Trustees
Trustees *Angela J Bothwell, Chair; Paul L James; Crispian M P Howard.*
CC Number 299056
Information available Information was on file at the Charity Commission.

The trust makes grants towards health, disability, conservation and older people's causes. In 2007/08 the trust had an income of £40,000 from rent and made grants totalling £46,000 to 25 organisations.

Grants were for amounts of either £1,000 or £2,500. Beneficiaries included: Arthritis Research Campaign, British Home and Hospital for Incurables, ECHO International Health Services Ltd, Friends of the Elderly, Leukaemia Research Fund, Parkinson's Disease Society, St Christopher's Hospice and Vitalise (£2,500 each); and Alzheimer's Society, British Trust for Conservation Volunteers, Children's Country Holiday Fund, Headway, National Autistic Society and Royal National Institute for Deaf People (£1,000 each).

Exclusions No grants for animal charities, overseas causes, individuals, or charities not registered with the Charity Commission.

Applications In writing to the correspondent. Distributions are usually made in February or March each year.

The Harry Bottom Charitable Trust

Religion, education and medical

£78,000 (2007/08)
Beneficial area UK, with a preference for Yorkshire and Derbyshire.

c/o Westons, Chartered Accountants, Queen's Buildings, 55 Queen Street, Sheffield S1 2DX
Correspondent J S Hinsley
Trustees *Revd J M Kilner; Prof. T H Lilley; Prof. I G Rennie; Prof. A Rawlinson.*
CC Number 204675
Information available Accounts were on file at the Charity Commission.

The trust states that support is divided roughly equally between religious, educational and medical causes. Within these categories grants are given to:

- religion – small local appeals and cathedral appeals
- education – universities and schools
- medical – equipment for hospitals and charities concerned with disability.

In 2007/08 the trust had assets of £5 million and an income of £560,000. Grants were made totalling £78,000 and were broken down as follows:

Category	Value
Religious activities	£31,000
Medical activities	£24,000
Educational and other activities	£23,000

Beneficiaries included: Yorkshire Baptist Trust (£25,000); University of Sheffield School of Medicine (£5,500); Cherry Tree Children's Home, Sheffield Association for Cerebral Palsy and St Luke's Hospice (£3,250 each); Sheffield Mencap (£2,800); and Heeley City Farm (£2,000).

Exclusions No grants to individuals.

Applications In writing to the correspondent at any time.

The A H and E Boulton Trust

Evangelical Christian

£154,000 (2007/08)
Beneficial area Worldwide.

c/o Moore Stephens, 110–114 Duke Street, Liverpool L1 5AG
Correspondent The Trustees
Trustees *Mrs J R Gopsill; F P Gopsill.*
CC Number 225328
Information available Accounts were on file at the Charity Commission.

The trust mainly supports the erection and maintenance of buildings to be used for preaching the Christian gospel, and teaching its doctrines. The trustees can also support other Christian institutions, especially missions in the UK and developing world.

In 2007/08 the trust had assets of £2.9 million and an income of £131,000. Grants totalled £154,000.

Beneficiaries included: Liverpool City Mission (£42,000); Holy Trinity Church (£22,000); the Slavic Gospel Association (£20,000); Bethesda Church and Pioneer People Wirral (£15,000 each); Operation Mobilisation (£12,000); Leprosy Mission (£6,000); Peel Beach Mission (£5,000); Salvation Army (£4,000); and Charles Thompson Mission (£3,000).

Applications In writing to the correspondent. The trust tends to support a set list of charities and applications are very unlikely to be successful.

P G and N J Boulton Trust

Christian

£66,000 (2007/08)
Beneficial area Worldwide.

PO Box 72, Wirral, Merseyside CH46 6AA
Website www.boultontrust.org.uk
Correspondent Andrew L Perry, Trustee
Trustees *Mr A L Perry, Chair; Miss L M Butchart; Mr P H Stafford; Mrs S Perry.*
CC Number 272525
Information available Accounts were on file at the Charity Commission

The trust describes its general funding policy on its website as follows:

Main Commitment – Our giving is largely restricted to organisations and activities that are of special interest to the trustees and this is largely concentrated in the area of Christian missionary work.

Other Areas – The trust has from time to time made donations in the following areas:

- disaster and poverty relief
- medical research and healthcare
- disability relief and care of older people.

In 2007/08 it had assets of £4.1 million, an income of £130,000 and made grants totalling £66,000.

Grants of £1,000 or more were made to 22 organisations and were listed in the accounts. Beneficiaries included: Children Alone (£11,000); New Life Centre (£10,000); Intercessors for Britain (£8,000); Longcroft Christian Trust (£6,000); Just Care and Shalom Christian Fellowship (£4,000 each); Barnabas Fund, Charles Thompson's Mission and Vision for China (£1,500 each); and Anglo-Peruvian Child Care Mission, New Tribes Mission and SAO Cambodia (£1,000 each).

Other donations of £1,000 or less totalled £4,000.

Exclusions No grants are made directly to individuals. No grants towards environment and conservation, culture and heritage, sport and leisure, animal welfare or church building repairs.

Applications The trust only makes donations to organisations with which it has existing commitments. Any new requests for funding will almost certainly be unsuccessful.

Sir Clive Bourne Family Trust

Jewish

£66,000 (2007/08)
Beneficial area UK.

134–136 High Street, Epping CM16 4AG
Correspondent Janet Bater
Trustees *Lady Bourne; Mrs Katie Cohen; Mrs Lucy Furman; Mrs Claire Lefton; Mrs Merryl Flitterman.*
CC Number 290620
Information available Full accounts were on file at the Charity Commission.

The trustees favour Jewish causes. A number of health and medical charities

(particularly relating to cancer) have also benefited.

In 2008/09 the trust's assets totalled £4.4 million and it had an income of £119,000. Grants were made totalling £66,000.

Beneficiaries included: Prostate Cancer Research Foundation (£17,000); Sydney Gold Trust (£12,000); Mossbourne Community Academy (£10,000); Norwood Ravenswood (£4,200); World Jewish Relief, WIZO UK and United Synagogue (£3,000 each); Drugsline (£2,500); the Langdon Foundation (£2,000); Maccabi Great Britain (£1,900); British WIZO (£1,000); Jewish Blind and Disabled (£500); Cancer Research (£300); UK Friends of AWIS (£250); Jewish Child's Day (£200); Walk the Walk (£150); and UJIA (£100).

Applications In writing to the correspondent.

Bourneheights Limited

Orthodox Jewish

£1.5 million (2006/07)
Beneficial area UK.

Flat 10, Palm Court, Queen Elizabeth's Walk, London N16 5XA
Correspondent Schloime Rand, Trustee
Trustees *Chaskel Rand; Esther Rand; Erno Berger; Yechiel Chersky; Schloime Rand.*
CC Number 298359
Information available Accounts were on file at the Charity Commission.

Registered with the Charity Commission in February 1998, in 2006/07 this charity had assets of £5.1 million and an income of £2.9 million including £2.6 million from donations. Its assets stood at £5.1 million.

Grants were made totalling £1.5 million. Beneficiaries included: Moreshet Hatorah (£378,000); Mercaz Torah Vahesed Ltd (£152,000); BFOT (£126,000); Belz Synagogue (£104,000); Telz Academy Trust (£95,000); Gevurath Ari Academy (£75,000); UTA (£34,000); Toreth Emeth (£30,000); Olam Chesed Yiboneh (£20,000); Before Trust (£12,000); Heaven Point (£10,000); Yeshivas Avas Torah (£5,000); and Lubavitch Mechina (£3,000).

Applications In writing to the correspondent.

The Bowerman Charitable Trust

Church, the arts, medical and young people

£509,000 (2007/08)

Beneficial area UK, with a preference for West Sussex.

Champs Hill, Coldwatham, Pulborough RH20 1LY

Correspondent D W Bowerman, Trustee

Trustees *D W Bowerman; Mrs C M Bowerman; Mrs J M Taylor; Miss K E Bowerman; Mrs A M Downham; J M Capper; M Follis.*

CC Number 289446

Information available Accounts were on file at the Charity Commission.

In 2007/08 the trust had assets of £11.9 million and an income of £189,000. Grants were made totalling £509,000 (£94,000 in the previous year) and included a one-off donation of £400,000 to St Margaret's Church – Angmering. Other donations were broken down as follows:

Category	Value
The arts	£52,000
Church activities	£21,000
Medical charities	£21,000
Youth work	£2,400
Other	£3,000

Beneficiaries included: Royal College of Music (£18,000); Macmillan Cancer Care (£13,000); British Youth Opera (£11,000); and St Helen's Bishopsgate (£10,000).

Applications In writing to the correspondent. The trustees have previously stated that they are bombarded with applications and unsolicited applications will not be considered.

The William Brake Charitable Trust

General

£283,000 (2007/08)

Beneficial area UK, with a preference for Kent.

c/o Gill Turner and Tucker, Colman House, King Street, Maidstone ME14 1JE

Correspondent The Trustees

Trustees *Philip R Wilson; Deborah J Isaac; Penelope A Lang; Michael Trigg.*

CC Number 1023244

Information available Accounts were on file at the Charity Commission.

The charity invites applications from the William Brake family for funding of worthy charitable causes each year, with a particular emphasis on local charities where the family know the charity's representative.

In 2007/08 the trust had assets of £9.3 million and an income of £78,000. The trust made 73 grants totalling £283,000.

Beneficiaries of the largest grants were: the Whitely Fund for Nature (£50,000); the Royal Masonic Benevolent Institution (£25,000); NSPCC (£14,000); the Duke of Edinburgh's Award (£11,000); and the Ecology Trust, the Friends of the V and A, Licensed Trade Charity, Mitchemp Trust, the Natural History Museum and Royal Academy of Arts (£10,000 each).

Other beneficiaries included: Wooden Spoon Society (£7,000); the Aurora Tsunami Orphanage, the Mike Collingwood Memorial Fund and the League of Remembrance (£5,000 each); the Friends of St Peter's Hospital Chertsey (£3,000); Canterbury Cathedral Development (£2,500); Cancer Research UK, Elimination of Leukaemia Fund, Maidstone Mencap Charitable Trust and RNLI (£2,000 each); and Alzheimer's Society, Breast Cancer Care, the Courtyard – Petersfield, the Dorothy Grinstead Memorial Fund, Macmillan Cancer Support, Portland College, the Save the Children Fund, Sustrans Limited and Wellbeing of Women (£1,000 each).

Applications In writing to the correspondent.

The Tony Bramall Charitable Trust

Medical research, ill health and social welfare

£222,000 (2007/08)

Beneficial area UK, with some preference for Yorkshire.

12 Cardale Court, Beckwith Head Road, Harrogate HG3 1RY

Tel. 01423 535300

Email johnholroyd64@hotmail.com

Correspondent The Trustees

Trustees *D C A Bramall; Mrs K S Bramall Odgen; Mrs M J Foody; G M Tate; Miss A Bramall.*

CC Number 1001522

Information available Full accounts were available at the Charity Commission.

The charity was established in 1988 by Mr D C A Bramall with an initial sum of £600,000. The charity is focussed on assisting persons less able to finance their medical/health needs, particularly children and particularly those causes based in the northern part of the country.

In 2007/08 the trust had assets of £3.8 million, an income of £217,000 and made grants totalling £222,000.

The largest donation went to Cancer Research UK (£200,000). Other beneficiaries included: Tamzin's Quest (£5,600); Henshaws Society for Blind People and Motor and Allied Trades Benevolent Fund (£5,000 each); Harrogate White Rose Theatre Trust Limited, Pondside Neighbours Group and Within Reach – Sheffield (£1,000 each); the Happy Wanderers Ambulance Association (£750); York and North Yorkshire Community Foundation (£500); Martin House Hospice (£300); and the Peter Hollis Memorial Fund (£250).

Applications In writing to the correspondent.

The Bransford Trust

General

£351,000 (2007/08)

Beneficial area Preference for the West Midlands.

PO Box 600, Worcester WR1 2XG

Correspondent The Trustees

Trustees C A Kinnear; Mrs B Kinnear; L E S Freeman; A J C Kinnear; A J Neil.

CC Number 1106554

Information available Accounts were on file at the Charity Commission.

Established in 2004, in 2007/08 the trust had assets of £147,000 and an income of £437,000. Grants totalled £351,000.

Beneficiaries included: the Leys School (£200,000); St Richard Hospice (£50,000); Acorns Children's Trust (£15,000); Prince's Trust and Worcester Festival and Worcester Porcelain Museum (£10,000 each); Noah's Ark Trust (£6,000); Dyslexia Association, Worcester Young Carers and Young Enterprise West Midlands (£5,000 each); and Elgar Birthplace Development Fund (£2,000).

Applications In writing to the correspondent.

The Breast Cancer Research Trust

Breast cancer research

£368,000 (2007/08)

Beneficial area UK.

48 Wayneflete Tower Avenue, Esher KT10 8QG

Tel. 01372 463235

Email bcrtoffice@aol.com

Website www.breastcancerresearchtrust.org.uk

Correspondent The Honorary Administrator

Trustees Dame Vera Lynn; Prof. Charles Coombes; Jean-Claude Gazet; Virginia Lewis-Jones; Bob Potter; Prof. Trevor J Powles; R M Rainsbury; Hon Mrs Justice Rafferty; Dr Margaret Spittle.

CC Number 272214

Information available Accounts on file at the Charity Commission.

The Breast Cancer Research Trust is a charity dedicated to funding clinical and laboratory project research, undertaken in recognised cancer centres or research institutions in the UK, directly aimed at improving the prevention, early diagnosis and treatment of breast cancer.

Limited grants are available up to a term of three years. Grants are reviewed annually.

In 2007/08 the trust had assets of over £583,000 and an income of £174,000. Grants were made to 12 organisations totalling £368,000. Of this, three grants were made to Imperial College.

Exclusions No grants to students.

Applications Application forms available only from the trust's website.

The Harold and Alice Bridges Charity

General

£90,000 (2007/08)

Beneficial area South Cumbria and North Lancashire (as far south as Preston)

Senior Calveley and Hardy Solicitors, 8 Hastings Place, Lytham FY8 5NA

Tel. 01253 733333

Email rnh@seniorslaw.co.uk

Correspondent Richard N Hardy, Trustee

Trustee Richard N Hardy.

CC Number 236654

Information available Accounts were obtained from the Charity Commission website.

The trustees normally make grants to local causes in the Lancashire and South Cumbria area with special preference to the River Ribble area and northwards, the Blackburn area, and the South Lakes area. Generally, grants are made to benefit younger and older people, and are mainly towards capital projects in connection with rural and village life, especially where there is associated voluntary effort.

In 2007/08 the trust had assets of £2.6 million and an income of £113,000. Grants to 50 organisations totalled £90,000. Donations ranged between £500 and £5,000.

Beneficiaries included: Bowland Pennine Mountain Rescue, Bryning with Warton Parish Council, St John the Baptist Church – Broughton, St John the Baptist Church – Tunstall and Storth Village Hall (£5,000 each); Early Mines Research Group Museum Trust (£4,000); Promenade Concert Orchestra (£3,000); Fylde Rugby Club (£2,500); British Red Cross Society and Ingleton Scout Group (£2,000 each); All Saints Grange Bowling Club, Lake District Summer Music and People's Dispensary for Sick Animals (£1,000 each); WRVS (£1,700); Steveley Village Enterprises (£1,500); Woodland Trust (£900); and Whitechapel Preschool Playgroup (£300).

Exclusions No grants to individuals.

Applications In writing to the correspondent, followed by completion of a standard application form. The trustees meet three times a year to discuss and approve grant applications and review finances. Cheques are sent out to those successful applicants within days of each meeting.

Briggs Animal Welfare Trust

Animal welfare

£100,000 (2007/08)

Beneficial area UK and overseas.

Little Champions Farm, Maplehurst Road, West Grinstead, West Sussex RH13 6RN

Correspondent The Trustees

Trustees Miss L M Hartnett; A P M Schouten.

CC Number 276459

Information available Accounts were on file at the Charity Commission.

This trust derives most of its income from shares in the company Eurotherm International plc. Although the original objects of the trust were general, but with particular support for animal welfare, the trust's policy is to now support only animal-welfare causes. There are five named beneficiaries in the trust deed: RSPCA, Reystede Animal Sanctuary Ringmer, Brooke Hospital for Animals – Cairo, Care of British Columbia House and the Society for the Protection of Animals in North Africa.

In 2007/08 it had assets of £779,000, an income of £37,000 and made grants totalling £100,000.

Applications In writing to the correspondent.

The British Council for Prevention of Blindness

Prevention and treatment of blindness

£229,000 (2007/08)
Beneficial area Worldwide.

4 Bloomsbury Square, London WC1A 2RP
Tel. 020 7404 7114
Email info@bcpb.org
Website www.bcpb.org
Correspondent The Trustees
Trustees A R Elkington; C Walker; S M Brooker; Prof. A Dick; Dr C Harper; R Jackson; R Porter; R Titley; Lady J Wilson.
CC Number 270941
Information available Full accounts were on file at the Charity Commission.

The BCPB's mission statement is to help prevent blindness and restore sight in the UK and developing world by:

- funding research (including fellowships) in UK hospitals and universities into the causes and treatments of the major eye diseases
- supporting practical treatment programmes and research in the developing world
- promoting vital skills, leadership, awareness and demand for the expansion of community eye health in the developing world through the education of doctors and nurses within communities.

The trust's policy is to divide its support equally between projects in the UK and abroad. Grants are given to hospitals, universities and health centres both in the UK and in developing countries. Grants are also given to individuals through the Boulter Fellowship Awards. Grants are usually for a maximum of £40,000 and given for a maximum of three years.

In 2007/08 the trust had an income of £409,000 and made grants totalling £229,000.

Exclusions BCPB do not deal with the individual welfare of blind people in the UK.

Applications Applications can be made throughout the year.

The British Dietetic Association General and Education Trust Fund

Dietary and nutritional issues

£20,000 (2007/08)
Beneficial area UK.

5th Floor, Charles House, 148–149 Great Charles Street, Queensway, Birmingham B3 3HT
Tel. 0121 200 8080
Email info@bda.uk.com
Website www.bda.uk.com
Correspondent The Secretary to the Trustees
Trustees Mrs P L Douglas, Chair; Dame Barbara Clayton; P Brindley; Miss E Elliot; W T Seddon; Mrs M Mackintosh.
CC Number 282553
Information available Accounts were on file at the Charity Commission.

The British Dietetic Association General and Education Trust exists 'to advance education and other purposes related to the science of dietetics'. The trust has an annual grant-giving budget of around £50,000 a year and can make grants to individuals and to recognised associations or groups of people engaged in dietetic research and associated activities.

In 2007/08 it had assets of £1.5 million and an income of £54,000. Grants were made totalling £20,000.

Exclusions Direct support of dietetic students in training or postgraduate qualifications for individuals, for instance, the trust will not pay postgraduate fees/expenses, or for elective/MSc study for doctors.

Applications Application forms can be downloaded from the trust's website.

British Humane Association

Welfare

£79,000 (2008)
Beneficial area UK.

Priory House, 25 St John's Lane, Clerkenwell, London EC1M 4PP
Correspondent The Trustees
Trustees H Gould, Chair; B Campbell-Johnston; C Campbell-Johnston; Sir Anthony Grant; J M Huntington; P Gee; D J Eldridge; D A Cantly; A H Chignell.
CC Number 207120
Information available Accounts were on file at the Charity Commission.

In 2008 the trust had an income of £126,000 and made 11 grants totalling £79,000. Assets stood at almost £3 million.

Beneficiaries included: Artists' General Benevolent Institution Guild of Freemen of the City of London (£34,000); St John of Jerusalem Eye Hospital (£7,000); Argyll and Bute Care and Repair, Challenging Behaviour, Children with Cancer and Leukaemia, City Gate Community, Extend and St Luke's Hospital for the Clergy (£5,000 each); and Church Lads' and Girls' Brigade and Neighbourhood Southall (£2,500 each).

Applications The trust only supports one new cause each year and applications are unlikely to be successful.

The Roger Brooke Charitable Trust

General

£194,000 (2007/08)
Beneficial area UK, with a preference for Hampshire.

Withers, 16 Old Bailey, London EC4M 7EG

Tel. 020 7597 6123

Correspondent J P Arnold, Trustee

Trustees *J P Arnold; C R E Brooke; Mrs N B Brooke; Ms J R Rousso; S H R Brooke.*

CC Number 1071250

Information available Accounts were on file at the Charity Commission.

Established in 1998, this trust has general charitable purposes, including medical research, support for carers and social action.

In 2007/08 the trust had assets of £1.3 million and an income of £481,000 including £480,000 from donations received. Grants totalled £194,000, of which £100,000 went to the Southampton University Development Fund.

Exclusions In general, individuals are not supported.

Applications In writing to the correspondent. Applications will only be acknowledged if successful.

The David Brooke Charity

Young people and medical

£91,000 (2007/08)

Beneficial area UK.

Cook Sutton, Tay Court, Blounts Court Road, Sonning Common RG4 9RS

Correspondent D J Rusman, Trustee

Trustees *D J Rusman; P M Hutt; N A Brooke.*

CC Number 283658

Information available Accounts were on file at the Charity Commission.

The trust supports youth causes, favouring disadvantaged young people, particularly through causes providing self-help programmes and outdoor-activity training. Grants are also given to medical organisations.

In 2007/08 the trust had assets of £1.9 million generating an income of £141,000. Grants were given to 35 organisations and totalled £91,000.

Grants were broken down into the following two categories and are shown here with examples of beneficiaries in each category:

Children and young people – 10 grants totalling £28,000
Great Ormond Street Hospital (£4,500); the Children's Society, Finchale Training College and YMCA (£3,500 each); Lord Wandsworth College and Stanbridge Earls School Trust (£3,000 each); NSPCC (£2,000); and Berkshire Girl Guides (£1,000).

Other – 25 grants totalling £64,000
Camphill Village Trust, the Fortune Riding Centre, RNID and the Salvation Army (£3,500 each); Alzheimer's Society, the Mission to Seafarers and Yorkshire Dales Millennium Trust (£3,000 each); Wyfold Riding for the Disabled (£2,500); the Kennet and Avon Canal Trust, RSPB and SSAFA Forces Help (£2,000 each); the Ramblers Association and the Sobriety Project (£1,500 each); and Hospice in the Weald (£500).

Applications The correspondent stated that the trust's annual income is not for general distribution as it is committed to a limited number of charities on a long-term basis.

Bill Brown's Charitable Settlement

Health and social welfare

£159,000 (2007/08)

Beneficial area UK.

BM Box 4567, London WC1N 3XX

Correspondent The Trustees

Trustees *G S Brown; A J Barnett.*

CC Number 801756

Information available Accounts were on file at the Charity Commission.

This settlement supports health and welfare causes, including those for older people.

In 2007/08 the trust had assets of £11 million and an income of £483,000. Grants to 20 organisations totalled £159,000. Grants are often recurrent. Future commitments were made to Churchill College and Moorfields Eye Hospital Development Fund totalling £493,000.

Beneficiaries included: Charities Aid Foundation Trust (£50,000 in two grants); Christ's Hospital Horsham (£32,000); Macmillan Cancer Relief and Salvation Army (£10,000 each); Alzheimer's Society, Cancer Research

UK, DebRA, Leonard Cheshire Foundation, Linden Lodge Charitable Trust, Princess Alice Hospice, St Christopher's Hospice and Treloar Trust (£5,000 each); the Scout Association (£4,000); and Barnardo's and NCH Action for Children (£2,500 each).

Exclusions No grants to individuals.

Applications In writing containing the following:

- aims and objectives of the charity
- nature of appeal
- total target if for a specific project
- contributions received against target
- registered charity number
- any other relevant factors.

Appeals should be accompanied by a set of the organisation's latest report and full accounts.

R S Brownless Charitable Trust

Disability, relief in need, ill health, accommodation and housing, education, job creation and voluntary work

£58,000 (2007/08)

Beneficial area Mainly UK and occasionally overseas.

Hennerton Holt, Wargrave, Reading RG10 8PD

Tel. 0118 940 4029

Correspondent Mrs P M A Nicolai, Trustee

Trustees *Mrs F A Plummer; Mrs P M Nicolai.*

CC Number 1000320

Information available Accounts were on file at the Charity Commission, without a list of grants.

The trust makes grants to causes that benefit people who are disabled, disadvantaged or seriously ill. Charities working in the fields of accommodation and housing, education, job creation and voluntary work are also supported. Grants are usually one-off, ranging between £100 and £2,000.

In 2007/08 the trust's assets totalled £1.2 million, it had an income of £58,000 all of which was given in grants.

Previous beneficiaries have included Alzheimer's Society, Camp Mohawk, Casa Allianza UK, Crisis, Foundation for Study of Infant Deaths, Prader-Willi Foundation, St Andrew's Hall, UNICEF, Wargrave PCC and Witham on the Hill PCC.

Exclusions Grants are rarely given to individuals for educational projects or to education or conservation causes or overseas aid.

Applications In writing to the correspondent. The trustees meet twice a year, but in special circumstances will meet at other times. The trust is unable to acknowledge all requests.

The T B H Brunner Charitable Settlement

Church of England, heritage, arts and general

£37,000 to organisations and individuals (2007/08)

Beneficial area UK with some preference for Oxfordshire.

Flat 4, 2 Inverness Gardens, London W8 4RN

Tel. 020 7727 6277

Correspondent T B H Brunner, Trustee

Trustees *Timothy Brunner; Helen Brunner; Dr Imogen Brunner.*

CC Number 260604

Information available Accounts were on file at the Charity Commission.

The trustees seek to make donations to other charities and voluntary bodies for the benefit of Church of England preservation projects and other charities dealing with historical preservation, both local to Oxfordshire and nationally. The trustees may also seek to make donations to other charities, voluntary bodies and individuals relating to the arts, music and also for general charitable purposes.

In 2007/08 this trust had an income of £43,000 and made grants to organisations and individuals totalling £37,000. Assets stood at £1.8 million.

There were 60 grants made during the year, of which 17 were for £1,000 or

more. Beneficiaries included: the Institute of Economic Affairs (£5,000 in two grants); Rotherfield Greys PCC (£2,500); Live Music Now (£2,000); St Mary's Church – Henley-on-Thames (£1,500); and Care International, IMS Prussia Grove, King Edward Hospital, the Minority Rights Group, the National Centre for Early Music, the National Trust, REFRESH, the Royal Theatrical Fund, Rugby Portobello Trust and St Mary – Chalgrove (£1,000 each).

Other beneficiaries included: the National Trust (£900); Rotherfield Greys PCC (£700); the London Library, the London School of Economics, the Oxfordshire Historic Churches Trust and Trinity College – Oxford (£500 each); the Children's Society and Sue Ryder Care (£250); the Greater London Fund for the Blind and the Royal British Legion (£200 each); and Friends of Covent Garden, Friends of Kensington Day Centre, Friends of Moorfields Eye Hospital and Venice in Peril Fund (£100 each).

Applications In writing to the correspondent.

Buckingham Trust

Christian purposes, relief of poverty and sickness and support for older people

£159,000 to organisations (2007/08)

Beneficial area UK and worldwide.

Foot Davson, 17 Church Road, Tunbridge Wells TN1 1LG

Tel. 01892 774774 **Fax** 01892 774775

Correspondent The Trustees

Trustees *R W D Foot; Mrs C T Clay.*

CC Number 237350

Information available A request for information received a reply stating that the trust are 'not able to assist in making a grant'.

In 2007/08 the trust had assets of £1 million and an income of £206,000. Grants were made totalling £164,000, broken down as follows:

Category	Value
Charities	£92,000
Churches	£67,000
Individuals	£5,600

Applications Unsolicited applications are not considered. A request for information received a reply stating that they were 'not able to assist in making a grant', so it would seem that correspondence is not considered.

Buckland Charitable Trust

General, international development, welfare and health research

£43,000 (2007/08)

Beneficial area UK and overseas.

Smith and Wllliamson Limited, 1 Bishops Wharf, Walnut Tree Close, Guildford GU1 4RA

Correspondent The Trustees

Trustees *Ali Afsari; Anna Bannister.*

CC Number 273679

Information available Accounts were on file at the Charity Commission.

In 2007/08 the trust had an income of £163,000 and grants to 36 organisations totalled £43,000. During the year the majority of the support was given to medical research and related activities as 'the trustees believe a good society is the product of a healthy mind and body'.

Beneficiaries included: Alzheimer's Disease Society (£2,500); Bishop Simeon Trust, Islamic Universal Association, Macmillan Cancer Relief, Médecins Sans Frontières, North Lakeland Hospice at Home and UNICEF (£2,000 each); Clinic of UK Africa Floods Children's Appeal, Eden Valley Hospice and The Smile Train (£1,500 each); the Bubble Foundation UK, the Hospice Foundation, Royal Holloway University of London and World Cancer Research Fund (£1,000 each); Barnardo's (£750); MIND (£500); IPCI (£250); and Children's Heart Unit Fund (£50).

Applications In writing to the correspondent.

The Bulldog Trust Limited

General

About £200,000 each year

Beneficial area Worldwide, with a preference for the south of England.

2 Temple Place, London WC2R 3BD

Website www.bulldogtrust.org

Correspondent The Trustees

Trustees *Patrick Burgess; Martin Riley; Brian Smouha; Mary Fagan; Charles Hoare.*

CC Number 1123081

Information available Accounts were available from the Charity Commission.

Operating since 1983, the Bulldog Trust has donated more than £3 million to a range of charities and in recent years has made grants totalling around £200,000 annually. The trust aims to support charity in ways which ensure that smaller donations provide maximum benefit. In the past we have pledged to start match funding campaigns; offered interest-free loans to tide charities through cash-flow crises; funded innovative pilot projects that could not access funding elsewhere and facilitated scholarships and bursaries in fields that we believed were being overlooked. The trustees have supported charities as diverse as Humanitarian Aid Relief Trust, the Prince's Trust and the University of Winchester.

Bulldog also runs two separately administered, smaller educational grants funds. The Bulldog Arts Fund offers grants to innovative and interesting arts projects. The Bulldog Educational Grants Fund makes small grants towards special educational needs.

The trust makes grants totalling about £200,000 each year. Previous beneficiaries have included Hampshire and Isle of Wight Foundation, National Playing Fields Association, David Robbie Charitable Trust, Portsmouth Cathedral Development Trust, the Prince's Trust, Royal National Theatre and University of Winchester.

Exclusions No grants are given to individuals or to unsolicited applications.

Applications The trust regrets that unsolicited applications cannot be accepted.

The Burden Trust

Christian, welfare, medical research, education and general

£175,000 (2007/08)

Beneficial area UK and overseas.

51 Downs Park West, Westbury Park, Bristol BS6 7QL

Tel. 0117 962 8611

Email p.oconor@netgates.co.uk

Correspondent Patrick O'Conor, Secretary

Trustees *A C Miles, Chair; R E J Bernays; Dr M G Barker; Prof. G M Stirrat; Bishop of Southwell and Nottingham; Prof. A Halestrap.*

CC Number 235859

Information available Accounts were on file at the Charity Commission.

The trust operates in accordance with various trust deeds dating back to 1913. These deeds provide grants for medical research, hospitals, retirement homes, schools and training institutions, homes and care for young people and people in need. The trust operates with an adherence to the tenets and principles of the Church of England.

In 2007/08 it had assets of £3.7 million, which generated an income of £167,000. Grants totalled £175,000, broken down as follows:

Neurological research – one grant of £80,000

This went to Burden Neurological Institute, which received the same amount in the previous year.

Schools and training institutions – seven grants totalling £69,000

All of these grants went to organisations supported in the previous year. Beneficiaries were: Trinity College – Bristol (£23,000); Langham Research Scholarships (£13,000); Oxford Centre for Mission Studies (£12,000); Union Biblical Seminary – Pune (£10,000); Association for Theological Education by Extension – Bangalore (£8,500); St Paul's Divinity College – Kenya (£2,000); and Redcliffe College (£1,500).

Organisations for care and training of young people – four grants totalling £25,000

Beneficiaries were: Easton Families Project (£12,000); Urban Saints and Prodigal Son Ministries (£5,000 each); and Crisis Centre Ministries (£2,800).

Clergy families' welfare – one grant totalling £1,000

This went to St Luke's Hospital for the Clergy, which received the same amount in the previous year.

Exclusions No grants to individuals.

Applications In writing to the correspondent. Financial information is required in support of the project for which help is requested. No application is responded to without a stamped, addressed envelope. Recipients of recurring grants are notified each year that grants are not automatic and must be applied for annually. Applications are considered at the annual trustees meeting.

Burdens Charitable Foundation

General

£72,000 (2007/08)

Beneficial area UK, but mostly overseas, with special interest in Sub-Saharan Africa.

St George's House, 215–219 Chester Road, Manchester M15 4JE

Correspondent A J Burden, Trustee

Trustees *A J Burden; G Burden; Mrs H Perkins; Mrs S Schofield; Dr A D Burden.*

CC Number 273535

Information available Accounts were on file at the Charity Commission.

There are no formal restrictions on the charitable activities that can be supported, but the trustees' main activities currently embrace the prevention and relief of acute poverty, substantially through the medium of education and healthcare and most especially in countries such as those of sub-Saharan Africa.

In 2007/08 the foundation had assets of £13 million, an income of £322,000 and made grants totalling £72,000 of which 74% was given overseas.

Beneficiaries included: Across (£10,000); Build-It (£5,000); Newtown Evangelical Church (£2,500); the Reid Foundation (£2,000); Safe Anchor Trust (£750); National Children's Homes and South Street Evangelical Church (£500 each); Tearfund (£350); Caring for Life (£250);

and St Andrew's Evangelical Mission (£100).

Exclusions Causes which rarely or never benefit from the foundation include animal welfare (except in less developed countries), the arts and museums, political activities, most medical research, preservation etc. of historic buildings and monuments, individual educational grants and sport, except sport for people with disabilities. No grants are made to individuals.

Applications In writing to the correspondent, accompanied by recent, audited accounts and statutory reports, coupled with at least an outline business plan where relevant. Trustees usually meet in March, June, September and December.

The Burry Charitable Trust

Medicine and health

£49,000 (2007/08)
Beneficial area UK, with a preference for Highcliffe and the surrounding and further areas.

261 Lymington Road, Highcliffe, Christchurch BH23 5EE
Correspondent R J Burry, Trustee
Trustees R J Burry; Mrs J A Knight; A J Osman: N J Lapage.
CC Number 281045
Information available Accounts were on file at the Charity Commission.

In 2007/08 the trust had an income of £628,000, of which £577,000 was from donations. Grants to 24 mainly local organisations totalled £49,000.

Beneficiaries included: Oakhaven Hospital Trust (£10,000); Not Forgotten Association and Wessex Cardiac Trust (£5,000 each); Ability Net and John Grooms Association (£2,500 each); Julia's House Hospice and Wessex Autistic Society (£2,000 each); Life Education Centres (£1,500); Cellular Pathology Charitable Fund (£1,100); British Red Cross, the Butterfly Appeal, Canine Partners, Meningitis UK, New Forest Mencap, St John's Ambulance and WRVS (£1,000 each); Myeloma UK (£500); Sway Welfare Aid Group and First Opportunities (£250 each).

Exclusions No grants to individuals or students.

Applications This trust states that it does not respond to unsolicited applications.

The Arnold Burton 1998 Charitable Trust

Jewish, medical research, education, social welfare and heritage

£286,000 (2007/08)
Beneficial area Worldwide.

c/o Trustee Management Ltd, 19 Cookridge Street, Leeds LS2 3AG
Correspondent The Trust Managers
Trustees A J Burton; J J Burton; N A Burton; M T Burton.
CC Number 1074633
Information available Accounts were on file at the Charity Commission.

Established in 1998, this trust gives special consideration to appeals from Jewish charities and projects related to medical research, education, social welfare and heritage. No grants are made to individuals. In 2007/08 it had assets of £5.2 million, an income of £180,000 and made grants totalling £286,000. Donations were broken down as follows:

Category	No. of grants	Amount
Jewish/Israel	21	£111,000
Health	97	£65,000
Social/welfare	105	£41,000
Developing world/ overseas	44	£37,000
Education	34	£23,000
Arts and amenities	31	£10,000

The following are examples of beneficiaries in each category:

Jewish/Israel
UJIA (£100,000); Harrogate Hebrew Congregation (£1,250); CST and University Jewish Chaplaincy Board (£1,000 each); Holocaust Educational Trust, Jewish Care, LJWB and Maccabi GB (£500 each); the Institute for Jewish Policy Research, Jewish Women's Week, Russian Immigrant Aid Fund, the Shalom Foundation and WIZO (£250 each); and Leeds Jewish Representative Council (£100).

Health
Breakthrough Breast Cancer, Fight for Sight and Royal College of Surgeons (£5,000 each); Henshaws Society for Blind People and RNIB (£2,500 each); Brain Research Trust (£2,000); British

Red Cross, Coronary Artery Research Association, Hospital Heartbeat Appeal, the National Hospital Development Foundation, St John's Catholic School for the Deaf and Sightsavers International (£1,000 each); Breast Cancer Haven Yorkshire, British Dental Health Foundation and Leonard Cheshire Disability (£500 each); Leukaemia Research Fund, Scope and the Smile Train (£250 each); British Heart Foundation and Four Paws (£100 each); and Cancer and Polio Research Fund (£50).

Social/welfare
The Children's Society (£2,500); Inkind Direct, NCH, NSPCC, South Yorkshire Community Foundation, St Gemma's Hospice and St William's Foundation (£1,000 each); Age Concern Norwich, BTCV, Caring for Life, Childhope, Dogs for the Disabled, the London Jewish Family Centre, Jubilee Sailing Trust, Princess Royal Trust for Carers, Meanwood Valley Urban Farm and Vitalise (£500 each); Crisis, Emmaus, Family Welfare Association, Barn Owl Trust, Salvation Army, Shaftesbury Society and SSAFA (£250 each); Church Urban Fund, IFAW, Project Trust and the ZSV Trust (£100 each); Royal British Legion (£25); and Sense (£10).

Developing world/overseas
JNF (£25,000); UNICEF (£1,000); JNF Charitable Trust (£750); Appropriate Technology Asia, Mercy Ships, Survival International, Tree Aid, Wells for India and WWF – UK (£500 each); Anti-Slavery International, Compassion in World Farming, Free Tibet Campaign, Medical Mission International and the Rainforest Foundation UK (£250 each); Action Ethiopia, Everychild, Grow Peace in Africa and the Tel Aviv Foundation (£100 each); and Galapogas Conservation Trust (£50).

Education
London Metropolitan University (£1,200); British Technion Society Weizmann UK and University Jewish Chaplaincy Board (£1,000 each); British Friends of the Jaffa Institute, British Technion Society, the Jennifer Trust, Olive Tree Educational Trust, Pestalozzi International Village Trust and Practical Action (£500 each); Institute of Jewish Policy Research, the Sheppard Trust and Wiener Library (£250 each); and British Schools Exploring Society and Project Trust (£100 each).

Arts and amenities
Historic Royal Palaces, Beth Shalom and the Jewish Museum (£1,000 each); the Alnwick Garden, Clean Rivers Trust, Imperial War Museum, Marine Conservation Society and Yorkshire

Wildlife Trust (£500 each); the Art Fund, the Civic Trust and the English Hedgerow Trust (£250 each); Ripon Cathedral Development Campaign and Wetherby Riverside Bandstand (£100 each); and American Museum in Britain (£20).

Applications In writing to the trust managers. Unsuccessful appeals will not necessarily be acknowledged.

The Geoffrey Burton Charitable Trust

General

£33,000 (2007/08)

Beneficial area UK, especially Suffolk and the Needham Market area.

Salix House, Falkenham, Ipswich IP10 0QY

Tel. 01394 448339

Email ericmaule@hotmail.com

Correspondent Eric Maule, Trustee

Trustees *Ted Nash; Eric Maule.*

CC Number 290854

Information available Accounts were on file at the Charity Commission.

In 2007/08 the trust had assets of £597,000 and an income of £37,000. Grants were made totalling £33,000. The trust continued to support the Green Light Trust with a contribution of £2,400 for general funding and the Mid-Suffolk Citizens Advice Bureau with a donation of £1,500 towards the cost of a specialist advisor.

Other grant beneficiaries included: Needham Market Community Centre (£7,500); Needham Market Bowls Club (£2,500); RSPB (£2,000); Mid-Suffolk Citizens Advice Bureau (£1,500); Alzheimer's Research Trust, Needham Market Crowley Park Play Scheme, Needham Market Scouts and Waveney Stardust (£1,000 each); University of Manchester – Blond McIndoe Research (£930); BREAK (£800); Listening Books (£750) Diss, Thetford and District CAB (£500); Jubilee Sailing Trust (£300); and RNIB and West Suffolk Voluntary Association for the Blind (£250 each).

Exclusions No grants to individuals.

Applications In writing to the correspondent.

The Bill Butlin Charity Trust

General

£69,000 (2007/08)

Beneficial area UK.

Eighth Floor, 6 New Street Square, London EC4A 3AQ

Tel. 020 7842 2000

Email bbct@rawlinson-hunter.com

Correspondent The Secretary

Trustees *Peter A Hetherington, Chair; Lady Sheila Butlin; Trevor Watts; Frederick T Devine; Sonia I Meaden; Terence H North.*

CC Number 228233

Information available Full accounts were on file at the Charity Commission.

This trust was established by Sir William E Butlin in 1963. It has a preference for organisations working with children, especially those with disabilities, and older people. The trust has a list of regular beneficiaries, to which only a few charities may be added each year.

In 2007/08 it had assets of £2 million, which generated an income of £86,000. There were 24 grants made totalling £69,000.

Beneficiaries included: Canadian Veterans Association of the UK (£15,000); Cancer Research UK, Home Farm Trust and South Buckinghamshire RDA Group (£5,000 each); Arundel Castle Cricket Foundation (£3,800); Grand Order of Water Rats, Lawrence Weston Community Farm, St Richard's Hospital – Chichester and Spinal Research (£3,000 each); and National Centre for Young People with Epilepsy and Saints and Sinners Club of London (£2,500); Entertainment Artistes Benevolent Fund, Camphill Village Trust Ltd, Royal Marsden Hospital, St Wilfred's Hospice and VSO (£1,000 each).

Applications In writing to the correspondent; unsuccessful applications do not receive a response. Trustees usually meet twice a year.

C and F Charitable Trust

Orthodox Jewish charities

£205,000 (2007/08)

Beneficial area UK and overseas.

c/o New Burlington House, 1075 Finchley House Road, London NW11 0PU

Correspondent The Trustees

Trustees *F H Kaufman; S Kaufman.*

CC Number 274529

Information available Accounts on file at the Charity Commission, without a list of grants.

The trust income derives mainly from investment properties and other investments. Grants are made to Orthodox Jewish charities.

In 2007/08 the trust had assets of £1.3 million, an income of £156,000 and made grants totalling £205,000.

Previous beneficiaries have included Community Council of Gateshead, Ezras Nitrochim, Gur Trust, Kollel Shaarei Shlomo, SOFT and Yetev Lev Jerusalem Trust.

Exclusions Registered charities only.

Applications In writing to the correspondent.

The Christopher Cadbury Charitable Trust

Nature conservation and general

£73,000 (2007/08)

Beneficial area UK, with a preference for the Midlands.

PKF (UK) LLP, New Guild House, 45 Great Charles Street, Queensway, Birmingham B3 2LX

Tel. 0121 212 2222

Correspondent The Trust Administrator

Trustees *R V J Cadbury; Dr C James Cadbury; Mrs V B Reekie; Dr T N D Peet; P H G Cadbury; Mrs C V E Benfield.*

CC Number 231859

Information available Accounts were on file at the Charity Commission.

In 2007/08 the trust had assets of £1.9 million and an income of £86,000. Grants totalled £73,000. The trustees have drawn up a schedule of commitments covering charities which they have chosen to support.

Beneficiaries included: Fircroft College and Island Conservation Society UK – Aride (£11,000 each); Playthings Past Museum Trust (£7,500); P H G Cadbury Charitable Trust (£7,000); Devon Wildlife Trust (£6,000); Norfolk Wildlife Trust (£5,000); Bower Trust, R V J Cadbury Charitable Trust, R A and V B Reekie Charitable Trust and Sarnia Charitable Trust (£4,000 each); Guide Association – Beaconfield Campsites (£2,000); Survival International (£1,000); and Avoncroft Arts Society and Selly Oak Nursery School (£500 each).

Exclusions No support for individuals.

Applications Unsolicited applications are unlikely to be successful.

The G W Cadbury Charitable Trust

Population control, conservation and general

£248,000 (2007/08)
Beneficial area Worldwide.

PKF (UK) LLP, New Guild House, 45 Great Charles Street, Queensway, Birmingham B3 2LX
Tel. 0121 212 2222
Correspondent The Trust Administrator
Trustees Miss J C Boal; Mrs L E Boal; P C Boal; Miss J L Woodroffe; Mrs C A Woodroffe; N B Woodroffe.
CC Number 231861

Information available Accounts were on file at the Charity Commission.

In 2007/08 the trust had assets of £6.3 million, generating an income of £271,000. There were 93 grants made totalling £248,000, given in the following geographical areas:

Area	Amount
USA	£115,000
UK	£110,000
Africa	£10,000
Canada	£5,100
Republic of Ireland	£2,000

There were 16 grants of £5,000 each or more listed in the accounts. Beneficiaries included: Pacific NorthWest Ballet (£46,000); Cancer Counselling Trust (£20,000); School of American Ballet (£13,000); AFRODAD – African Forum and Network on Debt and Development, Brook Northern Ireland, Joseph Rowntree Charitable Trust and World Development Movement Trust (£10,000 each); Brook Advisory Centre (£7,000); and Asylum Seekers in Islington Relief Trust, Fawcett Society, Haverford College and Help the Rural Children (£5,000 each).

A further 47 donations of between £1,000 and £5,000 each were made. Beneficiaries included: Amnesty International, Sustrans, Islington Boat Club and Planned Parenthood of New York City Inc. (£2,000 each); Bridge The Gap (£1,500); and American Friends Service Committee, One World Action, Refugee Council, Swaledale Festival, Woman's Sport Foundation, Womankind UK and Winchester A Better Chance (£1,000 each).

Other smaller grants of less than £1,000 were made to 30 organisations and totalled £5,800.

Exclusions No grants to individuals or non-registered charities, or for scholarships.

Applications In writing to the correspondent.

C J Cadbury Charitable Trust

Environment and conservation

£23,000 (2007/08)
Beneficial area UK.

Martineau, No. 1 Colmore Square, Birmingham B4 6AA
Correspondent The Clerk
Trustees Hugh Carslake; Joy Cadbury; Thomas Cadbury; Lucy Cadbury.
CC Number 270609

Information available Accounts were on file at the Charity Commission.

In 2007/08 the trust had assets of £730,000 and an income of £46,000. Grants totalled £23,000.

Beneficiaries included: Island Conservation Society UK (£13,000 in two grants); Kingfisher's Bridge Wetland Creation Trust (£5,500 in three grants); Bedfordshire, Cambridge and Northamptonshire Wildlife Trust (£2,000); and Plantlife International (£1,000).

Applications In writing to the correspondent. The trust does not generally support unsolicited applications.

Henry T and Lucy B Cadbury Charitable Trust

Quaker causes and institutions, health, homelessness, support groups and disadvantaged nations

£26,000 (2008)
Beneficial area Mainly UK, but also disadvantaged nations.

c/o B C M, Box 2024, London WC1 3XX
Correspondent The Secretary
Trustees Candia Carolan; C Ruth Charity; Suzannah Gibson; M Bevis Gillett; Tristram Hambly; Elizabeth Rawlins; Tamsin Yates.
CC Number 280314

Information available Accounts were on file at the Charity Commission.

In 2008 the trust had assets of £592,000, an income of £27,000 and made grants totalling £26,000.

Grant recipients are usually those that are personally chosen by one of the trustees. Among the 15 beneficiaries were: Quaker United Nations Office (£5,000); Battle Against Tranquillisers, British Pugwash Trust, the People's Kitchen and Slower Speeds Trust (£2,000 each); Action for ME, Money for Madagascar and Tools for Self Reliance (£1,500 each); and Calcutta Rescue Fund, Quaker Opportunity Playgroup and Youth Education Service Midnapore (£1,000 each).

Exclusions No grants to non-registered charities.

Applications The trust's income is committed each year and so unsolicited applications are not normally accepted. The trustees meet in March to consider applications.

P H G Cadbury Charitable Trust

General, arts, conservation and cancer-related causes

£31,000 (2007/08)

Beneficial area UK and overseas.

KS Carmichael, PO Box 4UD, London W1A 4UD

Tel. 020 7258 1577

Email dlarder@kscarmichael.com

Correspondent Derek Larder, Trustee

Trustees *Derek Larder; Peter Cadbury; Sally Cadbury.*

CC Number 327174

Information available Accounts were on file at the Charity Commission.

The trust makes grants to registered charities for general charitable purposes, with a preference for the arts, conservation and cancer-related causes. Grants range from between £25 and £3,000.

In 2007/08 the trust had assets of £625,000 and an income of £44,000. There were 43 grants made totalling £31,000, of which 15 were for £1,000 or more.

Beneficiaries included: the Art Fund, Helen and Douglas House, Natural History Museum and Sadlers Wells (£2,500 each); Dulwich Picture Gallery (£2,000); Magic Bus, Sir John Soames Museum and Trinity Hospice (£1,500 each); Garsington Opera (£1,250); and St Martins in the Fields and Watermill Theatre Trust (£1,000 each).

Applications The trust does not usually respond to unsolicited applications.

The George Cadbury Trust

General

£393,000 (2007/08)

Beneficial area Preference for the West Midlands, Hampshire and Gloucestershire.

PKF (UK) LLP, New Guild House, 45 Great Charles Street, Queensway, Birmingham B3 2LX

Tel. 0121 212 2222

Correspondent The Trust Administrator

Trustees *Mrs Anne L K Cadbury; Robin N Cadbury; Sir Adrian Cadbury; Roger V J Cadbury; Mrs A Janie Cadbury.*

CC Number 1040999

Information available Accounts were on file at the Charity Commission.

The trust was set up in 1924 and maintains a strong financial interest in the Cadbury company. In 2007/08 the trust had assets of £9.7 million and an income of £378,000. There were 219 donations made totalling £393,000.

The seven largest grants of £10,000 or more went to: National Star Centre Appeal (£30,000); National Youth Ballet and RSA Academy (£25,000 each); Dean and Chapter of Gloucester Cathedral (£20,000); and Armed Forces, Gloucestershire Community Foundation and Worcester Cathedral Music Appeal (£10,000 each).

Other beneficiaries included: Bower Trust, C James Cadbury Charitable Trust, P H G Cadbury Charitable Trust, R V J Cadbury Charitable Trust, R A and V B Reekie Trust and Sarnia Charitable Trust (£8,000 each); Alnwick Garden Trust (£5,500); RNLI (£5,300); Forum for the Future, Grace of God Church, London Library, Mission for Deep Sea Fishermen, North Hampshire Medical Fund, Oxford University, RAF Benevolent Fund and Symphony Hall Birmingham (£5,000 each); Action on Addiction (£3,000); DeafBlind UK (£2,500); RNIB (£2,000); Suzy Lamplugh Trust (£1,500); and Arthritis Research Campaign, Association of Wheelchair Children, Birmingham Settlement, CRISIS, Combat Stress, Dungannon Music and Drama Festival Association, Celia Hammond Animal Trust, High Sheriff of Gloucester Charity, the Prince's Trust, Royal London Society for the Blind and Winchester Cathedral (£1,000 each).

Exclusions No support for individuals for projects, courses of study, expeditions or sporting tours. No support for overseas appeals.

Applications In writing to the correspondent to be considered quarterly. Please note: very few new applications are supported due to ongoing and alternative commitments.

The Edward and Dorothy Cadbury Trust

Health, education and the arts

£104,000 (2007/08)

Beneficial area Preference for the West Midlands area.

Rokesley, University of Birmingham Selly Oak, Bristol Road, Selly Oak, Birmingham B29 6QF

Tel. 0121 472 1838

Correspondent Miss S Anderson, Trust Manager

Trustees *Mrs P A Gillett, Chair; Dr C M Elliott; Mrs P S Ward; Mrs S E Anfilogoff; Mrs J E Gillett; Mrs J A Cadbury.*

CC Number 1107327

Information available Accounts were on file at the Charity Commission.

This trust was registered in December 2004, and is the recipient of funds transferred from the now defunct Edward and Dorothy Cadbury Trust (1928), registered charity number 221441. The objects of the new trust remain the same: general charitable purposes in the West Midlands, with areas of work funded including music and the arts, children's charities, disadvantaged groups and support for the voluntary sector. The normal range of grants is between £500 and £2,500, with occasional larger grants made.

In 2007/08 it had assets of £4.6 million, which generated an income of £141,000. Grants totalled £104,000. The 95 donations made were broken down as follows and are shown below with examples of beneficiaries in each category.

Compassionate Support – 36 grants (£32,000)
Acorns Hospice – Worcester (£7,500); Bromsgrove Bereavement Counselling (£3,500); Breast Cancer Haven – Hereford, Council for Music in Hospitals, Edward's Trust – Birmingham, Macmillan Cancer Support, Royal National Institute of Blind People and Warwick Hospital Cancer Ward Appeal (£1,000 each); Children's Heart Federation (£650); Sightsavers International (£600); and British Institute for Brain Injured Children, Fight for Sight, Parkinson's

Disease Society, Winston's Wish and WRVS (£500 each).

Education and training – 12 grants (£32,000)
Sunfield Children's Home (£15,000); University of Cape Town (£7,000); Dodford Children's Holiday Farm – Bromsgrove (£5,000); National Playbus Association (£1,000); and Birmingham Centre for Arts Therapies, ICAN, Outward Bound Trust, Voices Foundation and Woodgate Valley Urban Farm – Birmingham (£500 each).

Community projects and integration – 27 grants (£25,000)
Age Concern, Bromsgrove and District (£5,000); South Birmingham Young Homeless Project (£3,000); Willow Trust (£2,000); Birmingham Settlement, Camphill Family – Botton Village, CARE International UK, Lickey Parish and Community Hall Development and Whizz-Kidz (£1,000 each); Ro-Ro Sailing Project (£600); and British Blind Sport, Canine Partnership, Jubilee Sailing Trust, Malvern Special Families, Noah's Ark – Worcester, Riding for the Disabled – Seecham, Send a Cow and Wheelpower (£500 each).

Arts and culture – 15 grants (£12,000)
Bromsgrove Festival (£3,750); Avoncroft Arts Society – Bromsgrove and Birmingham Royal Ballet (£1,000); Armonico Consort – Warwick (£750); Bromsgrove Choral Society (£700); and Big Brum Theatre in Education, Birmingham Music Festival, Lichfield Festival and National Youth Orchestra (£500 each).

Conservation and environment – 3 grants (£2,500)
Wildlife Trust for Birmingham & the Black Country (£1,500); and RSPB and Woodland Trust (£500 each).

Research – 2 grants (£1,000)
Arthritis Research Campaign and Meningitis Research Foundation (£500 each).

Exclusions No grants to individuals.

Applications In writing to the correspondent, giving clear, relevant information concerning the project's aims and its benefits, an outline budget and how the project is to be funded initially and in the future. Up-to-date accounts and annual reports, where available, should be included. Applications can be submitted at any time but three months should be allowed for a response. Applications that do not come within the policy as stated above may not be considered or acknowledged.

Calleva Foundation

General

£157,000 (2008)
Beneficial area UK and worldwide.

PO Box 22554, London W8 5GN
Correspondent The Trustees
Trustees *S C Butt; C Butt.*
CC Number 1078808
Information available Accounts were on file at the Charity Commission, without a list of grants.

Registered with the Charity Commission in January 2000, this trust can give in the UK and worldwide for general charitable purposes.

In 2008 it had an income of £194,000, including £150,000 from donations (total income in 2007 was £4,100). Assets stood at £43,000. Grants totalled £157,000, broken down as follows:

Category	Value
Social services	£64,000
Children's holidays	£28,000
Overseas/international relief	£25,000
Education	£19,000
Arts and culture	£16,000
Medical research	£3,500
Animal welfare	£500

Information on the size or type of grants, of the names of beneficiaries was not available.

Applications In writing to the correspondent.

The Calpe Trust

Relief work

£28,000 (2007/08)
Beneficial area Worldwide.

The Hideaway, Sandy Lane, Hatford Down, Faringdon SN7 8JH
Tel. 01367 870665
Email reggienorton@talktalk.net
Correspondent R Norton, Trustee
Trustees *R H L R Norton, Chair; B E M Norton; E R H Perks.*
CC Number 1004193
Information available Accounts were on file at the Charity Commission.

The trust makes grants towards registered charities benefiting people in need including refugees, homeless people, people who are socially disadvantaged, victims of war, victims of disasters and so on.

In 2007/08 the trust had assets of £1 million and an income of £32,000. It made 24 grants totalling £28,000.

Beneficiaries included: Ecumenical Project (£5,100); Salt of the Earth (£5,000); New Israel Fund (£4,000); OXFAM (£1,000); and CAFOD, International Refugee Trust, LEPRA, Survival International Charitable Trust, SSAFA, TRAX and UNICEF (£500 each).

Exclusions No grants towards animal welfare or to individuals.

Applications In writing to the correspondent. Applicants must contact the trust before making an application.

H and L Cantor Trust

Jewish and general

£33,000 (2007/08)
Beneficial area UK, with some preference for Sheffield.

3 Ivy Park Court, 35 Ivy Park Road, Sheffield S10 3LA
Correspondent Mrs Lilly Cantor, Trustee
Trustees *Mrs L Cantor; N Jeffrey.*
CC Number 220300
Information available Information was on file at the Charity Commission.

'The principal objective of the trust is to provide benefit for charities, with particular consideration given to Jewish charities.' In 2007/08 the trust had assets of £938,000 and an income of £27,000. There were 24 grants made totalling £33,000.

Beneficiaries included: Delamere Forest School Ltd (£31,000 in two grants); Sheffield Jewish Congregation & Centre (980 in seven grants); Sheffield Jewish Welfare Organisation (£150 in two grants); I Rescue, Jewish Childs Day, Sense and Share Zadek UK (£100 each); Brain Research Trust (£50); PDSA Sheffield (£25); and World Cancer Research (£10).

Applications Unsolicited applications are not considered.

Cardy Beaver Foundation

General

£118,000 (2007/08)

Beneficial area UK with preference for the Reading and Berkshire areas.

Clifton House, 17 Reading Road, Pangbourne RG8 7LU

Tel. 0118 984 4713

Correspondent G R Coia

Trustees *G R Coia, Chair; M G Cardy; S I Rice.*

CC Number 265763

Information available Accounts were on file at the Charity Commission.

Registered with the Charity Commission in May 1973, in 2007/08 the foundation had assets of £2.4 million and an income of £187,000. Grants totalled £118,000.

During the year 26 grants were made, of which 21 of the organisations were also supported in the previous year. All but three were for £4,500 each. Beneficiaries included: WAMPSAD (£9,000); Action Medical Research, Alzheimer's Disease Society, Berkshire Multiple Sclerosis Centre, the Cancer Counselling Trust, the Children's Transplant Foundation, Duchess of Kent House Trust, Newbury and District Cancer Care Trust, Pets as Therapy, Prostate Cancer Research Campaign UK, Reading Hospital's Cardiac Fund, RNLI, Thames Valley Air Ambulance, the Charlie Waller Memorial Trust, and the Watermill Theatre Appeal (£4,500 each); and St Matthew's Church – Midgham and St Peter's Church – Woolhampton (£2,500 each).

Applications In writing to the correspondent.

The D W T Cargill Fund

General

Around £200,000 a year

Beneficial area UK, with a preference for the west of Scotland.

Miller Beckett and Jackson Solicitors, 190 St Vincent Street, Glasgow G2 5SP

Correspondent Norman A Fyfe, Trustee

Trustees *A C Fyfe; W G Peacock; N A Fyfe; Mirren Elizabeth Graham.*

SC Number SC012703

Information available Despite making a written request for the accounts of this charity (including a stamped, addressed envelope) these were not provided. The following entry is based on information filed with the Office of the Scottish Charity Regulator.

This trust has the same address and trustees as two other trusts, W A Cargill Charitable Trust and W A Cargill Fund, although they all operate independently.

It supports 'any hospitals, institutions, societies or others whose work in the opinion of the trustees is likely to be beneficial to the community'.

In 2007/08 the fund had an income of £303,000. Grants have previously totalled around £200,000 a year.

Previous beneficiaries have included City of Glasgow Society of Social Service, Colquhoun Bequest Fund for Incurables, Crathie Opportunity Holidays, Glasgow and West of Scotland Society for the Blind, Glasgow City Mission, Greenock Medical Aid Society, North Glasgow Community Forum, Scottish Maritime Museum – Irvine, Scottish Episcopal Church, Scottish Motor Neurone Disease Association, Lead Scotland and Three Towns Blind Bowling/Social Club.

Exclusions No grants are made to individuals.

Applications In writing to the correspondent, supported by up-to-date accounts. Trustees meet quarterly.

The Carlton House Charitable Trust

Jewish, education and bursaries and general

£41,000 (2007/08)

Beneficial area UK and overseas.

Craven House, 121 Kingsway, London WC2B 6PA

Correspondent Stewart S Cohen, Trustee

Trustees *S Cohen; Mrs P G Cohen; Mrs F A Stein.*

CC Number 296791

Information available Accounts were on file at the Charity Commission.

In 2007/08 the trust had assets of £1.1 million and an income of £361,000, including over £300,000 from donations. Grants were made to 157 organisations totalling £41,000.

Beneficiaries of the 34 largest grants of £100 or more included: National Trust (£5,500); Godalfm Latymer School (£3,500); Bnai Brith First Lodge of England (£3,200); Westminster Advocacy Service (£3,000); Western Marble Arch Synagogue (£1,900); Academy of Creative Training, Bnai Brith Hillel Foundation, Community Security Trust, Imperial College, Jewish Care, Prostate Cancer Charity, Royal Academy of Dramatic Art, St Edmunds Hall and University of Bristol (£1,000 each); Jewish Music Institute (£900); Weiner Library (£800); London Philharmonic Orchestra (£750); Holocaust Centre, St Christopher's Hospice and United Jewish Israel Appeal (£500 each); British Friends of the Hebrew University (£250); and Army Benevolent Fund (£125).

Other donations of less than £100 each totalled £4,600.

Applications In writing to the correspondent.

The Carpenter Charitable Trust

Humanitarian and Christian outreach

£69,000 (2007/08)

Beneficial area UK and overseas.

The Old Vicarage, Hitchin Road, Kimpton, Hitchin SG4 8EF

Correspondent M S E Carpenter, Trustee

Trustees *M S E Carpenter; Mrs G M L Carpenter.*

CC Number 280692

Information available Accounts were on file at the Charity Commission.

The charity is established on wide grant giving terms. The trustees continue to pursue their 'preferred' list approach – a list of charities with which the trustees have developed a good relationship over the years.

In 2007/08 the trust's assets totalled £1.1 million and it had an income of £270,000 including £250,000 from donations. Grants totalled £69,000.

Among the 32 beneficiaries receiving grants during the year, 24 were also supported in the previous year. Beneficiaries included: Mission Aviation Fellowship Europe (£7,500); ORBIS Charitable Trust (£6,000); Andrew Christian Trust, Barnabas Fund, Help in Suffering UK and Relationships Foundation (£5,000 each); DEC Bangladesh (£2,500); Brooke Hospital for Animals, Crisis UK, Merlin and Salvation Army (£1,000 each); Blue Cross, Fight for Sight, Mercy Ships, Prison Fellowship, RSPB, Send a Cow and Tibet Relief (£500 each); and Cats Protection League (£250).

Three grants were made to individuals from the designated Monica Fund totalling £75.

Exclusions The trustees do not consider applications for church repairs (other than in respect of Kimpton Church), applications from individuals nor any applications received from abroad unless clearly 'sponsored' by an established charity based in England and Wales.

Applications In writing to the correspondent including sufficient details to enable a decision to be made. However, as about half the donations made are repeat grants, the amount available for unsolicited applications remains small.

The Carr-Gregory Trust

Arts, social welfare, health and education

£47,000 (2007/08)
Beneficial area UK.

56 Pembroke Road, Clifton, Bristol BS8 3DT
Correspondent Russ Carr, Trustee
Trustees *Russ Carr; Heather Wheelhouse; Linda Carr.*
CC Number 1085580
Information available Accounts were on file at the charity Commission.

In 2007/08 the trust had assets of £410,000 and an income of £47,000, including £23,000 from donations. Grants totalled £47,000.

Donations were broken down as follows:

Category	Value
Arts/culture	£17,000
Social welfare	£11,000
Health	£7,000
Education	£2,000
Other	£10,000

Beneficiaries included: the Royal National Theatre and St Thomas's – Goring on Thames (£10,000 each); Royal Shakespeare Company and St James Priory Project (£2,500 each); Alzheimer's Research Trust, Action on Disability and Development, the Cheltenham Ladies' College and Connect (£2,000 each); the Gate Theatre, the Holburne Museum, the Royal Marsden Cancer Campaign and Victoria and Albert Museum (£1,000 each); NSPCC (£800); and Alabare Christian Care Centres, Emmaus Bristol, Quartet Community Foundation, Prisoners' Education Trust and St Mungo's (£500 each).

Applications In writing to the correspondent.

The Carron Charitable Trust

Environment, education and medicine

£85,000 (2007/08)
Beneficial area UK and overseas.

c/o Rothman Panthall and Co., 10 Romsey Road, Eastleigh SO50 9AL
Correspondent The Trustees
Trustees *P G Fowler; W M Allen; D L Morgan.*
CC Number 289164
Information available Full accounts were on file at the Charity Commission.

'The trust was created for charitable purposes in connection with wildlife, education, medicine, the countryside and the printing and publishing trade.' Ongoing support is given to the St Bride's Church – Fleet Street.

In 2007/08 the trust's income was £77,000, including £60,000 from donations. Grants totalled £85,000. Assets totalled £214,000 at year end.

Beneficiaries included: St Bride's Church Appeal (£20,000); INTBAU (£10,000); Academy of Aviation and Space Medicine (£3,000); and Curwen Print Study Centre (£1,500).

Exclusions No grants to individuals.

Applications The trust does not invite applications from the general public.

The Leslie Mary Carter Charitable Trust

Conservation, environment and welfare

£101,000 (2008)
Beneficial area UK, with a preference for Norfolk, Suffolk and North Essex.

c/o Birketts, 24–26 Museum Street, Ipswich IP1 1HZ
Correspondent Sam Wilson, Trustee
Trustees *Miss L M Carter; S R M Wilson; Martyn Carr.*
CC Number 284782
Information available Accounts were on file at the Charity Commission.

The trust has a preference for welfare organisations and conservation/environment causes, with an emphasis on local projects including those in Suffolk, Norfolk and North Essex. Grants generally range from £500 to £5,000, but larger grants are sometimes considered.

In 2008 the trust had assets of £2.6 million, an income of £123,000 and made 27 grants totalling £101,000.

Beneficiaries included: East Coast Sail Trust and East Anglia Children's Hospices (£7,500 each); Barn Owl Trust, Field Studies Council – Flatford Mill Appeal, Motor Neurone Disease Association – Equipment Loan Service, RNID – Language Service Professional and YMCA Norfolk (5,000 each); Long Melford Church Appeal, Plantlife, Shelter – East Anglia and SSAFA Forces Help (£3,000 each); Acorn Village – Oakroom Project (£2,000); Royal Anglian Regiment Museum Appeal and Wildlife Trust – Awash with Wildlife (£1,000 each).

Trustees prefer well thought-out applications for larger gifts, than many applications for smaller grants.

Exclusions No grants to individuals.

Applications In writing to the correspondent. Telephone calls are not welcome. There is no need to enclose a stamped, addressed envelope unless applicants wish to have materials returned.

Applications made outside the preferred areas for grantgiving will be considered, but acknowledgements may not always be sent.

The Carvill Trust

General

£37,000 (2007/08)

Beneficial area UK.

5th Floor, Minories House,
2–5 Minories, London EC3N 1BJ

Tel. 020 7780 6900

Correspondent K D Tuson, Trustee

Trustees *R K Carvill; R E Pooley; K D Tuson.*

CC Number 1036420

Information available Accounts were on file at the Charity Commission.

The trust was established for general charitable purposes in 1994. In 2007/08 the trust had assets of £428,000 and an income of £121,000, including £100,000 from donations. Grants totalled £37,000.

Beneficiaries included: Irish Youth Foundation (£14,000); and Academy Ocean Reef and War Child (£10,000 each).

In 2006/07 the trust had an income of £16,000 and a total expenditure of £60,000. No further financial information was available for this year.

Applications In writing to the correspondent, although the trust states that it only supports beneficiaries known to or connected with the trustees. Unsolicited applications from individuals will not be supported.

The Casey Trust

Children and young people

£80,000 (2007/08)

Beneficial area UK and developing countries.

27 Arkwright Road, London NW3 6BJ

Correspondent Kenneth Howard, Trustee

Trustees *Kenneth Howard; Edwin Green; Hon. Judge Leonard Krikler.*

CC Number 1055726

Information available Full accounts were on file at the Charity Commission.

This trust was established to help children and young people in the UK and developing countries, by supporting new projects in a variety of countries.

In 2007/08 it had assets of £2.8 million, an income of £141,000 and made 41 grants totalling £80,000.

Beneficiaries included: Norwood (£10,000); Family Welfare Association and UNICEF Myanmar Cyclone Children's Appeal (£5,000 each); Rainbow Trust (£3,000); Hollybank Trust (£2,600); BLISS, EMMS International, Hope and Homes for Children and the Woodford Foundation (£2,500 each); Hope House (£2,000); Action for Kids, Pearson's Holiday Fund and Whizz Kidz (£1,500 each); Child Time, the Eyeless Trust, Harvest Trust, Hopscotch, Music as Therapy, the Hornsey Trust, National Holiday Fund, Pattaya Orphanage Trust and Rose Road Association (£1,000 each); Health Unlimited (£900); and Deep Impact Theatre (£750).

Exclusions Grants are not given to 'individual applicants requesting funds to continue studies or travel'.

Applications The following information is taken from the trust's accounts.

Not being a reactive trust, it is regretted that the trustees will be unable to respond to the majority of requests for assistance. In order to both reduce costs and administration the trustees will respond mainly to those charitable institutions known to them. There is no application form.

The Catholic Charitable Trust

Catholic

£53,000 (2007)

Beneficial area America and Europe.

Vernor, Miles and Noble, 5 Raymond Buildings, Gray's Inn, London WC1R 5DD

Correspondent J C Vernor Miles, Trustee

Trustees *J C Vernor Miles; W E Vernor Miles; D P Orr.*

CC Number 215553

Information available Accounts were on file at the Charity Commission.

The trust supports traditional Catholic organisations in America and Europe.

In 2007 it had assets of £1.7 million, which generated an income of £46,000. Grants were made to 14 organisations totalling £53,000.

Beneficiaries included: Society of Saint Pius X – England (£15,000); Society of Latin Mass Society (£5,100); Fraternity of St Pius X Switzerland and Little Sisters of the Poor (£5,000 each); Worth Abbey (£4,000); Cardinal Newman Library Project (£2,500); St Peter's Catholic Church and Society of the Grail (£2,000 each); and Carmelite Monastery Carmel California (£1,500).

Two grants were made to American organisations: the Carmelite Monastery Carmel California (US$4,000); and California Friends of the Society of St Pius X, (US$2,000 each).

Exclusions The trust does not normally support a charity unless it is known to the trustees. Grants are not made to individuals.

Applications Applications can only be accepted from registered charities and should be in writing to the correspondent. In order to save administration costs, replies are not sent to unsuccessful applicants. For the most part funds are fully committed.

The Catholic Trust for England and Wales

Catholic

£737,000 (2008)

Beneficial area England and Wales.

39 Eccleston Square, London SW1V 1BX

Tel. 020 7901 4810

Email secretariat@cbcew.org.uk

Website www.catholicchurch.org.uk

Correspondent Revd Marcus Stock

Trustees *Rt Revd Malcolm McMahon, Chair; Mgr Michael McKenna; Ben Andradi; Alison Cowdall; John Gibbs; Peter Lomas; Canon Nicholas Rothon; Robin Smith; Dr James Whiston.*

CC Number 1097482

Information available Accounts were on file at the Charity Commission.

The fund was established in 1968 and is concerned with 'the advancement of the Roman Catholic religion in England and Wales'. The trust achieves its objectives through the work of the various Committees of the Bishops' conference and various agencies such as the Catholic

Communications Service. Each committee is concerned with a different area of work of the Church. Grants are only given to organisations which benefit England and Wales as a whole, rather than local projects.

Five categories of grants have been agreed by the trustees in their annual report:

1) Small grants to charities that attract their major funding from other sources.
2) Grants to organisations, charities and projects that have a national role recognised by the Bishops' Conference and are therefore considered as being part of the national ecclesiastical structures.
3) Grants to organisations, charities and projects that either contribute to the life and work of the Catholic community in more than one diocese and require significant funding or require initial funding in order to develop the work of the Bishops' Conference.
4) Grants for purposes associated with social communications and media.
5) Grants to fulfil the purposes of the Lisbon Trust Fund.

In 2008 the trust had assets of £10.1 million and an income of £5.5 million, £1.7 million of which was from diocesan assessments. Grants and subscriptions totalled £737,000.

Beneficiaries included: CARITAS Social Action (£56,000); Linacre Centre (£50,000); Churches Legislation Advisory Service (£23,000); National Board of Catholic Women and National Confederation of Catholic Women (£12,000 each); Churches Media Council (£6,000); Lisbonia Society (£5,000); Churches Initiative Trust (£3,000); and Independent Catholic News (£1,000).

Exclusions No grants to individuals, local projects or projects not immediately advancing the Roman Catholic religion in England and Wales.

Applications In writing to the correspondent.

The Joseph and Annie Cattle Trust

General

£317,000 to organisations
(2007/08)

Beneficial area Worldwide, with a preference for Hull and East Yorkshire.

393–395 Anlaby Road, Hull HU3 6AB

Correspondent Roger Waudby, Administrator

Trustees *J A Collier; M T Gyte; P A Robins.*

CC Number 262011

Information available Full accounts were on file at the Charity Commission.

The object of the charity is to provide for general charitable purposes by making grants, principally to applicants in the Hull area. Older people and people who have disabilities or who are underprivileged are assisted wherever possible, and there is a particular emphasis on giving aid to children with dyslexia.

In 2007/08 the trust had assets of £8.2 million and an income of £432,000. Grants totalled £351,000 of which £34,000 was given to 63 individuals. The 211 grants to institutions were broken down into four main categories, shown here with examples of beneficiaries in each category.

Churches and missions
Holderness Road Methodist Church – the Bridge Community Project (£10,000); Boulevard Baptist Church and Christchurch – Cottingham and East Hull Presbyterian Church (£5,000 each); St John's Church – Newland (£3,000); Hull Churches Home from Hospital Service and St Matthew's Church (£2,000 each); and Amazing Grace Chapel, Crosslinks, East Hull United Reformed Church, Sutton Methodist Church and House of Light (£1,000 each).

Local societies and activities
Sobriety Project (£20,000); Dyslexia Action (£15,000); Archbishop Thurston Church of England School, Godfrey Robinson Home for the Disabled Bus Appeal and Melton Campsite (£5,000 each); Hull and East Riding Institute for the Blind (£3,000); Dads Against Drugs, Macmillan Cancer Appeal and Wold Primary School (£2,000 each); Edinburgh Street Community

Association (£1,500); and Andrew Marvell Youth Centre, Holme on Spalding Moor Village Hall, Hull Lighthouse Project, Prison Fellowship Hull and East Riding, St Leonard's Hospice and Withernsea and Holderness Play Action (£1,000 each).

National societies
Laser Trust Fund – Moghissi and UNICEF UK – Darfur (£5,000 each); Marie Curie Cancer Centre and Yorkshire Eye Research (£2,000 each); and Africa Equipment for Schools, Botton Village Appeal Fund, Cruse Bereavement Care, PDSA and Yorkshire Air Ambulance (£1,000 each).

Sponsoring and assisting local children and adults with disabilities and for training
Hull City Council Social Services received a major grants contribution of £80,000. Other grants awarded included those to individuals through organisations including: East Riding of Yorkshire Council, HMP Wolds, Humber Mental Health NHS Trust, Humbercare, Mobility Trust, National Probation Service, Perennial, SSAFA and Therapy Services Partnership NHS.

Exclusions Grants are very rarely given to individuals and are only supported through social services or relevant charitable or welfare organisations.

Applications In writing to the correspondent. Meetings are usually held on the third Monday of each month.

The Thomas Sivewright Catto Charitable Settlement

General

£211,000 (2007/08)

Beneficial area Unrestricted (for UK-based registered charities).

PO Box 47408, London N21 1YW

Correspondent The Secretary to the Trustees

Trustees *Lord Catto; Olivia Marchant; Zoe Richmond-Watson.*

CC Number 279549

Information available Accounts were on file at the Charity Commission.

This trust has general charitable purposes, making a large number of smaller grants to a wide range of organisations and a few larger grants of up to £20,000. Despite the large number of grants made, there appears to be no strong preference for any particular causes or geographical areas.

In 2007/08 the trust had assets of £3.2 million and an income of £193,000. There were 191 grants made totalling £211,000.

Beneficiaries included: Royal College of Music (£14,000) Royal Scottish Academy of Music and Drama (£12,000); Bowel Cancer Research and King VII's Hospital for Officers (£10,000 each); Haddo House Choral and Operatic Society and World YWCA (£5,000 each); Aviation for Paraplegics and Tetraplegics Trust (£2,000); NACRO (£1,500); Alzheimer's Research Trust, Elizabeth Finn Care, Concern Worldwide, the Fostering Network, Outward Bound Trust, Refugee Council, St Mungo's, Shelter and Charlie Waller Memorial Trust (£1,000 each); Crisis, Disabled Living Foundation, Matthew Trust, REACT and Royal London Society for the Blind (£750 each); and Clubs for Young People, Motability, Nepal Leprosy Trust, Prisoners' Advice Service, Queen Elizabeth's Foundation, Sportability and VSO (£500 each).

Exclusions The trust does not support non-registered charities, expeditions, travel bursaries and so on, or unsolicited applications from churches of any denomination. Grants are unlikely to be considered in the areas of community care, playschemes and drug abuse, or for local branches of national organisations.

Applications In writing to the correspondent, including a stamped, addressed envelope.

The Wilfrid and Constance Cave Foundation

Conservation, animal welfare, health, social welfare and general
£196,000 (2007/08)
Beneficial area UK, with preference for Berkshire, Cornwall, Devon, Dorset, Hampshire, Oxfordshire,

Somerset, Warwickshire and Wiltshire.

New Lodge Farm, Drift Road, Winkfield, Windsor SL4 4QQ
Correspondent The Secretary
Trustees Mrs T Jones; P Simpson; F H C Jones; Mrs J Archer; Mrs J Pickin; M Pickin; Mrs M Waterworth; Mrs N Thompson; R Walker; G Howells; W Howells; M Beckett.
CC Number 241900
Information available Accounts were on file at the Charity Commission.

The trust supports local and UK-wide organisations and has general charitable purposes.

In 2007/08 it had assets of £4.4 million which generated an income of £185,000. Grants were made to 44 organisations totalling £196,000, with Oxford Museum of Children's Literature receiving the largest grant of £60,000.

Other beneficiaries included: East Berkshire Women's Aid (£12,000); Northcott Theatre (£10,000); Royal Agricultural Benevolent Institution (£5,000); North Devon Hospice, Prospect Hospice and the West Country River Trust (£3,000 each); Countryside Foundation for Education, Dyslexia Institute, Exmoor Woodland Trust, Thames Restoration Trust and War Memorials Trust (£2,000 each); and Regain (£1,000).

Exclusions No grants to individuals.
Applications In writing to the correspondent a month before the trustees' meetings held twice each year, in May and October.

The Cayo Foundation

Medical research, crime, children and young people and general
£296,000 (2007/08)
Beneficial area UK.

7 Cowley Street, London SW1P 3NB
Correspondent Angela E McCarville
Trustees Angela E McCarville; Stewart A Harris.
CC Number 1080607
Information available Full accounts were on file at the Charity Commission.

The trust supports the fight against crime, medical research and training and children's charities.

In 2007/08 it had assets of £170,000. The income was £324,000, almost entirely from donations received. Grants to 16 organisations totalled £296,000 and were broken down as follows:

Children and young people – £160,000
Beneficiaries included: NSPCC (£125,000); PACT (£25,000); and Wessex Youth Trust (£10,000).

Medical research and training – £63,000
Beneficiaries included: the Disability Foundation and RNIB (£25,000 each); Christian Blind Mission (£6,000); Wellbeing of Women (£3,000); Royal Humane Society (£2,500); and Sue Ryder Care – St John's Hospice (£1,000).

Crime fighting – £3,100
The sole beneficiary was Crimestoppers.

Other – £71,000
Beneficiaries included: the Royal Opera House (£25,000); the Prince's Foundation (£20,000); SURF (£15,000); British WIZO (£5,000); Institute for Policy Research (£2,500); Erskine (£2,000); and Homes in Zimbabwe (£1,000).

Applications In writing to the correspondent.

Elizabeth Cayzer Charitable Trust

Arts
£63,000 (2007/08)
Beneficial area UK.

The Cayzer Trust Company Limited, Cayzer House, 30 Buckingham Gate, London SW1E 6NN
Tel. 020 7802 8422
Correspondent Helen D'Marco
Trustees The Hon. Elizabeth Gilmour; Diana Lloyd; Dominic Gibbs.
CC Number 1059265
Information available Accounts were on file at the Charity Commission, without a list of grants.

This charity was established by The Honourable Elizabeth Gilmour, who has made significant donations to the charity since 1996. In formulating policy the trustees have taken into account the wishes of the Settlor which are that the assets of the charity should be used in supporting and promoting activities relating to art.

In 2007/08 the trust had assets of £2 million with an income of £225,000 and made grants totalling £63,000, broken down as follows: education (£44,000); and conferences and exhibitions (£19,000).

Previous beneficiaries have included Elias Ashmole Trust, Dulwich Picture Gallery, the National Gallery and Sir John Soane's Museum.

Applications The following guidance is taken from the trustees' report.

The trustees identify the projects and organisations they wish to support and so do not consider grants to people or organisations who apply speculatively. The trust also has a policy of not responding to any correspondence unless it relates to grants it has agreed to make or to the general management of the trust.

The B G S Cayzer Charitable Trust

General

£80,000 (2007/08)
Beneficial area UK.

c/o Cayzer House, 30 Buckingham Gate, London SW1E 6NN

Correspondent Jeanne Cook

Trustees *P R Davies; Mrs M Buckley; Mrs A M Hunter; Mrs R N Leslie.*

CC Number 286063

Information available Accounts were on file at the Charity Commission, without a list of beneficiaries.

In 2007/08 the trust had assets of over £2.4 million, an income of £91,000 and made grants totalling £80,000, broken down as follows:

Category	Value
Education and training	£25,000
Heritage and conservation	£20,000
General	£16,000
Medical	£12,000
Relief of poverty	£5,500
Religion	£2,000

Previous beneficiaries have included: Friends of the National Maritime Museum, Hike for Hope, Marie Curie Cancer Care, RAFT, St Paul's Cathedral Foundation, Scottish Countryside Alliance Education Trust and Worshipful

Company of Shipwrights Charitable Fund.

Exclusions No grants to organisations outside the UK.

Applications The trust tends to support only people or projects known to the Cayzer family or the trustees. Unsolicited appeals will not be supported.

The Cazenove Charitable Trust

General

£47,000 (2007)
Beneficial area UK.

20 Moorgate, London EC2R 6DA

Correspondent The Secretary

Trustees *C R M Bishop; J Earl; E M Harley.*

CC Number 1086899

Information available Accounts were on file at the Charity Commission.

Established in 1969, this trust primarily supports the charitable activities sponsored by current and former Cazenove employees. In 2007 the trust had assets of £1.2 million and an income of £45,000. Grants totalled £47,000.

Beneficiaries included: Adam Cole Foundation (£5,500); St Michael's Church, Battersea and Samaritans (£5,000 each); Refuge (£3,900); Beormund School – Southwark and St Mungo's (£3,400 each); Cancer Research UK (£2,700); Kids Company (£1,300); and Whizz Kidz, Oxfam Great Britain and Macmillan Cancer Relief (£1,000 each).

Applications This trust does not respond to unsolicited applications.

The Cemlyn-Jones Trust

See below

£50,000 (2007/08)
Beneficial area North Wales and Anglesey.

59 Madoc Street, Llandudno LL30 2TW
Tel. 01492 874391

Email philip.brown@brewin.co.uk
Correspondent P G Brown, Trustee
Trustees *P G Brown; Mrs J E Lea; Mrs E G Jones.*

CC Number 1039164

Information available Accounts were on file at the Charity Commission.

This trust was registered in 1994, and has a welcome preference for making grants to small local projects in north Wales and Anglesey. Its objects, listed in the annual report, are:

1) conservation and protection of general public amenities, historic or public interests in Wales
2) medical research
3) protection and welfare of animals and birds
4) study and promotion of music
5) activities and requirements of religious and educational bodies.

In 2007/08 the trust's assets totalled £1.2 million, it had an income of £411,000 and made grants totalling £50,000.

Beneficiaries included: Bangor University (£20,000); UCNW Development Trust – Fellowship Fund (£6,600); UCNW Development Trust (£5,500); Menai Bridge Community Heritage Trust (£5,000); St David's Hospice (£4,500); Ty Gobaith (£4,000); Beaumaris Festival (£2,000); Ocean Youth Trust (£1,800); and Rowen Scout Camp (£1,000).

Exclusions No grants to individuals or non-charitable organisations.

Applications In writing to the correspondent.

The CH (1980) Charitable Trust

Jewish

£106,000 (2007/08)
Beneficial area UK and Israel.

30 Gresham Street, London EC2V 7PG

Correspondent The Administrator

Trustee *Kleinwort Benson Trustees Limited.*

CC Number 279481

Information available Accounts were on file at the Charity Commission.

Established in 1980, in 2007/08 the trust had assets of £1.8 million and an income of £139,000. Grants to 12 organisations totalled £106,000.

Beneficiaries included: Oxford Centre for Hebrew and Jewish Studies (£21,000); Jewish Care (£20,000); British ORT (£17,000); United Jewish Israel Appeal (£15,000); British Technion Society (12,000); Anglo Israel Association (£6,700); Friends of Boys Town Jerusalem in Great Britain (£5,000); West London Synagogue Charitable Fund (£3,000); Maccabi GB (£2,000); B'nai B'rith Hillel Foundation (£1,000); and British Friends of the Israel Guide Dogs Centre for the Blind (£500).

Applications In writing to the correspondent.

R E Chadwick Charitable Trust

General

£27,000 (2007/08)
Beneficial area UK.

19 Cookridge Street, Leeds LS2 3AG
Tel. 0113 244 6100
Email peter.chadwick@wrigleys.co.uk
Correspondent Peter Chadwick, Trustee
Trustees *Peter Chadwick; Esme Knowles; Paul Knowles; Ann Chadwick.*
CC Number 1104805
Information available Accounts were on file at the Charity Commission.

Set up in 2004, in 2007/08 the trust had assets of £883,000 and an income of £332,000. Grants to 47 organisations totalled £27,000.

Beneficiaries included: Grammar School at Leeds (£2,000); British Red Cross (£1,500); Crisis, Leeds Festival Chorus, Myasthenia Gravis Association and RNIB (£1,000 each); UNICEF (£750); Arthritis Research, CAFOD, the Country Trust, Friends of St Winifred's, Gloucester Choral Society, Leeds Parish Church Choral Foundation Appeal, Meanwood Valley Urban Farm, Muslim Hands, NSPCC, the Simon Community and Yorkshire Dales Millennium Trust (£500 each); and Landmark Trust, Mission to Deep Sea Fishermen, Nightstop and Royal Horticultural Society – Harlow Carr (£250 each).

Applications In writing to the correspondent.

The Amelia Chadwick Trust

General

£100,000 (2007/08)
Beneficial area UK, especially Merseyside.

Guy Williams Layton, Pacific Chambers, 11–13 Victoria Street, Liverpool L2 5QQ
Tel. 0151 236 7171
Correspondent J R McGibbon, Trustee
Trustees *J R McGibbon; J C H Bibby.*
CC Number 213795
Information available Accounts were on file at the Charity Commission.

The trust supports a wide range of charities, especially welfare causes. Although grants are given throughout the UK, there is a strong preference for Merseyside.

In 2007/08 the trust had assets of £3.7 million, an income of £133,000 and made 36 grants totalling £100,000.

Beneficiaries inlcuded: Merseyside Development Foundation (£31,000); Liverpool PSS (£12,000); St Helen's Women's Aid (£7,200); Oxfordshire Dyslexia Association and Phoenix Futures (£5,000 each); Volunteer Reading Help (£3,000); Alzheimer's Disease Society, St John's Hospice Wirral and the Sylvia Fund (£2,000 each); Sheila Kay Fund and Royal Liverpool Philharmonic Society (£1,500 each); Birkenhead YMCA, Claire House, Council for the Protection of Rural England and Oxfam (£1,000 each); Wirral Women's Aid (£750); the Fortune Centre (£500); and Neston Nomads (£250).

Applications All donations are made through Liverpool Council for Social Services. Grants are only made to charities known to the trustees, and unsolicited applications are not considered.

The Pamela Champion Foundation

General and disability

£29,000 (2007)
Beneficial area UK, with a preference for Kent.

Wiltons, Newnham Lane, Eastling, Faversham ME13 0AS
Tel. 01795 890233
Correspondent Elizabeth Bell, Trustee
Trustees *Miss M Stanlake; Mrs C Winser; Mrs E Bell; P M Williams.*
CC Number 268819
Information available Accounts were on file at the Charity Commission.

In 2007 the trust had assets of over £833,000 and an income of over £35,000. There were 28 grants made totalling £29,000.

Beneficiaries included: St Mary's Eastling (£2,500); Canterbury Cathedral Fund, Citizens Advice Maidstone, Independence at Home and Leonard Cheshire (£2,000 each); Demelza House (£1,500); Army Benevolent Fund, CHASE, Crimestoppers Kent, Royal British Legion Industries, Christian Lewis Trust, Anthony Nolan Trust, RUKBA and St Mary's Church Shackleford (£1,000 each); Grove Green Scout Group and Vauxhall City Farm (£750 each); 7th Petts Wood Scout Group, Barnados, Kent Wildlife Trust, Surrey Churches Preservation Trust and Whitstable Umbrella Community Centre (£500 each); and the Ripple Down House Trust (£250).

Exclusions No grants to non-registered charities.

Applications In writing to the correspondent.

The Chapman Charitable Trust

Welfare and general

£280,000 (2007/08)
Beneficial area Eastern and south east England, including London, and Wales.

Crouch Chapman, 62 Wilson Street, London EC2A 2BU

Tel. 020 7782 0007

Email cct@crouchchapman.co.uk

Correspondent Roger S Chapman, Trustee

Trustees *Roger Chapman; Richard Chapman; Bruce Chapman; Guy Chapman; Bryony Chapman.*

CC Number 232791

Information available Accounts were on file at the Charity Commission.

Established in 1963 with general charitable purposes, the trust mainly supports culture and recreation, education and research, health, social services, environment and heritage causes.

In 2007/08 the trust had assets of £6.3 million, an income of £282,000 and made grants totalling £280,000. A total of 140 grants were made totalling £280,000.

Beneficiaries included: Pesticide Action Network UK (£15,000 in two grants); Leonard Cheshire – Rustington, Methodist Homes for the Aged, NCH and Queen Alexandra Hospital Home (£12,000 in two grants each); Fragile X Society and TreeHouse Trust (£11,000 in two grants each); Aldeburgh Music (£6,000); Cambridge University Veterinary School, Fields in Trust, Longview and Phoenix Cinema Trust (£5,000 each); Action for Kids, Arthritis Research Campaign, Barbican Centre Trust, Breakthrough Breast Cancer, British Wheelchair Sports Foundation, Caxton House Community Centre – Islington, Children's Heart Federation, Connection at St Martin-in-the-Fields, Criccieth Festival, Dame Vera Lynn Trust, Diabetes UK, Foundation for Paediatric Osteopathy, Home-Start UK, In Kind Direct, Leukaemia Research Fund, Meningitis Research Foundation, Raynaud's and Scleroderma Association and Yvonne Arnaud Theatre – Guildford (£2,000 each); and Vitalise (£1,500).

There were 80 grants of £1,000 each and 1 of £500.

Exclusions No grants to or for the benefit of individuals, local branches of national UK charities, animal welfare, sports tours or sponsored adventure holidays.

Applications In writing at any time. The trustees currently meet to consider grants twice a year at the end of September and in March. They receive a large number of applications and regret that they cannot acknowledge receipt of them. The absence of any communication for six months would mean that an application must have been unsuccessful.

The Charter 600 Charity

General
£45,000 (2007/08)
Beneficial area UK.

Mercers' Hall, Ironmongers Lane, London EC2V 8HE

Website www.mercers.co.uk

Correspondent The Clerk

Trustee *The Mercers' Company.*

CC Number 1051146

Information available Accounts were on file at the Charity Commission.

The Charter 600 charity was established to commemorate the 600th anniversaries of the Grant of the Mercers' Company's first Charter in 1394 and of the first Mastership of Sir Richard Whittington in 1395. Established in 1994, it operates under a trust deed dated October 1995.

The trustee's aims are to support a range of organisations with the common theme of delivering charitable services and facilities to those in need and to local communities. The Charity has achieved these aims during the period by supporting community-based, grassroots organisations with particular emphasis on education, social and medical welfare support for young people and communities.

In 2007/08 the charity has assets of £753,000 and an income of £180,000. Grants made during the year totalled £45,000 and were distributed for the following purposes:

Category	%
Welfare	81
Education	8
Church	4
Conservation	4
Wildlife	2
Performing arts	1

Beneficiaries included: Scotts Project Trust (£2,400); World Pheasant Association (£2,000); 1st Headcorn Scout Group, Friends of Milstead and Frinsted School, Gwennili Trust, Project Peru and Walton-on-the-Hill Scout and Guide Association (£1,500 each); Braintree and Bocking Community Association, Farleigh Hospice, Great Bedwyn Swings and Slides, Queen Victoria School and Sinfield Nature Conservation Trust (£1,000 each); Crystal Palace Museum (£700); Look Good Feel Better and St Mary Magdalene PCC (£500 each); and Federation of London Youth Clubs (£250).

Exclusions Applications for charitable grants will only be accepted when put forward by a member of the Mercers' Company.

Applications The charity does not consider unsolicited applications.

The Worshipful Company of Chartered Accountants General Charitable Trust (also known as CALC)

General and education
£108,000 (2007/08)
Beneficial area UK.

Hampton City Services, Hampton House, High Street, East Grinstead RH19 3AW

Correspondent Peter Lusty, Clerk

Trustees *Ian Plaistowe; Rachel Adams; Colin Brown; John Cardnell; Michael Fowle; James Macnamara; David Allvey.*

CC Number 327681

Information available Full accounts were on file at the Charity Commission.

In general, the trust supports causes advancing education and/or benefiting disadvantaged people. It has a tendency to focus on a particular theme each year, as well as making grants to other causes and organisations of particular relevance to members of the company.

In 2007/08 the trust's assets stood at £1 million. It had an income of £130,000 and made grants totalling £108,000, which were broken down as follows:

Major grants were as follows.

- £30,000 to The Master's Project – Getting on Board.
- £35,000 to 20 Primary Schools to promote numeracy and literacy.

- £15,000 for a bursary for a member of the Institute of Chartered Accountants in England & Wales to study for a PhD in an accountancy related subject
- £10,000 for bursaries for students training at the Guildhall School of Music and Drama.
- £5,000 to MANGO, which provides management accounting support to Non Governmental Organisations, primarily in the developing world
- £2,500 to The Lord Mayors Appeal 2008.

Applications Applications must be sponsored by a liveryman of the company.

The Cheruby Trust

Welfare, education and general

£105,000 (2007/08)

Beneficial area UK and worldwide.

62 Grosvenor Street, London W1K 3JF

Tel. 020 7499 4301

Correspondent Mrs S Wechsler, Trustee

Trustees *A L Corob; L E Corob; T A Corob; C J Cook: S A Wechsler.*

CC Number 327069

Information available Full accounts were on file at the Charity Commission.

The trust's charitable objectives are the relief of poverty, the advancement of education and such other charitable purposes as the trustees see fit.

In 2007/08 the trust had assets of £43,000 and an income of £71,000, mostly from donations. There were 41 grants made totalling £105,000.

Beneficiaries included: Actionaid, Amnesty International, Children in Crisis, Concern Worldwide UK – Darfur, Crisis UK, HOPE Charity, ICELP, Save the Children, Sightsavers and WaterAid (£5,000 each); Help the Aged (£3,500); Alzheimer's Society, Breadline Africa, the Daneford Trust, Friends of the Earth and Sargent Cancer Care for Children (£3,000 each); Childhope and Family Welfare Association (2,500 each); APT Enterprise Development, International Service, Marie Curie Cancer Care, Motor Neurone Disease Association, SANE and Tibet Relief Fund (£2,000 each); British Deaf Association (£1,500); Camphill Family, Cruse Bereavement Care, Friends of Alyn, Norwood and Woodland Trust

(£1,000 each); Arthur Rank Hospice Charity (£500); London Wildlife Trust (£300); and Listening Books (£200).

Applications In writing to the correspondent.

The Chetwode Foundation

Education, churches and general

£60,000 (2007/08)

Beneficial area UK, with a preference for Nottinghamshire, Leicestershire and Derby.

Samworth Brothers (Holdings) Ltd, Chetwode House, 1 Samworth Way, Leicester Road, Melton Mowbray LE13 1GA

Tel. 01664 414500

Correspondent J G Ellis, Trustee

Trustees *J G Ellis; R N J S Price; A C Price.*

CC Number 265950

Information available Full accounts were on file at the Charity Commission.

This trust has general charitable purposes, giving without exclusion across the UK. Whilst it has preferences for education, churches and work in Nottinghamshire, Leicestershire and Derby, this is not at the expense of other causes.

In 2007/08 the trust had assets of £1.4 million and an income of £87,000. Grants totalling £60,000 were made to nine organisations.

Beneficiaries were: the Music Space Trust (£20,000); St Ann's Advice Centre (£11,000); the Zone Youth Project (£9,800); Think Children (£6,300); Weston Spirit (£5,000); Tythby and Cropwell Butler PCC (£3,000); Derby Toc H Children's Camp (£2,500); Newark and Nottinghamshire Agricultural Society (£2,400); and the National Trust for Scotland (£200).

Applications 'The foundation's grant making policy is to support a limited number of causes known to the trustees, particularly those supported by the settlor. Unsolicited applications are not normally considered.'

The Malcolm Chick Charity

Youth character building, armed forces welfare and medical research and care

£38,000 (2007/08)

Beneficial area UK.

White Horse Court, 25c North Street, Bishops Stortford CM23 2LD

Correspondent The Trust Administrator

Trustees *D J L Mobsby; R S Fowler; N D Waldman.*

CC Number 327732

Information available Full accounts were provided by the trust.

This trust has been in existence for some time with the trustees making small grants to organisations they were familiar with. On the death of one of the trustees, Malcolm Chick, the trust received part of his estate and has grown in size.

Grants are given in the following categories:

- youth character building
- armed service charities
- medical research and care.

In 2007/08 the trust's assets stood at £766,000, with an income of £30,000. Grants were made totalling £38,000.

Beneficiaries included: AHOY Centre and St Dunstan's (£9,000 each); Children's Heart Foundation (£4,000); Barts and the London Charity, the Daneforth Trust, Hove and the Adur Sea Cadet Unity and Tall Ships Youth Trust (£3,000 each); and Soft Power Education, Ocean Youth Trust South and Project Trust (£500 each).

Applications Applicants should write to ask for a copy of the criteria and application forms. Telephone calls are not welcomed. The trustees meet to consider applications in November and completed forms must be returned by the middle of October. There is a separate application form and guidance notes for individual applicants.

Child Growth Foundation

Institutions researching child/adult growth disorders, and people with such diseases

£177,000 (2007/08)
Beneficial area UK.

2 Mayfield Avenue, Chiswick W4 1PW
Tel. 020 8995 0257
Email info@childgrowthfoundation.org
Website www.childgrowthfoundation.org
Correspondent T Fry, Hon. Chair
Trustees *Tam Fry, Chair; Nick Child; Russell Chaplin; Simon Lane; Gillian McRobie; Rachel Pidcock; Linda Washington; Mark Coyle; Sue Davies.*
CC Number 274325
Information available Accounts were on file at the Charity Commission.

Among the objects of this foundation are to promote and fund research into the causes and cure of growth disorders in children within the area of benefit and to publish the results of such research.

In 2007/08 it had assets of £692,000 and an income of over £356,000. Out of a total expenditure of £300,000, grants were made totalling £177,000.

Applications In writing to the correspondent.

Children's Liver Disease Foundation

Diseases of the liver and biliary system in children

£230,000 (2007/08)
Beneficial area UK.

36 Great Charles Street, Queensway, Birmingham B3 3JY
Tel. 0121 212 3839 **Fax** 0121 212 4300
Email info@childliverdisease.org
Website www.childliverdisease.org
Correspondent Catherine Arkley, Chief Executive

Trustees *Tom Ross, Chair; Bob Benton; Nick Budd; Jayne Carroll; Kellie Charge; Mairi Everard; Michele Hunter; Ann Mowat; David Tildesley.*
CC Number 1067331
Information available Accounts were on file at the Charity Commission.

The Children's Liver Disease Foundation (CLDF) is a national registered charity founded in 1980. Its mission is to advance knowledge of childhood liver disease through:

- funding pioneering medical research
- providing effective education
- giving a professional and caring support service to families and young people with liver disease.

CLDF funds medical (basic and translational), nursing and social research connected with addressing the basic mechanisms, causes, prevention, diagnosis, cure and treatment of diseases of the liver and biliary system in children.

In 2007/08 the foundation had assets of £634,000, an income of £920,000 and a total expenditure of £917,000. Expenditure on research and grants totalled £230,000.

Exclusions The charity does not accept applications from organisations whose work is not associated with paediatric liver disease. No grants to individuals, whether medical professionals or patients. No grants for travel or personal education. No grants for general appeals.

Applications Applicants are strongly advised to look at the relevant pages on the Children's Liver Disease Foundation website.

The Children's Research Fund

Child health research

£120,000 (2008/09)
Beneficial area UK.

668 India Buildings, Water Street, Liverpool L2 0RA
Tel. 0151 236 2844
Website www.childrensresearchfund.org.uk
Correspondent The Trustees
Trustees *Hugh Greenwood, Chair; Gerald Inkin; Hugo Greenwood; Rt Hon. Lord Morris of Manchester; Elizabeth Theobald; David Lloyd.*

CC Number 226128
Information available Full accounts were on file at the Charity Commission.

The trust supports research into children's diseases, child health and prevention of illness in children, carried out at institutes and university departments of child health. The policy is to award grants, usually over several years, to centres of research. It will also support any charitable project associated with the well being of children.

In 2008/09 it had assets of £1.5 million, an income of £104,000 and made research grants totalling £120,000. Beneficiaries included: Great Ormond St Hospital (£75,000); Alder Hey Children's Hospital (£25,000); St James Hospital – Yorkshire Eye Research (£10,000); KIDSTEM International Conference (£5,000); and the Puffin Appeal and University of Cardiff (£1,000 each).

Exclusions No grants for capital projects.

Applications Applicants from child health research units and university departments are invited to send in an initial outline of their proposal; if it is eligible they will then be sent an application form. Applications are considered in March and November.

The Chownes Foundation

Religion, relief in need and social problems

£59,000 to organisations (2007/08)
Beneficial area UK, priority is given to charities based in Sussex, particularly in mid Sussex.

The Courtyard, Beeding Court, Shoreham Road, Steyning BN44 3TN
Tel. 01903 816699
Correspondent Sylvia Spencer, Secretary
Trustees *Mrs U Hazeel; The Rt Revd S Ortiger; M Woolley.*
CC Number 327451
Information available Accounts were on file at the Charity Commission.

The charity's objects are 'the advancement of religion, the advancement of education among the young, the amelioration of social problems, the relief of poverty amongst older people and the former employees of Sound Diffusion plc who lost their pensions when the company went into receivership and the furtherance of any other lawful charitable purpose'. Priority is given to charities based in Sussex, particularly in mid Sussex, being the former home of the founder. Preference will be given to projects where a donation by the Chownes Foundation may have some meaningful impact on an identified need rather than simply being absorbed into a larger funding requirement.

In 2007/08 the foundation had assets of £1.6 million and an income of £102,000. Grants totalled £114,000, of which £59,000 went to organisations and £55,000 to individuals.

Beneficiaries included: Worth Abbey (£7,000 in three grants); Amnesty International (£5,000 in two grants); St Anne's Convent (£4,000 in three grants); Fybromyalgia Support Group (£3,500); Burnside Amenity Fund (£3,000 in two grants); Burnside Social Club, Chestnut Tree House and Friends of the Samaritans (£2,000 in two grants each); 3H Fund, Association of Wheelchair Children and Streetmate (£2,000 each); Ace of Clubs, CamFed, FareShare Brighton and Hove, St Peter and St James Hospice and Trinity Hospice (£1,500 each); and Cancer Research UK, Mencap, NSPCC, St Paul's Church and Spinal Injuries Association (£1,000 in two grants each).

Applications In writing to the correspondent.

CLA Charitable Trust

People who are disabled or disadvantaged

£51,000 (2007/08)

Beneficial area England and Wales only.

Caunton Grange, Caunton, Newark NG23 6AB

Tel. 01636 636171

Website www.cla.org.uk

Correspondent Peter Geldart

Trustees *A Duckworth-Chad; A H Duberly; G E Lee-Strong; G N Mainwaring.*

CC Number 280264

Information available Accounts were on file at the Charity Commission.

The trust was founded in 1980 by CLA members. Its objects are threefold.

- To encourage education about the countryside for those who are disabled or disadvantaged, particularly youngsters from urban areas.
- To provide facilities for those with disabilities to have access to recreation in the countryside.
- To promote education in agriculture, horticulture and conservation for those who are disabled or disadvantaged.

It prefers to support smaller projects where a grant from the trust can make a 'real contribution to the success of the project'. It gives grants for specific projects or items rather than for ongoing running costs.

In 2007/08 it had assets of £288,000 and an income of £60,000. Grants totalled £51,000.

There were 24 grants of £1,000 or more listed in the accounts. Beneficiaries included: Harper Adams College (£3,000); Eden Rivers Trust (£2,500); Caring for Life (£2,100); Countryside Foundation, Hamelin Trust, Marrick Priory and NDFM (£2,000 each); Oxford Young Farmers and Royal School for the Deaf (£1,500 each); and Bridewell Organic Gardens (£1,100).

Other grants of less than £1,000 each totalled £5,600.

Exclusions No grants to individuals.

Applications In writing to the correspondent. Trustees meet four times a year.

J A Clark Charitable Trust

Health, education, peace, preservation of the earth and the arts

£348,000 (2006/07)

Beneficial area UK, with a preference for South West England.

PO Box 1704, Glastonbury, Somerset BA16 0YB

Correspondent Mrs P Grant, Secretary

Trustees *Tom Clark, Chair; Lance Clark; William Pym; Aidan Pelly.*

CC Number 1010520

Information available Full accounts were available from the Charity Commission.

In 2006/07 the trust had assets of £14 million and an income of £432,000. Grants to 26 organisations totalled £348,000.

Beneficiaries included: Eucalyptus Charitable Foundation (£64,000 in two grants); C&J Clark Property Fund (£35,000); Arts Education (£20,000); Conflicts Forum (£16,000); Pesticide Action, UK Theatre for a Change and UK Friends of Kwenco Kor (£15,000 each); Global Partnership (£14,000); Offscreen Education Programme (£12,000); Christian Aid and Open Bethlehem (£10,000 each); Adams Institute for Change, Camfed International and Watershed Arts Trust (£5,000 each); and Haiti Support Group (£1,200).

Applications This trust does not respond to unsolicited applications.

The Roger and Sarah Bancroft Clark Charitable Trust

Quaker and general

£2,500 (2007)

Beneficial area UK and overseas, with preference for Somerset and Scotland.

c/o KPMG LLP, 100 Temple Street, Bristol BS1 6AG

Correspondent The Trustees

Trustees *Mary P Lovell; Sarah C Gould; Roger S Goldby; Alice Clark; Robert B Robertson; Martin Lovell.*

CC Number 211513

Information available Full accounts were on file at the Charity Commission.

The objects of the trust are general charitable purposes with particular reference to:

- Religious Society of Friends and associated bodies
- charities connected with Somerset
- education (for individuals).

In 2007 it had assets of £1.2 million and an income of £49,000. Grants totalled £2,500 (£32,000 in 2006). The sole beneficiary was University of Edinburgh.

Previous beneficiaries have included Alfred Gillett Trust, Artlink Edinburgh, Bury St Edmunds Meeting House Appeal, Greenbank Swimming Pool, Holburne Museum of Art, Médecins Sans Frontières, Quaker Peace and Social Witness, Oxfam, Retreat York Ltd, Session's Book Trust, Society for the Protection of Ancient Buildings, Ulster Quaker Service Committee, Wilmington Friends School and Woodbrooke Quaker Study Centre.

Applications In writing to the correspondent. There is no application form and telephone calls are not accepted. Trustees meet about three times a year. Applications will be acknowledged if a stamped, addressed envelope is enclosed or an email address given.

The Cleopatra Trust

Mental health, cancer welfare/education, diabetes, physical disability, homelessness, addiction and children

£13,000 (2007/08)
Beneficial area Mainly UK.

c/o Charities Aid Foundation, King's Hill, West Malling ME19 4TA
Correspondent C H Peacock, Trustee
Trustees *Dr C Peacock; Mrs B Bond; C H Peacock.*
CC Number 1004551
Information available Accounts were on file at the Charity Commission.

The trust has common trustees with two other trusts, the Dorus Trust and the Epigoni Trust (see separate entries), with which it also shares the same aims and polices. All three trusts are administered by Charities Aid Foundation. Generally the trusts support different organisations each year.

The trust makes grants in the following areas:

- mental health
- cancer welfare/education – not research
- diabetes
- physical disability – not research
- homelessness

- addiction
- children who are disadvantaged.

There is also some preference for environmental causes. It only gives grants for specific projects and does not give grants for running costs or general appeals. Support is only given to national organisations, not for local areas or initiatives.

In 2007/08 it had assets of almost £3 million, which generated an income of £159,000. Grants were made totalling £13,000 (£117,000 in the previous year).

Beneficiaries included: Fairbridge (£11,000); All Star Youth Tennis Scholarship Trust and Finton House Educational Trust (£1,000 each); and Friends of Finton House Trust (£150).

Exclusions No grants to individuals, expeditions, research, scholarships, charities with a local focus, local branches of UK-wide charities or towards running costs.

Applications This trust no longer accepts applications.

Miss V L Clore's 1967 Charitable Trust

General, arts, social welfare, health and Jewish

£32,000 (2007/08)
Beneficial area UK.

Unit 3, Chelsea Manor Studios, Flood Street, London SW3 5SR
Tel. 020 7351 6061
Email info@cloreduffield.org.uk
Correspondent Sally Bacon
Trustees *Dame V L Duffield; David Harrel; Caroline Deletra.*
CC Number 253660
Information available Accounts were on file at the Charity Commission.

The trust has general charitable purposes, but broadly speaking is concerned with the performing arts, education, social welfare, health and disability. Grants usually range from £500 to £5,000. It is administrated alongside the much larger Clore Duffield Foundation, which gives well over 100 times more funds a year in grants.

In 2007/08 the trust had assets of £1.3 million, an income of £41,000 and made 16 grants totalling £32,000.

Beneficiaries included: Chelsea Physic Gardens, Family Friends and Maccabi GB (£5,000 each); North London Hospice (£4,000); West London Synagogue (£2,500); Friends of Castle of Mey, NSPCC, the Pearl Foundation and UF Elias Ashmole Trust (£1,000 each); and Institute for Polish-Jewish Studies and JTMM Mission (£500 each).

Exclusions No grants are given to individuals.

Applications In writing to the correspondent on one to two sides of A4, enclosing a stamped, addressed envelope.

The Clover Trust

Older people, young people, Catholic, health and disability

£197,000 (2007)
Beneficial area UK, and occasionally overseas, with a slight preference for West Dorset.

DTE Business Advisory Services Limited, Park House, 26 North End Road, London NW11 7PT
Correspondent G F D Wright
Trustees *N C Haydon; S Woodhouse.*
CC Number 213578
Information available Accounts were on file at the Charity Commission.

This trust supports organisations concerned with health, disability, young people, older people and Catholic activities. However, most grants are given to a 'core list' of beneficiaries and the trust states: 'the chances of a successful application from a new applicant are very slight, since the bulk of the income is earmarked for the regular beneficiaries, with the object of increasing the grants over time rather than adding to the number of beneficiaries.'

Grants are given towards general running costs. Unsolicited applications which impress the trustees are given one-off grants, although only a tiny percentage of the many applications are successful.

In 2007 the trust had assets of £4.7 million and an income of £240,000. Grants to 35 organisations totalled

£197,000. Grants ranged from £500 to £25,000, but were mainly for amounts of £5,000 or less. Beneficiaries of the largest grants were: Friends of Children in Romania (£25,000); and Action Medical Research, Cotswold Care, CAFOD and Cardinal Hume Centre (£10,000 each).

Other beneficiaries included: Childhood First and JOLT (£7,500 each); BIBIC, Demand, Dorset Association for the Disabled, Family Haven, Farms for City Children, Mary Hare Grammar School, Kidsactive and Sue Ryder Foundation (£5,000 each); CICRA, Disability Snowsport UK and Wireless for the Bedridden (£3,000 each); Essex Association of Boys' Clubs, MPS Society and National Eczema Society (£2,000 each); and English Catholic History Association (£500).

Exclusions The arts, monuments and non-registered charities are not supported. No grants are given towards building work.

Applications In writing to the correspondent. Replies are not given to unsuccessful applications.

The Robert Clutterbuck Charitable Trust

Service, sport and recreation, natural history and animal welfare and protection

£44,000 (2007/08)

Beneficial area UK, with preference for Cheshire and Hertfordshire.

28 Brookfields, Calver, Hope Valley S32 3XB

Tel. 01433 631308

Email secretary@clutterbucktrust.org.uk

Website www.clutterbucktrust.org.uk

Correspondent G A Wolfe, Secretary

Trustees *Maj. R G Clutterbuck; I A Pearson; R J Pincham.*

CC Number 1010559

Information available Accounts were on file at the Charity Commission.

The trust normally only makes grants to registered charities in the following areas:

- personnel within the armed forces and ex-servicemen and women
- sport and recreational facilities for young people benefiting Cheshire and Hertfordshire
- the welfare, protection and preservation of domestic animal life benefiting Cheshire and Hertfordshire
- natural history and wildlife
- other charities associated with the counties of Cheshire and Hertfordshire
- charities which have particular appeal to the founder, Major Robert Clutterbuck.

The trust prefers to make grants towards buying specific items rather than running costs. No grants are made below £500.

In 2007/08 the trust had assets of £1.2 million, an income of £43,000 and made 53 grants totalled £44,000.

Beneficiaries included: Music in Hospitals (£2,000); Nottinghamshire Wildlife Trust (£1,725); Queen Alexandra Hospital Home (£1,500); 11th Letchworth Scout Group, All Hallows Church – Cheadle, Culcheth Methodist Church, Filey Sea Cadets, Groundwork Cheshire, Hearing Dogs for Deaf People, Help for Heroes, Hertfordshire Gardens Trust, Northampton Air Cadets, Royal National Lifeboat, South Manchester Gymnastics, Whizz Kids and Youth with a Mission (£1,000 each); Buglife, Cricket Foundation, Independent Age, MENCAP Elstree and Rochdale Special Needs Cycling (£750 each); and Aspire Trust, Chester Sea Cadets, Hertfordshire Guide Centre, Marine Conservation Society, PDSA and Southern Uplands Partnership (£500 each).

Exclusions No grants to individuals.

Applications In writing to the correspondent. There are no application forms. Applications are acknowledged and considered by the trustees twice a year. The trustees will not normally consider appeals from charities within two years of a previous grant being approved.

The Francis Coales Charitable Foundation

Historical

£91,000 (2008)

Beneficial area UK, with a preference for Bedfordshire, Buckinghamshire, Hertfordshire and Northamptonshire.

The Bays, Hillcote, Bleadon Hill, Weston-super-Mare BS24 9JS

Tel. 01934 814009

Email enquiries@franciscoales.co.uk

Website franciscoales.co.uk

Correspondent Trevor Parker, Administrator

Trustees *H M Stuchfield, Chair; A G Harding; Revd B H Wilcox; I G Barnett.*

CC Number 270718

Information available Full accounts were on file at the Charity Commission.

The following information has been taken from the foundation's website:

In 1885 Francis Coales and his son, Walter John Coales, acquired a corn merchant's business in Newport Pagnell, Buckinghamshire. Over the years similar businesses were acquired, but after a major fire it was decided to close down the business. From the winding-up was established The Francis Coales Charitable Trust in 1975.

The objectives of the foundation are to provide grants for the structural repair of buildings (built before 1875) which are open to the public. Preference is given to churches in the counties of Bedfordshire, Buckinghamshire, Hertfordshire and Northamptonshire.

There is no territorial restriction in respect of the conservation of monuments and monumental brasses.

Grants are occasionally made towards publication of architectural and archaeological books and papers; towards the purchase of documents and items for record offices and museums; for archaeological research and related causes.

In 2008 it had assets of £2.3 million and an income of £759,000 including £649,000 from legacies. There were 35 grants made totalling £91,000.

Exclusions In respect of buildings, assistance is only given towards fabric repairs, but not to 'domestic' items such as heating, lighting, wiring, installation of facilities etc.

Applications An application form can be downloaded from the foundation's website. Trustees normally meet three times a year to consider grants.

In respect of a building or contents, include a copy of the relevant portion only of the architect's (or conservator's) specification showing the actual work proposed. Photographs illustrating this are a necessity, and only in exceptional circumstances will an application be considered without supporting photographs here.

It is of help if six copies of any supporting documentation are submitted in order that each trustee may have a copy in advance of the meeting.

The John Coates Charitable Trust

General, arts, children, environment and medical

£363,000 (2007/08)

Beneficial area UK, mainly southern England.

PO Box 529, Cambridge CB1 0BT

Correspondent Mrs R J Lawes, Trustee

Trustees *Mrs G F McGregor; Mrs C A Kesley; Mrs R J Lawes; Mrs P L Youngman; Mrs C P Cartledge.*

CC Number 262057

Information available Accounts were obtained from the Charity Commission website.

This trust has general charitable purposes. Grants are made to large UK-wide charities, or small charities of personal or local interest to the trustees.

In 2007/08 the trust had assets of £10.6 million, an income of £317,000 and made 74 grants totalling £363,000. About a third of organisations supported also received support in the previous year.

Beneficiaries of larger grants included: Action on Addiction, Age Concern, Changing Faces, CLAPA, Cutty Sark Trust, Exeter Cathedral, NSPCC, National Trust, Painshill Park Trust Limited, Royal Hospital for Neuro-Disability and Scope (£10,000 each);

Other beneficiaries included: the Landmark Trust (£8,000); Arthritis Care, the Cancer Resource Centre, Handel House Trust, Meningitis Research Foundation, Royal Marsden Hospital Charity and the Solent Protection Society (£5,000 each); Pimlico Opera and Tall Ships Youth Trust (£3,000 each); Whizz Kids (£2,500); InterAct Reading Service, National Literacy Trust and Two Moors Festival Limited (£2,000 each); Best Beginnings, Dreams Come True and Winchester and District Young Carers Project (£1,000 each); and Bury Church of England First School (£500).

Exclusions Grants are given to individuals only in exceptional circumstances.

Applications In writing to the correspondent. Small local charities are visited by the trust.

The Coats Foundation Trust

Textile and thread-related training courses and research

£74,000 to institutions (2007/08)

Beneficial area UK.

Coats plc, Pacific House, 70 Wellington Street, Glasgow G2 6UB

Correspondent The Secretary

Trustee *The Coats Trustee Company Limited.*

CC Number 268735

Information available Accounts were on file at the Charity Commission, without a list of grants.

Preference is given, but not specifically restricted, to applicants from textile and thread-related training courses.

In 2007/08 the foundation trust had assets of £1.8 million and an income of £84,000. Grants to institutions for educational purposes totalled £74,000. A further £66,000 was paid to individuals.

The following information was included in the trust's accounts regarding its grant making activity.

In total, 53 applicants were awarded grants ranging from £170 to £10,000 during the year and the trustee is actively seeking and approving more applications. During the

year, significant education payments totalling £20,000 were awarded to Copthall School. Copthall School will also benefit from future payments totalling a further £28,000 whilst Nottingham Trent University will benefit by £20,000 and Leeds University by £50,000.

Applications Please write, enclosing a CV and a stamped, addressed envelope, giving details of circumstances and the nature and amount of funding required. There is no formal application form. Only applicants enclosing a stamped, addressed envelope will receive a reply. Applications are considered four times a year.

The Cobalt Trust

General

£267,000 (2007/08)

Beneficial area UK and overseas.

17 New Row, London WC2N 4LA

Correspondent Stephen Dawson, Trustee

Trustees *Stephen Dawson; Brigitte Dawson; Jan Dawson.*

CC Number 1096342

Information available Accounts were on file at the Charity Commission.

This trust was set up in 2002 with general charitable purposes. The trustees do not respond to unsolicited applications.

The following is taken from the trust's 2007/08 report.

Criteria for grants are reviewed on a regular basis. The latest review has led to focussing a substantial proportion of the amounts donated on a small number of larger and regular donations. These are generally to organisations well known to the trustees or where the trustees have undertaken a thorough review before deciding to donate. The trustees have a preference in their strategic donations for smaller organisations where they feel their contribution will have a greater impact.

In 2007/08 the trust had assets of £1.5 million and an income of £90,000. Grants totalled £267,000.

Beneficiaries included: Impetus Trust (£200,000); Eating Disorders Association (£20,000); EVPA, Rosetrees Trust, Streats Limited and Tree Aid (£10,000 each); Banana Link, Bath Abbey, Care, Climate Group and Money for Madagascar (£1,000 each); Iford Arts (£350); and Avon Wildlife Trust and National Trust (£100 each).

The Vivienne and Samuel Cohen Charitable Trust

Jewish, education, health, medical, culture and general

£155,000 (2007/08)
Beneficial area UK and Israel.

9 Heathcroft, Hampstead Way, London NW11 7HH
Correspondent Dr Vivienne Cohen, Trustee
Trustees Dr V L L Cohen; M Y Ben-Gershon; J S Lauffer; Dr G L Lauffer; D G Cohen.
CC Number 255496
Information available Accounts were on file at the Charity Commission.

The majority of the trust's support is to Jewish organisations. In 2007/08 the trust had assets of £2.8 million and an income of £184,000. Grants totalled £155,000.

There were 237 grants made in the year which were broken down into the following categories:

Category	No.	Value
Medical care and welfare	86	£64,000
Care and welfare	22	£29,000
Cultural and recreation	75	£23,000
Education	22	£23,000
Religious activities and communal	32	£15,000

Beneficiaries included: Chai Cancer Care (£26,000 in two grants); University College London (£10,000); Ariel (£7,000); British Friends of Herzog Hospital (£5,000); SPNI Jerusalem (£4,700 in two grants); Yakar (£3,000); the Spiro Ark (£2,500 in two grants); Hamifal Education Children's Homes and University Jewish Chaplaincy Board (£2,000 each); Elimination of Leukaemia Fund, JNF Charitable Trust and Norwood Child Care (£1,000 each).

Exclusions No grants to individuals.

Applications In writing only, to the correspondent.

The Denise Cohen Charitable Trust

Health, welfare, arts, humanities, education, culture and Jewish

£98,000 (2007/08)
Beneficial area UK.

Berwin Leighton and Paisner, Adelaide House, London Bridge, London EC4R 9HA
Correspondent Martin Paisner, Trustee
Trustees Denise Cohen; Martin Paisner; Sara Cohen.
CC Number 276439
Information available Full accounts were on file at the Charity Commission.

In 2007/08 the trust had assets of £1 million and an income of £84,000. Grants were made to 87 charities totalling £98,000.

Grants of £1,000 or more were made to 35 organisations and included those to: Nightingale (£9,250); Chai Cancer Care (£8,000); Child Resettlement Fund and Community Security Trust (£5,000 each); British Technion Society and Jewish Women's Aid (£3,000 each); Central Synagogue (£2,750); Marie Curie Cancer Care (£2,000); Magen David Adom and Royal British Legion (£1,500 each); Almeida Theatre Company (£1,250); and Ben-Gurion University Foundation, British Friends of Herzog Hospital, British Friends of the Israeli War Disabled Trust, Donmar Warehouse Projects, Help for Heroes, Jewish Museum, Merlin Project, Royal Academy of Arts and Tate Gallery (£1,000 each);

Beneficiaries of smaller grants included: British Friends of Zaka (£750); Ataxia UK and Jewish Book Council (£500 each); Gateshead Yeshiva and Jewish Care (£400 each); Jewish Child's Day (£300); Youth Aliyah Child Rescue (£250); Salvation Army (£200); and Jewish Children's Holiday Fund (£100).

Applications In writing to the correspondent.

John Coldman Charitable Trust

General and Christian

£516,000 (2007/08)
Beneficial area UK, with a preference for Edenbridge in Kent.

Polebrook, Hever, Edenbridge TN8 7NJ
Tel. 01732 770660
Email charles.warner@warners-solicitors.co.uk
Correspondent C J Warner, Trustee
Trustees D J Coldman; G E Coldman; C J Warner.
CC Number 1050110
Information available Information was on file at the Charity Commission.

The trust gives grants to community and Christian groups in Edenbridge, Kent and UK organisations whose work benefits that community such as children's and medical charities and schools.

In 2007/08 the trust had assets of £362,000 and an income of £561,000, mainly from donations. Grants to 36 organisations totalled over £516,000.

Beneficiaries included: Oasis Community Learning (£290,000); Oasis International, India (£30,000); Institute of Cancer Research (£25,000); Hever Church of England Primary School (£23,000); NSPCC Special Investigation Unit and Prince's Trust (£20,000 each); Chiddingstone Church of England Primary School (£13,000); Great Ormond Street Hospital (£10,000); St Mary's Church Chiddingstone (£7,750); National Gardens Scheme – Kent (£6,900); Falkland Islands Memorial Chapel Appeal (£5,000); Africa Foundation (£4,000); the Avenues Trust and Headway – Tunbridge Wells and District (£2,500 each); Compaid Trust and Dig Deep (£1,000 each); Action Aid and National Autistic Society (£500 each); and Cancer Research UK (£250).

During the year an additional £39,000 went towards the running of the Holcot Residential Centre, which operates as a hostel, holiday centre and community centre for the use of young people and others.

Applications In writing to the correspondent.

The John and Freda Coleman Charitable Trust

Disadvantaged young people

£70,000 (2007/08)

Beneficial area Hampshire and Surrey and surrounding areas.

Alderney House, 58 Normandy Street, Alton GU34 1DE

Correspondent Paul Coleman, Chair

Trustees I Williamson; Mrs J L Bird; P H Coleman; B R Coleman.

CC Number 278223

Information available Accounts were on file at the Charity Commission.

The following information is taken from the trust's annual report and accounts.

The trust aims to provide an alternative to an essentially academic education, to encourage and further the aspirations of young people with talents to develop manual skills and relevant technical knowledge to fit them for satisfying careers and useful employment. The aim is to develop the self-confidence of individuals to succeed within established organisations or on their own account and to impress upon them the importance of service to the community, honesty, good manners and self discipline.

In 2007/08 the trust had assets of £906,000, an income of £37,000 and made 13 grants totalling £70,000.

The charitable donations this year have again been targeted at the core aims of the trust in helping young people to obtain the skills they need for both work and life. Principal donations are currently directed towards a number of organisations, in Surrey and Hampshire, focussed on providing practical training, skills and support where the normal education system has failed and young people are not reaching their full potential.

Beneficiaries included: Surrey SATRO (£11,000); Surrey Care Trust (£10,000); Surrey Community Development Trust (£8,000); Prince's Trust (£7,500); Guildford YMCA, Historic Royal Palaces and Treloar Trust (£5,000 each); Reigate and Redhill YMCA and Surrey Clubs for Young People (£3,000 each); Sayers Croft and Surrey Family Mediation Service (£2,500 each); and Surrey Council for Voluntary Youth Service (£2,000).

Exclusions No grants are made to students.

Applications In writing to the correspondent. Telephone calls are not welcome.

The E Alec Colman Charitable Fund Ltd

Religion, especially Jewish, children and social welfare

£44,000 (2007/08)

Beneficial area UK and worldwide.

Colman House, 6–10 South Street, Harborne, Birmingham B17 0DB

Tel. 0121 427 7700

Correspondent A N Carless, Secretary

Trustees S H Colman; Cecilia R Colman; M Harris; Susan R Stone.

CC Number 243817

Information available Accounts were on file at the Charity Commission.

In 2007/08 the trust had assets of £1 million and an income of £60,000. There were 58 grants made totalling £44,000, in the range of £150 and £5,000. Of the organisations supported, 21 also received grants in the previous year.

Beneficiaries included: World Jewish Relief (£5,000); Send a Cow (£2,500); Army Cadet Force Association, the Royal British Legion and RNIB (£2,000 each); Practical Action and St Dunstan's (£1,500 each); the Smile Train UK (£1,200); British Friends of Ohel Sarah, Institute for the Special Child, the Queen Alexandra Hospital Home, Rochdale Special Needs Cycling Club, the Salvation Army and Yad Vashem UK Foundation (£1,000 each); Brighton and Hove Parents and Children Group (£850); Operation New World and the Universal Beneficent Society (£750 each); 3H Fund, Amherst Heritage Centre, Deptford Action Group for the Elderly, Food Lifeline and the Tree Club (£500 each); At Risk Teenagers (£250); and 95th Birmingham Scout Group (£150).

Exclusions No grants to individuals.

Applications In writing to the correspondent; however, the trust has

stated that new beneficiaries are only considered in exceptional circumstances. The trust aims to pinpoint areas of interest and take the initiative in funding organisations working in these fields.

The Sir Jeremiah Colman Gift Trust

General

£109,000 (2007/08)

Beneficial area UK, with a preference for Hampshire, especially Basingstoke.

Malshanger, Basingstoke RG23 7EY

Correspondent Mrs V R Persson, Secretary to the Trustees

Trustees Sir Michael Colman; Lady Colman; Oliver Colman; Hon. Mrs Colman; Jeremiah Colman.

CC Number 229553

Information available Accounts were on file at the Charity Commission.

The trust makes grants for general charitable purposes with special regard to:

- advancement of education and literary scientific knowledge
- moral and social improvement of people
- maintenance of churches of the Church of England and gifts and offerings to the churches
- financial assistance to past and present employees/members of Sir Jeremiah Colman at Gatton Park, J and J Colman Ltd or other clubs and institutions associated with Sir Jeremiah Colman.

In 2007/08 the trust had assets of £4.3 million and an income of £134,000. Grants totalled £109,000 and were broken down as follows: 'annual' donations (£57,000); 'special' donations (£49,000); and 'extra' donations (£3,500).

Exclusions Grants are not made to individuals requiring support for personal education, or to individual families for welfare purposes.

Applications The trust has stated that funds are fully committed – unsolicited applications are therefore not welcomed.

Col-Reno Ltd

Jewish

£53,000 (2007/08)

Beneficial area UK and Israel.

15 Shirehall Gardens, London NW4 2QT

Correspondent The Trustees

Trustees M H Stern; A E Stern; K Davis; Mrs R Davis; C A Stern; Mrs L Goldstein.

CC Number 274896

Information available Accounts were on file at the Charity Commission.

The trust appears to support only Jewish organisations, with a preference for medical aid organisations and education.

In 2007/08 it had assets of £534,000 and an income of £91,000. Grants to 19 organisations totalled £53,000.

Beneficiaries included: Agudas Yisrael of California (£20,000); Hasmonean High School (£10,000); Society of Friends of the Torah (£8,000); Friends of Beis Yisrael Trust (£7,500); Jerusalem Library Fund (£1,900); Friends of Lubavitch Scotland (£1,000); Emuna (£750); Friends of Shabbaten Choir (£600); UK Friends of Meir Panim (£300); Chinuch Atzmai in Israel and Shaare Zedek UK (£200 each); and British Friends of Atid (£100).

Applications In writing to the correspondent.

The Coltstaple Trust

Medical, relief in need and education

£660,000 (2007/08)

Beneficial area Worldwide.

Pollen House, 10–12 Cork Street, London W1X 1PD

Correspondent Lord Oakshott of Seagrove Bay, Trustee

Trustees Lord Oakshott of Seagrove Bay; Dr P Oakshott; Lord Newby of Rothwell; B R M Stoneham; Mrs E G Colville.

CC Number 1085500

Information available Accounts were on file at the Charity Commission.

The trust was set up in 2001 with the following objects: 'the relief of persons in need, poverty or distress in developing countries and the relief of persons who are homeless or in housing need in the UK or any other part of the world'.

In 2007/08 the trust had assets of £5 million, an income of £234,000 and made grants totalling £660,000.

Category	Value
Medical and relief of poverty	£470,000
Educational	£190,000

The seven grants awarded went to: Oxfam (£400,000); St Mungo's (£150,000); Opportunity International (£40,000); North West University Whole School Development Programme, Portsmouth Housing Charity – E C Roberts Centre and Students Partnership (£20,000 each); and Sport for Life (£10,000).

Applications In writing to the correspondent.

Gordon Cook Foundation

Education and training

About £200,000

Beneficial area UK.

3 Chattan Place, Aberdeen AB10 6RB

Tel. 01224 571010 **Fax** 01224 571010

Email gordoncook@btconnect.com

Website www.gordoncook.org.uk

Correspondent Mrs Irene B Brown, Foundation Secretary

Trustees G Ross, Chair; D A Adams; Prof. B J McGettrick; Dr P Clarke; Dr W Gatherer; J Marshall; C P Skene.

SC Number SC017455

Information available Despite making a written request for the accounts of this foundation (including a stamped, addressed envelope) these were not provided. The following entry is based on information filed with the Office of the Scottish Charity Regulator.

This foundation was set up in 1974 and is dedicated to the advancement and promotion of all aspects of education and training which are likely to promote 'character development' and 'citizenship'. The following information is taken from the foundation's website.

In recent years, the foundation has adopted the term 'Values Education' to denote the wide range of activity it seeks to support. This includes:

- the promotion of good citizenship in its widest terms, including aspects of moral, ethical and aesthetic education, youth work, cooperation between home and school, and coordinating work in school with leisure time pursuits
- the promotion of health education as it relates to values education
- supporting relevant aspects of moral and religious education
- helping parents, teachers and others to enhance the personal development of pupils and young people
- supporting developments in the school curriculum subjects which relate to values education
- helping pupils and young people to develop commitment to the value of work, industry and enterprise generally
- disseminating the significant results of relevant research and development.

In 2008 the foundation had an income of £360,000. Previous research indicates that grants are made totalling around £200,000 each year. The foundation has previously stated that it supports projects, including 'consultations' organised by Institute of Global Ethics, Professional Ethics, Business Ethics, Enterprise Ethics and Values Education in the Four Home Nations. Grants usually range from around £1,000 to £30,000. Previous beneficiaries include Norham Foundation, Health Education Board for Scotland, Citizen Foundation, North Lanarkshire Council and Northern College.

Exclusions Individuals are unlikely to be funded.

Applications The trustees are proactive in looking for projects to support; however, unsolicited applications may be considered if they fall within the foundation's criteria and are in accordance with current programmes. Forms may be obtained from the correspondent.

The Cooks Charity

Catering and welfare

£224,000 (2007/08)

Beneficial area UK, especially City of London.

Coombe Ridge, Thursley Road, Churt, Farnham GU10 2LQ

Email clerk@cookslivery.org.uk

Correspondent Michael C Thatcher, Clerk and Solicitor

Trustees *H F Thornton; G A V Rees; B E G Puxley.*

CC Number 297913

Information available Accounts were on file at the Charity Commission.

The trust was established in 1989 to support educational and welfare projects concerned with people involved in catering, and any charitable purposes (with some sort of catering connection) in the City of London.

In 2007/08 it had assets of £4 million and an income of £372,000. Grants to 14 organisations totalled £224,000. Grants were broken down as follows and are shown here with examples of beneficiaries in each category:

Advancement of education (nine grants totalling £189,000)
Academy of Culinary Arts (£55,000); Food Education At Schools Today (£42,000); Hackney Community College (£30,000); Springboard (£25,000); Crisis Skylight Cafe (£12,000); Bournemouth University (£10,000); and Corpus Christi College (£3,400).

General Welfare (two grants totalling £10,000)
Broadway and Pembroke House (£5,000 each).

The City of London (three grants totalling £25,000)
Ironbridge Museum (£15,000); Treloar Trust (£5,000); and City University (£4,500).

Applications In writing to the correspondent. Applications are considered in spring and autumn.

The Catherine Cookson Charitable Trust

General

£292,000 (2007/08)

Beneficial area UK, with some preference for the north east of England.

Thomas Magnay and Co, 13 Regent Terrace, Gateshead, Tyne and Wear NE8 1LU

Tel. 0191 488 7459

Correspondent Peter Magnay, Trustee

Trustees *David S S Hawkins; Peter Magnay; Hugo F Marshall; Daniel E Sallows; Jack E Ravenscroft.*

CC Number 272895

Information available Accounts were available from the Charity Commission.

This trust was registered with the Charity Commission in February 1977.

In 2007/08 the trust had assets of £22 million and an income of just over £1.1 million, derived from investments and royalties from many of the literary works of Dame Catherine Cookson. Grants were made during the year totalling £292,000 and were broken down as follows:

Category	Value	No.
Medical, health and sickness	£103,000	16
Religious activities	£88,000	19
Education and training	£36,000	7
Disability	£16,000	11
Children and young people	£17,000	36
Arts and culture	£3,900	9
Animal welfare	£500	2
Other	£27,000	40

Beneficiaries of the largest grants included: St Paul's Church – Jarrow (£80,000); Kidney Research UK (£50,000); Royal Grammar School Newcastle (£35,000); Bubble Appeal (£30,000); and Heart Research UK and Riding for the Disabled Association (£10,000 each).

Other beneficiaries included: Berwick Upon Tweed Preservation Trust, Beadnell Parish Council, Leukaemia Research and Riding Mill Village Hall Trust (£5,000 each); Mining Museum – Cleveland and Royal Blind Society West Sussex (£2,000 each); Beadnell Village Playground, Help the Aged, Kings Church Darlington and Sunderland and North Durham Royal Society for the Blind (£1,000 each); Chernobyl Children Lifeline, Grove Hill Methodist Church – Middlesbrough, Hebburn Sea Scouts, National Missing Persons Helpline and Newcastle PROPS (£500 each); the Meningitis Trust (£400); Wildfowl and Wetlands Trust (£250); the Royal Regiment of Fusiliers (£200); and Albany Youth Project, All Saints Monkwearmouth, Children Community Safety Group, Hastings Writers' Group, the Royal British Legion and Spital Estate Community Association (£100 each).

Applications In writing to the correspondent.

Harold and Daphne Cooper Charitable Trust

Medical, health and Jewish

£138,000 (2007/08)

Beneficial area UK.

c/o Portrait Solicitors, 1 Chancery Lane, London WC2A 1LF

Correspondent T Miles

Trustees *Mrs S Roter; Miss Judith Portrait; T Roter; Miss A Roter; Ms M V Hockley.*

CC Number 206772

Information available Accounts were on file at the Charity Commission.

In 2007/08 it had assets of £1.7 million and an income of £158,000. Grants to 27 organisations were made totalling £138,000.

Beneficiaries included: Jewish Care (£75,000); Blond McIndoe Research Foundation (£5,000); Whizz Kidz (£3,000); Aidis Trust, Elimination of Leukaemia Fund and Macmillan Cancer Support (£2,000 each); Marie Curie Cancer Care (£1,500); and 3H Fund, Breast Cancer Campaign, Deafblind UK and the Shooting Star Children's Hospice (£1,000 each).

Exclusions No grants to individuals.

Applications In writing to the correspondent; applications are not acknowledged.

Mabel Cooper Charity

General

£19,000 (2007/08)

Beneficial area UK, with a possible interest in South Devon.

Lambury Cottage, East Portlemouth, Salcombe TQ8 8PU

Correspondent The Secretary

Trustees *A E M Harbottle; J Harbottle; I A Harbottle; D J Harbottle.*

CC Number 264621

Information available Accounts were obtained from the Charity Commission website.

In 2007/08 the charity had assets of just over £1.2 million and an income of £63,000. Grants were made totalling £19,000.

The sole beneficiary was East Portlemouth Village Hall.

Previous beneficiaries have included Christian Aid, Crisis, Devon Air Ambulance, East Portlemouth Village Hall, Farm Crisis Network, Macmillan Cancer Relief, National Children's Home, St Luke's Hospice, St Peter's Hospice and the Samaritans.

Exclusions No grants to individuals.

Applications The trust states that it does not welcome, or reply to, unsolicited applications.

The Marjorie Coote Animal Charity Trust

Wildlife and animal welfare
£174,000 (2007/08)
Beneficial area Worldwide.

Dykelands Farm, Whenby, York YO61 4SF

Email info@mcacharity.org.uk

Correspondent Mrs J P Holah, Trustees

Trustees *Sir Hugh Neill; Mrs J P Holah; Lady Neill; Mrs S E Browne.*

CC Number 208493

Information available Accounts were on file at the Charity Commission.

The trust was established in 1954 for the benefit of five named charities and any other charitable organisation which has as its main purpose the care and protection of horses, dogs or other animals or birds.

The trustees concentrate on research into animal health problems and on the protection of the species, whilst applying a small proportion of the income to general animal welfare, including sanctuaries.

In 2007/08 it had assets of £3.1 million and an income of £124,000. Grants paid totalled £174,000.

Ongoing support (£72,000 in 25 grants)
Grants were in the range of £500 and £10,000 and included those to: Animal Health Trust (£10,000); PDSA (£8,000);

Friends of Conservation (£7,000); WWF-UK (£6,000); the Whiteley Wildlife Conservation Trust (£4,000); Brooke Hospital for Animals, Sheffield Wildlife Trust and the Wildfowl and Wetlands Trust (£3,000 each); Mill House Sanctuary (£2,500); FRAME and Tusk Trust (£2,000 each); Devon Horse and Pony Sanctuary (£1,500); and the Barn Owl Trust, Greek Animal Welfare and SPANA (£1,000 each).

One-off grants (£102,000 in 5 grants)
By far the largest grant went to RSPCA Sheffield's Rebuild Project (£90,000). Other beneficiaries were: the Langford Trust for Animal Health and Welfare (£10,000); Save the Rhino International (£1,000); and Dog Lost and Yorkshire Swan Rescue (£500 each).

Exclusions No grants to individuals.

Applications In writing to the correspondent. Applications should reach the correspondent during September for consideration in October and November.

The Gershon Coren Charitable Foundation

Jewish, welfare and general
£131,000 (2007/08)
Beneficial area UK and the developing world.

3rd Floor, 7–10 Chandos Street, London W1G 9DQ

Correspondent The Trustees

Trustees *Muriel Coren; Anthony Coren; Walter Stanton.*

CC Number 257615

Information available Full accounts were on file at the Charity Commission.

The trust supports registered charities, particularly Jewish organisations.

In 2007/08 its assets totalled £2.5 million and it received an income of £114,000. Grants to 30 organisations totalled £131,000.

Beneficiaries included: Gategi Village Self Help Group (£40,000); Magen David Adom UK (£28,000); Aish UK and UJS Hillel (£6,000 each); Hadassah Medical Relief Association UK, Jewish Care and

Nightingale House (£5,000 each); B'nai B'rith UK and St Joseph's Hospice (£2,500 each); Smile Train (£1,100); Barnabas Fund, JAMI, Jewish Music Institute, One Voice and Zionist Federation (£1,000 each); and NSPCC, Spiro Ark and Whizz Kids (£500 each).

Applications In writing to the correspondent.

The Evan Cornish Foundation

General and overseas aid
£120,000 (2007/08)
Beneficial area UK and developing countries.

c/o Provincial House, Solly Street, Sheffield S1 4BA

Email contactus@ evancornishfoundation.org.uk

Correspondent The Trustees

Trustees *Ethel Cornish; Barbara Ward; Mary Cornish; Sally Cornish; Rachel Cornish.*

CC Number 1112703

Information available Accounts were on file at the Charity Commission.

The foundation was created by the widow and four daughters of businessman Evan Cornish who died in 2002. Support is given for 'charitable good causes'.

In 2007/08 the foundation had assets of £7.3 million and an income of £428,000. A total of 12 donations were made ranging from £5,000 to £15,000 totalling £120,000.

Beneficiaries were: Alzheimer's Society and Survival International (£15,000 each); Afghan Connection, Amnesty International UK, Field Studies Council, Jessie's Fund, Médecins Sans Frontières, Orbis UK, Tools for Self Reliance and the TreeHouse Trust – Parent Support Project (£10,000 each); and Asylum Seeker Support Initiative and Fydell House Centre (£5,000 each).

Applications The trustees will consider applications as well as seeking out causes to support. They normally meet at least four times a year.

The Duke of Cornwall's Benevolent Fund

General

£196,000 (2007/08)

Beneficial area UK, with a number of grants made in the Cornwall area.

10 Buckingham Gate, London SW1E 6LA

Tel. 020 7834 7346

Correspondent Robert Mitchell

Trustees *Hon. James Leigh-Pemberton; W R A Ross.*

CC Number 269183

Information available Accounts were on file at the Charity Commission.

The fund receives donations from the Duke of Cornwall (Prince Charles) based on amounts received by the Duke as Bona Vacantia (the casual profits of estates of deceased intestates dying domiciled in Cornwall without kin) after allowing for costs and ex-gratia payments made by the Duke in relation to claims on any estate.

The fund's objectives are the relief of people in need, provision of almshouses, homes of rest, hospitals and convalescent homes, advancement of education, advancement of religion, advancement of the arts and preservation for the benefit of the public of lands and buildings. Grants are made to registered charities only.

In 2007/08 the fund had assets of £2.8 million and an income of £139,000. Grants were made totalling £196,000.

Of the 142 grants made during the year, there were 21 grants of £1,000 or more listed in the accounts. Beneficiaries included: the Prince's Regenerations Trust (£105,000); the Prince's Foundation (£15,000); Bryher Community Association and Cornwall Buildings Preservation Trust (£5,000 each); Soil Association (£4,000); St Breward Parish Church Appeal (£2,500); Lifebuoy Charitable Trust (£2,000); and All Saints Church – Curry Mallet, Devon Country Agricultural Association, Launceston College, Menhemot Old School Trust, the Merchant Venturers, Royal Cornwall Agricultural Association and St Endellion Festival (£1,000 each).

Other donations of less than £1,000 each totalled £42,000. One grant of £500 was paid to an individual.

Applications In writing to the correspondent. Applicants should give as much detail as possible, especially information on how much money has been raised to date, what the target is and how it will be achieved. Applications can be made at any time. Trustees meet quarterly.

The Sidney and Elizabeth Corob Charitable Trust

General and Jewish

£216,000 (2007/08)

Beneficial area UK.

62 Grosvenor Street, London W1K 3JF

Correspondent The Trustees

Trustees *A L Corob; E Corob; C J Cook; J V Hajnal; S A Wechsler; S Wiseman.*

CC Number 266606

Information available Full accounts were on file at the Charity Commission.

The trust has general charitable purposes, supporting a range of causes including education, arts, welfare and Jewish charities.

In 2007/08 the trust had assets of £611,000 and an income of £34,000 (£168,000 in the previous year). There were 117 grants made totalling £216,000.

Beneficiaries of larger grants included: Oxford Centre for Hebrew and Jewish Studies (£47,000); Autism Speaks (£20,000); United Synagogue (£10,000); and British Technion Society, the HOPE Charity, Jewish Care and Magen David Adom UK, (£10,000 each).

Exclusions No grants to individuals or non-registered charities.

Applications In writing to the correspondent. The trustees meet at regular intervals.

The Corona Charitable Trust

Jewish

£42,000 (2007/08)

Beneficial area UK and overseas.

16 Mayfield Gardens, Hendon, London NW4 2QA

Correspondent A Levy, Trustee and Secretary

Trustees *A Levy; Mrs A Levy; B Levy.*

CC Number 1064320

Information available Accounts were on file at the Charity Commission.

In 2007/08 the trust had an income, mainly from donations of £43,000 and made grants totalling £42,000. Assets stood at £80,000 at the year end.

Beneficiaries included: Cosmos Belz Limited (£12,000); Hasmonean High School (£5,800); Friends of Tashbar Chazon Ish (£4,500); Raleigh Close Charitable Trust (£3,000); WST Charity Limited (£3,200); Ahavas Shalom Charity Fund (£800); Chana (£1,500); and Aish Hatorah, Emunah, the G M Trust, Gateshead Jewish Academy, Sasson Vesimcha Charitable Trust and Yeshivas Beis Hillel (£1,000 each).

Applications In writing to the correspondent.

The Costa Family Charitable Trust (formerly the Morgan Williams Charitable Trust)

Christian

£576,000 (2007/08)

Beneficial area UK.

50 Stratton Street, London W1J 8LL

Tel. 020 7352 6592

Correspondent K J Costa, Trustee

Trustees *K J Costa; Mrs A F Costa.*

CC Number 221604

Information available Full accounts were on file at the Charity Commission.

In 2007/08 the trust had assets of £101,000 and an income of £656,000 derived mostly from donations. Grants were made totalling £576,000, including £9,000 to individuals.

The largest grant of £500,000 went to Alpha International.

Other grants were: Great Ormond Street Hospital (£25,000); 24–7 Prayer (£10,000); The Message, Hope HIV and The Chasah Trust (£7,000 each); The Philo Trust (£5,000); Breakthrough Breast Cancer (£3,000); and St David's CTR (£1,000).

Applications The trust states that only charities personally connected with the trustees are supported and absolutely no applications are either solicited or acknowledged.

The Cotton Industry War Memorial Trust

Textiles

£131,000 (2008)

Beneficial area UK.

c/o 42 Boot Lane, Heaton, Bolton BL1 5SS

Correspondent The Trustees

Trustees *P Booth; C Trotter; Prof. A P Lockett; K Lloyd; K R Garbett; P Reid; D Babbs.*

CC Number 242721

Information available Accounts were on file at the Charity Commission.

This trust makes grants to educational bodies to assist eligible students in furtherance of their textile studies, to other bodies which encourage recruitment into or efficiency in the industry or organisations otherwise researching or benefiting the cotton industry. Major support has also been given to other causes, including those related to young people and people with disabilities.

In 2008 it had assets of £5.4 million and an income of £367,000. Grants totalled £131,000.

Beneficiaries included: Adventure Farm Trust (£35,000); Texprint – Contribution to Operating Costs of Exhibition (£30,000); Royal School for the Deaf and Communication Disorders (£20,000); Samuel Crompton Fellowship Award – Bursaries (£11,000); the Society of Dyers and Colourists (£10,000); Fusiliers Museum Bury (£9,800); the Jack Brown Scholarship Awards – Bursaries (£6,500); and Glasgow School of Art (£2,500).

Applications In writing to the correspondent.

The Cotton Trust

Relief of suffering, elimination and control of disease, people who have disabilities and disadvantaged people

£227,000 (2007/08)

Beneficial area UK and overseas.

PO Box 6895, Earl Shilton, Leicester LE9 8ZE

Tel. 01455 440917

Correspondent Mrs J B Congdon, Trustee

Trustees *J B Congdon; T E Cotton; E S Cotton; C B Cotton.*

CC Number 1094776

Information available Accounts were on file at the Charity Commission.

The trust's policy is the relief of suffering, the elimination and control of diseases and helping people of any age who are disabled or disadvantaged. Grants are primarily awarded for capital expenditure for specific projects or items of specialist equipment. A limited number of grants are awarded for running costs where the grant will provide direct support for a clearly identifiable charitable project.

The trust receives upwards of 600 applications each year. It awards about 80 to 100 grants to UK registered charities working both at home and overseas each year, ranging between £250 and £5,000. In exceptional cases the trust may award grants of between £10,000 and £15,000.

In 2007/08 the trust had assets of £5.7 million, an income of £198,000 and made grants totalling £227,000. A total

of 94 organisations were supported. Donations were broken down as follows.

- Specialist medical and therapeutic equipment, including mobility aids and medicines and emergency appeals (28 grants).
- Miscellaneous assistance and support costs for goods, services and materials (24 grants).
- Healthcare projects and HIV/Aids related charities, including health education, rehabilitation, training, safe water and sanitary provision, and assistance with means of transport (14 grants).
- Other equipment for specialist schools, supported accommodation/ education (13 grants).
- Counselling, therapy, advice and advocacy, support for help-lines and drop-in services and support for carers including respite breaks (11 grants).
- Holidays and activities for vulnerable, disabled and/or disadvantaged children and adults (8 grants).
- Support for hospices (2 grants).

Beneficiaries included: Leicester Charity Link towards support/equipment for families (£41,000); CamFed (£15,000); Merlin (£10,000); Africa Now (£5,000); Angels International (£4,000); John Fawcett Foundation, International Medical Corps and Leukaemia Research (£2,500 each); Harvest Help (£2,250); Edinburgh Young Carers Project and International Childcare Trust (£1,500 each); Shelter, St Giles Trust and Village Service Trust (£1,000 each); People for Animal Care Trust (£750); and Youth Action Wiltshire – young carers educational project (£580).

Exclusions Grants are only given to UK-registered charities that have been registered for at least one year. No grants to animal charities, individuals, students, further education, travel, expeditions, conservation, environment, arts, new building construction, the purchase of new buildings or 'circular' appeals. The trustees will only support the purchase of computer systems and equipment if it is to be directly used by people who are disadvantaged or have disabilities, but not general IT equipment for the running of organisations.

Applications In writing to the correspondent with latest accounts, evidence of charitable status, detailed budget, timetable and details of funds raised.

Guidelines are available with a stamped, addressed envelope. Deadlines for applications are the end of July and the end of January, with successful applicants being notified within three months of these dates. It is regretted that only successful applications can be answered. The trustees only accept one application in a 12 month period.

Country Houses Foundation

Preservation of buildings of historic or architectural significance

£231,000 (2007/08)
Beneficial area England.

The Manor, Sheephouse Farm, Uley Road, Dursley GL11 5AD

Tel. 0845 402 4102 **Fax** 0845 402 4103

Email david@countryhousesfoundation. org.uk

Website www.countryhousesfoundation. org.uk

Correspondent David Price, Company Secretary

Trustees Christopher Taylor, Chair; Oliver Pearcey; Nicholas Barber; Michael Clifton; Norman Hudson; Sir John Parsons.

CC Number 1111049

Information available Accounts are on file at the Charity Commission. Full guidelines are available on the foundation's website.

Registered with the Charity Commission in August 2005, the main aims of the foundation are to support the preservation of buildings of historic or architectural significance together with their gardens and grounds, for the public benefit. Beneficiaries can include registered charities, building preservation trusts and private owners.

In 2007/08 the foundation had assets of £14.4 million and an income of £1.4 million. Grants totalled £231,000.

The following information is taken from the foundation's accounts.

Since the launch of the grants scheme in February 2006, the number of applications for funding has increased significantly. At the end of the financial year [2007/08] the foundation was supporting 17 projects with grant offers in place totalling £1.6 million. In addition, 5 full applications were under consideration (total request £233,000) and a further 18 pre-applications had been received (£2.7 million).

Guidelines

These guidelines can be found on the foundation's website.

We aim to give grants for repairs and restoration work required to prevent loss or damage to historic buildings located in England, their gardens, grounds and any outbuildings. We would normally expect your building to be listed, scheduled, or in the case of a garden included in the English Heritage Register of Parks and Gardens. However, we may also make grants to projects which involve an unlisted building of sufficient historic or architectural significance or importance if it is within a conservation area.

In addition, to qualify for any grant you must be able to show the following.

- There is a compelling need for the work you want to undertake to be done within the next two to three years.
- The project will enhance our historic environment.
- There will be appropriate public access.
- The project will have a sustainable future.
- There is a financial need for the grant.
- The project can proceed within a reasonable time frame (one–two years).

We aim to make grants for projects which are ready to proceed (i.e. can be started within one–two years) but which either do not qualify for funding from any of the mainstream sources or have been awarded only partial funding and require significant further funds to complete the resource package.

We will also consider making grants to effectively 'kickstart' a project but will expect your other funding to be completed within one–two years.

Exclusions

As a general rule we do not offer grants for the following.

- Projects which do not have a heritage focus.
- Alterations and improvements.
- Routine maintenance and minor repairs.
- General running costs.
- Demolitions.
- Rent, loan or mortgage payments.
- Buying furniture, fittings and equipment except where they have an historic relationship with the site and are relevant to the project.
- Work carried out before a grant offer has been made in writing and accepted.

Applications

Pre-Application Forms can be completed online, or in a hard copy and returned by post. The foundation tries to respond to within 28 days of receipt. If a project fits the criteria then a unique reference number will be issued which must be quoted on the *Full Application Form*.

Applications can be made at anytime.

The Augustine Courtauld Trust

General

£64,000 (2007/08)
Beneficial area UK, with a preference for Essex.

Birkett Ballard, No. 1 Legg Street, Chelmsford, Essex CM1 1JS

Website www.augustinecourtauldtrust. org

Correspondent Bruce Ballard, Clerk

Trustees Revd. A C C Courtauld, Chair; The Lord Lieutenant of Essex; The Bishop of Chelmsford; Julien Courtauld; D E Fordham; Lt General Sir Anthony Denison-Smith; T J R Courtauld; W M Courtauld.

CC Number 226217

Information available Accounts were on file at the Charity Commission.

This trust was founded in 1956 by Augustine Courtauld, an Arctic explorer who was proud of his Essex roots. His charitable purpose was simple: 'my idea is to make available something that will do some good.' Among the main areas of work supported before his death in 1959 were young people, people with disabilities, the countryside, certain churches, Arctic exploration and the RNLI. The current guidelines are to support organisations that are:

- working within the historical boundaries of the county of Essex
- involved in expeditions to the Arctic and Antarctic regions
- known to one of the trustees.

Within Essex, the preference is to support disadvantaged young people, conservation projects and certain charities that the founder specifically wanted to help. Grants for projects and core costs and can be for multiple years, but only if the charity applies for a grant in consecutive years.

In 2007/08 the trust had assets of £1.2 million and an income of £56,000. The sum of £64,000 was given in 54 grants.

Beneficiaries included: Friends of Essex Churches (£7,000); Essex Association of Boys' Clubs (£4,500); the Cirdan Sailing Trust (£4,000); Rural Community Council of Essex (£2,400); Stubbers (£2,500); College of St Mark – Audley End and Prader-Willi Syndrome Association UK (£2,000 each); Depaul Trust, RNLI – Eastern Region and St Luke's Hospice – Basildon (£1,000 each); and Acorn Villages, Colchester Emergency Night Shelter, Michael Roberts Charitable Trust and the Victoria History of Essex Appeal Fund (£500 each).

The trust also supported five expeditions totalling £10,000.

Exclusions No grants to individuals. No grants to individual churches for fabric repairs or maintenance.

Applications Applications must be submitted via the online form on the trust's website. Written applications will not be accepted.

Coutts Charitable Trust

General and social need

£870,000 (2007/08)

Beneficial area UK. Preference is given to areas where Coutts and Co. has a physical presence, specifically London.

440 Strand, London WC2R 0QS

Tel. 020 7753 1000

Email carole.attwater@coutts.com

Correspondent Mrs C Attwater, Trust Administrator

Trustees *The Earl of Home, Peregrine Banbury, Mrs Sally Doyle, Gerald L Bailey; Mrs Wendy Butler*

CC Number 1000135

Information available Accounts were on file at the Charity Commission.

The trust was set up by the company Coutts and Co. which provides banking and allied services. It is funded by the bank under a deed of covenant equivalent to one half of 1 per cent of the bank's pre-tax profit with a minimum of £100,000.

In 2007/08 it had an income of £876,000 and made 1,124 grants totalling £870,000.

Grants are given to UK registered charities only and the trust prefers to support social need organisations in areas where the bank has a presence, mainly London.

Charities supported include those involved with helping the homeless, rehabilitation and teaching self-help (drugs; alcohol; young offenders), disabled (both physically and mentally) disadvantaged adults and children, youth organisations, older people, medical

research, heritage, education and the relief of poverty.

Most donations are in the range of between £500 and £1,000 'where a comparatively small amount can still make a great difference'. Many donations are between £1,000 and £2,000, with a portion of the charitable budget being used for larger donations.

Exclusions No response to circular appeals. No support for appeals from individuals or overseas projects.

Applications In writing to the Trust Administrator, at any time. Applications should include clear details of the purpose for which the grant is required. Grants are made regularly where amounts between £500 and £1,000 are deemed to be appropriate. The trustees meet quarterly to consider larger donations.

Cowley Charitable Foundation

Registered charities

£54,000 (2007/08)

Beneficial area Worldwide, with some preference for South Buckinghamshire and the Aylesbury area.

140 Trustee Co. Ltd, 36 Broadway, London SW1H 0BH

Correspondent The Secretary

Trustees *140 Trustee Co. Ltd; Mrs H M M Cullen.*

CC Number 270682

Information available Information was on file at the Charity Commission.

In 2007/08 the trust had assets of £866,000 and an income of £49,000. Grants to 35 organisations totalled £54,000.

Beneficiaries included: Thinking Foundation (£11,000); International Dark Sky Association – USA (£9,000); Chase – Christopher's Children's Hospice and War Memorials Trust (£5,000 each); Against Malaria Foundation, Alzheimer's Society, Médecins Sans Frontières, Royal Marsden Cancer Campaign and Wordsworth Trust (£1,500 each); Age Concern Buckinghamshire, Army Benevolent Fund, Coram Family, Live

Music Now! and John Soames Museum (£1,000 each); Pere Jean Zambe (£800); Association for International Cancer Research, Camphill Village Trust, Shelter, Trinity Hospice, Venice in Peril Fund and YMCA (£500 each); and Artists General Benevolent Fund (£200).

Exclusions No grants to non-registered charities. No grants to individuals, or for causes supposed to be serviced by public funds or with a scope considered to be too narrow.

Applications The trust states that unsolicited applications are not invited, and that the trustees carry out their own research into charities.

The Sir William Coxen Trust Fund

Orthopaedic hospitals or other hospitals or charities doing orthopaedic work

£79,000 (2007/08)

Beneficial area England.

The Town Clerk's Office, City of London, PO Box 270, Guildhall, London EC2P 2EJ

Correspondent The Trustees

Trustee *Six Aldermen appointed by the Court of Aldermen, together with the Lord Mayor.*

CC Number 206936

Information available Information was provided by the trust.

This trust was established following a bequest from the late Sir William Coxen in 1940. Expenditure is mainly applied for the support of orthopaedic hospitals or other hospitals or charities doing orthopaedic work.

In 2007/08 the trust had assets of £1.8 million and an income of £71,000. Grants were made to 19 organisations totalling £79,000.

Beneficiaries included: Action for Kids, Brainwave, Motability, Neuromuscular Centre, SCAT and Torch (£5,000 each); Bobath Centre, DEMAND, the Foundation for Conductive Education and Strongbones (£4,000 each); MERU and Pace Centre (£3,000 each); St Luke's

Hospital (£2,900); and Daisy Chain Children's Trust (£2,100).

Exclusions No grants to individuals or non-charitable institutions.

Applications In writing to the correspondent.

The Lord Cozens-Hardy Trust

Medical, health, education and general

£78,000 (2007/08)

Beneficial area UK with preference for Merseyside and Norfolk.

PO Box 28, Holt NR25 7WH

Correspondent The Trustees

Trustees *Hon. Beryl Cozens-Hardy; J E V Phelps; Mrs L F Phelps; J J P Ripman.*

CC Number 264237

Information available Full accounts were on file at the Charity Commission.

The annual report states that: 'The trustees' policy is to assist as many UK registered charities as possible but with particular interest in supporting medical and education causes in Norfolk and Merseyside.'

In 2007/08 the trust had assets of £2.7 million and an income of £144,000. Grants totalled £78,000 and were broken down as follows:

Category	Value
Medical	£54,000
Community	£16,000
Children, young people and education	£3,500
Other	£4,000

Beneficiaries included: Norfolk and Norwich Association for the Blind (£20,000); East Anglian Air Ambulance, North West Air Ambulance and YESU (£5,000 each); Raleigh International Trust (£1,250); and Breast Cancer Campaign, Liverpool School of Tropical Medicine, Norfolk and Norwich Association for the Blind, Princes Trust, Hospital of St John, Salvation Army and World Association of Girl Guides and Girl Scouts (£1,000).

Exclusions No grants to individuals.

Applications In writing to the correspondent. Applications are reviewed quarterly.

The Craignish Trust

Arts, education, environment and general

Around £100,000 each year

Beneficial area UK, with a preference for Scotland.

c/o Geoghegan and Co, 6 St Colme Street, Edinburgh EH3 6AD

Correspondent The Trustees

Trustees *Ms M Matheson; J Roberts; Ms C Younger.*

SC Number SC016882

Information available Despite making a written request for the accounts of this trust (including a stamped, addressed envelope) these were not provided. The following entry is based on information filed with the Office of the Scottish Charity Regulator.

This trust was established in 1961 by the late Sir William McEwan Younger; its funding criteria is summarised as follows:

- no grants to large national charities
- there is a Scottish bias, but not exclusively
- arts, particularly where innovative and/or involved in the community
- education
- environment
- organisations/projects of particular interest to a trustee.

In 2007/08 the trust had an income of £171,000.

Previous beneficiaries have included Art in Healthcare, Boilerhouse Theatre Company Ltd, Butterfly Conservation – Scotland, Cairndow Arts Promotions, Centre for Alternative Technology, Edinburgh International Book Festival, Edinburgh Royal Choral Union, Friends of the Earth Scotland, Human Rights Watch Charitable Trust and Soil Association Scotland.

Exclusions Running costs are not normally supported.

Applications There is no formal application form; applicants should write to the correspondent. Details of the project should be included together with a copy of the most recent audited accounts.

The Craps Charitable Trust

Jewish and general

£177,000 (2007/08)

Beneficial area UK, Israel.

3rd Floor, Bryanston Court, Selden Hill, Hemel Hempstead HP2 4TN

Correspondent The Trustees

Trustees *J P M Dent; Miss C S Dent; Miss L R Dent.*

CC Number 271492

Information available Accounts were on file at the Charity Commission.

This trust supports mostly Jewish charities, although medical and other organisations are also supported. There is a list of eight charities mentioned in the trust deed, although not all of these are supported every year and other groups in the UK and overseas can be supported.

In 2007/08 it had assets of £3.6 million, which generated an income of £259,000. Grants totalled £177,000.

There were 29 grants were made in the year, the largest of which went to: British Technion Society (£25,000); Jewish Care (£20,000); British WIZO and Nightingale House (£16,000 each); Friends of the Hebrew University (£14,000); JNF Charitable Trust (£13,000); the New Israel Fund (£12,000); and Jerusalem Foundation (£11,000).

Other beneficiaries included: CBF World Jewish Relief (£5,000); British Friends of Haifa University, Ben-Gurion University Foundation and Norwood Ravenswood (£4,000 each); Motor Neurone Disease Association (£2,000); Community Security Trust and London Jewish Cultural Centre (£1,500); and Amnesty International, B'nai B'rith Hillel Foundation, National Theatre and Shelter (£1,000 each).

Applications The trust states that 'funds of the trust are fully committed and the trust does not invite applications for its funds'.

The Crescent Trust

Museums, the arts, ecology and health

£109,000 (2007/08)
Beneficial area UK.

9 Queripel House, 1 Duke of York Square, London SW3 4LY
Correspondent Ms C Akehurst
Trustees J C S Tham; R A F Lascelles.
CC Number 327644
Information available Information had been file at the Charity Commission.

The trust concentrates on arts (especially larger museums), heritage and ecology. Smaller grants are mainly given in the medical field. Only specific charities of which the trustees have personal knowledge are supported.

In 2007/08 the trust had an income of £43,000, including £36,000 from donations. Assets stood at £333,000. Grants to 14 organisations totalled £109,000 (£65,000 in the previous year).

Beneficiaries included: the Fitzwilliam Museum (£45,000); National Gallery of Scotland (£40,000); the Louvre Museum (£10,000); the Attingham Trust and the Watts Gallery (£5,000 each); Museum of Garden History (£1,500); Broadway Central Office and Over the Wall (£1,000 each); Chase Hospice Care for Children, Chelsea Pensioners and Save the Children (£250 each); and AIDS Ark (£100).

Applications This trust states that it does not respond to unsolicited applications.

Criffel Charitable Trust

Christianity, welfare and health

£164,000 (2007/08)
Beneficial area UK and overseas.

Hillfield, 4 Wentworth Road, Sutton Coldfield B74 2SG
Correspondent Mr and Mrs J C Lees, Trustees
Trustees J C Lees; Mrs J E Lees; Mrs J I Harvey.

CC Number 1040680
Information available Accounts were on file at the Charity Commission.

The objectives of the trust are the advancement of Christianity and the relief of poverty, sickness and other needs. In 2007/08 it had assets of £1.4 million and an income of £74,000. Grants totalled £164,000 and were broken down as follows:

Category	Value
Relief of sickness	£74,000
Advancement of Christianity	£55,000
Relief in need	£22,000
Donations	£10,000
Miscellaneous	£3,900

Beneficiaries of the largest grants, over £2,000 each, were: St Giles Hospice (£61,000); Four Oaks Methodist Church (£28,000); Tear Fund (£11,000); and the Monkton Campaign (£10,000).

Applications All funds are fully committed. The trust states that no applications are considered or acknowledged. Please do not apply.

The Violet and Milo Cripps Charitable Trust

Prison and human rights

£272,000 (2007/08)
Beneficial area UK.

52 Bedford Row, London WC1R 4LR
Correspondent The Trustees
Trustees Anthony J R Newhouse; Richard J Lithenthal; Jennifer Beattie.
CC Number 289404
Information available Accounts were on file at the Charity Commission.

The trust supports large prison and human rights organisations. In 2007/08 it had assets of £1.4 million and an income of £458,000. Grants to seven organisations totalled £272,000.

Beneficiaries were: Prison Reform Trust (£115,000); European Educational Research Trust (£50,000); Corpus Christi College (£35,000); the Prison Advice and Care Trust (£25,000); the New Bridge and Trinity Hospice (£20,000 each); and St Bernadette's Church (£6,500).

Applications The trust states that unsolicited applications will not receive a response.

The Ronald Cruickshanks' Foundation

Welfare, education and general

£123,000 (2007/08)
Beneficial area UK, with some preference for Folkestone, Faversham and the surrounding area.

34 Cheriton Gardens, Folkestone CT20 2AX
Correspondent I F Cloke, Trustee
Trustees I F Cloke, Chair; J S Schilder; Mrs S E Cloke.
CC Number 296075
Information available Accounts were obtained from the Charity Commission website.

The settlor of this trust died in 1995 leaving his shareholding in Howe Properties Ltd to the foundation, under the terms of his will. The trust's objects are to provide general charitable and educational assistance as the trustees deem suitable with the knowledge of the wishes given to them by the settlor in his lifetime. The assistance is to include those in poverty and need in Folkestone and Faversham and surrounding areas.

In 2007/08 the foundation had assets of £1.8 million and an income of £223,000. There were 125 grants made, totalling £123,000. Donations ranged from £250 to £7,000.

Beneficiaries of larger grants included: Demelza House Children's Hospice and the Pilgrims Hospice – Canterbury (£7,000 each); Kent Air Ambulance (£3,500); Folkestone Town Mayor's Christmas Fund (£3,000); Jesuit Missions (£2,500); Canterbury Cathedral Appeal and Operation Sunshine (£2,000 each); Age Concern – Folkestone (£1,500); and Arthritis Research Campaign, British Red Cross, the Dystonia Society, Hope UK, Lupus UK, Morehall Primary School and St Joseph's – Cheriton (£1,000 each).

Other beneficiaries included: St Nicholas Church – Newington (£750); Action for Kids, Bus Shelter Project, Hospice in the Weald, Kent Autistic Trust, the Meningitis Trust and PDSA (£500 each); and Home-Start Shepway and Samaritans (£250 each).

Applications In writing to the correspondent. Applications should be received by the end of September for consideration on a date coinciding closely with the anniversary of the death of the founder, which was 7 December.

Cuby Charitable Trust

Jewish

£267,000 (2007/08)

Beneficial area UK, overseas.

16 Mowbray Road, Edgware HA8 8JQ

Correspondent C B Cuby, Secretary

Trustees *S S Cuby, Chair; Mrs C B Cuby.*

CC Number 328585

Information available Accounts are on file at the Charity Commission, but without a list of grants.

The main objectives of this charitable trust are 'providing charitable assistance in any part of the world and in particular for the advancement of Orthodox Jewish religious education'.

In 2007/08 the trust had assets of £234,000 and income of £311,000, mainly from donations. Grants totalled £267,000. No list of grants was provided with the accounts to indicate the size or number of beneficiaries during the year.

Applications In writing to the correspondent.

The Culra Charitable Trust

General

£27,000 (2007/08)

Beneficial area UK.

1 College Hill, London EC4R 2RA

Correspondent Stephen Tuck

Trustees *C Byam-Cook; P J Sienesi; G Needham; G Francis.*

CC Number 274612

Information available Full accounts were on file at the Charity Commission.

This trust has general charitable purposes, giving grants to a wide variety of active charitable organisations throughout the UK.

In 2007/08 the trust had an income of £29,000 and made grants totalling £27,000. Assets stood at £589,000.

During the year there were 37 grants awarded between £250 and £500 to local and UK charities, in addition the following two organisations received larger awards: Royal Air Force Benevolent Fund (£6,000); and Birchfield Educational Trust Ltd (£3,000).

Exclusions Grants are not given to non-registered charities or individuals.

Applications The trust tends to support organisations known to the trustees, rather than responding to unsolicited applications. The trustees meet twice a year.

The Cumber Family Charitable Trust

General

£56,000 (2007/08)

Beneficial area Worldwide, with a preference for the developing world and Berkshire and Oxfordshire.

Manor Farm, Marcham, Abingdon OX13 6NZ

Tel. 01865 391327

Correspondent Mrs M E Tearney, Trustee

Trustees *A R Davey; W Cumber; Mrs M J Cumber; Mrs M J Freeman; Mrs M E Tearney; Mrs J E Mearns.*

CC Number 291009

Information available Accounts were on file at the Charity Commission.

This trust has a preference for UK-wide needs, developing countries and local organisations in Oxfordshire and Berkshire. It favours the following causes: health, homelessness, disability, welfare, rural development, housing, overseas aid, Christian aid, agricultural development, young people and children's welfare and education. About 50% of the funding given is for work overseas.

In 2007/08 the trust had assets of £827,000, an income of £51,000 and a total of £56,000 was given in 64 grants. About 25% of grants were made to organisations not previously supported by the trust.

Beneficiaries included: RABI (£5,000); Vale and Ridgeway Trust (£3,000); Alzheimer's Research Trust and Maggie's Cancer Caring Centres (£2,000 each);

Build Africa, Door of Hope, Hand in Hand, Harvest Help, Home Start Southern Oxfordshire, Konnect 9 Worldwide, Maforga Christian Mission, the Respite Association and Tools for Self Reliance (£1,000 each); Sunningwell School of Art (£600); Independence at Home, Microloan Foundation, Oxfordshire Playbus and Slough Furniture Project (£500 each); and the Titus Trust (£250).

Exclusions No grants for animal welfare. Only very few to individuals with local connections and who are personally known to the trustees are supported. Local appeals outside Berkshire and Oxfordshire are not usually supported.

Applications In writing to the correspondent. The trustees usually meet twice a year.

The Dennis Curry Charitable Trust

Conservation and general

£84,000 (2007/08)

Beneficial area UK.

Alliotts, 5th Floor, 9 Kingsway, London WC2B 6XF

Correspondent N J Armstrong, Secretary to the Trust

Trustees *M Curry; Mrs A S Curry; Mrs M Curry-Jones; Mrs P Edmond.*

CC Number 263952

Information available Accounts were on file at the Charity Commission.

The trust has general charitable objects with special interest in the environment and education; occasional support is given to churches and cathedrals.

In 2007/08 it had assets of £3 million and an income of £94,000. Grants were made to 11 organisations totalling £84,000.

Beneficiaries included: Natural History Museum (£27,000); Durrell Wildlife Conservation Trust (£12,000); Galapagos Conservation Trust and University of Oxford – Wildlife Conservation Research Unit (£10,000 each); the Council for National Parks, New Hall and Royal Naval Museum (£5,000 each); British Trust for Ornithology (£2,000);

University of Glasgow Trinidad Expedition (£1,500); and Médecins Sans Frontières (£1,000).

Applications In writing to the correspondent.

The Manny Cussins Foundation

Older people, children, health, Jewish and general

£129,000 (2007/08)

Beneficial area Mainly UK, with some emphasis on Yorkshire.

c/o Ford Campbell Freedman, 34 Park Cross Street, Leeds, LS1 2QH

Correspondent Arnold Reuben, Trustee

Trustees *A Reuben; A Cussins; A J Cussins; J R Cussins; Mrs A Reuben.*

CC Number 219661

Information available Accounts were on file at the Charity Commission, without a list of grants.

The trust's objects are to support:

- the welfare and care of older people
- the welfare and care of children at risk
- health care in the Yorkshire region and abroad
- charities in Yorkshire and the former county of Humberside
- charitable need amongst Jewish communities in the UK and abroad
- general charitable purposes.

In 2007/08 the trust had assets of £837,000 and an income of £124,000. Grants totalled £129,000, which included a donation of £100,000 to Donisthorpe Hall.

Previous beneficiaries have included Angels International, Christie Hospital – Children Against Cancer, Forgiveness Project, Hadassah Lodge, Leeds International Piano Competition, Leeds Jewish Education Authority, Leeds Jewish Welfare Board, Lifeline for the Old Jerusalem, Martin House Hospice, United Jewish Israel Appeal, Wheatfields Hospice and Women's International Zionist Organisation.

Exclusions No grants to individuals.

Applications The correspondent states that applications are not sought as the trustees carry out their own research.

The Daily Prayer Union Charitable Trust Ltd

Evangelical Christian

£56,000 to organisations (2007/08)

Beneficial area UK.

12 Weymouth Street, London W1W 5BY

Correspondent Mrs C Palmer, Secretary

Trustees *Revd G C Grinham; Mrs F M Ashton; Mrs E D Bridger; Revd D J Jackman; Revd T J Sterry; Mrs A V Tompson.*

CC Number 284857

Information available Accounts were on file at the Charity Commission.

The trust supports evangelical Christian causes. Grants range from £1,000 to £7,000.

In 2007/08 the trust had assets of £226,000 and an income of £60,000. Grants totalled £99,000; of which £56,000 went to organisations and £43,000 to 12 individuals.

Beneficiaries included: Monkton Combe School (£14,000); UCCF (£6,700); Jerusalem Trust (£2,800); Anglican Mainstream, CARE, Careforce, Claypath Trust and Martyr's Memorial Trust (£2,000 each); London City Missions and Titus Trust (£1,400); Crosslinks, This Way Up and Wycliffe Bible Group (£1,200 each); and Adventure Plus, All Souls Clubhouse, IFES, Torbay Hospital and UCCF (£1,000 each).

Exclusions No grants for building projects.

Applications The trust supports causes already known to the trustees. Unsolicited applications are unlikely to be successful. Trustees meet at different times throughout the year, usually around March, June and October.

Oizer Dalim Trust

Jewish

£243,000 (2007/08)

Beneficial area UK and overseas.

68 Osbaldeston Road, London N16 7DR

Correspondent M Cik, Trustee

Trustees *B Berger; M Freund; M Cik.*

CC Number 1045296

Information available Accounts were on file at the Charity Commission, but without a list of grants.

The trustees' accounts state that 'the trust was established to help alleviate poverty amongst members of the Orthodox Jewish faith both in the UK and overseas. It assists also in the furtherance of Orthodox Jewish education throughout the world.'

In 2007/08 the trust had an income of £195,000 mostly from donations. Assets stood at £6,400. Grants were made for 'poverty alleviation' totalling £243,000. A list of grant beneficiaries was not available.

Applications In writing to the correspondent.

Davidson Charitable Trust

Jewish and general

£927,000 (2007/08)

Beneficial area UK.

58 Queen Anne Street, London W1G 8HW

Correspondent Eve Winer, Trustee

Trustees *G A Davidson; Maxine Y Davidson; Eve Winer.*

CC Number 262937

Information available Accounts were on file at the Charity Commission.

In 2007/08 this trust had assets of £207,000 and an income, mainly from donations, of £1.1 million. After very low administration costs of just £235, grants totalled £927,000.

Grants were awarded as follows:

Category	Value
Religious organisations	£695,000
Welfare	£80,000
International aid	£41,000
Medical	£40,000
The arts	£39,000
Education	£33,000

Beneficiaries included: Hampstead Synagogue Building Fund (£625,000); Holburne Museum (£24,000); Emunah (£20,000); Friends of Ohel Torah (£16,000); Royal Opera House (£10,000); Lubavitch UK, Maccabi GB, Magen David Adorn UK and Shaare Zedek UK

(£5,000 each); the Fairly House School (£4,000); and the Ashmolean Museum and Sarah Charitable Trust (£1,000).

Applications In writing to the correspondent.

Michael Davies Charitable Settlement

General

£94,000 to organisations (2007/08)

Beneficial area UK.

Lee Associates, 5 Southampton Place, London WC1A 2DA

Correspondent K Hawkins, Administrator

Trustees *M J P Davies; K A Hawkins.*

CC Number 1000574

Information available Full accounts were available from the Charity Commission.

In 2007/08 the settlement had assets of £555,000 and an income of £31,000. Grants were made to 14 organisations totalling £94,000.

Beneficiaries included: BTYC Sailsports Club (£15,000); Camden Arts Centre, Camp and Trek, Marie Curie Cancer Care, North London Hospice, School Aid India and Tools for Training Overseas (£10,000 each); Médecins du Monde and the Study Gallery (£5,000 each); Architects For Aid (£3,500); Thames Wharf Charity (£2,000); the Langford Trust for Animal Health and Welfare (£1,000); and the Architectural Association Inc. (£750).

Applications In writing to the correspondent.

The Wilfrid Bruce Davis Charitable Trust

Health

£60,000 (2007/08)

Beneficial area UK, but mainly Cornwall; India.

La Feock Grange, Feock, Truro TR3 6RG

Correspondent W B Davis, Trustee

Trustees *W B Davis; Mrs D F Davis; Mrs D S Dickens; Mrs C A S Peirce.*

CC Number 265421

Information available Accounts were on file at the Charity Commission.

The trust was set up in 1967, the objects being 'such charities as the settlor in his lifetime and the trustees after his death shall determine'. The trust presently concentrates on 'improving the quality of life for those who are physically disadvantaged and their carers'. The geographical area covered is almost exclusively Cornwall, however the main thrust of the trust's activities is now focused on India.

The trust is fully committed to its current beneficiaries.

In 2008/09 the trust had assets of £198,000 and an income of £31,000. Grants totalled £60,000.

Beneficiaries included: Pallium India (£35,000); Pain and Palliative Care Society Calicut (£15,000); Guwahati Pain Clinic (£5,000); Helford River Children's Sailing Trust and Jubilee Sailing Trust (£1,000 each); Cornwall Community Foundation (£525); Chernobyl Children's Holidays, Cornwall Blind Association and United Church of Zambia (£250 each); and NSPCC (£200).

Exclusions No applications from individuals are considered.

Applications No replies are made to unsolicited applications. The correspondent has stated that the budget is fully committed for many years to come and that the trust receives hundreds of applications, none of which can be supported.

The Helen and Geoffrey De Freitas Charitable Trust

Preservation of wildlife and rural England, conservation and environment and cultural heritage

£34,000 (2007/08)

Beneficial area UK.

Speechly Bircham LLP, 6 New Street Square, London EC4A 3LX

Correspondent Richard Kirby, Trustee

Trustees *R C Kirby; Frances de Freitas; Roger de Freitas.*

CC Number 258597

Information available Accounts were available from the Charity Commission.

The following information is taken from the annual reports.

The main object of the trust is to benefit UK charitable organisations and voluntary umbrella bodies which seek to:

- conserve countryside and environment in rural Britain
- preserve Britain's cultural heritage
- assist the underprivileged through community facilities and services, advice centres and community arts and recreation.

Once a year the trustees may respond to a national or international humanitarian crisis which may be outside the terms of reference of the trust.

Grants are usually one-off for feasibility studies, project and ocasionally for start-up costs and range from £500 to £5,000 each.

In 2007/08 the trust had assets of £659,000, an income of £25,000 and made grants totalling £34,000.

Beneficiaries included: Staffordshire Wildlife Trust and GINA (£5,000 each); Tarka Country Trust (£3,000); Dartington Hall Trust (£2,800); the Grasslands Trust, Marine Conservation Society, Nailsea Tithe Barn Trust and Suffolk Building Preservation Trust (£2,500 each); Devon Wildlife Trust (£1,500); St Michael and All Angels – London Fields (£1,500); and Community Can Cycle (£500).

Exclusions No grants to non-registered charities, individuals, or to charities on behalf of individuals. Definitely no support for charities concerned with medical or health matters, or with physical, mental or sensory impairments.

Applications In writing to the correspondent at the following address:

PO Box 18667
London
NW3 5WB

Trustees meet quarterly.

The De Laszlo Foundation

The arts and general

£366,000 (2007/08)
Beneficial area UK and worldwide.

5 Albany Courtyard, London W1J 0HF
Correspondent Christabel Wood
Trustees *Damon de Laszlo, Chair; Lucy Birkbeck; Robert de Laszlo; William de Laszlo.*
CC Number 327383
Information available Accounts were on file at the Charity Commission.

Registered with the Charity Commission in March 1987, the foundation has the following objects:

1) The advancement and promotion of education and interest in the visual arts with special reference to encouraging knowledge of the works of contemporary painters, in particular those of the late Philip de Laszlo.
2) To encourage research into the restoration of works of art and their preservation and the location of suitable venues for them.
3) To acquire and maintain a collection of the works of art of the late Philip de Laszlo and of appropriate works of art of the same or any other period.
4) To advance education and research generally in the areas of arts, science, economics and medicine.
5) To encourage the study reproduction and cataloguing of works of art and the publication of books and literature in connection therewith.
6) To promote the founding of scholarships and prizes related to the above.

It has increasingly been the policy of the trustees to make a small number of targeted large grants.

In 2007/08 it had assets of £2.3 million and an income of £774,000, including £453,000 from donations. Grants totalled £366,000.

Grants were broken down as follows and are shown here with examples of beneficiaries in each category:

Arts – 20 grants totalling £51,000
Gordonstoun School Arts Centre (£20,000); City and Guilds of London Art School (£6,500); Federation of British Artists (£3,000); Royal Academy of Arts (£2,250); National Youth Orchestra (£1,500); National Theatre (£1,250); Tate Foundation (£1,000); Cardboard Citizens (£500); and Chelsea Arts Club Trust (£450).

Medicine – 5 grants totalling £28,000
Royal Marsden (£10,000); Foundation for Liver Research (£8,000); and Southampton University (£5,000).

Education – 3 grants totalling £16,000
Durham University (£10,000); Treloar Trust (£5,500); and Chelsea Open Air Nursery School (£250).

Scholarships and grants – 7 grants totalling £16,000
European Foundation (£5,000); AGORA (£2,500); Purcell School (£1,900); and Chelsea Arts Club and Worldwide Volunteering (£1,000 each).

A further £188,000 was donated to the De Laszlo Archive Trust.

Applications The foundation informs us at the moment that funds are fully committed to existing long-term projects.

The Leopold De Rothschild Charitable Trust

Arts, Jewish and general

£475,000 (2007/08)
Beneficial area UK.

Rothschild Trust Corporation Ltd, New Court, St Swithin's Lane, London EC4P 4DU
Correspondent The Clerk
Trustee *Rothschild Trust Corporation Ltd.*
CC Number 212611

Information available Accounts were available at the Charity Commission.

The trust gives most of its support to the arts and has some preference for Jewish organisations, with limited support to other causes covering heritage, welfare, medical and children.

In 2007/08 the trust had assets of £1.4 million and an income of £71,000. Grants totalled £475,000, including £416,000 made from capital.

Beneficiaries included: Exbury Gardens Limited (£400,000); Countess of Munster Musical Trust and Solti Foundation (£10,000 each); Royal National Theatre and Trinity College Cambridge (£5,000 each); Jewish Music Institute and Royal College of Music (£2,000 each); Aldeburgh Foundation, Black Watch Heritage Appeal, English Chamber Orchestra and Music Society and London Philharmonic Orchestra (£1,000 each); Holly Lodge Centre, Interact (£500); Willow Trust (£250); and Friends of Holland Park and Streetwise Opera (£100 each).

Applications In writing to the correspondent.

William Dean Countryside and Educational Trust

Education in natural history, ecology and conservation

£48,000 (2007)
Beneficial area Principally Cheshire; also Derbyshire, Lancashire, Staffordshire and Wirral.

St Mary's Cottage, School Lane, Astbury, Congleton, Cheshire CW12 4RG
Tel. 01260 290194
Email bellstmarys@hotmail.com
Correspondent Mrs Brenda Bell
Trustees *David Daniel, Chair; William Crawford; John Ward; David Crawford; Margaret Williamson.*
CC Number 1044567
Information available Accounts were on file at the Charity Commission.

This trust gives grants towards enterprises in its immediate locality which promote education in natural history, ecology and the conservation of the natural environment.

In 2007 it had assets of £1.2 million, an income of £81,000 and made grants totalling £48,000.

There were 15 organisations in receipt of amounts of £1,000 or more, including: Cheshire Wildlife Trust (£16,000 in three grants); One Earth Festival (£2,000 in two grants); Bickerton Holy Trinity, Brereton C of E Primary and Friends of Westminster Park (£1,500 each); and Garden Organic, the Woodland Trust and St Stephens Church (£1,000 each).

Other beneficiaries included: Rossendale Trust (£750); Shropshire Barn Owls (£600 in two grants); Chester Cathedral Garden, Derbyshire Dry Stone Walling Association, St Mary's Primary School, Somerford Kindergarten, Staffordshire Wildlife Trust and Wild Flower and Wetlands Lancashire (£500 each); Believe to Achieve and Young People's Trust (£300 each); Congleton Cricket Club (£250); Butterfly Conservation (£200); and Astbury Parish Council and St Luke's Hospice (£100 each).

Exclusions The trust stated that education is not funded, unless directly associated with one of the eligible categories.

Applications In writing to the correspondent.

The Dellal Foundation

General and Jewish

£119,000 (2007/08)
Beneficial area UK.

25 Harley Street, London W1G 9BR
Correspondent The Administrator
Trustees J Dellal; E Azouz; J Azouz; G Dellal.
CC Number 265506
Information available Accounts were on file at the Charity Commission.

The trust states that it continues to give 'a significant proportion of the grants towards charities whose aim is the welfare and benefit of Jewish people'.

In 2007/08 the trust had assets of £604,000 and an income of £30,000. A total of £119,000 was given in grants.

Exclusions No grants to individuals.

Applications In writing to the correspondent.

The Delves Charitable Trust

Environment, conservation, medical and general

£170,000 (2007/08)
Beneficial area UK.

Luminary Finance LLP, PO Box 135, Longfield DA3 8WF
Correspondent The Trust Administrator
Trustees Elizabeth Breeze; John Breeze; George Breeze; Charles Breeze; Edward Breeze; Mark Breeze; Catharine Mackey.
CC Number 231860
Information available Accounts were available at the Charity Commission.

This trust has a list of organisations that receive an annual subscription from the trust, and also provides a small number of grants to other organisations.

In 2007/08 the trust had assets of £6.3 million, which generated an income of £279,000. Grants to 47 organisations totalled £170,000. These were broken down into 30 'subscriptions' (£147,000) and 17 'donations' (£23,000).

Beneficiaries of 'subscriptions' included: British Heart Foundation (£25,000); Action Medical Research and WaterAid (£10,000); Sequal Trust (£8,000); Macmillan Cancer Support (£6,500); Médecins Sans Frontières (£6,000); Liverpool School of Tropical Medicine (£5,500); Quaker Peace and Social Witness and Save the Children (£5,000 each); St Giles Hospice (£3,500); Motivation (£3,000); Tree Aid (£2,500); the Peace Museum and Sussex Wildlife Trust (£1,500 each); and Council for Music in Hospitals (£1,000).

Those in receipt of smaller 'donations' included: Centrepoint and International Childcare Trust (£3,000 each); Big Issue Foundation (£2,500); Charterhouse-in-Southwark and Samaritans (£1,000 each); Friends of London Transport Museum (£700); Bone Cancer Research Trust (£500); Action Aid (£300); and Sightsavers International and Liberty Foundation (£250 each).

Exclusions The trust does not give sponsorships or personal educational grants.

Applications 'The funds of the trust are currently fully committed and no unsolicited requests can therefore be considered by the trustees.'

The Demigryphon Trust

Medical, education, children and general

£57,000 (2007/08)
Beneficial area UK, with a preference for Scotland.

Pollen House, 10–12 Cork Street, London W1S 3LW
Correspondent The Secretary
Trustee The Cowdray Trust Ltd.
CC Number 275821
Information available Accounts were on file at the Charity Commission.

The trust supports a wide range of organisations and appears to have a preference for education, medical, children and Scottish organisations.

In 2007/08 the trust had assets of £2.6 million and an income of £82,000. Grants were made to 14 organisations totalling £57,000.

There was one major beneficiary during the year, the Third Viscount Cowdray's Charity Trust, which received £43,000 (£24,000 in the previous year).

Other beneficiaries included: the A-Z Trust and the Game Conservancy Trust (£5,000 each); Teenage Cancer Trust (£1,000); the Rainbow Trust Children's Charity, Royal Northern Countryside Initiative, Royal Scottish Agricultural Benevolent Institution and WCRF UK (£500 each); Breakthrough Breast cancer (£250); Children with Leukaemia (£200); and Cancer Research UK (£50).

A further 31 payments were made to pensioners.

Exclusions No grants to individuals; only registered charities are supported.

Applications In writing to the correspondent, including a stamped, addressed envelope. No application forms or guidelines are issued and there is no deadline. Only successful applications are acknowledged.

The Duke of Devonshire's Charitable Trust

General

£102,000 (2007/08)

Beneficial area UK, with a preference for Derbyshire.

Chatsworth, Bakewell DE45 1PP

Correspondent The Trustees

Trustees *Duke of Devonshire; Duchess of Devonshire; Earl of Burlington; Sir Richard Beckett.*

CC Number 213519

Information available Accounts were on file at the Charity Commission.

In 2007/08 the trust had assets of £10.4 million, an income of £290,000 and made grants totalling £102,000.

Grants are made to registered charities involved in a wide variety of charitable activities, with a preference to those working in Derbyshire.

During 2007/08 donations ranged in value from £100 to £8,000. There were 35 grants of £1,000 or more listed in the accounts.

Grants of £5,000 or more went to: Treasures Nursery (£8,000); Bolton Abbey PCC and Royal Agricultural Benevolent Fund (£7,000 each); and Atlantic Salmon Fishing Trust, Contact the Elderly, Hearing Dogs for Deaf People, Treetops Hospice, Weston Park Hospital Cancer Appeal and Wilsthorpe Business and Enterprise College (£5,000 each).

Other beneficiaries included: Edale Mountain Rescue Team and Pathways of Chesterfield (£4,000 each); Pilsley Church of England Trust Account (£2,500); Chesterfield and District Shopmobility (£2,000); and Army Benevolent Fund, Ashgate Hospice, Matlock Hospitals League of Friends and St John's Ambulance Derbyshire (£1,000 each).

Grants of less than £1,000 each totalled £8,900.

Exclusions Grants are only given to registered charities and not to individuals.

Applications In writing to the correspondent.

The Sandy Dewhirst Charitable Trust

General

£32,000 to organisations (2007)

Beneficial area UK, with a strong preference for East and North Yorkshire.

Addleshaw Goddard, 100 Barbirolli Square, Manchester M2 3AB

Correspondent The Secretary

Trustees *T C Dewhirst; P J Howell; J A R Dewhirst.*

CC Number 279161

Information available Accounts were on file at the Charity Commission.

The trust was established in 1979, firstly for the welfare of people connected through employment with I J Dewhirst Holdings Ltd or the settlor of the trust and secondly for general charitable purposes, with a strong preference for East and North Yorkshire.

In 2007 the trust had assets of £1.9 million and an income of £71,000. Grants totalled £38,000 with £6,000 of this distributed in two grants to individuals.

Local/regional charities
Committee of Huby and Weeton Pre-School (£2,000); Driffield Agricultural Society, Driffield Town Cricket and Recreation Club and York Minster Fund (£1,000); and All Saints Church Nafferton, All Saints Church – Kilham, Driffield Children's Outing Fund, Driffield Rotary Club, Filey Sea Cadets, Hull Sea Cadets Corps and St Catherine's Hospice (£500 each).

National
Samaritans (£10,000); St Mary's Church – Rievaulx (£5,000); Shrewsbury Drapers Co. (£2,000); Army Benevolent Fund and Salvation Army (£1,500 each); Action Medical Research and Friends of Chernobyl (£1,000 each); and Cancer Research (£250).

Applications The trust does not accept unsolicited applications.

DG Charitable Settlement

General

About £15,000 (2007/08)

Beneficial area UK.

PO Box 62, Heathfield TN21 8ZE

Correspondent Joanna Nelson

Trustees *D J Gilmour; P Grafton-Green; Ms P A Samson.*

CC Number 1040778

Information available Accounts are on file at the Charity Commission.

This trust makes regular donations to a fixed list of charities. In 2007/08 the trust had an income of £17,000 down from £336,000 in the previous year.

Previous beneficiaries have included Age Concern, Amnesty International, Battersea Home for Dogs, Crisis, Cancer Research UK, Environmental Investigation Agency Charitable Trust, Great Ormond Street Hospital, Greenpeace, IPPF Europe, Terrence Higgins Trust, Medical Foundation for Victims of Torture, Oxfam, Prisoners Abroad, Prisoners of Conscience Appeal Fund, Scope, St Richard's Hospital Charitable Trust and Shelter.

Applications This trust does not consider unsolicited applications.

The Laduma Dhamecha Charitable Trust

General

£68,000 (2007/08)

Beneficial area UK and overseas.

2 Hathaway Close, Stanmore HA7 3NR

Correspondent Pradip Dhamecha, Trustee

Trustees *K R Dhamecha; S R Dhamecha; P K Dhamecha.*

CC Number 328678

Information available Accounts were on file at the Charity Commission, without a list of grants.

The trust supports a wide range of organisations in the UK and overseas. The aims of the trust are listed in the annual report as being:

- to provide relief of sickness by the provision of medical equipment and the establishing or improvement of facilities at hospitals
- to provide educational establishments in rural areas to make children self-sufficient in the long term
- other general charitable purposes.

In 2007/08 the trust had assets of £1.7 million and an income of £279,000, including £202,000 from donations. Grants totalled £68,000. No information was available on the size or number of beneficiaries during this year.

Applications In writing to the correspondent.

Alan and Sheila Diamond Charitable Trust

Jewish and general

£57,000 (2007/08)
Beneficial area UK.

Regency House, 3 Grosvenor Square, Southampton S015 2BE
Correspondent The Trustees
Trustees A Diamond, Chair; Mrs S Diamond; J R Kropman; Ms K Goldberg.
CC Number 274312

Information available Accounts were available at the Charity Commission.

About two-thirds of the trust's grant-making is to Jewish organisations. The trust supports the same organisations each year which are listed in its trust deed, and cannot consider other applications.

In 2007/08 the trust had assets of £1.5 million and an income of £69,000. There were 59 grants made totalling £57,000.

Beneficiaries included: Norwood (£7,000); British WIZO (£5,300); Anglo Israel Association, British School of Osteopathy and Community Security Trust (£4,000 each); Sidney Sussex College and UJIA (£3,000 each); Youth Aliyah Child Rescue (£2,500); and Magen David Adorn (£2,100); British Friends of Bar-Ilan University and Holocaust Educational Trust (£1,000 each); British Technion Society (£600); British ORT and St Mary's Hospital (£500 each); Jewish Care (£250); and Demelza Hospice Care for Children,

Jewish Marriage Council, Kisharon, Weiner Library Endowment Trust and ZSV Trust (£100 each).

Exclusions No grants to individuals.

Applications The trust states that it will not consider unsolicited applications. No preliminary telephone calls. There are no regular trustees' meetings. The trustees frequently decide how the funds should be allocated. The trustees have their own guidelines, which are not published.

The Dickon Trust

General

£38,000 (2007/08)
Beneficial area North-east England and Scotland.

Dickinson Dees, St Anne's Wharf, 112 Quayside, Newcastle NE99 1SB
Tel. 0191 279 9698
Website www.dickontrust.org.uk
Correspondent Helen Tavroges
Trustees Mrs D L Barrett; Major-General R V Brims; R Y Barrett; M L Robson; A Copeman.
CC Number 327202

Information available Accounts were on file at the Charity Commission.

The trust has general charitable purposes giving grants to local groups in north-east England (from the Tees in the south to Cumbria in the west) and Scotland. The trustees in particular favour charities that are beneficial to young people.

In 2007/08 the trust had assets of £1.4 million and an income of £57,000. Grants to 37 organisations totalled £38,000.

All grants but five were for £1,000 each. Beneficiaries included: Burns Group Unit Support, Edinburgh Young Carers Project and MS Research Fund Newcastle University (£2,000 each); Alexandra Rose Day, British Red Cross – Northumbria Branch, Calvert Trust, Changing Faces, the Children's Charity, Headway, Mitford Church, National Talking Newspapers, Northumberland Association of Clubs for Young People, React, Spinal Injuries Association, the Yard and Whizz Kidz (£1,000 each); and Lothian Autistic Society Tyneside Challenge (£500 each).

Exclusions No support for individuals, unregistered charities or churches.

Applications Applications can be made online at the trust's website. The trustees meet twice a year in summer and winter to consider appeals. Any applications received by the end of October will be considered at the winter meeting and any applications made after that time, up to the end of May, will be considered at the summer meeting.

The Dinwoodie Settlement

Postgraduate medical education and research

£161,000 (2007/08)
Beneficial area UK.

c/o Thomas Eggar, The Corn Exchange, Baffins Lane, Chichester PO19 1GE
Correspondent The Clerk to the Trustees
Trustees William A Fairbairn; Dr John M Fowler; Miss Christian Webster; Rodney B N Fisher; John A Gibson.
CC Number 255495

Information available Accounts were on file at the Charity Commission.

The annual report states that 'the trustees endeavour to be proactive in pursuing the objectives of the charity by supporting eligible projects in the field of postgraduate medical education and research in England.'

The maximum grant towards a Postgraduate Medical Centres (PMCs) project in any one area is normally £1 million. Medical research is for no more than the salary of two research workers in any one year. The trust's funds can be committed for three years when supporting major projects.

In 2007/08 the trust had assets of £4.7 million and an income of £483,000. Grants to two organisations totalled £161,000. Beneficiaries were: Wolverhampton Medical Institute (£85,000); and Imperial College London (£76,000).

Exclusions Anything falling outside the main areas of work referred to above. The trustees do not expect to fund consumable or equipment costs or relieve the NHS of its financial responsibilities.

Applications The trustees state they are proactive rather than reactive in their grantgiving. Negotiating for new PMCs and monitoring their construction invariably takes a number of years.

Disability Aid Fund (The Roger and Jean Jefcoate Trust)

Disability

£141,000 to organisations
(2007/08)
Beneficial area UK.

2 Swanbourne Road, Mursley, Milton Keynes MK17 0JA

Correspondent Roger Jefcoate, Trustee

Trustees *Vivien Dinning, Chair; Roger Jefcoate; Valerie Henchoz; Rosemary McCloskey; Carol Wemyss.*

CC Number 1096211

Information available Accounts were on file at the Charity Commission.

The following is taken from the trust's report.

The trust was founded by Roger Jefcoate CBE in 1983 and reconstituted under a new trust deed in October 2002.

The trust supports disability, healthcare and medical organisations, also disabled individuals seeking special needs technology.

In partnership with other national, regional and local grantmakers we provide a wide range of technology like adapted computers and communication aids for people with physical, mental or multiple disabilities or hearing or visual impairment. People with poorly understood conditions are especially welcome to apply; examples include fibromyalgia, chronic fatigue syndrome or ME (myalgic encephalomyelitis), multiple chemical sensitivity, upper limb disorder or RSI (repetitive strain injury), dyslexia, post traumatic stress disorder, mental illness and similar, often hidden, disabilities which lack the compassion factor.

We also help people with progressive neurological conditions like muscular dystrophy, multiple sclerosis, Parkinson's disease, Friedreich's ataxia or motor neurone disease where there is often a total loss of speech. Providing an adapted portable computer or communication aid at this crucial time, when remaining lifespan is

limited, can be truly vital. We co-operate closely with local voluntary agencies and statutory services, usually arranging a personal visit by a specialist technology assessor who works with the disabled person and their family and local education and healthcare professionals to select and cost the most suitable equipment.

We also support well run local and regional and small national healthcare charities for adults which enjoy strong support from volunteers and service users, especially charities based in Buckinghamshire or Milton Keynes or adjacent counties.

In 2007/08 it had assets of £2.5 million, an income of £229,000 and made grants totalling £188,000 of which £141,000 went to 23 organisations and £47,000 to in 45 grants to individuals.

Beneficiaries included: Cancer and Bio-detection Dogs – Aylesbury, Canine Partners, ME Research UK – Perth and West Cumbria Society for the Blind (£10,000 each); British Sjogren's Association – Birmingham (£7,000); Cancer and Bio-detection Dogs – Aylesbury (£6,000); PACE – Aylesbury, SHARE Community – Wandsworth, Therapy Centre – Bedford and Woodrow High House – Amersham (£5,000 each); DIAL Northamptonshire – Daventry (£4,000); Multiple Sclerosis National Therapy Centres (£3,500); and MS Therapy Centre – Hereford (£1,000).

Applications In writing to the correspondent.

Dischma Charitable Trust

General, with a preference for education, arts and culture, conservation and human and animal welfare

£135,000 (2007)
Beneficial area Worldwide, with a strong preference for London and the south east of England.

Rathbone Trust Company Ltd, c/o 159 New Bond Street, London W15 2UD
Tel. 020 7399 0820
Email linda.cousins@rathbones.com
Correspondent Linda Cousins, The Secretary

Trustees *Simon Robertson; Edward Robertson; Lorna Robertson Timmis; Virginia Robertson; Selina Robertson; Arabella Brooke.*

CC Number 1077501

Information available Accounts were available at the Charity Commission.

Registered with the Charity Commission in September 1999, this trust has recently reviewed their grant-giving policy and have decided to support principally, but not exclusively, projects concerned with education, arts and culture, conservation and human and animal welfare.

In 2007 the trust had assets of £5.2 million and income of £83,000. Grants were made totalling £135,000 and were broken down as follows:

Category	Value
Wildlife and conservation	£27,000
General medical, mental health and disabilities	£22,000
Welfare of children and young people	£27,000
General	£20,000
Education	£21,000
Welfare of older people	£10,000
Sports-based charities	£9,000

Grants included those made to: the British Association for Adopting and Fostering, Treloar Trust, Trinity Hospice and World Wildlife Fund (£5,000 each); Happy Days Children's Charity and SANE (£3,500 each); Epic Arts and Acid Survivors Trust International (£3,000 each); International Animal Rescue (£2,500); and UK Sports Association (£2,000).

Exclusions The trust does not support charities who carry out medical research.

Applications The trustees meet half-yearly to review applications for funding. Only successful applicants are notified of the trustees' decision. Certain charities are supported annually, although no commitment is given.

The DLA Piper Rudnick Gray Cary Charitable Trust (previously known as the DLA Charitable Trust)

General

£132,000 (2008)

Beneficial area UK.

3rd Floor, Fountain Precinct, Balm Green, Sheffield S1 2JA

Tel. 0114 267 5594

Email godfrey.smallman@wrigleys.co.uk

Correspondent G J Smallman, Secretary

Trustees *N G Knowles; P Rooney.*

CC Number 327280

Information available Accounts were on file at the Charity Commission.

In 2008 this trust had assets of £236,000 and an income of £132,000, all of which was given in 96 grants.

Beneficiaries included: the Cutty Sark Trust (£10,000); Solicitors' Benevolent Association (£8,500); Christie's Hospital, Green Belt Movement International and the Prince's Trust (£5,000 each); and Yorkshire Air Ambulance and South Yorkshire Community Foundation Flood Disaster Relief Fund. A one-off donation of £51,000 was awarded to the University of Michigan Law School to fund the employment of a new professorial chair.

Other donations of less than £1,000 each totalled £17,000.

Exclusions No grants to individuals.

Applications In writing to the correspondent, for consideration every three months.

The DLM Charitable Trust

General

£106,000 (2007/08)

Beneficial area UK, especially the Oxford area.

Cloke and Co., Warnford Court, Throgmorton Street, London EC2N 2AT

Tel. 020 7638 8992

Correspondent J A Cloke, Trustee

Trustees *Dr E A de la Mare; Mrs P Sawyer; J A Cloke; Miss J E Sawyer.*

CC Number 328520

Information available Accounts were available from the Charity Commission.

The trust was established in 1990, after R D A de la Mare left 25 per cent of the residue of his estate for charitable purposes. It supports charities that were supported by the settler and local Oxford organisations 'where normal fundraising methods may not be successful'.

In 2007/08 the trust had assets of £4.9 million and an income of £150,000. Grants were given to 24 organisations totalling £106,000.

Beneficiaries included: the Ley Community (£20,000); Wildlife Research Conservation Unit and Pathway Workshop (£10,000 each); Prostate Cancer Charity and Bayworth Baptist Charity (£5,000 each); Oxford Youth Works (£2,500); Harvest Trust Holidays for Children and Christians Against Poverty (£2,000 each); and Oxfordshire Mind and Guide Dogs for the Blind (£1,000) each.

Exclusions No grants to individuals.

Applications In writing to the correspondent. Trustees meet in February, July and November to consider applications.

The Dorcas Trust

Christian, relief of poverty and advancement of education

£33,500 (2008/09)

Beneficial area UK.

Port of Liverpool Building, Pier Head, Liverpool L3 1NW

Tel. 0151 236 6666

Correspondent I Taylor

Trustees *J C L Broad; J D Broad; P L Butler.*

CC Number 275494

Information available Accounts were on file at the Charity Commission.

The trust has a preference for Christian causes, although other charities have also been supported. The trustees will also consider making loans to organisations and individuals.

In 2008/09 the trust had assets of £1.1 million and an income of £47,000. Grants were made totalling £33,500 (£39,500 in 2007/08). No further information regarding grant beneficiaries was available.

Previous beneficiaries have included: Dorcas Developments Limited (£103,000); Navigators (£15,000); Newmarket Day Centre (£14,000); World Vision (£5,000); Mildmay Mission (£3,000); Integra (£2,000); Shaftesbury Society and Moorlands Bible College (£1,000 each); Send a Cow (£500); Chernobyl Children's Lifeline (£100); and RNIB (£50).

Applications In writing to the correspondent, although the trust stated that applications cannot be considered as funds are already committed.

The Dorema Charitable Trust

Medicine, health, welfare, education and religion

£28,000 (2008)
Beneficial area UK.

4 Church Grove, Amersham HP6 6SH
Correspondent D S M Nussbaum, Trustee

Trustees *D S M Nussbaum; Mrs K M Nussbaum; S Murray Williams.*

CC Number 287001

Information available Information was available from the Charity Commission.

This trust supports medicine, health, welfare, education and religion.

In 2008 the trust had an income £63,000 and made grants totalling about £28,000. No further information was available.

Applications The trust strongly stated that unsolicited applications are not considered, describing such appeals as a waste of charitable resources.

The Dorus Trust

Health and welfare, disability, homelessness, addiction, children who are disadvantaged and the environment

£148,000 (2007)
Beneficial area Mainly UK.

c/o Charities Aid Foundation, Kings Hill, West Malling ME19 4TA
Tel. 01732 520028
Correspondent C H Peacock, Trustee

Trustees *C H Peacock; Mrs B Bond; A M Bond.*

CC Number 328724

Information available Full accounts were provided by the trust.

The trust has common trustees with two other trusts, the Cleopatra Trust and the Epigoni Trust (see separate entries) with which it also shares the same aims and polices. All three trusts are administered by Charities Aid Foundation. Generally the trusts support different organisations each year.

The trust makes grants in the following areas:

- mental health
- cancer welfare/education – not research
- diabetes
- physical disability – not research
- homelessness
- addiction
- children who are disadvantaged.

There is also some preference for environmental causes. It only gives grants for specific projects and does not give grants for running costs or general appeals. Support is only given to national organisations, not local areas or initiatives.

In 2007 the trust had assets of £3.1 million, which generated an income of £157,000. Grants were made to 22 organisations totalling £148,000.

Beneficiaries included: Dogs for the Blind (£13,000); British Liver Trust (£11,000); Epsom Medical Research, SeeAbility and Hearing Research Trust (£10,000 each); Heartline Association (£7,500); Tall Ships Youth Trust (£6,000); Crisis UK (£5,000); National Deaf Childrens' Society (£4,500); Exeter University Foundation (£3,000); and Christian Lewis Foundation (£2,500).

Exclusions No grants to individuals, expeditions, research, scholarships, charities with a local focus, local branches of UK charities or towards running costs.

Applications This trust no longer accepts applications.

Double 'O' Charity Ltd

General

£119,000 (2007/08)
Beneficial area UK and overseas.

c/o 4 Friars Lane, Richmond TW9 1NL
Correspondent The Trustees

Trustees *P D B Townshend; Mrs K Townshend.*

CC Number 271681

Information available Accounts were available at the Charity Commission.

The primary objective of the trust is to make grants towards the relief of poverty, preservation of health and the advancement of education. The trust considers all requests for aid.

In 2007/08 the trust had an income of £235,000 and assets of £113,000. Grants to organisations totalled £119,000, with a further £31,000 given to individuals.

Beneficiaries were: the National Association for People Abused in Childhood (£36,000); Bedales School (£32,000); Spirit of Recovery (£30,000); Richmond Bridge Friendship Club (£16,000); the Arvon Foundation (£5,000); and Elton John Aids Foundation (£1,000).

Exclusions No grants to individuals towards education or for their involvement in overseas charity work.

Applications In writing to the correspondent.

The Doughty Charity Trust

Orthodox Jewish, religious education and relief of poverty

£208,000 (2007)
Beneficial area England, Israel.

22 Ravenscroft Avenue, Golders Green, London NW11 0RY
Tel. 020 8209 0500
Correspondent Gerald B Halibard, Trustee

Trustees *G Halibard, Chair; Mrs M Halibard.*

CC Number 274977

Information available Full accounts were on file at the Charity Commission.

This trust appears to confine its giving to Orthodox Jewish causes. In 2007 the trust had an income of £244,000 and made grants totalling £208,000. Its assets stood at £75,000.

Beneficiaries included: Tomchai Shaarie Zion (£23,000); Bobor Institute and Keren Haschesed Trust (£10,000 each); Tiferes Ivi (£9,600); Friend of Kiryat Sefer (£5,000); Sinai Synagogue (£4,600); Beis Yaakov School (£3,400); and Jewish Rescue and Relief (£1,000).

Other grants of less than £250 each totalled £2,600.

Exclusions No grants to individuals.

Applications In writing to the correspondent.

The R M Douglas Charitable Trust

General

£34,000 to organisations (2007/08)

Beneficial area UK with a preference for Staffordshire.

68 Liverpool Road, Stoke-on-Trent ST4 1BG

Correspondent J R T Douglas, Trustee

Trustees *J R T Douglas; Mrs J E Lees; F W Carder.*

CC Number 248775

Information available Accounts were on file at the Charity Commission, without a list of grants.

The trust was set up for the relief of poverty (including provision of pensions) especially for present and past employees (and their families) of Robert M Douglas (Contractors) Ltd, and for general charitable purposes especially in the parish of St Mary, Dunstall. In practice, grants are only given to organisations previously supported by the trust. Grants range from £200 to £5,000, although only a few are for over £500.

In 2007/08 the trust had assets of £1.1 million and an income of £109,000. Grants were made totalling £34,000. A further £6,300 was distributed to individuals connected with the company.

Previous beneficiaries have included Bible Explorer for Christian outreach, British Red Cross for general purposes, Burton Graduate Medical College to equip a new lecture theatre, Four Oaks Methodist Church for its centenary appeal, Lichfield Diocesan Urban Fund for Christian mission, St Giles Hospice – Lichfield for development, SAT-7 Trust for Christian outreach and John Taylor High School – Barton in Needwood for a performing arts block.

Applications The trust has previously stated that its funds were fully committed.

The Drayson Foundation

Education and the relief of sickness

£47,000 (2007/08)

Beneficial area UK.

c/o Allen and Overy, One Bishops Square, London E1 6AO

Correspondent Clare Maurice

Trustees *Lord Drayson; Lady Drayson; Clare Maurice.*

CC Number 1076700

Information available Accounts were on file at the Charity Commission.

Set up in 1999, the main objects of the foundation are the relief of sickness, with particular emphasis on children and the advancement of education.

In 2007/08 it had assets of £3.3 million and an income of £92,000. Grants to three organisations totalled £47,000.

Beneficiaries were: National Centre for Young People with Epilepsy (£33,000); Children's Fire and Burn Trust (£10,000); and Macmillan Cancer Relief (£3,500).

Applications In writing to the correspondent.

Dromintee Trust

General

£112,000 (2007/08)

Beneficial area Worldwide.

The Manor House, Main Street, Thurnby, Leicester LE7 9PN

Tel. 0116 241 5100

Correspondent Hugh Murphy, Trustee

Trustees *Hugh Murphy; Margaret Murphy; Mary Murphy; Patrick Hugh Murphy; Robert Smith; Paul Tiernan.*

CC Number 1053956

Information available Accounts were available at the Charity Commission.

Established in March 1996, in 2007/08 the trust had assets of £1.2 million and an income of £240,000. Grants totalled £112,000.

The trust gives for people in need by reason of age, illness, disability or socio-economic circumstances; for charitable purposes connected with children's welfare in the United Kingdom and overseas; the advancement of health and education; research into rare diseases and disorders, in particular metabolic disorders and for general charitable purposes.

In 2007/08 the trust gave grants locally, nationally and in developing countries, which included donations to medical charities, health education and children's charities.

Beneficiaries were: Consolata Fathers (£30,000); CAFOD (£28,000); InterCare (£20,000); Loros and Rainbows Children's Hospital (£10,000 each); the Little Way Association (£5,000); and Breast Cancer Campaign, the MedicAlert Foundation, Mencap, Powerful Information and the World Medical Fund (£2,000 each).

Applications In writing to the correspondent.

The Dugdale Charitable Trust

Christian education, the advancement of Methodist education and the Catholic religion

£110,000 (2007/08)

Beneficial area UK, with a preference for Hampshire and West Sussex, and overseas.

Harmsworth Farm, Botley Road, Curbridge SO30 2HB

Correspondent R Dugdale, Trustee

Trustees *R A Dugdale; Mrs B Dugdale; J Dugdale; S Dugdale.*

CC Number 1052941

Information available Full accounts were on file at the Charity Commission.

The trust has general charitable purposes and supports the advancement of the Methodist religion and Christian education in the UK. Increasingly, the trust supports overseas mission and relief work, particularly in Africa and the Indian subcontinent.

In 2007/08 the trust had assets of £497,000 and an income of £94,000. Grants were made totalling £110,000.

Beneficiaries included: New Life Church (£10,000); Winchester Family Church (£9,000); Waltham Chase Methodist Church; Great Lakes Outreach,

Christians Against Poverty Mission Aviation Fellowship, Open Doors and Oriental Missionary Society International (£5,000 each); and Christian Action Research and Education (£2,000).

Grants were also given to a number of development projects in Uganda (£36,000) and South Africa (£5,000).

Applications This trust only supports causes known personally to the trustees. Unsolicited applications are not considered.

The Dumbreck Charity

General

£119,000 (2007/08)
Beneficial area Worldwide, especially the west Midlands.

7 Bridge Street, Pershore, Worcestershire WR10 1AJ
Correspondent A C S Hordern, Trustee
Trustees A C S Hordern; H B Carslake; Mrs J E Melling.
CC Number 273070
Information available Accounts were on file at the Charity Commission.

In 2007/08 the charity had an income of £103,000 and assets of £3.4 million. Grants to organisations totalled £119,000. A small number of new grants are awarded each year to charities in Worcestershire, Warwickshire and West Midlands.

Grants were broken downs as follows, with examples of beneficiaries:

Animal welfare/conservation
International/national – 8 grants totalling £12,000
Brooke Hospital for Animals Cairo (£3,000); International League for the Protection of Horses (£2,000); Greek Animal Welfare Fund and The Wildfowl Trust (£1,000 each).

Local – 5 grants totalling £8,000
Spear (£4,000); Redwing Horse Sanctuary, The Worcester Farming and Wildlife Advisory Group and Warwickshire Wildlife Trust (£1,000 each); Avon Cats Home (£500).

Children's welfare
National – 1 grant totalling £1,000
The sole beneficiary was ChildLine (£1,000).

Local – 3 grants totalling £3,000
Dr Barnados (West Midlands), Warwick Association of Youth Clubs and Warwickshire Clubs for Young People (£1,000 each).

Care of people who are older or have physical/mental disabilities
International/national – 8 grants totalling £8,000
The Injured Jockey's Fund, the Royal Agricultural Benevolent Institution, the Royal British Legion Poppy Appeal, Listening Books, Deafblind UK and the Ghurkha Welfare Trust (£1,000 each).

Local – 11 grants totalling £12,000
Myton Hospice (£2,000); and Warwickshire Association for the Blind, Birmingham Phab Camps, Dogs for the Disabled and Warwick Old People's Friendship Circle (£1,000 each).

Medical
Local - 9 grants totalling £12,500
British Red Cross Association – Hereford and Worcester Branch (£2,500); County Air Ambulance and Shipston Home Nursing (£2,000 each); and National Association for Chrohns and Colitis, Foundation for Conductive Education and Crossroads – Caring for Carers (£1,000 each).

Miscellaneous
International/national – 4 grants totalling £5,000
Countryside Alliance (£2,000); and Campaign to Protect Rural England and Hunt Servants Benefit Society and SSAFA (£1,000 each).

One-off donations
Donations were given in the following categories:

Category	No.	Value
Animal welfare/conservation	1	£500
Children's Welfare	3	£2,500
Care of older people and physically/ mentally disabled people	12	£12,500
Medical	12	£14,500
Miscellaneous	24	£28,000

Exclusions No grants to individuals.

Applications In writing to the correspondent. The trustees meet annually in April/May. Unsuccessful applications will not be acknowledged. In general, priority is given to applications from the Midlands.

The Houghton Dunn Charitable Trust

Medical, health, welfare, environment, wildlife, churches and heritage

£326,000 (2007/08)
Beneficial area UK, with an interest in Lancashire.

25 Clitheroe Road, Whalley, Clitheroe BD7 9AD
Correspondent D H Dunn, Trustee
Trustees D H Dunn; Mrs E Dunn; A M H Dunn; R C H Dunn.
CC Number 261685
Information available Accounts were on file at the Charity Commission, without a list of grants.

Support is given to organisations working in the Lancashire area or UK-wide. It mostly makes small recurrent grants towards core costs of small organisations to enable them to maintain and improve their services. Larger grants can also be made towards capital projects.

In 2007/08 the trust had assets of £7.1 million and an income of £328,000. Grants were made to 46 organisations totalling £326,000. Grants were broken down as follows:

Category	No.	Value
Medical and health – general	12	£86,000
Medical and health – research	9	£67,000
Medical and health – children	6	£46,000
Welfare in the community – children and young people	7	£44,000
Welfare in the community – blind and deaf	2	£10,000
Welfare in the community – general	4	£15,000
Environment and wildlife	5	£48,000
Church and heritage	1	£10,000

Grants totalling £99,000 were made to charities based in the Lancashire area and a further £15,000 worth of grants were channelled to national charities through their branches operating in Lancashire.

Previous beneficiaries have included: AMEND, Arthritis Research Campaign, Cancer BACUP, Cancer Research UK, Christie Hospital NHS Trust, East Lancashire Hospice Fund, Lancashire Wildlife Trust, Marie Curie Cancer Care, Macmillan Cancer Relief , National Eczema Society, National Trust Lake District Appeal and National Youth Orchestra.

Exclusions No grants to individuals.

Applications In writing to the correspondent. There is no set time for the consideration of applications, but donations are normally made in March each year.

Dunn Family Charitable Trust

Medical, general and conservation

£60,000 (2007/08)

Beneficial area UK, with a strong preference for Nottinghamshire.

Rushcliffe Developments, Tudor House, 13–15 Rectory Road, West Bridgford, Nottingham NG2 6BE

Tel. 0115 945 5300

Email nad@rushcliffe.co.uk

Correspondent The Trustees

Trustees *Graham R Dunn; Mrs Jacky R Dunn; Mrs Lisa J Dunn; Nigel A Dunn; Peter M Dunn; Richard M Dunn.*

CC Number 297389

Information available Full accounts were available at the Charity Commission.

This trust supports health, multiple sclerosis research, conservation, ecology and general community and voluntary organisations.

In 2007/08 the trust had an income of £74,000 and assets of £1.9 million. Grants to 30 organisations totalled £60,000.

Beneficiaries included: St Lukes Hospice (£4,500); Nottingham Multiple Sclerosis Therapy Centre Limited (£4,000); Disability Aid Fund (£3,500); Wildfowl and Wetlands Trust, Support Dogs and Friends of Brancaster Church (£3,000 each); Multiple Sclerosis Trust and National Association for Colitis and Crohns Disease (£2,500 each); Seafarers UK and Nottinghamshire Wildlife Trust (£2,000 each); Rainbow Children's Hospice and Parkinson's Disease Society (£1,500 each); and Age Concern and Macmillan Cancer Support (£1,000 each).

Exclusions No grants to individuals or unsolicited applications.

Applications In writing to the correspondent.

Mildred Duveen Charitable Trust

General

£40,000 (2007/08)

Beneficial area Worldwide.

Devonshire House, 60 Goswell Road, London EC1M 7AD

Tel. 020 7566 4000

Correspondent Peter Holgate, Trustee

Trustees *P Holgate; A Houlstoun; P Loose; J Shelford.*

CC Number 1059355

Information available Accounts were on file at the Charity Commission.

Registered with the Charity Commission in November 1996, in 1999/2000 this trust received a substantial income of £1.3 million. In 2007/08 the trust had assets of £1.2 million, which generated an income of £43,000. Grants to 23 organisations totalled £40,000.

Beneficiaries included: Whizz Kidz (£5,000); Monica Cantwell Trust (£4,000); Whittington Babies and Masterclass Trust (£2,500 each); National Deaf Children's Society, Tavistock Clinic Foundation, Almeida Theatre (£2,000 each); Help for Heroes (£1,500); and St Catherine's Hospice, PDSA, Brighton and Hove Parents Group and Sussex Air Ambulance (£1,000 each).

Applications In writing to the correspondent.

The Annette Duvollet Charitable Trust

General

£25,000 (2007/08)

Beneficial area UK.

18 Nassau Road, London SW13 9QE

Tel. 020 8748 5112

Correspondent Peter Clarke, Trustee

Trustees *Peter Clarke; Caroline Dawes; Richard Shuttleworth.*

CC Number 326505

Information available Accounts were on file at the Charity Commission.

Registered with the Charity Commission in 1984, this trust gives grants to charities whose work support young people aged 14 to 25. In 2007/08 the trust had assets of £1.2 million and an income of £40,000. Grants were given to eight organisations totalling £25,000.

Beneficiaries included: Norfolk and Norwich Scope Association (NANSA) (£7,400); Depaul Trust and SPEAR (£5,000 each); Centrepoint and Neuromuscular Centre (£3,000 each); Children's Trust (£1,750); and Island Trust (£1,050).

Applications In writing to the correspondent.

The Dwek Family Charitable Trust

General

£65,000 (2007/08)

Beneficial area UK, with a preference for the Greater Manchester area.

Suite One, Courthill House, 66 Water Lane, Wilmslow SK9 5AP

Correspondent J C Dwek, Trustee

Trustees *J C Dwek; J V Dwek; A J Leon.*

CC Number 1001456

Information available Information had been filed at the Charity Commission.

In 2007/08, this trust had an income of £93,000 and assets of £622,000. Charitable expenditure came to £65,000, however the trust's accounts were very brief and gave no information regarding beneficiaries.

Applications In writing to the correspondent.

The Dyers' Company Charitable Trust

General

£318,000 (2007/08)

Beneficial area UK.

Dyers' Hall, Dowgate Hill, London
EC4R 2ST

Correspondent The Clerk

Trustee *The court of The Dyers' Company.*

CC Number 289547

Information available Full accounts were on file at the Charity Commission.

In 2007/08 the trust had assets of £6 million generating an income of £876,000. Grants to organisations totalled £318,000 and were given in the following categories, shown with examples of beneficiaries in each category:

Education and young people – 29 grants totalling £64,000
Boutcher Church of England Primary School and St Saviours and St Olaves School (£15,000 each); Cirdan Sailing Trust, London Youth Trust and Northumbrian Coalition against Crime (£2,000 each); and Childhood First Foundation, Young Bristol and Trealoar Trust (£1,000 each).

'The craft' – 8 grants totalling £62,000
Heriot-Watt University (£22,000); Society of Dyers and Colourists (£19,000); University of Manchester (£8,000); Royal College of Art (£6,000); the Salters' Institute (£5,000); Stroudwater Textile Trust (£1,500); Edinburgh College of Art and Royal School of Needlework (£1,000 each).

Norwich School – £58,000
This organisation has also received substantial donations in previous years.

Health and welfare – 33 grants totalling £30,000
Beneficiaries included: Orchid Cancer Appeal and SPEAK Ability (£2,000 each); National Eczema Society, Dyslexia Action, East Anglia Children's Hospice and National Library for the Blind (£1,000 each); and Association for Post-Natal Illness, Bakewell and Eyam Community Transport, Motor Neurone Disease Association and Helen Arkell Dyslexia Trust (£500 each).

Services – 10 grants totalling £20,000
Airborne Museum Hartenstein and Help for Heroes (£5,000 each); British Limbless Ex-Service Men's Appeal, Combat Stress, Support our Paras and The Victory Services Association (£2,000); Scots Guards Charity (£1,000); 1475 Dulwich Squadron (£500); Royal British Legion Poppies Appeal and the Prince's Charities (£250 each).

The arts – 14 grants totalling £14,500
Royal Overseas League Music Competition and Grange Park Opera (£2,000 each); Ironbridge Gorge Museum Trust and Heritage of London Trust (£1,000 each); and The Actors' Charitable Trust and Birmingham Royal Ballet (£500 each).

Other – 10 grants totalling £10,500
Swan Lifeline – Windsor, Swan Sanctuary – Egham and College of Arms Trust (£1,500 each); Royal National Lifeboat Institution and Jubilee Sailing Trust (£1,000 each); and London Wildlife Trust and Frensham Pond Sailability (£500 each).

The church – 8 grants totalling £8,600
St James's Church, Garlickhythe and Charterhouse in Southwark (£2,000 each); Fowey Parish Church, Friends of St Paul's Cathedral, Historic Churches Preservation Trust and Mayfield Church Trust (£1,000 each); Binham Priory (£500); and The Trustees of the United Guilds' Services (£125).

Local community/City/Inner London – 4 grants totalling £7,200
City of London Police Widows and Orphans and Lord Mayor's Appeal (£2,000 each); City & Guilds of London Arts School and Guildhall School of Music and Drama (£1,000 each); Mansion House Scholarship Scheme and Sheriffs' and Recorder's Fund (£500 each); and City University (£200).

Exclusions No grants to individuals.

Applications The trust does not welcome unsolicited applications.

EAGA Partnership Charitable Trust

Fuel poverty

£246,000 (2007/08)

Beneficial area UK.

EAGA House, Archbold Terrace, Jesmond, Newcastle upon Tyne NE2 1DB

Tel. 0191 247 3800

Email eagact@aol.com

Website www.eagacharitabletrust.org

Correspondent Dr Naomi Brown, Trust Manager

Trustees *J Clough; V Graham; A Harvey; Prof. G Manners; G Ritzema; Dr J Wade; Prof. D Gordon.*

CC Number 1088361

Information available Accounts were on file at the Charity Commission.

The trust currently provides grants to fund research and other projects within two grant programmes.

- The first programme aims to clarify the nature, extent and consequences of fuel poverty and offer insights into the energy efficient and cost-effective relief of fuel poverty.
- The second programme aims to explore issues related to vulnerable consumers and their multiple needs and preferences. It explores the overlap between fuel poverty and wider deprivation, in order to develop a better understanding of different groups of vulnerable and/or deprived consumers.

The trust gives priority to funding proposals that have the potential to inform or influence national perceptions and policies and have a wide geographic focus. A project that operates at a local level will only be considered for a grant if it clearly demonstrates innovation, identifies the policy relevance of the project, has wide applicability and has well developed and accurately costed evaluation and dissemination plans.

The work funded by the trust can be divided into four categories:

- rigorous, policy-related research
- action projects (such as practical, community based initiatives which have wider applicability)
- the promotion of good practice (such as tool kits and workshops)
- practical resource materials and events (such as training and education resources).

In 2007/08 the trust had assets of £1.2 million, an income of £152,000 and approved new grants totalling £246,000. Grants included those to: Centre for Sustainable Energy (£70,000); Leeds Animation Workshop (£61,000); Changeworks (£52,000); Attend (£38,000); and Pett Projects (£24,000).

Exclusions No grants to individuals. No grants for general fundraising appeals; no grants for projects that comprise solely of capital works; no retrospective funding; no funding for energy advice provision materials; no funding towards the maintenance of websites; no grants for local energy efficiency/warm homes initiatives.

Applications The following information is taken from the trust's website:

Applicants are requested to complete an application form. All applications that are completed in full and fulfil the main aims of [the trust] will be assessed at a formal meeting of trustees. Meetings are held three times a year. The trustees review applications against specific criteria and objectives.

The Eagle Charity Trust

General, international and welfare

£39,000 (2007)

Beneficial area UK, in particular Manchester, and overseas.

Nairne Son and Green, 477 Chester Road, Cornbrook, Manchester M16 9HF

Tel. 0161 872 1701

Correspondent The Trustees

Trustees Mrs L A Gifford; Miss D Gifford; Mrs E Y Williams; Mrs S A Nowakowski; R M E Gifford.

CC Number 802134

Information available Information available at the Charity Commission.

The trust stated it supports a wide variety of charities, including UK and international charities and local charities in Manchester. There is a preference for those concerned with medicine and welfare. Grants are made on a one off basis, with no commitment to providing ongoing funding.

In 2007 the trust had assets of £968,000, an income of £35,000 and made 37 grants totalling £39,000.

Beneficiaries included: Oxfam – Darfur and Chad (£2,500); Médecins Sans Frontières, UNICEF and Shelter (£2,000 each); British Red Cross – Bangladesh and MacMillan Cancer Support (£1,500 each); Amnesty International, Sight Savers International and Samaritans (£1,000 each); and Turning Point, Claire House and Wateraid (£500 each).

Applications Unsolicited applications are not invited.

Audrey Earle Charitable Trust

General, with some preference for animal welfare and conservation charities

£57,000 (2007/08)

Beneficial area UK.

24 Bloomsbury Square, London WC1A 2PL

Tel. 020 7637 0661 **Fax** 020 7436 4663

Email psheils@mail.com

Correspondent Paul Sheils, Trustee

Trustees Paul Andrew Shiels; Roger James Weetch.

CC Number 290028

Information available Accounts were on file at the Charity Commission.

In 2007/08 the trust had assets of £3.6 million and an income of £62,000. Grants were made to 27 organisations totalling £57,000. Most of the beneficiaries are supported year after year.

Beneficiaries included: Wells and Hospital Hospice Trust (£10,000); Burnham Market and Norton Village Hall (£5,000); Action for Blind People, Age Concern England, British Red Cross Society and Blue Cross Animal Hospital (£2,000 each); and East Anglia Air Amubalance, RSPB and Wildfowl and Wetlands Trust (£1,000 each).

Applications In writing to the correspondent.

East Kent Provincial Charities

General, education, young and older people

£80,000 (2007/08)

Beneficial area UK, with a preference for Kent.

11 Boorman Way, Estuary View Business Park, Whitstable CT5 3SE

Tel. 01227 272944

Email office@ekpca.org.uk

Website www.ekpca.org.uk

Correspondent Patrick Flanagan, Secretary

Trustees Patrick Thomas, Chair; Graham Smith; John Edmondson; Peter Daniels; Peter Rodd; Brian Powell; Keith Pavey; Patrick Flanagan; Thomas Denne.

CC Number 1023859

Information available Accounts were obtained from the Charity Commission website.

In 2007/08 the trust had assets of £28,000 and an income of £470,000. Grants totalled £80,000 and were broken down as follows:

Category	Value
Care of people who are sick and older people	£12,000
Education	£4,000
General charitable purposes	£64,000

Beneficiaries included:

Masonic registered charities – £37,000
Provincial Grand Masters Lodge (£9,300); Kent Masonic Library and Museum (£7,500); Royal Masonic Benevolent Institution (£7,300); Kent Mark Benevolent Fund (£4,300); Canterbury Masonic Charities (£4,200); and New Masonic Samaritan Fund (£1,100).

Non-Masonic registered charities – £43,000
Kent Air Ambulance (£6,400); Pahar Trust (£4,000); Margate Swimming Club (£1,500); and Dover War Memorial, Sheppey Sea Cadets and Whitstable Umbrella Community Centre (£1,000 each).

Applications In writing to the correspondent.

The Ebenezer Trust

Evangelical Christianity and welfare

£74,000 (2007/08)

Beneficial area UK and overseas.

Longwood Lodge, Whites Hill, Stock, Ingatestone CM4 9QB

Tel. 01277 829893

Correspondent Nigel Davey, Trustee

Trustees Nigel Davey; Ruth Davey.

CC Number 272574

Information available Accounts are on file at the Charity Commission.

The trust gives grants to Evangelical Christian charities for education, medical, religion and welfare purposes.

In 2007/08 the trust had assets of £713,000, an income of £47,000 and made grants totalling £74,000 to 41 organisations.

Beneficiaries included: Brentwood Baptist Church (£11,000); TEAR Fund (£6,000); Baptist Missionary Society, Barnabas Trust, and Viz a Viz (£5,000 each); Brentwood Schools Christian Worker Trust (£4,000); Evangelical Alliance and Shatesbury Society (£2,000 each); Ethiopian Graduates School of Technology, Africa Inland Mission, Care Trust and Salvation Army (£1,000 each); and Stepping Stones Trust, London City Mission and Far Eastern Broadcasting Association (£500 each).

Exclusions No grants to individuals.

Applications The trust states that they 'are most unlikely to consider unsolicited requests for grants'.

The Gilbert and Eileen Edgar Foundation

General

£82,000 (2007)

Beneficial area UK (and a few international appeals).

c/o Chantrey Vellacott DFK, Prospect House, 58 Queens Road, Reading RG1 4RP

Website www.cvdfk.com

Correspondent Penny Tyson

Trustees *A E Gentilli; R S Parker.*

CC Number 241736

Information available Full accounts were on file at the Charity Commission.

Registered with the Charity Commission in 1965, the settler of this trust expressed the desire that preference be given to the following objects.

- Medical research – the promotion of medical and surgical science in all forms.
- Care and support – helping people who are young, old and in need.
- Fine arts – raising the artistic taste of the public in music, drama, opera, painting, sculpture and the fine arts.

- Education in the fine arts – the promotion of education in the fine arts.
- Religion – the promotion of religion.
- Recreation – the provision of facilities for recreation or other leisure time activities.

There is a preference for smaller organisations 'where even a limited grant may be of real value'. The majority of grants are around £500 to £1,000 each. Many of the organisations supported are regular beneficiaries.

In 2007 the foundation had assets of £1.9 million and an income of £82,000. Grants were made to 98 organisations totalling £82,000 and were broken down as follows:

Medical and surgical research – 19 grants totalling £12,000
Beneficiaries included: Cystic Fibrosis Trust and Prostate Cancer Research Charity, Multiple Sclerosis and Prostate Cancer Charity (£1,000 each); and Arthritis Research Campaign, Blond McIndoe Centre, Fight for Sight, Leukaemia Research Fund and Royal College of Surgeons of England (£500 each).

Care and support
Children and young people – 18 grants totalling £11,000
Beneficiaries included: Children in Crisis, Operation New World, NSPCC and Weston Spirit (£1,000); and ChildLine, National Institute of Conductive Education, New Start Africa and Books Abroad (£500 each).

Older people – 3 grants totalling £2,000
Beneficiaries included: Universal Beneficent Society (£1,000); and Ghurkha Welfare Trust and Nightingale House (£500 each).

People with special needs – 33 grants totalling £16,000
Beneficiaries included: Brains Trust (£2,000); Samaritans, National Missing Persons Helpline and Not Forgotten Association (£1,000 each); Deafblind UK, Reading Single Homeless Project, Alone in London Service, Headway, Reading Community Welfare Rights Unit, Reading Voluntary Action, and Victim Support (£500 each); and Hambledon Medical Surgery Fund (£250).

Fine arts – 3 grants totalling £6,500
Beneficiaries included: Royal National Theatre (£4,000); English National Ballet (£2,000); and Living Paintings Trust (£500).

Education in fine arts – 4 grants totalling £22,000
Beneficiaries included: Royal College of Music – Junior Fellowship (£9,000); Royal Academy of Arts – Scholarship (£6,000); Royal Academy of Dramatic Art – Scholarship (£5,000); and Elizabeth Harwood Memorial Trust – scholarship (£2,000).

Religion and recreation including conservation – 18 grants totalling £13,000
Beneficiaries included: Atlantic Salmon Trust, Landmine Action and Reading Chinese School (£1,000); and Wells for India, Survival for Tribal Peoples and Marine Conservation Society (£500 each).

Exclusions Grants for education in the fine arts are made by way of scholarships awarded by academies and no grants are made directly to individuals in this regard.

Applications In writing to the correspondent. There are no application forms.

Gilbert Edgar Trust

General

£108,000 (2007/08)

Beneficial area Predominantly UK, limited overseas.

c/o Cave Harper and Co., North Lee House, 66 Northfield End, Henley-on-Thames RG9 2BE

Tel. 01491 572565

Correspondent The Trustees

Trustees *S C E Gentilli; A E Gentilli; Dr R E B Solomons.*

CC Number 213630

Information available Accounts were available at the Charity Commission.

Registered with the Charity Commission in 1955, this trust supports organisations whose work is concerned with welfare of people in the UK and overseas.

In 2007/08 the trust had assets of £1.1 million, which generated an income of £59,000. Charitable expenditure came to £108,000 given in 177 grants, which are broken down as follows:

Children – £11,000
Beneficiaries included: NSPCC (£3,000); National Institute of Conductive Education (£2,000) and Early Bird Fund

93

and National Autistic Society (£1,000 each).

Deaf/Blind – £3,000
Beneficiaries included: Cambridge Hearing Trust, Fight for Sight and Sense (£1,000 each).

Disability – £13,000
Beneficiaries included: The Not Forgotten Association (£10,000); and Disabilities Trust, Robert Owen Communities and Woodcraft Folk (£1,000 each).

Drug Abuse – £4,000
Beneficiaries included: Broadreach House, Re-Solv, Release and Rhoserchan Project (£1,000 each).

Handicapped – £8,000
Beneficiaries included: Matthew Trust, Orchard Vale Trust, Shaftesbury Society and Willow Trust (£1,000 each).

Homeless – £24,000
Beneficiaries included: Marylebone Project (£10,000); and Centrepoint, Mind and Shelter (£3,000 each).

Medical – £4,000
Beneficiaries included: Macmillan Cancer Relief (£2,000); and Spinal Injuries Association and Pain Relief Foundation (£1,000 each).

Research – £6,500
Beneficiaries included: Prostate Cancer Charity (£2,000); and Anthony Nolan Trust, Barts Research Trust and Leukaemia Research Fund (£1,000 each).

Hospice – £13,000
Beneficiaries included: Shakespeare Hospice (£10,000); East Anglia's Children's Hospices, Hospice of St Francis and St Columba's Hospice (£1,000 each).

Social – £8,000
Beneficiaries included: Samaritans (£3,000); and Hambledon Church Council, St John's Ambulance and Police Foundation (£1,000 each).

Overseas – £10,000
Beneficiaries included: British Red Cross (£3,000); Save the Children Fund (£2,000); and Prisoners Abroad (£1,000).

Young people – £1,300
Beneficiaries included: YMCA, National Association of Clubs for Young People and Venturers Search and Rescue (£1,000 each).

Other – £100
The sole beneficiary in this category was the Worshipful Company of Clockmakers.

Exclusions No grants to individuals or non-registered charities.

Applications In writing to the correspondent, with a copy of a brochure describing your work.

The Edinburgh Trust, No 2 Account

Education and armed services

£66,000 (2007/08)

Beneficial area UK and worldwide.

Buckingham Palace, London SW1A 1AA

Tel. 020 7930 4832

Correspondent The Secretary

Trustees Sir Brian McGrath; C Woodhouse; Sir Miles Hunt-Davis.

CC Number 227897

Information available Full accounts were on file at the Charity Commission.

In 2007/08 the trust had assets of £2.2 million and an income of £94,000. Grants were given to 29 organisations totalling £66,000 and were broken down into the following categories:

Category	Value
General	£44,000
Armed Services	£18,000
Education	£4,000

Beneficiaries included: Edwina Mountbatten Trust (£2,750); Federation of London Youth Clubs and Royal Marines General Fund (£2,500 each); Outward Bound Trust and The Award Scheme (£2,000 each); Burman Star Association, The Maritime Trust and Royal Life Saving Society (£1,500 each); and British Heart Foundation, Interact Worldwide and The British Trust for Conservation Volunteers (£1,000 each).

Exclusions No grants to individuals; only scientific expeditions are considered with the backing of a major society. No grants to non-registered charities.

Applications In writing to the correspondent. The trustees meet to consider grants in April each year. Applications must be submitted by January.

Educational Foundation of Alderman John Norman

Education

£29,000 to organisations (2007/08)

Beneficial area Norwich and Old Catton.

Brown and Co, Old Bank of England Court, Queen Street, Norwich NR2 4TA

Tel. 01603 629871

Email n.saffell@brown-co.com

Correspondent N F Saffell, Clerk

Trustees Revd J Boston; R Sandall; Dr J Leach; Revd Canon M Smith; D S Armes; C D Brown; C I H Mawson; Mrs C I H Mawson; Mrs T Hughes; S Slack; J Hawkins; R Hughes; F Whymark.

CC Number 313105

Information available Accounts were on file at the Charity Commission.

The trust was originally founded by the terms of the will of Alderman Norman dated February 1720. It is currently regulated by schemes from 1972 and 1973. Grants made by the foundation are to assist the education of:

- young persons descended from Alderman John Norman
- young persons resident in the parish of Old Catton
- young persons resident in the city of Norwich and for the benefit of schools established for charitable purposes only or for the benefit of local authority schools for benefits not provided by local authority.

In 2007/08 the foundation had an income of £275,000 and assets of £6.1 million. Grants given to 14 organisations totalled £29,000.

Beneficiaries included: Norwich Cathedral Choir Endowment Fund (£6,000); The How Hill Trust (£5,000); Norfolk County Council EWS Activity Fund and West Norwich Partnership (£3,000 each); Mancroft Advice Project (£2,000); The Claimants Unity Trust (£1,700); and Football in the Community, Leeway Norwich Womens Aid and Norwich Sea Cadets (£1,000 each).

Exclusions No grants to non-registered charities. No applications from outside Norwich and Old Catton will be considered.

Applications In writing to the correspondent. Grants to organisations are considered at the trustees meeting in May/June, however the trustees usually meet three times each year, in February, May and October.

The W G Edwards Charitable Foundation

Care of older people

£102,000 (2007/08)
Beneficial area UK.

c/o 123a Station Road, Oxted RH8 0QE
Tel. 01883 714412 **Fax** 01883 714433
Email janetbrown@ wgedwardscharitablefoundation.org.uk
Website www. wgedwardscharitablefoundation.org.uk
Correspondent Janet Brown, Clerk to the Trustees
Trustees *Mrs Margaret E Offley Edwards; Prof. Wendy D Savage; Mrs G Shepherd Coates; Ms Yewande Savage.*
CC Number 293312
Information available Accounts were on file at the Charity Commission and well-detailed.

The foundation's policy statement is 'to assist with the provision of care for older people through existing charities, principally with capital projects but also innovative schemes for ongoing care'.

In 2007/08 the foundation had an income of £145,000 and assets of £3 million. A total of 195 applications were received, of which 22 were successful. Grants totalled £102,000 and were broken down as follows:

Category	Value
New Building	£6,100
Refurbishment	£46,000
Furniture/Equipment	£4,800
Recreational Activity	£17,000
Outreach/care projects	£22,000
Homeless	£4,400
Research	£2,100
Total	**£102,000**

Beneficiaries included: Age Concern Sevenoaks (£16,000); Deptford Action Group for the Elderly (£10,000); Action on Elder Abuse (£8,400); Extracare Charitable Trust, Coventry (£6,000);

London Mozarts Players and Northumberland Wildlife Trust (£5,000 each); Henshaws Society for Blind People (Northwest) and Age Exchange (£4,000 each); and Music in Hospitals – Scotland (£2,000).

Exclusions No grants to individuals.

Applications In writing to the correspondent, including: confirmation of charitable status (charity number on letterhead will suffice); brief details of the project; budget statement for the project; current fundraising achievements and proposals for future fundraising; items of expenditure within project costing approx £1,000 to £5,000 – trustees currently prefer to give towards a named item rather than into a pool building fund; and a copy of the latest accounts if available.

There are no forms or deadlines for applications. If your project fulfils the foundation's policy criteria, your details will be passed on to the trustees for consideration at their next meeting.

The Elephant Trust

Visual arts

£36,000 to organisations (2007/08)
Beneficial area UK.

512 Bankside Lofts, 65 Hopton Street, London SE1 9GZ
Email ruth@elephanttrust.org.uk
Correspondent Ruth Rattenbury
Trustees *Sarah Whitfield, Chair; Dawn Ades; Antony Forwood; Tony Penrose; Richard Wentworth; Polly Staple; Rob Tufnel.*
CC Number 269615
Information available Accounts were on file at the Charity Commission.

The trust makes grants to individual artists, arts organisations and publications concerned with the visual arts. It aims to extend the frontiers of creative endeavour, to promote the unconventional and the imaginative and, within its limited resources, to make it possible for artists and arts organisations to realise and complete specific projects.

In 2007/08 the trust's assets totalled £1.7 million, which generated an income of £66,000. Grants were awarded to 16 organisations totalling £36,000, with a

further £27,000 distributed to 16 individuals.

Beneficiaries included: Atlas Press and Studio Voltaire (£3,500 each); Camden Arts Centre and Matt's Gallery (£3,000 each); Book Works, The Common Guild and Ikon Birmingham, Institute of Contemporary Arts and S1 Art Space (£2,000 each); City Projects London Ltd (£1,800); and the Showroom (£1,000).

The trust also administers the George Melhuish Bequest, which has similar objectives.

Exclusions No education or other study grants.

Applications In writing to the correspondent. Guidelines are available. The trustees meet four times a year.

The George Elias Charitable Trust

Jewish and general

£251,000 (2007/08)
Beneficial area Some preference for Manchester.

Elitex House, 1 Ashley Road, Altrincham WA14 2DT
Tel. 0161 928 7171
Email textiles@kshaw.com
Correspondent N G Denton, Charity Accountant
Trustees *E C Elias; S E Elias.*
CC Number 273993
Information available Accounts were obtained from the Charity Commission website.

The trust states that it gives grants to charities supporting educational needs and the fight against poverty as well as organisations promoting the Jewish faith.

In 2007/08 the trust had an income of £263,000 and assets of £157,000. Grants were made to 104 organisations totalling £251,000.

Beneficiaries included: Ahavat Shalom (£43,000); Hale and District Hebrew Congregation (£26,000); Lubavitch South Manchester (£13,000); Jewish Humanitarian Foundation (£7,200); The Jewish Learning Exchange (£5,000); Chai Network (£4,700); South Manchester Mikva Trust (£4,000); Manchester Jewish Chaplaincy (£3,000); Christie Hospital (£1,900); and Jewish Agency (£1,000).

Applications In writing to the correspondent. Trustees meet monthly.

The Elizabeth Frankland Moore and Star Foundation

General

£90,000 (2007/08)

Beneficial area UK.

c/o Claydons Barns, 11 Towcester Road, Whittlebury NN12 8XU

Correspondent The Trustees

Trustees *Mrs J Cameron; R A Griffiths; Mrs A E Ely; Dr David Spalton.*

CC Number 257711

Information available Information was available from the Charity Commission website.

Registered with the Charity Commission in February 1969, in 2007/08 the trust had an income of £198,000, assets of £6.9 million and made grants to 26 organisations totalling £90,000.

Beneficiaries included: the Not Forgotten Association and Accord (£10,000 each); Prisoners Abroad and Riverside Museum Appeal (£5,000 each); Special Forces Benevolent Fund (£2,500); the Friends of Barnes Hospital (£2,000); the Barton Trust, Wiltshire Air Ambulance Appeal and Revive Scotland (£1,000 each); Scottish SPCA, Plan International UK and Wessex Multiple Sclerosis Therapy Centre (£500 each).

Applications In writing to the correspondent. Trustees meet twice a year.

Ellador Ltd

Jewish

£43,000 (2007/08)

Beneficial area UK.

Ellador Ltd, 20 Ashstead Road, London E5 9BH

Tel. 020 7242 3580

Correspondent J Schrieber, Trustee and Governor

Trustees *J Schrieber; S Schrieber; Mrs H Schrieber; Mrs R Schrieber.*

CC Number 283202

Information available Accounts were on file at the Charity Commission, but without a grants list.

The trust supports organisations benefiting Jewish people and also Jewish individuals, mainly for educational and religious purposes. In 2007/08 it had assets of £396,000 and an income of £43,000. Grants totalled £43,000, however a list of grants was not included in the accounts for this year.

Applications In writing to the correspondent.

The Ellerdale Trust

Children

£57,000 (2007/08)

Beneficial area Worldwide.

c/o Macfarlane and Co., Cunard Building, Water Street, Liverpool L3 1DS

Tel. 0151 236 6161

Correspondent The Trustees

Trustees *A T R Macfarlane; P C Kurthausen; S P Moores.*

CC Number 1073376

Information available Accounts were on file at the Charity Commission.

This trust was established to relieve poverty, distress or suffering in any part of the world; particularly children who are disadvantaged or in need.

In 2007/08 the trust had assets of £6.3 million and an income of £285,000. Grants were made to 11 organisations totalling £57,000.

Beneficiaries included: Sense (£18,000); Action for Kids (£10,000); Mind (£7,000); Psychiatric Research Trust and Nelson's Journey (£5,000 each); Fairbridge Merseyside and Martin Sailing Project (£3,000 each); Nightingales Romania (£2,000); and Music Alive (£1,000).

Applications In writing to the correspondent.

The Ellinson Foundation Ltd

Jewish

£358,000 (2007/08)

Beneficial area Worldwide.

Messrs Robson Laidler and Co, Fernwood House, Fernwood Road, Jesmond, Newcastle upon Tyne NE2 1TJ

Tel. 0191 281 8191

Correspondent The Trustees

Trustees *C O Ellinson; A Ellinson; A Z Ellinson; U Ellinson.*

CC Number 252018

Information available Full accounts were on file at the Charity Commission.

The trust supports hospitals, education and homelessness in the UK and overseas, usually with a Jewish-teaching aspect. The trust regularly supports organisations such as boarding schools for boys and girls teaching the Torah.

In 2007/08 the trust had assets of £2.9 million and an income of £1 million. Grants totalled £358,000.

The largest beneficiary continues to be the Tofrach Torah Centre (£241,000), a talmudical college in South Isreal, to which the trustees intend to donate a total of $1 million over the following years.

Other beneficiaries of grants over £1,000 included: Keser Yeshua Refua Uparnosa (£80,000); Kolel Ohel Torah (£9,000); British Friends of Jaffa Institute (£7,500); Friends of Yeshivas Brisk (£6,000); Institute of Torah and Charity (£3,000); and Rosecare Foundation (£1,000).

Grants of less that £1,000 each, unlisted in the accounts, totalled £1,900.

Exclusions No grants to individuals.

Applications In writing to the correspondent. However, the trust generally supports the same organisations each year and unsolicited applications are not welcome.

The Edith Maud Ellis 1985 Charitable Trust

Quaker, ecumenical, education, peace and international affairs and general

£34,000 (2007/08)

Beneficial area UK, Ireland and overseas.

c/o Heckford Norton, 18 Hill Street, Saffron Walden CB10 1JD

Tel. 01799 522636

Email hf@heckfordnorton.co.uk

Correspondent Mrs H Fuff, Administrator

Trustees *A P Honigmann; E H Milligan.*

CC Number 292835

Information available Accounts were on file at the Charity Commission.

The trust supports general charitable purposes including religious and educational projects (but not personal grants for religious or secular education nor grants for church buildings) and projects in international fields especially related to economic, social and humanitarian aid to developing countries.

In 2007/08 the trust had an income of £94,000 and gave grants totalling £34,000.

Beneficiaries included: Project Trust (£5,000); Friends World Committee for Consultation (£3,800); Dr Williams Charity, Women's International League and the Irish School of Ecumenics (£1,500 each); Wyndham Place Trust, Cape Town Peace Centre and Corrymeela Community (£1,000 each); and Dystonia Society and Budiriro Trust (£750 each).

Exclusions No grants to individuals.

Applications In writing to the correspondent.

The Elmgrant Trust

General charitable purposes, education, arts and social sciences

£46,000 to organisations (2007/08)

Beneficial area UK, with a preference for the south west of England.

The Elmhirst Centre, Dartington Hall, Totnes TQ9 6EL

Tel. 01803 863160

Correspondent Angela Taylor, Secretary

Trustees *Marian Ash, Chair; Sophie Young; Paul Elmhirst; David Young; Mark Sharman.*

CC Number 313398

Information available Accounts were on file at the Charity Commission.

This trust has general charitable purposes, but in particular aims to encourage local life through education, the arts and social sciences. Although there is a preference for south west England, grants to organisations are awarded throughout the UK.

In 2007/08 the trust had assets of £1.9 million and an income of £60,000. Grants paid to 84 organisations totalled £46,000. A further £2,100 was paid in ten grants to individuals. Donations were broken down as follows, shown with examples of organisations receiving support in each category:

Education and educational research – 42 grants totalling £20,000
Second Chance Trust for Devon and Cornwall (£3,000); Centre for Alternative Technology and Stallcombe House (£1,000 each); and Bristol Children's Help Society, Ecos Trust and Plymouth Guild (£500).

Arts and arts education – 22 grants totalling £12,000
Dartington International Summer School (£2,000); Wren and the Dartington Hall Trust (£1,000 each); Torbay Symphony Orchestra and Age Concern Exeter (£750 each); Playback Youth Theatre and Awards for Young Musicians (£500 each); and Anglo-Asian Cultural Centre (£200).

Social sciences and scientific grants – 23 grants totalling £12,000
Exeter Homeless Action Group (£1,000); the Prison Phoenix Trust (£700); Life Cycle UK and Refugee Support Group

Devon (£500); and Apollo Football Club (£200).

Pensions, donations and compassionate grants – 8 grants totalling £4,500
Kinergy (£1,000); the Eyeless Trust (£750); National Coastwatch Institution and St Peter's Hospice (£500 each); and National Blind Children's Society (£300).

Exclusions The following are not supported:

- large scale UK organisations
- postgraduate study, overseas student grants, expeditions and travel and study projects overseas
- counselling courses
- renewed requests from the same (successful) applicant within a two-year period.

Applications In writing to the correspondent, giving full financial details and, where possible, a letter of support. Initial telephone calls are welcome if advice is needed. There are no application forms. Guidelines are issued. A stamped, addressed envelope would be very helpful, although this is not obligatory. Currently, meetings are held three times a year in March, June and October. Applications need to be received one clear month prior to meeting.

Elshore Ltd

Jewish

£379,000 (2007/08)

Beneficial area Worldwide.

c/o Michael Pasha & Co., 220 The Vale, Golders Green, London NW11 8SR

Tel. 020 8203 1726

Correspondent H Lerner, Trustee

Trustees *H M Lerner; A Lerner; S Yanofsky.*

CC Number 287469

Information available Accounts were on file at the Charity Commission, but without a list of grants.

This trust appears to make grants solely to Jewish organisations. In 2007/08 it had an income of £452,000, mainly from donations. Grants were made totalling £379,000. The trust's assets came to £260,000. A grants list was not included with the accounts for this year.

Further information has been unavailable since 1994/95, when grants to 40 beneficiaries totalled £178,000. The larger grants were £26,000 to Eminor Educational Centre and £20,000 to Cosmon Belz. Grants of £10,000 were given to ten organisations, including Gur Trust and Marbe Torah Trust. Most other grants were less than £1,000, although some were for up to £8,000.

Applications In writing to the correspondent.

The Vernon N Ely Charitable Trust

Christian, welfare, disability, children and young people and overseas

£79,000 (2007/08)

Beneficial area Worldwide, with a preference for London borough of Merton.

Grosvenor Gardens House, 35–37 Grosvenor Gardens, London SW1W 0BY

Tel. 020 7828 3156

Email dph@helmores.co.uk

Correspondent Derek Howorth, Trustee

Trustees *J S Moyle; D P Howorth; R S Main.*

CC Number 230033

Information available Accounts were on file at the Charity Commission, but without a list of grants.

The trust makes grants to Christian, welfare, disability, children, young people and overseas charities. In 2007/08 the trust had assets of £1.6 million and an income of £73,000. Grants were made to 22 organisations totalling £79,000. The majority of grants (19) were given at £4,000.

Beneficiaries included: Age Concern, Cardiac Risk in the Young, the Samaritans, London Sports Forum for Disabled People, Christchurch URC, Polka Children's Theatre and Community Housing Therapy (£4,000 each); British Tennis Foundation (£1,750); and West Barnes Singers and Sobell Hospice (£500 each).

Exclusions No grants to individuals.

Applications In writing to the correspondent.

The Emerton-Christie Charity

Health, welfare, disability and the arts

£49,000 (2007/08)

Beneficial area UK.

c/o Cartmell Shepherd, Viaduct House, Carlisle CA3 8EZ

Tel. 01228 516666

Email jmj@cartmells.co.uk

Correspondent The Trustees

Trustees *A F Niekirk; Dr N A Walker; Dr C Mera-Nelson; Lt Col W D Niekirk; Dr S E Walker.*

CC Number 262837

Information available Accounts were on file at the Charity Commission.

The Emerton Charitable Settlement was established in 1971 by Maud Emerton, with additional funds subsequently added by Vera Bishop Emerton. In April 1996, it became the Emerton-Christie Charity following a merger with another trust, The Mrs C M S Christie Will Trust.

In 2007/08 it had assets totalling £2.4 million and an income of £69,000. Grants were made to 22 organisations totalling £49,000.

Beneficiaries included: RNLI and Trinity College of Music (£4,000 each); Médecins Sans Frontières and Westnell Nursery (£3,000 each); The Life Centre (£2,500); Alzheimers Research Trust, Cameroon Gardens Project, Roots and Shoots, National Eye Research Centre and British Forces Foundation (£2,000 each).

Exclusions Generally no grants to:

- individuals
- religious organisations
- restoration or extension of buildings
- start-up costs
- animal welfare and research
- cultural heritage
- environmental projects.

Applications In writing to the correspondent. A demonstration of need based on budgetary principles is required and applications will not be acknowledged unless accompanied by a stamped, addressed envelope. Trustees normally meet once a year in the autumn to select charities to benefit.

EMI Music Sound Foundation

Music education

£197,000 (2007/08)

Beneficial area UK and Ireland

27 Wrights Lane, London W8 5SW

Tel. 020 7795 7000 **Fax** 020 7795 7296

Email enquiries@ musicsoundfoundation.com

Website www.musicsoundfoundation. com

Correspondent Janie Orr, Chief Executive

Trustees *Eric Nicoli, Chair; Jim Beach; John Deacon; Paul Gambaccini; Leslie Hill; David Hughes; Rupert Perry; Tony Wadsworth; Christine Walter; Charles Ashcroft.*

CC Number 1104027

Information available Accounts were on file at the Charity Commission.

The following information is taken from the foundation's comprehensive website.

EMI Music Sound Foundation is an independent music education charity, established in 1997 to celebrate the centenary of EMI Records and to improve young peoples' access to music education in the UK & Ireland.

We are now the single largest sponsor of Specialist Performing Arts Colleges and have created vital bursaries at seven music colleges to assist music students in need of financial support. We have also helped hundreds of schools and individual students improve their access to music through the purchase or upgrade of instruments and music making equipment.

Together with the Specialist Schools and Academies Trust it has sponsored 36 schools to become Performing Arts Colleges. The foundation is the major sponsor in every case and still remains the largest single schools sponsor in this sector. Sponsorship has now been extended to Music Colleges as part of the foundation's ongoing support for specialist schools.

All enquiries for EMI Music Sound Foundation sponsorship must be made through the Specialist Schools and Academies Trust (Bidding Support Department 0207 802 2300) in the first instance, as initial recommendations are taken from them.

General Awards

EMI MSF is dedicated to the improvement of music education with a focus on young people. Preference is given to full-time students under the age of 25.

Support is given to:

- non-specialist schools to fund music education
- music students in full time education to fund instrument purchase
- music teachers to fund courses and training.

Previous beneficiaries have included North Leamington School, Churchfield School, Brentwood Ursulie Convent, Egglescliffe School, Guthlaxton College, Focus Events for the String of Pearls Millennium Festival, King William's College, Young Persons Concert Foundation and Music Wheel.

Bursary Awards

Every year EMI MSF awards bursaries to students at seven music colleges in the UK and Ireland. These bursaries are distributed at each college's discretion, based on criteria provided by EMI MSF. For more information, please contact the colleges directly (Birmingham Conservatoire, Drumtech/Vocaltech/GuitarX – London, Institute of Popular Music – Liverpool, Irish World Music Centre – Limerick, Royal Scottish Academy of Music and Drama – Glasgow, Royal Academy – London and Royal Welsh College of Music and Drama – Cardiff).

In 2007/08 the foundation had assets totalling £7.8 million and an income of £362,000. Grants totalled £197,000.

Exclusions No support for:

- applications from outside the United Kingdom and Ireland
- non-school based community groups, music therapy centres, etc.
- applications over £2,500.

Applications On a form which can be downloaded from the foundation's website.

The Emilienne Charitable Trust

Medical and education

£36,000 (2007/08)
Beneficial area Not defined.

Ashton House, 12 The Precinct, Winchester Road, Chandlers Ford, Eastleigh S053 3AP

Correspondent M Howson-Green, Trustee

Trustees *M Howson-Green; B M Baxendale; Mrs M A Howson-Green.*

CC Number 327849

Information available Accounts were on file at the Charity Commission.

Set up in 1988, the trustees are particularly interested in support for charities involved in the treatment of addiction and in promoting education.

In 2007/08 it had assets of £684,000 and an income of £41,000. Grants to seven organisations totalled £36,000.

Beneficiaries of grants over £1,000 each were: Streetscene (£25,000); Kids for Kids (£5,000); Southampton Society for the Blind (£2,500); and Wessex Cancer Trust (£2,000).

Applications In writing to the correspondent.

The Emmandjay Charitable Trust

Social welfare, medicine and young people

£389,000 (2007/08)
Beneficial area UK, with a special interest in West Yorkshire.

PO Box 88, Otley LS21 3TE
Correspondent Mrs A E Bancroft, Administrator

Trustees *Mrs Sylvia Clegg; John A Clegg; Mrs S L Worthington; Mrs E A Riddell.*

CC Number 212279

Information available Accounts were obtained from the Charity Commission website, but without a grants list.

The trustees' report gives the following information.

The trust gives most particularly to help disadvantaged people, but many different projects are supported – caring for the disabled and terminally ill, work with young people and medical research. The trust likes projects which reach a lot of people. The trustees are keen that grants are actually spent.

In 2007/08 the trust had assets of £3.8 million and an income of £229,000. Grants totalled £389,000. A grants list was not included in the accounts, although it contained a breakdown of the areas in which it gives grants as follows:

Category	Value
National charities	£288,000
Special schemes, workshops, disabilities	£32,000
Youth activities, schools	£21,000
Local community groups	£16,000
Children's charities and care	£12,000
Medical research	£10,000
Special overseas appeals	£5,800
Homeless	£1,800
Church, religious activities	£1,300
Counselling services	£1,000
Social services, probation services	£1,000
Advice centres	£700

Previous beneficiaries have included: Abbeyfield Bradford Society, Bradford's War on Cancer, British Heart Foundation, British Red Cross, Cancer Support Centre, Caring for Life – Leeds, Marie Curie Cancer Centre, Research into Ageing and West Yorkshire Youth Association.

Exclusions 'The trust does not pay debts, does not make grants to individual students, and does not respond to circulars.' Grants are only given, via social services, to individuals if they live in Bradford.

Applications In writing to the correspondent.

The English Schools' Football Association

Association football

£313,000 (2007)
Beneficial area England.

4 Parker Court, Staffordshire Technology Park, Stafford ST18 0WP

Tel. 01785 785970 **Fax** 01785 256246

Email dawn.howard@schoolsfa.com

Website www.esfa.co.uk

Correspondent Dawn Howard, Finance Officer

Trustees *Philip J Harding, Chair; Gerry Smith; Nigel Brown.*

CC Number 306003

Information available Accounts and annual report were provided by the association.

Support is given for the mental, moral and physical development and improvement of school children and students through the medium of association football. Assistance is also given to teachers' charities and 'other such charitable purposes'.

In 2007 the association had an income of £977,000. Charitable expenditure for the year totalled £313,000, and was broken down as follows:

Category	Value
National Competitions	£173,000
Council and AGM	£68,000
Coaching Courses	£43,000
Handbooks and Publications	£29,000

Exclusions Grants are restricted to membership and teaching charities.

Applications In writing to the correspondent. The deadline for applications for the 2008/09 season has closed – check the association's website for up-to-date information on future deadlines.

The Epigoni Trust

Health and welfare, disability, homelessness, addiction, children who are disadvantaged and the environment

£147,000 (2007/08)
Beneficial area UK.

c/o Charities Aid Foundation, King's Hill, West Malling ME19 4TA

Tel. 01732 520028

Correspondent Charles Peacock, Trustee

Trustees *C H Peacock; Mrs B Bond; A M Bond.*

CC Number 328700

Information available Full accounts were on file at the Charity Commission.

The trust has common trustees with two other trusts, the Cleopatra Trust and the Dorus Trust (see separate entries) with which it also shares the same aims and policies. All three trusts are administered by Charities Aid Foundation. Generally the trusts support different organisations.

The trust makes grants in the following areas:

- mental health
- cancer welfare/education – not research
- diabetes
- physical disability – not research
- homelessness
- addiction
- children who are disadvantaged.

There is also some preference for environmental causes. It only gives grants for specific projects and does not give grants for running costs or general appeals. Support is only given to national projects, not local areas or initiatives.

In 2007/08 it had assets of £3.1 million, which generated an income of £159,000. Grants to 19 organisations totalled £147,000.

Beneficiaries included: Refuge, Macmillan Cancer Support and Talking Books (£10,000 each); Family Matters (£9,400); Kidney Research UK (£8,100); Reality Adventure Works in Scotland Ltd (£7,700); Samaritans (£5,500); Treloar Trust (£4,700); and Winston's Wish and Sussex Snowdrop Trust (£4,000 each).

Exclusions No grants to individuals, expeditions, research, scholarships, charities with a local focus, local branches of UK charities or towards running costs.

Applications This trust no longer accepts applications.

The Equity Trust Fund

Theatre

£80,000 to organisations (2007/08)
Beneficial area UK.

222 Africa House, 64 Kingsway, London WC2B 6AH

Tel. 020 7404 6041

Correspondent Keith Carter, Secretary

Trustees *Colin Baker; Glen Barnham; James Bolam; Annie Bright; Jo Cameron Brown; Robin Browne; Oliver Ford Davies; Graham Hamilton; Frank Hitchman; Barbara Hyslop; Milton Johns; Harry Landis; Ian McGarry; Frederick Pyne; Gillian Raine; Jean Rogers; John Rubinstein; Rosalind Shanks; Ian Talbot; Josephine Tewson; Jeffry Wickham; Frank Williams; Johnny Worthy.*

CC Number 328103

Information available Accounts were on file at the Charity Commission.

The charity is a benevolent fund for professional performers and stage managers and their dependants. It offers help with welfare rights, gives free debt counselling and information and can offer financial assistance to those in

genuine need. It also has an education fund to help members of the profession with further training provided they have at least ten years' professional adult experience. It also makes grants and loans to professional theatres or theatre companies.

In 2007/08 the trust had assets of £9 million and an income of £364,000. Grants totalled £271,000, of which £80,000 was distributed to seven organisations.

Beneficiaries included: Dancers' Career Development (£45,000); Stage One (£15,000); The Mousetrap Foundation (£7,000); Bristol Old Vic Theatre and Kings Theatre Southsea (£5,000 each); Oval House Theatre (£2,000); Sherman Youth Theatre (£1,200).

Exclusions No grants to non-professional performers, drama students, non-professional theatre companies, multi-arts venues, community projects or projects with no connection to the professional theatre.

Applications In the first instance please call the office to ascertain if the application is relevant. Failing that, submit a brief letter outlining the application. A meeting takes place about every six to eight weeks. Telephone for precise dates. Applications are required at least two weeks beforehand.

The Ericson Trust

See below

£48,000 (2007/08)
Beneficial area UK, developing countries, Eastern and Central Europe.

Flat 2, 53 Carleton Road, London N7 0ET

Email claudia.cotton@googlemail.com

Correspondent The Trustees

Trustees *Miss R C Cotton; Mrs V J Barrow; Mrs A M C Cotton.*

CC Number 219762

Information available Full accounts were on file at the Charity Commission.

The trust provides grants to previously supported organisations in the following fields:

- older people
- community projects/local interest groups, including arts

- prisons, prison reform, mentoring projects, as well as research in this area
- refugees
- mental health
- environmental projects and research
- aid to developing countries provided by a UK-registered charity.

In 2007/08 the trust had assets of £810,000 and an income of £250,000, the majority of which came from donations (£220,000). Grants were made to 14 organisations totalling £48,000.

Beneficiaries were: Anti-Slavery International and Umalini Mary Brahma Charitable Trust (£6,000 each); Minority Rights Group (£4,000); Action on Elder Abuse, Ashram International, Bhopal Medical Appeal, Headway East London, Howard League for Penal Reform, The Koestler Trust, Psychiatric Rehabilitation Association, The Rainforest Foundation, The Relatives and Residents Association and Tools for Self Reliance (£3,000 each); and Quaker Social Action (£2,000).

Exclusions No grants to individuals or to non-registered charities. Applications from the following areas are generally not considered unless closely connected with one of the following: children's and young people's clubs, centres and so on; schools; charities dealing with illness or disability (except psychiatric); or religious institutions, except in their social projects.

Applications Unsolicited applications cannot be considered as the trust has no funds available. The correspondent stated: 'We are increasing worried by the waste of applicants' resources when they send expensive brochures at a time when we are unable to consider any new appeals and have, indeed, reduced some of our long standing grants due to the bad economic situation. It is particularly sad when we receive requests from small charities in Africa and Asia.'

The Esfandi Charitable Foundation

Jewish

£468,000 (2007/08)
Beneficial area UK and overseas.

36 Park Street, London W1K 2JE
Correspondent J Esfandi, Trustee

Trustees *J Esfandi; Mrs D Esfandi.*
CC Number 1103095
Information available Accounts were on file at the Charity Commission.

Set up in 2004, in 2007/08 the foundation had an income of £355,000 and made grants totalling £468,000

There were 29 donations of £1,000 or more, with the largest beneficiary by far being Norwood (£110,000).

Other beneficiaries included: British Friends of Migdal Ohr (£51,000); Colnel Chabad (£30,000); Winnicot Foundation (£27,000); Community Security Trust, Jewish Care and Lubavitch Foundation (£25,000 each); Association Des Israelites (£17,000); Jewish World Relief (£10,000); Western Marble Arch Synagogue (£7,100); Jerusalem Foundation and One Family UK (£5,000 each); National Hospital Development Foundation (£2,500); and Nightingale, TRIBE and UNICEF (£1,000 each).

Donations of £1,000 or less totalled £3,500.

Applications In writing to the correspondent.

The Essex Youth Trust

Young people and education of people under 25

£385,000 paid (2007/08)
Beneficial area Essex.

Gepp and Sons, 58 New London Road, Chelmsford CM2 0PA
Tel. 01245 493939 **Fax** 01245 493940
Email douglas-hughesj@gepp.co.uk
Correspondent J P Douglas-Hughes
Trustees *Richard Wenley; Julien Courtauld; Michael Dyer; Raymond Knappett; Revd Duncan Green; David Robson; Julia Denison-Smith; Claire Coltwell; Michael Biegel.*
CC Number 225768
Information available Accounts were on file at the Charity Commission.

The Essex Youth Trust comprises four charities administered under a scheme dated 24 February 1993. The four charities are Essex Home School for Boys, The Charity of George Stacey Gibson, The Charity of George Cleveley

and The Charity of Adelia Joyce Snelgrove.

The trust's objectives are the advancement of education for people under the age of 25 who are in need of assistance. According to the annual report and accounts, preference is given to those who are in need owing to 'being temporarily or permanently deprived of normal parental care or who are otherwise disadvantaged'.

The trustees favour organisations which develop young people's physical, mental and spiritual capacities through active participation in sports and indoor and outdoor activities. As a result they are particularly supportive of youth clubs and other organisations which provide facilities for young people to take active part in an assortment of activities as well as single activity organisations.

In 2007/08 the trust had assets of £7.9 million and an income of £490,000. Grants paid to 53 organisations in the year totalled £385,000.

Beneficiaries included: Cirdan Sailing Trust (£50,000 in two grants); Essex Association of Boys Clubs (£49,000 in four grants); Havering Crossroads (£10,000); Christian Adventure Trust (£6,000); Voice for the Child in Care and Depaul Trust (£5,000 each); Listening Books (£4,500); Whizzkids (£3,300); Dream Holidays and Strongbones Children's Charitable Trust (£1,000 each).

Exclusions No grants to individuals.

Applications On a form available from the correspondent. The trustees meet on a quarterly basis.

The Estelle Trust

Overseas aid

£69,000 (2007/08)
Beneficial area UK and Zambia.

Fisher Phillips, 170 Finchley Road, London NW3 6BP
Tel. 020 7483 6100
Correspondent Ged Ornstein, Trustee
Trustees *N A E Farrow; G R Ornstein; Mrs K-M Britain; Mrs S Farrow; D Wise.*
CC Number 1101299
Information available Accounts were on file at the Charity Commission.

Registered in December 2003, in 2007/08 the trust had assets of £1.4 million and an income of £302,000, the majority of which came from gifts and donations (£261,000).

Grants were made to 30 organisations totalling £69,000.

Beneficiaries included: Wind pump materials in Africa (£12,000); International Rescue Society (£10,000); Hand Around the World (£7,500); Malaysia Future Leap Project (£3,500); Chisamba Orphans Training Centre (£2,000); British Red Cross Disaster Fund, Action for Blind People, Shelter and Action Aid (£1,000 each); and Help for Heroes, Prostate Research Campaign UK and Sight Savers (£500 each).

Applications In writing to the correspondent.

The Evangelical Covenants Trust

Christian evangelism

£90,000 (2007/08)
Beneficial area UK, with a preference for Devon.

Mardon, 188b Exeter Road, Exmouth EX8 3DZ
Tel. 01395 273287
Correspondent Alfred W Tarring, Trustee
Trustees *C Desmond Gahan; Alfred W Tarring; Kathleen M Tarring.*
CC Number 285224
Information available Accounts were on file at the Charity Commission, without a list of grants.

The object of this trust is to distribute funds to Christian organisations of an evangelical nature, although any charitable cause will be considered.

In 2007/08 the trust had assets of £23,000 and an income of £91,000, mostly from covenants and Gift Aid donations. A total of £90,000 was distributed in grants, which are administered on a national basis, but with the majority of donors living in Devon.

Applications The trust stressed that unsolicited applications are not considered: 'Grants are made only on the request and recommendation of donors of the trust'.

The Alan Evans Memorial Trust

Preservation and conservation

£265,000 (2007/08)
Beneficial area UK.

Coutts and Co., Trustee Department, 440 Strand, London WC2R 0QS
Correspondent The Trust Manager
Trustees *Coutts and Co.; D J Halfhead; Mrs D Moss.*
CC Number 326263
Information available Full accounts were on file at the Charity Commission.

The objects of the trust 'are to promote the permanent preservation, for the benefit of the nation, of lands and tenements (including buildings) of beauty or historic interest and as regards land, the preservation (so far as practicable) of the natural aspect, features and animal and plant life'.

In 2007/08 the trust had assets of £1.8 million and an income of £72,000, with grants given to over 150 organisations totalling £265,000.

About two-thirds of the grants made were for amounts of £2,000, £1,500 or £1,000 each including those to the English Hedgerow Trust, the Landmark Trust and the Zoological Society of London (£1,000 each); St Wilfrid's Church – Leeds (£1,500); and Berkshire, Buckinghamshire and Oxfordshire Wildlife Trust and the Thatcham Charity (£2,000 each).

Other beneficiaries included: Cathedral Church of the Holy Spirit, Guildford, Surrey, the Peterborough Cathedral Development and Preservation Trust, Wells Cathedral – Somerset, Lincoln Cathedral – Lincolnshire, and the Church of Our Lord, St Mary and St Germaine – Selby Abbey (£5,000 each).

Exclusions No grants to individuals or for management or running expenses, although favourable consideration is given in respect of the purchase of land and restoration of buildings. Grants are given to registered charities only. Appeals will not be acknowledged.

Applications There is no formal application form, but appeals should be made in writing to the correspondent, stating why the funds are required, what funds have been promised from other sources (for example, English Heritage) and the amount outstanding. The trust

also told us that it would be helpful when making applications to provide a photograph of the project. Trustees normally meet four times a year, although in urgent cases decisions can be made between meetings.

The Eventhall Family Charitable Trust

General

£245,000 (2007/08)
Beneficial area Preference for north-west England.

PO Box 490, Altrincham WA14 2ZT
Correspondent The Trustees
Trustees *Julia Eventhall; David Eventhall.*
CC Number 803178
Information available Accounts were obtained from the Charity Commission website, but without a grants list.

In 2007/08 the trust had assets of £3 million and an income of £135,000, with grants totalling £245,000. A list of the beneficiaries was not available within the accounts.

In previous years other beneficiaries have included Aish Hatorah, ChildLine, Clitheroe Wolves Football Club, Community Security Trust, Greibach Memorial, Guide Dogs for the Blind, Heathlands Village, International Wildlife Coalition, JJCT, MB Foundation Charity, Only Foals and Horses Sanctuary, Red Nose Day, RNLI, Sale Ladies Society, Shelter and South Manchester Synagogue.

Exclusions No grants to students.

Applications In writing to the correspondent. Please note: previous research highlighted that the trust stated it only has a very limited amount of funds available. Telephone calls are not accepted by the trust. Trustees meet monthly to consider grants. A pre-addressed envelope is appreciated (stamp not necessary). Unsuccessful applicants will not receive a reply.

The Beryl Evetts and Robert Luff Animal Welfare Trust

Animal welfare

£136,000 (2007/08)
Beneficial area UK.

294 Earls Court Road, London SW5 9BB
Correspondent The Administrator
Trustees *Sir R Johnson; Revd M Tomlinson; Mrs J Tomlinson; R P J Price; B Nicholson; Lady Johnson; Ms G Favot; M Condon.*
CC Number 283944
Information available Full accounts were on file at the Charity Commission.

The principal objective of the trust is the funding of veterinary research and the care and welfare of animals. It appears to make substantial commitments to a few organisations over several years, whether to build up capital funds or to establish fellowships. The trust gives priority to research projects and bursaries. In practice, the trust supports the same beneficiaries each year.

In 2007/08 the trust had assets of £1.2 million with an income of £49,000 and made grants totalling £136,000.

Grants went to: Animal Welfare Trust (£65,000); Royal Veterinary College (£60,000); Mayhew Animal Home (£5,500); Blue Cross (£2,500); and Greek Animal Welfare Trust, National Equine Defence League, Battersea Dogs Home, Brooke Hospitals for Animals and World Land Trust Fund (£625 each).

Applications 'No applications, thank you.' The trust gives grants to the same beneficiaries each year and funds are often allocated two years in advance.

The Exilarch's Foundation

Jewish

£1.1 million (2007)
Beneficial area Mainly UK.

4 Carlos Place, Mayfair, London W1K 3AW
Tel. 020 7399 0850

Correspondent N E Dangoor, Trustee
Trustees *N E Dangoor; D A Dangoor; E B Dangoor; R D Dangoor; M J Dangoor.*
CC Number 275919
Information available Information was on file at the Charity Commission.

The foundation's annual report gives the following information.

The trustees have built up a designated reserve of £10 million for the specific purpose of assisting the setting up of educational and religious institutions in a future re-established Jewish community in Iraq. Once the position and security of that country has been stabilised it is anticipated that some Jews may choose to live in Iraq when they will be free to pursue their religious faith without fear of persecution and discrimination.

The funds now being specifically set aside are to be used to help rebuild synagogues and communal buildings, and to assist in providing Jewish schools in Iraq as and when the community's need arises, and when it becomes possible for Jews to again live there.

In 2007 the trust had assets of £52 million and an income of £9.1 million. Grants were made totalling £1.1 million, which were broken down as follows:

Category	Value
Education	£854,000
The arts	£125,000
Social welfare	£88,000
Individuals	£16,000
International	£1,500

Beneficiaries included: Westminster Academy (£600,000); The British Library £150,000; The Royal Albert Trust (£125,000); and ESC Educational Charity (£100,000).

Applications The trust stated that it does not respond to unsolicited applications for grants.

Extonglen Limited

Orthodox Jewish

£673,000 (2007)
Beneficial area UK.

New Burlington House, 1075 Finchley Road, London NW11 0PU
Tel. 020 8731 0777
Email ml@rowdeal.com
Correspondent The Trustees

Trustees *M Levine; Mrs C Levine; B Rapaport; I Katzenberg.*
CC Number 286230
Information available Accounts were on file at the Charity Commission.

Registered with the Charity Commission in January 1983, this trust accepts applications from representatives of Orthodox Jewish charities.

In 2007 it had assets of £14 million and an income of £1.2 million. Grants totalled £673,000 and included a major donation to Kol Halashon Education Programme (£470,000). Other listed beneficiaries were: Ahavas Chesed (£95,000); Pikuach Nefesh (£50,000); Kupath Gemach Chaim Bechesed Viznitz Trust (£40,000); British Friends of Nishmat Yisrael (£12,000); and Children's Town Charity (£3,600).

Donation under £1,000 each totalled £2,800.

Applications In writing to the correspondent.

The Fairway Trust

General

£34,000 (2007/08)
Beneficial area UK and worldwide.

The Gate House, Coombe Wood Road, Kingston-upon-Thames KT2 7JY
Correspondent Mrs J Grimstone, Trustee
Trustees *Mrs Janet Grimstone; Ms K V M Suenson-Taylor.*
CC Number 272227
Information available Accounts were on file at the Charity Commission.

The trust's accounts states it will continue support for charities engaged in the fields of education, religion and social welfare.

In 2007/08 the trust had an income, almost entirely from donations, of £36,000, most of which was given in grants. By far the largest grant was given to the Family Education Trust (£20,000).

Other beneficiaries included: Boys' and Girls' Clubs of Northern Ireland and Welsh National Opera (£2,000); Sight Savers (£1,500); Prayer Book Society (£1,300); KidsOut (£1,000); Kingston Theatre and Kingston University (£1,000 each); Grantchester PCC (£750); and Petersham Trust and ZANE (£500 each).

Exclusions No grants to medical charities.

Applications The trustees have an established list of charities which they support on a regular basis. Unsolicited applications are not therefore considered.

The Family Foundations Trust (also known as Mintz Family Foundation)

General and Jewish

£199,000 (2007/08)

Beneficial area UK.

Gerald Edelman, 25 Harley Street, London W1G 9BR

Tel. 020 7299 1400

Correspondent The Accountant to the Trustees

Trustees *R B Mintz; P G Mintz.*

CC Number 264014

Information available Information had been filed at the Charity Commission.

In 2007/08 the trust had assets of £564,000 and an income of £208,000. Grants were made to 45 organisations totalling £199,000.

Beneficiaries included: CIVITAS: Institute for the Study of Civil Society (£35,000); UK Jewish Israel Appeal (£30,000); UK Friends of AWIS (£25,000); World Jewish Relief and Community Security Trust (£10,000 each); Wellbeing of Women, Chai Cancer Care and Holocaust Education Trust (£5,000 each); Jewish Women's Aid (£3,500); the Roundhouse Trust (£3,000); National Hospital Development Foundation (£2,000); and Disability Foundation (£500).

Applications In writing to the correspondent.

Famos Foundation Trust

Jewish

£102,000 (2007/08)

Beneficial area UK and overseas.

4 Hanover Gardens, Salford M7 4FQ

Tel. 0161 740 5735

Correspondent Rabbi S M Kupetz, Trustee

Trustees *Rabbi S M Kupetz; Mrs F Kupetz.*

CC Number 271211

Information available Accounts were on file at the Charity Commission.

The trust supports a wide range of Jewish organisations, including those concerned with education and the relief of poverty. Many grants are recurrent and are of up to £5,000 each.

In 2007/08 it had assets of £1.5 million and an income of £312,000. Grants totalled £102,000, broken down into the following categories:

Category	Value
Relief of Poverty	£43,000
Education	£39,000
Places of Worship	£19,000
Medical	£1,400

Exclusions No grants to individuals.

Applications In writing to the correspondent, at any time. The trust does not accept telephone enquiries.

The Lord Faringdon Charitable Trust

Medical and general

£127,000 (2007/08)

Beneficial area UK.

The Estate Office, Buscot Park, Faringdon SN7 8BU

Tel. 01367 240786

Email estbuscot@aol.com

Correspondent J R Waters, Secretary to the Trustees

Trustees *A D A W Forbes, Chair; Hon. J H Henderson; R P Trotter.*

CC Number 1084690

Information available Accounts were on file at the Charity Commission.

This trust was formed in 2000 by the amalgamation of the Lord Faringdon first and second trusts. It supports:

- educational objectives
- hospitals and the provision of medical treatment for the sick
- purchase of antiques and artistic objects for museums and collections that have public access
- care and assistance of people who are older or infirm
- development and assistance of arts and sciences, physical recreation and drama
- research into matters of public interest
- relief of poverty
- support of matters of public interest
- maintaining and improving the Faringdon Collection.

In 2007/08 it had assets of £6.4 million, which generated an income of £186,000. Grants to 30 organisations totalled £127,000.

Beneficiaries of the largest grants were: Garsington Opera (£35,000); Faringdon Skateboard Track (£15,000); Canterbury Cathedral Development Ltd (£10,000 each).

Organisations in receipt of grants of £1,000 or more included: Faringdon Youth Centre, the James Wentworth-Stanley Memorial Fund, Oxford Playhouse Trust, Ashmolean Museum and Royal Choral Society (£5,000 each); Pembroke House Mission (£2,500); Stroke Association, Samaritans and Derma Trust (£2,000 each); and Migraine Trust, Listening Books and Prisoner's Advice Service (£1,000 each).

Exclusions No grants to individuals, just to registered charities.

Applications In writing to the correspondent.

Samuel William Farmer's Trust

Education, health and social welfare

£81,000 (2007)

Beneficial area Mainly Wiltshire.

71 High Street, Market Lavington, Devizes, Wiltshire SN10 4AG

Tel. 01380 813299

Correspondent Mrs M Linden-Fermor, Secretary

Trustees P G Fox-Andrews, Chair; Mrs J A Liddiard; W J Rendell; B J Waight; C K Brockis.

CC Number 258459

Information available Accounts were on file at the Charity Commission.

The trust was established in 1928 for: the benefit of poor people who through ill health or old age are unable to earn their own livelihood; for educational purposes; and for the benefit of hospitals, nursing and convalescent homes or other similar objects. The trustees apply a modern interpretation of these aims when assessing applications, supporting both individuals and organisations.

In 2007 the trust had assets of £2.4 million and an income of £81,000. 'Special' grants for this year totalled £75,000. An additional £6,000 was distributed in 'annual' grants to Royal Agricultural Benevolent Institution and Independent Age (£3,000 each). The sum of £400 went to individuals.

Special grants went to 50 organisations. Beneficiaries included: Devizes District Guiding Building Fund and the Community Foundation for Wiltshire and Swindon (£10,000 each); Wiltshire Air Ambulance Appeal (£7,000); Avon Wildlife Trust (£5,000); STARS Appeal and the Oundle School Mencap Holiday (£2,500 each); Fluency Trust, Helen and Douglas House Hospice, the Oundle School Foundation (£2,000); and Spinal Injuries Association, Larkrise Community Farm and National Osteoporosis Society (£1,000).

Exclusions No grants to students, or for schools and colleges, endowments, inner-city welfare or housing.

Applications In writing to the correspondent. Trustees meet half-yearly.

Farthing Trust

Christian and general

£139,000 to organisations and individuals (2007/08)

Beneficial area UK and overseas.

PO Box 277, Cambridge CB7 9DE

Correspondent The Trustees

Trustees C H Martin; Mrs E Martin; Miss J Martin; Mrs A White.

CC Number 268066

Information available Accounts were on file at the Charity Commission.

In 2007/08 the trust had assets of £3 million and an income of £118,000. Grants were made totalling £139,000, and were broken down as follows:

Category	Value
Christian Causes	£46,000
Churches	£30,000
Missionary Work	£26,000
Education	£20,000
Individuals in Need	£12,000
General Charities	£4,500
Local Grants	£1,300

Applications Applications and enquiries should be made in writing to the correspondent. Applicants, and any others requesting information, will only receive a response if a stamped, addressed envelope is enclosed. There would seem little point in applying unless a personal contact with a trustee is established.

The Fawcett Charitable Trust

Disability

£292,000 (2007/08)

Beneficial area UK with a preference for Hampshire and West Sussex.

Blake Lapthorn, Harbour Court, Compass Road, North Harbour, Portsmouth PO6 4ST

Correspondent Céline Lecomte

Trustees D J Fawcett; Mrs F P Fawcett; D W Russell.

CC Number 1013167

Information available Accounts were on file at the Charity Commission.

The trust was set up in 1991 by Derek and Frances Fawcett with an endowment of shares in their company with an initial value of £1.6 million.

According to the trust, it supports work aimed at increasing the quality of life of people with disabilities by facilitating and providing recreation opportunities. Preference is normally given to organisations and projects located in Hampshire and West Sussex.

In 2007/08 the trust had assets of £594,000, an income of £21,000 and made grants totalling £292,000 (£120,000 in the previous year).

Beneficiaries were: Chichester Harbour Trust (£75,000); RYA Sailability (£65,000); Naomi House (£50,000); Wessex Children's Hospice (£30,000); St Wilfrid's Hospice (£25,000); NSPCC (£20,000); Portsmouth Cathedral (£15,000); Sailing Academy and Jubilee Sailing Trust (£5,000 each); Bikeability (£1,000).

Exclusions Large national charities are excluded as a rule.

Applications In writing to the correspondent.

The John Feeney Charitable Bequest

Arts, heritage and open spaces

£50,000 (2007)

Beneficial area Birmingham.

Cobbetts Solicitors, One Colmore Square, Birmingham B4 6AJ

Tel. 0845 404 2404

Email martin.woodward@cobbetts.co.uk

Correspondent M J Woodward, Secretary

Trustees C R King-Farlow; D M P Lea; S J Lloyd; Mrs M F Lloyd; H B Carslake; J R L Smith; M S Darby; Mrs S R Wright.

CC Number 214486

Information available Accounts were available from the Charity Commission website.

The trust was set up in 1907 when John Feeney directed that one tenth of his residue estate be invested and the income used for the benefit of public charities in the city of Birmingham, for the promotion and cultivation of art in the city and for the acquisition and maintenance of parks, recreation grounds or open spaces in or near the city.

In 2007 the trust had assets of £1.6 million and an income of £72,000. There were 31 grants made to organisations totalling £50,000, which are broken down as follows and shown with examples of beneficiaries in each category:

Music – 10 grants totalling £20,000
Elmhurst Ballet School – Scholarship fund (£10,000); Birmingham Opera Company (£2,000); Armonico Consort and IKON Gallery (£1,000 each); and Operamus (£500).

Arts – 6 grants totalling £11,000
Memorial Arts Charity and Royal Birmingham Society of Artists (£2,000 each); Birmingham Royal Ballet (£1,000); and Artsense (£500).

General – 9 grants totalling £11,000
Birmingham Settlement (£3,000); Public Catalogue Foundation (£2,000); Lighthouse Group (£1,000); and Carrs Lane Counselling Centre Limited (£500).

Medical – 4 grants totalling £5,000
Birmingham Centre for Arts Therapies (£2,000); and Cerebral Palsy Midlands (£500).

Heritage and open spaces – 2 grants totalling £4,000
Warley Woods Community Trust (£3,000); and the Pen Room Museum and Learning Centre (£1,000).

Exclusions Applications will not be accepted: from, or on behalf of, individuals; which do not directly benefit the Birmingham area or Birmingham charitable organisations; which could be considered as political or denominational.

Additionally, applications from large national charities, even with a Birmingham base, are unlikely to succeed.

Applications Application forms are now available from the trust's website. When the form is completed please post or email it with a supporting letter and other documents to the correspondent.

The A M Fenton Trust

General
£132,000 (2007)
Beneficial area UK, preference for North Yorkshire, and overseas.

14 Beech Grove, Harrogate HG2 0EX
Tel. 01423 504442
Correspondent J L Fenton, Trustee
Trustees *J L Fenton; C M Fenton.*
CC Number 270353
Information available Accounts were obtained from the Charity Commission website.

The trust was created by Alexander Miller Fenton in 1975. After his death in 1977, the residue of his estate was transferred to the trust which was established for general charitable purposes.

In 2007 the trust had assets of £4.4 million and an income of £156,000. Grants to 78 organisations totalled £132,000.

Beneficiaries of the two largest grants were: Yorkshire County Cricket Club Charitable Youth Trust (£20,000); and Hipperholme Grammar School (£10,000).

Grants of £1,000 or more included those to: Dewsbury League of Friendship (£7,500); Yorkshire Dales Sailing Home (£5,000); Kenmore Leonard Cheshire Homes and St John of Jerusalem Eye Hospital (£2,500 each) Deaf Way, Disability Action Yorkshire, Ghurkha Welfare Trust and NSPCC (£2,000 each); Marie Curie Cancer Care and National Childrens Home (£1,500); and National Animal Welfare Trust, Crimestoppers Trust and Arthritis Research Campaign (£1,000 each).

Beneficiaries of smaller grants included: Association of WRENS, British Heart Foundation, Dyslexia Action, Safe Anchor Trust, Society for Abandoned Animals and War Memorials Trust.

Exclusions The trust is unlikely to support local appeals, unless they are close to where the trust is based.

Applications In writing to the correspondent.

Elizabeth Hardie Ferguson Charitable Trust Fund

Children, medical research, health and hospices
About £300,000
Beneficial area UK, with some interest in Scotland.

c/o 27 Peregrine Crescent, Droylsden, Manchester M43 7TA
Correspondent The Trustees
Trustees *Sir Alex Ferguson; Cathy Ferguson; Huw Roberts; Ted Way; Les Dalgarno; Paul Hardman; Jason Ferguson.*
SC Number SC026240
Information available Despite making a written request for the accounts of this trust (and including a stamped, addressed envelope), these were not provided. The following entry is based, therefore, on information filed with the Office of the Scottish Charity Regulator.

This trust was created by Sir Alex Ferguson in 1998 in memory of his mother. It supports a range of children's and medical charities. Grants range from £250 to £10,000 and can be recurrent. Various high-profile events have contributed to the trust's income in recent years. Grants are distributed in the areas where the income is raised.

In 2008 the trust had an income of £400,000 thus continuing the trend of it having doubled year on year since 2005. Grants totalled around £300,000.

Charities supported by the founder in his home town of Govan will continue to be supported through the trust. Recent beneficiaries have included the Govan Initiative and Harmony Row Boys' Club.

Exclusions Non-registered charities and individuals are not supported. The trust does not make grants overseas.

Applications An application form and guidelines should be requested in writing from the correspondent. The committee meets to consider grants at the end of January and July. Applications should be received by December and June respectively.

The Bluff Field Charitable Trust

General
Around £8,000 (2008)
Beneficial area UK.

8 The Little Boltons, London SW10 9LP
Tel. 020 7373 1863
Email bfct@btinternet.com
Correspondent Peter Field, Trustee
Trustees *Peter Field; Sonia Field; Stanley Salter.*
CC Number 1057992
Information available Accounts were on file at the Charity Commission.

Established in 1996, in 2008 this trust had an income of just £501 and a total expenditure of £8,100. In previous years it has received substantial income from donations and Gift Aid.

Previous beneficiaries have included Emmanuel Church Billericay, Leukaemia Research Fund, Risk Waters' World Trade Centre UK Appeal, St George's

Hospital Medical School and Wigmore Hall Trust.

Applications In writing to the correspondent.

The Doris Field Charitable Trust

General

£242,000 (2007/08)
Beneficial area UK, with a preference for Oxfordshire.

c/o Morgan Cole, Buxton Court, 3 West Way, Oxford OX2 0SZ
Tel. 01865 262183
Correspondent The Trustees
Trustees N A Harper; J Cole; Mrs W Church.
CC Number 328687
Information available Accounts were on file at the Charity Commission.

One-off and recurrent grants are given to large UK organisations and small local projects for a wide variety of causes. The trust states that it favours playgroups and local causes in Oxfordshire.

In 2007/08 the trust had assets of £7.7 million and an income of £397,000. Grants were made totalling £242,000 to 173 organisations. No grants were made to individuals in the year.

Beneficiaries of the largest grants included: Ucare (£45,000); Maintenance of Doris Field Memorial Park (£18,000); Oxford Radcliffe Hospital – Cancer Campaign (£10,000); and the Unicorn School (£5,000).

Beneficiaries of smaller grants included: Adventure Plus Limited (£3,000); Marie Curie Cancer Care, Jubilee Sailing Trust and Oxfordshire Samaritans (£2,000 each) Autism Speaks, Alzheimers Research Trust and Relate Oxfordshire (£1,000 each); and Abingdon Concert Band, British Blind Sport and Wellbeing of Women (£500 each).

Exclusions It is unlikely that grants would be made for overseas projects or to individuals for higher education.

Applications On a form available from the correspondent. Applications are considered three times a year or as and when necessary.

The Dixie Rose Findlay Charitable Trust

Children, seafarers, blindness and multiple sclerosis

£152,000 (2006/07)
Beneficial area UK.

HSBC Trust Co. (UK) Ltd, 10th Floor, Norwich House, Nelson Gate, Commercial Road, Southampton SO15 1GX
Tel. 023 8072 2231
Correspondent Samantha D'Ambrosio, Trust Manager
Trustee HSBC Trust Co. (UK) Ltd.
CC Number 251661
Information available Accounts were available at the Charity Commission.

The trust is concerned with children, seafarers, blindness, multiple sclerosis and similar conditions. In 2006/07 it had assets of £4.3 million and an income of £131,000. Grants were made to 44 organisations totalling £152,000.

Grants included those made to: Cassell Hospital, the Children's Society, Leukaemia Research, the Mission to Seafarers, Royal National Lifeboat Institution and Royal National Mission to Deep Sea Fishermen (£8,000 each); and Association of Wheelchair Children, Demand, Elizabeth Finn Care, Fighting Blindness, Motability and Treetops Hospice (£2,000 each).

Applications In writing to the correspondent.

Finnart House School Trust

Jewish children and young people in need of care and/or education

£149,000 (2007/08)
Beneficial area Worldwide.

PO Box 603, Edgware HA8 4EQ
Tel. 020 3209 6006
Email info@finnart.org
Website www.finnart.org

Correspondent Peter Shaw, Clerk
Trustees Dame Hilary Blume and David Fobel (co-Chairs); Robert Cohen; Lilian Hochhauser; Linda Paterson; Sue Leifer; Gideon Lyons; Dr Louis Marks; Mark Sebba.
CC Number 220917
Information available Accounts were available at the Charity Commission.

The trust supports the relief of children and young people who are of the Jewish faith and aged 21 and under. Bursaries and scholarships are given to Jewish secondary school pupils and university entrants who are capable of achieving, but would probably not do so because of family and economic pressures. Also supported is work concerned with people who are disaffected, disadvantaged socially and economically through illness or neglect, or in need of care and education.

In 2007/08 the trust had assets of £4.3 million, which generated an income of £178,000. Grants totalled £149,000.

The largest grants was made to Finnart Scholarship (£102,000), this included awards made during the period to 63 students for amounts of between £250 and £2,750 per annum for courses of three and four years.

Other grants went to: Jewish Free School (£12,000); King Solomon High School (£9,000); Hasmonean High School and the Club House (£3,000).

Applications By application form for organisations, which needs to be submitted together with a copy of the latest annual report and accounts.

For undergraduate students entering university there is a separate application form which has to be submitted with various supporting information.

Gerald Finzi Charitable Trust

Music

£13,000 to organisations (2007/08).
Beneficial area UK.

P O Box 137, Shaftesbury SP7 0WX
Tel. 01244 320300 **Fax** 01244 341200
Email admin@finzi.org.uk
Website www.geraldfinzi.org

Correspondent Elizabeth Pooley, Administator

Trustees *Robert Gower, Chair; Christian Alexander; Andrew Burn; Jean Finzi; Nigel Finzi; Jeremy Dale Roberts; Paul Spicer.*

CC Number 313047

Information available Full accounts were on file at the Charity Commission.

The trustees aim to reflect the ambitions and philosophy of the composer Gerald Finzi (1901–56), which included the general promotion of twentieth-century British music through assisting and promoting festivals, recordings and performances of British music. A limited number of modest grants are also offered to young musicians towards musical training.

In 2007/08 the trust had assets of £90,000 and an income of £66,000. Of a total charitable expenditure of £69,000, grants and scholarships were awarded totalling £37,000, after high support costs of £22,000.

Grants to seven organisations totalled £13,000, and were given to the following beneficiaries: National Youth Orchestra – composers course (£5,600); Bournemouth Symphony Orchestra (£3,000); Kenneth Leighton Trust (£1,600); Three Choirs Festival (£1,250); Music at Tradebigge and Ex Cathedra (£600 each); and Percy Young Scholarship (£500).

Other activities included a contribution of £16,000 in scholarships, £5,000 to individuals for the purchase of musical instruments and £3,200 towards music editing, publishing and publicity costs for the trust's projects.

Applications In writing to the correspondent.

Marc Fitch Fund

Humanities

£156,000 (2007/08)
Beneficial area UK.

PO Box 207, Chipping Norton OX7 3ZQ
Tel. 01608 811944
Email admin@marcfitchfund.org.uk
Website www.marcfitchfund.org.uk
Correspondent The Director
Trustees *A S Bell, Chair; Prof. D M Palliser; Prof. J Blair; Dr H Forde; A Murison; L Allason-Jones; Prof. D Hey.*
CC Number 313303

Information available Accounts were on file at the Charity Commission.

The trust makes grants to organisations and individuals for publication and research in archaeology, historical geography, history of art and architecture, heraldry, genealogy, use and preservation of archives, conservation of artefacts and other antiquarian, archaeological and historical studies. The primary focus of the fund is the local and regional history of the British Isles.

Grants range from relatively minor amounts to more substantial special project grants which may be paid over more than one year. In many cases, the awards enable work to be undertaken, or the results published either in print or online form, which would not otherwise be achieved.

In 2007/08 the trust had assets of £4.5 million and an income of £246,000. Grants to 24 organisations totalled £156,000, whilst £49,000 was given in research grants to individuals.

The largest grants were given to Victoria County History (£33,000); Bodleian Library (£28,000); Newcastle University (£17,000); and the Wallace Collection and Public Catalogue Foundation (£15,000 each).

Smaller grants were given to Berkshire Records Society (£10,000); Calendar of Papal Registers (£9,000); Henley Archaeological and Historical Group (£5,000); Royal Irish Academy (£3,000); Royal Albert Memorial Museum Exeter (£2,500); Ashmolean Museum (£2,000); National Museums Liverpool (£1,500); Watts Gallery (£1,250); the Trimontium Trust (£1,000); and Devonshire Association for Advancement of Science, Literature and Arts (£600).

Exclusions No grants are given towards foreign travel or for research outside the British Isles, unless the circumstances are very exceptional; no awards are made in connection with vocational or higher education courses or to people reading for higher degrees.

Applications In writing to the correspondent. The Council of Management meets twice a year, usually in April and September, to consider applications. The deadlines for receipt of completed applications and references are 1 March and 1 August.

The Fitton Trust

Social welfare and medical

£107,000 (2007/08)
Beneficial area UK.

PO Box 649, London SW3 4LA
Correspondent Mrs Rosalind Gordon-Cumming, The Secretary
Trustees *Dr R P A Rivers; D V Brand; R Brand; K J Lumsden; E M Lumsden; L P L Rivers.*
CC Number 208758

Information available Accounts were on file at the Charity Commission, but without a list of grants.

In 2007/08 the trust had assets of £1.8 million and an income of £126,000. The total amount given in 344 grants came to £107,000.

The majority of beneficiaries received £100 to £250. Only four organisations received £1,000 or more: King's Medical Research Trust (£2,100); and Young Peoples Trust for the Environment, Cancer Resource Centre and Sheffield Institute Foundation for Motor Neurone Disease (£1,000 each).

Exclusions No grants to individuals.

Applications In writing to correspondent. The trustees meet three times each year, usually in April, August and December. The trust states: 'No application considered unless accompanied by fully audited accounts. No replies will be sent to unsolicited applications whether from individuals, charities or other bodies.'

The Earl Fitzwilliam Charitable Trust

General

£91,000 (2007/08)
Beneficial area UK, with a preference for areas with historical family connections, chiefly in Cambridgeshire, Northamptonshire and Yorkshire.

Estate Office, Milton Park, Peterborough PE3 9HD
Tel. 01733 267740

Email agent@miltonestate.co.uk

Correspondent R W Dalgleish, Secretary to the Trustees

Trustees *Sir Philip Naylor-Leyland; Lady Isabella Naylor-Leyland.*

CC Number 269388

Information available Accounts were on file at the Charity Commission.

The trust tends to favour charities that benefit rural communities, especially those with a connection to Cambridgeshire, Peterborough, South Yorkshire and Malton in North Yorkshire where the Fitzwilliam family have held their landed estates for many centuries.

It was established in 1975 by the Rt Hon. Earl Fitzwilliam and has since had various capital sums and property gifted to it.

In 2007/08 it had assets of £7.2 million, an income of £218,000 and gave grants to 60 organisations totalling £91,000.

Grants tend to be given as one-off payments and range between £100 and £10,000. In this year, no grants exceeded £5,000.

Beneficiaries included: York Minster Fund, Peterborough Cathedral Trust and Liver Research Trust (£5,000 each); Ryedale In-Touch Group, Macmillan Cancer Support, Deafblind UK and Addenbrooke's Charitable Trust (£2,500 each); East Anglia's Children's Hospice, Northamptonshire Association for the Blind and Prince's Trust (£2,000 each); Helpston and Etton Community Association and Nene Valley Archaeological Trust (£1,000 each); Renewable Heritage Trust and Farm Crisis Network (£500); and Habitat for Humanity and Historic Churches Trust (£250 each).

Exclusions No grants to individuals.

Applications In writing to the correspondent. Trustees meet about every three months.

Bud Flanagan Leukaemia Fund

Leukaemia research and treatment

£11,000 (2007/08)
Beneficial area UK.

c/o Abbots, Printing House, 66 Lower Road, Harrow HA2 0DH

Website www.bflf.org.uk

Correspondent Sandra Clark, General Secretary

Trustees *S Coventry; K Kaye; A Rowden; G Till.*

CC Number 1092540

Information available Accounts were on file at the Charity Commission.

Established in 1969 from the estate of the late Bud Flanagan, the principle objects of the fund are 'the promotion of clinical research into the treatment and possible cure of leukaemia and allied diseases and the publication of the results of all such research'. The fund makes grants to hospitals and research institutions for research into the causes, diagnosis and treatment of leukaemia.

In 2007 it had assets totalling £562,000 and an income of £250,000, including £161,000 from fundraising events. Grants were made during the year totalling £11,000.

The three beneficiaries receiving grants were: The Royal Marsden Hospital (£10,000); St Christopher's Hospice (£500); and St Catherine's Hospice (£200).

Exclusions The fund does not normally make grants to welfare charities or to individuals.

Applications In writing to the correspondent.

The Rose Flatau Charitable Trust

Jewish and general

About £81,000 (2007/08)
Beneficial area UK.

5 Knott Park House, Wrens Hill, Oxshott, Leatherhead KT22 0HW

Correspondent M E G Prince, Trustee

Trustees *M E G Prince; A E Woolf; N L Woolf.*

CC Number 210492

Information available Accounts were available at the Charity Commission.

The trust supports Jewish organisations, although it also supports other organisations which particularly attract the interest of the trustees.

In 2007/08 the trust had assets of £1.7 million and an income of £50,000. Grants were made to 26 organisations totalling £81,000.

Beneficiaries included: World Jewish Relief (£10,000); Jewish Blind and

Disabled (£5,500); Multiple Sclerosis Society and Brantwoods Trust (£5,000 each); British Red Cross (£4,500); Institute of Cancer Research and the Childrens Trust (£2,500 each); Princess Alice Hospital and National Listening Library (£2,000 each); and Spinal Research (£1,000).

Exclusions No grants to individuals.

Applications The trust stated: 'Our funds are fully committed to the foreseeable future'. Speculative applications will therefore be fruitless.

The Ian Fleming Charitable Trust

Disability and medical

£48,000 to organisations
(2007/08)
Beneficial area UK.

haysmacintyre, Fairfax House, 15 Fulwood Place, London WC1V 6AY

Tel. 020 7969 5500

Email mjones@haysmacintyre.com

Correspondent A A I Fleming, Trustee

Trustees *A A I Fleming; N A M McDonald; A V W Baldwin; A H Isaacs.*

CC Number 263327

Information available Accounts were on file at the Charity Commission.

This trust's income is allocated equally between:

- UK charities actively operating for the support, relief and welfare of men, women and children who are disabled or otherwise in need of help, care and attention, and charities actively engaged in research on human diseases
- Music Education Awards under a scheme administered by the Musicians Benevolent Fund and advised by a committee of experts in the field of music.

In 2007/08 it had assets of £2 million, which generated an income of £114,000. Grants were made totalling £109,000, of which £48,000 was given in 34 grants to organisations and £61,000 in 17 music awards to individuals.

Beneficiaries included: Bowel and Cancer Research (£3,000); Arthritis Research Campaign, Dystonia Society, Royal British Legion and Gurkha Welfare Trust (£2,000 each); and British Forces

109

Foundation, Epilepsy Action, Scottish Society for Autism, Motability and Spinal Injuries Association (£1,500).

Exclusions No grants to individuals except under the music education award scheme. No grants to purely local charities.

Applications In writing to the correspondent.

The Joyce Fletcher Charitable Trust

Music and children's welfare

£71,000 (2007/08)

Beneficial area England, almost entirely the South West.

17 Westmead Gardens, Upper Weston, Bath BA1 4EZ

Tel. 01225 314355

Correspondent R A Fletcher, Trustee and Correspondent

Trustees R A Fletcher; W D R Fletcher; S C Sharp; S P Fletcher.

CC Number 297901

Information available Accounts were on file at the Charity Commission.

The policy of the trust is to support institutions and organisations that are registered charities, specialising in music in a social or therapeutic context, music and special needs, and children and young people's welfare. Other organisations which are supported outside these areas are usually known to the trustees and/or are in the South West. Grants usually range between £500 and £5,000. Occasionally more is given.

In 2007/08 the trust had assets of £2.2 million, an income of £83,000 and made grants totalling £71,000. Of the 41 organisations receiving support, 30 were based in the South West, eight were national charities, two were based in other UK regions and one was based overseas. Grants were broken down as follows:

Category	Value
Music education and performance	£31,000
Music in a social/therapeutic context	£20,000
Children and young people	£7,000
Disability and deprivation	£2,000
Organisations outside the immediate objectives	£11,000

Beneficiaries included: Live Music Now! (£5,500); Welsh National Opera (£4,000); Bath Festivals (£3,500); Iford Arts and Wiltshire Music Centre (£3,000 each); English Speak Union and Bath Area Play Project (£2,000 each); Project Trust and Hope and Homes for Children (£1,000 each); and Supporting Disabled in Need (£600).

Exclusions Grants to individuals and students are exceptionally rare; applications are not sought. No support for areas which are the responsibility of the local authority. No support is given to purely professional music/arts promotions. No support for purely medical research charities.

Applications In writing to the correspondent before 1 November each year. There are no application forms. Letters should include the purpose for the grant, an indication of the history and viability of the organisation and a summary of accounts. Preliminary telephone calls are accepted. Acknowledgements are only given if the application is being considered or if a stamped, addressed envelope is sent.

Florence's Charitable Trust

Education, welfare, sick and infirm and general

£99,000 to organisations (2007/08)

Beneficial area UK, with a preference for Rossendale in Lancashire.

E Suttons and Sons, PO Box 2, Riverside, Bacup OL13 0DT

Correspondent The Secretary to the Trustees

Trustees C C Harrison; A Connearn; G D Low; J Mellows; R D Uttley; K Duffy; S Holding.

CC Number 265754

Information available Accounts were on file at the Charity Commission.

The trust was formed, amongst other things, to:

- establish, maintain and support places of education and to give scholarships and other awards to encourage proficiency in education

- establish, maintain and support places providing relief for sickness and infirmity, and for older people
- relieve poverty of any person employed or formerly employed in the shoe trade
- provide general charitable public benefits.

In 2007/08 the trust had assets of £1.1 million and an income of £60,000. Grants to 89 organisations totalled £99,000, broken down as follows:

Category	No. of grants	Amount
Educational support	39	£29,000
General charitable purposes	35	£60,000
Relief for sickness and infirmity	12	£11,000

Beneficiaries included:

Educational support
Grants ranging from £150 to £1,000 were distributed to 41 local primary schools and playgroups, totalling £29,000.

General charitable purposes
Pioneer Community Club (£28,000); Whitworth Water Ski (£6,000); Bacup Family Centre (£5,000); Rossendale United Junior Football Club (£2,500); Rossendale Search and Rescue (£1,000); All Black Netball Fund (£500); and Sport Relief (£100).

Sickness and infirmity
North West Air Ambulance (£5,000); British Heart Foundation and Heart of Lancashire appeal (£1,000 each); Rochdale Special Needs (£750); Macmillan Cancer Support (£500); Children with AIDS and SENSE (£250 each); and Tenovus (£100).

Exclusions No grants to individuals educational fees, exchange visits or gap year activities.

Applications In writing only to the correspondent (no telephone calls please). To save on administration costs, unsuccessful applications will not be acknowledged even if a stamped, addressed envelope is provided.

The Florian Charitable Trust

General

£27,000 (2007/08)

Beneficial area UK.

Thomas Eggar LLP, The Corn Exchange, Baffins Lane, Chichester PO19 1GE

Correspondent R M G Thornely, Trustee

Trustees *V J Treasure; G A Treasure; R M G Thornely.*

CC Number 1043523

Information available Accounts were on file at the Charity Commission.

The 2005/06 annual report stated that:

The trustees meet bi-annually and are prepared to look at all applications received during the six months prior to the meeting. Particular emphasis has been placed on funding specific projects, and where possible supporting those charities geographically local to one or more of the trustees, so there can be personal contact between a trustee and the charity benefited. The majority, but by no means all, of the donations have supported medical and allied charities, with a particular focus on those helping disabled children.

In 2007/08 the trust had assets of £1.3 million and an income of £54,000. Grants totalled £27,000.

Grants of £3,000 were awarded to nine organisations: the Addenbrooke's Charitable Trust, Alzheimers Research Trust, Arthritis Research Campaign, BIME, the Brain Research Trust, Deafness Research Trust, Epilepsy Research UK, the Migraine Trust, Meningitis Research Campaign and the Multiple Sclerosis Society.

Applications In writing to the correspondent.

The Flow Foundation

Welfare, education, environment and medical

£98,000 (2007/08)
Beneficial area UK.

22 Old Bond Street, London W1S 4PY
Tel. 020 7499 9099
Correspondent Mrs Nita Sowerbutts, Trustee
Trustees *Mrs N Shashou; Mrs Nina Sowerbutts; H Woolf; Mrs J Woolf.*
CC Number 328274
Information available Full accounts were on file at the Charity Commission.

In 2007/08 it had an income of £20,000 and a total expenditure of £98,000.

Previous beneficiaries have included After Adoption, Brain Research Trust, British Friends of Haifa University, British ORT, Chicken Shed Theatre

Company, Honey Pot Charity, International Centre for Child Studies, Jewish Care, Norwood, Royal Pharmaceutical Society, Tate Gallery Foundation, Toynbee Hall Foundation, Unite for the Future, Variety Club Children's Charity, Weizmann Institute Foundation and West London Synagogue.

Applications In writing to the correspondent on one sheet of paper only.

The Gerald Fogel Charitable Trust

Jewish and general

£60,000 (2007/08)
Beneficial area UK.

Morley and Scott, Lynton House, 7–12 Tavistock Square, London WC1H 9LT
Correspondent J Clay, Accountant
Trustees *J G Fogel; B Fogel; S Fogel; D Fogel.*
CC Number 1004451
Information available Accounts were on file at the Charity Commission.

The trust stated in its annual report that its policy is 'to make a wide spread of grants', however mainly Jewish charities are supported in practice.

In 2007/08 the trust had assets of £908,000 and an income of £84,000, including £30,000 from donations. Grants totalled £60,000.

During the year 23 organisations received support of £1,000 or more, including: Chai Cancer Care (£12,000); Jewish Care (£10,000); Jewish Child's Day (£6,000); Nightingale House and Yad Vashem Foundation UK (£2,500 each); Alzheimers Society (£2,000); United Jewish Israel Appeal, London Jewish Cultural Centre and Oxfam (£1,000 each).

Small grants below £1,000 each totalled £4,900.

Exclusions No grants to individuals or non-registered charities.

Applications In writing to the correspondent.

The Follett Trust

Welfare, education and arts

£111,000 to organisations (2008/09)
Beneficial area UK and overseas.

17 Chescombe Road, Yatton, North Somerset BS49 4EE
Correspondent Brian Mitchell, Trustee
Trustees *Brian Mitchell; Ken Follett; Barbara Follett.*
CC Number 328638
Information available Accounts were on file at the Charity Commission.

The trust's policy is to: give financial assistance to organisations in the field of education and individual students in higher education including theatre; support organisations concerned with disability and health; support trusts involved with writers and publishing; respond to world crisis appeals for help.

In 2008/09 the trust had an income of £123,000. Grants totalled £140,000, of which £111,000 was given to organisations.

Grants of £1,000 or more were given to 26 organisations, with beneficiaries including: Canon Collins Trust (£21,000); Stevenage Citizens Advice Bureau (£14,000); Charities Aid Foundation, Dyslexia Action and Impilo Place of Safety (£10,000 each); Stevenage Community Trust (£7,000); National Campaign For The Arts (£5,000); MacMillan Cancer Relief (£3,400); Bedwell Community Centre (£3,000); Relate North Hertfordshire (£2,100); Stevenage Women's Resource Centre (£2,000); Stevenage Credit Union and International Medical Corps (£1,500 each); and Deafness Research, Tradecraft Exchange and One World Action (£1,000 each).

Grants of less than £1,000 totalled £7,200.

Applications The trust states, 'A high proportion of donees come to the attention of the trustees through personal knowledge and contact rather than by written application. Where the trustees find it impossible to make a donation they rarely respond to the applicant unless a stamped addressed envelope is provided'.

The Football Association National Sports Centre Trust

Play areas and community sports facilities

£42,000 (2007)

Beneficial area UK.

25 Soho Square, London W1D 4FA

Tel. 020 7745 4589 **Fax** 020 7745 5589

Email mike.appleby@thefa.com

Correspondent Mike Appleby, Secretary to the Trustees

Trustees *William T Annable; Raymond G Berridge; Barry W Bright; Geoff Thompson; Jack Perks.*

CC Number 265132

Information available Accounts were on file at the Charity Commission.

The trust supports the provision, maintenance and improvement of facilities for use in recreational and leisure activities. Grants are made to county football associations, football clubs and other sports associations.

In 2007, the trust had assets of £4.9 million and an income of £255,000. Grants totalled £42,000, however no grants were made in the previous financial year (2006). No further information was given regarding the beneficiaries or the size of grant they received.

In October 2008, the secretary of the trust clarified its current activities. A small grant aid scheme was introduced to assist clubs at the lower end of the FA's National League System. The maximum grant available was £10,000, which was designed to assist clubs seeking funding from other funding agencies such as the Football Foundation. The trustees allowed £500,000 for this project, which has now been fully allocated.

The trustees will however continue to consider applications from organisations for assistance towards the cost of community based projects.

Applications In writing to the correspondent.

The Forbes Charitable Foundation

Adults with learning disabilities

£38,000 (2007/08)

Beneficial area UK.

9 Weir Road, Kibworth, Leicestershire LE8 0LQ

Correspondent The Secretary to the Trustees

Trustees *Col. R G Wilkes, Chair; Major Gen. R L S Green; I Johnson; J C V Lang; C G Packham; N J Townsend; J M Waite; R Warburton.*

CC Number 326476

Information available Accounts were on file at the Charity Commission.

The trust supports charities involved with the care of adults with learning difficulties. It prefers to support capital rather than revenue projects.

In 2007/08 it had assets of £2.4 million, which generated an income of £90,000. Grants to 19 organisations totalled £38,000.

Beneficiaries included: Orchard Trust and L'Arche – Inverness (£5,000 each); Scope and Acorn Services – North Yorkshire (£2,500 each); Brain and Spinal Injuries Centre and the Fircroft Trust (£2,000 each); Break and the Norman Laud Association (£1,500 each); the Mayfield Trust (£1,250); Merseyside Tuesday and Thursday Clubs and Peter le Marchant Trust (£1,000 each); Cornerstone Community Care (£500); and Scope (£250).

Applications In writing to the correspondent. Applications are considered in June and November.

Forbesville Limited

Jewish and education

£38,000 (2007)

Beneficial area UK and overseas.

Holborn House, 219 Golders Green Road, London NW11 9DD

Tel. 020 8209 0355

Correspondent M Berger, Chair

Trustees *M Berger, Chair; Mrs J S Kritzler; D B Kritzler.*

CC Number 269898

Information available Brief information for this trust was available at the Charity Commission.

The trust makes grants to Orthodox Jewish organisations, educational and charitable institutions.

In 2007 the trust had an income of £20,000 and total expenditure of £38,000. Unfortunately no grants list was available for this period.

Applications In writing to the correspondent.

The Forces Trust

Military charities

£41,000 (2007/08)

Beneficial area UK.

c/o Hunters, 9 New Square, Lincoln's Inn, London WC2A 3QN

Correspondent Col. A F Niekirk, Trustee

Trustees *Col. A F Niekirk; Capt. A P C Niekirk; Lieu. Col. W D Niekirk; Brig. R E Nugee; B E V Bowater.*

CC Number 211529

Information available Accounts were on file at the Charity Commission.

The trust can only support military charities or institutions. The trustees prefer to support service charities that assist people rather than support buildings or property.

In 2007/08 it had assets of £1.1 million, which generated an income of £52,000. Grants totalling £41,000 were made to ten organisations.

Beneficiaries were: British Limbless Ex-Service Men's Association (£16,000); St David's Nursing Home (£8,000); League of Remembrance (£5,000); Erskine Hospital and Sir Oswald Stoll Foundation (£4,000 each); Scottish National Institution for the War Blinded (£2,000); and SSAFA Forces Help Cumbria and Gordon Highlanders London Association Benevolent Fund (£1,000 each).

Exclusions No grants to any non-naval or military charities, individuals, scholarships or education generally.

Applications In writing to the correspondent at any time, preferably on one side of A4.

Ford Britain Trust

Community service, education, environment, disability, schools, special needs education and young people

£137,000 (2007/08)

Beneficial area Local to the areas in close proximity to Ford Motor Company Limited's locations in the UK. These are Essex, East London, South Wales, Southampton, Daventry and Leamington Spa.

Room 1/445, Ford Motor Company Limited, Eagle Way, Brentwood, Essex CM13 3BW

Tel. 01277 252551

Email fbtrust@ford.com

Website www.ford.co.uk/fbtrust

Correspondent Andy Taylor

Trustees R M Blenkinsop; M J Brophy; M J Callaghan; J Calvert-Lee; A Dalvi; D S Russell; J L Tottingham.

CC Number 269410

Information available Accounts were available from the Charity Commission.

Registered with the Commission in 1975, the trust supports organisations in the areas where the Ford Motor Company is based, with special attention paid to projects that concern the trust's main objectives: education, the environment, children, disabilities, education of young people and projects that benefit the local communities that Ford operates in. When this is a town it will support the surrounding area, i.e. where the employees are likely to be living. There is also a preference for charities where a member of staff is involved. Grants are typically one-off, provided for specific capital projects or parts of a project, and fall into two categories:

- Small grants – for amounts up to £250, available four times a year
- Large grants – for amounts over £250 and usually up to £3,000, available twice a year

Applications for new Ford vehicles are considered when two-thirds of the purchase price is available from other sources. These grants are not usually more than £2,000, but registered charities may be able to arrange a reduction from the recommended retail price. Grants are not available for second-hand vehicles.

In 2007/08 the trust had assets of £187,000 and an income of £172,000, of which £120,000 came from a donation from the Ford Employee Benefit Trust. Grants totalled £137,000, broken down as follows:

Category	Value	No.
Community service	£44,000	64
Young people	£41,000	47
Schools/education	£25,000	21
Disability	£22,000	24
Special needs education	£4,000	4

Significant grants to individual charities were: Thames Gateway Youth Football Programme and London Borough of Barking and Dagenham (£20,000 each); and West Billericay Community Association (£5,000).

Grants of £3,000 each or less totalled £112,000.

Exclusions National charities are assisted rarely and then only when the purpose of their application has specific benefit to communities located in close proximity to Ford locations.

Applications in respect of sponsorship, individuals, research, overseas projects, travel, religious or political projects are not eligible. Applications for core funding and/or salaries, revenue expenses, and major building projects are rarely considered.

Applications In writing to the correspondent. Applications should include the following:

- purpose of the project
- whom it is intended to help and how
- why the project is important and necessary (how things were done before)
- how the project is to be carried out
- the project's proposed starting time and time of completion
- total cost of the project
- how much has been raised so far, sources of funding obtained and expected
- examples of fundraising activities by the organisation for the project
- the amount being asked for.

A brief résumé of the background of the charity is appreciated. Where appropriate copies of accounts should be provided.

Trustees meet in June and November each year. Applications are considered in order of receipt and it may take several months before an application is considered. The trust receives many more applications than it can help.

The Oliver Ford Charitable Trust

Housing and mental disability

£71,000 (2007/08)

Beneficial area UK.

Macfarlanes, 10 Norwich Street, London EC4A 1BD

Tel. 020 7831 9222

Correspondent Matthew Pintus

Trustees Derek Hayes; Lady Wakeham; Martin Levy.

CC Number 1026551

Information available Accounts were available at the Charity Commission.

The objects of the trust are to educate the public and advance knowledge of the history and techniques of interior decoration, the designs of fabric and other decorative materials and landscape gardening including Oliver Ford's own work. Income and capital not used for these purposes is used for the Anthroposophical Society of Great Britain, Camphill Village Trust, Norwood or any other charity providing housing, educational or training facilities for children, young persons or adults who have learning disabilities or learning difficulties.

In 2007/08 the trust had assets of £2.5 million and an income of £99,000. Grants to 14 organisations totalled £71,000.

Beneficiaries included: the Victoria and Albert Museum (£17,000); Mencap (£7,000); Fircroft Trust (£6,300); Fortune Centre of Riding Therapy, Norman Laud Association and Orchard Vale Trust (£5,000 each); Spadwork and Cornerstone Community Care (£3,000 each); Robert Owen Foundation (£2,300); Rose Road Association (£2,000); and the Furniture and History Society (£1,800).

Applications In writing to the correspondent. Trustees meet in March and October.

Fordeve Ltd

Jewish and general

£278,000 (2007/08)

Beneficial area UK.

c/o Gerald Kreditor & Co, Hallswelle House, 1 Hallswelle Road, London NW11 0DH

Tel. 020 8209 1535

Correspondent J Kon, Trustee

Trustees *J Kon; Mrs H Kon.*

CC Number 1011612

Information available Accounts were on file at the Charity Commission.

The trust makes grants to Jewish causes and for the relief of need.

In 2007/08, the trust had assets of £735,000, an income of £435,000 and gave grants totalling £278,000. No further information about the beneficiaries or the grants they received was available from this year's accounts.

Previous beneficiaries have included: the Gertner Charitable Trust; Lubavitch Foundation; the Yom Tov Assistance Fund; the Society of Friends of the Torah; Lolev Charitable Trust; Beth Jacob Grammar School for Girls.

Applications In writing to the correspondent.

The Forest Hill Charitable Trust

Mainly Christian causes and relief work

£196,000 (2007)

Beneficial area UK and overseas.

104 Summercourt Way, Brixham TQ5 0RB

Tel. 01803 852857

Email horacepile@tiscali.co.uk

Correspondent Mrs P J Pile, Secretary to the Trustees

Trustees *H F Pile, Chair; Mrs P J Pile; R S Pile; Mrs M S Tapper; M Thomas.*

CC Number 1050862

Information available Accounts were on file at the Charity Commission.

This trust gives grants mainly to Christian causes and for relief work (80%), although support is given to agencies helping people who are disabled, in need or sick.

In 2007 the trust had assets of £3.4 million and an income of £194,000. Grants to about 120 organisations were made totalling £196,000.

Beneficiaries included: LINX – two individual grants (£21,000); Great Parks Chapel – four individual grants (£12,000); Viz-a-Viz – two individual grants (£6,000); Leprosy Mission, Prison Fellowship and Life for the World (£2,000 each); Bible Network (£1,500); and Cambodian Trust, United Mission Nepal, Karen Hill Tribes Trust, World Villages Child and Farm Crisis Network (£1,000 each).

Applications The trustees have previously stated that their aim was to maintain regular and consistent support to the charities they are currently supporting. New requests for funding are therefore very unlikely to succeed.

The Anna Rosa Forster Charitable Trust

Medical research, animal welfare and famine relief

£82,000 (2007/08)

Beneficial area Worldwide.

Floor E, Milburn House, Dean Street, Newcastle upon Tyne NE1 1LF

Tel. 0191 230 1819

Correspondent R Napier, Trustee

Trustees *R Napier; A Morgan.*

CC Number 1090028

Information available Accounts were on file at the Charity Commission.

Registered with the Charity Commission in January 2002, in 2007/08 the trust had assets of £2.1 million and an income of £86,000. Grants totalled £82,000 with a third of funds going in each of the following areas.

Animal welfare – 8 grants
Grants of £3,400 each to the Cats Protection League, the Dogs Trust, the Donkey Sanctuary, PDSA, RSPCA, Animal Health Trust, International League for the Protection of Horses and World Society for the Protection of Animals.

Famine Relief – 8 grants
Grants of £3,400 each to British Red Cross, Farm Africa, Oxfam, Feed the Children, CARE International UK, Concern Worldwide (UK) Action Aid and World Medical Fund.

Medical research – 10 grants
Grants of £2,700 each included those to Alzheimer's Research Trust, Cancer Research UK, Cystic Fibrosis Trust, Prostate Research Campaign UK, British Cancer Research Trust, British Heart Foundation, International Spinal Research Trust, Arthritis Research Trust, Brain Research Trust and Motor Neurone Disease Association.

Applications In writing to the correspondent.

The Forte Charitable Trust

Roman Catholic, Alzheimer's disease and senile dementia

£120,000 a year

Beneficial area UK and overseas.

Lowndes House, Lowndes Place, London SW1X 8DB

Tel. 020 7235 6244

Email hmcconville@roccofortehotels.com

Correspondent Mrs Heather McConville

Trustees *Hon. Sir Rocco Forte; Hon. Mrs Olga Polizzi di Sorrentino; G F L Proctor; Lowndes Trustees Ltd.*

CC Number 326038

Information available Information was provided by the trust.

The trust has narrowed its areas of work down to those in relation to the Roman Catholic faith, Alzheimer's disease and senile dementia.

The trust stated that grants total about £120,000 a year.

Applications In writing to the correspondent.

Lord Forte Foundation

Hospitality

£60,000 (2007/08)
Beneficial area UK.

Lowndes House, Lowndes Place, Belgrave Square, London SW1X 8DB

Tel. 020 7235 6244

Email hmcconville@roccofortecollection. com

Correspondent Mrs Heather McConville

Trustees *Lord Janner, Chair; Hon Sir Rocco Forte; Hon. Mrs Olga Polizzi di Sorrentino; Viscount Montgomery of Alamein; G F L Proctor; T N Scade.*

CC Number 298100

Information available Accounts were on file at the Charity Commission.

This trust was set up in 1987, 'to encourage excellence in the fields of hospitality encompassing the hotel, catering, travel and tourism industries'. It does this by giving grants directly to educational establishments which provide training courses or carry out research projects in these fields.

In 2007/08 it had assets of £2 million, which generated an income of £68,000. Grants were made totalling £60,000 to six educational institutions providing training courses in the hospitality industry.

Beneficiaries were: Training for Life – the Hoxton Apprentice (£30,000); Thames Valley University (£10,000); and Leeds Thomas Danby, Llandrillo College, the Bournemouth and Poole College Foundation and Westminster Kingsway College (£5,000 each).

Applications In writing to the correspondent.

Foundation for Management Education

Management studies

£706,000 (2007/08)
Beneficial area UK.

TBAC Business Centre, Avenue Four, Station Lane, Witney OX28 4BN
Tel. 01993 848722

Email fme@lineone.net
Website www.management-education. org.uk
Correspondent The Director
Trustees *Geoffrey Armstrong; Valerie Boakes; Tim Boswell; Mary Chapman; Dr Charles Constable; Paula Graham; Prof. A G Hopwood; J L James; Robert Lintott; G C Olcott; David Thomas; C G C Vyvyan; Lord J E Tomlinson of Walsall; James Watson; John Wybrew.*

CC Number 313388

Information available Accounts were on file at the Charity Commission.

In 2007/08 the trust had an income of £390,000. Charitable expenditure amounted to £706,000, with grant beneficiaries including the universities of Surrey, Bath, Cambridge and Nottingham, and the London School of Economics.

Exclusions Individual applications for further studies cannot be supported.

Applications Unsolicited applications are not encouraged.

The Fowler, Smith and Jones Charitable Trust

Social welfare

£483,000 (2007/08)
Beneficial area Essex.

c/o Tolhurst Fisher, Marlborough House, Victoria Road South, Chelmsford CM1 1LN

Tel. 01245 216123

Email amason@tolhurstfisher.com

Correspondent Mrs A Mason, Secretary

Trustees *P J Tolhurst, Chair; W J Tolhurst; E C Watson.*

CC Number 259917

Information available Full accounts were on file at the Charity Commission.

The trust supports a few nominated charities on an annual basis, with the balance given to local charities in Essex. The trust concentrates its giving as follows:

- charities nominated by the original benefactors
- overseas projects
- church projects
- other Essex-related projects.

There is a fundamental criterion that any funding made must be matched by other funding or contributions.

In 2007/08 the trust had assets of £11.2 million, which generated an income of £582,000. There were 136 grants made totalling £483,000, which were broken down as follows:

Category	Value
Major Building	£165,000
Community	£79,000
Young people	£79,000
Medical/health	£68,000
Miscellaneous and 'top-up' grants	£68,000
Churches	£20,000
Overseas	£2,500
Arts	£2,000

Major Building – 3 grants totalling £165,000
PARC (£70,000); First Site (£65,000); and Brentwood Theatre (£25,000).

Community – 36 grants totalling £79,000
Age Concern – Southend (£4,000); Basildon Community Resource Centre, Family Support Clacton and Independent Age (£3,000 each); CAB Southend (£2,500); Trust Links and Cornerstone Trust (£2,000 each); and Copford Cricket Club and Essex Respite Association (£1,000 each).

Young people – 33 grants totalling £79,000
Special Needs and Parents Charity (£10,000); Depaul Trust (£5,000); Essex Association of Boys' Clubs (£4,000); Barnardo's, Maldon Carers Centre and Daycare Trust (£3,000 each); Positive Solutions Media and Express Link Up (£2,000 each); and Viz-a-Viz (£1,000).

Medical and health – 24 grants totalling £68,000
Marie Curie Cancer Care (£6,000); Alzheimers Society, Brainwave Essex and St Luke's Hospice (£5,000 each); Maldon MIND and Hamelin Trust (£3,000 each); Meningitis Trust, Aspire and British Lung Foundation (£2,000 each); Lupus UK and Motor Neurone Disease (£1,500); and Everyman (£1,000).

Miscellaneous and 'top-up' – 28 grants totalling £68,000
Anchor Staying Put, St Giles Trust and Scope (£5,000 each); Mencap and Volunteer Centre Uttlesford (£3,000 each); Maldon District CVS and Soundabout (£2,000 each); Relate and U Can Do IT (£1,500 each); and RDA Sadlers Farm (£1,000).

Churches – 10 grants totalling £20,000
Trinity Methodist Church and St Andrews Church (£3,000 each); St Margaret's Church and URC Witham (£2,000 each); and St Katherine's – Little Bardfield (£1,000).

Arts – 1 grant of £2,000
Pro Corda (£2,000).

Overseas – 1 grant of £2,500
Salesian Convent Welfare Centre (£2,500).

Exclusions No grants to individuals.

Applications In writing to the correspondent.

The Isaac and Freda Frankel Memorial Charitable Trust

Jewish and general

£134,000 (2007/08)

Beneficial area UK and overseas, particularly Israel.

33 Welbeck Street, London W1G 8EJ

Tel. 020 7872 0023

Correspondent M D Frankel, Secretary

Trustees *M D Frankel; G Frankel; J Steinhaus; J Silkin.*

CC Number 1003732

Information available Accounts were on file at the Charity Commission, without a list of grants.

The Isaac and Freda Frankel Memorial Charitable Trust was established in July 1991 by members of the Frankel family to support mainly Jewish causes.

In 2007/08 the trust had assets of £536,000 and an income of £108,000. Grants totalled £134,000. A list of beneficiaries was not included with the accounts filed at the Charity Commission.

Exclusions No grants to individuals or students, for expeditions or scholarships.

Applications In writing to the correspondent.

Sydney E Franklin Deceased's New Second Charity

Development

£36,000 (2007/08)

Beneficial area Worldwide. Priority, but not exclusively, to developing world projects.

c/o 39 Westleigh Avenue, London SW15 6RQ

Correspondent Dr R C G Franklin, Trustee

Trustees *Dr R C G Franklin; Ms N N Franklin; Ms C Holliday.*

CC Number 272047

Information available Accounts were on file at the Charity Commission.

The trust supports small charities with low overheads, focusing on developing world self-help projects, endangered species and people disadvantaged by poverty.

In 2007/08 the trust had assets of £541,000 and an income of £26,000. Grants totalled £36,000. A list of beneficiaries was unavailable from the accounts obtained from the Charity Commission.

Previous beneficiaries have included: Kerala Federation for the Blind; Water for Kids; Narwhal/Niaff; United Charities Fund; and Ashram International, Books Abroad, Children of the Andes, Kaloko Trust, Microloan Foundation, Tools for Self Reliance, Tree Aid and Window for Peace UK (£1,000 each).

Other smaller grants included those to: Forest Peoples Project (£750); African Initiatives, Lake Malawi Projects and World Medical Fund (£500 each); and Gwalior Children's Hospital (£250).

Applications Donations may only be requested by letter, including a copy of latest accounts, and these are placed before the trustees at their meeting which is normally held at the end of each year. Applications are not acknowledged.

The Jill Franklin Trust

Overseas, welfare, prisons and church restoration

£66,000 (2007/08)

Beneficial area Worldwide.

Flat 5, 17–19 Elsworthy Road, London NW3 3DS

Tel. 020 7722 4543

Email info@jill-franklin-trust.org.uk

Website www.jill-franklin-trust.org.uk

Correspondent N Franklin, Trustee

Trustees *Andrew Franklin; Norman Franklin; Sally Franklin; Sam Franklin; Tom Franklin.*

CC Number 1000175

Information available Accounts were available from the Charity Commission.

Grants are typically £500 to £1,000, and the trust has four areas in which it is soliciting grant applications:

- self-help groups, advice, training, and employment; to support people with a mental illness or learning difficulties, and their carers (parents etc.)
- respite care, and holidays (in the UK only). Grants for holidays are only given where there is a large element of respite care and only to registered charities, not to individuals
- organisations helping and supporting refugees and asylum-seekers coming to or in the UK
- the restoration (not 'improvement') of churches of architectural importance (half a page in Pevsner's *Buildings*) and occasionally to other buildings of architectural importance. The church should be open to visitors every day.

In 2007/08 it had assets of £1.6 million, an income of £78,000 and made grants totalling £66,000, broken down as follows.

Category	No.	Value	%
Church restoration	20	£12,000	17.5
Refugees	21	£11,000	16.4
Bereavement	2	£10,000	16.6
Prisoners	1	£8,800	13
Mental health and learning difficulties	16	£8,500	13.5
Respite/holidays	5	£8,000	12.2

Beneficiaries during the year included: Camden City Islington & Westminster Bereavement Services (£10,000); Prisoners Education Trust (£8,800); Marie Curie Cancer Cure (£5,600); Princess Royal Trust for Carers (£5,000); Buildings Book Trust (£3,000); Woodland Trust (£2,000); and

Powerhouse; Medical Foundation for Victims of Torture; North Somerset Crossroads Carers; and Respite Association (£1,000 each).

Exclusions Grants are not given to:

- appeals for building work
- endowment funds
- branches of a national organisations, and to the centre itself (unless it is a specific grant, probably for training in the branches)
- replace the duties of government, local authorities or the NHS
- encourage the 'contract culture', particularly where authorities are not funding the contract adequately
- religious organisations set up for welfare, education etc. of whatever religion, unless the service is open to and used by people from all denominations
- overseas projects
- heritage schemes
- animal charities
- students, nor to any individuals nor for overseas travel
- medical research.

Applications In writing to the correspondent, enclosing a copy of the latest annual report and accounts and a budget for the project. Organisations based outside the UK should provide the name, address and telephone number of a correspondent or referee in the UK.

The trust's report states that 'The trustees tend to look more favourably on an appeal which is simply and economically prepared: glossy, 'prestige' and mail sorted brochures do not impress the trustees'.

Unsolicited enquiries are not usually acknowledged. 'We have very little uncommitted cash, and so most applications are rejected, for the only reason that we have insufficient money'.

The Gordon Fraser Charitable Trust

Children, young people, environment and arts

£135,000 (2007/08)

Beneficial area UK, with a preference for Scotland.

Holmhurst, Westerton Drive, Bridge of Allan, Stirling FK9 4QL

Correspondent Mrs Margaret A Moss, Trustee

Trustees *Mrs Margaret A Moss; William F T Anderson.*

CC Number 260869

Information available Accounts were on file at the Charity Commission.

Currently the trustees are particularly interested in supporting children and young people in need, the environment and visual arts (including performance arts). Most grants are given within these categories. The trust states that 'applications from or for Scotland will receive favourable consideration, but not to the exclusion of applications from elsewhere'.

In 2007/08 the trust had assets of £2.9 million and an income of £239,000. Grants were made to 118 organisations totalling £135,000.

The trustees rarely make donations to the same charity more than once in the same year and a donation rarely exceeds £20,000 or is less than £100 although there are no minimum or maximum amounts for donations.

Beneficiaries included: Ballet West (£9,000); the MacRoberts Arts Centre (£7,000); the Aberlour Child Care Trust and Scottish Museums Council (£6,000 each); Scottish International Piano Competition (£5,500); Mull Theatre (£3,000); Kilmartin House Trust and National Library of Scotland (£2,000 each); and Paisley Festival Company, the Hebridean Trust and Sense Scotland (£1,000 each).

Exclusions No grants are made to organisations which are not recognised charities, or to individuals.

Applications In writing to the correspondent. Applications are considered in January, April, July and October. Grants towards national or international emergencies can be considered at any time. All applicants are acknowledged; a stamped, addressed envelope would, therefore, be appreciated.

The Louis and Valerie Freedman Charitable Settlement

General

£95,000 (2007/08)

Beneficial area UK, especially Burnham.

c/o Bridge House, 11 Creek Road, East Molesey KT8 9BE

Correspondent F H Hughes, Trustee

Trustees *M A G Ferrier; F H Hughes.*

CC Number 271067

Information available Accounts were on file at the Charity Commission.

The trust supports health, welfare and equine interests in which the Freedman family have a particular interest. Local education and charities for young people in Burnham are also supported.

In 2007/08 it had assets of £3.8 million, an income of £143,000 and made grants totalling £95,000.

Beneficiaries were: Burnham Health Promotion Trust (£50,000); Tavistock Aphasia Tryst, Prostate Research Campaign UK, British Heart Foundation, and Blakebrook School (£10,000 each); and Vitalise (£5,000 each).

Burnham Health Promotion Trust is a related charity, also established by Louis Freedman.

Exclusions No grants to individuals. Only registered charities are considered for support.

Applications There is no application form. Applications should be in writing to the correspondent and they will not be acknowledged. Notification of a failed application will only be given if a stamped, addressed envelope is enclosed.

The Friarsgate Trust

Health and welfare of young and older people

£72,000 (2007/08)

Beneficial area UK, with a strong preference for West Sussex, especially Chichester.

The Corn Exchange, Baffins Lane, Chichester PO19 1GE

Tel. 01243 786111 **Fax** 01243 775640

Correspondent Miss Amanda King-Jones

Trustees A C Colenutt; T J Bastow; Mrs V Higgins.

CC Number 220762

Information available Accounts were on file at the Charity Commission.

The objectives of the trust are as follows.

- To provide funds for the academic and general education of orphans and children (whether infant or adult) whose parents are in poor or reduced circumstances.
- To promote the mental, moral, physical, technical and social education of children, young persons and adults.
- To provide, equip and maintain for the purposes referred to above camping grounds, holiday camps, playing fields, club rooms or other accommodation and facilities.
- To provide for the relief and care of impotent persons including in that expression all persons suffering either temporarily or permanently from disease or disability of any kind affecting their body or mind.
- To provide for the relief of persons over the age of sixty years by the provision of maintenance, food, clothing and housing.
- To promote and support or aid any charitable institutions, purposes or projects in any way connected with the objects aforesaid or calculated to further such objects or any of them.

In 2007/08 the trust had assets of £3.1 million and an income of £106,000. Grants totalled £72,000, which were donated to 45 organisations.

Beneficiaries of the three largest grants were: West Sussex Association for Disabled People (£18,000); 12th Chichester Scout Group (£8,000); and Chichester Youth Adventure Trust (£5,200).

All other grants ranged between £500 and £2,000. Beneficiaries included: Christian Care Association, Fernhurst Youth Club and Chichester Community Transport (£2,000 each); Samaritans (£1,500); Remix Project and Impact Initiative (£1,100 each); the Dystonia Society, Independent Age and Southbourne Sea Scout Group (£1,000 each); and Farms for City Children, the National Society for Epilepsy and East Sussex Association for the Blind (£500 each).

Exclusions Local organisations outside Sussex are unlikely to be supported.

Applications In writing to the correspondent. Applicants are welcome to telephone first to check they fit the trust's criteria.

Friends of Biala Ltd

Jewish

£413,000 (2007/08)

Beneficial area UK and overseas.

c/o Sugarwhite Associates, 5 Windus Road, London N16 6UT

Correspondent The Secretary

Trustees B Z Rabinovitch; Mrs T Weinberg.

CC Number 271377

Information available Accounts were on file at the Charity Commission, but without a list of grants.

The trust supports religious education in accordance with the orthodox Jewish faith and registered welfare charities.

In 2007/08 the trust had assets of £3.2 million and an income of £426,000, mostly from donations.

Grants totalled £413,000 and were given to the following beneficiaries: Friends of Biala Israel (£227,000); Aguda Hadadit (£100,000); Yeshiva Beis Ephraim (£49,000); Gemach Ezra Hadadit (£27,000); and Freebee Foundation Limited (£10,000).

Applications In writing to the correspondent.

Friends of Boyan Trust

Orthodox Jewish

£207,000 (2007)

Beneficial area Worldwide.

23 Durley Road, London N16 5JW

Tel. 020 8809 6051

Correspondent Jacob Getter, Trustee

Trustees J Getter; M Freund; N Kuflik.

CC Number 1114498

Information available Accounts were on file at the Charity Commission.

Set up in 2006, 'the charity was formed for the advancement of the orthodox Jewish faith, orthodox Jewish religious education, and the relief of poverty in the orthodox Jewish community'; as stated in the annual report.

In 2007 the trust had income of £209,000 from donations and made grants totalling £207,000. The sum of £6,600 was carried forward at year end.

Beneficiaries included: Gomlei Chesed of Chasidei Boyan (£84,000); Mosdot Tiferet Yisroel Boyan (£31,000); Kimcha De'Pischa Boyan (£21,000); Kimcha De'Pischa Beitar Ilit (£13,000); Chevras Mo'oz Ladol (£12,000); Kolel Avrechim Boyan, Betar Ilit (£6,000); Ezer Mikoidesh Foundation (£2,000); Beis Rizhin Trust (£1,500); and Yad Vochessed (£1,000).

Applications In writing to the correspondent.

Friends of Wiznitz Limited

Jewish education

£827,000 (2007/08)

Beneficial area UK and overseas.

8 Jessam Avenue, London E5 9UD

Correspondent E Gottesfeld

Trustees H Feldman; E Kahan; R Bergman; S Feldman.

CC Number 255685

Information available Accounts were on file at the Charity Commission, without a list of grants.

This trust supports major educational projects being carried out by orthodox Jewish institutions.

In 2007/08 the trust had assets of just over £1 million and an income of £1.4 million. Grants were made totalling £827,000 divided between: education (£589,000); and relief of poverty (£237,000).

Beneficiaries listed in the accounts were: Mosdos Winitz (£280,000); Igud Mosdos Wiznitz (£209,000); Tzemach Tzadik (£35,000); LeHacahzicom V LeHachayosom (£198,000); and Kehal Ahavat Yisroel (£30,000).

Applications In writing to the correspondent.

The Frognal Trust

Older people, children, disability, blindness, ophthalmological research and environmental heritage

£75,000 (2007/08)
Beneficial area UK.

Steynings House, Summerlock Approach, Salisbury SP2 7RJ
Correspondent Donor Grants Officer
Trustees *Philippa Blake-Roberts; Jennifer Helen Fraser; P Fraser.*
CC Number 244444
Information available Accounts were on file at the Charity Commission.

The trust supports smaller charities rather than national organisations or local branches of large national charities.

In 2007/08 it had assets of £2 million, which generated an income of £80,000. Grants were made to 47 organisations totalling £75,000, which were broken down as follows:

Category	Value
Disability and blindness	£32,000
Medical research	£16,000
Children and young people	£11,000
Environmental heritage	£9,200
Older people	£7,000

Unfortunately a grants list was not available in this year's accounts.

Previous beneficiaries have included: Canniesburn Research Trust, Samantha Dickson Research Trust, Royal Liverpool and Broad Green University Hospitals, Aireborough Voluntary Services to the Elderly, Elderly Accommodation Counsel, Leeds Society for Deaf and Blind People, Action Medical Research,

Friends of the Elderly, Gloucestershire Disabled Afloat Riverboat Trust, National Rheumatoid Arthritis Society, Stubbers Adventure Centre, Wireless for the Bedridden Society, and Yorkshire Dales Millennium Project.

Exclusions The trust does not support:
- any animal charities
- the advancement of religion
- charities for the benefit of people outside the UK
- educational or research trips
- branches of national charities
- general appeals
- individuals.

Applications In writing to the correspondent. Applications should be received by February, May, August and November, for consideration at the trustees' meeting the following month.

T F C Frost Charitable Trust

Medical

£25,000 (2007/08)
Beneficial area UK and overseas.

Holmes and Co Accountants, 10 Torrington Road, Claygate, Esher KT10 0SA
Tel. 01372 465378
Correspondent John Holmes
Trustees *T A F Frost; M D Sanders; M H Miller.*
CC Number 256590
Information available Accounts were on file at the Charity Commission.

The trust supports research associates of recognised centres of excellence in ophthalmology, individuals and organisations benefiting academics, medical professionals, research workers and people with sight loss.

In 2007/08 it had assets of £2.7 million and an income of £91,000. Grants totalled £25,000.

The trust's report gives the following funding principles.

Our Founder's wish in establishing the Frost Charitable Trust, was to foster research into the prevention of blindness by supporting programmes submitted by senior trainees and by enhancing their horizons by underwriting the costs of educational or research periods of training at home or abroad at recognised centres.

Donations in this year were to: University of Southampton – Professor Andrew Lotery and University of Bristol – Chair in Experimental Ophthalmology (£10,000 each); and the Rayne Institute St Thomas' Hospital – Professor John Marshall (£5,000).

Exclusions No grants to individuals. There are no available resources for the relief of blind people or people suffering from diseases of the eye.

Applications In writing to the correspondent. Trustees meet twice a year.

Maurice Fry Charitable Trust

Medicine, health, welfare, humanities, environmental resources and international causes

£20,000 (2007/08)
Beneficial area UK and overseas.

98 Savernake Road, London NW3 2JR
Correspondent L E A Fry, Trustee
Trustees *L E A Fry; Mrs F Cooklin; Mrs L Weaks.*
CC Number 327934
Information available Accounts were on file at the Charity Commission.

The trust's main areas of interest are welfare, humanities, environmental resources and international causes, but it is not restricted to these.

In 2007/08 the trust had assets of £1.2 million and an income of £39,000. Grants to 14 organisations totalled £20,000.

Beneficiaries included: NSPCC (£2,500); Alone in London, Llanelli Dinefwr Hospice Appeal Fund and Lymphoma Association (£2,000 each); Amnesty International and The Maypole Project (£1,500 each); and Borders Forest Trust, Northumberland County Scout Council, Tree Aid and Scottish Borders Community Orchestra (£1,000 each).

Exclusions No grants to individuals.

Applications The trust states that it does not respond to unsolicited applications.

Mejer and Gertrude Miriam Frydman Foundation

Jewish and Jewish education

£33,000 (2007/08)

Beneficial area UK and overseas.

c/o Westbury Schotness and Co., 145–157 St John Street, London EC1V 4PY

Tel. 020 7253 7272

Correspondent G Frydman, Trustee

Trustees *L J Frydman; G B Frydman; D H Frydman.*

CC Number 262806

Information available Full accounts were available at the Charity Commission.

The trust supports new and established charitable projects for study and research, including scholarships, fellowships, professorial chairs, lectureships, prizes, awards and the cost of purchasing or erecting any building or land required for such projects.

In 2007/08 the foundation had assets of £85,000 and an income of £39,000. Grants were made to 18 organisations totalling £33,000.

Beneficiaries included: North West London Jewish Day School (£4,000); Jewish Care and Norwood Ravenswood (£3,500 each); Kisharon (£3,000); Chai Cancer Care (£2,000); Kesser Torah (£1,700); Friends of Yeshiva O H R Elchanan (£1,500); the Merephdi Foundation (£1,000); Institute for Higher Rabbinicial Studies (£700); and Talia Trust for Children (£500).

Exclusions No grants to individuals for scholarships or any other purpose.

Applications In writing to the correspondent.

The Fulmer Charitable Trust

Developing world and general

£422,000 (2007/08)

Beneficial area Worldwide, especially the developing world and Wiltshire.

Estate Office, Street Farm, Compton Bassett, Calne SN11 8SW

Tel. 01249 760410 **Fax** 01249 760410

Correspondent The Trustees

Trustees *J S Reis; Mrs S Reis; Mrs C Mytum; Miss E J Reis.*

CC Number 1070428

Information available Accounts were on file at the Charity Commission.

Most of the support is given in the developing world, although UK charities are also supported, especially those working in Wiltshire.

In 2007/08 the trust had assets of £8.7 million and an income of £442,000. Grants to 188 organisations totalled £422,000.

The largest donations included those to: Sight Savers (£14,000); Shelter, Sense and Save the Children (£12,000 each); the Sequal Trust and NSPCC (£9,000 each); Manna Society and Age Concern (£8,000 each); and the Brain Research Trust and Christian Aid (£7,000 each).

Other beneficiaries included: Coventry Cathedral Development Trust and World Medical Fund (£4,000 each); British Heart Foundation and Care International (£3,000 each); Farm Africa and Pump Aid (£2,500 each); Plan UK and Army Benevolent Fund (£2,000 each); Aid for Trade and Womankind (£1,500 each); Aid for Romanian Orphanages, Engineers without Borders UK and Medical Aid for Palestinians (£1,000 each); Zimbabwe Aids Orphans, Listening Books and Aplastic Anaemia Trust (£500 each); and Seeds for Africa and World Jewish Relief Fund (£250 each).

Exclusions No support for gap year requests. Very few unsolicited applications are accepted.

Applications In writing to the correspondent.

The Fuserna Foundation

Relief in need, children, older people and mental and physical illness

£478,000 (2007/08)

Beneficial area UK and overseas.

Sixth Floor, 6 Chesterfield Gardens, Mayfair, London W1J 5BQ

Tel. 020 7409 3900

Email info@fusernafoundation.org

Website www.fusernafoundation.org

Correspondent The Trustees

Trustees *Ariadne Getty; Justin Williams; Fran Hollywood; Susan Bartkowiak; Owen Clutton.*

CC Number 1107895

Information available Accounts were on file at the Charity Commission.

The Fuserna Foundation was formed in February 2005 and its charitable objects are stated as follows in the annual report.

- To revitalise existing charities and individual charitable projects that are failing in their objectives due to financial constraints and or lack of exposure and publicity. This will include vital projects that have difficulty in raising funds to continue in their operations or get off the ground and without any form of reserve, good contacts or patrons to assist them.
- To fund projects that intend to alleviate poverty and financial hardship, to relieve sickness and poor health. The emphasis will be on self help and community.
- To enable individuals to reach their potential despite their social, physiological or environmental limitations. This will include providing new opportunities and experiences for children and older people that they may not otherwise have access to.
- To assist, promote, encourage sustainable projects that create long-term benefits for disadvantaged local communities that are trying to improve their area. This will include the making of grants to projects that assist individuals who by reason of their youth, age, infirmity or disablement, financial hardship or social and economic circumstances have need of such facilities, particularly projects which assist young people in the long term through education and training.
- To assist in the treatment and care of individuals suffering from mental or physical illness or those in need of rehabilitation as a result of such illness. This will include projects for the mentally ill, drug, alcohol and other addictions.

The trustees of the Fuserna Foundation have an informal policy that they will not generally support charities that have annual incoming resources in excess of £3 million or charities that have a high level of publicity through high profile patrons. The foundation focuses on supporting smaller charities and unpopular causes where any donation made can make a real and sustained impact.

The trustees have in the past made exceptions to this policy and have donated to charities with higher levels of incoming resources and publicity but this is not regarded by them as their core focus.

Grants are usually of between £5,000 and £15,000 each.

In 2007 the charity had an income of £697,000, mostly from voluntary income, and made grants totalling £478,000.

Beneficiaries were: Clinton Climate Initiative (£245,000); Project Walk (£172,000); Global Heritage Fund (£40,000); Amaudo UK (£10,000); Santa Monica Mountains & Seashore (£7,700); SeeSaw (£2,100); and Moving Mountains (£1,000).

Exclusions The foundation will not generally consider projects that include the following:

- animals
- religious activities/institutions
- general appeals.

Applications The foundation asks for all initial applications to be in writing and to include the following:

- background information about the charity or charitable project in question
- details of the project that currently requires funding, including the objective of the project and full operational details of how that objective will be achieved
- a copy of your most recent financial statutory accounts
- details of the budget outlined in respect of the project
- details of existing sources of finance, including donations from other charitable trusts and details of other fundraising activities in place in respect of raising the funds needed for the project.

Upon receipt of the above information, a member of the foundation's day to day operational staff may wish to visit the charity prior to presenting its application to the trustees or alternatively to commence discussions with you. Further to this your application will be put forward to the trustees of the Fuserna Foundation for their consideration.

The G D Charitable Trust

Animal welfare, the environment, disability and homelessness

£97,000 (2007)

Beneficial area Worldwide.

c/o Bircham Dyson Bell LLP, 50 Broadway, Westminster, London SW1H 0BL

Tel. 020 7227 7000

Correspondent The Trustees

Trustees *George Lincoln Duffield; Natasha Velvet Duffield; Alexander Seamus Fitzgibbons.*

CC Number 1096101

Information available Accounts were on file at the Charity Commission.

Registered in February 2003, the trust aims to support the following charitable areas:

- the relief of animal suffering
- the preservation of the environment
- the promotion of equal opportunities for people who are disabled
- the relief of people who are homeless.

In 2007 the trust had assets of £3.7 million, an income of £110,000 and made grants totalling £97,000.

Beneficiaries were: Marine Conservation Society (£51,000); George Adamson Wildlife Preservation Trust (£25,000); Society for the Protection of Animals Abroad (£13,000); The Children's Hospice South West – Bristol (£5,000); Born Free (£3,500); and Wild Horse Welfare (£500).

Exclusions No grants to individuals.

Applications In writing to the correspondent.

Gableholt Limited

Jewish

£81,000 to organisations and individuals (2007/08)

Beneficial area UK.

115 Craven Park Road, London N15 6BL

Tel. 020 8802 4782

Correspondent Mrs E Noe, Secretary

Trustees *S Noe; Mrs E Noe; C Lerner; P Noe; A E Bude.*

CC Number 276250

Information available Accounts were on file at the Charity Commission.

Set up as a limited company in 1978, the trust gives practically all of its funds to Jewish institutions, particularly those working in accordance with the orthodox Jewish faith.

In 2007/08 it had an income of £1.7 million and made grants to organisations and individuals totalling £81,000. The sum of £16 million was carried forward to the next year.

Unfortunately no information on grants was included with the trust's accounts that were on file at the Charity Commission. In previous years beneficiaries have included: Afula Society, Child Resettlement, Friends of Harim Establishment, Friends of the Sick, Gur Trust, Mengrah Grammar School, Rachel Charitable Trust and Torah Venchased Le'Ezra Vasad.

Applications In the past this trust has stated that 'in the governors' view, true charitable giving should always be coupled with virtual anonymity' and for this reason they are most reluctant to be a party to any publicity. Along with suggesting that the listed beneficiaries might also want to remain unidentified, they also state that the nature of the giving (to orthodox Jewish organisations) means the information is unlikely to be of much interest to anyone else. Potential applicants would be strongly advised to take heed of these comments.

The Galanthus Trust

Medical, developing countries, environment and conservation

£106,000 (2007/08)

Beneficial area UK and overseas.

West Farm House, Newton Toney, Salisbury SP4 0HF

Tel. 01980 629345

Email galanthustrust@yahoo.co.uk

Correspondent Mrs J M Rogers, Trustee

Trustees *S F Rogers; Mrs J M Rogers.*

CC Number 1103538

Information available Accounts were on file at the Charity Commission, without a list of grants.

This trust was registered with the Charity Commission in April 2004. The following information is taken from the trustees' annual report.

Our aim is to help finance a variety of smaller local projects and good causes, in addition to supporting the work of existing organisations, both in the UK and abroad.

There are several areas of particular interest to the trustees:

- Medical and healthcare needs including research, and patient support (for example, stroke, MS, heart disease and cancer). This might also include help for disability access, support groups or individuals with special needs resulting from illness or injury.
- Projects in developing countries: health, education, water supplies and sustainable development. Here the intention is to fund on-going projects being managed by charitable organisations in the developing world.
- Environmental and wildlife concerns, including the restoration and maintenance of the UK's natural habitats, such as local woodlands and chalk downland. The trust will also give grants for the creation of new footpaths, particularly those facilitating access for disabled people.
- Conservation and preservation projects of historic and cultural value (for example, the National Trust's work at Tyntesfield).

In 2007/08 the trust had assets of £871,000 and an income of £51,000. Charitable donations totalled £106,000 and were broken down by the trust as follows:

Category	Value
Medical and healthcare	£79,000
Projects in the developing world	£36,000
Environment and welfare	£11,000

Applications In writing to the correspondent. 'All requests for grants are considered carefully by the trustees. The trustees decide whether to donate and the amount to donate'.

The Gale Family Charitable Trust

General

£165,000 (2006/07)

Beneficial area UK, mainly Bedfordshire.

Garner Associates, Northwood House, 138 Bromham Road, Bedford MK40 2QW

Tel. 01234 354 508 **Fax** 01234 349 588

Email ggg@garnerassociates.co.uk

Correspondent G Garner

Trustees G D Payne, Chair; J Tyley; J Williams; A J Ormerod; Mrs D Watson; R Beard; W Browning; D Stanton.

CC Number 289212

Information available Accounts were on file at the Charity Commission.

The trust gives support in three areas:

- for churches and church ministries, with emphasis on Bunyan Meeting Free Church in Bedford and the ministries of the Baptist Union in England and Wales
- donations to charities and organisations active in the community life of Bedford and Bedfordshire
- donations to UK charities and organisations active in community life.

In 2006/07 the trust had assets of £4.2 million and an income of £166,000. Grants totalled £165,000 and were broken down as follows, shown here with examples of beneficiaries in each category.

Church donations – 14 grants totalling £42,500
Bunyan Meeting Free Church (£17,000); Baptist Union (£8,000); St Paul's Church – Bedford (£7,000); Odell Parish Council and St Owen's Church – Bromham (£1,000 each); and Clapham Methodist Church (£500).

Local donations – 51 grants totalling £69,000
Prebend Day Centre (£5,000); North Beds. Hospice Day Care (£4,000); Bedford Home Start and Keech Cottage (£3,000 each); Road Victim Support (£2,000); and Bedfordshire Youth Theatre (£500).

General donations – 47 grants totalling £50,000
RNLI, Spinal Injuries Association and Starlight Children's Foundation (£2,000 each); 3H Fund, Barnardo's, Cancer Research UK and War Memorials Trust (£1,000 each).

Exclusions Grants are rarely given to individuals.

Applications In writing to the correspondent. Grants are distributed once a year and applications should be made by May for consideration in July.

The Angela Gallagher Memorial Fund

Children and young people, Christian, humanitarian and education

£34,000 (2007)

Beneficial area UK and international organisations based in the UK.

Church Cott, The Green, Mirey Lane, Woodbury EX5 1LT

Tel. 01395 232097

Correspondent Mrs D R Moss, Secretary

Trustees N A Maxwell-Lawford; P Mostyn; P A Wolrige Gordon; A Swan.

CC Number 800739

Information available Full accounts were on file at the Charity Commission.

The aim of the fund is to help children within the UK. The fund will also consider Christian, humanitarian and educational projects worldwide, although international disasters are only aided through British Red Cross or CAFOD. Small charities which do not have access to large corporate donors are given priority.

In 2007 the trust had assets of £1.2 million and an income of £38,000. Grants to 64 organisations totalled £34,000.

Four grants of £1,000 each were made to Anglo-Peruvian Child Care Mission, Kidz R Us, Dream Holidays Handicapped Children and Order of the Assumption – India. Remaining donations were mostly for £500 each and included those to Rochdale Cycling Club, Penguins Playgroup, Alliance Youth Works, Rutland Sailability, Wells for India, Sussex Autistic Society, Seeds of Hope and Combat Stress.

Exclusions Donations will not be made to the following: older people; scientific research; hospitals and hospices; artistic and cultural appeals;

animal welfare; or building and equipment appeals. No grants to individuals.

Applications In writing to the correspondent, for consideration at trustees' meetings twice a year. Applicants must include a set of accounts or the appeal will not be considered. Applications are not acknowledged without a stamped, addressed envelope.

The Gamlen Charitable Trust

Legal education and general

£11,000 (2007/08)
Beneficial area UK.

c/o Thomas Eggar LLP, Newbury House, 20 Kings Road West, Newbury RG14 5XR
Tel. 01635 571000
Correspondent R G Stubblefield, Trustee
Trustees *R G Stubblefield; P G Eaton; J W M Chadwick.*
CC Number 327977
Information available Accounts were on file at the Charity Commission.

Established in 1988; in 2007/08 this trust had assets of £1.5 million and an income of £251,000. Grants to four organisations totalled £11,000.

Beneficiaries were: Newbury Spring Festival (£7,500); City Solicitors Educational Trust (£2,700); and Cancer Research UK and Bampton Classical Opera (£500 each).

Applications In writing to the correspondent.

The Gamma Trust

General

About £60,000
Beneficial area UK, with a possible preference for Scotland.

c/o Mazars CYB Services Limited, 90 St Vincent Street, Glasgow G2 5UB

Correspondent The Trust Secretary
CC Number The Gamma Trust
Information available Information was provided by the trust.

This trust has general charitable purposes. It appears that new grants are only given to UK-wide organisations although most grants are ongoing commitments to local organisations in Scotland. It has a grant total of about £60,000 a year.

Previous beneficiaries have included British Red Cross, British Heart Foundation, Cancer Research Campaign and Erskine Hospital.

Exclusions No grants to individuals.

Applications In writing to the correspondent for consideration quarterly.

Garrick Charitable Trust

Theatre, music, literature and dance

£192,000 (2007/08)
Beneficial area UK.

15 Garrick Street, London WC2E 9AY
Tel. 020 7395 4136
Email alans@garrickclub.co.uk
Correspondent The Secretary
Trustees *Anthony Hamilton Doggart; John Nigel Newton; Geoffrey Dyson Palmer; David A Sigall; Stephen Waley-Cohen.*
CC Number 1071279
Information available Accounts were available at the Charity Commission.

This trust supports institutions which are seeking to further the profession of theatre (including dance), literature or music. Grants are usually for amounts of around £2,500, only in exceptional circumstances will they exceed £10,000.

In 2007/08 the trust had assets of £4.8 million, which generated an income of £182,000. Grants totalled £192,000 and were broken down as follows, with examples of beneficiaries:

Theatrical – 14 grants totalling £39,000
Paines Plough (£5,000); Cherub Company London, Talawa Theatre Company and Shakespeare at the Tobacco Factory (£2,500 each);

Stonecrabs Productions Ltd (£2,000); and Catherine Wheels Theatre Company (£1,000).

Music – 36 grants totalling £130,000
Montiverdi Choir and Orchestra Ltd (£11,000); Music in Prisons, Young Concert Artists Trust and Manchester Camerata (£5,000 each); Voices of British Ballet (£4,000); Music in Hospitals (£2,900); Southwark Sinfonia, Lake Music Festival and Early Opera Company (£2,500 each); and Yorkshire Bach Choir (£1,000).

Literature – 4 grants totalling £15,500
Asham Literary Endowment Trust and Childrens Discovery Centre (£5,000 each); Spread the Word (£3,000); and National Academy of Writing (£2,500).

Dance – 1 grant of £7,500
The sole beneficiary was Henri Oguike Dance Company.

Applications Initial applications are reviewed by the trustees who decide whether or not to send an application form. Trustees meet quarterly.

Garvan Limited

Jewish

£228,000 (2007/08)
Beneficial area UK.

Flat 9, Windsor Court, Golders Green Road, London NW11 9PP
Correspondent The Trustees
Trustees *A Ebert; L Ebert.*
CC Number 286110
Information available Accounts were on file at the Charity Commission, but without a list of grants.

This trust makes grants to Jewish organisations. In 2007/08 it had assets of £839,000 and an income of £460,000. Grants totalled £228,000. Unfortunately, no further information was available on the size or number of beneficiaries for this year.

Applications In writing to the correspondent.

Jacqueline and Michael Gee Charitable Trust

Health and education (including Jewish)

£60,000 (2007/08)

Beneficial area UK.

27 Berkeley House, Hay Hill, London W1J 8NS

Tel. 020 7493 1904 **Fax** 020 7499 1470

Email trust@sherman.co.uk

Correspondent Michael J Gee, Trustee

Trustees *M J Gee; J S Gee.*

CC Number 1062566

Information available Accounts were on file at the Charity Commission.

This charity's policy is to benefit almost exclusively health and educational charities. In practice this includes many Jewish organisations.

It was created in 1997 by the settlement of £50 from the Archie Sherman Charitable Trust. In 2007/08 the trust had assets of £64,000, an income of £101,000, made up mostly from donations, and made grants totalling £60,000. Grants were broken down as follows, shown here with examples of beneficiaries receiving £1,000 or more:

Medical, health and sickness – 21 grants totalling £29,000

Chai Lifeline Cancer Care (£7,800); Sheffield Institute Foundation for Motor Neurone Disease (£5,000); St George's Medical School (£3,000); the TreeHouse Trust (£2,000); Nightingale House (£1,500); Heart Cells Foundation (£1,300); and Children with Leukaemia (£1,000).

Arts and culture – 7 grants totalling £15,000

SJP Charity Trust Ltd (£10,000); Garsington Opera Limited (£1,250); and Almeida Theatre Company Limited and Hampstead Theatre Limited (£1,000 each).

General – 11 grants totalling £12,000

Central Synagogue General Charities Fund (£4,100); Tel Aviv Foundation (£2,000); and Maccabi GB (£1,000).

Education and training – 6 grants totalling £4,100

The Jewish Museum London (£1,400).

Applications In writing to the correspondent.

Generations Charitable Trust

Children and overseas projects

About £140,000 (2007/08)

Beneficial area UK, Merton and overseas.

36 Marryat Road, Wimbledon, London SW19 5BD

Tel. 020 8946 7760

Email rfinch@rfinch.plus.com

Website www.generationsct.co.uk

Correspondent Rohini Finch, Trustee

Trustees *Robert Finch, Stephen Finch; Rohini Finch.*

CC Number 1110565

Information available Accounts were filed at the Charity Commission. The following excerpt is taken from the trust's website.

Generations Charitable trust was set up in July 2005 by the Finch Family. The Trust is funded by the family and aims to provide a better quality of life for children who need it the most; those who are disabled, disadvantaged, or struggle with ill health. The trust supports local causes in the Borough of Merton where the family are resident and also works abroad in developing countries. The trust also supports projects for environmental protection and conservation; the central aim being to leave a gift for future generations.

In 2007/08 the trust had an income of £13,000 and a total expenditure of £147,000. No list of beneficiaries was available.

Previous beneficiaries have included Born Free Foundation, the Friends of the Mothers Programme, Hampton House – Northampton, Hopes and Homes for Children, Kids Company, Mothers2Mothers, Over the Wall, Royal Institute for the Blind, the Spring Centre, Youth Cancer Trust and Velocity Wheelchair Racing.

Applications In writing to the correspondent.

The Gibbs Charitable Trust

Methodism, international and arts

£130,000 (2007/08)

Beneficial area UK with a preference for the south of England and worldwide.

8 Victoria Square, Clifton, Bristol BS8 4ET

Email jamesgibbs@btinternet.com

Website www.gibbstrust.org.uk

Correspondent Dr James M Gibbs, Trustee

Trustees *John N Gibbs, Chair; James Gibbs; Andrew Gibbs; Celia Gibbs; Elizabeth Gibbs; Jessica Gibbs; John E Gibbs; Juliet Gibbs; Patience Gibbs; Rebecca Gibbs; William Gibbs; James D Gibbs.*

CC Number 207997

Information available Accounts were on file at the Charity Commission.

The trust supports Methodist churches and organisations, other Christian causes (especially those of an ecumenical nature) and creative arts, education and social and international causes. It has a slight preference for projects which can be easily visited by the trustees and it also occasionally supports overseas applications.

In 2007/08 the trust had assets of £2.2 million, an income of £79,000 and made grants totalling £130,000 which were broken down as follows:

International – 21 grants totalling £51,000

Christian Aid – Afghanistan and Climate Change and Oxfam Mozambique (£10,000 each); Tree Aid (£4,000); Practical Action (£3,000); Solar Aid (£2,500); Hope and Homes for Children – Sierra Leone (£2,000); and World Medical Fund, Harvest Help, YCare – Education in Southern Sudan and Appropriate Technology Asia (£1,000 each).

Other Christian Initiatives – 7 grants totalling £12,000

Biblical Illiteracy, St John's College, Durham (£5,000); West London Churches, Homeless Concern (£2,000); and L'Arche Brecon and St David's Cathedral (£1,000 each).

Arts, Drama and Music – 8 grants totalling £11,000
Blackheath Conservatoire (£3,000); Welsh National Opera – community outreach (£2,000); Shakespeare at the Tobacco Factory and Cardiff Singer of the World – educational programme (£1,000 each); and Tara Arts and Circomedia (£500 each).

Social, educational and medical need – 7 grants totalling £9,800
Broadway Trust and YMCA West Kent (£2,000 each); and Families and Friends of Camphill and African Initiatives for African Voices (£1,000 each);

Other Methodist Initiatives – 9 grants totalling £9,400
Pentecost Festival Share Jesus International (£2,000); Old Rectory Epworth and Midland Road Methodist (£1,000) and Parkway Methodist Church – Gospel Choir (£500).

Designated fund – 1 grant of £30,000
The sole beneficiary in this category was Methodist Church Fund for Ministerial Training.

Exclusions A large number of requests are received by the trust from churches undertaking improvement, refurbishment and development projects, but only a few of these can be helped. In general, Methodist churches are selected, sometimes those the trustees have particular knowledge of.

No unsolicited applications from individuals and no animal charities.

Applications The trust has no application forms, although an application cover sheet is available on the trust's website along with a policy and guidelines page. Requests should be made in writing to the correspondent. The trustees meet three times a year, after Christmas, near Easter and late summer. Unsuccessful applicants are not normally notified. The trustees do not encourage telephone enquiries or speculative applications. They also state that they are not impressed by applicants that send a huge amount of paperwork.

The B and P Glasser Charitable Trust

Health, disability, Jewish and welfare
£65,000 (2007/08)

Beneficial area UK and worldwide.

Stafford Young Jones, The Old Rectory, 29 Martin Lane, London EC4R 0AU

Correspondent B S Christer

Trustees J D H Cullingham; M J Glasser; J A Glasser.

CC Number 326571

Information available Accounts were on file at the Charity Commission.

This trust makes grants mainly to health and disability-related charities and Jewish charities, but also for other social-welfare purposes.

In 2007/08 the trust had an income of £85,000 with assets of £1.6 million. Grants to 31 organisations totalled £65,000.

Beneficiaries included: Practical Action (£8,000); Nightingale House (£7,500); RNIB and Sight Savers International (£5,000 each); British Council Shaare Zedek Medical Centre, Jewish Deaf Association, Macmillan Cancer Relief – Hertfordshire and UNICEF (£2,000 each); Action Aid, British Red Cross and Friends of St Francis Hospice (£1,000 each); and Tring and District Patients Medical Fund (£500).

Exclusions No grant to individuals or students.

Applications In writing to the correspondent. To keep administrative costs to a minimum the trust is unable to reply to unsuccessful applicants.

GMC Trust

Medical research, healthcare and general
£232,000 (2007/08)

Beneficial area UK, predominantly in the West Midlands.

4 Fairways, 1240 Warwick Road, Knowle, Solihull, West Midlands B93 9LL

Tel. 01564 779971 **Fax** 01564 770499

Correspondent Rodney Pitts, Secretary

Trustees Sir Adrian Cadbury; B E S Cadbury; M J Cadbury.

CC Number 288418

Information available Accounts were on file at the Charity Commission.

The trust supports medical research and causes related to inner city disadvantage. Income is substantially committed to a range of existing beneficiaries.

In 2007/08 the trust had assets of £2.5 million and an income of £167,000. Grants to 69 organisations totalled £232,000.

Beneficiaries included: Cancer Research UK and Mental Health Foundation (£50,000 each); ZANE (£11,000); Mind and Prostate Cancer Research Centre (£10,000 each); CORE – Digestive Disorders Foundation (£5,000); Age Concern (£2,500); Schools Outreach and King's Lynn Arts Centre (£2,000 each); NSPCC, Depaul Trust and Birmingham Royal Ballet (£1,000 each); British Lung Foundation and Musicians Benevolent Fund (£500 each); and British-Nigeria Educational Trust and Lymphoma Association (£100 each).

Exclusions No grants to individuals, or to local or regional appeals outside the West Midlands. The trust does not respond to national appeals, except where there are established links.

Applications In writing to the correspondent. The trust will only consider written applications and applications outside the trust's remit will not be acknowledged.

The GNC Trust

General
£312,000 (2007)

Beneficial area UK, with preferences for Birmingham and Cornwall.

c/o PricewaterhouseCoopers, Cornwall Court, 19 Cornwall Street, Birmingham B3 2DT

Tel. 0121 265 5000

Correspondent Mrs P M Spragg

Trustees G T E Cadbury; R N Cadbury; Mrs J E B Yelloly.

CC Number 211533

Information available Accounts were obtained from the Charity Commission's website.

In 2007 the trust had assets of £1.5 million and an income of £73,000. Grants were made totalling £312,000.

Support is given to registered charities in which the trustees have special interest, knowledge of or association. With the exception of one large grant to Downing College for £250,000, most grants were made in the region of £1,000 to £10,000. Grants were broken down as follows, with examples of beneficiaries:

Furtherance of education
Downing College (£250,000); Oxford Peace Research Trust (£5,000); Downs Light Railway Trust (£2,500); and League of Venturers Search and Rescue (£1,000).

Social welfare
Oxford Research Group (£10,000); Lansbury Trust Fund (£5,000); and Crisis at Christmas and Worcestershire Community Foundation (£1,000 each).

Religious interests
Grace of God Church (£4,000); Orthodox Church (£2,500); and Overseas Mission Fellowship (£750).

Medical Causes
Marie Curie Cancer Care and Association for International Cancer Research (£1,000 each); and Primrose Hospice (£750).

Performing arts
Dyson Perrins Museum Trust and the Art Fund (£1,000 each).

Disability
Alzheimers Society and Treloar Trust (£1,000 each).

Animal Welfare
Hampshire and Isle of Wight Wildlife Trust (£1,000).

Exclusions No grants are made to national appeals, London-based charities or to individuals.

Applications In writing to the correspondent at any time. There are no application forms and applications are not acknowledged.

The Sydney and Phyllis Goldberg Memorial Charitable Trust

Medical research, welfare and disability

£102,000 (2007/08)
Beneficial area UK.

Coulthards Mackenzie, 17 Park Street, Camberley GU15 3PQ
Tel. 01276 65470
Correspondent M J Church, Trustee
Trustees *H G Vowles; M J Church; C J Pexton.*
CC Number 291835
Information available Full accounts were on file at the Charity Commission.

The income for the trust comes from its investments which are mainly held in Syona Investments Limited. Phyllis Goldberg initially bequeathed her shareholding in Syona Investments Limited to the trust and since then the trust has bought the balance of the shares.

In 2007/08 the trust had assets of £3.1 million with an income of £544,000 and made seven grants totalling £102,000.

Grants were: £13,500 each to Children of St Mary's Intensive Care Department of Child Health, the British Stammering Association, the Dystonia Society, Children with Special Needs Foundation, Life Centre and the Prostate Cancer Charity; and £7,500 to the Isaac Goldberg Charity Trust.

Applications In writing to the correspondent. Telephone requests are not appreciated. Applicants are advised to apply towards the end of the calendar year.

Golden Charitable Trust

Preservation, conservation and medical research

£155,000 (2007/08)
Beneficial area UK with a preference for West Sussex.

Little Leith Gate, Angel Street, Petworth GU28 0BG
Tel. 01798 342434
Correspondent Lewis Golden, Secretary to the Trustees
Trustees *Mrs S J F Solnick; J M F Golden.*
CC Number 263916
Information available Accounts were on file at the Charity Commission.

The trust appears to have a preference in its grantmaking for organisations in West Sussex in the field of the preservation and conservation of historic articles and materials, church restoration and medical research charities.

In 2007/08 the trust had assets of £1 million and an income of £116,000. Grants were made to 26 organisations totalling £155,000.

The three largest grants were given to: Westminster Synagogue (£100,000); Petworth Cottage Nursing Home (£20,000); and the Music Mind Spirit Trust (10,000).

All other grants ranged between £100 and £2,500 and beneficiaries included: the Wordsworth Trust (£2,500); the Langdon Foundation (£2,000); Chichester Cathedral Trust (£1,750); Royal School of Needlework and Inter-Cultural Youth Exchange (£1,000 each); Reform Foundation Trust (£700); the Macmillan Cancer Trust and Dermatitis and Allied Diseases Research Trust (£500 each); Helen and Douglas House (£250); and Cancer Research UK (£100).

Exclusions No grants to individuals.

Applications In writing to the correspondent.

The Jack Goldhill Charitable Trust

Jewish and general

£104,000 (2007)
Beneficial area UK.

85 Kensington Heights, Campden Hill Road, London W8 7BD
Tel. 020 7727 4326
Correspondent Jack Goldhill, Trustee
Trustees *G Goldhill; J A Goldhill; M L Goldhill.*
CC Number 267018
Information available Accounts were on file at the Charity Commission.

In 2007 the trust had assets of £2.9 million and an income of £113,000. Grants were made totalling £104,000, however no details of beneficiaries were provided in the trust's accounts.

Previous beneficiaries have included CST, City and Guilds of London School of Art, Jack Goldhill Award Fund, JNF Charitable Trust, Jewish Care, Joint

Jewish Charitable Trust, Nightingale House, Royal Academy of Arts, Royal London Hospital, Tate Gallery, Tricycle Theatre Co., West London Synagogue and Atlantic College.

Exclusions No support for individuals or new applications.

Applications The trustees have a restricted list of charities to whom they are committed and no unsolicited applications can be considered.

The Goldmark Trust

General

£60,000 (2007/08)
Beneficial area UK.

30 St Giles, Oxford OX1 3LE
Correspondent Graham Cole
Trustees *A O M Goldsmith; P L Luckett; M J Snell.*
CC Number 1072901
Information available Accounts were on file at the Charity Commission.

Registered with the Charity Commission on 10 December 1998, in 2007/08 the trust had assets of £2.3 million, an income of £135,000 and made grants to 28 organisations totalling £60,000. The trustees' report stated that this level of giving would continue in the future.

Beneficiaries included: Sight Savers International – Eye Care programme in Sierra Leone and After Adoption (£5,000 each); Rainbow Trust, Fostering Network and Diabetes UK (£2,500 each); Noah's Ark Trust (£2,000); and Tuberous Sclerosis Association, British Blind Sport, Bikeability and Jubilee Sailing Trust (£1,000 each).

Applications In writing to the correspondent. The trustees meet at least twice a year.

The Golsoncott Foundation

The arts

£53,000 (2007/08)
Beneficial area UK.

53 St Leonord's Rd, Exeter EX2 4LS

Tel. 01392 252855
Email golsoncott@btinternet.com
Correspondent Hal Bishop, Administrator
Trustees *Penelope Lively, Chair; Josephine Lively; Stephen Wick; Dr Harriet Harvey Wood.*
CC Number 1070885
Information available Accounts were on file at the Charity Commission.

The trust states its objects in its annual report as follows:

to promote, maintain, improve and advance the education of the public in the arts generally and in particular [...] the fine arts and music. The fostering of the practice and appreciation of the arts, especially amongst young people and new audiences, is a further specific objective.

Grants vary according to context and are not subject to an inflexible limit, but they are unlikely to exceed £5,000 and are normally given on a non-recurrent basis.

In 2007/08 the foundation had assets of £1.8 million and an income of £74,000. Grants to 59 organisations totalled £53,000 and ranged between £200 and £3,000.

Beneficiaries included: Elias Parish Alvars Festival (£3,000); Jessie's Fund (£2,700); Wales Millenium Centre and English Touring Opera (£2,000 each); Lowry Centre, Southbank Sinfonia, Young Persons Theatre and London Children's Ballet (£1,000 each); Leicestershire Chorale and National Student Drama Festival (£500 each); and New Street Productions (£350).

Exclusions No grants to individuals.

Applications The trustees meet quarterly to consider applications, in February, May, August and November. Applications should be sent to the correspondent by the end of the month preceding the month of the trustees meeting. They should include the following:

- A clear and concise statement of the project, whether the award sought will be for the whole project or a component part. Is the applicant organisation of charitable status?
- Evidence that there is a clear benefit to the public. Does the project conform with the declared object of the trust?
- The amount requested should be specified, or a band indicated. Is this the only source of funding being sought? All other sources of funding should be indicated, including those that have refused funding.

- If the grant requested is part of the match-funding required by the Heritage Lottery Foundation (HLF) following an award, state the amount of that award and the percentage of match-funding required by the HLF and the completion date.
- Wherever possible an annual report and accounts should accompany the application, as may other supporting information deemed relevant.

Second or further applications will not be considered until a minimum of 12 months has elapsed since determination of the previous application, whether successful or not.

Golubovich Foundation

Arts

£166,000 (2007/08)
Beneficial area Not defined.

15a High Street, Battle TN33 0AE
Correspondent Tim Lewin
Trustees *A Golubovich; Mrs O Mirimskaya; A Lisyanski.*
CC Number 1113965
Information available Accounts were on file at the Charity Commission.

Set up in 2006, in 2007/08 the foundation had an income of £195,000 and made grants totalling £166,000.

Beneficiaries were: University of the Arts London (£77,000); Trinity College of Music London (£75,000); Jewish Community Centre for Moscow (£10,000); and Imperial War Museum (£4,500).

Applications In writing to the correspondent.

The Good Neighbours Trust

People with mental or physical disabilities

£77,000 (2007)
Beneficial area UK, with preference for Bristol, Somerset and Gloucestershire.

127

16 Westway, Nailsea, Bristol BS48 2NA

Tel. 01275 851051

Email gntbristol@aol.com

Correspondent P S Broderick, Secretary

Trustees G V Arter, Chair; J C Gurney; P S Broderick; J L Hudd.

CC Number 201794

Information available Accounts were on file at the Charity Commission.

The present policy of the trust is to principally support registered charities whose activities benefit people who are physically or mentally disabled. It mainly gives one-off grants for low-cost specific projects such as purchase of equipment or UK holidays for people with disabilities.

In 2007 the trust had assets of £2.8 million and an income of £95,000. Grants totalling £77,000 were made to 124 organisations, ranging from £250 to £10,000. Donations were broken down as follows:

Local Grants (£41,000)
Beneficiaries included: Children's Hospice South West – Bristol (£10,000); Avon Riding Centre for the Disabled – Bristol, British Wireless for the Blind – Chatham, National Eye Research Centre – Bristol Eye Hospital and Willow Trust – Cirencester (£1,000 each); Vitalise – Redhill (£750); Theatre Royal Bath, Macmillan Cancer Support – Bristol, Bristol Area Stroke Foundation and Disabled on Line – Trowbridge (£500 each); and Talking Newspaper Association – Sussex, Charity Search, Avonmouth and British MS Parents and Toddlers (£250 each).

National Grants (£35,000)
Beneficiaries included: Help The Hospices – London (£2,500); Army Benevolent Fund – London, Eyeless Trust – Beaconsfield, Neuro-muscular Centre – Winsford and Rochdale Special Needs Cycling Club (£1,000 each); Local Solutions – Liverpool, Sensory Trust – St Austell, MedEquip4Kids – Manchester, Children's Adventure Farm Trust – Cheshire and Dogs for the Disabled – Banbury (£500 each); and Caring for Life – Leeds, Independence at Home – Harrow, Challenging Behaviour Foundation – Rochester and Dystonia Society – London (£250 each).

Exclusions Support is not given for:

- overseas projects
- general community projects*
- individuals
- general education projects*
- religious and ethnic projects*
- projects for unemployment and related training schemes*

- projects on behalf of offenders and ex-offenders
- projects concerned with the abuse of drugs and/or alcohol
- wildlife and conservation schemes*
- general restoration and preservation of buildings, purely for historical and/or architectural reasons.

(* If these projects are mainly or wholly for the benefit of people who have disabilities then they may be considered.)

Ongoing support is not given, and grants are not usually given for running costs, salaries, research and items requiring major funding. Loans are not given.

Applications The trust does not have an official application form. Appeals should be made in writing to the secretary. Telephone calls are not welcome. The trust asks that the following is carefully considered before submitting an application:

Appeals must:

- be from registered charities
- include a copy of the latest audited accounts available (for newly registered charities a copy of provisional accounts showing estimated income and expenditure for the current financial year)
- show that the project is 'both feasible and viable' and, if relevant, give the starting date of the project and the anticipated date of completion
- include the estimated cost of the project, together with the appeal's target figure and details of what funds have already been raised and any fundraising schemes for the project.

The trustees state in their report that 'where applicable, due consideration will be given to evidence of voluntary and self-help (both in practical and fundraising terms) and to the number of people expected to benefit from the project'. They also comment that their decision is final and 'no reason for a decision, whether favourable or otherwise, need be given' and that 'the award and acceptance of a grant will not involve the trustees in any other commitment'.

Appeals are dealt with on an ongoing basis, but the trustees meet formally four times a year, usually in March, June, September and December.

Nicholas and Judith Goodison's Charitable Settlement

Arts and arts education
£153,000 (2007/08)
Beneficial area UK.

PO Box 2512, London W1A 5ZP

Correspondent Sir N Goodison, Trustee

Trustees *Sir Nicholas Goodison; Lady Judith Goodison; Miss Katharine Goodison.*

CC Number 1004124

Information available Accounts were on file at the Charity Commission.

The trust supports registered charities in the field of the arts and arts education. Grants are also given to institutions in instalments over several years towards capital projects.

In 2007/08 it had assets of £1.8 million, which generated an income of £217,000. Grants were made to 34 organisations totalling £153,000. Management and administration expenses for the year were very low at just £650.

The largest grants were to Wigmore Hall and Handel House Trust (£25,000); V and A – Medieval (£20,000); and the Courtauld Institute (£15,000).

Other grants included: Fitzwilliam (£6,900); Academy of Ancient Music, English National Opera and London Library (£5,000 each); Victoria and Albert Museum (£2,700); British Museum (£2,000); Attingham Trust, Royal Academy Exhibitions and Tate Foundation (£1,000 each); National Life Story Collection (£850); Crafts Council (£500); and World Monuments Fund (£350).

Exclusions No grants to individuals.

Applications The trust states that it cannot respond to unsolicited applications.

The Everard and Mina Goodman Charitable Foundation

Jewish and general

£273,000 (2007/08)

Beneficial area UK and Israel.

Flat 5, 5 Bryanston Court, London W1H 7HA

Tel. 020 7355 3333

Correspondent Dr Everard Goodman, Trustee

Trustees *Dr Everard Goodman; Mina Goodman; Michael Goodman; Suzanne Goodman; David Goodman.*

CC Number 220474

Information available Accounts were available from the Charity Commission.

As well as supporting causes related to the Jewish faith, this trust also makes grants for: the relief of poverty; the advancement of education; children and young people; medicine and health; and rehabilitation and training. Grants are predominantly small, totalling less than £500. Although, larger grants of around £15,000 are also made.

In 2006 the foundation's income increased significantly due to a substantial donation from the settlor, Everard Goodman, former chief executive of property company Tops Estates. Although, a substantial part of this went to the Faculty of Life Sciences at Bar-Ilan University in Israel (£2 million), which is now named after the settler and his wife, the foundation's increase in income has allowed the level of general grantmaking to rise significantly.

In 2007/08 the foundation had assets of £1.8 million and an income of £59,000. Grants were made totalling £273,000. No grants list was available.

Previous beneficiaries include: British Friends of Bar-Ilan University – Life Sciences Faculty, Variety Club – Sunshine Coach Appeal, British Friends of Laniado Hospital, Child Resettlement Fund, Institute for Jewish Policy Research, Western Marble Arch Synagogue, Smile Train UK, Jewish Women's Aid, National Autistic Society and High Blood Pressure Foundation.

Exclusions No grants to individuals or organisations which are not registered charities.

Applications In writing to the correspondent.

The Goodman Foundation

General, social welfare, older people, health and disability

£336,000 (2007/08)

Beneficial area England, Wales and the Republic of Ireland.

c/o APB, Unit 6290, Bishops Court, Solihull Parkway, Birmingham Business Park, Birmingham B37 7YB

Correspondent The Trustees

Trustees *L J Goodman; C Goodman; R M Cracknell; L Tidd.*

CC Number 1097231

Information available Accounts were on file at the Charity Commission, but without a list of grants.

Registered in April 2003, in 2007/08 the foundation had assets of £8.7 million and an income of £2.3 million, including £2 million from voluntary income. Grants to 32 organisations totalled £336,000 and were broken down in the accounts as follows:

Category	Value	No.
Poverty, older people, illness and disability	£159,000	14
Developing countries and disasters	£93,000	7
Other	£53,000	6
Children's charities	£31,000	5

Applications In writing to the correspondent.

Leonard Gordon Charitable Trust

Jewish religious, educational and welfare organisations

£87,000 (2007/08)

Beneficial area England and Wales.

17 Park Street, Salford M7 4NJ

Tel. 0161 792 3421

Correspondent Leonard Gordon, Chair

Trustees *Leonard Gordon, Chair; Michael Gordon; Jan Fidler.*

CC Number 1075185

Information available Information was on file with the Charity Commission, without a list of grants.

Established in 1999, in 2007/08 the trust had assets of £196,000 and an income of £30,000. Grants were made totalling £87,000. No list of donations was included with the accounts.

Applications In writing to the correspondent.

The Gough Charitable Trust

Young people, Episcopal and Church of England, preservation of the countryside and social welfare

£7,100 (2007/08)

Beneficial area UK, with a possible preference for Scotland.

Lloyds TSB Private Banking Ltd, UK Trust Centre, 22–26 Ock Street, Abingdon OX14 5SW

Tel. 01235 232712

Correspondent The Trust Manager

Trustee *Lloyds Bank plc.*

CC Number 262355

Information available Accounts were on file at the Charity Commission.

The trust has previously shown a preference for Scotland, however it is not clear if this is still the case.

In 2007/08, the trust had an income of £43,000 and made grants totalling £7,100.

During the year the trust made grants to nine organisations. No indication was given on the size of these donations. Beneficiaries were: Irish Guards Lieutenant Colonels Fund, Prince of Wales Lodge No 259 Benevolent Fund, The Lifeboat Service Memorial Book Trust, National Army Development Trust, Household Brigade Benevolent Fund, Lloyds Charities Fund, Lloyds Benevolent Fund, Crown and Manor Boys Club and Trinity Hospice.

Exclusions No support for non-registered charities and individuals including students.

Applications In writing to the correspondent at any time. No acknowledgements are sent. Applications are considered quarterly.

The Gould Charitable Trust

General

£62,000 (2007/08)

Beneficial area UK, Israel and the Philippines.

Cervantes, Pinner Hill, Pinner HA5 3XU

Correspondent S Gould, Trustee

Trustees *Mrs J B Gould; L J Gould; M S Gould; S Gould; S H Gould.*

CC Number 1035453

Information available Accounts were available at the Charity Commission.

In 2007/08 the trust had assets of £951,000, which generated an income of £53,000. Grants to 44 organisations totalled £62,000, with the largest donation made to UJIA for £40,000.

Other beneficiaries included: One to One (£5,000); Alzheimers Research Trust, NSPCC and FCED Foundation Philippines (£2,000 each); Child Hope (£600); Médecins Sans Frontières, Friends of Hebrew University, and New Israel Fund (£500 each); SOS Children and Jewish World Relief (£300 each); and Project Trust and Hackney Quest (£200 each).

Exclusions No support for non-registered charities. No grants to individuals.

Applications In writing to the correspondent, although the trust states: 'We never give donations to unsolicited requests on principle.'

The Grace Charitable Trust

Christian, general, education, medical and social welfare

£303,000 to organisations (2007/08)

Beneficial area UK.

Rhuallt House, Rhuallt, St Asaph, Denbighshire LL17 0TG

Tel. 01745 583141 **Fax** 01745 585243

Correspondent Mrs G J R Payne, Trustee

Trustees *Mrs G J R Payne; E Payne; Mrs G M Snaith; R B M Quayle.*

CC Number 292984

Information available Accounts were available from the Charity Commission, but without a list of beneficiaries.

Established in 1985, the trust generally gives grants of £1,000 to £10,000 each with a preference for Christian organisations.

In 2007/08 the trust had assets of £3.5 million and an income of £80,000. Grants were made to organisations totalling £303,000, which were broken down as follows:

Category	Value
Christian based activities	£141,000
Education	£97,000
Social and medical causes	£65,000
General charitable purposes	£8,800

Beneficiaries included: Alpha (£25,000); the International Christian College (£25,000); and Euroevangelism (£52,000). A further £8,900 was given in grants to individuals.

Applications The trust states: 'Grants are made only to charities known to the settlors and unsolicited applications are, therefore, not considered.'

The Grahame Charitable Foundation Limited

Jewish

£311,000 (2008)

Beneficial area UK and worldwide.

5 Spencer Walk, Hampstead High Street, London NW3 1QZ

Tel. 020 7794 5281

Correspondent Mrs G Grahame, Secretary

Trustees *A Grahame; J M Greenwood.*

CC Number 1102332

Information available Accounts were on file at the Charity Commission, but without a grants list.

The trustees' report states that: 'The charity's objects and its principal activities are that of the advancement of education, religion and the relief of poverty anywhere in the world and to act as a charitable fund.'

In 2008 the trust's assets totalled £1.4 million. It had an income of £206,000, including £103,000 in covenants and donations. Grants totalled £311,000, with only two beneficiaries listed in the accounts: British Friends of the Shaare Zedek Medical Centre (£60,000); and United Jewish Israel Appeal (£38,000).

Exclusions No grants to individuals.

Applications The trustees allocate funds on a long-term basis and therefore have none available for other applicants.

Grand Charitable Trust of the Order of Women Freemasons

General in the UK and overseas

£500,000 to non-Masonic charities (2007/08)

Beneficial area UK and overseas.

27 Pembridge Gardens, London W2 4EF

Tel. 020 7229 2368

Website www.owf.org.uk

Correspondent Mrs Joan Sylvia Brown, Trustee

Trustees *B I Fleming-Taylor; M J P Masters; B Wildman; H I Naldrett; J S Brown; Z D Penn.*

CC Number 1059151

Information available Accounts were available at the Charity Commission, but without a list of beneficiaries.

This trust donates about half its grant total to causes related to the Order of Women Freemasons, including individual members and their dependants. The remaining half is donated to external charities.

In 2007/08 the trust had assets of £691,000, an income of £311,000 and made grants totalling £557,000.

The two largest grants of £250,000 each were awarded to Cancer Research UK and Macmillan Nurses. A payment of £49,000 went to Adelaide Litten Charitable Trust, who provide support to individual Masons who are in need. A further £15,000 went directly to individuals.

Applications In writing to the correspondent. Applications should be submitted by the end of July each year for consideration by the trustees.

The Grand Order of Water Rats Charities Fund

Medical equipment and theatrical

£83,000 (2007)

Beneficial area UK.

328 Gray's Inn Road, London WC1X 8BZ

Tel. 020 7407 8007

Email charities@gowr.net

Website www.gowr.net

Correspondent John Adrian, Secretary

Trustees Chas McDevitt, Chair; Wyn Calvin; Roy Hudd; Kaplan Kaye; Keith Simmons; Ken Joy.

CC Number 292201

Information available Accounts were on file at the Charity Commission, but without a list of grants.

The trust was established to assist members of the variety and light entertainment profession and their dependants who, due to illness or age, are in need. The fund also buys medical equipment for certain institutions and for individuals who have worked with or who have been closely connected with the same profession.

In 2007 the trust had an income of £199,000 and assets of £1.5 million, with income coming mainly from the profit gained from functions organised by the members of the Grand Order of Water Rats. Grants totalled £83,000, which included £12,000 listed as donations, £58,000 in monthly allowances, grants and gifts, £6,000 in expenses and £2,500 for fruit and flowers.

In 1997, the last year in which grant information was available, the largest grants went to Cause for Hope

(£11,000), Bud Flanagan Leukaemia Fund (£6,700) and Queen Elizabeth Hospital for Children (£3,000). There were six grants of between £1,000 and £2,000 including those to Actors Church Union, British Legion Wales and Northwick Park Hospital.

Exclusions No grants to students.

Applications In writing to the correspondent. The trustees meet once a month.

The Constance Green Foundation

Social welfare, medicine, health and general

£297,000 (2007/08)

Beneficial area Mainly England, with a preference for West Yorkshire. Some grants are made to charities operating overseas.

FCM Limited, Centenary House, La Grande Route de St Pierre, St Peter, Jersey JE3 7AY

Tel. 01534 487757 **Fax** 01534 485261

Email management@fcmtrust.com

Correspondent Mrs S Hall

Trustees M Collinson; Col. H R Hall; Mrs M L Hall; Mrs S Collinson.

CC Number 270775

Information available Accounts were on file at the Charity Commission.

The foundation makes grants mainly in the fields of social welfare and medicine. There is a special emphasis on the needs of young people and people who are mentally or physically disabled. Preference is given to making grants to assist in funding special projects being undertaken by charities rather than grants to supplement funds used for general purposes.

In 2007/08 the trust had assets of £7.5 million and an income of £356,000. Grants were made to 92 organisations totalling £297,000 and were broken down as follows:

Category	Value
Medical and social care	£106,000
Disabled and older people	£79,000
Children and young persons	£67,000
Homeless	£26,000
Church and community projects	£20,000

Beneficiaries included: Avalon Breakaway, Teenage Cancer Trust and Martin House – Wetherby (£10,000 each); Salvation Army and Leonard Cheshire (£7,500 each); Act4Africa, Children of the Andes, British Association for Adopting and Fostering and Save The Children – Bangladesh Cyclone Appeal (£5,000 each); Sports Aid and the Olive Branch (£3,000 each); West Yorkshire Playhouse, Older Peoples Action in the Locality and Huntingdon's Disease Association (£1,500 each); and Autism Initiatives UK, British Red Cross and Chernobyl Children in Need (£1,000 each).

Exclusions Sponsorship of individuals is not supported.

Applications At any time in writing to the correspondent (no special form of application required). Applications should include clear details of the need the intended project is designed to meet, plus an outline budget.

The Barry Green Memorial Fund

Animal welfare

£63,000 (2006/07)

Beneficial area UK, with a preference for Yorkshire and Lancashire.

c/o Fitzgerald-Harts, Claro Chambers, Bridge Street, Boroughbridge, York YO51 9LD

Tel. 01423 322 312

Correspondent The Clerk to the Trustees

Trustees Richard Fitzgerald-Hart; Mark Fitzgerald-Hart.

CC Number 1000492

Information available Accounts were on file at the Charity Commission.

The trust was created under the Will of Mrs E M Green. It supports animal welfare charities concerned with the rescue, maintenance and benefit of cruelly treated animals and also the prevention of cruelty to animals. There is a preference for small charities.

In 2006/07 the trust had assets of £1.5 million and an income of £197,000. Grants totalled £63,000.

Beneficiaries included: Assisi Animal Sanctuary (£8,000); Brooke Hospital for Animals and HACK (£5,000 each);

Dumfries & Galway Canine Rescue Centre (£4,000); Animal Health Trust and Hearing Dogs for the Deaf (£3,000 each); Albert's Horse Sanctuary and Greyhound Awareness League (£2,000 each); Hollyfield Wild Bird Hospital and Margaret Green Foundation Trust (£1,000 each); and Cotton Tails Rabbit and Guinea Pig Rescue and London Wildlife Trust (£500 each).

Exclusions No expeditions, scholarships, work outside the UK or individuals.

Applications In writing to the correspondent including a copy of the accounts.

The Philip Green Memorial Trust

Young and older people, people with disabilities and people in need

£355,000 (2007/08)

Beneficial area UK and overseas, particularly Israel and Nepal.

301 Trafalgar House, Grenville Place, Mill Hill, London NW7 3SA

Tel. 020 8906 8732

Email info@pgmt.org.uk

Website www.pgmt.org.uk

Correspondent The Committee

Trustees C Paskin; M Campbell; S Paskin; I Rondel; P Green; M Parsons; D Calderhead.

CC Number 293156

Information available Accounts were on file at the Charity Commission.

The trust's 2007/08 accounts stated that the objectives of the charity are 'raising money to help young people, older people, people with disabilities, and the needy in the community at large'.

During the year it had an income of £570,000, mainly raised through means such as annual dinners, a quiz night and the London Marathon. Grants to 32 organisations totalled £355,000.

The largest grants during the year were made to several schools: Colnbrook School (£70,000); Norwood (£31,000); Jewish Community Secondary School (£30,000); and Royal School for the Deaf (£27,000).

Other beneficiaries included: Community Security Trust (£14,000);

Ayrshire Hospice (£11,000); Sail Africa (£10,000); Namaste Children's Home – Nepal and Jewish Care (£5,000 each); Chai Lifeline Cancer Care Centre, Human Development and Community Services – Nepal and Searchlight Educational Trust (£3,000 each); Project Harar and London ExBoxers Association (£2,000 each); and National Hospital Development Fund and Cancer Research UK (£1,000 each).

Applications In writing to the correspondent.

Philip and Judith Green Trust

Christian and missions

£61,000 (2007/08)

Beneficial area UK and Africa.

Marchfield, Flowers Hill, Pangbourne RG8 7BD

Correspondent Philip Green, Trustee

Trustees P N Green; J A Green.

CC Number 1109933

Information available Accounts were on file at the Charity Commission.

Registered with the Charity Commission in 2005, the trust states its objects in its accounts as follows.

The charity's objects are to advance the education and support the development of pupils in underprivileged communities both overseas and in the UK and to advance the Christian faith for the benefit of the public by supporting missionaries and to include the upkeep and provision of places of worship both overseas and in the UK.

In 2007/08 it had assets of £151,000 and an income of £101,000, most of which came from donations (£94,000). Grants were made totalling £61,000.

Beneficiaries included: Lambeth Partnership and the Bible Society (£10,000 each); Africa Enterprises (£9,300); Greyfriars Church (£7,200); Stewardship SVS (£6,200); and Mission Aviation (£2,400). Other grants of smaller amounts were made totalling £16,000, however these were not listed in the charity's accounts.

Applications In writing to the correspondent.

Mrs H R Greene Charitable Settlement

General, particularly at risk-groups, poverty and social isolation

£73,000 (2007/08)

Beneficial area UK, with a preference for Norfolk and Wistanstow in Shropshire.

c/o Birketts, Kingfisher House, 1 Gilder's Way, Norwich NR3 1UB

Correspondent N G Sparrow

Trustees A C Briggs; Revd J B Boston; D A Moore.

CC Number 1050812

Information available Accounts were on file at the Charity Commission.

The founder of this trust lived in Wistanstow in Shropshire and the principal trustee was for many years based in Norwich. Both these factors influence the grantmaking of the trust, with several grants given in both the parish of Wistanstow and in the Norfolk area. The trust has an additional preference for supporting organisations helping at-risk groups and people who are disadvantaged by poverty or socially isolated.

In 2007/08 the trust had assets of £2.2 million, an income of £79,000 and made grants totalling £73,000 which included £3,400 in Christmas gifts. This is the only information available for this year. The most recent grants list available comes from 1997/98, when it had an income of £61,000, a total expenditure of £72,000 and gave £60,000 in grants. This includes £6,700 given to individuals, plus £3,500 in Christmas gifts and poultry. The rest was given to 43 organisations, in grants ranging between £170 and £6,000.

The largest grant in 1997/98 was £6,000 to St Michael's Hospital Bartestree, followed by a grant of £2,500 to Norfolk and Norwich Clergymen's Widows' and Children's Charity. Grants of £2,000 were given to Brittle Bone Society, Children's Food Fund, Landau, Macmillan Cancer Relief, Muscular Dystrophy Group and Orbis.

The grants list did not mention the geographical location of most of the charities. It was possible to distinguish that some are based in Norfolk, as follows: Beeston Church Organ (£1,000);

Friends of Norwich Cathedral (£500); Horsford and St Faith's Scout Group (£400); and Litcham Parochial Church Council (£300); also see the second largest grant, above. It was not obvious from the grants list that the trust gave any grants in Wistanstow, Shropshire in 1997/98, although a couple of charities appeared on the grants list that were in the bordering county of Herefordshire (such as the largest grant).

Applications The trust states that it does not respond to unsolicited applications.

The Gretna Charitable Trust

General

£35,000 (2007/08)

Beneficial area UK, with a preference for Hertfordshire and London.

Imperial London Hotels Limited, Russell Square, London WC1B 5BB

Correspondent The Trustees

Trustees H R Walduck; Mrs S M C Walduck; A H E P Walduck; C B Bowles.

CC Number 1020533

Information available Accounts were on file at the Charity Commission.

This trust gives grants to a wide range of voluntary organisations in the UK, with a preference for Hertfordshire and London.

In 2007/08 the trust had assets of just over £1.2 million, an income of £68,000 and made 50 grants totalling £35,000, all of which were for £2,500 or less.

Beneficiaries included: St Mary's Essendon (£2,500); the Mixed Group and the Tibet Foundation (£2,000 each); St Albans Cathedral (£1,600); High Sheriffs Fund – Hertfordshire (£1,500); Charlie Waller Memorial Trust, Crimebeat – Hertfordshire, Potters Bar Youth Marching Blues, Museum of Garden History and Victim Support Hertfordshire (£1,000 each); National Children's Hospital, Action on Addiction and Zurich Appeal (£500 each); and Hertford Museum and Busoga Trust (£250 each).

Exclusions The trust will not provide support to fund salaries or administration costs.

Applications This trust does not encourage applications.

The Greys Charitable Trust

General

£74,000 (2007/08)

Beneficial area UK and locally in Oxfordshire.

c/o Lawrence Graham LLP, 4 More London Riverside, London SE1 2AU

Correspondent The Trustees

Trustees J S Brunner; T B H Brunner.

CC Number 1103717

Information available Accounts were on file at the Charity Commission.

Registered in May 2004, this charity's trust fund consists solely of shares in the Brunner Investment Trust plc and cash.

The following is taken from the annual report.

The trustees seek to make donations to other charities and voluntary bodies for the benefit of Church of England preservation projects, other charities dealing with historical preservation, both local to Oxfordshire and nationally, and may seek to make donations to the arts.

In 2007/08 it had assets of £1.2 million, an income of £31,000 and made 17 grants totalling £74,000.

Beneficiaries included: Trinity College – Oxford (£20,000); Conservation International and Oxfordshire Historic Churches Trust (£10,000 each); Rotherfield Greys PCC (£6,000); St Mary's Church – Henley-on-Thames (£5,000); the Landmark Trust (£3,500 in two grants); the Royal Opera House (£1,500); the Art Fund, Ripon College Cuddesdon (£1,000); and Army Benevolent Fund (£500).

Applications In writing to the correspondent, the trustees usually meet twice a year.

Grimmitt Trust

General

£234,000 (2007/08)

Beneficial area Birmingham and district and areas where trustees have a personal connection.

4a St Catherines Road, Blackwell B60 1BN

Tel. 0121 445 2197

Email admin@grimmitt-trust.org.uk

Correspondent The Secretary

Trustees P W Welch; Mrs M E Welch; T N P Welch; Revd C Hughes Smith; Dr A D Owen; Mrs S L Day; L Murray; J M Dickens; Mrs S J Wilkey.

CC Number 801975

Information available Accounts were obtained from the Charity Commission website.

Grants are given to organisations in the Birmingham area. Local branches of UK organisations are supported, but larger UK appeals are not. Over half of the grant total is given in grants of less than £500 each.

In 2007/08 it had assets of £6.9 million and an income of £294,000. There were 188 grants made in the year totalling £234,000, broken down as follows:

Category	No.	Value
Community	65	£79,000
Cultural and Educational	28	£28,000
Children and Young people	38	£39,000
Overseas	11	£47,000
Medical and Health	20	£18,000
Older people	8	£25,000
Benevolent and small grants	18	£2,100

Beneficiaries included: Go Africa – Sudan schools and Lench's Trust (£20,000 each); Birmingham County Scout Council (£12,000); the Methodist Art Collection and WaterAid (£10,000 each); Birmingham Bach Choir (£6,000); Birmingham Childrens Hospital, Birmingham Law Centre, Komera Project and Barnardo's Midlands (£5,000 each); Edwards Trust (£3,500); Barton Training Trust and Prisoners Education Trust (£3,000 each); and Lozells Project (£2,500).

Smaller grants of less than £2,500 were made to 167 organisations, totalling £82,000, and a grant was made to one individual during the year.

Applications In writing to the correspondent.

The GRP Charitable Trust

Jewish and general

£172,000 (2007/08)
Beneficial area UK.

Kleinwort Benson Trustees Ltd, PO Box 57005, 30 Gresham Street, London EC2V 7PG

Tel. 020 3207 7356

Correspondent The Secretary

Trustee *Kleinwort Benson Trustees Ltd.*

CC Number 255733

Information available Full accounts were on file at the Charity Commission.

The GRP of the title stands for the settlor, George Richard Pinto, a London banker who set up the trust in 1968. Most of the grants are given to Jewish organisations.

In 2007/08 the trust had assets of £4.5 million and an income of £166,000. A total of £172,000 was given in 20 grants, broken down as follows:

Jewish causes – 7 grants totalling £106,000

Oxford Centre for Hebrew & Jewish Studies (£80,000); Jerusalem Foundation (£14,000); British Friends of the Israel Philharmonic Orchestra (£5,000); Community Security Trust (£3,000); Anglo-Israel Association (£2,000); Simon Marks Jewish Primary School Trust (£1,000); and British Friends of Haifa University (£500).

General – 13 grants totalling £67,000

Traditional Alternatives Foundation (£25,000); Wallace Collection (£18,000); Trinity College (£10,000); Politics and Economics Research Trust and Council of Christians and Jews (£5,000 each); Friends of Courtauld Institute of Art and Gurkha Regimental Trust (£1,000 each); Royal British Legion, Chicken Shed Theatre Company and Woolf Institute (£500 each); and Arrhythmia Alliance (£200).

Exclusions No grants to individuals.

Applications In writing to the correspondent. However, the trustees prefer to provide medium-term support for a number of charities already known to them, and unsolicited applications are not acknowledged. Trustees meet annually in March.

The Walter Guinness Charitable Trust

General

£117,000 (2007/08)
Beneficial area UK with a preference for Wiltshire and overseas.

Biddesden House, Andover SP11 9DN

Correspondent The Secretary

Trustees *Hon. F B Guinness; Hon. Mrs R Mulji; Hon. Catriona Guinness.*

CC Number 205375

Information available Accounts were on file at the Charity Commission.

The trust was established in 1961 by Bryan Walter, the second Lord Moyne, in memory of his father, the first Lord Moyne. Most grants are given to a number of charities which the trust has been consistently supporting for many years. In 2007/08 the trust had assets of £6 million and an income of £135,000. There were 106 grants made totalling £117,000.

Grants were broken down as follows.

- Medical – £27,000 (21)
- Disability – £17,300 (21)
- Communities/community – £13,500 (11)
- Young people – £13,000 (7)
- Education – £12,500 (7)
- Mental health/addictions – £6,000 (5)
- Overseas – £5,000 (8)
- Older people – £5,900 (6)
- Children – £5,500 (4)
- Prisoners – £2,000 (3)
- Animals – £2,000 (1)
- Medical research – £2,000 (1)
- Refugees – £1,000 (1)
- Overseas education – £1,000 (1)
- Carers – £1,000 (1)
- Marine – £1,000 (2)
- Culture – £600 (3)
- Other – £300 (1)
- Ecology – £116 (2)

There were 100 grants of £250 or more listed in the accounts. Beneficiaries included: British Red Cross, Fairbridge and Textile Conservation Centre Foundation (£5,000 each); Andover Mind, Ludgershall Scouts Hall and National Children's Homes (£3,000); Friends of the Elderly, Help for Heroes, Inspire Foundation and Prospect Hospice (£2,000 each); and Octobus Project, Reach Inclusive Arts, Refugee Therapy Centre, RNIB and SCOPE (£1,000 each).

Six unlisted grants under £250 each totalled £430.

Exclusions No grants to individuals.

Applications In writing to the correspondent. Replies are only sent when there is a positive decision. Initial telephone calls are not possible. There are no application forms, guidelines or deadlines. No stamped, addressed envelope is required.

The Gunter Charitable Trust

General

£130,000 (2007/08)
Beneficial area UK.

c/o Forsters, 31 Hill Street, London W1J 5LS

Tel. 020 7863 8333

Correspondent The Trustees

Trustees *J de C Findlay; R G Worrall.*

CC Number 268346

Information available Full accounts were on file at the Charity Commission.

The trust gives grants to a wide range of local and UK organisations, including countryside, medical and wildlife causes.

In 2007/08 the trust had assets of £2.4 million, an income of £133,000 and made 48 grants totalling £130,000.

The largest grants made were for £18,000 each to the Disaster Emergency Committee for the Bangladesh Cyclone Appeal and the Darfur and Chad Crisis Appeal.

Other grants included: Liverpool School of Tropical Medicine (£9,500); Dandelion Trust (£9,000); Marie Stopes International (£7,000); Medical Foundation for the Care of Victims of Torture (£5,800); Friends of Doctor Peary Lal Hospital (£3,900); Médecins Sans Frontières (£3,000); St Nicholas Church – Charlwood, Sense and Alzheimer's Disease Society (£2,000 each); Work Aid and the Prostate Cancer Charity (£1,000 each); and Plantlife International and Rainforest Concern (£500 each).

Exclusions No support for unsolicited applications.

Applications Applications are considered by the trustees twice a year. No unsolicited applications are accepted, and all such applications are immediately returned to the applicant.

The Gur Trust

Jewish causes

£46,000 (2007/08)
Beneficial area Worldwide.

5 Windus Road, London N16 6UT
Tel. 020 8880 8910
Correspondent The Trustees
Trustees *I M Cymerman; M Mandel; S Morgenstern.*
CC Number 283423
Information available Accounts were on file at the Charity Commission.

In 2007/08 the trust had assets of £1.4 million and an income of £60,000. Grants were made totalling £46,000, however a list of beneficiaries was not available in this year's accounts.

Previous beneficiaries have included Beis Yaacov Casidic Seminary, Beth Yaacov Town, Bnei Emes Institutions, Central Charity Fund, Gur Talmudical College, Kollel Arad, Yeshiva Lezeirim, Pri Gidulim, Maala and Mifal Gevura Shecehessed.

Applications In writing to the correspondent. The trust has previously stated that: 'Funds are raised by the trustees. All calls for help are carefully considered and help is given according to circumstances and funds then available.'

The H and M Charitable Trust

Seafaring

£114,000 (2007/08)
Beneficial area UK, with some preference for Kent.

Abbey House, 342 Regents Park Road, London N3 2LJ
Tel. 020 8445 9104
Correspondent David Harris, Trustee
Trustees *Mrs P M Lister; D Harris; J Lister*
CC Number 272391
Information available Accounts were on file at the Charity Commission.

The trust supports charities concerned with seamanship, divided between educational and welfare causes. In 2007/08 the trust had assets of £2.6 million and an income of £37,000. Grants to 12 organisations totalled £114,000.

Beneficiaries were: Arethusa Venture Centre (£36,000); Jubilee Sailing Trust (£15,000); Royal Engineers Association, North London Hospice and Guide Dogs for the Blind (£10,000 each); Fairbridge – Kent (£6,000); Royal Star and Garter Home, R.S.P.C.A and Royal National Lifeboat Association (£5,000 each); Kent Air Ambulance (£4,000); and Hand in Gillingham (£2,000).

The trust has previously stated that 'resources are committed on a regular annual basis to organisations who have come to rely upon us for their funding'.

Applications The trustees said they do not wish their trust to be included in this guide since it leads to disappointment for applicants. Unsolicited applications will not be successful.

The H P Charitable Trust

Orthodox Jewish

£352,000 (2007/08)
Beneficial area UK.

26 Lingwood Road, London E5 9BN
Tel. 020 8806 2432
Correspondent Aron Piller, Trustee
Trustees *A Piller; Mrs H Piller; A Zonszajn.*
CC Number 278006
Information available Accounts were on file at the Charity Commission, but without a grants list.

The H P Charitable Trust was created by Hannah Piller in 1979 and makes grants to orthodox Jewish charities. In 2007/08 its assets totalled £1.4 million and it had an income of £361,000. Grants totalled £352,000, however a list of beneficiaries was not available with this year's accounts.

Previous beneficiaries included: Craven Walk Charities, Emuno Educational Centre Ltd, Gur Trust, Ponivez, Yad Eliezer, Yeshuas Caim Synagogue and Yetev Lev.

Applications In writing to the correspondent.

The Edith Winifred Hall Charitable Trust

General

£1.3 million (2007/08)
Beneficial area UK, with a preference for Northamptonshire.

Spratt Endicott, 52–54 South Bar Street, Banbury OX16 9AB
Tel. 01295 204000
Correspondent D Endicott, Trustee
Trustees *D Reynolds; D Endicott; P P Reynolds; L C Burgess-Lumsden.*
CC Number 1057032
Information available Full accounts were on file at the Charity Commission.

This trust has stated that it wants its funds to make a difference. It prefers to make a small number of large grants.

In 2007/08 the trust had assets of £3.4 million and an income of £141,000. Grants to 11 organisations totalled £1.3 million.

Beneficiaries included: Northamptonshire Association of Youth Clubs (£300,000); Age Concern Northamptonshire and St Peter's School (£250,00 each); the Countryside Alliance Foundation (£150,000); University of Northampton Foundation (£138,000); Creation Theatre Company (£80,000); St Peter's Church – Walgrave and Luton Churches Education Trust (£35,000 each); St Mary Magdelene (£7,200); and Northamptonshire Community Foundation (£5,000).

Applications In writing to the correspondent.

The Hamamelis Trust

Ecological conservation and medical research

£78,000 (2007/08)
Beneficial area UK, but with a special interest in the Godalming and Surrey areas.

c/o Penningtons Solicitors LLP, Highfield, Brighton Road, Godalming GU7 1NS

Tel. 01483 791800

Correspondent Mrs L Dadswell, Trustee

Trustees *Mrs L Dadswell; Dr A F M Stone; Ms L J Stone.*

CC Number 280938

Information available Full accounts were available from the Charity Commission.

The trust was set up in 1980 by John Ashley Slocock and enhanced on his death in 1986. The main areas of work are medical research and ecological conservation. Grants are occasionally made to other projects. Preference is given to projects in the Godalming and Surrey areas.

In 2007/08 the trust had assets of £2.3 million and an income of £101,000. Grants totalled £78,000, and were awarded to four beneficiaries: Chiddingfold PCC St Marys Church (£50,000); Bedfordshire, Cambridge and Northamptonshire Wildlife Trust (£25,000); Berkshire, Buckinghamshire and Oxfordshire Wildlife Trust (£2,500); and Rodborough Technology School (£500).

Exclusions Projects outside the UK are not considered. No grants to individuals.

Applications In writing to the correspondent. All applicants are asked to include a short summary of the application along with any published material and references. Unsuccessful appeals will not be acknowledged.

Dr Adam Stone, one of the trustees, who is medically qualified, assesses medical applications.

The Sue Hammerson Charitable Trust

Health care, education and religion

£276,000 (2007/08)

Beneficial area UK, with a preference for London.

H W Fisher and Co, Acre House, 11–15 William Road, London NW1 3ER

Tel. 020 7388 7000

Correspondent R Watson

Trustees *Sir Gavin Lightman; Mrs Patricia A Beecham; Anthony Bernstein;*

David B Hammerson; Peter S Hammerson; Anthony J Thompson.

CC Number 235196

Information available Accounts were available at the Charity Commission.

The objects of the trust are to advance medical learning and research and the relief of sickness and poverty; it also supports a range of other charities including a number of Jewish and arts organisations.

In 2007/08 it had assets of £8.4 million and an income of £300,000. Grants were made to 156 organisations totalling £276,000, and were broken down as follows:

Category	Value
Arts and culture	£21,000
Education, international and religious causes	£24,000
Healthcare and relief of poverty	£217,000

The largest beneficiary by far was Lewis W Hammerson Memorial Home, to which the trust makes an donation of £200,000 each year.

Other beneficiaries included: Royal Albert Hall and WLS Jewish Futures (£5,000 each); Royal Opera House (£4,400); National Theatre (£3,500); Hampstead Synagogue, Musequality, and the Rix Centre (£2,000 each); Youth Cancer Trust (£1,500); Tate Foundation and Royal Academy of Arts (£1,000 each); and World Emergency Relief, Holocaust Educational Trust, Ethiopiaid and British Heart Foundation (£250 each).

Exclusions No grants to individuals.

Applications In writing to the correspondent. The trust states, however, that its funds are fully committed.

The Hammonds Charitable Trust

General

£72,000 (2007/08)

Beneficial area Mainly Birmingham, London, Leeds, Bradford and Manchester.

Hammonds Solicitors, Rutland House, 148 Edmund Street, Birmingham B3 2JR

Email linda.sylvester@hammonds.com

Website www.hammonds.com

Correspondent Linda Sylvester

Trustees *S M Gordon; J S Forrest; S R Miller; S Kelly*

CC Number 1064028

Information available Accounts were on file at the Charity Commission.

The trust (formerly known as The Hammond Suddards Edge Charitable Trust) usually makes donations to charitable organisations based locally to the trust.

In 2007/08 the trust 'supported a number of national charities in a wide variety of areas, but in particular the trustees were pleased to support smaller charities working within the areas in which its firm's offices are based – situated in Birmingham, London, Leeds and Manchester.'

During the year, the trust had assets of £138,000, an income of £78,000 and made grants to 102 organisations totalling £72,000.

Beneficiaries included: Business in the Community (£8,800); Jane's Appeal (£4,200); Crisis UK (£3,600); Cancer Research UK (£2,300); Eureka, The National Children's Museum, Global Angels Foundation and Orchid Cancer Appeal (£1,000 each); Leukaemia Research Fund and Cross-Cultural Solutions (£500 each); and Shelter, Oxfam and Acorns Children's Hospice (£250 each).

Applications This trust does not accept unsolicited applications.

Beatrice Hankey Foundation Ltd

Christian

£28,000 (2007)

Beneficial area UK and overseas.

11 Staverton Road, Werrington, Peterborough PE4 6LY

Tel. 01733 571794

Correspondent Mrs M Churchill, Secretary

Trustees *Rev S Barnes; H W Bright; E F Dawe; J G Green; Rev Canon P Gompertz; L Grafin zu Lynar; T Halliday; P Sargeant; Revd D Savill; A Y Stewart; H Walker; G Vye; R Woodcock*

CC Number 211093

Information available Full accounts were available at the Charity Commission.

Grants are made to individuals and groups known personally to the foundation members and carrying out activities that will promote the values of Christian teaching. It gives mostly small grants of up to £5,000 each.

In 2007 the foundation had assets of £1.2 million and an income of £48,000. Grants were made to 16 organisations totalling £28,000.

Beneficiaries included: Lagan College (£14,000); Corrymeela Community (£3,500); St Alfege's School Project (£3,000); Cornerstone Community (£2,000); the Dalitso Trust and Community Meeting Point – Harpenden (£1,000 each); Christian Solidarity Worldwide, the Light House and Hope in Christ (£500 each); and Rugby Youth for Christ (£200).

Exclusions No grants for buildings or equipment.

Applications Unsolicited applications cannot be considered.

The Hanley Trust

Social welfare and people who are disadvantaged

£29,000 (2007/08)

Beneficial area UK, with a preference for Corby and Rutland.

21 Buckingham Gate, London SW1E 6LS

Correspondent Hon. Mrs Sarah Price, Trustee

Trustees *Hon. Sarah Price, Chair; Hon. James Butler; Nicholas Smith.*

CC Number 299209

Information available Full accounts were available from the Charity Commission website.

The trust states that it has various funding priorities, for social welfare and people who are disadvantaged. It makes grants to registered charities only, usually small, up to a maximum of £4,000.

In 2007/08 the trust had assets of £1.1 million and an income of £36,000. Grants to 79 organisations totalled £29,000 and ranged between £500 and £2,500.

Beneficiaries included: Butler Trust and Irene Taylor Trust (£2,500 each); Helen Arkell Dyslexia Centre, Howard League for Penal Reform, Pembroke

College Cambridge and Shelter (£1,000 each); and Amnesty International, Deafness Research UK, Mind, Project Trust and Kurdish Aid Foundation (£500 each).

Exclusions Grants are not made to individuals or to non-registered charities.

Applications In writing to the correspondent.

Harbo Charities Limited

General, education and Jewish causes

£118,000 (2007/08)

Beneficial area UK.

c/o Cohen Arnold and Co., New Burlington House, 1075 Finchley Road, London NW11 0PU

Correspondent The Trustees

Trustees *Harry Stern; Barbara J Stern; Harold Gluck.*

CC Number 282262

Information available Accounts were on file at the Charity Commission, but without a grants list.

In 2007/08 the trust had assets of £759,000, an income of £87,000 and made grants totalling £118,000.

Previous beneficiaries have included Beis Chinuch Lebonos Girls School, Beth Rochel d'Satmar, Bobov Trust, Chevras Maoz Ladol, Craven Walk Charitable Trust, Edgware Yeshiva Trust, Keren Yesomim, Kollel Shomrei HaChomoth, Tevini Limited, Tomchei Shabbos, Yad Eliezer, Yesode Ha Torah School and Yeshiva Chachmay Tsorpha.

Applications In writing to the correspondent.

The Harbour Charitable Trust

General

£62,000 (2007/08)

Beneficial area UK.

c/o Barbican House, 26–34 Old Street, London EC1V 9QQ

Correspondent The Trustees

Trustees *Mrs B B Green; Mrs Z S Blackman; Mrs T Elsenstat; Mrs E Knobil.*

CC Number 234268

Information available Accounts were on file at the Charity Commission, but without a list of grants.

The trust makes grants for the benefit of childcare, education and healthcare and to various other charitable organisations.

In 2007/08 it had assets of £3 million and an income of £157,000. Grants were made totalling £62,000. These were categorised by the trust as follows: Joint Jewish Charitable Trust (£39,000); education (£16,000); healthcare (£2,000); childcare (£900); and other donations (£2,000).

No further information was available on the charities supported.

Exclusions Grants are given to registered charities only.

Applications In writing to the correspondent.

The Harbour Foundation

Jewish and general

£291,000 (2007/08)

Beneficial area Worldwide, with a preference for London.

The Courtyard Building, 11 Curtain Road, London EC2A 3LT

Tel. 020 7456 8180

Correspondent The Trustees

Trustees *D Harbour; Rex Harbour; Anthony C Humphries; Susan Harbour.*

CC Number 264927

Information available Accounts were on file at the Charity Commission.

The principal activities of the trust are providing relief among refugees and people who are homeless, the advancement of education, learning and research, and to make donations to any institution established for charitable purposes throughout the world.

In 2007/08 the foundation had assets of £29 million and an income of £1.2 million. There were 86 grants made totalling £291,000, which were broken down into the following categories:

137

Category	No.	Value
Social Organisations	36	£107,000
Education	16	£54,000
Music	14	£36,000
Medical	12	£34,000
Religious Bodies	4	£19,000
Relief	4	£41,000

The following is taken from the trustee's report:

The foundation's current and future charitable programme is directed towards general support for charities and individuals involved in work to aid those in need and to helping with programmes of education both generally and in technology and music. Support will be given to help musical organisations and musically talented individuals with their training. Donations are also made to wider community charities engaged on both social and educational work as well as to organisations of the Jewish community and other bodies.

Educational support is directed to mainly postgraduate university level and to those who have been failed by educational system. To enable greater levels of donation to be made it is, therefore, essential to continue to build up reserves of the foundation to a level sufficient to ensure a reliable high level of financial support to such providers.

In order that the foundation can provide the required level of donations on a consistent and ongoing basis it continues to invest surplus funds in investments generating attractive returns. In the meantime the foundation has sufficient available resources to fulfil its obligations.

Previous beneficiaries included: Hope Charity (£37,000); Inspire (£10,000); ACIM (£7,500); Belsize Park Synagogue (£7,000); East London Business Alliance (£5,500); Wigmore Hall Trust (£3,000); St Marys Church (£2,000); and Countess Mountbatten Hospice and Sisters of Charity (£1,000 each).

Applications In writing to the correspondent. Applications need to be received by February, as trustees meet in March.

The Harding Trust

Arts and general charitable purposes

£117,000 (2007/08)
Beneficial area Mainly, but not exclusively, north Staffordshire and surrounding areas.

Brabners Chaffe Street, 1 Dale Street, Liverpool L2 2ET

Tel. 0151 600 3000

Correspondent The Administrator

Trustees G G Wall; J P C Fowell; M N Lloyd; G B Snow.

CC Number 328182

Information available Accounts were on file at the Charity Commission.

The aim of this trust is 'to promote, improve, develop and maintain public education in, and appreciation of, the art and science of music, by sponsoring or by otherwise supporting public concerts, recitals and performances by amateur and professional organisations'.

In 2007/08 the trust had assets of £3.8 million and an income of £171,000. Grants were made totalling £117,000 as follows:

Music donations – 17 grants (£111,000)
Beneficiaries included: Stoke on Trent Festival (£30,000); Harding Trust Piano Recitals (£17,000); Wolverhampton Civic Hall Orchestra (£10,000); Stoke on Trent Music School – Education Scheme (£5,000); Patrons Victoria Hall Organ (£2,500); and Wolverhampton Recital Series (£1,000).

Other donations – 4 grants (£5,500)
Grants went to Douglas Macmillan Hospice, Katharine House Hospice and Donna Louise Trust (£1,500 each); and St John Ambulance (£1,000).

Applications In writing to the correspondent. The trustees meet annually in spring/early summer. Accounts are needed for recurrent applications.

The Hare of Steep Charitable Trust

General

£50,000 (2007/08)
Beneficial area UK, with preference for the south of England, especially Petersfield and East Hampshire.

56 Heath Road, Petersfield GU31 4EJ

Tel. 01730 267953

Correspondent Mrs S M Fowler, Hon. Secretary

Trustees P L F Baillon; J S Grenfell; J R F Fowler; S M Fowler; S E R Johnson-Hill.

CC Number 297308

Information available Accounts were on file at the Charity Commission.

In 2007/08 the trust had assets of £128,000 and an income of £102,000. Grants were made to 40 organisations and totalled £50,000. The trust made only one donation greater than 5 per cent of the total distributed, a grant of £4,000 paid to The Petersfield Heart Medequip Trust. There is a preference for local charities and other community projects in the south of England particularly in East Hampshire.

Unfortunately an exact breakdown of the grant beneficiaries was not provided by the trust. Previous grants have been made to Alzheimer's Disease Society, Arthritis and Rheumatism Council – Petersfield, British Heart Foundation, Rainbow House Trust and SSAFA.

Exclusions No funding for overseas charities, students, visits abroad or political causes.

Applications 'The trustees already support as many charities as they could wish and would certainly not welcome any appeals from others. Unsolicited requests are not acknowledged.'

The Harebell Centenary Fund

General, education, medical research and animal welfare

£54,000 (2007)
Beneficial area UK.

50 Broadway, London SW1H 0BL

Tel. 020 7227 7000

Email pennychapman@bdb-law.co.uk

Correspondent Ms P J Chapman

Trustees P J Chapman; M I Goodbody; F M Reed.

CC Number 1003552

Information available Accounts were on file at the Charity Commission.

Established in 1991, this trust provides funding towards the promotion of neurological and neurosurgical research and the relief of sickness and suffering amongst animals, as well as holding an interest in the education of young people.

The current policy of the trustees is to concentrate on making donations to charities that do not receive widespread public support. For this reason the trustees have decided to make donations only to registered charities and not to individuals.

In 2007 it had assets of £2.2 million, which generated an income of £78,000. Grants totalling £54,000 were made to 29 organisations, many of which were hospices. Management and administration fees were high at £11,000.

All grants ranged between £1,500 and £2,500 each. Beneficiaries included: Crathie School (£2,500); the Cats Protection League, Bluebell Hospice, Motor Neurone Disease Association and Ro-Ro Sailing Project (£2,000 each); and Trinity Hospice, Martin's House Children's Hospice and Helen House Hospice (£1,500 each).

Exclusions No grants are made towards infrastructure or to individuals.

Applications In writing to the correspondent. Unsolicited applications are not requested, as the trustees prefer to make donations to charities whose work they have come across through their own research.

The Hargrave Foundation

General, medical and welfare

£43,000 (2007/08)
Beneficial area Worldwide.

47 Lamb's Conduit Street, London WC1N 3NG
Correspondent Stephen Hargrave, Trustee
Trustees Stephen Hargrave; Dominic Moseley; Mark Parkin.
CC Number 1106524
Information available Accounts were on file at the Charity Commission.

Registered with the Charity Commission in November 2004, in its first year of operation this trust received income of £2.8 million.

In 2007/08 it had assets of £2.8 million, an income of £166,000 and made grants totalling £43,000.

Beneficiaries included: Journalism Education and Reform (£10,000 each); St Giles Hospice (£6,000); and Rainforest Concern and The Gentlemen's 'Night Out' (£5,000 each).

Applications In writing to the correspondent.

The Harris Family Charitable Trust

Health and sickness

£132,000 (2007/08)
Beneficial area UK.

65 New Cavendish Street, London W1G 7LS
Correspondent R M Harris, Trustee
Trustees R M Harris; L Harris; C E Harris.
CC Number 1064394
Information available Accounts were on file at the Charity Commission. The notes to the accounts stated that 'a list of grants paid during the year can be obtained from the trustees on request'. Despite a request being made in writing, we were unable to see a list of donations made during the year.

Set up in 1997, the trust makes grants to organisations dealing with health issues and the alleviation of sickness.

In 2007/08 it had an income of £570,000, mostly from donations and legacies and assets stood at £1.3 million. The sum of £132,000 was distributed in grants.

Applications 'The charity invites applications for funding of projects through various sources. The applications are reviewed by the trustees who ensure that they are in accordance with the charity's objectives'.

The Alfred And Peggy Harvey Charitable Trust

See below

£79,000 (2007/08)
Beneficial area UK.

c/o Manches LLP, Aldwych House, 81 Aldwych, London WC2B 4RP
Correspondent The Trustees
Trustees Colin John Russell; John Duncan; Kevin James Custis.
CC Number 1095855
Information available Accounts were on file at the Charity Commission.

The following information is taken from the accounts.

The trustees hold the capital and income of the trust fund upon trust to apply the income and all or such part or parts of the capital for or towards:

1) the advancement and funding of medical and surgical studies and research
2) the care of older people and the provision of accommodation for older people
3) the care of and provision of financial support for disabled children and young people and for children and young people suffering from the lack of stable family upbringing or other social or educational disadvantages
4) the care of blind and deaf people.

In 2007/08 the trust had assets of £500,000 and an income of £119,000. Grants to 36 organisations totalled £79,000.

One large grant of £89,000 was made to St Christopher's Hospice, and other beneficiaries included: Children's Adventure Farm Trust (£24,000); Country Holidays For Inner City Kids (£23,000); Starlight Children's Foundation (£20,000); Lighthouse Educational Scheme (£7,200); Beat Bullying (£7,000); the Eyeless Trust (£5,000); Deafblind UK (£4,000); Learning Through Action (£3,000); Action for Kids (£2,000); and Sunflower Trust (£1,000).

Applications In writing to the correspondent.

Haskel Family Foundation

Jewish, social-policy research, arts and education

£26,000 (2007)
Beneficial area UK.

12 Rosemont Road, Richmond-upon-Thames TW10 6QL

Tel. 0208 948 7711

Correspondent The Trustees

Trustees *A M Davis; S P Haskel; M Nutman; Lord Haskel.*

CC Number 1039969

Information available Full accounts were on file at the Charity Commission.

The charity funds projects concerned with social-policy research, Jewish communal life, arts and education.

In 2007 it had assets of £556,000 and an income of £33,000. Grants totalled £26,000 and were: Aldeburgh Music (£12,000); the Orange Tree Theatre (£5,000); Liberal Judaism and the Jewish Quarterly (£3,000 each); Aldeburgh Productions (£2,000); and Rainford Trust and Watford Mencap (£500 each).

Applications This trust states that it does not respond to unsolicited applications.

Hasluck Charitable Trust

Health, welfare, disability, young people and overseas aid

£102,000 (2007/08)

Beneficial area UK.

Thring Townsend Lee & Pembertons, Kinnaird House, 1 Pall Mall East, London SW1Y 5AU

Tel. 020 7766 5600

Email solicitors@ttuk.com

Correspondent John Billing, Trustee

Trustees *Matthew James Wakefield; John Philip Billing.*

CC Number 1115323

Information available Accounts were on file at the Charity Commission.

Registered with the Charity Commission on 14 July 2008, 'the trustees allocate half of the income received to eight charities [Barnardo's, Mrs R H Hotblacks Michelham Priory Endowment Fund, International Fund for Animal Welfare, Macmillan Cancer Relief, the Riding for the Disabled Association, RNLI, RSPB and Scope], which are of particular interest to the settlor. The remaining monies are distributed to such charitable bodies as the trustees decide.'

In 2007/08 the trust had assets of £1.1 million and an income of £152,000. Grants totalled £102,000.

The sum of £50,000 was given to the trust's eight primary beneficiaries. There were a further 30 grants made in the range of £1,000 to £2,000. Beneficiaries included 3H Fund, the John Aspinall Foundation, British Blind Sport, Combat Stress, Deafblind UK, Give Youth a Break, Opera North, Papworth Trust, the Smile Train, Starlight Children's Foundation, the Stroke Association, Sustrans, World Vision-Bangladesh Appeal, Whirlow Hall Farm Trust, Whizz Kidz and Women's Aid.

Applications In writing to the correspondent. 'Distributions are generally made in January and July, although consideration is given to appeals received at other times of the year.'

The M A Hawe Settlement

General

£252,000 to organisations (2007/08)

Beneficial area UK, with a preference for the north west of England, particularly the Fylde coast area.

94 Park View Road, Lytham St Annes FY8 4JF

Tel. 01253 796888

Correspondent M A Hawe, Trustee

Trustees *M A Hawe; Mrs G Hawe; M G Hawe.*

CC Number 327827

Information available Accounts were on file at the Charity Commission.

In 2007/08 the trust had assets of £5.4 million and an income of £314,000. Grants to organisations totalled £254,000 with £1,700 being distributed to individuals.

As usual, the largest grant was to Kensington House Trust Ltd, which received £251,000. This company was established to run a property bought by the trust in 1993, as accommodation on a short-stay basis for young homeless people. It now also provides furniture and equipment to people in need, shelter for victims of domestic violence and holidays for children who are deprived. The trust has decided to close

Kensington House in 2008, but will still use the proportionate funding to continue activities in a different accommodation.

The remaining grants ranged between £60 and £860. Beneficiaries were Holy Cross Church and Soup Kitchen (£860); Clarenden Street School (£240); and Impulse Dance Troup (£60).

Applications In writing to the correspondent.

The Hawthorne Charitable Trust

General

£196,000 (2007/08)

Beneficial area UK, especially Hereford and Worcester.

c/o Baker Tilly, Lancaster House, 7 Elmfield Road, Bromley BR1 1LT

Tel. 020 8461 8068

Correspondent Roger Clark, Trustee

Trustees *Mrs A S C Berington; R J Clark; T P M Berington; R White.*

CC Number 233921

Information available Full accounts were on file at the Charity Commission.

The trust supports a wide range of organisations, particularly health and welfare causes but also charities concerned with animal welfare, disability, heritage and young people.

In 2007/08 it had assets of £6.7 million, which generated an income of £206,000. Grants were made to 93 organisations totalling £196,000. Donations were broken down into the following categories:

Category	Value	No.
Other	£57,000	30
Medical and health	£55,000	26
Environment, conservation and heritage	£32,000	11
Disability	£22,000	10
Caring for animals	£17,000	9
Relief of poverty	£16,000	7

All grants were made in the region of £250 to £8,000 and beneficiaries included: The Dyson Perrins Museum Trust (£8,000); Army Benevolent Fund and Welland Pre-school (£5,000 each); Motor Neurone Disease Association, Battersea Dogs and Cats Home and National Trust (£3,000 each); London Library, Combat Stress and Hospice Care Kenya (£2,500 each); Woodland Trust, Crusaid and Mobility Trust (£2,000 each); Dogs Trust, SPACE and Music

Space West Midlands (£1,000 each); and Cambridge Cancer Research Fund, Prostate Appeal and Herefordshire Mind (£250 each).

A number of the above beneficiaries have been supported in previous years.

Exclusions Grants are given to registered charities only. No grants to individuals.

Applications In writing to the correspondent, including up-to-date accounts. Applications should be received by October for consideration in November.

The Dorothy Hay-Bolton Charitable Trust

Deafness and blindness

£35,000 (2007/08)

Beneficial area UK, with a preference for the south-east of England and overseas.

c/o F W Stephens, 3rd Floor, 24 Chiswell Street, London EC1Y 4YX

Tel. 020 7382 1820

Email brian.carter@fwstephens.co.uk

Correspondent Brian E Carter, Trustee

Trustees Brian E Carter; Stephen J Gallico.

CC Number 1010438

Information available Accounts were on file at the Charity Commission.

The trust makes grants towards charities working with people who are deaf or blind, particularly children, young people and older people. In 2007/08 the trust had assets of £855,000 and an income of £31,000. Grants to organisations totalled £35,000.

Beneficiaries included: Hearing Dogs for the Deaf (£3,500); Action for Blind People, Sussex Lantern and Telephones for the Blind (£2,500 each); Eyeless Trust (£1,500); British Blind Sport and Esther Benjamin's Trust (£1,250 each); East Sussex Association for the Blind (£1,000); the Seeing Ear (£750); and East Kent Cycling Club (£250).

Exclusions The trust states that it does not generally give to individuals.

Applications In writing to the correspondent.

The Haydan Charitable Trust

Jewish and general

About £33,000 (2008)

Beneficial area UK.

1 Manchester Square, London W1U 3AB

Tel. 020 3219 2600

Correspondent Neil Bradley

Trustees Christopher Smith; Irene Smith; Anthony Winter; Neil Bradley.

CC Number 1003801

Information available Accounts were on file at the Charity Commission.

This trust was set up in 1990 it has a clear relationship with its namesake company, Haydan Holdings Ltd. The trust states that it gives recurrent grants to a few organisations and does not invite applications.

In 2008 the trust had an income of £52,000 and a total expenditure £38,000. Grants were made totalling about £33,000. No further information was available for the year.

Previous beneficiaries include: Jewish Communal Fund (£83,000); Babes in Arms, Greater London Fund for the Blind and Anthony Nolan Trust (£10,000 each); Beth Jacob Grammar School for Girls, Leukaemia Research Fund and Nordoff Robbins Music Trust (£5,000 each); and Cancer Research UK (£1,600).

Exclusions No grants are given for projects overseas.

Applications Unsolicited applications are not considered.

The Haymills Charitable Trust

Education, medicine, welfare and young people

£195,000 to organisations and individuals (2007/08)

Beneficial area UK, but particularly the west of London and Suffolk, where the Haymills group is sited.

7 Wildwood, Northwood HA6 2DB

Tel. 01923 825989

Email ian.w.ferres@btinternet.com

Correspondent I W Ferres, Secretary

Trustees W G Underwood, Chair; E F C Drake; I W Ferres; K C Perryman; J A Sharpe; J L Wosner.

CC Number 277761

Information available Accounts were on file at the Charity Commission, but without a list of grants.

'The trustees endeavour to make the best use of the monies available from the funds of the trust. In particular donations are made to projects they believe to be inadequately supported.'

In the past, grants have fallen into four main categories.

- Education: grants to schools, colleges and universities.
- Medicine: grants to hospitals and associated institutions and to medical research.
- Welfare: primarily to include former Haymills' staff, and to those who are considered to be 'in necessitous circumstances' or who are otherwise distressed or disadvantaged.
- Young people: support for training schemes to assist in the education, welfare and training of young people.

In 2007/08 it had assets of £5.9 million and an income of £219,000. Grants totalled £195,000 and were broken down as follows:

Category	Value
Young people and welfare	£108,000
Medical	£55,000
Education	£33,000

Unfortunately no list of grants was included with the accounts on file at the Charity Commission, however some information on beneficiaries was given for each category of grants:

Educational
Grants were given to various educational establishments, especially towards bursaries, prizes and scholarships. The largest grant given was awarded to Merchant Taylor's Company for the Geoffrey Cox Scholarships (£26,500), with the next highest going to a primary school for sports facilities (£4,000) and a further four grants given to schools and universities for prize funds and awards (£2,300).

Medical
Medical grants were given to 24 organisations, with the highest grant going to the Royal College of Physicians (£5,000), a regular grant that has been made for many years. Other organisations supported included League of Friends at Ealing, Central Middlesex and Bournemouth Eye Hospitals and research societies of Cancer, Parkinsons and Meningitis.

141

Young people and welfare

Payments to support retired employees of Haymills Contractors Ltd, which totalled £4,800 in the year.

An additional £103,000 was distributed between 50 organisations, with the highest grants going to the Universal Beneficent Society (£6,000) and British Red Cross Society and the Sea Cadets (£5,000 each). Further grants were also given to Prince's Trust, Project Trust, Raleigh International, Young Enterprise and Greater London Scouts. Hospices in London and East Anglia were also supported.

Exclusions No personal applications will be considered unless endorsed by a university, college or other appropriate authority.

Applications In writing to the correspondent, but note the comments earlier in the section. Trustees meet at least twice a year, usually in March and October. Applications are not acknowledged.

May Hearnshaw's Charity

General

£73,000 (2007/08)

Beneficial area UK, particularly South Yorkshire, North Nottinghamshire, Derbyshire, East Lancashire or Cheshire areas.

Barber Harrison and Platt, 2 Rutland Park, Sheffield S10 2PD

Correspondent J Rowan, Trustee

Trustees J Rowan; D C Law; Mrs M West; M Ferreday; R Law; W Munro.

CC Number 1008638

Information available Accounts were on file at the Charity Commission.

This trust was set up by the will of the late May Hearnshaw who died in 1988. It was her wish that the trust be used for the promotion of education, advancement of religion and relief of poverty and sickness. Support is mostly given to children's organisations within these themes. Grants are made to UK-wide charities or local charities working in the South Yorkshire, North Nottinghamshire, Derbyshire, East Lancashire or Cheshire areas.

In 2007/08 the trust had an income of £81,000 and made grants to 42 organisations totalling £73,000. The main beneficiaries were Alzheimers Society Sheffield, Ripley Methodist Church and Whirlow Hall Farm Trust (£5,000 each). Other beneficiaries included: MIND (£4,000); Culcheth Methodist Church, Dore Youth Worker Trust and St Laurence Education Trust (£3,000 each); Derbyshire Children's Holiday Centre, Dyslexic Action and Cystic Fibrosis Trust (£2,000 each); the Living Paintings Trust, the Mercian Trust and Royal British Legion (£1,000 each); and the Elizabeth Foundation (£500).

Applications 'The trustees usually decide on and make grants to charitable organisations at least once a year but may decide to make grants at any time. They do not include in their consideration appeals received direct from individuals.'

The Heathcoat Trust

Welfare and local causes to Tiverton, Devon

£78,000 to organisations (2007/08)

Beneficial area Mainly Tiverton, Devon.

The Factory, West Exe, Tiverton EX16 5LL

Tel. 01884 254949

Website www.heathcoat.co.uk

Correspondent Mr E W Summers, Secretary

Trustees Sir Ian Heathcoat Amory; M J Gratton; J Smith; Mr C Dunster; Mr S Butt.

CC Number 203367

Information available Accounts were on file at the Charity Commission.

The trust was established in 1945. Its objectives as stated in the 2006 accounts are 'for the relief of financial hardship, for education and training, for building or making grants to health institutions, and in certain circumstances for making contributions to any charity but mostly in Tiverton in Devon and its neighbourhood, or in places where the firms John Heathcoat and Company Limited and Lowman Manufacturing Company Limited and their subsidiaries carry on business. In so far as the income cannot be applied towards the objects specified in the trust deed, it may be applied for any charitable purpose.'

Over 100 grants a year, mostly under £1,000 each, are made to organisations and nearly all to local causes around the Tiverton area. Other grants are made to individuals, employees and pensioners of the Heathcoat group of companies. Educational grants are given to children of those employees or pensioners and also to local students attending schools and colleges in Tiverton, or beyond if courses are not available locally.

In 2007/08 the trust had assets of £19 million and an income of £612,000. Grants totalled £560,000 of which £78,000 went to organisations and £483,000 to individuals.

Applications In writing to the correspondent. There are application forms for certain education grants.

The Charlotte Heber-Percy Charitable Trust

General

£210,000 (2007/08)

Beneficial area Worldwide, with a preference for Gloucestershire.

Rathbones, 159 New Bond Street, London W1S 2UD

Tel. 020 7399 0820

Correspondent The Administrator

Trustees Mrs C S Heber-Percy; Mrs J A Prest.

CC Number 284387

Information available Full accounts were on file at the Charity Commission.

The trust has a stated preference for Gloucestershire. In addition to local appeals, non-local applications are accumulated and considered annually by the trustees. In 2007/08 the trust had assets of £5.3 million and an income of £222,000. Grants were made to 47 organisations totalling £210,000. Categories of charities supported are as follows:

- international charities – £65,000
- medical, cancer and hospices – £45,000
- local organisations – £34,000
- education and children – £32,000

- the arts and museums – £16,000
- general charitable organisations – £13,000
- animal welfare and the local environment – £6,000.

Grants recipients included: Funds for Refugees in Slovenia (£22,000); the Royal Ballet School (£15,000); the Family Survival Trust, Gloucestershire Community Foundation and Longborough Festival Opera (£10,000 each); British Yemeni Society and Help for Heroes (£5,000 each); Canine Partners and Independent Age (£3,000 each); Royal Scots Dragoon Guards Association (£2,000); Songbird Survival (£1,000); and Friends of St Mary Magdalene Church – Adelstrop (£500).

Exclusions No grants to individuals.

Applications The correspondent stated that unsolicited applications are not required.

Percy Hedley 1990 Charitable Trust

General charitable purposes

£40,000 (2007/08)

Beneficial area UK with a preference for Northumberland and Tyne and Wear.

10 Castleton Close, Newcastle upon Tyne NE2 2HF

Tel. 0191 281 5953

Correspondent J Armstrong, Trustee

Trustees *G W Meikle; J R Armstrong; Mrs F M Ruffman.*

CC Number 1000033

Information available Accounts were on file at the Charity Commission.

In 2007/08 the trust had assets of £1.4 million and an income of £53,000. Grants totalling £40,000 were distributed to 58 institutions.

Unfortunately a grants list was not available from this years accounts. However, previous beneficiaries have included: Newcastle Theatre Royal Trust (£5,000); Percy Hedley Foundation and Newcastle Royal Grammar School – Bursary Fund (£3,000 each); National Playing Fields Association, the Anaphylaxis Campaign, Samaritans of Tyneside and Marie Curie Foundation –

Newcastle (£1,000 each); Salvation Army and Northumberland Wildlife Trust (£500 each); and Listening Books and Pets as Therapy (£250 each).

Applications In writing to the correspondent. Trustees meet twice a year.

The Hellenic Foundation

Greek education in the UK

£16,000 to organisations (2007)

Beneficial area UK.

St Paul's House, Warwick Lane, London EC4M 7BP

Tel. 020 7251 5100

Correspondent The Secretary

Trustees *Tryphon E Kendros, Hon. Chair; Stamos J Fafalios, Chair; George A Tsavliris; Nicos H Sideris; Irene M Monios; Dr Eleni Yannakakis; Zenon K Mouskos; Constantinos I Caroussis; Mary Bromley; Irene J Fafalios-Zannas; Angela K Kulukundis; George A Lemos; George D Lemos; Louisa Williamson; Despina M Moschos; Anna S Polemis-Alisafakis.*

CC Number 326301

Information available Full accounts were on file at the Charity Commission.

As stated in the trustees' report, the foundation was set up in 1982 to 'advance and propagate education and learning in Great Britain in the cultural tradition and heritage of Greece and particularly in the subjects involving education, research, music and dance, books and library facilities and university symposia'.

In 2007 the trust's assets totalled £470,000 and it had an income of £26,000. Grants totalled £16,000 and were distributed to three organisations. The sum of £500 went to individuals.

Beneficiaries were: Royal Academy Byzantine exhibition (£15,000); Theatro Technis (£1,000); and Aghia Shophia School (£200).

Exclusions The foundation is unable to offer scholarships or grants to cover tuition fees and living expenses.

Applications In writing to the correspondent.

The Michael and Morven Heller Charitable Foundation

University and medical research projects and the arts

£203,000 (2007/08)

Beneficial area Worldwide.

Carlton House, 22a St James's Square, London SW1Y 4JH

Tel. 020 7415 5000 **Fax** 020 7415 0611

Correspondent M A Heller, Trustee

Trustees *Michael Heller; Morven Heller; W S Trustee Company Limited.*

CC Number 327832

Information available Accounts were on file at the Charity Commission.

This trust was established in 1972 and funds specific projects relating to medical research, science and educational research. This usually involves making large grants to universities for research purposes, particularly medical research. In practice, there appears to be some preference for Jewish organisations.

In 2007/08 the trust had assets of £4.6 million and an income of £305,000. Grants totalled £204,000, broken down as follows: education (£141,000); humanitarian (£47,000); and research (£17,000).

Exclusions No support for individuals.

Applications In writing to the correspondent.

The Simon Heller Charitable Settlement

Medical research, science and educational research

£292,000 (2007/08)

Beneficial area Worldwide.

143

Carlton House, 22a St James' Square,
London SW1Y 4JH

Tel. 020 7415 5000

Correspondent The Trustees

Trustees *M A Heller; Morven Heller; W S Trustee Company Limited.*

CC Number 265405

Information available Accounts were on file at the Charity Commission, without a list of grants.

This trust was established in 1972, and funds specific projects relating to medical research, science and educational research. This usually involves making large grants to universities for research purposes, particularly medical research. In practice, there appears to be some preference for Jewish organisations.

In 2007/08 the trust had assets of £8.6 million and an income of £400,000. Grants were made totalling £292,000. Broken down as follows: humanitarian (£153,000); education (£72,000); and research (£68,000). No list of grants was included with the accounts filed at the Charity Commission.

The 2000/01 accounts listed 19 grants over £1,000 each. UJIA received the largest single grant of £35,000 with Institute for Jewish Policy Research receiving the same amount in two grants of £25,000 and £10,000. Other major beneficiaries were Jewish Care (£30,000), Aish Hatora (£15,000 in two grants), Spiro Institute (£13,000), Scopus (£12,000 in two grants) and Chief Rabbinate Charitable Trust (£10,000).

Exclusions No grants to individuals.

Applications In writing to the correspondent.

Help the Homeless Ltd

Homelessness

£120,000 (2007/08)

Beneficial area UK only.

6th Floor, 248 Tottenham Court Road, London W1T 7QZ

Email hth@help-the-homeless.org.uk

Website www.help-the-homeless.org.uk

Correspondent The Secretary

Trustees *F J Bergin; T S Cookson; L A Bains; T Rogers; P Fullerton; J Rose.*

CC Number 271988

Information available Accounts were on file at the Charity Commission.

The trust makes small grants to smaller or new voluntary organisations, who are registered charities, for items of capital expenditure directly related to the provision of housing for people who are single and homeless. Grants do not normally exceed £3,000.

Trustees will also consider applications for larger pump priming grants for major and innovative projects. Applicants should enquire about the status of the Large Grants Programme before making an application.

In 2007/08 the trust had assets of £1.2 million and an income of £102,000. Grants were made totalling £120,000.

The largest grant made during the year was given to Emmaus Sheffield (£50,000). Other beneficiaries included: Slough Homeless Our Concern (£10,000); Emmaus Cambridge and Byker Bridge Housing Association (£5,000 each); Oasis Church Trust, Save the Family and Healthy Living Projects (£3,000 each); Freedom Centre (£2,500); Nightsafe (£2,000); and Harlow Homeless Centre (£560).

Exclusions Charities with substantial funds are not supported. No grants to individuals.

Applications Application forms can be downloaded from the trust's website. Trustees meet to consider grants four times a year.

Help the Hospices

Hospices

£996,000 (2007/08)

Beneficial area UK.

34–44 Britannia Street, London WC1 9JG

Tel. 020 7520 8200

Email grants@helpthehospices.org.uk

Website www.helpthehospices.org.uk

Correspondent David Praill, Chief Executive

Trustees *Dr Helen Clayson; Rt Hon Lord Newton; Sally Taylor; David Clark; Bay Green; Beverley Brooks; Graham Elderfield; Gary Hawkes; Judith Hodgson; Peter Holliday; Marina Phillips; Sheila Tonge; Isabel Whaite.*

CC Number 1014851

Information available Accounts were on file at the Charity Commission.

The objects of the charity are as follows.

- To facilitate and promote the relief, care and treatment of the sick, especially of the dying, and the support and care of their families and carers and of the bereaved.
- To facilitate and promote the charitable activities of independent hospices.
- To provide or facilitate education and training for professionals and volunteers engaged in palliative care and increase awareness among the general public of the values, principles and practise of hospice and palliative care.

These objectives are met by providing education and training as well as funding hospices and palliative care units through a number of grant schemes. See www.helpthehospices.org.uk for up-to-date details of current programmes.

In 2007/08 the trust had assets of just under £5 million and an income of £6.1 million, including over £5 million from voluntary income.

Out of a total charitable expenditure of £5.1 million, grants to organisations were made totalling £996,000, of which given £557,000 was given to 128 hospices through various grant programmes. A further £409,000 was distributed among 1,067 individuals.

Applications Generally on a form available from the Grants Officer, from whom further information is also available. For major grant programmes, potential applicants should request details first as policies change. The trust's website contains detailed information of the grant-making policy and should be viewed before an application is considered. For emergency grants, applicants should write directly to the chief executive.

The Christina Mary Hendrie Trust for Scottish and Canadian Charities

Young people, older people and general

£272,000 (2007/08)

Beneficial area Scotland and Canada.

Anderson Strathern Solicitors, 1 Rutland Court, Edinburgh EH3 8EY

Tel. 0131 270 7700 **Fax** 0131 270 7788

Correspondent Alan Sharp, Secretary

Trustees *Sir Alistair Irwin, Chair; Anthony Cox; Arabella Cox; Charles Cox; Mary-Rose Grieve; Susie Hendrie; Miss Caroline Irwin; John K Scott-Moncrieff.*

SC Number SC014514

Information available Accounts supplied by the trust

The trust was established in 1975 following the death in Scotland of Christina Mary Hendrie. The funds constituting the trust originated in Canada. Grants are distributed to charities throughout Scotland and Canada, although the majority are now given in Scotland. There is a preference for charities connected with young or older people, although other groups to receive grants include cancer charities. In 2007/08 the trust had assets of £6.4 million and an income of £124,000. Grants were made totalling £272,000. Beneficiaries of grants included: Outfit Moray (£150,000); Beannachar Ltd (£50,000); Lilias Graham Trust (£35,000); Erskine (£30,000); Combat Stress and Prison Phoenix Trust (£15,000 each); Lord Roberts Workshop (£10,000); Rock Trust (£5,000); and Scottish Cot Death (£2,500).

Exclusions Grants are not given to individuals. Only organisations known to the trustees can be considered.

Applications In writing to the correspondent.

Philip Henman Trust

General

£45,000 (2007/08)

Beneficial area Worldwide.

16 Pembury Road, Tonbridge TN9 2HX

Tel. 01732 362227

Email info@pht.org.uk

Website www.pht.org.uk

Correspondent D J Clark, Trustee

Trustees *J C Clark; D J Clark; J Duffey.*

CC Number 1054707

Information available Accounts were on file at the Charity Commission.

The Philip Henman Trust offers grants to major UK based overseas development organisations requiring partnership funding for projects lasting between three and five years. These grants are split into annual payments (normally between £3,000 and £5,000 per annum) with a maximum total of £25,000. Once the grant has been approved the organisation will be guaranteed an annual grant for the duration of the project, as long as receipts and reports are sent back to the trust. Once a grant has been given, the organisation cannot apply for a grant in respect of a project for which they have already received funding.

The trust only has resources to guarantee an average of two new long-term grants a year, and therefore it is important to be sure any project fits our criteria before applying. Successful applications are normally those that prove the following.

- The project is being run professionally by an established major UK registered charity (normally defined as having an income of over £100,000 per annum).
- The project is concerned with long-term overseas development.
- The project is a project and will start and finish within five years. We do not fund ongoing concerns.
- The funding from the Philip Henman Trust is important to the project (normally requires the grant funding to account for between 20% and 80% of the total project budget).
- The project will provide a lasting beneficial impact to the people or environment it seeks to help.
- The project is being partly funded by other sources. Voluntary work and central office administration costs can be counted as other source funding.

Please note: from 2007 the trust is no longer offering one-off grants.

In 2007/08 the trust had assets of £1.9 million and an income of £65,000. Grants totalled £45,000, and were broken down as follows:

Category	Value
Overseas aid	£29,000
Child aid	£5,000
Medical and community work	£5,000
Social welfare	£5,000
Other	£200

Unfortunately, a list of beneficiaries was not included in the trusts accounts.

Applications Applications are only considered once a year – the deadline is always 10 September. Applications are no longer accepted by post. Please use the online form to submit applications.

The G D Herbert Charitable Trust

Medicine, health, welfare and environmental resources

£72,500 (2007/08)

Beneficial area UK.

Barnards Inn, 86 Fetter Lane, London EC4A 1AD

Tel. 020 7405 1234

Correspondent J J H Burden, Trustee

Trustees *M E Beaumont; J J H Burden.*

CC Number 295998

Information available Full accounts were on file at the Charity Commission.

The trust makes grants in the areas of medicine, health, welfare and environmental resources. It mainly gives regular grants to a set list of charities, with a few one-off grants given each year.

In 2007/08 this trust had assets of £1.8 million and an income of £60,000. Grants totalled £72,500 of which 25 were regular donations totalling £58,500.

Beneficiaries of special donations included: Ashford and Tenterden Samaritans, Children's Fire and Burn Trust, The Queen Alexandra Hospital Home, National ME Centre for Fatigue Syndromes, The Rainbow Centre, St Raphael's Hospice and Deafness Research UK (£2,000 each).

Beneficiaries of regular donations included: The National Trust, Friends of the Elderly, Marie Curie Cancer Care,

PDSA, Royal College of Surgeons of England, Royal Hospital for Neuro-Disability and The Woodland Trust (£2,500 each); Ogbourne St Georges PCC and Wiltshire Wildlife Trust (£500 each).

Applications In writing to the correspondent. No applications are invited other than from those charities currently supported by the trust.

The Joanna Herbert-Stepney Charitable Settlement (also known as The Paget Charitable Trust)

General

£243,000 (2007/08)

Beneficial area Worldwide, with an interest in Loughborough.

Old Village Stores, Dippenhall Street, Crondall, Farnham GU10 5NZ

Correspondent Joanna Herbert-Stepney, Trustee

Trustees *Joanna Herbert-Stepney; Lesley Mary Blood; Meg Williams.*

CC Number 327402

Information available Information was on file at the Charity Commission.

The trust supports both UK and local charities for general charitable purposes. Priorities include international aid and development, children who are disadvantaged, older people, animal welfare and environmental projects. The trust states that there is a preference for the 'unglamorous' and 'projects where a little money goes a long way'. In many cases ongoing support is given to organisations.

In 2007/08 the trust had assets of £6.8 million and an income of £310,000. Out of a total expenditure of £298,000, grants totalled £243,000.

Grants were made to 173 organisations, of which the two largest grants went to Belton Church Restoration (£50,000);

and Dawson and Fowler Foundation (£20,000). Other beneficiaries included: Second Chance (£5,000); Oxfam (£4,000); Farms for City Children and Soil Association (£3,000 each); Childhood First, Ethiopiaid, and Pattaya Orphanage Trust (£2,000 each); the Organic Research Centre, World Medical Fund, Task Brasil, Southwark Community Education Council and Mission Romania (£1,000 each); and Coventry City Farm, Asthma UK and Anglo-Peruvian Child Care Mission (£500 each).

Exclusions The trust states that 'sheer need is paramount, in practice, nothing else is considered'. Grants are only given to registered UK charities. Overseas projects can only be funded via UK charities; no money can be sent directly overseas. The trust does not support individuals (including students), projects for people with mental disabilities, medical research or AIDS/HIV projects.

Applications In writing to the correspondent; there is no application form. The trustees meet in spring and autumn. The trust regrets that it cannot respond to all applications.

The Hesed Trust

Christian

£73,000 to organisations

(2007/08)

Beneficial area UK and overseas.

14 Chiltern Avenue, Cosby, Leicester LE9 1UF

Tel. 0116 286 2990

Email glynrawlings@btopenworld.com

Correspondent G Rawlings, Secretary

Trustees *P Briggs; R Eagle; G Rawlings; C Smith.*

CC Number 1000489

Information available Accounts were on file at the Charity Commission.

The trust's objectives are:

- the advancement of the Christian faith
- the relief of persons who are in conditions of need, hardship or distress or who are older or sick
- the provision of instruction the Christian faith at any educational establishment
- the provision of facilities for recreation for persons in need of, for the benefit of the public at large with the object of improving the conditions of life for such persons.

In 2007/08 the trust had net assets of £94,000, total income of £173,000 and had a charitable expenditure of £175,000. This included £73,000 in grants to charitable organisations and £100,000 in ministry support costs.

Organisations to benefit were: Ministries Without Borders (45,000); Aquila Ministries (£14,000); Iglesia Cuba (£11,000); Scripture Knowledge (£3,000); and Rainbow Africa (£100).

Exclusions No support for expeditions and individual requests.

Applications The trust states that no applications are now being considered.

The Bernhard Heuberger Charitable Trust

Jewish

£161,000 (2007/08)

Beneficial area Worldwide.

12 Sherwood Road, London NW4 1AD

Correspondent The Trustees

Trustees *D H Heuberger; S N Heuberger.*

CC Number 294378

Information available Accounts were on file at the Charity Commission.

This trust was established in 1986. In 2007/08 it had assets of £2.3 million and an income of £111,000. During the year 17 grants totalling £161,000 were approved compared with 21 grants totalling £179,000 in the previous year. Donations were broken down as follows, shown here with examples of beneficiaries in each category:

Education/training – £31,500
Shuvo Yisroel and Yesoday Hatorah Schools (£10,000 each); Enzer North West (£5,000); JFS School (£3,500); Institute for Higher Rabbinical Studies (£2,000); and Beth Yaakov Seminary for Girls (£1,000).

Medical/health/sickness – £25,000
Notzar Chesed Central Aid Fund (£20,000); and Down's Syndrome Association (£5,000).

General – £104,000
Beis Ahron Trust, Tchabe Kollel Limited and C.M.M (£25,000 each); WST Charity Limited (£10,000 each); C.M.Z. Limited (£5,000); Kemble Charitable Trust (£3,500); Emunah (£2,500); Hendon

United Synagogue (£2,400) and other small charitable donations (£5,800).

Applications In writing to the correspondent.

The P and C Hickinbotham Charitable Trust

Social welfare

£71,000 (2007/08)

Beneficial area UK, with a preference for Leicestershire and Rutland.

9 Windmill Way, Lyddington, Oakham LE15 9LY

Tel. 01572 821236

Email rogerhick@gmail.com

Correspondent Roger Hickinbotham, Trustee

Trustees *Catherine Hickinbotham; Roger Hickinbotham; Rachel Hickinbotham; Anna Hickinbotham.*

CC Number 216432

Information available Accounts were available from the Charity Commission.

Grants are generally not recurrent and are largely to social welfare organisations, with some churches and Quaker meetings also receiving support. Grants are mainly under £500, with some smaller grants made to a variety of registered charities. The trust gives occasional, one-off larger grants usually between £5,000 and £20,000.

In 2007/08 the trust had assets of £3.2 million, which generated an income of £636,000. Grants were made totalling £71,000.

Beneficiaries included: Voluntary Action – Rutland (£15,000); Worgan Trust and Rainbows Children's Hospice (£10,000 each); Belgrave Playhouse (£2,500); National Trust for Egryn – North Wales and the Woodland Trust (£2,000 each); Society of Friends – Leicester PM (£1,400); and Cruise Bereavement Care, RSPB and New Futures Project (£1,000 each).

Exclusions No grants to individuals applying for bursary-type assistance or to large UK charities.

Applications In writing to the correspondent, giving a brief outline of the purpose of the grant. Replies will not be sent to unsuccessful applicants.

Highcroft Charitable Trust

Jewish and poverty

£76,000 (2007/08)

Beneficial area UK and overseas.

15 Highcroft Gardens, London NW11 0LY

Correspondent Rabbi R Fischer, Trustee

Trustees *Rabbi R Fischer; Mrs S L Fischer.*

CC Number 272684

Information available Accounts were on file at the Charity Commission.

The trust supports the advancement and study of the Jewish faith and the Torah, and also the relief of poverty and advancement of education among people of the Jewish faith. Grants have previously ranged between £150 and £5,000.

In 2007/08 the trust had assets of £434,000 and an income of £102,000. Grants totalled £76,000.

Unfortunately, a list of beneficiaries was not available in this year's accounts, however previous beneficiaries have included: Friends of Beer Miriam, Institute For Higher Rabbinic Studies and Kollel Ohr Yechiel (£5,000 each); Kollel Chibas Yerushalayim (£4,200); Craven Walk Charity Trust (£2,500); London Friends of Kamenitzer (£2,000); Hachzakas Torah Vachesed Charity (£1,900); Amutat Shaarei Harama, Beis Yaacov High School and Tashbar Manchester (£1,000 each); Belt Haknesset Kehilat Yaacov (£700); and British Friends of College Technology and Delamere Forest School (£100 each).

Applications In writing to the correspondent.

The Holly Hill Charitable Trust

Environmental education, conservation and wildlife

£201,000 (2007/08)

Beneficial area UK.

Unit No. 525, Citibox Kensington, 2 Old Brompton Road, London SW7 3DQ

Correspondent The Trustees

Trustees *M D Stanley; A Lewis.*

CC Number 1044510

Information available Accounts were on file at the Charity Commission.

This trust was established in 1995 to support environmental education, conservation and wildlife organisations.

In 2007/08 it had assets of £986,000 and an income of £29,000, made from investments. Grants were made totalling £201,000.

The largest grant by far went to Rainforest Concern (£65,000). Other beneficiaries included: Eden River Trust (£30,000); Devon Wildlife Trust (£20,000); West Country Rivers Trust and Kasanka Trust (£15,000 each); Cuenca Limon Costa Rica (£7,700); True Nature Films, Aberdeen University and St Columban's Environmental Report (£5,000 each); Sussex University (£4,000); Ecology Project (£2,600); and Ecuador Community Workshop (£1,500).

Other small donations were made totalling £20,000.

Exclusions No grants to individuals.

Applications In writing to the correspondent. Applications need to be received in April and September, and trustees meet in June and November.

The Derek Hill Foundation

Arts and culture

£52,000 (2007/08)

Beneficial area UK.

c/o Northern Trust Fiduciary Services UK Ltd, 50 Bank Street, Canary Wharf, London E14 5NT

Correspondent The Trustees

Trustees *Northern Trust Fiduciary Services (UK) Limited; Rt Hon. Alexander Patrick Greysteil Hore Ruthven, Earl of Gowrie; Lord Armstrong of Ilminster; Mrs Josephine Batterham.*

CC Number 801590

Information available Accounts were on file at the Charity Commission.

This trust was set up in 1989, by the writer and artist Derek Hill. Following his death in 1990, a specific legacy was left to the foundation including properties, furniture and pieces of art. In

2007/08 it had assets of £1.6 million and an income of £55,000. Grants totalled £76,000, of which £52,000 went to organisations.

Beneficiaries included: Artes Mundi – funding to provide education and develop public interest in contemporary visual art (£10,000); the British School at Rome – scholarship (£8,000); Future Talent – to fund opportunities for young musicians in state sector education and Welsh National Opera – contribution to the Songlines 2008 project (£7,500 each); Festival of Muslim Cultures – funding to promote a better understanding between Muslims and Memorial Arts Charity – to fund part of the living costs of an apprentice (£5,000); Royal Northern College of Music – travel bursaries and Watts Gallery Summer School – bursaries (£3,000 each); and Royal Academy of Music – travel bursaries (£1,500).

The sum of £14,000 went to seven individuals.

Applications In writing to the correspondent.

The Charles Littlewood Hill Trust

Health, disability, service and children (including schools)

£167,000 (2008)

Beneficial area UK, with a preference for Nottinghamshire and Norfolk.

Berryman Shacklock LLP, Park House, Friar Lane, Nottingham NG1 6DN

Tel. 0115 945 3700 **Fax** 0115 948 0234

Correspondent W F Whysall, Trustee

Trustees C W L Barratt; W F Whysall; T H Farr; N R Savory.

CC Number 286350

Information available Accounts were on file at the Charity Commission.

The trust supports schools, disability, health, service and children's organisations. It gives UK-wide, although particular preference is given to applications from Norfolk and Nottinghamshire.

In 2008 the trust had assets of £3.3 million, which generated an income of £200,000. Grants were made totalling £167,000 and were broken down as follows, shown here with examples of beneficiaries in each category:

Norfolk – 19 grants totalling £61,000
The Norfolk and Norwich Association for the Blind (£13,000); Catholic Cathedral of East Anglia (£10,000); The Norfolk Churches Trust (£5,000); Norfolk Eating Disorders Association and St Martin's Housing Trust (£3,000); Norfolk Community Foundation (£2,500); All Hallows Hospital (£2,000); and Samaritans Great Yarmouth (£1,000).

Nottinghamshire – 23 grants totalling £59,000
St John Waterwing (£6,000); Beaumond House Community Hospice, Nottinghamshire Wildlife Trust and Peter Le Marchant Trust (£5,000 each); Family Care (£3,000); Nottingham University Hospitals Charity (£2,500); and Nottingham Regional Society for Adults & Children with Autism and Nottingham Sea Cadet Unit (£2,000 each).

Elsewhere – 21 grants totalling £29,000
ExtraCare (£5,000); Royal Anglian Regiment Museum Appeal (£2,500); National Centre for Young People with Epilepsy (£2,000); and Brainwave, British Lung Foundation, the Gurkha Welfare Trust, the Prostate Cancer Charity, Tiny Tickers and the Queen Alexandra Hospital Home (£1,000 each).

Other grants in aggregate totalled £18,000.

Exclusions Applications from individuals are not considered. Grants are seldom made for repairs of parish churches outside Nottinghamshire.

Applications In writing to the correspondent, including the latest set of audited accounts, at least one month before trustees' meetings in March, July and November. Unsuccessful applications will not be notified.

R G Hills Charitable Trust

General

£120,000 (2007/08)

Beneficial area UK and overseas.

Furley Page, 39 St Margaret's Street, Canterbury CT1 2TX

Tel. 01227 763939

Correspondent H M S Barrett, Trustee

Trustees D J Pentin; H M S Barrett.

CC Number 1008914

Information available Full accounts were on file at the Charity Commission.

This trust was dormant until Mrs E M Hill's death in March 1996, when she left three-quarters of the residue of her estate to the trust. The balance was received in June 1999.

In 2007/08 the trust had assets of £2.8 million and an income of £120,000, all of which was distributed in grants to 50 organisations.

Beneficiaries included: Canterbury Theatre and Festival Trust, Arthritis Care and Disability Challengers Ltd (£5,000 each); Health for All and Leonard Cheshire (£4,000 each); Hope UK and Sumatran Orangutan Society (£3,000 each); Build Africa, Kent Wildlife Trust and Macmillan Cancer Support (£2,000 each); and British Blind Sport and Bowland Pennine Mountain Rescue Team (£1,000 each).

Applications In writing to the correspondent.

Hinchley Charitable Trust

Mainly evangelical Christian

£142,000 (2007/08)

Beneficial area UK and overseas.

Watersmeet, 56 Barton Road, Haslingfield, Cambridge CB3 7LL

Tel. 01223 741120

Email bs217@cam.ac.uk

Correspondent Dr Brian Stanley, Chair

Trustees Dr B Stanley; J D Levick; S P Dengate; R Northcott.

CC Number 1108412

Information available Accounts were on file at the Charity Commission.

The trust give grants in the following categories: training; education; overseas; famine relief; religious activity; young people; and medical (primary ancillary care). The trust states that most grants are given to organisations with an 'Evangelical ethos'.

In 2007/08 the trust had assets of £2.7 million and an income of £166,000.

Grants to 30 organisations totalled £142,000.

Beneficiaries included: Associated Bus Ministries (£12,000); International Needs and Lighthouse Group (£10,000 each); Central Eurasian Partners, Wycliffe Bible Translators and Nehemiah Project (£5,000 each); Scripture Union (£3,000); Mission Aviation Fellowship and Kids Church (£2,500 each); Cross Roads Christian Counselling (£2,000); Reach for Rwanda (£1,500); and Timios Trust (£1,000).

Applications The trust states that it does not respond to unsolicited applications. Replies will rarely, if ever, be made to applications for grants by post or on the telephone, as existing funds are all fully committed to charities which are regularly supported.

Stuart Hine Trust

Evangelical Christianity

£130,000 (2007/08)
Beneficial area UK and overseas.

Cherith, 23 Derwent Close, Hailsham BN27 3DA
Tel. 01323 843948
Correspondent Raymond Bodkin, Trustee
Trustees *Raymond Bodkin; Nigel Coltman; Amelia Gardner; Philip Johnson.*
CC Number 326941
Information available Accounts were on file at the Charity Commission.

The trust gives grants to evangelical Christian organisations that have been supported by the trustees or by the settlor during his lifetime and that are known to the trustees. In 2007/08 the trust had an income of £163,000, mainly from royalties received from the song 'How Great Thou Art' written by Stuart Hine. Grants totalled £130,000.

A detailed grants list was not available, although the trust did inform us that the bulk of the grant total was given to Wycliff Bible Translators (£99,000). Grants to other organisations totalled £31,000.

Applications The trust states that 'unsolicited requests for funds will not be considered'. Funds are basically distributed in accordance with the wishes of the settlor.

The Hinrichsen Foundation

Music

£42,000 to organisations and individuals (2007)
Beneficial area UK.

PO Box 309, Leatherhead KT22 2AT
Email hinrichsen.foundation@ editionpeters.com
Website www.hinrichsenfoundation.org.uk
Correspondent The Secretary
Trustees *P Standford, Chair; T Berg; Dr J Cross; Dr Linda Hirst; Sue Lubbock; K Potter; P Strang; Prof S Walsh; Mrs T Estell.*
CC Number 272389
Information available Accounts were on file at the Charity Commission.

The following statement is currently (November 2009) posted on the foundation's website:

The trustees have decided with much regret that the foundation is deferring its grant-giving programme for the time being, largely as a result of the present uncertainty in world markets and the weakness of its investment currency. The foundation's advisers will reappraise the situation at the end of 2009.

The foundation's trustees have previously stated:

The Hinrichsen Foundation is a charity devoted to the promotion of music. Although the objects of the trust are widely drawn, the trustees have decided for the time being to concentrate on assisting in the 'written' areas of music, that is, assisting contemporary composition and its performance and musical research.

However, in the near future it hopes to widen its activities beyond this area.

Support is given to the public performance of living composers; grants include those to performing ensembles for concerts and festivals. Organisations supported include both UK organisations and local groups throughout the UK.

In 2007 the foundation had an income of £32,000 almost entirely from donations received. Grants were approved to 41 organisations/individuals totalling £42,000.

Beneficiaries included: Huddersfield Contemporary Music Festival (£5,000); Dartington International Summer School and Spitalfields Festival (£2,000 each);

Birmingham Contemporary Music Group and Kettle's Yard (£1,500 each); Swaledale Festival and York Late Music Festival (£1,000 each); the Red Violin (£750); Dmitri Ensemble (£500); and Pro Nobis Singers (£450).

Exclusions The foundation does not:
- fund the commissioning of new works
- make donations towards the costs of making recordings, either by private or commercial companies
- as a general rule, finance degree courses. The aim is to encourage composition and research, but not to finance the acquisition of basic skills in these subjects
- consider applications for assistance in purchasing musical instruments or equipment including the electronic or computer variety
- make grants retrospectively.

Applications On a form which can be downloaded from the foundation's website.

The trustees have noted that in a number of applications they have been invited to make a grant equal to the total cost of the project where a commercial organisation has a specific interest whether as a publisher or as an impresario. While the trustees are prepared to consider making grants in such circumstances towards the cost of a project which is essentially non-commercial, they will always have greater sympathy for those projects where the organisation involved is making some contribution towards the risk.

The trustees will be pleased to receive applications for assistance with projects that fall within these terms, and such applications may come from individuals, organisations, or other charities. The trustees do not wish to consider applications for which there are existing official schemes of help, but rather to devote their efforts to areas at present neglected.

The Henry C Hoare Charitable Trust

General

£181,000 (2007/08)
Beneficial area UK.

C Hoare and Co, 37 Fleet Street, London EC4P 4DQ
Trustees *Henry C Hoare; Messrs Hoare Trustees.*

CC Number 1088669

Information available Accounts were on file at the Charity Commission.

This trust was established in 2001 with general charitable purposes. One-off and annual donations are made.

In 2007/08 it had an income of £186,000 and made grants totalling £181,000. Assets stood at £3.1 million.

Donations were broken down as follows:

Category	Value
Health	£53,000
Education	£48,000
Animal welfare	£29,000
Young people, older people, ill health, disability and financial hardship	£26,000
Environment protection and improvement	£14,000
Citizenship and community development	£8,300
Religion	£3,500
Arts	£500

Beneficiaries of grants of £5,000 or more were: Trinity College Cambridge (£25,000); Transform Drug Policy Foundation (£20,000); Autism Research Centre, European Squirrel Initiative, Mental Health Foundation, Prospect Burma and Reform Research Trust (£10,000 each); Tree Aid (£7,500); and Okeford Fitzpaine Church of England Primary School (£7,000).

Applications In writing to the correspondent.

Hockerill Educational Foundation

Education, especially Christian education

£210,000 to organisations (2009/10)

Beneficial area UK, with a preference for the dioceses of Chelmsford and St Albans.

3 The Swallows, Harlow CM17 0AR

Tel. 01279 420855 **Fax** 0560 3140931

Email info@hockerillfoundation.org.uk

Website www.hockerillfoundation.org. uk

Correspondent Derek J Humphrey, Secretary

Trustees *Revd C W Herbert; Ven T P Jones. Four ex-officio trustees; four diocesan trustees; seven nominative trustees; one co-opted trustee.*

CC Number 311018

Information available Accounts were available from the Charity Commission.

The foundation was set up in 1978 following the closure of Hockerill College, which was established in 1852 to train women teachers who 'would go to schools in the service of humanity'. When the Secretary of State for Education and Science decided in 1976 to wind down Hockerill College, the proceeds of the sale of its assets were given to this foundation to use for the purposes for which the college was created.

The foundation's current priorities are as follows.

- Grants to individual teachers and others in an educational capacity, either training to teach or seeking to develop their professional abilities and qualifications, particularly in Religious Education.
- Grants to individuals taking other first degree or further education courses, excluding courses which lead directly to careers other than teaching.
- Training and support for the church's educational work in the dioceses of Chelmsford and St Albans.
- Research, development and support grants to organisations in the field of religious education.

Grants are also made to organisations for projects and research likely to enhance the Church of England's contribution to higher and further education or religious education in schools. The trustees will normally consider applications from corporate bodies or institutions associated with education on Christian principles. There is a religious dimension to all education, but the trustees would expect any activity, course, project or research supported to be of real benefit to religious education and/or the church's educational work. They will give priority to imaginative new projects which will enhance the Church of England's contribution to higher and further education and/or promote aspects of religious education in schools.

In 2008/09 the foundation made grants to individuals and organisations totalling £210,000. Further information for this financial year was not available.

In 2007/08 the foundation had assets of £5.6 million and a total income of £305,000. Grants were made totalling £246,000 and were distributed as follows:

Area	Value
Diocese of St Albans	£87,000
Diocese of Chelmsford	£80,000
Individuals	£42,000
Research and development in education	£37,000

Exclusions Grants are not given for general appeals for funds, 'bricks and mortar' building projects or purposes that are the clear responsibility of another body.

With regard to individuals, grants will not normally be considered for:

- teachers who intend to move out of the profession
- those in training for ordination or for other kinds of mission
- clergy who wish to improve their own qualifications, unless they are already engaged in teaching in schools and/or intend to teach in the future
- students of counselling, therapy or social work
- undergraduates or people training for other professions, such as accountancy, business, law or medicine
- people doing courses or visits abroad, including 'gap' year courses (except as an integral part of a course, or a necessary part of research)
- children at primary or secondary school.

Applications On a form available from the correspondent, to be submitted by 30 April each year. Results of applications will be communicated in June. Receipt of applications are not acknowledged. Applications which do not fit the criteria do not normally receive a reply.

The Sir Julian Hodge Charitable Trust

General

£73,000 (2007/08)

Beneficial area UK.

Ty Gwyn, Lisvane Road, Lisvane, Cardiff CF14 0SG

Correspondent Margaret Cason, Trustee

Trustees *Lady Hodge; Robert J Hodge; Joyce Harrison; Derek L Jones; Margaret Cason; Eric M Hammonds.*

CC Number 234848

Information available Accounts on file at the Charity Commission

The trust was established by a gift from Sir Julian Hodge and in 2006 received a further substantial bequest under the terms of his will. In 2007/08 the trust had assets of £1.3 million and an income of £81,000. Grants were made totalling £73,000 and were broken down as follows:

Category	Value
Medical	£28,000
Other	£24,000
Education	£19,000
Religion	£3,000

Beneficiaries included: Techniquest (£3,000); Royal Vetenary College and Dogs for the Disabled (£2,500 each); Brittle Bone Society, Deafblind UK and Royal School for the Deaf & Communication Disorders (£2,000 each); the Firefighters Charity (£1,500); Watford & Three Rivers Furniture Recycling Scheme, The Royal National Institute for Deaf People and SENSE (£1,000 each).

Exclusions No grants to individuals or companies.

Applications In writing to the correspondent.

The J G Hogg Charitable Trust

Welfare, animal welfare and general

£57,000 (2007/08)
Beneficial area UK.

Chantrey Vellacott DFK, Russell Square House, 10–12 Russell Square, London WC1B 5LF

Tel. 020 75099000

Email cjones@cvdfk.com

Correspondent C M Jones, Trustees' Accountant

Trustees *Sarah Jane Houldsworth; Joanna Wynfreda Turvey.*

CC Number 299042

Information available Information was on file at the Charity Commission

The trust states that it has no set policy on the type of charity supported, but would give favourable consideration to those based primarily in the UK that support the relief of human and animal suffering.

In 2007/08 the trust had assets of £724,000 and an income of £24,000. Grants totalled £57,000 and were made to the following organisations: Kids Company and Oxfam (£15,000 each); Medicinema and Teddy Bear Air Care (£10,000 each); and Addiction Recovery Foundation (£7,000).

Exclusions No grants to individuals. Registered charities only are supported.

Applications In writing to the correspondent. To keep administration costs to a minimum, the trust is unable to reply to unsuccessful applicants.

The Holden Charitable Trust

Jewish

£213,000 (2007/08)
Beneficial area UK, with a preference for the Manchester area.

c/o Lopian Gross Barnett and Co., Cardinal House, 20 St Mary's Parsonage, Manchester M3 2LG

Tel. 0161 832 8721

Correspondent The Clerk

Trustees *David Lopian; Marian Lopian; Michael Lopian.*

CC Number 264185

Information available Accounts were on file at the Charity Commission website.

The trustees' report states:

The Holden Charitable Trust exists to receive and distribute charitable donations to worthy causes primarily within the Jewish community.

In 2007/08 the trust had assets of £1 million and an income of £158,000 and made grants totalled £213,000.

There were 34 grants of £1,000 or more listed in the accounts. Beneficiaries included: Friends of Beis Eliyohu Trust (£23,000); Broughton Jewish Cassel Fox Primary School (£20,000); Broom Foundation (£18,000); Talmud Torah Trust (£11,000); Yeshayh Adler Memorial Fund (£10,000); King David Schools (£7,400); Manchester Jewish Grammar School (£5,000); Ohr Yerushalayim (£4,300); Manchester Eruv Committee (£3,000); The Forum (£2,500); Manchester Junior Girls School (£2,000); and Aish UK (£1,000).

Donations of less than £1,000 each totalled £47,000.

Applications In writing to the correspondent.

The Dorothy Holmes Charitable Trust

General

£65,000 (2007/08)
Beneficial area UK, with a preference for Dorset.

Smallfield Cody and Co., 5 Harley Place, Harley Street, London W1G 8QD

Tel. 0207 636 6100

Correspondent Michael Kennedy

Trustees *Mrs B M Cody; Miss M Cody; Dr S Roberts; J Roberts.*

CC Number 237213

Information available Accounts were on file at the Charity Commission.

The trust's policy is to make a substantial number of relatively small donations to groups working in many charitable fields – including those involved in medical research, disability, older people, children and young people, churches, the disadvantaged, the environment and the arts. The trust can give throughout the UK but has a preference for Dorset, especially Poole. In practice nearly all grants are given to either national charities or those based in Dorset.

In 2007/08 the trust had an income of £29,000 and an expenditure of £77,000, of which £65,000 was given in grants to 30 organisations.

All grants ranged from £300 to £6,000, with beneficiaries including: Wallingford School (£6,000); Children in Touch, Crisis and Christmas and RNLI (£5,000 each); Hyman Cen Foundation (£4,000); Army Benevolent Fund (£3,000); Action on Elder Abuse and Clic Sargeant Cancer Fund (£2,000 each); National Autistic Society and Raleigh International (£1,000 each); and Royal Free Hospital Retirement Fellowship (£300).

Exclusions Only applications from registered charities will be considered.

Applications In writing to the correspondent, preferably in January to March each year.

The Holst Foundation

Arts

£213,000 to individuals and organisations (2004/05) see below
Beneficial area UK.

179 Great Portland Street, London
W1W 5LS

Tel. 020 8673 4215 (answerphone only)

Email holst@dpmail.co.uk

Correspondent The Grants Administrator

Trustees *Prof. Arnold Whittall, Chair; Noel Periton; Rosamund Strode; Peter Carter; Andrew Clements; Julian Anderson.*

CC Number 283668

Information available Accounts were on file at the Charity Commission.

The trust has two objects: firstly, to promote public appreciation of the musical works of Gustav and Imogen Holst; and secondly, to encourage the study and practice of the arts.

In practice the trust tends to be proactive. Funds are available almost exclusively for the performance of music by living composers. The trust has historical links with Aldeburgh in Suffolk and is a major funder of new music at the annual Aldeburgh Festival. It also promotes the recording of new music by means of substantial funding to the recording label NMC, which the foundation also provided the funds to set up.

In 2007/08 it had assets of almost £2 million and an income of £97,000. Grants totalling £213,000 were made to individuals and organisations. There were 19 grants of £1,000 or more listed in the accounts.

By far the largest donation of £120,000 went to NMC Recordings. Other beneficiaries included: Aldeburgh Music (£30,000); BCMG (£8,800); Aldeburgh Productions (£6,000); Andre Heller (£5,000); BMIC (£3,000); Tête à Tête Productions and Opera North (£2,500); Huddersfield Festival and Spitalfield Festival (£2,000 each); and Cheltenham Music Society, Chandos Records, Pro Corda Trust and Prestiegne Festival (£1,000 each).

A further 42 unlisted grants totalled £20,000.

Royalties from the Holst Estate have largely ceased since the copyright expired at the end of 2004. From 2006 both the number and the size of grants have been greatly reduced as a result.

Exclusions No support for the recordings or works of Holst that are already well supported, nor for capital projects. No grants to individuals for educational purposes.

Applications In writing to the correspondent. Trustees meet four times a year. There is no application form. Seven copies of the application should be sent. Applications should contain full financial details and be as concise as possible. Funding is not given retrospectively.

P H Holt Foundation

General

£130,000 (2007/08)
Beneficial area UK, with a preference for Merseyside.

India Buildings, Liverpool L2 0RB

Tel. 0151 473 4693 **Fax** 0151 473 4693

Correspondent Roger Morris, Secretary

Trustees *Neil Kemsley, Chair; Tilly Boyce; Martin Cooke; Paige Earlam; Nikki Eastwood; Anthony Hannay; Derek Morris; Ken Ravenscroft.*

CC Number 1113708

Information available Accounts were on file at the Charity Commission.

The foundation makes a large number of mostly small grants, about three quarters of them in Merseyside. This foundation is a welcome and exceptional example of Liverpool shipping money staying in and around the city. It organises its giving in two established grant programmes concerned with Merseyside and the 'Holt tradition.'

In 2007/08 the foundation had assets of £12.9 million and an income of £262,000. Grants committed during the year totalled £130,000, categorised as follows:

Activity 2007/08

	Merseyside	'Holt tradition'
No. of applications received	255	26
No. of grants made	61	15
of which		
recipients previously supported	34	13
recipients supported for the first time	24	2
consortium projects	3	nil
total value of commitments made	£121,000	£8,000
average size of grant	£2,000	£550

Grants by category 2007/08

	Total	Merseyside	'Holt' tradition
Community development and participation	£47,000	£44,000	£3,000
Social welfare	£17,000	£16,000	£500
Education	£32,000	£29,000	£2,500
Visual and performing arts	£32,000	£31,000	£500
Heritage and built environment	£1,800	£1,050	£750
Natural environment	£1,750	£750	£1,000
Medical research	Nil	Nil	Nil
Total committed in year	£129,000	£121,000	£8,000

Merseyside

Major grants included those made to: Rotters Community Composting (£7,000); Plaza Community Cinema (£6,000); Fuse New Theatre for Young People, Liverpool Arts Interface, Liverpool Carnival Company and Merseyside Dance Initiative (£5,000 each); Merseyside Family Support Association and Toxteth Community College (£3,000 each); the Basement Drop Night Drop-in Centre and Yambi Africa (£2,000 each); and the Bluecoat, China Pearl and Urban Strawberry Lunch (£1,000 each).

There were also 17 routine grants to organisations with which the foundation has regular contact.

The 'Holt Tradition'

Smaller grants included those made to: Lake Malawi Projects – for a programme to help develop agriculture and eradicate malnutrition and food insecurity in Likoma District (£1,500); Liverpool School of Tropical Medicine – for a follow-up oral history project about the health of former Far East Prisoners of War (£1,000); and International Journal of Maritime History – for publication of research about mercantile society in nineteenth-century Liverpool (£500).

There were also 12 routine grants to organisations with which the foundation has regular contact.

Exclusions No grants to individuals. Grants are not usually given to organisations outside Merseyside.

Applications In writing to the correspondent at any time. Full and detailed guidance notes are available from the foundation.

The Homelands Charitable Trust

The New Church, health and social welfare

£270,000 (2007/08)
Beneficial area UK.

c/o Alliotts, 4th Floor, Imperial House, 15 Kingsway, London WC2B 6UN

Tel. 020 7240 9971

Correspondent N J Armstrong, Trustee

Trustees *D G W Ballard; N J Armstrong; Revd C Curry; R J Curry.*

CC Number 214322

Information available Accounts were on file at the Charity Commission.

The trust was established in 1962, the settlors were four members of the Curry family and the original endowment was in the form of shares in the Curry company.

In 2007/08 it had assets of £6.6 million and a total income of £260,000. Grants were made totalling £270,000. Unfortunately, a list of beneficiaries was not included in the trust's accounts.

Previously, beneficiaries have included: General Conference of the New Church (£45,000); Bournemouth Society of the New Church (£20,000); Broadfield Memorial Benevolent Trust (£11,000); New Church College (£7,500); Asbah (£5,000); RNLI (£4,000); Action Medical Research, Fellowship Afloat, Jubilee Sailing Trust, Manic Depression Fellowship and National Children Homes (£3,000 each); and Action for the Blind, Bliss, Child Accident Prevention Trust, Dreams Come True, Hope House, Mencap, RNID, Seeability, Survival International, Trinity Hospice, University College London, Wessex Children Hospice Trust and YMCA (£2,000 each).

The following was included under the heading 'Future plans and commitments' in the annual report:

The trustees intend to continue supporting registered charities with a bias towards:

1) General Conference of the New Church
2) medical research
3) care and protection of children
4) hospices

The trustees are aware of the proposed extension and refurbishment of the New Church's residential centre in the Midlands at an estimated cost of £1.5 million and have set up a designated fund of £250,000 to contribute towards this project.

Exclusions No grants to individuals.

Applications In writing to the correspondent.

The Homestead Charitable Trust

Medical, health and welfare, animal welfare and the arts

£54,000 (2007/08)
Beneficial area UK.

7 Clarence Gate Gardens, Glentworth Street, London NW1 6AY

Tel. 020 7258 1051

Correspondent Lady Nina Bracewell-Smith, Trustee

Trustees *Sir C Bracewell-Smith; Lady N Bracewell-Smith.*

CC Number 293979

Information available Accounts were on file at the Charity Commission.

The trust makes grants towards medical, health and welfare, animal welfare, Christianity and the arts.

In 2007/08 it had assets of £5 million and an income of £241,000. The trust fund of the Sir Charles Bracewell-Smith Voluntary Settlement, worth £1.6 million, was transferred to the trust in October 2004. Grants given to individuals and institutions totalled £54,000.

Beneficiaries included: City of Joy Foundation (£10,000); Crusade, PAVA Foundation and Angel Covers USA (£5,000 each); EKTA Project (£3,600); Hope and Homes for Children, Vedanta Institute and Francis Home Hospice (£2,000 each); and Vet Aid, CRY and Gwalior Children's Home (£1,000 each).

Applications In writing to the correspondent.

The Hope Trust

Temperance and Reformed Protestant churches

About £150,000 (2008)
Beneficial area Worldwide, with a preference for Scotland.

Drummond Miller, 31–32 Moray Place, Edinburgh EH3 6BZ

Tel. 0131 226 5151

Email rmiller@drummond-miller.co.uk

Correspondent The Secretary

Trustees *Prof. G M Newlands; Prof. D A S Ferguson; Revd G R Barr; Revd Dr Lyall; Carole Hope; Revd Gillean McLean.*

SC Number SC000987

Information available Despite making a written request for the accounts of this trust (and including a stamped, addressed envelope), these were not provided. The following entry is based, therefore, on information filed with the Office of the Scottish Charity Regulator.

The trust was established to promote the ideals of temperance in the areas of drink and drugs, and Protestant church reform through education and the distribution of literature. PhD students of theology studying at Scottish universities are also supported.

In 2008 its income was £187,000. Grants totalled around £150,000.

Previous beneficiaries have included Church of Scotland Priority Areas Fund, World Alliance of Reformed Churches, National Bible Society for Scotland, Feed the Minds and Waldensian Mission Aid.

Exclusions No grants to gap year students, scholarship schemes or to any individuals, with the sole exception of PhD students of theology studying at Scottish universities. No grants for the refurbishment of property.

Applications In writing to the correspondent. The trustees meet to consider applications in June and December each year. Applications should be submitted by mid-May or mid-November each year.

The Cuthbert Horn Trust

Environment, people with disabilities or special needs and older people

£55,000 (2007)

Beneficial area UK.

Capita Trust Company Limited, Phoenix House, 18 King William Street, London EC4N 7HE

Tel. 020 7800 4126

Email trusts@capitatrust.co.uk

Correspondent Laurie Wilson, Trust Manager

Trustees *Alliance Assurance Company Ltd; A H Flint.*

CC Number 291465

Information available Accounts were on file at the Charity Commission.

The trust's main aims are to support charities helping older people and charities undertaking practical work in supporting the conservation and preservation of the environment.

In 2007 the trust had assets of £1.4 million and a total income of £343,000. Grants were made to 15 organisations totalling £55,000.

Beneficiaries included: Farms for City Children (£6,000); Progressive Farming Trust (£5,000); International Bee Research Association, Norfolk Wherry Trust and Sevenoaks Symphony Orchestra (£4,000 each); Ovingdean Hall School, The Charleston Trust, The Fishermans Mission and MS National Therapy Centres (£3,000 each); Norwegian Locomotive Trust (£2,500); and The Grasslands Trust (£2,000).

Exclusions No grants are made to individuals.

Applications There are no application forms to complete; applicants should provide in writing as much background about their charity or cause as possible. Applications need to be received by December as the trustees meet as soon as possible after the financial year end. Only successful applications will be notified.

The Horne Trust

Hospices

£416,000 (2007/08)

Beneficial area UK and the developing world.

Kingsdown, Warmlake Road, Chart Sutton, Maidstone ME17 3RP

Tel. 01622 842638

Email mail.jh@horne-trust.org.uk

Correspondent J T Horne, Trustee

Trustees *J T Horne; J L Horne; N J Camamile.*

CC Number 1010625

Information available Accounts were on file at the Charity Commission.

The trust supports homelessness charities and hospices, particularly children's hospices. Grants can also be given to medical support charities and organisations helping to develop self-reliant technology in Africa and the developing world.

In 2007/08 it had assets of £6.6 million and an income of £212,000. Grants to 70 organisations and totalled £416,000.

Beneficiaries included: Demelza House Children's Hospice, Humberstone Hydrotherapy Pool and World Medical Fund (£10,000 each); AbilityNet, Share Community and Woodlands Hospice – Liverpool (£7,500); Laura Campbell-Preston Trust (£6,700); Deafblind UK, FACT, and Fisherman's Mission (£5,000 each); and Winfield Trust, Disability Aid Fund and Whitby Dog Rescue (£1,000 each).

Applications Normally in writing to the correspondent, although the trust has stated that currently unsolicited applications cannot be supported.

The Hospital Saturday Fund

Medical and health

£307,000 to organisations (2008)

Beneficial area UK, the Republic of Ireland and overseas.

24 Upper Ground, London SE1 9PD

Tel. 020 7928 6662

Email charity@hsf.eu.com

Correspondent K R Bradley, Chief Executive

Trustees *John Greenwood, Chair; M Boyle; David Thomas; Mrs J L Dalton; Mr G R M Hind; Mr K Lawrey; Mr J Randel.*

CC Number 1123381

Information available Full accounts were on file at the Charity Commission.

The Hospital Saturday Fund is a healthcare cash plan organisation, which was founded in 1873. In 1987 it established a charitable trust to support a wide range of hospitals, hospices and medical charities for care and research, as well as welfare organisations providing similar services. The trustees continue to provide support to smaller, lesser-known charities connected with diseases and disabilities about which there is little public awareness. Individuals can also be supported by the trust, usually for special equipment to relieve their condition or in cases where their health has contributed to their financial hardship, although sponsorship can be given to people studying for a medically-related career.

In 2008 it an income of £166,000, mostly through donations from its parent company. Grants were made to organisations totalling £307,000 and to individuals totalling £22,000. Grants to organisations were broken down as follows:

- medical charities – £201,000
- hospices – £101,000.

Unfortunately a grants list was not available with this years accounts, however previous beneficiaries have included: Alzheimer's Society (£3,000); Teenage Cancer Trust and International Glaucoma Association (£1,500 each); BasicNeeds UK Trust, LEPRA, Motivation Quality of Life (£750 each); and Age Concern England, Brain Tumour UK, Childline, DebRA, the Ear Foundation, Friends of the Elderly, the National Autistic Society, OCD Action, Rethink, the Shaftesbury Society, the Sunflower Trust, Terrence Higgins Trust and Wellbeing of Women (£500 each).

Exclusions Unless there are exceptional circumstances, organisations are not supported in successive years.

Applications Hospitals, hospices and medically-related charities are invited to write detailed letters or to send a brochure with an accompanying letter. There is a form for individuals to complete available from the personal assistant to the trust administrator.

Houblon-Norman/George Fund

Finance

£81,000 (2007/08)

Beneficial area UK.

MA Business Support Unit HO-2, Bank of England, Threadneedle Street, London EC2R 8AH

Tel. 020 7601 3778 **Fax** 020 7601 4423

Email ma-hngfund@bankofengland.co.uk

Website www.bankofengland.co.uk/about/fellowships

Correspondent The Secretary

Trustees C R Bean; Brendan Barber; Hon. Peter Jay.

CC Number 213168

Information available Accounts were on file at the Charity Commission.

The trust supports research into the interaction and function of financial and business institutions, the economic conditions affecting them, and the dissemination of knowledge thereof. Fellowships are tenable at the Bank of England. The research work to be undertaken is intended to be full-time work, and teaching or other paid work must not be undertaken during the tenure of the fellowship, without the specific consent of the trustees. In considering applications the trustees will pay particular regard to the relevance of the research to current problems in economics and finance.

In 2007/08 the trust had assets of £2 million, an income of £116,000 and made grants totalling £81,000 in the form of three fellowships.

Applications On an application form available from the website.

The Reta Lila Howard Foundation

Children, arts and environment

£718,000 (2007/08)

Beneficial area UK and Republic of Ireland.

Jamestown Investments Ltd, 4 Felstead Gardens, Ferry Street, London E14 3BS

Tel. 020 7537 1118

Email jamestown@btinternet.com

Correspondent The Company Secretary

Trustees Emma Adamo; Christian Bauta; Alannah Weston; Charles Burnett; Graham Weston; Garfield Mitchell; Tamara Rebanks; Kim Abell.

CC Number 1041634

Information available Accounts were on file at the Charity Commission, without a list of grants, which was provided separately by the foundation.

The founder of this trust had an interest in children's charities and the trust's grant-making focus is 'to support a few innovative projects that benefit children up to the age of 16 within the British Isles'. Funds are directed to selected projects, 'to support the education of young people or to ameliorate their physical and emotional environment'. In practice the trust also supports arts and environmental organisations. Donations are given over a finite period, with the aim that the project can be self-supporting when funding has ended.

In 2007/08 the trust had assets of £14 million and an income of £268,000. Grants were made to 25 organisations totalling £718,000 (2006/07: £353,000).

Beneficiaries included: Countryside Education Trust (£70,000); Barnardo's (£68,500); Civitas (£60,000); the Tree Council (£53,000); Farms for City Children (£40,000); Children's Hospice Association Scotland (£35,000); Teach First (£30,000); New Forest Museum & Library (£20,000); the Bridge End Community Centre (£15,000); and, Bibles for Children (£10,000).

Exclusions Grants are not given to individuals, organisations which are not registered charities, or towards operating expenses, budget deficits, (sole) capital projects, annual charitable appeals, general endowment funds, fundraising drives or events, conferences, or student aid.

Applications The trust states that it does not accept unsolicited applications, since the trustees seek out and support projects they are interested in.

The Daniel Howard Trust

Jewish causes

£178,000 (2005/06)

Beneficial area UK and Israel.

c/o Principle Capital, 9 Savoy Street, London WC2E 7ER

Tel. 020 7340 3222

Correspondent Mrs Sarah Hunt

Trustees Dame Shirley Porter; Mrs Linda Streit; Steven Nigel Porter; Brian Padgett; Andrew Peggie.

CC Number 267173

Information available Accounts were on file at the Charity Commission.

The trust states that it supports projects concerned with education, culture, the environment and welfare. In practice, most grants are made to Jewish or Israeli organisations.

In 2005/06 the trust had assets of £10.8 million, which generated an income of only £264,000. Grants were made totalling £178,000. Recent accounts were overdue at the Charity Commission.

Major beneficiaries included: World Jewish Relief – Metuna (£30,000); The Israel Family Therapy Advancement Fund (£25,000); Friends of Daniel for Rowing (£20,000); International Scholarship Foundation Charitable Trust (£20,000 in two grants); British Friends of the IGDCB and The British Friends of Israel Philharmonic (£15,000 each); and Tel Aviv University and Weizmann Institute Foundation (£10,000 each).

Exclusions Grants are only made to registered charities. No grants to individuals.

Applications In writing to the correspondent.

155

Clifford Howarth Charity Trust

General

£34,000 (2007/08)

Beneficial area UK, with a preference for Lancashire (Burnley/Rossendale).

14A Hall Garth, Kelbeck, Barrow in Furness LA13 0QT

Correspondent James Howarth, Trustee

Trustees *James Howarth; Judith Howarth; Mary Fenton.*

CC Number 264890

Information available Accounts were on file at the Charity Commission.

The charity has general charitable purposes assisting local and UK charities supported by the founder. This is generally for work within Burnley and Rossendale.

In 2007/08 the charity had assets of £593,000, an income of £28,000 and made eight grants totalling £34,000.

Beneficiaries were: Cumbria Cerebral Palsy (£15,000); St Mary's Hospice (£5,000); St Nicholas Church – Newchurch (£3,000); Hospice in Rossendale (£2,500); and Ulverstone Inshore Rescue, Beaver Scouts, Spurgeons and Burnley Garrick Club (£2,000 each).

Exclusions Only registered charities will be supported. No grants to individuals, for scholarships or for non-local special projects.

Applications The charity states that grants are only made to organisations known to the trustees, and that applications are unlikely to be successful.

The Hudson Foundation

Older people and general

£218,000 (2007/08)

Beneficial area UK, with a preference for the Wisbech area.

1–3 York Row, Wisbech, Cambridge PE13 1EA

Correspondent D W Ball, Trustee

Trustees *H A Godfrey; D W Ball; S G Layton.*

CC Number 280332

Information available Accounts were obtained from the Charity Commission website.

The object of the foundation is the relief of infirm and/or older people, in particular the establishment and maintenance of residential accommodation for relief of infirm and/or older people and to make donations to other charitable purposes with a preference for the Wisbech area. The accounts state that 'whilst the trustees do make contributions to revenue expenditure of charitable organisations, they prefer to assist in the funding of capital projects for the advancement of the community of Wisbech and district'.

In 2007/08 the foundation had assets of £1.7 million and an income of £913,000. Grants to nine organisations totalled £218,000.

Beneficiaries were: Wisbech Parish Church of St Peter and St Paul (£80,000); Ely Diocesan Board of Finance (£64,000); Wisbech St Mary Sports and Community Centre (£30,000); Wisbech Grammar School (£29,000); Wisbech Swimming Club (£8,400); Methodist Homes for the Aged (£6,200); Alzheimer's Society (£1,200); Wisbech and Fenland Museum (£250); and Wisbech Music Society (£150).

Applications In writing to the correspondent. Trustees meet quarterly.

The Huggard Charitable Trust

General

£82,000 (2007/08)

Beneficial area UK, with a preference for South Wales.

Blacklands Farm, Five Mile Lane, Bonvilston, Cardiff CF5 6TQ

Correspondent S J Thomas, Trustee

Trustees *Mrs A Helme; S J Thomas.*

CC Number 327501

Information available Accounts were on file at the Charity Commission.

In 2007/08 the trust had assets of £1.8 million and an income of £52,000. Grants totalled £82,000.

Beneficiaries of the largest grants were: Bro Morgannwg NHS Trust (£12,000);

Whitton Rosser Trust – Vale of Glamorgan (£8,000); Laparoscopy Laser Fund – UHW (£6,000); SWS Cymru (£5,000); Amelia Methodist Trust, Vale of Glamorgan (£4,500); and CURE Fund, Cardiff (£4,000).

Other donations under £4,000 each totalled £43,000.

Applications The trustees are not inviting applications for funds.

The Geoffrey C Hughes Charitable Trust

Nature conservation, environment and performing arts

£16,000 (2007/08)

Beneficial area UK.

c/o Mills & Reeve, Francis House, 112 Hills Road, Cambridge CB2 1PH

Tel. 01223 222290

Correspondent P C M Solon, Trustee

Trustees *J R Young; P C M Solon; W A Bailey.*

CC Number 1010079

Information available Accounts were on file at the Charity Commission.

This trust is essentially interested in two areas: nature conservation, environment and performing arts, particularly ballet or opera with a preference towards modern work.

In 2007/08 the trust had an income of £15,000 and total expenditure of £16,000. In the previous year expenditure was £515,000.

Exclusions No grants to individuals.

Applications In writing to the correspondent.

The Humanitarian Trust

Education, health, social welfare and Jewish

£80,000 to organisations (2007/08)

Beneficial area Worldwide, mainly Israel.

27 St James's Place, London SW1A 1NR

Tel. 0207 409 1376

Correspondent Mrs M Myers, Secretary

Trustees *Jacques Gunsbourg; Pierre Halban; Anthony Lerman.*

CC Number 208575

Information available Accounts were on file at the Charity Commission.

The trust was founded in 1946. In the early years donations were made overwhelmingly to educational causes in Israel. Now the trust is giving to a wider range of causes, still mainly Jewish, but some smaller grants are given to non-Jewish organisations.

The report states that 'the trustees consider grant applications from organisations and individuals in the UK and abroad, especially in the fields of education, health, social welfare, civil society, Jewish communal life and general charitable purposes.'

In 2007/08 it had assets of £4.1 million and an income of £121,000. Grants totalled £80,000 and were broken down as follows.

The two largest grants went to one organisation, Friends of the Hebrew University of Jerusalem towards: the Humanitarian Trust Fellowship and the M Gunsbourg Memorial Scholarships (£10,000 each).

Other beneficiaries included: New Israel Fund (£6,000); Institute for Jewish Policy Research (£5,000); University of Oxford (£4,500); Jerusalem Foundation Bilingual School, Association for Civil Rights in Israel and The Samaritans (£2,000 each); and King's College London, University of Dundee and University of Birmingham (£500 each).

Applications In writing to the correspondent, including annual report and accounts, projected budgets and future plans. Applications are considered at trustees' meetings in March and October.

The Michael and Shirley Hunt Charitable Trust

Prisoners' families, animal welfare

£54,000 (2007/08)

Beneficial area UK and overseas.

Ansty House, Henfield Road, Small Dole BN5 9XH

Tel. 01903 817116 **Fax** 01903 879995

Correspondent Mrs D S Jenkins, Trustee

Trustees *W J Baker; C J Hunt; S E Hunt; D S Jenkins; K D Mayberry.*

CC Number 1063418

Information available Accounts were on file at the Charity Commission.

The trust makes grants for the benefit of prisoners' families, and also animals which are unwanted, sick or ill-treated.

In 2007/08 it had assets of £5.1 million and an income of £338,000. Grants were made totalling £54,000, broken down as follows and shown with examples of beneficiaries:

Relief of hardship of prisoners and prisoner's families – 6 grants totalling £14,000
Prisoners Abroad (£3,000); Action for Prisoners Families (£2,500); and NCH Styal Prison Baby Support Unit (£1,000).

Grants to 75 individuals totalled £6,800.

Relief of suffering of Animals – 19 grants totalling £16,000
Animal Care and Sheffield Animal Shelter (£2,000 each); and Hack Horse Sanctuary, Yorkshire Swan Rescue Hospital and British Divers Marine Life Rescue (£1,000 each).

Grants to 11 other organisations of less than £1,000 each totalled £6,300.

'Other deserving causes' – 9 grants totalling £24,000
Martletts Hospice Hove (£6,000); CNCF and St Barnabus Hospice (£5,000 each); Nursery Playgroup (£2,000); and Mobility Trust and YMCA Lancaster (£1,000 each).

Exclusions No grants for fines, bail, legal costs, rent deposits and so on.

Applications In writing to the correspondent.

The Hutton Foundation

Christian

£366,000 (2007)

Beneficial area Worldwide.

Spring Cottage, Cranes Road, Sherborne St John RG24 9HY

Correspondent Graham Hutton, Trustee

Trustees *Graham Hutton; Amanda Hutton; Richard Hutton; James Hutton.*

CC Number 1106521

Information available Accounts were on file at the Charity Commission.

Set up in 2004, in 2007 the foundation had an income of £2.8 million, mostly from donations. Grants totalled £366,000. Assets stood at £2.4 million at year end.

Beneficiaries of the largest grants were: Catholic Trust for England and Wales and Emmaus Hampshire (£100,000 each); NSPCC (£34,000); Catholic Bishops Conference (£25,000); Aid to the Church in Need (£25,000); and International Theologies Institute (£21,000).

Applications In writing to the correspondent.

The Huxham Charitable Trust

Christianity, churches and organisations and development work

£38,000 to individuals and organisations (2007/08)

Beneficial area UK and Eastern Europe, especially Albania and Kosova.

Thatcher Brake, 37 Whidborne Avenue, Torquay TQ1 2PG

Tel. 01803 380399

Correspondent Adrian W Huxham

Trustees *Revd Deryck Markham; Revd Percy; Mr Corney; Mrs Angela Huxham.*

CC Number 1000179

Information available Accounts were on file at the Charity Commission.

In 2007/08 the trust had assets of £151,000 and an income of £50,000.

Grants to organisations and individuals totalled £38,000.

Applications Grants cannot be made to unsolicited applicants. The trust states that it now concentrates solely on its own projects.

The Nani Huyu Charitable Trust

Welfare

£137,000 (2007/08)

Beneficial area UK, particularly but not exclusively within 50 miles of Bristol.

Rusling House, Butcombe, Bristol
BS40 7XQ

Tel. 01275 474433

Email maureensimonwhitmore@btinternet.com

Correspondent The Trustees

Trustees *Simon Whitmore; Ben Whitmore; Charles Thatcher; Maureen Whitmore.*

CC Number 1082868

Information available Accounts were on file at the Charity Commission, without a list of grants.

The trust was registered with the Charity commission in October 2000. Its aims are to assist people who are underprivileged, disadvantaged or ill, young people in matters of health, accommodation and training and those requiring assistance or medical care at the end of their lives, principally within Bristol and its surroundings.

In 2007/08 the trust had assets of £2.9 million and an income of £153,000. Grants totalled £137,000. No list of donations was included with the accounts on file at the Charity Commission.

Applications In writing to the correspondent.

The P Y N and B Hyams Trust

Jewish, general

£331,000 (2007/08)

Beneficial area Worldwide.

Lubbock Fine, Russell Bedford House, City Forum, 250 City Road, London EC1V 2QQ

Tel. 020 7490 7766

Correspondent Mrs M Hyams, Trustee

Trustees *Mrs M Hyams; D Levy; N Shah.*

CC Number 268129

Information available Accounts were on file at the Charity Commission, but without a narrative report or a list of grants.

In 2007/08 the trust had assets of £1.3 million and an income of £105,000. Grants to organisations totalled £331,000. No list of grants was included with the accounts.

In previous years, grants have been mostly given to Jewish organisations, although other causes are also funded.

Applications In writing to the correspondent, but please note, the trust states that funds are fully committed and unsolicited applications are not welcomed.

The Hyde Charitable Trust – Youth Plus

Disadvantaged children and young people

£307,000 (2007/08)

Beneficial area The areas in which the Hyde Group operates (currently London, Kent, Surrey, Sussex and Hampshire).

Youth Plus, Hyde Charitable Trust, Hollingsworth House, 181 Lewisham High Street, London SE13 6AA

Tel. 020 8297 7575

Email youthplus@hyde-housing.co.uk

Website www.youthplus.co.uk

Correspondent Janet Grant

Trustees *Peter Matthew; Stephen Hill; Patrick Elliott; Geron Walker; Martin Wheatley; Derrick Biggs; Kishwer Falkner.*

CC Number 289888

Information available Accounts were available from the Charity Commission.

Hyde Charitable Trust is a company limited by guarantee established in 1984. It 'works to help improve the condition and quality of life of people from the poorest communities.'

Youth Plus works throughout the areas where the Hyde Group, one of the biggest housing association groups in the country, currently operates (London, Kent, Surrey, Sussex and Hampshire).

Youth Plus aims to support disadvantaged children and young people in communities suffering high social deprivation in London and the South East of England. Each year, approximately £70,000 is available for distribution to projects that meet the Youth Plus objectives.

Youth Plus is supported by Hyde Plus, Hyde's economic and community regeneration arm. Hyde Plus administers the grants and supports groups in the development of projects seeking Youth Plus funding.

What have we funded previously and why?

We are mainly interested in innovative projects seeking to address problems faced by children and young people in areas typified by social deprivation. These areas will often have high levels of unemployment and disenchantment within the community and offer very few prospects for young people.

We are keen to hear about projects that demonstrate a partnership approach and which are committed to involving children and young people in both the planning and delivery of their services.

Grants of up to £200 each can also be made to young Hyde residents (16 years or under) for education or development training and equipment under the Hyde Young Pride Award.

In 2007/08 the trust had assets of £2.8 million and an income of £314,000. Grants were made totalling £307,000 to various youth-related charitable projects.

Beneficiaries included: Young Pride Awards (£26,000); Holiday Play Fund (£19,000); and Sports Fund (£12,000).

Exclusions No funding for the following.

- Projects outside of the area where Hyde is working. No areas outside the south east of England.
- Sporting, social or fundraising events.
- Medical research, hospices, residential homes for older people.
- Any other projects which the trustees deem to fall outside the trust's main criteria.

Applications The trust has recently informed us that it can no longer accept unsolicited applications.

The Idlewild Trust

Performing arts, culture, restoration and conservation and occasionally arts education

£123,000 (2008)
Beneficial area UK.

1a Taylors Yard, 67 Alderbrook Street, London SW12 8AD

Tel. 020 8772 3155

Email info@idlewildtrust.org.uk

Website www.idlewildtrust.org.uk

Correspondent Mrs Angela Hurst, Administrator

Trustees *Lady Judith Goodison, Chair; J A Ford; M Wilson; J Ouvry; Dr T Murdoch.*

CC Number 268124

Information available Accounts were on file at the Charity Commission.

The trust was founded in 1974 by Peter Brissault Minet, who had previously set up the Peter Minet Trust. Its policy is to support charities concerned with the encouragement of performing and fine arts and preservation for the benefit of the public of lands, buildings and other objects of beauty or historic interest. Occasionally support is given to bodies for educational bursaries in these fields or for conservation of the natural environment. The trust prefers to support UK charities and it is unlikely to support a project of local interest only.

In 2008 the trust had assets of £3.3 million, an income of £188,000 and made grants totalling £123,000.

Grants were categorised in the trust's annual report as follows:

Category	No.	Value
Preservation and Restoration	21	£42,000
Performing Arts	16	£33,000
Fine Art	8	£18,000
Education	8	£17,000
Museums and Galleries	6	£14,000

Beneficiaries included: National Children's Orchestra, Tate Gallery and the Council for Music in Hospitals (£3,000 each); National Youth Theatre of Great Britain (£2,500); London Symphony Orchestra and Young Musicians Symphony Orchestra (£2,000 each) Edinburgh World Heritage (£1,800); Nottinghamshire Wildlife Trust and Spitalfields Festival (£1,500 each); and Trees for Cities (£1,000).

Exclusions Grants to registered charities only. No grants are made to individuals. The trust will not give to:

- repetitive UK-wide appeals by large charities
- appeals where all, or most, of the beneficiaries live outside the UK
- local appeals unless the artistic significance of the project is of more than local importance
- appeals whose sole or main purpose is to make grants from the funds collected
- endowment or deficit funding.

Applications On a form available from the correspondent, or as a download from the trust's website. This can be sent via post or emailed as a Microsoft Word file. Applications should include the following information:

- budget breakdown (one page)
- most recent audited accounts
- a list of other sponsors, including those applied to
- other relevant information.

Potential applicants are welcome to telephone the trust on Tuesdays or Wednesdays between 10am and 4pm to discuss their application and check eligibility. Trustees meet twice a year usually in March and November.

All eligible applications, which are put forward to the trustees, are acknowledged; other applications will not be acknowledged unless a stamped, addressed envelope is enclosed. Applications from organisations within 18 months of a previous grant will not be considered.

The Iliffe Family Charitable Trust

Medical, disability, heritage and education

£254,000 (2007/08)
Beneficial area UK and Worldwide.

Barn Close, Yattendon RG18 0UX

Tel. 01635 203929

Correspondent The Secretary to the Trustees

Trustees *N G E Petter; G A Bremner; Lord Iliffe; Hon. Edward Iliffe.*

CC Number 273437

Information available Full accounts were on file at the Charity Commission.

The trust gives grants towards groups concerned with medical causes, disability, heritage and education. The bulk of the grants made are to charities already known to the trustees, to which funds are committed from year to year. Other donations are made for a wide range of charitable purposes in which the trust has a special interest.

In 2007/08 the trust had assets of £1.2 million and an income of £195,000. Grants totalled £254,000 and were broken down as follows, shown with examples of beneficiaries in each category:

Welfare (£72,000 in 13 grants)
Marine Society & Sea Cadets (£25,000); Berkshire Community Foundation (£15,000); Arthur Rank Centre (£12,000); Jubilee Sailing Trust (£8,000); Army Benevolent Fund (£3,000); Farm Africa (£1,000); and The Bruce Trust (£750).

Education (£66,000 in 7 grants)
Yattendon PCC (£40,000); Bradfield Foundation (£10,000); Douai Library Appeal (£6,000); Tennis Foundation (£5,000); The Scout Association (£1,500); and Upton Court Education Trust (£500).

Heritage (£40,000 in 4 grants)
Royal Shakespeare Company (£20,000); Royal Horticultural Society and Belgrade Theatre (£10,000 each); and National Trust (£400).

Medical (£32,000 in 7 grants)
CF Alice Martineau Appeal (£25,000); Prior's Court Foundation (£5,000); Jennifer Trust for SMA (£1,000); British Neurological Research (£250); and Adelaide Cancer Ward (£150).

Religious (£25,000 in 4 grants)
St Bride's Appeal (£20,000); Yattendon and Frilsham Christian Stewardship (£3,000); Holy Trinity Church Appeal (£2,000); and All Saints' Church (£250).

Conservation (£19,000 in 3 grants)
Game Conservancy Trust (£15,000); John Simond's Trust (£3,300); and North Atlantic Salmon Fund (£1,000).

Exclusions No grants to individuals and rarely to non-registered charities.

Applications In writing to the correspondent. Only successful applications will be acknowledged. Grants are considered at ad hoc meetings of the trustees, held throughout the year.

The Indigo Trust

Prisons and criminal justice

£31,000 (2007/08)

Beneficial area UK and overseas.

Allington House, 1st Floor, 150 Victoria Street, London SW1E 5AE

Tel. 020 7410 0330 **Fax** 020 7410 0332

Website www.sfct.org.uk

Correspondent Alan Bookbinder, Director

Trustees *Francesca Sainsbury; Dominic Flynn; Bernard Chi-Chung Fung.*

CC Number 1075920

Information available Annual report and accounts were available from the Charity Commission.

This is one of the Sainsbury Family Charitable Trusts, which share a joint administration. They have a common approach to grantmaking which is described in the entry for the group as a whole (in the first volume of this guide), and which is generally discouraging to organisations not already in contact with the trust concerned, but some appear increasingly open to unsolicited approaches.

The trust's 2007/08 accounts offer the following analysis of its grant-making policy:

Last year the trustees decided to focus their grant-making entirely in the field of criminal justice. During the course of this year the trustees have concentrated on researching parts of the sector where support from the Indigo Trust could have significant impact and create sustained change. As a result of this work, the trustees are likely to wish to fund programmes in the areas of:

- improved use of resources in the sector, particularly in resettlement and education
- the development of innovation and best practice in the sector, particularly in terms of the use of the web and new technologies
- research and dissemination to support the areas above.

Over the next year the trustees will make a small number of grants to organisations or programmes that have the potential to bring about systematic change both in prisons and within the criminal justice system more widely.

Proposals are generally invited by the trustees or initiated at their request. Unsolicited applications are not encouraged and are unlikely to be successful. Grants are not normally made to individuals.

In 2007/08 the trust had assets of £8.1 million and a significantly lower income of £391,000 (£5.8 million in 2006/07). However, the high income in the previous year was mainly due to a large gift of £5.5 million from the settlor. This has since been invested by the trust and the higher returns generated should allow for increased grantmaking in future years.

Grants payable during the current year totalled £31,000 (£826,000 in 2006/07).

Beneficiaries were: Anne Peaker Centre for Arts in Criminal Justice and We Are What We Do (£40,000 each); Ashden Awards (£20,000); and HM YOI Huntercombe (£9,400).

Please note: cancelled grants and changes in date of payment meant that a total of £79,000 was not actually paid during the year.

Exclusions Grants are not usually made to individuals.

Applications See the guidance for applicants in the entry for the Sainsbury Family Charitable Trusts in volume one. A single application will be considered for support by all the trusts in the group. However, please see comments in the 'General Information' section regarding the selection of beneficiaries.

The Ingram Trust

General

£766,000 (2007/08)

Beneficial area UK and overseas, with a local preference for Surrey.

c/o 8th Floor, 101 Wigmore Street, London W1U 1QU

Email theingramtrust@sandaire.com

Correspondent Joan Major, Administrator

Trustees *C J Ingram; Mrs J E Ingram; Ms C M Maurice.*

CC Number 1040194

Information available Accounts were on file at the Charity Commission.

The trust's policies are as follows:

- it selects a limited number of charities which it commits itself to support for three to five years
- it prefers to support specific projects which can include identifiable costs for special services provided by the charity or equipment that is required

- beneficiaries will generally be major UK-wide or international charities together with some local ones in the county of Surrey
- the majority of grants will be made for periods of three to four years at a time in order to better assess grant applications and monitor progress
- the only overseas aid charities which are considered are those dedicated to encouraging self-help and providing more permanent solutions to problems
- no animal charities are considered except those concerned with wildlife conservation.

In 2007/08 the trust had assets of £14 million, an income of £366,000 and made grants to 31 organisations totalling £766,000.

Beneficiaries included: The Centre of the Cell (£75,000); Shelter and ActionAid (£50,000 each); the Prince's Trust (£30,000); Almeida Theatre Company Limited (£25,000); Farm Africa (£20,000); CHASE (£17,000); ChildLine, Disability Challengers and the Woodland Trust (£10,000 each); and the Princess Alice Hospice Trust Ltd (£3,000).

Exclusions No grants to non-registered charities or to individuals. No charities specialising in overseas aid are considered except those dedicated to encouraging self help or providing more permanent solutions. No animal charities except those concerned with wildlife conservation.

Applications In writing to the correspondent, although the trust states that it receives far more worthy applications than it is able to support.

The Inland Waterways Association

Inland waterways

£27,000 (2008)

Beneficial area UK and Ireland.

Island House, Moor Road, Chesham HP5 1WA

Tel. 01923 711114 **Fax** 01923 897000

Email iwa@waterways.org.uk

Website www.waterways.org.uk

Correspondent The Chairman of the IWA Restoration Committee

Trustees *The Council of the Association; Doug Beard; Ray Carter; Leslie Etheridge; John Fletcher; Anthony Harrison; Michael Palmer; John Pomfret; Paul Strudwick; Vaughan Welch; Ian West.*

CC Number 212342

Information available Accounts were on file at the Charity Commission.

The trust supports organisations promoting the restoration of inland waterways (that is, canal and river navigations).

It makes grants for:

1) construction – especially works relating to the restoration of navigation such as locks, bridges, aquaducts, culverts, weirs, pumps, excavation, dredging, lining and so on

2) administration – support for a particular purpose, such as a project officer, a funding appeal or for promotional literature or events

3) professional services – such as funding of feasibility studies or detailed work on engineering, economic or environmental issues

4) land purchase

5) research on matters affecting waterway restoration – including original research, reviews of research undertaken by others and literature reviews

6) education – such as providing information to local authorities or agencies to promote the nature and benefits of waterway restoration.

In 2008 charitable activities came to £788,000, of which £27,000 was given in grants.

Grant beneficiaries were: the Driffield Navigation Trust (£7,500); Lichfield & Hatherton Canals Restoration Trust and Caldon & Uttoxeter Canal Trust (£5,000 each); British Waterways (£2,500); Rolle Canal and North Devon Waterways Society, Wiltshire and Berkshire Canal Trust and Foxton Locks Partnership (£2,000 each); and River Gipping Trust (£1,000).

Exclusions No grants to individuals. No retrospective grants for projects where expenditure has already been incurred or committed.

Applications In writing to the correspondent. Applications should comply with the 'Guidelines for Applicants', also available from the correspondent. Each applicant should provide a full description of its proposal, show that the organisation can maintain a satisfactory financial position and demonstrate that it is capable of undertaking the proposed project.

Applications for up to £2,000 are assessed under a simplified procedure – each application should demonstrate that the grant would be used to initiate or sustain a restoration scheme or significantly benefit a specific small project.

Applications for over £2,000 should demonstrate that the grant would be applied to one of the types of projects (1–6). Applicants should also demonstrate the extent to which the project satisfies one or more of the following conditions:

● the grant would unlock (lever) a grant several times larger from another body

● the grant would not replace grants available from other sources

● the project does not qualify for grants from major funding sources

● the grant would enable a key project to be undertaken which would have a significant effect on the prospect of advancing the restoration and gaining funds from other sources for further restoration projects

● the result of the project would have a major influence over the progress of a number of other restoration projects

● The Inland Waterways Association Restoration Committee would have a major influence in the management of the project, including monitoring of expenditure.

The Inlight Trust

Religion

£148,000 (2007/08)

Beneficial area UK.

PO Box 2, Liss, Hampshire GU33 6YP

Tel. 01730 894120

Correspondent The Trustees

Trustees *Sir T Lucas; Mrs W Collett; S Neil; R Wolfe; D Hawkins; Mrs J Hayward.*

CC Number 236782

Information available Accounts were on file at the Charity Commission.

The trust makes grants for the advancement of religion only. It states in its report that its funding priorities are: 'To make donations on an undenominational basis to charities providing valuable contributions to spiritual development and charities concerned with spiritual healing and spiritual growth through religious retreats.'

Grants are usually one-off for a specific project or part of a project. Bursary schemes may also be supported. Core funding and/or salaries are rarely considered.

In 2007/08 it had assets of £5.2 million, which generated an income of £237,000, through which 14 grants were made totalling £148,000.

The main beneficiaries were: Samye Ling Rokpa Trust – 4 grants totalling £60,000; and White Eagle Lodge – 2 grants totalling £31,000.

Other beneficiaries were: Kagyu Samye Dzong (£20,000); Burrswood, Tunbridge Wells (10,000); White Eagle Lodge (£7,500); FWBO – Buddhafield, Meditation Centre and the Magga Bhavaka Trust (5,000 each); Christians in Care (£3,000); and Manchester Reform Synangogue (£1,500).

Exclusions Grants are made to registered charities only. Applications from individuals, including students, are ineligible. No grants are made in response to general appeals from large national organisations. Grants are seldom available for church buildings.

Applications In writing to the correspondent including details of the need the intended project is designed to meet plus an outline budget and the most recent available annual accounts of the charity. Only applications from eligible bodies are acknowledged. Applications must be accompanied by a copy of your trust deed or of your entry in the Charity Commission register. They are considered four times a year. Only successful applicants are informed.

The Inman Charity

See below

£262,000 (2008)

Beneficial area UK.

Payne Hicks Beech, 10 New Square, Lincoln's Inn, London WC2A 3QG

Correspondent The Trustees

Trustees *A L Walker; Miss B M A Strother; M R Mathews; Prof. J D Langdon.*

CC Number 261366

Information available Full accounts were on file at the Charity Commission.

The following is taken from the trust's accounts.

The directors operate a grant giving policy, providing funds for such charitable object or institution as the directors think fit. In addition to supporting a wide range of charitable organisations, the charity makes a regular payment (normally £15,000 per annum) to the Victor Inman Bursary Fund at Uppingham School of which the settlor had been a lifelong supporter.

The directors aim to make grants totalling approximately £250,000 per year. Previously grants have been given in the areas of social welfare, disability, older people and hospices.

In 2008 it had assets of £4.4 million generating an income of £204,000. Grants to 64 organisations totalled £262,000.

Beneficiaries included: Victor Inman Bursary Fund at Uppingham School (£20,000); Vitalise and Help the Hospices (£8,000 each); the Roy Castle Lung Cancer Research, Bowel Disease Research Foundation and the Inspire Foundation (£5,000 each); the Anthony Nolan Trust, DeafBlind UK and Gurkha Welfare Trust (£4,000 each); The Manna Society and West Suffolk Voluntary Association for the Blind (£3,000 each); Tax Volunteers (£2,000); Mind (£1,500); and Tools for Self Reliance (£1,000).

Exclusions No grants to individuals.

Applications In writing to the correspondent accompanied by the charity's latest report and full accounts. Applications should contain the following: aims and objectives of the charity; nature of the appeal; total target if for a specific project; contributions received against target; registered charity number and any other relevant factors.

The Worshipful Company of Innholders General Charity Fund

General
See below
Beneficial area UK.

Innholders' Hall, 30 College Street, London EC4R 2RH

Tel. 020 7236 6703 **Fax** 020 7236 0059
Email mail@innholders.co.uk
Correspondent The Clerk
Trustee *The Worshipful Company of Innholders.*
CC Number 270948
Information available Accounts were on file at the Charity Commission.

This trust supports children and young people, older people and education and training, particularly regarding the hotel industry. In recent years, the trust's income and expenditure have fluctuated between £10,000 and £60,000, however it usually gives around £30,000 in grants annually.

Previously, most of the funds were given towards the 'welfare of the young' (£33,000) and Master Innholders' Scholarships (£20,000).

Exclusions No grants to individuals.

Applications In writing to the correspondent, including the reason for applying and current financial statements and so on.

The International Bankers Charitable Trust (The Worshipful Company of International Bankers)

The recruitment and development of employees in the financial services
£73,000 (2007/08)
Beneficial area UK with preference for inner London.

3rd Floor, 12 Austin Friars, London EC2N 2HE
Tel. 020 7374 0214
Email tim.woods@internationalbankers.co.uk
Website www.internationalbankers.co.uk

Correspondent Tim Woods, Clerk
Trustee *The Worshipful Company of International Bankers.*
CC Number 1087630
Information available Accounts were on file at the Charity Commission.

The following information is taken from the website.

As a representative of the major commercial activity in the city, banking and financial services, the company combines the traditions of the City Livery Companies with a modern outlook on the financial services sector. With more than 600 members, drawn from over 250 companies and institutions and with almost 50 nationalities represented, the company has a truly international character.

Set up in 2001, 'The company will seek to promote recruitment and development of employees in the financial services industry with particular emphasis on those younger people in the immediate area of the city who would not normally be able to aspire to a city job.' Grants are made to registered charities only.

The company may support:

1) Specific projects where a donation from the company would cover either a significant proportion of the cost or an identified element of it.
2) Long-term funding of scholarships and/or bursaries.

In 2007/08 the trust had an income of £180,000, including £118,000 in donations from members of the Worshipful Company of International Bankers. Grants totalled £73,000. The sum of £796,000 was carried forward at year end.

Beneficiaries included: Brokerage Citylink Grant (£30,000); Chinese Earthquake Donation (£6,400); City of London School for Boys and City of London School for Girls (£5,000 each); Lord Mayor's Appeal and Mansion House Scholarship Scheme (£2,500 each); and CHICKS and Reed's School Helping Hands Scheme (£1,000 each).

Exclusions The following areas are excluded from company grants:

- large projects towards which any contribution from the company would have limited impact
- general appeals or circulars
- replacement of statutory funds
- salaries
- counselling
- course fees for professionals
- medical research
- fundraising events and sponsorship.

Applications On a form with can be downloaded from the trust's website. Previous grant recipients must allow two years from the date the original grant was awarded to reapply.

The Inverforth Charitable Trust

General

£155,000 (2007)
Beneficial area UK.

58a Flood Street, London SW3 5TE

Tel. 0870 770 2657

Correspondent The Secretary

Trustees *Elizabeth Lady Inverforth; Dr Andrew Weir; Mrs Clarinda Kane.*

CC Number 274132

Information available Accounts were on file at the Charity Commission.

For the three year period commencing January 2008, the trustees have decided to support 12 selected charities with annual donations. The charities concerned have been notified. Charities supported in the past who have not been selected have also been notified, and for the next three years the funds of the Inverforth Charitable Trust will be fully committed. Charities which have not been selected for donations should not apply to the Inverforth Charitable trust; any unsolicited applications made in 2008 and thereafter will be discarded and no acknowledgement will be sent.

In 2007 it had assets of £3.9 million, which generated an income of £195,000. Grants were made to 129 organisations totalling £155,000, broken down as follows:

Category	No.	Value
Phyical and mental health	32	£37,000
Hospices	20	£26,000
Music and the arts	19	£21,000
Disability and older people	17	£19,000
Young people and education	11	£13,000
Churches and heritage	8	£9,000
Other (including international)	24	£31,000

Beneficiaries included: Help for Heroes (£5,000); Helriot Hospice Homecare and CHASE Hospice Care for Children (£2,000 each); the ART Fund, British Lung Foundation, Voluntary Services Overseas and National Youth Orchestra of Great Britain (£1,500 each); National Playbus Association, Kidscape, Contact the Elderly and Farms for City Children (£1,000 each); and Book Aid International, Bowel Cancer UK and the Gurkha Welfare Trust (£500 each).

Applications No applications are being accepted for the three year period commencing January 2008.

The Ireland Fund of Great Britain

Welfare, community, education, peace and reconciliation and the arts

£489,000 (2007)
Beneficial area Ireland and Great Britain.

2nd Floor, Wigglesworth House, 69 Southwark Bridge Road, London SE1 9HH

Tel. 0845 872 5401

Email greatbritain@irlfunds.org

Website www.irlfunds.org/great_britain

Correspondent The Trustees

Trustees *Peter Sutherland, Chair; Kingsley Aikins; Seamus McGarry; Basil Geoghegan; Peter Kiernan; John Rowan; Hon Kevin Pakenham; Ruth McCarthy.*

CC Number 327889

Information available Accounts were on file at the Charity Commission.

Founded in 1976 by Sir Anthony O'Reilly and a number of key American businessmen, *The Ireland Funds* is an international charitable organisation operating in 11 countries and has raised over $300 million for worthy causes in Ireland.

The Ireland Fund of Great Britain (IFGB) is dedicated to raising funds to support programmes of peace and reconciliation, arts and culture, education and community development in Ireland and the United Kingdom.

In 2007 the fund had assets of £643,000 an income of £1.1 million, mainly from fundraising events. Grants totalled £489,000 and were broken down as follows:

Category	Value
Community development and relief of poverty	£364,000
Sharing and developing Irish arts and culture	£84,000
Education	£41,000

Beneficiaries were: Louvain Trust (£175,000); GOAL International (£140,000); Wexford Festival Foundation

(£84,000); Young Christian Workers (£25,000); Linacre (£20,000); Alfaner (£15,000); All Hallows College (£14,000); Lifestart (£10,000); and Belvedere College (£2,000).

A further £3,800 was given in unnamed restricted grants.

IFGB supports projects in the following categories:

- arts and culture
- community development
- education
- peace and reconciliation.

Each category is accorded equal importance.

Arts and culture
IFGB wishes to support excellence and innovation in the arts and culture and especially projects that make the arts more accessible to the wider community. In particular, the IFGB will focus on the following:

- arts/cultural activities applied in settings of socio-economic disadvantage
- arts/cultural activities applied in educational or health settings
- arts/cultural activities promoting tolerance and reconciliation.

Community Development/Relief of Poverty
IFGB is seeking ways to promote an inclusive and integrated society and to ensure the regeneration of marginalised sections of the Irish community. IFGB sees the following areas as priorities:

- increasing the capacity of the social economy
- promotion of social inclusion
- promotion of tolerance and diversity.

Education
Investment in education is investment in the future. Economic and social development depends on a well-educated population. For this reason, IFGB will focus on programmes supporting:

- access and progression to further education
- pre-school education
- lifelong learning
- tolerance through education.

Peace and Reconciliation
IFGB seeks to support communities working together towards a shared future. The skills and culture of negotiation and compromise need to be honed politically and organisationally within and between communities. To this end, programmes supporting the following areas have been prioritised for assistance:

- citizenship and participation

163

- a greater understanding of cultural identity within and between communities
- social inclusion.

Exclusions Grants are generally not given for: general administration costs; travel or accommodation costs; payments for buildings or land; general appeals, that is, applications must be made for clearly specified purposes; other grant making trusts; payments for vehicles; medical expenses. No multi-annual awards.

Applications Application forms and full details of how to apply are available from the IFGB website.

The Irish Youth Foundation (UK) Ltd (incorporating The Lawlor Foundation)

Irish young people

£253,000 (2008)

Beneficial area UK.

The Irish Cultural Centre, 3 Blacks Road, Hammersmith, London W6 9DT

Tel. 020 8748 9640

Email info@iyf.org.uk

Website www.iyf.org.uk

Correspondent Linda Tanner

Trustees *John O'Neill, Chair; John Dwyer; Fred Hucker; Virginia Lawlor; Mary Clancy; Mark Gilbert; David Murray; Jim O'Hara.*

CC Number 328265

Information available Accounts were on file at the Charity Commission, but without a full list of grantees.

Irish Youth Foundation (UK) Ltd merged with the Lawlor Foundation (effective from 30 June 2005). The work of the Lawlor Foundation, towards the advancement of education in Northern Ireland, continues with support for Irish students and educational organisations.

The foundation supports organisations anywhere in the UK working with young Irish people aged up to 25 who are socially, educationally or culturally disadvantaged.

A wide range of projects are supported which include: training/counselling; drug rehabilitation; advice/advocacy; youth work; family support; homelessness; educational, cultural and social activities; cross-community initiatives; travellers and disability.

Grant range from £500 to £25,000 and are awarded annually. Grants for organisations in England, Scotland and Wales fall into the following three categories:

- Small grants for up to £2,500
- Medium grants for over £2,500 and under £12,000
- Large grants for one year or more ranging from £12,000 to £25,000.

The Irish Youth Foundation (UK) and the Irish Youth Foundation (Ireland) have established a joint fund to provide support for community and voluntary groups in Northern Ireland. Grants for organisations in Northern Ireland are up to £5,000.

In 2008 the foundation had assets of £2.3 million and an income of £274,000. Grants totalled £253,000.

Beneficiaries in the UK (excluding Northern Ireland) included: Brent Adolescent Centre – London (£15,000 in two grants for three years); Irish Community Care – Merseyside (£12,000); London Gypsy and Traveller Unit (£9,000); Irish Arts Foundation – Leeds (£4,000); Warwickshire Schools Gaelic Athletics Association (£2,000); and Liverpool Irish Festival Society (£1,000).

Beneficiaries in Northern Ireland included: The National Deaf Children's Society, Northern Ireland (£4,500); Artillery Youth Centre – Belfast (£4,000); Drake Music Project – Newry (£3,500); Down Community Arts – Downpatrick (£3,000); Headliners – Derry (£2,500); and Our Lady Queen of Peace Youth Club – Belfast (£1,000).

Exclusions The foundation generally does not support: projects for people over 25; general appeals; large/national charities; academic research; alleviating deficits already incurred; individuals; capital bids; or overseas travel.

Applications Applications are assessed on an annual basis and application forms are only available during the annual round either on the website or by request. The application period is short as forms are only available during December and January, with grant awards being made the following April.

Applications are assessed on the following requirements: need; continuity; track record/evaluation; disadvantaged

young people; innovativeness; funding sources; and budgetary control. Faxed or emailed applications are not considered. Unsolicited applications outside the annual round of grant applications will not be considered or acknowledged.

The Ironmongers' Foundation

General

£184,000 to organisations (2007/08)

Beneficial area UK with some preference for inner London.

Ironmongers' Hall, Barbican, London EC2Y 8AA

Tel. 020 7776 2311 **Fax** 020 7600 3519

Email helen@ironhall.co.uk

Website www.ironhall.co.uk

Correspondent Helen Sant, Charities Administrator

Trustee *Worshipful Ironmongers' Company.*

CC Number 238256

Information available Accounts were available from the Charity Commission.

'The Ironmongers' Company aims to help people who are disadvantaged to improve their ability to make the most of life. We wish to support projects that develop and nurture the motivation and skills necessary to take advantage of opportunities.'

Grants will be made for projects that meet all of the following criteria:

1) Children and young people up to the age of 25
2) Educational activities
3) Specific projects with clear aims and objectives to be met within a planned timescale.

Most grants are in the region of £1,000 to £5,000. The trustees will consider making grants over more than one year to longer term projects, subject to a satisfactory evaluation of progress at the end of each year. The company's support should make a recognisable difference, therefore preference will be given to requests which cover a significant element of the cost and to those from smaller organisations.

In 2007/08 the fund had assets of £2.1 million, an income of £167,000 and made grants to organisations totalling £184,000.

The accounts listed beneficiaries in receipt of awards over £1,000 each, with examples of beneficiaries, divided as follows:

City of London organisations – £87,000
King Edward's School (£75,000); Guildhall School Trust (£3,200); Sea Cadets (£2,400); Museum of London (£2,000); and St Boltoph's Church (£1,000).

Ironwork – £40,000
Chelsea Pensioners' Appeal (£12,000); St Paul's Cathedral (£10,000); Friends of Arnold Circus (£5,900); Shoots and Roots (£5,000); Crossness Engines Trust (£4,000); and Chapel Street Nursery (£1,300).

Universities and industry – £27,000
Institute of Cast Metal Engineers (£3,800); and Birmingham, Cambridge, Oxford, Sheffield and Manchester Universities and Imperial College (£3,000 each).

Relief in Need – £25,000
Westminster Bangladeshi Association (£7,000); Aurora Orchestra and Markfield Project (£5,000 each); and the Rona Trust (£2,000).

Grants of less than £1,000 for 'crafts' totalled £475 and grants to 'iron education' were also made to Engineering Education Scheme Wales (£2,000); and Arkwright Scholarship (£1,800). The foundation also gave £100,000 to its own bursary scheme.

Exclusions No grants towards:

- Large projects towards which any contribution from the Company would have limited impact.
- General appeals or circulars.
- Replacement of statutory funds.
- General running costs. (A reasonable proportion of overheads will be accepted as part of project costs).
- Counselling.
- Course fees for professionals.
- Medical research.
- Fundraising events and sponsorship.
- Retrospective appeals and projects starting before the date of the relevant committee meeting.

Applications The Company's 'Grant Application Summary Sheet' must be completed and returned including a description of the project, of no more than three A4 pages. Summary sheets can be downloaded from the fund's website.

The Appeals Committee meets twice a year in March and October. The

deadlines for receipt of applications are 31 January and 31 August respectively. Please note: applications are not accepted by email.

Grants must be spent within twelve months from the date of the award.

The ISA Charity

Arts, health and education
£46,000 (2007/08)
Beneficial area UK.

Bourton House, Bourton On The Hill, Moreton-In-Marsh GL56 9AE
Tel. 01386 700121
Website www.isacharity.org
Correspondent R Paice, Trustee
Trustees *R Paice; Mrs M Paice; Miss A Paice.*
CC Number 326882
Information available Accounts were on file at the Charity Commission, but without a list of grants. Detailed information is available on the charity's website.

Founded in 1985 by Richard Paice, the ISA Charity supports causes related to the arts, health and education in the broadest sense. This can include both UK and overseas initiatives. The charity selects various organisations which help to find the individual beneficiaries. Up to £50,000 is distributed each year.

In 2007/08 the charity had assets of £1.5 million and an income of £195,000, including £100,000 from ISA Holdings Limited. Grants totalled £46,000.

Unfortunately a list of the beneficiaries was not available.

Applications The charity's website included the following statement: 'The charity adopts a venture philanthropy approach and identifies its own projects. It does not accept funding requests from individuals, organisations or other charities. As a consequence it will not acknowledge any unsolicited funding requests.'

J Issacs Charitable Trust

General
£457,000 (2007/08)
Beneficial area England and Wales.

c/o Touch Group plc, Saffron House, 6–10 Kirby Street, London EC1N 6TS
Email peter.katz@touchgroupplc.com
Correspondent P Katz
Trustees *J M Isaacs: Mrs J M Isaacs; Helen Eastick.*
CC Number 1059865
Information available Accounts were on file at the Charity Commission.

Registered with the Charity Commission in 1996, the trust states that it strives to support causes connected to the following:

- children
- respite for parents/children
- cancer
- sponsorship for causes supported by Lehman employees
- London-based organisations.

In 2007/08 it had an income of £8 million, raised mainly from donations made by J Isaacs, a trustee of the J Isaac Charitable Trust. Grants totalled £457,000 and funds of £14.5 million were carried forward.

There were 29 grants made during the year, with the two largest grants went to United Jewish Israel Appeal and Shlomi High School (£100,000 each).

Other beneficiaries included: Jewish Museum London and Trinity Hospice (£50,000 each); Lehman Brothers Foundation Europe (£40,000); Oxford Centre for Hebrew Jewish Studies and Greenhouse Schools Project (£25,000 each); Norwood (£14,000); One Family UK (£11,000); Hospital for Special Surgery (£7,600); London Jewish Forum and the Children Foundation (£5,000 each); Young People Foundation, Alone in London, Cancer Research UK and Cystic Fibrosis Foundation (£2,500 each); and Myeloma UK (£1,500).

Applications In writing to the correspondent.

J A R Charitable Trust

Roman Catholic, education and welfare

£64,000 (2007/08)

Beneficial area Worldwide.

c/o Vernor Miles and Noble, 5 Raymond Buildings, Gray's Inn, London WC1R 5DD

Tel. 020 7242 8688

Correspondent Philip R Noble, Trustee

Trustees *Philip R Noble; Revd William Young; Revd Paschal Ryan.*

CC Number 248418

Information available Accounts were on file at the Charity Commission.

The trust states in its annual report that it makes grants towards: Roman Catholic missionaries, churches and other causes; education for people under 30; and food and clothing for people over 55 who are in need. In practice, the trust gives regular grants to support mainly Roman Catholic organisations.

In 2007/08 the trust had assets of £2.2 million which generated an income of £75,000. Grants were made to 40 organisations totalling £64,000.

Beneficiaries included: Westminster Cathedral (£5,000); The Passage (£4,000); Liverpool Archdiocesan Youth Pilgrimage, Venerable English College and St Joseph's Hospice (£3,000 each); Anchor House, Jesuit Volunteers and Aid to the Church in Need (£2,000 each); and Tongabezi Trust School, Marriage Care and Dans La Rue (£1,000 each).

Exclusions The trust does not normally support a charity unless it is known to the trustees and it does not support individuals.

Applications In writing to the correspondent. Please note: the trust's funds are fully committed to regular beneficiaries and it states that there is very little, if any, for unsolicited appeals. In order to save administration costs replies are not sent to unsuccessful applicants.

The J R S S T Charitable Trust

Democracy and social justice

£67,000 paid (2007/08)

Beneficial area UK.

The Garden House, Water End, York YO30 6WQ

Tel. 01904 625744 **Fax** 01904 651502

Email info@jrrt.org.uk

Website www.jrrt.org.uk

Correspondent Tina Walker

Trustees *Christine J Day; Christopher J Greenfield; David T Shutt (Lord Shutt of Greetland); Paedar Cremin; Mandy Cormack; Danny G Alexander; Pam Giddy; Andrew Neal.*

CC Number 247498

Information available Accounts were on file at the Charity Commission.

The trust was originally endowed by the non-charitable Joseph Rowntree Reform Trust Ltd. It will consider and sometimes instigate charitable projects which relate specifically to the work of The Joseph Rowntree Reform Trust Ltd in supporting the development of an increasingly democratic and socially-just society in Great Britain.

In 2007 the trust had assets of £3.5 million and an income of £167,000. After high support costs of £24,000, grants paid to organisations totalled £67,000.

Beneficiaries of grants approved during the year included: IDASA/Zimbabwe Institute (£104,000); British Documentary Film Foundation (£49,000); Democratic Audit (£29,000); Reuters Institute for the Study of Journalism (£24,000); Foreign Policy Centre and Scottish Votepods (£5,000 each); Centre for Women & Democracy (£4,800); Scottish Social Enterprise Coalition (£4,400); and Lesbian & Gay Foundation (£2,400).

Exclusions No student grants are funded.

Applications The trustees meet quarterly. They do not invite applications.

Jacobs Charitable Trust

Jewish charities and the arts

£264,000 (2007/08)

Beneficial area Unrestricted.

9 Nottingham Terrace, London NW1 4QB

Tel. 020 7486 6323

Correspondent The Rt Hon the Lord Jacobs, Chair

Trustees *Lord Jacobs, Chair; Lady Jacobs.*

CC Number 264942

Information available Accounts were on file at the Charity Commission.

In 2007/08 the trust had an income of £3,500 and a total expenditure of £264,000.

Previous beneficiaries have included: Central Synagogue Central Charities Fund (£36,000); Jewish Care (£30,000); Haifa University and London School of Economics (£28,000 each); Norton Museum of Art (£27,000); Tate Foundation (£25,000); Community Security Trust (£20,000): Israel Philharmonic Orchestra Foundation (£14,000); Royal Academy of Arts and Royal Opera House (£10,000 each); Norwood Ltd (£7,500); Board of Deputies of British Jews (£5,000); American Friends of the Israel Museum (£2,900); Council for a Beautiful Israel (£1,800); and Barnardo's, MDA UK, Princess Alice Hospice, Saving Faces and Tribe (£1,000 each).

Applications In writing to the correspondent.

The Ruth and Lionel Jacobson Trust (Second Fund) No 2

Jewish, medical, children and disability

£38,000 (2007/08)

Beneficial area UK, with a preference for north east England

14 The Grainger Suite, Dobson House, The Regent Centre, Gosforth, Newcastle upon Tyne NE3 3PF

Correspondent The Trustees

Trustees *Anne Jacobson; Malcolm Jacobson.*

CC Number 326665

Information available Accounts were on file at the Charity Commission.

The trust supports UK charities and organisations based in the north east of England. The trust states that it supports the advancement of Jewish religious education and healthcare charities. Charities outside the north east of England are supported whenever possible.

In 2007/08 the trust had assets of £1.2 million, an income of £51,000 and made grants totalling £38,000.

The four main grants in the year went to: United Jewish Israel Appeal (£25,000); Lupus UK (£5,000); and WIZO UK (£3,000).

Grants to other institutions not exceeding £500 each totalled £5,000.

Exclusions No grants for individuals. Only registered charities will be supported.

Applications In writing to the correspondent. Please enclose a stamped, addressed envelope. Applications are considered every other month.

The James Trust

Christianity

£82,000 (2008/09)

Beneficial area UK and overseas.

27 Radway Road, Upper Shirley, Southampton SO15 7PL

Tel. 023 8078 8249

Correspondent R J Todd, Trustee

Trustees *R J Todd; G Blue.*

CC Number 800774

Information available Accounts were on file at the Charity Commission.

Principally, the trust has a preference for supporting Christian organisations. It operates primarily as a channel for the giving of a small group of donors. Grants are primarily to churches and Christian organisations involved in overseas development and work with young people.

In 2008/09 it had an income of £50,000 and made grants to 52 organisations totalling £82,000. Donations were in the range of £30 and £10,000 and were broken down as follows:

Category	Value
Organisations working overseas	£29,000
Organisations working in the UK	£26,000
Churches and church organisations	£18,000
Development and relief work	£10,000
Individuals	£650

During the year donations were made to the local churches of the donors and to a wide range of Christian organisations. The main beneficiaries were Above Bar Church, Ambassadors in Sport, Food for the Hungry, UCCF and Wycliffe Translators.

Unfortunately a full grants list was not provided in this year's set of accounts, however previous beneficiaries have included: Archbishops Council (£10,000); Above Bar Church (£7,700); Food For the Hungrey (£5,000); UCCF (£3,600); Crusaders (£4,100); Tearfund (£1,900); Christian Aid (£1,300); Bible Society (£800); Church Missionary Society (£500); and Cancer Research (£200).

Exclusions No grants to individuals not personally known to the trustees.

Applications In writing to the correspondent. Unsolicited applications are not acknowledged.

The John Jarrold Trust

Social welfare, arts, education, environment, conservation, medical research and churches

£132,000 to organisations (2007/08)

Beneficial area Norfolk.

Jarrold and Sons Ltd, Whitefriars, Norwich NR3 1SH

Tel. 01603 677360

Email caroline.jarrold@jarrold.com

Website www.jarrold.com

Correspondent Caroline Jarrold, Secretary

Trustees *A C Jarrold, Chair; R E Jarrold; P J Jarrold; Mrs D J Jarrold; Mrs J Jarrold; K W Jarrold; Caroline Jarrold; Mrs W A L Jarrold.*

CC Number 242029

Information available Full accounts were available from the Charity Commission.

The trust supports a wide range of organisations including churches, medical, arts, environment, conservation and welfare. It prefers to support specific projects, rather than contribute to general funding. In practice, most of the funds are given in Norfolk. In 2007/08 the trust had assets of £1.4 million and an income of £129,000. Grants made to 112 organisations totalled £132,000, and were broken down as follows:

Category	Value
Arts	£40,000
Social and Welfare	£29,000
Education	£14,000
Churches and historic buildings	£14,000
Developing countries	£8,000
Health and Medical	£7,500
Environment	£4,400

Beneficiaries included:

Arts – 16 grants totalling £40,000
Norwich Theatre Royal Limited (£23,000); Norfolk and Norwich Festival (£5,000); Northern Ballet (£2,500); East Anglia Art Fund (£1,500); and Friends of Norfolk County Youth Orchestra (£750).

Social and Welfare – 31 grants totalling £29,000
YMCA Norfolk (£15,000); EACH, Corton House Limited and Norfolk and Norwich Association for the Blind (£2,000 each); NCH (£1,500); City of Norwich Swimming Club, East Anglia Air Ambulance and Matthew Project (£1,000 each); and the Big Issue Foundation, Irene Taylor Trust and Strong Roots (£500 each).

Education – 16 grants totalling £14,000
Arkwright Scholarship Trust (£3,600); City of Norwich School Association and Notre Dame HIgh School (£2,000 each); Thorpe St Andrew School Development Trust (£1,000); and Teacher Scientist Network (£500).

Churches and Historic Buildings – 16 grants totalling £14,000
Dragon Hall (£3,000); Catholic Cathedral of East Anglia Preservation and Development, Erpingham PCC and Pinham Priory Trust (£1,000 each); and Arts Alive in Norfolk Churches (£600).

Developing Countries – 13 grants totalling £8,000
Rotary Club of Norwich – Bansang Appeal (£1,500); Sight Savers International, Uganda Support Fund and British Red Cross Darfur Appeal (£1,000 each); Harvest Help (£500); and Feed the Minds (£250).

Health and Medical – 13 grants totalling £7,500

Breast Cancer Campaign, National Society for Epilepsy and NANSA (£1,000 each); the British Stammering Association, Meningitis Trust and Blood Pressure Association (£500 each); and Aspergers East Anglia (£250).

Environment – 7 grants totalling £4,400

Norfolk Wildlife Trust (£1,300); RSPB (£1,000); Green Light Trust (£500); and Little Ouse Headwaters Project (£250).

Exclusions Educational purposes that should be supported by the state will not be helped by the trust. Local groups outside Norfolk are very unlikely to be supported unless there is a personal connection to the trust. Individual educational programmes and gap year projects are not supported.

Applications Trustees meet in January and June each year and applications should be made in writing by the end of November and April respectively. Grants of up to £250 can be made between meetings.

Rees Jeffreys Road Fund

Road and transport research and education

£211,000 (2008)

Beneficial area UK.

Merriewood, Horsell Park, Woking GU21 4LW

Tel. 01483 750758

Email briansmith@reesjeffreys.co.uk

Website www.reesjeffreys.org

Correspondent Brian Smith, Fund Secretary

Trustees David Bayliss, Chair; M N T Cottell; T Depledge; A Frye; Prof S Glaister; D Hutchinson; M Shaw; Prof J Wootton.

CC Number 217771

Information available Report and accounts with full grants list, explanation of grants, and descriptions of the trust's history and objects provided by the trust.

The late William Rees Jeffreys established the trust in 1950, shortly after he wrote 'The King's Highway'. He campaigned extensively for the improvement of better roads and transport and was described by Lloyd George as 'the greatest authority on roads in the United Kingdom and one of the greatest in the world', due to his unrivalled expertise in this field.

In 2008 the fund had assets of £5.2 million and an income of £128,000. Grants totalled £211,000 and were broken down as follows:

- Research and general – £89,000
- Education – £92,000
- 'Physical Projects' – £28,000
- Other Education Projects – £23,000.

The fund gives financial support for research to improve the quality and efficiency of roads and their use by vehicles, cyclists, pedestrians and public transport.

The trust's priorities are as follows.

- Education of transport professionals, largely through financial support for teaching staff and bursaries for postgraduate studies. The trust is concerned about the supply of trained professionals and has launched a study of future requirements.
- Appropriate research into all aspects of roads, road usage and road traffic, in accordance with the fund's objectives – this commands a large share of the fund's budget. The trust develops its own research programmes as well as responding to proposals from recognised agencies and researchers. Proposals are assessed against prevailing transport issues, such as environmental questions, congestion, modal choice and resource development.
- Roadside environment. Applications for the provision of roadside rests are welcome, while support for the work of country wildlife trusts for improving land adjoining main roads is also maintained. The trust is not normally able to buy land or to fund improvements to roads, footpaths or cycle tracks.

The trust will support projects and pump priming for longer-term ventures for up to a maximum of five years. Operational or administrative staff costs are rarely supported. In almost all cases applicants are expected to provide or arrange match funding.

Research and General

Grants ranged from £500 to £20,000, with examples including: Road Safety Foundation and ITC (£20,000 each); Transport Planning Society (£15,000); and Heathcote and Barr (£5,000).

Education

This category included a total £92,000 for academic funding; eight postgraduate studentships were awarded for the following institutions: Leeds University, Imperial College, Cardiff University and University College London. Funding was also given to the Disabilities Trust and Riverside Museum – Glasgow. Unfortunately an individual breakdown of this academic funding total was unavailable.

'Physical Projects'

Grants were given in this category to a number of wildlife and conservation projects, ranging between £500 and £6,400. Beneficiaries included: Norfolk Wildlife Trust (£6,400); Surrey Wildlife Trust (£5,000); Heywoods Initiative (£3,000); St George's Flower Bank (£2,500); and Butterfly Conservation (£2,000).

Exclusions Grants are not given to environmental projects not related to highways, individual works for cycle tracks or works of only local application. Also, operational and administrative staff costs are rarely considered.

Applications There is no set form of application for grants; brief details should be submitted initially to the trustees either by telephone or post. The trustees meet five times in the year, usually in January, April, July, September and November. Trustees 'favour proposals where the outcome will have a national impact rather than local application and where costs are shared with other funding partners'. In general, 'project expenditure (excluding overheads and core funding) is grant aided'.

The Jenour Foundation

General

£119,000 (2007/08)

Beneficial area UK, with a special interest in Wales.

Deloitte and Touche, Blenhein House, Fitzalan Court, Newport Road, Cardiff CF24 0TS

Tel. 02920 264348

Correspondent The Trustees

Trustees Sir P J Phillips; G R Camfield; D M Jones.

CC Number 256637

Information available Accounts were on file at the Charity Commission.

This foundation has general charitable purposes, with a preference for Welsh causes.

In 2007/08 the foundation had assets of £3.1 million, an income of £157,000 and made 37 grants totalling £119,000.

Beneficiaries included: Atlantic College and Cancer Research Wales (£8,000 each); Welsh National Opera and British Heart Foundation (£7,000 each); Red Cross International and Army Benevolent Fund (£6,000 each); Wales Council for the Blind and George Thomas Society (£4,000 each); Wales Millenium Centre and Bath Institute of Medical Engineering (£3,000 each); the Gurkha Welfare Trust and Multiple Sclerosis Society (£2,000 each); and Society for Welfare of Horses and Ponies (£1,000).

Exclusions No support for individuals.

Applications Applications should be in writing and reach the correspondent by February for the trustees' meeting in March.

The Jephcott Charitable Trust

Alleviation of poverty in developing countries and general

£200,000 (2007/08)
Beneficial area UK, developing countries.

Cotley, Streatham Rise, Exeter EX4 4PE
Tel. 01392 841160
Website www.jephcottcharitabletrust. org.uk
Correspondent Mrs Meg Harris, Secretary
Trustees *Lady Jephcott, Chair; Judge A North; M L Jephcott; K Morgan; Mrs D Adler; Mrs C Thomas.*
CC Number 240915
Information available Accounts were on file at the Charity Commission.

The trust's funding priorities are:

- **Population control** – The trust is prepared to consider support for schemes, particularly educational ones, which help to control excessive growth in population.
- **The natural environment** – The trust has supported a number of projects involved in conserving the natural environment. It does not support projects involving animal welfare or heritage sites or buildings.
- **Education** – Projects will be considered benefiting people of all ages and backgrounds. They may be able to provide formal education, to teach vocational skills to enhance the possibility of employment, to enhance computer skills, health awareness, distance learning.
- **Health** – A wide range of healthcare projects are supported.

The trust prefers to support projects which are pump-priming – helping to get an organisation up and running, or make a significant step forward. The trustees state in their annual report that they 'like to make grants which will make a difference, preference will be given to charities or projects which are having difficulty getting started, or raising funds from other sources. This often means that the trust is funding capital projects, for example, for equipment or materials, rather than running costs.' It is not usual to make more than one grant to any organisation, preferring to help many new projects get started.

Grants are made in the range of £2,000 to £10,000, and in exceptional cases only, up to £20,000.

In 2007/08 the trust had assets of £4.8 million, an income of £290,000 and made 22 grants totalling £200,000. Examples of grants listed in the accounts included:

The natural environment – £14,600
Green Light Trust (£8,000); and Berkeley Reforestation Trust (£6,600).

Education – £134,000
Riding School for the Disabled of Cornwall (£25,000); African Child Education Programme (£15,000); Ugandan Rural School Initiative (£11,000); China Candlelight Education Fund (£10,000); Youth Education Service (£6,600); and African Village Support (£4,000).

Health – £52,000
Depaul Foundation (£15,000); Hailer Foundation (£12,500); Action Water (£5,100); and Lowe Syndrome Trust (£1,500).

Exclusions The trust does not support:

- organisations whose administrative expenses form more than 15% of their annual income
- individuals
- animal welfare
- heritage.

Projects which require long-term funding are not normally considered.

The trust prefers to make one-off donations to get many projects started, rather than support fewer projects charities over a long period.

Applications Full and detailed guidelines and application forms can be downloaded from the trust's website. Trustees meet twice a year (in April and October) and must have detailed financial information about each project before they will make a decision. Only applications from eligible bodies are acknowledged, when further information about the project may be requested. Monitoring of grant expenditure is usually required.

The Jewish Youth Fund

Jewish youth work

£162,000 (2007/08)
Beneficial area UK.

24 Chiswell Street, London EC1Y 4YX
Tel. 020 7443 5169
Email info@jyf.org.uk
Correspondent Peter Shaw, Secretary
Trustees *Leo E Gestetner; Richard McGratty; Lady Morris of Kenwood; Miss Wendy F Pollecoff; Adam D Rose; Stephen B Spitz; Phillipa Strauss.*
CC Number 251902
Information available Accounts were on file at the Charity Commission.

The fund's objectives are to promote and protect religious, moral, educational, physical and social interests of young members of the Jewish community in the UK.

In 2007/08 the trust had assets of £3.8 million and an income of £93,000. Grants totalling £162,000 went to 16 organisations.

Grants ranged from £2,500 to £50,000.

Beneficiaries were: Federation of Zionist Youth (£50,000); New North London Synagogue (£18,000); LJY Netzer (£11,000); B'nei Akiva, Norwood, The Northwest Clubhouse and JAT (£10,000); Noam Masorti Youth (£8,000); The Youth Project Manchester (£6,000); R S Y Netzer (£5,600); Brady Maccabi Youth & Community Centre, Habonim Dror and Bushey Youth Scene (£5,000 each); Camp Simcha (£4,900); and Chaverim Youth Organisation and

St Albans Masorti Jewish Youth Charity (£2,500).

Exclusions Grants are not made in response to general appeals. Formal education is not supported.

Applications On an application form available from the correspondent, enclosing a copy of the latest accounts and an annual report.

The JMK Charitable Trust

Art, music and religions and their relations with other faiths

£75,000 (2008)
Beneficial area Worldwide.

Chantrey Vellacott DFK, Prospect House, 58 Queen's Road, Reading RG1 4RP
Tel. 0118 952 4700
Correspondent The Trustees
Trustees Mrs J M Karaviotis; J Karaviotis.
CC Number 274576
Information available Accounts were on file at the Charity Commission.

This trust supports registered charities, with a current preference for those concerned with the appreciation of art and music. 'We also assist religious organisations to help relations with other faiths.'

In 2007/08 the trust had assets of almost £2 million and an income of £83,000. Grants to 22 organisations totalled £75,000.

The two largest grants went to: Royal College of Music (£30,000); and English Touring Opera (£9,000).

Other beneficiaries included: National Theatre (£7,500); Les Azuriales Opera House (£4,500); Royal Opera House (£4,200); Magen David Adom UK (£3,000); Get Kids Going, Philharmonia Trust, Starlight and West London Synagogue (£1,000 each); and Classic Opera Company and RCR Cancer Appeal (£500 each).

Applications In writing to the correspondent. No acknowledgement of receipt is given.

The Norman Joels Charitable Trust

Jewish causes and general

£45,000 (2007/08)
Beneficial area UK, Israel and the Middle East.

Grunberg and Co, 10–14 Accommodation Road, Golders Green, London NW11 8ED
Tel. 020 8458 0083 **Fax** 0208 458 0783
Correspondent Henry Freedman
Trustees Jessica L Joels; Norman Joels; Harold Joels; Myriam Joels.
CC Number 206325
Information available Accounts were on file at the Charity Commission.

In 2007/08, the trust's assets totalled £1.3 million and it had an income of £57,000. Grants totalled £45,000, however a list of grant beneficiaries was not available with the accounts.

Previous beneficiaries have included: Friends of Magen David Action in Great Britain, Jewish Aid Committee, Jewish Care, Joint Jewish Charitable Trust, New London Synagogue, Norwood Ravenswood, The Spiro Institute and World Jewish Relief.

Applications In writing to the correspondent.

The Harold Joels Charitable Trust

Jewish

£56,000 (2007/08)
Beneficial area UK and overseas.

11a Arkwright Road, Hampstead, London NW3 6AA
Email hjoles7@aol.com
Correspondent H Joels, Trustee
Trustees H Joels; Dr N Joels; Mrs V Joels; N E Joels.
CC Number 206326
Information available Full accounts were on file at the Charity Commission.

The trust makes grants to Jewish organisations in the UK and US.

In 2007/08 the trust had assets of over £778,000, an income of £36,000 and made grants to 75 organisations totalling £56,000.

Beneficiaries in the US included: Womens Resource Centre of Sarasota County (£20,000); Young Judea (£15,000); Florida Studio Theatre (£12,000); Jewish Family and Children's Service (£6,300); Emunah of America (£3,000); Florida Holocaust Museum (£2,000); Temple Beth Sholom (£1,600); Gocio Elementary School (£1,000); Family Law Connection (£250); World Jewish Congress (£170); and the American Jewish Committee (£100).

Beneficiaries in the UK included: Jewish Care (£5,200); World Jewish Relief (£5,000); the Tel Aviv Foundation (£2,000); Bet Elazraki Home (£1,500); United Synagogue (£1,400); National Theatre (£1,300); Royal Academy of Arts (£1,000); I Rescue (£500); Tricycle Theatre Co Ltd (£400); Hampstead Synagogue and British Friend of the Hebrew University (£300 each); and Chai Cancer Care (£100).

Applications In writing to the correspondent.

The Nicholas Joels Charitable Trust

Jewish, medical welfare and general

£33,000 (2007/08)
Beneficial area UK and overseas.

66 Wigmore Street, London W1U 2SB
Tel. 01923 841376
Correspondent N Joels, Trustee
Trustees N Joels; H Joels; Mrs C Joels.
CC Number 278409
Information available Information had been filed at the Charity Commission.

The trust makes grants to registered charities only, and from the list of beneficiaries it appears to support Jewish causes and medical and welfare charities.

In 2007/08 it had assets of £494,000, an income of £26,000 and made grants to 48 organisations totalling £33,000.

Beneficiaries included: World Jewish Relief (£9,000); Norwood (£5,300); Emunah (£4,300); United Jewish Israel Appeal (£3,800); Jewish Care (£2,000);

Zionist Federation (£1,000); United Synagogue (£900); I Rescue (£750); Chinese Disaster Fund (£500); Jewish Women's Aid (£200); and Friends of the Tate Gallery (£100).

Applications In writing to the correspondent.

The Lillie Johnson Charitable Trust

Children, young people who are blind or deaf and medical

£204,000 (2007/08)

Beneficial area UK, with a preference for the West Midlands.

Heathcote House, 136 Hagley Road, Edgbaston, Birmingham B16 9PN

Tel. 0121 454 4141

Correspondent J W Desmond, Trustee

Trustees *V M C Lyttle; P W Adams; J W Desmond; Mrs V C Adams.*

CC Number 326761

Information available Accounts were obtained from the Charity Commission website.

In 2007/08 the trust had assets of £5.6 million and an income of £275,000. Grants to 138 organisations were made totalling £204,000.

Donations under £1,000 were made to 85 organisations. Beneficiaries of grants of £1,000 or more included: LEC – Worcester (£40,000); West House School – Bursary (£23,000); Web Care (£18,000); Peter Allis Wheelchair Appeal (£7,500); and Family Care Trust (£7,000).

Exclusions No support for individuals.

Applications Applications are only considered from charities which are traditionally supported by the trust. The trust stated that it is inundated with applications it cannot support and feels obliged to respond to all of these.

The Johnson Foundation

Education, health and relief of poverty

£359,000 (2007/08)

Beneficial area Merseyside.

Westmount, Vyner Road South, Birkenhead, Wirral CH43 7PN

Tel. 0151 653 1700

Correspondent P R Johnson, Trustee

Trustees *P R Johnson; C W Johnson.*

CC Number 518660

Information available Accounts were available at the Charity Commission.

The objects for which the foundation was established are:

- to promote any charitable purposes for the benefit of the City of Liverpool or the immediate neighbourhood at the discretion of Liverpool City Council
- to promote any charitable purposes and in particular the advancement of education, the preservation and protection of health and relief of poverty and sickness.

In 2007/08 the trust had assets of £1.9 million and an income of £152,000. Grants totalled £359,000.

Beneficiaries included: Liverpool JMU University Trust (£200,000); NSPCC – Hargreaves Centre (£100,000); Birkenhead School Scholarship (£25,000); NSPCC Safe Place Appeal (£11,000); Claire House Hospice (£7,000); New Brighton Rugby Youth Training (£5,000); Wirral Schools Concert Band (£1,300); and Olivia Newton John Cancer Charity, Prostate Cancer Charity and Gilbrook Special School (£1,000 each).

Other grants and donations of less than £1,000 each totalled £6,800.

Exclusions Grants are not normally given to individuals.

Applications In writing to the correspondent. The trustees meet monthly.

Dezna Robins Jones Charitable Foundation

Medical and general

£720,000 (2007/08)

Beneficial area Preference for Wales.

Greenacres, Laleston, Bridgend, Mid Glamorgan CF32 OHN

Tel. 01656 768584

Correspondent Bernard Jones, Trustee

Trustees *B W R Jones; A C Cooke; A L C Boobyer.*

CC Number 1104252

Information available Accounts were on file at the Charity Commission.

Registered in June 2004, the main object of the foundation is to support local medical charities. It has an ongoing relationship with Cancer Care Cymru.

In 2007/08 this trust had assets of £4.7 million and an income of £129,000. Grants totalled £720,000.

Beneficiaries were: Cancer Care Cymru (£462,000); University Hospital of Wales – Cardiff (£138,000); Cory band (£72,000); and Performance Arts Education (£48,000).

Applications In writing to the correspondent. Trustees meet at least twice a year.

The Marjorie and Geoffrey Jones Charitable Trust

General

£49,000 (2007/08)

Beneficial area UK, preference for the south west of England.

Carlton House, 30 The Terrace, Torquay TQ1 1BS

Tel. 01803 213251

Email nigel.wollen@hooperwollen.co.uk

Correspondent N J Wollen, Trustee

Trustees *N J Wollen; W F Coplestone Boughey; P M Kay.*

CC Number 1051031

Information available Full accounts were on file at the Charity Commission.

The trust was set up under the terms of the will of Rose Marjorie Jones, who died in 1995, leaving the gross of her estate amounting to £2.2 million for grant-making purposes. In her will she donated amounts of £15,000 and £10,000 to charities based in Devon, such as the Donkey Sanctuary – Sidmouth, Paignton Zoological and Botanical Gardens Limited, the Rowcroft Hospital – Torquay, the Torbay Hospital League of Friends and RNIB – Torquay. Other organisations named in the will were UK-wide, such as RNLI, RSPCA and NSPCC – although grants were probably given to local branches.

In 2007/08 the trust had assets of £2 million and an income of £74,000. After high management and administration costs of £29,000, grants to 25 organisations totalled £49,000.

Beneficiaries included: Torbay Coast and Countryside Trust (£4,000); Pilgrim BM45 Trust Ltd, Living Paintings and Teign Heritage (£3,000 each); Children's Hospice South West and Fire Services Benevolent Fund (£2,500); Deafblind UK and West Country Rivers (£2,000 each); and Rural Stress South West, The Two Moors Festival and Apollo Football Club (£1,000 each).

Applications In writing to the correspondent. The trustees meet four times a year to consider applications.

The J E Joseph Charitable Fund

Jewish

£122,000 (2007/08)

Beneficial area London, Manchester, Israel, India and Hong Kong.

Flat 10, Compass Close, Edgware HA8 8HU

Tel. 020 8958 0126

Correspondent Roger J Leon, Secretary

Trustees *F D A Mocatta, Chair; P Sheldon; J H Corre; J S Horesh; Abe Simon.*

CC Number 209058

Information available Information was on file at the Charity Commission.

The trust was established for the benefit of Jewish communities for any purposes, mainly in the fields of education,

disability and the relief of poverty. In 2007/08 it had assets of £4.2 million, an income of £152,000 and made grants totalling £122,000.

Grants were broken down as follows, shown with examples of beneficiaries in each category:

Israeli (15 grants totalling £56,000)
The Future Generation Fund (£15,000); Tishma School Centre for Autistic Children (£5,000); Alyn Pediatric & Adolescence Rehabilitation Centre (£4,500); Melabev (£4,000); and Or Hachayim Girls College (£2,500).

Home – general (12 grants totalling £38,000)
University Jewish Chaplaincy Board (£5,500); Spanish and Portuguese Synagogue Welfare Board (£5,000); Edinburgh House (£4,500); Jacob Benjamin Elias Synagogue (£3,000); and Jewish Lads & Girls Brigade (£1,500).

Home – schools (4 grants totalling £14,000)
Kisharon Day School (£5,000); Simon Marks Jewish Primary School, Jewish Free School and Jewish Preparatory School (£3,000 each); and Michael Sobell Sinai School (£1,500).

Eastern (2 grants totalling £9,500)
Sir Jacob Sassoon Charity Trust (£6,500); and Ahva (£3,000).

Exclusions No grants to individuals. No support for capital projects.

Applications In writing to the correspondent, including a copy of the latest accounts. The trustees respond to all applications which are first vetted by the secretary. The trust stated that many applications are unsuccessful as the number of appeals exceeds the amount available from limited income.

The Lady Eileen Joseph Foundation

People who are disadvantaged by poverty or socially isolated, at-risk groups, welfare, medical causes and general charitable purposes

£116,000 (2007/08)

Beneficial area UK.

Colbrans Farm, Cow Lane, Laughton BN8 6BZ

Correspondent Thurlstan W Simpson, Trustee

Trustees *Judith M Sawdy; Thurlstan W Simpson; Ninette J Thornton.*

CC Number 327549

Information available Full accounts were available from the Charity Commission.

The trust was registered in 1987. It supports people who are disadvantaged by poverty or who are socially isolated. Medical causes are also supported.

In 2007/08 the foundation had assets of £943,000 and an income of £39,000. Grants to 43 organisations totalled £116,000.

Beneficiaries included: Second Chance (£7,500); Coldstream Guards Association (£6,500); Alzheimers Research Trust and Friends of the Home Physiotherapy Service (£5,000 each); Havens Hospices (£4,500); Ellenor Foundation and Queen Alexandra Hospital (£3,000 each); Independent Age and Wellbeing of Women (£2,000 each); and Cystic Fibrosis Trust, Foundation for the Prevention of Blindness and Action for Kids (£1,000 each).

Other grants of less than £1,000 amounted to £7,600.

Applications In writing to the correspondent, although the trust states that unsolicited requests will not be considered.

The Judith Trust

Mental health and learning disabilities with some preference for women and Jewish people

£37,000 (2007/08)

Beneficial area UK.

5 Carriage House, 88–90 Randolph Avenue, London W9 1BG

Tel. 020 7266 1073 **Fax** 020 7289 5804

Email judith.trust@lineone.net

Website www.judithtrust.org.uk

Correspondent Dr A R Lawson, Trustee

Trustees Dr Annette Lawson; Peter Lawrence; George Lawson; Charlotte Collins; Geraldine Holt; Colin Samson.

CC Number 1063012

Information available Accounts were on file at the Charity Commission. The following publication is available from the trust: Joined Up Care: good practice in services for people with learning disabilities and mental health needs.

The Judith Trust aims to improve the quality of life of people who have both learning disabilities and mental health needs. The Judith Trust was founded in 1997 by Judith's family and set up to ensure the concerns of the trustees would closely follow the nature of Judith's own problems, her background and personal characteristics.

The trust's website gives an account of Judith's history.

It is because Judith has both learning and mental health problems that the trust explores how to improve the quality of life with and for people with both these issues. It is because Judith is a woman and our background is Jewish that we take a particular interest in the needs and concerns of women and Jewish people ... we have learned how much is also still shared with people of all ages in varied backgrounds with these problems. And with their families, carers and friends.

The trust supports multi-disciplinary, preventative and innovative approaches and pays particular attention to the needs of women and Jewish people.

The Judith Trust:

- commissions and carries out research supports innovative projects
- forms strategic alliances with government departments, voluntary organisations and academic institutions

- brings together groups of professionals and others, including service users, for specific purposes
- campaigns on behalf of and with people with learning disabilities and mental health needs
- promotes examples of good practice and the sharing of knowledge in its publications, seminars and conferences.

In 2007/08 the trust had assets of £581,000 and an income of £28,000. Grants were made totalling £37,000 to Living in the Community Project (£26,000) and 'Healthcare needs and experiences of care' (£11,000).

The trust has awarded a grant for a two year period to Dr Laurence Taggart of the University of Ulster. The project will explore to what extent successful living in the community after the move from long-stay hospitals is affected by the diagnosis of both learning disabilities and mental health problems, posing answers to the question: 'Having moved from long-stay hospitals, how well do women who have serious and enduring mental health problems, as well as a learning disability, succeed at living in the community, as compared with those who do not have additional mental health problems?'.

Exclusions No grants to individuals.

Applications In writing to the correspondent; however, please note: most grants are made through experts and advisors. The trust does not accept unsolicited applications for funding, but is pleased to hear from organisations who wish the trust to be aware of their work.

Jusaca Charitable Trust

Jewish, arts, research, religion and housing

£132,000 (2007/08)

Beneficial area UK, Israel and worldwide.

17 Ashburnham Grove, London SE10 8UH

Correspondent The Trustees

Trustees Ralph Neville Emanuel; Sara Jane Emanuel; Carolyn Leonora Emanuel; Maurice Seymour Emanuel; Diana Clare Franklin; Donald Franklin; Rachel Paul.

CC Number 1012966

Information available Accounts were on file at the Charity Commission, without a list of grants.

The following is taken from the trustees' report:

The trust aims to give grants to alleviate poverty, promote health and education, to support the arts, research, religious activities and the provision of decent housing. The objective is to distribute at least 50 per cent of donations to Jewish charities (in the UK, overseas and Israel), of the remainder about 40 per cent to be donation to charities operating in the UK and about 60 per cent outside the UK.

In 2007/08 the trust had an income of £1.4 million from donations. Grants to 77 organisations totalled £132,000, of which 31 grants exceeded £1,000. The sum of £1.4 million was carried forward at year end.

Donations were broken down as follows:

Category	No.	Value
Welfare	25	£61,000
Overseas	11	£19,000
Education	11	£18,000
Religious	5	£8,700
Housing	3	£8,500
Health	9	£7,800
Community relations	8	£7,300
General	2	£1,800
Arts	3	£1,000

Applications Grants are made at the discretion of the trustees.

The Bernard Kahn Charitable Trust

Jewish

£130,000 (2007/08)

Beneficial area UK and Israel.

18 Gresham Gardens, London NW11 8PD

Correspondent The Trustees

Trustees Mrs C B Kahn; S Fuehrer; Y E Kahn.

CC Number 249130

Information available Accounts were on file at the Charity Commission.

In 2007/08 the trust had assets of £1.8 million and an income of £118,000. Grants were made to 32 organisations totalling £130,000.

Beneficiaries of the largest grants were: Achiezer, Jewish Educational Trust, Orthodox Council of Jerusalem Limited, the Gevurath Ari Torah Academy Trust and the Telz Talmudical Academy and Talmud Torah Trust (£20,000 each).

Other beneficiaries included: Achisomoch Aid Company Ltd (£10,000); the Menorah Primary School (£4,800); Whinney House Limited (£4,500); Arachim Limited (£3,000); Beth Hamedrash Elyon Golders Green Limited (£2,100); Shaare Zedek UK (£500); Society for the Transmission of the Jewish Heritage (£200); and Manchester Jewish Grammar School (£100).

Applications In writing to the correspondent.

The Stanley Kalms Foundation

Jewish charities, general including arts, education and health

Around £199,000 (2007/08)

Beneficial area UK and overseas.

84 Brook Street, London W1K 5EH

Tel. 020 7499 3494

Correspondent Mrs Jane Hunt-Cooke

Trustees Lord Stanley Kalms; Lady Pamela Kalms; Stephen Kalms.

CC Number 328368

Information available Accounts were on file at the Charity Commission.

Established in 1989 by Lord Stanley Kalms, the president of DSG International plc (formerly Dixons Stores Group plc), this charity states its objectives as the encouragement of Jewish education in the UK and Israel. Other activities include support for the arts and media and other programmes, both secular and religious.

In 2007/08 the foundation had an income of £15,000 and a total expenditure of £199,000. No further information was available.

Previous grants have been to mainly Jewish organisations (social and educational) with grants also going to the arts, education and health.

Beneficiaries have included: Dixons City Academy (£25,000); Milliken Community High (£23,000); Royal Opera House Foundation (£17,000); Jewish Care (£14,000); Jewish National

Fund (£12,000); Norwood (£7,600); British Friends of Haifa University (£7,200); Keren Klita (£7,000); Civitas, Centre for Social Justice, Institute of Economic Affairs, Jewish Policy Research and Royal Academy Trust (£5,000 each); Stephen Wise Temple (£4,500); the Kabbalah Centre (£2,900); Anglo Israel Association (£2,000); British ORT (£1,500); and St James Conversation Trust (£1,000).

Applications In writing to the correspondent, but note that most of the trust's funds are committed to projects supported for a number of years.

The Boris Karloff Charitable Foundation

General

£66,000 (2007/08)

Beneficial area Worldwide.

Peachey and Co., 95 Aldwych, London WC2B 4JF

Tel. 0207 316 5200

Correspondent The Trustees

Trustees I D Wilson; P A Williamson; O M Lewis.

CC Number 326898

Information available Full accounts were on file at the Charity Commission.

This foundation was set up in 1985, by Evelyn Pratt (Karloff), wife of the famous horror actor, Boris Karloff (whose real name was William Henry Pratt). When Evelyn Pratt died in June 1993, she bequeathed over £1.4 million to the assets of the foundation.

In 2007/08 the trust had assets of £2.2 million and an income of £82,000. Grants to 11 organisations totalled £66,000.

Beneficiaries were: RADA – Boris Karloff Scholarship Fund, Royal Theatrical Fund and Cinema and Television Fund (£10,000 each); Shakespeare Globe Trust (£6,500); Cambridge Film Festival and Surrey County Cricket (2 grants); and the English Touring Theatre and LAMDA (£5,000 each).

Exclusions Charities with large resources are not supported.

Applications In writing to the correspondent.

The Ian Karten Charitable Trust

Technology centres for people who are disabled

£207,000 to organisations (2007/08)

Beneficial area Great Britain and Israel, with some local interest in Surrey and London.

The Mill House, Newark Lane, Ripley GU23 6DP

Tel. 01483 225020 **Fax** 01483 222420

Email iankarten@btinternet.com

Website www.karten-network.org.uk

Correspondent Timothy Simon

Trustees Ian H Karten, Chair; Mrs Mildred Karten; Tim Simon; Angela Hobbs.

CC Number 281721

Information available Accounts were on file at the Charity Commission.

The trusts states its objects in its 2007/08 accounts:

The objects of the trust are to carry out legally charitable purposes for the relief of poverty, the advancement of education or religion or otherwise for the benefit of the community.

The trust currently concentrates on

- Improving the quality of life and independence of people with severe physical, sensory, cognitive disability or mental health problems by providing for them Centres for Computer-aided Training, Education and Communication (CTEC Centres). These are typically established by and located in colleges of further education or (mainly residential) host charities concerned with rehabilitation and education, especially vocational, of people with one or more of the above mentioned disabilities.
- the support of higher education by funding studentships for postgraduate studies and research at selected universities in the UK.

The trust also has a separate modest budget from which it makes small donations to other selected registered charities, mostly local to the trust (London or Surrey).

In 2007/08 it had assets of £7.7 million and an income of £312,000. Grants paid to organisations totalled £207,000, broken down as follows and shown with examples of beneficiaries:

CTEC Centres – 5 grants totalling £87,000
Schonfeld Square Foundation (£38,000); Cantraybridge (£27,000); and Aspire (£20,000).

Large grants – 11 grants totalling £6,700
Jewish Care (£1,500); Commonwealth Jewish Trust and Yad Vashem UK Foundation (£1,000 each); World Jewish Relief and UJIA Foundation for Education (£650 each); Spiro Ark (£500); Speech Language and Hearing Centre, Institute for Jewish Policy Research, Community Security Trust (£300); and Anne Frank Educational Trust (£250).

A grant of £107,000 was awarded to Southampton University to fund an Outreach teaching fellow for five years, and the sum of £5,800 was also given in small grants.

A further £52,000 was distributed to six institutions for scholarships.

Exclusions No grants to individuals.

Applications The trust currently only considers grants to charities supported in the past. Individual scholarships are no longer available directly to students, instead the trust's chosen universities select the Karten Scholarships themselves. The trustees meet every six weeks to consider applications.

The Kasner Charitable Trust

Jewish
£95,000 (2007/08
Beneficial area UK and Israel.

1a Gresham Gardens, London NW11 8NX
Tel. 020 8455 7830
Correspondent Josef Kasner, Trustee
Trustees *Elfreda Erlich; Baruch Erlich; Josef Kasner; Judith Erlich.*
CC Number 267510
Information available Accounts were on file at the Charity Commission.

In 2007/08 the trust had assets of £741,000, an income of £127,000 and made grants to over 150 organisations totalling £95,000. Unfortunately a list of

beneficiaries was not available in this year's accounts.

Previous beneficiaries have included: Friends of Bar Ilan University and UJIA (£10,000 each); UTA (£5,100); Gateshead Academy for Jewish Studies, RS Trust and Yeshivat Maharash Engel Radomshitz (£5,000 each); Beth Abraham Synagogue and Emunoh Educational Trust (£3,000 each); British Friends of Bnei Brak Hospital and Friends of Arad (£2,000 each); Society of Friends of Torah (£1,500); Ponevez (£1,400); and Chevras Maoz Ladal (£1,200).

Applications In writing to the correspondent.

The Kass Charitable Trust

Welfare, education and Jewish
£40,000 to organisations (2007/08)
Beneficial area UK.

37 Sherwood Road, London NW4 1AE
Tel. 020 8371 3111
Correspondent D E Kass, Trustee
Trustees *David Elliot Kass; Mrs Shulamith Malkah Sandler.*
CC Number 1006296
Information available Accounts were on file at the Charity Commission, but without a list of grants.

The trust now focuses on 'poverty and education for disadvantaged children'.

In 2007/08 it had assets of £28,000 and an income of £92,000 mostly from donations received. Grants totalled £66,000, of which £40,000 was given in grants to organisations.

Unfortunately a list of grant beneficiaries was not included with the accounts, however the trust stated that approximately 400 donations were made to institutions during the year, mostly for small amounts and were provided for educational purposes or relief of poverty.

The largest beneficiary was Torah Temimah School (£11,000), for the promotion of education.

Applications In writing to the correspondent.

The Kathleen Trust

Musicians
£35,000 (2007/08)
Beneficial area UK, with a preference for London.

Currey and Co, 21 Buckingham Gate, London SW1E 6LS
Tel. 020 7828 4091
Correspondent E R H Perks, Trustee
Trustees *E R H Perks; Sir O C A Scott; Lady P A Scott; Mrs CN Withington.*
CC Number 1064516
Information available Accounts were on file at the Charity Commission.

Established in 1997, it is the policy of the trustees to 'assist young and impecunious musicians'.

In 2007/08 it had assets of £1.2 million and an income of £31,000. Grants were made totalling £35,000, given mainly to 16 individuals. A further £10,000 was given to Oxford Chamber Music Festival, and £1,000 was given to British Kidney Patient Association (Young Clarinetist).

Applications In writing to the correspondent.

The Michael and Ilse Katz Foundation

Jewish, music, medical and general
About £109,000 (2007/08)
Beneficial area Worldwide.

The Counting House, Trelill, Bodmin PL30 3HZ
Tel. 01208 851814
Correspondent Osman Azis, Trustee
Trustees *Norris Gilbert; Osman Azis.*
CC Number 263726
Information available Information had been filed at the Charity Commission.

Established in 1971, this foundation supports many Jewish organisations, although musical and medical charities have also received funds.

In 2007/08 it had assets of £867,000 and an income of £109,000. Grants to organisations totalled £109,000, of which £12,000 was allocated in grants not exceeding £1,000 each.

Beneficiaries included: Jewish Care (£20,000); University College London (£15,000); Community Security Trust (£12,000); Norwood Children and Families First and Bournemouth Orchestral Society (£10,000 each); The Worshipful Company of Butchers (£5,000); Nightingale House for Aged Jews (£3,000); New Israel Fund of Great Britain and Magen David Adorn UK (£2,000 each); Bournemouth Reform Synagogue and Hannah Levy House Trust (£1,200 each); and MacMillan Cancer Relief, Holocaust Education Trust and Tel Aviv Sourasky Medical Centre (£1,000 each).

Applications In writing to the correspondent.

The Katzauer Charitable Settlement

Jewish

£77,000 (2007/08)
Beneficial area UK, but mainly Israel.

c/o Devonshire House, 1 Devonshire Street, London W1W 5DR
Tel. 020 7304 2000
Email walter.lian@citroenwells.co.uk
Correspondent Gordon Smith, Trustee
Trustees *G C Smith; Mrs E Moller; M S Bailey; W Lian.*
CC Number 275110
Information available Full accounts were on file at the Charity Commission.

In 2007/08 the trust had assets of £921,000, with an income of £98,000, which was mainly derived from donations and investment income. Grants totalled £77,000.

Beneficiaries were: Chabad Ra'anana (£26,000); Moriah Community and Meir Hospital (£10,000); Nahalat Yehiel (£6,000); Mercaz Hatorah (£4,000); Rabbi K Gross (£3,800); KollelRalanana (£3,200); Friends of Lubavitch (£2,900); and Beit Hatavshil (£1,000).

Grants of under £1,500 each totalled £9,500.

Applications In writing to the correspondent.

The C S Kaufman Charitable Trust

Jewish

£133,000 (2007/08)
Beneficial area UK.

162 Whitehall Road, Gateshead, Tyne and Wear NE8 1TP
Correspondent C S Kaufman
Trustees *I I Kaufman; Mrs L L Kaufman; J J Kaufman; S Kaufman.*
CC Number 253194
Information available Accounts were on file at the Charity Commission.

In 2007/08 this trust had assets of £863,000, an income of £76,000 and a grant total of £133,000. About 90 grants were made in the year.

Recipients of grants over £1,000 were: Vaad Lehatzole and Mifalei Tzedoko Vochesed Israel (£30,000 each); Centre for Torah Educational Trust (£25,000); Matono (£20,000); Kollel Sha'arei Schlomo and Association Cerfi (£4,000 each); Achiezer (£2,500); Jewish Teachers Training Course (£1,700); and TAT Family Relief Fund (£1,500).

Many organisations received more than one grant.
Exclusions No grants to individuals.
Applications In writing to the correspondent.

The Geoffrey John Kaye Charitable Foundation

Jewish and general

£17,000 to organisations (2007/08)
Beneficial area UK and overseas.

7 St John's Road, Harrow HA1 2EY
Tel. 020 8863 1234
Email charity@mmrca.co.uk
Correspondent R J Freebody, Accountant
Trustees *G J Kaye; Mrs S Rose; J Pears.*

CC Number 262547
Information available Accounts are on file at the Charity Commission.

In 2007/08 the trust had assets of £855,000, an income of £51,000 and made three grants totalling £17,000. Grants are largely recurrent and are made to Jewish organisations.

Beneficiaries were: WJA (£4,900); and Friends of Nightingale House (£1,000).

A further £11,000 went to one individual.

Applications In writing to the correspondent, but please note that the foundation has previously stated that funds were fully committed.

The Emmanuel Kaye Foundation

Medical research, welfare and Jewish organisations

£59,000 (2007/08)
Beneficial area UK and overseas.

Oakleigh House, High Street, Hartley Wintney RG27 8PE
Tel. 01252 843773
Correspondent The Secretary to the Trustees
Trustees *David Kaye; Lady Kaye; John Forster; Michael Cutler.*
CC Number 280281
Information available Full accounts were provided by the trust.

The trust supports organisations benefiting medical professionals, research workers, scientists, Jewish people, at risk groups, people who are disadvantaged by poverty and socially isolated people.

In 2007/08 it had assets of £1 million, generating an income of £57,000. Grants totalled £59,000.

Beneficiaries listed in the accounts were: St James Conservation Trust (£6,000); Imperial College London and Nightingale (£5,000 each); Royal Academy of Arts and St Michaels Hospice – North Hampshire (£2,500 each); Jewish Care, the Holocaust Education Trust, Shaare Zedek UK, Community Links Trust, Laniado UK and UK Friends of Magen David Adom (£2,000 each); and Caius (£1,500).

Unlisted grants of less than £1,000 each totalled £25,000.

Exclusions Organisations not registered with the Charity Commission are not supported.

Applications In writing to the correspondent.

Caron Keating Foundation

Support of small cancer charities

£173,000 (2007/08)
Beneficial area UK.

PO Box 122, Sevenoaks TN13 1UM
Email info@caronkeating.org
Website www.caronkeating.org
Correspondent The Secretary
Trustees *M Keating; G Hunniford.*
CC Number 1106160
Information available Information was obtained from the foundation's website.

Registered with the Charity Commission in October 2004, this foundation is a fundraising charity that aims to target and financially assist small but significant cancer charities and support groups.

The foundation's overall aim is to help small cancer charities in their work with professional carers, complimentary healing practitioners as well as groups that provide support and advice to cancer patients and the people closest to them who are affected by the disease.

It will also financially help a number of cancer charities with their ongoing quest for prevention, early detection and hopefully ultimate cure.

In 2007/08 the foundation had assets of £527,000 and an income of £275,000. Grants totalled £173,000, which included £98,000 made in small grants of less than £20,000.

Grants included those made to: Jersey Hospice Care (£30,000); Action Cancer (£25,000); and SCAT Bone Cancer (£20,000).

Previous beneficiaries have included organisations such as the Lavendar Touch, the Rosemary Foundation, the Sarah Lee Trust and the Rainbow Centre

for children affected by cancer and bereavement.

Exclusions No grants to individuals.

Applications In writing to the correspondent.

The Soli and Leah Kelaty Trust Fund

General, education, overseas aid and religion

£57,000 (2007/08)
Beneficial area Not defined.

Block O, OCC Building, London N4 1TJ
Tel. 020 8800 2000
Email freddy.kelaty@asiatic.co.uk
Correspondent F S Kelaty, Secretary
Trustees *David Lerer; Fredrick Kelaty; Sharon Mozel Kelaty.*
CC Number 1077620
Information available Accounts were on file at the Charity Commission, without any details of grants.

Registered with the Charity Commission in September 1999, grants can be made to organisations and individuals.

In 2007/08 the trust had assets of £820,000 and an income of £60,000, including £71,000 from donations. Grants were made totalling £57,000, however a list of beneficiaries was not provided with the accounts.

Applications In writing to the correspondent.

The Kennel Club Charitable Trust

Dogs

£824,000 (2008)
Beneficial area UK.

1–5 Clarges Street, Piccadilly, London W1J 8AB
Tel. 020 7518 1037
Email dholford@the-kennel-club.org.uk
Website www.mad4dogs.org.uk
Correspondent Doug Holford

Trustees *M Townsend, Chair; M Herrtage; W H King; J Spurling; Mrs J Ziman.*
CC Number 327802
Information available Accounts were on file at the Charity Commission.

The trust describes its objects as 'science, welfare and support'. It supports the furthering of research into canine diseases and hereditary disorders of dogs and also organisations concerned with the welfare of dogs in need and those which aim to improve the quality of life of humans by promoting dogs as practical or therapeutic aids.

The trust gives both ongoing and one-off grants, generally up to £35,000 each a year for research, and of up to £10,000 each for support of dogs and those who care for them or benefit from them.

Kennel Club Charitable Trust worked in conjunction with Pedigree on the Pedigree Adoption Drive, which in 2008 raised over £496,000 for distribution by the trust. The trust was selected for its expertise and experience in allocating funds and the money has been distributed through its welfare initiative to organisations in the United Kingdom and Republic of Ireland. The drive was re-run in 2009 and at the time of writing (Autumn 2009) had raised a further £564,000.

In 2008 the trust had assets of £2.6 million and an income of £1.3 million. 34 grants were made under the trust's charitable objectives, totalling £328,000. These were divided into 'scientific and research project support' which amounted to £157,000, and 'other grants' totalling £171,000. In addition, the £496,000 donated by Pedigree was disbursed to UK and Irish canine welfare and rescue bodies. Payments were made to 150 applicants and details of the groups receiving these grants can be found in the 2008 annual report and accounts and on the trust's website.

Beneficiaries of the trust's annual grant-making included: Animal Health Trust – DNA research into canine eye conditions (£83,000) and analysis/reporting of health survey (£30,000); the Blue Cross (£30,000); University of Glasgow – research into canine arthritis (£19,000); Dogs for the Disabled (£14,300); Stokenchurch Dog Rescue (£10,000); Waggy Tails Rescue (£8,000); Mayhew Animal Rescue Home (£7,000); Doris Banham Sanctuary, Exmoor Search & Rescue Team, Hereford & Worcester Animal Rescue and Rotherham Dog Rescue (£5,000); Greyhound & Lurcher Welfare & Rescue (£2,500); and Staffordshire Bull Terrier Rescue (£750).

Exclusions The trust does not give grants directly to individuals; veterinary nurses can apply to the British Veterinary Nursing Association where bursaries are available. The trustees tend not to favour funding the costs of building work.

Applications In writing to the administrator, including latest accounts. Please state clearly details of the costs for which you are requesting funding, and for what purpose and over what period the funding is required. The trustees meet three or four times a year.

The Nancy Kenyon Charitable Trust

General

£45,000 to organisations
(2007/08)
Beneficial area UK.

Meads Barn, Ashwell Business Park, Ilminster TA19 9DX
Tel. 01460 259852
Correspondent The Trustees
Trustees *Lucy Phipps; Maureen Kenyon; Christopher Kenyon; Sally Kenyon; Peter Kenyon.*
CC Number 265359
Information available Accounts were on file at the Charity Commission.

The trust makes grants primarily for people and causes known to the trustees.

In 2007/08 the trust's assets totalled around £1.4 million. It had an income totalling £45,000, all of which was distributed in grants to individuals and organisations.

Beneficiaries in the year included: Nancy Oldfield Trust (£11,000); the Rainbow Farm Trust (£8,500); St Nicholas Church – Ashchurch (£3,500); Essex Association of Boys' Clubs and the Nehemiah Project (£3,000 each); Cheltenham Youth for Christ and the Starfish Cafe – Cambodia (£2,000 each); and the Family Haven, National Star Centre for Disabled Youth and Emthonjeni Trust (£1,000 each).

Exclusions No grants to individuals.

Applications In writing to the correspondent at any time. Applications for causes not known to the trustees are considered annually in December.

Kermaville Ltd

Jewish

£26,000 (2007/08)
Beneficial area UK.

3 Overlea Road, London E5 9BG
Tel. 020 8806 5783
Correspondent M Freund
Trustee *L Rabinowitz.*
CC Number 266075
Information available Accounts were on file at the Charity Commission.

The trust makes grants to Jewish organisations and towards those concerned with general charitable purposes.

In 2007/08 the trust had assets of £228,000 and an income of £27,000. Grants totalled £26,000, however a list of beneficiaries was not available in this years accounts.

Previous beneficiaries have included: Yeshivas Imrei Chaim Spinka (£60,000); Bais Rochel D'Satmar (£16,000); Keren Tzedoka Vechessed (£7,500); Kollel Congregation Yetev Lev (£6,100); Kollel Atzei Chaim (£5,000); United Talmudical Association (£4,000); Ponevez Beth Hamedrash (£4,000); and Lolev Charitable Trust (£3,000).

Applications In writing to the correspondent.

E and E Kernkraut Charities Limited

General, education and Jewish

£736,000 (2007/08)
Beneficial area UK.

c/o New Burlington House, 1075 Finchley Road, London NW11 0PU
Tel. 0208 806 7947
Correspondent E Kernkraut, Chair
Trustees *E Kernkraut, Chair; Mrs E Kernkraut; Joseph Kernkraut; Jacob Kernkraut.*
CC Number 275636

Information available Accounts were on file at the Charity Commission, but without a list of grants.

The trust states that it makes grants for educational, Jewish and other charitable purposes. It did not provide a list of grants with its accounts or further details of its grant-making criteria, so we were unable to tell what type of charity is likely to be supported by this trust.

In 2007/08 it had an income of £1 million from donations. Grants totalled £736,000.

Applications In writing to the correspondent.

The Peter Kershaw Trust

Medical research, education and social welfare

£269,000 (2007/08)
Beneficial area Manchester and the surrounding district only.

22 Ashworth Park, Knutsford WA16 9DE
Tel. 01565 651086
Email pkershawtrust@btinternet.com
Correspondent Bryan Peak, Secretary
Trustees *R P Kershaw, Chair; Mrs H F Kershaw; Mrs M L Rushbrooke; D Tully; Mrs R Adams; T Page.*
CC Number 268934
Information available Accounts were on file at the Charity Commission.

The principal activities of the trust continue to be those of funding medical research, grants to medical and other institutions and to schools in respect of bursaries.

In 2007/08 the trust had assets of £6.5 million and an income of £301,000. Grants were made totalling £269,000 and were broken down as follows, shown here with examples of grants in each category:

Social welfare institutions (£128,000 in 29 grants)
Copperdale Trust (£14,000); Brentwood Middleton Day Centre (£12,000); Fairbridge, Life Share, Jigsaw and Broughton House (£10,000 each); Stockport Cerebral Palsy Society (£8,000); Mosses Centre (£7,500); Willow Wood Hospice (£5,000); Knutsford Methodist Church (£3,000);

Farms for City Children (£2,300); Independent Options (£1,500); and Bobby Moore Fund (£250).

Memorial bursary (84,000 in 5 grants)
Chorlton Youth Project (£25,000); Reach Out (£20,000); Royal School for Deaf and Communications Disorder (£15,000); and M13 Youth Project (£10,000).

Medical research (£21,000 in 1 grant)
Charnley Research Institute – hip replacement surgery research (£21,000).

School bursaries (£37,000 in 7 grants)
Withington Girls' School (£9,600); Manchester High School for Girls (£7,300); King's School – Macclesfield (£5,500); and Bury Grammar Schools and Manchester Grammar School (£3,300 each).

Exclusions No grants to individuals or for building projects.

Applications In writing to the correspondent, however the trust is always oversubscribed. The trustees normally meet twice a year in May and November to consider recommendations for grant aid which will be disbursed in June and December respectively.

The Kessler Foundation

General and Jewish

£46,000 (2007/08)
Beneficial area UK.

25 Furnival Street, London EC4A 1JT
Correspondent L R Blackstone
Trustees *L Blackstone, Chair; Mrs J Jacobs; Prof. M Geller; Mr N P J Saphir; Mrs J F Mayers; P Morgenstern.*
CC Number 290759
Information available Accounts were on file at the Charity Commission.

The foundation makes grants for general charitable causes, with particular emphasis on supporting Jewish organisations. Generally the trust will support relatively small institutions (with an income of less than £100,000 a year) which do not attract funds from the larger charities. In exceptional circumstances, grants to individuals will be considered. The foundation's funds depend upon dividends from its shareholdings in the Jewish Chronicle and grants made by the newspaper. Grants generally range from £250 to

£2,000 each, mostly at the lower end of this scale.

The foundation will assist organisations which may be devoted to:

- the advancement of Jewish religion, learning, education and culture
- the improvement of inter-faith, community and race relations, and the combating of prejudice
- the alleviation of the problems of minority and disadvantaged groups
- the protection, maintenance and monitoring of human rights
- the promotion of health and welfare
- the protection and preservation of records and objects with special significance to the Jewish and general community
- the encouragement of arts, literature and science including archaeology, natural history and protection of the environment with special reference to the Jewish community.

In 2007/08 the foundation had assets of £238,000 and an income of £29,000. Grants were made to 45 organisations totalling £46,000.

Beneficiaries included: Jewish Council for Racial Equality, Asylum Aid and Bedouin Women for Themselves (£2,000 each); International Council of Jewish Women (£1,500); Project Harar Ethiopia (£1,200); Peace Child Israel, Makor Charitable Trust, Jewish Bereavement Counselling Service and Theatre Objektiv (£1,000 each); Friends of Israel Educational Foundation and Quest New London Synagogue (£750 each); Ipswich Community Playbus and Aid for Romanian Orphanages (£500 each); and Arts to Share (£250).

Exclusions In general the foundation will not support the larger, well-known charities with an income in excess of £100,000, and will not provide grants for social, medical and welfare projects which are the responsibility of local or national government.

Applications On a form available from the correspondent. The trustees meet at least twice a year in June and December. Applicants will be notified of decisions as soon as possible after then.

The Kiawah Charitable Trust

Young people whose lives are vulnerable due to health and/or education issues

£354,000 (2007/08)
Beneficial area Primarily sub-Saharan Africa and southern India.

c/o Farrer and Co., 65–66 Lincoln's Inn Fields, London WC2A 3LH
Correspondent The Trustees
Trustees *Peter Smitham; Lynne Smitham; Vic Miles.*
CC Number 1107730
Information available Accounts were on file at the Charity Commission.

Registered in January 2005, in 2007/08 it had assets of over £1 million and an income of £285,000. Grants totalled £354,000.

Beneficiaries included: Hope and Homes for Children (£177,000); Playpumps (£50,000); Sight Savers International (£45,000); Noah and Railway Children (£30,000 each); Pratham UK Limited (£10,000); EOPD (£7,500); and Dreamnight and Walk the Walk Worldwide (£1,000 each).

Applications 'The trustees consider any applications received for grants and adopt a proactive approach in seeking worthy causes requiring support.'

The King/ Cullimore Charitable Trust

General

£111,000 (2007/08)
Beneficial area UK.

52 Ledborough Lane, Beaconsfield HP9 2DF
Tel. 01494 678811
Correspondent P A Cullimore, Trustee
Trustees *P A Cullimore; C Gardner; C J King; A G McKechnie.*
CC Number 1074928
Information available Accounts were on file at the Charity Commission.

This trust has general charitable purposes and was registered with the Charity Commission on 30 March 1999.

In 2007/08 it had assets amounting to £5.1 million and an income of £317,000. Grants were made to 10 organisations totalling £111,000.

Organisations to benefit in the year were: Amerderm Research Trust (£25,000); Countryside Foundation for Education (£15,000); Music in Hospitals (£11,000); Duke of Edinburgh Award, Thames Valley Hospice, Lorica St Patrick's, Crisis, Age Concern (£10,000 each); and Practical Action in Nepal and Orangutan Foundation (£5,000 each).

Applications In writing to the correspondent.

Kinsurdy Charitable Trust

General

£73,000 (2007/08)
Beneficial area UK.

Cheviot Asset Management Limited, 90 Long Acre, London WC2E 9RA
Correspondent The Trustees
Trustees *R P Tullett; A H Bartlett.*
CC Number 1076085
Information available Accounts were on file at the Charity Commission.

Registered in June 1999, in 2007/08 this trust had assets of £1.4 million and an income of £270,000. Grants to 18 organisations totalled £73,000.

Beneficiaries included: R.N.L.I. and Alzheimer's Society (£5,000 each); Parkinson's Disease Society, Help the Aged, MacMillan Cancer Support, the Childrens Trust, the British Red Cross and Save the Children (£4,000 each); and League of friends – West Berkshire Hospice (£2,000 each).

Applications In writing to the correspondent.

The Richard Kirkman Charitable Trust

General

£86,000 (2007/08)
Beneficial area UK, with a preference for Hampshire.

Ashton House, 12 The Precinct, Winchester Road, Chandlers Ford, Eastleigh S053 2GB
Tel. 023 8027 4555 **Fax** 023 8027 5766
Correspondent M Howson-Green, Trustee
Trustees *M Howson-Green; Mrs F O Kirkman; B M Baxendale; D A Hoare.*
CC Number 327972
Information available Accounts were on file at the Charity Commission.

This trust supports a range of causes with a preference for Hampshire, especially Southampton. The trustees have stated that they are considering financing various plans for alleviating drug addiction.

In 2007/08 the trust had assets of £1.6 million and an income of £70,000. Grants were made to 70 organisations totalling £86,000.

There were 20 grants of £1,500 or more listed in the accounts. Beneficiaries included: Vermont School (£7,000); Streetscene, Rose Road Association and British Limbless Ex-Servicemen Association (£4,000 each); Leukeamia Busters, Marwell Preservation Trust and Alresford Citizens Advice Bureau (£3,000 each); British Diabetic Association, Jubilee Sailing Trust and Stroke Association (£2,000 each); and Wessex Childrens Hospice Trust, Haemophilia Society and Police Dependants' Trust (£1,500 each).

There were 50 further grants to institutions of £1,000 or less, totalling £33,000.

Applications The trust carries out its own research for beneficiaries and does not respond to applications by post or telephone.

Kirschel Foundation

Jewish and medical

£386,000 (2007/08)
Beneficial area UK.

131 Edgware Road, London W2 2AP
Tel. 020 7437 4372
Correspondent The Trustees
Trustees *Laurence Grant Kirschel; Ian Lipman; Steven Pinshaw.*
CC Number 1067672
Information available Accounts were on file at the Charity Commission.

This trust states its aims and objectives are 'to provide benefits to underprivileged persons, who may be either disabled or lacking resources'. In practice this includes many Jewish organisations.

In 2007/08 the foundation had an income, mainly from donations, of £537,000 and made grants to 48 organisations totalling £386,000.

There were 48 grants of £1,000 or more listed in the accounts. Beneficiaries included: Ahavat Shalom Charity Fund (£50,000); Jewish Learning Exchange (£46,000); Moracha Limited (£40,000); TreeHouse Trust (£25,000); Friends of Lubavitch Scotland (£17,000); Yakar Education Foundation (£10,000); Evelina Children's Hospital Appeal (£8,000); Friends of Yeshiva Hazon Mei (£5,000); Noam Primary School (£4,300); National Autistic Society (£3,500); Rays of Sunshine (£3,000); Cholel Chabad (£2,500); WST Charity Limited (£2,000); and the BST Charitable Trust, Jewish Care and Kisharon (£1,000 each).

The total of all other donations, individually less than £1,000 each, was £7,800.

Applications In writing to the correspondent.

The Marina Kleinwort Charitable Trust

Arts

£58,000 (2007/08)
Beneficial area UK.

30 Gresham Street, London EC2V 7PG
Correspondent The Secretary
Trustees *Miss Marina Rose Kleinwort, Chair; David James Roper Robinson; Miss Zenaida Yanowsky; Mrs Tessa Elizabeth Bremner.*
CC Number 1081825
Information available Accounts were on file at the Charity Commission.

In 2007/08 it had assets of £1.4 million and an income of £65,000. Grants totalling £58,000 were made to 15 organisations.

Beneficiaries included: National Theatre (£6,000); Old Vic (£5,500); Almeida Theatre Co Ltd, Central School of Ballet, Dance Umbrella and Music Theatre Wales (£5,000 each); Gate Theatre Company Limited (£4,000); English Chamber Orchestra and Music Society (£3,200); Blindart, Bonachela Dance Company, Conquest Art, Endymion Ensemble Ltd and London Children's Ballet (£3,000 each); and Chicken Shed Theatre Company and Classical Road Show (£2,000 each).

Exclusions No grants to individuals.

Applications In writing to the correspondent.

The Kobler Trust

Arts, Jewish and general

£242,000 (2007/08)
Beneficial area UK.

c/o Lewis Silkin LLP, 5 Chancery Lane, Clifford's Inn, London EC4A 1BL
Correspondent Ms J L Evans, Trustee
Trustees *A Xuereb; A H Stone; Ms J L Evans; J W Israelsohn.*
CC Number 275237
Information available Accounts were available at the Charity Commission.

The Kobler Charitable Trust was established in 1963 by the settlor, Fred Kobler, for charitable purposes in the UK. In 2007/08 the trust had assets of £3.3 million and an income of £148,000 from investments. Grants totalling £242,000 were given to 54 organisations.

Beneficiaries included: Beth Shalom (£50,000); Jewish AIDS Trust (£20,000); Chicken Shed Theatre Company, Royal Academy of Music and UK Jewish Film Festival (£10,000 each); Naz Project London (£6,000); Cued Speech Association and South West London Law Centre (£5,000 each); Action for Blind People and St Giles Trust (£2,000 each); Merseyside Thursday Club and Surrey Care Trust (£1,000 each); and Age Concern (£500).

Exclusions Grants are only given to individuals in exceptional circumstances.

Applications Applications should be in writing and incorporate full details of the charity for which funding is requested. Acknowledgements are not generally sent out to unsuccessful applicants.

The Kohn Foundation

Scientific and medical projects, the arts – particularly music, education and Jewish charities

£620,000 (2007)
Beneficial area UK and overseas.

c/o Wilkins Kennedy, Bridge House, London Bridge, London SE1 9QR
Correspondent Dr R Kohn, Trustee
Trustees *Dr Ralph Kohn, Chair; Zahava Kohn; Anthony A Forwood.*
CC Number 1003951
Information available Full accounts were on file at the Charity Commission.

The foundation supports advancement of scientific and medical research, promotion of the arts – particularly music, general educational projects and Jewish charities.

In 2007 the foundation had assets of £1.1 million, an income of £46,000 and made grants totalling £620,000. Donations were broken down as follows, shown here with examples of beneficiaries in each category:

Medical and scientific – 9 grants totalling £331,000
The Royal Society (£275,000); Chai Cancer Care (£20,000); and Imperial College Ernst Chain Prize (£18,000).

Performing Arts – 14 grants totalling £245,000
Royal Academy of Music (£114,000); Wigmore Hall Song Contest (£81,000); and English Chamber Orchestra and Hampstead and Highgate Festival (£1,000 each).

Advancement of the Jewish religion, education and charitable institutions – 36 grants totalling £44,000
Israel Philharmonic Orchestra Foundation (£12,000); Emunah (£10,000); and Hasmonean High School (£6,000).

Applications In writing to the correspondent.

Kollel and Co. Limited

Jewish and relief of poverty

£1.5 million (2007/08)
Beneficial area Worldwide.

Lieberman and Co, 2L Cara House, 339 Seven Sisters Road, London N15 6RD
Correspondent A Low, Secretary
Trustees *S Low; J Lipschitz; Z Rothschild.*
CC Number 1077180
Information available Accounts were on file at the Charity Commission, without a list of grants.

Set up in 1999, the objects of the charity are the:

- advancement of education and religion in accordance with the doctrines of the Jewish religion
- relief of poverty.

In 2007/08 it had an income of £1.3 million including £1.1 million from donations. Grants totalled £1.5 million. Assets stood at £2.2 million at year end.

The main areas of support were: education (£608,000); religious institutions (£267,000); advancement of religion (£205,000); relief of poverty (£145,000); and synagogues (£129,000). The sum of £128,000 was given under the category 'general'.

Applications 'Grants are made upon application by the charity concerned. Grants are made in amounts thought appropriate by the directors/trustees'.

The Kreditor Charitable Trust

Jewish, welfare and education

£68,000 (2007/08)

Beneficial area UK, with preferences for London and North East England.

Gerald Kreditor and Co., Chartered Accountants, Hallswelle House, 1 Hallswelle Road, London NW11 0DH

Tel. 020 8209 1535 **Fax** 020 8209 1923

Email admin@gerald-kreditor.co.uk

Correspondent Paul M Kreditor

Trustees *Paul M Kreditor; Merle P Kreditor.*

CC Number 292649

Information available Accounts are on file at the Charity Commission, without a list of grants.

This trust was established in 1985 for general charitable purposes, including the relief of poverty and the advancement of the Jewish religion.

In 2007/08 the trust had assets of £88,000 and an income of £69,000. Grants totalled £68,000.

In previous years, grants have been mostly for less than £100 and have been given mainly to Jewish organisations working in education and social and medical welfare. Beneficiaries have been scattered across London and the north east of England. The vast majority of grants were for less than £100. Recipients have included Academy for Rabbinical Research, British Friends of Israel War Disabled, Fordeve Ltd, Jerusalem Ladies' Society, Jewish Care, Jewish Marriage Council, Kosher Meals on Wheels, London Academy of Jewish Studies, NW London Talmudical College and Ravenswood. Non-Jewish organisations supported included British Diabetic Association, RNID and UNICEF UK.

Applications In writing to the correspondent.

Kupath Gemach Chaim Bechesed Viznitz Trust

Jewish

£56,000 to organisations (2008/09)

Beneficial area UK and Israel.

171 Kyverdale Road, London N16 6PS

Tel. 020 8442 9604

Correspondent S Weiss, Trustee

Trustees *I Kahan; S Weiss; A Pifko.*

CC Number 1110323

Information available Accounts were on file at the Charity Commission.

The charity was established by Deed of Trust dated 18 May 2005.

The objects of the charity are:

- the relief of the poor, sick, feeble and frail throughout the world and in particular, but not exclusively, amongst members of the Jewish faith
- the advancement of the Orthodox Jewish faith
- the advancement of the Orthodox Jewish religious education.

In 2008/09 the trust had an income of £237,000 from donations and made grants to organisations totalling £56,000, which were broken down as follows:

Category	Value
Religious education	£42,000
Advancement of religion	£8,000
Relief of poverty	£4,500
General	£2,000

Organisations to benefit included: Kehal Chasidei Wiznitz (£32,000); and Yesodey Hatorah School (£10,000).

During the year, a further £58,000 went to individuals.

Applications In writing to the correspondent.

The Kyte Charitable Trust

Medical, disadvantaged and socially isolated people

£126,000 (2007/08)

Beneficial area UK.

Business Design Centre, 52 Upper Street, London N1 0QH

Correspondent The Trustees

Trustees *D M Kyte; T M Kyte; J L Kyte; I J Kyte.*

CC Number 1035886

Information available Accounts were on file at the Charity Commission, without a list of grants.

The trust supports organisations benefiting medical professionals and research workers. Support may go to organisations working with at-risk groups, and people who are disadvantaged by poverty or socially isolated.

In 2007/08 the trust had assets of £27,000 and an income of £146,000 from covenants and Gift Aid received. Grants were made totalling £126,000, and were broken down into the following categories:

Category	Value
Community support	£57,000
Healthcare	£38,000
International aid	£14,000
Arts, culture and heritage	£5,000
Children	£1,800
Sports	£1,300
Educational support	£1,000
Miscellaneous	£8,200

Organisations recieving grants during the year were: United Jewish Israel Appeal (£25,000); Jewish Care (£20,000); Myeloma UK (£15,000); and Community Security Trust (£12,000).

Applications In writing to the correspondent.

Sir Pierce Lacy Charity Trust

Roman Catholic and general

About £24,000 (2007/08)

Beneficial area UK and overseas.

Norwich Union, Trustee Department, Pitheavlis, Perth PH2 0NH

Tel. 01738 895590 **Fax** 01738 895903

Correspondent P Burke, Head of Trustee Management

Trustee *CGU Insurance plc*

CC Number 1013505

Information available Information was obtained from the Charity Commission website.

In 2007/08 the trust had an income of £25,000 and gave grants totalling

£24,000. Grants are only made to Roman Catholic and associated institutions. Newly established and UK organisations are supported; benefiting children, young adults, older people, Roman Catholics, at-risk groups, carers, people who are disabled and people disadvantaged by poverty.

Grants are made in the areas of medicine and health, welfare, education, religion and for general charitable purposes. The trust particularly supports charities working in the field of infrastructure development, residential facilities and services, Christian education, Christian outreach, Catholic bodies, charity or voluntary umbrella bodies, hospices, rehabilitation centres, advocacy, education and training, community services and community issues.

Recurrent small grants of £1,000 or less are made, and grants can be for buildings, capital, core costs, project, research and start-up costs. Funding for more than three years may be considered.

Exclusions The trust only supports the Roman Catholic Church or associated institutions.

Applications In writing to the correspondent, at any time.

John Laing Charitable Trust

Education, community regeneration, young people, homelessness and environment

£1.4 million to organisations (2008)

Beneficial area UK.

33 Bunns Lane, Mill Hill, London NW7 2DX

Tel. 020 8959 7321

Email michael.a.hamilton@laing.com

Website www.laing.com/lct.htm

Correspondent Michael Hamilton, Secretary

Trustees *C M Laing; Sir Martin Laing; D C Madden; R I Sumner; P Jones; D Whipp; L Krige.*

CC Number 236852

Information available Accounts were on file at the Charity Commission.

The John Laing Charitable Trust has always tried to match its areas of donations to sectors allied to the Company's business.

More recently, the trust has concentrated its support on charities which support the following main themes:

- education
- community regeneration
- disadvantaged young people
- homelessness with a particular emphasis on day centres
- environment.

The John Laing Charitable Trust takes a proactive role in seeking charities that fit the criteria.

Donations range from £250 to £25,000 with up to 12 charities receiving more than £10,000. Usually, charities receive one-off donations, but a small number are supported for an agreed period, often up to three years.

In 2008 the trust had an income of £2 million and made grants totalling £2.2 million of which £1.4 million went to organisations, with a further £741,000 distributed to about 645 individuals whom were either current or former employees of John Laing plc.

Beneficiaries of the largest grants included: National Communities Resource Centre (£50,000); ContinYou (£35,000); Young Enterprise London (£30,000); Prince's Trust (£26,000); Homeless Link and Learning Through Landscapes (£25,000 each); Hertfordshire Groundwork, University Hospital of Leicester and National Literacy Trust (£20,000 each); Atlantic College (£18,000); Business in the Community and Springboard for Children (£15,000 each); and Citizenship Foundation, Duke of Edinburgh's Award, Fairshare, Forum for the Future, Groundswell, Princess Royal Trust for Carers and Tomorrow's People (£10,000 each).

Other beneficiaries included: Grounds for Learning (£9,500); Depaul Trust (£7,500); Essex Wildlife Trust (£6,000); Shekinah Torbay (£5,000); Ashburnham Community School, Child Victim of Crime, the Connection at St Martins, Crime Concern, Maryland Primary School and Voice (£5,000 each); Gwyl Gregynog Festival (£3,500); and First Stop Darlington, Rock Trust, Scarborough Homeless Support Services and Thanet Trust C4WS Project (£2,500 each).

Exclusions No grants to individuals (other than to Laing employees and/or their dependants).

Applications In writing to the correspondent. The trust does not have

an application form and applicants are asked to keep the initial request as brief as possible. There is no deadline for receipt of applications. All applications are dealt with on a rolling basis. The trust says that all applications are acknowledged.

Christopher Laing Foundation

Social welfare, environment, culture, health and children and young people

£160,000 (2007/08)

Beneficial area UK, with an interest in Hertfordshire.

c/o TMF Management UK Ltd, 400 Capability Green, Luton LU1 3AE

Tel. 01582 439200

Email sarah.martin@tmf-group.com

Correspondent Sarah Martin, Trust Consultant

Trustees *Christopher M Laing; John Keeble; Peter S Jackson; Diana C Laing.*

CC Number 278460

Information available Accounts were available from the Charity Commission.

In 2007/08 the trust had assets of £6.5 million, which generated an income of £223,000. Grants totalled £160,000 and were broken down by category and beneficiary as follows:

Children and young people (£40,000) The Lord's Taverners (£25,000); NCH – Action for Children, The Orpheus Centre and Youth Create (£5,000 each).

Culture and environment (£57,500) Fields in Trust – National Playing Fields Association (£25,000); Groundwork, Hertfordshire (£20,000); Global Action Plan (£10,000); and Forum for the Future (£2,500).

Health and medicine (£10,000) Hertfordshire Air Ambulance (£10,000).

Social welfare (£22,500) Hertfordshire Community Foundation (£20,000); and St Peter's Church (£2,500).

Charities Aid Foundation (£30,000) For disbursement amongst smaller charities.

Exclusions Donations are only made to registered charities.

Applications In writing to the correspondent.

Martin Laing Foundation

General, environment and conservation, disadvantaged young people and older people

£130,000 (2007/08)

Beneficial area UK and worldwide, particularly Malta.

33 Bunns Lane, London NW7 2DX

Tel. 020 8238 8890

Correspondent Ms Elizabeth Ann Harley

Trustees *Sir John Martin Laing; Colin Fletcher; Edward Charles Laing; Nicholas Gregory; Lady Stephanie Stearn Laing.*

CC Number 278461

Information available Accounts were on file at the Charity Commission.

Most of the trust's support is given to organisations and projects with which the trustees have a personal connection. A small number of larger grants are made, including one to the Charities Aid Foundation (CAF) which is then disbursed in smaller grants to a large number of organisations 'at the Settlor's discretion'.

In 2007/08 the foundation had assets of £7 million, which generated an income of £260,000. Management and administration charges totalled £28,000, while the investment manager's charges totalled £17,000. Grants were made totalling £130,000 of which £25,000 was distributed through CAF.

Grants made directly by the foundation were broken down as follows, shown with examples of grants in each category:

Education (£40,000)
Foundation for the College of St George.

Religion (£20,000)
Coptic Orthodox Church Centre.

Culture and environment (£15,000)
WWF UK (£10,000); and the Marine Stewardship Council (£5,000).

Children and young people (£10,000)
St Loys C of E Primary School and the Pushkin Prizes (£5,000 each).

Overseas (£8,000)
Student Education Trust.

Social welfare (£7,500)
John Laing Charitable Trust.

Health and medicine (£5,000)
Diabetes UK.

Applications The trust states that 'the trustees receive an enormous and increasing number of requests for help. Unfortunately the trustees are only able to help a small proportion of the requests and consequently they limit their support to those charities where they have an interest in their activities.'

The trustees meet twice a year.

David Laing Foundation

Young people, disability, the arts and general

£179,000 (2007/08)

Beneficial area Worldwide, with an apparent preference for the south of England

Fermyn Woods Hall, Brigstock NN14 3JA

Tel. 01536 373886

Correspondent David E Laing, Trustee

Trustees *David Eric Laing; John Stuart Lewis; Richard Francis Dudley Barlow; Frances Mary Laing.*

CC Number 278462

Information available Accounts were on file at the Charity Commission.

The foundation has general charitable purposes with an emphasis on young people, disability and the arts. Previous information has shown the foundation to make large grants to a wide and varied number of organisations as well as donating smaller grants through Charities Aid Foundation.

In 2007/08 the foundation had assets of around £4.7 million and an income of £150,000. Grants totalled £179,000 and were broken down into the categories shown below.

Category	Value
Children and young people inc. education	£88,000
Medical, health and sickness	£47,000
General	£16,000
Sport and recreation	£15,000
Arts and culture	£7,000
Overseas aid	£4,800
Education and training	£450
Social welfare	£200

Exclusions No grants to individuals.

Applications In writing to the correspondent. Trustees meet in March, June, October and December, although applications are reviewed weekly. Due to the large number of applications received, and the relatively small number of grants made, the trust is not able to respond to all requests.

The Lambert Charitable Trust

Health, welfare, education, disability and Jewish

£70,000 (2007/08)

Beneficial area UK and Israel.

Mercer & Hole, 72 London Road, St Albans AL1 1NS

Tel. 01727 869141

Correspondent George Georghiou

Trustees *M Lambert; Prof. H P Lambert; H Alexander-Passe; Jane Lambert; O E Lambert; D J R Wells.*

CC Number 257803

Information available Accounts were on file at the Charity Commission.

The trust usually uses half of its funds supporting Jewish and Israeli causes and half for medical, welfare and arts causes.

In 2007/08 the trust had assets of £2.9 million and an income of £107,000. After administration costs of £25,000, grants totalled £70,000.

Donations were broken down as follows, shown here with examples of beneficiaries in each category.

Israel (£6,700 in 9 grants)
British Friends of Rambah Medical Centre (£1,250); Operation Wheelchairs Committee (£1,000); and Sanhedria Children's Homes and Educational Centre (£500).

Jewish Faith in the United Kingdom (£22,000 in 7 grants)
Jewish Care (£15,000); Nightingale House (£2,000); and Jewish Blind and Disabled (£1,000).

Other charitable purposes (£41,000 in 27 grants)
Action on Addiction (£4,000); Dreamstore (£3,000); Headway and Meningitis Research Foundation (£2,000 each); and Friends of War Memorials and Ro-Ro Sailing Project (£1,000).

Applications In writing to the correspondent before July for payment by 1 September.

Lancashire Environmental Fund

Environment and community

£613,000 (2007)
Beneficial area Lancashire

The Barn, Berkeley Drive, Bamber Bridge, Preston PR5 6BY

Tel. 01772 317 247 **Fax** 01772 628 849

Email andyrowett@lancsenvfund.org.uk

Website www.lancsenvfund.org.uk

Correspondent Andy Rowett, Administration Officer

Trustees *Cllr A C P Martin, Chair; P Greijenberg; D Tattersall; P Taylor.*

CC Number 1074983

Information available Accounts were available from the Charity Commission.

This fund was established in June 1998 from a partnership of four organisations: SITA (Lancashire) Ltd, Lancashire County Council, the Wildlife Trust for Lancashire, Manchester and North Merseyside and Community Futures. The fund enables community groups and organisations throughout the country to take advantage of the funding opportunities offered by landfill tax credits. It achieves this by supporting organisations and projects based within Lancashire, or nationwide research or development with a relevance to Lancashire, which are managed by an Enrolled Environmental Body, as recognised by Entrust.

The fund operates three funding schemes:

Community Chest
The Community Chest is available as a small grant for a small scheme usually to support groups who are seeking one-off funding for a project. Applications are accepted for grants between £3,000 and £15,000. The overall cost of the project should not exceed £30,000. The fund may act as Environmental Body for the project and administer the paperwork required by the regulator.

Strategic Fund
The Strategic Fund is available to organisations that are registered as Environmental Bodies with Entrust, the scheme regulator. Applications are accepted for grants up to £30,000 but the overall cost should not exceed £250,000.

Dirtworks
The Dirtworks programme is funding to encourage young people to volunteer and get involved with practical environmental schemes. Applications are invited from organisations with the capacity to supervise and deliver a high quality project with young people. Schemes should cost up to £25,000 with the Fund contributing £20,000. The capital works element of the project should be at least 40 per cent of the cost.

Please note: The fund does not normally consider applications for 100 per cent funding therefore, support from other grant sources is welcome.

In 2007 the fund had assets of £3.4 million and an income of £813,000. Grants (paid and payable) totalled £613,000.

At the April 2009 meeting of the board grants totalling £224,000 were approved in support of 11 projects. The beneficiaries were: Parbold Scout Group and Holton Youth and Community Centre (£30,000 each); Lancashire Wildlife Trust (£28,000); Hawthorne Park Trust, West View Community Association and Pilling Memorial Hall (£25,000 each); Heritage Trust for the North West (£19,000); Bolton le Sands Village Hall and Saheli Community Garden (£15,000 each); Freckleton Parish Council (£8,500); and Elswick and District Village Hall (£3,000).

Exclusions Funding is not given for the following:

- core cost of an organisation
- retrospective funding
- projects in school grounds
- allotment or food growing projects
- car parks and public conveniences
- recycling projects
- projects within the unitary authority districts of Blackpool and Blackburn.

All projects must satisfy at least one objective of the Landfill Communities Fund. For more information about the scheme contact Entrust, the regulatory body, by visiting their website (www.entrust.org.uk) or by telephoning 0161 972 0074.

Applications Guidance notes and application forms for each funding strands are available from the correspondent or may be downloaded from the fund's website. Completed forms should contain all possible relevant material including maps, photographs, plans, and so on.

The board meets quarterly in January, April, July and October.

Staff are willing to have informal discussions before an application is made. Potential applicants are strongly advised to visit the website before contacting the trust.

LandAid Charitable Trust

Homelessness, relief of need

£40,000 available (2008/09)
Beneficial area UK

7th Floor, 1 Warwick Row, London SW1E 5ER

Tel. 020 7802 0117

Email enquiries@landaid.org

Website www.landaid.org

Correspondent Rosie Groves, Grants Officer

Trustees *Robin Broadhurst, Chair; Steven Ossack; Michael Slade; Mike Hussey; Liz Peace; Jeremy Newsum; David Taylor; Sherin Aminossehe; Robert Bould; Lynette Lackey.*

CC Number 295157

Information available Information was provided by the trust.

We are a charity established by the property industry to bring the expertise, resource and influence of the industry together in promoting effective charitable work. Our grantmaking reflects our commitment to giving those who are less advantaged an opportunity to transform their lives and achieve their full potential.

Small Grants Programme
Our Small Grants programme supports homeless people by funding projects which:

- provide accommodation or assist in meeting accommodation needs
- refurbish or renew facilities
- deliver training, life skills or other educational programmes.

We will not normally consider funding staff costs, unless the project is of limited duration or the applicant has shown how such costs will be met on an ongoing basis.

In 2008/09 LandAid will distribute up to £40,000 to appropriate specialist agencies. Applications are invited for awards ranging from £5,000 to £40,000. The trustees will consider whether to award several grants of different sizes or a single grant for the full amount available for an exceptional project.

Past beneficiaries have included: Marylebone Project (£25,000); New Horizon Youth Centre (£20,000); Upper Room (£15,000); Derbyshire Housing Aid (£13,500); Canaan Trust (£8,200); Emmaus Hampshire and St Mungo's (£8,000 each); Haven House (£5,500); and Booth Centre and the Genesis Trust (£5,000 each).

In addition to the above, the trust donated £500,000 in support of 'Foundations for Life'.

[This is] an innovative partnership between LandAid and Centrepoint which aims to deliver real help to homeless young people in order to turn their lives around and progress to independent adulthood, with their own career and home.

The programme will, over a four year period, provide up-to-date learning facilities, courses of training in useful skills for life and work, support in getting into work with training in the property industry and in finding and moving into a new home in the private sector.

Exclusions No grants to individuals.

Applications In writing to the correspondent. The applicant should set out clearly the aims of the project and the intended outcomes in no more than 500 words. The trust needs to know how the full cost of the project will be met, how the project will be managed effectively and how the applying organisation will report on its progress and success. A budget for the project must be provided together with a copy of the organisation's most recent annual report and accounts. (Please mark the envelope 'application for funding'.)

Applications should be submitted between 1 December and 31 January each year. A decision on grant allocation will be made by the committee towards the end of March. Information on the next round of funding will be posted on the charity's website when it becomes available.

Before reaching a decision to fund the committee and/or its representatives may wish to visit the project/organisation.

The Langdale Trust

Social welfare, Christian, medical and general

£140,000 (2006/07)

Beneficial area Worldwide, but with a special interest in Birmingham.

c/o Cobbetts Solicitors, One Colmore Circus, Birmingham B4 6AJ

Tel. 0845 404 2404

Correspondent Martin J Woodward, Trustee

Trustees *Jethro Elvin; Timothy R Wilson; Mrs Teresa Whiting; Martin J Woodward.*

CC Number 215317

Information available Accounts were available at the Charity Commission.

The trust was established in 1960 by the late Antony Langdale Wilson. There is a preference for local charities in the Birmingham area and those in the fields of social welfare and health, especially with a Christian context.

In 2006/07 the trust had assets of £4.2 million, which generated an income of £135,000. Grants were made to 47 organisations totalling £140,000.

Grants included those made to: Barnardo's – Amazon Project, Birmingham and UNICEF – Water and Wells (£8,000 each); The Leprosy Mission and Save the Children Fund (£4,000 each); Birmingham Settlement, Fairbridge West Midlands and The Grasslands Trust (£3,000 each); National Playing Fields Association and Quaker Social Action (£2,000 each); and The TreeHouse Trust (£1,000).

Applications In writing to the correspondent. The trustees meet in July.

The Langley Charitable Trust

Christian and general

£2,300 to organisations (2007)

Beneficial area UK and worldwide, with a preference for the West Midlands

Wheatmoor Farm, 301 Tamworth Road, Sutton Coldfield, West Midlands B75 6JP

Tel. 0121 308 0165

Correspondent The Trustees

Trustees *J P Gilmour; Mrs S S Gilmour.*

CC Number 280104

Information available Accounts were available from the Charity Commission

The trust makes grants to evangelical Christian organisations and to other charities in the fields of welfare, medicine and health. It makes grants in the UK and worldwide, but appears to have a small preference for the West Midlands. It operates My Word, a trading book shop and rents out the first floor of its offices to other charities to supplement its income.

In 2007 the trust had assets of £5.2 million and an income of £492,000. Grants were made totalling £4,000 of which £2,300 went to organisations. Unfortunately, a list of beneficiaries was not included in the accounts.

Exclusions No grants to animal or bird charities.

Applications In writing to the correspondent. 'The trustees only reply where they require further information and so on. Neither telephone calls nor correspondence will be entered into concerning any proposed or declined applications.'

The Lanvern Foundation

Education and health, especially relating to children

£95,000 (2007)

Beneficial area UK.

P O Box 34475, London W6 9YB

Tel. 020 8741 2930

Correspondent J C G Stancliffe, Trustee

Trustees *J C G Stancliffe; A H Isaacs.*

CC Number 295846

Information available Accounts were on file at the Charity Commission.

The foundation was established in 1986. The trustees state that it supports registered charities working primarily in the fields of education and health, with particular emphasis on children. There are never any grants to individuals.

In 2007 it had assets of £3.5 million, an income of £125,000 and made ten grants totalling £95,000. The beneficiaries were:

Moorfields Eye Hospital (£25,000); Childhood First, ICAN, The Joint Educational Trust, Marchant-Holliday School and Odiham Cottage Hospital Redevelopment Trust (£10,000 each); and Brathay Hall Trust, Edinburgh University – Botanic Productions, Theodora Children's Trust and Winchester Young Carers (£5,000 each).

Exclusions Absolutely no grants to individuals.

Applications In writing to the correspondent.

The R J Larg Family Charitable Trust

Education, health, medical research and arts – particularly music
About £100,000
Beneficial area UK but generally Scotland, particularly Tayside.

Whitehall House, Yeaman Shore, Dundee DD1 4BJ
Correspondent The Trustees
Trustees R W Gibson; D A Brand; Mrs S A Stewart.
SC Number SC004946
Information available Information was provided by the trust.

The trust has an annual income of approximately £140,000. Grants, which total about £100,000 each year, range between £250 and £6,000 and are given to a variety of organisations.

These include organisations concerned with cancer research and other medical charities, youth organisations, university students' associations and amateur musical groups. No further recent information was available.

Previous beneficiaries include High School – Dundee, Whitehall Theatre Trust, Macmillan Cancer Relief – Dundee and Sense Scotland Children's Hospice.

Exclusions Grants are not available for individuals.

Applications In writing to the correspondent. Trustees meet to consider grants in February and August.

Laufer Charitable Trust

Jewish
£8,600 (2007/08)
Beneficial area UK.

342 Regents Park Road, London N3 2LJ
Tel. 020 8343 1660
Correspondent S W Laufer, Trustee
Trustees S W Laufer; Mrs D D Laufer; S C Goulden; R Aarons; M Hoffman.
CC Number 275375
Information available Accounts were on file at the Charity Commission

The trust makes grants mainly to Jewish organisations and has a list of charities which it has a long-term commitment to and supports annually or twice a year. It rarely adds new charities to the list.

In 2007/08 the trust had assets of £755,000 and an income of £99,000. Grants were made totalling £8,600 as the trust sought to consolidate its reserves following the exceptional donations totalling £1.1 million made in the previous year.

Unfortunately, we have no information regarding the beneficiaries.

Exclusions No grants to individuals, as grants are only made to registered charities.

Applications New beneficiaries are only considered by the trust in exceptional circumstances, as the trustees seek to maintain support for an existing group of charities. In view of this it is suggested that no applications be made.

The Lauffer Family Charitable Foundation

Jewish and general
£191,000 (2007/08)
Beneficial area Commonwealth countries, Israel and USA.

Clayton Stark & Co, 5th Floor, Charles House, 108–110 Finchley Road, London NW3 5JJ

Tel. 020 7431 4200
Correspondent J S Lauffer, Trustee
Trustees Mrs R R Lauffer; J S Lauffer; G L Lauffer; R M Lauffer.
CC Number 251115
Information available Accounts were on file at the Charity Commission.

The trust has general charitable purposes, supporting Jewish causes in the UK, Commonwealth, Israel and USA.

In 2007/08 it had assets of £4.7 million, which generated an income of £148,000. Grants totalled £191,000. Management and administration costs were high at £47,000.

Grants were broken down as follows:

Category	Grants	Value
Education	51	£80,000
Welfare and care of children and families	79	£59,000
Religious Activities	19	£22,000
Medical Healthcare	26	£18,000
Recreation and Culture	17	£11,000
Environment	7	£1,900

Beneficiaries included: Jewish Learning Exchange (£12,000); Society of Friends of Torah (£11,000); Spiro Ark (£9,000); United Joint Israel Appeal (£6,000); Ballet West and Jewish Deaf Association (£5,000 each); Ulpan Akiva Netanya (£3,900); Kisharon School (£2,100); Young Jewish Care (£1,300); and British Friends of the Jaffa Institute (£1,000).

Exclusions No support for individuals.

Applications In writing to the correspondent; applications are considered once a year.

Mrs F B Laurence Charitable Trust

Social welfare, medical, disability and environment
£92,000 (2007/08)
Beneficial area Worldwide.

B M Box 2082, London WC1N 3XX
Correspondent The Trustees
Trustees Mrs Caroline Fry; Mrs Camilla Carr; Ms Elizabeth Lyle.
CC Number 296548
Information available Accounts were on file at the Charity Commission.

The trust produces guidelines which state the following.

The trustees' preference is to make grants for the care and improvements of conditions experienced by disadvantaged members of society both within the United Kingdom and overseas for whom the United Kingdom owes a duty of care.

The trustees are willing to support small organisations and those that by the nature of their work, find it difficult to attract funding.

The trust gives for general charitable purposes, including many service, medical and welfare charities, as well as hospices and environmental groups.

In 2007/08 the trust had assets of £2.4 million and a total income of £92,000. Grants were made totalling £113,000. Management and administration expenses were high at £21,000, including a payment of £18,000 to a firm in which one of the trustees is a partner. Whilst wholly legal, these editors always regret such payments unless, in the words of the Charity Commission, 'there is no realistic alternative'.

Major beneficiaries included: Stroke Association (£15,000); and St Christopher's Hospice (£5,000).

Other grant recipients were Alzheimer Society – Haslemere, Breakthrough Breast Cancer, the Gurkha Welfare Trust and Halow (£2,000 each); the Brooke and Coram (£1,500 each); and CRY (£1,250). Other grants of £1,000 or less totalled £52,000.

Exclusions No support for individuals. The following applications are unlikely to be considered:

- appeals for endowment or sponsorship
- overseas projects, unless overseen by the charity's own fieldworkers
- maintenance of buildings or landscape
- provision of work or materials that are the responsibility of the state
- where administration expenses, in all their guises, are considered by the trustees to be excessive
- where the fundraising costs in the preceding year have not resulted in an increase in the succeeding years' donations in excess of these costs.

Applications In writing to the correspondent, including the latest set of accounts, as filed with the Charity Commission. The guidelines state:

Write to us on not more than two sides of A4 paper with the following information:

- who you are
- what you do
- what distinguishes your work from others in your field

- where applicable describe the project that the money you are asking for is going towards and include a business plan/budget
- what funds have already been raised and how
- how much are you seeking from us
- how do you intend to measure the potential benefits of your project or work as a whole?

Trustees usually meet in April and November. Please submit your application by 1 February for the April meeting and by 1 August for the October meeting.

To save on our administration costs, we will only notify the successful applicants.

The Kathleen Laurence Trust

Heart disease, arthritis, mental disabilities, medical research, older people and children

£114,000 (2007/08)
Beneficial area UK.

Coutts and Co, Trustee Department, 440 Strand, London WC2R 0QS

Tel. 020 7753 1000 **Fax** 020 7753 1090

Correspondent David Breach, Assistant Trust Manager

Trustee *Coutts and Co.*

CC Number 296461

Information available Accounts were on file at the Charity Commission.

Donations are given to a wide range of institutions, particularly favouring smaller organisations and those raising funds for specific requirements, such as for the caring and support of the mentally disabled, arthritic and rheumatoid research, cancer research, research into respiratory and cardiac illnesses, and children's charities.

In 2007/08 the trust had assets of £3.1 million and an income of £129,000. Grants were made to 52 organisations totalling £114,000.

As in previous years the largest grants were to Arthritis Research Campaign, British Heart Foundation, MENCAP, Elizabeth Finn Trust, Battersea Dogs Home, Cancer Research Campaign and NSPCC, each of whom received £8,500.

Smaller grants included: Blood Pressure Association, Guideposts Trust and

Independent Age (£2,000 each); the Dame Vera Lynn Trust and the Sick Children's Trust (£1,500 each); Action for Kids and Birmingham Settlement (£1,000 each); Endeavour Training and Second Chance (£750 each); and the Bognor Fun Bus (£400).

Exclusions No donations are made for running costs, management expenses or to individuals.

Applications In writing to the correspondent. Trustees meet in January and June.

The Law Society Charity

Law and justice

£319,000 (2006/07)
Beneficial area Worldwide.

113 Chancery Lane, London WC2A 1PL

Tel. 020 7316 5597

Website www.lawsociety.org.uk

Correspondent Andrew Dobson, Company Secretary

Trustee *The Law Society Trustees Ltd.*

CC Number 268736

Information available Accounts were on file at the Charity Commission.

As the name suggests, this trust is concerned with causes connected to the legal profession, particularly in advancing legal education and access to legal knowledge. Organisations protecting people's legal rights and lawyers' welfare are also supported, as are law-related projects from charities without an identifiable legal connection.

In 2006/07 the trust had assets of £1.9 million and an income of £99,000. Grants totalling £319,000 were made to 21 organisations.

The largest grant was for £90,000 to The Citizenship Foundation. Other major beneficiaries included: LawCare Limited (£82,500); Howard League for Penal Reform (£17,500); Environmental Law Foundation and Solicitors' Benevolent Society (£15,000 each); Nottinghamshire Law Society and Working Families (£10,000 each); Asylum Support Appeals Project (£7,500); Book Aid International (£6,400); Peace Brigades International and YouthNet UK (£5,000 each).

Applications In writing to the correspondent. Applications are considered at quarterly trustees'

meetings, usually held in April, July, September and December.

Further details of the aims and objectives of the charity, together with an application form, can be downloaded from the website.

The Edgar E Lawley Foundation

Older people, disability, children, community, hospices and medical

£174,000 (2007/08)

Beneficial area UK, with a preference for the West Midlands.

Lower Wakefield, 116 Foley Road, Claygate KT10 0NA

Tel. 01372 805 760

Email frankjackson1945@yahoo.com

Website www.edgarelawleyfoundation. org.uk

Correspondent F S Jackson, Trustee

Trustees J H Cooke, Chair; Mrs G V H Hilton; P J Cooke; F S Jackson.

CC Number 201589

Information available Accounts were on file at the Charity Commission.

The foundation currently funds six broad areas to ensure balance in its grant-giving programme. These areas are: hospices, children and young people, older people, community, disabled people, medical, research and other miscellaneous projects. There is a preference for the West Midlands.

In 2007/08 the foundation had assets of £4.3 million and an income of £225,000. Grants were made to 97 organisations and totalled £174,000.

Beneficiaries were listed in the accounts, but without any indication of the size of grant received. In the West Midlands, beneficiaries included: Birmingham Boys' and Girls' Union; Birmingham St Mary's Hospice; ChildLine West Midlands; Macmillan Cancer Support (Birmingham); Walsall Society for the Blind; and YWCA (Wolverhampton).

Beneficiaries elsewhere included: Autism Initiative UK; Belfast Central Mission; Bolton Lads & Girls Club; Cotswold Care Hospice; South Bucks Hospice; and Youth Action Wiltshire.

Exclusions No grants to individuals.

Applications Applications should be made in writing to the correspondent, usually before the end of April (please check the foundation's website to confirm this). Applicants should outline the reasons for the grant request and the amount of grant being sought. Any supporting information that adds to the strength of the application should be included.

Successful applicants will receive the approved grants by the end of July or early August. The foundation regrets that it is not possible, unless a stamped addressed envelope has been provided, to communicate with unsuccessful applicants and the fact that a grant has not been received by mid August indicates that it has not been possible to fund it.

The Lawson Beckman Charitable Trust

Jewish, welfare, education and arts

£143,000 (2007/08)

Beneficial area UK.

A Beckman plc, PO Box 1ED, London W1A 1ED

Tel. 020 7637 8412 **Fax** 020 7436 8599

Correspondent Melvin Lawson, Trustee

Trustees M A Lawson; F C Katz; L R Stock.

CC Number 261378

Information available Accounts were on file at the Charity Commission.

The trust gives grants for the 'relief of poverty, support of the arts and general charitable purposes'. Grants are allocated two years in advance.

In 2007/08 the trust had assets of £1.9 million and an income of £123,000. A total of £143,000 was distributed in 15 grants broken down as follows:

Medical, health and sickness – £130,000 in 8 grants
Jewish Care (£100,000); Nightingale House (£13,500); Norwood Ravenswood (£10,000); Chai Lifeline Cancer Care (£3,000); UCH Hospital Charity (£1,500); Hatzola Trust (£1,000); Juvenile Diabetes Research Foundation

(£500); and Heart Cells Foundation (£250).

General charitable purposes – £8,000 in 4 grants
UJIA (£5,000); Central Synagogue General Charities Fund (£2,000); Bernard and Lucy Lyons Charitable Trust (£750); and Talking Newspapers (£250).

Education and training – £5,000 in 1 grant
Project SEED.

Relief of poverty – £150 in 1 grant
Child Resettlement Trust Fund.

Exclusions No grants to individuals.

Applications In writing to the correspondent, but please note that grants are allocated two years in advance.

The Raymond and Blanche Lawson Charitable Trust

General

£90,000 (2006/07)

Beneficial area UK, with an interest in West Kent and East Sussex.

28 Barden Road, Tonbridge TN9 1TX

Tel. 01732 352 183 **Fax** 01732 352 621

Correspondent Mrs P E V Banks, Trustee

Trustees John V Banks; Mrs P E V Banks; Mrs Sarah Hill.

CC Number 281269

Information available Accounts were on file at the Charity Commission.

The trust has a preference for local organisations and generally supports charities within the following categories:

- local voluntary organisations
- preservation of buildings
- local hospices
- care in the community
- assistance for people who are disabled
- armed forces and benevolent funds

In 2006/07 the trust had assets of £1.6 million, an income of £123,000 and made grants totalling £90,000.

The largest grant was for £5,000 and went to the Hospice in the Weald. Other large grants went to: Poppy Appeal

(£4,000); Langton Green Village Hall and Heart of Kent Hospice (£3,000 each); and Kent Music School and the National Trust (£2,000 each).

Smaller grants included: British Lung Foundation and Childhood First (£1,000 each); Independent Age and Kent Youth (£750 each); and Micro Anophtamimic Children's Society and the Eyeless Trust (£500 each).

Exclusions No support for churches or individuals.

Applications In writing to the correspondent.

The Carole and Geoffrey Lawson Foundation

Child welfare, poverty, arts, education, research and Jewish organisations

£273,000 (2007/08)

Beneficial area Worldwide, in practice UK.

Stilemans, Munstead, Godalming GU8 4AB

Tel. 01483 420757

Correspondent Geoffrey Lawson, Trustee

Trustees *Geoffrey C H Lawson; Hon Carole Lawson; Harold I Connick; Edward C S Lawson; Jeremy S Lawson.*

CC Number 801751

Information available Accounts were available at the Charity Commission.

This trust was established in 1989 for general charitable purposes and focuses on child welfare, relief of poverty, the advancement of education, the arts, research and Jewish organisations.

In 2007/08 the trust had assets of £222,000 and a total income of £116,000. Grants were made to 24 organisations totalling £273,000.

By far the largest grant was to World ORT Trust (£113,000). Other large grants were made to: the Prince's Trust (£33,000); Chase Children's Hospice Service (£29,000); St David's Care in the Community (£15,000); and Jewish Care (£13,000).

Other beneficiaries included: Community Security Trust and World Jewish Relief (£10,000 each); Nightingale Home (£8,000); King Silver Lining Appeal (£5,000); Young Enterprise (£3,500); Meath Epilepsy Trust (£2,000); and Royal Opera House, the Sanctuary and Coexistence Trust (£1,000 each).

One grant was made to an individual for research into Rheumatology (£25,000).

Exclusions In principal, no grants to individuals.

Applications In writing to the correspondent.

The Leach Fourteenth Trust

Medical, disability, environment, conservation and general

£88,000 (2007/08)

Beneficial area UK, with some preference for south west England and overseas only via a UK charity.

Barron & Barron, Chartered Accountants, Bathurst House, 86 Micklegate, York Y01 6LQ

Tel. 01904 628 551 **Fax** 01904 623 533

Email info@barronyork.co.uk

Correspondent Guy Ward, Trustee

Trustees *W J Henderson; Mrs J M M Nash; G S Ward; Roger Murray-Leach.*

CC Number 204844

Information available Accounts were on file at the Charity Commission.

Although the trust's objectives are general, the trustees tend towards medical and disability organisations. The trust also has a preference for conservation (ecological) organisations. In practice there is a preference for south-west England and the Home Counties.

A few charities receive regular donations. The trustees prefer to give single grants for specific projects rather than towards general funding and also favour small organisations or projects.

In 2007/08 the trust had assets of £2.8 million, an income of £105,000 and gave 74 grants totalling £88,000.

Beneficiaries for the year included: Durrell Wildlife Conservation Trust (£5,000); the Princess Royal Trust for Carers (£4,000); Salvation Army (£3,000); Merlin (£2,800); Afghan Aid (£2,500); British Red Cross (£2,200); Children in Crisis (£2,000); Orbis and the Country Trust – Suffolk (£1,500 each); and UK Sports Association (£1,000).

Exclusions Only registered charities based in the UK are supported (the trust only gives overseas via a UK-based charity). No grants to: individuals, including for gap years or trips abroad; private schools other than for people with disabilities or learning difficulties; or pet charities.

Applications In writing to the correspondent. Applications for a specific item or purpose are favoured. Only successful appeals can expect a reply. A representative of the trust occasionally visits potential beneficiaries. There are bi-annual meetings of trustees in summer and late autumn. Grants tend to be distributed twice a year, but exceptions are made.

The David Lean Foundation

Film production

£426,000 to organisations (2008)

Beneficial area UK.

KJD, Churchill House, Regent House, Stoke-on-Trent ST1 3RQ

Tel. 01782 202 020 **Fax** 01782 266060

Email aar@kjd.co.uk

Website www.davidleanfoundation.org

Correspondent The Trustees

Trustees *A A Reeves; J G Moore.*

CC Number 1067074

Information available Accounts were on file at the Charity Commission.

The foundation was registered on 23 December 1997 and was given rights to royalties of four of the major films directed by the late Sir David Lean. This provides the foundation's principal, current and future source of income.

The foundation's grant-making policy is to achieve its objects by making awards:

- to other charitable institutions whose aims include aims similar to those of the foundation

- to the National Film and Television School for student scholarships on recommendations of the school
- to institutions/individuals for film literature and research with associations with the work of Sir David Lean associations.

In 2008 the foundation had an income of £318,000 and made grants totalling £426,000. A further £65,000 was distributed in scholarships/awards to individuals.

The beneficiaries were: British Film Institute (£311,000 for film restoration); National Film and Television School (£73,000 for library/fiction direction lectures); British Academy of Film and Television Arts (£20,000 for lectures); Royal Academy of Arts (£10,000 for lectures); Literary Research (£9,000); and David Lean Trailer (£3,600).

Future commitments totalling £341,000 were also made in 2008, including those to the following organisations – British Film Institute, BAFTA, NFTS and the Royal Academy of Arts.

Applications Scholarship grants for students attending the National Film and Television School, Royal Holloway or Leighton Park School, are normally only awarded on the recommendation of the course provider with the trustees.

Other applications for grants that would meet the aims of the foundation are invited in writing, enclosing full details of the project and including financial information and two references.

The Leche Trust

Preservation and restoration of Georgian art, music and architecture

£187,000 to organisations (2007/08)

Beneficial area UK.

84 Cicada Road, London SW18 2NZ

Tel. 020 8870 6233 **Fax** 020 8870 6233

Email info@lechetrust.org

Website www.lechetrust.org

Correspondent Mrs Louisa Lawson, Secretary

Trustees *Dr Ian Bristow; The Hon. Mrs Felicity Guinness; Simon Jervis; Lady Greenstock; Martin Williams; Simon Wethered; Mrs Caroline Laing.*

CC Number 225659

Information available Accounts were on file at the Charity Commission.

The trust was founded and endowed by the late Mr Angus Acworth in 1950. As stated in its accounts, the trust supports the following categories:

1) the promotion of amity and good relations between Britain and developing countries by financing visits to such countries by teachers or other appropriate persons, or providing financial assistance to students from overseas especially those in financial hardship during the last six months of their postgraduate doctorate study in the UK or those engaged in activities consistent with the charitable objects of the trust

2) assistance to academic, educational or other organisations concerned with music, drama, dance and the arts

3) the preservation of buildings and their contents and the repair and conservation of church furniture (including such items as monuments, but excluding structural repairs to the church fabric); preference is to be given to buildings and objects of the Georgian period

4) assistance to conservation in all its aspects, including in particular museums and encouraging good practice in the art of conservation by supporting investigative and diagnostic reports

5) the support of charitable bodies or organisations associated with the preservation of the nation's countryside, towns, villages and historic landscapes.

In 2007/08 the trust had assets of £6 million and an income of £275,000. Grants approved to organisations and individuals totalling £215,000 were broken down as follows:

Historic buildings – 11 grants totalling £46,000
These included: London Historic Parks and Gardens Trust (£6,000); Chawton House Library, National Trust for Scotland – Little Houses in Peterhead and Octavia Hill's Birthplace House – Wisbech (£5,000 each); Paxton House – Berwick upon Tweed (£3,000); and the Hebridean Trust – Isle of Tree (£2,500).

Churches – 23 grants totalling £63,000
These included: Chapel at Stansted Park – Hampshire and St Patrick's Catholic Church – Soho Square, London (£5,000 each); St Mary's Church – Molland, Devon (£4,000); St Margaret's Church – Owthorpe, Nottingham (£2,500); Church of St James the Great – Aslackby, Lincolnshire (£2,000); and St Mary the Virgin Church – Offwell, Devon (£1,600).

Institutions and museums – 10 grants totalling £25,000
These included: The Watts Gallery – Compton, Surrey (£5,000); College of Arms – London (£3,000); British School of Rome (£2,000); Gainsborough' House – Sudbury, Suffolk (£1,500); Wisbech and Fenland Museum (£1,000); and The Quilters' Guild – York (£900).

Arts – 27 grants totalling £57,000
These included: the Opera Group – London (£5,000); Scottish Ballet – Glasgow (£3,400); Oxford Philomusica and The Watermill Theatre – Newbury (£2,000 each); Fressingfield Music Festival – Suffolk (£1,600); and Wonderful Beast (£1,000).

Education (individuals) – 2 grants totalling £3,000
These were made in the form of bursaries to West Dean College and Guildhall School of Music.

Overseas students – 19 grants totalling £25,000
These were given to students who are in the final six months of their PhD courses. The average grant was just over £1,300.

Exclusions No grants are made for: religious bodies; overseas missions; schools and school buildings; social welfare; animals; medicine; expeditions; or British students other than music students.

Applications In writing to the secretary. Trustees meet three times a year, in February, June and October; applications need to be received the month before.

The Arnold Lee Charitable Trust

Jewish, educational and health

£89,000 (2007/08)

Beneficial area UK.

Hazlems Fenton LLP, Palladium House, 1–4 Argyll Street, London W1F 7LD

Tel. 020 7487 5757

Correspondent A Lee, Trustee

Trustees *Helen Lee; Alan Lee.*

CC Number 264437

Information available Accounts were on file at the Charity Commission, but without an up-to-date grants list.

The policy of the trustees is to distribute income to 'established charities of high repute' for any charitable purpose or object. The trust supports a large number of Jewish organisations.

In 2007/08 the trust had assets of £1.9 million and an income of £96,000. Grants were made to 34 institutions totalling £89,000. No information regarding the beneficiaries was available.

Previous beneficiaries have included Joint Jewish Charitable Trust, Project SEED, Jewish Care, Lubavich Foundations, The Home of Aged Jews, Yesodey Hatorah School and Friends of Akim.

Exclusions Grants are rarely made to individuals.

Applications In writing to the correspondent.

Morris Leigh Foundation

Jewish and general

£27,000 (2006/07)

Beneficial area UK.

40 Portland Place, London W1B 1NB

Tel. 020 7908 6000

Correspondent Tina Grant-Brook

Trustees *Martin D Paisner; Howard D Leigh.*

CC Number 280695

Information available Accounts were on file at the Charity Commission, but without an up-to-date grants list.

The foundation has general charitable purposes, mostly supporting Jewish, welfare and arts organisations.

In 2006/07 the foundation had assets of £1.6 million and an income of £47,000. Grants totalling £27,000 were made during the year, but we have no details of the beneficiaries.

Previously, grants have been made to the Royal College of Music, London Business School, Rycolewood College, Institute for Jewish Policy Research, Ronald Raven Cancer Trust, London Symphony Orchestra, London Philharmonic Orchestra, Somerset House Arts Fund, Sussex University, Community Service Trust, Chicken Shed Theatre, Holocaust Educational Fund, British ORT, Cancerkin – Women Gala, Commonwealth Jewish Trust, London Jewish Culture Centre, Reading Hebrew

Congregation, UJIA, Medical Foundation and Inspire Foundation.

Applications In writing to the correspondent.

The Leigh Trust

Addiction, children and young people, criminal justice, asylum seekers, racial equality and education

£144,000 (2007/08)

Beneficial area UK and overseas.

Begbies Chettle Agar, Epworth House, 25 City Road, London EC1Y 1AR

Tel. 020 7628 5801 **Fax** 020 7628 0390

Correspondent The Trustees

Trustees *Hon. David Bernstein; Dr R M E Stone; Caroline Moorehead.*

CC Number 275372

Information available Accounts were available from the Charity Commission.

The Leigh Trust was registered in 1978. Its current policy is to distribute investment revenue and a proportion of capital gains. The trust makes grants to a variety of registered charities concerned with:

- drug and alcohol rehabilitation
- criminal justice
- asylum seekers/racial equality
- education.

'The policy of the trustees is to support those organisations which they believe to be in greatest need. The trustees can respond favourably to very few applicants.'

In 2007/08 the trust had assets of nearly £3 million and an income of £93,000. Grants totalling £144,000 were categorised by the trust as follows:

Category	Value	No.
Addiction	£60,000	15
Criminal justice	£45,000	11
Asylum seekers and racial equality	£33,000	11
Overseas	£5,000	1
Children and young people	£1,000	1

Major beneficiaries included: Action on Addiction, Asylum Support Appeal Project, Care for Prisoners Overseas Organisation, Church Action on Poverty, Nazareth House, New Hope Leeds and Stonebridge City Farm (£5,000 each); Ipswich Housing Action Group, New Bridge Foundation and Student Action for Refugees (£3,000 each); BID Deaf

Prison Project (£2,500); Ice & Fire Theatre Company (£2,000); and Alnwick Garden Trust and Marylebone High School (£1,000 each).

Exclusions The trust does not make grants to individuals.

Applications Organisations applying for grants must provide their most recent audited accounts, a registered charity number, a cash flow statement for the next 12 months, and a stamped addressed envelope.

Applicants should state clearly on one side of A4 what their charity does and what they are requesting funding for. They should provide a detailed budget and show other sources of funding for the project.

The P Leigh-Bramwell Trust 'E'

Methodist and general

£115,000 (2007/08)

Beneficial area UK, with a preference for Bolton

W and J Leigh and Co., Tower Works, Kestor Street, Bolton BL2 2AL

Tel. 01204 521771

Correspondent Mrs L Cooper, Secretary

Trustees *Mrs H R Leigh-Bramwell; Mrs J Leigh Hardyment; B H Leigh-Bramwell.*

CC Number 267333

Information available Accounts were on file at the Charity Commission.

The objects of the charity are to 'advance Christian religion, education, the RNLI and any other legal charitable institution'.

In 2007/08 the trust had assets of £2.2 million, an income of £116,000 and made grants totalling £115,000. Distributions were made to both regular beneficiaries and six additional charitable organisations.

The largest grant was given to King's College School (£30,000). Other large beneficiaries included: Leigh-Bramwell Fund (£23,000); the Methodist Church – Bolton (£11,000); Rivington Parish Church (£7,500); the Unicorn School (£7,000); and the Methodist Church – Delph Hill and the Methodist Church – Breightmet (£3,400 each).

Smaller grant beneficiaries included Barnabus, Bolton Choral Union, Bolton Deaf Society, ChildLine North West, NCH Bypass, West London Mission and YWCA (£500 each).

Exclusions No grants to individuals.

Applications In writing to the correspondent; however, please note that previous research suggests that there is only a small amount of funds available for unsolicited applications and therefore success is unlikely.

The Leonard Trust

Christian and overseas aid

£33,000 to organisations (2007)
Beneficial area Overseas and UK, with a preference for Winchester.

18 Edgar Road, Winchester SO23 9TW
Tel. 01962 854 800
Correspondent Tessa E Feilden
Trustees *Dominic Gold; Mrs N A Gold.*
CC Number 1031723
Information available Accounts were available from the Charity Commission, but without a narrative report.

The trust informed us that it makes grants totalling about £30,000 each year, ranging between £1,000 and £5,000 each. It supports Christian and overseas aid organisations. In 2007 the trust had an income of £35,000 and made grants to 16 organisations totalling £33,000.

Grant recipients included: VIVA Network – Street Children South America (£10,500); Christian Aid (£5,000); Chernobyl Children in Need (£2,300); Care in the Family, Frontier Youth, Tear Fund and Tower Hamlets (£2,000 each); L'Arche and YMCA (£1,000 each); and Brendon Care (£800).

Exclusions No grants to individuals. Medical research and building projects are no longer supported.

Applications Unsolicited applications cannot be considered.

The Leverhulme Trade Charities Trust

Charities benefiting commercial travellers, grocers or chemists

£312,000 to organisations (2008)
Beneficial area UK.

1 Pemberton Row, London EC4A 3BG
Tel. 020 7822 6825
Email pread@leverhulme.ac.uk
Website leverhulme-trade.org.uk
Correspondent Paul Read, Secretary
Trustees *Sir Michael Perry, Chair; N W A Fitzgerald; P J-P Cescau; A S Ganguly; P Polman.*
CC Number 288404
Information available Accounts were on file at the Charity Commission.

The Leverhulme Trade Charities Trust derives from the will of the First Viscount Leverhulme, who died in 1925. He left a proportion of his shares in Lever Brothers Ltd upon trust and specified the income beneficiaries to include certain trade charities. In 1983, the Leverhulme Trade Charities Trust itself was established, with its own shareholding in Unilever, and with grantmaking to be restricted to charities connected with commercial travellers, grocers or chemists, their wives, widows or children. The trust has no full-time employees, but the day-to-day administration is carried out by the director of finance at The Leverhulme Trust.

Grants are only made to:

* trade benevolent institutions supporting commercial travellers, grocers or chemists
* schools or universities providing education for them or their children.

In 2008 the trust had assets of £39 million and an income of £1.5 million. Grants to organisations totalled £312,000. A further £548,000 was given in 113 undergraduate and postgraduate bursaries.

The largest single grant of £240,000 went to Commercial Travellers' Institution. The only other organisation to benefit was the Provision Trade Institution, which received £72,000 over three years.

Exclusions No capital grants. No response is given to general appeals.

Applications By letter to the correspondent. All correspondence is acknowledged. The trustees meet in February and applications need to be received by the preceding October.

Undergraduate and postgraduate bursary applications should be directed to the relevant institution

Lewis Family Charitable Trust

Research into cancer, head injuries and birth defects, health, education and Jewish

£1.4 million (2008)
Beneficial area UK and Israel.

Chelsea House, West Gate, London W5 1DR
Tel. 020 8991 4601
Correspondent The Secretary
Trustees *David Lewis; Julian Lewis.*
CC Number 259892
Information available Accounts were on file at the Charity Commission.

The trust's annual report states the following.

The Lewis Family Charitable Trust was established to give expression to the charitable intentions of members of the families of David, Bernard, Geoffrey and Godfrey Lewis and certain companies which they control. The legally permitted objectives are very wide and cover virtually every generally accepted charitable object. However, in practice the causes to which the trustees have devoted the bulk of their resources in recent years have been medical research and support with particular reference to the following:

* research into possible treatments for cancer
* head injuries
* birth defects
* rehabilitation following amputation and physical disability
* Jewish community general charities
* educational funding.

In 2007/08 the trust had assets of £7.9 million and an income of £3.47 million. Grants were made totalling £1.4 million broken down as follows: Medical – general support (£570,000); Educational funding (£260,000); General charitable funding

(£160,000); Medical research (£140,000); Support for older people (£110,000); Jewish religious support (£70,000); Childcare (£50,000); and Poverty relief (£30,000).

The vast majority of beneficiaries had a Jewish connection, support was also given to a number of non-Jewish organisations. Beneficiaries within each category included:

Childcare – Norwood Ravenswood (£4,500) and Action for Kids Charitable Trust (£1,500).

Education – Citizens for True Social Justice (£39,500) and Oxford Centre for Hebrew and Jewish Studies (£10,000).

General – The Community Security Trust (£30,000) and Demand (£5,000).

Jewish religious support – Westminster Synagogue (£10,000) and The Jewish Leadership Council (£5,000).

Medical general – Birth Defects Foundation (£100,000) and Meningitis UK (£2,000).

Medical research – The Institute of Cancer Research (£40,000) and Children's Liver Disease Foundation (£5,000).

Poverty relief – Kenya Red Cross Society (£25,000) and British WIZO (£1,000).

Support for older people – Jewish Care (£106,000).

Exclusions No grants to individuals.

Applications In writing to the correspondent.

The John Spedan Lewis Foundation

Natural sciences, particularly horticulture, environmental education, ornithology and conservation

£79,000 (2007/08)
Beneficial area UK.

Partnership House, Carlisle Place, London SW1P 1BX
Tel. 020 7592 6121
Email bridget_chamberlain@johnlewis.co.uk

194

Correspondent Ms Bridget Chamberlain, Secretary
Trustees *Charlie Mayfield, Chair; Ken Temple; Dr Vaughan Southgate; Simon Fowler; Miss Tessa Colman.*
CC Number 240473
Information available Accounts were on file at the Charity Commission.

The trust makes grants in the areas of horticulture, environmental education, ornithology and conservation, and to associated educational and research projects. Donations are mainly one-off.

In 2007/08 the foundation had assets of £2.3 million, which generated an income of £92,000. Grants were made to 13 organisations totalling £79,000.

The beneficiaries included: Royal Botanic Gardens – Kew (£12,000); University of Oxford Botanic Gardens and Harcourt Arboretum (£9,000); the Tree Council, Devon Bird Watching and Preservation Society and British Trust for Ornithology (£5,000 each); Fauna and Flora International and Farming and Countryside Education (£4,500 each); the English Hedgerow Trust (£3,000); RSPB Northern Ireland (£1,000); and London Children's Flower Society (£60).

Exclusions No grants to individuals (including students), local branches of national organisations, or for salaries, medical research, welfare projects, building works or overseas expeditions.

Applications In writing to the correspondent with latest report and accounts and a budget for the proposed project.

The Sir Edward Lewis Foundation

General

£191,000 (2007/08)
Beneficial area UK and overseas, with a preference for Surrey.

Messrs Rawlinson and Hunter, The Lower Mill, Kingston Road, Ewell, Surrey KT17 2AE
Tel. 020 7451 9000
Correspondent Mrs Sandra Frankland
Trustees *R A Lewis; K W Dent; Christine J A Lewis; Sarah J N Dorin.*
CC Number 264475

Information available Accounts were available from the Charity Commission.

The trust was established in 1972 by Sir Edward Roberts Lewis. The trust has revised its policy and now plans to make one substantial donation every two or three years to an appropriate cause as well as smaller donations on an annual basis. Therefore it will not distribute all its income every year. The trustees prefer to support charities known personally to them and those favoured by the settlor.

In 2007/08 the foundation had assets of £7.2 million, an income of £470,000 and made grants to 100 organisations totalling £191,000.

Major beneficiaries included: Fareshare (£38,000); the Children's Trust – Tadworth (£10,000); and Gurkha Welfare Trust, the David Shepherd Wildlife Trust, Global Diversity Foundation and Ridgegate Home (£5,000 each).

Other beneficiaries included: the Rugby Clubs (£4,000); Council for Music in Hospitals (£3,000); Ophthalmic Aid to Eastern Europe and Musicians Benevolent Fund (£2,500 each); UK Antarctic Heritage Trust and Telephones for the Blind (£2,000 each); Cary Dickinson Breast Cancer and Shipwrecked Fisherman's Society (£1,500); Newspaper Press Fund and Walk the Walk Worldwide (£1,000 each); and Compaid Trust and the Uphill Ski Club (£500 each).

Exclusions Grants are only given to charities, projects or people known to the trustees. No grants are given to individuals.

Applications In writing to the correspondent. The trustees meet every six months.

Lifeline 4 Kids

Equipment for children with disabilities

£215,000 (2008)
Beneficial area Worldwide.

215 West End Lane, West Hampstead, London NW6 1XJ
Tel. 020 7794 1661 **Fax** 020 7794 1161
Website www.lifeline4kids.org
Correspondent The Investigations Officer

CC Number 200050

Information available Accounts were on file at the Charity Commission, but without a list of grants. Information was available on its website.

This charity supports children who are disabled up to 18 years old. The following description is taken from its website:

We are a London based children's charity established in 1961. Originally known as 'The Handicapped Children's Aid Committee', our working name has now changed to Lifeline 4 Kids. Our members work on an entirely voluntary basis and we have no paid staff.

We were formed for one purpose – to provide essential equipment to help improve the quality of life for children with disabilities and special needs irrespective of their race or creed.

- Schools, children's hospices, respite care homes and support centres throughout the UK receive our help with equipment including playground equipment, soft play and multi-sensory rooms and special beds.
- For the individual child we provide the full spectrum of specialised equipment such as electric wheelchairs, mobility aids and varying items including specialised computers. We are also one of the only UK charities prepared to help a special needs child from a low-income family with essential smaller items such as shoes, clothing, bedding and specialist toys.
- We are able to give emergency and welfare appeals immediate approval within the authorised limits of our welfare sub-committee.
- We also help equip hospital neonatal units with the latest incubators, infusion pumps and ultrasonic monitors amongst other life saving equipment.
- No appeal is too large or too small for us to consider.

In 2008 the charity had assets of £698,000, an income of £94,000 and gave £215,000 in response to appeals. Details of the successful applicants were not included with the accounts.

Please note: the trust does not give financial support, but purchases equipment directly for and on behalf of the beneficiary.

Assistance given in 2006 included that to: Central Middlesex Hospital, towards equipment for its outdoor play area (£5,000); the Living Paintings Trust, funding the production of 20 copies of a new Living Picture Book (£2,500); the New Jumbulance Travel Trust, providing two portable instant resuscitation packs (£2,400); Vision Aid, providing a specialised flat screen video magnifier (£2,000); and the Lothian Autistic Society, for equipment for its various play schemes (£1,500).

Exclusions Building projects, research grants and salaries will not be funded.

Applications Applications for help indicating specific requirements and brief factual information must initially be made in writing, addressed to the correspondent, or by email (appeals@lifeline4kids.org).

The charity states on its website that:

Each request will be acknowledged and provided it meets our criteria, an application form will be sent by post or email. The form contains comprehensive questions relating to the child/children's medical condition and requires backup information from health professionals together with a financial statement of the applicant/organisation.

After we have received the completed application form, if appropriate, the appeal will be investigated personally by one of our members.

The majority of appeals are discussed and decided upon at our monthly meetings. If approved, a maximum sum is allocated and we take full responsibility for the purchase and safe delivery of the approved item.

Initial telephone calls from applicants are not welcome.

The Limbourne Trust

Environment, welfare and arts

£91,000 (2007/08)

Beneficial area UK and overseas.

Downs Farm, Homersfield, Harleston, Norwich IP20 0NS

Correspondent Elisabeth Anne Thistlethwayte, Trustee

CC Number 1113796

Information available Accounts were on file at the Charity Commission.

The trust was set up in 2006. The following is taken from its website.

The trust has wide charitable objects, which encompass the benefit of communities throughout the world, and in particular the advancement of education, the protection of health, and the relief of poverty, distress and sickness.

The charity will also seek to challenge all forms of oppression and inequality, and will prioritise funding for groups who assist people who are unable to take a full role in society due to economic, political and social disadvantage.

The charity will seek to achieve these objectives by providing grant funding for other Charities working in the following fields:

- research into renewable energy sources
- development of organic farming methods
- development of environmentally sustainable projects
- overcoming adverse effects of climate change
- community projects to assist those at disadvantage
- protection and conservation of the environment
- promote the public education in and appreciation of literature, music and drama
- other charitable purposes as the trustees from time to time may decide.

In 2007/08 the trust had assets of £2.4 million and an income of £114,000. Grants totalled £91,000.

Beneficiaries included: Chicks (£12,000); Journey of a Lifetime Trust and Sinfield Nature Conservation Trust (£11,000 each); the Hand Partnership and Magdalene Group (£10,000 each); Norfolk and Norwich Families House (£7,500); the Poetry Trust (£7,100); Aldeburgh Music, BEAT – the Eating Disorders Association, Whirlow Hall Farm Trust and Vauxhall City Farm (£5,000 each).

Applications 'The trustees will seek to identify those projects where the greatest and widest benefit can be attained, and usually will only consider written applications and, where necessary, make further enquiries.' Trustees meet three times a year.

Limoges Charitable Trust

Animals, services and general

About £50,000 (2007/08)

Beneficial area UK, with a preference for Birmingham.

Tyndallwoods Solicitors, 29 Woodbourne Road, Edgbaston, Birmingham B17 8BY

Tel. 0121 693 2222 **Fax** 0121 693 0844

Correspondent Mrs J A Dyke, Trustee

Trustees *Mike Dyer; Albert Kenneth Dyer; Judy Ann Dyke; Andrew Milner.*

CC Number 1016178

Information available Full accounts were available at the Charity Commission.

The trust has general charitable purposes, although there are preferences for animal and service organisations. Many of the beneficiaries are based in Birmingham.

In 2007/08 the trust had an income of £17,000 and expenditure of £53,000. No further information was available.

Previous beneficiaries have included Edward's Trust (£3,000); Birmingham Midland Limbless Ex-Service (£1,500); Holy Cross Community Centre (£1,000); Early Childhood Intervention, Heart Failure Foundation and Hereford Cathedral (£500 each); and Kids Like Us, Spear and the Donkey Sanctuary (£250 each).

Applications In writing to the correspondent.

The Lind Trust

Social action, community and Christian service

£231,000 to organisations and individuals (2007/08)

Beneficial area UK.

Tithe Barn, Attlebridge, Norwich NR9 5AA

Tel. 01603 262 626

Correspondent Gavin Croft Wilcox, Trustee

Trustees *Leslie C Brown; Dr Graham M Dacre; Gavin C Wilcock; Mrs Julia*

M Dacre; Russell B Dacre; Samuel E Dacre

CC Number 803174

Information available Accounts were on file at the Charity Commission.

In 2007/08 the trust had assets of £17.1 million and an income of £6.9 million. Grants were made to charities, organisations and individuals totalling £231,000. No breakdown of this was available.

Applications In writing to the correspondent at any time. However, the trust commits most of its funds in advance, giving the remainder to eligible applicants as received.

Lindale Educational Foundation

Roman Catholic and education

£86,000 (2007/08)

Beneficial area UK and overseas.

1 Leopold Road, Ealing Common, London W5 3PB

Tel. 020 7229 7574

Correspondent J Valero

Trustees *Netherhall Educational Association; Dawliffe Hall Educational Foundation; Greygarth Association.*

CC Number 282758

Information available Accounts were on file at the Charity Commission.

The foundation supports the Roman Catholic religion and the advancement of education. Its aims are to:

- train priests
- establish, extend, improve and maintain churches, chapels, oratories and other places of worship
- establish, extend, improve and maintain university halls and halls of residence for students of all nationalities
- arrange and conduct courses, camps, study centres, meetings, conferences and seminars
- provide financial support for education or research by individuals or groups of students
- provide financial support for other individuals or institutions which meet the trust's criteria, including the corporate trustees.

In 2007/08 the foundation had an income of £84,000 and made grants totalling £86,000, as detailed in the examples below.

The main emphasis was on the training of priests, with a grant of £35,000 being made to Collegio Romano della Santa Croce.

Other grants included those to: Wickenden Manor and the Netherhall Educational Association Centre for Retreats and Study (three grants totalling £21,000); Thornycroft Hall (three grants totalling £23,000); and Pontifical University (£1,200).

Exclusions No grants to individuals.

Applications In writing to the correspondent, but please note that most funds are already committed.

The Linden Charitable Trust

Medical, healthcare and the arts

£113,000 (2007/08)

Beneficial area UK, with a preference for West Yorkshire

c/o Baker Tilly, 2 Whitehall Quay, Leeds LS1 4HG

Tel. 0113 285 5000

Correspondent The Trustee

Trustee *Miss M H Pearson.*

CC Number 326788

Information available Information was obtained from the Charity Commission website.

Currently, the trust's policy is to benefit charities specialising in cancer relief and research, those particularly involved with hospices, those involved in arts and also a wider range of charities based in and around Leeds, West Yorkshire.

In 2007/08 the trust had assets of £2.6 million and an income of £80,000. Grants were made totalling £113,000. Beneficiaries included: Leeds International Pianoforte Competition (£20,000); Macmillan Cancer Relief (£10,000); Marie Curie Cancer Care (£7,000); Leeds Lieder, Martin House Hospice and Mission for Seafarers (£4,000 each); Caring for Life (£3,000); Opera North Foundation (£2,000); Live Music Now and York Glaziers Trust (£1,000 each); Listening Books (£600);

and Second World War Experience Centre (£500).

Exclusions No grants to individuals.

Applications In writing to the correspondent.

The Linmardon Trust

General

£38,000 (2007/08)

Beneficial area UK, with a preference for the Nottingham area.

HSBC Trust Company (UK) Limited, Norwich House, Nelson Gate, Commercial Road, Southampton SO15 1GX

Tel. 023 8072 2240

Correspondent The Secretary

Trustee *HSBC Trust Company Limited.*

CC Number 275307

Information available Accounts were on file at the Charity Commission.

The trust supports charities in the UK with a preference for those in the Nottingham area.

In 2007/08 it had assets of £1.2 million and an income of £195,000. Grants totalling £38,000 were made to 39 organisations.

Beneficiaries included: Association for Spina Bifida and Hydrocephalus, Changing Faces, Prostate Cancer Research Foundation, The Meningitis Trust and The Stroke Association (£3,000 each); Action Medical Research, British Institute for Brain Injured Children, Community of the Holy Fire and Leap Confronting Conflict (£1,000 each); and Get Connected, Sunny Days Children's Fund and The Manna Society (£500 each).

Exclusions Grants are made to registered charities only. No support to individuals.

Applications In writing to the correspondent. The trustees meet quarterly, generally in February, May, August and November.

The Ruth and Stuart Lipton Charitable Trust

Jewish and general

£92,000 (2007/08)

Beneficial area UK and overseas

Lewis Golden and Co., 40 Queen Ann Street, London W1G 9EL

Tel. 020 7580 7313

Correspondent N W Benson, Trustee

Trustees *Sir S Lipton; Lady Lipton; N W Benson.*

CC Number 266741

Information available Accounts were on file at the Charity Commission.

The trust was founded by property and art mogul Stuart Lipton and his wife in 1973.

In 2007/08 the trust had assets of £550,000 and an income of £76,000. Grants totalled £92,000.

Grant beneficiaries included: Glyndebourne (£30,000); Nightingale (£15,000); Royal Opera House and Community Security Trust (£10,000 each); the Winnicot Foundation (£2,500); Cancer Research UK and The Facial Surgery Research Foundation (£1,000 each); Crafts Council (£500); Give Youth A Break (£250); and Cycle to Cannes (£100).

Exclusions No grants to individuals.

Applications In writing to the correspondent.

The Lister Charitable Trust

Outdoor activities for disadvantaged young people

£111,000 (2008/09)

Beneficial area UK.

c/o Apperley Limited, Market Street, Maidenhead SL6 8BE

Tel. 01628 477 879

Correspondent Nicholas Yellowlees

Trustees *Noel A V Lister; David A Collingwood; Penny A Horne; Paul A Lister; Sylvia J Lister.*

CC Number 288730

Information available Accounts were on file at the Charity Commission.

The trust's annual report and accounts for 2008/09 included the following statement:

The trust formerly had strong links to the UK Sailing Academy but this is now primarily supported by the Whirlwind Charitable Trust having been seeded with £4m capital sum by the trust in June 2007. This has enabled the Lister Charity to have greater impact in other areas of charitable support as demonstrated by the list of donations made during the year.

In 2008/09 the trust had assets of £5.8 million and an income of £230,000. Grants were made during the year totalling £111,000.

The beneficiaries during the year were: the European Nature Trust (£46,000); Oak Lodge School and the Chemical Dependency Centre (£20,000 each); the Challenger Trust (£10,000); and Action of Addiction, the Children's Trust and Ray of Sunshine (£5,000 each).

Exclusions Applications from individuals, including students, are ineligible. No grants are made in response to general appeals from large UK organisations or to smaller bodies working in areas outside its criteria.

Applications In writing to the correspondent. Applications should include clear details of the need the intended project is designed to meet, plus an outline budget. Only applications from eligible bodies are acknowledged, when further information may be requested.

The Second Joseph Aaron Littman Foundation

General

£256,000 (2007/08)

Beneficial area UK.

Manor Farm, Mill Lane, Charlton Mackrell, Somerton TA11 7BQ

Tel. 01458 223 650

Correspondent R J Littman, Trustee

Trustees *Mrs C C Littman; R J Littman; Glenn Hurstfield.*

CC Number 201892

Information available Accounts were on file at the Charity Commission.

This trust has general charitable purposes with special preference for academic and medical research.

In 2007/08 it had assets of £5.3 million and an income of £283,000. Grants were made to totalling £256,000.

The main beneficiary, as in previous years, was Littman Library of Jewish Civilisation which received £220,000. There were 10 further donations of £1,000 or more listed in the accounts. Beneficiaries included: Foundation of Circulatory Health, Lubavitch Senior Girls School and The Spiro Ark (£5,000); University College London and Westminster Synagogue (£2,000 each); Dorset & Somerset Air Ambulance and Marie Curie Nurses (£1,500 each); and Juvenile Diabetes (£1,000).

Sundry donations of less than £1,000 each totalled £6,000.

Exclusions Applications from individuals are not considered.

Applications The trust's funds are fully committed and no new applications are considered.

Jack Livingstone Charitable Trust

Jewish and general

£109,000 (2007/08)

Beneficial area UK and worldwide, with a preference for Manchester.

Westholme, The Springs, Park Road, Bowdon, Altrincham WA14 3JH

Tel. 0161 928 3232

Correspondent Mrs Janice Livingstone, Trustee

Trustees Mrs J V Livingstone; Terence Livingstone; Brian White.

CC Number 263473

Information available Accounts were on file at the Charity Commission.

In 2007/08 the trust had assets of £1.8 million, an income of £95,000 and made grants totalling £109,000. The largest grant of £31,000 went to United Jewish Israel Appeal. Other large grant beneficiaries included: Manchester City Art Gallery (£15,000); Rainscough (£6,000); the Jerusalem Foundation and Community Security Trust (£10,000

each); Bowen Trust, King David School and Royal Exchange (£5,000 each); Christies (£2,000); and Southport Jewish Aged Home, Stockdales and World Jewish Relief (£1,000 each).

Other grants of £1,000 or less each totalled £7,500.

Applications The trust does not respond to unsolicited applications.

The Elaine and Angus Lloyd Charitable Trust

General

£70,000 to organisations (2007/08)

Beneficial area UK, with a preference for Surrey, Kent and the south of England.

Messrs Badger Hakim Chartered Accountants, 10 Dover Street, London W1S 4LQ

Correspondent Ross Badger

Trustees C R H Lloyd; A S Lloyd; J S Gordon; Sir Michael Craig-Cooper; Mrs V E Best; J S Lloyd; Mrs Philippa Satchwell Smith; Revd R J Lloyd.

CC Number 237250

Information available Accounts were on file at the Charity Commission.

In 1992, the Elaine Lloyd Charitable Trust and the Mr Angus Lloyd Charitable Settlement were amalgamated and are now known as the Elaine and Angus Lloyd Charitable Trust. Many grants are recurrent, some may be paid quarterly. Grants are mainly to UK charities and local organisations in the Surrey and Kent area and elsewhere in the south of England. Grants are given in practice to those charities known to one or more of the trustees. Donations are made to:

- any charitable institution whether incorporated or not
- any individual recipients to assist them in meeting education expenses either for themselves or their children
- any individual recipients whose circumstances are such they come within the legal conception of poverty.

In 2007/08 the trust had assets of £2.4 million and an income of £105,000. Grants to organisations totalled £70,000 and grants to individuals totalled £5,600.

Donations to organisations included: Rhemal Religious & Charitable Trust (£5,000); EHAS (£4,200); Alive and Kicking (£2,500); Diabetes UK and Skillway (£2,000 each); Barry Vale Community Aid, Community Life Trust, Martha Trust, Monday to Wednesday Club and Salvation Army (£1,500 each); and Dandelion Trust and St Clements – Sandwich (£1,000 each).

Exclusions No support for overseas aid.

Applications In writing to the correspondent. The trustees meet regularly to consider grants.

The Charles Lloyd Foundation

Construction, repair and maintenance of Roman Catholic buildings, the advancement of Roman Catholic religion and music

About £2,000 (2007/08)

Beneficial area The Roman Catholic Dioceses of Menevia and Wrexham.

8–10 Grosvenor Road, Wrexham, Clwyd LL11 1SD

Tel. 01978 291 000 **Fax** 01978 290493

Email vincentryan@allingtonhughes.co.uk

Correspondent Vincent Ryan, Trustee

Trustees Revd C D S Lloyd; P Walters; T V Ryan; R C A Thorn.

CC Number 235225

Information available Accounts were on file at the Charity Commission.

The trust supports the construction, repair or maintenance of Roman Catholic churches, houses, convents and monasteries, the advancement of Roman Catholic charities in the beneficial area and the promotion and advancement of music, either religious or secular, for public appreciation in or towards national Catholic charities operating in the area of benefit. It prefers to give one-off donations for specific projects.

In 2007/08 it had assets of £1.4 million and an income of £55,000. One grant was made during the year. This was for

£2,000 and went to Caernarfon Catholic Church.

Applications In writing to the correspondent. The trust asks for 'evidence of hardship'. Unsuccessful applications are not acknowledged.

Lloyd's Charities Trust

General

£383,000 (2008)

Beneficial area UK, with particular interest in East London.

One Lime Street, London EC3M 7HA

Tel. 020 7327 6075 **Fax** 020 7327 6368

Email communityaffairs@lloyds.com

Website www.lloyds.com

Correspondent Mrs Vicky Mirfin, Secretary

Trustees *Ms Holly Bellingham; Grahame Chilton; Brian Pomeroy; Anthony Townsend; Graham White; David Gittings; Lawrence Holder; John Spencer; Iain Wilson; Ms Sue Langley.*

CC Number 207232

Information available Accounts were available from the Charity Commission.

The charity was set up in 1953, and is the charitable arm of Lloyd's insurance market in London. In 2008 the trust had assets of nearly £2 million and an income of £507,000. Grants were made in the form of donations and bursaries totalling £383,000. Grantmaking during the year is described in the 2008 report as follows:

Lloyd's Partner Charities (2007–2010)

The trust works with and supports three partner charities over a three year period. The theme for 2007–2010 is 'At Risk' and the partner charities have been selected on the basis of providing innovative projects to support some of those most at risk at home and abroad, with an emphasis on protection of those involved and a focus on prevention of further issues. The current partner charities for 2007–2010 are Coram; FARM-Africa and Samaritans. Grants of £150,000 will be provided to each of the charities over a three year period [a total of £450,000 in all].

The trust aims to promote and support further activities throughout the Lloyd's market to raise additional funds and awareness for the charities' work.

General fund

The majority of the trust's funds are committed to the above three partners. However, ad hoc donations may be made (funds permitting) to international emergencies and other appeals from organisations working in the following areas:

- environmental
- social welfare
- medical/disability
- children and young people
- emergency relief.

In 2008 around 275 unsolicited applications were received and reviewed by the trust. Of these, only seven were able to be given a grant. these were broken down as follows: Emergency relief (three grants totalling £30,000); Children and young people (two grants totalling £12,000); and Medical/disability (two grants totalling £10,000).

Please note: the following statement was included on the trust's website as at end November 2009 – At this time we are not inviting new applications for funding. We will update these pages if an opportunity arises for charities to put forward applications.

Cuthbert Heath Centenary Fund

This is a sub-fund of the trust and aims to provide bursaries at nine named schools. The participating schools are Aldenham, Bishops Stortford, Bradfield, Brighton, Charterhouse, Felsted, Reed's School, Queenswood and Westminster.

During 2008, bursaries totalling nearly £46,000 were made to the above schools. A review of the fund was planned to take place during 2009.

Lloyd's Community Programme

Lloyds Community Programme (LCP) aims to meet its objective of improving the opportunities and the environment for communities in Tower Hamlets and neighbouring East London boroughs by mobilising the support and involvement of individuals and companies in the Lloyds market, primarily through volunteering. LCP also funds local organisations in the field of education, employability and enterprise.

In 2008, over 940 employees from the Lloyds markets took time out to volunteer for various schemes such as: Reading partners; Student Mentoring; Team Challenges; and Sports Volunteering. A total of £99,000 was given in funding during the year to organisations such as: Tower Hamlet Education Business Partnership (£40,000); East London Business Alliance (£18,000); and East London Small Business Centre (£15,000). Other beneficiaries were Inspire!, The National Theatre and Music Platform.

Lloyd's Special Award

This annual award provides a one-off donation of £50,000 to a charity making a positive contribution to an issue of interest to the Lloyd's Market. In 2008, the recipient of the award was the e-Learing Foundation.

Lloyd's Market Charity Awards

These provide employees within the Lloyd's markets to apply for donations of £1,000 on behalf of their chosen charities. Due to the positive response the awards received, the number of donations was increased from the intended 20 to 32 making a total of £32,000 donated.

Exclusions No grants for any appeal where it is likely that the grant would be used for sectarian purposes or to local or regional branches of charities where it is possible to support the UK organisation. Support is not given to individuals.

Applications Lloyd's Charities Trust makes ad hoc donations, however the majority of funds are committed to supporting the partnership charities the trust works with. The trust has previously stated that as funds are committed over a three-year period. 'We are unable to respond positively to the numerous appeals we receive'. Applications are not being invited for partner charity status.

Llysdinam Charitable Trust

General

£119,000 (2007/08)

Beneficial area Wales.

Rees Richards and Partners, Druslyn House, De La Beche Street, Swansea SA1 3HH

Tel. 01792 650 705 **Fax** 01792 468 384

Email post@reesrichards.co.uk

Correspondent The Trustees

Trustees *Mrs M J Elster; N O Tyler; Mrs E S Birkmyre.*

CC Number 255528

Information available Full accounts were on file at the Charity Commission.

In 2007/08 the trust had assets of £4.5 million and an income of £195,000. Grants totalled £119,000.

Beneficiaries included: University of Wales – Cardiff (£16,000); Central Beacons Mountain Rescue Team (£15,000); Christ College Brecon Scholarship (£8,000); Powys Art Forum

(£5,000); Swansea Rugby Foundation (£4,000); Bobath Cymru Children's Therapy (£3,000); Cystic Fibrosis Unit – Singleton Hospital (£2,000); the Sequel Trust (£1,500); Fire Services National Benevolent Unit (£1,000); and Wakes Air Ambulance (£270).

Exclusions No grants to individuals.

Applications The trust stated that it was overloaded with applications and does not welcome unsolicited applications.

Localtrent Ltd

Jewish, education and religion

£118,000 (2007/08)

Beneficial area UK, with some preference for Manchester.

Lopian Gross Barnett and Co., 6th Floor, Cardinal House, 20 St Mary's Parsonage, Manchester M3 2LG

Tel. 0161 832 8721 **Fax** 0161 835 3085

Correspondent A Kahan

Trustees *Mrs M Weiss; B Weiss; P Weiss; Mrs Y Weiss; Mrs Z Weiss; H Weiss.*

CC Number 326329

Information available Full accounts were on file at the Charity Commission.

The trust was established in 1983 for the distribution of funds to religious, educational and similar charities for the advancement of the Jewish religion.

In 2007/08 the trust had assets of £271,000 and an income of £81,000. Grants totalling £118,000 were described as being made 'to a number of institutions which carry out activities such as providing Orthodox Jewish education and other activities which advance Jewish religion in accordance with the Orthodox Jewish faith (e.g. The Chasdei Yoel Charitable Trust: grant £39,360).'

Previous beneficiaries have included: Modos Belz and Yeshivas Sharei Zion (£2,900 each); Congregation Beth Medrash Chemed (£2,300); 3 Pillars Charity, Asser Bishvil and BAT (£1,500 each); and Manchester Killel and Talmudical Torah Yetev Lev (£1,000 each).

Applications In writing to the correspondent.

The Locker Foundation

Jewish

£477,000 (2007/08)

Beneficial area UK and overseas.

28 High Road, East Finchley, London N2 9PJ

Tel. 020 8455 9280

Correspondent The Trustees

Trustees *I Carter; M Carter; Mrs S Segal.*

CC Number 264180

Information available Accounts were on file at the Charity Commission.

The trust mainly supports Jewish organisations. In 2007/08 it had assets of £4.3 million and an income of £708,000. It made 37 grants totalling £477,000.

The largest grant was £57,000 to Kahal Chassidim Bobov. Other major grant beneficiaries included: British Friends of Ezer Mizion and Magen David Adorn (£50,000 each); Supporters of Israel Dependents (£25,000); British Friends of Israel War Disabled (£21,000); British Friends of Rambam Medical Centre (£20,600); Chai Cancer Care and Wizo (£20,150 each); Emunah (£20,000 and Friends of Bnei Akiva (£18,600).

Smaller grants of between £100 and £1,000 were made to Bottoms Up, Friends of Laniado UK, Jewish Child's Day, Jewish Women, Rosh Pinah Primary School and The Swaminarayan Hindu Mission.

Applications In writing to the correspondent.

The Loftus Charitable Trust

Jewish

£355,000 (2007/08)

Beneficial area UK and overseas.

Asher House, Blackburn Road, London NW6 1AW

Tel. 020 7604 5900

Correspondent Anthony Loftus, Trustee

Trustees *R I Loftus; A L Loftus; A D Loftus.*

CC Number 297664

Information available Full accounts were on file at the Charity Commission.

The trust was established in 1987 by Richard Ian Loftus. Its objects are the:

- advancement of the Jewish religion
- advancement of Jewish education and the education of Jewish people
- relief of the Jewish poor.

In 2007/08 the trust had an income of £289,000 and made grants totalling £355,000. These were categorised as follows: religious organisations (£193,000); education (£77,000); and relief of poverty and ill-health (£85,000).

The largest grants were to: South Hampstead Synagogue (£101,000); Lubavitch Foundation (£25,000); Jewish Care (£24,500); Immanuel College (£16,000); Community Security Trust (£15,000); and JNF Charitable Trust (£13,000).

Smaller grants of £5,000 each included those made to the following: British Friends of Tikva Odessa, Shalom Foundation, The Holocaust Foundation, Camp Simcha, Chai Cancer Care and Nightingale House.

Applications The trustees state that all funds are committed and unsolicited applications are not welcome.

The Lolev Charitable Trust

Orthodox Jewish

£241,000 to organisations (2008)

Beneficial area Worldwide.

14a Gilda Crescent, London N16 6JP

Correspondent Abraham Tager, Trustee

Trustees *Abraham Tager; Eve Tager; Michael Tager.*

CC Number 326249

Information available Accounts were on file at the Charity Commission, without a list of grants.

The objects of the charity are the relief of the sick and needy and the support of Orthodox Jewish education.

In 2008 the trust had an income of £3.4 million, mainly from donations. All of the income was distributed in grants during the year.

Most of the trust's charitable expenditure was given towards the relief of sick and needy individuals (£3.1 million), with £241,000 in total awarded to organisations. This naturally indicates that funding individuals is a priority, however it may be the case that eligible applications from educational organisation are considered just as favourably.

Grants to organisations were broken down as follows:

Category	Value
Religious education	£130,000
Poor and needy	£59,000
Medical	£26,000
Schools	£26,000

Applications In writing to the correspondent.

The London Law Trust

Health and personal development of children and young people

£134,000 (2007/08)

Beneficial area UK.

Hunters, 9 New Square, Lincoln's Inn, London WC2A 3QN

Tel. 020 7412 0050

Email londonlawtrust@ hunters-solicitors.co.uk

Website www.thelondonlawtrust.org

Correspondent G D Ogilvie, Secretary

Trustees *Prof. Anthony R Mellows; R A Pellant; Sir Michael Hobbs; Sir Ian Gainsford.*

CC Number 1115266

Information available Accounts were on file at the Charity Commission.

The trust's aims are to support charities which:

- prevent or cure illness and disability in children and young people – via seed-corn grants and grants towards small research projects
- alleviate or reduce the causes or likelihood of illness and disability in children and young people – via grants for new ventures and small support groups for children and young people suffering from more obscure conditions
- encourage and develop in young people the qualities of leadership and service to the community – via grants to national organisations for specific purposes.

In 2007/08 the trust had assets of £3.7 million and an income of £568,000. Grants averaging £3,000 were made to 63 organisations and totalled £134,000. The

beneficiaries were not listed in the accounts.

Previous beneficiaries have included: BRIC, British Lung Foundation, Deans & Canons of Windsor, Great Ormond Street and St George's Hospital Medical School (£5,000 each); Envision (£3,000); Activenture and Swan Syndrome (£2,500 each); and Circomedia (£1,000).

Exclusions Applications from individuals, including students, are ineligible.

Applications In writing to the correspondent. The trustees employ a grant advisor whose job is to evaluate applications. Grant applicants are requested to supply detailed information in support of their applications. The grant advisor makes on-site visits to all applicants and makes a written report.

The directors of the trust meet around May and December to consider the grant advisor's individual visit reports together with the application form, latest accounts and other supporting information. Most applications are considered in December, with payment being made in the following months.

The best time to apply is between January and March.

The William and Katherine Longman Trust

General

£255,000 (2007/08)

Beneficial area UK.

Charles Russell LLP, 8–10 New Fetter Lane, London EC4A 1RS

Tel. 020 7203 5124

Correspondent Paul Harriman, Trustee

Trustees *W P Harriman; J B Talbot; A C O Bell.*

CC Number 800785

Information available Accounts were on file at the Charity Commission.

The trust supports a wide range of organisations with grants ranging from £1,000 to £30,000 each, mostly at the lower end of the scale.

In 2007/08 it had assets of £4 million, which generated an income of £119,000. Grants were made totalling £255,000. Management and administration charges were relatively high at £28,000.

There were 53 grants made during the year. Beneficiaries of grants of £10,000 or more included: Vanessa Grant Trust (£30,000); Chelsea Festival and World Child Cancer Fund (£20,000 each); Care (£12,000); and Hope Education Trust and RADA (£10,000 each).

Other beneficiaries included: Action for ME (£5,000); the Children's Society (£4,500); Age Concern – Kensington & Chelsea (£3,500); RSPCA – Harmsworth Hospital (£3,000); St Mungo's (£2,500); and Prisoners Abroad (£1,000).

Exclusions Grants are only made to registered charities.

Applications The trustees believe in taking a proactive approach in deciding which charities to support and it is their policy not to respond to unsolicited appeals.

The Loseley and Guildway Charitable Trust

General

£35,000 (2007/08)

Beneficial area International and UK, with an interest in Guildford.

The Estate Offices, Loseley Park, Guildford GU3 1HS

Tel. 01483 405 114 **Fax** 01483 302 036

Email charities@loseleypark.co.uk

Website www.loseley-park.com/charities. asp

Correspondent Mrs Julia Barnes, Secretary

Trustees *Maj. James More-Molyneux, Chair; Mrs Susan More-Molyneux; Michael More-Molyneux; Glye Hodson.*

CC Number 267178

Information available Accounts were available from the Charity Commission.

The trust was founded in 1973, when 'the More-Molyneux family injected private capital and transferred five of their own properties to the trust'. The rent of these properties provides about half the trust's present income. Two of these properties have now been sold in order to finance the purchase of land on which CHASE Children's Hospice has now been built.

The trust's accounts state that: 'the objects of the charity are widely drawn to include making grants to charitable associations, trusts, societies and corporations whether they are local, national or international. The major part of the available funds tend to be distributed locally to charitable institutions which the trustees consider to be particularly worthy of support'. In effect this means that major grants tend to be given to charities with which various members of the More-Molyneux family and trustees are associated.

In 2007/08 the trust had assets of £1.2 million, an income of £63,000 and made grants totalling £35,000. Only the top ten grants were listed in the accounts. These were: CHASE and Disability Challengers (£5,000 each); and Brooke Hospital, Cherry Trees, Dame Vera Lynn Trust, Gurkha Welfare Trust, National Society for Epilepsy, Phyllis Tuckwell Hospice and Send a Cow (£1,000 each).

Exclusions No grants to individuals or non-registered charities.

Applications In writing to the correspondent. The trustees meet in February, May and September to consider applications. However, due to commitments, new applications for any causes are unlikely to be successful.

The Lotus Foundation

Children and families, women, community, animal protection, addiction recovery and education

£224,000 (2007)

Beneficial area UK, especially London and Surrey; occasionally overseas.

c/o Startling Music Ltd, 90 Jermyn Street, London SW1Y 6JD

Tel. 020 7930 5133

Website www.lotusfoundation.com

Correspondent Mrs B Starkey, Trustee

Trustees *Mrs B Starkey; R Starkey; Mrs E Turner.*

CC Number 1070111

Information available Accounts were on file at the Charity Commission.

The trust was established in 1998 and aims to make grants to other established and newly-formed charities. The primary

objectives of the trust are 'to support those charities that fall within our aims, [i.e.] children and young people, medical, substance abuse and domestic violence, education, animal welfare and community charities'.

In 2007 the trust had an income of £172,000 and made grants to 47 organisations totalling £224,000. Grants ranged from £200 to £21,000 and included the following major beneficiaries: WaterAid (£21,000); Training the Teachers of Tomorrow (£20,000); RAPT (£16,000); Médicins Sans Frontières (£11,000); and Shorefields School – Liverpool and Tower Hamlets Mission (£10,000 each).

Beneficiaries of smaller grants included: Fine Cell Work (£5,000); Scope (£3,000); World Horse Welfare (£2,000); the National Police Community Trust (£1,000); Children with Leukaemia (£400); and Motor Neurone Disease Association (£200).

Exclusions No response to circular appeals. No grants to individuals, non-registered charities, charities working outside of the foundation's areas of interest, or for research purposes.

Applications In writing to the correspondent giving a brief outline of the work, amount required and project/programme to benefit. The trustees prefer applications which are simple and economically prepared rather than glossy 'prestige' and mail sorted brochures.

Please note: In order to reduce administration costs and concentrate its efforts on the charitable work at hand, unsolicited requests will no longer be acknowledged by the foundation.

C L Loyd's Charitable Trust

General

£111,000 (2007/08)

Beneficial area UK, with a preference for Berkshire and Oxfordshire.

Betterton House, Lockinge, Wantage OX12 8QL

Tel. 01235 833 265

Correspondent C L Loyd, Trustee

Trustees *C L Loyd; T C Loyd.*

CC Number 265076

Information available Accounts were on file at the Charity Commission.

The trust supports UK charities and local charities (in Berkshire and Oxfordshire) involved in welfare, animals, churches, medical/disability, children/young people and education.

In 2007/08 the trust had assets of £2.5 million, an income of £91,000 and made grants totalling £111,000.

The accounts only listed beneficiaries of grants of £1,000 or more. These were: Country Buildings Protection Trust (£49,000); Ashmolean Museum (£15,000); Wantage Town Governors Appeal and Wantage Vale and Downland Museum (£10,000 each); Ardington and Lockinge Tennis Club (£5,000); British Red Cross (£3,200); King Alfred Education (£3,000); Christian Aid (£2,100); Ardington and Lockinge PCC (£1,140); and East Hendred PCC and PACE (£1,000 each).

Exclusions No support for individuals or medical research.

Applications In writing to the correspondent. Grants are made several times each month.

Henry Lumley Charitable Trust

General, medical, educational and relief of poverty or hardship

£136,000 (2008)

Beneficial area England and Wales.

Grove End, Bagshot GU1 5HY

Tel. 01276 472273

Correspondent Peter Lumley, Trustee

Trustees *Henry Lumley; Peter Lumley; Robert Lumley; James Porter.*

CC Number 1079480

Information available Accounts were on file at the Charity Commission.

Registered in February 2000, the income of the trust is derived from the dividends and interest received from shares in the private company Edward Lumley Holdings Ltd. Charities supported should be known to at least one trustee. Aside from the founder's initial list of beneficiaries, new charities have been added as funds permit and are usually of a one-off nature to assist medical or educational projects.

In 2008 the trust had assets of £2.9 million and an income of £109,000. Grants totalling £136,000 were made to 29 organisations, most of which were recurring in nature. Although established as a general charitable trust, grants effectively cover three main areas, namely, medical, educational and relief of poverty and hardship which were broken down as follows:

Category	No.	Value
Medical	29	£113,000
Educational	2	£11,000
Relief of poverty and hardship	4	£10,000
Other	1	£2,000

Beneficiaries included: Royal College of Surgeons (£20,000); Eton College Foundation (£10,000); Action on Addiction, British Liver Trust, Discs, International Spinal Research, Northwick Park Institute, and Tuberous Sclerosis Association (£5,000 each); Parity, Royal British Legion and Royal Star and Garter Home for Disabled Ex-service Men and Women (£2,500 each); and Outward Bound Trust (£1,000).

Applications In writing to the correspondent.

Paul Lunn-Rockliffe Charitable Trust

Christianity, poverty, infirm people and young people

£39,000 (2007/08)

Beneficial area UK and Developing World.

4a Barnes Close, Winchester SO23 9QX

Tel. 01962 852 949 **Fax** 01962 852 949

Correspondent Mrs J M Lunn-Rockliffe, Secretary

Trustees *Mrs Jacqueline Lunn-Rockliffe; Victor Lunn-Rockliffe; James Lunn-Rockliffe.*

CC Number 264119

Information available Accounts were on file at the Charity Commission.

The following is taken from the 2007/08 annual report.

The object of the charity is to make grants to any charity or for any charitable purpose, at the trustees discretion, but preferably to those recipients likely to further Christianity,

support the relief of poverty and assist the aged and infirm.

The charity has supported 75 separate charities during the year... [and] maintains a database of details and financial data for the charities supported. The latest financial information for recipient charities is reviewed and their achievements assessed, prior to donating further funds.

The trustees have a policy of restricting the total number of recipient charities in order to ensure that each receives a more significant donation and has a preference for smaller and locally based charities, or those known to the trustees or members of their families.

The trustees allocate a proportion of the funds for donation to be applied to charities not previously supported and for special one-off causes.

In 2007/08 the trust had assets of £869,000 and an income of £41,000. Grants totalled £39,000 and were made within the following categories: older people; children; disabled people; education and students; family; mission; those in need, drug users, homeless and unemployed people; prisoners; radio/mission; developing world; and 'others'.

Beneficiaries included: Christians Against Poverty (£1,100); Winchester Night Shelter (£1,000); Bible Society and Care (£800 each); Action for Elder Abuse, Children Country Holiday Fund, Fusion, Salvation Army, Spastics Society of India and Touchstones 12 (£500 each); Way of Life (£400); and Gateway Club (£300).

Exclusions The trustees will not fund individuals; for example, student's expenses and travel grants. Repair and maintenance of historic buildings are also excluded for support.

Applications The trust encourages preliminary phone calls to discuss applications. It will generally only reply to written correspondence if a stamped, addressed envelope has been included.

The Ruth and Jack Lunzer Charitable Trust

Jewish, children, young adults, education and the arts

£57,000 (2007/08)

Beneficial area UK.

c/o Berwin Leighton Paisner, Adelaide House, London Bridge, London EC4R 9HA

Tel. 020 7760 1000

Correspondent M D Paisner, Trustee

Trustees *J V Lunzer; M D Paisner.*

CC Number 276201

Information available Accounts were on file at the Charity Commission.

The trust says it makes grants to organisations benefiting children, young adults and students; primarily educational establishments. In practice many such beneficiaries are Jewish organisations.

In 2007/08 the trust had assets of £44,000 and an income of £60,000, with grants totalling £57,000.

The largest grants went to Kahal Chassidim Bobov (£11,000) and Yesoday Hatorah Schools (£10,000).

Other beneficiaries included: Chai Cancer Care (£5,250); Hampstead Heath (£2,900); North West London Communal Mikvah (£2,000); Central Square Minyan and GGBH Congregation (£1,500 each); Jerusalem Foundation and Royal College of Music (£1,000 each); Three Faiths Forum and Lambeth Palace Gallery (£500 each); and Glyndebourne Arts Trust (£250).

Applications In writing to the correspondent. Unsuccessful applicants are not acknowledged.

Lord and Lady Lurgan Trust

Medical charities, older people, children and the arts

£61,000 (2007)

Beneficial area UK and South Africa.

c/o Pemberton Greenish, 45 Pont Street, London SW1X 0BX

Tel. 020 7591 3515

Email charitymanager@pg-aw.co.uk

Correspondent Mrs Diana Burke

Trustees *Simon David Howard Ladd Staughton; Andrew John Francis Stebbings; Diana Sarah Graves*

CC Number 297046

Information available Accounts were on file at the Charity Commission.

The registered objects of this trust are:

- the relief and medical care of older people
- medical research, in particular cancer research and the publication of the useful results of such research
- the advancement of education including education in the arts for the public benefit by the establishment of educational and artistic bursaries
- other charitable purposes at the discretion of the trustees.

There is also special interest in: South Africa (due to the settlors spending the latter part of their lives there) with about one quarter of the funds available being distributed there; in music; and in Northern Ireland because of family origins.

In 2007 the trust had assets of £1.5 million and an income of £45,000. Grants totalling £61,000 were made to 49 beneficiaries.

Grant distribution is divided into two key areas:

Institutional grants in the UK (excluding Scotland) – 32 grants totalling £44,000 including those to: Royal College of Music (£10,000); English National Opera and Queen's University – Belfast (£2,000 each); Greater Shankhill Business Forum (£1,540); and Deafblind UK, Help the Aged, Macmillan Cancer Relief, Oesophageal Patients Association, St Joseph's Hospice and Water Aid (£1,000 each).

South Africa – 17 grants of about £1,000 each, including those to Blind SA, The Community Chest Trust, Deaf Federation of South Africa, Forest Town School for Cerebral Palsied Children, Princess Alice Adoption Home and Woodside Sanctuary.

Applications In writing to the correspondent.

The Lyndhurst Trust

Christian

£66,000 (2007)

Beneficial area UK and overseas, with preferences for north east England and the developing world.

PO Box 615, North Shields, Tyne and Wear NE29 1AP

Correspondent The Secretary

Trustees *Revd Dr R Ward; Mrs Jane Hinton; Ben Hinton; Mrs Sally Tan.*

CC Number 235252

Information available Accounts were on file at the Charity Commission.

The trust's accounts stated the following.

The trustees have continued to support opportunities to promote and advance the spreading of the Christian religion in any part of the world. The policy has been continued of supporting regularly charities that are promoting the awareness of the Christian gospel, in those areas of the World where people are prevented from hearing it through normal channels of communication. Agencies operating in difficult circumstances are given special consideration.

The trustees have continued their policy of making funds available to the disadvantaged in the United Kingdom. In addition, the trustees give special consideration to charities involved in supporting members of the persecuted church around the world. Churches in the north east of England have been given increased support due to the particular needs of the communities where they are operating.

During 2007 it had assets of £1.6 million and an income of £48,000. Grants totalled £66,000 and were broken down as follows:

Category	No. of grants	£	% of total
North east of England	9	44,000	67.0
Developing countries	12	17,000	25.5
United Kingdom	3	4,000	6.0
Europe/Rest of World	1	1,000	1.5

Grants in the UK and north east of England included: NE1 (Just 10) – Tyneside (£20,000); St Aidan's Community Church – Middlesbrough (£6,000); Bible Reading Fellowship – Tyneside (£5,000); Friends International (£2,000); and David Pawson Teaching Trust and Urban Saints – Crusaders (£1,000 each).

Exclusions No support for individuals or buildings.

Applications In writing to the correspondent, enclosing a stamped, addressed envelope if a reply is required. Requests are considered half-yearly.

The Lynn Foundation

General

£283,000 (2007/08)

Beneficial area UK and overseas.

Blackfriars, 17 Lewes Road, Haywards Heath RH17 7SP

Tel. 01444 454 773 **Fax** 01444 456 192

Correspondent Guy Parsons, Chairman of the Trustees

Trustees *Guy Parsons, Chair; J F Emmott; Dr P E Andry; P R Parsons; Ian Fair; John Sykes.*

CC Number 326944

Information available Accounts were on file at the Charity Commission, but without any narrative.

The trust has previously stated that it supports a very wide range of organisations, including those in the areas of music, the arts, Masonic charities, disability, older people and children.

During 2007/08 grants were made to 491 organisations and totalled £283,000. Details of individual beneficiaries were not available, although the total was broken down as follows:

Category	No. of grants	£
Music and the arts	119	88,000
Disabled children	141	73,000
Disabled adults	121	63,000
Youth sponsorship	43	27,000
Medical research	35	17,000
Hospices	32	16,000
Sundry	0	0

Applications In writing to the correspondent.

The Lyons Charitable Trust

Health, animals and children

£95,000 (2007/08)

Beneficial area UK.

74 Broad Walk, London N21 3BX

Tel. 020 8882 1336

Correspondent Michael Gibbon

Trustees *M S Gibbon; J Gibbon; G Read.*

CC Number 1045650

Information available Accounts were on file at the Charity Commission.

The trust in particular makes grants in the fields of health, medical research, animals and children in need. The same 11 charities are supported each year.

In 2007/08 it had assets of £1.5 million and an income of £394,000. Grants were made totalling £95,000.

The beneficiaries each year are: The Royal Marsden Hospital and Macmillan Cancer Relief (£20,000 each); Helen House (£12,000); St Thomas Hospital and Streetsmart (£10,000 each); CLIC and One25 Ltd. (£5,000 each); Cambridge Curwen Print Study Centre, Cats Protection League, Children with Aids and Walthamstow Stadium Greyhounds (£3,000 each).

Applications The trust has stated that it is closed to new applications.

The Sir Jack Lyons Charitable Trust

Jewish, arts and education

£122,000 (2007/08)
Beneficial area UK and Israel.

Sagars, 3rd Floor, Elizabeth House, Queen Street, Leeds LS1 2TW
Tel. 0133 297 6789
Correspondent Paul Mitchell
Trustees *Lady Roslyn Marion Lyons; M J Friedman; D S Lyons; Miss A R J Maude-Roxby; P D Mitchell.*
CC Number 212148
Information available Full accounts were on file at the Charity Commission.

This trust shows a particular interest in Jewish charities and also a consistent interest in the arts, particularly music. In 2007/08 it had assets of £3.6 million and an income of £224,000. Grants were made to 11 organisations totalling £122,000.

The four largest grants went to: Youth Futures in Beer Sheva (£50,000); UJIA (£25,000); Naeh Youth Centre (£24,000); and Ben-Gurion University (£7,500).

The remaining grants went to: London Symphony Orchestra (£7,000); The Technion Israel and University of Haifa Israel (£2,500 each); York Early Music Festival (£1,500); and Aldeburgh Festival and Jewish Institute of Music (£500 each).

Exclusions No grants to individuals.
Applications In writing to the correspondent. In the past the trust has stated: 'In the light of increased pressure for funds, unsolicited appeals are less welcome and would waste much time and money for applicants who were looking for funds which were not available'.

Malcolm Lyons Foundation

Jewish

£51,000 (2007/08)
Beneficial area UK.

BDO Stoy Hayward, 55 Baker Street, London W1U 7EU
Tel. 020 7893 2602
Correspondent Jeremy Newman, Trustee
Trustees *M S Lyons; Mrs J Lyons; J S Newman.*
CC Number 1050689
Information available Full accounts were on file at the Charity Commission.

This trust supports Jewish and Israeli organisations. In 2007/08 it had assets of £80,000 and an income of £102,000 mainly from donations. Grants totalled £51,000.

There were 14 grants listed in the accounts. Beneficiaries included: Sage (£20,000); L'Ecole Juive du Cannes (£7,000); Chai Cancer Care (£5,500); Lubavitch Foundation (£4,000); Child Resettlement Fund (£2,300); Noam Primary School (£1,500); British Friends of Ezer Mizion and Jewish Care (£500 each); Camp Simcha (£100); and British Emunah (£10).

Applications The trust states that it will not consider unsolicited applications.

The M and C Trust

Social welfare and Jewish

£161,000 (2006/07)
Beneficial area UK.

c/o Chantrey Vellacott DFK, Russell Square House, 10–12 Russell Square, London WC1B 5LF
Tel. 020 7509 9000 **Fax** 020 7509 9219
Correspondent Chris Jones, Secretary
Trustees *Lord Bernstein; Rachel J Lebus; Joyce Kemble.*
CC Number 265391
Information available Accounts were on file at the Charity Commission.

The trust's primary charitable objects are Jewish causes and social welfare.

In 2006/07 the trust had assets of £5.2 million and an income of £140,000. Grants totalled £161,000.

The three largest grants went to Jewish Care and Norwood (£20,000 each) and Jerusalem Foundation (£15,000).

Other beneficiaries included: Jewish Children's Holiday Fund, Marchant Holiday School and One Voice Europe (£10,000 each); Nightingale House (£7,500); Parentline (£7,000); Institute for Jewish Policy Research and TreeHouse (£5,000 each); Break (£4,000); and Chicken Shed Theatre (£3,000).

The trust is connected with Quercus Trust, being under the same administration and having similar objectives.

Exclusions No grants to individuals.
Applications In writing to the correspondent, but the trust states that funds are currently earmarked for existing projects. In order to keep administration costs to a minimum, they are unable to reply to any unsuccessful applications.

The M D and S Charitable Trust

Jewish

£301,000 (2007/08)
Beneficial area UK and Israel.

15 Riverside Drive, Golders Green Road, London NW11 9PU
Tel. 020 7272 2255
Correspondent Martin D Cymerman, Trustee
Trustees *M D Cymerman; Mrs S Cymerman.*
CC Number 273992

Information available Full accounts were on file at the Charity Commission.

The trust supports Jewish organisations in the UK and has general charitable purposes in Israel.

In 2007/08 the trust had assets of £2.4 million and an income of £301,000. Grants to 22 organisations totalled £301,000.

The largest grants went to: Kolel Breslaw (£26,000); Beit Yisroel Benevolent Fund (£24,000); United Torah Institutions of Gur (£23,000); and Kolel Rashbi (£21,000).

Other beneficiaries included: Ponevez Aid and Benevolence Trust (£17,000); Chovat Hatalmidim Fund (£14,000); Gevurath Ari Academy Trust (£10,000); Kolel Polin (£9,000); TAT Family Relief Fund (£5,000); and Lovlev Trust (£4,000);

Applications In writing to the correspondent.

The E M MacAndrew Trust

Medical, children and general

£58,000 (2007/08)

Beneficial area UK.

J P Thornton and Co., The Old Dairy, Adstockfields, Adstock, Buckingham MK18 2JE

Tel. 01296 714886 **Fax** 01296 714711

Correspondent J P Thornton, Administrator

Trustees *Amanda Nicholson; J K Nicholson; Sally Grant; Verity Webster.*

CC Number 290736

Information available Accounts were on file at the Charity Commission.

The trust is mainly interested in medical and children's charities. In 2007/08 it had assets of £1.2 million and an income of £62,000. Grants totalling £58,000 were made to 32 organisations.

Major beneficiaries included: Buckinghamshire County Agricultural Association and Buckinghamshire Foundation (£5,000 each); Action 4 Youth, Bletchley Park Trust and Calibre Audio Library (£3,000 each); Cystic

Fibrosis Trust and Smile Train UK (£2,000 each); RAF Benevolent Fund and Willen Hospice (£1,000); and Crossroads (£500).

Applications The trustees state that they do not respond to any unsolicited applications under any circumstances, as they prefer to make their own decisions as to which charities to support.

The Macdonald-Buchanan Charitable Trust

General

£111,000 (2008)

Beneficial area UK, with a slight preference for Northamptonshire.

Rathbone Trust Co. Ltd, 159 New Bond Street, London W1S 2UD

Tel. 020 7399 0820

Email linda.cousins@rathbone.com

Correspondent Miss Linda Cousins

Trustees *Capt. John Macdonald-Buchanan, Chair; A J Macdonald-Buchanan; A R Macdonald-Buchanan; H J Macdonald-Buchanan; Mrs M C A Philipson.*

CC Number 209994

Information available Accounts were on file at the Charity Commission.

The Hon. Catherine Macdonald-Buchanan set up this trust in 1952 for general charitable purposes and endowed it with 40,000 shares in the then Distillers Company.

In 2008 the trust had assets of £2.8 million and an income of £139,000. Grants totalled £111,000.

Overall, grants by category of the recipient charity were broken down as follows:

Category	Value
General welfare	£44,800
Medical and research	£17,600
Forces welfare charities	£15,900
Welfare of young people	£9,800
Disabled charities	£8,600
Welfare of older people	£4,600
Animal welfare	£4,300
Hospices	£3,500
Religion	£1,700

The largest grants included those made to: Carriejo Charity and Orrin Charitable Trust (£15,000 each); Ghurka Welfare, Help for Heroes and Skill Force (£5,000 each); and Charities Aid Foundation (£4,000).

Smaller grants of £500 each went to: Artists' General Benevolent Institution, Hearing Dogs for the Deaf, Migraine Trust, Order of St John, Salvation Army and Wheel Power.

Exclusions No grants to individuals.

Applications In writing to the correspondent, for consideration once a year. Appeals will not be acknowledged.

The Macfarlane Walker Trust

Education, the arts, social welfare and general

£15,000 to organisations (2007/08)

Beneficial area UK, with priority for Gloucestershire.

60 Flask Walk, London NW3 1HE

Correspondent Miss C Walker, Secretary

Trustees *D F Walker; N G Walker.*

CC Number 227890

Information available Accounts were on file at the Charity Commission.

This trust has a particular interest in the provision of facilities for recreation and social welfare in Gloucestershire, the relief of poverty and hardship among employees and former employees of Walker Crosweller and Co Ltd, the provision of educational facilities particularly in scientific research and the encouragement of music, drama and the fine arts. The trust also prefers to support small projects where they believe their 'contribution will be significant.'

In 2007/08 the trust had assets of £628,000, an income of £33,000 and made grants to 11 organisations totalling £15,000.

Beneficiaries included: Gloucestershire Association for Mental Health and National Star College (£2,000 each); Gloucester Choral Society, North Cotswolds Voluntary Help Centre, Prestbury & Pittville Youth and St Peters Church of England Primary School (£1,000 each); CVOPHA – Home for Independent Elderly Residents (£500); and Help The Aged – Podsmead Neighbourhood Project (£100).

Exclusions No grants for expeditions, medical expenses, nationwide appeals, animal charities or educational fees.

Applications In writing to the correspondent giving the reason for applying, and an outline of the project with a financial forecast. A stamped, addressed envelope must accompany the initial application.

The Mactaggart Third Fund

General

£414,000 (2008/09)

Beneficial area UK and abroad.

One Red Place, London W1K 6PL

Website www.mactaggartthirdfund.org

Correspondent The Trustees

Trustees Sandy Mactaggart; Robert Gore; Fiona Mactaggart; Andrew Mactaggart; Sir John Mactaggart.

SC Number SC014285

Information available Accounts were available to download from the charity's website.

The Mactaggart Third Fund is a grant-making charity, established in 1968 by Deed of Trust granted by Western Heritable Investment Company Limited. The objectives of the trust are to distribute funds by way of charitable donations to suitable charities in the United Kingdom and abroad. The trustees have decided to take a proactive approach to their grantmaking. Their present policy is to make grants to those charities whose aims they support and who they believe have demonstrated excellence in their achievements. Please note the fund does not accept unsolicited applications.

The trust aims to make grants of circa £250,000 each year and since its inauguration it has made grants of over £4 million to a range of charitable organisations.

In 2008/09 it had assets of almost £9.5 million and an income of £506,000. Grants totalled £414,000. Major beneficiaries included: St Mary's Paddington Charitable Trust (£50,000); Amazon Conservation Team – Orito Sanctuary Project (£28,000); WPSI – UK (£25,000); Bahamas National Trust (£16,000); Friends of the Environment (£15,000); Mactaggart Community Cybercafe (£11,000).

Other beneficiaries included: Ella Edgar School of Dancing (£6,300); Angling for

Youth Development (£5,200); Medical Aid for Palestinians (£3,000); Scottish Countryside Alliance Education Trust (£2,000); the Red Squirrel Survival Trust (£1,000); and Seeing Ear (£750).

Applications 'The trustees are solely responsible for the choice of charitable organisations to be supported. Trustees are proactive in seeking out charities to support and all projects are chosen on the initiative of the trustees. Unsolicited applications are not supported.'

Ian Mactaggart Trust

Education and training, culture, welfare and disability

£322,000 (2008/09)

Beneficial area UK, with a preference for Scotland.

One Red Place, London, W1K 6PL

Website www.ianmactaggarttrust. org/index.htm

Correspondent The Trustees

Trustees Sir John Mactaggart; P A Mactaggart; Jane L Mactaggart; Fiona M Mactaggart; Lady Caroline Mactaggart.

SC Number SC012502

Information available Accounts were available on the trust's website.

The Ian Mactaggart Trust is a grant-making charity, established in 1984. The objectives of the trust are to distribute funds by way of charitable donations to suitable charities in the United Kingdom and abroad. The trustees have decided to take a proactive approach to their grantmaking. Their present policy is to make grants to those charities whose aims they support and who they believe have demonstrated excellence in their achievements.

In 2008/09 grants totalled £322,000. Major beneficiaries were: Robin Hood Foundation (£52,000); St Mary's Paddington Charitable Trust (£50,000); Oxfordshire Community Foundation (£22,000); Groundwork Thames Valley (£15,000); Toynbee Hall (£12,000); Islay, Jura and Community Enterprise Trust and Macmillan Cancer Support (£10,000 each).

Other beneficiaries included: Billy's Appeal – CLIC Sargent (£8,000); Medical Foundation for the Victim's of Torture

(£3,000); the English Stage Co. Ltd (£2,000); For Dementia (£1,000); Enable Glasgow (£500); and Quaker Social Action (£250).

Applications The trustees are committed to seeking out charitable organisations that they wish to support and therefore they do not respond to unsolicited applications.

The Magen Charitable Trust

Education and Jewish

£44,000 (2007/08)

Beneficial area UK.

New Riverside, 439 Lower Broughton, Salford M7 2FX

Tel. 0161 792 2626

Correspondent The Trustees

Trustees Jacob Halpern; Mrs Rose Halpern.

CC Number 326535

Information available Accounts were on file at the Charity Commission, but without a list of grants.

In the accounts the trust's aims were stated as making donations to charitable and educational institutions. In 2007/08 the trust had assets of £1.4 million and an income of £56,000. Grants were made totalling £44,000.

Previous beneficiaries have included Manchester Yeshiva Kollel, Talmud Educational Trust, Bnos Yisroel School and Mesifta Tiferes Yisroel.

Applications In writing to the correspondent.

Mageni Trust

Arts

£22,000 to organisations
(2007/08)

Beneficial area UK.

5 Hyde Vale, Greenwich SE10 8QQ

Tel. 020 8469 2683

Email garfcollins@gmail.com

Correspondent Garfield Collins, Trustee

Trustees G L Collins; Mrs G L Collins; S J Hoare.

CC Number 1070732

Information available Accounts were on file at the Charity Commission.

In 2007/08 the trust had assets of £1.2 million, an income of £63,000 and made grants to the total of £28,000. This included two single grants to individuals totalling £6,000.

There were 22 donations made in the year, including those to: LPO Thomas Beecham Group (£3,000); National Youth Orchestra (£2,500); A Feast of Music for Beckenham (£2,350); Crisis (£2,000); Extra Care, Marie Curie Cancer Care and National Theatre (£1,000 each); Opera Rara (£500); Maternity Worldwide (£370); Hope for the World (£200); and Cancer Research and YMCA (£100 each).

Applications In writing to the correspondent.

Mahavir Trust (also known as the K S Mehta Charitable Trust)

General, medical, welfare, relief of poverty, overseas aid and religion

£220,000 (2007/08)
Beneficial area UK.

19 Hillersdon Avenue, Edgware, Middlesex HA8 7SG
Tel. 020 8958 4883
Email mahavirtrust@googlemail.com
Correspondent Jay Mehta
Trustees *Jay Mehta; Pravin Mehta; Kumud Mehta; Mrs Sheena Mehta Sabharwal; Nemish Mehta; Mrs P H Mehta; Mrs Sudha Mehta; Humar Mehta.*
CC Number 298551
Information available Accounts were on file at the Charity Commission.

In 2007/08 the trust had assets of £324,000 and an income of £120,000, mainly from donations and gifts. Grants totalled £220,000 and were broken down as follows:

- Jain religion – £127,000
- advancement of education in rural areas – £56,000

- relief of poverty, sickness and distress – £22,000
- promotion of humane behaviour towards animals and vegetarianism – £14,000
- relief of financial need for victims of natural disasters – £1,000.

Applications The trust states that it does not accept unsolicited applications.

Malbin Trust

Jewish and general

£78,000 (2006/07)
Beneficial area Worldwide.

8 Cheltenham Crescent, Salford M7 0FE
Tel. 0161 792 7343
Correspondent B Leitner, Trustee
Trustees *B Leitner; M Leitner; J Waldman.*
CC Number 1045174
Information available Accounts were on file at the Charity Commission, but without a list of beneficiaries.

In 2006/07 the trust had assets of £502,000 and an income of £115,000. Grants totalled £78,000. No details of the beneficiaries were included with the accounts.

Applications In writing to the correspondent.

The Mandeville Trust

Cancer, young people and children

£58,000 (2007/08)
Beneficial area UK.

The Hockett, Hockett Lane, Cookham Dean, Berkshire SL6 9UF
Tel. 01628 484 272
Correspondent R C Mandeville, Trustee
Trustees *Robert Cartwright Mandeville; Pauline Maud Mandeville; Peter William Murcott; Justin Craigie Mandeville.*
CC Number 1041880
Information available Accounts were on file at the Charity Commission.

In 2007/08 the trust had an income of £58,000 and made grants totalling

£58,000. The grant beneficiaries were: University College London (£26,000) and Imperial College (£20,000) for research purposes; and the Berkshire Community Foundation (£10,000). Other smaller grants totalled £2,500.

Applications In writing to the correspondent.

Maranatha Christian Trust

Christian, relief of poverty and education of young people

£100,000 to organisations and individuals (2007/08)
Beneficial area UK and overseas.

208 Cooden Drive, Bexhill-on-Sea TN39 3AH
Tel. 01424 844 741
Correspondent The Secretary
Trustees *A C Bell; Revd L Bowring; Rt Hon. Viscount Brentford.*
CC Number 265323
Information available Accounts were on file at the Charity Commission.

The trust's objectives are the promotion of education among young persons and the relief of poverty, particularly among those professing the Christian religion or working to promote such religion.

In 2007/08 the trust had assets of £1 million and an income of £34,000. Grants were made to various organisations and seven individuals and totalled just under £100,000. Grants of less than £1,000 each were not listed, but accounted for £5,500 of the total given.

The largest grants were to Christian Action Research and Education (£17,000 in three grants) and £10,000 to The Vanessa Grant Memorial Trust.

Other beneficiaries included: Cafe Africa Trust and Micah Trust (£7,000 each); Friends of St Andrew's Church (£5,000); The Office for International Diplomacy (£3,500); Concordis International (£3,000); Cheer (£2,500); Re Source (£2,000); and Forty-Three Trust and Christians in Entertainment (£1,000 each).

Applications In writing to the correspondent, but please note, the trust does not consider unsolicited applications.

Marbeh Torah Trust

Jewish education and religion, and the relief of poverty

£142,000 (2007)

Beneficial area UK and Israel.

116 Castlewood Road, London N15 6BE

Correspondent M C Elzas, Trustee

Trustees *Moishe Chaim Elzas; Jacob Naftoli Elzas; Simone Elzas.*

CC Number 292491

Information available Accounts were on file at the Charity Commission.

The trust's objects are to further and support Jewish education and religion, as well as the relief of poverty.

In 2007 the trust had an income of £162,000, almost entirely comprised of donations received. Grants were made to nine organisations and totalled £142,000. Major beneficiaries were Yeshiva Marbeh Torah (£72,000), Yad Gershon (£22,000), Kol Yaakov (£12,000), Chazon Avraham Yitzchak, Mishkenos Yaakov and Tashbar (£10,000 each).

Smaller grants went to Shaarei Limud (£2,600), Beis Dovid (£2,500) and Nechomas Isser Israel (£2,000).

Applications In writing to the correspondent.

The Marchday Charitable Fund

Education, health, social welfare, support groups and overseas aid

£184,000 (2008)

Beneficial area UK, with a preference for south-east England.

c/o Marchday Group plc, Lingfield Point, McMullen Road, Darlington DL1 1RW

Tel. 0845 888 7070

Correspondent Mrs Rose Leigh, Trustee

Trustees *Alan Mann; Lyndsey Mann; Dudley Leigh; Rose Leigh; Maureen Postles; Graham Smith; John Orchard; Priyen Gudka.*

CC Number 328438

Information available Accounts were on file at the Charity Commission.

The trust was established in 1989 to support charities and projects in a broad spectrum of education, health, social welfare, support groups and overseas aid. The trustees wish to assist small charities where a grant will support a particular project or make a difference to the continuation of the charity. There is a preference for charities in the south east of England. The trust also prefers to commit itself to three years' support rather than give a one-off grant, and revenue funding is preferred. The trustees like to have continual involvement with supported charities.

In 2008 the fund had assets of £404,000 and an income of £97,000 of which £75,000 was received in gift aid from Marchday Group plc. However, the company has stated that in the current economic climate it will not be supporting the fund. Grants were made to 22 organisations (the majority of which have been supported in previous years) and totalled £184,000.

Beneficiaries included: Tunbridge Wells Mental Health (£11,000); Prisoners Advice Service, Refugee Support Group – Devon and Warwickshire Women's Refuge (£10,000 each); Bridewell Organic Gardens (£9,000); Kidscape (£8,000); After Adoption and Pimlico Toy Library (£7,000 each); and Magic Lantern and Red R (£5,000 each).

Exclusions The trust prefers not to support local organisations outside the south east of England. No grants to individuals or towards building projects or for religious activities.

Applications In writing to the correspondent. Replies cannot be sent to all requests. Trustees meet quarterly.

Marchig Animal Welfare Trust

Animal welfare

£332,000 (2007)

Beneficial area Worldwide.

10 Queensferry Street, Edinburgh EH2 4PG

Tel. 0131 225 6039 **Fax** 0131 220 6377

Email info@marchigtrust.org

Website www.marchigtrust.org

Correspondent The Trustees

Trustees *Madame Jeanne Marchig; Dr Bill Jordan; Colin Moor.*

CC Number 802133

Information available Accounts were on file at the Charity Commission. Further information is available via the website.

The objects of the trust are to protect animals and to promote and encourage practical work in preventing cruelty. There are no restrictions on the geographical area of work, types of grants or potential applicants, but all applications must be related to animal welfare and be of direct benefit to animals. Projects supported by the trust have included mobile spay/neuter clinics, alternatives to the use of animals in research, poster campaigns, anti-poaching programmes, establishment of veterinary hospitals, clinics and animal sanctuaries.

There are no restrictions on the geographical area of the work, the type of grant, or the applicant. All applications meeting the following criteria will be considered by the trust.

- Those encouraging initiatives designed to improve animal welfare.
- Those promoting alternative methods to animal experimentation and their practical implementation.
- Those promoting and encouraging practical work in alleviating suffering and preventing cruelty to animals.

As well as giving grants, the trust also makes Jeanne Marchig Awards. These awards, which take the form of a financial donation in support of the winner's animal welfare work, are given in either of the following two categories.

- The development of an alternative method to the use of animals in experimental procedures and the practical implementation of such an alternative resulting in a significant reduction in the number of animals used in experimental procedures.
- Practical work in the field of animal welfare resulting in significant improvements for animals either nationally or internationally.

In 2007 the trust had assets of £14.3 million, an income of £500,000 and made grants totalling £332,000.

Grants in 2007
The trust's website gives many examples of projects that have been supported worldwide recently, although the amounts awarded are not given.

Projects included: the rescue and subsequent care of various species of animals in Lebanon, South Africa,

Philippines, Israel, Egypt, Romania, India, Greece, Poland, Mauritius, Italy, Czech Republic and the UK; spay/neuter programmes and their promotion in Turkey, Greece, Portugal, Spain, Cyprus, South Africa, the UK, Eire, Sri Lanka, Romania, Israel, Malta, Brazil, France, Indonesia and India; providing on-going support for the activities of a mobile clinic in Turkey and grants to establish mobile clinic's and other veterinary/care vehicles in India, Lebanon, South Africa, Kenya, Thailand and the UK; assisting with the construction, renovation, maintenance and ongoing operations of animal shelters in Thailand, Greece, Romania, the UK, Bolivia, South Africa, Israel, India and Belgium; support was given for the promotion internationally of various education programmes relating to the care, responsible ownership and importance of animal birth control measures; in addition, support was given for the campaign against canned hunting in South Africa, investigations into the live export trade of animals from Australia to the Middle East and wildlife anti-poaching measures; veterinary medicines to relieve the suffering of animals was provided to various organisations in a number of countries.

Exclusions The trust will reject any application failing to meet its criteria. Additionally, applications relating to educational studies or other courses, expeditions, payment of salaries, support of conferences and meetings, or activities that are not totally animal welfare related, will also be rejected.

Applications On an application form available from the correspondent or via the trust's website.

All applications must be completed in full and include:

- a detailed account of the purpose for which the grant is required
- a copy of your most recent financial accounts
- a copy of your latest annual report.

Any incomplete applications received or those which fail to meet our criteria (as outlined above) will be rejected.

The Stella and Alexander Margulies Charitable Trust

Jewish, the arts and general

£384,000 (2007/08)

Beneficial area UK.

c/o Time Products Ltd, 34 Dover Street, London W1S 4NG

Tel. 020 7343 7200 **Fax** 020 7343 7201

Email marcus@timeproducts.co.uk

Correspondent M J Margulies, Trustee

Trustees *Marcus J Margulies; Martin D Paisner; Sir Stuart Lipton; Alexander M Sorkin; Leslie D Michaels.*

CC Number 220441

Information available Accounts were on file at the Charity Commission.

Established in 1962, the trust has general charitable purposes, with a preference for Jewish organisations.

In 2007/08 it had assets of £8.1 million, which generated an income of £257,000. Grants were made to 16 organisations and totalled £384,000.

The two largest grants for the year went to UJIA (£256,000) and Shaare Zedek UK (£88,000).

Other, non-Jewish, beneficiaries were: Royal Opera House Foundation (£25,000); Nightingale House (£3,000); Royal Academy Trust and Tate Foundation (£1,000 each); Enfield Centre for Natural Health (£180); NSPCC (£100); and British Heart Foundation (£50).

Applications In writing to the correspondent.

Mariapolis Limited

Christian ecumenism

£544,000 (2007/08)

Beneficial area UK and overseas.

38 Audley Road, London W5 3ET

Tel. 020 8991 2022 **Fax** 020 8991 9053

Email timking@focolare.org.uk

Correspondent Tim King

Trustees *Timothy M King; Manfred Kochinky; Barry Redmond.*

CC Number 257912

Information available Accounts were on file at the Charity Commission.

The trust promotes the international Focolare Movement in the UK, and grantmaking is only one area of its work. It works towards a united world and its activities focus on peace and cooperation. It has a related interest in ecumenism and also in overseas development. Activities include organising conferences and courses, and publishing books and magazines.

In 2007/08 assets stood at £2.2 million and income, mostly from various donations received and earned income, at £510,000. Grants totalling £544,000 were made to the following: Focolare Trust (£362,000); Pia Associazione Maschile Opera di Maria (£174,000); Family Welfare Grants (£5,800); and Anglican Priests Training Fund (£1,500).

Applications In writing to the correspondent.

The Michael Marks Charitable Trust

Culture and environment

£190,000 (2008/09)

Beneficial area UK and overseas.

5 Elm Tree Road, London NW8 9JY

Tel. 020 7286 4633 **Fax** 020 7289 2173

Correspondent The Secretary

Trustees *Marina, Lady Marks; Prof. Sir Christopher White; Noel Annesley.*

CC Number 248136

Information available Full accounts were on file at the Charity Commission.

The trust supports the arts (including galleries and museums), and environmental groups, with grants generally ranging from £1,000 to £25,000, although larger grants have been given.

In 2008/09 it had assets of £4.6 million and an income of £333,000. Grants totalling £190,000 were made to 26 organisations many of which are supported annually.

Beneficiaries of the largest grants included: Tate Britain (£25,000); The London Library (£20,000); British Library (£14,000); the De Laszlo Foundation and Zoological Society of London (£12,000 each); and Norwich Theatre Royal (£10,000).

Other beneficiaries included: St Pancras Community Trust (£8,000); Academy of Ancient Music (£7,000); Campaign for Drawing (£6,000); Oxford Philomusica Trust (£5,000); BTCV/Green Gym (£2,000); and London Song Festival (£1,000).

Exclusions Grants are given to registered charities only. No grants to individuals or profit organisations.

Applications In writing to the correspondent before July. Applications should include audited accounts, information on other bodies approached and details of funding obtained. Requests will not receive a response unless they have been successful.

The Hilda and Samuel Marks Foundation

Jewish and general

£193,000 (2007/08)
Beneficial area UK and Israel.

1 Ambassador Place, Stockport Road, Altrincham WA15 8DB

Tel. 0161 941 3183 **Fax** 0161 927 7437

Email davidmarks@mutleyprperties.co.uk

Correspondent D L Marks, Trustee

Trustees S Marks; Mrs H Marks; D L Marks; Mrs R D Selby.

CC Number 245208

Information available Accounts were on file at the Charity Commission.

The foundation mainly gives support to UK charities and to charities based in Israel. The 2007/08 annual report states that:

The object of the foundation is to provide relief and assistance to poor and needy persons; for the advancement of education, religion or for other purposes beneficial to the community.

As stated in previous years, the foundation has supported a number of organisations on a long-term basis.

In 2007/08 the foundation had assets of £3.2 million and an income of £172,000 – including a combined donation of £20,000 from Mutley Property (Holdings) Limited and Mutley Properties Limited, companies in which all trustees are shareholders and directors. Grants totalling £193,000 were made during the year.

In line with the trustee's general rule to not comment on individual donations, grants were broken down as follows

- community/education £40,000 (20.8%)
- health £112,000 (58.00%)
- welfare £41,000 (21.2%).

However, notwithstanding this, the following observations were made by the trustees in their annual report:

Over the year in question donations totalling £72,475 were given to UK Charities and £118,600 for Israel-based charities. The residue of £2,100 was given to projects in other countries.

During the year under review the emphasis of the grants was to support health-based charities (primarily in Israel). This included donations given to celebrate the 90th birthday of one of the settlors.

The two donations each of £25,000 was given to the, ALYN Paediatric and Adolescent Rehabilitation Centre in Jerusalem.

Exclusions No grants to individuals.

Applications The trust primarily supports projects known to the trustees and its funds are fully committed. Therefore unsolicited applications are not being sought.

The Ann and David Marks Foundation

Jewish and general

£39,000 (2007)
Beneficial area Worldwide with a preference for Manchester.

Mutley House, 1 Ambassador Place, Stockport Road, Altrincham WA15 8DB

Tel. 0161 941 3183

Email davidmarks@mutleyproperties.co.uk

Correspondent D L Marks, Trustee

Trustees D L Marks; Mrs A M Marks; Dr G E Marks; A H Marks; M Marks.

CC Number 326303

Information available Accounts were obtained from the Charity Commission website, but without a list of grants.

The trust mainly supports Jewish charities, especially in the Manchester area. It has a number of regular commitments and prefers to distribute to charities known to the trustees.

In 2007 the foundation had assets of £524,000 and an income of £52,000. Grants totalled £39,000. Unfortunately a list of grants was unavailable. Previous beneficiaries included: the North Cheshire Jewish Primary School (£2,600); the United Jewish Israel Appeal (£2,500); and the Manchester Jewish Federation (£2,000).

Applications Previous research suggested that the trust's funds are mostly committed and unsolicited applications are not welcome.

Marmot Charitable Trust

'Green' organisations and conflict resolution

£53,000 (2007/08)
Beneficial area Worldwide.

c/o BM Marmot, London WC1N 3XX

Correspondent The Secretary

Trustees Jean Barlow; Martin Gillett; Jonathan Gillett.

CC Number 1106619

Information available Accounts were on file at the Charity Commission.

The trust was registered with the Charity Commission in November 2004. It has general charitable purposes. The following is taken from the trustees' report.

In practice, a policy reflecting the interests of the settlors has been implemented along with the interests of the late David Gillett, who left a major legacy to the trust. There is a concentration on funding 'green' organisations that support changes that will pave the way for a sustainable future. In addition, there is an interest n supporting peace organisations that are seeking new ways of dealing with conflict particularly at an international level and lessening the dependence on armaments including the eventual elimination of nuclear weapons.

In 2007/08 it had assets of £2.3 million and an income of £93,000. Grants totalling £53,000 were made to 14 organisations.

Beneficiaries included: Earth Resources Research (£12,000); Oxford Research Group (£8,200); Soil Association – Richard Young Antibiotics Project (£5,000); the University of Essex and the University of London School of Oriental and African Studies (£4,000 each); Sustrans and the Martin Ryle Trust – Scientists for Global Responsibility (£2,000 each); Tree Aid and Sustain – Vivid Picture Collective (£1,000 each); and Anaphylaxis Campaign (£500).

Applications In writing to the correspondent.

The Marr-Munning Trust

Overseas aid

£101,000 (2007/08)

Beneficial area Worldwide, mainly developing world.

9 Madeley Road, Ealing, London W5 2LA

Tel. 020 8998 7747 **Fax** 020 8998 9593

Email dongleeson@tiscali.co.uk

Correspondent Donford Gleeson

Trustees *Glen Barnham; Marianne Elliott; Julian Kay; Guy Perfect; Richard Tomlinson; David Strachan; Pierre Thomas.*

CC Number 261786

Information available Accounts were on file at the Charity Commission.

The trust was founded in 1970 by the late Frank Harcourt-Munning. An extract from the trust deed encapsulates its purposes:

To support charities giving overseas aid for the relief of poverty suffering and distress particularly those inhabitants so qualified of such territories as appear to the managing trustees to be economically underprivileged through want of development or of support of the necessities of life or of those commodities and facilities which enhance human existence enriched by education and free from the threat of poverty disease under nourishment or starvation.

Income is derived primarily from the letting of property. The trustees have been addressing its historically low proportion of charitable expenditure by modernising the management of its

assets and the effects are already being seen in an increased level of grant.

In 2007/08 the trust had assets of £12.5 million and an income of £515,000. Grants totalling £101,000 were made to organisations working overseas and were broken down as follows:

- Helping natural disaster victims (£33,500)
- Providing shelter to destitute people (£33,180)
- Providing healthcare to poor people (£12,000)
- Supporting self-sustaining projects (£11,850)
- Providing educational support (£10,750).

Major beneficiaries were: Oxfam (£21,000); Marr-Munning Asram – India (£12,000); and CAFOD – Zimbabwe (£10,000).

Recipients of smaller grants included: Gram Niyojon Kendra – India (£5,100); Harvest Help – West Africa (£4,300); Homeless International – India (£4,000); Gondor University Hospital – Ethiopia (£2,000); and Action Force – Gambia, Build Africa – Kenya, Deafway – Nepal, Franciscan Missionaries Hospital, Human Need and UNICEF – African Flood Children Appeal (£1,000 each).

Exclusions No grants to individuals or for work taking place within the UK.

Applications The trustees meet quarterly on average and usually review applications twice yearly, in the spring and autumn. Sometimes a request may be carried forward to a later meeting. However, emergency appeals may be considered at any meeting.

Applications should be concise, ideally limited to no more than two sides of A4 plus a project description, budget and summary accounts or annual report. Clear financial information is essential, and applications from small or new organisations may benefit from reference to any better-known supporters or partners. Charitable or equivalent status of the applicant organisation should be made clear.

Please note: Any other supporting literature should be kept to a minimum. Do not waste stamps on a stamped, addressed envelope; the trust regrets that it does not have the administrative resources at present to return papers or respond to telephone or email enquiries (a website is under consideration). A trustee has agreed to look at the requests each month and where necessary seek further information. Otherwise, applicants will normally only hear if their bid has been successful which may

be more than six months from receipt of application.

The Marsh Christian Trust

General

£162,000 (2007/08)

Beneficial area UK.

2nd Floor, 36 Broadway, London SW1H 0BH

Tel. 020 7233 3112

Website www.marshchristiantrust.org

Correspondent Brian Peter Marsh, Trustee

Trustees *B P Marsh; R J C Marsh; Miss N C S Marsh; Mrs L A Ryan.*

CC Number 284470

Information available Full accounts were available from the Charity Commission.

The trust was established in 1981 and has increased steadily in size with each passing year. In 2007/08 the trust had assets of £5.7 million and an income of £215,000. Grants and awards were made to 277 organisations and totalled £162,000. Support costs stood at £63,000.

Grants/awards were broken down as follows:

- social welfare: £96,000
- literature, arts and heritage: £54,000
- environment causes and animal welfare: £42,000
- miscellaneous £16,000
- healthcare and medical research: £7,000
- overseas appeals: £6,000
- education and training: £5,000.

Please note: The above figures include supports costs.

Charitable donations

Grants generally range from £250 to £4,000, with responses to new applications being at the lower end of this scale. The trust engages in long-term core funding and prefers to build up the level of grantmaking over time.

Grants of £1,000 or more included: English Speaking Union of the Commonwealth (£6,000); Industry and Parliament Trust (£5,000); Wildlife Information Network (£3,000); Refugee Council, Royal College of Music and The British Museum Friends (£2,000 each); and Christians Against Poverty, Holy

Trinity Brompton General Charity, National AIDS Trust and Prisoners Abroad (£1,000 each).

Grants of under £1,000 each included: Addaction (£800); Care (£700); Jolt (£650); Cued Speech Association UK (£600); Dystonia Society and Garden Organic (£500 each); Local Solutions (£450); Not Forgotten Association (£350); Society of Archivists (£275); and UK Antarctic Heritage Trust (£100).

The following information is from the trust's website.

Marsh Awards
The trust runs a portfolio of awards with a number of internationally and nationally recognised organisations such as Barnardo's, the National Trust and the Zoological Society of London. The awards seek to recognise unsung heroes who all aim to improve the world we live in. Recipients of Marsh Awards range from scientists working in conservation biology and ecology, to authors and sculptors from the arts world, and those who give their time unselfishly to work with the young, older people, people with mental health issues and for our heritage.

These partners recommend a short-list of worthy award winners, but the final decision lies with the award trustees, ensuring complete independence and giving real value to the winners in terms of the recognition earned.

The Marsh Awards now total 32 and continue to grow. The main areas of focus for the awards include conservation, science, the arts, heritage, literature and volunteering.

22 awards were made during the year and totalled £30,000.

Exclusions No grants can be made to individuals or for sponsorships. No start-up grants. No support for building funds, ordinary schools, colleges, universities or hospitals, or research.

Applications In writing to the correspondent. All applications for grants must be accompanied by a copy of the most recent audited accounts. The trustees currently receive about 8,000 applications every year, of which 7,800 are new. Decisions are made at monthly trustee meetings.

The trustees attempt to visit each long-term recipient at least once every three years to review the work done, to learn of future plans and renew acquaintance with those responsible for the charity.

The Charlotte Marshall Charitable Trust

Roman Catholic and general
£115,000 (2007/08)
Beneficial area UK.

c/o C and C Marshall Limited, Sidney Little Road, Churchfields Industrial Estate, St Leonards-on-Sea TN38 9PU

Tel. 01424 446 262

Correspondent The Trustees

Trustees *Mrs E M Cosgrave; J Cosgrave; K B Page; J M Russell.*

CC Number 211941

Information available Accounts were on file at the Charity Commission.

The trust has general charitable purposes in the UK, mainly supporting educational, religious and other charitable purposes for Roman Catholics.

In 2007/08 the trust had assets of £584,000 and an income of £121,000. The latter was derived from investment income and a donation of £60,000 (2005: £60,000) from C & C Marshall Limited due to the cessation of trading of Tufflex Limited in May 2000 and the subsequent loss of dividend income.

During the year, grants were made to 87 organisations and totalled £115,000. Of this, £80,000 went towards Roman Catholic activities and £35,000 towards other charitable activities. Grants were further broken down as follows:

- educational – 11 grants totalling £26,000
- disability and illness – 29 grants totalling £22,000
- homelessness – 11 grants totalling £21,000
- parents, children and young people – 14 grants totalling £21,000
- needy and underprivileged – 7 grants totalling £6,000
- abuse, addition, refugee and torture – 4 grants totalling £5,000
- older people – 4 grants totalling £2,000
- other charitable activities – 7 grants totalling £12,000.

Beneficiaries included: St Winifred's Centre – Sheffield (£8,000); St Gregory's Youth and Community Centre – Liverpool and St Mary's Star of the Sea (£6,000 each); Sacred Heart Primary School and St Mary Magdalen Catholic

School (£5,000 each); Scottish Marriage Care (£4,000); St James Priory Project – Bristol and Westminster Children's Society (£3,000 each); Speak Out Hounslow (£1,500); Independent Age (£1,000); and Birmingham Settlement (£500).

Exclusions No grants are given to individuals.

Applications On a form available from the correspondent. Completed forms must be returned by 31 December for consideration in March.

The Jim Marshall Charitable Trust

General
£95,000 (2007)
Beneficial area Milton Keynes.

Simpson Wreford and Co, Wellesley House, Duke of Wellington Avenue, London SE18 6SS

Tel. 020 8317 6460

Email carl.graham@simpsonwreford.co.uk

Correspondent Carl Graham

Trustees *Dr James Marshall, Chair; Kenneth Saunders; Brian Charlton; Jonathon Ellery; Victoria Marshall.*

CC Number 328118

Information available Accounts were on file at the Charity Commission.

Established in 1989 by the founder of Marshall Amplification plc, this trust supports organisations concerned with children, young people, families and people who are sick or have disabilities and the local community generally. Grants are also made directly to individuals.

In 2008 the trust had an income of £8,900 and a total expenditure of £90,000. No further details were available.

In 2007 the trust had assets of £135,000 and an income of just £11,000. Grants were made totalling £95,000 (2006: £1.1 million).

During the year there were ten beneficiaries receiving more than £1,000 each. Grants went to: MK Victors Boxing Club, Luton and Bedfordshire Youth Association and Action 4 Youth (£25,000 each); Foundation for Promoting the Art

213

of Magic (£5,000); Comedians' Golfing Society (£2,500); Hazeley School Charitable Trust (£2,000); Nathan Edwards Mobility Bike Fund (£1,100); and Music Alive, Brainwave and Music for All (£1,000 each). Grants of less than £1,000 each totalled £6,000.

Applications In writing to the correspondent at any time.

John Martin's Charity

Religious activity, relief in need and education

£199,000 to schools and organisations (2008/09)

Beneficial area Evesham and certain surrounding villages only.

16 Queen's Road, Evesham WR11 4JP

Tel. 01386 765 440 **Fax** 01386 765 340

Email enquiries@johnmartins.org.uk

Website www.johnmartins.org.uk

Correspondent John Daniels, Clerk

Trustees N Lamb, Chair; Mrs J Turner; J Smith; C Scorse; R Emson; Mrs D Raphael; Mrs F S Smith; Mrs J Westlake; J Wilson; Mrs C Evans; Revd B Collins; Revd A Spurr; Revd A Binney; Mrs G Falkner.

CC Number 527473

Information available Accounts were available from the Charity Commission.

The charity was created following the death of John Martin of Hampton, Worcestershire in 1714. His property was left for the benefit of local residents, and over the years some of this property has been sold to generate income to enable the charity to carry out its objectives in accordance with his wishes. It was formally registered with the Charity Commission in 1981.

Aims and objectives

Under the terms of the original will and the amended Charity Commission Scheme, the overall aim of the charity is to benefit the residents of the town and neighbourhood of Evesham, Worcestershire.

It does this through the implementation of four specific aims:

- propagation of the Christian Gospel (religious support)
- relief in need

- promotion of education
- health.

Objectives

- religious support – to assist the Vicars and Parochial Church Councils within the town of Evesham
- relief in need – to assist individuals and organisations within the town of Evesham who are in conditions of need, hardship and distress
- promotion of education – to promote education to persons who are or have a parent residing within the town of Evesham and to provide benefits to schools within Evesham
- health – the trustees have wide-ranging authority within the scheme to provide such charitable purposes as they see fit, for either assisting beneficiaries within the town of Evesham or within the immediate neighbourhood. The trustees currently utilise this authority to support people with chronic health problems and other related health issues.

Any unspent income at the end of the financial year can be used for the relief of conditions arising from health problems or medical needs either within the town of Evesham or certain designated villages.

In 2008/09 the charity had assets of £14.6 million and an income of £751,000. Grants were made to organisations (including schools) totalling £199,000, broken down as follows:

- promotion of education – £298,000
- relief in need – £225,000
- religious support – £77,000
- health – £40,000.

Beneficiaries included: St Peter's PCC – Bengeworth (£30,000); Wychavon Citizens Advice Bureau (£20,000); All Saints' PCC – Evesham, St Andrew's PCC – Hampton and St Richard's Hospice (£18,000 each); Prince Henry's High School (£11,000); Evesham Splash Club (£6,500); Noah's Ark Trust (£4,000); Vale of Evesham Special School (£2,500); and Youth Music Festival (£1,300).

Grants were also made to individuals across all four categories totalling £441,000.

Exclusions No grants for the payment of rates or taxes, or otherwise to replace statutory benefits.

Applications Grant applications are considered from organisations in, or supporting, the town of Evesham where the requested support is considered to fit within the governing schemes of the charity. Application periods close on

1 March, 1 June, 1 September and 20 November. Forms are available from the correspondent or via the charity's website.

Details of the application procedure for individuals are also contained on the trust's website.

The Mary Homfray Charitable Trust

General

£54,000 (2006/07)

Beneficial area UK, with a preference for Wales.

c/o Blenheim House, Fitzalan Court, Newport Road, Cardiff CF24 0TS

Tel. 0292 048 1111

Correspondent Angela Homfray, Trustee

Trustees Angela Homfray; George Gibson.

CC Number 273564

Information available Accounts were on file at the Charity Commission.

The trust supports a wide range of organisations, including many in Wales.

In 2006/07 it had assets of £1.8 million and an income of £64,000. Grants were made to 27 organisations totalling £54,000 and were mostly recurrent. Unfortunately more recent financial information was unavailable.

Beneficiaries included: Age Concern, NSPCC, Prince's Trust – Cymru, Salvation Army and Wallich Clifford Community (£3,000 each); National Botanic Garden of Wales, PDSA, Urdd Gobaith Cymru, and Wales Millennium Centre (£2,000 each); and RSPB and Y Bont (£500 each).

Applications In writing to the correspondent. Applications should be made towards the end of the year, for consideration at the trustees' meeting in February or March each year.

The Mason Porter Charitable Trust

Christian

£90,000 (2007/08)
Beneficial area UK.

Liverpool Charity and Voluntary Services, 151 Dale Street, Liverpool L2 2AH

Tel. 0151 227 5177

Correspondent The Secretary

Trustees *Sue Newton, Chair; Mark Blundell; Dil Daly; Richard Fassam; Charles Feeny; William Fulton; Prof. Phillip Love; Andrew Lovelady; Christine Reeves; Hilary Russell; Heather Akehurst.*

CC Number 255545

Information available Accounts were on file at the Charity Commission.

The trust supports mainly Christian causes in the UK, including those which provide relief or missionary work overseas.

In 2007/08 the trust had assets of £1.7 million and an income of £107,000. Grants to organisations totalled £90,000.

Grants of £1,000 and over were made to: St Luke's Methodist Church – Hoylake (£24,000); Abernethy Trust Ltd, Just Care and NXT Ministries (£10,000 each); Proclaim Trust (£5,500); St John's Hospice – Wirral and Share Jesus International (£5,000 each); the Messengers (£1,300); and the Mukuru Project (£1,000).

Other grants totalled £18,300.

Applications The trust states that it only makes grants to charities known to the settlor and unsolicited applications are not considered.

Matliwala Family Charitable Trust

Islam and general

£567,000 (2007/08)
Beneficial area UK and overseas, especially Bharuch – India.

9 Brookview, Fulwood, Preston PR2 8FG

Tel. 01772 706501

Correspondent A V Bux, Trustee

Trustees *Ayub Vali Bux; Usman Salya; Abdul Aziz Vali Patel; Yousuf Bux; Ibrahaim Vali Patel.*

CC Number 1012756

Information available Full accounts were on file at the Charity Commission.

The trust's areas of giving are:

- the advancement of education for pupils at Matliwala School Of Bharuch in Gujarat – India, and other schools, including assisting with the provision of equipment and facilities
- the advancement of the Islamic religion
- the relief of sickness and poverty
- the advancement of education.

In 2007/08 the trust had assets of £4.5 million and an income of £874,000. Grants totalled £567,000 of which the vast majority went towards supporting various projects in Bharuch, Gujarat – India. These included the building of a school, hospital care, purchase of educational books and materials, provision of clothing for the poor and the supply of free medicine.

In support of the trust's other objectives £36,000 went towards advancing education – overseas, £4,300 towards education and Islamic schools – UK, £4,000 towards the relief of poverty – overseas and £3,500 towards the advancement of Islamic schools – overseas.

Applications In writing to the correspondent.

The Matt 6.3 Charitable Trust

Christian

£441,000 (2007/08)
Beneficial area UK.

Progress House, Progress Park, Cupola Way, Scunthorpe DN15 9YJ

Tel. 01724 863 666

Correspondent I H Davey

Trustees *Christine Ruth Barnett; Doris Dibdin; T P Dibdin; R O Dauncey.*

CC Number 1069985

Information available Accounts were on file at the Charity Commission.

Established in 1998, this trust mainly supports Christian organisations.

In 2007/08 the trust had assets of £6.4 million and an income of £240,000. Grants totalling £441,000 were broken down as follows:

- promotion of Christian faith (£299,000)
- Christian broadcasting (£109,000)
- education (£10,000)
- building (£10,000)
- relief of poverty (£8,000)
- grants to individuals (£5,000).

No further information regarding the beneficiaries was available.

Applications The trust does not accept unsolicited applications. Funds are committed to ongoing projects.

The Violet Mauray Charitable Trust

General, medical and Jewish

£65,000 (2007/08)
Beneficial area UK.

HWCA Limited, 3rd Floor, 7–10 Chandos Street, Cavendish Square, London, W1G 9DQ

Correspondent John Stephany, Trustee

Trustees *Mrs A Karlin; John Stephany; Robert Stephany.*

CC Number 1001716

Information available Accounts were on file at the Charity Commission.

The trust supports general charitable causes, with preference for medical charities and Jewish organisations.

In 2007/08 the trust had assets of £1.8 million and an income of £57,000. Grants totalled £65,000.

Beneficiaries included: New North London Synagogue (£6,000); Cherry Lodge Cancer Care, Mango Tree and Opportunities International (£5,000 each); Aqua Box and Shelter Box (£4,000 each); Wells for India (£3,000); Jewish Children (£2,000); and Help the Aged and LEPRA (£1,000 each).

Exclusions No grants to individuals.

Applications In writing to the correspondent.

215

Evelyn May Trust

Children, older people, medical and natural disaster relief

Around £25,000 (2007)
Beneficial area Worldwide.

c/o Messrs Pothecary Witham Weld, White Horse Court, North Street, Bishop's Stortford CM23 2LD
Tel. 01279 5064210
Correspondent Ms Kim Gray
Trustees *Mrs E Tabersham; Ms K Gray; Ms J Tabersham*
CC Number 261038
Information available Accounts were on file at the Charity Commission.

Registered in 1970, this trust supports a variety of charities but appears to focus on specific areas every couple of years. One-off grants are given for specific projects but general funding is also considered.

In 2007 the trust had an income of £24,000 and total expenditure of £29,000. No information regarding grant beneficiaries was available.

Previous beneficiaries include: APT Enterprise Development, British Red Cross in response to the Iraq Crisis Appeal, Listening Books, Respite Association – Essex, Wells for India, Richard House Children's Hospice and Teen Talk Drop-in Centre.

Exclusions No grants to individuals, including students, or to general appeals or animal welfare charities.

Applications In writing to the correspondent.

The Mayfield Valley Arts Trust

Arts, especially chamber music

£116,000 (2007/08)
Beneficial area Unrestricted, but with a special interest in Sheffield and South Yorkshire.

Hawsons, Pegasus House, 463a Glossop Road, Sheffield S10 2QD

Tel. 0114 266 7141
Correspondent P J Kennan, Administrator
Trustees *A H Thornton; J R Thornton; Mrs P M Thornton; D Whelton; D Brown; J R Rider.*
CC Number 327665
Information available Accounts were on file at the Charity Commission.

Established in 1987, the objects of this trust are the advancement of education by the encouragement of art and artistic activities of a charitable nature, especially music and the promotion and preservation of concerts and other musical events and activities.

In 2007/08 the trust had assets of £2.3 million and an income of £137,000. Grants totalling £116,000 were made as follows: Sheffield Chamber Music in the Round (£30,000); Live Music Now (£28,500); York Early Music Foundation (£27,500); Wigmore Hall (£25,000); and Prussia Cove (£5,000).

Exclusions No grants to students.

Applications The trust states that no unsolicited applications are considered.

Mazars Charitable Trust

General

£224,000 (2007)
Beneficial area UK, overseas.

1 Cranleigh Gardens, South Croyden CR2 9LD
Tel. 020 8657 3053
Correspondent Bryan K Rodgers, Trust Administrator
Trustees *Peter Hyatt; Alan Edwards; David Evans; Bob Neate.*
CC Number 287735
Information available Accounts were on file at the Charity Commission.

The trust acts as a conduit for the charitable giving of the Mazars firm of chartered accountants (formerly Mazars Neville Russell). Up to ten per cent of the funds raised from each of the regional branches can be given to local organisations at the discretion of the managing partner; the rest of the funds are given by the trustees for general charitable causes. From April 2004 onwards, it was determined that grants will be broadly split between those

received with a personal commendation of team members of Mazars LLP, the donor firm, and those which are aligned to the LLP's corporate ethos.

The trust states it prefers to support specific projects (e.g. capital expenditure, research, an event) rather than normal revenue expenditure, although the latter will be considered provided that the applicant appears to be launching a strategic initiative and is financially sound.

The following is taken from the trust's annual report.

The trust supports charities which reflect the corporate ethos of our donor, the UK firm of Mazars. This ethos is being developed over time, but encapsulates the following sorts of charitable activity, associated with organisations which:

- will benefit significantly from receipt of a grant (i.e. the trust rarely supports large national charities)
- support professionals of whom our team are members (e.g. Chartered Accountants Benevolent Association)
- support disadvantaged people in the communities near which our offices are based
- seek to place people into employment and assist in housing (essential if a job is to be held down)
- seek to relieve hardship in deprived areas of the world in crisis situations
- our clients are encouraging us to support (subject always to careful adherence to independence criteria).

In 2007 the trust had assets of £91,000 and an income of £240,000. Grants were made to 118 organisations and totalled £224,000.

The largest grants were to: The Thana Trust (£19,000); Starfish (£17,000); EdUKaid (£12,000); International Needs Network (£11,000); and Allergy UK (£10,000). Other beneficiaries included: British Deaf Sports Council (£5,000); Abigail Project (£3,000); Shelter (£1,500); and Marie Curie Cancer Care (£1,000).

In addition to the above, 90 other grants of between £55 and £800 each were made totalling £29,000.

Exclusions No grants to individuals, large national charities (rarely), applications from a particular national charity within three years of an earlier grant, or for on-going funding. Unsolicited appeals are rarely considered.

Applications The trustees operate through a management committee which meets annually to consider applications for major grants which fit with the stated criteria. Some monies are allocated to five regional 'pot' holders who approve minor grant applications from within their own region. Applicants for a national grant must be known to the team members of Mazars LLP.

National and regional criteria are regularly reviewed but, in general, the trustees consider that the national grant-making policy should avoid core funding and other activities that require funding over a number of years. Most national grants are therefore made towards one-off projects.

A copy of these criteria is available upon request to the Trust Administrator.

The Robert McAlpine Foundation

Children with disabilities, older people, medical research and welfare

£505,000 (2007/08)
Beneficial area UK.

Eaton Court, Maylands Avenue, Hemel Hempstead HP2 7TR

Tel. 01442 233444

Correspondent Brian Arter

Trustees *Hon. David McAlpine; Malcolm H D McAlpine; Kenneth McAlpine; Cullum McAlpine; Adrian N R McAlpine.*

CC Number 226646

Information available Full accounts were on file at the Charity Commission.

This foundation generally supports causes concerned with children with disabilities, older people, medical research and social welfare. A small number of other charities are also supported through a long-term connection with the foundation and therefore no new beneficiaries are considered from outside the usual areas.

In 2007/08 the trust had assets of £12.6 million and had an income of £600,000. Grants paid or payable totalled £505,000.

There were 34 grants paid during the year. Major beneficiaries included: The Ewing Foundation (£90,000); Contact the Elderly (£26,000); Age Concern (£25,000); Merchants Academy –

Withywood and Community Self Build Agency (£20,000 each); and National Eye Research Centre (£17,000).

Other beneficiaries were Eyeless Trust (£15,000); Greenfingers Appeal and Hi Kent (£10,000 each); Rochdale Special Needs Cycling Club (£5,000); Hillfields Park Baptist Church (£4,000); and Grateful Society (£2,500).

Exclusions The trust does not like to fund overheads. No grants to individuals.

Applications In writing to the correspondent at any time. Considered annually, normally in November.

McGreevy No 5 Charitable Settlement

General

£38,000 (2007/08)

Beneficial area UK, with a preference for the Bristol and Bath area.

KPMG, 100 Temple Street, Bristol BS1 6AG

Tel. 0117 905 4000

Correspondent Karen Ganson

Trustees *Avon Executor and Trustee Co. Ltd; Anthony M McGreevy; Elise McGreevy-Harris; Katrina Paterson.*

CC Number 280666

Information available Accounts were on file at the Charity Commission.

The trust was established in 1979 by Anthony M McGreevy. In previous years there has been a preference for charities based in the former county of Avon.

In 2007/08 the trust had assets of £2.3 million, generating an income of £210,000. Grants were made to four organisations totalling £38,000. The beneficiaries were: NSPCC (£25,000); London Library (£10,000); Mucopolysaccharide Diseases (£2,000); and Prostate Cancer Charity (£1,000).

Exclusions No support for individuals.

Applications In writing to the correspondent.

The McKenna Charitable Trust

Health, disability, education, children and general

£378,000 to organisations
(2007/08)
Beneficial area England and Wales.

c/o Buzzacott, 12 New Fetter Lane, London EC4A 1AG

Tel. 020 7319 4000

Correspondent The Trustees

Trustees *P A McKenna; Mrs M E A McKenna; J L Boyton; H R Jones.*

CC Number 1050672

Information available Accounts were on file at the Charity Commission.

The trust's aims are to:

- assist with education, medical welfare and relief of need amongst people with disabilities
- provide funds for education as a means of relieving poverty
- make grants to children's charities
- make grants for general charitable purposes.

In 2007/08 the trust had assets of £72,000 and an income of £108,000. Grants were made to nine beneficiaries and totalled £378,000. The beneficiaries were: The Young Vic Company (£307,000); SNAP – Special Needs and Parents (£26,000); St Joseph the Worker Primary School (£20,000); Aldeburgh Music (£10,000); BEAT, The Cure Parkinson's Trust and RYL Humane Society (£5,000 each); Little Haven Hospice (£520); and Dumfries and Galloway Museum (£80).

Applications The 2007/08 trustees report and accounts states: 'The trustees will consider applications for grants from individuals and charitable bodies on their merits but will place particular emphasis on the educational needs and the provision of support for disabled people'.

Martin McLaren Memorial Trust

General

About £20,000 (2006/07)
Beneficial area UK.

c/o Charles Russell Solicitors, 5 Fleet Place, London EC4M 7RD

Tel. 020 7203 5269

Correspondent Michaiel McFadyen

Trustees *Mrs Nancy Gordon McLaren; Nicholas Durlacher; Michael Robert Macfadyen; Revd Richard Francis McLaren; Sir Kenneth Carlisle; William Francklin.*

CC Number 291609

Information available Information was taken from the Charity Commission website.

In 2006/07 the trust had an income of £22,000 and expenditure of £24,000. No further information was available.

Previously, in 2001/02, the trust's assets totalled £629,000 generating an income of £26,000. Grants were £11,900 to Art and Christianity Enquiry Trust, £10,000 to Horticultural Scholarships Fund, £4,800 to European Gardens and £2,000 to St John's Smith Square.

Further grants under £500 were to: Combe PCC, ESU Music Scholarship Fund (£500 each); Queen Mary's Clothing Guild (£200); Macmillan Cancer Relief, The PCC Busbridge Church (£100 each); and Fairbridge Garden Society (£50).

Applications In writing to the correspondent.

The Helen Isabella McMorran Charitable Foundation

General and Christian

About £40,000 (2007/08)
Beneficial area UK and overseas.

NatWest Trust Services, 5th Floor, Trinity Quay 2, Avon Street, Bristol BS2 0PT

Tel. 0117 940 3283

Correspondent NatWest Trust Services

Trustee *NatWest Trust Services*

CC Number 266338

Information available Accounts on file at the Charity Commission.

The trust makes one-off grants towards older people's welfare, Christian education, churches, the arts, residential facilities and services, social and moral welfare, special schools, cultural and religious teaching, special needs education, health, medical and religious studies, conservation, animal welfare, bird sanctuaries and heritage.

In 2007/08 the foundation had an income of £22,000 and a total expenditure of £42,000.

Previous beneficiaries included: Christian Aid, Marine Conservation, Moon Bear Rescue, National Association for Crohn's Disease, National Children's Bureau, React, St Matthews PCC, St Nicholas Church, Sense International and Stoneham Housing Association.

Exclusions No grants to individuals.

Applications In writing to the correspondent. Brief guidelines are available. The closing date for applications is February each year.

D D McPhail Charitable Settlement

Medical research, disability and older people

£70,000 (2007/08)
Beneficial area UK.

PO Box 285, Pinner HA5 3FB

Correspondent Mrs Sheila Watson, Administrator

Trustees *Ian McPhail; Mrs Patricia Cruddas; Mrs Julia Noble; Mrs C Charles-Jones; Tariq Kazi.*

CC Number 267588

Information available Accounts were on file at the Charity Commission.

Although the trust's income and assets have remained fairly stable over recent times, donations have fallen significantly in the last few years.

In 2007/08 it had assets of £8.3 million and an income of £273,000. Grants were made totalling just under £70,000, of which the major beneficiary was the Sir William Burrough School which received £20,000.

Other grant recipients included: Community Links (£7,500); DebRA (£5,000); Spina Bifida & Hydracephalus Association (£3,000); Bliss, I-CAN and RNID (£2,000 each); and the Barbara Bus Fund, International League for the Protection of Horses and the Samaritans – Harrow (£1,000 each).

Applications In writing to the correspondent.

The Anthony and Elizabeth Mellows Charitable Settlement

National heritage and Church of England churches

£86,000 (2008/09)
Beneficial area UK.

22 Devereux Court, Temple Bar, London WC2R 3JJ

Tel. 020 7583 8813

Correspondent Prof. Anthony Mellows, Trustee

Trustees *Prof. Anthony R Mellows; Mrs Elizabeth Mellows.*

CC Number 281229

Information available Accounts were on file at the Charity Commission.

The trust gives support to charities in four main areas:

- the arts and national heritage
- churches of the Church of England
- hospitals and hospices
- the training and development of children and young people.

The trust states that it aims: 'To further the charitable work of the operational charities supported by grants. The grants for the arts and national heritage are made only to national institutions and, save in exceptional circumstances, grants for churches of the Church of England are only made on a recommendation from the Council for the Care of Churches'.

In 2008/09 the trust had assets of £498,000 and an income of £94,000. Grants were made totalling £86,000 and were broken down as follows:

- hospitals, hospices and welfare (£52,000)
- the arts and national heritage (£21,000)
- Church of England (£12,000)
- churches – Council for the Care of Churches (£1,000).

Major beneficiaries included: The Order of St John (£51,000); St John Ambulance Museum (£10,000); the Lambeth Fund and St Martin-in-the-Fields (£5,000 each); Royal Academy Trust (£4,500); and Royal Opera House Foundation (£4,000).

Exclusions Applications from individuals, including students, are ineligible.

Applications Applications are considered when received, but only from UK institutions. No application forms are used. Grants decisions are made three times a year when the trustees meet to consider applications.

Melodor Ltd

Jewish and general

£156,000 (2007/08)

Beneficial area UK and overseas.

10 Cubley Road, Salford M7 4GN

Tel. 0161 720 6188

Correspondent Bernardin Weiss, Secretary

Trustees H Weiss; Mrs Y Weiss; Mrs Z Weiss; Mrs E Henry; Mrs J Bleier; Mrs M Freidlander; Mrs M Weiss; Mrs R Rabinowitz; P Weiss; P Neumann; E Neumann; H Neumann; M Neumann; Mrs R Delange; Mrs R Ollech.

CC Number 260972

Information available Full accounts were on file at the Charity Commission.

The trust supports religious, educational and similar causes, with most grants going to Jewish organisations.

In 2007/08 it had assets of £855,000 and an income of £180,000. Grants to organisations totalled £156,000. A list of beneficiaries was not available.

Previously, beneficiaries of the largest grants have been Centre for Torah

Education Trust (£30,000), Beis Rochel (£19,000) and Chasdei Yoel (£12,000).

Other beneficiaries included: Beth Hamedrash Hachodosh (£6,100); Yeshivas Ohel Shimon (£5,300); Beis Minchas Yitzhok (£4,000); Talmud Torah Education Trust (£3,000); Dushinsky Trust (£1,900); Kollel Chelkas Yakov and Yetev Lev (£1,500 each); Delman Charitable Trust (£1,100); and Ovois Ubonim and Friends of Viznitz (£1,000 each).

Sundry Donations under £1,000 each totalled £39,000.

Applications In writing to the correspondent.

Melow Charitable Trust

Jewish

£870,000 (2006/07)

Beneficial area UK and overseas.

21 Warwick Grove, London E5 9HX

Tel. 020 8806 1549

Correspondent J Low

Trustees Miriam Spitz; Esther Weiser.

CC Number 275454

Information available Accounts were on file at the Charity Commission.

The trust makes grants to Jewish charities both in the UK and overseas. In 2006/07 it had assets of £4.3 million and an income of £1.1 million. Grants totalled £870,000 and were broken down as follows:

- needy persons (£376,000)
- education (£215,000)
- religious organisations (£179,000)
- synagogues (£39,000)
- Talmudical colleges (£35,000)
- general (£12,000)
- care for older people (£10,000)
- youth clubs (£4,000)
- community organisation and integrated nursery (£1,000).

The largest grants were awarded to: Lovlev Charitable Trust (£109,000); Edupoor Ltd (£73,000); Keren Zedokah Foundation (£53,000); Havenpoint Ltd (£50,000); Keren Hachesed Trust (£48,000); and Shalom Torah Centres (£33,000).

Applications In writing to the correspondent.

Meningitis Trust

Meningitis in the UK

£330,000 to organisations (2007/08)

Beneficial area UK.

Fern House, Bath Road, Stroud GL5 3TJ

Tel. 01453 768000 **Fax** 01453 768001

Email helpline@meningitis-trust.org

Website www.meningitis-trust.org

Correspondent Tracy Lewendon, Financial Grants & Helpline Administrator

Trustees Lesley Green; Mrs Bernadette Julia McGhie; Mrs Gillian Mae Noble; James William Edward Wilson; Michael Anthony Hall; Peter James Johnson; Robert Johnson; Suzanne Devine; Mike Carroll; James Kilmister; Richard Greenhalgh.

CC Number 803016

Information available Accounts were on file at the Charity Commission.

The Meningitis Trust is an international charity with a strong community focus, fighting meningitis through the provision of support, education and awareness and research.

In 2007/08 the trust had an income of £3.5 million and a total charitable expenditure of £2.5 million. Grants to organisations for research purposes totalled £330,000. The sum of £193,000 was distributed to individuals in support grants.

Applications Application forms are available from the correspondent. Requests for financial support are reviewed regularly by the Financial Grants Review Panel.

Menuchar Ltd

Jewish

£352,000 (2007/08)

Beneficial area UK.

c/o Barry Flack & Co., Knight House, 27–31 East Barnet Road, Barnet EN4 8RN

Tel. 020 8275 5186

Correspondent The Trustees

Trustees N Bude; Mrs G Bude.

CC Number 262782

Information available Accounts were on file at the Charity Commission, but without a list of grants.

The main objects of the trust are the advancement of religion in accordance with the orthodox Jewish faith and the relief of people in need.

In 2007/08 the trust had assets of £155,000 and an income of £281,000. Grants 'to religious organisations' totalled £352,000. Unfortunately, a list of beneficiaries was not available.

Exclusions No grants to non-registered charities or to individuals.

Applications In writing to the correspondent.

Brian Mercer Charitable Trust

Welfare, medical and visual arts in UK and overseas

£193,000 (2007/08)
Beneficial area UK and overseas.

c/o Waterworths, Central Buildings, Richmond Terrace, Blackburn BB1 7AP
Tel. 01254 686 600
Email arowntree@waterworths.co.uk
Correspondent A T Rowntree, Trustee
Trustees Mrs C J Clancy; K J Merrill; A T Rowntree; R P T Duckworth; Mrs A E T Clitheroe.
CC Number 1076925
Information available Accounts were on file at the Charity Commission.

The trust's objectives are:

- the advancement of education and in particular, but not restricted to, the provision of grants for the promotion of medical and scientific research and the dissemination of the useful results thereof
- the furtherance and promotion of any other exclusively charitable objects and purposes in any part of the world as the trustees may in their absolute discretion think fit.

The following information is taken from the trustees' report.

Amongst other objects, the causes which they [the trustees] will most seek to benefit will be:

- the prevention, treatment and cure of diseases effecting eyesight
- the prevention, treatment and cure of cancer, particularly liver cancer
- the promotion of the visual arts.

The trustees are seeking to develop close relationships with a number of charities with a view to working in partnership with those charities on specific projects and thus being in a position to influence the manner in which funds are expended in order to ensure that maximum benefit is derived from them. The trustees envisage that it may take some time yet to fully develop these relationships.

In 2007/08 the trust had assets of £21 million and an income of £604,000. Grants, many of which are recurrent, were made to 18 organisations and totalled £193,000.

The beneficiaries included: Fight for Sight (£50,000); SightSavers International and British Council for the Prevention of Blindness (£20,000 each); Macular Disease Society, Marie Curie Cancer Care and The Living Paintings Trust (£10,000 each); Orbis Charitable Trust and Ro Ro Sailing Trust (£5,000 each); Royal British Society of Sculptors (£2,700); and Blackburn College (£1,500).

Applications In writing to the correspondent. Trustees meet at least twice yearly to allocate grants.

The Merchant Taylors' Company Charities Fund

Education, training, church, medicine and general

£99,000 (2007)
Beneficial area UK.

30 Threadneedle Street, London EC2R 8JB
Tel. 020 7450 4440
Email charities@merchant-taylors.co.uk
Website www.merchanttaylors.co.uk
Correspondent Nick Harris, Clerk to the Trustees
Trustees Richard W E Charlton; Peregrine T E Massey; The Earl of Stockton; Christopher M Keville.
CC Number 1069124

Information available Full accounts were available from the Charity Commission.

Grants are considered for the arts, social care and community development, disability, older people, poverty, medical studies and research, chemical dependency, homelessness, children, and education, with priority for special needs.

In 2007 the trust had assets of £276,000 and an income of £94,000. Grants were made totalling £99,000 and were broken down as follows:

Educational awards
17 grants totalling £57,000 were given for Outward Bound/Sail Training Association awards, prizes and bursaries via nine schools associated with Merchant Taylors' Company. The schools were Merchant Taylors' School – Norwood, St John's School, Merchant Taylors' School Crosby – Boys, Merchant Taylors' School Crosby – Girls, Wolverhampton Grammar School, Foyle College – Londonderry, Walingford School – Oxford, St Helen's School and Haymills.

Training awards
Grants were made to three organisations totalling £17,000 and went to: Textile Conservation Centre (£10,000); Guildhall School of Music (£6,000); and St Paul's Cathedral Choir School (£500).

Church and clergy
Grants to five organisations and totalled £5,000. Beneficiaries were: St Helen's Church – Bishopgate (£2,000); St Paul's Cathedral of Friends and St Margaret's Church – Lee (£1,000 each); and St Michael's – Cornhill and St Paul's Church – Swanley & St Peter's – Huxtable (£500 each).

Miscellaneous
There were three grants made totalling £2,500. Beneficiaries were: CREATE – Deptford Churches Centre (£1,700); Walk the Walk (£500); and Brandram Road Community Centre (£300).

Livery and Freemen Fund
Grants were made to three organisations from this designated fund. The beneficiaries were: Dartford Methodist Mission (£7,500); and Deafblind UK and National Youth Orchestra (£5,000 each).

Applications Awards are restricted at present to charities nominated by the Livery Committee.

The Merchants' House of Glasgow

General

About £60,000 to organisations a year

Beneficial area Glasgow and the west of Scotland.

7 West George Street, Glasgow G2 1BA

Tel. 0141 221 8272 **Fax** 0141 226 2275

Email theoffice@merchantshouse.org.uk

Website www.merchantshouse.org.uk

Correspondent The Directors

Trustee *The Directors.*

SC Number SC008900

Information available Accounts were provided by the trust.

As stated in its annual report and accounts, the charity's main activities included paying: 'pensions to pensioners, who may or may not have membership qualifications, and to provide assistance in the form of grants to charitable institutions within and around Glasgow'. It will normally consider applications from the following:

- organisations providing care and assistance to people with disabilities, older people, people who are terminally ill and people who have been socially deprived
- organisations providing for the care, advancement and rehabilitation of young people
- universities, colleges of further education and schools
- organisations connected with the arts, including music, theatre and the visual arts
- institutions that are connected with and represented by the Merchants' House.

The charity has an income of around £750,000 and makes grants to organisations of about £60,000 a year.

Previous grant recipients have included: Erskine Hospital, the National Youth Orchestra of Scotland, Scottish Motor Neurone Disease, the Castle Howard Trust, Delta, the National Burns Memorial Homes, Quarriers Village and Shelter.

Exclusions The trust will not, unless in exceptional circumstances, make grants to:

- individuals
- churches other than Glasgow Cathedral

- organisations that have received support in the two years preceding an application.

Applications In writing to the correspondent at any time, supported by copy of accounts and information about the organisation's principal activities.

Mercury Phoenix Trust

AIDS and HIV

£243,500 (2007/08)

Beneficial area Worldwide.

22 Cottage Offices, Latimer Park, Latimer, Chesham HP5 1TU

Tel. 01494 766 799

Email mercuryphoenixtrust@idrec.com

Website www.mercuryphoenixtrust.com

Correspondent Peter Chant

Trustees *M Austin; H J Beach; B H May; R M Taylor.*

CC Number 1013768

Information available Accounts were on file at the Charity Commission.

The trust was set up in memory of Freddie Mercury by the remaining members of the rock group, Queen, and their manager. It makes grants to 'help relieve the poverty, sickness and distress of people with AIDS and HIV and to stimulate awareness and education in connection with the disease throughout the world'.

The following information is taken from the trust's website.

Since 1992 the Mercury Phoenix Trust have been responsible for donating more than £8 million in the fight against AIDS making over 600 grants to charities worldwide. Applications for grants have come in from many countries around the world and collaboration has been realised with groups as far removed as the World Health Organisation to grass-root organisations run partly by voluntary workers in Uganda, Kenya, South Africa, Zambia, Nepal, India and South America. The trust is following the latest developments in drug therapies and adapting funding policy to the changing needs of those affected by HIV/AIDS, and currently concentrating its efforts on education and awareness in the Developing World.

In 2007/08 the trust had assets of £1.2 million and an income of £287,000. Grants were made totalling £243,500.

Major beneficiaries included: Care International – Niger/Ivory Coast, Y Care International – India and Christian Aid – India (£10,000); Mfesane – South Africa (£8,500); Childhope UK – India and GAPA – Brazil (£7,000 each); CAF – Kenya (£6,000); Nepal International, Group 12 – Zamia and Social Welfare – Nepal (£5,000 each).

Applications In writing to the correspondent.

The Metropolitan Drinking Fountain and Cattle Trough Association

Provision of pure drinking water

£29,000 (2008)

Beneficial area UK, mainly London, and overseas.

Oaklands, 5 Queenborough Gardens, Chislehurst BR7 6NP

Tel. 020 8467 1261

Email ralph.baber@tesco.net

Website www.drinkingfountains.org

Correspondent R P Baber, Secretary

Trustees *J E Mills, Chair; R P Baber; Mrs S Fuller; Sir J Smith; M W Elliott; M Nations; A King; M Bear; Mrs L Erith.*

CC Number 207743

Information available Accounts were on file at the Charity Commission.

The objectives of the association are to promote the provision of drinking water for people and animals in the United Kingdom and overseas, and the preservation of the association's archive materials, artefacts, drinking fountains, cattle troughs and other installations.

Over the years the association has recognised a need for supplying fountains to schools throughout the United Kingdom. The association typically gifts a Novus drinking fountain to a school on the condition that the school pays £25 to join the association. Generally one fountain is donated per 100 children. The school is responsible for the installation and the maintenance of the fountain.

In 2008 the trust had assets of £541,000 and an income of £44,000. Grants totalling around £29,000 were made to organisations. Beneficiaries included: Brooke Animal Hospital, The Busoga Trust, UK Youth and World Vision (£2,000 each); Spana (£1,500); and World Horse Welfare (£1,000 each). 25 schools received grants not exceeding £1,000 and totalling £12,000.

Applications In writing to the correspondent. In addition, in considering an application for a grant, trustees also require the following information:

- a copy of the most recent audited accounts
- how has the cost of the project been ascertained, for example, qualified surveyor?
- how many people/animals is it estimated would use the fountain/ trough in a day?
- will the charity supervise the project? If not who would?
- where is it anticipated the remainder of the funds to complete the project will come from?

T and J Meyer Family Foundation Limited

Education, healthcare and environment

£164,000 (2007)

Beneficial area UK and overseas.

3 Kendrick Mews, London SW7 3HG

Email info@tjmff.org

Correspondent The Trustees

Trustees *A C Meyer-Ahoulyek; J D Meyer; Q H Meyer; I T Meyer; M M Meyer.*

CC Number 1087507

Information available Accounts were on file at the Charity Commission.

Set up in 2001, this foundation focuses primarily on education, healthcare and the environment. The criteria for donee charities are:

- organisations which alleviate the suffering of humanity through health, education and environment
- organisations with extremely high correlation between what is gifted and what the beneficiary receives
- organisations which struggle to raise funds either because either they are new, their size or their access to funds is constrained
- organisations which promote long-term effective sustainable solutions.

In 2007 the foundation had assets of £17.1 million and an income of £239,000. Grants to 11 organisations totalled £164,000.

Beneficiaries included: University of Oregon (£100,000); Sisters of Sacred Heart of Jesus and Mary (£40,000); Cancer Active (£7,000); Hope and Homes for Children (£5,000); Living Heart – Peru (£4,000); Bowel Cancer UK (£1,500); Dreamscheme Network (£1,000); and Children's Fire and Burns Trust (£750).

Applications In writing to the correspondent.

Mickleham Charitable Trust

Relief in need

£108,000 (2007/08)

Beneficial area UK, with a preference for Norfolk.

c/o Hansells, 13–14 The Close, Norwich NR1 4DS

Tel. 01603 615 731

Email philipnorton@hansells.co.uk

Correspondent Philip Norton, Trustee

Trustees *P R Norton; S F Nunney; Mrs J A Richardson.*

CC Number 1048337

Information available Accounts were on file at the Charity Commission.

Set up in 1995, the trust's main objects are relief in need, particularly relating to young people and people who are blind.

In 2007/08 the trust had assets of £3.1 million and an income of £143,000.

Grants totalling £108,000 were made to 55 organisations, many of which had been supported in the previous year. Beneficiaries included: Orbis International (£10,000); Motability – Norfolk (£6,000); Defeating Deafness, East Anglian Children's Hospice,

Norfolk & Norwich Association for the Blind and YESU (£5,000 each); SCOPE (£4,000); Age Concern – Norwich (£3,000); Foundation for Conductive Education (£2,000); and British Blind Sport (£1,000).

Applications In writing to the correspondent.

The Gerald Micklem Charitable Trust

General and health

£96,000 (2008)

Beneficial area UK and East Hampshire

Bolinge Hill Farm, Buriton, Petersfield GU31 4NN

Tel. 01730 264 207

Email mail@geraldmicklemct.org.uk

Website www.geraldmicklemct.org.uk

Correspondent Mrs S J Shone, Trustee

Trustees *Susan J Shone; Joanna L Scott-Dalgleish; Helen Ratcliffe.*

CC Number 802583

Information available Information was available from the Charity Commission

The trust was established in November 1989 with a bequest left in the will of Gerald Micklem. The trust states it is most interested in UK charities working on a national basis in the following areas:

- Disability
- Deafness and blindness
- Medical conditions affecting both adults and children
- Medical research, but not in substitution of NHS spending
- People with learning disabilities
- Children and young people, especially the disadvantaged
- Environment and wildlife.

On occasion, the trust will make grants to charities working in East Hampshire outside the above fields. It does not make grants to local charities operating elsewhere in the UK. Donations are generally for between £2,000 and £3,000.

In 2008 the trust had assets of £514,000 and an income of £121,000. Grants totalling £96,000 were broken down as follows:

Blindness – 1 grant of £2,000.

Carers/older people – 1 grant of £2,000.

Children/young people – 5 grants totalling £11,000.

Disabled – 4 grants totalling £9,000.

Education/schools – 1 grant of £2,000.

Environment/wildlife – 2 grants totalling £3,000.

General community – 2 grants totalling £4,000.

Hospices – 4 grants totalling £11,000.

Medical conditions/research/hospitals – 13 grants totalling £39,000.

Mental disability – 2 grants totalling £5,000.

Overseas aid/international – 3 grants totalling £8,000.

Major beneficiaries included: Penny Brohn Cancer Care, Osteopathic Centre for Children and the Rosemary Foundation (£4,000 each); Against Breast Cancer, BRACE, British Schools Exploring Society, Cecily's Fund and Motor Neurone Disease Association (£3,000 each); Hope UK, Open Sight and UK Sports Association for People with Learning Disability (£2,000 each); and Little Ouse Headwaters Project (£1,000).

Exclusions The trust does not make grants to individuals, does not enter into sponsorship arrangements with individuals and does not make grants to organisations that are not UK-registered charities.

The following exclusions are taken from the trust's helpful website.

The areas of charitable activity that fall outside the trust's current funding priorities are: drug/alcohol abuse and counselling; museums, galleries and heritage; performing arts and cultural organisations; churches; and, overseas aid.

Applications Applications may be made to the correspondent by letter – not by email. Enquiries prior to any application may be made by email.

There is no application form. Applications may be made at any time, but preferably not in December, and should be accompanied by the latest report and accounts of the applicant organisation.

Applicants should note that, at their main meeting early in the calendar year, the trustees consider applications received up to 31 December each year, but do not carry them forward. Having regard for the time of year when this meeting takes place, it makes sense for applications to be made as late as possible in the calendar year so that the information they contain is most up to date when the trustees meet.

Please note: The trustees receive a very substantial number of appeals each year. It is not their practice to acknowledge appeals, and they prefer not to enter into correspondence with applicants other than those to whom grants are being made or from whom further information is required. Only successful applicants are notified of the outcome of their application.

Full details are available on the trust's website.

The Migraine Trust

Study of migraine

£184,000 in research grants (2008/09)

Beneficial area UK and overseas.

2nd Floor, 55–56 Russel Square, London WC1B 4HP

Tel. 0207 462 6604

Email info@migrainetrust.org

Website www.migrainetrust.org

Correspondent Adam Speller

Trustees *Andrew Jordan, Chair; J P S Wolff-Ingham; Prof. P J Goadsby; Ms S Hammond; H McGregor QC; Dr Anne McGregor; Mrs Jennifer Mills; Dr Mark Wetherall; Dr Brendan Davies; Ian Watmore; Mrs Suzanne Marriot.*

CC Number 1081300

Information available Accounts on file at the Charity Commission.

Amongst other objects in relation to the study of migraine, the trust provides research grants, fellowships and studentships (studentships should be applied for by host institution only). Funds provide for research into migraine at recognised institutions, such as hospitals and universities.

In 2008/09 the trust had assets of £372,000, an income of £555,000 and made grants for research purposes totalling £184,000.

Applications By application form available from the trust. Applications will be acknowledged.

Millennium Stadium Charitable Trust

Sport, the arts, community and environment

£244,000 (2007/08)

Beneficial area Wales.

c/o Fusion, Loft 2, Ocean House, Clarence Road, Cardiff Bay CF10 5FR

Tel. 029 2049 4963 **Fax** 029 2049 4964

Email msct@fusionuk.org.uk

Website www.millenniumstadiumtrust.co.uk

Correspondent The Trust Officer

Trustees *Gerallt Hughes; Peredur Jenkins; Russell Goodway; Paul Glaze; Wendy Williams; Michael John; Ian Davies; Simon Wakefield; John Lloyd-Jones; Louise Cassella; Gerald Davies.*

CC Number 1086596

Information available Accounts were on file at the Charity Commission, without a list of beneficiaries.

The trust was established by an agreement between the Millennium Commission and the Millennium Stadium plc. Its income is generated through a levy on every ticket purchased for public events at the stadium.

The following information is taken from the trust's website.

The trust's aims
Through its grant funding the trust aims to improve the quality of life of people who live and work in Wales. In particular the trust aims to promote education, history, language and culture, particularly for those who face disadvantage or discrimination.

Wales is a country rich in culture, history, language and sporting successes. In today's era of globalisation people often forget what is in their locality. As a result the trust is keen to help young people learn more about their country via exchange programmes and has made provision to support youth exchange programmes which fall in to any of the funding categories of the trust.

In 2007/08 the trust had an income of £460,000, mainly from donations from the Millennium Stadium. Grants were made totalling £244,000.

Guidelines
The trust has chosen to make grants in the following four categories:

223

Sport

Sport embraces much more than traditional team games and competition. Sport can mean physical activity or the improvement of physical fitness and mental well-being, and can assist in the formation of social relationships and individual and team confidence.

The trust is particularly interested in supporting projects that improve the quality of life of people and communities facing disadvantage.

Funding Priorities

The trust strives to make a difference to sporting organisations throughout Wales and appreciates that sport relies heavily on volunteers.

The trust is keen to support volunteer-based projects, particularly from ethnic minorities and people with disabilities. In addition, the trust recognises the difference that coaching can make to the development of a sport and is keen to fund equipment and coaching costs if the need has been clearly identified.

The arts

The trust is keen to support arts projects that are creative, unique and work with the disadvantaged or deprived individuals and groups throughout Wales. In particular, the trust wishes to develop and improve the knowledge and practice of the arts and to increase opportunities for people to see and participate in the arts throughout Wales.

Funding Priorities

The trust aims to give more people the opportunity to enjoy the diversity of performing and visual arts in Wales. The trust particularly favours proposals which expand and improve arts provision in parts of the country less well served than others and will give priority to organisations which strive to work together to share experiences, practices and ideas.

The environment

The environment of Wales varies dramatically between the north, south, east and west of the country. From the mountains of the north to the valleys of the south, the trust welcomes applications relating to environmental groups from both rural and urban areas in Wales.

Funding Priorities

The trust encourages applications relating to recycling, developing green spaces, the development and promotion of green practices and the promotion of public transport schemes. Projects that improve the quality of Wales' environment, protect and create a vibrant countryside, and develop and promote sustainable land-use planning will be a priority for support.

The trust aims to fund programmes that protect and enhance Wales' natural heritage and promote its sustainable use and enjoyment in a way which contributes to local economic prosperity and social inclusion.

The community

The trust is keen to target local communities suffering from greatest disadvantage in Wales.

Funding Priorities

The trust will give priority to organisations that are looking to tackle social, personal, economic or cultural barriers within their own communities. In particular projects that lead to greater independence and give people more control over their lives will be given priority. The trust welcomes applications that give people a voice to express their needs and hopes.

The trust is keen to help disabled people to challenge barriers and to be active and visible in their local communities.

Youth Exchange Programmes

The trust will give priority to projects [in the above categories] that foster greater understanding and friendship among the young people of Wales through exchange programmes. Organisations may wish to consider applying for costs towards travel and accommodation to visit another similar group in Wales. Examples of projects such as this may include one football club in Wales travelling to visit another football club to undertake a sporting and social weekend. In particular the trust is keen to support youth programmes that bring together 11 to 25 year olds through sporting or cultural exchanges. Exchange projects should demonstrate long-term benefits for the groups and communities involved and must be between groups based within Wales. These benefits will be as a result of new experiences that are educative, participative, empowering and expressive. The trust recognises that such exchanges can lead to a better appreciation of the different cultural, linguistic and social characteristics that make up the communities of Wales.

The trust supports:

- not-for-profit organisations
- properly constituted voluntary organisations
- charitable organisations
- voluntary groups working with local authorities (applicant cannot be the local authority)
- applications from groups of any age.

Priority is given to organisations serving groups and communities suffering from the greatest disadvantage.

The trust issues funding according to the size of geographical area that an organisation has a remit to cover.

Exclusions The trust does not support:

- projects outside of Wales
- day-to-day running costs
- projects that seek to redistribute grant funds for the benefit of third party organisations
- payments of debts/overdrafts
- retrospective requests
- requests from individuals
- payment to profit-making organisations
- applications made solely in the name of a local authority.

Please note: In addition to the above, successful applicants may not re-apply to the trust until a three year period from the date of grant offer has elapsed. The grant offer letter will advise applicants of the date when they will be eligible to re-apply.

Applications The trust asks that all applicants call or email the trust office to discuss their application.

Deadline dates can be found on the trust's website, along with full guidelines and application forms.

The Miller Foundation

General

About £150,000

Beneficial area UK, with a preference for Scotland, especially the west of Scotland.

Maclay Murray and Spens, 151 St Vincent Street, Glasgow G2 5NJ

Correspondent The Secretary

Trustees C Fleming-Brown; G R G Graham; J Simpson; G F R Fleming-Brown.

SC Number SC008798

Information available Despite making a written request for the accounts of this foundation (and including a stamped, addressed envelope), these were not provided. The following entry is based, therefore, on information filed with the Office of the Scottish Charity Regulator.

The foundation supports a wide range of charitable activities, primarily in Scotland, but also in other parts of the UK. Grants previously range from £500 to £2,000, with the majority of them recurrent.

In 2007/08 the foundation had a gross income of £195,000. Grants are made totalling around £150,000 each year. No further information was available.

Exclusions No grants to individuals.

Applications The foundation stated in summer 2008 that it was closed to applications.

The Millfield House Foundation

Social disadvantage and social policy

£156,000 (2007/08)

Beneficial area North-east England particularly Tyne and Wear.

19 The Crescent, Benton Lodge, Newcastle upon Tyne NE7 7ST

Tel. 0191 266 9429

Email finley@lineone.net

Website www.mhfdn.org.uk

Correspondent Terence Finley, Administrator

Trustees *Rosemary Chubb; George Hepburn; Grigor McClelland; Jen McClelland; Stephen McClelland; Sheila Spencer; Jane Streather.*

CC Number 271180

Information available Accounts were on file at the Charity Commission.

The Millfield House Foundation (MHF) helps to tackle poverty, disadvantage and exclusion and to promote social change in the north east of England, particularly Tyne and Wear. It funds projects that inform discussion and influence public policy and attitudes, with the aim of diminishing social deprivation and empowering communities.

The following information is taken from the foundation's website.

Projects supported might for example seek to:

- give a voice to excluded groups
- bring first hand experience of poverty to opinion formers and policy makers
- promote social policy discussion in the region
- campaign on local social issues.

MHF aims to provide, alone or in partnership with other funders, significant and medium-term support to a small number of carefully selected projects or organisations. It is unlikely to have more than about 6 to 12 grants in payment at the same time and can therefore approve only a small number of new grants in any one year. One-off grants may be between £5,000 and £50,000.

Grants for more than one year could be between £20,000 and £30,000 per annum for two or three years.

MHF will support national as well as local bodies, provided that projects are based in the north east of England (includes regional and sub-regional projects; projects which are locally based may be considered so long as they are of wider benefit).

The financial resources of MHF are a tiny fraction of the total available for charitable activity in the North East. The trustees therefore wish to concentrate their resources on projects which most other funding bodies can not or will not support.

As a charity, the foundation must confine its grants to purposes accepted in law as charitable. However, official guidance makes it clear that charities may include a variety of political and campaigning activities to further their purposes. [See 'Speaking Out – Guidance on Political Activity and Campaigning by Charities' published by the Charity Commission].

The foundation welcomes applications from stand-alone projects, from organisations which sponsor or manage projects, or from two or more projects applying jointly.

In certain cases, and strictly subject to compliance with the Charity Commission's guidance, the foundation may be willing to support proposals which involve non-violent direct action.

The trustees may consider an additional element of grant to allow for support from a consultant to assist with campaigning, lobbying, media and public relations.

In 2007/08 the foundation had assets of £6.3 million and an income of £168,000. Grants were made to seven organisations totalling £156,000. Beneficiaries were: Institute for Public Policy Research (£60,000); Regional Refugee Forum North East (£30,000); Prison Reform Trust – Smart Justice (£24,000); St Chad's College, Durham University (£19,000); Living Streets (£15,000); Mental Health North East (£5,000); and Church Action on Poverty North East (£3,500).

Exclusions The foundation 'will not fund straightforward service provision, nor mainline university research, nor the wide range of other projects that are eligible for support elsewhere'.

Applications Initial outline proposals should be made in writing to the correspondent. If the application meets the stated guidelines the administrator may request further information or arrange a meeting. Applications unconnected with Tyne and Wear are not acknowledged.

The trustees meet twice a year, in May and November so completed applications should arrive by the end of March or end of September. The administrator is willing to provide guidance for the preparation of final applications, but not without first receiving an outline proposal.

Applications should include:

- Full contact details, including email address if available. A covering letter containing a brief summary of the purpose of the project and the amount sought from MHF, and a substantive paper of no more than four pages. All other information should be provided as appendices.
- A description of the project including its aims and intended outcomes, with specific reference to possible policy implications, an action programme and proposed timescale for delivery.
- A budget for the project giving a breakdown of total expenditure and of sources of anticipated income.
- A copy of the most recent annual report and audited accounts for the project and/ or the sponsoring body.
- The constitution of the responsible body.
- Details of the organisation's policy and procedures for equal opportunities and diversity.
- If appropriate, plans for dissemination of the results of the project. (Research reports should be summarised in a format similar to that of the 'Findings' series produced by the Joseph Rowntree Foundation).
- Details of arrangements for monitoring and evaluation.
- If funding is sought towards the costs of a salaried post, a job description.
- The names of two independent referees (references may not be taken up in every case).

For further information, potential applicants are strongly advised to visit the trust's website.

The Millfield Trust

Christian

£66,000 to organisations (2007/08)

Beneficial area UK and worldwide.

Millfield House, Bell Lane, Liddington, Swindon SN4 0HE

Tel. 01793 790 181

Correspondent D Bunce, Trustee

Trustees D Bunce; P W Bunce; S D Bunce; A C Bunce; Mrs R W Bunce.

CC Number 262406

Information available Accounts were on file at the Charity Commission.

The trust was set up to provide grants to Christian organisations, and has supported a number of missionary societies for the last 50 years. Grants are given solely to organisations known to the trust and new applications are not considered.

In 2007/08 the trust had assets of £138,000 and an income of £79,000, including £62,000 in Gift Aid donations from three of its trustees. Grants to organisations totalled £66,000. A further £3,800 was given in grants to individual missionaries and evangelists, and £260 in gifts to older people.

Major beneficiaries included: Gideon's International (£12,500); Mark Gillingham Charitable Trust (£9,200); Ashbury Evangelical Free Church (£3,700); and Mission to Europe and Tear Fund – Evangelical Alliance Relief Fund (£3,000 each).

Grants of up to £1,000 each included those to: Swindon Youth for Christ (£1,000); Gospel Printing Mission (£800); Liverpool School of Tropical Medicine (£500); Anglo Peruvian Childcare Mission (£400); Family in Trust (£300); and Spanish Gospel Mission (£100).

Applications No replies to unsolicited applications.

The Millhouses Charitable Trust

Christian, overseas aid and general

£28,000 (2007/08)

Beneficial area UK and overseas.

c/o MacFarlane and Co., Cunard Building, Water Street, Liverpool L3 1DS

Tel. 0151 236 6161

Correspondent The Trustees

Trustees Revd Jeanetta S Harcus; Dr A W Harcus; Dr J L S Alexander; Ms Penelope A Thornton; Mrs Fiona J van Nieuwkerk.

CC Number 327773

Information available Accounts were on file at the Charity Commission.

In 2007/08 the trust had assets of £845,000 and an income of £44,000. Grants to 20 organisations totalled £28,000.

Beneficiaries included: NSPCC and Christian Solidarity (£5,000 each); Release International and Barnabus Fund (£2,500 each); Children's Society, Crisis and Oasis (£1,000 each); Rehab UK and Medical Foundation (£500 each); and Mercy Ships, Operation Mobilisation and Smile (£250 each).

Exclusions Grants are made to registered charities only; no grants to individuals.

Applications In writing to the correspondent, but note that most of the grants given by this trust are recurrent. If new grants are made, they are usually to organisations known to the trustees.

The Millichope Foundation

General

£295,000 (2007/08)

Beneficial area UK, especially the West Midlands and Shropshire.

Millichope Park, Munslow, Craven Arms SY7 9HA

Tel. 01584 841 234

Email sarah@millichope.com

Correspondent Mrs S A Bury, Trustee

Trustees L C N Bury; Mrs S A Bury; Mrs B Marshall.

CC Number 282357

Information available Accounts were on file at the Charity Commission.

The foundation makes donations to a wide range of different organisations including:

- UK charities
- local charities serving Birmingham and Shropshire
- arts and culture
- conservation/heritage
- education.

In 2007/08 the foundation had assets of £6.8 million and an income of £493,000. Grants were made to organisations totalling £295,000.

The largest grants given during the year were in support of Lady Willington Hospital – Manila (£20,000) and Hope &

Homes for Children, Shropshire Historic Churches Trust and St Laurence – Special Music Projects (£10,000 each).

Other beneficiaries included: Animal Health Trust, Brazilian Atlantic Rainforest Trust, Prince's Trust – Shrewsbury and Shropshire Wildlife – Hollies Appeal (£5,000 each); Cambridge Foundation (£4,000); Birmingham City Mission and Sandwell MultiCare (£2,000 each); and Ludlow Music Society (£200).

Exclusions No grants to individuals or non-registered charities.

Applications In writing to the correspondent.

The Millward Charitable Trust

Social welfare, performing arts, medical research and animal welfare

£181,000 (2007/08)

Beneficial area UK and overseas

c/o Burgis & Bullock, 2 Chapel Court, Holly Walk, Leamington Spa CV32 4YS

Tel. 01926 451 000

Correspondent John Hulse, Trustee

Trustees Maurice Millward; Sheila Millward; John Hulse.

CC Number 328564

Information available Accounts were on file at the Charity Commission.

The trust has general charitable purposes and during the year supported a variety of causes including social welfare, performing arts, medical research and animal welfare.

In 2007/08 the trust had assets of £2.1 million and an income of £72,000. Grants were made totalling £181,000 and were broken down as follows:

- social welfare – 33 grants totalling £84,000
- performing arts – 10 grants totalling £86,000
- medical research – 2 grants totalling £750
- animal welfare – 8 grants totalling £11,000.

Institutional grants greater than £1,000 each included: Birds Eye View (£36,000 in three grants); Music in the Round (£32,000 in two grants); Interface

226

Uganda and L.I.F.E (£20,0000 each); City of Birmingham Symphony Orchestra (£10,000 in two grants); RSPCA (£8,000 in two grants); St Paul's Church (£6,000 in four grants); Leamington Music (£5,000); and Adoramus and Hillside Animal Sanctuary (£1,000 each).

Applications In writing to the correspondent.

The Edgar Milward Charity

Christian and humanitarian

£56,000 (2007/08)

Beneficial area UK and overseas, with an interest in Reading.

53 Brook Drive, Corsham SN13 9AX

Correspondent A S Fogwill, Secretary

Trustees *J S Milward, Chair; Mrs M V Roberts; G M Fogwill; S M W Fogwill; A S Fogwill; Mrs F Palethorpe; Mrs J C Austin.*

CC Number 281018

Information available Accounts were on file at the Charity Commission.

The object of the charity is to distribute all of its income as it arises as follows:

- one-half for the furtherance of the Christian religion within the UK and throughout the world
- two-fifths for general charitable purposes
- one-tenth for educational purposes within a 15-mile radius of the Civic Centre in Reading.

Within this, the trust's grant-making policy is to support a limited number of causes known to the trustees, particularly those supported by the settlor.

In 2007/08 the charity had assets of £995,000 and an income of £59,000. Grants were made totalling £56,000 and were distributed as follows:

Christian religion – 36 grants totalling £27,000, including those to: Goal Ministries (£2,500); Bible Society (£2,000); Christian Solidarity Worldwide, Lee Abbey and Urban Saints (£1,000 each).

General charitable purposes – 35 grants totalling £24,000, including those to: Interserve (£1,500); Agape Asia, Eurovision and Time for God (£1,000 each).

Educational purposes – six grants totalling £5,500 including those to: REinspired (£1,500); Bibles for Children, Kendrick School and Reading School Workers Trust (£1,000) each).

Exclusions No new applications will be supported.

Applications Unsolicited applications cannot be considered.

The Peter Minet Trust

General, children, young people, health, disability and community

£182,000 (2007/08)

Beneficial area Mainly south east London boroughs, particularly Lambeth and Southwark.

1a Taylors Yard, 67 Alderbrook Road, London SW12 8AD

Tel. 020 8772 3155

Email info@peterminet.org.uk

Website www.peterminet.org.uk

Correspondent The Administrator

Trustees *J C B South, Chair; Mrs R L C Rowan; Ms P C Jones; R Luff; Revd Bruce Stokes; Mrs L Cleverly.*

CC Number 259963

Information available Accounts were on file at the Charity Commission.

In the mid-sixties, the Minet family sold much of their property to local councils. Part of the proceeds were used by Peter Brissault Minet to set up the trust in 1969.

The trust gives priority to registered charities (not individuals) working with people in the boroughs of Lambeth and Southwark, and particularly those working with young people, the sick, disabled, disadvantaged, older people, the arts and the environment. Most grants are for between £1,000 and £3,000 each, although there is also a small grants scheme (£50 to £500 each) to which applications can be made throughout the year.

In 2007/08 the trust had assets of £3.8 million, an income of £192,000 and made grants totalling £182,000. Grants were distributed in the following categories:

Children and young people (£42,000 in 22 grants) – for playschemes, holidays, youth clubs, adoption agencies and sports programmes.

Health and disability (£29,000 in 16 grants) – for counselling projects, holidays for people with disabilities, medical education and information and access projects.

Community projects (£50,000 in 22 grants) – for projects providing information, advice and support to various groups including ex-offenders, homeless people, single parents and unemployed people.

General and cultural (£18,000 in 7 grants).

Small grants (£12,000 in 30 grants).

Grants for less than £1,000 each were made totalling £14,000.

Exclusions The trust does not make grants directly to individuals, nor normally make grants for:

- national appeals by large charities for large sums of money
- appeals where all, or most of the beneficiaries live outside the UK
- appeals whose sole or main purpose is to make grants from collected funds
- endowment or deficit funding
- medical or other research
- local appeals, outside the inner city boroughs of south London.

Applications Application forms along with guidelines are available either by post from the correspondent or by downloading them from the trust's website.

The form should be submitted along with your latest audited accounts, details of the project (no more than two sides of A4), a budget breakdown, money raised so far, and a list of other bodies to which you have applied for funding. Meetings are usually held in February, June and October. Unsuccessful applicants will not be acknowledged unless a stamped, addressed envelope is enclosed.

If you would like to speak to someone about your proposed application then you should telephone 020 8772 3155 between 9am and 3pm on Monday or Tuesday each week.

Minge's Gift and the Pooled Trusts

Medical, education, disadvantage and disability

£48,000 (2007/08)
Beneficial area UK.

The Worshipful Company of Cordwainers, Clothworkers' Hall, Dunster Court, Mincing Lane, London EC3R 7AH

Tel. 020 7929 1121 **Fax** 020 7929 1124

Email office@cordwain.co.org

Website www.cordwainers.org

Correspondent John Miller, Clerk

Trustee *The Master and Wardens of the Worshipful Company of Cordwainers.*

CC Number 266073

Information available Accounts were on file at the Charity Commission.

Minge's Gift – The trust was established for general charitable purposes as directed by the Master and Wardens of the Worshipful Company of Cordwainers. The income of Minge's Gift is generally allocated for the support of educational and medical establishments with which the company has developed long-term relationships, ex-service organisations and towards assistance for disabled and/or disadvantaged young people.

In 2007/08 the trust had assets of £1.2 million and an income of £101,000. Grants were made to organisations totalling £48,000, broken down as follows:

Standard grants – £47,000 in 21 grants, the largest of which were those to: University of Northamptonshire (£10,000); London College of Fashion – prizes and scholarships (£7,000); Footwear Friends (£6,500); and Capel Manor College (£5,000). Other beneficiaries included: University of Arts (£3,000); Royal London Society for the Blind (£2,500); and Centrepoint, Guildhall School of Music and Drama, Leather Conservation Centre and St Dunstan-in-the-West Church (£1,000 each).

Master's gifts – £1,400 in four grants to Haringey Sea Cadets (£1,000), King's College (£250), City of London Festival (£100) and Keen London (£50).

In addition to the above, £10,500 was spent on the upkeep of company almshouses in Chesham.

Pooled Trusts – Also included in the accounts for Minge's Gift, were details of the giving of the Common Investment Fund (Pooled Trusts). This combines a number of small trusts which are administered by the Worshipful Company of Cordwainers for the benefit of scholars, the blind, deaf, clergy widows, spinsters of the Church of England, ex-servicemen and their widows and those who served in the merchant services. It also provides for the upkeep of the Company's five almshouses in Shorne, Kent.

Exclusions Grants to individuals are only given through the Pooled Trusts. Generally, only UK-based charitable organisations are supported.

Applications In writing to the correspondent.

The Minos Trust

Christian and general

Around **£35,000** (2007/08)
Beneficial area UK and overseas.

Kleinwort Benson Trustees Ltd, 30 Gresham Street, London EC2V 7PG

Tel. 020 8207 7356 **Fax** 020 8207 7665

Correspondent The Trustees

Trustees *Revd K W Habershon; Mrs E M Habershon; Mrs D M Irwin-Clark.*

CC Number 265012

Information available Accounts were not on file at the Charity Commission.

Previously we were advised that the trust gives most of its support to Christian charities in grants ranging up to £15,000. Remaining funds are given to other causes, with a preference for animals and wildlife, although these grants tend to be less than £1,000. Many of the organisations receiving the larger grants are regularly supported by the trust.

In 2007/08 the trust had an income of £23,000 and a total expenditure of £36,000. This is in line with previous years when its expenditure has regularly exceeded its income. Further information was not available.

Previous beneficiaries include: £3,000 each to Care Trust and Tigers Club Project. Other large grants included those to Care Trust (£2,500), Tearfund (£2,000) and Ashburnham Christian

Trust (£1,500), with £1,000 each to Bible Society, Friends of the Elderly and Youth with a Mission.

Grants under £1,000 were given to Christian organisations in the UK and overseas including: Africa Christian Press (£400), Aid to Russian Christians (£300) and Gideons International (£100). Other grants included those to Worldwide Fund for Nature (£450) and Sussex Farming Wildlife Advisory Group and RSPB (£50 each).

Applications In writing to the correspondent, for consideration on an ongoing basis.

Minton Charitable Trust

General

£200,000 to organisations and individuals (2007/08)
Beneficial area UK.

26 Hamilton House, Vicarage Gate, London W8 4HL

Correspondent Sir Anthony Armitage Greener, Trustee

Trustees *Sir Anthony Armitage Greener; Richard J Edmunds; Lady Audrey Greener.*

CC Number 1112106

Information available Accounts were on file at the Charity Commission, without a list of grants.

Set up in 2005, in 2007/08 the trust had assets of £671,000 and an income of £387,000, mostly from donations. Grants totalled £200,000.

Applications In writing to the correspondent.

The Mirianog Trust

General

£63,000 (2007/08)
Beneficial area UK.

Moorcote, Thornley, Tow Law, Bishop Auckland DL13 4NU

Correspondent Canon W E L Broad, Chair

Trustees *Canon William Broad, Chair; Daphne Broad; Elizabeth Jeary.*

CC Number 1091397

Information available Accounts were on file at the Charity Commission.

Set up in 2002 with general charitable purposes, currently the trustees give preference to:

- relief of poverty
- overseas aid and famine relief
- accommodation and housing
- environment, conservation and heritage.

In 2007/08 the trust had assets of £725,000 and an income of £69,000 including £29,000 from donations. Grants totalled £63,000.

Beneficiaries included: Newcastle University (£22,000); Justice First (£10,000); Sea Change and START (£5,000 each); Medical Foundation for the Victims of Torture and Practical Action (£4,000 each); Butterwick Hospice and St Giles (£3,000 each); Fauna and Flora (£1,500); and Cancer Connections (£1,000).

Applications In writing to the correspondent. The trustees meet twice each year.

The Laurence Misener Charitable Trust

Jewish and general

£178,000 (2007/08)

Beneficial area UK.

1 Printing Yard House, London E2 7PR

Tel. 020 7739 8780

Correspondent David Lyons

Trustees *Mrs J Legane; Capt. G F Swaine.*

CC Number 283460

Information available Accounts were on file at the Charity Commission.

In 2007/08 the trust had assets of £2.9 million and an income of £137,000. Grants were made totalling £178,000.

The largest grants were to: Jewish Association for the Physically Handicapped, Jewish Care and Nightingale House (£15,000 each); Robert Owen Foundation (£12,000); and Royal College of Surgeons of England (£10,000).

Other grants included: Cancer Research UK (£9,000); Jewish Temporary Shelter (£8,000); Great Ormond Street Children's Hospital fund (£7,000); Age Concern, SSAFA and St George's Church, Dittisham (£6,000 each); and Imperial War Museum Trust (£5,000).

Applications In writing to the correspondent.

The Mishcon Family Charitable Trust

Jewish and social welfare

£96,000 (2007/08)

Beneficial area UK.

Summit House, 12 Red Lion Square, London WC1R 4QD

Correspondent The Trustees

Trustees *P A Mishcon; R O Mishcon; Mrs J Landau.*

CC Number 213165

Information available Full accounts were on file at the Charity Commission.

The trust supports mainly Jewish charities, but also gives grants to general social welfare and medical/disability causes, especially children's charities.

In 2007/08 the trust had assets of £1.9 million, which generated an income of £87,000. Grants were made to over 100 organisations totalling £96,000.

The largest grant went to the United Jewish Israel Appeal (£45,000). Other large grants of £1,000 or more included those to: One Voice Europe (£10,000); Misholim (£4,000); Norwood, Sick Children's Trust and United Synagogue (£2,500 each); and Chai Cancer Care, Katherine Domandy Trust and Motivation Charitable Trust (£1,000 each).

Remaining grants were in the range of £20 and £950. Beneficiaries included: London Jewish Cultural Centre (£750); Friends of Alyn (£600); Acorn Hospice, The Genesis Appeal and One World Action (£500 each); Dream Holidays (£350); Myeloma UK (£250); Listening Books (£100); Help the Aged (£50); Joely Bear Appeal (£30); and Sports Relief (£20).

Applications In writing to the correspondent.

The Misselbrook Trust

General

£31,000 (2007/08)

Beneficial area UK with a preference for the Wessex area.

Ashton House, 12 The Central Precinct, Winchester Road, Chandlers Ford, Eastleigh SO53 2GB

Tel. 023 8027 4555

Correspondent M Howson-Green, Trustee

Trustees *M Howson-Green; B M Baxendale; D A Hoare; Mrs M A Howson-Green.*

CC Number 327928

Information available Full accounts were available from the Charity Commission.

In 2007/08 the trust had assets of £575,000 and an income of £29,000. Grants were made totalling £31,000.

Grants of more than £500 went to 14 organisations including: Marwell Preservation Trust (£3,000); and AIDS Trust, Blond McIndoe Centre, Canine Partner Independence, Fairbridge – Solent, Hampshire Autistic Society, Honeypot Charity, Rainbow Centre, Royal Star & Garter Home, Southampton Churches Rent Bond Scheme and Southampton Women's Aid (£1,000 each).

Other grants of £500 or less were made to 30 institutions and totalled £15,000.

Applications In writing to the correspondent.

The Mitchell Charitable Trust

Jewish and general

£141,000 (2008/09)

Beneficial area UK, with a preference for London, and overseas.

28 Heath Drive, London NW3 7SB

Tel. 020 7794 5668

Correspondent Ashley Mitchell, Trustee

Trustees *Ashley Mitchell; Elizabeth Mitchell; Antonia Mitchell; Keren Mitchell.*

CC Number 290273

Information available Accounts were on file at the Charity Commission.

The trust was established in 1984. It has general charitable purposes but in practice appears to have a strong preference for welfare charities, Jewish organisations and health charities.

In 2008/09 the trust had assets of £942,000 and an income of £50,000. There were 27 grants made during the year totalling £141,000, broken down as follows:

Category	Amount
Arts and Culture	£750
Community and welfare	£25,000
Education	£1,750
Medical and disability	£105,000
Overseas Aid	£9,250

The main beneficiaries during the year were: Hammersmith Clinical Research (£38,000); Ovarian Cancer Care (£33,000); Prostate Cancer Research Foundation (£25,000); Jewish Care (£13,000); World Jewish Relief (£8,000); and The National Organisation for Foetal Alcohol Syndrome (£8,000).

Smaller grants were paid to: Women to Women International UK (£1,500); University of Nottingham Karnival (£900); LSE Students Union (£750); St Michael's Church Restoration Fund (£500); Tricycle Theatre (£200); and Spiroark (£50).

Exclusions No grants to individuals or for research, education, overseas appeals or non-Jewish religious appeals. Applicants from small charities outside London are unlikely to be considered.

Applications In writing to the correspondent. Applications must include financial information. The trust does not reply to any applications unless they choose to support them. Trustees do not meet on a regular basis, thus applicants may not be advised of a grant for a considerable period.

Keren Mitzvah Trust

General and Jewish

£881,000 (2007)
Beneficial area UK.

1 Manchester Square, London W1U 3AB
Tel. 020 3219 2600
Correspondent The Trustees
Trustees *A McCormack; M Weiss; N Bradley.*

CC Number 1041948
Information available Accounts were on file at the Charity Commission.

In 2007 the trust had an income of £819,000, mainly from donations. Grants totalled £881,000.

Grants of £5,000 or more were made to 30 organisations and were listed in the accounts. Beneficiaries included: Lezion Berina Institute (£120,000); CML (£54,000); Wiseheights (£45,000); Ahaavat Shalom Charity (£43,000); Torah & Chesed (£34,000); ETC Youth (£18,000); Gateshead Jewish Academy (£14,000); Project Seed (£10,000); The Jewish Literacy Foundation (£8,000); and Jewish Learning Exchange (£5,000).

Unlisted smaller grants totalled £113,000.

Applications The trust stated that the trustees support their own personal charities.

The Mizpah Trust

General

£61,000 (2007/08)
Beneficial area UK and overseas.

Foresters House, Humbly Grove, South Warnborough, Basingstoke RG29 1RY
Correspondent A C O Bell, Trustee
Trustees *A C O Bell; Mrs J E Bell.*
CC Number 287231
Information available Full accounts were on file at the Charity Commission.

The trust is proactive and makes grants to a wide range of organisations in the UK and, to a lesser extent, overseas.

In 2007/08 the trust had assets of £200,000 and an income of £11,000. Grants were made to 13 organisations totalling £61,000. A further £1,500 was given to individuals.

The major beneficiaries were The Vanessa Grant Trust (£20,000) and CURE International (£15,000). Smaller grants included those to: Kenya Outreach Account (£7,000); World Vision (£5,000); The Brentford Trust (£4,000); CARE and Meah Trust (£3,000 each); Lambeth Partnership (£1,000); SOS Children's Villages (£500); and The Treloar Trust (£50).

Applications The trust has stated that 'no applications will be considered'.

The Modiano Charitable Trust

Arts, Jewish and general

£79,000 (2007/08)
Beneficial area UK and overseas

Broad Street House, 55 Old Broad Street, London EC2M 1RX
Tel. 020 7012 0000
Correspondent G Modiano, Trustee
Trustees *G Modiano; Mrs B Modiano; L S Modiano; M Modiano.*
CC Number 328372
Information available Accounts are on file at the Charity Commission.

In 2007/08 the trust had an income of £100,000 and made grants totalling £79,000. Although in previous years around 30–40 per cent of the trust's income has been given in grants to Jewish organisations, this year saw support mainly going to arts organisations. However, its core charities were not neglected, whilst a number of new recipients were added.

The largest grants were to: Philharmonia Orchestra (£20,000); Weiznam Institute Foundation (£7,500); and UJIA and World Jewish Relief (£5,000 each).

Smaller grants went to: Photos of Turkish Synagogues Project (£2,500); The Queen Alexandra Hospital Home (£2,000); Help the Aged (£1,500); European Union Youth Orchestra (£1,000); Inter Act Reading Service (£500); and The Keyboard Charitable Trust (£100).

Applications In writing to the correspondent.

The Moette Charitable Trust

Education and Jewish

£63,000 (2006/07)
Beneficial area UK and overseas.

1 Holden Road, Salford M7 4NL
Tel. 0161 832 8721
Correspondent Simon Lopian, Trustee
Trustees *Simon Lopian; Pearl Lopian; David Haffner.*
CC Number 1068886

Information available Accounts were on file at the Charity Commission.

The principal activity of the trust is the provision of support of the poor and needy for educational purposes.

In 2006/07 the trust had assets of £391,000 and an income of £31,000. Grants to 'various worthwhile causes' totalled £63,000. A list of beneficiaries was unavailable.

Previous grants have included: Finchley Road Synagogue (£15,000); King David Schools – Manchester and Manchester Charitable Trust (£2,500 each); The Purim Fund (£2,000); Yad Voezer and Yeshivas Lev Aryeh (£1,000 each); Hakalo and London School of Jewish Studies (£500 each); Manchester Jewish Federation (£400); and Manchester Seminary for Girls (£50).

Applications In writing to the correspondent.

Mole Charitable Trust

Jewish and general

£320,000 (2007/08)
Beneficial area UK, with a preference for Manchester.

2 Okeover Road, Salford M7 4JX
Tel. 0161 832 8721
Email martin.gross@lopiangb.co.uk
Correspondent Martin Gross, Trustee
Trustees *M Gross; Mrs L P Gross.*
CC Number 281452
Information available Accounts were on file at the Charity Commission.

The objects of the charity are to make donations and loans to educational institutions and charitable organisations, and for the relief of poverty.

In 2007/08 the trust had assets of £2.8 million and an income of £53,000. Grants totalling £320,000 were broken down as follows:

- education (£165,000)
- religious institutions and charitable organisations (£154,000).

A list of beneficiaries for the year was unavailable.

Grants have previously included those to: Three Pillars Charity (£60,000); Manchester Jewish Grammar School (£26,000); Chasdei Yoel Charitable Trust

and United Talmudical Associates Limited (£20,000 each); Binoh of Manchester (£6,000); Beis Ruchel Girls School (£3,000); Manchester Jewish Federation (£2,500); and Our Kids (£1,000).

Applications The trust has stated that it does not wish to receive any new applications.

The D C Moncrieff Charitable Trust

Social welfare and environment

£38,000 (2007/08)
Beneficial area UK and worldwide, with a preference for Norfolk and Suffolk.

8 Quinnell Way, Lowestoft NR32 4WL
Correspondent D J Coleman, Trustee
Trustees *D J Coleman; R E James; M F Dunne.*
CC Number 203919
Information available Accounts were on file at the Charity Commission.

The trust was established in 1961. It supports a number of large UK organisations but tends to concentrate on charities local to Norfolk and Suffolk.

In 2007/08 the trust had assets of £1.8 million and an income of £50,000. Grants were made to organisations totalling £38,000. A list of beneficiaries for the year was unavailable.

Previous grants have included those to: All Hallows Hospital , East Anglia's Children's Hospice and The Society for Lincolnshire History and Archaeology (£2,000 each); Hemley Church PCC, Lowestoft Girl Guides Association and The Scouts Association (£1,000 each); and, BREAK, Strongbones Children's Charitable Trust and East Anglian Air Ambulance Association (£500 each).

Exclusions No grants for individuals.

Applications In writing to the correspondent. The trust has previously stated that demand for funds exceeds available resources; therefore no further requests are currently invited.

Monmouthshire County Council Welsh Church Act Fund

General

£140,000 to organisations (2007/08)
Beneficial area Blaenau Gwent, Caerphilly, Monmouthshire, Torfaen and Newport

Treasurer's Department, Monmouthshire County Council, County Hall, Croesyceiliog, Cwmbran NP44 2XH
Tel. 01633 644644 **Fax** 01633 644260
Correspondent S K F Greenslade
Trustee *Monmouthshire County Council.*
CC Number 507094
Information available Accounts on file at the Charity Commission.

An annual budget set by the authority for grant payments is split between the administrative areas of Blaenau Gwent, Caerphilly, Monmouthshire, Torfaen and Newport on a population basis. A committee set up by the authority approves grant applications on a quarterly basis. The trust supports individuals or organisations that are known to the trustees. It has supported a wide variety of causes including education, people who are blind, sick or in need, older people, medical and social research, recreation, culture and the arts, historic buildings, churches and burial grounds, emergencies and disaster appeals.

In 2007/08 the trust had assets totalling £5 million and an income of around £590,000. Grants to organisations during the year totalled £140,000 of which £87,000 was spent on purposes beneficial to the community and £54,000 on the advancement of religion.

Previous beneficiaries include: Parish Church Llandogo, Parish Church Llangybi, Bridges Community Centre, St David's Foundation Hospice Care and North Wales Society for the Blind.

Applications On a form available from the correspondent, which must be signed by a county councillor. They are considered in March, June, September and December.

The Montague Thompson Coon Charitable Trust

Children with disabilities

£47,000 (2007/08)

Beneficial area UK.

Old Rectory, Church Lane, Colton, Norwich NR9 5DE

Tel. 07766 072592

Correspondent Mrs Philippa Blake-Roberts, Trustee

Trustees *P A Clarke, Chair; J P Lister; Mrs P Blake-Roberts*

CC Number 294096

Information available Accounts were on file at the Charity Commission.

This trust was registered with the Charity Commission in 1986. Grants are made to projects involving children with disabilities, particularly those providing opportunities for recreation and access to the countryside.

In 2007/08 the trust had assets of £1.2 million and an income of £52,000. There were 13 grants made in the year totalling £47,000.

Beneficiaries included: Treloar Trust (£8,800 in two grants); Action Medical Research (£7,500); Cultivations, Fairfields School, SCOPE and The Pasque Charity (£5,000 each); The Springhead Trust (£4,000); The PACE Centre (£3,000); and 3H Fund (£2,000).

Exclusions No grants to individuals.

Applications In writing to the correspondent.

The Colin Montgomerie Charitable Foundation

General

Around £40,000 to organisations (2007)

Beneficial area UK.

c/o Catella, Chiswick Gate, 3rd Floor, 598–608 Chiswick High Road, London W4 5RT

Correspondent Miss Donna Cooksley, Trustee

Trustees *Colin Montgomerie; Guy Kinnings; Jonathan Dudman; Miss Donna Cooksley.*

CC Number 1072388

Information available Information was obtained from the Charity Commission, but was limited.

Set up in November 1998, the foundation aims to support the relief of poverty, the advancement of education and religion, and any other charitable purposes as decided by the trustees.

In 2007 the trust had an income of £12,000 and a total expenditure of £50,000. Grants totalled around £40,000. Details on beneficiaries were not available for the year. However, previous recipients have included British Lung Foundation, Cancer Vaccine Institute, NSPCC for the Full Stop Campaign and University of Glasgow MRI Scanner Fund.

Applications In writing to the correspondent.

The George A Moore Foundation

General

£635,000 (2007/08)

Beneficial area Principally Yorkshire and the Isle of Man.

Mitre House, North Park Road, Harrogate HG1 5RX

Website www.gamf.org.uk

Correspondent Mrs A L James, Chief Administrator

Trustees *George A Moore; Mrs E Moore; J R Moore; P D Turner*

CC Number 262107

Information available Accounts were on file at the Charity Commission

The trustees of the foundation select causes and projects from applications received during the year, as well as using independent research to identify specific objectives where they wish to direct assistance.

In 2007/08 the trust had assets of £7.4 million and an income of £550,000. A total of £635,000 was distributed in grants, the majority of which were for £5,000 or less.

The largest grant of £140,000 went to Macmillan Cancer Relief. Other major beneficiaries included: Henshaws College – Living Life Campaign (£27,000); The Ear Trust and Gateway Action (£25,000 each); and King James School – Knaresborough and Knaresborough Players – Frazer Theatre (£20,000 each).

Other grants went to: Teeside Hospice Care Foundation (£10,000); The Woodland Trust (£8,000); British Association for Adoption and Fostering, Harrogate Homeless Project Ltd, Life Education Centres, Ocean Youth Trust – North East and Yorkshire Yoga and Therapy Centre (£5,000 each); Brainwave (£3,000); Ilkley & District CVS (£2,000); Horsforth Live at Home Scheme (£1,000); Blood Pressure Association and Parent Lifeline (£500 each); and Sulby Horticultural Show (£200).

Exclusions No assistance will be given to individuals, courses of study, expeditions, overseas travel, holidays, or for purposes outside the UK. Local appeals for UK charities will only be considered if in the area of interest. Because of present long-term commitments, the foundation is not prepared to consider appeals for religious property or institutions.

Applications In writing to the correspondent. No guidelines or application forms are issued. The trustees meet approximately four times a year, on variable dates, and an appropriate response is sent out after the relevant meeting.

The Nigel Moores Family Charitable Trust

Arts

£540,000 (2007/08)

Beneficial area UK, but mostly Liverpool and Wales.

c/o Macfarlane and Co., 2nd Floor, Cunard Building, Water Street, Liverpool L3 1DS

Tel. 0151 236 6161 **Fax** 0151 236 1095

Correspondent P Kurthausen, Accountant

Trustees *J C S Moores; Mrs P M Kennaway.*

CC Number 1002366

Information available Accounts were on file at the Charity Commission.

The trustees have determined that their principal objective should be the raising of the artistic taste of the public, whether in relation to music, drama, opera, painting, sculpture or otherwise in connection with the fine arts, the promotion of education in the fine arts and academic education, the promotion of the environment, the provision of facilities for recreation or other leisure time occupation and the advancement of religion.

In 2007/08 the trust had assets of £90,000 and an income of £376,000. Grants during the year totalled £540,000, the major beneficiary of which was The A Foundation which received a grant of £525,000 (the trustees of the trust are also trustees of The A Foundation). The other grant recipients were: London Library (£20,000); Mostyn Gallery (£10,000); University of York (£6,750); Art School Palestine (£1,000); and Matts Gallery (£500).

Applications In writing to the correspondent.

The Morel Charitable Trust

General

£48,000 (2005/06)

Beneficial area UK and the developing world.

34 Durand Gardens, London SW9 0PP

Tel. 020 7582 6901

Correspondent S E Gibbs, Trustee

Trustees *J M Gibbs, Chair; W M Gibbs; S E Gibbs; B M O Gibbs; Dr T Gibbs; Dr Emily Parry; Mrs Susanna Coan.*

CC Number 268943

Information available No accounts on file at the Charity Commission since 2003.

The trust supports: the arts, particularly drama; organisations working for improved race relations; inner-city projects and developing-world projects. Also supported are: culture and recreation; health; conservation and environment; education and training; and social care and development.

Previous beneficiaries included: Child2Child – Ecuador and Oxfam –

South African drought (£3,000 each); Planned Parenthood Action – Ghana (£2,500); Harvest Help – Zambia (£2,000); Pecan – UK (£1,000); and Youth Music Theatre (£500).

Exclusions No grants to individuals.

Applications In writing to the correspondent. The trustees normally meet three times a year to consider applications.

The Morgan Charitable Foundation

Welfare, hospices, medical, Jewish and general

£76,000 (2008)

Beneficial area UK.

MCF, PO Box 57749, London NW11 1FD

Tel. 079 6882 7709

Correspondent The Trustees

Trustees *The Morgan Charitable Foundation Trustees Ltd. (A Morgan; L Morgan; Mrs C Morgan).*

CC Number 283128

Information available Accounts were on file at the Charity Commission.

The Morgan Charitable Foundation (previously known as The Erich Markus Charitable Foundation) was established in 1979 when, following Erich Markus's death, half of his residual estate was left to the trust. The original capital was made up of 355,000 ordinary 25p shares in Office and Electronic Machines Ltd.

In 2008 the foundation had assets at £3.2 million and an income of £41,000. Grants were made to 25 organisations and totalled £76,000.

The two largest grants went to Magen David Adom and World Jewish Relief (£8,000 each). Other major beneficiaries included: Chai Cancer Care, JNF Charitable Trust and Mango (£5,000 each).

All other grants were for £4,000 or less. Recipients included: Jewish Care and One to One Children's Fund (£4,000 each); Duke of Edinburgh Award and London Pro Arte Choir (£2,000 each); and In Kind Direct Charity and South East Cancer Help Centre (£1,000 each).

Exclusions No grants to individuals.

Applications In writing to the correspondent. Applications will only be considered if accompanied by a copy of the charitable organisation's latest report and accounts. Trustees meet twice a year, usually in April and October. No telephone enquiries.

Diana and Allan Morgenthau Charitable Trust

Jewish and general

£119,000 (2007/08)

Beneficial area Worldwide.

Flat 27, Berkeley House, 15 Hay Hill, London W1J 8NS

Tel. 020 7493 1904

Correspondent Allan Morgenthau, Trustee

Trustees *Allan Morgenthau; Diana Morgenthau.*

CC Number 1062180

Information available Accounts were on file at the Charity Commission.

Registered with the Charity Commission in April 1997, grants are made to a range of Jewish, medical, education and arts organisations. In 2007/08 the trust had an income of £126,000, of which £125,000 came from the Archie Sherman Charitable Trust. Grants totalling £119,000 were broken down as follows:

- general donations and overseas aid (£88,000)
- education and training (£13,000)
- arts and culture (£10,000)
- medical, health and sickness (£8,000).

The four largest grants were to: The British Friends of the Jaffa Institute (£20,000); The Central British Fund for World Jewish Relief (£15,000); and United Jewish Israel Appeal and JNF Charitable Trust (£10,000 each).

Other beneficiaries included: Rays of Sunshine (£5,000); The Hope Centre for Cognitive Education (£2,000); Royal National Theatre (£1,000); London Master Class (£500); British WIZO (£250); and Rishon MS Society (£150).

Applications In writing to the correspondent.

The Oliver Morland Charitable Trust

Quakers and general

£114,000 (2007/08)

Beneficial area UK.

Thomas's House, Stower Row, Shaftesbury SP7 0QW

Tel. 01747 853524

Correspondent J M Rutter, Trustee

Trustees *Priscilla Khan; Stephen Rutter; Joseph Rutter; Jennifer Pittard; Kate Lovell; Charlotte Jones; Simon Pittard.*

CC Number 1076213

Information available Accounts were on file at the Charity Commission.

The trustees state that the majority of funds are given to Quaker projects or Quaker-related projects, which are usually chosen through the personal knowledge of the trustees. In 2007/08 the trust had assets of £1.5 million, an income of £103,000 and made grants totalling £114,000.

Grants were broken down as follows:

Quaker and schools – 25 grants totalling £91,000
Beneficiaries included: Quaker Peace and Service (£30,000); Quaker Home Service – children and young people (£16,000); Quaker Social Action (£5,000); Ulster Quaker Service (£4,000); Peter Bedford Trust (£2,000); and The Leaveners (£1,000).

Health and social care – 9 grants totalling £7,600
Beneficiaries included: Refugee Council (£2,000); Sightsavers International (£1,500); Glade (£1,000); Relate – Dorset (£500); Bishop Creighton House (£350); and Pilsdon Community (£250).

International and environment – 3 grants totalling £3,800
Beneficiaries included: Pakistan Environmental Protection Foundation (£3,000); SOS Sahel (£750); and Henry Doubleday Association (£45).

Animals and nature – 6 grants totalling £5,500
Beneficiaries included: Dorset Wildlife Trust, Hestercombe Gardens, National Trust, Somerset Wildlife Trust, and Woodland Trust (£1,000 each); and Kingcombe Trust (£500).

Meeting house appeals – 4 grants totalling £2,000
Meeting houses in Adel, Aireton, Thirsk and Worcester received grants of £500 each.

Sundry – 6 grants totalling £4,400
Beneficiaries included: Bristol Mediation and Medical Aid for Palestine (£1,000 each); Mendip CAB (£900); Bethlehem Link, Community of the Holy Fire and Praxis (£500 each).

Exclusions No grants to individuals.

Applications 'Most of our grants are for continuing support of existing beneficiaries (approx 90 per cent) so there is little left for responding to new appeals. We receive unsolicited applications at the rate of six or seven each week, 99 per cent are not even considered.'

S C and M E Morland's Charitable Trust

Quaker, sickness, welfare, peace and development overseas

£34,000 (2007/08)

Beneficial area UK.

Gable House, Parbrook, Glastonbury BA6 8PB

Tel. 01458 850 804

Correspondent J C Morland, Trustee

Trustees *J C Morland; Ms J E Morland; Miss E Boyd; H N Boyd.*

CC Number 201645

Information available Accounts were on file at the Charity Commission.

The trust states in its annual report and accounts that it 'gives to Quaker, local and national charities which have a strong social bias, and also to some UK-based international charities'. Also, that it supports those charities concerned with the relief of poverty and ill health, and those promoting peace and development overseas.

The trust generally makes grants to charities it has supported on a long-term basis, but each year this list is reviewed and new charities may be added.

In 2007/08 the trust had assets of £947,000 and an income of £42,000. Grants to 101 charities totalled £34,000.

Only two grants of £1,000 or over were made and thus required listing in the accounts. These were to Britain Yearly Meeting (£7,000) and Oxfam (£1,000).

Exclusions The trust does not usually give to animal welfare, individuals or medical research.

Applications In writing to the correspondent. The trustees meet twice a year to make grants, in March and December. Applications should be submitted in the month before each meeting.

The Bernard Morris Charitable Trust

General

£60,000 (2007/08)

Beneficial area UK.

5 Wolvercote Green, Oxford OX2 8BD

Tel. 01865 516 593

Correspondent Simon Ryde, Trustee

Trustees *Simon Ryde; Judith Silver; Simon Fineman.*

CC Number 266532

Information available Information was available from the Charity Commission.

In 2007/08 the trust had an income of £9,000 and made grants totalling around £60,000. No details of the beneficiaries were available.

Previous grant recipients included: Oxford Synagogue (£16,000); Dragon School Trust (£12,000); One Voice (£2,500); OCJHS – Oxford Centre for Jewish and Hebrew Studies (£2,000); Soundabout (£1,000); the Story Museum (£500); and Centrepoint Homeless (£200).

Applications In writing to the correspondent.

The Willie and Mabel Morris Charitable Trust

Medical and general

£116,000 (2007/08)

Beneficial area UK.

41 Field Lane, Letchworth Garden City SG6 3LD

Tel. 01462 480 583

Correspondent Angela Tether

Trustees *Michael Macfadyen; Alan Bryant; Peter Tether; Andrew Tether; Angela Tether; Suzanne Marriott.*

CC Number 280554

Information available Full accounts were on file at the Charity Commission.

The trust was established in 1980 by Mr and Mrs Morris. It was constituted for general charitable purposes and specifically to relieve physical ill-health, particularly cancer, heart trouble, cerebral palsy, arthritis and rheumatism. Grants are usually only given to registered charities.

In 2007/08 the trust had assets of £3.4 million and an income of £117,000. Grants were made totalling £116,000.

The largest grants were those to: Paul Strickland – Mount Vernon Hospital (£15,000); Brickwell and Miller Charity, St John's Hospice and University of Cambridge (£10,000 each). Medium-sized grants of £5,000 each were given to Covent Garden Cancer Research Trust, East Anglian Air Ambulance, The High Blood Pressure Foundation, MS Trust, St Thomas Trust and the Stroke Association.

Smaller grants included: The Bedford Hospital Charity (£2,000); Hospices at Home (£1,000); The Dorchester Abbey Preservation Trust (£750); The Royal British Legion (£500); Lowe Syndrome Trust (£250); and The Scleroderma Society (£100).

Exclusions No grants for individuals or non-registered charities.

Applications The trustees 'formulate an independent grants policy at regular meetings so that funds are already committed'.

The Morris Charitable Trust

Relief of need, education, community support and development

£98,000 (2007/08)

Beneficial area UK, with a preference for Islington.

c/o Management Office, Business Design Centre, 52 Upper Street, London N1 0QH

Tel. 020 7359 3535 **Fax** 020 7226 0590

Email info@morrischaritabletrust.com

Website www.morrischaritabletrust.com

Correspondent Jack A Morris, Trustee

Trustees *Jack A Morris, Chair; Paul B Morris; Alan R Stenning.*

CC Number 802290

Information available Accounts were on file at the Charity Commission.

The Morris Charitable Trust was established in 1989 to provide support for charitable causes. It was founded by the Morris Family, whose principal business – The Business Design Centre Group Ltd – is based in Islington, London. The group contributes a proportion of its annual profits to facilitate the trust's charitable activities.

The trust has general charitable purposes, placing particular emphasis on alleviating social hardship and deprivation, supporting national, international and local charities. There is a preference for supporting causes within the borough of Islington.

In 2007/08 the trust had assets of £180,000 and an income of £106,000, mainly from donations received from the above mentioned company. Grants totalling £98,000 were made to 171 beneficiaries, the majority of which (134) received a grant of less than £500 each. 14 organisations received a grant of between £1,000 and £5,000, whilst one received a grant for £7,500. No further information was available.

Exclusions No grants for individuals. No repeat donations are made within 12 months.

Applications By application form available from the trust or downloadable from its website. The completed form should be returned complete with any supporting documentation and a copy of your latest report and accounts.

The trustees generally meet monthly.

The Peter Morrison Charitable Foundation

Jewish and general

£87,000 (2007/08)

Beneficial area UK.

Begbies Chettle Agar Chartered Accountants, Epworth House, 25 City Road, London EC1Y 1AR

Tel. 020 7628 5801

Correspondent J Payne

Trustees *M Morrison; I R Morrison; Mrs J Morrison; Mrs L Greenhill.*

CC Number 277202

Information available Full accounts were on file at the Charity Commission.

In the trust's annual report it states:

The trustees are concerned to make donations to charitable institutions which in the opinion of the trustees are most in need and which provide a beneficial service to the needy.

In 2007/08 the trust had assets of £960,000 and an income of £27,000. Grants totalling £87,000 were made during the year, mostly for £500 each or less.

The largest grants were those to: World Jewish Relief (£10,000); St Giles Church (£6,400); St Johns and Highwoods Community Association (£6,300); Project 2005 (£4,800); RNLI (£4,300); and Spinal Injuries Association (£4,200).

Smaller grants included those to: Donkey Sanctuary (£1,000); Jewish Blind and Disabled (£500); MIND (£300); Prisoners Education Trust (£250); Starlight Children's Foundation (£100); and Tate Friends (£75).

Applications In writing to the correspondent.

G M Morrison Charitable Trust

Medical, education and welfare

£153,000 (2007/08)

Beneficial area UK.

235

Currey and Co., 21 Buckingham Gate, London SW1E 6LS

Tel. 020 7802 2700

Correspondent A E Cornick, Trustee

Trustees *N W Smith, Chair; A E Cornick; J A Hunt; E H Morrison.*

CC Number 261380

Information available Full accounts were on file at the Charity Commission.

Grants are given to a wide variety of activities in the social welfare, medical and education/training fields. The trust maintains a list of beneficiaries that it has regularly supported.

In 2007/08 the trust had assets of £7.3 million and a total income of £847,000. Grants were made to 236 organisations totalling £153,000 and ranged from £400 to £10,000 each. The average size of grant was £650.

By far the largest grant was £10,000 to University of Aberdeen Development Trust. Other large grants included those to: British Red Cross and Christian Aid (£3,000 each); The Circulation Foundation (£2,200); Practical Action Bangladesh Emergency Appeal (£2,000); Ninewells Hospital (Dundee) Cancer Campaign (£1,200); and Royal Academy of Music (£1,000).

Grants under £1,000 each included those to: Schools Outreach (£950); Corporation for the Sons of the Clergy (£750); Family Welfare Association (£650); British Vascular Foundation (£550); Prisoners Abroad (£450); and Liverpool School of Tropical Medicine (£400).

Exclusions No support for individuals, charities not registered in the UK, schemes or activities which are generally regarded as the responsibility of statutory authorities, short-term projects or one-off capital grants (except for emergency appeals).

Applications The trust's annual report states:

Beneficiaries of grants are normally selected on the basis of trustees' personal knowledge and recommendation. The trust's grantmaking is however of a long-term recurring nature and is restricted by available income. The trustees have decided that for the present, new applications for grants will only be considered in the most exceptional circumstances; any spare income will be allocated to increasing the grants made to charities currently receiving support. In the future this policy will of course be reviewed. Applicants who understanding this policy nevertheless wish to apply for a grant should write to the [correspondent].

Monitoring is undertaken by assessment of annual reports and accounts which are required from all beneficiaries, and by occasional trustee visits.

Moshal Charitable Trust

Jewish

£76,000 (2007/08)

Beneficial area UK.

c/o S Yodaiken & Co., 40a Bury New Road, Prestwich, Manchester M25 0LD

Correspondent The Trustees

Trustees *D Halpern; L Halpern.*

CC Number 284448

Information available Accounts were on file at the Charity Commission.

In 2007/08, the trust had assets of £526,000 and an income of £307,000 mainly from donations and the sale of investments. Grants during the year totalled £76,000 but no grants list was included in the file at the Charity Commission.

Applications In writing to the correspondent.

Vyoel Moshe Charitable Trust

Education and the relief of poverty

1 million (2007/08)

Beneficial area UK and overseas.

2–4 Chardmore Road, London N16 6HX

Tel. 020 7806 2598

Correspondent J Weinberger, Secretary

Trustees *J Frankel; B Berger; S Seidenfeld.*

CC Number 327054

Information available Accounts were on file at the Charity Commission, but without a list of grants or a narrative report.

In 2007/08 the trust's assets totalled £56,000 and it had an income, mainly from donations, of £1.1 million. Grants were made totalling £1 million and were broken down as follows: Overseas

(£984,000); and Zorchei yom tov – UK (£43,000).

Applications In writing to the correspondent.

The Moshulu Charitable Trust

Humanitarian and evangelical

£99,000 (2007/08)

Beneficial area UK.

Devonshire Road, Heathpark, Honiton EX14 1SD

Correspondent H J Fulls, Trustee

Trustees *H J Fulls; D M Fulls; G N Fulls; S M Fulls; G F Symons.*

CC Number 1071479

Information available Accounts were on file at the Charity Commission.

Set up in September 1998, in 2007/08 the trust had an income of £81,000 including £73,000 from donations and made grants totalling £99,000. Assets stood at £183,000.

Beneficiaries included: Seaway Trust (£40,000); Christ Church (£15,000); SWYM (£12,000); Vineyard (£6,000); Tear Fund (£5,200); Open Door Centre (£2,900); and Care for the Family (£2,500).

Applications In writing to the correspondent.

Brian and Jill Moss Charitable Trust

Jewish and healthcare

£178,000 (2007/08)

Beneficial area Worldwide.

c/o Deloitte, Blenheim House, Fitzalan Court, Newport Road, Cardiff CF24 0TS

Correspondent The Trustees

Trustees *Brian Peter Moss; Jill Moss; David Paul Moss; Sarah Levy.*

CC Number 1084664

Information available Accounts were on file at the Charity Commission.

Established in 2000, this trust makes grants for capital projects and towards 'ordinary charity expenditure'. In 2007/08 it had assets of almost £3 million and an income of £281,000. Grants to 20 organisations totalled £178,000.

Beneficiaries included: United Jewish Israel Appeal (£43,000); Magen David Adom UK (£31,000); Jewish Care (£16,000); World Jewish Relief (£15,000); Norwood (£13,000); Chai Cancer Care (£12,000); United Synagogue-Tribe (£11,000); Cancer Backup (£6,300); WIZO UK (£6,000); National Jewish Chaplaincy Board (£5,500); Prostate Cancer Charitable Trust (£5,000); Jewish Association for the Mentally Ill (£3,500); Myeloma UK (£3,000); Holocaust Centre and Israel Folk Dance Institute (£500 each); and Jewish Museum and Operation Wheelchairs (£250 each).

Exclusions Donations are made to registered charities only.

Applications In writing to the correspondent. 'Appeals are considered as they are received and the trustees will make donations throughout the year.'

The Moss Charitable Trust

Christian, education, poverty and health

£81,000 to organisations (2007/08)

Beneficial area Worldwide, with an interest in Dorset, Hampshire and Sussex.

7 Church Road, Parkstone, Poole BH14 8UF

Tel. 01202 730002

Correspondent P D Malpas

Trustees *J H Simmons; A F Simmons; P L Simmons; D S Olby.*

CC Number 258031

Information available Information was provided by the trust.

The objects of the trust are to benefit the community in the county borough of Bournemouth and the counties of Hampshire, Dorset and Sussex, and also the advancement of religion in the UK and overseas, the advancement of education and the relief of poverty, disease and sickness.

The trust achieves this by providing facilities for contributors to give under Gift Aid or direct giving and redistributes them according to their recommendations. The trustees also make smaller grants from the general income of the trust.

In 2007/08 the trust had assets of £59,000, an income of £90,000 and made 140 grants totalling £86,000. These were categorised by the trust as follows:

- UK institutions (£79,000)
- overseas institutions (£1,500)
- UK individuals (£3,000)
- overseas individuals (£2,300).

Beneficiaries receiving grants of £1,000 or more, included: Tabitha Trust (£8,000); Walking on Water Trust (£6,500); Christ Church – Westbourne (£6,400); Tamil Church (£2,500); Chichester Counselling Service and St James – Poole (£2,000 each); Barnabus Fund (£1,600); European Christian Mission (£1,300); Ebenezer Emergency Fund (£1,200); and Yapton PCC (£1,000).

Applications No funds are available by direct application. Because of the way in which this trust operates it is not open to external applications for grants.

J P Moulton Charitable Foundation

Medical, education, training and counselling

£1.2 million (2008)
Beneficial area UK.

The Mount, Church Street Shoreham, Sevenoaks TN14 7SD

Tel. 01959 524 008

Correspondent J P Moulton, Trustee

Trustees *J P Moulton; Mrs P M Moulton; Sara Everett.*

CC Number 1109891

Information available Accounts were on file at the Charity Commission.

As described in the foundation's report, the foundation provides 'charitable donations for community service projects of any kind and to further the aims of the community by promoting education, training, counselling for disadvantaged persons of any age; to provide donations to hospitals, hospices,

medical and care projects of any kind and to generally promote the relief of suffering.'

In 2008 the trust had assets of £8.4 million and an income of £1.2 million. Grants were made totalling £1.2 million of which roughly half went towards funding medical research projects. Major beneficiaries included: Imperial College (£126,000); University of Manchester (£76,000); Meningitis Research Foundation (£57,000); University College London and the University of Leicester (£55,000 each); and South Manchester University Hospital (£53,000).

Other donations included those made to: St Martin-in-the-Fields and The Stoke-on-Trent and North Staffordshire Theatre Trust (£100,000 each); Marlborough Primary School (£50,000); Muir Maxwell Trust (£24,000); St Christopher's Hospice (£5,000); and Action on Addiction (£500).

Applications In writing to the correspondent.

Mountbatten Festival of Music

Royal Marines and Royal Navy charities

£123,000 (2007/08)
Beneficial area UK.

The Corps Secretariat, Building 32, HMS Excellent, Whale Island, Portsmouth PO2 8ER

Tel. 02392 547 201

Email royalmarines.charities@charity. vfree.com

Website www.royalmarinesregimental. co.uk

Correspondent Lt Col I W Grant, Corps Secretary

Trustees *Commandant General Royal Marines; Director of Royal Marines; Naval Personnel Team (RM) Team Leader*

CC Number 1016088

Information available Information was on file at the Charity Commission.

The trust was set up in 1993 and is administered by the Royal Marines. It raises funds from band concerts, festivals of music and Beating Retreat.

Unsurprisingly, the main beneficiaries are service charities connected with the Royal Marines and Royal Navy. The only other beneficiaries are those hospitals or rehabilitation centres and so on, which have recently directly aided a Royal Marine in some way, and Malcolm Sergeant Cancer Care. One-off and recurrent grants are made.

In 2008/09 the trust had an income of £263,000 and expenditure of £294,000. No further information was available for this accounting year.

In 2007/08 the trust had assets of £159,000 and an income of £292,000. Grants were made totalling £123,000.

Major beneficiaries during the year were: Malcolm Sergeant Cancer Fund (£20,000); Metropolitan Police Benevolent Trust (14,000); RN Benevolent Fund, RNRMC and RM Museum (£10,000 each).

Beneficiaries of smaller grants included: Wrens Benevolent Trust, Seafarers UK, Royal British Legion, The 'Not Forgotten' Society, Queen Ann Hospital Home, and Scottish Veterans Residences (£1,000 each).

Exclusions Charities/organisations unknown to the trustees.

Applications Unsolicited applications are not considered as the trust's income is dependent upon the running and success of various musical events. Any money raised by this means is then disbursed to a set of regular beneficiaries.

Information available Full accounts were on file at the Charity Commission.

The trust was set up in 1979 to honour the ideals of the Admiral of the Fleet, the Earl Mountbatten of Burma. It supports charities and causes 'working to further the humanitarian purposes with which he was associated in his latter years'. The trust mainly focuses on making grants towards the development of technical aids for people with disabilities. A previous focus has also been to support the United World Colleges movement, which has the aim of providing a broad education to students from around the world and grants continue to be given to Atlantic College.

Following the merger with the Mountbatten Community Trust in January 2008, grants are now also made to aid the young and disadvantaged in various communities throughout Britain.

In 2007/08 the trust had assets of £520,000 and an income of £51,000. Grants totalling £73,000 were made to the following organisations: Atlantic College (£57,000); Soundabout, Soundaround and Seeing Ear (£3,000 each); St Saviour's Youth Club – Nottingham (£4,000); and St Mary's Youth Club – Stratton (£2,500).

Exclusions No grants are made towards the purchase of technology to assist people with disabilities.

Applications In writing to the correspondent, at any time.

The trust was established in 1960 to honour the causes Edwina, Countess Mountbatten of Burma, was involved with during her lifetime. Each year support is given to St John Ambulance (of which she was superintendent-in-chief) for work in the UK and the Commonwealth, and Save the Children (of which she was president) for the relief of children who are sick, distressed or otherwise in need. Nursing organisations are also supported, as she was the patron or vice-president of a number of nursing organisations. Grants, even to the core beneficiaries, are only given towards specific projects rather than core costs.

In 2007 the trust had assets of £3.4 million and an income of £99,000. Grants totalling £97,000 were made to 12 organisations.

The two major beneficiaries were: Save the Children (£32,000) and St John Ambulance – Romsey (£21,000).

Other grant recipients included: Homestart and St Jerusalem Eye Hospital (£9,000 each); Independent Age UK, Target TB and Whizz Kidz (£5,000 each); Ashram International (£3,000); and Changing Faces and Well Child (£2,000 each).

Exclusions No grants for research or to individual nurses working in the UK for further professional training.

Applications In writing to the correspondent. The trustees meet once a year, generally in September/October.

The Mountbatten Memorial Trust

Technological research in aid of disabilities

£73,000 (2007/08)
Beneficial area Mainly UK, but some overseas.

The Estate Office, Broadlands, Romsey SO51 9ZE

Tel. 01794 529 750

Correspondent John Moss, Secretary

Trustees *Countess Mountbatten of Burma; Lady Pamela Hicks; Ben Moorhead; Ashley Hicks; Hon. Michael John Knatchbull; Hon. Philip Knatchbull.*

CC Number 278691

The Edwina Mountbatten Trust

Medical

£97,000 (2007)
Beneficial area UK and overseas.

Estate Office, Broadlands, Romsey SO51 9ZE

Tel. 01794 529 750

Correspondent John Moss, Secretary

Trustees *Countess Mountbatten of Burma, Chair; Hon. Alexandra Knatchbull; Lord Brabourne; Peter H T Mimpriss; Dame Mary Fagan.*

CC Number 228166

Information available Full accounts were on file at the Charity Commission.

The F H Muirhead Charitable Trust

Hospitals and medical research institutes

About £35,000 (2007/08)
Beneficial area UK.

Merlin House, 6 Boltro Road, Haywards Heath RH16 1BB

Tel. 01444 411 333

Correspondent S J Gallico

Trustees *Dr M J Harding; S J Gallico; Dr R C D Staughton; Prof. D Leslie.*

CC Number 327605

Information available Information was previously provided by the trust.

The trust makes grants for specific items of medical equipment for use in hospitals and medical research institutes. Priority is given to applications from smaller organisations.

In 2007/08 the trust had an income of £20,000 and an expenditure of £48,000. Grants totalled about £35,000. No further information was available.

Previous beneficiaries included: Defeating Deafness (£11,000); Cystic Fibrosis Trust (£9,300); Bath Institute of Medical Engineering (£9,100); Ehlers-Danlos Support Group (£8,000); The David Tolkien Trust for Stoke Mandeville NBIC (£7,700); Covent Garden Cancer Research Trust (£6,400); and High Blood Pressure Foundation (£4,700).

Exclusions No grants to non-charitable bodies. No grants for equipment for diagnostic or clinical use.

Applications On a form available from the correspondent. This should be returned with details of specific items of equipment for which a grant is required. Trustees meet twice a year in March and October. Application forms are to be received at least three weeks before the meeting.

Murphy-Newmann Charity Company Limited

Older and young people with disabilities

£28,500 (2007/08)

Beneficial area UK, predominantly the South, South East and the Midlands.

Hayling Cottage, Upper Street, Stratford-St-Mary, Colchester CO7 6JW

Tel. 01206 323 685 **Fax** 01206 323686

Email mnccl@keme.co.uk

Correspondent M J Lockett, Trustee

Trustees *M J Lockett; Colette Safhill; M Richman.*

CC Number 229555

Information available Accounts were on file at the Charity commission

The trustees state that: the objects of the charity are to support projects aimed at helping those in society who suffer economic or social disadvantages; aid charities working to alleviate chronic illness and disabling diseases among all age groups; and help fund research into medical conditions for which there is not yet a cure.

In 2007/08 the trust had assets of £747,000 and an income of £36,000. Grants were made totalling £28,500 and ranged between £250 and £1,750. Most, however, were for between £500 and £1,500.

The major beneficiaries were Contact the Elderly and Evening Argus Christmas Appeal (£1,750 each) and Elizabeth Finn Trust, Haemophilia Society, RUKBA, Invalids at Home, Norwood Children's and Families Trust, RNIB Sunshine House Nursery School, South East Cancer Help Centre and North London Hospice (£1,000 each).

Other grant recipients included: British Home and Hospital for Incurables and Chicks Camping Holidays (£750 each); REACT and Lowe Syndrome Trust (£500 each); and Dream Makers and 2 Care (£250 each).

Exclusions No grants to individuals, or non-registered charities.

Applications In writing to the correspondent, in a letter outlining the purpose of the required charitable donation. Telephone calls are not welcome. There are no application forms, guidelines or deadlines. No stamped, addressed envelope is required. Grants are usually given in November and December.

The Mushroom Fund

General

£35,000 (2007/08)

Beneficial area UK and overseas, with a preference for St Helens.

Liverpool Charity and Voluntary Services, 151 Dale Street, Liverpool L2 2AH

Tel. 0151 227 5177

Email enquiries@charitycheques.org.uk

Website www.merseytrusts.org.uk

Correspondent The Trustees

Trustees *G Pilkington; Mrs R Christian; Mrs J Wailing; J Pilkington; H Christian; Liverpool Charity and Voluntary Services.*

CC Number 259954

Information available Accounts were available at the Charity Commission.

The trust has general charitable purposes, usually supporting causes known to the trustees.

In 2007/08 the trust had assets of £977,000 and an income of £39,000, gained from investments. Grants were made totalling £35,000.

Beneficiaries receiving grants of £1,000 or more each included: World Society for the Protection of Animals (£3,000); Hearing Dogs for Deaf People (£2,500); Born Free Foundation and UROLINK (£2,000 each); and Bicester Intrepid Scout Group, Buckley and Mold Lions Club, Patterdale Mountain Rescue, Rowans Hospice – Purbrook, Topps Training and Walk the Walk Worldwide (£1,000 each).

Exclusions No grants to individuals or to organisations that are not registered charities.

Applications The trust does not consider or respond to unsolicited applications.

The Music Sales Charitable Trust

Children, young people and musical education

£36,000 (2007)

Beneficial area UK, but mostly Bury St Edmunds and London.

Music Sales Ltd, Dettingen Way, Bury St Edmunds IP33 3YB

Tel. 01284 702 600

Email neville.wignall@musicsales.co.uk

Correspondent Neville Wignall, Clerk

Trustees *Robert Wise; T Wise; Ian Morgan; Christopher Butler; David Rockberger; Mrs Mildred Wise; A E Latham.*

CC Number 1014942

Information available Accounts were on file at the Charity Commission, but without a list of grants.

The trust was established in 1992 by the company Music Sales Ltd. It supports registered charities benefiting children and young adults, musicians, people who

239

are disabled and people disadvantaged by poverty, particularly those resident in London and Bury St Edmunds. The trust is also interested in helping to promote music and musical education, again with a particular interest in children attending schools in London and Bury St Edmunds.

In 2007 the trust had assets of £7,000 and an income of £20,000. During the year grants were made totalling £36,000. No further information was available.

Previous beneficiaries have included: The Purcell School Scholarship (£45,000 in three grants); Suffolk County Council, Music Department (£15,000); Westminster Synagogue (£10,000 in two grants); and St Edmundsbury Borough Council 2005 Festival (£6,000).

Exclusions No grants to individuals.

Applications In writing to the correspondent. The trustees meet quarterly, generally in March, June, September and December.

The Mutual Trust Group

Jewish, education and poverty

£211,000 (2008).
Beneficial area UK.

12 Dunstan Road, London NW11 8AA
Tel. 020 8458 7549
Correspondent B Weitz, Trustee
Trustees *B Weitz; M Weitz; A Weisz.*
CC Number 1039300
Information available Brief accounts were on file at the Charity Commission.

In 2008 the trust had an income of £180,000 and made grants totalling £211,000. The largest grant went to Yeshivat Shar Hashamaym which received £168,000 'to further education'. Other grants recipients were: Yeshivat Kesser Hatalmud (£38,000); Congregation Beis Hamedrash (£4,000); and 'other' (£400).

Applications In writing to the correspondent.

MYA Charitable Trust

Jewish

£142,000 to organisations
(2007/08)
Beneficial area Worldwide.

Medcar House, 149a Stamford Hill, London N16 5LL
Tel. 020 8800 3582
Correspondent M Rothfield, Trustee
Trustees *M Rothfeld; Mrs E Rothfeld; Mrs H Schraiber; J D Pfeffer.*
CC Number 299642
Information available Accounts were on file at the Charity Commission.

In 2007/08 the trust had assets of £893,000 and an income of £191,000. Grants totalled £151,000 of which £9,000 was paid in total to individuals. No further information was available.

Previous beneficiaries have included: ZSV Trust (£3,500); KZF (£3,300); Beis Rochel and Keren Zedoko Vochesed (£2,500 each); London Friends of Kamenitzer Yeshiva and Maos Yesomim Charitable Trust (£2,000 each); Bikkur Cholim De Satmar (£1,100); and Keren Mitzva Trust and Wlodowa Charity Rehabilitation Trust (£1,000 each).

Applications In writing to the correspondent.

MYR Charitable Trust

Jewish

£86,000 (2007)
Beneficial area In practice, Israel, USA and England.

50 Keswick Street, Gateshead, Tyne and Wear NE8 1TQ
Correspondent Z M Kaufman, Trustee
Trustees *Z M Kaufman; S Kaufman; A A Zonszajn; J Kaufman.*
CC Number 1104406
Information available Accounts were on file at the Charity Commission, but without a list of beneficiaries.

In 2007 the trust had assets of £404,000, an income of £103,000 and made grants totalling £86,000. No further information was available.

Previous beneficiaries have included: Cong Beth Joseph (£26,000); HP Charitable Trust (£2,300); UTA (£2,200); Gateshead Jewish Boarding School (£2,000); Keren Eretz Yisorel (£1,800); SCT Sunderland (£1,400) and GJLC (£1,000).

Applications In writing to the correspondent.

The Kitty and Daniel Nabarro Charitable Trust

Welfare, education, medicine, homelessness and general

£82,000 (2007/08)
Beneficial area UK.

PO Box 7491, London N20 8LY
Email nabarro.charity@gmail.com
Correspondent D J N Nabarro, Trustee
Trustees *D J N Nabarro; Katherine Nabarro; Allan Watson.*
CC Number 1002786
Information available Accounts were on file at the Charity Commission.

The trust makes grants towards the relief of poverty, advancement of medicine and advancement of education, with some preference for work with homeless people. This trust will consider funding: information technology and computers; support and self-help groups; nature reserves; environmental issues; IT training; literacy; training for work; vocational training; and crime prevention schemes.

In 2007/08 the trust had assets of £790,000 and an income of £23,000. Grants were made totalling £82,000 as follows: New North London Synagogue – building fund (£50,000); OCD Action (£13,000); and other grants (£19,000).

Exclusions No grants to individuals.

Applications In writing to the correspondent. However, the trustees allocate grants on an annual basis to an existing list of charities. The trustees do not at this time envisage awarding grants to charities which are not already on the list. This trust states that it does not respond to unsolicited applications.

The Nadezhda Charitable Trust

Christian

£83,000 (2007/08)

Beneficial area UK and worldwide, particularly Zimbabwe.

C/o Ballard Dale Syree Watson LLP, Oakmore Court, Kingswood Road, Hampton Lovett, Droitwich Spa WR9 0GH

Correspondent Mrs Jill Kingston, Trustee

Trustees *William M Kingston; Mrs Jill M Kingston; Anthony R Collins; Ian Conolly.*

CC Number 1007295

Information available Accounts were on file at the Charity Commission.

The trust makes grants to projects for the advancement of Christianity in the UK and overseas, especially in Zimbabwe.

In 2007/08 the trust had assets of £36,000, an income of £66,000 and made grants totalling £83,000. Of this £52,000 came from restricted funds which are designated for use in Zimbabwe. The beneficiaries of this were: Bible Society – Zimbabwe Ndebele Bibles Project (£17,000); Friends of the Theological College of Zimbabwe in the USA (£12,000); Ebenezer Project (£10,000); Evangelical Fellowship of Zimbabwe (£7,000); and Bulawayo Orphanage (£5,000).

Grants totalling £32,000 were made from the unrestricted fund, including those to CHIPS (£5,000), All Saints' Worcester (£2,000) and Friends of George Whitefield College (£1,500).

Exclusions No grants to individuals.

Applications The majority of funds are presently directed to supporting the Christian Church in Zimbabwe. The trust does not, therefore, respond to unsolicited applications.

The Willie Nagel Charitable Trust

Jewish and general

£17,000 (2007/08)

Beneficial area UK.

Lubbock Fine, Russell Bedford House, City Forum, 250 City Road, London EC1V 2QQ

Tel. 020 7490 7766

Email anthonysober@lubbockfine.co.uk

Correspondent A L Sober, Trustee

Trustees *W Nagel; A L Sober.*

CC Number 275938

Information available Accounts were available at the Charity Commission, but without a full narrative report or a grants list.

The trust makes grants to registered charities, committing its income before the funds have been generated.

In 2007/08 it had assets of £14,000 and an income of £26,000, almost entirely from donations. Grants were made totalling £17,000. No further information on the size or type of grants, or any details of the beneficiaries was available.

Previous beneficiaries included Board of Deputies Charitable Trust, Friends of Wiznitz, Israel Music Foundation, National Children's Home and Victoria and Albert Museum.

Applications In writing to the correspondent.

The Naggar Charitable Trust

Jewish, the arts and general

£421,000 (2007/08)

Beneficial area UK and overseas.

61 Avenue Road, London NW8 6HR

Tel. 020 7834 8060

Correspondent Mr and Mrs Naggar, Trustees

Trustees *Guy Naggar; Hon. Marion Naggar; Marc Zilkha.*

CC Number 265409

Information available Accounts were on file at the Charity Commission.

The trust mainly supports Jewish organisations and a few medical charities. Arts organisations also receive some support.

In 2007/08 the trust had assets of £109,000, an income of £527,000 and made grants totalling £421,000.

Major grant beneficiaries were: The Tate Gallery (£100,000); Society of Friends of the Torah (£98,000); British Friends of the Art Museums of Israel (£85,000); The Jerusalem Foundation (£70,000); Office of the Chief Rabbi (£20,000); and London Jewish Cultural Centre and United Synagogue Tribe (£10,000 each).

Other beneficiaries included: Tate Foundation – New York (£5,000); The Prince's Foundation – children (£2,500); Camden Arts Centre and Royal Opera House Foundation (£1,000 each); Cancer Research UK (£500); Jewish Music Institute (£250); and The Conservative Party (£80).

Applications In writing to the correspondent.

The Eleni Nakou Foundation

Education and international understanding

Around **£60,000** (2007/08)

Beneficial area Worldwide, mostly Continental Europe.

c/o Kleinwort Benson Trustees Ltd, 30 Gresham Street, London EC2V 7PG

Email chris.gilbert@kbpb.co.uk

Correspondent Chris Gilbert, Secretary

Trustee *Kleinwort Benson Trustees Ltd.*

CC Number 803753

Information available Basic information was available from the Charity Commission.

The main aim of the trust is to advance the education of the people of Europe in each other's culture.

In 2007/08 the foundation had an income of £649 and an expenditure of £66,000. No further details were available.

Previous beneficiaries have included: Danish Institute at Athens (£45,000); Hellenic Foundation (£17,500); Eleni Nakou Scholarship Athens (£9,000); and Scandinavian Society for Modern Greek Studies (£1,100).

Applications In writing to the correspondent. Applications are considered periodically. However, the trustees state: 'It is unusual to respond favourably to unsolicited appeals'.

The Janet Nash Charitable Settlement

Medical, hardship and general

£74,000 to organisations
(2007/08)

Beneficial area UK.

Ron Gulliver and Co. Ltd, The Old Chapel, New Mill Lane, Eversley RG27 0RA

Tel. 01189 733 194

Correspondent R Gulliver, Trustee

Trustees *Ronald Gulliver; M S Jacobs; Mrs C E Coyle.*

CC Number 326880

Information available Full accounts were on file at the Charity Commission.

The trust has general charitable purposes, although it mostly supports medical and social welfare organisations. In 2007/08 the trust had assets of £75,000 and an income of £452,000. Grants were made totalling £378,000, of which £74,000 went to organisations and £304,000 went to individuals.

Four of the largest grants were made to: Shirley Medical Centre (£16,000); The Get A-Head Charitable Trust (£15,000); and Crimestoppers Trust and Martha Trust – Hereford (£10,000 each).

Other grants included those to Aide Au Pere Pedro Opeka (£9,000), Dyslexia Institute (£6,000) and London Philharmonic Orchestra and Vision Charity (£4,000 each).

Grants to individuals totalled £265,000 and were given in two categories:

- medical – £238,000
- hardship relief – £66,000.

Applications Absolutely no response to unsolicited applications. The trustees have stated: 'The charity does not, repeat not, ever consider any applications for benefit from the public'. Furthermore, that: 'Our existing charitable commitments more than use up our potential funds and were found personally by the trustees themselves, never as a result of applications from third parties'.

Nathan Charitable Trust

Evangelical Christian work and mission

£72,000 (2008/09)

Beneficial area UK and overseas.

The Copse, Sheviock, Torpoint PL11 3EL

Tel. 01503 230 413

Correspondent T R Worth, Trustee

Trustees *T R Worth; Mrs P J Worth; G A Jones.*

CC Number 251781

Information available Accounts were on file at the Charity Commission.

In 2008/09 the trust made grants totalling £72,000 many of which receive a grant biennially.

Beneficiaries included: Operation Mobilisation (£11,000); Carrot Tops, Leprosy Mission and Mission Aviation Fellowship (£10,000 each); Open Doors (£6,000); African Inland Mission, Bridges for Peace and Open Air Campaigners (£4,000 each); Rhema Theatre Company (£3,000); and Christian Friends of Israel (£1,000).

Applications Funds are fully committed to current beneficiaries.

The National Manuscripts Conservation Trust

Conservation of manuscripts

£102,000 (2008)

Beneficial area UK.

c/o The National Archives, Ruskin Avenue, Kew TW9 4DU

Tel. 020 8392 5218

Email nmct@nationalarchives.gov.uk

Website www.nationalarchives.gov.uk/preservation/trust/

Correspondent Dr Anna Bulow, Secretary to the Trustees

Trustees *Lord Egremont; B Naylor; C Sebag-Montefiore.*

CC Number 802796

Information available Full accounts were available from the Charity Commission website.

The object of the trust is to advance the education of the public by making grants towards the cost of conserving manuscripts which are of historic or educational value.

The following information is taken from the trust's website.

Grants are awarded in June and December, usually for 50% of the cost of conservation of manuscripts held by any records office, library, capital tax exempt individual or charitable trust. The trustees take into account the significance of the manuscript or archive, the suitability of the storage conditions, the applicant's commitment to continuing good preservation practice, and the requirement for the public to have reasonable access to it.

In 2008 the trust had assets of £1.6 million and an income of £118,000. Grants were made totalling £102,000 of which approximately three-quarters came from the trust's own resources and the balance from the Welsh Assembly Government as part of an initiative to fund preservation projects in Wales.

Beneficiaries during the year included: The Fitzwilliam Museum – towards the Founder's Library Conservation Project (£20,000); Cheshire County Council – towards conservation of the Wyatt and associated architectural drawings at Tatton Park (£18,000); Aberystwyth University – towards the conservation of the Library Planning Archive (£11,000); London Metropolitan Archives – towards the conservation of personal record books from Training Ship Exmouth (£10,000); Dean and Chapter, Exeter Cathedral – towards the conservation of the cathedral's archives (£8,000); and The Library and Museum of Freemasonry – towards the conservation of Building Blocks: The Manuscript Old Charges of British Freemasonry (£1,600).

The trust is administered by the National Archives.

Exclusions The following are not eligible: public records within the meaning of the Public Records Act; official archives of the institution or authority applying except in the case of some older records; loan collections unless exempt from capital taxation or owned by a charitable trust; and photographic, audio-visual or printed materials.

Applications Applicants must submit six copies of the application form including six copies of a detailed description of the project. The applicant should also submit one copy of their most recent annual reports and accounts and details of its constitution.

Visit the trust's website for full details of how to apply.

The Nazareth Trust Fund

Christian, in the UK and developing countries

£28,000 to organisations (2007/08)

Beneficial area UK and developing countries.

Barrowpoint, 18 Millennium Close, Odstock Road, Salisbury SP2 8TB

Tel. 01722 349 322

Correspondent Dr Robert W G Hunt, Trustee

Trustees *Dr Robert W G Hunt; Mrs E M Hunt; Revd David R G Hunt; Mrs Elma R L Hunt; Philip R W Hunt; Mrs Nicola Mhairi Hunt.*

CC Number 210503

Information available Full accounts were available from the Charity Commission website.

The trust funds churches, Christian missionaries, Christian youth work and overseas aid. Grants are only made to people or causes known personally to the trustees.

In 2007/08 the trust had an income of £44,000 and made grants totalling around £32,000. Grants made to organisations totalled £28,000. Major beneficiaries included: Bridge Project, Crusaders, Harnham Free Church, Northwood Hills Evangelical Church, Scripture Union and World Vision.

Exclusions No support for individuals not known to the trustees.

Applications In writing to the correspondent, although the trust tends to only support organisations it is directly involved with.

Ner Foundation

Orthodox Jewish

£222,000 (2007/08)

Beneficial area UK and Israel.

309 Bury New Road, Salford, Manchester M7 2YN

Correspondent A Henry, Trustee

Trustees *A Henry; N Neumann; Mrs E Henry.*

CC Number 1104866

Information available Accounts were on file at the Charity Commission, without a list of grants.

Set up in July 2004 as a company limited by guarantee, 'the objects of the charity are the relief of poverty amongst older people or persons in need, hardship or distress in the Jewish Community; the advancement of the orthodox Jewish religion and the advancement of education according to the tenets of the orthodox Jewish faith', as stated in the annual report.

In 2007/08 the foundation had assets of £431,000 and an income of £34,000. Grants totalling £222,000 were broken down as follows:

- relief of poverty – £104,000
- schools – £64,000
- yeshivos and seminaries – £23,000
- advancement of religion – £14,000
- kollel – £10,000
- grants under £1,000 each – £7,500.

Applications In writing to the correspondent.

Nesswall Ltd

Jewish

£110,000 (2007/08)

Beneficial area UK

28 Overlea Road, London E5 9BG

Tel. 020 8806 2965

Correspondent Mrs R Teitelbaum, Secretary

Trustees *I Teitelbaum, Chair; Mrs R Teitelbaum; I Chersky; Mrs H Wahrhaftig.*

CC Number 283600

Information available Accounts were on file at the Charity Commission but without a recent list of grants.

In 2007/08 the trust had assets of £625,000 and an income of £154,000.

Grants and donations totalled £110,000. A list of grants was not available. Previous beneficiaries have included Friends of Horim Establishments, Torah Vochesed L'Ezra Vesaad and Emunah Education Centre.

Applications In writing to the correspondent, at any time.

Newby Trust Limited

Welfare

£415,000 to organisations and individuals (2007/08)

Beneficial area UK.

Hill Farm, Froxfield, Petersfield GU32 1BQ

Tel. 01730 827 557 **Fax** 01730 827938

Email info@newby-trust.org.uk

Website www.newby-trust.org.uk

Correspondent Miss W Gillam, Secretary, Secretary

Trustees *Mrs S A Charlton; Mrs J M Gooder; Dr R D Gooder; Mrs A S Reed; R B Gooder; Mrs A L Foxell.*

CC Number 227151

Information available Full accounts were available from the Charity Commission website.

The following information regarding the trust's work is taken from its 2007/08 annual report and accounts.

The company works nationally, in particular to promote medical welfare, education, training and research, and the relief of poverty. The company does not provide funding for non UK activities or education, but takes steps to ensure the grants disbursed are spread as widely as possible to those in need within the United Kingdom.

Medical welfare

To help alleviate physical and mental suffering within the United Kingdom, the company provides:

- small grants to individuals towards essential equipment, such as mobility aids, specialist chairs and beds
- larger grants on occasions, to registered charities for medical research, equipment, building improvements, and so on. These are often related to the company's annual special category, as noted below.

Education, training and research

Widening Participation policies within the United Kingdom have led to an increased demand for postsecondary school education and training. The company assists those individuals in need of additional funding with educational grants. These are not hardship funds, but recognition of merit in relation to need. The company promotes education by providing:

- grants (to a maximum of £1,000 per annum) to students who have a record of academic achievement within the United Kingdom and a confirmed placement
- larger grants to registered charities and educational establishments for educational, cultural, sporting, or other projects. Once again these are often associated with the annual special category (see below).

Relief of poverty

Recognising that there is widespread poverty and privation within the United Kingdom, some of which manifests itself as crime, violence, bullying, or domestic intimidation, the company makes:

- small grants to individuals for home comforts, clothing, school uniforms, footwear, white goods, flooring, and so on
- larger grants to registered charities for community projects, refurbishment of community halls and buildings, the alleviation of homelessness, and so on, again often related to the company's annual special category.

Annual Special Category

Under the general headings above, the directors have a policy of selecting one category for special support each year:

- in 2008/09 it was respite support for carers of older people or those incapacitated
- for 2009/10 (6 April – 5 April) it is projects and/or training that encourage artisan skills, for example sculpture, printing, thatching, weaving, and so on.

In 2007/08 the trust had assets of £13.3 million and an income of £398,000. 485 grants were made to organisations and individuals following 1,622 applications and totalled £415,000. Grants were broken down as follows:

- **education, training and research (£335,000)**
- **relief of poverty (£58,000)**
- **medical welfare (£22,000).**

Please note: Within 'Education, training and research', £216,000 came under the annual special category award. Overall around £69,000 went to organisations in support of individuals.

Major beneficiaries included: I CAN, InterAct, Liverpool Cathedral, The Martlets Hospice, Rowan Tree Trust and The Social Mobility Foundation (£10,000 each); Echoes of Service (£7,000); Amani Foundation, Blenheim Scout Group,

Chance to Shine – the Cricket Foundation, The Hardman Trust, National Literacy Trust and Theatre Royal Bath (£5,000 each); Tall Ships Youth Trust (£4,000); The Michael Palin Centre for Stammering Children (£3,600); Citizenship Foundation and Glasgow Social Work (£3,000 each); British Athletic Charitable Trust (£2,500); Bolton Lads and Girls Club and Groundwork – Cheshire (£2,000 each); and No Limits Theatre (£1,000).

Applications The application procedure differs between each category as follows:

Annual special category – unsolicited applications will not be considered;

Education, training and research – the trust currently has four selected institutions (City University, London, The London School of Economics & Political Science, The University of Edinburgh and The University of Manchester). Grants are awarded at the discretion of these universities subject to guidelines related to the purposes of the trust.

Medical welfare and *Relief of poverty* – Social Services or similar organisations may apply only online on behalf of individuals in need using the pre-application screening form.

The Richard Newitt Fund

Education

£75,000 (2006/07)
Beneficial area UK.

Kleinwort Benson Trustees Ltd, 30 Gresham Street, London EC2V 7PG

Tel. 020 3207 7356

Correspondent The Administrator

Trustees *Kleinwort Benson Trustees Ltd; D A Schofield; Prof. D Holt; Baroness Diana Maddock.*

CC Number 276470

Information available Full accounts were on file at the Charity Commission.

In 2007/08 the trust had an income of £69,000 and expenditure of £2.2 million. No further information regarding the beneficiaries was available.

In 2006/07 the trust had assets of £2.4 million and an income of £67,000. Grants were made totalling £75,000 as follows: University of Southampton –

existing bursaries (£65,000); and Bristol Old Vic Theatre School and Royal Northern School of Music (£5,000 each).

Exclusions No grants to individuals.

Applications Requests for application forms should be submitted by 1 April in any one year; applicants will be notified of the results in August. Unsolicited applications are unlikely to be considered, educational institutional applications by invitation only.

Mr and Mrs F E F Newman's Charitable Trust

Christian, overseas aid and development

£37,000 (2007/08)
Beneficial area UK and overseas.

c/o David Quinn Associates, Southcroft, Caledon Road, Beaconsfield HP9 2BX

Tel. 01494 674 396

Correspondent David Quinn, Administrator

Trustees *Frederick E F Newman; Margaret C Hayes; Canon Newman; Michael R F Newman; George S Smith.*

CC Number 263831

Information available Full accounts were on file at the Charity Commission.

In 2007/08 the trust had assets of £236,000 and an income of £47,000. Grants were made totalling £37,000 and were distributed from two funds as follows:

Donations – 'A' Fund

Grants were made to 15 organisations, ranging from £25 to £300. Beneficiaries included: Christian Aid (£300 in two grants); Prostate Cancer Research (£250); Church Urban Fund, Help the Aged and Music as Therapy (£100 each); and Horsell Common Preservation Society (£25).

Donations – 'B' Fund

Grants were made to 27 organisations, ranging from £500 to £7,000. Beneficiaries included: Tear Fund (£7,000 in two grants); Resource (£5,500 in two grants); Teso Development (£3,500); Church Missionary Society (£2,000); and Amnesty International and Traidcraft Exchange (£500 each).

Exclusions No grants to individuals.

Applications In writing to the correspondent.

Newpier Charity Ltd

Jewish and general

£536,000 (2007/08)
Beneficial area UK.

186 Lordship Road, London N16 5ES
Correspondent Charles Margulies, Trustee
Trustees *C M Margulies; Mrs H Knopfler; Mrs R Margulies.*
CC Number 293686
Information available Accounts were on file at the Charity Commission, but without a list of grants.

The main objectives of the charity are the advancement of the orthodox Jewish faith and the relief of poverty.

In 2007/08 it had assets of £4.3 million and an income of £916,000. Grants totalling £536,000 wee made during the year. Unfortunately, no list of grantees was included with the accounts at the Charity Commission.

Applications In writing to the correspondent.

The Chevras Ezras Nitzrochim Trust

Jewish

£50,000 to organisations (2008)
Beneficial area UK, with a preference for London.

53 Heathland Road, London N16 5PQ
Tel. 020 8800 5187
Correspondent Hertz Kahan, Trustee
Trustees *Joseph Stern; Hertz Kahan.*
CC Number 275352
Information available Accounts were on file at the Charity Commission, without a list of grants.

The trustees' report states that 'the objects of the charity are the relief of the poor, needy and sick and the advancement of Jewish religious education.' There is a preference for Greater London, but help is also given further afield. The majority of grants are made to individuals.

In 2008 the trust had assets of £1,000 and an income of £249,000. Grants totalled £245,000, of which £195,000 went to individuals and £50,000 went to organisations. No details of beneficiaries during the year were available.

Previous beneficiaries included Mesifta, Kupas Tzedoko Vochesed, Beis Chinuch Lenonos, Hachzokas Torah Vochesed Trust, Ezras Hakohol Trust, Woodstock Sinclair Trust, Side by Side, Yeshivas Panim Meiros, Yeahuas Chaim Synagogue, TYY Trust, Square Yeshiva and Stanislow.

Applications In writing to the correspondent.

NJD Charitable Trust

Jewish

£125,000 to organisations and individuals (2006/07)
Beneficial area UK and Israel.

35 Frognal, Hampstead, London NW3 6YD
Tel. 020 7435 6883
Email info@igpinvest.com
Correspondent J C Dwek, Trustee
Trustees *J C Dwek; Mrs N L Dwek; J P Glaskie; J Wolf.*
CC Number 1109146
Information available Accounts were on file at the Charity Commission, without a list of beneficiaries.

Set up in 2005, the objects of this trust are:

- the relief of poverty and hardship of members of the Jewish faith
- the advancement of Jewish religion through Jewish education.

In 2007/08 the trust had assets of £101,000, an income of £103,000 and made grants totalling £125,000. A list of beneficiaries was unavailable.

Applications In writing to the correspondent.

The Noel Buxton Trust

Child and family welfare, penal matters and Africa

£117,000 (2008)
Beneficial area UK, eastern and southern Africa.

PO Box 393, Farnham, Surrey GU9 8WZ
Website www.noelbuxtontrust.org.uk/index.htm
Correspondent Ray Waters, Secretary
Trustees *Richenda Wallace; Joyce Morton; Simon Buxton; Jon Snow; Jo Tunnard; John Littlewood; Brendan Gormley; Miss Emma Ponsonby; Miss Katie Aston.*
CC Number 220881
Information available Accounts were on file at the Charity Commission.

Grants are made for the following:

- the welfare of children in disadvantaged families and of children in care. This will normally cover families with children of primary school age and younger, although work with children in care will be considered up to the age at which they leave care. (Grants are not given for anything connected with physical or mental disability or any medical condition).
- the prevention of crime, especially work with young people at risk of offending; the welfare of prisoners' families and the rehabilitation of prisoners (housing of any kind is excluded).
- education and development in eastern and southern Africa.

The trust is a small one and seldom makes grants of more than £4,000, often considerably less. The average grant in 2008 was around £1,650. The trust will fund core costs and will consider making a series of annual grants for up to three years. Due to the size of grant, appeals whose major component is salary costs will not be considered.

The trustees very much welcome appeals from small local groups in England, Scotland and Wales. The emphasis of their giving is on areas outside London, south-east England and Northern Ireland. The trust does not respond to appeals from large and well-supported charities or to general appeals.

In 2008 the trust had assets of £2 million and an income of £144,000. Donations were made totalling £117,000. They were broken down as follows and are shown here with examples of beneficiaries:

Africa – 16 grants totalling £40,000
Self Help Africa (£5,000); International Network of Street Papers (£4,000); Tirrim Development Programme (£3,600); Africa Christian Fellowship Reading (£3,000); Dig Deep (£2,000); and Phapphama Initiatives (£1,100).

Family – 32 grants totalling £30,000
Young People taking Action – Bury St Edmunds (£2,000); Behind Closed Doors – Leeds and Fun in Action for Children (£1,500 each); Campus Children's Holiday – Liverpool (£1,000); and Just 42 – Woodbridge (£500).

Penal – 22 grants totalling £38,000
Prison Reform Trust (£4,000); North Eastern Prison After Care Society (£2,500); Fair Shares and Footprints Project (£2,000 each); Halow – Birmingham (£1,500); and Church Housing Trust (£1,000).

Exclusions The trust does not give to: academic research; advice centres; animals; the arts of any kind; buildings; conferences; counselling; development education; drug and alcohol work; older people; the environment; expeditions, exchanges, study tours, visits, and so on, or anything else involving fares; housing and homelessness; human rights; anything medical or connected with illness or mental or physical disability; anywhere overseas except eastern and southern Africa; peace and disarmament; race relations; young people (except for the prevention of offending); and unemployment. Grants are not made to individuals for any purpose.

Applications By letter, setting out the reasons why a grant is being requested. Applications should include the applicant's charity registration number and the name of the organisation to which cheques should be made payable if different from that at the head of the appeal letter. Applications should include: budget for current and following year; details of funding already received, promised or applied for from other sources; and latest annual report/accounts in the shortest available form.

Applications may be made at any time and are not acknowledged. Successful applicants will normally hear from the trust within six months. The trust will not discuss applications on the telephone or correspond about rejected appeals.

The Noon Foundation

General, education, relief of poverty, community relations, alleviation of racial discrimination

£62,000 to institutions (2007)
Beneficial area UK.

25 Queen Anne's Gate, St James' Park, London SW1H 9BU
Tel. 020 7654 1600
Email grants@noongroup.co.uk
Correspondent The Trustees
Trustees Sir Gulam Noon; Akbar Shirazi; Mrs Zeenat Harnal; A M Jepson; D Robinson; Mrs Zarmin N Sekhon.
CC Number 1053654
Information available Full accounts were available from the Charity Commission website.

The trust was set up in 1996 by Sir Gulam Noon, the founder of Noon Products. In 2007 the trust had assets of £3.8 million and an income of £194,000. Grants were made totalling £62,000, summarised as follows:

- **education** – £55,000
- **sickness** – £7,000
- **community relations** – £50.

The beneficiaries of grants of £1,000 or more during the year were: Birkbeck University of London (£50,000); Shonia-Stem cell treatment in China (£5,000); University of Coventry (£3,000); London School of Economics (£2,000); and The Calamus Foundation and Well Being of Women (£1,000 each).

The trust's annual report and accounts commented on its current and future grantmaking as follows.

During the year the trust supported Birkbeck University of London and the trustees have agreed to make further grants of £50,000 per annum for the next three years. Birkbeck University of London are working in conjunction with the University of East London and these grants will finance bursaries and top up grants for students in the East London area. The funding provided by the Noon Foundation will provide 35 full year bursaries and 60 top up grants for mainly evening work based courses to enhance employment prospects in some of the most deprived areas of London suffering from the lowest participation rate in higher education.

Plans for future periods
Since the end of the period under review, the trustees have made a substantial grant for the establishment of a scholarship fund at the Oxford Centre for Islamic Studies which promotes the scholarly study of Islam and of contemporary Muslim societies; pursuing academic excellence through teaching, research and publication.

Applications All applications and queries should be made by email.

The Norda Trust

Prisoners, asylum seekers and disadvantaged communities

£140,000 (2008)
Beneficial area UK.

The Shieling, St Agnes TR5 0SS
Tel. 01871 553822
Email enquiries@thenordatrust.org.uk
Website www.thenordatrust.org.uk/
Correspondent Martin Ward, Administrator
Trustees J N Macpherson; P Gildener.
CC Number 296418
Information available Accounts were on file at the Charity Commission.

The trustees allocate funds principally in support of those working for the rehabilitation of prisoners both before and after release, and support for the partners and families of prisoners. Trustees are actively looking into how effective support for those working with asylum seekers can be expanded. As funds permit, the trust can also support small local charities whose primary aim should be to improve the quality of life for the most severely disadvantaged communities or individuals. The majority of awards are made on a one-off basis, with very few commitments made over two or more years.

The trustees have a particular interest in helping to support new initiatives where there is a high level of volunteer involvement.

When funds allow, applications will be considered from charities and organisations who, by the nature of the work they undertake, do not attract popular support.

In 2008 the trust's assets stood at £2.7 million. It had an income of

£190,000 and made grants totalling £140,000. Grants were made in four categories as follows:

Category	No.	Value
Prisoners and their families	£113,000	23
Asylum seekers and refugees	£17,000	4
Homelessness and poverty	£5,000	1
General	£5,000	2

Beneficiaries included: Christian Care (£10,000); Castle Gate Family Trust (£7,000); Derbyshire Housing Aid (£6,000); 999 Club, Apex Charitable Trust, Burnbake Trust, City Gate Community Project, Dover Detainee Visitor Group, Nehemiah Project, Prisoners Advice Service, Refugee Support Group Devon, Routeways Centre, St Edmund's Society and Wildwood (£5,000 each); London Detainee Support Group, Open Gate and SOFA Project (£4,000 each); Enterprise Education Trust (£3,100); Sudden Productions (£3,000); and Family Medication Scotland and HMP Highpoint (£2,000 each).

Exclusions The following areas are not funded by the trust:

- medical causes
- animal causes
- individuals
- school fees
- proselytising.

Applications Via letter or email, outlining the appeal. The trust will then make contact to request any further information they need.

The Norman Family Charitable Trust

General

£347,000 (2008/09)

Beneficial area Primarily Cornwall, Devon and Somerset

14 Fore Street, Budleigh Salterton EX9 6NG

Tel. 01395 446 699 **Fax** 01395 446698

Email enquiries@normanfct.plus.com

Website www.nfct.org

Correspondent R J Dawe, Chairman of the Trustees

Trustees R J Dawe, Chair; Mrs M H Evans; M B Saunders; Mrs M J Webb; Mrs C E Houghton.

CC Number 277616

Information available Accounts were available from the Charity Commission.

In 2008/09 the trust had assets of £8 million and an income of £433,000. Grants totalling £347,000 were made to 317 organisations and were mainly for less than £5,000 each. Grants were broken down by category as follows:

Category	£	No. of grants
Community, sport and leisure	103,000	83
Medical (inc. research)	53,000	40
Environmental and conservation	39,000	14
Young people	37,000	27
Older people	36,000	10
Blind, deaf, physically disabled	29,000	50
Children	22,000	45
Animals	10,000	14
Homeless	7,000	10
Drugs, alcohol and prison	6,500	9
Mentally disabled	6,000	14
Other	250	1

Major beneficiaries were: RNLI (£37,000); Devon Wildlife Trust (£30,000); Resthaven (£25,000); Kenn Parish Hall and Men's Club (£15,000); Sports Aid – South West (£10,000); and Budleigh Youth Project (£7,500).

Other beneficiaries included: Devon Air Ambulance, Hospiscare – Exeter, Marie Curie Cancer Care and Shelter Box (£5,000 each); Prince's Trust (£4,000); Cats Protection League and Devon Farming and Wildlife Advisory (£2,500 each); and Adventure Trust for Girls, Blue Cross, Devon County Association for the Blind and Jubilee Sailing Trust (£2,000 each).

Exclusions No grants to individuals. No funding for religious buildings or to assist any organisations using animals for live experimental purposes or generally to fund overseas work.

Applications In writing to the correspondent. A sub-committee of trustees meet regularly to make grants of up to £5,000. Grants in excess of £5,000 are dealt with at one of the quarterly meetings of all the trustees.

The Duncan Norman Trust Fund

General

£35,000 (2007/08)

Beneficial area UK, with a preference for Merseyside.

Liverpool Charity and Voluntary Services, 151 Dale Street, Liverpool L2 2AH

Tel. 0151 227 5177

Email enquiries@charitycheques.org.uk

Correspondent The Trustees

Trustees R K Asser; Mrs C Chapman; Mrs V S Hilton; Mrs C E Lazar; W Stothart; C Venner.

CC Number 250434

Information available Accounts were obtained from the Charity Commission website.

The trust has general charitable purposes, but particularly supports organisations in the Merseyside area.

In 2007/08 the trust had assets of £799,000 and an income of £35,000. Grants were made totalling nearly £35,000. Grants over £1,000 were made to: The Campaign for Drawing (£5,000); PCC of St Gwenfaen Church, Rhoscolyn (£2,000); Army Benevolent Fund, Combat Stress and Royal Star and Garter Home (£1,500 each); and Breast Cancer Haven – London, Help for Heroes and PCC of SS Peter & Paul Church – Swalcliffe (£1,000 each). Grants of less than £1,000 each totalled £21,500.

Exclusions No grants to individuals.

Applications The trust states that it only makes grants to charities known to the settlor and unsolicited applications are not considered.

The Normanby Charitable Trust

Social welfare, disability and general

£175,000 (2007/08).

Beneficial area UK, with a special interest in North Yorkshire and north east England.

52 Tite Street, London SW3 4JA

Correspondent The Trustees

Trustees The 5th Marquis of Normanby; The Dowager Marchioness of Normanby; Lady Lepel Kornicki; Lady Evelyn Buchan; Lady Peronel Phipps de Cruz; Lady Henrietta Burridge.

CC Number 252102

Information available Accounts were available from the Charity Commission website.

The trustees state in their report 'that only exceptionally will they help individuals in the future, and that they will confine their assistance for the moment, to mainly North Yorkshire and the North East of England.' The trust concentrates its support upon general charitable purposes, however previous research has suggested a preference for supporting social welfare, disability and the arts. The trust has occasionally considered giving grants for the preservation of religious and secular buildings of historical or architectural interest.

In 2007/08 the trust had assets of £8.7 million and an income of £339,000. Grants to 33 organisations were made totalling £175,000. The largest grants included those to: The Ashmolean Museum and Ryedale Festival (£20,000 each); and Action Trust for the Blind, Child Bereavement Charity, Scarborough Theatre Trust and Trinity Annual Fund (£10,000 each).

Other grants included: Scarborough and Ryedale Mountain Rescue (£7,500); Children's Country Holiday Fund (£5,000); Tom Carpenter Centre and Whitby Archive Heritage Centre (£2,000 each); Bognor Fun Bus Co. Ltd (£500); and Esk Moors Active Ltd (£250).

Exclusions No grants to individuals, or to non-UK charities.

Applications In writing to the correspondent. There are no regular dates for trustees' meetings. Please note: only successful applications will be acknowledged.

The Earl of Northampton's Charity

Welfare

£9,000 to organisations (2008/09)
Beneficial area England, with a preference for London and the South East.

Mercers' Company, Mercers' Hall, Ironmonger Lane, London EC2V 8HE
Tel. 020 7726 4991 **Fax** 020 7600 1158
Email mail@mercers.co.uk
Website www.mercers.co.uk
Correspondent M McGregor, Clerk to the Mercers' Company
Trustee *The Mercers' Company.*

CC Number 210291
Information available Full accounts were on file at the Charity Commission.

In 2008/09 the charity's assets stood at £18.9 million. It had an income of £1.6 million. Most of the charity's expenditure (£528,000) went towards maintaining its almshouses for older people. This and its commitment to redeveloping the old almshouses at Greenwich, meant grants to other charitable causes for the year were low at £9,000.

The recipients were Trinity Hospital – Clun (£4,000), Trinity Hospital – Castle Rising (£3,000); Jubilee Trust Almshouses (£2,000); and St Michael's Church Framlingham (£250).

The Charity of Sir Richard Whittington received £22,000 to distribute to individuals through its relief in need programme.

Applications In writing to the correspondent.

The Norton Foundation

Young people under 25 years of age (Currently restricted to the areas of Birmingham, Coventry and the County of Warwick)

£103,000 to organisations (2007/08)
Beneficial area UK, with a preference for Birmingham, Coventry and the County of Warwick.

PO Box 10282, Redditch B97 9ZA
Tel. 01527 544 446
Email correspondent@ nortonfoundation.org
Website www.nortonfoundation.org
Correspondent Richard C Perkins, Correspondent
Trustees *R H Graham Suggett, Chair; Alan Bailey; Michael R Bailey; Parminder Singh Birdi; Mrs Jane Gaynor; Mrs Sarah V Henderson; Richard G D Hurley; Brian W Lewis; Robert K Meacham; Richard C Perkins; Mrs Louise Sewell.*
CC Number 702638

Information available Accounts were obtained from the Charity Commission website.

The foundation was created in 1990. Its objects are to help children and young people under 25 who are in 'need of care or rehabilitation or aid of any kind, particularly as a result of delinquency, deprivation, maltreatment or neglect or who are in danger of lapsing or relapsing into delinquency'.

Once every five years the foundation intends making a donation of £100,000 to a capital project. A designated fund has been created for this purpose and it is anticipated that the next such grant will be made in 2010/11.

In 2007/08 the foundation had assets of £4 million and an income of £145,000. Grants totalling £113,000 were made to individuals (£10,000) and organisations (£103,000). The latter amount included £28,000 in 'discretionary awards' to organisations which, at their discretion, the trustees can make grants to individuals. Grants were made to institutions for the following purposes: social work (£30,000); leisure activities (£16,000); medical (£14,000); education and training (£12,000); and holidays (£3,000).

Beneficiaries of grants of £1,000 or more included: South Birmingham Young Homeless Project (£10,000); Playbox Theatre Company (£4,000); The Wellchild Trust (£3,750); 20th Walsall Scouts Group – St Margaret's (£3,500); Heatlands Church – Stratford (£3,000); Tiny Tim's Children's Centre (£2,500); Birmingham Settlement and The Quizone Centre (£2,000 each); and Birmingham Royal Ballet, Rotary Club of Coventry Breakfast, Training Ship – Sutton Coalfield and Warwickshire Clubs for Young People (£1,000 each).

Exclusions No grants for the payment of debts that have already been incurred. Grants are not made for further education (except in very exceptional circumstances).

Applications By letter which should contain all the information required as detailed in the guidance notes for applicants. Guidance notes and application forms are available from the correspondent or from the foundation's website. Applications from organisations are normally processed by the trustees at their quarterly meetings.

Norwood and Newton Settlement

Christian

£335,000 (2007/08)
Beneficial area England and Wales.

126 Beauly Way, Romford RM1 4XL
Tel. 01708 723 670
Correspondent David M Holland, Trustee
Trustees *P Clarke; D M Holland; Mrs Stella Holland; W W Leyland; Mrs Susan Newsom.*
CC Number 234964
Information available Full accounts were on file at the Charity Commission.

The trust supports Methodist and other mainline Free Churches and some other smaller UK charities in which the founders had a particular interest. As a general rule, grants are for capital building projects which aim to improve the worship, outreach and mission of the church.

Where churches are concerned, the trustees take particular note of the contribution and promised contributions towards the project by members of the church in question.

In 2008/09 the settlement had an income of £396,000 and expenditure of £312,000. No further details were available.

In 2007/08 the settlement had assets of £7.8 million and an income of £374,000. Grants were made to 50, mainly Methodist, organisations and totalled £335,000.

The largest grants made included those to: Holmes Chapel Methodist Church – Cheshire and Maulden Baptist Church – Bedford (£13,000 each); and Bishops Cleave Methodist Church – Cheltenham, Chew Magna Baptist Church – Bristol, Kidlington Baptist Church – Oxon, Southwick Christian Community Church – West Sussex, Tools With a Mission – Ipswich and Youth for Christ HQ – Halesowen (£10,000 each).

Other grants made included those to: Etherley Methodist Church – County Durham (£7,500); Worsley Road URC – Manchester (£6,000); Bury St Edmunds Friends Meeting House and Museum of Army Flying (£5,000 each); Wrenthorpe Methodist Church – Wakefield (£3,000); and Wardle Village Church (Meth/CofE) – Rochdale (£1,000).

Exclusions Projects will not be considered where an application for National Lottery funding has been made or is contemplated. No grants to individuals, rarely to large UK charities and not for staff or running costs, equipment, repairs or general maintenance.

Applications In writing to the correspondent. In normal circumstances, the trustees' decision is communicated to the applicant within seven days (if a refusal), and if successful, immediately after the trustees' quarterly meetings.

The Sir Peter O'Sullevan Charitable Trust

Animal welfare

£300,000 (2007/08)
Beneficial area Worldwide.

The Old School, Bolventor, Launceston PL15 7TS
Tel. 01566 880 292
Email nigel@earthsummit.demon.co.uk
Website www.thevoiceofracing.com
Correspondent Nigel Payne, Trustee
Trustees *Christopher Spence; Lord Oaksey; Sir Peter O'Sullevan; Nigel Payne; Geoffrey Hughes; Bob McCreery; Michael Dillon.*
CC Number 1078889
Information available Accounts were on file at the Charity Commission.

Registered with the Charity Commission in January 2000, in 2007/08 the trust had assets of £107,000 and an income of £372,000 (mainly from fundraising events). Grants were made totalling £300,000.

A total of six grants of £50,000 each were made, as in previous years, to Blue Cross, Brooke Hospital for Animals, Compassion in World Farming, International League for the Protection of Horses, the Racing Welfare Charities and the Thoroughbred Rehabilitation Centre.

Applications In writing to the correspondent.

The Oak Trust

General

£28,000 (2007/08)
Beneficial area UK.

Essex House, 42 Crouch Street, Colchester CO3 3HH
Email bruce.ballard@birkettlong.co.uk
Website www.oaktrust.org.uk
Correspondent Bruce Ballard, Clerk
Trustees *Revd A C C Courtauld; J Courtauld; Dr Elizabeth Courtauld; Miss C M Courtauld.*
CC Number 231456
Information available Full accounts were available from the Charity Commission website.

The trust has a preference for supporting those charities that it has a special interest in, knowledge of or association with and with a turnover of below £1 million. In 2007/08 the trust had assets of £517,000 and an income of £28,000. Grants were made to 36 organisations totalling £28,000, of which over half received £500 each.

Grant recipients included: The Cirdan Sailing Trust (£3,000); Christian Aid and Prader-Willi Syndrome Association UK (£2,000 each); Children's Overseas Relief Fund and Voice (£1,000 each); Cambridge Society for the Blind and Partially-Sighted, Detention Advice Service, Practical Action – Darfor Appeal, The Swiften Charitable Trust and Westcott House (£500 each); and, Grace of God Church – Malawi and Maranatho Orphanage Ministries – Malawi (£250 each).

Exclusions No support to individuals.

Applications Written applications will no longer be accepted. Applications must be submitted via the online form.

Details of the next submission date are included on the application form. Applicants will receive an acknowledgement of their application and notification of the outcome within 10 days of the review meeting by email.

The Oakdale Trust

Social work, medical and general

£166,000 (2007/08)

Beneficial area UK, especially Wales, and overseas.

Tansor House, Tansor, Oundle, Peterborough PE8 5HS

Email oakdale@tanh.demon.co.uk

Correspondent Rupert Cadbury

Trustees *Brandon Cadbury; Mrs Flavia Cadbury; Rupert Cadbury; Bruce Cadbury; Mrs Olivia Tatton-Brown; Dr Rebecca Cadbury.*

CC Number 218827

Information available Accounts were on file at the Charity Commission.

The trust's main areas of interest, as listed in its accounts, include:

- Welsh-based social and community projects
- medical support groups operating in Wales and UK-based research projects
- UK-based charities working in the third world
- environmental conservation in the UK and overseas
- penal reform.

Some support is also given to the arts, particularly where there is a Welsh connection. The average grant is approximately £750.

In 2008/09 the trust had an income of £226,000 and expenditure of £159,000. No further information was available.

In 2007/08 the trust had assets of £5.6 million and an income of £226,000. Grants were made totalling £166,000 with the two major beneficiaries being The Brandon Centre (£15,000) and Concern Universal (£10,000).

Other grant recipients included: Medical Foundation for Care of Victims of Torture (£5,000); Radnorshire Wildlife Trust (£3,000); Cambridge Female Education Trust (£2,000); Howard League for Penal Reform (£1,500); The Penllergare Trust, Shakespeare Link, Simon Community and Y Care International (£1,000 each); Prisoners Abroad and Sherman Cymru (£500 each); and Adel Quaker Appeal and SOS Africa (£250 each).

Exclusions No grants to individuals, holiday schemes, sport activities or expeditions.

Applications An official application form is available on request. However applicants are free to submit requests in any format so long as applications are clear and concise, covering aims, achievements, plans and needs supported by a budget. Applicants applying for grants in excess of £750 are asked to submit a copy of a recent set of audited annual accounts (which can be returned on request).

The trustees meet twice a year in April and October to consider applications and to award grants. No grants are awarded between meetings. The deadline for the April meeting is 1 March and for the October meeting 1 September.

The trust is administered by the trustees at no cost, and owing to a lack of secretarial help and in view of the numerous requests received, no applications are acknowledged even when accompanied by a stamped addressed envelope.

The Oakmoor Charitable Trust

General

£49,000 (2007/08)

Beneficial area UK.

Rathbone Trust Company Limited, 159 New Bond Street, London W1S 2UD

Tel. 020 7399 0811

Correspondent The Administrator, Rathbone Trust Company Limited

Trustees *Rathbone Trust Company Ltd; P M H Andreae; Mrs R J Andreae.*

CC Number 258516

Information available Full accounts were available from the Charity Commission website.

Established in 1969 the trust receives regular donations from the settlor, Peter Andreae.

In 2007/08 the trust had assets of £1.3 million and an income of £32,000. Grants were made to 26 organisations totalling £49,000 and were categorised by the trust as follows:

- the arts and museums – £19,000
- young people and education – £16,200
- other national and international charities – £9,500
- local charities and hospices – £3,250
- religious organisations – £1,000.

The four largest grants were made to: The London Library and Mary Rose Trust (£10,000 each); Save Britain's Heritage (£7,500); and CAFOD (£5,000).

Other beneficiaries included: Institute of Economic Affairs (£3,000); Downe House Trust (£2,000); Armed Forces Memorial, Elias Ashmole Group and Hampshire Country Learning (£1,000 each); Bembridge Harbour Trust and Convent of St Lucy – Chichester (£500 each); Cancer Research (£250); and Friends of the Royal Opera House Foundation (£100).

Exclusions No grants to individuals.

Applications The trust states that it does not respond to unsolicited applications.

The Odin Charitable Trust

General

£157,000 (2007/08)

Beneficial area UK.

PO Box 1898, Bradford-on-Avon BA15 1YS

Correspondent Mrs S G P Scotford, Trustee

Trustees *Mrs S G A P Scotford; Mrs A H Palmer; Mrs D L Kelly; Mrs P C Cherry.*

CC Number 1027521

Information available Accounts were on file at the Charity Commission.

In 2007/08 the trust had assets of £5.2 million and an income of £480,000. Grants were made to 71 organisations and totalled £157,000.

Although the objects of the charity are wide, the trust has a preference for making grants towards: furthering the arts; providing care for people who are disabled and disadvantaged; supporting hospices, the homeless, prisoners' families, refugees, gypsies and 'tribal groups'; and furthering research into false memories and dyslexia.

The trustees are more likely to support small organisations and those, that by the nature of their work, find it difficult to attract funding.

A number of beneficiaries received a recurrent grant which ran from 2007 to 2009. These were: Action for Prisoners' Families (£3,000 a year); Hartlepool and District Hospice (£3,000 a year); Interact

Reading Scheme (£2,500 a year); and Asylum Link Merseyside (£2,000 a year).

Other beneficiaries included: Blaen Wern Farm Trust and Survival (£3,000 each); Clothing Solutions for Disabled People and Space Trust (£2,500 each); Ellenor Foundation, Jessie's Fund, Prison Fellowship and Willow Wood Hospice (£2,000 each); Lewisham Churches for Asylum Seekers and 9 Lives Furniture Scheme (£1,500 each); and Cherished Memories and Knowsley Carers Centre (£1,000 each).

Exclusions Applications from individuals are not considered.

Applications In writing to the correspondent.

The Ogle Christian Trust

Evangelical Christianity

£125,000 (2008)
Beneficial area Worldwide.

43 Woolstone Road, Forest Hill, London SE23 2TR
Tel. 020 8699 1036
Correspondent Mrs F J Putley, Trustee
Trustees D J Harris, Chair; R J Goodenough; S Proctor; Mrs F J Putley; Mrs L M Quanrud.
CC Number 1061458
Information available Accounts were on file at the Charity Commission.

The trust mainly directs funds to new initiatives in evangelism worldwide, support of missionary enterprises, publication of scriptures and Christian literature, pastor training and famine and other relief work.

In 2008 it had assets of £2.2 million and an income of £132,000. Grants totalled £125,000. There were 179 grants made in the year of which 42 were for £1,000 or more as listed in the accounts.

By far the largest grant, as in previous years, went to Operation Mobilisation (£18,000). Other beneficiaries included: Tear Fund (£6,000); Translation Trust (£4,000); Chessington Evangelical Church, Elm Foundation School – Nigeria, Global Care, The Lighthouse Group and The Source – China (£3,000 each); France Mission Trust, Middle East Concern, PECAN, Stepping Stones Trust and The Thana Trust (£2,000 each); and CARE, Caring for Life, Make Jesus

Known and Rhema Theatre Company (£1,000 each).

Unlisted grants totalled £12,500.

Exclusions Applications from individuals are discouraged; those granted require accreditation by a sponsoring organisation. Grants are rarely made for building projects. Funding will not be offered in response to general appeals from large national organisations.

Applications In writing to the correspondent, accompanied by documentary support and a stamped, addressed envelope. Trustees meet in May and November, but applications can be made at any time.

The Oikonomia Trust

Christian

£48,000 (2007/08)
Beneficial area UK and overseas.

98 White Lee Road, Batley WF17 8AF
Tel. 01924 502 616
Email c.mountain@ntlworld.com
Correspondent Colin Mountain, Trustee
Trustees D H Metcalfe; R H Metcalfe; S D Metcalfe; C Mountain; Revd R O Owens.
CC Number 273481
Information available Full accounts were on file at the Charity Commission.

The trust supports evangelical work, famine and other relief through Christian agencies. The trust is not looking for new outlets as those it has knowledge of are sufficient to absorb its available funds.

In 2007/08 it had assets of £396,000 and an income of £32,000. Grants were made to 20 organisations and totalled £48,000.

Beneficiaries included: Barnabus Trust (£5,500); Slavic Gospel Association (£5,000); Bethel Church (£4,000); Asia Link, Association of Evangelists and Caring for Life (£3,000 each); Japan Mission (£2,500); Starbeck Mission (£2,000); People International (£1,000); and Carey Outreach Ministries (£500).

Exclusions No grants made in response to general appeals from large national organisations.

Applications In writing to the correspondent, although the trust has

previously stated that known needs are greater than the trust's supplies. If an applicant desires an answer, a stamped, addressed envelope should be enclosed. Applications should arrive in January.

The Old Broad Street Charity Trust

General

£98,000 to organisations (2007/08)
Beneficial area UK and overseas.

Rawlinson and Hunter, Eighth Floor, 6 New Street Square, London EC4A 3AQ
Tel. 020 7482 2000
Correspondent Simon Jennings, Secretary to the Trustees
Trustees Mrs Evelyn J Franck; Mrs Martine Cartier-Bresson; Adrian T J Stanford; Peter A Hetherington; Christopher J Sheridan; Clare Gough.
CC Number 231382
Information available Accounts were on file at the Charity Commission.

The objects of the trust are general, although most of the funds are given towards the arts. It was the wish of Louis Franck, the founder, that part of the income should be used to fund scholarships, preferably for UK citizens, to reach the highest levels of executive management in banking and financial institutions. It gives around half of its grant total each year to the Louis Franck Scholarship Fund for this purpose (£35,000 in six scholarships in 2007/08).

In 2007/08 it had assets of £1.9 million and an income of £79,000. Grants totalling £98,000 were made to 10 organisations; all but one was supported in the previous year.

Beneficiaries were: Foundation Henri Cartier-Bresson (£49,000); Grant Life – Moscow (£15,000); Société Française le Lutte contre la Cécité et contre le Tranchome (£10,700); Bezirksfursorge – Saanen (£8,600); Camphill Village Trust (£5,000); International Menuhin Music Academy (£4,300); Royal Academy of Arts (£2,500); The National Gallery Trust (£2,000); Tate Gallery Foundation (£1,000); and Artangel (£400).

Exclusions The trustees only support organisations of which they personally have some knowledge.

Applications In writing to the correspondent. Unsolicited applications are not considered.

Old Possum's Practical Trust

General

£287,000 to organisations and individuals (2007/08)
Beneficial area UK.

PO Box 5701, Milton Keynes MK9 2WZ
Email generalenquiry@ old-possums-practical-trust.org.uk
Website www. old-possums-practical-trust.org.uk
Correspondent The Trustees
Trustees *Mrs Esme Eliot; Mrs Judith Hooper; Mrs D Simpson; Clare Reihill.*
CC Number 328558
Information available Full accounts were on file at the Charity Commission.

The report states that 'the primary object of the trust is to increase knowledge and appreciation of any matters of historic, artistic, architectural, aesthetic, musical or theatrical interest. The trust however is not limited to that primary object and considers all worthwhile causes carefully'

The trust states that grants are more likely to be given to projects that involve children or young people; disabled or disadvantaged people; and communities.

In 2007/08 the trust had assets of £7.9 million and an income of £514,000. Grants were made £287,000 and were broken down into the following categories:

Educational support
Grants were awarded to three organisations in this category totalling around £27,000. The beneficiaries were: First Story (£20,000); Snowflake School (£4,000); and Listening Books (£1,000).

The arts and historical conservation
Grants were made to 40 organisations. The six largest grants in this category were given to: High Tide Festival (£25,000); Shakespeare School Festival (£20,000); Poetry Book Society – T S Eliot Poetry Prize costs (£17,500); Arete and Victoria & Albert Museum (£15,000 each); and Poetry Book Society – Children's Competition (£12,000). A total of £25,000 was also awarded to the T S Eliot Poetry Prize winners.

Other beneficiaries included: MK City Orchestra, St Bride Foundation and Wordsworth Trust (£10,000 each); Little Angel Theatre and London Film School (£7,500 each); Queens University Belfast Festival and the Mousetrap Foundation (£5,000 each); Finchley Children's Music Group (£3,000); Classworks Theatre (£2,000); Welsh Youth Classical Music Foundation (£1,000); Leeds Metropolitan University – The Big Draw (£500); and St Mary's Woburn Flower Festival (£250).

Support for the disabled and disadvantaged
Grants were awarded to 13 organisations. The two largest grants went to Dogs for the Disabled (£20,000) and The Book Trade Benevolent Society (£10,000). Other beneficiaries included: Farms for City Children (£5,000); Strongbones Children's Charitable Trust and Octopus (£3,000 each); Felixstowe Youth Group (£2,000); Hospice in the Weald (£1,500); and Manzini Youth Centre (£1,000).

Exclusions The trust does not support the following:

- activities or projects already completed
- capital building projects
- individuals
- personal training and education for example tuition or living costs for college or university
- projects outside the UK
- medical care or resources, feasibility studies, national charities having substantial amounts of potential funding likely from other sources.

Applications Online submission is the preferred method of application. Faxed or emailed applications will be rejected but you may post your application if you have a good reason why you cannot submit your request online.

To download the printable version you require which you can complete and send by post, click either 'Individual' or 'Charity' on the 'Apply for Funding' page.

Please note: in so doing you will be required to explain why you cannot use the online application process.

The John Oldacre Foundation

Research and education in agricultural sciences
£126,000 (2007/08)
Beneficial area UK.

Hazleton House, Hazleton, Cheltenham GL54 4EB
Tel. 01451 860 752
Correspondent Henry Shouler, Trustee
Trustees *H B Shouler; S J Charnock; D G Stevens.*
CC Number 284960
Information available Full accounts were on file at the Charity Commission.

Grants are made to universities and agricultural colleges towards the advancement and promotion, for public benefit, of research and education in agricultural sciences and the publication of useful results.

In 2007/08 the foundation had assets of £7.4 million and an income of £122,000. Grants were made to five organisations and an individual and totalled £126,000.

Beneficiaries were Royal Agricultural College (£40,000 in two grants), University of Bristol (£30,000), Nuffield Fanning Trust (£15,000), Harper Adams University College (£16,500), TAG Arable Group (£14,000) and NIAB (£7,500).

A grant to an individual was made for £2,500.

Exclusions No grants towards tuition fees.

Applications In writing to the correspondent.

The Olga Charitable Trust

Health, welfare, youth organisations, children's welfare and carers' organisations
£51,000 (2007/08)
Beneficial area UK and overseas.

Mercer & Hole, London International Press Centre, 76 Shoe Lane, London EC4A 3JB

Tel. 020 7353 1597

Correspondent Adam Broke, Accountant

Trustees *HRH Princess Alexandra; James Robert Bruce Ogilvy.*

CC Number 277925

Information available Accounts were on file at the Charity Commission.

The trust supports health, welfare and youth organisations, children's welfare and carers' organisations. All must be known to the trustees.

In 2007/08 the trust had assets of £1 million and an income of £186,000, including £128,000 from Gift Aid. Grants totalling £51,000 were made to 23 organisations including: Columba 1400 (£12,000); Holy Trinity Church (£8,250); Kingston Hospital and St Andrew's Church – Ham (£5,000 each); Maggie's (£2,000); Arundel Castle Cricket Club, Foundation Recal and Piggy Bank Kids (£1,000 each); and Castle of Mey Trust and Walsingham Appeal (£500 each).

Applications In writing to the correspondent, although the trust states that its funds are fully committed and applications made cannot be acknowledged.

Onaway Trust

General

£95,000 (2008)

Beneficial area UK, USA and worldwide.

275 Main Street, Shadwell, Leeds LS17 8LH

Tel. 0113 265 9611

Email david@onaway.org

Website www.onaway.org

Correspondent David Watters, Trust Administrator

Trustees *J Morris; A Breslin; C Howles; Ms Annie Smith; Ms V A Worwood; Ms Elaine Bradley; D Watters.*

CC Number 268448

Information available Full accounts were available from the Charity Commission website.

This trust's objects are stated on its website as follows.

To relieve poverty and suffering amongst indigenous peoples by providing seed grants for (small) self-help, self-sufficiency and environmentally sustainable projects. This is expressed in many areas and includes the protection of the environment, the support of children and adults with learning difficulties, the assistance of smaller charities whose aim is to safeguard sick, injured, threatened or abandoned animals and emergency relief for victims of disaster.

In 2008 the trust had assets of £3.8 million and an income of £177,000. Grants were made to 31 organisations totalling £95,000 and awarded in the following categories:

Indigenous – America (£23,000)
All but one of the six grants awarded went to Plenty USA for separate projects totalling £20,000. The other beneficiary was Centre of Sacred Studies which received £3,000.

Indigenous – Rest of the world (£52,000)
The largest grants were given to Institute for Development Exchange – India and Jeel Al Amal – Middle East (£9,000 each). Other recipients included: Fundacion Redes De Santas (£8,000); Rainforest Foundation UK (£5,000); Lotus Children's Centre Charitable Trust (£4,500); The Gorilla Organisation (£3,000); Vetaid Africa (£2,000); and Yellow House – China (£1,000).

Environmental (£5,000)
Beneficiaries were WaterAid (£3,000) and Greenpeace and Sea Shepherd (£1,000 each).

Animal welfare (£3,000)
Two grants were made, one to Magic of Life Butterfly House – UK (£2,000) and AISPA (£1,000).

Other Onaway projects (£12,000)
Beneficiaries included: Opera North (£4,000); World Medical Fund for Children (£2,400); St John's Eye Hospital (£2,000); The Seekers Trust (£1,000); and Deafway – Nepal and The Simon Community (£500 each).

Exclusions No grants for administration costs, travel expenses or projects considered unethical or detrimental to the struggle of indigenous people.

Applications In writing to the correspondent, enclosing a stamped, addressed envelope.

The Ormsby Charitable Trust

General

£62,000 (2007/08)

Beneficial area UK, London and the South East.

Wasing Old Rectory, Shalford Hill, Aldermaston, Reading RG7 4NB

Tel. 0118 981 9663

Correspondent Mrs K McCrossan, Trustee

Trustees *Rosemary Ormsby David; Angela Ormsby Chiswell; Katrina Ormsby McCrossan.*

CC Number 1000599

Information available Accounts were on file at the Charity Commission.

In 2007/08 the trust had assets of £1.6 million and an income of £57.000. Donations were made to 25 organisations totalling £62,000 and ranged from £500 to £6,000 each.

Beneficiaries included: The Royal Marsden Hospital Charity (£6,000); Honey Pot House and In Kind Direct (£4,000 each); Breast Cancer Haven, Seeability – Royal Society for the Blind and Wessex Children's Hospice Trust (£3,200 each); Newbury Community Resource Centre, The Stroke Association and The Woodland Trust (£2,000 each); RSPB (£1,000); and The Living Paintings Trust and Thrive (£500 each).

Exclusions No grants to individuals, animals or religious causes.

Applications In writing to the correspondent.

The Ouseley Trust

Choral services of the Church of England, Church in Wales and Church of Ireland and choir schools

£94,000 (2008)

Beneficial area England, Wales and Ireland.

PO Box 281, Stamford PE9 9BU

Tel. 01780 752 266

Email ouseleytrust@btinternet.com

Website www.ouseleytrust.org.uk

Correspondent Martin Williams, Clerk

Trustees *Dr Christopher Robinson, Chair; Dr J A Birch; Rev Canon Mark Boyling; Dr S M Darlington; Prof B W Harvey; Mrs Gillian Perkins; Martin Pickering; Adam Ridley; Dr John Rutter; Revd A F Walters; Richard White; Sir David Willcocks.*

CC Number 527519

Information available Full accounts were available from the Charity Commission website.

The trust administers funds made available from trusts of the former St Michael's College, Tenbury. Its object is 'projects which promote and maintain to a high standard the choral services of the Church of England, the Church in Wales and the Church of Ireland', including contributions to endowment funds, courses, fees and the promotion of religious, musical and secular education for pupils connected to the churches and observing choral liturgy.

In 2008 the trust had assets of £3 million and an income of £161,000. Grants were made totalling £94,000 broken down as follows:

Category	No. of grants	£
Fees	24	63.000
Endowments	3	35,000
Other	3	11,000
Music	2	1,500
Courses	1	500

Please note: two grants worth a total of £16,500 were not taken up or were refunded.

Grants will be awarded only where there is a clear indication that an already acceptable standard of choral service will be raised. Under certain circumstances grants may be awarded for organ tuition. Each application will be considered on its merits, keeping in mind the specific terms of the trust deed. Unique, imaginative ventures will receive careful consideration.

The trust does not normally award further grants to successful applicants within a two-year period. The trustees' policy is to continue making grants to cathedrals, choral foundations and parish churches throughout England, Wales and Ireland.

Exclusions Grants will not be awarded to help with the cost of fees for ex-choristers, for chant books, hymnals or psalters. Grants will not be made for the purchase of new instruments or for the installation of an instrument from another place of worship where this involves extensive reconstruction. Under normal circumstances, grants will not be awarded for buildings, cassettes, commissions, compact discs, furniture, pianos, robes, tours or visits. No grants are made towards new organs or the installation of one which involves extensive reconstruction.

Applications Applicants are strongly advised to refer to the trust's guidelines and frequently asked questions section of its website before drafting an application. Applications must be submitted by an institution on a form available from the correspondent. Closing dates for applications are 31 January for the March meeting and 30 June for the October meeting.

The Owen Family Trust

Christian and general

£59,000 (2008/09)

Beneficial area UK, with a preference for West Midlands.

c/o Rubery Owen Holdings Limited, PO Box 10, Wednesbury WS10 8JD

Tel. 0121 526 3131

Correspondent A D Owen, Trustee

Trustees *Mrs H G Jenkins; A D Owen.*

CC Number 251975

Information available Full accounts were available from the Charity Commission website.

Grants are given to independent and church schools, Christian youth centres, churches, community organisations, arts, conservation and medical charities. Support is given throughout the UK, with a preference for the West Midlands.

In 2008/09 the trust had assets of £1.1 million and an income of £47,000. During the year 27 grants were made totalling £59,000.

The largest grants were made to: Oundle School Foundation (£15,000); Black Country Museum Development Trust, Lichfield Cathedral and NAYC – Pioneer Centre (£5,000 each).

Other beneficiaries included: Acorns, Birmingham Federation of Clubs for Young People and Lozells Project Trust (£3,000 each); Chaplaincy Plus, The Public Catalogue Foundation and St Giles Hospice (£1,000 each); The Army Benevolent Fund – Birmingham and Ben Uri Gallery (£500 each); and Dorothy Parkes Centre and St Peter's Little Aston PCC (£250 each).

Exclusions The trust states 'No grants to individuals unless part of a charitable organisation'.

Applications In writing to the correspondent including annual report, budget for project and general information regarding the application. Organisations need to be a registered charity; however an 'umbrella' body which would hold funds would be acceptable. Only a small number of grants can be given each year and unsuccessful applications are not acknowledged unless a stamped, addressed envelope is enclosed. The trustees meet quarterly.

The Doris Pacey Charitable Foundation

Jewish, medical, educational and social

£298,000 (2007/08)

Beneficial area UK and Israel.

30 Old Burlington Street, London W1S 3NL

Tel. 020 7468 2600

Correspondent J D Cohen, Trustee

Trustees *J D Cohen; R Locke; L Powell.*

CC Number 1101724

Information available Accounts were on fie at the Charity Commission.

In 2007/08 the foundation had assets of £6.2 million and an income of £204,000. Grants totalled £298,000 of which by far the largest went to British Friends of Bar Ulan University (£138,000).

Other beneficiaries included: Magen David Adom (£60,000); Jewish Chaplaincy (£36,000); UJIA – Palmach Club (£19,000); Courtaulds Institute of Art and World Jewish Relief (£15,000 each); Simon Marks School (£10,000); and One Family UK and St Christopher's Hospice (£1,000 each).

Applications Unsolicited applications are not considered.

The Pallant Charitable Trust

Church music

£42,000 to organisations and individuals (2006/07)

Beneficial area UK, with a preference for areas within 50 miles of Chichester.

c/o Thomas Eggar, The Corn Exchange, Baffins Lane, Chichester PO19 1GE

Tel. 01243 786 111 **Fax** 01243 532 001

Correspondent Simon Macfarlane, Trustee

Trustees *A J Thurlow; S A E Macfarlane; C Smyth; C J Henville.*

CC Number 265120

Information available Information was available from the Charity Commission website.

The trust's objective is to promote mainstream church music both in choral and instrumental form. Consideration will be given for schemes that provide training and opportunities for children or adults in the field of church music and with an emphasis on traditional services. Such schemes may include:

- vocal or instrumental (in particular organ) training
- choral work in the context of church services
- the training of choir leaders, organists or directors
- the provision and the purchase of equipment necessary for the above.

In 2007/08 the trust had an income of £40,000 and expenditure of around £49,000. No further information was available.

Previous beneficiaries include: Chichester Cathedral Choristers Scholarships – Prebendal School Fees (£33,000 for four individuals); Friends of St Mary's Church – Stoughton (£7,000); Bosham PCC (£1,000); and RSCM Sussex area (£750).

Exclusions No grants to individuals, or for computer equipment or sponsorship for concerts.

Applications In writing to the correspondent. Applications should be submitted by recognised organisations such as churches, schools, colleges or charities working in the field of church music.

The Panacea Society

Christian religion and relief of sickness

£284,000 (2008)

Beneficial area UK, with a strong preference for Bedford and its immediate region.

14 Albany Road, Bedford MK40 3PH

Tel. 01234 359 737

Email admin@panacea-society.org

Website www.panacea-society.org

Correspondent David McLynn, Business Administrator

Trustees *G Allan; L Aston; Revd Dr Jane Shaw; Prof. C Rowland; Dr J Meggitt.*

CC Number 227530

Information available Full accounts were available from the Charity Commission website.

The work of this Christian charity, established in 1926, is informed by the teachings of Joanna Southcott. In meeting its charitable objects the society from time to time makes grants out of its income.

Funding criteria
The trustees have agreed the following policy criteria should apply in all cases for a funding application to be selected for further consideration. The purpose of the funding should be:

- work related to the advancement of the religious beliefs of the society as defined by its original charitable objects
- sponsoring the writing, publication, and distribution of religious works associated with The Visitation
- undertaking the duties and responsibilities incumbent on being the custodian of Joanna Southcott's Box of Sealed Writings
- sponsoring research by recognised academic institutions into the history and theology of the society and its antecedents
- supporting the work of the Church of England in advancing the Christian religion especially in the Bedford area, or in aspects of theology or liturgy that relate to the society's specific interests
- supporting recognised local organisations dealing with the relief of sickness within the Bedford area.

The trust states that grants will be made for charitable purposes to UK-based organisations only. Priority will be given

to funding requests that promote the religious aims of the society, benefit large numbers of people and are made on behalf of organisations rather than individuals.

In 2008 the society had assets of £20.3 million and an income of £654,000. Grants were made totalling £284,000 broken down as follows:

- Oxford University Prophecy Project – £181,000
- other universities research and conference grants – £34,000
- miscellaneous scholarship/educational grants – £2,000
- religious grants – £3,000
- health/social grants – £64,000.

Beneficiaries under the last category included: Pasque Charity – Keech Children's Hospice (£30,000 over three years); CHUMS (£10,000); Road Victims Trust (£4,600); Retirement Education Centre Bedford Ltd (£3,500); Friendship Link Action Group (£2,000); Bedford Cerebral Palsy (£1,500); and Yarls Wood Befrienders Group (£1,000).

Exclusions The society will not consider funding:

- political parties or political lobbying
- pressure groups
- commercial ventures
- non-charitable activities
- that which could be paid out of central or local government funds.

Applications The trust has previously stated that it receives many applications that they are unable or unwilling to support. Please read the grant criteria carefully before submitting an application. Unsolicited applications are not responded to.

Any organisation considering applying for funding support should make a formal application in writing to the correspondent. The application should set out the purpose for which the funding is required, and explain how it falls within the funding criteria and complies with their requirements. Full information on the work of the applicant body together with details of how the proposed funding will be applied should be given.

The correspondent will acknowledge receipt of an application, and indicate if the application falls within their parameters. At this point the society may call for additional information, or indicate that it is unable to consider the application further. Most applications fail because they fall outside the criteria, however the society does not provide additional reasons why it is unable to support a particular application.

When all relevant information has been received the application will be discussed at the next meeting of the society's trustees. The trustees may at that meeting refuse or defer any application or request further information without giving reasons. Applicants will be advised in writing of the trustees' decision.

For full details visit the society's website.

Panahpur Charitable Trust

Missionaries and general

£213,000 to organisations (2008)

Beneficial area UK, overseas.

Jacob Cavenagh and Skeet, 5 Robin Hood Lane, Sutton SM1 2SW

Tel. 020 8643 1166

Email bob.moffett@panhpur.org

Correspondent The Trust Department

Trustees *P East; Miss D Haile; D Harland; A Matheson; A E Perry; J Perry.*

CC Number 214299

Information available Full accounts were on file at the Charity Commission.

The following is taken from the trust's accounts.

The trust was established for the distribution of funds to Christian charities and other Christian organisations and individuals, both in the UK and overseas. In the past the trust has sought to support a wide range of Christian missionary organisations. Over the last few years it has sought to not only form partnerships with a small number of organisations and people, but to work with them in a more meaningful relationship and over a greater period of time.

In 2007/08 the trust had assets of £6.6 million and an income of £275,000. Grants to organisations and individuals totalled £257,000 and were broken down as follows:

- missionary work – overseas (£148,000)
- missionary work – UK (£65,000)
- individuals – four grants (£44,000)
- direct preaching of the Gospel (£500).

The largest grants were those to: Oasis International (£38,000); Operation Agape (£25,000); 180 Degrees – Viva Network (£23,000); Ambassadors in Sport and European Christian Mission (£15,000 each); and EMMS International (£10,000).

Other grantees included: World Radio (£8,000); Retrack (£7,000); Global Connection (£4,000); St Stephen's Society (£2,000); SOMA UK (£1,000); Redcliffe College (£500); and Cloud Trust (£475).

Applications The trustees do their own research and do not respond to unsolicited applications.

Panton Trust

Animal wildlife worldwide and environment of the UK

£53,000 to organisations (2007/08)

Beneficial area UK and overseas.

Ramsay House, 18 Vera Avenue, Grange Park, London N21 1RB

Tel. 020 8370 7700

Correspondent Laurence Slavin, Trustee

Trustees *L M Slavin; R Craig.*

CC Number 292910

Information available Full accounts were on file at the Charity Commission.

The trust states that it is 'concerned with any animal or animals or with wildlife in any part of the world, or with the environment of the UK or any part thereof. The trustees consider applications from a wide variety of sources and favour smaller charities which do not have the same capacity for large-scale fundraising as major charities in this field.'

In 2007/08 the trust had assets of £216,000 and an income of £66,000. Grants were made totalling £53,000. Beneficiaries included: Gonville and Caius (£6,000); St Tiggywinkles Wildlife Hospital, Whales and Dolphin Conservation Society and Wroxton Abbey Charitable Trust (£5,000 each); Royal Botanic Garden Kew and Zoological Society (£3,000 each); and Arrow Riding Centre and Association for Protection of Animals – Algone (£2,500 each).

Other grants of less than £1,000 totalled £5,250.

Applications In writing to the correspondent.

The Paragon Trust

General

£98,000 (2007/08)

Beneficial area UK and overseas.

c/o Thomson Snell and Passmore Solicitors (ref: 1211), 3 Lonsdale Gardens, Tunbridge Wells TN1 1NX

Tel. 01892 701 211

Correspondent Mrs Kathy Larter

Trustees *The Lord Wrenbury; Revd Canon R Coppin; Miss L J Whistler; P Cunningham; Dr Fiona Cornish.*

CC Number 278348

Information available Full accounts were on file at the Charity Commission.

In 2007/08 the trust had assets of £1.9 million and an income of £104,000. Grants totalled £98,000. The majority of donations are standing orders.

Grants of £1,000 or more included those to: Compassion in World Farming (£5,000); Army Benevolent Fund (£4,000); British Red Cross (£3,000); Holy Cross Centre Trust and Demelza House Children's Hospice (£2,000 each); Mary Fielding Guild (£1,500); and The Art Fund, Buildings at Risk, National Autistic Society and Mines Advisory Group (£1,000 each).

Grants of less than £1,000 included those to: Whizz-Kidz, Church Housing Trust and Cystic Fibrosis (£750 each); and The Canon Collins Educational Trust for Southern Africa, South London Industrial Mission and St Dunstan's (£500 each).

Applications The trust states that it does not respond to unsolicited applications; all beneficiaries 'are known personally to the trustees and no attention is paid to appeal literature, which is discarded on receipt. Fundraisers are therefore urged to save resources by not sending literature.'

The Park Charitable Trust

Jewish, patient care – cancer and heart conditions and hospitals

£991,000 (2007/08)
Beneficial area UK.

69 Singleton Road, Salford M7 4LX
Correspondent E Pine, Trustee
Trustees *D Hammelburger; Mrs M Hammelburger; E Pine.*
CC Number 1095541
Information available Accounts were on file at the Charity Commission, without a list of grants.

The following is taken from the annual report.

The objects of the charity are the advancement of the Jewish Faith; the advancement of Jewish education; the relief of poverty amongst the Jewish community; the relief of patients suffering from cancer and heart conditions; giving financial support to hospitals and furthering such other charitable purposes as the trustees may from time to time determine in support of their charitable activities.

Registered in January 2003, in 2007/08 the trust had assets of £3.8 million, an income of £1.1 million and made grants totalling £991,000.

Grants were broken down as follows:

Category	Value
Relief of poverty	£382,000
Community projects	£372,000
Schools	£148,000
Yeshivot and seminaries	£60,000
Grants paid under £1,000	£20,000
Kollelim	£10,000

Applications In writing to the correspondent.

The Park House Charitable Trust

Education, social welfare and ecclesiastical

£278,000 (2008)
Beneficial area UK and overseas, with a preference for the Midlands, particularly Coventry and Warwickshire.

Dafferns, Queen's House, Queen's Road, Coventry CV1 3DR
Tel. 024 7622 1046
Correspondent Paul Varney
Trustees *N P Bailey; Mrs M M Bailey; P Bailey; Dr M F Whelan.*
CC Number 1077677
Information available Information was available from the Charity Commission website.

The trust was established in September 1999. In 2006 it had assets of £1.1 million and an income of £270,000. Grants totalled £278,000 and were categorised as follows:

Social Welfare (£207,000) – Beneficiaries included: Mary's Meals (£60,000); St Joseph and the Helper's Charity (£35,000); Life (£30,000); Society for the Protection of Unborn Children (£15,000); CAFOD and Serenity (£10,000 each); Ear Foundation (£5,000); and Coventry Jesus Centre, International Rescue Committee UK and Malawi Link Trust (£2,000 each).

Education (£65,000) – Krizevac Project (£50,000) and Maryvale Institute (£15,000).

Medical (£4,000) – Operation Smile and Tiny Tim's Children's Centre (£2,000 each).

Arts (£2,000) – to the sole beneficiary, Armonico Consort.

Exclusions No grants to individuals.

Applications In writing to the correspondent. The trust has stated that it does not expect to have surplus funds available to meet the majority of applications.

The Frank Parkinson Agricultural Trust

British agriculture

£29,000 (2008)
Beneficial area UK.

11 Alder Drive, Pudsey LS28 8RD
Tel. 0113 257 8613
Email janet.pudsey@live.co.uk
Correspondent Miss Janet Smith, Secretary to the Trustees

Trustees *Prof. J D Leaver; C Bourchier; J S Sclanders; Prof. Paul Webster.*
CC Number 209407
Information available Accounts were on file at the Charity Commission.

The trust's principal object is the improvement and welfare of British agriculture. Its aims are:

- the improvement and welfare of British agriculture
- the undertaking of agricultural research or the provision of grants for such means
- the establishment of scholarships, bursaries and exhibitions at any university, college or other technical institution in any branch of the agricultural industry
- the granting of financial assistance to young people of ability who are in need of assistance and are working in the agricultural industry to improve their education and experience by working, training or otherwise
- the encouragement and assistance of the social and cultural welfare of people working in the agricultural industry
- the making of grants to any charity or organisation which is carrying on any work in connection with the provision of any such benefits as aforesaid.

In 2008 it had assets of £1.1 million and an income of £59,000. Grants were made to four organisations and totalled £29,000. The beneficiaries were: Nuffield Farming Scholarships Trust (£15,000 in four payments); Institute of Agricultural Management Leadership Development Programme (£8,000); St George's House – Windsor Castle (£5,000); and AgriFood Charities Partnership (£500).

Exclusions Grants are given to corporate bodies and the trust is not able to assist with financial help to any individuals undertaking postgraduate studies or degree courses.

Applications In writing to the correspondent. The trustees meet annually in April and applicants are expected to make an oral presentation. Further details of the whole application process can be found in the useful 'Guidelines for Grant Applications' which is available from the trust. However, please note 'The chairman has the authority to approve small grants between annual meetings, but these are only for minor sums and minor projects.'

The Samuel and Freda Parkinson Charitable Trust

General

£100,000 (2007/08)
Beneficial area UK.

Thomson Wilson Pattinson, Trustees' Solicitors, Stonecliffe, Lake Road, Windermere LA23 3AR

Tel. 01539 442 233 **Fax** 01539 488 810

Correspondent Trust Administrator

Trustees *D E G Roberts; Miss J A Todd; M J Fletcher.*

CC Number 327749

Information available Accounts were on file at the Charity Commission.

This trust was established in 1987 with £100. The fund stayed at this level until 1994/95 when £2.1 million worth of assets were placed in the trust on the death of the settlor. It supports the same eight beneficiaries each year, although for varying amounts.

In 2007/08 it had assets of £2.5 million, an income of £126,000 and made grants totalling £100,000. The beneficiaries were: Salvation Army (£25,000); Leonard Cheshire Foundation (£24,000); Church Army (£20,000); RNLI (£10,000); RSPCA (£6,000); and Animal Concern, Animal Rescue and Animal Welfare (£5,000 each).

Applications The founder of this charity restricted the list of potential beneficiaries to named charities of his choice and accordingly the trustees do not have discretion to include further beneficiaries, although they do have complete discretion within the stated beneficiary list.

The Constance Paterson Charitable Trust

Medical research, health, welfare of children, older people and service people

£19,000 (2008/09)
Beneficial area UK.

Royal Bank of Canada Trust Corporation Limited, 71 Queen Victoria Street, London EC4V 4DE

Tel. 020 7653 4756

Email anita.carter@rbc.com

Correspondent Miss Anita Carter, Administrator

Trustee *Royal Bank of Canada Trust Corporation Ltd.*

CC Number 249556

Information available Full accounts were on file at the Charity Commission.

The trust makes grants in support of medical research, healthcare, welfare of older people and children (including accommodation and housing) and service people's welfare.

In 2008/09 the trust had assets of £1.2 million and an income of £40,000. Grants were made to 10 organisations totalling £19,000. The grant recipients were: Ataxia – Telangiectasia Society, Changing Faces, Havens Hospices, Theodora Children's Trust and Orchid (£2,220 each); and Children 1st, CLAPA, The Jennifer Trust, Charity Search and Medical Engineering Resource Unit (£1,550 each).

Exclusions No grants to individuals.

Applications In writing to the correspondent, including covering letter and the latest set of annual report and accounts. The trust does not have an application form. Deadlines for applications are June and December.

Arthur James Paterson Charitable Trust

Medical research and welfare of older people and children

£36,000 (2007/08)
Beneficial area UK.

Royal Bank of Canada Trust Corporation Limited, 71 Queen Victoria Street, London EC4V 4DE

Tel. 020 7653 4756

Email anita.carter@rbc.com

Correspondent Anita Carter

Trustee *Royal Bank of Canada Trust Corporation Ltd.*

CC Number 278569

Information available Accounts were on file at the Charity Commission.

In 2007/08 the trust had assets of £1.7 million with an income of £58,000. Grants to 13 organisations totalled £36,000.

The grants were to: Glenalmond College and Worcester College (£4,700 each); The Children's Trust, Elderly Accommodation Counsel, MDF The Bipolar Organisation, Demand, London Air Ambulance and Tommy's (£3,415 each); and Children First, Dance Umbrella, Jubilee Sailing Trust, Leukaemia and Polka Children's Theatre (£1,175 each).

Applications There are no application forms. Send your application with a covering letter and include the latest set of report and accounts. Deadlines are February and August.

Miss M E Swinton Paterson's Charitable Trust

Church of Scotland, young people and general

About £40,000 a year.
Beneficial area Scotland.

Lindsays' Solicitors, Calendonian Exchange, 19a Canning Street, Edinburgh EH3 8HE

Correspondent The Trustees

Trustees *Michael A Noble; J A W Somerville; C S Kennedy; R J Steel.*

SC Number SC004835

Information available Despite making a written request for the accounts of this trust (and including a stamped, addressed envelope), these were not provided. The following entry is based, therefore, on information filed with the Office of the Scottish Charity Regulator.

The trust was set up by the will of Miss M E Swinton Paterson who died in October 1989. The objectives of the trust are the support of charities in Scotland, specifically including schemes of the Church of Scotland.

The trust has an income of around £50,000 a year and makes grants totalling about £40,000 annually.

Previous beneficiaries included: L'Arche Edinburgh Community (£2,000); Livingstone Baptist Church, Lloyd Morris Congregational Church, Haddington West Parish Church, Acorn Christian Centre, Stranraer YMCA, Care for the Family, Boys' and Girls' Clubs of Scotland, Fresh Start, Friends of the Elms, Iona Community, Edinburgh Young Carers' Project and Epilepsy Scotland (£1,000 each); and Stoneykirk Parish Church, Scotland Yard Adventure Centre, Atholl Centre, Scottish Crusaders, Disablement Income Group Scotland and Artlink (£500 each).

Exclusions No grants to individuals or students.

Applications In writing to the correspondent. Trustees meet once a year in July to consider grants.

The Susanna Peake Charitable Trust

General

£165,000 (2007/08)

Beneficial area UK, with a preference for the south west of England, particularly Gloucestershire.

Rathbone Trust Company Limited, 159 New Bond Street, London W1S 2UD

Tel. 020 7399 0820

Correspondent The Administrator

Trustees *Susanna Peake; David Peake.*

CC Number 283462

Information available Full accounts were on file at the Charity Commission.

This is one of the Kleinwort family trusts. It was set up by Susanna Peake in 1981 for general charitable purposes and has a preference for charities based in the Gloucestershire area. In addition, non-local appeals when received are accumulated and considered by the trustees annually.

In 2007/08 the trust had assets of £5.2 million and an income of £188,000. Grants were made to 45 organisations totalling £165,000 and were broken down as follows:

- medical, cancer and hospices – £41,000

- local charitable organisations – £35,000
- education and children – £34,000
- international and overseas charities – £25,000
- general and animal charitable organisations – £24,000
- older people – £7,000.

Grants generally ranged from £500 to £5,000 although there were exceptions to this. Beneficiaries included: Chipping Norton Theatre and Friends Group and The Nelson Trust (£10,000 each); Fine Cell Work, Gurkha Welfare Trust and The Museum of London (£5,000 each); Interact Reading Service and Pain Relief Foundation (£3,000 each); Gloucestershire Historic Churches and Tax Aid (£2,000 each); The Gloucestershire Society (£1,000); Charity Aid Fund (£750); and Canine Partners (£500).

Exclusions No grants to individuals.

Applications In writing to the correspondent. 'The trustees meet on an ad hoc basis to review applications for funding, and a full review is undertaken annually when the financial statements are available. Only successful applications are notified of the trustees' decision.'

The David Pearlman Charitable Foundation

Jewish and general

£160,000 (2007/08)

Beneficial area UK.

New Burlington House, 1075 Finchley Road, London NW11 0PU

Tel. 020 8731 0777

Correspondent M R Goldberger, Trustee

Trustees *D A Pearlman; M R Goldberger; S Appleman; J Hager.*

CC Number 287009

Information available Accounts were on file at the Charity Commission, but without a grants list.

Set up in 1983, in 2007/08 the foundation had assets of £1.3 million and an income of £72,000. Grants totalled £160,000. Further information was unavailable via the Charity Commission.

Previous recipients of grants of £500 or more have included: British Friends of Igud Hakolelim B'Yerushalayim (£60,000); Lolev Charitable Trust (£30,000); Jewish Care (£16,000); Chevras Mo'oz Ladol (£15,000); Norwood (£12,000); the Duke of Edinburgh Trust (£7,000); Community Security Trust (£6,000); Life's 4 Living Trust Ltd (£6,400); Children Number One Foundation (£3,750); the Variety Club Children's Charity (£2,750); London Academy of Jewish Studies (£1,500); Jewish Music Institute and United Jewish Israel Appeal (£1,000 each).

Applications In writing to the correspondent.

Pearson's Holiday Fund

Young people who are disadvantaged

£36,000 to organisations (2008)

Beneficial area UK.

PO Box 3017, South Croydon CR2 9PN

Tel. 020 8657 3053

Website www.pearsonsholidayfund.org

Correspondent The General Secretary

Trustees *A John Bale, Chair; John S Bradley; David P Golder; John F Gore; Mark A Hutchings; Ms Jan Elbourn.*

CC Number 217024

Information available Accounts were available from the Charity Commission website with good commentary.

The fund was founded in 1892 as 'The Fresh Air Fund' by Cyril Arthur Pearson, who, in 1900, founded and edited the Daily Express. In 1920, the fund was registered under the Companies Act as 'Pearson's Fresh Air Fund' with trustees who were then all connected with the newspaper trade. In 1981 the fund's name was changed to its present form.

The present activity of the fund is the making of small grants to assist financially disadvantaged children and young people living in the United Kingdom to have holidays, outings, or to take part in group respite activities in the United Kingdom.

In reviewing its activities for 2008 the fund noted how its lack of 'underlying wealth' had not been helped by a decline in donations from grant-making trusts and companies. Support from individuals, nevertheless, did rise, due in part to 26 donations being enhanced by Gift Aid declarations in favour of the fund. In addition, the fund was aware of the need to restrict the number and amount of future grants to some geographical areas in order to achieve a more even distribution of funds.

Application guidance notes

Grants are awarded for the benefit of children and young people aged between 4 and 16 (inclusive) who, regardless of race, colour, creed or sex, meet the fund's criteria of being disadvantaged. The consideration of applications is made with regard to criteria set out in the frequently revised *Guidance Notes re: Applications for Grants*.

The extract below is taken from the 2009 version of the notes and sets out the criteria that must be met by applicants.

[Besides helping] children and young people of families on benefit-level income, those children and young people may, in addition, have:

- learning difficulties
- physical disabilities or other heath related problems
- experienced abuse or violence in the home or are regarded as being at risk
- disabled or older parents to care for
- other problems, e.g. refugees, homeless, and so on.

The following conditions must also be met in all cases:

- the child/children/young person(s) must live in the United Kingdom
- the holiday, outing or group activity must be in the United Kingdom
- the child/children/young person(s) must be aged 4 to 16 years (inclusive) at the time of the holiday/outing.

Where a family with a disadvantaged child/young person are taking a holiday together, we normally regard all the children/young people in the family, within our age range, participating in the holiday as meeting our criteria.

- the maximum grant we can offer is £75 per individual qualifying child/young person
- the maximum grant for the children/young people in any one family is £500.

In 2008 the fund had assets of £117,000 and an income of £61,000, the majority of which came from donations. 194 grants totalling £36,000 were made to the benefit of 504 individuals. No grants were made towards group activities during the year.

Applications Guidance notes for potential applicants can be viewed and/or downloaded from the fund's website and should be read fully before submitting an application.

Applications for grants must be submitted by an appropriate third party referring agency (e.g. social workers, health visitors, teachers, doctors, ministers of religion, organisers of holiday activities/projects, and so on). Applications must be in the form of a letter addressed and posted to The General Secretary, Pearson's Holiday Fund, PO Box 3017, South Croydon, Surrey, CR2 9PN accompanied by a stamped addressed or prepaid envelope for our reply. Any applications submitted by facsimile or email will not be considered.

We do not act upon direct applications from families.

Subject to the availability of funds, grants are awarded on a first come, first served, basis once all the information we require is complete. Consideration of any application that does not provide all the required information (and a prepaid envelope) will almost inevitably be delayed and may result in no grant being available by the time all the details have been provided. It is advisable to check the news page of our website (www.pearsonsholidayfund.org) as to the availability of funds before submitting any application to us.

In respect of the above, the fund pointed out in its 2008 annual report and accounts that some 78 applications were rejected on the grounds of not meeting the necessary criteria and a further 213 declined after available funds had been exhausted.

Peltz Trust

Arts and humanities, education and culture, health and welfare and Jewish

£234,000 (2007/08)

Beneficial area UK and Israel.

Berwin Leighton Paisner, Adelaide House, London Bridge, London EC4R 9HA

Tel. 020 7760 1000

Correspondent Martin D Paisner, Trustee

Trustees *Martin D Paisner; Daniel Peltz; Hon. Elizabeth Wolfson Peltz.*

CC Number 1002302

Information available Full accounts were available from the Charity Commission website.

In 2007/08 the trust had assets of £306,000 and an income of £513,000. Grants were made to 37 organisations totalling £234,000, broken down into the following categories:

Medical, health and sickness – 8 grants totalling £53,000
Including: CLIC Sargent (£11,000); Levka 2000 (£6,000); Willow Foundation (£5,000); and Wellbeing of Women (£4,500).

Economic and community development – 4 grants totalling £52,000
Including: Norwood Ravenswood and St Stephen's Trust (£20,000 each); Community Security Trust (£7,000); and Nightingale House (£5,000).

General charities – 8 grants totalling £43,000
Including: Jewish Care (£12,500); Central Synagogue General Charities (£10,000); One Family (£5,000); and War Memorials Trust (£2,500).

Education and training – 6 grants totalling £42,000
Including: City of London School Bursary Trust and Oxford Centre for Hebrew and Jewish Studies (£10,000 each); Facing History and Ourselves Ltd (£5,000); and Greenhouse Schools Project (£4,000).

Religious activities – 7 grants totalling £20,000
Including: Lubavitch Foundation (£10,000); Beth Shalom Ltd (£5,000); Tikun (£2,000); and Westminster Synagogue Memorial Scrolls (£1,000).

Arts and culture – 2 grants totalling £19,000
Hampstead Theatre (£18,000) and Shakespeare Globe Trust (£1,000).

Relief of poverty – 1 grant of £6,250
INF Charitable Trust (£6,250).

Exclusions No grants to individuals for research or educational awards.

Applications In writing to the correspondent. The trustees meet at irregular intervals during the year to consider appeals from appropriate organisations.

The Pennycress Trust

General

£54,000 (2007/08)

Beneficial area UK and worldwide, with a preference for Cheshire and Norfolk.

Flat D, 15 Millman Street, London WC1N 3EP

Tel. 020 7404 0145

Correspondent Mrs Doreen Howells, Secretary to the Trustees

Trustees *Lady Aline Cholmondeley; Anthony J M Baker; C G Cholmondeley; Miss Sybil Sassoon.*

CC Number 261536

Information available Accounts were available from the Charity Commission website, but without a list of beneficiaries.

The trust's policy is to make donations to smaller charities and especially those based in Cheshire and Norfolk, with some donations to UK and international organisations.

In 2007/08 the trust had assets of £2 million and an income of £91,000. During the year 191 donations were made totalling £54,000. These were mostly between £100 and £500, with one of £3,000 and two of £1,000 each. A list of beneficiaries was not included with the latest accounts.

Previous beneficiaries have included All Saints' Church – Beeston Regis, Brain Research Trust, Brighton and Hove Parents' and Children's Group, British Red Cross, Crusaid, Depaul Trust, Elimination of Leukaemia Fund, Eyeless Trust, Genesis Appeal, Help the Aged, Matthew Project, RUKBA, St Peter's – Eaton Square Appeal, Salvation Army, Tibet Relief Fund, West Suffolk Headway, Women's Link and Youth Federation.

Exclusions No support for individuals.

Applications In writing to the correspondent. 'No telephone applications please.' Trustees meet regularly. They do not have an application form as a simple letter will be sufficient.

B E Perl Charitable Trust

Jewish and general

£100,000(2007/08)

Beneficial area UK.

Foframe House, 35–37 Brent Street, Hendon, London NW4 2EF

Correspondent B Perl, Chair

Trustees *B Perl, Chair; Dr S Perl; Jonathan Perl; Joseph Perl; Naomi Sorotzkin; Mrs R Jeidal.*

CC Number 282847

Information available Accounts were on file at the Charity Commission, but without a list of beneficiaries.

The trust states that it makes grants for the advancement of the Orthodox Jewish faith as well as for other charitable purposes.

In 2007/08 the trust had assets of £11.7 million and an income of £1.3 million of which £940,000 was gift-aided from three related companies. Grants totalled £100,000 and were categorised as follows:

- educational – £62,000
- other charitable purposes – £25,000
- advancement of religion – £12,000
- relief of poverty and illness – £1,000.

Previously, a grant of £1.6 million went to Huntingdon Foundation Limited. Other beneficiaries receiving grants of £1,000 each or more included Kisharon, Gateshead Yeshiva, Talmud Torah School, Hertsmere Jewish High School, The Harav Lord Jacobovits Torah Institute of Contemporary Issues, Gateshead Jewish Academy for Girls, Or Chadash Children's Town, British Friends of Shuvu and the Before Trust.

This statement is taken from the trust's accounts.

Plans for future periods
The trustees have considered and approved plans for the establishment of a major educational project in the UK. It is anticipated that the cost of this project will be in the order of £5 million and it is the intention of the trustees to accumulate this amount over the next 10 years. During the year an amount of £500,000 (2007-£500,000) was transferred to a designated reserve in order to fund this project.

The designated reserve for this purpose stands at £1 million as at April 2008.

Applications In writing to the correspondent.

The Persson Charitable Trust (formerly Highmoore Hall Charitable Trust)

Christian mission societies and agencies

£254,000 (2007/08)

Beneficial area UK and overseas.

Long Meadow, Dark Lane, Chearsley, Aylesbury HP18 0DA

Correspondent P D Persson, Trustee

Trustees *P D Persson; Mrs A D Persson; J P G Persson; A S J Persson.*

CC Number 289027

Information available Accounts were on file at the Charity Commission.

The trust's accounts state that 'the trustees have a policy of awarding grants to charitable, not-for-profit, organisations which are predominantly involved in promoting the Christian faith and in humanitarian aid.'

In 2007/08 the trust had an income of £344,000, including £240,000 from Gift Aid. Grants totalled £254,000, broken down as follows:

Category	Value
Home missions	£148,000
Overseas missions	£100,000
Other charities	£6,000

The five largest grants were those to Bible Reading Fellowship – Foundations 21 course and Tearfund – Christian Relief (£50,000 each), Alpha International (£40,000), Christian Solidarity Worldwide (£21,000) and Reaching the Unchurched (£20,000). Other listed grants included those to Integral Alliance – networking Christian relief (£12,500) and Jubilee Centre Trust – encouraging and resourcing Christians (£10,000).

Smaller grants totalled almost £50,000.

Exclusions No grants to non-registered charities.

Applications The trust states that it does not respond to unsolicited applications. Telephone calls are not welcome.

The Persula Foundation

Homeless, disablement, human rights and animal welfare

£622,000 (2007/08)

Beneficial area Predominantly UK; overseas grants are occasionally given.

Unit 3/4, Gallery Court, Hankey Place, London SE1 4BB

Tel. 020 7357 9298 **Fax** 020 7357 8685

Email fiona@persula.org

Website www.persula.org

Correspondent Fiona Brown, Chief Executive

Trustees *J Richer; D Robinson; D Highton; Mrs R Richer; Mrs H Oppenheim.*

CC Number 1044174

Information available Accounts were available from the Charity Commission website.

The trust works in collaboration with organisations to support projects that are innovative and original in the UK and worldwide.

The foundation has core charity interests which they call Generic Research Projects (GRPs) and from this base, they decide on the charity and amount they donate.

These are:

- animal welfare
- disabilities (blind and visually impaired, deaf and hard of hearing, learning disabilities, mental health, physical disabilities)
- human welfare (bullying, children and young people, homeless, welfare)
- human rights.

The following information is taken from the 'Guidelines for Applicants' on the foundation's website.

We consider applications which fit our broad criteria, but they must also fulfil the following:

1) They must come from a registered charity or other appropriate organisation.

2) The project should be an original idea, and not duplicating an existing service or suchlike.

3) The project should be or have the potential to be of national application, rather than local to one area.

4) We will not consider applications from charities that have substantial financial reserves (three to six months running costs), and ask to see an annual report from any charity making an application.

5) Any charity with whom we work must be prepared to co-operate in a professional manner, for example, meet deadlines, return calls, perform mutually agreed work, in short, to behave 'commercially'.

6) The project, in most cases, must fall within the remit of one or more GRPs.

7) They must provide value for money.

This list is by no means exhaustive, nor is it final. We will attempt to consider every application but, in general, the above should apply.

In 2007/08 the trust had an income of £469,000. Of this, £406,000 was donated by Richer Sounds plc of which Julian Richer is the founder. Grants were made totalling £622,000 the largest listed of which went to Tapesense (£47,000). This project was set up a few years ago by the foundation and offers subsidised equipment and accessories to blind and visually impaired people.

Previous beneficiaries have included Action for ME, African Children's Educational Trust, the Aidis Trust, the Backup Trust, The Helen Bamber Foundation, Bullying Online, Disability Challengers, Dogs Trust, Emmaus, Humane Slaughter Association, Interact Worldwide, Kidscape, League Against Cruel Sports, The Mango Tree, the MicroLoan Foundation, National Deaf Children's Society, Practical Action, Prisoners Abroad, Prison Reform Trust, Respect for Animals, RNIB, RNID, St Mungos, SOS Children, Stonewall, VIVA! and WSPA.

Exclusions No grants to individuals, including sponsorship, for core costs, buildings/building work or to statutory bodies.

Applications In writing to the correspondent. Trustees meet every two months. Full guidelines can be downloaded form the foundation's website.

The Pestalozzi Overseas Children's Trust

Secondary education of deprived children

£804,000 (2008)

Beneficial area Worldwide, especially Asia and Africa.

15 Ebner Street, Wandsworth, London SW18 1BT

Tel. 020 8704 4455

Email info@pestalozziworld.com

Website www.pestalozziworld.com

Correspondent Simon Wakely

Trustees *Lady Butler; J J Dilger; S P Pahlson-Moller; F Von Hurter.*

CC Number 1046599

Information available Accounts were available from the Charity Commission website.

Pestalozzi Overseas Children's Trust – POCT is the co-ordinating entity of Pestalozzi World – the working alliance of several organisations working in Africa and Asia.

Pestalozzi World seeks to address all barriers to education, be it poverty, distance, lack of infrastructure or prejudice against children (especially girls) receiving schooling.

The 2008 accounts stated that:

The trust's mission is to provide a practical secondary education (age about 10 onwards) to deprived children in some of the poorest countries in Africa and Asia. It focuses on the brightest children, especially girls. The uniqueness of the programme is that the children once educated by Pestalozzi help provide education for the other children similar to themselves. This produces an ongoing ripple effect.

The accounts continued to detail the trust's work as follows:

The Trust and the Pestalozzi US Children's Charity Inc. now fund the education of 411 children in India, (including exiled Tibetans), Nepal, Malawi, Thailand and Zambia. A new group of 25 children joined the Asian Village in Northern India, bringing the total to 120 and a similar increase in the number of children is planned in each of the next three years.

A new database for scholars and alumni was commissioned enabling us to track the progress of Pestalozzi scholars from selection through to their adult lives and careers. this will be an important resource for measuring the impact of Pestalozzi World and demonstrating our success.

In 2008 the trust had assets of £2.4 million and an income of £915,000. Charitable expenditure totalled £804,000 comprising capital projects of £525,000 and school fees totalling £279,000.

Exclusions The trust emphasised that funding is not available to individuals, including students.

Applications Applications cannot be made to this trust. It works in partnerships with local organisations it identifies through its own research and networks and grants are given proactively by the trust. The trust will contact organisations it wants to support proactively.

The Petplan Charitable Trust

Welfare of dogs, cats, horses and rabbits

£517,000 (2008)
Beneficial area UK.

Great West House GW2, Great West Road, Brentford TW8 9EG

Tel. 020 8580 8013 **Fax** 020 8580 8186

Email catherine.bourg@allianz.co.uk

Website www.petplantrust.org

Correspondent Catherine Bourg, Administrator

Trustees David Simpson, Chair; Clarissa Baldwin; Patsy Bloom; John Bower; Ted Chandler; George Stratford.

CC Number 1032907

Information available Full accounts were available from the Charity Commission website.

The trust was established by a pet insurance company by adding an optional £1.50 a year to the premiums paid by its members.

The trust provides grants towards the welfare of dogs, cats, horses and rabbits by funding clinical veterinary investigation, education and welfare projects. The trust does not and will not consider applications which involve experimental or invasive surgery.

The principal activity of the trust is to make grants from donations received to fund clinical veterinary investigation, education and welfare projects. Two rounds of grants are awarded each year, welfare and

scientific. Capital grants for major projects may also be awarded to veterinary schools when funds allow, from time to time.

In 2008 the trust had assets of £179,000 and an income of £530,000. There were 39 grants made (29 welfare and 10 scientific) totalling £517,000.

The largest grants for scientific purposes were awarded to the University of Glasgow – £200,000 to a small animal hospital campaign and £103,000 towards research into the role of undetectable bacteria in the aetiopathogenesis of feline lymphocytic/plasmacytic gingivostomatitis.

Smaller scientific grants were made varying from £3,000 to £9,000 including those to: Animal Health Trust (£9,250); University of Cambridge (£8,800); and Royal Veterinary College (£3,100).

The three largest welfare grants were those paid to Hampshire Fire and Rescue – towards the purchase and fitting of a new animal rescue vehicle (£65,000) and Cats Protection – neutering campaign in Northern Ireland and Mayhew Animal Home – 'Save Our Staffies' neutering (£10,000 each).

Other smaller grants included: Stokechurch Dog Rescue – kennel renovation (£7,500); Cat Chat – dedicated web server (£6,000); Assisi Animal Sanctuary – assistance with veterinary costs (£5,000); Exmoor Search and Rescue – towards dog/handler training and welfare (£3,000); and Cotton Tails (rabbit and guinea pig rescue) – towards rabbit neutering and vaccination (£2,000).

Exclusions No grants to individuals or non-registered charities. The trust does not support or condone invasive procedures, vivisection or experimentation of any kind.

Applications Closing dates for scientific and welfare applications vary so please check the trust's website first. Grant guidelines and application forms can be downloaded from the trust's website.

The Phillips and Rubens Charitable Trust

General and Jewish

£340,000 (2007/08)
Beneficial area UK.

Fifth Floor, Berkeley Square House, Berkeley Square, London W1J 6BY

Tel. 020 7491 3763 **Fax** 020 7491 0818

Correspondent M L Phillips, Trustee

Trustees Michael L Phiiips; Mrs Ruth Philips; Martin D Paisner; Paul Philips; Gary Philips; Carolyn Mishon.

CC Number 260378

Information available Full accounts were on file at the Charity Commission.

The trust supports a wide range of causes, including medical research, education, disability, old age, poverty, sheltered accommodation and the arts. In practice, almost all the grants are made to Jewish/Israeli organisations.

In 2007/08 the trust had assets of £9.8 million and an income of £145,000. Grants were made totalling £340,000.

By far the largest grant was the £110,000 donated to the connected Phillips Family Charitable Trust, followed by those to United Jewish Israel Appeal (£41,000), and Charities Aid Foundation and Jewish Community Secondary School (£25,000 each).

Other beneficiaries included: Royal Opera House Foundation (£11,000); Holocaust Educational Trust (£10,000); British ORT (£7,500); Nightingale House (£5,000); Wizo Charitable Foundation (£2,000); and City of London School (£1,000).

Grants to organisations of less than £1,000 each totalled £5,400.

Exclusions No grants are made to individuals.

Applications In writing to the correspondent at any time.

The Phillips Family Charitable Trust

Jewish charities, welfare and general

£94,000 (2008/09)
Beneficial area UK.

Berkeley Square House, Berkeley Square, London W1J 6BY

Tel. 020 7491 3763

Correspondent Paul S Phillips, Trustee

Trustees *Michael L Phillips; Mrs Ruth Phillips; Martin D Paisner; Paul S Phillips; Gary M Phillips.*

CC Number 279120

Information available Full accounts were available from the Charity Commission website.

This trust stated that it makes grants to Jewish organisations and to a range of other causes, including older people, children and refugee charities and educational establishments.

In 2008/09 the trust had assets of £26,000 and an income of £90,000. Grants were made totalling £94,000 the largest of which were made to UJIA (£15,000) and Holocaust Educational Trust (£10,000 in two grants).

Other beneficiaries included: Jewish Leadership Council (£7,000 in two grants); Chief Rabbinate Trust and Community Security Trust (£5,000 each); Elephant Family (£3,500); Lubavitch Foundation (£3,000); Maccabi GB (£2,000); President's Club Charitable Trust (£1,500); and Royal National Institute for the Blind and Windsor Jewish Cultural Centre (£1,000 each).

Exclusions No grants to individuals.

Applications In writing to the correspondent. Please note: the trust informed us that there is not much scope for new beneficiaries.

The David Pickford Charitable Foundation

Christian and general

£34,000 (2006/07)

Beneficial area UK (with a preference for Kent and London) and overseas.

Elm Tree Farm, Mersham, Ashford TN25 7HS

Tel. 01233 720 200 **Fax** 01233 720 522

Correspondent D M Pickford, Trustee

Trustees *D M Pickford; C J Pickford; Mrs E J Pettersen;*

CC Number 243437

Information available Accounts were on file at the Charity Commission.

The general policy is to make gifts to Christian organisations, especially those helping young people, and those with special needs in the UK and overseas.

In 2006/07 the foundation had assets of £833,000 and an income of £24,000. Grants were made totalling £34,000. Beneficiaries included: CARE (£5,000); Chaucer Trust (£4,000); Oasis Trust (£2,500); Brighter Future and Pastor Training international (£1,000 each); Toybox (£750); Alpha International, Flow Romania and Mersham Parish Curch (£500 each); Compassion (£300); Samaritans (£250); and Lionhart (£15).

Exclusions No grants to individuals. No building projects.

Applications In writing to the correspondent. Trustees meet every other month from January. Applications will not be acknowledged. The correspondent states: 'It is our general policy only to give to charities to whom we are personally known. Those falling outside the criteria mentioned above will be ignored'.

The Bernard Piggott Trust

General

£69,000 (2007/08)

Beneficial area North Wales and Birmingham.

4 Streetsbrook Road, Shirley, Solihull, West Midlands B90 3PL

Tel. 0121 744 1695 **Fax** 0121 744 1695

Correspondent Miss J P Whitworth

Trustees *D M P Lea; N J L Lea; R J Easton; Archdeacon of Bangor.*

CC Number 260347

Information available Full accounts were available from the Charity Commission website.

This trust provides one-off grants for Church of England, Church of Wales, educational, medical, drama and youth organisations in Birmingham and North Wales only. In 2007/08 the trust's assets stood at £1.3 million. It had an income of £102,000 and made grants totalling £69,000. Grants ranged from £250 to £4,000.

Grant recipients included: The Black Country Living Museum (£4,000); Cynllun Efe (£3,000); St Tanwg Church – Llandanwg (£2,500); Acorns, Cure

Leukaemia, Parkinson's Disease Society and Sunfield (£2,000 each); Conway County District Scouts, DebRA and Listening Books (£1,500 each); Birmingham Focus on Blindness, British Stammering Association, Karis Neighbourhood Scheme and St John Wales (£1,000 each); and City of Birmingham Choir and Weoley Castle Community Church (£500 each).

Exclusions No grants to individuals.

Applications The trustees meet in May/June and November. Applications should be in writing to the secretary including annual accounts and details of the specific project including running costs and so on. General policy is not to consider any further grant to the same institution within the next two years.

The Cecil Pilkington Charitable Trust

Conservation, medical research and general

£93,000 (2007/08)

Beneficial area UK, particularly Sunningwell in Oxfordshire and St Helens.

Duncan Sheard Glass, Castle Chambers, 43 Castle Street, Liverpool L2 9TL

Correspondent The Administrator

Trustees *A P Pilkington; R F Carter Jonas; M R Feeny.*

CC Number 249997

Information available Accounts were on file at the Charity Commission.

This trust supports conservation and medical research causes across the UK, supporting both national and local organisations. It also has general charitable purposes in Sunningwell in Oxfordshire and St Helens, Merseyside.

In 2007/08 the trust's assets stood at £6.8 million. It had an income of £257,000 and made grants to 40 organisations totalling £93,000.

Beneficiaries included: Peninsular Medical School Foundation (£12,000); St Leonard's Church Restoration (£10,000); Alzheimer's Research Trust (£6,000); SANE (£5,000); RABI and Willowbrooke Hospice (£3,000 each); Compassion in World Farming, Global Canopy Foundation and Lepus UK

(£2,000 each); Barn Owl Trust, Diabetes UK, PEACH and Rare Breeds Survival Trust (£1,000 each) and Agro Forestry Research Trust (£500).

Exclusions No grants to individuals or non-registered charities.

Applications The trust does not respond to unsolicited appeals.

The Sir Harry Pilkington Trust

General

£177,000 (2007/08)

Beneficial area UK, with a preference for Merseyside.

Liverpool Charity And Voluntary Services, 151 Dale Street, Liverpool L2 2AH

Correspondent The Trustees

Trustee *Liverpool Charity and Voluntary Services.*

CC Number 206740

Information available Accounts were on file at the Charity Commission.

In 2007/08 the trust had assets of £5.1 million and an income of £207,000. Grants were made totalling £183,000, those of £1,000 or more were made to 53 organisations and were listed in the accounts.

Beneficiaries included: Liverpool Council for Voluntary Service (£50,000); Shopmobility St Helens (£3,200); Black and Equality Merseyside Network, Dingle Community Theatre, Everton Red Triangle ABC, Merseyside Dance Initiative and Youth Communications Network (£3,000 each); St John's Youth and Community Centre (£2,500); Henshaws Society for the Blind, Toxteth Learning and Unity Theatre – Homotopia (£2,000 each); the Activate Project (£1,600); Kuumba Imani Millennium Centre and Southport Flower Show (£1,500 each); and Coast International Artists Limited and Listening Ear – Merseyside (£1,000 each).

Applications In writing to the correspondent.

Austin and Hope Pilkington Trust

Categories of funding repeated in a three-year rotation

£313,000 (2007)

Beneficial area Unrestricted, but see exclusions field.

PO Box 124, Stroud, Gloucestershire GL6 7YN

Email admin@austin-hope-pilkington. org.uk

Website www.austin-hope-pilkington. org.uk

Correspondent Karen Frank, Administrator

Trustees *Jennifer Jones; Deborah Nelson; Penny Shankar.*

CC Number 255274

Information available Full accounts were available from the Charity Commission website.

The trustees welcome applications for projects within the following areas for the next three years. These categories are then repeated in a three-year rotation.

- 2009 – community; disability.
- 2010 – children; young people; older people; medical.
- 2011 – music and the arts; overseas.

Please note that, for 2010, only medical research projects dealing with the ageing population will be considered. The other priorities – children, young people and older people – as well as other non-research based medical work are still welcome.

Registered charities only. National projects are preferred to those with a local remit. Grants are usually between £1,000 and £10,000, with the majority being £5,000 or less. Exceptionally, grants of up to £20,000 are made, but these are usually for medical research projects. Grants are usually awarded for one year only.

In 2007 the trust had assets of £9.5 million and an income of £283,000. Grants were made totalling £313,000.

Exclusions Grants only to registered charities. No grants to individuals, including individuals embarking on a trip overseas with an umbrella organisation. Overseas projects can only be supported in the stated year. Charities working in the following areas are not supported: religion (including repair of Church fabric), and animals (welfare and conservation).

Applications Applicants are strongly advised to visit the trust's website as projects supported and eligibility criteria change from year to year. Grants are made twice a year, with deadlines for applications being 1 June and 1 November.

Applications should be made in writing to the correspondent. To apply for a grant, submit the following material.

- A letter summarising the application, including acknowledgement of any previous grants awarded from the trust.
- A maximum of two sides of A4 (including photographs) summarising the project.
- A detailed budget for the project.
- A maximum of two sides of A4 (including photographs) summarising the charity's general activities.
- The most recent accounts and annual report.

Please do not send CDs, DVDs, or any other additional information. If we require further details, we will contact the charity directly. Charities are therefore advised to send in applications with sufficient time before the June or November deadlines to allow for such enquiries.

With the increased level of applications, the trust has stated that all successful applicants will in future be listed on their website on the 'recent awards' after each trustee meeting. All applicants will still be contacted by letter in due course.

The Col W W Pilkington Will Trusts – The General Charity Fund

Medical, arts, social welfare, international charities, drugs misuse and environment

£41,000 (2007/08)

Beneficial area Mainly UK, with a preference for Merseyside.

PO Box 8162, London W2 1GF

Correspondent The Clerk

Trustees *Arnold Pilkington; Hon. Mrs Jennifer Jones; Neil Pilkington Jones.*

CC Number 234710

Information available Accounts were on file at the Charity Commission.

The trust gives grants to registered charities only, with a preference for the Merseyside area.

In 2007/08 the trust had assets of £1.7 million and an income of £57,000. Grants were made to 24 organisations totalling £41,000 and were broken down into the following categories:

Category	No.
Medical	7
Environment	6
Arts	4
International	4
Welfare	2
Drugs	1

Beneficiaries included: Exeter University Postgraduate Medical School (£8,000); No Panic, Marie Stopes International and Windows Project (£2,000 each); and British Friends of Neve Shalom, Farm Africa, Lupus UK, Marine Conservation Society, Merseyside Dance Initiative, Royal British Legion, Soil Association and WISH (£1,000 each).

Exclusions No support for non-registered charities, building projects, animal charities or individuals.

Applications In writing to the correspondent.

Miss A M Pilkington's Charitable Trust

General

About £150,000 (2008/09)

Beneficial area UK, with a preference for Scotland.

Carters Chartered Accountants, Pentland House, Saltire Centre, Glenrothes, Fife KY6 2AH

Correspondent The Clerk

SC Number SC000282

Information available Despite making a written request for the accounts of this trust (including a stamped, addressed envelope) these were not provided. The following entry is based on information filed with the Office of the Scottish Charity Regulator.

The trust supports a wide variety of causes in the UK, with few causes excluded (see exclusions). In practice there is a preference for Scotland – probably half the grants are given in Scotland. There is a preference for giving recurring grants, which normally range from £500 to £1,500.

In 2008/09 the trust had an income of £152,000.

Exclusions Grants are not given to overseas projects or political appeals.

Applications The trustees state that, regrettably, they are unable to make grants to new applicants since they already have 'more than enough causes to support'.

Mrs Pilkington's Charitable Trust

Equine animals, older people, the infirm and the poor

£199,000 (2006/07)

Beneficial area UK.

Taylor Wessing, Carmelite, 50 Victoria Embankment, London EC4Y 0DX

Tel. 020 300 7000

Correspondent Lord Brentford

Trustees *Mrs Caroline Doulton, Chair; Mrs Tara Economakis; Revd Rob Merchant; Mrs Helen Timpany.*

CC Number 278332

Information available Accounts were available from the Charity Commission website.

This trust supports small specific projects of a capital nature which benefit equines and older people in need.

In 2006/07 the trust's assets stood at £3.5 million. It had an income of £97,000 and made 25 grants totalling £199,000, broken down as follows:

- to prevent cruelty to equine animals – £85,000
- to provide help for older people, the infirm or poor – £115,000

A list of beneficiaries was not available.

Applications In writing to the correspondent.

The Platinum Trust

Disability

£516,000 (2007/08)

Beneficial area UK.

Sedley Richard Laurence Voulters, Kendal House, 1 Conduit Street, London W1S 2XA

Correspondent The Secretary

Trustees *G K Panayiotou; S Marks; C D Organ.*

CC Number 328570

Information available Accounts were on file at the Chaity Commission.

This trust gives grants in the UK for the relief of children with special needs and adults with mental or physical disabilities 'requiring special attention'.

In 2007/08 the trust had an income of £492,000 mainly from donations and assets stood at £151,000. Grants to 28 organisations totalled £516,000.

Beneficiaries included: UKDPC (£45,000); Disability, Pregnancy and Parenthood International (£40,000); Centre for Studies on Inclusive Education (£32,000); Disability Equality in Education (£25,000); Alliance for Inclusive Education (£22,000); Parents for Inclusion (£20,000); Independent Panel for Special Education Advice (£15,000); Vassal Centre Trust (£10,000); Multiple Sclerosis Trust and VSO (£5,000 each); SENSE (£3,000); the Snowdon Award Scheme (£2,500); and the Simon Paul Foundation (£1,200).

Exclusions No grants for services run by statutory or public bodies, or from mental health organisations. No grants for: medical research/treatment or equipment; mobility aids/wheelchairs; community transport/disabled transport schemes; holidays/exchanges/holiday playschemes; special-needs playgroups; toy and leisure libraries; special Olympic and Paralympics groups; sports and recreation clubs for people with disabilities; residential care/sheltered housing/respite care; carers; conservation schemes/city farms/horticultural therapy; sheltered or supported employment/community business/social firms; purchase/construction/repair of buildings; and conductive education/other special educational programmes.

Applications The trust does not accept unsolicited applications; all future grants will be allocated by the trustees to groups they have already made links with.

G S Plaut Charitable Trust Limited

Sickness, disability, Jewish, older people, Christian and general

£25,000 (2007/08)

Beneficial area Predominantly UK.

39 Bay Road, Wormit, Newport-on-Tay, Fife DD6 8LW

Correspondent Dr R A Speirs, Secretary

Trustees *Mrs A D Wrapson, Chair; W E Murfett; Miss T A Warburg; Dr A M S Shaw; Mrs B A Sprinz.*

CC Number 261469

Information available Accounts were on file on at the Charity Commission, without a list of grants.

This trust appears to make grants across the whole spectrum of the voluntary sector, however it may have some preference for charities in those fields listed above.

In 2007/08 the trust's assets totalled £1.1 million, it had an income of £227,000 and grants totalled £25,000.

Previous beneficiaries have included Book Aid International, British Deaf Association, Down's Syndrome Association, Friends of Meals on Wheels Service – Liverpool, Gurkha Welfare Trust, Hull Jewish Community Care, Liverpool School of Tropical Medicine, Nightingale Home for Aged Jews, Rehearsal Orchestra, RNIB Talking Book Services, St George's Crypt – Leeds, Southend Riding Club for the Disabled, TOC H and VSO.

Exclusions No grants to individuals or for repeat applications.

Applications In writing to the correspondent. Applications are reviewed twice a year. A stamped, addressed envelope should be enclosed. Applications will not be acknowledged.

The J S F Pollitzer Charitable Settlement

General

£21,000 (2007/08)

Beneficial area UK and overseas.

Mary Street House, Mary Street, Taunton TA1 3NW

Tel. 020 7388 7000

Correspondent P Samuel, Accountant

Trustees *R F C Pollitzer, Chair; Mrs J F A Davis; Mrs S O'Farrell*

CC Number 210680

Information available Accounts were on file at the Charity Commission.

The trust supports a range of UK and local charities. In 2007/08 the trust had assets of £677,000 and an income of £11,000. Grants were made to 21 organisations totalling £21,000, all grants were for amounts of £1,000 each, with the exception of one grant totalling £500. Grants were broken down into the following categories:

Category	Value
Health	£5,000
Overseas aid	£5,000
Social and community welfare	£3,000
Children and young people	£2,000
Disabled	£2,000
Blind	£1,000
Cultural	£1,000
Hospices	£1,000
Religion	£1,000

Beneficiaries included: Casa Allianza, Children's Hospice South West, Comex, the Community Furniture Project, Disability Snowsport UK, the Eyeless Trust, Foundation for the Relief of Disabled Orphans, Free the Way, Headway, Help for Heroes, Mercy Corps, the Spiro Ark, Spinal Injuries Association, Steps, the Theatres Trust Charitable Fund, Tolerance International and Youth Net.

Exclusions No grants to individuals or students.

Applications In writing to the correspondent. Grants are distributed twice a year, usually around April/May and November/December.

The George and Esme Pollitzer Charitable Settlement

Jewish and general

£110,000 (2007/08)

Beneficial area UK.

Saffery Champness, Beaufort House, 2 Beaufort Road, Clifton, Bristol B58 2AE

Correspondent J Barnes, Trustee

Trustees *J Barnes; B G Levy; R F C Pollitzer.*

CC Number 212631

Information available Full accounts were on file at the Charity Commission.

This trust has general charitable purposes with no exclusions. Most funds are given to Jewish causes.

In 2007/08 the settlement's assets stood at £3 million. It had an income of £116,000 and made grants to 55 organisations totalling £110,000. A large proportion of grants were for £1,000 and £1,500 each.

Beneficiaries included: Royal School for Needlework (£15,000); Royal Hospital for Neuro Disability (£5,000); Deafblind UK (£3,000); Jewish Children's Holidays Fund, London Youth Support Trust and the Weiner Library (£2,000 each); Apex Trust, Atlantic College, the Foundation for Conductive Education, Independent Age, Mencap, Pestalozzi International Village Trust and the Prostate Cancer Charity (£1,500 each); Contact the Elderly (£1,000); and Crimestoppers Trust (£500).

Applications In writing to the correspondent.

Edith and Ferdinand Porjes Charitable Trust

Jewish and general

£85,000 (2007/08)

Beneficial area UK and overseas.

Adelaide House, London Bridge, London EC4R 9HA

Correspondent M D Paisner, Trustee

Trustees *M D Paisner; A S Rosenfelder; H Stanton.*

CC Number 274012

Information available Full accounts were on file at the Charity Commission.

Although the trust has general charitable purposes, the trust is inclined to support applications from the Jewish community in the UK and overseas. The trustees have set aside a fund, referred to as the 'British Friends of the Art Museums of Israel Endowment Fund' with the specific aim of supporting the British Friends of the Art Museums of Israel.

In 2007/08 the trust had assets of £1.5 million and an income of £64,000 with grants to seven organisations totalling £85,000.

Beneficiaries were: London School of Jewish Studies (£30,000); the Jewish Museum (£25,000); Queen Mary University of London (£15,000); the Cancer Treatment and Research Trust and European Jewish Publication Society (£5,000 each); British Friends of the Art Museums of Israel (£3,000); and British Friends of OHEL Sarah (£2,000).

Applications In writing to the correspondent.

The Porter Foundation

Jewish charities, environment, arts and general

£225,000 (2007/08)

Beneficial area Israel and the UK.

5a Jewry St, Winchester SO23 8RZ

Tel. 01962 849684

Email theporterfoundation@btinternet.com

Correspondent Paul Williams, Executive Director

Trustees *David Brecher; Albert Castle; Dame Shirley Porter; Steven Porter; Sir Walter Bodmer; John Porter; Linda Streit.*

CC Number 261194

Information available Accounts were on file at the Charity Commission.

The foundation supports 'projects in the fields of education, the environment, culture and health and welfare, which encourage excellence, efficiency and innovation and enhance the quality of people's lives'.

During recent years it has cut back on the number of beneficiaries supported and is making fewer, larger grants, mainly to the connected Porter School of Environmental Studies at Tel Aviv University, or the university itself, and to other causes in Israel. This has led to a temporary reduction in UK-based activity. A limited number of community awards continue to be given, though usually to organisations already known to the foundation.

The foundation was set up in 1970 by Sir Leslie Porter and Dame Shirley Porter, a former leader of Westminster City Council and daughter of Sir John Cohen, the founder of Tesco.

In 2007/08 the foundation had assets of £48 million and an income of £1.3 million. During the year the trust made uncommitted charitable donations totalling £225,000 and paid £753,000 in respect of binding charitable commitments. No new commitments were entered into.

Beneficiaries of uncommitted grants included: Friends of Daniel for Rowing Association (49,000); Tel Aviv Foundation (£27,000); New Israel Fund (£25,000); British Friends of the Verbier Festival and Academy (£12,000); Imperial War Museum (£10,000); Royal Opera House Foundation (£8,000); Trinity Laban (£6,000); Norwood Ravenswood (£5,000); ESRA Community Fund (£2,900); and Wigmore Hall Trust (£1,000).

Exclusions The foundation makes grants only to registered charitable organisations or to organisations with charitable objects that are exempt from the requirement for charitable registration.

Grants will not be made to:

- general appeals such as direct mail circulars
- charities which redistribute funds to other charities
- third-party organisations raising money on behalf of other charities
- cover general running costs.

No grants are made to individuals.

Applications An initial letter summarising your application, together with basic costings and background details on your organisation, such as the annual report and accounts, should be sent to the director. Speculative approaches containing expensive publicity material are not encouraged.

If your proposal falls within the foundation's current funding criteria you may be contacted for further information, including perhaps a visit from the foundation staff. There is no need to fill out an application form.

Applications fulfilling the criteria will be considered by the trustees, who meet three times a year, usually in March, July and November. You will hear shortly after the meeting whether your application has been successful. Unfortunately, it is not possible to acknowledge all unsolicited applications (unless a stamped, addressed envelope is enclosed). Due to limits on funds available, some excellent projects may have to be refused a grant. In such a case the trustees may invite the applicant to re-apply in a future financial year, without giving a commitment to fund.

The Portrack Charitable Trust

General

£47,000 (2007/08)

Beneficial area Some preference for Scotland.

Butterfield Bank, 99 Gresham Street, London EC2V 7NG

Correspondent The Trustees

Trustees *Charles Jencks; Keith Galloway; John Jencks.*

CC Number 266120

Information available Accounts were on file at the Charity Commission.

In 2007/08 the trust had assets of £2.1 million and an income of £46,000. Grants were made totalling £47,000. The majority of the 36 grants made were for £500.

Beneficiaries included: Maggie's Cancer Caring Centres (£10,000); Royal Institute for British Architects (£5,000); Medical Aid for Palestinians (£1,500); Carers UK, Listening Books, National Museums Scotland and Princess Royal Trust for Carers (£1,000 each); and Contact the Elderly, Forum for the Future, Holywood Church, Human Rights Watch, Musicians Benevolent Fund, Scottish Youth Theatre and the Tricycle Theatre (£500 each).

Exclusions Grants are not given to individuals.

Applications In writing to the correspondent.

The J E Posnansky Charitable Trust

Jewish charities, health, social welfare and humanitarian

£145,000 (2007/08)

Beneficial area UK and overseas.

Sobell Rhodes, Monument House, 215 Marsh Road, Pinner, London WA5 5NE

Tel. 020 7431 0909 **Fax** 020 7435 1516

Correspondent Mr N S Posnansky, Trustee

Trustees *Mrs G Raffles; A Posnansky; P A Mishcon; Mrs E J Feather; N S Posnansky.*

CC Number 210416

Information available Accounts were available at the Charity Commission.

The trust was created in 1958 for general charitable purposes in the UK and elsewhere and grant giving now concentrates on the areas of Jewish, health, education, social welfare and humanitarian causes. The trust incorporates the A V Posnansky Charitable Trust.

In 2007/08 the trust had assets of £3.7 million and an income of £155,000. Grants totalled £145,000.

Beneficiaries included: Magen David Adom UK and UKIA (£20,000 each); British WIZO and Friends of Alyn (£15,000 each); the Jewish Aid Committee and Jewish Care (£7,500 each); Ben Gurion University Foundation (£5,000); Nightingale House (£3,000); Sight Savers International and Water Aid (£2,500 each); Amnesty International (£1,000); British Limbless Ex-Servicemen (£1,000); and Kisharon Day School Charity Trust and St Luke's Hospice (£500 each).

Exclusions No grants to individuals.

Applications Unsolicited applications will not be considered.

The David and Elaine Potter Foundation

Advancement of education and scientific research

£212,000 (2007)

Beneficial area UK and overseas with particular emphasis on the developing world.

10 Park Crescent, London W1B 1PQ

Tel. 020 7291 3993

Website www.potterfoundation.com

Correspondent Mrs Angela Seay, Director

Trustees *M S Polonsky; M Langley; D Potter; E Potter; S Potter.*

CC Number 1078217

Information available Accounts were on file at the Charity Commission.

This foundation was registered with the Charity Commission in November 1999. It has general charitable objectives but focuses on supporting education, science, human rights, and the general strengthening of civil society. Most grants are made for:

- scholarships and other related activities that will improve understanding, governance and the promotion of a civil society
- research through the creation of institutions and other means
- human rights activism
- initiatives that support democratic governance
- agencies and charities carrying out development, research and educational projects.

In 2007 the trust had assets of £18 million and an income of £1.2 million. Grants were made to 18 organisations totalling £212,000.

The largest grants were made to: Open Trust – China Dialogue (£58,000); Centre of Investigative Journalism (£51,000); Performa (£50,000); International Alert (£45,000); Royal Society Edinburgh and Canon Collins Trust (£30,000 each); the Howard League (£20,000); and Reform Research (£15,000).

Other grants made included those to: HemiHelp (£7,500); Donmar Warehouse Projects (£3,000); Variety Club Children's Charity and Almeida Theatre (£1,000 each); and Wellbeing for Women (£500).

Applications 'The trustees' policy is to consider all applications received, but they prefer to seek projects that they wish to support rather than to receive unsolicited applications.'

Prairie Trust

Developing countries, the environment and conflict prevention

£70,000 (2007/08)

Beneficial area Worldwide.

83 Belsize Park Gardens, London NW3 4NJ

Correspondent The Administrator

Trustees *Dr Frederick Mulder; Hannah Mulder.*

CC Number 296019

Information available Accounts were available from the Charity Commission.

The trust does not consider unsolicited applications and instead develops its own programme to support a small number of organisations working on issues of developing countries, the environment and conflict prevention, particularly to support policy and advocacy work in these areas. The trustees are also interested in supporting innovative and entrepreneurial approaches to traditional problems.

In 2007/08 the trust had an income of £1.4 million received under Gift Aid and made 18 grants totalling £70,000. Assets stood at £1.6 million at year end.

Beneficiaries included: the Funding Network London (£31,000); Oxford Research Group (£10,000); Global Democratic Citizens Union and Women in Dialogue (£5,000 each); Bedouin Wool Project (£4,700); the Funding Network Leeds (£3,000); the Funding Network Toronto (£2,800); Women in Need – India leprosy project (£2,500); Pegasus Theatre (£1,000); British Institute Florence (£500); CIVA and Peace Direct (£250 each); and Merseyside Community Federation for Adult Dyslexia, Stroke Association and Willow Foundation (£100 each).

Exclusions No grants to individuals, for expeditions or for capital projects.

Applications The trust states: 'As we are a proactive trust with limited funds and administrative help, we are unable to consider unsolicited applications'.

The W L Pratt Charitable Trust

General

£61,000 (2007/08)

Beneficial area UK, particularly York, and overseas.

Grays, Duncombe Place, York YO1 7DY

Tel. 01904 634771

Email christophergoodway@ grayssolicitors.co.uk

Correspondent C C Goodway, Trustee

Trustees *J L C Pratt; C M Tetley; C C Goodway.*

CC Number 256907

Information available Accounts were on file at the Charity Commission.

The trust divides its grant giving between overseas charities, local charities in the York area and UK national charities. UK and overseas grants are restricted to well-known registered charities.

Support is given:

- in the UK: to support religious and social objectives with priority for York and district, including health and community services
- overseas: to help the developing world by assisting in food production and relief of famine and disease.

In 2007/08 the trust's assets stood at £1.7 million. It had an income of £60,000 and made 55 grants totalling £61,000, broken down into the following categories and shown here with examples of beneficiaries in each category:

York and district charities – 20 grants totalling £22,000

York Diocesan Board of Finance (£4,300); St Leonard's Hospice (£2,300); Wilberforce Trust (£2,200); York Minster Fund (£1,800); the Army Benevolent Fund North Region (£1,300); York CVS (£1,100); Yorkshire Air Ambulance (£1,000); and Abbeyfield York Society, British Red Cross – North Yorkshire Branch, Camphill Village Trust – Croft Community, Sue Ryder Foundation, WRVS and York Sea Cadets (£500 each).

UK charities – 15 grants totalling £11,000

Barnados and Salvation Army (£1,100 each); Guide Dogs for the Blind, RNLI and St John Ambulance (£1,000 each); and Action Research, Age Concern, CARE, Marie Curie Memorial Foundation, Live Music Now!, NSPCC, SSAFA and Shelter (£500 each).

Overseas charities – 7 grants totalling £10,000

Christian Aid and Sight Savers International (£2,200 each); Save the Children (£1,800); and British Humanitarian Aid Limited, British Red Cross and Oxfam (£500 each).

One-off donations – 13 grants totalling £18,000

York Minster Development Campaign (£10,000); Alzheimer's Research, African Mission, Community Furniture Store – York and York Arc Light (£1,000 each); Crisis, Lepra and Yorkshire Young Musicians (£500 each); York and North Yorkshire Community (£250); and Royal Northumberland Fusiliers (£100).

Exclusions No grants to individuals. No grants for buildings or for upkeep and preservation of places of worship.

Applications In writing to the correspondent. Applications will not be acknowledged unless a stamped, addressed envelope is supplied. Telephone applications are not accepted.

Premierquote Ltd

Jewish and general

£650,000 (2007/08)

Beneficial area Worldwide.

18 Green Walk, London NW4 2AJ

Correspondent D Last, Trustee

Trustees *D Last; Mrs L Last; H Last; M Weisenfeld.*

CC Number 801957

Information available Accounts were on file at the Charity Commission, but without a list of grants.

The trust was established in 1985 for the benefit of Jewish organisations, the relief of poverty and general purposes. In 2007/08 it had assets of £7.3 million and an income of £1.1 million. There were 49 grants made totalling £650,000.

Previous beneficiaries have included Achisomoch, Belz Yeshiva Trust, Beth

Jacob Grammar School for Girls Ltd, British Friends of Shuvu, Friends of Ohel Moshe, Friends of Senet Wiznitz, Friends of the United Institutions of Arad, Kehal Chasidel Bobov, Meadowgold Limited, Menorah Primary School, North West London Communal Mikvah and Torah Vedaas Primary School.

Applications In writing to the correspondent.

Premishlaner Charitable Trust

Jewish

£99,000 (2007/08)

Beneficial area UK and worldwide.

186 Lordship Road, London N16 5ES

Correspondent C M Margulies, Trustee

Trustees *C Freudenberger; C M Margulies.*

CC Number 1046945

Information available Accounts were on file at the Charity Commission.

This trust was founded in 1995; its principal objects are:

- to advance orthodox Jewish education
- to advance the religion of the Jewish faith in accordance with the Orthodox practice
- the relief of poverty.

Previous beneficiaries included: Gateshead Jewish Primary School, Shaat Ratzon, TTBA and Zichron Yechezkel Trust (£10,000 each); J and R Charitable Trust (£8,000); and Hadras Kodesh and Kehal Yisroel (£5,000 each).

Applications In writing to the correspondent.

The Primrose Trust

General

£235,000 (2007/08)

Beneficial area UK.

Blenheim House, Fitzalan Court, Newport Road, Cardiff CF24 0TS

Tel. 0292 021 4873

Correspondent M G Clark, Trustee

Trustees *M G Clark; Susan Boyes-Korkis.*

CC Number 800049

Information available Full accounts were on file at the Charity Commission.

The trust was established in 1986 with general charitable purposes. In 2007/08 the trust had assets of £3.6 million and an income of £143,000. Grants were made to three organisations totalling £235,000.

Grant recipients were: Murry Foundation (£210,000); Bill Jordan Foundation for Wildlife (£15,000); and Langford Trust (£10,000).

Exclusions Grants are given to registered charities only.

Applications In writing to the correspondent, including a copy of the most recent accounts. The trust does not wish to receive telephone calls.

The Princess Anne's Charities Trust

Children, medical, welfare and general

£128,000 (2007/08)
Beneficial area UK.

Buckingham Palace, London SW1A 1AA

Correspondent Capt. N Wright

Trustees *Hon. M T Bridges; Rear Admiral T J H Laurence; B Hammond.*

CC Number 277814

Information available Accounts were available from the Charity Commission website.

This trust has general charitable purposes, with a preference for charities or organisations in which the Princess Royal has a particular interest. In 2007/08 the trust had assets of £4.8 million and an income of £162,000. Grants were made to 33 organisations totalling £128,000, broken down as follows:

Category	Value	No.
Social welfare	£43,000	13
Children and young people	£28,000	3
Medical	£16,000	7
Environment and wildlife	£13,000	4
Armed forces	£7,500	3
Religion	£5,000	1
General	£17,000	1

Previous beneficiaries have included: Butler Trust, the Canal Museum Trust Cranfield Trust, Dogs Trust, Dorothy House Foundation, Durrell Wildlife Conservation Trust, the Evelina

Children's Hospital Appeal, Farms for City Children, Farrer and Co Charitable Trust, Fire Services National Benevolent Fund, the Home Farm Trust, Intensive Care Society, International League for the Protection of Horses, King Edward VIII Hospital-Sister Agnes, National Autistic Society, Minchinhampton Centre for the Elderly, Mission to Seafarers, Princess Royal Trust for Carers, REDR, RYA Sailability, Save the Children Fund, Scottish Field Studies Association, Scottish Motor Neurone Disease Association, SENSE, Spinal Injuries Association, Strathcarron Hospice, Transaid, London Bombing Relief Charitable Fund, Victim Support, VSO and Women's Royal Navy Benevolent Trust.

Exclusions No grants to individuals.

Applications 'The trustees are not anxious to receive unsolicited general applications as these are unlikely to be successful and only increase the cost of administration of the charity.'

The Priory Foundation

Health and social welfare, especially children

£741,000 (2007)
Beneficial area UK.

c/o Cavendish House, 18 Cavendish Square, London W1G 0PJ

Correspondent The Trustees

Trustees *N W Wray; L E Wray; T W Bunyard; D Poutney.*

CC Number 295919

Information available Accounts were on file at the Charity Commission.

The trust was established in 1987 to make donations to charities and appeals that directly benefit children.

In 2007 it had assets of £1.9 million and an income of £143,000. Grants totalled £741,000.

There were 46 grants listed in the accounts of £1,000 or more. Beneficiaries included: Saracens Foundation (£34,000); Infer Trust and Ovarian Cancer Action (£30,000 each); London Borough of Barnet (£29,000); Wellbeing (£25,000); Arundel Castle Cricket Foundation (£24,000); Watford Palace Theatre (£21,000); Get-A-Head Appeal

(£19,000); Barnet CAB (£6,500); Barnet Primary Care NHS Trust (£3,400); Children for Peace (£2,500); Tim Parry Jonathan Ball Foundation for Peace and Dame Vera Lynn Trust (£2,500 each); and Disability Aid Fund and Mill Hill School (£1,000 each).

Applications In writing to the correspondent.

Prison Service Charity Fund

General

£149,000 (2008)
Beneficial area UK.

The Lodge, 8 Derby Road, Garstang, Preston PR3 1EU

Correspondent The Trustees

Trustees *A N Joseph, Chair; P Ashes; J Goldsworthy; R Howard; P McFall; Ms C F Smith; K Wingfield.*

CC Number 801678

Information available Full accounts were available from the Charity Commission website.

In 2008 the fund's assets stood at £500,000. It had an income of £151,000 and made 144 grants totalling £149,000, the majority of which were for less than £1,000 each.

Beneficiaries included: the Robbie James Trust and Women for Women Fund (£3,000 each); Michael Charlton Appeal (£2,600); Breast Cancer Care (£2,500); Teenage Cancer Trust and Phyllis Tuckwell Hospice (£2,400); Cancer Research UK and Motor Neurone Disease Association (£2,300 each); Riding for the Disabled Association and Yorkshire Disabled Powerlifting (£2,000 each); Friends of Abbey Hill and Walton Hall School (£1,500 each); Earl Mountbatten Hospice, Children with Leukaemia, Great North Air Ambulance and Prison Service Special Games (£1,000 each); Neuroblastoma Society (£800); St Anne's Hospice (£600); Cystic Fibrosis Trust and National Autistic Society (£500 each); Great North Air Ambulance (£400); Dysphasia Society (£200); and Breast Care Awareness (£80).

Applications The trust does not accept outside applications – the person making the application has to be a member of staff.

271

The Puebla Charitable Trust

Community development work and relief of poverty

See below

Beneficial area Worldwide.

Ensors, Cardinal House, 46 St Nicholas Street, Ipswich IP1 1TT

Tel. 01473 220 022

Correspondent The Clerk

Trustees *J Phipps; M A Strutt.*

CC Number 290055

Information available Accounts were on file at the Charity Commission.

The trust has stated that: 'At present, the council limits its support to charities which assist the poorest sections of the population and community development work – either of these may be in urban or rural areas, both in the UK and overseas.'

Grants are normally in the region of £5,000 to £20,000, with support given over a number of years where possible. Most of the trust's income is therefore already committed, and the trust rarely supports new organisations.

In 2007/08 the trust's assets stood at £2.5 million and it had an income of £155,000. No grants were paid during the year. During 2006/07 the trust committed to pay grants of £450,000 over a three year period, and this commitment was recognised in the accounts for that year.

Recent beneficiaries have included: Action on Disability and Development, the Cambodia Trust, Child Poverty Action Group, Family Welfare Association, Mines Advisory Group, Shelter, South West London Law Centres, Immigrants Aid and Zimbabwe Benefit Foundation.

Exclusions No grants for capital projects, religious institutions, research or institutions for people who are disabled. Individuals are not supported and no scholarships are given.

Applications In writing to the correspondent. The trustees meet in July. The trust is unable to acknowledge applications.

The Richard and Christine Purchas Charitable Trust

Medical research, medical education and patient care

£140,000 (2007/08)

Beneficial area UK.

46 Hyde Park Gardens Mews, London W2 2NX

Correspondent Daniel Auerbach, Trustee

Trustees *Daniel Auerbach; Mrs Pauline Auerbach; Dr Douglas Rossdale; Robert Auerbach.*

CC Number 1083126

Information available Accounts were on file at the Charity Commission.

Registered with the Charity Commission in October 2000, in 2007/08 the trust had assets amounting to £2.5 million and an income of £139,000. Grants totalled £140,000.

No list of grants was included with the accounts filed at the Charity Commission. Previously the trust has part-funded the post of Consultant Speech Therapist at the Charing Cross Hospital in association with Macmillan Cancer Relief.

Applications In writing to the correspondent.

The Pyne Charitable Trust

Christian and health

£101,000 (2008)

Beneficial area UK and overseas, particularly Malawi, Moldova, Slovakia and Ukraine.

26 Tredegar Square, London E3 5AG

Correspondent Pauline Brennan, Secretary

Trustees *Michael Brennan; Pauline Brennan; Mike Mitchell.*

CC Number 1105357

Information available Accounts were on file at the Charity Commission.

In 2008 the trust had an income of £90,000, mostly from voluntary income. Grants to organisations totalled £101,000. Assets stood at £19,000.

Beneficiaries included: Good Shepherd Mission (£60,000); Amersham Christian Housing Association (£34,000); Teen Challenge London and Wings of Eagles Trust (£2,400 each); Crossroads Christian Counselling (£1,200); Release International (£600); Serpentine Gallery (£500); and Cancer Research UK and Lawrence's Roundabout Well Appeal (£100 each).

Applications Ongoing support appears to be given to projects selected by the trustees.

The Queen Anne's Gate Foundation

Educational, medical and rehabilitative charities and those that work with underprivileged areas of society

£398,000 (2007/08)

Beneficial area UK and overseas.

WillcoxLewis LLP, The Old Coach House, Bergh Apton, Norwich NR15 1DD

Correspondent The Trustees

Trustees *N T Allan; J M E Boyer; I G Lewis.*

CC Number 1108903

Information available Accounts were on file at the Charity Commission.

The annual report states:

The foundation seeks to support projects and charities within the following broad criteria. It seeks to make a contribution that is meaningful in the context of the project/charity with which it is working. It tries to focus in particular on projects which might be said to make potentially unproductive lives productive. This tends to mean a bias towards educational, medical and rehabilitative charities and those that work with underprivileged areas of society. There is an attempt to focus a significant proportion of donations on Asia, Malawi and the UK.

In 2007/08 the foundation had an income of £4 million, mostly from voluntary income. Donations to other charities totalled £398,000. The sum of £4.6 million was carried forward at year end.

Previous beneficiaries included Hackney Music Development Trust, Merlin, Udavum Karangal and World Medical Fund.

Applications In writing to the correspondent.

Quercus Trust

Arts and general

About £100,000 (2007/08)
Beneficial area UK.

Chantrey Vellacott, Russell Square House, 10–12 Russell Square, London WC1B 5LF
Correspondent The Trustees
Trustees Lord Bernstein; Lady Bernstein; Kate E Bernstein.
CC Number 1039205
Information available Full accounts were on file at the Charity Commission.

In February 1999 the trustees declared by deed that distributions would in future be directed principally (but not exclusively) to the arts and any other objects and purposes which seek to further public knowledge, understanding and appreciation of any matters of artistic, aesthetic, scientific or historical interest.

In 2007/08 the trust had an income of £156,000 and a total expenditure of £131,000.

Recent beneficiaries have included: Almedia Theatre Company, British Friends of the Art Museums of Israel, Central School of Ballet, English Stage Company, George Piper Dances, Kangyur Rinpoche Foundation, Random Dance Company, Sadler's Wells Trust, Siobahn Davies' Dance Company, Tate Foundation and Wigmore Hall Trust.

Exclusions No grants to individuals.

Applications In writing to the correspondent, but please note, the trust states: 'All of the trust's funds are currently earmarked for existing projects. The trust has a policy of not making donations to individuals and the trustees regret that, in order to keep administrative costs to a minimum, they are unable to reply to any unsuccessful applicants.'

The R D Crusaders Foundation

General

£3.8 million (2008)
Beneficial area Worldwide.

The Northern and Shell Building, No. 10 Lower Thames Street, London EC3R 6EN
Correspondent The Trustees
Trustees R C Desmond; Mrs J Desmond.
CC Number 1014352
Information available Accounts were on file at the Charity Commission.

The trust gives one-off and recurrent grants for core, capital and project funding for general charitable purposes, especially for the relief of poverty and sickness amongst children.

In 2008 the trust had an income of £4.7 million, most of which came via a concert organised through R D Crusaders Limited, and made 93 grants totalling £3.8 million (£412,000 in 2007).

There were 56 grants of £1,000 or more listed in the accounts. Beneficiaries included Marie Curie Cancer Care (£1 million); Moorfields Eye Hospital Development Fund (£500,000); Jewish Care (£435,000); Fight for Sight (£100,000); Maggie's – Joy of Living Campaign (£25,000); Variety Club Children's Charity (£20,000); Zoe's Place Hospice (£15,000); COSMIC and the Healing Foundation (£10,000 each); Ovarian Cancer Action and UK Jewish Film Festival (£5,000 each); World Jewish Affairs Fund (£3,000); and Cued Speech Association Centre, Magen David Adom and RISE Foundation (£1,000 each).

A further 37 grants of less than £1,000 each totalled £12,000.

Applications In writing to the correspondent.

R S Charitable Trust

Jewish and welfare

£485,000 (2006/07)
Beneficial area UK.

138 Stamford Hill, London N16 6QT
Correspondent Max Freudenberger, Trustee
Trustees Harvey Freudenberger; Max Reudenberger; Michelle Freudenberger; Stuart Freudenberger; Max Freudenberger.
CC Number 1053660
Information available Accounts for year ending 2007/08 were overdue at the Charity Commission. Those filed for 2006/07 included no details of beneficiaries.

Established in 1996, this trust states that it supports Jewish organisations and other bodies working towards the relief of poverty. In 2006/07 the trust had assets of £2 million and an income of £668,000. Grants were made to 15 organisations totalling £485,000.

Previous beneficiaries have included British Friends of Tshernobil, Forty Ltd, NRST, Society of Friends of the Torah, Talmud Hochschule, Viznitz, Yeshiva Horomo and Yeshivas Luzern.

Applications In writing to the correspondent.

The R V W Trust

Music education and appreciation

£281,000 (2008)
Beneficial area UK.

7–11 Britannia Street, London WC1X 9JS
Email helen@rvwtrust.org.uk
Website www.rvwtrust.org.uk
Correspondent Ms Helen Faulkner, Administrator
Trustees Hugh Cobbe, Chair; Dr Michael Kennedy; The Lord Armstrong of Ilminster; Andrew Hunter Johnston; Sir John Manduell; Jeremy Dale Roberts; Musicians Benevolent Fund.
CC Number 1066977
Information available Accounts were available from the Charity Commission website.

The trust's current grant-making policies are as follows:

1) To give assistance to British composers who have not yet achieved a national reputation.
2) To give assistance towards the performance and recording of music by neglected or currently unfashionable twentieth-century

British composers, including performances by societies and at festivals which include works by such composers in their programmes.

3) To assist UK organisations that promote public knowledge and appreciation of twentieth and twenty-first-century British music.

4) To assist education projects in the field of music.

5) To support postgraduate students of composition taking first Masters degrees at British universities and conservatoires.

In 2008 the trust's assets stood at £1.1 million with an income of £431,000. Grants were made totalling £281,000, broken down as follows:

Category	Value	No.
Public performance	£140,000	75
Music festivals	£70,000	25
Public education	£86,000	22
Education grants	£21,000	8

Beneficiaries included: British Music Information Centre, Society for the Promotion of New Music and Vaughan Williams Memorial Library (£25,000 each); Huddersfield Contemporary Music Festival and Park Lane Group (£15,000 each); Royal Philharmonic Society Composition Prize (£7,000); Birmingham Contemporary Music Group, Corsham Festival, Opera Circus, Opera Group, Orchestra of the Swan, Presteigne Festival, Royal Northern College of Music, Frederic Cox Award, Scottish Opera, Spitalfields Festival, University of York and Worcester Three Choirs Festival (£5,000 each); Hampstead and Highgate Festival and London Sinfonietta (£4,000 each); English Music Festival, Brighton Festival and London Festival of Contemporary Church Music (£3,000 each); and Cheltenham Music Society, Deal Festival and Music Theatre Wales (£2,000 each).

Exclusions No grants for local authority or other government-funded bodies, nor degree courses, except first Masters' degrees in musical composition. No support for dance or drama courses. No grants for workshops without public performance, private vocal or instrumental tuition or the purchase or repair of musical instruments. No grants for concerts that do not include music by twentieth and twenty-first-century composers or for musicals, rock, pop, ethnic, jazz or dance music. No grants for the construction or restoration of buildings. The trust is not able to make grants towards the music of Ralph Vaughan Williams.

Applications All potential applicants should contact the trust for further details of current grant-making policy and details of how to apply by emailing the secretary. The trust holds three main grant-making meetings a year. Closing dates for applications are 2 January, 1 May and 1 September. Applicants are notified of the results approximately eight weeks after these dates.

The Monica Rabagliati Charitable Trust

Children, Humanitarian, medical and general

£60,000 (2007/08)

Beneficial area UK.

S G Hambros Trust Company Limited, S G House, 41 Tower Hill, London EC3N 4SG

Website www.rabagliati.org.uk

Correspondent The Administrator

Trustees *S G Hambros Trust Company Limited; R L McLean*

CC Number 1086368

Information available Accounts were available from the Charity Commission website.

The trust was registered with the Charity Commission in April 2001. It makes grants in support of 'organisations that focus on the alleviation of child suffering and deprivation'. The trust also supports humanitarian and medical causes. 'The trustees have decided to prioritise small/medium sized organisations where possible.'

In 2007/08 the trust had assets of £1.9 million and an income of £49,000. Grants to 33 organisations were made totalling £60,000 and were broken into the following categories:

Category	No.
Children's projects	26
Medical	4
Humanitarian	1
General	2

Beneficiaries included: St Joseph Priestly Scholarships (£10,000); Children in Distress (£4,000); International Childcare Trust (£3,500); Centrepoint, DebRA and U-Turn (£2,500 each); RNLI (£2,000); and Children's Hope Foundation, the Children's Voice, CHICKS, Kid Connect, Place2Be, Refuge and Surrey Care Trust (£1,000 each).

Applications In writing to the correspondent. 'The trustees assess grant applications and make appropriate grants twice yearly.'

The Radcliffe Trust

Music, crafts and conservation

£282,000 (2007/08)

Beneficial area UK.

6 Trull Farm Buildings, Tetbury GL8 8SQ

Tel. 01285 841900

Email radcliffe@thetrustpartnership.com

Website www.theradcliffetrust.org

Correspondent The Secretary to the Trustees

Trustees *Felix Warnock, Chair; Sir Henry Aubrey-Fletcher; Lord Balfour of Burleigh; Christopher Butcher; Dr Ivor Guest; Mary Ann Sieghart.*

CC Number 209212

Information available Accounts were on file at the Charity Commission.

The Radcliffe Trust was founded in 1714 by the will of Dr John Radcliffe, the most prominent physician of his day, who left his residuary estate for the income to be applied for general charitable purposes.

The trustees' present grant-making policy is concentrated in two main areas – music and the crafts – but they may consider applications which do not fall within those two categories.

The following information is taken from the trust's annual report.

Music
The Radcliffe Trust supports classical music performance and training especially chamber music, composition and music education. Particular interests within music education are music for children and adults with special needs, youth orchestras and projects at secondary and higher levels, including academic research.

Craft
The Radcliffe Trust supports craft training among young people both at the level of apprenticeship and also at the post-graduate and post-experience levels. Crafts are broadly defined, including building conservation skills, rural skills and traditional creative craft skills.

The trustees are also concerned to promote a standard of excellence through support for conservation and craft projects involving traditional or innovative craft skills.

Direct applications for the restoration or conservation of old or otherwise interesting buildings are accepted only in exceptional circumstances.

In 2007/08 the trust had assets of £13.7 million, which generated an income of £376,000. Grants were made totalling £282,000, broken down as follows and shown with examples of beneficiaries:

Music – £161,000 (35 grants)
The Allegri String Quartet (£20,000); Royal Academy of Music and Trinity College of Music (£12,000 each); National Youth Orchestra (£10,000); Aldeburgh Productions, Chamber Music at the Purcell School, Handel House Museum, Kettles Yard University and London Philharmonic Orchestra (£5,000 each); Dartington International Summer School (£3,000); Birmingham Music Group (£2,500); Lake District of Summer Music and Liverpool Cathedral Centenary Fund (£2,000 each); Newark and Sherwood College (£1,100); and the Royal Northern College of Music (£200).

Crafts – £122,000 (24 grants)
National Library of Scotland (£15,000); Edward Barnsley Education Trust (£11,000); Scottish Lime Centre (£10,000); Meridian Trust Association (£7,000); Courtauld Institute of Art (£5,000); Orton Trust (£3,500); Salisbury Cathedral and Wells Cathedral (£2,000 each); Worcester Cathedral Development and Restoration Trust (£1,500); and Edinburgh and Lothians Greenspace Trust (£1,000).

Miscellaneous – £2,400 (3 grants)
Radcliffe Science Library (£1,500); St Bartholomew's Hospital (£900); and Radcliffe School Welfare Fund (£15).

Exclusions No grants to individual applicants. No retrospective grants are made, nor for deficit funding, core costs, general appeals or endowment funds. No new building appeals.

Applications Trustees meet twice yearly to administer the charity. There is a music panel of advisers who also meet twice a year to consider music applications. The deadlines for music applications are 31 January for the spring panel and 31 August for the autumn panel. The deadlines for craft applications are 30 April for the June meeting and 31 August for the November meeting. Please note that it is advisable to submit an application well in advance of the deadline.

An application should include:

- A cover letter, which should include official address, telephone number, email address and charity registration number. The applicant should make clear their position in the charity.
- No more than two pages outlining the proposal and the specific request to the trust. Please note that it is important to give an indication of the timing of the project, as the trustees do not make retrospective grants.
- Other relevant supporting information, but applicants should be aware that additional information may not be circulated to trustees.
- A budget, which must include the total cost of the project; the amount requested, and other income secured or requested.
- An indication of past grants from the trust.

The Bishop Radford Trust

Church of England
£485,000 (2007/08)
Beneficial area UK.

Devonshire House, 1 Devonshire Street, London W1W 5DR

Correspondent The Secretary

Trustees *Stephen Green; Janian Green; Suzannah O'Brien; Ruth Dare.*

CC Number 1113562

Information available Accounts were on file at the Charity Commission.

The trust was set up in 2006 to help 'promote the work of the Christian church in a manner consistent with the doctrines and principles of the Church of England'. During 2007/08 it received income of £3.4 million, mostly from donations and grants, totalled £485,000. Assets stood at £3.5 million at year end.

Donations were broken down as follows:

Category	Value	No.
Church-related projects (including church renovation/construction/ maintenance)	£199,000	2
Education of priests and other church workers	£40,000	1
Support of church ministry	£246,000	7

Beneficiaries included: Anglican Investment Agency Trust (£154,000); Tearfund (£56,000); St Luke's Hospital for the Clergy and World Vision (£50,000 each); Diocese of Liverpool (£45,000); Bible Reading Fellowship (£40,000); St Barnabas PCC (£20,000);

and Bible Reading Fellowship and the Quiet Garden Trust (£10,000 each).

Applications In writing to the correspondent.

The Rainford Trust

Social welfare and general
£191,000 (2007/08)
Beneficial area Worldwide, with a preference for areas in which Pilkington plc have works and offices, especially St Helens and Merseyside.

c/o Pilkington plc, Prescot Road, St Helens, Merseyside WA10 3TT

Tel. 01744 20574

Email rainfordtrust@btconnect.com

Correspondent W H Simm, Secretary

Trustees *Dr F Graham; Mrs A J Moseley; H Pilkington; Lady Pilkington; D C Pilkington; R G Pilkington; S D Pilkington; Mrs I Raziu; Mrs L F Walker.*

CC Number 266157

Information available Accounts were obtained from the Charity Commission website.

The trust's accounts stated that its objectives are to:

apply money for charitable purposes and to charitable institutions within the St Helens MBC area, and other places in the UK or overseas where Pilkington has employees. This does not prejudice the trustees' discretion to help charities that operate outside those areas.

Further to this the trust's charitable purposes are to support:

- the relief of poverty, the older generation, the sick, helpless and disabled, and the unemployed.
- the advancement of education including the arts, and other purposes with wide benefit for the community such as environmental and conservation projects.

In 2007/08 the trust had assets of £6.8 million and an income of £198,000, generated from investments. Grants were made totalling £191,000 and were broken down as follows and are shown here with examples of beneficiaries:

Humanities – £62,000 in 6 grants
The Citadel Arts Centre (£49,000 in two grants); St Helens Open Art Exhibition

(£2,000); St Helens Concert Band (£800); and St Helens MBC – the Godfrey Pilkington Gallery (£500).

Welfare – £57,000 in 59 grants

Canine Partners for Independence and Prison Reform Trust (£2,500 each); British Institute for Brain Injured Children and Eccleston Mere Primary School (£2,000 each); Skill Force (£1,500); the Boys' Brigade North West District, Penny Brohn Cancer Care, Caring for Life, Changing Faces, Listening Books, National Talking Newspapers and Magazines, St Helens CVS, Seeing Hands Nepal, Tools for Self Reliance, and the Wingate Special Children's Trust (£1,000 each); Sutton Village Church (£750); Jubilee Sailing Trust (£630); and Motability and Wheelchair Dance Association (£500 each).

Education – £29,000 in 15 grants

Clonter Opera (£15,000); WASOT UK (£5,000); Book Aid International and Voluntary Service Overseas (£1,000 each); War Memorials Trust (£750); the Cricket Foundation (£600); and Action Transport Theatre Company Limited and Volunteer Reading Help (£500 each).

Medical – £13,000 in 10 grants

Alzheimer's Research Trust and British Association for Performing Arts Medicine (£2,000); the Swinfen Charitable Trust (£1,500); the Leprosy Mission and North West Air Ambulance (£1,000 each); the Pancreatitis Supporters Network (£750); and Stepping Stones (£500).

Environmental – £7,250 in 7 grants

Marine Stewardship Council (£2,500); Lowe House Heritage and Development Group, Marine Conservation Society and Women's Environmental Network Trust (£1,000 each); the Barn Owl Trust (£750); and Agroforestry Research Trust and Landlife (£500 each).

Exclusions Funding for the arts is restricted to St Helens only. Applications from individuals for grants for educational purposes will be considered only from applicants who are normally resident in St Helens.

Applications On a form available from the correspondent. Applications should be accompanied by a copy of the latest accounts and cost data on projects for which funding is sought. Applicants may apply at any time. Only successful applications will be acknowledged.

The Peggy Ramsay Foundation

Writers and writing for the stage

£28,000 to organisations (2007/08)

Beneficial area British Isles.

Harbottle and Lewis Solicitors, Hanover House, 14 Hanover Square, London W1S 1HP

Tel. 020 7667 5000 **Fax** 020 7667 5100

Email laurence.harbottle@harbottle.com

Website www.peggyramsayfoundation. org

Correspondent G Laurence Harbottle, Trustee

Trustees *G Laurence Harbottle; Simon P H Callow; Michael Codron; Sir David Hare; John Tydeman; Harriet Walter; Tamara C Harvey; Dominic L Cavendish.*

CC Number 1015427

Information available Accounts were obtained from the Charity Commission website.

This trust was established in 1992, in accordance with the will of the late Peggy Ramsay.

Peggy Ramsay was one of the best-known play agents in the United Kingdom during the second half of the Twentieth Century. When she died in 1991 her estate was left for charitable purposes to help writers and writing for the stage.

The objects of the trust are:

- the advancement of education by the encouragement of the art of writing
- the relief of poverty among those practising the arts, together with their dependants and relatives, with special reference to writers
- any charitable purpose which may, in the opinion of the trustees, achieve, assist in, or contribute to, the achievement of these objectives.

Grants are made to:

- writers who have some writing experience who need time to write and cannot otherwise afford to do so
- companies which might not otherwise be able to find, develop or use new work
- projects which may facilitate new writing for the stage.

The main priority of the trust is to support semi-professional writers who fulfil the trust's application criteria. The trust also supports organisations and projects, which they review annually. Please visit the trust's website for further information.

In 2008 the trust had assets of £4.1 million and an income of £270,000. Grants were made totalling £217,000, of which £28,000 went to six organisations.

Beneficiaries were: Pearson Playwrights (£7,000); Polka Theatre (£6,000); High Tide Festival Limited and Talawa (£5,000 each); Society of Authors (£3,000); and the New Works (£1,500).

The sum of £190,000 was distributed in 86 grants to individuals.

Exclusions No grants are made for productions or writing not for the theatre. Commissioning costs are often considered as part of production costs. Course fees are not considered. Aspiring writers without some production record are not usually considered.

Applications Applications should be made by writing a short letter, when there is a promising purpose not otherwise likely to be funded and which will help writers or writing for the stage. Grants are considered at four or five meetings during the year, although urgent appeals can be considered at other times. All appeals are usually acknowledged.

The Joseph and Lena Randall Charitable Trust

General

£100,000 (2007/08)

Beneficial area Worldwide.

Europa Residence, Place des Moulins, Monte-Carlo MC98 000

Correspondent The Secretary

Trustee *Rofrano Trustee Services Ltd.*

CC Number 255035

Information available Accounts were on file at the charity Commission, without a list of grants.

It is the policy of this trust to provide regular support to a selection of charities.

In 2007/08 the trust's assets totalled £1.8 million, it had an income of £99,000 and 51 grants were made totalling £100,000.

The following is taken from the Report of Trustees:

As always most of our awards went to organisations committed to the relief of hardship, suffering and poverty, particularly of minorities. The balance was directed to supporting initiatives dedicated to providing medical, educational and cultural facilities.

Previous beneficiaries have included: Cancer Research UK, Community Security Trust, Diabetes UK, Downe House 21st Century Appeal, Holocaust Educational Trust, Jewish Care, Jewish Deaf Association, LPO, LSE Foundation, Motor Neurone Disease Association, ROH Foundation and Transplant Trust.

Exclusions No grants to individuals.

Applications The trust has stated that funds are fully committed and that it was 'unable to respond to the many worthy appeals'.

The Ranworth Trust

General

£272,000 (2006/07)

Beneficial area UK and developing countries, with a preference for Norfolk.

The Old House, Ranworth, Norwich NR13 6HS

Correspondent Hon. Mrs J Cator, Trustee

Trustees *Hon. Mrs J Cator; F Cator; C F Cator; M Cator.*

CC Number 292633

Information available Accounts were obtained from the Charity Commission website.

In 2006/07 the trust's assets stood at £5.5 million. It had an income of £250,000 and made grants to 32 organisations from income, totalling £272,000.

Beneficiaries included: Limbourne Trust (£66,000); Jubilee Sailing Trust (£25,000); Water Aid (£20,000); Cancer Research UK and East Anglia's Children's Hospice (£15,000 each); BREAK and the Reach Foundation (£10,000 each); the Game Conservancy Trust (£4,000); Norfolk Wherry Trust (£2,500); Coeliac Society (£2,000); East Anglia Art Fund, Hearing Dogs for Deaf People and Musical Keys (£1,000 each); and Teenage Cancer Trust (£500).

A further donation was made from capital funds to the Limbourne Trust, a registered charity in which Mrs E A Thistlethwayte, a former trustee of the Ranworth Trust and a daughter of the Hon. Mrs J Cator and Mr F Cator, is both settlor and trustee.

Exclusions No grants to non-registered charities.

Applications The trust does not respond to unsolicited applications.

The Fanny Rapaport Charitable Settlement

Jewish and general

£21,000 (2007/08)

Beneficial area North-west England.

Kuit Steinart Levy, 3 St Mary's Parsonage, Manchester M3 2RD

Correspondent J S Fidler, Trustee

Trustees *J S Fidler; N Marks.*

CC Number 229406

Information available Information was obtained from the Charity Commission website.

The trust supports mainly, but not exclusively, Jewish charities and health and welfare organisations, with preference for the north west of England.

In 2007/08 the charity had assets of £787,000, an income of £28,000 and made grants totalling £21,000.

Previous beneficiaries included Brookvale, Christie Hospital NHS Trust, Community Security Trust, Delamere Forest School, the Heathlands Village, King David Schools, Manchester Jewish Federation, South Manchester Synagogue, United Jewish Israel Appeal and World Jewish Relief.

Exclusions No grants to individuals.

Applications Trustees hold meetings twice a year in March/April and September/October with cheques for donations issued shortly thereafter. If the applicant does not receive a cheque by the end of April or October, the application will have been unsuccessful. No applications are acknowledged.

The Ratcliff Foundation

General

£218,000 (2007/08)

Beneficial area UK, with a preference for local charities in the Midlands, North Wales and Gloucestershire.

Clement Keys, 39–40 Calthorpe Road, Edgbaston, Birmingham B15 1TS

Tel. 0121 456 4456

Email chris.gupwell@btinternet.com

Correspondent Christopher J Gupwell, Secretary and Trustee

Trustees *David M Ratcliff, Chair; Edward H Ratcliff; Carolyn M Ratcliff; Gillian Mary Thorpe; James M G Fea; Christopher J Gupwell.*

CC Number 222441

Information available Accounts were on file at the Charity Commission.

The foundation was established in 1961, by Martin Rawlinson Ratcliff. Grants are made to any organisation that has charitable status for tax purposes.

In 2007/08 it had assets of £3.6 million and an income of £244,000. There were 90 grants made totalling £218,000, of which 54 were for £2,000 or more each.

Beneficiaries included: Organic Research Centre (£12,000); Warwickshire and Northamptonshire Air Ambulance (£7,000); Avoncroft Museum of Historic Buildings, Myton Hospices and SSAFA Forces Help (£5,000 each); Harbury Village Hall (£4,000); Meningitis Trust and Music for Youth (£3,000 each); Motability (£2,800); and Cruse Bereavement, Carem Foundation for Conductive Education, Lighthorne PCC, Multiple Births Foundation, Wildfowl and Wetlands Trust (£2,000 each).

There were 36 grants of less than £2,000 each that totalled £45,000.

Exclusions No grants to individuals.

Applications In writing to the correspondent.

The E L Rathbone Charitable Trust

Social work

£47,000 (2007/08)

Beneficial area UK, with a strong preference for Merseyside.

Rathbone Investment Management Ltd, Port of Liverpool Building, Pier Head, Liverpool L3 1NW

Tel. 0151 236 6666

Correspondent The Secretary

Trustees *J B Rathbone; Mrs S K Rathbone; Mrs C E Rathbone; R S Rathbone.*

CC Number 233240

Information available Accounts were on file at the Charity Commission.

The trust has a special interest in social work charities. There is a strong preference for Merseyside with local beneficiaries receiving the major funding.

In 2007/08 the trust had assets of £2.1 million and an income of £85,000. Grants were made to 26 organisation totalling £47,000.

Beneficiaries included: Shaftesbury Youth Club, Tranmere Alliance and Wirral Community Narrowboat Trust (£3,000 each); Huntingdon's Disease Association, Liverpool Cathedral, Merseyside Holiday Service, RASA and RNCM (£2,000 each); No Panic (£1,500); PSS (£1,000); and Sprowston High School (£150).

Exclusions No grants to individuals seeking support for second degrees.

Applications In writing to the correspondent.

The Eleanor Rathbone Charitable Trust

Merseyside, women and 'unpopular causes'

£253,000 (2007/08)

Beneficial area UK, with the major allocation for Merseyside; also international projects (Africa, the Indian Sub Continent, plus exceptionally Iraq and Palestine).

546 Warrington Road, Rainhill, Merseyside L35 4LZ

Email eleanor.rathbone.trust@tinyworld.co.uk

Correspondent Mrs Liese Astbury, Administrator

Trustees *William Rathbone; Jenny Rathbone; Andrew Rathbone; Lady Morgan; Mark Rathbone.*

CC Number 233241

Information available Accounts were on file at the Charity Commission, without a list of grants.

The trust concentrates its support largely on the following:

- charities and charitable projects focused on Merseyside
- charities benefiting women and unpopular and neglected causes but avoiding those with a sectarian interest
- charities with which any of the trustees have a particular knowledge or association or in which it is thought Eleanor Rathbone or her father William Rathbone VI would have had a special interest
- charities providing holidays for disadvantaged people from Merseyside.

International Grants

The trust also makes international grants which are governed by the following criteria.

- The trust will only consider projects from Africa, the Indian Sub Continent, plus exceptionally Iraq and Palestine.
- Applications will be considered only from small or medium sized charities.
- Projects must be sponsored and monitored by a UK-based charity. In addition, projects must meet one or more of the following criteria: (i) they will benefit women or orphaned children; (ii) they will demonstrate local involvement in scoping and delivery, except where skills required are not currently available, for example eye surgeons in remote rural areas; (iii) they will aim to repair the damage in countries recently ravaged by international or civil war; (iv) they will deliver clean water.

In 2007/08 the trust's assets stood at £7.6 million. It had an income of £289,000 and made grants totalling £253,000, which are broken down as follows:

Category	Value	No.
Merseyside	£136,000	45
International	£67,000	44
National/Regional	£43,000	16
Holidays	£6,800	6

Most donations are on a one-off basis, although requests for commitments over two or more years are considered. Grants are made in the range £100 to £3,000 and exceptionally higher.

Exclusions Grants are not made in support of: any activity which relieves a statutory authority of its obligations; individuals, unless (and only exceptionally) it is made through a charity and it also fulfils at least one of the other positive objects mentioned above; overseas organisations without a sponsoring charity based in the UK.

The trust does not generally favour grants for running costs, but prefers to support specific projects, services or to contribute to specific developments.

Applications There is no application form. The trust asks for a brief proposal for funding including costings, accompanied by the latest available accounts and any relevant supporting material. It is useful to know who else is supporting the project.

To keep administration costs to a minimum, receipt of applications is not usually acknowledged. Applicants requiring acknowledgement should enclose a stamped, addressed envelope.

Trustees currently meet three times a year on varying dates (contact the administrator for information on the latest deadlines).

The Rayden Charitable Trust

Jewish

£64,000 (2008/09)

Beneficial area UK.

c/o Vantis Group Ltd, 82 St John Street, London EC1M 4JN

Correspondent The Trustees

Trustees *S Rayden; C Rayden; P Rayden.*

CC Number 294446

Information available Accounts were on file at the Charity Commission.

In 2008/09 the trust had an income from donations of £76,000 and made grants totalling £64,000. Assets stood at £12,000.

Over 200 grants were made in the year, of which 26 were for £1,000 or more. Beneficiaries of these larger grants included: Or Chadash (£7,500); Western Marble Arch (£3,800); Yesodey Hatorah (£2,600); Carl Bach Shul Trust and City of London School (£2,500 each); AISH, Hampstead Theatre and London School of Economics (£2,000 each); UK Friends Awis (£1,500); Lolev Trust (£1,200); and British Technion Society and St John's Wood Synagogue (£1,000 each).

Applications In writing to the correspondent.

The Roger Raymond Charitable Trust

Older people, education and medical

£226,000 (2007/08)

Beneficial area UK (and very occasionally large, well-known overseas organisations).

Suttondene, 17 The South Border, Purley CR8 3LL

Tel. 020 8660 9133

Email russell@pullen.cix.co.uk

Correspondent R W Pullen, Trustee

Trustees *R W Pullen; P F Raymond; M G Raymond.*

CC Number 262217

Information available Accounts were on file at the Charity Commission.

The accounts state that 'the Roger Raymond Charitable Trust owns 100% of the issued share capital of Shaw White Estates Limited whose principle business is that of property investment. Any profits attributable to the subsidiary undertaking are covenanted up to the Roger Raymond Charitable Trust.'

In 2007/08 the trust had assets of £12.6 million and an income of £264,000. Out of a total expenditure of £283,000, grants totalled £226,000.

The principal beneficiary during the year, as in previous years, was Bloxham School, which received a donation of £172,000.

Other beneficiaries included: Nanyuki Children's Home (£3,500); and the Brain Research Trust, Great Ormond Street Hospital Children's Charity, NSPCC, MacMillan Cancer Nurses Foundation,

Project Trust and Sight Savers International (£2,000 each).

Exclusions Grants are rarely given to individuals.

Applications The trust stated that applications are considered throughout the year, although funds are not always available.

The Rayne Trust

Jewish organisations, older and young people and people disadvantaged by poverty or social isolation

£554,000 (2007/08)

Beneficial area Israel and UK.

Carlton House, 33 Robert Adam Street, London W1U 3HR

Website www.raynefoundation.org.uk

Correspondent Tim Joss, Director

Trustees *Lady Jane Rayne; the Hon. Robert A Rayne.*

CC Number 207392

Information available Accounts were available at the Charity Commission.

The Rayne Trust was established by Lord Rayne to support organisations in which its trustees (Lady Rayne and the Hon. Robert A Rayne) have a close personal interest. Its annual expenditure is approximately £400,000.

The trust shares the Rayne Foundation's (Charity Commission No: 216291) overall theme of bridge building. It focuses its contributions on these two areas:

• Social welfare and arts charities known to trustees and working in the UK to help young and older people and others disadvantaged by poverty or social isolation. Unsolicited applications for work in the UK will not be considered.
• Projects in Israel. (Due to a major donation in 2008, the trust's resources in this area were heavily committed. Details about future grant-making strategy was to be posted on its website as soon as it was known.

In 2007/08 it had assets of £21 million and an income of £385,000. Grants totalled £554,000.

Grants relating to UK-based charities – £293,000
Chicken Shed Theatre Trust and Topolski Memoir (£25,000 each); North London Hospice and Schonfeld Square Home for the Elderly (£20,000 each); and Jewish Care (£12,500).

Grants relating to Israel-based charities – £261,000
The Jewish Joint Distribution Committee (£60,000); Jerusalem Cinematheque (£25,000); Forward Thinking and Windows for Peace (£15,000); and Jerusalem Foundation, the Jewish-Arab Community Association, Marianne's Early Childhood and Family Centre, Shluvim, the St John of Jerusalem Eye Hospital and Workers Advice Centre (£10,000 each).

Exclusions No grants to individuals or non-registered charities.

Applications If you are considering applying to the trust you should first discuss your proposal with the Grants Manager, Susan O'Sullivan: tel. 020 7487 9630 or email: sosullivan@raynefoundation.org.uk.

The John Rayner Charitable Trust

General

£34,000 (2007/08)

Beneficial area England, with a preference for Merseyside and Wiltshire.

Manor Farmhouse, Church Street, Great Bedwyn, Marlborough SN8 3PE

Correspondent Mrs J Wilkinson, Trustee

Trustees *Mrs J Wilkinson; Dr J M H Rayner; Mrs A L McNeilage.*

CC Number 802363

Information available Accounts were available from the Charity Commission website.

This trust has general charitable purposes in the UK, with a preference for Merseyside and Wiltshire. Support is given to small organisations.

In 2007/08 the trust had assets of £838,000 and an income of £35,000. Grants were made totalling £34,000.

Beneficiaries were: Breast Cancer Haven and Help for Heroes (£5,000 each); BIME, Carers UK and Music in Hospitals (£4,000 each); the Country

Trust and Jubilee Sailing Trust (£3,000 each); Bootle YMCA (£2,000); and Dressability, Kennet Furniture Recycling, the Sand Rose Project and University of Liverpool – The Reader (£1,000 each).

Exclusions No grants to individuals or non-registered charities.

Applications In writing to the correspondent by 31 January each year. Trustees meet to allocate donations in February/March. Only successful applicants will be contacted. There are no application forms or guidelines.

The Albert Reckitt Charitable Trust

General and Quaker

£74,000 (2007/08)
Beneficial area UK.

7 Derrymore Road, Willerby, Hull HU10 6ES
Correspondent John Barrett, Secretary
Trustees J Hughes-Reckitt, Chair; Mrs S C Bradley; Mrs G M Atherton; P C Knee; Dr A Joy; W Russell.
CC Number 209974
Information available Accounts were on file at the Charity Commission, without a list of grants.

The trust states its objects are to make grants to a wide variety of registered charities, including non-political charities connected with the Society of Friends. It tends to support UK organisations rather than local groups, giving grants of £250 to £750 each.

In 2007/08 it had assets of £2.8 million, which generated an income of £96,000. Grants totalled £74,000, given as £52,000 in subscriptions (annual grants), the rest in donations (one-off grants). No further information for the year was available.

Exclusions No support to individuals. No grants for political or sectarian charities, except for non-political charities connected with the Society of Friends.

Applications In writing to the correspondent. Trustees meet in June/July and applications need to be received by the end of March.

Eva Reckitt Trust Fund

Welfare, relief in need, extension and development of education and the victims of war

£53,000 (2008)
Beneficial area UK and overseas.

1 Somerford Road, Cirencester GL7 1TP
Email davidbirch50@googlemail.com
Correspondent David Birch, Trustee
Trustees Anna Bunney; Chris Whittaker; David Birch; Diana Holliday.
CC Number 210563
Information available Accounts were on file at the Charity Commission.

Registered in October 1962, in 2008 the trust had an income from investments of £33,000 and made 59 grants totalling £53,000.

Beneficiaries included: Medical Foundation for the Care of Victims of Torture (£4,000); Water and Sanitation for the Urban Poor (£3,000); Prisoners of Conscience Appeal Fund (£2,000); Children of the Andes, One World Action, St John of Jerusalem Eye Hospital, St Mungo's and World Development Movement (£1,000 each); and Christian Engineers in Development, Computer Aid International, Crisis, Stephen Lawrence Charitable Trust, Orbis, Send a Cow and Traidcraft (£500 each).

Applications In writing to the correspondent.

The Red Rose Charitable Trust

Older people and people with disabilities

£45,000 (2007/08)
Beneficial area UK with a preference for Lancashire and Merseyside.

c/o Rathbones, Port of Liverpool Building, Pier Head, Liverpool L3 1NW
Correspondent J N L Packer, Trustee
Trustees James N L Packer; Jane L Fagan.
CC Number 1038358
Information available Full accounts were on file at the Charity Commission.

This trust was established in 1994. It has a preference for supporting charities working with older people and people who have physical or mental disabilities. Grants are also made to individuals within these categories.

In 2007/08 the trust's assets stood at £1.1 million. It had an income of £53,000 and made 34 grants totalling £45,000.

Beneficiaries included: Liverpool Cathedral Centenary Fund (£5,000); the Barnstondale Centre (£2,000); Help the Aged, the National Autistic Society, Sense and Wirral Autistic Society (£1,000 each); and Local Solutions, McIntyre Housing Association and Neuromuscular Centre (£500 each).

Applications In writing to the correspondent.

The C A Redfern Charitable Foundation

General

£226,000 (2007/08)
Beneficial area UK.

PricewaterhouseCoopers, 9 Greyfriars Road, Reading RG1 1JG
Correspondent The Trustees
Trustees Cecil Redfern, Chair; Sir Robert Clark; William Maclaren; David Redfern; Terence Thornton; Simon Ward.
CC Number 299918
Information available Accounts were on file at the Charity Commission.

This trust supports a wide range of organisations with some preference for those concerned with health and welfare. In 2007/08 the foundation had assets of £5.3 million and an income of £230,000. Grants were made totalling £226,000. Grants ranged from £250 to £50,000, with the majority of grants totalling less than £5,000 each.

Beneficiaries included: South Buckinghamshire Riding for the Disabled (£50,000); Saints and Sinners (£30,000); Ghurkha Welfare Trust (£7,000); Live Music Now! and St Botolph without

Bishopsgate (£5,000 each);
St Christopher's Hospice (£4,000); BEN (£3,000); Breast Cancer Haven and Fight for Sight (£1,000 each); Cancer Resource Centre and St Mary's of Paddington Charitable Trust (£5,000 each); CRUSE (£3,000); NSPCC (£500); and Hope House Hospice (£250).

Exclusions No grants for building works or individuals.

Applications The trust does not accept unsolicited applications.

Redfern Charitable Trust

General

£79,000 (2008/09)
Beneficial area UK.

Hedges Solicitors, The Glass Tower, 6 Station Road, Didcot OX11 7LL
Correspondent The Trustees
Trustees *Miss M D Roe; M St Clair Thomas; A S Hatt.*
CC Number 1090647
Information available Accounts were on file at the Charity Commission.

In 2008/09 the trust had assets of £901,000 and an income of £48,000. Grants to 13 organisations totalled £79,000.

Beneficiaries included: Age Concern, Arthritis Rheumatism Council, British Red Cross, NSPCC, Stroke Association, RNIB, RNID and World Wildlife Fund (£7,500 each); CLIC (£2,500); and Crisis and DES – Bangladesh Flood (£500 each).

Applications In writing to the correspondent.

The Max Reinhardt Charitable Trust

Deafness and fine arts promotion

£28,000 (2007/08)
Beneficial area UK.

c/o BSG Valentine, Lynton House, 7–12 Tavistock Square, London WC1H 9BQ
Correspondent The Secretary
Trustees *Joan Reinhardt; Veronica Reinhardt.*
CC Number 264741
Information available Accounts were on file at the Charity Commission, without a list of grants.

The trust supports organisations benefiting people who are deaf, as well as fine arts promotion. In 2007/08 the trust had assets of £519,000 and an income of £45,000. Grants were made totalling £28,000.

Previous beneficiaries have included the Art Fund, Art in Healthcare, Concern Worldwide, Delta, St George's Medical School, NDCS, Paintings in Hospitals, RNID, Salvation Army, Sound Seekers and Top Banana.

Exclusions No grants to individuals.

Applications In writing to the correspondent.

REMEDI

Research into disability

£113,000 (2007/08)
Beneficial area UK.

Elysium House, 126–128 New Kings Road, London SW6 4LZ
Tel. 020 7384 2929
Email research@remedi.org.uk
Website www.remedi.org.uk
Correspondent Rosie Wait, Director
Trustees *Dr Anthony K Clarke, Chair; James Mosley; Brian Winterflood; Dr Adrian H M Heagerty; Colin Maynard; Dr I T Stuttaford; Dr Anthony B Ward; Mrs Karin Russell; Michael Hines.*
CC Number 1063359
Information available Accounts were available from the Charity Commission website.

REMEDI supports pioneering research into all aspects of disability in the widest sense of the word, with special emphasis on the way in which disability limits the activities and lifestyle of all ages.

The trust receives most of its income from companies and other trusts, which is then given towards researchers carrying out innovative and original work who find it difficult to find funding from larger organisations. Grants are generally for one year, although funding

for the second year is considered sympathetically and for a third year exceptionally. There is a preference for awarding a few sizeable grants rather than many smaller grants.

In 2007/08 the trust's assets stood at £252,000. It had an income of £326,000 and made grants totalling £113,000.

Exclusions Cancer and cancer-related diseases are not supported.

Applications By email to the correspondent. Applications are received throughout the year. They should initially include a summary of the project on one side of A4 with costings. The Chair normally considers applications on the third Tuesday of each month with a view to inviting applicants to complete an application form by email. For further information please visit the trust's website.

The Rest-Harrow Trust

Jewish and general

£53,000 (2007/08)
Beneficial area UK.

c/o Portrait Solicitors, 1 Chancery Lane, London WC2A 1LF
Tel. 020 7320 3890
Correspondent Miss Judith S Portrait
Trustees *Mrs J B Bloch; Miss J S Portrait; Mr D B Flynn; H O N and V Trustee Limited.*
CC Number 238042
Information available Accounts were available from the Charity Commission website.

This trust was established in 1964, its main objectives are to distribute grants from its income for education, housing and to assist the deprived and older people.

In 2007/08 the trust had an income of £75,000 and made grants totalling £53,000. Its assets stood at £896,000. There were 218 grants of which the vast majority were under £500 each.

The largest grants were those made to: Nightingale House (£5,500); Jewish Care (£2,500); World Jewish Relief (£2,000); British Friends of the Hebrew University (£1,500); JNF Charitable Trust (£1,000); and Weizmann Institute Foundation (£1,000).

Smaller grants included those made to: British Friends of Neve Shalom, Cheltenham Ladies College (for Bursaries Fund), Jewish Deaf Association and St Christopher's Hospice (£500 each); Action for Kids, Age Concern, Appropriate Technology Asia and Breast Cancer Care (£200 each); and Back to Work for the Over 40s, Canine Partners for Independence, Heartline and Princess Royal Trust for Carers (£100 each).

Exclusions No grants to non-registered charities or to individuals.

Applications In writing to the correspondent. Applications are considered quarterly. Only submissions from eligible bodies are acknowledged.

The Rhododendron Trust

Overseas aid and development, social welfare and culture

£44,000 (2007/08)
Beneficial area UK and overseas.

Lewis House, 12 Smith Street, Rochdale OL16 1TX
Correspondent P E Healey, Trustee
Trustees *Peter Edward Healey; Dr Ralph Walker; Mrs Sarah Ray; Mrs Sarah Oliver.*
CC Number 267192
Information available Accounts were available from the Charity Commission website.

It is the current policy of the trustees to divide donations as follows:

- 50% to charities whose work is primarily overseas
- 40% for UK social welfare charities
- 10% for UK cultural activities.

In 2007/08 the trust had assets of £1.4 million and an income of £79,000. Grants of £500 or £1,000 are made generally to charities which have been supported in the past although a few new beneficiaries are included each year. In 2007/08 the trust made 94 grants totalling £44,000.

Grant recipients included, Find Your Feet, Sound Seekers, MAG, Health Unlimited and C.A.S.A. Alianzia (£1,000 each) and Cambodia Trust, Survival

International, Young Actors Theatre, Africa Equipment for Schools and Children in Crisis (£500 each).

Exclusions The trust does not support medical research, individual projects, or local community projects in the UK.

Applications In writing to the correspondent at any time. The majority of donations are made in March. Applications are not acknowledged.

Daisie Rich Trust

General

£83,000 to organisations (2007/08)
Beneficial area UK, with a priority for the Isle of Wight.

The Hawthorns, School Lane, Arreton, Newport, Isle of Wight PO30 3AD
Tel. 07866 449 855
Email daisierich@yahoo.co.uk
Correspondent Mrs L Mitchell, Administrator
Trustees *A H Medley; Mrs A C Medley; M J Flux; D J Longford.*
CC Number 236706
Information available Accounts were on file at the Charity Commission.

The trust makes grants to former employees, or their spouses, of Upward and Rich Limited. Further grants are made mainly to Isle of Wight institutions, charities and individuals.

In 2007/08 the trust had assets of £3.2 million and an income of £169,000. Grants totalled £120,000 of which £36,000 went to ex-employees of Upward and Rich Ltd and their dependants and £730 to 'other individuals'. The remaining £83,000 was distributed in 58 grants ranging between £150 and £30,000.

The largest grant again went to the Earl Mountbatten Hospice (£30,000). Beneficiaries also included: Macmillan Cancer Relief, Marie Curie Nurses and SSAFA Isle of White (£3,000 each); Isle of White RCC 'Helping Hands', Isle of White Youth Trust and St Vincent's Residential Home (£2,000 each); and Haig Homes and Island Women's Refuge (£1,500 each).

Smaller grants included those to: Carisbrooke Priory Trust and Semi-Colon Group (£1,000 each); Challenge

and Adventure and Isle of White Hospital Broadcasting Association (£500 each); Isle of White Gateway Club and RNID – Isle of White Sound Advice (£250 each); and Rope Walk Social Club (£150).

Applications In writing to the correspondent. The trustees hold regular meetings to decide on grant applications and are assisted by information gathered by the administrator.

C B Richard Ellis Charitable Trust

General

£62,000 (2007/08)
Beneficial area Unrestricted

St Martin's Court, 10 Paternoster Row, London EC4M 7HP
Tel. 020 7182 3452 **Fax** 020 718 22001
Email anaftis@cbhillierparker.com
Correspondent A C Naftis, Secretary to the Trustees
Trustees *M D A Black; F G Morris; K Bramley; L Patel; M J Prentice; N R Martel.*
CC Number 299026
Information available Accounts were on file at the Charity Commission.

The aim of the trust is primarily to respond to clients of C B Richard Ellis Ltd requests for support and to provide sponsorship to staff who are personally involved in fundraising activities. The trust will also consider applications from any other party with whom C B Richard Ellis has a significant relationship.

In 2007/08 the trust had assets of £28,000 and an income of £77,000. Grants were made totalling £62,000 to 115 organisations in a wide range of areas including health, welfare, churches and overseas development.

Donations ranged from £50 to £10,000, but were mostly under £1,000. Beneficiaries included: Riders for Health (£11,000); The Story of Christmas (£3,300); Cancer Research UK (£2,400); British Heart Foundation (£1,200); Child Rights, You UK and Wellbeing of Women (£1,000 each); and Walk the Walk Worldwide (£600).

Exclusions No grants to third parties, such as fundraising organisations or publication companies producing charity awareness materials.

Applications In writing to the correspondent.

The trust stated that in recent years they have received as many as two hundred unsolicited requests for support that do not meet with the above donations criteria. Given the size of the trust, a response to such requests is not always possible.

The Violet M Richards Charity

Older people, ill health, medical research and education

£88,000 (2007/08)

Beneficial area UK, with a preference for East Sussex, particularly Crowborough.

c/o Wedlake Bell, 52 Bedford Row, London WC1R 4LR

Tel. 020 7395 3155 **Fax** 020 7395 3100

Email chicks@wedlakebell.com

Correspondent Charles Hicks, Secretary

Trustees Mrs E H Hill; G R Andersen; C A Hicks; Mrs M Burt; Dr J Clements; Miss M K Davies.

CC Number 273928

Information available Full accounts were provided by the trust.

The trust's objects are the relief of age and ill health, through the advancement of medical research (particularly into geriatric problems), medical education, homes and other facilities for older people and those who are sick. Applications from East Sussex, particualrly the Crowborough area, are favoured by the trustees. The trustees are happy to commit themselves to funding a research project over a number of years, including 'seed corn' projects. However, the trust has stated that for the next two to three years it will be focusing on a small number of medical research projects and is unlikely to have any surplus funds to support external applications.

In 2007/08 the trust had assets of £2.2 million and an income of £79,000. Grants were made to three organisations totalling £88,000.

The beneficiaries were: British Liver Trust (£51,000); Stroke Association (£32,000); and Lee Smith Foundation (£5,000).

Exclusions No support for individuals.

Applications In writing to the correspondent, however the trust states in its accounts that the trustees 'prefer to be proactive with charities of their own choice, rather than reactive to external applications.' The trustees generally meet to consider grants twice a year in the spring and the autumn. There is no set format for applying and only successful applications are acknowledged. Due to the change of grant policy to focus on a smaller number of projects, external applications are unlikely to be successful and are therefore discouraged.

The Clive Richards Charity

Churches, schools, arts, disability and poverty

£730,000 (2007/08)

Beneficial area UK, with a preference for Herefordshire.

Lower Hope, Ullingswick, Hereford HR1 3JF

Tel. 01432 820557 **Fax** 01432 820772

Email anna@crco.co.uk

Correspondent Anna Lewis, Trustee

Trustees Anna Lewis; Clive Richards; Sylvia Richards.

CC Number 327155

Information available Accounts were available from the Charity Commission website.

The trust gives predominantly to schools, churches and organisations which support disability and the arts. Help is also available to individuals, particularly those who suffer from disabilities.

In 2007/08 the trust had assets of £199,000 and an income of £55,000. Grants were made to over 50 organisations totalling £730,000.

The largest grants made included those to: the Vesey Foundation (£250,000); John Kyrle School (£100,000); Queen Elizabeth High School (£50,000); Luctonians Youth Development (£35,000); Chance to Shine Appeal (£20,000); and the Worshipful Company of Gunmakers (£10,000).

Grants of less than £10,000 each included those made to: Royal Shakespeare Company (£5,000); Hereford Police Choir (£3,000); Royal

Naval Museum (£2,500); and Deafblind UK (£1,000). Other grants of less than £1,000 each totalled £19,000.

Applications In writing to the correspondent. The trustees meet monthly to consider applications. Please note: the trust has previously stated that due to its resources being almost fully committed, it is extremely selective in accepting any requests for funding.

The Muriel Edith Rickman Trust

Medical research and education

£1.1 million (2006/07)

Beneficial area UK.

12 Fitzroy Court, 57 Shepherds Hill, London N6 5RD

Correspondent H P Rickman, Trustee

Trustees H P Rickman, Chair; A S Purcell; Prof J Waxman; R Tallis.

CC Number 326143

Information available Accounts for 2007/08 were overdue at the Charity Commission.

The trust makes grants to medical research organisations towards research and equipment. The trust prefers to support physical disabilities rather than mental illnesses.

In 2006/07 it had assets of £118,000 and an unusually high income of £1 million, mostly from donations. Grants to eleven organisations totalled £1.1 million.

The major beneficiary was University of Manchester (£1 million) and others included: Cancer Research (£40,000); Leukaemia Busters and Kings College (£10,000); Neuro Disability Research Trust (£3,000); and Great Ormond Street (£100).

Exclusions The trustees will not respond to individual students, clubs, community projects or expeditions.

Applications There are no guidelines for applications and the trust only replies if it is interested at first glance; it will then ask for further details. Trustees meet as required.

The Ripple Effect Foundation

General, particularly disadvantaged young people, the environment and developing countries

£66,000 (2007/08)

Beneficial area UK, with a preference for the south west of England.

Marlborough Investment Consultants Ltd, Wessex House, Oxford Road, Newbury RG14 1PA

Tel. 01635 814 470

Correspondent Caroline D Marks, Trustee

Trustees *Caroline D Marks (Chairman); I R Marks; I S Wesley.*

CC Number 802327

Information available Accounts were on file at the Charity Commission.

The accounts of this charity state: 'The objectives of the trustees are to support a range of charitable causes over a few years that meet their funding criteria. They proactively seek out projects that meet their criteria and do not respond to unsolicited applications.'

In 2007/08 the trust had assets of £1.6 million, which generated an income of £43,000. Grants to three organisations totalled £66,000.

This included an award of £50,000 to the Devon Community Foundation to help identify and fund community initiatives which support vulnerable young people. A further £11,000 was given to the Network for Social Change. Through this, funding was passed on to other organisations largely for environmental work, both in the UK and overseas and to the 'Smart Justice' campaign (now in its sixth and final year of funding). A one-off grant of £5,000 was also made to Homestart UK to assist ten families in being able to access the West Devon Family Group.

Exclusions No grants are made to individuals.

Applications The trust states that it does not respond to unsolicited applications.

The Sir John Ritblat Family Foundation

Jewish and general

£384,000 (2007/08)

Beneficial area UK.

Baker Tilly, 1st Floor, 46 Clarendon Road, Watford WD17 1JJ

Tel. 01923 816400

Correspondent The Clerk

Trustees *J H Ritblat; N S J Ritblat; C B Wagman; J W J Ritblat.*

CC Number 262463

Information available Full accounts were on file at the Charity Commission.

In 2007/08 the trust had assets of £1.2 million and an income of £61,000. Grants were made to 48 organisations totalling £384,000.

Beneficiaries included Southbank Centre (£175,000); Imperial College (£100,000); Weizman UK (£42,000); Jewish Care and Norwood (£11,000 each); Tate Foundation (£5,000); St Richard's Hospital and Tennis and Racquets Association (£1,000 each); UK Jewish Film Festival (£500); and Barnardo's (£300).

The trust makes grants primarily to long-established organisations. Please note: the trust was previously known as The John Ritblat Charitable Trust No. 1.

Exclusions No grants to individuals.

Applications The trust has previously stated that its funds are fully committed.

The River Farm Foundation

General, education, welfare, medical, disability and overseas aid

£16,000 (2007/08)

Beneficial area UK.

The Old Coach House, Bergh Apton, Norwich NR15 1DD

Tel. 01508 480100

Email info@willcoxlewis.co.uk

Correspondent M D Willcox, Trustee

Trustees *M Haworth; Mrs E Haworth; M D Willcox.*

CC Number 1113109

Information available Accounts were on file at the Charity Commission.

The foundation was set up in February 2006. In 2007/08 it had assets of £1.8 million, an income of £467,000 and made three grants totalling £16,000.

Beneficiaries were: Busoga Trust (£10,500); and Noah's Ark Children's Hospice and Buliding for Babies (£2,500 each).

Applications 'The trust is very selective in the grant-making process and applications are reviewed by the trustees personally.'

The River Trust

Christian

£78,000 (2006/07)

Beneficial area UK, with a preference for Sussex.

c/o Kleinwort Benson Trustees Ltd, PO Box 57005, 30 Gresham Street, London EC2V 7PG

Tel. 020 3207 7337 **Fax** 020 3207 7665

Correspondent The Trustees

Trustee *Kleinwort Benson Trustees Ltd.*

CC Number 275843

Information available Accounts were obtained from the Charity Commission website.

Gillian Warren formed the trust in 1977 with an endowment mainly of shares in the merchant bank Kleinwort Benson. It is one of the many Kleinwort trusts. The River Trust is one of the smaller of the family trusts. It supports Evangelical Christian causes. In 2006/07 the trust had assets of £656,000 and an income of £92,000. Grants were made to 39 organisations totalling £78,000. These were divided into the following categories:

Advancement of Christian Faith – 7 grants totalling £26,000
Grant recipients included: Youth with a Mission (£13,000); Harrow Development Trust (£5,000); Youth with a Mission Scotland (£3,000); Tear Fund (£2,700); and Stewards Trust (£750).

Religious Education – 13 grants totalling £21,000
Beneficiaries included: Chasah Trust (£5,000); Interhealth (£3,000); The R Foundation and Scriptural Knowledge

Institute (£1,500 each); and Fusion UK (£370).

Church Funds – 6 grants totalling £16,000

Grants awarded include those made to: Barcombe Parochial Church (£7,000); St Mary's Church PCC Barcombe (£5,000); and St Barnabus Church (£1,000).

Religious Welfare Work – 9 grants totalling £13,000

Grants made included those to: Ironmongers Foundation (£5,000); Care for the Family (£3,700); St Barnabas Hospices (£1,000); and Open Door UK (£500).

Missionary Work – 4 grants totalling £2,000

Beneficiaries included: St Stephen's Society, African Enterprise, ICCOWE and Mitchell Ministries (£500 each).

Exclusions Only appeals for Christian causes will be considered. No grants to individuals. The trust does not support 'repairs of the fabric of the church' nor does it give grants for capital expenditure.

Applications In writing to the correspondent. It is unusual for unsolicited appeals to be successful. Only successful applicants are notified of the trustees' decision. Some charities are supported for more than one year, although no commitment is usually given to the recipients.

Riverside Charitable Trust Limited

Health, welfare, older people, education and general

£136,000 to individuals and organisations (2007/08)
Beneficial area Mainly Lancashire.

Riverside, Bacup OL13 0DT
Tel. 01706 874 961
Correspondent F Drew, Trustee
Trustees B J Lynch; I B Dearing; J A Davidson; F Drew; H Francis; A Higginson; G Maden; L Clegg; B Terry.
CC Number 264015

Information available Accounts were obtained from the Charity Commission website.

The trust's objects are to support the following: poor, sick and older people; education; healthcare; the relief of poverty of people employed or formerly employed in the shoe trade; and other charitable purposes.

In 2007/08 the trust had an income of £111,000 and made 185 grants totalling £136,000. Its assets stood at £2.4 million. Grants were broken down into the following categories:

- **Relief for sickness, infirmity and for older people** - 26 grants totalling £34,000
- **General charitable public benefits** – 72 grants totalling £57,000
- **Relief of poverty** – 71 grants totalling £40,000
- **Death grants** – 15 grants totalling £3,400
- **Educational support** – 1 grant totalling £1,000.

Exclusions No grants for political causes.

Applications In writing to the correspondent.

The Daniel Rivlin Charitable Trust

Jewish and general
£20,000 (2007/08)
Beneficial area UK.

Manor House, Northgate Lane, Linton, Wetherby LS22 4HN
Tel. 01937 589645
Correspondent D R Rivlin, Trustee
Trustees D R Rivlin; N S Butler; M Miller.
CC Number 328341

Information available Accounts were on file at the Charity Commission

In 2007/08 the trust had an income of £6,000. Grants were made totalling £20,000.

Previous beneficiaries include: Donisthorpe Hall; Friends of Israel; Hay on Wye Festival of Literature; Makor Charitable Trust; Make a Dream; Pocklington and Market Weighton Rotary Club; UJIA; and Yad Vashem.

Applications The trust states that funds are fully committed and does not welcome unsolicited applications.

Rix-Thompson-Rothenburg Foundation

Learning disabilities
£97,500 (2008)
Beneficial area UK.

12 York Gate, Regent's Park, London NW1 4QS
Correspondent The Trustees
Trustees Lord Rix; Sir Anthony S Jolliffe; Joss Nangle; Walter Rothenberg; Loretto Lambe; Fred Heddell; Barrie Davis; Jonathan Rix; Brian Baldock.
CC Number 285368

Information available Accounts were on file on the Charity Commission.

The following information is taken from the accounts:

The foundation is dedicated to supporting projects connected with the care, education, training, development and leisure activities of people with a learning disability.

It makes grants to a variety of organisations which aim to benefit people with a learning disability and their carers. A special emphasis is given to grants that will enhance opportunity and lifestyle.

Set up in 1982, in 2008 the foundation had assets of £1.2 million and an income of £141,000, including £76,000 from donations. Grants totalled £97,500.

Beneficiaries included: Centre 404, and Dundee Independent Advocacy Service (£5,000 each); Accessible Arts and Media, Artslink Central Limited, Colchester Gateway Clubs, Enable Ability and Half Moon Young People's Theatre Limited (£4,000 each); and Oswestry and District Mencap (£1,000).

The foundation maintains a close relationship with the Baily Thomas Charitable Fund which gives it substantial donations towards the annual grant-making activity.

Applications In writing to the correspondent.

RJM Charitable Trust

Jewish

£165,000 (2007/08)

Beneficial area UK and worldwide.

84 Upper Park Road, Salford M7 4JA

Tel. 0161 720 8787

Email joshua@broomwell.com

Correspondent J Rowe, Trustee

Trustees *J Rowe; Mrs M B Rowe.*

CC Number 288336

Information available Accounts were available from the Charity Commission website.

In 2007/08 the trust had assets of £223,000 and an income of £160,000. Grants were made to 74 organisations totalling £165,000.

Beneficiaries of the largest grants included: UJIA (£55,000); Aish Hatorah Rabbi Schiff (£16,000); KD AD Min (£11,000); and CRT and CST (£10,000 each).

Beneficiaries of smaller grants included: Friends of Brei Akiva (£6,000); Jewish Hum Foundation and Manchester Eruv (£5,000 each); the Fed (£3,000); MJS (£2,000); Our Kids and Gateshead Tal College Rabbi Z Cohen (£1,000 each); Jew Chap (£500); BFIWD (£200); and Child Resettlement (£100).

Applications In writing to the correspondent.

Thomas Roberts Trust

Medical, disability and relief in need

£38,000 to organisations (2007/08)

Beneficial area UK.

5–6 The Square, Winchester SO23 9WE

Tel. 01962 843 211 **Fax** 01962 843 223

Email trtust@thomasroberts.co.uk

Correspondent James Roberts, Trustee

Trustees *R E Gammage; J Roberts; Mrs G Hemmings.*

CC Number 1067235

Information available Accounts were on file at the Charity Commission.

Established in November 1997, this trust mainly makes grants to medical (particularly cancer support and research), disability and welfare organisations. Applications from employees and former employees of the Thomas Roberts Group Companies are also considered. In 2007/08 the trust had an income of £24,000 and assets of £1 million. Grants were made to over 40 organisations totalling £38,000. A further £7,800 was distributed to 29 individuals.

Beneficiaries include: Cancer Research UK (£6,000); Macmillan Cancer Relief and Marie Curie Cancer Care (£3,000 each); Age Concern (£2,100); Winchester Churches Nightshelter (£750); Diabetes UK and Riding for the Disabled (£500 each); Parkinson's Disease Society (£250); and Breast Cancer Campaign (£100).

Applications In writing to the correspondent. Applicants are required to provide a summary of their proposals to the trustees, explaining how the funds would be used and what would be achieved.

The Alex Roberts-Miller Foundation

Education, sport and social opportunities for disadvantaged young people

£57,000 (2006/07)

Beneficial area UK.

PO Box 104, Dorking RH5 6YN

Tel. 01306 741 368

Email alexrmfoundation@mac.com

Website www.alexrmfoundation.org.uk

Correspondent The Trustees

Trustees *Will Armitage; David Avery-Gee; Emma Temple; Richard Roberts-Miller; Fiona Roberts-Miller; Jo Roberts-Miller; Beth Roberts-Miller.*

CC Number 1093912

Information available Accounts were available from the Charity Commission and further information was taken from the trust's website.

The foundation was established in 2002. Its main goal is to help provide educational, sporting and social opportunities for disadvantaged young people. It aims to target funds where they will have a direct and significant impact on the lives of those people the trust is trying to help. The foundation also promotes causes related to road safety.

In 2006/07 the trust had an income of £117,000 and assets of £160,000. Grants were made totalling £57,000.

Grants were made to seven organisations: Back-up Trust (£25,000); SeeAbility (£9,000); Red Balloon (£8,000); Capital Kids Cricket (£5,500); Sutton Trust (£4,000); CCB&H Young Carers (£3,000); and RoadPeace (£2,000).

Exclusions No grants to individuals.

Applications The foundation researches its own beneficiaries. The trust states: 'if you represent a registered charity with goals consistent with ours, you are welcome to write or email, but please understand that our resources are limited and we already receive many applications – far more than we are able even to acknowledge'.

Edwin George Robinson Charitable Trust

Medical research

£47,000 (2007/08)

Beneficial area UK.

71 Manor Road South, Hinchley Wood KT10 0QB

Tel. 020 8398 6845

Correspondent E C Robinson, Trustee

Trustees *E C Robinson; Mrs S C Robinson.*

CC Number 1068763

Information available Information was obtained from the trust's annual accounts.

The trust supports organisations which provide care for people with disabilities and older people, particularly in the area of medical research. Grants tend to be made for specific research projects and are not usually made to fund general operating costs. In 2007/08 the trust had an income of £15,000 and assets of £303,000. Grants were made to over 30 organisations totalling £47,000.

Beneficiaries included: Marie Curie Cancer Care (£6,500); Diabetes UK (£5,000); Bath Institute of Medical Engineering (£4,000); Deafness Research (£2,000); Brainwave, Action for Medical Research and Ness Foundation (£1,000 each); Cure Parkinsons and Holly Lodge Centre (£500 each); and Salvation Army (£25).

Exclusions No grants to individuals or for general running costs for small local organisations.

Applications In writing to the correspondent.

Robyn Charitable Trust

General and young people

£17,000 (2007/08)
Beneficial area UK and overseas.

c/o Harris and Trotter, 65 New Cavendish Street, London W1G 7LS

Tel. 020 7467 6300

Correspondent The Trustees

Trustees *Malcolm Webber; Mark Knopfler; Ronnie Harris.*

CC Number 327745

Information available Accounts were on file at the Charity Commission.

This trust was established in 1988 to advance education and relieve need amongst children in any part of the world.

In 2007/08 the trust had an income of £38,000 and assets of £286,000. Grants were made totalling £17,000.

Previous beneficiaries have included: One to One Children's Fund, The Purcell School, Variety Club, The Honeypot Charity, Malawi Against Aids and Teenage Cancer Trust.

Exclusions No grants to individuals.

Applications In writing to the correspondent.

The Rock Foundation

Christian ministries and charities

£96,000 to organisations (2007/08)
Beneficial area Worldwide.

Park Green Cottage, Barhatch Road, Cranleigh GU6 7DJ

Correspondent The Trustees

Trustees *Richard Borgonon; Andrew Green; Kevin Locock; Jane Borgonon; Colin Spreckley.*

CC Number 294775

Information available Accounts were on file at the Charity Commission.

Formed in 1986, this charity seeks to support charitable undertakings which are built upon a clear biblical basis and which, in most instances, receive little or no publicity. It is not the intention of the foundation to give widespread support, but rather to specifically research and invest time and money in the work of a few selected Christian ministries. As well as supporting such ministries, grants are also made to registered charities.

In 2007/08 the foundation had an income of £207,000 and made grants totalling £167,000, of which £96,000 went to 34 organisations.

There were 12 grants of £1,000 or more listed in the accounts. Beneficiaries were: Cranleigh Baptist Church (£21,000); Proclamation Task (£15,000); Proclamation Trust (£11,000); Crosslinks (£6,000); Simon Trust (£4,900); Friends International (£4,700); City Partnership (£4,500); Harare Central Baptist Church (£4,000); Lahore Evangelical Ministries (£3,700); British Urological Foundation (£2,500); Agape (£1,500); and Truth Mission (£1,100).

The sum of £71,000 was distributed to 18 individuals.

Applications The trust has previously stated: 'the trust identifies its beneficiaries through its own networks, choosing to support organisations it has a working relationship with. This allows the trust to verify that the organisation is doing excellent work in a sensible manner in a way which cannot be conveyed from a written application. As such, all appeals from charities the foundation do not find through their own research are simply thrown in the bin. If a stamped, addressed envelope is included in an application, it will merely end up in the foundation's waste-paper bin rather than a post box.'

The Rock Solid Trust

Christian causes

£47,500 to organisations (2007/08)
Beneficial area Worldwide.

7 Belgrave Place, Clifton, Bristol BS8 3DD

Correspondent J D W Pocock, Trustee

Trustees *J D W Pocock; T P Wicks; T G Bretell.*

CC Number 1077669

Information available Accounts were on file at the Charity Commission.

This trust supports:

- Christian charitable institutions and the advancement of Christian religion
- the maintenance, restoration and repair of the fabric of any Christian church
- the education and training of individuals
- relief in need.

In 2007/08 it had assets amounting to £626,000, an income of £25,500 and made grants totalling £59,500, including £12,000 to individuals.

The sum of £47,500 was distributed to organisations. Beneficiaries included: Christchurch Clifton and Sherborne School Foundation (£20,000 each); Bristol University (£5,000); Chain of Hope and London School of Theology (£500 each); and RNLI (£100).

Applications In writing to the correspondent.

The Rofeh Trust

General and religious activities

£46,000 (2007/08)
Beneficial area UK.

44 Southway, London NW11 6SA

Tel. 020 8458 7382

Correspondent The Trustees

Trustees *Martin Dunitz; Ruth Dunitz; Vivian Wineman; Henry Eder.*

CC Number 1077682

Information available Accounts were on file at the Charity Commission, but without a list of grants.

In 2007/08 the trust had an income of £76,000 and made grants totalling £46,000. Its assets stood at £866,000. Unfortunately no list of grants was included with accounts on file at the Charity Commission.

Applications In writing to the correspondent.

Richard Rogers Charitable Settlement

General

£127,000 (2007/08)

Beneficial area UK.

Lee Associates, 5 Southampton Place, London WC1A 2DA

Tel. 020 7025 4600

Correspondent K A Hawkins

Trustees *Lord R G Rogers; Lady R Rogers.*

CC Number 283252

Information available Accounts were available from the Charity Commission website.

In 2007/08 the trust had assets of £992,000 and an income of £80,000. Grants were made to 40 organisations totalling £127,000.

The largest grants went to: National Communities Research Centre (£50,000); the Constant Gardener Trust and the National Community Resource Ltd (£13,000 each); Serpentine Gallery (£11,000); Refuge (£10,000); Tree House (£6,400); and Crisis (£1,000).

Smaller grants of less than £1,000 each went to: Trafford Hall (£900); British Heart Foundation (£500); Scientists for Global Responsibility (£330); Walk the Walk Worldwide (£300); and The RSA (£95).

Applications In writing to the correspondent.

Rokach Family Charitable Trust

Jewish and general

Around **£500,000** (2005/06)

Beneficial area UK.

20 Middleton Road, London NW11 7NS

Tel. 020 8455 6359

Correspondent Norman Rokach, Trustee

Trustees *N Rokach; Mrs H Rokach; Mrs E Hoffman; Mrs M Feingold; Mrs A Gefilhaus; Mrs N Brenig.*

CC Number 284007

Information available No accounts received at the Charity Commission since those for 2005/06.

This trust supports Jewish and general causes in the UK. In 2005/06 the trust had an income of £507,000 and a total expenditure of £697,000. No other information was available.

Previous beneficiaries have included: Before Trust, Kisharon Charitable Trust, Cosmon Limited; Moreshet Hatorah Ltd, Belz Synagogue and Friends of Wiznitz.

Applications In writing to the correspondent.

The Sir James Roll Charitable Trust

General

£185,000 (2007/08)

Beneficial area UK.

5 New Road Avenue, Chatham ME4 6AR

Tel. 01634 830 111

Correspondent N T Wharton, Trustee

Trustees *N T Wharton; B W Elvy; J M Liddiard.*

CC Number 1064963

Information available Full accounts were on file at the Charity Commission.

The trust's main objects are the:

- promotion of mutual tolerance, commonality and cordiality in major world religions
- promotion of improved access to computer technology in community based projects other than political parties or local government

- funding of projects aimed at early identification of specific learning disorders
- other charitable projects as the trustees see fit.

In 2007/08 the trust had assets totalling £4.2 million and an income of £234,000. Grants were made to 163 beneficiaries totalling £185,000. Grants ranged from £1,000 to £10,000, although most were for £1,000.

The largest grants were: DEC Bangladesh Cyclone Appeal and DEC Darfur and Chad Crisis Appeal (£10,000 each); and CRISIS at Christmas (£5,000).

Grants of £1,000 went to a variety of organisations including Cricket Foundation, Computer Aid International, Family Holiday Association, Help the Hospices, Howard League for Penal Reform, Kent Association for the Blind, Jubilee Sailing Trust, SSAFA, Support Dogs Ltd, Whizz-Kidz, and Shelter.

Applications In writing to the correspondent. The trustees usually meet around four times a year to assess grant applications.

The Helen Roll Charitable Trust

General

£128,000 (2007/08)

Beneficial area UK.

30 St Giles, Oxford OX1 3LE

Tel. 01865 559 900

Correspondent F R Williamson, Trustee

Trustees *Christine Chapman; Paul Strang; Christine Reid; Jennifer Williamson; Dick Williamson; Stephen G Williamson; Patrick Stopford.*

CC Number 299108

Information available Accounts were available from the Charity Commission website.

The accounts state that 'one of the trustees' aims is to support work for which charities find it difficult or impossible to obtain funds from other sources. Some projects are supported on a start-up basis, others involve funding over a longer term'.

The charities supported are mainly those whose work is already known to the trustees and who report on both their needs and achievements. Each year a handful of new causes are supported. However the trust has previously stated that 'the chances of success for a new application are about 100–1'.

In 2007/08 the trust had assets of £1.6 million and an income of £63,000. Grants were made to 38 organisations totalling £128,000.

Beneficiaries of the largest grants were: Home Farm Trust (£13,500); Pembroke College Oxford (£10,000); Oxford University Ashmolean Museum (£7,500); Sick Children's Trust (£6,000); and Purcell School (£5,000).

Beneficiaries of smaller grants included: Canine Partners for Independence (£4,000); Alzheimer's Research Trust (£3,000); SeeSaw (£2,000); and Gerald Moore Award, Carers UK and Barn Owl Trust (£1,000 each).

Exclusions No support for individuals or non-registered charities.

Applications In writing to the correspondent during the first fortnight in February. Applications should be kept short, ideally on one sheet of A4. Further material will then be requested from those who are short-listed. The trustees normally make their distributions in March.

The Cecil Rosen Foundation

Welfare, especially older people, infirm people and those who are mentally or physically disabled

£327,000 (2007/08)
Beneficial area UK.

22 Lisson Grove, London NW1 6TT
Correspondent M J Ozin, Trustee
Trustees *M J Ozin; J A Hart; P H Silverman.*
CC Number 247425
Information available Accounts were on file at the Charity Commission, but without a list of grants and only a limited review of activities.

Established in 1966, the charity's main object is the assistance and relief of the poor, especially older people, the infirm, or people who are disabled.

The correspondent has previously stated that almost all the trust's funds are (and will always continue to be) allocated between five projects. The surplus is then distributed in small donations between an unchanging list of around 200 organisations. 'Rarely are any organisations added to or taken off the list.'

In 2007/08 the foundation had an income of £643,000 and had assets of £5.4 million. Grants were made totalling £327,000. Unfortunately, a list of grants was not included in the accounts.

The foundation has previously made grants to Jewish Blind and Disabled and The Cecil Rosen Charitable Trust (a charity with the same trustees as this foundation).

Exclusions No grants to individuals.

Applications The correspondent has previously stated that 'no new applications can be considered'. Unsuccessful applications are not acknowledged.

The Rothermere Foundation

Education and general

£348,000 to organisations (2007/08)
Beneficial area UK.

Beech Court, Canterbury Road, Challock, Ashford TN25 4DJ
Correspondent V P W Harmsworth, Secretary
Trustees *Rt Hon. Viscount Rothermere; Viscountess Rothermere; V P W Harmsworth; J G Hemingway; Hon. Esme Countess of Cromer.*
CC Number 314125
Information available Information was on file at the Charity Commission.

This trust was set up for: the establishment and maintenance of 'Rothermere Scholarships' to be awarded to graduates of the Memorial University of Newfoundland to enable them to undertake further periods of study in the UK; and general charitable causes.

In 2007/08 the foundation had assets of £16.6 million and an income of £765,000. Grants totalled £348,000, broken down in the following categories:

Medical research
Beneficiaries included: Tick Tock Club (£75,000); and WISE Communities (£5,000).

Educational and children's charities
Beneficiaries included: Sandroyd School (£90,000); Corams' Field (£10,000); Child Bereavement Trust (£5,000); and Chicken Shed Theatre (£1,200).

Religious organisations
Beneficiaries included: St Brides Church (£4,000); and Farm Street Church (£2,500).

The arts and sport
Beneficiaries included: Princess Waterski Club (£5,600); The Cheribium Music Trust (£5,000); and RADA (£1,000).

Other charitable donations
Beneficiaries included: Kings Rifles & East African Forces Association and Museum of Garden History (£10,000 each); Help for Heroes (£5,000) and Southbank Centre (£1,000).

Three fellowship grants were awarded totalling £128,000.

Applications In writing to the correspondent.

The Rowan Charitable Trust

Overseas aid, social welfare and general

£637,000 (2007/08) see below
Beneficial area UK, with a preference for Merseyside, and overseas.

Mr Jonathan C M Tippett, c/o Morley Tippett, White Park Barn, Loseley Park, Guildford GU3 1HS
Tel. 01483 575193
Correspondent Mr Jonathan C M Tippett
Trustees *C R Jones; Reva J R Pilkington; Mrs M C Pilkington.*
CC Number 242678
Information available Accounts were available from the Charity Commission.

The trust focuses on projects that will benefit disadvantaged groups and communities and generally allocates two-thirds of its grant funds to overseas projects and one-third to United Kingdom based projects. It gives a mix of one-off and recurrent grants, although the trustees have started to make more effort to identify projects which require longer term funding rather than one-off donations. It has regularly given grants to a limited number of large national organisations and development agencies, but also gives grants to smaller organisations and locally based projects.

In 2007/08 the trust had assets of £5.1 million and an unusually large income of £1.3 million, which was due primarily to a significant donation received during the year. Grants were made totalling £637,000, with £438,000 going to overseas organisations and £199,000 to groups in the UK.

Beneficiaries of UK grants included: 9 Lives Furniture, Duke of Edinburgh Award – Merseyside and Whizz-Kidz (£10,000 each); Housing Justice (£8,000); Combat Stress (£7,000); Wirral Autistic Society (£5,000); Where Next Association (£2,000); and Bibic (£1,000).

Beneficiaries of overseas grants included: Christian Aid and Practical Action (£50,000 each); CMS – Samaritans, Rurcon and Wateraid (£20,000 each); Find Your Feet (£15,000); Sense International (£10,000); Quakers (£5,000); the Rainforest Foundation (£3,000); and Children of the Andes (£1,000).

Exclusions The trust does not give grants for:

- individuals
- buildings, building work or office equipment (including IT hardware)
- academic research and medical research or equipment
- expeditions
- bursaries or scholarships
- vehicle purchases
- animal welfare charities.

Applications In writing to the correspondent. No application forms are issued but applicant guidelines are available on request.

Applications should include:

- a brief description (two sides of A4 paper) of, and a budget for, the work for which the grant is sought
- the organisation's annual report and accounts (this is essential).

The applications need to provide the trustees with information about:

- the aims and objectives of the organisation
- its structure and organisational capacity
- what the funds are being requested for and how much is being requested
- how progress of the work will be monitored and evaluated.

Trustees meet twice a year. The closing dates for applications are usually in June and December.

The trust has previously stated that: 'unfortunately the volume of applications received precludes acknowledgement on receipt or notifying unsuccessful applicants. The trust emphasises that it is unable to make donations to applicants who are not, or do not have links with, a UK-registered charity.'

The Rowing Foundation

Water sports
£26,000 (2007)
Beneficial area UK.

6 Lower Mall, Hammersmith, London W6 9DJ
Tel. 020 8878 3723 **Fax** 020 8878 6298
Email p.churcher@sky.com
Website www.ara-rowing. org/rowing-foundation
Correspondent Pauline Churcher, Secretary
Trustees *Iain Reid, Chair; John Buchan; Simon Goodey; Philip J Phillips; Roger S Smith; John Chick.*
CC Number 281688
Information available Accounts were available from the Charity Commission.

The Rowing Foundation was set up in 1981 to generate and administer funds for the aid and support of young people (those under 18 or 23 if still in full-time education) and people who are disabled of all ages, through their participation in water sports, particularly rowing. Its income is mainly dependent on donations from the rowing fraternity.

Grants are made in the range of £500 and £2,000 to support youth and adaptive rowing and particularly to pump-prime projects. The foundation is anxious to help organisations and clubs whose requirements may be too small or who may be otherwise ineligible for an approach to the Big Lottery Fund or other similar sources of funds. It has also helped to get rowing started in areas where it did not exist or was struggling. Grants are not restricted to boats/sculls and have also been made for buoyancy aids, splash suits, canoes and 'taster' rowing courses.

In 2007 the foundation had assets of £295,000 and an income of £36,000. Grants were made totalling £26,000.

The largest grant made during the year went to Headway, which received £4,800. Other beneficiaries during the year included London Youth (£3,000); Cranmore School RC (£2,000); University of Derby and Oarsport – Sculls (£1,200 each); and Back Up Trust (£900).

Exclusions The foundation does not give grants to individuals, only to clubs and organisations, and for a specific purpose, not as a contribution to general funds.

Applications Applications should be made on a form, available to download from the Amateur Rowing Association website.

The Rowland Family Foundation

Relief in need, education, religion and community
£264,000 (2007/08)
Beneficial area UK and overseas.

Harcus Sinclair, 3 Lincoln's Inn Fields, London WC2A 3AA
Tel. 020 7242 9700
Email lucy.gibson@harcus-sinclair.co.uk
Correspondent Lucy Gibson
Trustees *Mrs A M Rowland; N G Rowland.*
CC Number 1111177
Information available Accounts were on file at the Charity Commission.

The foundation was registered with the Charity Commission on 5 September 2005. Its principal objectives are the relief of poverty, the advancement of education, the advancement of religion or other purposes beneficial for the community.

In 2007/08 it had assets of £5.4 million and an income of £154,000. Grants totalled £264,000.

Beneficiaries during the year were: Hope and Homes for Children (£212,000); Balikpapan Orangutan Survival Foundation and Child Welfare Scheme (£25,000 each); and Light from Africa (£2,000).

Applications In writing to the correspondent.

The Rowlands Trust

General, but mainly medical research, social welfare, music, the arts and the environment

£363,000 (2007)

Beneficial area West and South Midlands including Hereford and Worcester, Gloucester, Shropshire and Birmingham.

c/o Mills and Reeve, 78–84 Colmore Row, Birmingham B3 2AB

Tel. 0121 456 8341 **Fax** 0121 200 3028

Email nicola.fenn@mills-reeve.com

Correspondent Ms N Fenn, Clerk to the Trustees

Trustees *A C S Hordern, Chair; Mrs F J Burman; Mrs A M I Harris; G B G Hingley; K G Mason.*

CC Number 1062148

Information available Accounts were available from the Charity Commission website.

The trust primarily has an interest in supporting projects in the West Midlands and the South Midlands, including Hereford and Worcester, Gloucester, Shropshire and Birmingham. Grants are given in the following areas:

- research, education and training in the broadest sense with special regard to medical and scientific research
- sick, poor, disabled and older people
- music and the arts
- the environment.

In 2007 the trust had assets of £6.8 million and an income of £230,000. Grants were made totalling £363,000.

Research, education and training in the broadest sense with special regard to medical and scientific research – £102,000 (41 grants)

The largest grants went to: Worcester Acute Hospitals NHS Trust – Islet Research Laboratory (£15,000); City Technology College (£14,000); and Baverstock Foundation School (£11,000).

Grants of £5,000 or less included those to: Malverns District Scout Council (£5,000); Age Concern – Hereford and

Worcester (£3,000); Relate – Worcester (£2,000); and Voices Foundation (£400).

Sick, poor, handicapped and older people – £89,000 (42 grants)

Grant recipients included: Royal Star and Garter Homes (£10,000); Myton Hospices (£5,000); Cerebral Palsy, West Midlands (£3,000); and St Lukes Community Project, Kingstanding (£1,000).

Music and the Arts – £22,000 (7 grants)

Beneficiaries included: Belgrade Theatre Trust (£10,000); Worcester Cathedral Music & Light Appeal (choral scholarship) (£5,000); Elmhurst School for Dance (£3,000); and Langley Band (£750).

Environment – £51,000 (8 grants)

Grants were made to: Worcestershire Wildlife Trust (25,000); Hereford and Worcester Gardens Trust (£20,000); and Plantlife International (£1,000).

Exclusions No support for individuals or to animal charities. No support is given for revenue funding.

Applications Applications forms are available from the correspondent and are the preferred means by which to apply. Completed forms should be returned with a copy of the most recent accounts. The trustees meet to consider grants four times a year.

Royal Artillery Charitable Fund

Service charities

£163,000 to organisations (2007)

Beneficial area UK and overseas.

Artillery House, Artillery Centre, Larkhill SP4 8QT

Tel. 01980 845698

Email AC-RHQRA-RACF-WelfareClk2@mod.uk

Website www.forums.theraa.co.uk

Correspondent The Welfare Secretary

Trustees *Brig. A Gordon; Col. G Gilchrist; Col. A Jolley; Col. C Fletcher-Wood; Lieut. Col. M J Darmody; Maj. A T G Richards; Maj. A J Dines; Brig. R P M Weighill; Brig. N D Ashmore; Col. P R L Lane; Col. C J Nicholls; Lieut. Col. I A Vere Nicoll.*

CC Number 210202

Information available Accounts were on file at the Charity Commission.

In 2007 the trust had assets of £14 million and an income of £1.4 million. Grants were made totalling £904,000, of which £163,000 was given to organisations and the remaining £741,000 was distributed to individuals.

Grants were made to nine organisations as follows: Royal Artillery Institution (£55,000); Army Benevolent Fund (£50,000); Regiment and Batteries (£22,000); Gunner Magazine (£20,000); RAA Grants (£7,000); Ex Service Fellow Centre (£3,500); Not Forgotten Association (£3,000); King Edward VII Hospital (£2,800); and Independent Age (£1,000).

Applications In writing to the correspondent.

Royal Masonic Trust for Girls and Boys

Children and young people

£218,000 to non-Masonic charities (2007)

Beneficial area UK.

Freemasons' Hall, 60 Great Queen Street, London WC2B 5AZ

Tel. 020 7405 2644 **Fax** 020 7831 4094

Email info@rmtgb.org

Website www.rmtgb.org

Correspondent W Bro Les Hutchinson, Chief Executive

Trustees *Rt Hon. Earl Cadogan; P A Marsh; O N N Hart; C F Harris.*

CC Number 285836

Information available Accounts were available from the Charity Commission website.

This trust was established in 1982 and is largely focused on making grants to individual children of Freemasons who are in need. However, grants are also made to UK non-Masonic organisations working with children and young people and to support bursaries at cathedrals and collegiate chapels.

In 2007 the trust had assets of £127 million and an income of £6.6 million. Grants made to non-Masonic charities totalled £218,000. Other grants totalled £5 million, and a further £413,000 went to individuals through the TalentAid programme.

The non-Masonic grants were divided between the Choral Bursaries (£204,000) and Ripon Cathedral Development (£14,000). The trust stated in its annual accounts that in 2007 it, 'continued to limit its non-Masonic activities to its existing Choral Bursary project, as there were insufficient funds available to make donations to other charities'.

Applications In writing to the correspondent.

Please note: the trust states on its website that, 'at present, the trust's resources are sufficient only to support its primary beneficiaries and its existing projects. It is not able to consider applications for new non-Masonic grants at this time'.

Any change to this policy will be noted on the trust's website.

The RRAF Charitable Trust

General, medical research, children who are disadvantaged, religious organisations, aid for the developing world and support for older people

£178,000 (2007/08)
Beneficial area UK and the developing world.

Rathbone Trust Company Limited, 159 New Bond Street, London W1S 2UD

Tel. 020 7399 0807

Correspondent The Administrator

Trustees *Rathbone Trust Company Limited; Claire Tufnell; Emilie Astley-Arlington; Joanne Mcarthy; Rosemary Mcarthy; Elizabeth Astley-Arlington.*

CC Number 1103662

Information available Accounts were on file at the Charity Commission.

This trust was established in 2004. In 2007/08 it had assets of £700,000 and an income of £25,000. Grants were made to seven organisations totalling £178,000.

Beneficiaries during the year were: Extra Care Charitable Trust and Southwell Cathedral Chapter (£50,000 each); Ethiopiaid, Mums for Mums – FECIN and Trinity Church (£25,000 each);

Methodist Homes for the Aged (£2,000); and Sightsavers International (£500).

Applications In writing to the correspondent. Only successful applicants are notified of the trustees' decision.

William Arthur Rudd Memorial Trust

General in the UK, and selected Spanish charities

£41,000 (2007)
Beneficial area In practice UK and Spain.

12 South Square, Gray's Inn, London WC1R 5HH

Tel. 020 7405 8932

Email mail@mmandm.co.uk

Correspondent Miss A A Sarkis, Trustee

Trustees *Miss A A Sarkis; D H Smyth; R G Maples.*

CC Number 326495

Information available Accounts were on file at the Charity Commission, without a narrative report or a list of beneficiaries.

In 2007 the trust had assets of £903,000, an income of £40,000 and made grants totalling £41,000. The trust's accounts state that donations were made to registered charities in the UK and to selected Spanish charities; however, no grants list was provided.

Applications As the trust's resources are fully committed, the trustees do not consider unsolicited applications.

The Russell Trust

General

Around £200,000 (2007/08)
Beneficial area UK, especially Scotland.

Markinch, Glenrothes, Fife KY7 6PB

Tel. 01592 753311

Email russelltrust@trg.co.uk

Correspondent Iona Russell, Administrator and Trustee

Trustees *Fred Bowden; Mrs Cecilia Croal; Graeme Crombie; David Erdal; Don Munro; Ms Iona Russell; Alan Scott.*

SC Number SC004424

Information available Accounts were provided by the trust.

This family trust was established in 1947 in memory of Capt. J P O Russell who was killed in Italy during the Second World War. The trustees prefer to make grants to pump-prime new projects, rather than giving on an ongoing basis. Grants of up to £10,000 can be distributed; however, generally the amounts given are for between £250 and £2,000. Three or four larger grants of up to £20,000 may be awarded annually.

In 2007/08 the trust had an income of £273,000. No grants list was available, but previously donations have been broken down as follows:

- Music and the Arts – £36,000
- Education – £26,000
- St Andrew's University – £24,000
- Archaeology – £21,000
- Health and Welfare – £19,000
- National Trust for Scotland – £15,000
- Youth work – £15,000
- Preservation work – £12,000
- Local – £9,000
- Church – £7,000
- General – £5,500
- The Iona Community – £5,000

Exclusions Only registered charities or organisations with charitable status are supported.

Applications On a form available from the correspondent. A statement of accounts must be supplied. Trustees meet quarterly, although decisions on the allocation of grants are made more regularly.

Ryklow Charitable Trust 1992 (also known as A B Williamson Charitable Trust)

Education, health, environment and welfare

£34,000 to organisations

(2007/08)

Beneficial area Worldwide.

c/o Robinsons Solicitors, 10–11 St James Court, Friar Gate, Derby DE1 1BT

Tel. 01332 291 431 **Fax** 01332 254 141

Email stephen.marshall@ robinsons-solicitors.co.uk

Website ryklowcharitabletrust.org

Correspondent Stephen F Marshall

Trustees *A Williamson; E J S Cannings: P W Hanson; Mrs S Taylor.*

CC Number 1010122

Information available Accounts were on file at the Charity Commission.

The trust says that its guidelines for applicants: 'have been compiled to help applicants understand how best it is felt the trust can be operated and the constraints of time under which the (unpaid) trustees must work. It will help enormously if you try to ensure that your application follows these guidelines if at all possible'.

Applications will only be considered for activities if they meet the following descriptions:

- medical research, especially that which benefits children
- assistance to students from overseas wishing to study in the UK or for UK students volunteering for unpaid work overseas
- projects in the developing world – especially those which are intended to be self-sustaining or concerned with education
- help for vulnerable families, minorities and the prevention of abuse or exploitation of children
- conservation of natural species, landscape and resources.

In 2007/08 the trust had assets of £1.6 million and an income of £694,000.

Grants were made to 66 organisations totalling £34,000 and were distributed as follows:

Category	No. of grants	Amount
Medical research	6	£3,000
Projects in the developing world	24	£12,000
Help for vulnerable families, minorities and children	28	£14,500
Conservation of natural species, landscape and resources	8	£4,000

No grants list was available but previous beneficiaries have included: Ark Trust, BLISS, Books Abroad, Care International UK, Children in Crisis, Interact Worldwide, International Otter Survival Fund, Motor Neurone Research, Nepal Trust, Soil Association, Sun Seed (Tanzania) Trust, Water Aid, Wildlife Conservation Research Unit, Wolf Trust and Young Minds.

One grant of £500 was made to an individual.

Applications On a form available from the correspondent or to download from the trust's website. Applications should be brief and include an audited financial report (or at least a statement of finances).

Forms should be submitted between 1 September and 31 December. The trustees usually make a decision once a year in March, with grants being awarded by the end of the month. Only in cases of real emergency will applications be considered at other times.

Only successful applicants will be notified.

The Michael Sacher Charitable Trust

General: including arts, culture and heritage; medical and disability; community and welfare; education, science and technology; children and young people; and religion

£126,000 (2007/08)

Beneficial area UK and Israel.

16 Clifton Villas, London W9 2PH

Tel. 020 7289 5873

Correspondent John Sacher

Trustees *Simon John Sacher; Jeremy Michael Sacher; Hon. Mrs Rosalind E C Sacher; Mrs Elisabeth J Sacher.*

CC Number 206321

Information available Full accounts were on file at the Charity Commission.

This trust has general charitable purposes, with a particular interest in Jewish/Israeli organisations. In 2007/08 the trust had assets of £4.5 million and an income of £153,000. Grants were made to 29 organisations totalling £126,000 and were broken down into the following seven categories:

Arts, culture and heritage – 14 grants (£66,000)

The largest grant was made to Royal College of Music (£31,000). Other grants included: the National Gallery (£10,000); Royal Opera House (£6,250); and London Masterclass (£670).

Medical and disability – 3 grants (£23,000)

Grants went to: Anna Freud Centre (£22,000); and Motor Neurone Disease Association and Children's Neurosurgery Ward – Southampton Hospital (£500 each).

Community and welfare – 2 grants (£9,600)

Grants were made to Friends of the Hebrew University (£8,600) and British Friends of Kishorit (£1,000).

Education, science and technology – 1 grant (£10,000)

One grant was made to Kings College London (£10,000).

Children and young people – 1 grant (£250)

One grant was made to Chain of Hope (£250).

Religion – 1 grant (£10,000)

One grant was made to the Jerusalem Foundation (£10,000).

General – 3 grants (£7,100)

Beneficiaries were: FEROP (£6,600); St Johns Smith Square (£360); and New Israel Fund (£120).

Applications In writing to the correspondent at any time.

The Michael Harry Sacher Charitable Trust

General, arts, education, animal welfare, Jewish, health and social welfare

£101,000 (2007/08)

Beneficial area UK and overseas

c/o H W Fisher and Co, 11–15 William Road, London NW1 3ER

Tel. 020 7388 7000

Correspondent The Trustees

Trustees *Nicola Shelley Sacher; Michael Harry Sacher.*

CC Number 288973

Information available Accounts were on file at the Charity Commission.

The trust was established in 1984 and makes donations to registered charities which support a wide range of causes. Grants are only made to charities known personally to the trustees and generally range from £250 to £30,000.

In 2007/08 the trust had assets of £2.3 million and an income of £71,000. Grants were made to 30 organisations totalling £101,000 and were broken down into these key areas:

Culture and arts (£14,000)
Among the 7 beneficiaries were: Royal Opera House Foundation (£11,000); National Gallery Trust (£10,000); Royal National Theatre (£7,500); and Donmar Warehouse Projects Ltd (£1,500).

Overseas aid (£4,500)
One grant went to Friends of the Hebrew University.

Education (£22,000)
Beneficiaries were: INSTEAD UK Trust for European Management Education (£11,000); Goldsmith College (£9,300); and One to One (£2,500).

Community care (£6,000)
Grants went to: Jewish Care and Community Security Trust (£2,500 each); and Nightingale House (£1,000).

Animals (£14,000)
Grants were made to: Singapore Zoo (£8,500); Whale and Dolphin Conservation Society (£3,300); World Society for the Protection of Animals (£1,500); and Safe Haven for Donkeys in the Holy Land (£500).

Children and young people (£2,000)
As in the previous year Norwood Ltd again received the sole grant in this category.

Health (£3,800)
Beneficiaries were: Friends of Alyn (£2,000); MDA UK (£1,000); Crusaid (£500); and Kidney Cancer UK (£250).

Religious organisations (£2,700)
Beneficiaries were: West London Synagogue and New West End Synagogue (£1,000 each); and United Synagogue Membership (£730).

General (£3,100)
The sole grant in this category was made to Jeremy and John Sacher Charitable Trust.

Exclusions No grants to individuals or organisations which are not registered charities.

Applications In writing to the correspondent.

Dr Mortimer and Theresa Sackler Foundation

Arts and culture, science and medical

£1.7 million (2007)

Beneficial area UK.

9th Floor, New Zealand House, 80 Haymarket, London SW1Y 4TQ

Tel. 020 7930 4944

Correspondent Christopher B Mitchell, Trustee

Trustees *Dr Mortimer Sackler; Theresa Sackler; Christopher Mitchell; Raymond Smith; Ilene Lefcourt Sackler; Marissa Sackler; Peter Stormonth Darling.*

CC Number 327863

Information available Accounts were on file at the Charity Commission.

The foundation was set up in 1988 to support 'the advancement of the public in the UK and elsewhere in the fields of art, science and medical research generally'. In 2007 it had assets of £5 million and an income of £3.1 million. Grants were made totalling £1.7 million.

There were 20 grants of £10,000 or more. Beneficiaries included: Edinburgh

and Glasgow Universities (joint grant of £500,000); Museum of London (£333,000); Watermill Theatre (£160,000); National History Museum (£125,000); Dulwich Picture Gallery Centre for Arts Education (£70,000); Chiswick House and Gardens Trust (£50,000); Capital City Academy (£25,000); and Charity Global (£12,000).

Donations under £10,000 each totalled £92,000.

Applications In writing to the correspondent.

The Ruzin Sadagora Trust

Jewish

£528,000 (2007/08)

Beneficial area UK and Israel.

269 Golders Green Road, London NW11 9JJ

Correspondent Rabbi I M Friedman, Trustee

Trustees *Rabbi I M Friedman; Mrs S Friedman.*

CC Number 285475

Information available Accounts were on file at the Charity Commission.

In 2007/08 the trust had assets of £529,000 with an income of £636,000 and grants totalling £528,000.

Grants listed in the accounts were: Beth Israel Ruzin Sadagora (£196,000); Friends of Ruzin Sadagora (£180,000); Beth Kaknesset Ohr Yisroel (£91,600); Mosdos Sadigur (£40,000); Yeshivas Torah Temimah (£9,000); Chevras Moaz Lodol (£6,500); and Pardes House (£2,000).

'Sundry donations' totalled £2,600.

Applications In writing to the correspondent.

The Jean Sainsbury Animal Welfare Trust

Animal welfare

£318,000 (2007)

Beneficial area UK registered charities.

PO Box 50793, London NW6 9DE

Tel. 020 7602 7948

Website jeansainsburyanimalwelfare.org.uk

Correspondent Madeleine Orchard, Administrator

Trustees Colin Russell; Gillian Tarlington; James Keliher; Mark Spurdens; Evelyn Jane Winship; Valerie Pike.

CC Number 326358

Information available Accounts were on file at the Charity Commission.

The trust was established in 1982 with the objective of benefiting animals and protecting them from suffering. The policy of the trustees is to support smaller charities concerned with the following areas:

- benefiting or protecting animals
- relieving animals from suffering
- conserving wildlife
- encouraging the understanding of animals.

Grants are given towards general running costs, veterinary fees, neutering campaigns and major items such as vehicles, veterinary equipment, kennels and cattery units. Capital building projects will be considered under certain circumstances. Charities must be registered in the UK, though their work can take place overseas. However, at least 90 per cent of the trust's donated income must be given to those who operate in the UK.

In 2007 the trust had assets of £13.7 million and an unusually large income of nearly £5 million. This was the due to the £4.5 million legacy left to the trust by Jean Sainsbury on her death in February 2007. Grants were made to 75 organisations totalling £318,000.

Beneficiaries of larger grants of £1,000 or more included: Gambia Horse and Pony Trust and Danaher Animal Home (£12,000 each); North Clwyd Animal Rescue and Greyhound Rescue West of England (£10,000 each); Lluest Horse and Pony Trust (£7,000); Shropshire Cat Rescue and Three Owls (£5,000 each); Exotic Pet Refuge (£3,000); Bunny Burrows (£2,000); and Maggie's Pet Rescue (£1,000).

Smaller grants of £1,000 or less included those to: Safe Haven for Donkeys in the Holy Land (£750); Greek Cat Welfare Society and Mountains Animal Sanctuary (£500 each); Hollyfield Wild Bird Hospital and Withington Hedgehog Care – Manchester (£300 each); and Trinity Hospice (£100).

Exclusions No grants are given to charities which:

- are mainly engaged with the preservation of specific species of wild animals
- have available reserves equal to more than one year's running costs (unless it can be demonstrated that reserves are being held for a designated project)
- are offering sanctuary to animals, with no effort to re-home, foster or rehabilitate
- do not have a realistic policy for animals that cannot be given a reasonable quality of life
- are involved with assistance animals e.g. Hearing Dogs for the Deaf, Riding for the Disabled etc
- spend more than a reasonable proportion of their income on administration or cannot justify their costs per animal helped
- are registered outside the UK.

No support is given to veterinary schools (unless the money can be seen to be directly benefiting the type of animals the trust would want to support). No individuals are supported.

Applications On a form available from the correspondent or to download from the trust's website. Applicants should complete and return seven copies of the form, their latest set of audited accounts and any other information which may be relevant to the application. Please note: the trust requests that you do not send originals as these cannot be returned.

There are three trustees' meetings every year, usually in March, July and November and applications should be submitted by 1 February, 1 June and 1 October respectively. Further application information and policy guidelines are available by visiting the website.

Saint Luke's College Foundation

Research and studies in theology

£144,000 (2007/08)

Beneficial area UK and overseas, with some preference for Exeter and Truro.

Heathayne, Colyton EX24 6RS

Tel. 01297 552281 **Fax** 01297 552281

Correspondent Professor Michael Bond, Director

Trustees The Bishop of Exeter; The Dean of Exeter; Diocesan Director of Education; Chairman of Diocesan Board of Finance; Revd David Moss; Prof Grace Davie; Dr Michael Wykes; Prof Mark Overton; Revd Canon Bruce Duncan; Prof Dame Margaret Turner Warwick; Dr Barbara Wintersgill.

CC Number 306606

Information available Accounts were available from the Charity Commission website.

This foundation encourages original work and imaginative new projects by educational and training bodies. Grants are only made for research or studies in theology and religious education and normally only at postgraduate level.

In 2007/08 the foundation had assets of £3.9 million and an income of £164,000. Grants were made totalling £144,000 which was broken down as follows:

- Chapel and chaplaincy (£77,100)
- University of Exeter – Chair of Theology (£31,000)
- Personal and corporate grants (£35,500).

Exclusions Grants are not made for studies or research in fields other than religious studies, or for buildings or schools (except indirectly through courses or research projects undertaken by Religious Education teachers). Block grants to support schemes or organisations are not made. Grants are not normally made for periods in excess of three years.

Applications Requests for application packs, and all other correspondence, should be sent to the correspondent. Applications are considered once a year and should be received by 1st May.

Saint Sarkis Charity Trust

Armenian churches and welfare and offenders

£289,000 (2007/08)

Beneficial area UK and overseas.

98 Portland Place, London W1B 1ET

Tel. 020 7908 7604 **Fax** 020 7908 7582

Email info@saintsarkis.org.uk

Website www.saintsarkis.org.uk

Correspondent Louisa Hooper, Secretary

Trustees *Martin Sarkis Essayan; Boghos Parsegh Gulbenkian; Rita Alice Vartoukian; Robert Brian Todd.*

CC Number 215352

Information available Accounts were available from the Charity Commission website.

The Saint Sarkis Charity Trust funds the following organisations:

- the Armenian Church of Saint Sarkis in London
- the Gulbenkian Library at the Armenian Patriarchate in Jerusalem
- registered charities concerned with the Armenian community in the UK and/ or overseas
- UK-registered charities developing innovative projects to support prisoners in the UK and so reduce the rates of re-offending; in particular, the trust is interested in helping people with short-term sentences to cope on their release from prison, women offenders and the families of offenders.

In 2007/08 the trust had an income of £356,000 and made grants totalling £289,000. Its assets stood at £7 million. Grants were divided into two categories:

Armenian projects (£239,000)
The largest grants were made to: Armenian Church of Saint Sarkis (£123,000); Friends of Armenia (£48,000); Fonds Armenia de France (£25,000); and Centre for Armenian Information and Advice (£15,000).

Smaller grants of less than £10,000 each included those made to: London Armenian Poor Relief (£8,000); Armenian Patriarchate – Jerusalem Library (£6,600); and Armenian Institute (£800).

Other projects – (£50,000)
Beneficiaries included: Revolving Doors Agency and Action for Prisoners (£10,000 each); Howard League for Penal Reform (£5,000); Send Family Link (£1,000); Safe Ground (£800); and SPODA (£500).

Exclusions The trust does not give grants to:

- individual applicants
- organisations that are not registered charities
- registered charities outside the UK, unless the project benefits the Armenian community in the UK and/ or overseas.

The trust does not fund:

- general appeals
- core costs or salaries (as opposed to project costs)
- projects concerning substance abuse
- medical research.

Applications In writing to the correspondent. There is no standard application form so applicants should write a covering letter including the following:

- an explanation of the exact purpose of the grant
- how much is needed, with details of how the budget has been arrived at
- details of any other sources of income (firm commitments and those still being explored)
- the charity registration number
- the latest annual report and audited accounts
- any plans for monitoring and evaluating the work.

The Saintbury Trust

General

£269,000 (2007)

Beneficial area West Midlands and Warwickshire (which the trust considers to be post code areas B, CV, DY, WS and WV), Worcestershire, Herefordshire and Gloucestershire (post code areas WR, HR and GL).

P O Box 464, Abinger Hammer, Dorking RH4 9AF

Tel. 01306 730119

Correspondent Mrs J P Lewis, Trustee

Trustees *Victoria K Houghton; Anne R Thomas; Jane P Lewis; Amanda E Atkinson-Willes; Harry O Forrester.*

CC Number 326790

Information available Accounts were on file at the Charity Commission.

The trust gives grants for general charitable purposes, although the trust deed states that no grants can be given to animal charities. Grants are made to registered charities in Gloucestershire, West Midlands and Worcestershire.

In 2007 the trust had assets of £7.2 million and an income of £282,000. Grants were made to 67 organisations totalling £269,000. They ranged from £500 to £40,000 and were made in the following categories:

Addiction (£21,000)
Beneficiaries included: RAPt (£15,000); and Nelson Trust (£5,000).

Arts and leisure (£108,000)
The largest grant in this category again went to the Midlands Arts Centre (£90,000). Other beneficiaries included: UCE Birmingham Conservatoire (£5,000); Sudden Productions (formerly the Deep Impact Theatre Company) (£2,000); and Gloucester Choral Society (£500).

Care of the dying (£15,000)
Grants went to: St Richard's Hospice Foundation (£5,000); Myton Hamlet Hospice Trust (£4,000); and Freshwinds (£2,000).

Children and young people (£12,000)
Grants included those made to: Sunfield Children's Home Ltd. (£4,000); and Adoption Support (£1,000).

Community work (£21,000)
Grant recipients included: Trinity Winchester (£10,000); Sahil Project (£2,000); and Family Mediation Worcestershire Ltd (£1,000).

Disability (£31,000)
Beneficiaries included: Foundation for Conductive Education and Tiny Tim's Children's Centre (£5,000 each); Phoenix Centre (£2,000); and Blind Art (£1,000).

Education (£2,000)
The sole beneficiary was Tettenhall Wood School Fund (£2,000).

Environment (£2,000)
One grant was given to the Good Gardeners' Foundation (£2,000).

Health (£26,000)
Grants included those made to: Birmingham Children's Hospitals Charities (£20,000); Alzheimer's Research Trust (£2,000); and MacMillan Cancer Support (£1,000).

Heritage (£3,000)
Grant recipients included: Kings Norton PCC Restoration (£2,000); and Bristol Aero Collection.

Homelessness (£6,000)
Beneficiaries included: St Basil's (£2,000); and Oasis Church Trust Birmingham (£1,000).

Old age (£17,000)
Grants went to: the Royal Surgical Aid Society (£15,000); and Age Concern Malvern and District and Independent Age (£1,000 each).

Other special needs (£1,000)
One grant was made to Hop Skip and Jump – Cotswold (£1,000).

Prisons (£5,000)
The sole beneficiary was Pimlico Opera (£5,000).

Exclusions No grants to animal charities, individuals (including individuals seeking sponsorship for challenges in support of charities), 'cold-calling' national charities or local branches of national charities. The trust only gives grants to charities outside its beneficial area if the charity is personally known to one or more of the trustees.

Applications In writing to the correspondent. Applications are considered twice a year, usually in April and November.

The Saints and Sinners Trust

General, welfare and medical

£75,000 (2007/08)
Beneficial area Mostly UK.

Lewis Golden and Co., 40 Queen Anne Street, London W1G 9EL
Tel. 020 7580 7313
Correspondent N W Benson, Trustee
Trustees *N W Benson; Sir Donald Gosling; N C Royds; I A N Irvine.*
CC Number 200536
Information available Accounts were available from the Charity Commission website.

This trust supports welfare and medical causes through the proceeds of its fundraising efforts. In 2007/08 the trust had assets of £328,000 and an income of £152,000. Grants were made to 31 organisations totalling £75,000.

Beneficiaries included: Royal Opera House (£10,000); South Buckinghamshire Riding for the Disabled Association and White Ensign Association Limited (£5,000 each); Marine Conversation Society and AJET (£3,000 each); Police Rehabilitation Trust and Sandy Gall's Afghanistan Appeal (£2,000 each); and British Limbless Ex-service Men's Association, Spinal Injuries Association and Foundation for the Study of Infant Deaths (£1,000 each).

Exclusions No grants to individuals or non-registered charities.

Applications Applications are not considered unless nominated by members of the club.

The Salamander Charitable Trust

Christian and general

£81,000 (2007/08)
Beneficial area Worldwide.

Threave, 2 Brudenell Avenue, Canford Cliffs, Poole BH13 7NW
Tel. 01202 706661
Correspondent John R T Douglas, Trustee
Trustees *J R T Douglas; Sheila M Douglas.*
CC Number 273657
Information available Accounts were available from the Charity Commission website.

Founded in 1977, the principal objects of the trust are the:

- relief and assistance of people who are poor or in need
- advancement of education and religion
- relief of sickness and other exclusively charitable purposes beneficial to the community.

In 2007/08 the trust had assets of £2 million and an income of £65,000. Grants were made to 99 organisations totalling £81,000, ranging from £250 to £3,000. A list of beneficiaries was not available.

Previous beneficiaries have included SAT-7 Trust, All Nations Christian College, All Saints in Branksome Park, Birmingham Christian College, Christian Aid, Churches Commission on overseas students, FEBA Radio, International Christian College, London Bible College, Middle East Media, Moorland College, St James PCC in Poole, SAMS, Trinity College and Wycliffe Bible Translators.

Exclusions No grants to individuals. Only registered charities are supported.

Applications The trust's income is fully allocated each year, mainly to regular beneficiaries. The trustees do not wish to receive any further new requests.

The Salters' Charities

General

£148,000 (2007/08)
Beneficial area Greater London and the UK

The Salters' Company, Salters' Hall, 4 Fore Street, London EC2Y 5DE
Tel. 020 7588 5216 **Fax** 020 7638 3679
Email diane@salters.co.uk
Website www.salters.co.uk
Correspondent Diane Bundock, Administrator
Trustee *The Salters' Company.*
CC Number 328258
Information available Accounts were available from the Charity Commission.

The trust makes donations for a range of charitable purposes including, children and young people, health, homelessness, Christian aid, the developing world, the environment and members of the armed forces. Priority is given to funding small nationwide charities and organisations connected with the City of London, where the trust's contribution would make a 'real difference'. As a livery company, the trust pays particular interest to charities a liveryman is involved with. In previous years, grants of around £2,000 have been given to around 80 charities each year. Many beneficiaries have received grants over a number of years.

In 2007/08 the trust had an income of £162,000 and made grants totalling £148,000. Its assets stood at £800.

Armed forces – 5 grants (£7,500)
These went to London Sea Cadet Corps – District 5 – NE and the King's Royal Hussars Regimental Association (£2,000 each); The Royal Naval Benevolent Trust and South West London Army Cadet Force (£1,500 each); and HMS Vengeance Welfare Fund and Crew Prize (£500).

**Children, schools and young people –
9 grants (£22,000)**
Beneficiaries included: Arkwright
Schools Scholarships (£5,400);
Wheelpower (£3,000); Rainbow Trust
(£2,000); and the National Deaf
Children's Society (£1,000).

Christian aid – 1 grant (£1,000)
The sole beneficiary was again WPF
Westminster Pastoral Foundation.

City of London – 10 grants (£20,000)
Grant recipients included: Lord Mayor
Treloar Trust (£3,000); Sheriffs' and
Recorders' Fund and Community Links
(£2,000 each); and City University
London (£1,000).

**Environment and developing countries
– 4 grants (£16,000)**
Grants were made to: UNEP – WCMC
(£9,000); TEAR Fund (£3,000); and
Educaid and the African Scholars' Fund
(£2,000 each).

Medical – 21 grants (£42,000)
Beneficiaries included: Cure Parkinson's
Trust and Mildmay (£3,000 each); Blind
in Business, Diabetes UK and Queen
Elizabeth's Foundation (£2,000 each);
and Thames Hospice Care (£1,000).

Homelessness – 3 grants (£8,000)
Grants went to Centrepoint – for the
Salters' City Foyer Project and
Providence Row/Just Ask – Counselling
& Advisory Service (£3,000 each); and
the Passage (£2,000).

Other donations – 19 grants (£25,000)
Grants made included those to: The
Lord Todd Memorial Bursary (£3,200);
University of Ulster Step Up programme
(£3,000); Care International UK and
Chelsea Pensioner's Appeal (£1,000
each).

Exclusions Grants are not normally
made to charities working with people
who are homeless unless there is some
connection with a liveryman of the
company or with the Salters' City Foyer
and the charities involved.

Applications In writing to the
correspondent. Please note: the trust
states that email requests for funding
will not be considered.

The Andrew Salvesen Charitable Trust

General
About £100,000
Beneficial area UK, with a
preference for Scotland.

c/o Meston Reid and Co., 12 Carden
Place, Aberdeen AB10 1UR

Tel. 01224 625554

Correspondent The Trustees

Trustees *A C Salvesen; Ms K Turner;
V Lall.*

SC Number SC008000

Information available Despite making a
written request for the accounts of this
trust (and including a stamped,
addressed envelope), these were not
provided. The following entry is based,
therefore, on information filed with the
Office of the Scottish Charity Regulator.

The trust gives grants for general
charitable purposes; in particular it will
support the arts, education/training,
medical sciences and welfare of people
who are young, older or ill.

In 2007/08 the trust had an income of
£110,000 and made grants totalling
around £100,000.

Previous beneficiaries have included
Bield Housing Trust, William Higgins
Marathon Account, Multiple Sclerosis
Society in Scotland, Royal Zoological
Society of Scotland, Sail Training
Association, Scottish Down's Syndrome
Association and Sick Kids Appeal.

Exclusions No grants to individuals.

Applications The trustees only
support organisations known to them
through their personal contacts. The
trust has previously stated that all
applications sent to them are 'thrown in
the bin'.

The Sammermar Trust

General
£248,000 (2007)
Beneficial area UK and overseas.

Swire House, 59 Buckingham Gate,
London SW1E 6AJ

Tel. 020 7834 7717

Correspondent Mrs Yvonne Barnes

Trustees *Lady Judith Swire; M Dunne;
M B Swire; Mrs M V Allfrey; S C Swire.*

CC Number 800493

Information available Accounts were
available from the Charity Commission
website.

The trust, formerly known as the Adrian
Swire Charitable Trust, was established
in 1988 with general charitable purposes.
In 2007 the trust had assets of
£7.6 million and an income of £244,000.
Grants were made totalling £248,000.

The largest grants were those made to:
Wantage Nursing Home Charitable
Trust (£125,000); Mango Tree (£12,000);
and Book Aid International, Sparsholt
PCC and Vulcan to the Sky Trust
(£10,000 each).

Smaller grants of £5,000 or less were
made to: YMSO and Oxford Nature
Conservation Forum (£5,000 each);
Griffin Hall (£4,000); Warwickshire
Firefighters Families Fund (£3,000);
Headington School (£2,500); Myton
Hospice (£2,000); and Nilgiris Adivasi
Trust, Head and Neck Cancer Research
Trust and Guild of Air Pilots and Air
Navigators (£1,000 each).

Other grants of less than £1,000 each
were made totalling £7,800.

Applications In writing to the
correspondent. The trust states that:
'although the trustees make some grants
with no formal applications, they
normally require organisations to submit
a request saying how the funds could be
used and what would be achieved'. The
trustees usually meet monthly.

Coral Samuel Charitable Trust

General, with a preference for educational, cultural and social support
£138,000 (2007/08)
Beneficial area UK.

c/o Smith and Williamson, 25 Moorgate,
London EC2R 6AY

Correspondent Mrs Coral Samuel,
Trustee

Trustees *Coral Samuel; P Fineman.*

CC Number 239677

Information available Accounts were on file at the Charity Commission.

This trust was established in 1962 and makes grants to educational, cultural and socially supportive charities, plus a number of other charities.

In 2007/08 the trust had assets totalling £4.9 million and an income of £244,000. Grants were made to 17 institutions totalling £138,000.

The largest grants went to: South Bank Foundation (£50,000); Victoria and Albert Museum (£25,000); and Natural History Museum Development Trust, Royal Opera House Foundation and SAVE (£10,000 each).

The remaining, smaller grants ranged from £500 to £5,000. Beneficiaries included: Chelsea Physic Garden (£5,000); Maccabi GB (£2,000); Royal British Legion and Mercers' Charitable Foundation (£1,000 each); and European Union Youth Orchestra (£500).

Exclusions Grants are only made to registered charities.

Applications In writing to the correspondent.

The Peter Samuel Charitable Trust

Health, welfare, conservation and Jewish care

£95,000 (2007/08)

Beneficial area UK, with some preference for local organisations in south Berkshire, Highlands of Scotland and East Somerset.

The Estate Office, Farley Hall, Castle Road, Farley Hill RG7 1UL

Tel. 0118 973 0047 **Fax** 0118 973 0385

Email emma@farleyfarms.co.uk

Correspondent Miss Emma Chapman, Trust Administrator

Trustees Hon. Viscount Bearsted; Hon. Michael Samuel.

CC Number 269065

Information available Full accounts were available from the Charity Commission website.

The trust was established in 1975 and supports medical sciences, Jewish

concerns, heritage, forestry/land restoration and the quality of life in local areas (south-central Berkshire, east Somerset and the highlands of Scotland).

In 2007/08 the trust had assets of £3.4 million, which produced an income of £103,000. Grants were made to 30 organisations totalling £95,000.

The largest grant went to Game Conservancy (£25,000).

Other grants made included those to: Marie Curie, Outreach and Anna Freud Centre (£5,000 each); Cancer Research (£3,000); St Mary's Paddington Charitable Trust (£2,500); NSPCC, Highland Hospice and I Can (£2,000 each); London String Quartet and Chicken Shed Theatre Company (£1,000 each); National Talking Newspapers & Magazines and Oxford University Jewish Society (£500 each); and BBONT (£200).

Exclusions No grants to purely local charities outside Berkshire, east Somerset or the highlands of Scotland, or to individuals.

Applications In writing to the correspondent. Trustees meet twice-yearly.

The M J Samuel Charitable Trust

General and Jewish

£287,000 (2007/08)

Beneficial area UK and overseas.

35 Connaught Square, London W2 2HL

Correspondent The Secretary

Trustees Hon. Michael Samuel; Hon. Mrs Julia A Samuel; Viscount Bearsted.

CC Number 327013

Information available Accounts were available at the Charity Commission.

The trust supports a wide range of causes, many of them Jewish, environmental or concerned with mental health.

In 2007/08 the trust had assets of almost £3 million, which generated an income of £102,000. There were 28 grants made totalling £287,000.

Beneficiaries of grants of £1,000 or more included: Anna Freud Centre (£250,000); Institute Trust Fund (£5,000); Liver Research Trust (£4,000); Atlantic Salmon Trust (£3,500); the Children's Hospice (£3,000); BAAF, Brogdale Horticultural Trust and the Wheelyboat Trust (£2,500

each); Chicken Shed Theatre Company (£2,000); the Tyne Rivers Trust (£1,500); and TATE Foundation, Valid Nutrition and the Henry van Straubenzee Memorial Fund (£1,000 each).

Exclusions No grants to individuals.

Applications In writing to the correspondent.

The Camilla Samuel Fund

Medical research

Around £25,000 (2007/08)

Beneficial area UK.

40 Berkerly Square, London W1J 5AL

Correspondent The Secretary to the Trustees

Trustees Sir Ronald Grierson; Hon. Mrs Waley-Cohen; Dr Hon. J P H Hunt.

CC Number 235424

Information available Information was obtained from the Charity Commission website.

The trust supports medical research projects in a discipline agreed by the trustees at their annual meetings.

In 2007/08 the trust had an income of £17,000 and a total expenditure of £31,000. Further information was not available. Previous beneficiaries have included Imperial Cancer Research Fund and EORTC.

Exclusions Individuals and general appeals.

Applications The trustees will request written applications following the recommendation of a suitable project by the medical trustees. However, please note: as all the money available, together with the fund's future income, has been earmarked for four years for an important research project, the fund will not be in a position to consider any applications for grants during this period.

The Sandhu Charitable Foundation

General

£25,000 (2007/08)
Beneficial area Worldwide.

First Floor, 21 Knightsbridge, London SW1X 7LY
Correspondent The Trustees
Trustees *B S Sandhu, Chair; S Carey.*
CC Number 1114236
Information available Accounts were on file at the Charity Commission.

The foundation was established in 2006 as a focus for the philanthropic activities of Bim and Pardeep Sandhu and their family.

In 2007/08 it had an income of £397,000, mostly from donations. Assets stood at over £1 million at year end. The trustees made three grants totalling £25,000 to Grand Bahama Children's Home, Emmaus Hampshire and Young Enterprise.

Applications 'The charity is to support individual charities or charitable causes, mainly on a single donation basis, which they themselves identify'.

Jimmy Savile Charitable Trust

General

£77,000 (2007/08)
Beneficial area UK.

Stoke Mandeville Hospital, Mandeville Road, Aylesbury HP21 8DL
Correspondent The Trustees
Trustees *Sir James Savile; James Collier; Luke Lucas; Dr Roger Bodley.*
CC Number 326970
Information available Accounts were available from the Charity Commission website.

The trust provides funds for the relief of poverty, sickness and other charitable purposes which are beneficial to the community, including the provision of recreational and other facilities for people with disabilities. Grants are made to charitable organisations and individuals.

In 2007/08 the trust had assets of £3.5 million and an income of £176,000. Grants were made totalling £77,000. The largest grant of £48,000 went to the University of Leeds for the Lure Scholarships.

Grants of £1,000 or more went to: Laniado Hospital (£5,000); and Across, Royal Marines Atlantic Challenge, RMA Jubilee Fund, Scope and William Merritt Disabled Living Centre (£1,000 each).

Grants of less than £1,000 included those to: Music in Hospitals, Walk the Walk Worldwide, Kidney Research UK and Dame Vera Lynn Trust (£500 each); Hops and Sick Children's Trust (£250); and University of Bradford – IK Hospital Fund (£100).

Applications The trust does not respond to unsolicited applications.

The Scarfe Charitable Trust

Churches, arts, music and the environment

£64,000 to organisations (2007/08)
Beneficial area UK, with an emphasis on Suffolk.

Salix House, Falkenham, Ipswich IP10 0QY
Tel. 01394 448 339 **Fax** 01394 448 339
Email ericmaule@hotmail.com
Correspondent Eric Maule, Trustee
Trustees *N Scarfe; E Maule; John McCarthy.*
CC Number 275535
Information available Accounts were available from the Charity Commission website.

The trust was established in 1978 by W S N Scarfe and supports mainly art and musical projects and the restoration of churches in Suffolk.

In 2007/08 the trust had an income of £75,000 and made grants totalling £66,000. Its assets stood at £1.2 million. Grants were made as follows:

Churches – 15 grants (£10,800)
Beneficiaries included: St Peters PCC Bruisyard (£2,500); Shadingfield PCC (£2,000); Dunwich PCC and Ickworth Church Conservation Trust (£1,000 each); St John Campsea Ashe Bells project (£700); St Peter and St Paul PCC Clare (£500); and Friends of Kirton Church (£150).

Grants to organisations – 52 grants (£54,000)
Grant recipients included: Aldeburgh Music (£19,000); MacMillan Cancer Support and Mahogany Opera (£2,000 each); Red Rose Chain (£1,250); Poetry Trust, City of London Sinfonia and RSPB (£1,000 each); Terrence Higgins Trust (£600); and Blyth Valley Chamber Music (£200).

Two grants were also made to individuals totalling £1,800.

Applications In writing to the correspondent by post or email. The trustees meet quarterly to consider applications.

The Schapira Charitable Trust

Jewish

£379,000 (2007)
Beneficial area UK.

2 Dancastle Court, 14 Arcadia Avenue, Finchley, London N3 2JU
Tel. 020 8371 0381
Email londonoffice@istrad.com
Correspondent The Trustees
Trustees *Issac Y Schapira; Michael Neuberger; Suzanne L Schapira.*
CC Number 328435
Information available Accounts were available from the Charity Commission website.

This trust was established in 1989 and has a policy of supporting Jewish organisations. Applications from the fields of health and education may also be considered but in practice grants seem to be made exclusively to Jewish charities.

In 2007 the trust had assets of £7 million and an income of £443,000. Grants were made to 44 organisations totalling £379,000.

The largest grants made included those to: Friends of Tashbar Chazon Ish (£136,000); Emuno Education Centre (£48,000); KSH (£38,000); and SOFT (£33,000).

Smaller grants of less than £10,000 each included those made to: the New

Rachmistrivke Synagogue (£9,000); Trustees of Bais Rizhin Trust and Friends of Horim (£7,700 each); T and S Trust (£5,000); Mercaz Hatorah (£2,000); Stanislow (£1,000); and Kiryat Sanz Jerusalem (£500).

Applications In writing to the correspondent.

The Annie Schiff Charitable Trust

Orthodox Jewish education

£69,000 (2007/08)
Beneficial area UK, overseas.

8 Highfield Gardens, London NW11 3HB
Tel. 020 8458 9266
Correspondent J Pearlman, Trustee
Trustees *J Pearlman; Mrs R Pearlman.*
CC Number 265401
Information available Full accounts were on file at the Charity Commission.

The trust's objectives are:

- relief of poverty, particularly amongst the Jewish community
- advancement of education, particularly the study and instruction of Jewish religious literature
- advancement of religion, particularly Judaism.

In 2007/08 the trust had assets of £244,000 and an income of £69,000. Grants were made to 16 organisations totalling £69,000.

Grant recipients included: Friends of Beis Yisrael Trust (£20,000); Friends of Seret Wiznitz (£7,500); Yeshivo Horomo Talmudical College and Tiferes High School (£5,000 each); Jewish Learning Exchange (£4,000); Menorah Grammar School Trust (£2,000); and Sassoon Memorial (£600).

Exclusions No support for individuals and non-recognised institutions.

Applications In writing to the correspondent. Grants are generally made only to registered charities.

The Schmidt-Bodner Charitable Trust

Jewish and general

£112,000 (2007/08)
Beneficial area UK and overseas.

55 Baker Street, London W1U 7EU
Tel. 020 7486 5888
Correspondent Daniel Dover
Trustees *Daniel Dover; Martin Paisner; Mrs E Schmidt-Bodner.*
CC Number 283014
Information available Full accounts were on file at the Charity Commission.

This trust mainly supports Jewish organisations though it has also given a few small grants to medical and welfare charities. In 2007/08 the trust had assets of £925,000 and an income of £39,000. Grants were made to 12 organisations totalling £112,000.

The largest grants went to: Lubavitch Foundation (£35,000); Nightingale House and Jewish Care (£15,000 each); and World Jewish Relief (£11,000).

Smaller grants of £10,000 or less went to: Community Security Trust and UJIA (£10,000 each); Yesodey Hatorah School (£5,000); HGSS Friends of Lvov (£4,000); British Friends of Or Chadash (£3,000); British Emunah (Child Resettlement Fund) (£2,000); Holocaust Educational Trust (£1,000); and United Synagogue (£250).

Applications In writing to the correspondent.

The R H Scholes Charitable Trust

General, including children and young people who are disabled or disadvantaged, hospices, preservation and churches

£32,000 (2007/08)
Beneficial area England.

Fairacre, Bonfire Hill, Southwater, Horsham RH13 9BU

Email roger@rogpat.plus.com
Correspondent R H C Pattison, Trustee
Trustees *R H C Pattison; Mrs A J Pattison.*
CC Number 267023
Information available Accounts were available from the Charity Commission website.

This trust currently only supports organisations in which the trustees have a special interest, knowledge of or association with. Both recurrent and one-off grants are made depending upon the needs of the beneficiary. Core costs, project and research grants are made. Funding for more than three years will be considered.

In 2007/08 the trust had assets of £795,000 and an income of £225,000. Grants were made to 96 organisations totalling £32,000.

Grants of £1,000 each went to the Church of England Pensions Board, the Friends of Lancing Chapel, Historic Churches Preservation Trust, St Catherine's Hospice, St Luke's Hospital for the Clergy and the Children's Country Holidays Fund. All other grants were between £100 and £800 each.

Exclusions Grants only to registered charities. No grants to individuals, animal charities, expeditions or scholarships. The trust tries not to make grants to more than one charity operating in a particular field, and does not make grants to charities outside England.

Applications Due to a lack of funds the trust is not currently accepting unsolicited applications from organisations it is not already supporting.

The Schreiber Charitable Trust

Jewish with a preference for education, social welfare and medical

£175,000 (2007/08)
Beneficial area UK.

PO Box 35547, The Exchange, 4 Brent Cross Gardens, London NW4 3WH
Email graham@schreibers.com
Correspondent G S Morris, Trustee

301

Trustees *Graham S Morris; David A Schreiber; Sara Schreiber.*

CC Number 264735

Information available Accounts were on file at the Charity Commission.

In 2007/08 the trust had assets of £3.6 million and an unusually large income of £698,000, which was due to a special dividend of £500,000 received from Schreiber Holdings Ltd. Grants were made totalling £175,000.

The largest grants again went to Friends of Rabbinical College Kol Tora Jerusalem (£50,000); SOFT (£12,000); Gateshead Talmudical College (£11,000); and British Friends of Gesher (£10,000).

Smaller grants included those to made to Ner Israel Educational Trust (£9,000); and Aish Hatorah UK Limited, Seed and Menorah High School for Girls (£5,000 each).

Other grants of less than £5,000 totalled £68,000.

Applications The trust states that the trustees 'regularly appraise new opportunities for direct charitable expenditure and actively seek suitable causes to reduce the unrestricted fund to the appropriate level'.

Schroder Charity Trust

Medicine and health, older people, social welfare, education, humanities, arts, environment, international causes and general charitable purposes

£232,000 (2008/09)

Beneficial area Worldwide, in practice mainly UK.

31 Gresham Street, London EC2V 7QA

Correspondent Sally Yates, Secretary

Trustees *Claire Fitzalan Howard; Charmaine Mallinckrodt; Bruno Schroder; T B Schroder; Leonie Fane; Jessica Schroder.*

CC Number 214050

Information available Accounts were available at the Charity Commission.

The trust was established in 1944 and currently makes grants towards medical charities, international relief, social welfare, older people, environment and the arts. Preference is given to UK registered charities with a proven track record or those in which the trust has a special interest.

In 2008/09 the trust had assets of £4.3 million and an income of £182,000. 98 grants were made totalling £232,000.

Beneficiaries included: Royal Chapel – Windsor and Prostate Cancer Research Centre (£25,000 each); Cirencester Parish Church (£15,000); Muscular Dystrophy Campaign (£5,000); Place2Be (£4,000); Tearfund (£3,000); Almshouse Association (£2,000); HemiHelp (£1,500); Children in Crisis (£1,000); and Farms for City Children (£600).

Exclusions No grants to individuals.

Applications In writing to the correspondent. Applicants should briefly state their case and enclose a copy of their latest accounts or annual review. Requests will be acknowledged in writing. The trust does not have the capacity to correspond with organisations on the progress of their application. Therefore, if you have not heard from the trust after six months, you can assume that the application has not been successful.

The Scotshill Trust

General, particularly health, arts, conservation, education, social needs, animal welfare and conservation

£277,000 (2007/08)

Beneficial area UK and overseas.

Trustee Management Limited, 19 Cookridge Street, Leeds LS2 3AG

Tel. 0113 243 6466

Correspondent The Trust Manager

Trustees *Amanda Claire Burton; Paul Howard Burton; Deborah Maureen Hazan; Jeremy John Burton.*

CC Number 1113071

Information available Accounts were on file at the Charity Commission.

Donations are made at the discretion of the trustees and grants are normally made for the following objects:

1) the advance of education of all members of the public in the arts, but in particular those that are disadvantaged by reason of poverty, disability, ill health, youth or age and those attending performing arts colleges
2) to educate the public in matters pertaining to animal welfare in general and the prevention of cruelty and suffering among animals
3) the advancement of education and relief of poverty for those who are disadvantaged by reason of youth, age, ill health, disability, financial hardship or other disadvantage
4) to promote for the benefit of the public the conservation, protection and improvement of the physical and natural environment
5) the advancement of health for the saving of lives
6) such other charitable purposes for the benefit of the community.

In 2007/08 the trust had assets of £5 million and an income of £449,000. Grants to organisations totalled £277,000. There were 36 grants made during the year. Beneficiaries of £1,000 or more included:

Social and welfare (£147,000 in 16 grants)
UJIA (£30,000); Samaritans (£25,000); Crisis (£20,000); Big Issue, Richmond Fellowship and Salvation Army (£10,000 each); Demand and SNAP (£5,000 each); Nightstop (£2,500); and Amber Trust (£1,500).

Developing countries and human rights (£100,000 in 10 grants)
Oxfam (£50,000); Amnesty International, Medical Foundation and Médecins Sans Frontières (£10,000 each); CARE International (£5,000); and Prisoners Abroad (£1,000).

Animal welfare (£13,000 in 4 grants)
Amarderm Research Trust (£10,000); the Horse Trust and Redwings Horse (£1,000 each); and ILPH (£500).

Arts (£10,000 in 2 grants)
Queens Park (£5,000); and SoundAbout (£5,000).

Disability (£8,000 in 4 grants)
Canine Partners (£5,000); Opportunities Trust (£2,000); Pace Centre (£500); and Happy Wonderers (£250).

Exclusions No grants to individuals.

Applications Appeals should be in writing only to the trust managers. Unsuccessful appeals will not necessarily be acknowledged.

Scott (Eredine) Charitable Trust

Service and ex-service charities, medical and welfare

£155,000 (2008)

Beneficial area Not defined.

40 Victoria Embankment, London EC4Y OBA

Correspondent The Trustees

Trustees *M B Scott; K J Bruce-Smith; A J Scott.*

CC Number 1002267

Information available Accounts were on file at the Charity Commission.

Set up in 1999, in 2008 the trust had an income of £169,000 and made 60 grants totalling £155,000.

By far the largest grant went to Scots Guards Charitable Funds (£28,000). Other grants included those to: Hampshire Youth Options (£7,000); Combat Stress (£5,100); Army Benevolent Fund, BLESMA and SSAFA (£4,600 each); the Tall Ships Trust (£3,000); Age Concern and Starlight Children's Foundation (£1,800 each); and the Born Free Foundation, EIA Charitable Trust, Send a Cow and Wheely Boat Trust (£500 each).

Applications In writing to the correspondent.

The Scott Bader Commonwealth Ltd

General

£112,000 (2007)

Beneficial area UK, France, South Africa, Croatia, Dubai, USA, Czech Republic, Sweden, Spain.

Wollaston Hall, Wellingborough NN29 7RL

Tel. 01933 666755 **Fax** 01933 666608

Email commonwealth_office@ scottbader.com

Website www.scottbader.com

Correspondent Sue Carter, Secretary

Trustee *The Board of Management: Angela Miller, Jon Wiles, Celia Clayson,*

Kevin Hendrikse, Richard Stillwell, Heather Puddephatt, Paul Palmer, Sylvia Brown.

CC Number 206391

Information available Accounts were on file at the Charity Commission.

The charity fulfils its objects by making grants to charitable organisations around the world whose purposes are to help young and disadvantaged people, that is, those who suffer deprivation and discrimination. For example, poor, homeless, vulnerable children, women and minority communities and people affected by poverty, hunger and disease.

In 2007 the charity made grants totalling £112,000. The Global Charity Fund is divided into two categories:

Local Funds
The money in this category is shared between the Companies in the Scott Bader Group, for them to support charities where they are located i.e. UK, Eire, France, South Africa, Dubai, Croatia, USA, Czech Republic, Sweden, Spain. Some of the grants made in 2007 were:

- UK – Play Therapy (£5,000); Ro-Ro Sailing Project (£2,000); and June and Brian Cox Educational Trust (£1,000)
- France – continued supporting Kuborroto School, Guinea Bissau and gave aid to the flood victims in Ethopia (£7,000)
- Croatia – Firefly and SNAGA (£2,000 each); and Association of Parents of Children with Special Needs and Croatian Association of the Blind (£1,000)
- Sweden – Handikappidrott Falkenberg who provide sport programmes for the disabled (£400)
- Czech Republic – School of Hearing for Handicapped Children in Liberec (£500)
- Spain – Casa Dels Infants Del Raval, a school for troubled children (£300)
- South Africa – Fulton School for the Deaf (£3,000); Thusang HIV/AIDS Project for Orphans and Open Door Crisis Centre (£1,000 each); and VEMA (£350)
- USA – donations to Children's Museum of Cleveland, Stewart's Caring Place, Big Brothers Big Sisters of Greater Cleveland and the Gathering Place totalled £600
- Dubai – Dubai Cares Campaign (£5,000).

Central Fund
Currently this fund is to support two large community based environmental/ educational projects to the value of £25,000 each. In 2007, Tools for Self Reliance and Children in Crisis – DRC,

received the grants from this fund. The process and deadline for applications is posted on the website at the beginning of each year.

Exclusions No support for charities concerned with the well-being of animals, individuals in need or organisations sending volunteers abroad. It does not respond to general appeals or support the larger well-established national charities. It does not provide grants for medical research. It does not make up deficits already incurred, or support the arts, museums, travel, adventure, sports clubs or the construction, renovation or maintenance of buildings.

Applications In writing or by email to the correspondent. Trustees meet quarterly in February, May, September and November.

Sir Samuel Scott of Yews Trust

Medical research

£107,000 (2007/08)

Beneficial area UK.

c/o Currey and Co, 21 Buckingham Gate, London SW1E 6LS

Tel. 020 7802 2700 **Fax** 020 7828 5049

Correspondent The Secretary

Trustees *Lady Phoebe Scott; Hermione Stanford; Edward Perks.*

CC Number 220878

Information available Accounts were available from the Charity Commission website.

In 2007/08 the trust had assets of £5.4 million and an income of £145,000. There were 30 grants made to organisations totalling £107,000.

The largest grants made included those to: Prostate Cancer Charity (£15,000); Meningitis UK, Royal United Hospital – Bath Cancer Research, BIME – Bath Institute of Medical Engineering and Breast Cancer Campaign (£10,000 each); and British Orthopaedic Association, Islet Research Laboratory NHS Trust, Research into Ageing and RNID (£5,000 each).

Smaller grants of less than £5,000 each included those made to: DebRA (£3,000); Fight for Sight, FSID, Kings College London – Professor Paul Ciclitira (£2,000 each); and Tommy's The Baby Charity, Research Institute for the Care of the Elderly and Foundation for Conductive Education (£1,000 each).

Exclusions No grants for: core funding; purely clinical work; individuals (although research by an individual may be funded if sponsored by a registered charity through which the application is made); research leading to higher degrees (unless the departmental head concerned certifies that the work is of real scientific importance); medical students' elective periods; or expeditions (unless involving an element of genuine medical research).

Applications In writing to the correspondent. Trustees hold their half-yearly meetings in April and October and applications have to be submitted two months before. There are no special forms, but applicants should give the following information: the nature and purpose of the research project or programme; the names, qualifications and present posts of the scientists involved; reference to any published results of their previous research; details of present funding; and if possible, the budget for the next 12 months or other convenient period.

All applications are acknowledged and both successful and unsuccessful applicants are notified after each meeting of the trustees. No telephone calls.

The Scouloudi Foundation

General

£212,000 (2007/08)

Beneficial area UK charities working domestically or overseas.

c/o Haysmacintyre, Fairfax House, 15 Fulwood Place, London WC1V 6AY

Tel. 020 7969 5500 **Fax** 020 7969 5600

Correspondent The Administrators

Trustees *Sarah Stowell; David Marnham; James Sewell.*

CC Number 205685

Information available Full accounts were available from the Charity Commission website.

The foundation has three types of grants:

- Historical grants are made each year to the Institute of Historical Research at University of London for fellowships, research and publications, to reflect the interests of the settlor, Irene Scouloudi, who was a historian

- Regular grants, generally of £1,300 each, are made to organisations on a five-year cycle
- Special grants are one-off grants in connection with capital projects.

In 2007/08 the foundation had assets of £5.9 million and an income of £284,000 generated mostly from investment income. Grants were made totalling £212,000, broken down as follows:

- Humanities – £81,000
- Medicine, health and hospices – £27,000
- Disability – £20,000
- Famine relief and overseas aid – £20,000
- Social welfare – £15,000
- Children and young people – £14,000
- Environment – £8,000
- Older people – £9,000
- Welfare of armed forces and sailors – £10,000.

By far the largest donation was a historical grant made to the University of London – Institute of Historical Research (£81,000).

Other grants included those made to: British Red Cross Disaster Fund (£10,000); Action for Prisoners' Families, Barnardo's, Christina Noble Children's Foundation, Friends of the National Libraries, Gurkha Welfare Trust and Great Ormond Street Hospital (£2,300 each); and Art Fund – National Art Collections Fund, British and International Sailors' Society, British Records Association, Landmark Trust, Shooting Star Children's Hospice, Tree Council, WaterAid and Sightsavers International – Royal Commonwealth Society for the Blind (£1,300 each).

Exclusions Donations are not made to individuals, and are not normally made for welfare activities of a purely local nature. The trustees do not make loans or enter into deeds of covenant.

Applications Only Historical grants are open to application. Copies of the regulations and application forms for 'Historical Awards' can be obtained from: The Secretary, The Scouloudi Foundation Historical Awards Committee, c/o Institute of Historical Research, University of London, Senate House, Malet Street, London WC1E 7HU.

Seamen's Hospital Society

Seafarers

£253,000 to organisations (2007)

Beneficial area UK.

29 King William Walk, Greenwich, London SE10 9HX

Tel. 020 8858 3696 **Fax** 020 8293 9630

Email admin@seahospital.org.uk

Website www.seahospital.org.uk

Correspondent Peter Coulson, General Secretary

Trustees *J Guthrie, Chair; Capt. D Glass; Capt. P M Hambling; J C Jenkinson; Dr J F Leonard; P McEwan; R Chichester; A R Nairne; Capt. A J Speed; S Todd; Capt. C Stewart; G Ellis; J Newton; Dr C Mendes.*

CC Number 231724

Information available Accounts were on file at the Charity Commission.

This trust makes grants to medical, care and welfare organisations working with seafarers and to individual seafarers and their dependants. In 2007 the society had assets of £9.5 million and an income of £495,000. Over £253,000 was distributed to organisations helping seafarers, with a further £101,000 going to individuals.

The largest grant went to the Seafarers' Benefits Advice Line (£128,000) which the society operates to help provide free confidential advice and information on welfare benefits, housing, consumer problems, legal matters, credit and debt, matrimonial and tax.

Other beneficiaries included: NUMAST Welfare Fund – Mariners' Park (£45,000); Merchant Seamen's War Memorial Society and Royal Alfred Seafarers' Society (£25,000 each); Royal National Mission to Deep Sea Fishermen (£13,000); Queen Victoria Seamen's Rest (£10,000); and Mission to Seafarers – Dreadnought Visitor and Scottish Nautical Welfare Society (£4,000 each). Other grants totalled £100.

Applications On a form available from the correspondent. Grants are awarded in November of each year.

The Searchlight Electric Charitable Trust

General

£99,000 (2007/08)

Beneficial area UK, with a preference for Manchester.

Searchlight Electric Ltd, 900 Oldham Road, Manchester M40 2BS

Email heh@slightdemon.co.uk

Correspondent H E Hamburger, Trustee

Trustees *D M Hamburger, Chair; H E Hamburger; M E Hamburger.*

CC Number 801644

Information available Accounts were obtained from the Charity Commission website.

This trust has general charitable purposes, although most grants are given to Jewish organisations. A large number of grants are made in the Manchester area.

In 2007/08 the trust had assets of £1.3 million and an income of £176,000. Grants were made totalling £99,000.

The largest grants included those made to: UJIA (£45,000); CST (£6,000); Bnei a Kivah Sefer Torah (£5,000); Guide Dogs for the Blind (£4,000); Young Israel Synagogue (£2,600); the Federation (£2,000); and Langdon College (£1,500).

Smaller grants of £1,000 or less included those made to: Heathlands, Lubavitch Manchester and Manchester Eruv Committee (£1,000 each); Reshet and the Purim Fund (£750 each); and Sense, Nightingales and Chabad Vilna (£500 each).

Grants of less than £500 totalled £15,000.

Exclusions No grants for individuals.

Applications In writing to the correspondent, but please note that in the past the trustees have stated that it is their policy to only support charities already on their existing list of beneficiaries or those already known to them.

The Searle Charitable Trust

Youth development with a nautical basis

£54,000 (2007/08)

Beneficial area UK.

30 Watling Street, St Albans AL1 2QB

Correspondent Sarah Sharkey

Trustees *Andrew D Searle; Victoria C Searle.*

CC Number 288541

Information available Full accounts were on file at the Charity Commission.

This trust was established in 1982 by Joan Wynne Searle. Following the death of the settlor in 1995 the trust was split into two. One half is administered by the son of the settlor (Searle Charitable Trust) and the other half by her daughter (Searle Memorial Trust).

The Searle Charitable Trust only supports projects/organisations for youth development within a nautical framework.

In 2007/08 the trust had assets of £3.5 million and an income of £118,000. Grants totalled £54,000. By far the largest grant was £53,000 to RONA Trust, also a major beneficiary in previous years. One small grant of £1,000 was made to Royal National Institute for the Deaf.

Exclusions No grants for individuals or for appeals not related to sailing.

Applications In writing to the correspondent.

The Helene Sebba Charitable Trust

Medical, disability and Jewish

£173,000 (2007/08)

Beneficial area UK, Canada and Israel.

PO Box 326, Bedford MK40 3XU

Tel. 01234 266657

Correspondent David L Hull

Trustees *Mrs N C Klein; Mrs J C Sebba; L Sebba.*

CC Number 277245

Information available Full accounts were available from the Charity Commission website.

The trust supports disability, medical and Jewish organisations and in the past has made grants to causes in the UK, Canada and Israel. In 2007/08 the trust had assets of £2.6 million and an income of £65,000. Grants were made totalling £173,000 divided between two categories:

Welfare, health and medical research – 33 grants (£166,000)

The largest grants in this category went to: Menorah Primary School (£40,000); Friends of Israel Sports Centre for the Disabled (£25,000); Ehlers-Danlos and Connective Tissue Disorders Research Fund (£15,000); and Care Education Trust (£10,000).

Smaller grants included those made to: SAS Success After Stroke (£7,000); Ferring Country Centre and AKIM – Wings of Love (£5,000 each); Prostate Cancer Charity (£3,500); Friends of Morris Fienmann Homes and Brainstrust (£3,000 each); Scope and Beth Hayeled (£2,000 each); Breakthrough Breast Cancer and Age Concern (£1,000 each); and AKIM (£500).

Other – 3 grants (£7,000)

Grants went to: Jersey Heritage Trust (£5,000); Royal Geographical Society (£1,500); and National Jewish Chaplaincy (£500).

Applications In writing to the correspondent.

The Seedfield Trust

Christian and relief of poverty

£82,000 (2007)

Beneficial area Worldwide.

3 Woodland Vale, Lakeside, Ulverston LA12 8DR

Tel. 01768 777 377

Correspondent The Trustees

Trustees *Paul Vipond; Keith Buckler; David Ryan; Revd Lionel Osborn; Janet Buckler; Valerie James.*

CC Number 283463

Information available Accounts were on file at the Charity Commission.

The trust's main objects are the furthering of Christian work and the relief of poverty. The trust rarely makes grants towards core funding or for activities that may require funding over a number of years, preferring to make one-off grants for projects which are also receiving support from other sources.

In 2007 the trust had assets of £2.7 million and an income of £106,000. Grants to 33 organisations totalled £82,000.

A small number of beneficiaries favoured by the settlors are supported on a regular basis, including: Dorothea Trust (£11,000); and European Christian Mission, International and Overseas Missionary Fellowship (£10,000 each).

Other grants included those to: Gideons International (£8,000); Mullers (£6,000); Mercy Ships (£5,000); Churches Child Protection Advisory Service (£3,000); Anglo-Peruvian Childcare Mission, Hope 2008 and St Mary's PCC – for Vision Ignition (£2,000 each); Interhealth and Care for the Family (£1,000 each); OMS International (£800); and Christians Against Poverty (£500).

Exclusions No grants to individuals.

Applications In writing to the correspondent, for consideration by the trustees who meet twice each year. Please enclose a stamped, addressed envelope for acknowledgement.

Leslie Sell Charitable Trust

Scout and guide groups

£168,000 (2007/08)

Beneficial area UK and worldwide.

Ashbrittle House, 2a Lower Dagnall Street, St Albans AL3 4PA

Tel. 01727 843 603 **Fax** 01727 843 663

Email admin@iplltd.co.uk

Website www.lesliesellct.org.uk

Correspondent Sharon Long, Secretary

Trustees *Mrs M R Wiltshire; A H Sell; J Byrnes.*

CC Number 258699

Information available Accounts were on file at the Charity Commission.

Established in 1969 by the late Leslie Baden Sell, the trust mainly supports scout and guide groups. Most grants are made towards small projects such as building repair works, transport or equipment. Grants are also available to individuals making trips in the UK and overseas.

In 2007/08 the trust had an income of £179,000 and assets totalling £3 million. Grants were made totalling £168,000. No grants list was available.

Applications In writing to the correspondent. Applications should include clear details of the project or purpose for which funds are required, together with an estimate of total costs and details of any funds raised by the group or individual for the project. The trust states that: 'Applications are usually treated sympathetically provided they are connected to the Scouting or Guide movement'.

Sellata Ltd

Jewish and welfare

£6,500 (2007/08)

Beneficial area UK.

29 Fontayne Road, London N16 7EA

Correspondent E S Benedikt, Trustee

Trustees *E S Benedikt; N Benedikt; P Benedikt; J Stern.*

CC Number 285429

Information available Accounts were on file at the Charity Commission, but without a list of grants.

The trust says it supports the advancement of religion and the relief of poverty. In 2007/08 the trust had assets of £436,000 and an income of £190,000. Grants were made totalling £6,500. A list of beneficiaries was not available.

Applications In writing to the correspondent.

SEM Charitable Trust

General, with a preference for educational special needs and Jewish organisations

£77,000 (2007/08)

Beneficial area Mainly South Africa, Israel and UK.

Reeves and Neylan, 37 St Margaret's Street, Canterbury CT1 2TU

Tel. 01227 768231

Correspondent The Trustees

Trustees *Sarah Radomir; Michael Radomir.*

CC Number 265831

Information available Accounts were available from the Charity Commission website.

The trust operates in two main ways:

- supporting and operating educational and training initiatives in South Africa
- making grants to organisations in the UK and Israel, particularly those supporting educational special needs.

In 2007/08 the trust had assets of £1.2 million and an income of £177,000. A significant amount of this (£55,000) was spent on support costs. Grants were made to 27 organisations totalling £77,000.

Beneficiaries included: Natal Society for Arts (£46,000); Play Action Ltd (£8,000); the Valley Trust (£3,000); Ezrath Nasiim Herzog Hospital (£2,000); Art & Power Community, Council of Kwazulu Natal Jewry and Ipswich Community (£1,000 each); and Local Solutions and Ilan Israel Foundation for Handicapped Children (£500 each).

Exclusions No grants to individuals.

Applications In writing to the correspondent.

The Ayrton Senna Foundation

Children's health and education

£146,000 (2007)

Beneficial area Worldwide, with a preference for Brazil.

8th Floor, 6 New Street Square, London EC4A 3AQ

Tel. 020 7842 2000

Correspondent Christopher Bliss, Trustee

Trustees *Viviane Lalli; Milton Guerado Theodoro da Silva; Neyde Joanna Senna da Silva; Leonardo Senna da Silva; Christopher Bliss; Stephen Howard Ravenscroft.*

CC Number 1041759

Information available Accounts were available from the Charity Commission website.

The trust was established in 1994 by the father of the late Ayrton Senna, in memory of his son, the racing driver. The trust was given the whole issued share capital of Ayrton Senna Foundation Ltd, a company set up to license the continued use of the Senna trademark and copyrights. The trust supports the relief of poverty and the advancement of education, religion and health, particularly the provision of education, healthcare and medical support for children.

In 2007 the trust had assets of £2.7 million, an income of £303,000 and a total expenditure of £234,000. A significant amount of the trust's expenditure (£56,000) was spent on 'governance costs, including foreign exchange movements'. There was one grant made to Instituto Ayrton Senna totalling £146,000.

Exclusions No grants to individuals.

Applications In writing to the correspondent.

The Seven Fifty Trust

Christian

£54,000 (2007/08)
Beneficial area UK and worldwide.

All Saints Vicarage, Church Road, Crowborough TN6 1ED

Tel. 01892 667384

Correspondent Revd Andrew C J Cornes, Trustee

Trustees Rev Andrew C J Cornes; Katherine E Cornes; Peter N Collier; Rev Susan M Collier.

CC Number 298886

Information available Full accounts were on file at the Charity Commission.

This trust is for the advancement of the Christian religion in the UK and throughout the world. In 2007/08 it had assets of £1.9 million and an income of £60,000. Grants were made totalling £54,000.

The largest grant again went to All Saints Church – Crowborough (£15,000). Other beneficiaries included: St Matthew's – Fulham (£4,700); the Langham

Partnership (£4,200); Christian Fellowship (£3,400); Church Mission Society (£2,700); Overseas Missionary Fellowship (£2,600); Care for the Family (£1,700); and Church Resources Ministries (£530).

Exclusions No support for unsolicited requests.

Applications Unsolicited applications will not be considered.

SFIA Educational Trust Limited

Education

£282,000 (2007/08)
Beneficial area UK.

Tectonic Place, Holyport Road, Maidenhead SL6 2YE

Tel. 01628 502040 **Fax** 01628 502049

Email admin@plans-ltd.co.uk

Website www.plans-ltd.co.uk/trusts

Correspondent Anne Feek, Chief Executive

Trustees Beatrice Roberts; Anthony Hastings; David Prince; John Rees; Hugh Monro.

CC Number 270272

Information available Full accounts were available from the Charity Commission website.

The trust is focused on the furtherance of education for children and young people under 18. Grants are only awarded to schools/educational organisations towards bursaries to cover part fees for pupils with the following needs:

- special learning difficulties
- social deprivation
- emotional/behavioural difficulties
- physical disabilities
- gifted in a specialist area
- boarding need.

Grants are also given towards educational projects, books, equipment and school trips to promote the advancement of learning. Grants will only be considered for specific projects. Recipients will be asked to complete a declaration confirming that the funds will be used for the nominated purpose. No applications will be considered from individuals or from schools or

organisations in respect of pupils/students over the age of 18.

In 2007/08 the trust had assets of £5.6 million and an income of £164,000. Grants were made to 80 institutions totalling £282,000 and were divided as follows:

Educational organisations – 50 grants (£154,000)
Grants included those to: Emmott Foundation (£30,000); Frank Buttle Trust (£12,000); Rubella Association (£10,000); Choir Schools' Association (£8,000); Awards for Young Musicians (£5,000); Jessie's Fund (£2,000); Royal London Society for the Blind (£1,000); and Butterflies (£500).

Primary Schools – 7 grants (£6,500)
Beneficiaries included: Puzzle Pre-School (£2,000); Etwall Primary School (£1,000); and Talley County Primary School (£500).

Schools – 23 grants (£121,000)
Grants included those to: King Edward's School Witley (£15,000); Shebbear College (£10,000); Royal Welsh College of Music and Drama (£5,000); and Thomas Hepburn Community School (£1,000).

Exclusions No applications will be considered from individuals or from schools or organisations in respect of pupils/students over the age of 18.

Applications Application forms are available on the trust's website. All applications should be received by 31 January accompanied by the most recent set of audited accounts. Applications are considered in March/April each year. After the meeting, all applicants will be informed of the outcome as soon as possible.

The Cyril Shack Trust

Jewish and general

£85,000 (2007/08)
Beneficial area UK.

c/o Lubbock Fine, Chartered Accountants, Russell Bedford House, City Forum, 250 City Road, London EC1V 2QQ

Tel. 020 7490 7766

Correspondent The Clerk

Trustees J Shack; C C Shack.

CC Number 264270

Information available Accounts were on file at the Charity Commission, but without a list of grants.

In 2007/08 the trust's assets totalled £682,000. It had an income of £74,000 and made grants totalling £85,000. Jewish organisations are mainly supported.

Jewish organisations previously supported have included Finchley Road Synagogue, Nightingale House and St John's Wood Synagogue. UK organisations to benefit have included Breakthrough Breast Cancer, Crisis, Golf Aid, Hampstead Theatre, Hartsbourne Ladies Charity, London Library, Prisoners of Conscience, Samaritans, St John's Hospice and University of the Third Age – London.

Exclusions No grants for expeditions, travel bursaries, scholarships or to individuals.

Applications In writing to the correspondent.

The Jean Shanks Foundation

Medical research and education

£307,000 (2007/08)

Beneficial area UK.

Peppard Cottage, Peppard Common, Henley on Thames RG9 5LB

Email barbara.sears@ukgateway.net

Website jeanshanksfoundation.org

Correspondent Mrs B Sears

Trustees *Prof. Sir Dillwyn Williams; Dr Julian Axe; Alistair Jones; Eric Rothbarth; Prof. Dame Lesley Rees; Prof. Andrew Carr; Prof. Sir James Underwood; Prof. Sir Nicholas Wright.*

CC Number 293108

Information available Accounts were on file at the Charity Commission.

Registered with the Charity Commission in November 1985 this foundation supports medical research and education, particularly in the area of pathology. Grants are made to fund medical students who wish to have an extra research year at medical school and also to other research projects the trustees consider worthwhile.

In 2007/08 the foundation had assets amounting to £16 million and an

income of £725,000. Grants were made to 31 institutions totalling £307,000.

The largest grants went to: Royal London Hospital (£50,000); Royal College of Pathologists (£42,000); University of Oxford (£30,000); University of Cambridge (£20,000); and University of Leeds and University of Leicester (£15,000 each).

Grants of £7,500 each went to: Keele University, St George's, University of London, Queen's University Belfast, Brighton and Sussex Medical School and University of Manchester.

Exclusions No grants for capital items. No grants for research which is already supported by another grant-giving body or for projects of the type normally dealt with by bodies such as the MRC or Wellcome Trust.

Applications In writing to the correspondent. Please note: full grant guidelines are available on the foundation's website.

The Shanley Charitable Trust

Relief of poverty

£55,000 (2007/08)

Beneficial area Worldwide.

Knowles Benning Solicitors, 32 High Street, Shefford SG17 5DG

Correspondent S J Atkins, Trustee

Trustees *C A Shanley; R F Lander; S J Atkins.*

CC Number 1103323

Information available Accounts were on file at the Charity Commission, without a list of grants.

In 2007/08 the trust had assets of £1.4 million, an income of £70,000 and made grants totalling £55,000.

Applications In writing to the correspondent.

The Shanti Charitable Trust

General, Christian and international development

£185,000 (2007/08)

Beneficial area UK, with preference for West Yorkshire, and developing countries (especially Nepal).

Baker Tilly, The Waterfront, Salts Mill Road, Saltaire, Shipley BD17 7EZ

Tel. 01274 536 400

Correspondent Timothy Parr, Trustee

Trustees *Barbara Gill; Timothy Parr; Ross Hyett.*

CC Number 1064813

Information available Accounts were available from the Charity Commission website.

This trust is a long-term supporter of the International Nepal Fellowship, although other funding is given. The trust states that most of the beneficiaries are those which the trustees already have links with and this priority also influences them in giving to local branches of national organisations.

In 2007/08 the trust had assets of £220,000 and an income of £151,000. Grants were made to 17 organisations totalling £185,000.

The largest grant was made to St John's Church – Aiden Project (£100,000).

Other grants were made to: Missionaries of Charity (£40,000); International Nepal Fellowship (£12,000); Protac/Theotac, Nepal (£8,000); Development Associates International and CBRS (£5,000 each); Tear Fund (£3,000); Urban Vision (£2,500); Sue Ryder – Manorlands (£1,000); and Kidz Klub Bradford and Nepal Leprosy Trust (£500 each).

Exclusions No grants to gap year students, or political or animal welfare causes.

Applications In writing to the correspondent. Please note: most beneficiaries are those the trustees already have contact with.

The Linley Shaw Foundation

Conservation

£79,500 (2007/08)
Beneficial area UK.

Natwest Trust Services, 5th Floor, Trinity Quay 2, Avon Street, Bristol BS2 0PT
Tel. 0117 940 3283 **Fax** 0117 940 3275
Correspondent The Trust Section
Trustee *National Westminster Bank plc.*
CC Number 1034051
Information available Brief accounts available at the Charity Commission

The foundation supports charities working to conserve, preserve and restore the natural beauty of the UK countryside for the public benefit.

Generally the trustees prefer to support a specific project, rather than give money for general use. In his will, Linley Shaw placed particular emphasis on those charities which organise voluntary workers to achieve the objects of the foundation. This may be taken into account when considering applications. Grants can be given towards any aspect of a project. Previous examples include the cost of tools, management surveys and assistance with the cost of land purchase.

In 2007/08 the trust had assets of £1.5 million and an income of £62,000. Grants were made totalling £79,500. Beneficiaries included: Durham Wildlife; Gazen Salts Nature Reserve; Little Ouse Project; and Wales Wildlife Trust.

Exclusions No grants to non-charitable organisations, or to organisations whose aims or objects do not include conservation, preservation or restoration of the natural beauty of the UK countryside, even if the purpose of the grant would be eligible. No grants to individuals.

Applications In writing to the correspondent. All material will be photocopied by the trust so please avoid sending 'bound' copies of reports and so on. Evidence of aims and objectives are needed, usually in the forms of accounts, annual reports or leaflets, which cannot be returned. Applications are considered in February/early March and should be received by December/early January.

The Sheldon Trust

General

£171,000 (2007/08)
Beneficial area West Midlands.

White Horse Court, 25c North Street, Bishop's Stortford CM23 2LD
Tel. 01279 506 421
Email charities@pwwsolicitors.co.uk
Website www.pwwsolicitors.co.uk
Correspondent The Trust Administrator
Trustees *Mrs R M Bagshaw; A Bidnell; Revd R S Bidnell; J K R England; R V Wiglesworth; Mrs R Beatton; Mrs R Gibbins.*
CC Number 242328
Information available Full accounts were on file at the Charity Commission.

The trust's geographical area of giving is the West Midlands, with particular emphasis on the areas of Birmingham, Coventry, Dudley, Sandwell, Solihull, Wolverhampton and Warwickshire. The main aims continue to be the relief of poverty and distress in society, concentrating grants on community projects as well as those directed to special needs groups, especially in deprived areas. The trustees review their policy and criteria regularly and 'although they have a central policy, flexibility is retained to allow for reaction to changes in the environment and the community alike'.

In 2007/08 the trust had assets of £3.8 million, which generated an income of £194,000. Grants were made to 38 organisations totalling £171,000. The average grant size was £4,000.

Grants were broken down in the accounts as follows:

Holiday projects – Grants of £4,000 each for holiday projects were awarded to: Bethany Christian Fellowship, Birmingham Phab Camps, Harvest Trust, Vitalise, African Caribbean Community Initiative, Barton Training Trust, Birmingham Mental Health Leisure Forum and Kids Adventure.

Grants for special needs groups – Beneficiaries included: Birmingham Centre for Arts Therapies, Birmingham Rathbone Society and Birmingham Focus on Blindness (£5,000 each); Sound It Out Community Music and the Living Paintings Trust (£4,000 each); Edward's Trust (£3,400); Solihull Action Through Advocacy (£2,800); and Dystonia Society (£1,300).

Community Projects – Organisations supported during the year included: Edenbridge Music and Arts (£5,000); Great Bridge Community Forum (£4,700); Home-Start Dudley, Warwickshire Clubs for Young People and Age Concern Dudley (£3,000 each); and the Friendship Project for Children (£2,000).

Continuing Grants – Six new continuing grants were approved by the Trustees: St Basils, Nuneaton and Bedworth Doorway and Sutton Coldfield YMCA (£15,000 each); Wolverhampton Asylum Seeker and Refugee Services (£9,000); St James Community Support and Advice Centre (£6,000); and Acorn Trust (£3,000).

One Special Grant of £5,000 was also made to Shelterbox, who provide humanitarian aid worldwide.

Exclusions The trust does not consider general appeals from national organisations and does not usually consider appeals in respect of the cost of buildings.

Applications Application forms are available from the correspondent but the trust prefers applicants to complete and submit their application online. The trustees meet three times a year, in April, August and November. Application forms, including the most recent signed accounts, a project budget and a job description (if applying for a salary) should be received at least six weeks before the date of the next meeting.

Successful organisations will be sent a grant offer and any conditions. Unsuccessful applicants will have to wait two years before re-applying.

Please note: a designated sum is set aside for the holiday grants programme and applications are considered in April each year. Applications should be submitted by the end of February.

P and D Shepherd Charitable Trust

General

£199,000 to organisations (2007/08)
Beneficial area Worldwide, particularly the north of England and Scotland.

5 Cherry Lane, Dringhouses, York
YO24 1QH

Correspondent The Trustees

Trustees *Mrs P Shepherd; Mrs
J L Robertson; Patrick M Shepherd;
D R Reaston; I O Robertson; Mrs
C M Shepherd; M J Shepherd;
J O Shepherd; R O Robertson.*

CC Number 272948

Information available Full accounts
were on file at the Charity Commission.

The trust makes grants through
charitable organisations to benefit people
in need and society in general. There is a
preference for supporting charities in the
north of England and Scotland, or those
connected with the trustees.

In 2007/08 the trust had assets of
£520,000 and an income of £146,000.
Grants were made to organisations
totalling almost £199,000 and one grant
of £70 was made to an individual.

Beneficiaries of grants of £1,000 or more
during this period included: St Peter's
School Foundation (£100,000);
St Edward the Confessor Church
(£25,000); Henshaw's College (£10,000);
Army Cadet Fund, York Minster Fund
and Yorkshire Cadet Trust (£5,000
each); and Hearing Dogs for the Deaf
(£1,000).

Applications In writing to the
correspondent.

The Archie Sherman Cardiff Foundation

Health, education, training, overseas aid, community and Jewish

£125,000 (2007/08)

Beneficial area UK, Canada,
Australia, New Zealand, Pakistan, Sri
Lanka, South Africa, India, Israel, USA
and other parts of the British
Commonwealth.

Rothschild Trust Corp Ltd, New Court,
St Swithins Lane, London EC4P 4DU

Tel. 020 7280 5000

Correspondent The Trustees

Trustee *Rothschild Trust Corporation
Ltd.*

CC Number 272225

Information available Full accounts
were available from the Charity
Commission website.

Established in 1976, this foundation
supports health and educational charities
in the UK and overseas. The foundation
is empowered to distribute its income as
it sees fit but it tends to pay special
regard to the following organisations:
Society of Friends of the Jewish
Refugees, UJIA, British Organisation for
Rehabilitation and Training, JNF
Charitable Trust, British Council of the
Shaare Zedek Hospital, British Technion
Society and Friends of the Hebrew
University.

In 2007/08 the foundation had assets of
£2.5 million and an income of £165,000.
Grants were made totalling £125,000,
broken down as follows:

**Education and training – 1 grant
(£35,000)**
Friends of the Hebrew University of
Jerusalem.

Overseas aid – 3 grants (£80,000)
Beneficiaries were: JNF Charitable Trust
(£48,000); Tel Aviv Foundation
(£20,000); and WIZO (£12,000).

Community – 1 grant (£10,000)
Central British Fund for World Jewish
Relief.

Exclusions No grants to individuals.

Applications In writing to the
correspondent.

The Barnett and Sylvia Shine No 2 Charitable Trust

General

£45,000 (2007/08)

Beneficial area Worldwide.

Berwin Leiton Paisner, Adelaide House,
London Bridge, London EC4R 9HA

Tel. 020 7760 1000 **Fax** 020 7760 1111

Correspondent M D Paisner, Trustee

Trustees *M D Paisner; Barbara
J Grahame; Prof R Grahame.*

CC Number 281821

Information available Accounts were
on file at the Charity Commission.

In 1980, half the assets of the No 1
Charitable Trust (see separate entry)

were transferred to the No 2 Charitable
Trust. In 1981, the executors of the
estate of the late Sylvia Shine transferred
several paintings, jewellery and cash to
the trusts. The No 2 fund has some
preference for organisations working
with children and young adults, older
people and people with disabilities.

In 2007/08 the trust had assets of
£1.3 million and an income of £59,000.
One grant was made to the One-to-One
Children's Fund – Vygrond Community
Development Trust totalling £45,000.

Exclusions No grants to individuals.

Applications In writing to the
correspondent.

The Bassil Shippam and Alsford Trust

Young and older people, health, education, learning disabilities and Christian

£158,000 to organisations and
individuals (2007/08)

Beneficial area UK, with a
preference for West Sussex.

Thomas Eggar, The Corn Exchange,
Baffins Lane, Chichester PO19 1GE

Tel. 01243 786111 **Fax** 01243 775640

Correspondent Simon MacFarlane,
Clerk to the Trustees

Trustees *J H S Shippam; C W Doman;
S A E MacFarlane; S W Young; Mrs
M Hanwell; R Tayler; Mrs S Trayler.*

CC Number 256996

Information available Full accounts
were available from the Charity
Commission website.

This trust supports charities active in the
fields of care for young and older people,
health, education and religion. Many of
the organisations supported are in West
Sussex. In 2007/08 the trust had assets of
£3.8 million and an income of £136,000.
Grants were made totalling £158,000.

The largest grants included those made
to: Chichester Boys Club (£38,000);
Donnington House Care Home Ltd.
(£12,000); Friends of Cobnor (£9,000);
Outset Youth Action South West Sussex
(£7,200); St Wilfrid's Hospice (£5,000);
Christian Care Association (£4,000);

West Sussex Learning Links (£2,000); and Life Education Centre (£1,000).

Grants of £500 or less included those made to: Chichester Art Trust, Careforce and Bognor Regis Youth Wing (£500 each); Scripture Union (£300); Bognor Can, Dreams Come True and Bikeability (£250 each); and Wellspring West Sussex (£100).

Applications In writing to the correspondent, including a copy of the latest set of reports, accounts and forecasts. The trustees meet three times a year to consider applications.

The Shipwrights' Company Charitable Fund

Maritime or waterborne connected charities

Around £100,000 (2007/08)

Beneficial area UK, with a preference for the City of London.

Ironmongers' Hall, Shaftesbury Place, Barbican, London EC2Y 8AA

Tel. 020 7606 2376 **Fax** 020 7600 8117

Email clerk@shipwrights.co.uk

Website www.shipwrights.co.uk

Correspondent The Clerk

Trustees *The Worshipful Company of Shipwrights; Richard Sayer; Simon Sherrard; Sir Jock Slater; Alan Marsh; The Hon. Jeffery Evans; Graham Clarke.*

CC Number 262043

Information available Accounts were available from the Charity Commission.

The Shipwrights' Company is a Livery Company of the City of London and draws its members from all the various aspects of marine commerce and industry in the UK. Its charitable interests therefore focus on the maritime, with an emphasis on young people, church work and the City.

Applications from individuals or, for example, schools to join sail training voyages are considered. It supports sailing for people with disabilities, with both the Jubilee Sailing Trust and the Challenger class.

In 2007/08 the trust had assets of £2.8 million and an income of £392,000.

Grants to organisations and individuals totalled around £100,000 and are categorised as general donations and outdoor activity bursaries.

Grant recipients included: Sea Cadets, Sea Scout Association, Cutty Sark Trust, Fairbridge Volunteer Bosun Traineeship, Royal Society of Marine Artists, Westminster Boating Base, Meridian Trust Association, British Maritime Federation and Ahoy Centre.

Exclusions Any application without a clear maritime connection.

Applications In writing to the correspondent. Applications and guidelines are available from the trust's website. Applications are considered in February, June and November.

The Charles Shorto Charitable Trust

General

£163,000 (2007/08)

Beneficial area UK.

c/o Taylors, Mercury House, 1 Mason Road, Redditch B97 5DA

Tel. 01527 544 221

Email tom@taylorssolicitors.com

Correspondent T J J Baxter

Trustees *Joseph A V Blackham; Brian M Dent.*

CC Number 1069995

Information available Accounts were on file at the Charity Commission.

This trust was established under the will of Edward Herbert Charles Shorto with general charitable purposes. Whilst welcoming applications, the trustees also like to identify causes that they know Charles Shorto had an interest in.

In 2007/08 the trust had assets of £4.5 million, which generated an income of £211,000. Management and administration expenses were quite high at £59,000. Grants were made to 15 organisations totalling £163,000.

The largest grants were made to: Arnold Foundation for Rugby School (£53,000); Oxford Youth Works (£35,000); Cumnor PCC (£29,000); and Exmouth & District Community Transport Group (£10,000).

Smaller grants went to: All Saints Church East Budleigh (£5,200); Brecon

Cathedral Choir Endowment Fund (£5,000); St Basils (£2,000); and Extra Care Charitable Trust – Coventry, Warwickshire & Northamptonshire Air Ambulance and Grassland Trust (£1,000 each).

Applications In writing to the correspondent at any time. The trustees meet four times a year.

The Barbara A Shuttleworth Memorial Trust

People with disabilities

£42,000 (2007/08)

Beneficial area UK, with a preference for West Yorkshire.

Baty Casson Long, Shear's Yard, 21 Wharf Street, The Calls, Leeds LS2 7EQ

Tel. 0113 242 5848 **Fax** 0013 247 0342

Email baty@btinternet.com

Correspondent John Baty, Chair

Trustees *John Alistair Baty, Chair; Barbara Anne Shuttleworth; John Christopher Joseph Eaton; William Fenton.*

CC Number 1016117

Information available Information was obtained from the Charity Commission website.

The trust gives grants to organisations that aim to improve the circumstances of people who are disabled, and particularly those helping children. The trust prefers to make grants for what it calls 'hard' benefits such as equipment, premises or other permanent facilities but it will consider funding 'soft' benefits like holidays, training courses and visits.

In 2007/08 the trust had assets of £526,000 and an income of £25,000. Grants were made totalling £42,000.

Beneficiaries included: National Deaf Children's Society (£2,300); Chapel Grange Special School and Children's Liver Disease Foundation (£2,000 each); Aidis Trust (£1,500); United Response – York and Sunny Days Children's Charity (£1,000 each); St James's Hospital for 'Chemo Ducks' (£900); Muscular Dystrophy Group (£600); Symbol Trust (£500); Rutland House School for Parents (£350); and British Diabetic Association (£250).

311

Applications In writing to the correspondent.

The Leslie Silver Charitable Trust

Jewish and general

£129,000 (2007/08)

Beneficial area UK, but mostly West Yorkshire.

Bentley Jennison, 2 Wellington Place, Leeds LS1 4AP

Tel. 0113 244 5451 **Fax** 0113 242 6308

Correspondent Ian J Fraser, Trustee

Trustees *Leslie H Silver; Mark S Silver; Ian J Fraser.*

CC Number 1007599

Information available Full accounts were available from the Charity Commission website.

This trust principally supports Jewish-based charities and appeal funds launched in the West Yorkshire area. In 2007/08 the trust had assets of £547,000 and an income of £27,000. Grants were made totalling £129,000.

The largest grants included those made to: Donisthorpe Hall (£55,000); Leeds Centre for Deaf and Blind People (£16,000); and Holocaust Centre and Variety Club Children's Charity (£10,000 each).

Other grants included those made to: UJIA and Jewish National Fund (£5,000 each); the Zone (£4,000); Children in Crisis and Lord Mayor's Charity Appeal (£2,000 each); Second World War Experience (£1,000); and Holocaust Educational Trust (£500).

Exclusions No grants to individuals or students.

Applications In writing to the correspondent following a specific format. Please note: the trust has previously stated that, 'the recipients of donations are restricted almost exclusively to the concerns in which the trustees take a personal interest and that unsolicited requests from other sources, although considered by the trustees, are rejected almost invariably'.

The Simpson Education and Conservation Trust

Environmental conservation

£64,000 (2007/08)

Beneficial area UK and overseas, with a preference for the neotropics (South America).

Honeysuckle Cottage, Tidenham Chase, Chepstow, Gwent NP16 7JW

Tel. 01291 689423 **Fax** 01291 689803

Correspondent N Simpson, Chair

Trustees *Dr R N F Simpson, Chair; Prof. D M Broom; Dr J M Lock; Prof. S Chang; Dr K A Simpson.*

CC Number 1069695

Information available Accounts were on file at the Charity Commission.

Established in 1998, the main objectives of this trust are:

- the advancement of education in the UK and overseas, including medical and scientific research
- the conservation and protection of the natural environment and endangered species of plants and animals with special emphasis on the protection of forests and endangered avifauna in the neotropics (South America).

The trust receives its income from Gift Aid donations, which totalled £76,000 in 2007/08. Its priority for this year was again to support the Jocotoco Foundation in Equador. This charity is dedicated to the conservation of endangered special birds through the acquisition of forest habitat. The chair of this trust, Dr RNF Simpson, an expert in ornithology and conservation, is also on the board of trustees for Jocotoco Conservation Foundation (JCF).

In 2007/08 JCF received a grant of £62,000. Grants of £1,000 were also made to Lord Trealor Trust and Friends of RBG Kew (for Tanzania).

Exclusions No grants to individuals.

Applications In writing to the correspondent. The day-to-day activities of this trust are carried out by email, telephone and circulation of documents, since the trustees do not all live in the UK.

The Simpson Foundation

Roman Catholic

Around £25,000 (2007/08)

Beneficial area UK.

70 St George's Square, London SW1V 3RD

Tel. 020 7821 8211 **Fax** 020 7630 6484

Correspondent P J O Herschan, Trustee

Trustees *C E T Bellord; P J M Hawthorne; P J O Herschan.*

CC Number 231030

Information available Accounts on file at the Charity Commission.

The trust supports charities favoured by the founder in his lifetime and others with similar objects; mainly Catholic charities. Only registered charities are supported.

In 2007/08 it had an income of £18,000 and a total expenditure of £30,000. No information on grant beneficiaries for this year was available.

Beneficiaries in previous years have included: Venerable Collegio Inglese, St Benedict's Abbey, Sisters of Charity of Jesus and Mary, The Access Partnership, Congregation of the Blessed Sacrament and Providence Row Night Refuge and Home.

Exclusions No grants to non-registered charities or individuals.

Applications In writing to the correspondent, at any time. No telephone applications will be considered.

The Huntly and Margery Sinclair Charitable Trust

General

£39,000 (2007/08)

Beneficial area UK.

c/o Vernor-Miles and Noble Solicitors, 5 Raymond Buildings, Gray's Inn, London WC1R 5DD

Tel. 020 7242 8688 **Fax** 020 7242 3192

Email wilfridvm@vmn.org.uk

Correspondent Wilfrid Vernor-Miles, Administrator

Trustees *Mrs A M H Gibbs; Mrs M A H Windsor; Mrs J Floyd.*

CC Number 235939

Information available Full accounts were available from the Charity Commission website.

This trust has general charitable purposes at the discretion of the trustees. However, the trust states that nearly all grants are made to organisations already known to the trustees so unsolicited applications are rarely successful.

In 2007/08 the trust had assets of £1.3 million and an income of £48,000. Grants were made to 31 organisations totalling £39,000.

Recipients of the largest grants included: Priors Court School (£6,000); Starlight Children's Fund and St Patrick's Catholic Church (£3,000 each); Old Etonian Masonic Lodge (£2,000); and Eddies, PDSA and County Air Ambulance (£1,000 each).

Smaller donations of less than £1,000 went to: Army Benevolent Fund and NSPCC (£500 each); Elkstone Church PCC (£400); Coeliac (£350); and Breast Cancer Haven (£200).

Applications Unsolicited applications are rarely successful and due to the high number of such requests, the trust is not able to respond to them or return any printed materials supplied.

Sino-British Fellowship Trust

Education

£263,000 (2007)

Beneficial area UK and China.

Flat 23 Bede House, Manor Fields, London SW15 3LT

Tel. 020 8788 6252

Correspondent Mrs Anne Ely

Trustees *Prof. H D R Baker; Mrs A E Ely; P J Ely; Prof. Sir B Heap; Dr J A Langton; Mrs L Thompson; Prof. Sir D Todd; Lady P Youde.*

CC Number 313669

Information available Full accounts were available from the Charity Commission website.

The trust makes grants to institutions benefiting individual postgraduate students. It does this through: scholarships to Chinese citizens to enable them to pursue their studies in Britain;

grants to British citizens in China to educate/train Chinese citizens in any art, science or profession.

In 2007 the trust had assets of £13 million and an income of £553,000. Grants were made totalling £316,000. Grants were divided between British and Chinese organisations:

UK Institutions – 8 grants (£187,000)
Grants went to: Royal Society (£82,000); British Library (£23,000); British Academy and Universities China Committee (£20,000 each); Great Britain China Educational Trust and School of Oriental & African Studies (£15,000 each); Needham Research Institute (£6,800); Institute of Archaeology (£6,000).

Overseas Institutions – 5 grants (£76,000)
Grants went to: China Scholarship Council (£21,000); Chinese University of Hong Kong and Open University of Hong Kong (£16,500 each); Hong Kong University (£15,000); and Lingnan University (£7,500).

Grants totalling £38,000 were also made to individuals.

Applications On a form available by writing to the address below.

The Charles Skey Charitable Trust

General

£114,000 (2007/08)

Beneficial area UK.

Flint House, Park Homer Road, Colehill, Wimborne BH21 2SP

Correspondent J M Leggett, Trustee

Trustees *C H A Skey, Chair; J M Leggett; C B Berkeley; Revd J H A Leggett.*

CC Number 277697

Information available Accounts were available from the Charity Commission website.

The trust's 2007/08 annual report states: 'The trustees support causes on an annual basis, irregularly and on a one-off basis. For those charities receiving annual donations, the amount to be given is reviewed annually. For those receiving periodic donations, the trustees are the judge of when a further grant should be made. For one-off donations,

the trustees examine the requests which have been received and have sole authority as to which to support. In general, the trust supports those causes where the grant made is meaningful to the recipient'.

In 2007/08 the trust had assets of £3.2 million and an income of £234,000. Grants were made totalling £114,000 and were broken down as follows:

Education, training, medical, health, sickness and disability – 27 grants
Beneficiaries included: Lloyds Patriotic Fund (£60,000); Trinity Hospice (£7,500); Children's Trust (£5,000); Stepping Stones Trust (£4,500); Camphill Village Trust (£3,000); St Dunstans (£2,000); Poole Hospital NHS Trust and Institute of Cancer Research (£1,000 each); and Salisbury Spinal Injuries Trust (£500).

General purposes – 2 grants
Grants went to the Christian Care Association and the Royal British Legion (£2,000 each).

Environmental, conservation and heritage – 3 grants
Grants went to: Roses Charitable Trust (£4,000); Water Aid (£2,000); and Heritage of London Trust (£1,000).

Religious activities – 1 grant
The sole beneficiary was the Dagenham Gospel Trust (£1,000).

Applications The trust has previously stated that no written or telephoned requests for support will be entertained.

The John Slater Foundation

Medical, animal welfare and general

£177,000 (2007/08)

Beneficial area UK, with a strong preference for the north west of England especially West Lancashire.

HSBC Trust Services, 10th Floor, Norwich House, Nelson Gate, Commercial Road, Southampton SO15 1GX

Tel. 023 8072 2231 **Fax** 023 8072 2250

Correspondent Colin Bould

Trustee *HSBC Trust Co. Ltd.*

CC Number 231145

Information available Accounts were obtained from the Charity Commission website.

The foundation gives grants for £1,000 to £5,000 to a range of organisations, particularly those working in the fields of medicine or animal welfare.

In 2007/08 it had assets of £3.9 million and an income of £153,000. Grants were made to 99 organisations totalling £177,000.

Beneficiaries included: Blackpool Ladies Sick Poor Association (£9,100); Grand Theatre Blackpool (£7,300); Adlington Community Centre (£7,200); Bury Grammar School for Girls (£5,500); Fleetwood and Wyre Mencap (£3,700); Redwings Horse Sanctuary, Cancer Care – Lancaster, Liverpool School for Tropical Medicine and Christ's Church – Thornton (£1,800 each); and Mersey Inshore Rescue (£1,000).

Exclusions No grants to individuals.

Applications In writing to the correspondent, including accounts. Applications are considered twice a year, in May and November.

Rita and David Slowe Charitable Trust

General

£68,000 (2007/08)
Beneficial area UK and overseas.

32 Hampstead High Street, London NW3 1JQ
Tel. 020 7435 7800
Correspondent R L Slowe, Trustee
Trustees *R L Slowe; Mrs E H Douglas; J L Slowe; G Weinberg.*
CC Number 1048209
Information available Full accounts were available from the Charity Commission.

The trust makes grants to a range of registered charities. In 2007/08 the trust had an income of £64,000 and made grants to nine organisations totalling £68,000. Its assets stood at £652,000.

Grants went to: Shelter (£13,000); Computer Aid International, David Baum Foundation and Big Issue Foundation (£10,000 each); Wells for India, Action Aid, Books Abroad, Excellent Development and Send a Cow (£5,000 each).

Exclusions No grants are made to individuals (including gap year students) or religious bodies.

Applications In writing to the correspondent.

The SMB Charitable Trust

Christian and general

£201,000 (2007/08)
Beneficial area UK and overseas.

15 Wilman Rd, Tunbridge Wells TN4 9AJ
Tel. 01892 537 301 **Fax** 01892 618 202
Correspondent Mrs B M O'Driscoll, Trustee
Trustees *E D Anstead; P J Stanford; Barbara O'Driscoll; J A Anstead; Claire Swarbrick.*
CC Number 263814
Information available Accounts were on file at the Charity Commission.

The trust supports charities which meet one of the following criteria:

- support of the Christian faith
- provision of social care in the UK and abroad
- provision of famine or emergency aid
- protection of the environment and wildlife
- support of education or medical research.

Grants are generally of £1,000 each, although this can vary. The trustees make regular grants to a large number of 'core' charities, so while new applications are considered, only a small minority are likely to be successful. The founder's preferences are taken into account when deciding which of the applicants will be supported.

In 2007/08 the trust had assets of £8.8 million and an income of £335,000. Grants were made to over 150 organisations totalling £201,000.

Beneficiaries included: London City Mission and Pilgrim Homes (£4,000 each); Salvation Army and Hope Now (£3,000 each); Baptist Missionary Society and British Red Cross (£2,500 each); All Nations Christian College, Dentaid and Scripture Union (£2,000 each); Shaftesbury Society (£1,500); People International (£1,000); and St Andrews Leyland (£500).

Exclusions Grants to individuals are not normally considered, unless the application is made through a registered charity which can receive the cheque.

Applications In writing to the correspondent, including the aims and principal activities of the applicant, the current financial position and details of any special projects for which funding is sought. Application forms are not used. Trustees normally meet in March, June, September and December and applications should be received before the beginning of the month in which meetings are held. Because of the volume of appeals received, unsuccessful applicants will only receive a reply if they enclose a stamped, addressed envelope. Unsuccessful applicants are welcome to reapply.

The N Smith Charitable Settlement

General including social work, medical research, education, environment, animals, arts and overseas aid

£162,000 (2007/08)
Beneficial area Worldwide.

Linder Myers, Phoenix House, 45 Cross Street, Manchester M2 4JF
Tel. 0161 832 6972 **Fax** 0161 834 0718
Correspondent Anne E Merricks
Trustees *T R Kendal; Miss A E Merricks; J H Williams-Rigby; G Wardle.*
CC Number 276660
Information available Full accounts were available from the Charity Commission website.

This trust was established in 1978. In 2007/08 the trust had assets of £4.2 million and an income of £168,000. Grants were made totalling £162,000 and were broken down into the following categories:

Social work – £59,000
Beneficiaries included: Action For Kids and Contact a Family (£750 each); Beechwood Cancer Care Centre (£650); Deafway and Core (£550 each); and Rainbow Centre for Children (£500).

Overseas aid – £47,000
Grants made included those to: Oxfam GB (£5,000); Books Abroad, ChildHope and Tree Aid (£1,000 each); and Y Care International (£750).

Medical research – £35,000
Alzheimer's Research Trust, Christie Hospital NHS Trust, Brain Research Trust, Deafness Research UK, Leukaemia Research Fund, Genesis Appeal and Tommy's Campaign all received £2,000 each.

Education – £9,000
Grants were made to British Dyslexics, John Rylands University Library, National Institute for Conductive Education and Manchester Outward Bound Association (£1,000 each).

Arts – £7,000
Beneficiaries included: Masterclass Media Foundation (£1,000); Artlink, Derby Playhouse and Rehearsal Orchestra (£600 each); and Birmingham Royal Ballet (£500).

Environment and animals – £6,300
Grants went to Soil Association (£750) and WWF-UK, Royal Botanic Gardens Kew and Fauna and Flora International (£500 each).

Exclusions Grants are only made to registered charities and not to individuals.

Applications In writing to the correspondent. The trustees meet twice a year.

The Amanda Smith Charitable Trust

General

Around £25,000 (2008)
Beneficial area UK.

1 Manchester Square, London W1U 3AB
Tel. 020 3219 2600
Correspondent Neil Bradley
Trustees *C Smith, Chair; Ms A Smith.*
CC Number 1052975
Information available Information was obtained from the Charity Commission website.

This trust was established in 1996. The trust's income is derived mainly from the rent of a shopping centre and a housing estate. The trust stated that this

is gradually decreasing. The trust makes grants irregularly.

In 2008 the trust had an income of just £19 and a total expenditure of £36,000. Further information was not available. Previous beneficiaries have included Cedar School and Nordoff Robbins Music Therapy.

Applications In writing to the correspondent.

The Smith Charitable Trust

General

£124,000 (2007/08)
Beneficial area UK and overseas.

c/o Moon Beever, Solicitors, 24 Bloomsbury Square, London WC1A 2PL
Tel. 020 7637 0661
Correspondent Paul Shiels, Trustee
Trustees *A G F Fuller; P A Sheils; R I Turner; R J Weetch.*
CC Number 288570
Information available Accounts were available from the Charity Commission website.

The trust supports registered charities, which are usually larger well-known UK organisations. Beneficiaries are chosen by the settlor and he has a set list of charities that are supported twice a year. Other charities are unlikely to receive a grant.

In 2007/08 the trust had assets of £5.1 million and an income of £89,000. Grants were made totalling £124,000.

Grants included those made to: Sue Ryder Care (£12,000); Research Institute for the Care of the Elderly and Macmillan Cancer Relief (£8,000 each); St Nicholas' Hospice and NCH (£6,000 each); and the Marine Society and Sea Cadets, MIND, Royal British Legion and SCOPE (£4,000 each).

Exclusions No grants to animal charities or to individuals.

Applications Unsolicited applications are not considered.

The E H Smith Charitable Trust

General

£68,000 (2007/08)
Beneficial area UK, some preference for the Midlands.

Westhaven House, Arleston Way, Shipley, West Midlands B90 4LH
Tel. 0121 706 6100
Correspondent K H A Smith, Trustee
Trustees *K H A Smith; Mrs B M Hodgskin-Brown; D P Ensell.*
CC Number 328313
Information available Full accounts were available from the Charity Commission website.

This trust has general charitable purposes and supports a range of local and national organisations. In 2007/08 it had assets of £228,000 and an income of £87,000. Grants were made totalling £68,000, the largest of which went to Severn Valley Railway (£5,000).

Other beneficiaries included: Romania Challenge (£4,900); Betel (£2,500); Solihull Hall (£1,500); Cancer Research UK (£900); County Air Ambulance (£700); Smile Train UK (£600); and Crash Christmas Cards, NSPCC and Junior Heybridge Swifts FC (£500 each).

Exclusions No grants to political parties. Grants are not normally given to individuals.

Applications In writing to the correspondent at any time.

The Martin Smith Foundation

Art, music, sport and education

£1.1 million (2007/08)
Beneficial area UK.

4 Essex Villas, London W8 7BN
Tel. 020 7937 0027
Correspondent Martin Smith
Trustees *Martin G Smith, Chair; Elise Smith; Jeremy J G Smith; Katherine Wake; Elizabeth F C Buchanan; B Peerless.*

CC Number 1072607

Information available Accounts were available at the Charity Commission.

This trust mainly gives to projects and organisations connected to art, music, sports and education. In 2007/08 the trust had assets of £3.2 million and an unusually high income of £4.2 million. This was due to a large donation from Martin Smith. Grants were made to 23 organisations totalling £1.1 million.

The three largest grants went to: National Museum of Science and Industry (£750,000); Orchestra of the Age of Enlightenment – Smith Challenge (£165,000); and Royal Academy of Music (£106,000).

Other grants of £15,000 or less included those made to: Bath Mozartfest (£15,000); Tetbury Music Festival (£7,500); Royal Philharmonic Society (£5,900); International Musicians Seminar Prussia Cove (£2,800); Ashmolean Museum (£1,000); and Wellbeing of Women (£250).

Grants totalling £31,000 were also made to individuals.

Applications This trust does not consider unsolicited applications.

The Leslie Smith Foundation

General

£110,000 (2007/08)

Beneficial area UK with a preference for Wiltshire, Norfolk, Middlesex, London and Dorset.

c/o Willcox & Lewis, The Old Coach House, Sunnyside, Bergh Apton, Norwich NR15 1DD

Tel. 01508 480100 Fax 01508 480001

Email info@willcoxlewis.co.uk

Correspondent The Directors

Trustees M D Willcox; H L Young Jones.

CC Number 250030

Information available Accounts were obtained from the Charity Commission website.

The foundation, which regularly reviews its grant-making policy, is currently focusing on:

- children with illnesses, both terminal and non-terminal, in the UK, excluding respite care and research
- orphans

- schools, specifically special needs schools based in the UK.

In 2007/08 the trust had an income of £305,000 and made grants totalling £110,000. Its assets stood at £4.1 million. Grants were broken down as follows:

- health and allied services – £52,000
- children's welfare – £18,000
- counselling services – £15,000
- ex-servicemen's welfare – £10,000
- miscellaneous – £16,000

Grants included those made to: Gaddum Centre, Joseph Weld Hospice and Royal British Legion (£10,000 each); Manna House Counselling Services, Shooting Star Children's Hospice and London Youth (£5,000 each); Community Fund Wiltshire and Swindon (£2,500); Norfolk Accident Rescue Service and Wooden Spoon Society (£2,000 each); Bingham Chapel Project (£1,100); and St Peter and St Paul Bergh Apton (£500).

Exclusions Grants are given to registered charities only. No grants for individuals.

Applications In writing to the correspondent, including a summary of the project and a copy of the latest accounts. Only successful applications are acknowledged.

The Stanley Smith UK Horticultural Trust

Horticulture

£93,000 (2007/08)

Beneficial area UK and overseas.

Cory Lodge, PO Box 365, Cambridge CB2 1HR

Tel. 01223 336 299 Fax 01223 336 278

Correspondent James Cullen, Director

Trustees C D Brickell; Lady Renfrew; J B E Simmons; A De Brye; P R Sykes; Dr D A H Rae; E Reed.

CC Number 261925

Information available Accounts were on file at the Charity Commission.

Established by deed in 1970, the trust's objects are the advancement of horticulture. In particular, the trustees have power to make grants for the following purposes:

- horticultural research
- the creation, development, preservation and maintenance of public gardens
- the promotion of the cultivation and wide distribution of plants of horticultural value/other value to mankind
- the promotion of the cultivation of new plants
- publishing books and work related to horticultural sciences.

In 2007/08 the trust had assets of £3.2 million and an income of £136,000. Grants to 25 organisations and individuals totalled £93,000.

Beneficiaries from the general fund included: Anglo-Greek Collaboration (£8,000); Dundee University Botanic Garden and Grounds (£6,000); Botanic Gardens Conservation International, Friends of Urchfront Gardens – Wiltshire and Galapagos Conservation Trust (£2,500 each); and Plants for Life – Kenya and Cambridgeshire Gardens Trust (£1,000 each).

The director continues to provide advice to actual and potential applicants, and to established projects which have already received grants. Any grant provided by the trust bears the condition that the recipient should provide within six months, or some other agreed period, a report on the use of the grant.

Exclusions Grants are not made for projects in commercial horticulture (crop production) or agriculture, nor are they made to support students taking academic or diploma courses of any kind, although educational institutions are supported.

Applications In writing to the correspondent. Guidelines for applicants are available from the trust. The director is willing to give advice on how applications should be presented.

Grants are awarded twice a year, in spring and autumn. To be considered in the spring allocation, applications should reach the director before 15 February of each year; for the autumn allocation the equivalent date is 15 August. Potential recipients are advised to get their applications in early.

Philip Smith's Charitable Trust

Welfare, older people and children

£81,000 (2007/08)

Beneficial area UK with a preference for Gloucestershire.

Bircham Dyson Bell, 50 Broadway, London SW1H 0BL

Tel. 020 7783 3685 **Fax** 020 7222 3480

Email helendmonte@bdb-law.co.uk

Correspondent Helen D'Monte

Trustees *Hon. Philip R Smith; Mary Smith.*

CC Number 1003751

Information available Accounts were obtained from the Charity Commission website.

The trustees have adopted a policy of donating to those charities within the Gloucestershire area and also national charities supporting the environment, older people, children and the needy.

In 2007/08 the trust had assets of £1.2 million and an income of £48,000. Grants were made to 35 organisations totalling £81,000.

Grants included those made to: NSPCC (£20,000); Star Appeal, Gloucester Community Foundation and Gloucestershire Flood Relief Fund (£5,000 each); Salvation Army (£2,500); Wester Ross Fisheries Trust (£2,000); Merlin (£1,000); Pied Piper Appeal (£500); St Richards Hospice (£350); and Royal Green Jackets (£100).

Applications In writing to the correspondent. The trustees meet regularly to consider grants. A lack of response can be taken to indicate that the trust does not wish to contribute to an appeal.

Solev Co Ltd

Jewish

£827,000 (2007/08)

Beneficial area UK.

Romeo House, 160 Bridport Road, London N18 1SY

Correspondent R Tager, Trustee

Trustees *R Tager; S Tager; J Tager; C M Frommer.*

CC Number 254623

Information available Accounts were on file at the Charity Commission, but without a grants list.

In 2007/08 the charity had assets of £4.1 million and an income of £1.6 million. Grants were made totalling £827,000. No information on beneficiaries has been included in the accounts in recent years.

Previous beneficiaries include: £100,000 to the Dina Perelmam Trust Ltd, a charitable company of which Mr Perelman and Mr Grosskopf are governors; and £40,000 to Songdale Ltd, a charity of which Mr M Grosskopf is a governor.

Other previous beneficiaries include: Society of Friends of the Torah (£3,900); Finchley Road Synagogue (£2,300); NW London Talmudical College (£1,500); Yesodey Hatorah School (£700); and Gateshead Talmudical College (£400).

Applications In writing to the correspondent.

The Solo Charitable Settlement

Jewish and general

£81,000 (2007/08)

Beneficial area UK and Israel.

c/o Randall Greene, 32–34 London Road, Guildford GU1 2AB

Tel. 01483 230440

Correspondent The Trustees

Trustees *Peter D Goldstein; Edna A Goldstein; Paul Goldstein; Dean Goldstein; Jamie Goldstein; Tammy Ward.*

CC Number 326444

Information available Full accounts were obtained from the Charity Commission website.

Peter David Goldstein established the trust in 1983. The main object of the trust is to support Jewish charities, and where possible, to concentrate their efforts on the relief of suffering and poverty, and on education. The majority of grants were given to organisations that focused on Jewish related causes, medical research, the arts and palliative care.

In 2007/08 the trust had assets of £5.2 million and an income of £256,000.

Grants were made to 25 organisations totalling £81,000, which were broken down as follows:

The largest grants of £1,000 or more went to: Jewish Care (£30,000); Community Security Trust (£11,000); Norwood Ravenswood (£10,000); Nightingale House (£5,500); Holocaust Education Trust (£2,500); Royal Opera House Campaign (£2,400); Eve Appeal (£2,000); and Cancer Research (£1,000).

Other beneficiaries included: English Stage Company (£500); Chai Cancer Care (£300); One Family UK (£250); and Walk the Walk (£100).

Applications In writing to the correspondent.

David Solomons Charitable Trust

Mental disability

£148,000 (2007/08)

Beneficial area UK.

Jasmine Cottage, 11 Lower Road, Breachwood Green, Hitchin SG4 8NS

Tel. 01438 833254

Email g.crosby@waitrose.com

Correspondent Graeme Crosby, Administrator

Trustees *J L Drewitt; J J Rutter; W H McBryde; Dr R E B Solomons; M T Chamberlayne; Dr L B Cooke; D J Huntingford.*

CC Number 297275

Information available Accounts were on file at the Charity Commission.

This trust supports research into the treatment and care of people with mental disabilities, with a preference for smaller or localised charities. Most grants range from £1,000 to £2,000, although larger and smaller amounts are given. Administrative expenses and large building projects are not usually funded, although grants can be made towards furnishing or equipping rooms.

In 2007/08 the trust had assets of £2.2 million, an income of £102,000 and made grants to 168 organisations totalling £148,000.

The largest grant was made to Down's Syndrome Association (£11,000).

Other grants included: Kids Care (£2,500); Birmingham Royal Ballet, Camphill Communities and Mencap

(£2,000 each); TACT and Play Matters (£1,500 each); Royal School for Deaf and Communications Disorder and Sleep Scotland (£1,000 each); and Our Choice (£750).

Smaller donations of £500 or £250 each included those to Edenbridge & District Mencap, Friends of Beverley School, Grosby & District Out of School Club, Medical Engineering Resource Unit, Parents United and Grosby & District Out of School Club.

Exclusions No grants to individuals.

Applications In writing to the correspondent. The trustees meet three times a year to consider applications.

Songdale Ltd

Jewish and education

£234,000 (2007/08)

Beneficial area UK and Israel.

6 Spring Hill, London E5 9BE

Tel. 020 8806 5010

Correspondent M Grosskopf

Trustees *M Grosskopf; Mrs M Grosskopf; Y Grosskopf.*

CC Number 286075

Information available Accounts were on file at the Charity Commission.

In 2007/08 the trust had assets of £2.9 million and an income of £519,000. Grants were made totalling £234,000. No up-to-date grants list was available.

Previous beneficiaries included: Cosmon Belz Ltd (£53,000); Kollel Belz (£50,000); BFOT (£27,000); Ezras Yisroel (£20,000); Forty Limited (£17,000); Darkei Ovois (£10,400); Germach Veholachto and Keren Nedunnia Lchasanim (£10,000 each); Belz Nursery (£9,500); and Bais Chinuch (£9,000).

Applications In writing to the correspondent.

The E C Sosnow Charitable Trust

Mainly education and arts

£41,000 (2007/08)

Beneficial area UK and overseas.

PO Box 13398, London SW3 6ZL

Correspondent The Trustees

Trustees *E R Fattal; Mrs F J M Fattal.*

CC Number 273578

Information available Full accounts were on file at the Charity Commission.

The trust makes grants mainly to organisations working in education and the arts. Other potential areas of interest mentioned in its annual report are the underprivileged, healthcare and emergency relief. In 2007/08 the trust had assets of £1.9 million and an income of £79,000. Grants were made to 24 organisations totalling £41,000.

Grants included those made to: HET (£5,500); London Youth and Nightingale House (£3,000 each); Griffins Society, Place to Be, Worldwide Volunteering and Chicken Shed Theatre (£2,000 each); NSPCC and Brent Adolescent Centre (£1,000 each); Woodstock Sinclair Trust (£500); and Ohel Sarah (£200).

Exclusions No grants are made to individuals.

Applications In writing to the correspondent.

The South Square Trust

General

£150,000 to organisations (2007/08)

Beneficial area UK, with a preference for London and the Home Counties.

PO Box 169, Lewes BN7 9FB

Tel. 01825 872264

Website www.southsquaretrust.org.uk

Correspondent Mrs Nicola Chrimes, Clerk to the Trustees

Trustees *A E Woodall; W P Harriman; C P Grimwade; D B Inglis; R S Baldock.*

CC Number 278960

Information available Accounts were on file at the Charity Commission.

General donations are made to registered charities working in the fields of older people, medical research and equipment, support groups, community groups, horticulture, green issues and other projects connected with the fine and applied arts.

The trust also gives grants to students for full-time postgraduate or undergraduate courses within the UK connected with the fine and applied arts, including drama, dance, music, but particularly related to gold and silver work. Help is given to various colleges in the form of bursary awards. A full list is available from the correspondent. Where a school is in receipt of a bursary, no further assistance will be given to individuals as the school will select candidates themselves.

In 2007/08 the trust had assets of £3.4 million, which generated an income of £187,000. Grants were made totalling £164,000 of which £150,000 went to organisations and £14,000 to individuals.

Grants were broken down as follows:

Annual donations to charities – £19,000
These consisted of three grants of £1,000 each and 31 grants of £500 each. Further information was not available.

General charitable donations – £38,000
A total of 59 grants were made, of which three were for amounts over £1,000 each: Hertfordshire Community Foundation (£2,000); and Gordonstoun School Ltd and Monkton Combe School (£1,500 each).

Bursaries and scholarships to schools/ colleges – £94,000
Ten institutions were supported by these schemes, including: St Paul's School (£23,000); Royal Academy of Music (£15,000); Royal College of Art (£12,000); Royal Northern College of Music (£8,000); and London Contemporary Dance School (£3,000).

Directly aided students and single payment grants – £14,000
These were made to 23 individuals.

Exclusions No support for building projects, salaries or individuals wishing to start up a business. No grants given to individuals under 18 or those seeking funding for expeditions, travel, courses outside the UK, short courses or courses not connected with fine and applied arts.

Applications Registered charities: In writing to the correspondent with details about your charity and the reason for requesting funding. Applications are considered three times a year, in November, March and June, and should be submitted at least one month before the next meeting. It is advisable to telephone the correspondent for up-to-date information about the criteria for funding.

Individuals: Standard application forms are available from the correspondent. Forms are sent out between January and

April only, to be returned by the end of April for consideration for the following academic year.

The Stephen R and Philippa H Southall Charitable Trust

General

£38,000 (2007/08)

Beneficial area UK, but mostly Herefordshire.

Porking Barn, Clifford, Hereford HR3 5HE

Tel. 01497 831243

Correspondent Philippa Southall, Trustee

Trustees *Stephen Readhead Southall; Philippa Helen Southall; Anna Catherine Southall; Candia Helen Compton.*

CC Number 223190

Information available Accounts were obtained from the Charity Commission website.

This trust has general charitable purposes, with a preference for promoting education and conservation of the natural environment and cultural heritage. A large number of grants are made in Herefordshire.

In 2007/08 the trust had assets of £2.2 million and an income of £59,000. Grants were made to 24 organisations totalling £38,000.

Beneficiaries included: Hereford Waterworks Museum Trust (£23,000); National Museum and Galleries for Wales and Tobacco Factory Arts Trust (£5,000 each); National Trust (£500); Dogs for the Disabled and Home Start Herefordshire (£250 each); Herefordshire Historical Churches Trust (£200); British Legion (£100); and RNLI (£20).

Applications The trust makes several repeat donations and has previously stated that: 'no applications can be considered or replied to'.

The W F Southall Trust

Quaker and general

£324,000 (2007/08)

Beneficial area UK and overseas.

c/o Rutters Solicitors, 2 Bimport, Shaftesbury SP7 8AY

Tel. 01747 852377 **Fax** 01747 851989

Email southall@rutterslaw.co.uk

Correspondent The Secretary

Trustees *Donald Southall, Chair; Joanna Engelkamp; Claire Greaves; Mark Holtom; Daphne Maw; Annette Wallis; Richard Maw; Hannah Engelkamp.*

CC Number 218371

Information available Accounts were available from the Charity Commission website.

This trust prefers to support innovative projects from smaller charities where the grant will make a more significant difference. Areas of work supported are: Society of Friends; peace-making and conflict resolution; alcohol, drug abuse and penal affairs; environmental action; homelessness; community action; and overseas development.

In 2007/08 the trust had assets of £8 million and an income of £326,000. Grants were made totalling £324,000 and were broken down as follows:

Quaker and Society of Friends Charities (£93,000)
Grant recipients included: Yearly Meeting – Society of Friends (£55,000); Friends World Committee for Consultation and Woodbrooke Quaker Study Centre (£10,000 each); and West Midlands Quaker Peace Education Project (£3,000). There were seven other grants of up to £3,000 made totalling £15,000.

Peace and reconciliation (£44,000)
Beneficiaries included: Responding to Conflict (£7,600); International Voluntary Services (£6,500); Peace Museum (£5,000); Corrymeela Community (£3,000). There were six other grants of less than £3,000 made totalling £10,000.

Overseas development (£34,000)
Beneficiaries included: Oxfam (£6,500); Salt of the Earth (£4,000); and International Service (£3,000). There were twelve other grants of up to £3,000 totalling £26,000.

Environmental action (£20,000)
Grants included those to Seeds for Change thru Climate Outreach &

Information Network and John Muir Trust (£3,000 each). There were eight other grants of less than £3,000 totalling £16,000.

Community action (£44,000)
Grants included: Quaker Social Action (£5,000); Refugee Council (£4,000); and Asylum Welcome and Confidential & Local Mediation (£3,000 each). There were twelve other grants under £3,000 totalling £21,000.

Alcohol and drug abuse and penal affairs (£75,000)
Grants went to St Giles Trust (£46,000) and Counselling in Prison (£25,000). There were three other grants under £3,000 totalling £4,300.

Homelessness (£3,000)
One grant was made under this category.

Exclusions No grants to individuals or large national charities.

Applications In writing to the correspondent (via post or email), requesting an application form. Applications are usually considered in February/March and November. Applications received between meetings are considered at the next meeting.

R H Southern Trust

Education, disability, relief of poverty, environment and conservation

£195,000 (2007/08)

Beneficial area Worldwide.

23 Sydenham Road, Cotham, Bristol BS6 5SJ

Tel. 0117 942 5834

Correspondent The Trustees

Trustees *Marion Valiant Wells; Charles Sebastian Rivett Wells; Charles James Long Bruges; Colkin Trustee Company Limited.*

CC Number 1077509

Information available Accounts were on file at the Charity Commission.

This trust was registered with the Charity Commission in 1999. Grants tend to be made to a small number of organisations, mostly for long-term core funding and special projects. The trust's objects are:

- the advancement of education (including medical and scientific research)
- the relief of poverty
- disability
- the preservation, conservation and protection of the environment.

In 2007/08 the trust had assets of £3.4 million and an income of £156,000. Grants were made to 16 organisations totalling £195,000 and were broken down as follows:

Education (£63,000)
Grants made to Feasta amounted to £30,000. Other grants made included New Economics Foundation (£20,000) and Corporate Europe Observatory (£5,000).

Environment (£45,000)
Beneficiaries included: Soil Association (£15,000 in two grants); and Oxford Research Group and Friends of the Earth (£10,000 each).

Poverty (£49,000)
Grants included those made to Action Village India and Just Change – Oxfam (£10,000 each) and E I Rural Links – Tam Wed (£8,500).

Disabilities (£38,000)
Grants were made to Equal Adventure (£23,000 in two grants) and Motivation (£15,000).

Applications In writing to the correspondent.

Spar Charitable Fund

General, with a preference for children and young people

£364,000 (2007/08)
Beneficial area UK.

Mezzanine Floor, Hygeia Building, 66 – 68 College Road, Harrow HA1 1BE
Tel. 020 8426 3700
Email philip.marchant@spar.co.uk
Correspondent P W Marchant, Director and Company Secretary
Trustee *The National Guild of Spar Ltd.*
CC Number 236252
Information available Full accounts were on file at the Charity Commission.

This trust tends to choose one main beneficiary, which receives most of its funds, with smaller grants being made to other beneficiaries each year. In 2007/08 the trust had assets of £975,000 and an income of £374,000. Grants were made totalling £364,000.

The main beneficiary was the NSPCC, which received £344,000. Grants were also made to the Woodland Trust (£12,000) and Business in the Community (£8,800).

Applications In writing to the correspondent.

The Spear Charitable Trust

General, with some preference for animal welfare, the environment and health

£109,000 to organisations (2007)
Beneficial area UK.

Roughground House, Old Hall Green, Ware SG11 1HB
Tel. 01920 823071 **Fax** 01920 823071
Correspondent Hazel E Spear, Secretary
Trustees *P N Harris; F A Spear; H E Spear; N Gooch.*
CC Number 1041568
Information available Full accounts were on file at the Charity Commission.

Established in 1994 with general charitable purposes, this trust has particular interest in helping employees and former employees of J W Spear and Sons plc and their families and dependants.

In 2007 the assets totalled £4.9 million and generated an income of £145,000. Grants were made to 44 organisations totalling £109,000, whilst ex-employees received £26,000 in total. Management and administration charges were quite high at £18,000.

Beneficiaries included: RSPCA – Enfield (£8,000); Friends of the Earth (£5,000); Fuerth Jewish Cemetery (£6,900); Imagine – Mozambique (£6,000); British Philatelic Trust and East-Side Educational Trust (£2,500 each); Devon Wildlife Trust and Trees for Life (£2,000 each); and Greyhounds Compassion, Bowel Disease Research Foundation and Greater Shankhill Youth Initiative (£1,000 each).

Exclusions Appeals from individuals are not considered.
Applications In writing to the correspondent.

Spears-Stutz Charitable Trust

Welfare causes

Around £35,000 (2007/08)
Beneficial area Worldwide.

4 More London Riverside, London SE1 2AU
Tel. 020 7759 6734
Correspondent The Trustees
Trustees *Glenn Hurstfield; Jonathan Spears.*
CC Number 225491
Information available Information was obtained from the Charity Commission website.

This trust was previously known as the Roama Spears Charitable Settlement. It states that it makes grants to organisations towards the relief of poverty worldwide. In practice it appears to support a range of organisations including a number of museums and arts organisations. It has some preference for Jewish causes.

In 2007/08 the trust had an income of £24,000 and a total expenditure of £43,000. Further information was not available.

Previous beneficiaries included Cancer Macmillan Fund, Royal Academy Trust, Royal Academy of Arts, Wellbeing, King Edward Hospital, Help the Aged and Westminster Synagogue.

Applications In writing to the correspondent.

The Worshipful Company of Spectacle Makers' Charity

Visual impairment, City of London and general

£53,000 (2007/08)

Beneficial area Worldwide, with a preference for the City of London.

Apothecaries Hall, Blackfriars Lane, London EC4V 6EL

Tel. 020 7236 2932

Email clerk@spectaclemakers.com

Website www.spectaclemakers.com

Correspondent John Salmon, Clerk

Trustees Michael Barton; David Burt; John Marshall; Brian Mitchell; Christine Tomkins.

CC Number 1072172

Information available Accounts were on file at the Charity Commission.

Registered with the Charity Commission in October 1998, this livery company supports causes related to visual impairment and the City of London, however it has also supported a wide range of other projects worldwide. Grants tend to be made for specific projects, not general funds, and to national campaigns rather than local causes.

In 2007/08 the charity had assets of £657,000 and an income of £63,000. Grants were made to organisations totalling £53,000.

The charity's website lists a number of beneficiaries, without details of the value of individual grants. These included: Action for Blind People, Blind in Business, Childhood Eye Cancer Trust, Eyeless Trust, St John's Eye Hospital in Jerusalem, Prison Fellowship, Optical Workers' Benevolent Fund, British Council for the Prevention of Blindness, Vision 2020 UK, Livings Paintings Trust, Vision Aid Overseas, Macular Disease Society, British Blind Sport and the Talking Newspaper Association.

Exclusions No grants are made to individuals.

Applications In writing to the correspondent including details of how the grant will be used and a copy of the latest audited accounts. Please note: the trustees meet in early spring to decide on grants, meaning that applications received between June and March are unlikely to be addressed quickly.

The Jessie Spencer Trust

General

£119,000 to organisations (2007/08)

Beneficial area UK, with some preference for Nottinghamshire.

Berryman Shacklock LLP, Park House, Friar Lane, Nottingham NG1 6DN

Tel. 0115 945 3700 **Fax** 0115 948 0234

Correspondent The Trustees

Trustees V W Semmens; R S Hursthouse; Mrs J Galloway; Mrs B Mitchell.

CC Number 219289

Information available Accounts were available from the Charity Commission website.

The trust supports a range wide of causes, including welfare, religion and the environment amongst others. Whilst grants are made UK-wide, there is a preference for work in Nottinghamshire.

In 2007/08 the trust had assets of £3.5 million and an income of £147,000. Grants were made totalling £119,000 and were broken down as follows:

Medical and disabled (£38,000)
Beneficiaries included: Nottingham University Hospitals Charity and Core – Digestive Disorders Foundation (£5,000 each); Nottinghamshire Hospice (£2,000); Vitalise (£1,500); Deafness Research UK (£1,000); and Headway (£500).

Welfare (£28,000)
Grants included those made to: Charis Life Church (£5,000); the Hardman Trust (£1,000); Nottingham Pregnancy Crisis Centre (£750); Open Minds and Think Children (£500 each); and People's Dispensary for Sick Animals (£250).

Churches (£15,000)
Grant recipients included: Nottinghamshire Historic Churches Trust (£10,000); Our Lady and All Saints Church – Annesley (£1,000); Sherwood United Reformed Church (£500); and Linby and Papplewick PCC (£100).

Education (£15,000)
Beneficiaries included: Rutland House School (£6,000); Rutland House School for Parents (£5,000); Community of the Holy Fire (£1,000); and Literacy Volunteers (£500).

Other (£1,800)
Grants included those made to: Bromley House Library (£1,000); Project Trust (£500); and Sherwood Rise Residents' Association (£250).

Accommodation (£6,000)
Grants went to: Framework Housing Association (£2,000); and Shelter – Nottinghamshire and the Oaklands (£1,000 each).

Groups and clubs (£3,500)
Grant recipients included: Arnold St Mary's Community Youth Club (£1,000), Oliver Hind Club and Muslim Community Organisation (£500 each).

Arts (£5,500)
Grants included: Shakespeare Youth Festival (£1,000); Armonico Consort (£750); and Magdala (£500).

Environment (£1,500)
Grants went to: Farming and Wildlife Advisory Group – Nottinghamshire, RSPB Midlands and Nottinghamshire Wildlife Trust (£500 each).

Services (£500)
One grant was made to SSAFA (£500).

Heritage (£3,000)
Grants went to Binns Organ Trust (£2,000) and St Mary's Church Nottingham – War Memorial (£1,000).

Individuals (£1,600)
Grants totalled £1,600.

Exclusions Grants are rarely made for the repair of parish churches outside Nottinghamshire.

Applications In writing to the correspondent, including the latest set of audited accounts, at least three weeks before the trustees' meetings in March, June, September and December. Unsuccessful applications will not be notified.

The Moss Spiro Will Charitable Foundation

Jewish welfare

Around £25,000 (2008/09)

Beneficial area UK.

Crowndean House, 26 Bruton Lane, London W1J 6JH

Tel. 020 7491 9817 **Fax** 020 7499 6850

Email trevor@assassin.co.uk

Correspondent Trevor Spiro, Trustee

Trustees *Trevor David Spiro; Melvin Clifford Kay; David Jeremy Goodman.*

CC Number 1064249

Information available Information was obtained from the Charity Commission website.

The trust makes grants towards Jewish welfare. In 2008/09 the trust had an income of £2,300 and a total expenditure of £26,000. Further information was not available.

Previous beneficiaries have included American Friends of Yershivas Birchas Ha Torah, Lubavitch Foundation, J T Tannenbaum Jewish Cultural Centre, Friends of Neve Shalom, Jewish Care and HGS Emunah.

Applications In writing to the correspondent.

W W Spooner Charitable Trust

General

Around £100,000 (2006/07)

Beneficial area UK, with a preference for Yorkshire especially West Yorkshire.

Tree Tops, Main Street, Hawksworth, Leeds LS20 8NX

Correspondent M H Broughton, Chair and Trustee

Trustees *M H Broughton; Sir James F Hill; J C Priestley; T J P Ramsden; Mrs J M McKiddie; J H Wright.*

CC Number 313653

Information available The latest accounts available from the Charity Commission website were for year ending 2006/07.

The trust will support charities working in the following areas:

- Young people – for example, welfare, sport and education including school appeals and initiatives, clubs, scouting, guiding, adventure training, individual voluntary service overseas and approved expeditions
- Community – including churches, associations, welfare and support groups
- Healing – including care of people who are sick, disabled or underprivileged, welfare organisations, victim support, hospitals, hospices and selected medical charities and research
- The countryside – causes such as the protection and preservation of the environment including rescue and similar services and preservation and maintenance of historic buildings
- The arts – including museums, teaching, performing, musical and literary festivals and selective support for the purchase of works of art for public benefit.

The trust has a list of regular beneficiaries that receive grants each year and also supports around 40 to 50 one-off applications. Grants can range from £200 to £2,000, although they are usually for £250 to £350.

In 2006/07 the trust had an income of £82,500 and a total expenditure of £106,800.

Previous beneficiaries have included Wordsworth Trust – Grasmere, Parish of Tong and Holme Wood, Guide Dogs for the Blind, St Margaret's PCC – Ilkley, Abbeyfield Society, All Saints' Church – Ilkley, Ardenlea, Hawksworth Church of England School, Leith School of Art, Martin House Hospice, North of England Christian Healing Trust, St Gemma's Hospice, St George's Crypt, Wheatfield House and Yorkshire Ballet Seminar.

Exclusions 'No grants for high-profile appeals seeking large sums.' Most donations are for less than £500.

Applications In writing to the correspondent.

Stanley Spooner Deceased Charitable Trust

Children and general

£52,000 (2007/08)

Beneficial area UK.

The Public Trustee (Ref. G5361), Official Solicitor and Public Trustee, 81 Chancery Lane, London WC2A 1DD

Tel. 020 7911 7073

Email suzanne.marks@offsol.gsi.gov.uk

Correspondent Miss Suzanne Marks, Trust Officer

CC Number 1044737

Information available Accounts were on file at the Charity Commission.

The trust mainly makes grants to charities listed in the trust deed and only a small part of its grantmaking is discretionary. In 2007/08 the trust had an income of £94,000 and made grants totalling £52,000. Its assets stood at £1.4 million. A list of grants was not available.

In previous years the three regular beneficiaries have been the Children's Society, Docklands Settlement and Metropolitan Police Courts Poor Boxes (Drinan Bequest). Each of these beneficiaries received three-tenths of the income. The remaining tenth is given to similar charities at the trustee's discretion. Previous beneficiaries of this fund have included Barnados and National Children's Home.

Applications In writing to the correspondent.

Rosalyn and Nicholas Springer Charitable Trust

Welfare, Jewish, education and general

£136,000 (2007/08)

Beneficial area UK.

Flat 27, Berkeley House, 15 Hay Hill, London W1J 8NS

Tel. 020 7493 1904

Correspondent Nicholas Springer, Trustee

Trustees *Rosalyn Springer; N S Springer; Judith Joseph.*

CC Number 1062239

Information available Full accounts were on file at the Charity Commission.

This trust supports the relief and assistance of people in need, for the advancement of education, religion and other purposes. Grants were made in the following categories: medical, health and sickness, education and training, arts and culture, religious activities, relief of poverty and for general charitable purposes. In 2007/08 the trust had assets of £36,000 and an income of £125,000. Grants were made totalling £136,000.

Beneficiaries included: UJIA (£35,000); North London Collegiate (£22,000); MDA UK (£13,000); Community

Security Trust (£4,000); Maccabi GB and Cancerkin (£2,500 each); West London Synagogue (£2,400); Ovarian Cancer Action (£1,300); Royal Opera House Foundation (£1,100); British Wizo (£1,000); Coram Family (£750); and Resources for Autism (£350).

Applications The trust has previously stated that it only supports organisations it is already in contact with. 99% of unsolicited applications are unsuccessful and because of the volume it receives, the trust is unable to reply to such letters. It would therefore not seem appropriate to apply to this trust.

The Spurrell Charitable Trust

General

£83,000 (2007/08)

Beneficial area UK, with some preference for Norfolk.

16 Harescroft, Moat Farm, Tunbridge Wells TN2 5XE

Tel. 01892 541565

Correspondent A T How, Trustee

Trustees *Alan T How; Richard J K Spurrell; Mrs Inge H Spurrell; Martyn R Spurrell.*

CC Number 267287

Information available Accounts were on file at the Charity Commission.

The trust has previously stated that grants are only distributed to charities known personally to the trustees and that its funds are fully committed.

In 2007/08 the trust had assets of £2.2 million and an income of £92,000. Grants were made totalling £83,000.

Larger grants were made to: East Anglian Air Ambulance (£7,500); Merlin (£5,000); Donna's Dream House (£4,500); Royal Agricultural Benevolent Institution (£4,000); the Rowans Hospice (£2,000); and Break (£1,500).

Smaller grants included: Alzheimer's Research Trust, Brooke Hospital for Animals and Camphill Village Trust (£1,000 each); Caister Volunteer Rescue Service (£750); Dream Makers and Church Urban Fund (£500 each); and North Norfolk District 1st Rural Scout Group (£250).

In 2008/09 the trust's income fell to £80,000 and is still falling. Existing commitments are likely to be reduced as a result.

Applications Unsolicited applications are not considered.

The Geoff and Fiona Squire Foundation

General

£1 million (2007/08)

Beneficial area UK.

Home Farm House, Hursley, Winchester SO21 2JL

Correspondent Fiona Squire, Trustee

Trustees *G W Squire; Fiona Squire; B P Peerless.*

CC Number 1085553

Information available Accounts were on file at the Charity Commission.

Registered with the Charity Commission in March 2001. In 2007/08 the trust had assets of £13 million and an income of £345,000. Grants were made totalling £1 million.

The largest grants included those made to: Friends of Hursley School (£230,000); Naomi House – Wessex Children's Hospice Trust (£194,000); Changing Faces (£114,000); Hillier Arboreteum (£80,000); Grange Park Opera (£60,000); and Lord's Taverners (£29,000).

Other grants included those made to: Animal Health Trust, Sportability and Cancer Research UK (£5,000 each); RNIB (£4,800); Strong Bones Children's Charitable Trust (£2,000); St Johns Ambulance (£750); and Brendencare Club (£500).

Applications The trust has previously stated: 'the trustees have in place a well-established donations policy and we do not therefore encourage unsolicited grant applications, not least because they take time and expense to deal with properly.'

St Andrew Animal Fund

Animal welfare

About £25,000 (2008)

Beneficial area UK and overseas, with a preference for Scotland.

10 Queensferry Street, Edinburgh EH2 4PG

Tel. 0131 225 2116 **Fax** 0131 220 6377

Email info@advocatesforanimals.org

Website www.advocatesforanimals.org

Correspondent Secretary to the Trustees

Trustees *Murray McGrath, Chair; David Martin; Dr Jane Goodall; Heather Petrie; Rebecca Ford; Shona McManus; Stephen Blakeway; Emma Law; Audrey Fearn; Duchess of Hamilton; Virginia Hay; Les Ward; Sheelagh Graham.*

SC Number SC005337

Information available Despite making a written request for the accounts of this fund (and including a stamped, addressed envelope), these were not provided. The following entry is based, therefore, on information filed with the Office of the Scottish Charity Regulator.

The fund was formed in 1969 to carry out charitable activities for the protection of animals from cruelty and suffering. Grants are awarded only to fund or to part-fund a specific project, for example building work, renovation, repairs etc.; an animal project – spaying/ neutering, re-homing etc.; or animal rescue/animal sanctuary – providing care for unwanted, ill or injured animals.

Previously, activities have included making grants and awards to further animal welfare projects in the UK and overseas. The fund continued its involvement in a project dealing with the force feeding of ducks and geese in the production of foie gras, and with Focus on Alternatives, a group promoting the development, acceptance and use of humane alternatives to animals in research.

The trustees consider that the priorities for the charity in the next few years are support for the development of non-animal research techniques, funding farm animal, companion animal and wildlife projects to improve and enhance the welfare of animals.

In 2007/08 the charity had an income of £34,000 and made grants totalling around £25,000.

Past recipients of grants of £1,000 or more, include: Lawrence and Beavan

323

Website Project (£11,000); Tinto Kennels (£3,000); InterNICHE and Uist Hedgehog Rescue (£2,000 each); and Captive Animals Protection Society and Norwegian School of Veterinary Science (£1,200 each).

Beneficiaries of smaller grants included ATLA Abstracts, Friends of the Ferals – Devon, Muirhead Animal Fund – Edinburgh, Cat Register and Rescue Centre – Falkirk and The Sanctuary – Morpeth.

Exclusions No support for routine day-to-day expenses.

Applications In writing to the correspondent. The trustees meet in April and applications must reach the fund by 28 February for consideration at the next meeting. Applications should include a copy of the latest accounts, the name and address of a referee (for example, veterinary surgeon or an animal welfare organisation), the purpose for which any grant will be used and, where relevant, two estimates. Receipts for work carried out may be requested and the fund states that visits by representatives of the fund to those organisations receiving grants will be made at random.

St Gabriel's Trust

Higher and further religious education

£46,000 to organisations (2007)
Beneficial area Mainly in the UK.

Ladykirk, 32 The Ridgeway, Enfield EN2 8QH

Tel. 020 8363 6474

Correspondent Peter Duffell, Clerk

Trustees *Dr Priscilla Chadwick, Chair; Arthur Pendlebury-Green; Susanna Ainsworth; Prof Andrew Wright; James Cowen; Linda Borthwick; Jan Ainsworth; Colin Alves; John Keast; Jessica Giles; Barbara Lane; Mary Halvorson; David Stephenson.*

CC Number 312933

Information available Accounts were available from the Charity Commission.

The trust is concerned with the advancement of higher and further education in one or more of the following ways:

- promotion of the education and training of people who are, or intend to become, engaged as teachers or otherwise in work connected with religious education
- promotion of research in, and development of, religious education
- promotion of religious education by the provision of instruction, classes, lectures, books, libraries and reading rooms
- granting of financial assistance to institutions of higher or further education established for charitable purposes only
- provision and conduct of a chapel and chaplaincy providing religious worship, care and instruction.

In 2007 the trust had assets of £7.5 million and an income of £269,000. Grants totalling £213,000 were made comprising £46,000 in 'corporate awards', £142,000 to St Gabriel's Programme (see below) and £25,000 in total to 21 individuals.

The five corporate beneficiaries were: ACCT Virtual RE Centre (£23,000); ACCT – Teach RE (£7,500); Lambeth Palace Library (£5,500); and St Paul's Cathedral Foundation (£1,600).

The trustees have committed funds for several corporate projects including:

- an initiative to develop a virtual RE Centre, in conjunction with other trusts
- the St Gabriel's Programme, an ongoing venture which has been run jointly with The Culham Institute, 'to develop thought and action in support of RE teachers'.

Awards to individuals are given towards course fees and expenses for teachers taking part-time RE courses whilst continuing their teaching jobs. Occasional grants have been given to those undertaking specialist research that will clearly benefit the religious education world.

Exclusions Grants are not normally available for: any project for which local authority money is available, or which ought primarily to be funded by the church – theological study, parish or missionary work – unless school RE is involved; and research projects where it will be a long time before any benefit can filter down into RE teaching. No grants are made to schools as such; higher and further education must be involved.

Applications In writing to the correspondent with a stamped, addressed envelope. Applicants are asked to describe their religious allegiance and to provide a reference from their minister of religion. Applications need to be received by the beginning of January, April or September as trustees meet in February, May and October.

St James' Trust Settlement

General

£81,000 (2007/08)
Beneficial area Worldwide, with a preference for the UK and USA.

Epworth House, 25 City Road, London EC1Y 1AR

Tel. 020 7628 5801

Correspondent The Trustees

Trustees *Jane Wells; Cathy Ingram; Simon Taffler.*

CC Number 280455

Information available Full accounts were on file at the Charity Commission.

The trust's main aim is to make grants to charitable organisations that respond to areas of concern which the trustees are involved or interested in. In the UK, the main concerns are health, education and social justice; in the USA the main areas are in education, especially to the children of very disadvantaged families, and in community arts projects. Grants are made by the trustees through their involvement with the project. Projects are also monitored and evaluated by the trustees.

In 2007/08 the trust had assets of £3.6 million and an income of £113,000. Grants were made totalling £81,000, which went to eight organisations the UK amounting to £35,000 and 25 in the USA amounting to £47,000.

In the UK grants went to: Blackstock Trust (£12,000); Prisoners Abroad and Yakar Educational Foundation (£10,000 each); Joshua Foundation (£7,300); CARIS, South East Cancer Centre and Enfant du Monde (£5,000 each); and Friends of Israel Trust (£2,500).

In the USA, grants included those to: Trevor Day School (£9,600); Global Grassroots (£7,300); VH1 Save the Music (£4,000); One Kid One World (£2,500); Dramatists Guild Fund for Kitty Hart (£1,200); Aids Walk New York (£490); and Naked Mind Productions (£250).

Exclusions No grants to individuals.

Applications The trust states that it 'does not seek unsolicited applications for grants and, without paid staff, are unable to respond to such applications'.

St Michael's and All Saints' Charities

Health and welfare

£52,000 (2007)

Beneficial area City of Oxford.

St Michael's Church Centre, St Michael at the North Gate, Cornmarket Street, Oxford OX1 3EY

Tel. 01865 240940

Email robert.hawes@smng.org.uk

Correspondent Robert J Spencer Hawes

Trustees *P Beavis; C Burton; Rev H Lee; D Frostick; Prof. P Langford; M Lear; Lord Krebs; The Ven J Hubbard; Dr J Maddicott; Ruth Loseby.*

CC Number 202750

Information available Accounts were obtained from the Charity Commission website.

Income of the charity is applied to relieve, either generally or individually, persons resident in the city of Oxford who are in conditions of need, hardship or distress. Grants may be made to institutions or organisations which provide services or facilities for such people.

In 2007 the trust had assets of £1.1 million and an income of £54,000. Grants were made to 12 organisations totalling £52,000.

Beneficiaries included: Leys Youth Programme (£7,500); Cowley Child Contact Centre (£5,700); Oxford Christian Institute for Counselling (£4,000); Elmore Community Services and Abbeyfield Society (£3,000 each); Asylum Welcome (£2,500); and Archway and Oxford Young Cruse (£2,000 each).

Exclusions Individuals are very rarely supported.

Applications In writing to the correspondent.

St Monica Trust Community Fund

Older people and disability

£139,000 (2007)

Beneficial area Preference for the south west of England, particularly Bristol and the surrounding area.

Cote Lane, Westbury-on-Trym, Bristol BS9 3UN

Tel. 0117 949 4003 **Fax** 0117 949 4044

Email kate.stobie@stmonicatrust.org.uk

Website www.communityfund.stmonicatrust.org.uk

Correspondent Kate Stobie, Community Fund Manager

Trustees *Revd Robert Grimley Dean Of Bristol; Timothy Thom; Robert Bernays; Revd Ian Gobey; Jane Edwards Cork; Peter Sherwood; Trevor Smallwood; Mary Prior Lord Lieutenant of Bristol; John Laycock; Gillian Camm; Charles Hunter; Judith Pearce; Prof. Patricia Broadfoot; Dr. Pippa Marsh.*

CC Number 202151

Information available Accounts were on file at the Charity Commission.

This St Monica Trust has provided accommodation, care and support for older and disabled people for over 85 years. Another branch of its work, the St Monica Trust Community Fund, gives grants to individuals and organisations to help improve the daily lives of people with a physical or sensory impairment or long-term physical health problem.

Grants of up to £10,000 each are available to organisations. Grants may be awarded for small capital items and/or for running costs. To be considered, organisations must meet all five of the following criteria:

1) Benefit people (over 16 years old) who have a physical or sensory impairment or long-term physical health problem, including those with infirmities due to old age.
2) Benefit people living in Bristol or the surrounding area (North Somerset, Somerset, South Gloucestershire, Gloucestershire, Bath and North East Somerset and Wiltshire).
3) Make a real difference to people's daily lives.
4) Be both properly constituted and a not-for-profit organisation.

5) Fit in with the fund's current theme (see below).

Each year has a different theme – the 2009 grants scheme was open to organisations working with older people living with a long-term physical disability, impairment or physical health problem where substance misuse has been a contributing factor. Please see the fund's website for up-to-date information.

In 2007 the trust gave grants to 34 organisations totalling £139,000. Beneficiaries included: Citizen's Advice Bureau (£9,800); St Peter's Hospice, Headway Bristol and Motor Neurone Disease Association (£7,500 each); IT Help@Home (£5,000); the New Place (£3,900); Bristol and Avon Chinese Women's Group (£2,000); Bath Institute of Medical Engineering (£1,500); and Western Active Stroke Group (£1,000).

The trust accepts applications from organisations that it has previously funded.

Exclusions No grants to fund buildings, adaptations to buildings or minibus purchases.

Applications On a form available from the correspondent, or to download from the fund's website. All applicants must submit a form together with additional information that is requested, for example, an annual report.

Applications are considered once a year; please see the fund's website for deadline dates.

All applications will be considered by the Community Fund Committee of the fund. Notification of the outcome will be made in writing.

The fund states: 'we receive many more requests than we have funds available. For example, in 2009 we received 35 applications with requests totalling over £318,000: well above the £110,000 we had available. In practice this means that we do not give grants to organisations which do not fully meet our criteria'.

The Late St Patrick White Charitable Trust

General

£35,000 (2007/08)

Beneficial area UK, with a possible preference for Hampshire.

HSBC Trust Co UK Ltd, Norwich House, Nelson Gate, Commercial Road, Southampton SO15 1GX

Tel. 023 8072 2240

Correspondent Lee Topp, Trust Manager

Trustee *HSBC Trusts Co. (UK) Ltd.*

CC Number 1056520

Information available Accounts were available from the Charity Commission website.

The objects of the charity are in perpetuity to pay or to apply the income from the trust fund for the benefit of Barnardo's, Guide Dogs for the Blind, The Salvation Army, Age Concern and other charities benefiting the blind, cancer research, arthritis and rheumatism research.

In 2007/08 the trust had assets of £2.1 million and an income of £53,000. Grants were made totalling £35,000. Beneficiaries included: Age Concern, Arthritis Concern, Barnardo's, Guide Dogs for the Blind Association and The Salvation Army (£5,000 each); Prostate Cancer and Tuberous Sclerosis Association (£2,500 each); and Braille Chess Association, National Blind Children's Society and The Seeing Ear (£1,000 each).

Applications In writing to the correspondent. Applications are considered in February, May, August and November.

St Teilo's Trust

Evangelistic work in the Church in Wales

Around £40,000 (2007/08)

Beneficial area Wales.

Capel Isaf, Manordeilo, Llandeilo, Carmarthenshire SA19 7BS

Tel. 01558 822273

Correspondent Rev P Mansel Lewis

Trustees *P C A Mansel Lewis, Chair; Mrs C Mansel Lewis; Revd Canon S R Bell; Revd Dr W A Strange; Revd P A Bement; Revd Bob Capper.*

CC Number 1032405

Information available Accounts on file at the Charity Commission.

The trust supports evangelistic work in the Church in Wales. For example, it provides funding towards the cost of evangelistic initiatives in parishes, Alpha courses, evangelistic events and literature distribution. Grants are usually one-off and range from £50 to £1,000.

In 2007/08 the trust had an income of £13,000 and made grants totalling about £40,000. No grants list was available.

Previous beneficiaries include: Llandeilo PC, Gobaith Gymru, St Michael's Aberyswyth, Cilcoed Christian Centre, Parish of Bargoed, Postal Bible School and St David's Diocesan Council.

Applications In writing to the correspondent. Trustees meet in February, May and September. Applications should be sent by January, April and August. Guidelines are available from the trust.

Miss Doreen Stanford Trust

General

£22,000 to organisations and individuals (2007)

Beneficial area UK.

26 The Mead, Beckenham BR3 5PE

Tel. 020 8650 3368

Correspondent Mrs G M B Borner, Secretary

Trustees *T Carter; R S Borner; T Butler; D Valder; Miss M Winter.*

CC Number 1049934

Information available Full accounts were available from the Charity Commission.

The trust states that its aims are to provide grants to individuals in need through charities, to further their education and help them or the public in the appreciation of the learned arts or sciences, to help towards holidays and to help those in conditions of hardship or distress.

In 2007 the trust had assets of £781,000 and an income of £42,000. Grants were made totalling £22,000.

Beneficiaries included: Happy Days (£2,700); Deafblind (£2,000); Harvest Trust (£1,500); British Wireless for the Blind (£1,300); Fulham Good Neighbours (£1,000); Sense (£650); Sailors Families Society (£300); and Access to Arts (£210).

The trust also awarded two bursaries for tuitions fees with the Cheltenham Ladies College totalling £2,000.

Exclusions No grants are given towards building repairs, alterations to property, electrical goods, floor coverings, holidays for individuals or towards household furniture or equipment.

Applications In writing to the correspondent, enclosing a stamped, addressed envelope. Allocations of grants are made once a year in March at the trustees' meeting.

The Stanley Foundation Ltd

Older people, medical care and research, education and social welfare

£141,000 (2007/08)

Beneficial area UK.

Flat 3, 19 Holland Park, London W11 3TD

Tel. 020 7792 3854

Email nick@meristan.com

Correspondent N Stanley, Secretary

Trustees *N Stanley, Chair; S R Stanley; Mrs E Stanley; S H Hall.*

CC Number 206866

Information available Full accounts were on file at the Charity Commission.

The trust has traditionally supported medical care and research, education and social welfare charities. In 2007/08 it had assets of £3.7 million and an income of £98,000. Grants were made to 47 organisations totalling £141,000. Support and governance costs were high at £59,000.

Beneficiaries included: Share Community, Friends of the Fitzwilliam Museum and King's College Cambridge (£10,000 each); Penny Brohn Cancer

Care (£7,000); Homes for Heroes (£5,000); Royal Hospital for Neuro Disability (£3,000); Tusk (£2,500); Killing Cancer (£2,000); and PSP Association, Museum of Garden History and Wells Cathedral Girls Chorister Trust (£1,000 each).

Donations of less than £1,000 each totalled £3,500 (7 charities).

Exclusions No grants to individuals.

Applications In writing to the correspondent.

The Star Charitable Trust

General

Around £20,000 (2007/08)

Beneficial area UK.

2nd Floor, 16–18 Hatton Garden, London EC1N 8AT

Tel. 020 7404 2222 **Fax** 020 7404 3333

Correspondent The Trustees

Trustees *D D Fiszman; P I Propper; D A Rosen.*

CC Number 266695

Information available Information was obtained from the Charity Commission website.

Connected to the star Diamond Group of companies, this trust was established in March 1974. In 2007/08 the trust had an income of £12,000 and a total expenditure of £22,000. Further information was not available.

Applications In writing to the correspondent.

The Starfish Trust

Sickness and medical

£120,000 to organisations (2007/08)

Beneficial area Within a 25-mile radius of Bristol.

PO Box 213, Patchway, Bristol BS32 4YY

Tel. 0117 970 1756 **Fax** 0117 970 1756

Correspondent Robert Woodward

Trustees *Charles E Dobson; Mary Dobson.*

CC Number 800203

Information available Full accounts were on file at the Charity Commission

Priority is given to appeals from individuals and charitable organisations living or based within a 25-mile radius of central Bristol with the following objects:

- direct assistance to people who are disabled
- direct assistance to people for the relief of illness or disease
- medical research and welfare in the above areas.

The following information is taken from trust's 2007/08 report and accounts:

It is the trustees' policy that they should give priority to providing direct assistance to individuals and to identifying and evaluating specific projects when giving to charitable organisations. Where appropriate, matched funding is encouraged.

It is the trustee's future policy that they will not make grants in excess of £10,000 to capital projects.

It is the trustee's policy not to provide grants to NHS Trusts.

In 2007/08 the trust had assets of £1.3 million and an income of £81,000. Grants totalling £145,000 were made, of which £25,000 was paid to 23 individuals. Grants to organisations included the following:

Direct assistance to the disabled – Hop, Skip and a Jump – the Seven Springs Foundation (£45,000); Ridgeway Care and Repair (£2,000); Swansea University (£1,500); and Mobility Trust (£1,000).

Medical research and welfare – Meningitis UK (£48,000); SWALLOW (£15,000); Cirencester Opportunity Group (£10,000); Bristol Music Space (£1,600); Carousel Community Base (£500); and Penpole Residents Association (£250).

Exclusions Individuals and charitable organisations outside a 25-mile radius of Bristol or not working in the areas defined above.

Applications In writing to the correspondent.

The Peter Stebbings Memorial Charity

General

£178,000 to institutions (2007/08)

Beneficial area UK and developing countries.

45 Pont Street, London SW1X 0BX

Tel. 020 7591 3333

Correspondent Andrew Stebbings, Trustee

Trustees *A J F Stebbings; N F Cosin; Mrs J A Clifford.*

CC Number 274862

Information available Accounts were available from the Charity Commission website.

The trust makes grants for a range of charitable purposes and the objects of the trust are to fund, in particular, medical research and education, and the welfare of those who are poor, old or sick.

In 2007/08 the charity had assets of £7.2 million and an income of £241,000. Grants were made to institutions totalling £178,000.

Beneficiaries included: Westminster Patrol Found (£100,000); Maya Centre (£30,000); Berkeley Reafforestation Trust (£20,000); Koestler Trust (£10,000); Tools for Self Reliance and CanSupport (£5,000 each); TB Alert (£1,500); and Multiple Birth Foundation (£1,000).

Exclusions No grants to individuals, non-registered charities or for salaries.

Applications It is the trustee's policy to make more substantial grants to a limited number of charities. Please note: the trust has previously stated that it does not respond to unsolicited applications and that its funds are fully committed.

The Cyril and Betty Stein Charitable Trust

Jewish causes

£294,000 (2007/08)

Beneficial area UK and Israel.

c/o Clayton Stark and Co., 5th Floor, Charles House, 108–110 Finchley Road, London NW3 5JJ

Tel. 020 7431 4200

Correspondent The Trustees

Trustees *Mrs B Stein; C Stein; D Stein; L Curry.*

CC Number 292235

Information available Accounts were on file at the Charity Commission.

The trust makes a number of grants each year, primarily for the advancement of the Jewish religion and the welfare of Jewish people.

In 2007/08 the trust had an income of £225,000. Grants were made to 151 institutions totalling £294,000.

Beneficiaries included: the Institute for the Advancement of Education in Jaffa (£111,000); Jewish National Fund (£55,000); Bar Amana (£25,000); Mizrahi Charitable Trust (£13,000); Friends of Bnei David (£12,000); New Heritage Foundation (£10,000); British Friends of Tikva Odessa (£4,900); Western Marble Arch Synagogue (£2,700); and Chief Rabbinate Charitable Trust (£1,000).

There were 93 other grants of less than £1,000 each totalling £12,000.

Applications In writing to the correspondent.

The Steinberg Family Charitable Trust

Jewish and health

£226,000 (2006/07)

Beneficial area UK, with a preference for Greater Manchester.

Lime Tree Cottage, Bollingway, Hale, Altrincham WA15 0NZ

Tel. 016 903 8851

Email admin@steinberg-trust.co.uk

Correspondent The Trustees

Trustees *D Burke, Chairman; Lady Steinberg; J Steinberg; D K Johnston; Mrs L Rochelle Attias.*

CC Number 1045231

Information available Accounts for 2007/08 were overdue at the Charity Commission.

Whilst the objects of the founding deed are very wide, the trust is primarily concerned with the support of charities located in the North West region or active within the Jewish Community (whether in the North West or Israel), particularly those involved with the provision of social or health services. There is a particular emphasis on the needs of children and young people within those areas.

In 2006/07 the trust had an income of £308,000 and expenditure of £307,000. At the time of writing (November 2009), subsequent accounts were overdue at the Charity Commission.

Previous beneficiaries include: Netanya Supporters of Laniado Hospital and Women's UJIA (£20,000 each); Community Security Trust, Imperial War Museum and North West Cancer (£10,000 each); Hale Adult Hebrew Education Trust (£8,000); National Library for the Blind (£6,000 in two grants); Alzheimer's Society, RNIB and World Jewish Relief (£5,000 each); Auditory Verbal UK, Studley Royal Cricket Club and Zichron Manachem (£2,000 each); Dreams Come True Charity (£1,500); Manchester YMCA (£1,000); and Rochdale Special Needs Cycling Club (£500).

Exclusions Registered charities only.

Applications In writing to the correspondent, including evidence of charitable status, the purpose to which the funds are to be put, evidence of other action taken to fund the project concerned, and the outcome of that action.

The Sigmund Sternberg Charitable Foundation

Jewish, inter-faith causes and general

£252,000 (2007/08)

Beneficial area Worldwide.

Star House, 104/108 Grafton Road, London NW5 4BA

Tel. 020 7431 4200

Correspondent Sir S Sternberg, Trustee

Trustees *Sir S Sternberg; V M Sternberg; Lady Sternberg; Rev M C Rossi Braybrooke; M A M Slowe; R Tamir; M D Paisner.*

CC Number 257950

Information available Full accounts were on file at the Charity Commission.

This trust supports the furtherance of the inter-faith activities to promote racial and religious harmony, in particular between Christian, Jewish and Muslim faiths, and the education in, and understanding of, their fundamental tenets and beliefs. Most grants are made to Jewish and Israeli charities. The trust makes a small number of large grants, generally of £10,000 to £80,000 each, and a large number of smaller grants.

In 2007/08 the trust had an income of £244,000 and made 161 grants totalling £252,000. Its assets stood at £4.7 million.

Beneficiaries included: Three Faiths Forum (£86,000); the Reform Synagogues of Great Britain (£70,000); the Board of Deputies Charitable Foundation (£18,000); National Portrait Gallery (£10,000); the Interreligious Coordinating Council in Israel (£6,800); Brighton Islamic Mission (£2,300); World Jewish Aid (£2,000); Institute of Business Ethics (£1,000); and Age Exchange Theatre Trust (£430).

There were 74 grants of less than £1,000 each, totalling £9,700.

Exclusions No grants to individuals.

Applications In writing to the correspondent.

Stervon Ltd

Jewish

£317,000 (2007)
Beneficial area UK.

c/o Stervon House, 1 Seaford Road, Salford M6 6AS

Tel. 0161 737 5000

Correspondent A Reich, Secretary

Trustees *A Reich; G Rothbart.*

CC Number 280958

Information available Accounts were on file at the Charity Commission.

'The principal objective of the company is the distribution of funds to Jewish, religious, educational and similar charities.' In 2007 the trust had assets of £75,000 and an income of £347,000. Grants were made totalling £317,000. No grants list was available.

Previous beneficiaries include: Eitz Chaim, Rehabilitation Trust, Chasdei Yoel, Beis Yoel, Friends of Horeinu, Beis Hamedrash Hachadash, Tashbar, Tov V' Chessed, Beth Sorah Schneirer and Asser Bishvil.

Applications In writing to the correspondent.

Stevenson Family's Charitable Trust

Culture and arts, conservation and heritage, health, education and general charitable purposes

£179,000 (2007/08)
Beneficial area Worldwide, in practice mainly UK.

Old Waterfield, Winkfield Road, Ascot SL5 7LJ

Correspondent Hugh Stevenson

Trustees *Hugh Stevenson; Catherine Stevenson; Sir Jeremy Lever.*

CC Number 327148

Information available Accounts were available at the Charity Commission.

This is the family trust of Hugh and Catherine Stevenson. A well known City of London figure, Mr Stevenson was formerly the chairman of one of London's largest investment management companies. The trust is operated personally with no premises or salaried staff of its own and is probably best seen simply as the vehicle for the personal donations of Mr and Mrs Stevenson, rather than as an institution with an independent existence.

The current policy of the trustees is in the main to support charitable causes in the fields of culture and the arts, conservation and heritage, and education, but they can exercise their discretion to make donations for other charitable purposes. In accordance with this policy the main donations made by the trustees during the year were in favour of places of culture and arts.

In 2007/08 the trust had assets of £2.7 million and an income of £110,000. The trust made 30 grants totalling £179,000.

Grants are categorised as follows:

Culture and arts – 10 grants totalling £102,000
Beneficiaries included: Holbourne Museum Limited (£50,000); Order of St John (£25,000); Glyndebourne Productions (£15,000); Royal Opera House Foundation (£6,500); British Museum Society (£1,500); and Marie Curie Cancer Care (£500).

Conservation and heritage – 5 grants totalling £37,000
Beneficiaries were: National Trust for Scotland (£25,000); Historic Royal Places (£10,000); Charleston Trust (£1,000); National Gardens Scheme (£820); Berkshire, Buckinghamshire and Oxon Wildlife Trust (£500).

General charitable purposes – 7 grants totalling £20,000
Beneficiaries included: St Michael and All Angels – Sunninghill (£15,000); Facing the World, St Mungo's and Ross Goobey Charitable Trust (£1,000 each); and CVT Appeal (£500).

Health and medicine – 7 grants totalling £19,000
Beneficiaries included: PSP Association and Changing Faces (£5,000 each); Sense (£2,000); Kids Kidney Research (£1,000); and Haven House Foundation (£500).

Education and training – 1 grant of £250
The sole beneficiary was Reed's School Foundation Appeal.

Applications 'No unsolicited applications can be considered as the charity's funds are required to support purposes chosen by the trustees.'

The Stewards' Charitable Trust

Rowing

£305,000 (2007/08)
Beneficial area Principally the UK.

Regatta Headquarters, Henley-on-Thames RG9 2LY

Tel. 01491 572153 **Fax** 01491 575509

Website www.hrr.co.uk

Correspondent Daniel Grist, Secretary

Trustees *M A Sweeney; C G V Davidge; C L Baillieu; R C Lester; Sir S Redgrave.*

CC Number 299597

Information available Accounts were on file at the Charity Commission.

The following information is taken from the trust's website:

The Stewards' Charitable Trust was formally established by the governing body of the Henley Regatta in June 1988. The principal objective of the trust was to provide funds to encourage and support young people (still receiving education or undergoing training) to row or scull.

The trust receives the bulk of its money from substantial annual donations made by Henley Royal Regatta and its trading arm, Henley Royal Regatta Limited, but also benefits from the generosity of other donors, both corporate and individual, including several members of the Stewards' Enclosure.

The trust makes grants to organisations and clubs benefiting boys and girls involved in the sport of rowing. It supports rowing at all levels, from grassroots upwards; beneficiaries should be in full-time education or training. Support is also given to related medical and educational research projects. The trust works closely with the ARA and plans to offer long-term support to their various coaching schemes. Grants can be one-off or recurring and are especially made where matched funds are raised elsewhere.

In 2007/08 the trust had assets of £4.4 million and an income of £420,000, including £227,000 in donations received from Henley Royal Regatta Limited. Grants were made totalling £305,000.

The beneficiaries were: ARA Scholarships (£194,000); ARA London Youth Rowing (£25,000); River and Rowing Museum and Project Oarsome – Boat Refurbishment (£20,000 each); Rowing Foundation (£15,000); ARA Regional Sculling Camps (£12,000); Upper Thames Rowing Club – Junior Development (£10,000); Mark Lees

Foundation (£5,000); and Ball Cup Regatta (£3,500).

Exclusions No grants to individuals or for building or capital costs.

Applications In writing to the correspondent. Applications are usually first vetted by the Amateur Rowing Association.

The Andy Stewart Charitable Foundation

General

£40,000 (2008)
Beneficial area Worldwide.

c/o Cenkos Securities plc, 6–8 Tokenhouse Yard, London EC2R 7AS
Tel. 020 7397 8900
Correspondent The Trustees
Trustees *Andy Stewart; Ivonne Cantu; Nicholas Weston Wells.*
CC Number 1114802
Information available Accounts were on file at the Charity Commission, without a list of beneficiaries.

This trust was set up in 2006. During 2008 it had assets of £629,000 and an income of £102,000. Grants to 14 charities and totalled £40,000. A list of beneficiaries was unavailable.

During the year the foundation supported the following:

Category	%
Healthcare related	59
Children	20
Animals	14
Other	7

Applications In writing to the correspondent.

The Stoller Charitable Trust

Medical, children and general

£353,000 (2007/08)
Beneficial area UK, with a preference for the Greater Manchester area.

PO Box 164, Middleton, Manchester M24 1XA
Tel. 0161 653 3849
Correspondent Alison M Ford, Secretary
Trustees *Norman K Stoller, Chair; Roger Gould; Jan Fidler; Sheila M Stoller.*
CC Number 285415
Information available Accounts were available from the Charity Commission website.

The trust supports a wide variety of charitable causes, but with particular emphasis on those that are local (Greater Manchester), medically related or supportive of children. It also endeavours to maintain a balance between regular and occasional donations and between large and smaller grants. Grants can be considered for buildings, capital costs, projects, research costs, recurring costs and start-up costs. As well as one-off grants, funding may also be given for up to three years.

In 2007/08 the trust had assets of £6.7 million and an income of £130,000. Grants were made to 130 organisations totalling £353,000.

Grants included those made to: Broughton House and Farmers Help Farmers (£20,000 each); Brathay Hall Trust and Live Music Now (£10,000 each); Life Education Centres North West (£6,000); Christie Hospital (£5,000); Duke of Edinburgh Golf Society (£3,000); Diggle & Uppermill Ecumenical Youth Project, Ambassadors in Sport and Opera North (£1,000 each); St Ann's Hospice (£500); and Rotary Club of Windermere and Sight Savers (£250 each).

Exclusions No grants to individuals.

Applications In writing to the correspondent. Applications need to be received by February, May, August or November. The trustees usually meet in March, June, September and December.

The M J C Stone Charitable Trust

General

£259,000 (2007)
Beneficial area UK.

Estate Office, Ozleworth Park, Wotton-under-Edge GL12 7QA
Tel. 01453 845591
Correspondent Michael Stone, Trustee
Trustees *Michael Stone; Louisa Stone; Charles Stone; Andrew Stone; Nicola Farquhar.*
CC Number 283920
Information available Accounts were available from the Charity Commission.

While the trust has general charitable objects, giving to a range of causes, it stated that its main area of interest is the advancement of education. In 2007 the trust had assets of £693,000 and an income of £39,000. Grants were made totalling £259,000 and were broken down as follows:

Education (£116,000)
Grants included those made to: Westonbirt School (£50,000); Bradfield Foundation (£26,000); Civitas (£15,000); Countryside Foundation for Education (£12,000); Ufton Court Educational Trust (£10,000); Noah's Ark Childrens Venture (£1,000); and GlosCat Catering Academy (£250).

Health and medical (£48,000)
Grant recipients included: Great North Air Ambulance (£26,000); Maggie Keswick Jencks Cancer (£10,000); Macmillan Cancer Relief (£2,800); Leukaemia Research (£2,000); Dean Forest Hospital (£1,300); Penny Brohn Cancer Care (£1,000); and Hearing Dogs for Deaf People (£350).

Environment and countryside (£25,000)
Grants included those to: African Parks Foundation (£10,000); National Trust (£5,000); Royal Horticultural Society (£3,500); Gloucestershire Wildlife Trust (£1,000); Game Conservancy Trust (£250); and Song Bird Survival (£20).

Relief of poverty (£2,300)
Grants went to: Zimbabwe Rhodesia Relief and Gloucestershire Society (£1,000 each); and CDTR – Peruvian Appeal (£250).

Religion (£1,500)
Beneficiaries included: St Clements Church – Kaloleim Project (£1,000); and Tewkesbury Abbey Appeal Trust (£250).

Others (£66,000)
Grants included those to: Wotton Under Edge Community Sports Fund (£20,000); Gloucestershire Community Foundation and Infobuzz (£10,000 each); IEA (£5,000); Stow Food Foundation (£2,500); Rainbow Centre (£1,000); Tyndale Choral Society (£500); and the Royal British Legion (£250).

Applications The trust does not accept unsolicited applications.

The Stone-Mallabar Charitable Foundation

Medical, arts, religion, overseas appeals, welfare and education

£103,000 (2007/08)
Beneficial area UK.

41 Orchard Court, Portman Square, London W1H 6LF
Email jmls@ymail.com
Correspondent Jonathan Stone, Trustee
Trustees *Jonathan Stone; Thalia Stone; Robin Paul; Graham Hutton.*
CC Number 1013678
Information available Accounts were on file at the Charity Commission.

The foundation supports a range of charitable purposes including the arts, religion, overseas appeals, welfare and education, but tends to have a preference for medical causes.

In 2007/08 the foundation had assets of £892,000 and an income of £78,000. Grants were made totalling £103,000.

There were 11 donations of £1,000 or more listed in the accounts. Beneficiaries were: Sheffield Institute Foundation for Motor Neurone Disease (£53,000); Brain Research Trust (£25,000); Trinity Laban (£4,000); Bolshoy Ballet School (£3,800); Zimbabwe Benefit Foundation and Thalidomide at 50 (£2,500 each); R Ziegler – Thalidomide Research (£2,000); National Trust (£1,100); and Beating Bowel Cancer Awareness Education & Support, Dermatrust and West London Mission (£1,000 each).

Unlisted grants of less than £1,000 each totalled £5,600.

Exclusions No grants to individuals.
Applications In writing to the correspondent.

The Samuel Storey Family Charitable Trust

General

£116,000 (2007/08)
Beneficial area UK, with a preference for Yorkshire.

21 Buckingham Gate, London SW1E 6LS
Tel. 020 7802 2700
Correspondent Hon. Sir Richard Storey, Trustee
Trustees *Hon. Sir Richard Storey; Wren Hoskyns Abrahall; Kenelm Storey.*
CC Number 267684
Information available Accounts were available from the Charity Commission website.

This trust has general charitable purposes, supporting a wide range of causes, including the arts, children, gardens and churches. The grants list shows a large number of beneficiaries in Yorkshire. In 2007/08 the trust had assets of £4.8 million and an income of £156,000. Grants were made to 115 organisations totalling £116,000.

The largest grant again went to Hope and Homes for Children (£27,000). Other beneficiaries included: Cancer Vaccine Institute (£10,000); Giles Worsley Travel Fellowship (£5,000); Paint a Smile (£3,300); Pebbles Project and Rhino Rescue Trust (£2,000 each); Ryedale Festival Friends (£1,300); Tadcaster Community Swimming and Woodland Trust (£1,000 each); WSPA (£500); World Monument Fund in Britain (£350); Yorkshire Historic Churches Trust (£250); and Horse Trust (£25).

Exclusions The trust does not support non-registered charities or individuals.

Applications In writing to the correspondent.

Peter Stormonth Darling Charitable Trust

Heritage, medical research and sport

£54,000 (2008)
Beneficial area UK.

Soditic Ltd, Wellington House, 125–130 Strand, London WC2R 0AP
Correspondent Peter Stormonth Darling
Trustees *Tom Colville; John Rodwell; Peter Stormonth Darling; Elizabeth Cobb; Arabella Johannes; Christa Taylor.*
CC Number 1049946
Information available Full accounts were on file at the Charity Commission.

The trust makes grants towards heritage, education, healthcare and sports facilities. In 2008 it had assets of £2.1 million and an income of £174,000. Grants were made to 14 organisations totalling £54,000.

The largest grants were made to the Black Watch Heritage Appeal (£12,000) and Friends of East Sussex Hospices (£10,000).

Smaller grants included those to: Reed's School (£4,000); Rainbow Trust and Chelsea Physic Garden (£3,000 each); Wintershall Charitable Trust and Perth College Development Trust (£2,500 each); and National Gallery, Christ Church Chelsea and Leonard Cheshire Disability (£2,000 each).

Exclusions No grants to individuals.

Applications This trust states that it does not respond to unsolicited applications.

Peter Storrs Trust

Education

£70,000 (2007/08)
Beneficial area UK.

Smithfield Accountants, 117 Charterhouse Street, London EC1M 6AA
Tel. 020 7253 3757
Correspondent J A Fordyce, Trustee
Trustees *G V Adams; A R E Curtis; J A Fordyce.*

CC Number 313804

Information available Accounts were on file at the Charity Commission, but without a list of beneficiaries.

The trust makes grants to registered charities working for the advancement of education in the UK. In 2007/08 the trust had assets of £2.5 million and an income of £106,000. Grants were made totalling £70,000, unfortunately further information including a list of grant beneficiaries was not available.

Applications In writing to the correspondent. Applications are considered every three to six months. Please note: the trust receives far more applications than it is able to support, many of which do not meet the criteria outlined above. This results in a 'heavy waste of time and expense' for both applicants and the trust itself.

The Strawberry Charitable Trust

Jewish and young people

£138,000 (2007/08)

Beneficial area Not defined but with a preference for Manchester.

4 Westfields, Hale, Altrincham WA15 0LL

Email anthonysula@hotmail.com

Correspondent Anthony Leon, Trustee

Trustees *Emma Myers; Laura Avigdori; Anthony Leon.*

CC Number 1090173

Information available Accounts were on file at the Charity Commission.

Set up in January 2000, this trust supports the relief of poverty and hardship amongst Jewish persons and the advancement of the Jewish religion.

In 2007/08 the trust had an income of £290,000, including a £253,000 gift of shares. Grants were made totalling £138,000. There were 13 grants made during the year.

Beneficiaries included: Community Security Trust (£32,000); United Jewish Israel Appeal (£30,000); Christies (£20,000); Manchester Jewish Federation (£11,000); Philip Green Memorial Trust (£6,300); Manchester Jewish Community Care (£5,100); World Jewish Relief (£5,000); Belz (£3,000); and Jewish Care and Heathlands Animal Sanctuary (£2,500 each).

Smaller grants of less than £1,000 were not listed individually, but totalled £11,000.

Applications In writing to the correspondent.

The W O Street Charitable Foundation

Education, people with disabilities, young people, health and social welfare

£410,000 (2007)

Beneficial area Worldwide. In practice UK, with a preference for the north west of England and Jersey.

c/o Barclays Bank Trust Company Ltd, PO Box 15, Osborne Court, Gadbrook Park, Northwich CW9 7UR

Tel. 01606 313 173

Correspondent The Trust Officer

Trustees *Barclays Bank Trust Co. Ltd; Mr C D Cutbill.*

CC Number 267127

Information available Accounts were available at the Charity Commission.

In considering grants, the trustees pay close regard to the wishes of the late Mr Street who had particular interests in education, support for people with financial difficulties (particularly older people, people who are blind or who have other disabilities), health and social welfare generally. Special support is given to the north west of England and Jersey.

A proportion of the available income annually, not exceeding 10%, is paid by grant to the W 0 Street Jersey Charitable Trust. Arrangements have also been made for a limited number of small local grants to be made, particularly in the Bury area of the North West. In addition the foundation supports the Combined Trusts Scholarship Trust (a separate registered charity – numbered 295402). It also provides grants to assist with fee-paying schooling where there is unexpected financial difficulty.

In 2007 the trust had assets of nearly £18 million and an income of £490,000. Grants were made totalling £410,000 broken down as follows:

Category	£
Education	90,000
Disability	89,000
Miscellaneous	80,000
Jersey grants	42,000
Family and social welfare	40,000
Ill health/relief of suffering/addiction	35,000
Poverty/homelessness	24,000
Older people	10,000

Within the above were the following named beneficiaries: DEG educational bursaries (£48,000); W O Street Jersey Charitable Trust (£42,000); Combined Trusts Scholarship (35,000); and Community Foundation for Greater Manchester (£22,000).

Exclusions No grants towards:

- schools, colleges or universities
- running or core costs
- religion or church buildings
- medical research
- animal welfare
- overseas projects or charities
- NHS trusts.

Applications directly from individuals are not considered.

Applications In writing to the correspondent. Applications are considered on a quarterly basis, at the end of January, April, July and October.

The A B Strom and R Strom Charitable Trust

Jewish and general

£54,000 (2007/08)

Beneficial area UK.

c/o 11 Gloucester Gardens, London NW11 9AB

Tel. 020 8455 5949

Email m@michaelpasha.worldonline.co.uk

Correspondent Mrs R Strom, Trustee

Trustees *Mrs R Strom; Mrs D Weissbraun.*

CC Number 268916

Information available Accounts were on file at the Charity Commission.

The objects of the charity are stated as follows:

- the advancement of education according to the tenets of the orthodox Jewish faith
- the relief of poverty and sickness.

However, according to the correspondent 'the trust only supports a set list of charities working with older people, schools/colleges, hospitals and Christian causes. It does not have any money available for any charities not already on the list.'

In 2007/08 the trust had assets of £549,000 with an income of £113,000. Grants totalled £54,000. No further information was available.

Previously, grants in excess of £1,000 each were made to Yeshivas Hanegev (£10,000), JRRC (£10,000 in two grants) and Redcroft and Russian Immigrants (£5,000 each).

Applications Please note: the same organisations are supported each year, therefore the trust does not wish to receive any applications for funding.

Sueberry Ltd

Jewish and welfare

£163,000 (2007/08)
Beneficial area UK and overseas.

18 Clifton Gardens, London N15 6AP
Correspondent Mrs M Davis, Trustee
Trustees J Davis, Chair; Mrs H Davis; Mrs M Davis; D S Davis; C Davis; A D Davis; S M Davis; Y Davis.
CC Number 256566
Information available Accounts were on file at the Charity Commission but without a list of beneficiaries.

The trust makes grants to Jewish organisations and also to other UK welfare, educational and medical organisations benefiting children and young adults, at risk groups, people who are disadvantaged by poverty, or socially isolated people.

In 2007/08 the trust had assets of £62,000 and an income of £246,000. Grants were made totalling £163,000. A list of beneficiaries was not available. In previous years the trust has supported educational, religious and other charitable organisations.

Applications In writing to the correspondent.

The Alan Sugar Foundation

Jewish charities and general

£1.3 million (2007/08)
Beneficial area UK.

Sterling House, Langston Road, Loughton IG10 3TS
Tel. 020 3225 5560
Email colin@amsprop.com
Correspondent Colin Sandy, Trustee
Trustees Sir Alan Sugar; Colin Sandy; Simon Sugar; Daniel Sugar; Louise Baron.
CC Number 294880
Information available Accounts were available from the Charity Commission website.

This trust was established by the well-known ex-chair of Tottenham Hotspur FC, and gives a small number of substantial grants each year. Grants are made to registered charities that are of current and ongoing interest to the trustees.

In 2007/08 the trust had assets of £235,000 and an unusually large income of £1.1 million (£542,000 in 2006/07). This was due to a substantial donation of over £1 million from Sir Alan Sugar and his family. Grants were made totalling £1.3 million, again much more than the previous year (£262,000 in 2006/07).

Beneficiaries were: Great Ormond Street Hospital (£500,000); Jewish Community Secondary School Trust and Cancer Research UK (£250,000 each); Jewish Care (£200,000); LIV – Cystic Fibrosis (£75,000); Myeloma (£10,000); Second Space (£5,200); the Drugs Line (£5,000); Prostate Cancer Charitable Fund (£2,000); and Cancerbackup (£1,000).

Exclusions No grants for individuals or to non-registered charities.

Applications This trust states that it does not respond to unsolicited applications. All projects are initiated by the trustees.

The Adrienne and Leslie Sussman Charitable Trust

Jewish and general

£71,000 (2007/08)
Beneficial area UK, in practice Greater London, particularly Barnet.

25 Tillingbourne Gardens, London N3 3JJ
Correspondent Adrienne Sussman
Trustees Adrienne Sussman; Leslie Sussman; Martin Paisner.
CC Number 274955
Information available Accounts are on file at the Charity Commission, without a list of grants.

The trust supports a variety of Jewish, medical and social welfare organisations, including many in the Greater London area. In 2007/08 the trust had assets of £1.7 million and an income of £194,000. Grants were made totalling £71,000.

A list of beneficiaries was not available, however previous beneficiaries have included; BF Shvut Ami, Chai – Lifeline, B'nai B'rith Hillel Fund, Child Resettlement, Children and Youth Aliyah, Finchley Synagogue, Jewish Care, Nightingale House, Norwood Ravenswood and Sidney Sussex CLL.

Exclusions No grants to branches of UK charities outside Barnet, non-registered charities or individuals.

Applications In writing to the correspondent.

The Sutasoma Trust

Education and general

£105,000 (2007/08)
Beneficial area UK and overseas.

PO Box 1118, Cottenham, Cambridge CB24 8WQ
Tel. 07768 245384
Email sutasoma.trust@ntlworld.com
Correspondent Jane M Lichtenstein
Trustees Dr Angela R Hobart; Marcel A Burgauer; Jane M Lichtenstein; Prof.

Bruce Kapferer; Dr Sally Wolfe; Dr Piers Vitebsky.

CC Number 803301

Information available Accounts were available from the Charity Commission.

The trust's objects are 'to advance education and humanitarian activities by providing bursaries and support to institutions in the field of social sciences, humanities and humanitarian activities'. General grants may also be made. 'The trustees have indicated in the past that they prefer that annual donations should be made available to organisations on a recurring basis for the mid to long term'.

In 2007/08 the trust had assets of £2.3 million and an income of £113,000. Grants were made totalling £105,000. The largest grants went to Lucy Cavendish College Fellowship (£16,000) and University of Bergen (£12,000).

Other grants included those made to: LACP Zambia (£7,000); Practical Action Disappearing Lands (£6,000); Emslie Horniman Fund and School of Oriental and African Studies (£5,000 each); Merlin Medical Relief (£3,000); Corporation of Haverford and Link Literacy Training (£2,000 each); Harmony House Kerala (£1,000); and Anti-Slavery International (£500).

Applications In writing to the correspondent.

The Suva Foundation Limited

General

£258,000 (2007/08)

Beneficial area Unrestricted with a preference for Henley-on-Thames.

c/o 89 New Bond Street, London W1S 1DA

Correspondent The Trustees

Trustees *Mrs A Nicoll; P Nicoll.*

CC Number 1077057

Information available Accounts were on file at the Charity Commission.

Set up in 1999, the following was taken from the foundation's 2007/08 annual report:

The charity's principal activity during the year was the support of charities through the payments of donations. The objects of the charity are to promote any charitable

purpose or support any charity selected by the directors. It is expressly contemplated that the Arbib Foundation (Charity Commission no. 296358) may be the beneficiary of the application of some or all funds or other benefits by the charity.

In 2007/08 the foundation had assets of almost £9 million and an income of £246,000. Grants totalled £258,000 of which £255,000 went to the Arbib Foundation.

Other beneficiaries included: Pangbourne College and the Thames Valley and Cheltenham Ambulance Fund (£1,000 each); Langalanga Scholarship Fund and Remenham PCC (£500 each); and Friends of Henley Festival Society (£250).

Applications This trust does not accept unsolicited applications.

Swan Mountain Trust

Mental health and penal concerns

£32,000 (2007/08)

Beneficial area UK.

7 Mount Vernon, London NW3 6QS

Tel. 020 7794 2486

Correspondent Janet Hargreaves, Trustee

Trustees *Dodie Carter; Janet Hargreaves; Peter Kilgarriff; Calton Younger.*

CC Number 275594

Information available Accounts were on file with the Charity Commission.

The following information is take from the annual report and accounts.

The main charitable activities undertaken consist of the making of grants to organisations which are actively involved in the fields of mental health and penal affairs, the current principal focus of the trustees of the charity. Provision is also made to help prisoners with educational needs. Grants are made to meet specific needs and rarely exceed £1,500.

The trust has previously stated in its advice to applicants:

We are a very small grant-making trust; as such we like to ensure that our limited resources are used as effectively as possible. We do not consider contributing to a large appeal but would rather consider a piece of equipment or an activity for which we can

consider meeting the total cost, somewhere around £500. Alternatively, we will consider meeting the final amount of a larger appeal when most of the rest has been found.

In 2007/08 the trust had assets of £994,000 and an unusually large income of £106,000. This increase was due to a substantial legacy donation of £71,000. Grants were made to 28 organisations totalling £32,000.

Beneficiaries included: AVID – Association of Visitors to Immigrant Detainees (£2,000); Sheffield MIND (£1,600); Prision Advice and Care Trust – London (£1,500); HMP Morton Hall (£1,200); Community Action Halfway Home (£1,000); Foundation for the Arts and Mental Health (£940); Lifecraft – Cambridge and Corner House Resource Centre (£750 each); and Wigan and Leigh CVS – Freebirds Mental Health Group (£450).

Exclusions No grants for annual holidays, debt repayment, large appeals or for causes outside the trust's two main areas of work.

Applications In writing to the correspondent, enclosing an up-to-date report on your fundraising, and a copy of your most recent annual report and accounts (or any financial information you have). The trustees meet in early February, June and October each year, but can occasionally reach decisions quickly in an emergency. Applications should be made at least four weeks before the trustees' next meeting. The trust tries to be as responsive as it can be to appropriate applicants.

The Swan Trust

General, arts and culture

£30,000 (2007/08)

Beneficial area Overseas and the UK, with a preference for East Sussex, Kent, Surrey and West Sussex.

Pollen House, 10–12 Cork Street, London W1S 3LW

Tel. 020 7439 9061

Email charity@mfs.co.uk

Correspondent Laura Gosling

Trustee *The Cowdray Trust Limited.*

CC Number 261442

Information available Accounts were on file at the Charity Commission.

The trust makes grants to a range of organisations including a number that are arts and culture related. Priority is given to grants for one year or less; grants for up to two years are considered. Grants range from £20 up to around £10,000, but the majority tend to be below £1,000.

In 2007/08 the trust had assets of £1.1 million and an income of £27,000. Grants were made to 60 organisations totalling £30,000.

Beneficiaries included: Withyham Parochial Church Council (£11,000); Royal National Theatre (£1,500); Royal Academy Trust (£1,300); Blond McIndoe Centre (£1,000); Bowles (£500); Chichester Cathedral Restoration and Development Trust (£350); Combat Stress (£250); London Philharmonic Orchestra (£120); Southbank Centre (£45); and Friends of Friendless Churches (£20).

Exclusions No grants to individuals or non-registered charities.

Applications In writing to the correspondent. Acknowledgements will only be sent if a grant is being made.

The John Swire (1989) Charitable Trust

General
£425,000 (2007)
Beneficial area UK.

John Swire and Sons Ltd, Swire House, 59 Buckingham Gate, London SW1E 6AJ
Tel. 020 7834 7717
Correspondent Michael Todhunter, Charities Administrator
Trustees *Sir John Swire; J S Swire; B N Swire; M C Robinson; Lady Swire.*
CC Number 802142
Information available Full accounts were on file at the Charity Commission.

Established in 1989 by Sir John Swire of John Swire and Sons Ltd, merchants and ship owners, the trust supports a wide range of organisations including some in the area of arts, welfare, education, medicine and research.

In 2007 the trust had assets of £14 million and an income of £721,000. Grants were made totalling £425,000. The largest grants included those to: Canterbury Cathedral Developments Ltd (£80,000); Rod Kesson Benefit Fund

(£50,000); The Sir John Swire St Nicholas School and Educational Trust (£30,000); DISCS (£15,000); St John of Jerusalem Eye Hospital (£12,000); Inge Wakehurst Trust (£11,000); and Demelza – Hospice Care for Children and Prior's Court Foundation (£10,000 each).

Other grants included those to: Bird Atlas (£5,000); Action for ME (£4,000); Edenbridge Hospital (£3,000); Order of St John of Kent (£2,000); and Atlantic Salmon Trust, Downs Syndrome Association, Irish Guards Benevolent Fund, National Back Pain Association, Royal Association for Deaf and Dumb and Sustrans – National Cycle Network (£1,000 each).

Applications In writing to the correspondent.

The Swire Charitable Trust

General
£477,000 (2007)
Beneficial area Worldwide.

John Swire and Sons Ltd, Swire House, 59 Buckingham Gate, London SW1E 6AJ
Tel. 020 7834 7717
Correspondent Michael Todhunter, Charities Administrator
Trustees *Sir J Swire; Sir Adrian Swire; B N Swire; M J B Todhunter; P A Johansen; J S Swire.*
CC Number 270726
Information available Full accounts were on file at the Charity Commission.

In 2007 the trust had an income of £479,000 – almost entirely from donations received from John Swire & Sons Limited. Grants totalled £477,000.

Grants of £1,000 or more were listed in the accounts. Beneficiaries of the six largest grants were: Marine Society & Sea Cadets and Wantage Nursing Home Charitable Trust (£50,000 each); Neck & Head Cancer Research Trust (£25,000); Air League Educational Trust (£23,000); and Children in Crisis and Prior's Court Foundation (£20,000 each).

Other beneficiaries included: Breast Cancer Haven (£15,000); Head First (£10,000); Brooklands Museum Trust Limited (£5,000); Chelsea & Westminster Health Charity (£3,000); Warwickshire Firefighters Families Fund (£2,000); and The Cardinal Hume Centre (£1,000).

Grants of less than £1,000 each totalled £6,450.

Applications In writing to the correspondent. Applications are considered throughout the year.

The Hugh and Ruby Sykes Charitable Trust

General, medical, education and employment
£104,000 (2007/08)
Beneficial area Principally South Yorkshire, also Derbyshire.

The Coach House, Brookfield Manor, Hathersage, Hope Valley S32 1BR
Tel. 01433 651190
Email info@brookfieldmanor.com
Correspondent Brian Evans, Administrator
Trustees *Sir Hugh Sykes; Lady Ruby Sykes.*
CC Number 327648
Information available Accounts were on file at the Charity Commission, but without a list of grants.

This trust was set up in 1987 for general charitable purposes by Sir Hugh Sykes and his wife Lady Sykes. It supports local charities in South Yorkshire and Derbyshire, some major UK charities and a few medical charities.

In 2007/08 the trust had assets of £2.3 million and an income of £136,000. Grants were made totalling £104,000. A list of beneficiaries was not included in the accounts.

Exclusions No grants are made to individuals. Most grants are made to organisations which have a connection to one of the trustees.

Applications Applications can only be accepted from registered charities and should be in writing to the correspondent. In order to save administration costs, replies are not sent to unsuccessful applicants. If the trustees are able to consider a request for support, they aim to express interest within one month.

The Sylvanus Charitable Trust

Animal welfare and Roman Catholicism

£33,000 in Europe (2007)

Beneficial area Europe and North America.

Vernor Miles and Noble, 5 Raymond Buildings, Gray's Inn, London WC1R 5DD

Tel. 020 7242 8688

Correspondent John C Vernor Miles, Trustee

Trustees *John C Vernor Miles; Alexander D Gemmill; Wilfred E Vernor Miles; Gloria Taviner.*

CC Number 259520

Information available Full accounts were on file at the Charity Commission.

This trust was established in 1968 by the Countess of Kinnoull, who spent the last 40 years of her life in California, and supports animal welfare, prevention of animal cruelty and the teachings and practices of the Roman Catholic Church pre Second Vatican Council. Organisations in North America and Europe are supported, with the trust splitting its finances into two sections, namely, the sterling section (Europe) and the Dollar section (North America) to avoid currency troubles.

As the dollar section focuses solely on US giving (and information on it was unavailable), only the sterling section is described here.

In 2008 it had assets of £1.7 million and an income of £50,000. Grants were made to 17 organisations totalling £33,000.

The beneficiaries included: Mauritian Wildlife Foundation and Save the Elephants (£5,000 each); Durrell Wildlife Conservation Trust and Fauna & Flora International (£2,000 each); Mayhew Animal Home and Prevent Unwanted Pets (£1,500 each); and Blue Cross, Help in Suffering, Newcastle Dog and Cat Shelter and Society for Abandoned Animals (£1,000 each).

Exclusions No grants for expeditions, scholarships or individuals.

Applications In writing to the correspondent. The trustees meet once a year.

T and S Trust Fund

Orthodox Jewish

£92,000 (2007/08)

Beneficial area Greater London, Gateshead and Manchester City.

96 Whitehall Road, Gateshead, Tyne and Wear NE8 4ET

Tel. 0191 482 5050

Correspondent A Sandier, Trustee

Trustees *A T Sandler; Mrs S Sandler; E Salomon.*

CC Number 1095939

Information available Accounts were on file at the Charity Commission.

The following information is taken from the fund's annual report:

The objects of the charity are the advancement of education according to the tenets of the orthodox Jewish faith, the advancement of the orthodox Jewish religion and the relief of poverty amongst older people or persons in need, hardship and distress in the Jewish community.

In 2007/08 the trust had assets of £621,000 and an income of £43,000. Grants were made to eight organisations and totalled £92,000.

The beneficiaries were: Stervon Ltd and Tomchei Yotzei Anglia (£23,000 each); VHLT (£16,000); Y Y Gemach (£2,000); Bnos Yisroel School (£1,500); and Gateshead Hebrew Congregation, Manchester Talmudical College and Sameach (£1,000 each).

In addition to the above there were 'relief of poverty grants' (£15,000) and 'educational grants' (£5,600). Donations of under £1,000 each totalled £3,350.

Applications In writing to the correspondent.

The Tabeel Trust

Evangelical Christian

£113,000 (2007/08)

Beneficial area Worldwide with a preference for Clacton (Essex).

Dairy House Farm, Little Clacton Road, Great Holland, Frinton-on-Sea CO13 0EX

Tel. 01255 812130

Correspondent Douglas K Brown, Secretary

Trustees *Douglas K Brown; Pauline M Brown; Barbara J Carter; Dr Mary P Clark; Jean A Richardson; James Davey; Sarah Taylor; Nigel Davey.*

CC Number 266645

Information available Full accounts were on file at the Charity Commission.

This trust primarily supports evangelical Christian activities and projects which are either based in Clacton or are personally known to one or more of the trustees. In 2007/08 it had assets amounting to £870,000 and an income of £46,000. Grants were made to 38 organisations totalling £113,000.

Beneficiaries included: St George's Crypt – Leeds (£30,000); Essex County Evangelists' – Accommodation Trust (£10,000); ZACS (£6,000); Radio Worldwide (£5,000); Barnabas Fund (£4,000); Viz a Viz (£3,000); Tabernacle Baptist Church – Penarth (£2,000); Christian Institute (£1,000); and Upesi and Salvation Army – Clacton (£500 each).

Applications Only charities with which a trustee already has contact should apply. Grants are considered at trustees' meetings in May and November.

Tadlus Limited

Orthodox Jewish

Nil (2007/08)

Beneficial area UK and Israel.

6 Spring Hill, London E5 9BE

Correspondent J Grosskopf

Trustees *J M Grosskopf; M Grosskopf; C S Grosskopf.*

CC Number 1109982

Information available Accounts were on file at the Charity Commission, with no details of grantmaking.

Set up in 2005, this trust supports the advancement of religion in accordance with the orthodox Jewish faith. Grants are made to promote and maintain institutions, organisations and individuals involved in religious education and worship, and for the relief of individuals in need.

In 2007/08 the trust had assets of £1 million and an income £76,000. No grants were made during the year, for which no explanation was given in the accounts. However, the trust has experienced 'unusual and unexpected' problems with both of its investment properties during the year, which could account for the lack of grantmaking. In 2006/07 grants were made totalling £89,000.

Applications In writing to the correspondent.

The Gay and Keith Talbot Trust

Overseas aid, health and famine relief

£41,000 (2008/09)
Beneficial area Worldwide.

Fold Howe, Kentmere, Kendal LA8 9JW
Correspondent Keith Talbot
Trustees *Gay Talbot; Keith Talbot.*
CC Number 1102192
Information available Accounts were on file at the Charity Commission.

Established in 2004, this trust mainly supports charities working in developing countries. In 2008/09 it had an income of £148,000, made up of voluntary income (£147,000) and investment income (£270). Assets stood at £131,000. Grants to nine organisations totalled £41,000.

Beneficiaries were: Medical Missionaries of Mary – Uganda and Nigeria (£12,000); Cystic Fibrosis Trust (£10,000); SVP – Sudan, Impact Foundation – Bangladesh and Uganda Childbirth Injury Fund (£5,000 each); Rwanda Group Trust (£1,500); CAFOD – Sudan and Door of Hope (£1,000 each); Our Lady of Windermere and St Herbert (£500).

Applications In writing to the correspondent.

The Talbot Village Trust

General

£593,000 (2008)
Beneficial area The boroughs of Bournemouth, Christchurch and Poole; the districts of East Dorset and Purbeck.

Dickinson Manser, 5 Parkstone Road, Poole BH15 2NL
Tel. 01202 673071
Email garycox@dickinsonmanser.co.uk
Correspondent Gary S Cox, Clerk
Trustees *Christopher Lees, Chair; James Fleming; Sir George Meyrick; Sir Thomas Salt; Russell Rowe; Earl of Shaftesbury.*
CC Number 249349
Information available Accounts were on file at the Charity Commission.

Support is given to 'other charitable bodies, churches, schools and the like for projects which support young people, older people and the disadvantaged in the boroughs of Bournemouth, Christchurch and Poole and the districts of East Dorset and Purbeck.' In addition, the trust also gives extensive support to charities in the form of loans. The charity owns and manages land and property at Talbot Village, Bournemouth, including almshouses which it maintains through an associated trust. There is a strong property focus to much of the trust's work.

As part of the trust's rolling five year plan it aims to make grants and loans averaging £800,000 per annum, in addition to its regular support of St Mark's Church, St Mark's School, the University Chaplaincy and others. The majority of grants are made for capital costs such as, equipment, refurbishment and building extensions.

In 2008 the trust had assets of £28 million and an income of £1.9 million of which nearly £1.1 million was obtained from rents. Grants authorised and paid during the year totalled £270,000 whilst donations authorised but left unpaid totalled £354,000. Allowing for two lapsed grants, this gave a grant total of £593,000. The trust acknowledges that this is less than the objective of £800,000 per annum, but expects that this will average out over the next three to five years.

Grants authorised and paid during the year included those to: Bournemouth

War Memorial Homes (£38,000); Butterfly Appeal (£35,000); Kinson Community Centre (£25,000); Lighthouse Family Church (£20,000); Deanery Youth Worker Project (£16,000); International Care Network (£10,000); Purbeck Strings (£6,000); St Luke's Church Hall (£4,000); Children's Heart Foundation (£2,500); and Embassy Youth Centre (£1,300).

Exclusions No grants for individuals.

Applications In writing to the correspondent.

Talteg Ltd

Jewish and welfare

£361,000 (2008)
Beneficial area UK, with a preference for Scotland.

90 Mitchell Street, Glasgow G1 3NQ
Tel. 0141 221 3353
Correspondent F S Berkeley, Trustee
Trustees *F S Berkeley, Chair; M Berkeley; A N Berkeley; M Berkeley; Miss D L Berkeley.*
CC Number 283253
Information available Accounts were on file at the Charity Commission, but without a grants list or a narrative report.

In 2008 the trust had assets totalling £3.4 million and an income of £512,000. Grants were made during the year totalling £361,000.

Previous beneficiaries include British Friends of Laniado Hospital, Centre for Jewish Studies, Society of Friends of the Torah, Glasgow Jewish Community Trust, National Trust for Scotland, Ayrshire Hospice, Earl Haig Fund – Scotland and RSSPCC.

Applications In writing to the correspondent.

The Lady Tangye Charitable Trust

Catholic, overseas aid and general

£29,000 (2007/08)

Beneficial area UK and worldwide, with some preference for the Midlands.

55 Warwick Crest, Arthur Road, Birmingham B15 2LH

Correspondent Colin Ferguson Smith, Trustee

Trustees *Gitta Clarisse Gilzean Tangye; Colin Ferguson Smith; Michael Plaut.*

CC Number 1044220

Information available Accounts are on file at the Charity Commission.

This trust has general charitable purposes, with a preference for work in the Midlands and the developing world. Christian and environmental causes are well represented in the grants list.

In 2007/08 it had assets of £583,000, which generated an income of £30,000. Grants were made to 21 organisations totalling £29,000.

Beneficiaries included: West Midland Urban Wildlife Trust (£3,000); Spana, ChildLine – Midlands and Aid to the Church in Need (£2,000 each); Amnesty International, Priest Training Fund and Crew Trust (£1,500 each); St Saviour's Church, Walsall and District Samaritans, Life and European Children's Trust (£1,000 each); and Charity Ignite – Big Ideal (£500).

Applications In writing to the correspondent.

The Tanner Trust

General

£382,000 (2007/08)

Beneficial area UK, with a slight preference for the south of England, and overseas.

c/o Blake Lapthorn Tarlo Lyons, Harbour Court, Compass Road, Portsmouth PO6 4ST

Tel. 02392 221 122 **Fax** 02392 221 123

Correspondent Celine Lecomte, Trust Administrator

Trustees *Alice P Williams; Lucie Nottingham.*

CC Number 1021175

Information available Full accounts were on file at the Charity Commission.

This trust has general charitable purposes, supporting organisations worldwide. The grants list shows no cause or geographical regions favoured or missing, although there appear to be many organisations concerned with young people, welfare and relief work.

In 2007/08 the trust had assets of £5.2 million, an income of £431,000 and made about 140 grants totalling £382,000.

Beneficiaries included: Help for Heroes (£7,000); Foresta 2000 – Din L-Art Helwa and National Trust (£6,000 each); Yorkshire Dales Millenium Trust and Truro Cathedral Music (£5,000 each); Holton Lee (£4,500); Practical Action (£4,000); Homeopaths without Borders (£3,000); Cooltan Arts (£2,800); Book Power (£2,000); and Elliot Foundation (£500).

Exclusions No grants to individuals.

Applications The trust states that unsolicited applications are, without exception, not considered. Support is only given to charities personally known to the trustees.

The Lili Tapper Charitable Foundation

Jewish

£39,000 (2007/08)

Beneficial area UK.

Yew Tree Cottage, Artists Lane, Nether Alderley, Macclesfield SK10 4UA

Correspondent Michael Webber

Trustees *Michael Webber; Dr Jonathan Webber.*

CC Number 268523

Information available Accounts were available from the Charity Commission, without a list of grants.

The trust primarily supports organisations benefiting Jewish people.

In 2007/08 it had assets of £2.9 million, which generated an income of £156,000.

Grants were made to 18 organisations totalling £39,000. No details of grant beneficiaries were available.

Previous beneficiaries include: UJIA, CST, Manchester Jewish Foundation, Teenage Cancer Trust, Keshet Eilon, Israel Educational Foundation, Chicken Shed Theatre Company and Jewish Representation Council.

Exclusions No grants to individuals.

Applications The trust states that it does not respond to any unsolicited applications.

The Tay Charitable Trust

General

£216,000 (2007/08)

Beneficial area UK, with a preference for Scotland, particularly Dundee.

6 Douglas Terrace, Broughty Ferry, Dundee DD5 1EA

Correspondent Mrs E A Mussen, Trustee

Trustees *Mrs E A Mussen; Mrs Z C Martin; G C Bonar.*

SC Number SC001004

Information available Accounts were provided by the trust.

This trust has general charitable purposes and supports a wide range of causes. Grants are generally made to UK-wide charities or organisations benefiting Scotland or Dundee, although local groups elsewhere can also be supported.

In 2008/09 the trust had assets of £4.1 million and an income of £231,000. Grants were made to 241 charities totalling £216,000.

Beneficiaries of grants of £1,000 or more included: Dundee Heritage Trust and RNLI (£5,000 each); Boarders Forest Trust, DermaTrust, Edinburgh World Heritage Trust, Maritime Volunteer Service and Univeristy of St Andrews – Low Scholarship (£3,000 each); Bowel Cancer UK, High Blood Pressure Foundation, John Muir Trust and National Trust for Scotland (£2,000 each); Princess Royal Trust for Carers (£1,500); and Army Benevolent Fund, Changing Faces, Dundee Symphony Orchestra, Guide Dogs for the Blind, Lincoln Cathedral, Samaritans, Scottish Countryside Alliance Trust, Skillforce

Development and Tayside Council on Alcohol (£1,000 each).

Exclusions Grants are only given to charities recognised by the Inland Revenue. No grants to individuals.

Applications No standard form; applications in writing to the correspondent, including a financial statement. A stamped, addressed envelope is appreciated.

C B and H H Taylor 1984 Trust

Quaker and general

£261,000 (2007/08)

Beneficial area West Midlands, Ireland and overseas.

c/o Home Farm, Abberton, Pershore WR10 2NR

Correspondent William James Taylor, Trustee

Trustees *Clare H Norton; Elizabeth J Birmingham; John A B Taylor; William James Taylor; Constance M Penny; Thomas W Penny; Robert J Birmingham; Simon B Taylor.*

CC Number 291363

Information available Accounts were on file at the Charity Commission.

The trust's geographical areas of benefit are:

- organisations serving Birmingham and the West Midlands
- organisations outside the West Midlands where the trust has well-established links
- organisations in Ireland
- UK-based charities working overseas.

The general areas of benefit are:

- the Religious Society of Friends (Quakers) and other religious denominations
- healthcare projects
- social welfare: community groups; children and young people; older people; disadvantaged people; people with disabilities; homeless people; housing initiatives; counselling and mediation agencies
- education: adult literacy schemes; employment training; youth work
- penal affairs: work with offenders and ex-offenders; police projects

- the environment and conservation work
- the arts: museums and art galleries; music and drama
- Ireland: cross-community health and social welfare projects
- UK charities working overseas on long-term development projects.

About 60% of grants are for the work and concerns of the Religious Society of Friends (Quakers). The trust favours specific applications. It does not usually award grants on an annual basis for revenue costs. Applications are encouraged from minority groups and women-led initiatives. Grants, which are made only to or through registered charities, range from £500 to £5,000. Larger grants are seldom awarded.

In 2007/08 the trust had assets of £7.6 million and an income of £260,000. Grants to 131 organisations totalled £261,000.

The two largest grants went to Britain Yearly Meeting (£27,000) and Bournville Almshouses (£25,000).

Other beneficiaries included: Warwickshire Monthly Meeting (£9,500); Friends of Swanirvar (£6,000); Tiny Tim's Children's Centre (£5,000); Fry Housing Trust (£4,000); Community Initiative Programme (£3,000); Medical Aid for Palestinians (£1,500); Bees Abroad (£1,000); Christ's Church Selly Park (£850); Circul-8 Credit Union (£200); and Dudley Association of Community Networks (£100).

Exclusions The trust does not fund: individuals (whether for research, expeditions, educational purposes and so on); local projects or groups outside the West Midlands; or projects concerned with travel or adventure.

Applications There is no formal application form. Applicants should write to the correspondent giving the charity's registration number, a brief description of the charity's activities, and details of the specific project for which the grant is being sought. Applicants should also include a budget of the proposed work, together with a copy of the charity's most recent accounts. Trustees will also wish to know what funds have already been raised for the project and how the shortfall will be met.

The trust states that it receives more applications than it can support. Therefore, even if work falls within its policy it may not be able to help, particularly if the project is outside the West Midlands.

Trustees meet twice each year, in May and November. Applications will be acknowledged if a stamped, addressed envelope is provided.

The Cyril Taylor Charitable Trust

Education

£32,000 (2007/08)

Beneficial area Generally in Greater London.

Penningtons, Abacus House, 33 Gutter Lane, London EC2V 8AR

Tel. 020 7457 3000 **Fax** 020 7457 3240

Email chris.lintott@penningtons.co.uk

Correspondent Christopher Lintott, Trustee

Trustees *Sir Cyril Taylor, Chair; Clifford D Joseph; Robert W Maas; Peter A Tchereprine; Stephen Rasch; Christopher Lintott; Lady June Taylor; Jonathan Berry; William Gertz; Marcie Schneider.*

CC Number 1040179

Information available Accounts were on file at the Charity Commission.

This trust makes grants to organisations benefiting students in particular those studying at Richmond College and the American International University in London.

In 2007/08 the trust had assets of £39,000 and an income of £64,000. Grants were made totalling £32,000.

Beneficiaries were: Richmond Foundation (£25,000); Institute of Economic Affairs and the British Friends of Harvard Business School (£3,000 each); and Trinity Hall, Cambridge (£1,000).

Applications In writing to the correspondent.

Rosanna Taylor's 1987 Charity Trust

General

£54,000 (2007/08)

Beneficial area UK and overseas, with a preference for Oxfordshire and West Sussex.

The Cowdray Trust Ltd, Pollen House, 10–12 Cork Street, London W1S 3LW

Tel. 020 7439 9061

Email charity@mfs.co.uk

Correspondent Laura Gosling

Trustee *The Cowdray Trust Limited.*

CC Number 297210

Information available Accounts were on file at the Charity Commission.

The trust has general charitable purposes, including support for medical, cancer, child development and environmental charities.

In 2007/08 the trust had assets of £1.2 million, an income of £34,000 and made grants totalling £54,000. Donations were made to the Charities Aid Foundation (£28,000) and Pearson Taylor Trust (£26,000).

Exclusions No grants to individuals or non-registered charities.

Applications In writing to the correspondent. Acknowledgements are not sent to unsuccessful applicants.

Tegham Limited

Orthodox Jewish faith and welfare

£372,000 (2007/08)

Beneficial area UK.

1 Hallswelle Road, London NW11 0DH

Correspondent Mrs S Fluss, Trustee

Trustees *Mrs S Fluss; Miss N Fluss.*

CC Number 283066

Information available Accounts were on file at the Charity Commission but without a list of grants.

This trust supports the promotion of the orthodox Jewish faith and the relief of poverty.

In 2007/08 the trust had assets of £1.6 million, an income of £279,000 and made grants totalling £372,000. Unfortunately no grants list was available for this period.

Applications The trust has stated that it has enough causes to support and does not welcome other applications.

Thackray Medical Research Trust

History of medical products and of their supply trade

£157,000 (2007/08)

Beneficial area Worldwide.

c/o Thackray Museum, Beckett Street, Leeds LS9 7LN

Correspondent The Chair of the Trustees

Trustees *S Warren, Chair; J Campbell; W Mathie; M S Schweiger; C Thackray; W M Wrigley.*

CC Number 702896

Information available Accounts were on file at the Charity Commission.

The trust is a registered charity and was established by Paul Thackray with the principal aims being:

- to set up a museum dedicated to the history of medicine
- to support research into the same subject, particularly into the history of the medical supply trades
- to provide support for charitable organisations which specialise in supplying medical equipment to or within developing countries.

Over the last few years, the majority of the funds available have been devoted to setting up the Thackray Museum in Leeds. The museum is a charity largely independent of the trust and with its own board of trustees.

In 2007/08 it had assets of almost £6 million and an income of £234,000. Grants awarded totalled £157,000, of which £131,000 went to the Thackray Museum.

Applications In writing to the correspondent. The trustees usually meet twice a year.

The Thames Wharf Charity

General

£260,000 (2007/08)

Beneficial area UK.

Thames Wharf Studios, Rainville Road, London W6 9HA

Correspondent The Trustees

Trustees *Avtar Lotay; Patrick Burgess; Graham Stirk.*

CC Number 1000796

Information available Accounts were on file at the Charity Commission.

In 2007/08 the charity had an income of £548,000 and made grants to about 150 organisations totalling £260,000. Assets totalled £838,000.

The largest grants went to Goldschmied Foundation (£62,000), Glebe Court Residents Support Group (£16,000) and Architectural Association – Stephen Lawrence Scholarship Fund (£10,000).

Beneficiaries included: Ellenor Foundation Ltd (£6,800); Amnesty International (£6,600); Clinical Science Foundation and Mossbourne Academy (£5,000 each); Medical Aid for Palestinians (£3,000); British Heart Foundation (£2,800); BUKKA Education and Research Trust (£2,500); Scope and Willow Foundation (£1,500 each); Zoological Society (£1,300); Art Academy, Bedford Pentecostal Church and Foresight (£1,000 each); National Gallery (£600); Cornwall Hospice, Human Rights Watch Charitable Trust and Tibet Relief Fund (£500 each); Hope Hospice (£450); Greenpeace Environmental Trust and Royal Marsden Hospital Charity (£400 each); and Macintyre Charitable Trust (£100).

Exclusions No grants for the purchase of property, motor vehicles or holidays.

Applications In writing to the correspondent.

The Thistle Trust

Arts

£65,000 (2007/08)

Beneficial area UK.

PO Box 57005, 30 Gresham Street, London EC2P 2US

Correspondent Nicholas Kerr-Sheppard, Secretary

Trustees *Madeleine, Lady Kleinwort; Nigel Porteous; Neil Morris; Donald McGilvray; Nicholas Kerr-Sheppard.*

CC Number 1091327

Information available Accounts were on file at the Charity Commission.

This trust was established in 2002, and during the following year it received a £1 million endowment from the settlor. Its main objects are to promote study and research in the arts and to further public knowledge and education of art.

In 2007/08 the trust had assets of £1.3 million and an income of £49,000. Grants totalled £65,000.

Beneficiaries included: Juventus Lyrica Asociación (£8,000); Prix de Lausanne (£6,000); the Opera Group, the Place, Wells Cathedral School and Whitechapel Art Gallery (£5,000 each); Yvonne Arnaud Theatre (£3,500); Welsh Youth Classical Music (£3,000); Royal Liverpool Philharmonic (£2,500); Blindart, Grid Iron Theatre Co Ltd, Making Music and Somerset House Trust (£2,000 each); Bampton Classical, Conquest Art Centre, Late Music Festival, Polka Children Theatre Ltd, Scottish Opera and Sheffield Mencap and Gateway (£1,000 each); Heather Music Festival (£500); and Deep Impact Theatre Co. (£200).

Exclusions No grants to individuals.

Applications In writing to the correspondent including most recent report and financial accounts. The trustees meet at least once a year with only successful applicants notified of the trustees' decision.

The Loke Wan Tho Memorial Foundation

Environment, conservation, medical causes and overseas aid

£63,000 (2007/08)
Beneficial area Worldwide.

Abacus Financial Services Ltd, La Motte Chambers, St Helier, Jersey JE1 1BJ

Correspondent The Secretary

Trustees *Lady Y P McNeice; Mrs T S Tonkyn; A P Tonkyn.*

CC Number 264273

Information available Accounts were on file at the Charity Commission.

The trust supports environment/conservation organisations, medical causes and overseas aid organisations. In 2007/08 it had assets of £5.5 million and an income of £153,000. Grants totalled £63,000.

Beneficiaries included: Opportunity International (£5,000); Alzheimer's Disease International, Brooke Hospital for Animals, Plantlife, Rainforest Concern, SPANA, Tree Aid and University of Bristol – Animal Welfare Group (£4,000 each); Cancer Research UK (£3,000); and THRIVE (£2,000).

Applications In writing to the correspondent.

The Thomas Wall Trust

Education and welfare

£32,000 to organisations
(2007/08)
Beneficial area UK.

PO Box 52781, London EC2P 2UT

Email information@thomaswalltrust.org.uk

Website www.thomaswalltrust.org.uk

Correspondent Prof. G Holt, Director

Trustees *Dr G M Copland, Chair; Mrs M A Barrie; P Bellamy; C R Broomfield; Miss A S Kennedy; Miss A-M Martin; Mrs A Mullins; J Porteous; Revd Dr R Waller.*

CC Number 206121

Information available Accounts on file at the Charity Commission.

This trust makes grants to both individuals and charitable organisations. 'The applying organisation, movement or institution has to be a registered charity with objects in a broad sense educational and/or concerned with social service'.

Please note: on grants to individuals: 'The trustees consider applications from UK nationals only who are in financial need and who wish to undertake educational courses at any level and duration, especially courses which are vocational or are concerned with social service in a broad sense and which will lead to paid employment.'

In 2007/08 the trust had assets of £2.7 million and an income of £123,000. Grants to organisations totalled £32,000 and to individuals over £37,000.

Beneficiaries included: Konnect9 Worldwide, Octobus Project and Seafood Training Centre (£2,000 each); Back to Work (£1,500); the Asha Centre (£1,200); and Acorn Christian Ministries, Barton Training Trust, Cleveland Housing Advice Centre, Derby Toc H Children's Camp, Dressability, the Dystonia Society, Federation of Artistic and Creative Therapy, Island Advice Centre, Volunteer Centre North Warwickshire, Where Next Association and Wildwood Trust (£1,000 each).

Exclusions Grants are not made: towards the erection, upkeep or renovation of buildings; to hospitals, almshouses or similar institutions; for objects which are purely medical; for projects outside of the UK.

Applications There is no application form for charitable organisations to use except that all applicants must complete a cover sheet which can be downloaded from the trust's website. A copy of the latest available set of accounts for the charity should be included along with a stamped, addressed envelope, to acknowledge receipt of application.

The trustees meet twice a year, in July and November. Applications for the July meeting must be received by mid-May and for the November meeting by end of September.

The Maurice and Vivien Thompson Charitable Trust

General

£29,000 (2007/08)
Beneficial area UK.

2 The Orchard, London W4 1JX

Correspondent M N B Thompson, Trustee

Trustees *M N B Thompson; Mrs V Thomson; P Rhodes.*

CC Number 1085041

Information available Accounts were on file at the Charity Commission.

341

In 2007/08 the trust had assets of £1.3 million and an income of £239,000, including £211,000 from donations. Grants to eight organisations totalled £29,000.

Beneficiaries were: Beacon Fellowship Charitable Trust (£15,000); Martin Johnson Development Scholarship (£7,500); Pelican Cancer Foundation (£3,000); Leicester and Rutland Crimebeat (£1,800); Shackleton Foundation and Sight for Africa (£1,000 each); RIED (£200); and Bridge2Aid (£100).

Applications In writing to the correspondent.

The Sue Thomson Foundation

Christ's Hospital School and education

£106,000 (2007/08)

Beneficial area UK, Sussex, London and Surrey.

Furners Keep, Furners Lane, Henfield BN5 9HS

Tel. 01273 493461

Email thesuethomsonfoundation@ macdream.net

Correspondent Jane Akers, Administrator

Trustees *Susan M Mitchell, Chair; Timothy J Binnington; Charles L Corman; Kathleen Duncan; Susannah Holliman.*

CC Number 298808

Information available Accounts were on file at the Charity Commission.

The foundation exists to support children in need in the UK, mainly by helping Christ's Hospital and the school in Horsham which caters specifically for children in need. Other areas of support include educational and self-help organisations and projects. Grants are awarded within one of three categories:

- major grants which are above £5,000
- regular grants which can be from £500 to £5,000
- special grants which can be for up to £3,000.

In 2007/08 the trust had assets of £2.6 million and an income of £434,000. Grants paid totalled £106,000, divided

between education (£80,000) and welfare (£26,000).

Major grants

The majority of the funds went to Christ's Hospital, which received £82,000. The foundation nominates one new entrant each year from a needy background to the school, subject to the child meeting Christ's Hospital's own admissions criteria academically, socially and in terms of need. The foundation commits to contributing to the child's costs at a level agreed with Christ's Hospital for as long as each of them remains in the school.

Regular grants

It is the policy of the trustees to provide up to 10% of the foundation's available income each year for grants in this category, subject to the foundation's commitments to Christ's Hospital having been satisfied. Charities eligible for consideration for grants at this level include:

- charities related to Christ's Hospital including the sister school, King Edward's – Witley
- UK booktrade charities, including the charities of the Worshipful Company of Stationers and Newspaper Makers
- suitable grant-making charities selected in recognition of pro-bono professional work done for the foundation by its trustees or others
- special situations or other applications at the trustees' discretion.

Grants in this category may be spread over a period of years.

Special grants

It is the policy of the trustees to set aside a further 10% of available income each year for this programme, subject to its commitments in the major and medium categories and other financial needs having been met. Special grants are awarded to up to four small charities at any one time. They are confined to charities in Sussex, Surrey and London that support young and older people in need through no fault of their own, often via well run small self-help organisations.

Donations included: the Sussex Snowdrop – Chichester (£3,000); Brighton and Hove Parents and Children Group and Streets Alive Theatre Company – Lambeth (£2,000 each); the National Literacy Trust – London (£1,400); and the St Bride Foundation – London (£500).

Exclusions No grants to large, national charities (except Christ's Hospital) or individuals, except as part of a specific scheme. No research projects, charities

concerned with animals, birds, the environment, gardens or historic buildings.

Applications In writing to the correspondent, or preliminary telephone enquiry. Unsolicited applications are not acknowledged, unless accompanied by a stamped, addressed envelope or an email address.

The Thornton Foundation

General

£275,000 (2007/08)

Beneficial area UK.

Stephenson Harwood, 1 St Paul's Churchyard, London EC4M 8SH

Correspondent A H Isaacs

Trustees *R C Thornton, Chair; A H Isaacs; H D C Thornton; Mrs S J Thornton.*

CC Number 326383

Information available Accounts are on file at the Charity Commission.

The object of the foundation is to make grants to charities selected by the trustees. The principal guideline of the trust is to use the funds to further charitable causes where their money will, as far as possible, act as 'high powered money', in other words be of significant use to the cause. Only causes that are known personally to the trustees and/or that they are able to investigate thoroughly are supported. The trust states it is proactive rather than reactive in seeking applicants.

In 2007/08 the trust had assets of £4.1 million, which generated an income of £74,000. Grants totalling £275,000 were made to 19 organisations, of which many were supported in the previous year.

Beneficiaries included: the Marine Society and Sea Cadets (£130,000); St Dunstan-in-the-West (£50,000); the Tick Tock Club (£32,000); Stowe School Foundation (£10,000); The Cirdan Sailing Trust (£7,500); Helen House (£6,000); Action for Blind People, Books Abroad, Keble College – Oxford and Reed's School Foundation (£5,000 each); the Tait Memorial Trust (£3,000); BREAK Prisoners of Conscience and St Paul's Church Knightsbridge (£2,000 each); and Bishop's Castle Hospital

Patient's Fund and the Handel Society (£1,000 each).

Applications The trust strongly emphasises that it does not accept unsolicited applications, and, as it states above, only organisations that are known to one of the trustees will be considered for support. Any unsolicited applications will not receive a reply.

The Thornton Trust

Evangelical Christianity, education, relief of sickness and poverty

£218,000 (2007/08)
Beneficial area UK and overseas.

Hunters Cottage, Hunters Yard, Debden Road, Saffron Walden CB11 4AA
Correspondent D H Thornton, Trustee
Trustees D H Thornton; Mrs B Y Thornton; J D Thornton.
CC Number 205357
Information available Accounts were on file at the Charity Commission.

This trust was created in 1962 for 'the promotion of and furthering of education and the Evangelical Christian faith, and assisting in the relief of sickness, suffering and poverty'.

In 2007/08 it had assets of £1.2 million and an income of £80,000. Grants were made to 79 organisations totalling £218,000.

Beneficiaries included: Christian Action Research and Education (£53,000); Africa Inland Mission (£23,000); Saffron Walden Baptist Church (£11,000); London School of Theology (£7,000); Tyndale House (£6,000); Bible Society, Keswick Convention (£5,000); Mildmay Mission Hospital (£4,500); Send a Cow (£3,000); Stort Valley Schools Trust (£2,500); Criccieth HC Evangelism Trust, International Fellowship of Evangelical Students and Salvation Army (£2,000 each); National Library for the Blind (£1,000); ChildLine (£200); Hertford Museum (£150); and CIOB Benevolent Fund (£50).

Applications The trust states: 'Our funds are fully committed and we regret that we are unable to respond to the many unsolicited calls for assistance we are now receiving.'

The Three Oaks Trust

Welfare

£149,000 to organisations (2007/08)
Beneficial area UK and overseas, with a preference for West Sussex.

PO Box 243, Crawley RH10 6YB
Email contact@thethreeoakstrust.co.uk
Website www.thethreeoakstrust.co.uk
Correspondent The Trustees
Trustees Mrs M E Griffin; Mrs C A Johnson; Mrs P A Wilkinson; Dr P Kane; Mrs S A Kane.
CC Number 297079
Information available Accounts were on file at the Charity Commission.

Grants are made to organisations that promote the welfare of individuals and families. Grants are also made to individuals via statutory authorities or voluntary agencies. The trust regularly supports the same welfare organisations in the UK and overseas each year.

In 2007/08 the trust had assets of £5.9 million and a total income of £227,000. Grants were made totalling £212,000 of which £149,000 was donated to organisations and £63,000 to individuals. Grants were broken down as follows, shown here with examples of beneficiaries:

Within the UK – 19 grants totalling £103,000
Crawley Open House and MIND (£10,000 each); Dalesdown and Raynauds Association (£7,500 each); Abilitynet, Adoption Support UK and Coventry Cyrenians (£5,000 each); and Adur Information Shop (£2,500).

Overseas aid – 12 grants totalling £46,000
British Yemeni Society, CECO, Janeve Foundation and Kaloko Trust UK (£5,000 each); and CFDP (£1,000).

Exclusions No direct applications from individuals. Applications from students for gap year activities are not a priority and will not be funded.

Applications 'The trustees intend to continue supporting the organisations that they have supported in the past and are not planning to fund any new projects in the near future. To save administrative costs, the trustees do not respond to requests, unless they are considering making a donation.'

The Thriplow Charitable Trust

Higher and further education and research

£83,000 (2007/08)
Beneficial area Preference for British institutions.

PO Box 225, Royston SG8 1BG
Correspondent Mrs C Walston
Trustees Sir Peter Swinnerton-Dyer, Chair; Dr Harriet Crawford; Prof. Christopher Bayly; Sir David Wallace; Dame Jean Thomas.
CC Number 1025531
Information available Accounts were on file at the Charity Commission, without a list of grants.

The charity was established by a trust deed in 1983. Its main aims are the furtherance of higher and further education and research, with preference given to British institutions.

Projects that have generally been supported in the past include contributions to research study funds, research fellowships, academic training schemes, computer facilities and building projects. Specific projects are preferred rather than contributions to general running costs. The trust prefers to support smaller projects where grants can 'make a difference'.

In 2007/08 it had an income of £94,000 and gave grants totalling £83,000.

Previous beneficiaries have included Cambridge University Library, Centre of South Asian Studies, Computer Aid International, Fight for Sight, Fitzwilliam Museum, Foundation for Prevention of Blindness, Foundation of Research Students, Hearing Research Trust, Inspire Foundation, Loughborough University, Marie Curie Cancer Care, Royal Botanic Gardens, Royal College of Music, Transplant Trust and University of Reading.

Exclusions Grants can only be made to charitable bodies or component parts of charitable bodies. In no circumstances can grants be made to individuals.

Applications There is no application form. A letter of application should specify the purpose for which funds are sought and the costings of the project. It should be indicated whether other applications for funds are pending and, if the funds are to be channelled to an individual or a small group, what degree of supervision over the quality of the work would be exercised by the institution. Trustee meetings are held twice a year – in spring and in autumn.

The Tinsley Foundation

Human rights, poverty and homelessness and health education in underdeveloped countries

£153,000 (2007/08)
Beneficial area UK and overseas.

14 St Mary's Street, Stamford PE9 2DF
Tel. 01780 762056 **Fax** 01780 767594
Email hctinsley@aol.com
Correspondent Henry C Tinsley, Trustee
Trustees *H C Tinsley; Mrs R C Tinsley; T A Jones.*
CC Number 1076537
Information available Accounts were on file at the Charity Commission.

The foundation was founded by Henry Tinsley in 1999 and will support:

- charities which promote human rights and democratisation and/or which educate against racism, discrimination and oppression
- charities which promote self-help in fighting poverty and homelessness
- charities which provide reproductive health education in underdeveloped countries, but specifically excluding charities whose policy is against abortion or birth control.

In 2007/08 the foundation had assets of £2.6 million, an income of £207,000 and made 20 grants totalling £153,000.

Beneficiaries included: Jubilee Action (£42,000); Human Rights Watch Charitable Trust (£22,000); Network for Africa (£20,000); the Carter Centre UK Foundation (£13,000); Peace Brigades International UK (£11,000); Business Solutions to Poverty (£10,000); Reprieve (£8,500); Conciliation Resources (£4,200); Learning for Life, Marie Stopes International, Prisoners of Conscience, Refugee Council and World Vision (£2,500 each); Fairtrade Foundation (£1,500); and English National Opera, Royal Star and Garter Home (£1,000 each).

Applications 'While the charity welcomes applications from eligible potential grantees, the trustees seek out organisations that will effectively fulfil our objectives.'

The Tisbury Telegraph Trust

Christian, overseas aid and general

£398,000 (2007/08)
Beneficial area UK and overseas.

35 Kitto Road, Telegraph Hill, London SE14 5TW
Correspondent Mrs E Orr, Trustee
Trustees *Alison Davidson; John Davidson; Eleanor Orr; Roger Orr; Sonia Phippard.*
CC Number 328595
Information available Accounts were on file at the Charity Commission.

In 2007/08 it had assets of £114,000 and an income of £343,000, mostly from donations. Grants were made totalling £398,000.

Beneficiaries included: World Vision (£160,000); Romania Care (£54,000); Friends of Kiwoko Hospital (£50,000); Practical Action (£49,000); St Mary's Building Fund (£15,000); Tear Fund (£12,000); All Saints Church (£9,000); Church Mission Society (£3,000); Bible Society (£2,500); Crisis and Salvation Army (£1,000 each); and Lee Abbey and Shelter (£500 each).

Exclusions Grants are only made to registered charities. No applications from individuals for expeditions or courses can be considered.

Applications In writing to the correspondent. However, it is extremely rare that unsolicited applications are successful and the trust does not respond to applicants unless a stamped, addressed envelope is included. No telephone applications please.

TJH Foundation

Social welfare, medical and racing welfare

£1.1 million (2007/08)
Beneficial area England and Wales with some preference for organisations based in the north west of England.

Gleadhill House, Dawbers Lane, Euxton, Chorley PR7 6EA
Correspondent J C Kay, Trustee
Trustees *T J Hemmings, Chair; Mrs M Catherall; J C Kay; Ms K Revitt.*
CC Number 1077311
Information available Accounts were on file at the Charity Commission.

The TJH Foundation was established in 1999. In 2007/08 it had assets of £1.9 million and an income of £1.1 million, mostly from donations (total income was £108,000 in the previous year). Grants totalled £1.1 million, which mostly went to the Princess Royal Trust for Carers.

Beneficiaries, listed by category, included:

Social welfare
The Princess Royal Trust for Carers (£1 million in six grants); Maggie's Centres (£25,000); Leyland Methodist Church (£10,000); Royal Lancashire Agricultural Society (£4,300); the Marina Dalglish Appeal (£3,000); British Red Cross (£1,500); Little Sisters of the Poor (£1,000); St David's Care in the Community (£250); and the Lambourn Valley Housing Trust (£100).

Medical
Macmillan Cancer Relief (four grants totalling £7,000); Cancer Vaccine Institution (£2,500); St Catherine's Hospice (£1,000); Cancer Research UK (£350); and Starlight Children's Foundation (£100).

Racing welfare
Injured Jockeys Fund (£500 in two grants); Racing Welfare (£150 in two grants); and Moorcroft Racehorse Welfare Centre (£100).

Applications In writing to the correspondent.

Tomchei Torah Charitable Trust

Jewish
£288,000 (2007/08)
Beneficial area UK.

36 Cranbourne Gardens, London NW11 0HP
Correspondent The Trustees
Trustees I J Kohn; S M Kohn; A Frei.
CC Number 802125
Information available Full accounts were on file at the Charity Commission.

This trust supports Jewish educational institutions. Grants usually average about £5,000.

In 2007/08 the trust had an income of £1.5 million mainly from donations. Grants totalled £288,000 and were made to mainly Jewish organisations. There were 74 grants made during the year which were broken down as follows:

Category	Value
Education	£233,000
Religion and community	£35,000
Poor, needy and others	£20,000

Beneficiaries included: Friends of Mir (£122,000); MST College (£35,000); Friends of Sanz Institutions (£25,000); United Talmudical Associates (£15,000); Ezer North West and Menorah Grammar School (£10,000 each); Friends of Torah Ohr (£5,000); Ruzin Sadagora Trust (£4,000); Achisomoch Aid Co (£3,600); and Chesed Charity Trust (£2,600).

Applications In writing to the correspondent at any time.

The Torah Temimah Trust

Orthodox Jewish
£78,000 (2007/08)
Beneficial area UK.

16 Reizel Close, Stamford Hill, London N16 5GY
Correspondent Mrs E Bernath, Trustee
Trustees Mrs E Bernath; M Bernath; A Grunfeld.
CC Number 802390
Information available Accounts were on file at the Charity Commission, without a list of grants.

This trust was set up in 1980 to advance and promote orthodox Jewish religious education and religion. In 2007/08 it had an income mainly from donations of £63,000 and grants totalled £78,000.

Applications In writing to the correspondent.

Toras Chesed (London) Trust

Jewish and education
£208,000 (2007/08)
Beneficial area Worldwide.

14 Lampard Grove, London N16 6UZ
Correspondent A Langberg, Trustee
Trustees A Stenn; S Stern; A Langberg.
CC Number 1110653
Information available Accounts were on file at the Charity Commission, without a list of grants

Set up in 2005, the objects of the charity are outlined in the trustee's report:

1) the advancement of the Orthodox Jewish faith
2) the advancement of Orthodox Jewish religious education
3) the relief of poverty and infirmity among persons of the Jewish faith
4) to provide a safe and user friendly environment to share mutual problems and experiences
5) to encourage active parental participation in their children's education.

The charity achieves its objectives by making grants to quantifying institutions and individuals.

In 2007/08 the trust had an income of £198,000 and made grants totalling £208,000. Assets stood at £10,000.

Applications 'Applications for grants are considered by the trustees and reviewed in depth for final approval.'

The Tory Family Foundation

Education, Christian and medical
£74,000 (2007/08)
Beneficial area Worldwide, but principally Folkestone.

The Estate Office, Etchinghill Golf Club, Folkestone CT18 8FA
Correspondent Paul N Tory, Trustee
Trustees P N Tory; J N Tory; Mrs S A Rice.
CC Number 326584
Information available Accounts were on file at the Charity Commission, without a list of grants.

The trust has stated:

The charity was formed to provide financial help to a wide range of charitable needs. It is currently supporting causes principally in the locality of Folkestone. These causes include education, religious, social and medical subjects and the donees themselves are often registered charities.

The charity does not normally aim to fund the whole of any given project, and thus applicants are expected to demonstrate a degree of existing and regular support.

In 2007/08 the foundation had assets of £3.2 million, an income of £121,000 and made grants totalling £74,000. These were broken down as follows:

Category	Value
Overseas	£19,000
Local	£16,000
Health	£15,000
Education	£12,000
Churches	£7,250
Older people	£500
Other	£5,000

Previous beneficiaries have included: Ashford YMCA, Bletchley Park, Canterbury Cathedral, Concern Worldwide, Deal Festival, Disability Law Service, Folk Rainbow Club, Foresight, Friends of Birzett, Gurkha Welfare, Kent Cancer Trust, Royal British Legion, Uppingham Foundation and Youth Action Wiltshire.

Exclusions Grants are given to registered charities only. Applications outside Kent are unlikely to be considered. No grants are given for further education.

Applications In writing to the correspondent. Applications are considered throughout the year. To keep costs down, unsuccessful applicants will not be notified.

The Toy Trust

Children

£306,000 (2008)

Beneficial area UK.

c/o British Toy and Hobby Association, 80 Camberwell Road, London SE5 0EG

Website www.btha.co.uk

Correspondent The Secretary

Trustees *The British Toy and Hobby Association; Roger Dyson, Chair; Nick Austin; Clive Jones; Christine Nicholls.*

CC Number 1001634

Information available Accounts were on file at the Charity Commission.

This trust was registered in 1991 to centralise the giving of the British Toy and Hobby Association. Prior to this, the association raised money from the toy industry, which it pledged to one charity on an annual basis. It was felt that the fundraising activities of the association were probably more than matched by its individual members, and that the charitable giving of the toy industry to children's charities was going unnoticed by the public. The trust still receives the majority of its income from fundraising activities, donating the proceeds to children's charities and charitable projects benefiting children.

In 2008 the trust had an income of £228,000, mostly in donations received and grants were made totalling £306,000. Assets stood at £236,000.

Beneficiaries included: Great Ormond Street Hospital (£47,000); the National Autistic Society (£30,000); the Friends of Baale Mane Gopalapura (£28,000); Action Force for Africa (£5,900); Cerebra, Cystic Fibrosis Dream Holidays, Lennox Children's Cancer Fund and Whizz Kids (£5,000 each); Rays of Sunshine Children's Charity (£4,800); and PACE, South Tyneside Football Trust and YWCA England and Wales (£4,000 each).

Applications In writing to the correspondent.

Annie Tranmer Charitable Trust

General and young people

£121,000 to organisations (2007/08)

Beneficial area UK, particularly Suffolk and adjacent counties.

51 Bennett Road, Ipswich IP1 5HX

Correspondent Mrs M R Kirby, Clerk to the Trustees

Trustees *J F F Miller; V A Lewis; N J Bonham-Carter.*

CC Number 1044231

Information available Accounts were obtained from the Charity Commission website.

The objectives of the trust are to:

- make grants in the county of Suffolk and adjacent counties
- make grants to national charities according to the wished of Mrs Tranmer during her lifetime
- advance education and historical research relating to the national monument known as Sutton Hoo burial site and Sutton Hoo estate
- protect and preserve the Sutton Hoo burial site
- to further the education of children and young people in Suffolk
- make grants for general charitable purposes.

In 2007/08 the trust had assets of £3.5 million and an income of £131,000. Grants were made totalling £131,000 of which £121,000 was donated to 60 organisations and £12,000 to individuals.

Beneficiaries included: East Anglian Air Ambulance and the Suffolk Punch Trust (£10,000 each); Hope House Suffolk (£6,400); Great Ormond Street Hospital (£6,000); the Seckford Foundation (£5,000); Independent Age and Motor Neurone Disease (£3,000 each); Children with Leukaemia (£2,500); Bowel Cancer UK (£2,250); St Elizabeth Hospice (£2,000); Ipswich Furniture Project, the National Autistic Society and RNIB (£1,000 each); Listening Books (£600); Suffolk Family Carers and Wellchild (£500 each); and Bredfield Youth Project (£250).

Applications This trust does not accept unsolicited applications.

Anthony Travis Charitable Trust

General

£53,000 (2008/09)

Beneficial area UK.

86 Drayton Gardens, London SW10 9SB

Correspondent Anthony Travis

Trustees *E R A Travis; M J Travis; P J Travis.*

CC Number 1095198

Information available Accounts were on file at the Charity Commission.

Registered in 2003, in 2008/09 the trust had assets of £1.6 million and an income of £95,000. Grants totalled £53,000.

Beneficiaries included: Chetham's School of Music, Maggie's Cancer Caring Centres, the Three Miracles Fund and Volunteer Reading Help (£5,000 each); St Mary's School Ascot Development Fund (£3,000); Dyslexia Teaching Centre (£2,500); the Berkley Reforestation Trust, Derry Hill Trust (£2,000); Compassion in World Farming (£1,000); Children's Hospital Trust Fund (£500); Cancer Research UK (£200); and Filipino Club at Westminster Cathedral (£100).

Applications In writing to the correspondent. The trustees meet on a regular basis to consider what grants they will make.

The Treeside Trust

General

£108,000 (2007/08)

Beneficial area UK, but mainly local in Oldham

4 The Park, Grasscroft, Oldham OL4 4ES

Tel. 01457 876422

Correspondent John Gould, Trustee

Trustees *Mrs C C Gould; J R B Gould; J R W Gould; Mrs D M Ives; R J Ives; Mrs B Washbrook.*

CC Number 1061586

Information available Accounts were on file at the Charity Commission, but without a list of grants.

The trust supports mainly small local charities, and a few UK-wide charities which are supported on a regular basis.

The majority of grants are made as a result of half-yearly reviews. In the main, the trustees' policy is to make a limited number of substantial grants each year, rather than a larger number of smaller ones, in order to make significant contributions to some of the causes supported.

In 2007/08 the trust had assets of £1.2 million and an income of £158,000. Grants totalling £108,000 were made during the year, 'none of which exceeded £12,000'. A list of grants for this year was not available.

Applications The trust has stated that they 'do not welcome unsolicited applications'.

The Tresillian Trust

Overseas aid and welfare

£56,000 (2007/08)
Beneficial area Worldwide.

Old Coach House, Sunnyside, Bergh Apton, Norwich NR15 1DD
Correspondent M D Willcox, Trustee
Trustees G E S Robinson; P W Bate; M D Willcox.
CC Number 1105826
Information available Accounts were on file at the Charity Commission.

Registered with the Charity Commission in September 2004, in 2007/08 this trust had an income of £1.3 million, mostly from donations and made grants to 15 organisations totalling £56,000. The sum of £2.3 million was carried forward at year end.

Beneficiaries included: International Rescue Committee (£20,000); Sightsavers International, the Bishop Simeon Trust and Street Child Africa (£5,000 each); SOS Enfants (£3,000); Avert, Families of Spinal Muscular Atrophy, One Ummah Foundation and Saigon Children's Charity (£2,000 each); and the Condor Trust for Education and Contact the Elderly (£1,000 each).

Applications In writing to the correspondent. The trust is very selective in the grant making process and applications are reviewed by the trustees personally.

Truedene Co. Ltd

Jewish

£1.1 million (2007/08)
Beneficial area UK and overseas.

c/o Cohen Arnold and Co., 1075 Finchley Road, London NW11 0PU
Correspondent The Trustees
Trustees Sarah Klein, Chair; Samuel Berger; Solomon Laufer; Sije Berger; Zelda Sternlicht.
CC Number 248268
Information available Accounts were on file at the Charity Commission but without a list of grants.

In 2007/08 this trust had assets of almost £4.1 million and an income of £1 million. Grants were made totalling £1.1 million.

Previous beneficiaries have included: Beis Ruchel D'Satmar Girls School Ltd, British Friends of Tchernobyl, Congregation Paile Yoetz, Cosmon Belz Limited, Friends of Mir, Kolel Shomrei Hachomoth, Mesifta Talmudical College, Mosdos Ramou, Orthodox Council of Jerusalem, Tevini Limited, United Talmudical Associates Limited, VMCT and Yeshivo Horomo Talmudical College.

Applications In writing to the correspondent.

The Truemark Trust

General

£284,000 (2007/08)
Beneficial area UK.

PO Box 2, Liss GU33 6YP
Correspondent The Trustees
Trustees Sir T Lucas; S Neil; Mrs W Collett; D Hawkins; Mrs J Hayward; R Wolfe.
CC Number 265855
Information available Accounts were on file at the Charity Commission.

The trustees' report states that 'the trust's purpose is to make grants to other charitable bodies for the relief of all kinds of social distress and disadvantage.'

Donations are to mostly made to 'small local charities dealing with all kinds of disadvantage, with preferences to neighbourhood based community projects and for innovatory work with less popular groups.'

Grants are usually one-off for a specific project or part of a project. Core funding and/or salaries are rarely considered. The average size of grants is £1,000.

In 2007/08 it had assets of £10.4 million which generated an income of £480,000, including £223,000 from rental income. Grants totalled £284,000.

There were 116 grants made in the year. Beneficiaries included: Inner Yoga Trust – Petersfield (£5,000); Jumbulance (£4,000); Acorn to Oak Children's Trust and Winchester Youth Counselling (£3,000 each); Children's Chronic Arthritis Association (£2,500); Access to Art, Clothing Solutions, Norfolk Association for the Disabled, Norris Green Youth Centre Ltd and Sussex Autistic Society (£2,000 each); Different Strokes, East Didsbury Methodist Church and Hertfordshire Gardens Trust (£1,500 each); and Brighton Unemployed Centre Families Project, Citylife, Olive Branch Counselling and Wishing Well Waters (£1,000 each).

Exclusions Grants are made to registered charities only. Applications from individuals, including students, are ineligible. No grants are made in response to general appeals from large national charities. Grants are seldom available for churches or church buildings or for scientific or medical research projects.

Applications In writing to the correspondent, including the most recent set of accounts, clear details of the need the project is designed to meet and an outline budget. Trustees meet four times a year. Only successful applicants receive a reply.

Truemart Limited

General, Jewish and welfare

£72,000 (2006/07)
Beneficial area UK-wide and overseas, with a preference for Greater London.

347

34 The Ridgeway, London NW11 8QS

Correspondent Mrs S Heitner, Secretary

Trustees *I Heitner; I M Cymerman; B Hoffman.*

CC Number 1090586

Information available Accounts were on file at the Charity Commission, without a list of grants.

The trust was set up to promote:

- the advancement of religion in accordance with the Orthodox Jewish faith
- the relief of poverty
- general charitable purposes.

In 2006/07 it had an income from donations of £57,000. Grants totalled £72,000. Unfortunately a list of beneficiaries was not included with the accounts.

Applications In writing to the correspondent.

Trumros Limited

Jewish

£316,000 (2008)

Beneficial area UK.

282 Finchley Road, London NW3 7AD

Correspondent Mrs H Hofbauer, Trustee

Trustees *R S Hofbauer; Mrs H Hofbauer.*

CC Number 285533

Information available Full accounts were on file at the Charity Commission.

In 2008 the trust had assets of £6.6 million and a total income of £984,000. A total of £316,000 was given in about 126 grants.

Beneficiaries included: Achisomoch Aid Co. (£39,000); MST College (£25,000); Before Trust (£22,000); Hamayon (£20,000); Entondale (£18,000); Beis Auraham Synagogue (£12,000); and Jewish Learning Eachange, Lelov Charitable Trust and Yad Vo Chessed (£10,000 each).

Applications In writing to the correspondent, but please note that the trust states it is already inundated with applications.

Tudor Rose Ltd

Jewish

£219,000 (2006/07)

Beneficial area UK.

c/o Martin and Heller, 5 North End Road, London NW11 7RJ

Correspondent Samuel Taub, Secretary

Trustees *M Lehrfield; M Taub; A Taub; S Taub; S L Taub.*

CC Number 800576

Information available Accounts were on file at the Charity Commission.

This trust works for the promotion of the orthodox Jewish faith and the relief of poverty. Accounts for year ending 2007/08 were overdue at the Charity Commission.

In 2006/07 it had assets of £2.8 million. Total income was £360,000, mainly from property income (the sum of £117,000 was spent on these properties during the year). Grants were made totalling £219,000.

Beneficiaries included: Lolev Charitable Trust (£58,000); Woodlands Charity (£32,000); KTV (£14,000); Bell Synagogue (£11,000); Hatzola (£10,000); Lubavitch Centre (£5,000); and TCT (£4,000).

Applications In writing to the correspondent.

The Tufton Charitable Trust

Christian

£334,000 (2008)

Beneficial area UK.

c/o Baker Tilly, 4th Floor, 65 Kingsway, London WC2B 6TD

Correspondent The Trustees

Trustees *Sir Christopher Wates; Lady Wates; J R F Lulham.*

CC Number 801479

Information available Accounts were on file at the Charity Commission.

This trust supports Christian organisations, by providing grants as well as allowing them to use premises leased by the trust for retreats.

In 2008 the trust had an income of £612,000, including £385,000 from gifts and donations and grants totalled £334,000. Assets stood at £423,000.

There were 18 grants listed in the accounts. Beneficiaries included: the Church of England (£137,000); Nuffield Hospitals (£37,000); Martha Trust (£30,000); the Dorothy Kerin Trust (£25,000); Alpha International and London Institute of Christianity (£10,000 each); Bible by the Beach, Relationships Foundation and Right to Life (£7,500 each); and Catholic Foundation and St John Ambulance (£5,000 each).

Exclusions No grants for repair or maintenance of buildings.

Applications In writing to the correspondent, including a stamped, addressed envelope.

The R D Turner Charitable Trust

General

£164,000 (2008/09)

Beneficial area UK, with a preference for the Worcestershire area.

3 Poplar Piece, Inkberrow, Worcester WR7 4JD

Tel. 01386 792014

Email timpatrickson@hotmail.co.uk

Correspondent Timothy J Patrickson, Administrator

Trustees *J M Del Mar, Chair; D P Pearson; S L Preedy; P J Millward; J M G Fea.*

CC Number 263556

Information available Accounts were on file at the Charity Commission.

This trust has general charitable purposes, particularly in the Worcestershire area, with a specific preference for the villages of Arley and Upper Arley.

In 2008/09 it had assets of £25 million, which generated an income of £708,000. Most of this was spent on the upkeep of the Ardley Estate (£419,000), with grants to 42 organisations totalling £164,000. Grants were broken down as follows, shown here with examples of grants in each category:

Older people (2 grants)
Kidderminster Disabled Club (£2,500); and Age Concern Droitwich (£2,000).

Medical research (1 grant)
Breast Cancer Campaign (£5,000).

Children and young people (6 grants)
Pioneer Centre (£5,000); Howley Grange Scots Halestown (£4,000); Mentor Link and St James's Primary School PTS (£3,000 each); and Sunfield Children's Homes (£2,000).

Environment and heritage (3 grants)
Worcestershire and Dudley Historic Churches Trust (£12,000); St Peter's Church Upper Arley (£4,000); and All Saints Wribbenhall (£2,000).

The arts (4 grants)
Worcester Live (£5,000); Voices Foundation (£2,000); and Arley Memorial Hall Opera (£100).

Work in the community (10 grants)
British Red Cross Hereford and Worcester (£10,000); Cookley Playing Fields Association and Ombersley Memorial Hall (£5,000 each): County Air Ambulance Trust and Relate Worcestershire (£3,000); and Batchley Support Group and St George's Kidderminster (£2,000 each).

Social support (2 grants)
Asha Worcester and Fine Cell Work (£2,000 each).

Disabled and health (8 grants)
ARCOS, Cobalt Appeal Fund and Motor Neurone Disease Association (£5,000 each); BIBIC (£3,000); Where Next? (£2,000); Listening Books (£1,000); and Talking Newspapers of the UK (£500).

Hospices (5 grants)
St Richard's Hospice (£15,000); Kemp Hospice (£6,000); Primrose Hospice Bromsgrove (£5,000); and Breast Cancer Haven Hereford (£2,000).

Exclusions No grants to non-registered charities or to individuals.

Applications In writing to the correspondent with a copy of your latest annual report and accounts. There are no application forms. The trustees meet in February, May, August and December to consider applications, which should be submitted in the month prior to each meeting. Telephone enquiries may be made before submitting an appeal.

The Florence Turner Trust

General

£161,000 (2007/08)
Beneficial area UK, but with a strong preference for Leicestershire.

c/o Harvey Ingram Owston, 20 New Walk, Leicester LE1 6TX
Correspondent The Trustees
Trustees *Roger Bowder; Allan A Veasey; Caroline A Macpherson.*
CC Number 502721
Information available Accounts were on file at the Charity Commission.

This trust has general charitable purposes, giving most of its support in Leicestershire. Grants are made to organisations and individuals. Smaller projects are favoured where donations will make a 'quantifiable difference to the recipients rather than favouring large national charities whose income is measured in millions rather than thousands.' Grants are made for the benefit of individuals through a referring agency such as social services, NHS trusts or similar responsible bodies.

In 2007/08 it had assets of £5.2 million which generated an income of £199,000. Grants totalled £161,000.

There were 161 grants made in the year, of which 58 were listed in the accounts. Beneficiaries included: Leicester Charity Organisation Society (£12,000); Leicester Grammar School – Bursary (£8,800); Age Concern – Leicestershire, Leicestershire Scout Council, Mosaic and Vista (£2,300 each); Shelter Housing Aid and Research Project (£2,000 each); Guide Dogs for the Blind Association – Leicester (£1,800); Elizabeth Finn Care (£1,500); Barnardo's (£1,300); and the Carers Centre – Leicestershire and Rutland and Vitalise (£1,000 each).

A further 103 grants below £1,000 each totalled £56,000.

Exclusions The trust does not support individuals for educational purposes.

Applications In writing to the correspondent. Trustees meet every eight or nine weeks.

The TUUT Charitable Trust

General, but with a bias towards trade-union-favoured causes

£81,000 (2007/08)
Beneficial area Worldwide.

Congress House, Great Russell Street, London WC1B 3LQ
Tel. 020 7637 7116 **Fax** 020 7637 7087
Email info@tufm.co.uk
Website www.tufm.co.uk
Correspondent Ann Smith, Secretary
Trustees *Lord Christopher; A Tuffin; M Walsh; M Bradley; B Barber; Lord Brookman; E Sweeney.*
CC Number 258665
Information available Accounts were on file at the Charity Commission.

The following information is taken from their website.

The TUUT Charitable Trust was set up by the trade union movement in 1969 for the sole purpose of owning TU Fund Managers Limited. The intention was – and still is – that profits distributed by the company should go to good causes rather than individual shareholders.

It is a requirement of the Trust Deed that all the trustees must be trades unionists, the intention being to ensure that causes benefiting should broadly be those that would be supported by the movement. Trade unions – and indeed individuals – are free to nominate favoured causes, all of which are reviewed by the trustees before any payment is made.

The trust considers requests from 'small to medium sized non-religious charitable organisations based in the UK'.

In 2007/08 the trust had assets of £2.3 million and an income of £114,000. Grants were made totalling £81,000, including a Fellowship Award of £7,000.

Beneficiaries included: NACRO (£40,000); Alma Hospital and PFA Centenary Fund (£5,000 each); Macmillan Cancer Relief (£3,000); Evelina Children's Hospital Appeal (£2,300); CCA, Concern Worldwide and Scrap Poverty in Africa (£2,000 each); UK Sports Association and Woking Hospice (£1,000 each); and World Development Movement Trust, Hope and Homes for Children, Cruse Bereavement Care and the Respite Association (£500 each).

Exclusions No grants to individuals or to charities based overseas.

Applications 'To apply for a grant, charitable organisations should apply for a Form of Request and submit this, duly completed. The Trustees meet three times a year to consider requests received.'

Ulting Overseas Trust

Theological training

£107,000 to organisations (2007/08)

Beneficial area The developing world (mostly, but not exclusively, Asia, Africa and South and Central America).

Pothecary Witham Weld, 70 St George's Square, London SW1V 3RD

Correspondent T B Warren, Trustee

Trustees A J Bale, Chair; Mrs M Brinkley; D Ford; J C Heyward; J Kapolyo; Dr J B A Kessler; N Sylvester; T B Warren.

CC Number 294397

Information available Accounts were on file at the Charity Commission.

The trust exists solely to provide bursaries, normally via grants, to Christian theological training institutions or organisations with a training focus, for those in the developing world who wish to train for the Christian ministry, or for those who wish to improve their ministry skills. It gives priority to the training of students in their home countries or continents.

In 2007/08 it had assets of £3.7 million and an income of £141,000. There were 31 grants made in the year totalling £107,000. A further grant was made to an individual of £1,000.

Beneficiaries included: IFES (£16,000); Scripture Union International (£14,000); Langham Trust (£13,000); Oxford Centre for Mission Studies (£7,500 in two grants); Pan African Christian College (£6,300 in two grants); Asian Theological Seminary and Discipleship Training College – Singapore (£4,800 each); Cornerstone Christian College (£2,000); Buenos Aires Bible Institute (£1,000); and Bangladesh Bible School Sim UK (£700).

Exclusions No grants are given for capital projects such as buildings or library stock, nor for training in subjects other than biblical, theological and missionary studies. Grants are only made to institutions to pass on to their students; direct grants to individuals cannot be made.

Applications The funds of the trust are already committed. Unsolicited applications cannot be supported.

The Ulverscroft Foundation

Visually impaired people (blind and partially sighted)

£243,000 (2007/08)

Beneficial area Worldwide.

1 The Green, Bradgate Road, Anstey, Leicester LE7 7FU

Tel. 0116 236 1595 **Fax** 0116 236 1594

Email foundation@ulverscroft.co.uk

Website www.foundation.ulverscroft.com

Correspondent Joyce Sumner, Secretary

Trustees A W Leach, Chair; P H F Carr; M K Down; D Owen; R Crooks.

CC Number 264873

Information available Accounts were available at the Charity Commission.

Ulverscroft Large Print Books Limited, was formed in 1964. The company republished existing books in large type to sell to libraries and donate the profits to sight-related charitable causes. In 1972 The Ulverscroft Foundation was created.

The foundation supports projects which will have a positive effect on the quality of life of visually impaired people (blind and partially sighted). Funding is channelled via recognised organisations which help the visually impaired, for example, libraries, hospitals, clinics, schools and colleges, and social and welfare organisations.

In 2007/08 the foundation had a total income of £13.5 million, including £12.9 million from trading income. Out of a total expenditure of £12.3 million, grants totalled £243,000.

Beneficiaries included: Vision Research Group – Great Ormond Street Hospital (£107,000); Ulverscroft IFLA Award 2007

(£20,000); Calibre (£4,200); Kenya Albino Child Support (£3,300); National Blind Children's Society (£3,000); Accrington and District Blind Society, Force Foundation UK and Look Essex (£2,000 each); National Eye Research Council (£2,000); and Computer Aid international, East Sussex Association for the Blind, Queen Alexandra Hospital Home and St John of Jerusalem Eye Hospital (£1,000 each).

Exclusions Applications from individuals are not encouraged. Generally, assistance towards salaries and general running costs are not given.

Applications In writing to the correspondent including the latest annual report and accounts, there is no application form. Proposals should be as detailed as possible, including: details of the current service provided to the visually impaired (if any) and how the proposed project will be integrated or enhanced; an estimate (if possible) of how many visually impaired people use/will use the service; the amount of funding obtained to date (if any); and the names of any other organisations to whom funding applications have been made.

Trustees meet quarterly to consider appeals in January, April, July and October each year; deadlines for appeals are the last day of the previous month.

Due to the large number of appeals received, the foundation will not consider fresh appeals until a period of 12 to 18 months has elapsed since the last application. The success of any appeal is dependent on the level of funding available at the time of consideration.

The Union of Orthodox Hebrew Congregation

Jewish

£285,000 to organisations (2007)

Beneficial area UK.

140 Stamford Hill, London N16 6QT

Correspondent The Administrator

Trustees B S F Freshwater; I Cymerman; C Konig; Rabbi A Pinter.

CC Number 249892

Information available Accounts were on file at the Charity Commission, without a list of grants.

The operational charity works to protect and to further in every way the interests of traditional Judaism in Great Britain and to establish and support such institutions as will serve this object.

In 2007 it had assets of £1.6 million and an income of £1.3 million comprising principally 'grants and donations' and 'community levies'. Out of a total charitable expenditure of £1.3 million, grants to organisations totalled £285,000, with £3,200 donated to individuals.

Previous beneficiaries have included: Addas Yisoroel Mikva Foundation, Achieve Trust, Atereth Shau, Beis Malka, Beis Shmuel, Belz Nursery, Bnos Yerushaim, Chesed Charity Trust, London Board of Schechita, Mutual Trust, Maoz Ladol, North West London Mikvah, Needy Families and Poor Families Pesach, Society of Friends of the Torah, Talmud Centre Trust and VMCT.

Applications In writing to the correspondent.

United Trusts

General

£365,000 (2007/08)

Beneficial area Unrestricted, in practice mainly organisations operating in north-west England and north Wales.

Liverpool Charity and Voluntary Services, 151 Dale Street, Liverpool L2 2AH

Tel. 0151 227 5177

Email information@unitedtrusts.org.uk

Correspondent The Secretary

Trustees *Liverpool Charity and Voluntary Services, Susan Newton; Harry Williams.*

CC Number 327579

Information available Accounts were obtained from the Charity Commission website.

United Trust's main objective is to promote tax-free payroll giving to workplace charity funds, where gift distributions can be made by a workplace charity fund committee. We operate nationwide, but our main areas of activity are north-west England and north Wales. In addition we operate the Give As You Earn elective payroll giving service that enables individual donors, at the time the payroll deductions are authorised, to

nominate which charities are to receive their gifts.

In 2007/08 the trust had assets of £292,000 and an income of £400,000. Grants were made totalling £365,000. Information on individual beneficiaries was not available.

The breakdown of resources expended by the trust was as follows:

Local United Trusts Funds accounts
- Merseyside – £51,000
- Cumbria – £1,300
- Other districts – £34,000.

United Trusts Workplace Trust accounts
- Merseyside – £189,000
- Lancashire – £22,000
- Cumbria – £19,000
- Cheshire – £9,900
- Greater Manchester – £4,500
- Other districts – £33,000.

Exclusions Individuals. Grants to individuals, called 'people for people funds', are made through umbrella charities.

Applications It is requested that applications should be made to the secretary of the local United Trust Fund or Workplace Charity Fund concerned. If the address is not know, applicants are advised to telephone the correspondent of the trust.

The David Uri Memorial Trust

Jewish and general

£103,000 (2007/08)

Beneficial area Worldwide.

Suite 511, 19–21 Crawford Street, London W1H 1PJ

Correspondent The Trustees

Trustees *Mrs S Blackman; Mrs B Roden; B Blackman.*

CC Number 327810

Information available Accounts were on file at the Charity Commission, but without a list of grants since those for 1991/92.

In 2007/08 the trust's assets totalled £2.5 million, it had an income of £375,000, mainly from property investment revenue and made grants to organisations totalling £103,000.

Previous beneficiaries have included: National Jewish Chaplaincy Board, Age Concern, Crisis at Christmas, Jefferies

Research Wing Trust, NSPCC and Yakar Education Foundation.

Exclusions No grants to individuals.

Applications In writing to the correspondent.

Vale of Glamorgan – Welsh Church Fund

General

£42,000 (2007/08)

Beneficial area Vale of Glamorgan and City of Cardiff council areas.

The Vale of Glamorgan Council, Civic Offices, Holton Rd, Barry CF63 4RU

Tel. 01446 709250

Email adwilliams@valeofglamorgan.gov.uk

Correspondent A D Williams, Director of Finance, ICT and Property

Trustee *Vale of Glamorgan County Borough Council.*

CC Number 506628

Information available Accounts were on file at the Charity Commission

The charitable purposes to which the fund may be applied are:

- educational
- relief in sickness
- relief in need
- libraries, museums, art galleries
- social and recreational
- protection of historical buildings
- medical and social research treatment
- probation
- older people
- blind people
- places of worship and burial grounds
- emergencies or disasters
- other charitable purposes.

In 2008/09 it had assets of £2.9 million and an income of £59,000. Grants to 26 organisations were made totalling £42,000.

Grants are given on a one-off basis. Whilst no maximum/minimum grant levels are stipulated, awards are usually in the region of £1,500.

Beneficiaries included: St Augustine's Parish Community Hall – Penarth (£10,000); Bonvilston Parochial Church Council (£3,000); Coastlands Family

Church – Barry (£2,500); St Cadoc's Church – Pendoylan and St Paul's Church – Grangetown (£2,000 each); St Paul's Community Church – Butetown (£1,500); Bethel Evangelical Chapel – Rhoose and St Illtud's Church – Llantwit Major (£1,000 each); and Ararat Baptist Church – Whitchurch, Llandaff Cathedral and St Canna's Church, Llangan (£500 each).

Exclusions No grants to individuals.

Applications For organisations based in the Vale of Glamorgan, further information can be obtained from A D Williams at the address given in this entry. For organisations based in Cardiff, please contact R Anthony at Cardiff County Council (Tel. 0292 087 2395).

The Albert Van Den Bergh Charitable Trust

Medical research, disability, community and general

£95,000 (2008/09)

Beneficial area UK and overseas.

Trevornick Farmhouse, Holywell Bay, Newquay TR8 5PW

Correspondent Mrs J Hartley, Trustee

Trustees *Mrs J M Hartley; Mrs N Glover; B Hopkins.*

CC Number 296885

Information available Accounts were on file at the Charity Commission, without a list of grants.

The trust was established in 1987. In 2008/09 its assets stood at £2.5 million and it had an income of £103,000. Grants to 79 organisations totalled £95,000 and were broken down as follows:

Category	Value
Medical research, care and support	£27,000
Help in the community	£20,000
Hospices	£8,000
Disability	£7,000
Overseas	£7,000
Older people	£4,600
Disadvantaged	£3,000
Outward bound	£3,000
Conservation	£2,000
Homelessness	£2,000
Cultural	£1,000
Services	£1,000
Other	£9,000

Previous beneficiaries have included BLISS, Bishop of Guildford's Charity, British Heart Foundation, Counsel and Care for the Elderly, Leukaemia Research Trust, Multiple Sclerosis Society, Parentline Surrey, National Osteoporosis Society, RNID, Riding for the Disabled – Cranleigh Age Concern, SSAFA, St John Ambulance and United Charities Fund – Liberal Jewish Synagogue.

Applications In writing to the correspondent, including accounts and budgets.

The Van Neste Foundation

Welfare, Christian and developing world

£265,000 (2007/08)

Beneficial area UK (especially the Bristol area) and overseas.

15 Alexandra Road, Clifton, Bristol BS8 2DD

Correspondent Fergus Lyons, Secretary

Trustees *M T M Appleby, Chair; F J F Lyons; G J Walker; J F Lyons; B M Appleby.*

CC Number 201951

Information available Accounts were on file at the Charity Commission.

The trustees currently give priority to the following:

- developing world
- disabled or older people
- advancement of religion and respect for the sanctity and dignity of life
- community and Christian family life.

These objectives are reviewed by the trustees from time to time but applications falling outside them are unlikely to be considered.

In 2007/08 the trust had assets of £6.7 million and an income of £248,000. Grants were made totalling £265,000.

Donations were broken down as follows and are shown here with examples of beneficiaries in each category:

Community and Christian family life – 14 grants totalling £155,000
St James Priory Project (£75,000); CHAS Bristol (£30,000); Families for Children, Housing Justice and the Withywood Centre (£10,000 each); Colston Society (£3,000); Salvation Army (£1,000); SOFA Project (£500); and Avon Outward Bound Association (£400).

Developing world – 5 grants totalling £46,000
CAFOD (£29,000); Sisters of Mercy (£10,000); MAP (£3,000); and the Karuna Trust (£1,000).

Respect for dignity and sanctity of life – 4 grants totalling £35,000
Avon and Bristol Law Centre (£15,000); the Linacre Centre (£10,000); and Polish RC Church (£5,000).

Disability/older people – 8 grants totalling £22,000
St Peter's Hospice and Spadework (£5,000 each); Dressability and Stepping Out (£3,000 each); St Angela's Home for the Elderly (£1,000); and the Matthew Trust (£500).

Religion – 5 grants totalling £8,300
Emmaus House Bristol (£5,000); St Bridget's Church Chelvey and Walsingham Trust (£1,000 each); and St Mary's RC Church Cardiff (£250).

Exclusions No grants to individuals or to large, well-known charities. Applications are only considered from registered charities.

Applications Applications should be in the form of a concise letter setting out the clear objectives to be obtained, which must be charitable. Information must be supplied concerning agreed funding from other sources together with a timetable for achieving the objectives of the appeal and a copy of the latest accounts. The foundation does not normally make grants on a continuing basis. To keep overheads to a minimum, only successful applications are acknowledged. Appeals are considered by the trustees at their meetings in January, June and October.

Mrs Maud Van Norden's Charitable Foundation

General

£43,000 (2008)

Beneficial area UK.

BM Box 2367, London WC1N 3XX

Correspondent The Trustees

Trustees *Ena Dukler; John Gordon; Elizabeth Humphryes; Neil Wingerath.*

CC Number 210844

Information available Accounts were on file at the Charity Commission.

Established in 1962, in 2008 the trust had assets of £860,000 and an income of £44,000. There were 28 grants made totalling £43,000.

All but one of grants made were for £1,500 each. Beneficiaries included: Royal Hospital for Neuro-Disability (£2,500); and Changing Faces, Church Urban Fund, Cured Speech Association UK, the Daisy Trust, Help for Heroes, Humane Slaughter Association, National Rheumatoid Arthritis Society, Police Community Clubs of Great Britain, Royal British Legion, the Samaritans, Victim Support and Women's Link (£1,500 each).

Exclusions No grants to individuals, expeditions or scholarships. The trustees make donations to registered UK charities only.

Applications All appeals should be by letter containing the following:

- aims and objectives of the charity
- nature of the appeal
- total target, if for a specific project
- contributions received against target
- registered charity number
- any other factors.

Letters should be accompanied by a copy of the applicant's latest reports and accounts.

The Vandervell Foundation

General

£291,000 to organisations (2008)
Beneficial area UK.

Hampstead Town Hall Centre, 213 Haverstock Hill, London NW3 4QP
Correspondent Valerie Kaye, Administrator
Trustee *The Vandervell Foundation Limited Trustee Company.*
CC Number 255651
Information available Full accounts were on file at the Charity Commission.

This trust has general charitable purposes, supporting both individuals and organisations. A wide range of causes has been supported, including schools, educational establishments, hospices and other health organisations, with the trust stating there are no real preferences or exclusions. Grants

generally range from £1,000 to £5,000 each.

In 2008 the trust had assets of £6 million and an income of £372,000. Grants were made totalling £308,000, of which £291,000 went to organisations, broken down as follows:

Category	No.	Value
Advancement of education	24	£162,000
Social welfare	43	£74,000
Medical research	5	£24,000
Performing arts	7	£19,000
Environmental regeneration	7	£13,000

Beneficiaries included: Royal College of Surgeons and Prisoners Educational Trust (£20,000 each); Oxford Medical School (£18,000); Arts Education School Tring Park (£15,000); Guildhall School Trust, King's College London School of Medicine, PMS Foundation and University of Leeds School of Medicine (£10,000 each); Fareshare, Royal National Theatre and St George's Youth Club (£5,000 each).

The sum of £17,000 was distributed in 55 grants to individuals.

Applications In writing to the correspondent. Trustees meet every two months to consider major grant applications; smaller grants are considered more frequently.

Roger Vere Foundation

General

About £200,000 (2007/08)
Beneficial area UK and worldwide, with a special interest in High Wycombe.

19 Berwick Road, Marlow SL7 3AR
Correspondent Peter Allen, Trustee
Trustees *Mrs Rosemary Vere, Chair; Mrs Marion Lyon; Peter Allen.*
CC Number 1077559
Information available Accounts had been filed at the Charity Commission.

This trust was established in September 1999 and it supports, worldwide:

- the relief of financial hardship in and around, but not restricted to, High Wycombe
- advancement of education
- advancement of religion
- advancement of scientific and medical research

- conservation and protection of the natural environment and endangered plants and animals
- relief of natural and civil disasters
- general charitable purposes.

In 2007/08 the trust had an income of £298,000 and a total expenditure of £232,000.

Previous beneficiaries have included Cord Blood Charity, the Leprosy Mission, Claire House Children's Hospice, Angels International, SignAlong Group, Changing Faces, Women's Aid, St John Water Wing, UK Youth and Jubilee Plus.

Applications In writing to the correspondent.

The Nigel Vinson Charitable Trust

Economic and community development, employment and general

£225,000 (2007/08)
Beneficial area UK, with a preference for north-east England.

Hoare Trustees, 37 Fleet Street, London EC4P 4DQ
Correspondent The Trustees
Trustees *Mrs Rowena A Cowan; Rt Hon. Lord Vinson of Roddam Dene; Thomas O C Harris; Hon. Miss Bettina C Witheridge; Hon. Mrs Antonia C Bennett.*
CC Number 265077
Information available Full accounts were on file at the Charity Commission.

This trust was established in 1972. It supports economic/community development and employment as well as making grants to other causes.

In 2007/08 the trust had assets of £4.1 million and an income of £272,000. Grants were made totalling £225,000.

There were 16 grants of £1,000 or more listed in the accounts. Beneficiaries included: Institute for Policy Research (£73,000); Renewable Energy Foundation (£47,000); Civitas (£30,000); Institute of Economic Affairs (£11,000); Electoral Reform Society (£10,000); Foundation for Social and Economic Thinking (£8,000); the Almshouse Association,

Hampden Trust and Hart Charity (£5,000 each); Christian Institute and Reform Research Trust (£4,000 each); International Policy Network (£2,000); and Christian Fellowship (£1,000).

Applications In writing to the correspondent. The trustees meet periodically to consider applications for grants of £1,000 and above. All grants below £1,000 are decided by The Rt. Hon. Nigel Lord Vinson on behalf of the trustees.

The William and Ellen Vinten Trust

Science and technology education

£65,000 (2007/08)

Beneficial area UK, but mostly Bury St Edmunds.

80 Guildhall Street, Bury St Edmunds IP33 1QB

Correspondent The Chair of the Trustees

CC Number 285758

Information available Accounts were obtained from the Charity Commission website.

The 2007/08 trustees' report stated that:

The principal activity of the trust during the year was continuing to pursue initiatives to increase the interest of schools and college students in the Bury St Edmunds' area in science and technology subjects, with a view to increasing the numbers who might consider careers related to the subjects and improving their attainment.

In 2007/08 the trust had assets of £1.4 million and an income of £71,000. Grants were made totalling £65,000 of which £52,000 was given towards education and £13,000 towards training.

Applications The trust stated that as a proactive charity it does not seek unsolicited applications. Such applications are now so significant in number that the trust has decided not to respond to them, however discourteous this may seem.

Vision Charity

Children who are blind, visually impaired or dyslexic

£130,000 (2007/08)

Beneficial area UK and overseas.

PO Box 553, Chatham ME4 9AN

Website www.visioncharity.co.uk

Correspondent The Trustees

Trustees *Herbert Brenninkmeijer, Chair; Bill Bohanna; Larry Davis; David Pacy.*

CC Number 1075630

Information available Accounts were on file at the Charity Commission.

The objects of the charity are to combine the fundraising efforts of companies and individuals who use or benefit from, or work in, the visual communications industry for the benefit of children who are blind, visually impaired or dyslexic.

The following information is taken from the charity's annual report.

The monies raised are used expressly to purchase equipment, goods or specialist services. The Vision Charity will make cash donations only in very exceptional circumstances, as approved by its Board of Trustees.

Vision is keen to emphasize its increasing international focus, both in terms of its fundraising activities and in directing its donations.

In 2007/08 it had assets of £239,000 and an income of £477,000, most of which came from donations received and various fundraising events organised by the charity. A total of £205,000 was spent on fundraising activities. Grants were made totalling £130,000.

There were nine grants of £1,000 or more listed in the accounts. Beneficiaries included: London Society for the Blind – Dorton House School (£45,000); Dyslexia Action (£24,000); New College – Worcester (£14,000); the Eyeless Trust (£10,000); Milton Margai School (£9,000); SENSE (£8,000); Joseph Clark School (£5,000); and See Ability (£3,600).

Applications A brief summary of the request should be sent to the correspondent. If the request is of interest to the trustees, further details will be requested. If the request has not been acknowledged within three months of submission, the applicant should assume that it has not been successful. The charity is interested to receive such applications but regrets that it is not able to acknowledge every unsuccessful submission.

Vivdale Ltd

Jewish

£127,000 (2007/08)

Beneficial area UK.

17 Cheyne Walk, London NW4 3QH

Correspondent D H Marks, Trustee

Trustees *D H Marks; L Marks; F Z Sinclair.*

CC Number 268505

Information available Accounts were available at the Charity Commission, without a list of grants.

In 2007/08 the trust's assets totalled £2.4 million, it had an income of £123,000 and donations totalled £127,000.

Previous beneficiaries have included: Achisomach Aid Company Ltd, Beis Soroh Schneirer, Beis Yaakov Town, Beis Yisroel Tel Aviv, Comet Charities Ltd, Friends of Harim Bnei Brak, Jewish Teachers Training College Gateshead, Mosdos Bnei Brak, Torah Vechesed Ashdod and Woodstock Sinclair Trust.

Applications In writing to the correspondent.

The Viznitz Foundation

Jewish

£74,000 (2007/08)

Beneficial area UK and abroad.

23 Overlea Road, London E5 9BG

Correspondent H Feldman, Trustee

Trustees *H Feldman; E Kahan.*

CC Number 326581

Information available Accounts were on file at the Charity Commission, without a list a of grants.

The following is taken from the trustees' report:

The objects of the charity are to pay and apply and appropriate the whole of the trust fund to those purposes both in the UK and abroad recognised as charitable by English Law and in accordance with the trust deed and the wishes of the Grand Rabbi of Viznitz.

In 2007/08 the foundation had assets of £1.6 million, an income of £199,000 and made grants totalling £74,000. Unfortunately a list of grants was not available for this period.

Applications In writing to the correspondent.

The Scurrah Wainwright Charity

Social reform

£86,000 (2007/08)
Beneficial area Preference for Yorkshire, South Africa and Zimbabwe.

16 Blenheim Street, Hebden Bridge HX7 8BU

Email admin@wainwrighttrusts.org.uk

Website www.wainwrighttrusts.org.uk

Correspondent Kerry McQuade, Administrator

Trustees *M S Wainwright, Chair; R R Bhaskar; H P I Scott; H A Wainwright; J M Wainwright; P Wainwright; T M Wainwright.*

CC Number 1002755

Information available Full accounts were available from the Charity Commission website.

The following information is taken from the trust's website.

The Wainwright family runs two trusts, one charitable [The Scurrah Wainwright Charity], one non-charitable [The Andrew Wainwright Reform Trust Ltd]. The trusts are based on the family's traditions of liberal values and support for the socially disempowered. The trustees are all family members, based in West Yorkshire.

- The charity funds projects in England, primarily in Yorkshire and the north of England, as well as Zimbabwe and Southern Africa. It rarely funds work in any other part of the world.
- It looks for innovative work in the field of social reform, with a preference for 'root-cause' rather than palliative projects.
- It favours causes that are outside the mainstream, and unlikely to be funded by other charities.
- It will contribute to core costs.

Typically, grants are between £1,000 and £5,000, but in cases of exceptional merit larger grants may be awarded.

In 2007/08 the trust had assets of £1.8 million, an income of £58,000 and made 42 grants totalling £86,000.

Beneficiaries included: Asylum Support Housing Advice, Fairshare Education Foundation and Refugee Action (£5,000 each); Domestic Violence Service (£4,500); Actionaid, Open Democracy and War on Want (£3,000 each); Mustard Seed Communities (£3,000); International Children's Trust (£2,500); Bradford Nightstop, Catch 21 Productions, Leeds Christian Community, Next Steps Ryedale, Oxford Research Group and St Wilfred's Centre (£2,000 each); Sheffield Theatres (£1,500); Bradford Family Support Network (£1,300); and Bradford Action for Refugees, Ethical Consumer Research Association, Fairtrade Foundation, Peace Brigade International and Ravenscliffe Community Development (£1,000 each).

Exclusions No support is given to:

- individuals
- animal welfare
- buildings
- medical research or support for individual medical conditions
- substitution for Government funding (e.g. in education and health)
- charities who send unsolicited general appeal letters.

Applications In writing to the correspondent, covering the following (taken from the website):

- background information about you and/or your organisation
- the nature of the project you wish to pursue and what it seeks to achieve
- your plans for practical implementation of the work and a budget
- your most recent accounts and details of any additional sources of funding already secured or to be sought
- whether you will accept a contribution to the amount requested
- where you heard about the charity
- a summary on no more than two sides of A4, using a font no smaller than 12-point.

Trustees meet in March, July and November. Applications should be received by the first day of the preceding month. For further information please visit the trust's website. Applicants may contact the administrator by email, for any clarification.

Wakeham Trust

Community development, education and community service by young people

£85,000 (2007/08)
Beneficial area UK.

Wakeham Lodge, Rogate, Petersfield GU31 5EJ

Tel. 01730 821748

Email wakehamtrust@mac.com

Website www.wakehamtrust.org

Correspondent The Trustees

Trustees *Harold Carter; Barnaby Newbolt; Tess Silkstone.*

CC Number 267495

Information available Accounts were on file at the Charity Commission. Full and detailed guidelines (summarised here) can be found at the trust's website.

We provide grants to help people rebuild their communities. We are particularly interested in neighbourhood projects, community arts projects, projects involving community service by young people, or projects set up by those who are socially excluded.

We also support innovative projects to promote excellence in teaching (at any level, from primary schools to universities), though we never support individuals.

We aim to refresh the parts that other funding sources can't reach, especially new ideas and unpopular causes. Because we don't appeal to the public for funds, we can take risks.

Because we are mostly run by volunteers, we can afford to make very small grants, without our funds being eaten up by administration costs.

We favour small projects – often, but not always, start-ups. We try to break the vicious circle whereby you have to be established to get funding from major charities, but you have to get funding to get established. Grants are normally given where an initial £75 to £750 can make a real difference to getting the project up and running.

In 2007/08 the trust's assets totalled £1.6 million and it had an income of £48,000. There were 193 grants made totalling £85,000.

Beneficiaries included: De Montford University (£8,000); Sharana – India (£5,000); Unite (£1,500); Bristol Cathedral Trust and Streatham Youth and Community Centre (£600 each); BUGS and the Initiative (£500 each);

Bexley Trust for Adult Students (£400); Darlington Boys Club (£300); Brighton and Hove Unemployed Centre (£250); Dyslexia Action, Rising Brook Writers and South Tyneside Football Trust (£200 each); Springtime Lunch Club, Tree the Way and Waterloo Housing Society (£150 each); and Bridestone Village Hall (£100).

Exclusions No grants to individuals or large, well-established charities, or towards buildings and transport.

Applications By letter or by filling in the online form. The trust prefers online applications. Full guidelines are available on the trust's website.

Wallace and Gromit's Children's Foundation

Improving the quality of life for sick children

£183,000 (2007/08)
Beneficial area UK.

PO Box 2186, Bristol BS99 7NT

Email info@wrongtrousersday.org

Website www.wallaceandgromitfoundation.org

Correspondent The Company Secretary

Trustees I Hannah, Chair; S Cooper; P Lord; J Moule; N Park; D Sproxton.

CC Number 1096483

Information available Accounts were on file at the Charity Commission.

Wallace & Gromit's Children's Foundation is a national charity raising funds to improve the quality of life for children in hospitals and hospices throughout the UK.

'We are the only national charity raising funds for local children's hospitals and hospices to improve the quality of life for sick children across the UK.'

The foundation provides funding to support projects such as:

- arts, music play and entertainment programmes to stimulate young minds and divert attention away from illness
- providing welcoming and accessible environments and surroundings, designed specifically for children in a fun and engaging way

- funding education and information programmes to educate young people and recognising the importance of self help and health related issues
- helping to fund the acquisition of medical facilities, which can help to improve diagnosis and treatment of a wide range of conditions and illnesses in children
- sustaining family relationships helping to keep families together during emotionally difficult times
- helping to meet the cost of care in a children's hospice where children and their families are cared for during good days, difficult days and last days
- supporting children with physical and emotional difficulties empowering and increasing confidence.

Wallace and Gromit's Wrong Trousers Day is the foundation's primary fundraising event which encourages the general public to wear the wrong trousers for the day and donate funds raised to the foundation. In 2007/08 it had an income of £190,000 and Grants to 24 organisations totalled £183,000.

Beneficiaries included: Aberdeen Children's Hospital, Acorns Children's Hospice Birmingham, Alder Hey Children's Hospital, Belfast Children's Hospital, Bristol Children's Hospital, Butterwick Children's Hospice – Stockton-on-Tees, Edinburgh Children's Hospital, Glasgow Children's Hospital, Naomi House Children's Hospice – Winchester, Oxford Children's Hospital, St Oswald's Children's Hospice – Newcastle and the Whittington Hospital (£10,000 each); Addenbrooke's Hospital – Cambridge and SeeSaw (£7,000 each); MedEquip4Kids (£2,100); Rainbows Children's Hospice (£2,000); and Hope House Children's Hospice and Shooting Star Hospice (£1,000 each).

Exclusions
- Charities not supporting children's healthcare.
- Organisations that do not have charitable status.
- Animal, religious or international charities.
- Retrospective funding.
- Organisations that do not work within a hospital or hospice environment.
- Organisations that provide excursions, holidays or away days.
- No grants will be made to individuals.

Applications Grants are distributed on an annual basis. Application forms and guidelines are posted on the foundation's website from October and the closing date for applications is usually in December. All awards are made by the end of March.

The F J Wallis Charitable Settlement

General

£41,000 (2007/08)
Beneficial area UK, with some interest in Hampshire and Surrey.

c/o Bridge House, 11 Creek Road, Hampton Court, East Molesey KT8 9BE

Correspondent F H Hughes, Trustee

Trustees F H Hughes; A J Hills; Revd J J A Archer.

CC Number 279273

Information available Accounts were on file at the Charity Commission.

In 2007/08 the settlement had assets of £1.2 million and an income of £60,000. Grants to 40 organisations totalled £41,000. The majority of grants given were for £1,000 each.

Grants in 2007/08 were broken down as follows and are shown with examples of beneficiaries in each category:

Hospices – 9 grants totalling £12,000
Naomi House Children's Hospice and Princess Alice Hospice (£2,000 each); and Association of Children's Hospices, Chase Hospice Care for Children, Hope House Children's Hospice, St John's Hospice and Trinity Hospice (£1,000 each).

Community – 12 grants totalling £11,000
Crisis, GASP, Independent Age, My Life Project, RNLI, Relate, Watermill Theatre Education Trust and Winchester Youth Counselling (£1,000 each); and Forget Me Not (£250).

Disability – 8 grants totalling £8,000
The Children's Trust, Combat Stress, Down's Syndrome Association, Headway, National Talking Newspapers, the Sick Children's Trust and UK Sport Association (£1,000 each).

Children – 3 grants totalling £3,000
British Association for Adopting and Fostering, Disability Challengers and Sunflower Trust (£1,000 each).

Medical – 4 grants totalling £2,750
CLIC Sargent and Great Ormond Street Hospital Children's Charity (£1,000 each); Cystic Fibrosis Trust (£500); and Leukaemia Research (£250).

Animals – 2 grants totalling £2,000
Dogs for the Disabled and Hampshire Animal Rescue Team (£1,000 each)

Appeals – 1 grant of £1,000
DEC Bangladesh Cyclone Appeal.

Foreign – 1 grant of £1,000
Ulla Rapazote-Akin-Nepal.

Exclusions No grants to individuals or to local charities except those in Surrey or in Hampshire. The same organisation is not supported twice within a 24-month period.

Applications In writing to the correspondent. No telephone calls. Applications are not acknowledged and unsuccessful applicants will only be contacted if a stamped, addressed envelope is provided. Trustees meet in March and September and applications need to be received the month prior to the trustees' meeting.

Sir Siegmund Warburg's Voluntary Settlement

Arts
£1 million (2008/09)
Beneficial area UK, especially London.

c/o 33 St Mary Axe, London EC3A 8LL
Correspondent The Secretary
Trustees Hugh A Stevenson, Chair; Doris E Wasserman; Dr Michael J Harding; Christopher Purvis.
CC Number 286719
Information available Accounts were available from the Charity Commission.

The trust has recently changed the focus of its grantmaking from health and medicine to the arts.

In 2008/09 the trust had assets of £10 million, an income of £488,000 and made eight grants totalling over £1 million.

Beneficiaries included: Charleston Trust and National Gallery (£250,000 each); Ashmolean Museum (£200,000); Wordsworth Trust (£120,000); Garsington Opera (£105,000); Wallace Collection (£100,000); London Handel Festival (£10,000) and St Paul's Girls' School (£2,000).

Exclusions No grants to individuals.

Applications In writing to the correspondent.

The Ward Blenkinsop Trust

Medicine, social welfare, arts, education and general
£367,000 (2007/08)
Beneficial area UK, with a special interest in Merseyside and surrounding counties.

PO Box 28840, London SW13 0WZ
Correspondent Charlotte Blenkinsop, Trustee
Trustees A M Blenkinsop; Ms S J Blenkinsop; Ms C A Blenkinsop; Mrs F A Stormer; Mrs H E Millin.
CC Number 265449
Information available Information was on file at the Charity Commission, without a list of grants.

The trust currently supports charities in the Merseyside area and charities of a medical nature, but all requests for funds are considered.

In 2007/08 the trust had an income of £477,000 and made grants totalling £367,000.

By far the largest grant was £100,000 to Clatterbridge Cancer Research.

Previous beneficiaries have included Action on Addiction, BID, Chase Children's Hospice, Clatterbridge Cancer Research, Clod Ensemble, Comic Relief, Depaul Trust, Fairley House, Give Youth a Break, Halton Autistic Family Support Group, Hope HIV, Infertility Network, George Martin Music Foundation, Royal Academy of Dance, St Joseph's Family Centre, Strongbones Children's Charitable Trust, Walk the Walk, Winchester Visitors Group and Wirral Holistic Care Services.

Exclusions No grants to individuals.

Applications In writing to the correspondent.

The Barbara Ward Children's Foundation

Children
£506,000 (2008)
Beneficial area England and Wales.

5 Great College Street, London SW1P 3SJ
Website www.bwcf.org.uk
Correspondent The Trustees
Trustees Mrs B I Ward, Chair; D C Bailey; J C Banks; A M Gardner; K R Parker; B M Walters.
CC Number 1089783
Information available Accounts were on file at the Charity Commission.

This foundation makes grants to organisations working with children who are seriously or terminally ill, disadvantaged or otherwise. Grants made can range from one-off grants to project-related grants that run for two or three years.

In 2008 it had assets of £6.5 million and an income of £485,000. Grants to 70 organisations totalled £506,000.

The largest grants were made to: the Rainbow Centre (£37,000); MERU (£35,000); TreeHouse (£33,000); Richard House Children's Hospice (£28,000); WellChild (£23,000); Dame Vera Lynn Trust (£22,000); New College Worcester (£20,000); the Ellenor Foundation (£14,000); the Bobath Centre (£13,000); and National Blind Children's Society and PARC (£10,000 each).

Other beneficiaries included: Dogs for the Disabled and Rainbow Trust (£8,500 each); React (£8,000); the Ear Foundation (£6,700); Hop, Skip and Jump – South West (£6,000); Army Cadet Force Association, Federation of Artistic and Creative Therapy, Happy Days, Huntington's Disease Association, Network 81, Over the Wall, the Ellen MacArthur Trust, the Roundabout Trust, the Sailors' Families' Society, Stubbers Adventure Centre, WheelPower and the Wingate Special Children's Trust (£5,000 each); Kids Enjoy Exercise Now (£4,900); Ipswich Community Playbus (£4,000); Deafway, Edinburgh Young Carers and Fun in Action for Children (£3,000 each); the Rose Road Association (£2,500); and the Asha Centre (£500).

Applications In writing to the correspondent including latest set of audited financial statements. The trustees usually meet quarterly.

G R Waters Charitable Trust 2000

General

£14,000 (2007/08)

Beneficial area UK, also North and Central America.

Finers Stephens Innocent, 179–185 Great Portland Street, London W1W 5LS

Correspondent Michael Lewis

Trustees *M Fenwick; A Russell.*

CC Number 1091525

Information available Accounts were on file at the Charity Commission.

This trust was registered with the Charity Commission in 2002, replacing Roger Waters 1989 Charitable Trust (Charity Commission number 328574), which transferred its assets to this new trust. (The 2000 in the title refers to when the declaration of trust was made). Like the former trust, it receives a share of Pink Floyd's royalties as part of its annual income. It has general charitable purposes throughout the UK, as well as North and Central America.

In 2007/08 the trust had assets of £1.5 million, an income of£124,000 and made four grants totalling £14,000 (£70,000).

Beneficiaries were: Dream Holidays and React (£5,000 each); British Volunteer Fireman (£2,600); and Lance Armstrong Foundation (£1,700).

Applications In writing to the correspondent.

Blyth Watson Charitable Trust

UK-based humanitarian organisations and hospices

£72,000 (2007/08)

Beneficial area UK.

50 Broadway, Westminster, London SW1H 0BL

Correspondent The Trustees

Trustees *Edward Brown; Ian McCulloch.*

CC Number 1071390

Information available Accounts were on file at the Charity Commission.

The trust dedicates its grant-giving policy in the area of humanitarian causes based in the UK. A number of hospices are supported each year.

In 2007/08 the trust had assets of £2.8 million and an income of £98,000. Grants to 32 organisations totalled £72,000.

Previous beneficiaries have included: Army Benevolent Fund, Breast Cancer Haven, Children's Fire and Burns Trust, King Edward VII Hospital, Over the Wall Gang Camp, Pace Centre, Regalla Aid, Society for the Relief of Distress, St John's Hospice, St John of Jerusalem Eye Hospital, St Leonard's Hospice, St Luke's Hospital, St Martin in the Fields Christmas Appeal, Vision Aid Overseas, Waterways Trust and Wavemakers.

Applications In writing to the correspondent. Trustees usually meet twice during the year.

Weatherley Charitable Trust

General

£58,000 (2007/08)

Beneficial area Unrestricted.

Northampton Science Park Ltd, Newton House, Kings Park Road Moulton Park, Northampton NN3 6LG

Correspondent Christine Weatherley, Trustee

Trustees *Christine Weatherley; Richard Weatherley; Steven Chambers.*

CC Number 1079267

Information available Accounts were on file at the Charity Commission, without a list of grants.

This trust was established in 1999 for general charitable purposes. In 2007/08 it had assets amounting to £723,000 and an income of £37,000. Grants were made totalling £58,000. A list of grants was not included with the accounts.

Applications This trust does not accept unsolicited applications.

The Weavers' Company Benevolent Fund

Helping disadvantaged young people, offenders and ex-offenders

£333,000 (2008)

Beneficial area UK.

The Worshipful Company of Weavers', Saddlers' House, Gutter Lane, London EC2V 6BR

Tel. 020 7606 1155 **Fax** 020 7606 1119

Email charity@weaversco.co.uk

Website www.weavers.org.uk

Correspondent John Snowdon, Clerk

Trustee *The Worshipful Company of Weavers.*

CC Number 266189

Information available Accounts were on file at the Charity Commission. Guidelines for applicants can be found on the Weavers' Company website.

This benevolent fund was set up in 1973 with funds provided by the Worshipful Company of Weavers, the oldest of the City of London Livery Companies. Its priorities, adapted from the website, are:

1) Helping disadvantaged young people

The object of the fund is to support projects working with disadvantaged young people to ensure that they are given every possible chance to meet their full potential and to participate fully in society. We normally define young people as being aged from 5 to 30 years.

2) Offenders and ex-offenders, particularly those under 30 years of age

Many offenders and ex-offenders suffer from a variety of difficult and complex problems and they are amongst the most vulnerable members of society. We will fund work that addresses the social and economic problems faced by this group and their families, and provide them with support, life skills training and a way back into education, training and/ or employment, so that they may reintegrate and make a positive contribution to society.

We are especially interested in helping smaller organisations which offer direct services. They must be registered charities or in the process of applying for registration. Our grants are relatively modest, usually with an upper limit of £15,000 per annum, and to make sure grants of this size have an impact, we will not fund large organisations.

Applicants must show that they have investigated other sources of funding and made plans for the future, which should include replacement funding if appropriate.

What is funded?
Size of organisation – To be eligible for funding, local organisations such as those working in a village, estate or small town should normally have an income of less than about £100,000. Those working across the UK should normally have an income of not more than about £250,000.

Funding limit – Grants are usually up to £15,000 per annum but smaller applications are also welcomed.

Duration – Grants may be awarded for up to three years.

Pump-priming – We particularly welcome applications for pump-priming grants from small community-based organisations where a grant would form a major element of the funding. It prefers to support projects where our grant will be used for an identified purpose.

Core costs – We will consider applications for core funding, such as general administration and training that enable an organisation to develop and maintain expertise.

Innovative or pioneering work – We like to encourage new ideas and to fund projects that could inspire similar work in other areas of the country.

Continuation funding – We appreciate the importance of providing ongoing funding for successful projects, which have proved their worth.

Salaries – We normally fund salaries for up to three years but payment of the second and third year grants are subject to satisfactory progress reports.

Emergency or deficit funding – In exceptional circumstances, we may provide emergency or deficit funding for an established organisation. Applicants most likely to be granted emergency funding are charities which the company knows or has previously supported.

In 2008 the trust had assets of £5.7 million, an income of £360,000 and made grants totalling £333,000. Major support was given to: Weavers' Company Education Fund (£70,000); and Weavers' Company Millennial Fund (£35,000).

Other beneficiaries included: Emmanuel Youth Club, Straight Talking Peer Education – Surrey, Synergy Theatre and Project Voice UK (£15,000 each); Upper Room (£12,000); Northumbria Coalition Against Crime, Strood Community Project and Zone Youth Project (£10,000 each); People and Drugs – Northumberland (£5,200); Safety Zone – Glasgow (£5,000); Guildhall School of Music and Drama (£3,000); Jim Bareham Minibus Trust (£1,000); the Prison Phoenix Trust (£500); and City of London Freemen's School and St Luke's Hospital for the Clergy (£250 each).

Exclusions
- Long-term support – We will not normally provide long-term support.
- General appeals – We will not support sponsorship, marketing or other fundraising activities.
- Endowment funds – We will not support endowment funds, nor bursaries or long-term capital projects.
- Grant-giving charities.
- Retrospective funding – We will not make grants for work that has been completed or will be completed while the application is being considered.
- Replacement funding – We will not provide grants for work that should be covered by statutory funding.
- Building projects – We will not fund building work but may help with the cost of equipment or furnishings.
- Disability Discrimination Act – We will not fund capital projects to provide access in compliance with the DDA.
- Personal appeals – We will not make grants to individuals. Applicants must be registered charities, in the process of registering, or qualified as charitable.
- Umbrella bodies or large, established organisations – We will not normally support projects in which the charity is collaborating or working in partnership with umbrella bodies or large, established organisations.
- Overseas – We will not support organisations outside the UK, nor overseas expeditions or travel.

Work that we cannot normally support includes:
- Work with children under five years of age.
- Universities or colleges.
- Medical charities or those involved in medical care.
- Organisations of and for disabled people.
- Environmental projects.
- Work in promotion of religious or political causes.

Applications Detailed *Guidelines for Applicants* are available from the the Weavers' Company website.

Application forms can be downloaded from the fund's website, or requested by post or email.

The grants committee meets in February, June and October of each year, it may take up to four months for applications to be processed.

Webb Memorial Trust

Education, politics and social policy
£70,000 per year
Beneficial area UK and Eastern Europe.

Mount Royal, Allendale Road, Hexham NE46 2NJ
Website www.webbmemorialtrust.org.uk
Correspondent Mike Parker, The Hon. Secretary
Trustees *Richard Rawes, Chair; Mike Parker; Robert Lloyd-Davies; Dianne Hayter; Mike Gapes; Barry Knight.*
CC Number 313760
Information available Information was provided by the trust.

The Webb Memorial Trust is a registered charity; it was established in 1947 as a memorial to the socialist pioneer Beatrice Webb.

The trust is set up with the aims of the advancement of education and learning with respect to the history and problem of government and social policy (including socialism, trade unionism and co-operation) in Great Britain and elsewhere by:

1) research
2) lectures, scholarships and educational grants
3) such other educational means as the trustees may from time to time approve.

Since 1987 the trust has provided £70,000 a year to fund a variety of projects in the UK and Eastern Europe.

Beneficiaries have included Ruskin College, Fabian Society, Institute of Contemporary British History, Socialist Health Association, Transport 2000, Westminster Foundation for Democracy and Unison.

Half of the trust's grant expenditure goes towards funding students from Eastern Europe attending Ruskin College – Oxford to study courses relevant to the trust's objects. The rest goes on projects either within the UK or overseas in Europe.

Exclusions No grants in support of any political party.

Applications See the trust's website for details of availability.

The David Webster Charitable Trust

Ecological and broadly environmental projects

£174,000 (2007/08)

Beneficial area UK.

Marshalls, Marshalls Lane, High Cross, Ware SG11 1AJ

Correspondent The Trustees

Trustees *T W D Webster; Mrs N Thompson.*

CC Number 1055111

Information available Accounts were on file at the Charity Commission.

Set up in 1995, in 2007/08 the trust had assets of £2.8 million, an income of £236,000 and made 11 grants totalling £174,000.

Beneficiaries included: Bird Life International (£100,000); Wells Cathedral (£25,000); Hertfordshire and Middlesex Wildlife Trust (£15,000); St George's Church (£13,000); National Trust, Nottingham Wildlife Trust and Oxford Arboretum (£5,000 each); Bat Conservation Trust and Norfolk Wherry Trust (£2,000 each); and Bettisfield Church (£1,000).

Applications In writing to the correspondent.

The Weinberg Foundation

General

£166,000 (2007/08)

Beneficial area UK and overseas.

2nd Floor, Manfield House, 1 Southampton Street, London WC2R 0LR

Correspondent The Trustees

Trustees *N H Ablitt; C L Simon.*

CC Number 273308

Information available Accounts were on file at the Charity Commission.

In 2007/08 the trust had assets of £819,000, which generated an income of £34,000. Grants were made totalling £166,000.

There were 21 donations of £1,000 or more listed in the accounts. Beneficiaries included: Natan Foundation (£23,000); Friends of EORTC (£20,000); Amnesty International (£15,000); Community Security trust (£12,500); Ability Net, Philharmonia Orchestra, the Royal Shakespeare Theatre and St James's Palace Foundation (£10,000 each); University of Cambridge (£5,000); UJIA Campaign (£4,000); South Bank Foundation (£2,000); and Elton John AIDS Foundation (£1,000).

Applications In writing to the correspondent.

The Weinstein Foundation

Jewish, medical and welfare

£52,000 (2007/08)

Beneficial area Worldwide.

32 Fairholme Gardens, Finchley, London N3 3EB

Correspondent M L Weinstein, Trustee

Trustees *Stella Weinstein; Michael Weinstein; Philip Weinstein; Leanne Newman.*

CC Number 277779

Information available Full accounts were on file at the Charity Commission.

This trust mostly supports Jewish organisations, although it does have general charitable purposes and supports a wide range of other causes, notably medical-related charities.

In 2007/08 the foundation had assets of £1.6 million, an income of £53,000 and made grants totalling £52,000.

There were 10 grants of £1,000 each or more listed in the accounts, beneficiaries included: Chevras Evas Nitzrochim Trust (£8,000); Friends of Mir (£6,000); SOFT UK (£2,200); Chesed Charitable Trust and Hachnosas Torah Vechesed Charity (£1,500 each); and Youth Aliyah (£1,000).

Donations under £1,000 each totalled £22,000.

Exclusions No grants to individuals.

Applications In writing to the correspondent.

The Weinstock Fund

General

Around £250,000 (2007/08)

Beneficial area Unrestricted, but with some local interest in the Wiltshire and Newbury area.

PO Box 17734, London SW18 3ZQ

Correspondent Miss Jacqueline Elstone, Trust Administrator

Trustees *Susan G Lacroix; Michael Lester; Laura H Weinstock.*

CC Number 222376

Information available Accounts were on file at the Charity Commission.

The trustees support a wide range of charitable causes, particularly in the field of welfare, children, education, medicine and arts. Only UK registered charities are considered.

In 2007/08 grants totalled around £250,000.

Previous beneficiaries have included: Army Benevolent Fund, Ashmolean Museum, British Friends of Hatzolah Israel, British ORT, Chicken Shed Theatre Company, CLIC Sargent, Community Security Trust, Delamere Forest School, Donmar Warehouse, Dorothy House Foundation, Home Warmth for the Aged, Garsington Opera, Hampstead Theatre, Jewish Care Oxford Synagogue, Jewish Centre, Multiple Sclerosis Society, NICHS, National Gallery Trust, Holocaust Educational Trust, London Symphony Orchestra, Rainbow Trust, St Hilda's College, St Paul's Girls School Development Trust, Save the Children Fund, Royal Opera House Foundation, UK Youth, Winchester College Development Fund and Yetev Lev Youth Club.

Exclusions No grants to individuals or unregistered organisations.

Applications In writing to the correspondent. There are no printed details or applications forms. Previous information received stated 'Where nationwide charities are concerned, the trustees prefer to make donations centrally.' Donations can only be made to registered charities, and details of the registration number are required before any payment can be made.

The James Weir Foundation

Welfare, education and general

£254,000 (2008)

Beneficial area UK, with a preference for Ayrshire and Glasgow.

84 Cicada Road, London SW18 2NZ

Correspondent The Secretary

Trustees *Simon Bonham; William Ducas; Elizabeth Bonham.*

CC Number 251764

Information available Accounts were on file at the Charity Commission.

The foundation has general charitable purposes, giving priority to schools and educational institutions; Scottish organisations, especially local charities in Ayrshire and Glasgow; and charities with which either James Weir or the trustees are particularly associated. These preferences, however, do not appear to be at the expense of other causes, UK-wide charities or local organisations outside of Scotland. The following six charities are listed in the trust deed as potential beneficiaries:

- The Royal Society
- The British Association for Advancement of Science
- The RAF Benevolent Fund
- The Royal College of Surgeons
- The Royal College of Physicians
- The University of Strathclyde.

In 2008 the trust had an income of £268,000 and made 81 grants totalling £254,000. Assets stood at £6.8 million.

In total, 81 grants were made, the largest of which were given to the six organisations listed in the trust deed: University of Strathclyde (£8,500); and British Association for the Advancement of Science, National Trust for Scotland, RAF Benevolent Fund, Royal College of Surgeons and Royal College of Physicians (£5,000 each).

Other beneficiaries included: Action for Blind People, Bowel Cancer UK, Roy Castle Lung Cancer Foundation, Contact the Elderly, Cystic Fibrous Trust, Disabled Living Foundation, Dressability, Elizabeth Finn Care, Jubilee Sailing Trust, National Autistic Society,

SSAFA Forces Help and ZANE (£3,000 each); and American Museum in Bath and Prostate UK (£1,000 each).

Exclusions Grants are given to recognised charities only. No grants to individuals.

Applications In writing to the correspondent. Distributions are made twice-yearly in June and November when the trustees meet. Applications should be received by May or October.

The Barbara Welby Trust

General

£40,000 (2007/08)

Beneficial area UK, with a preference for Lincolnshire.

Hunters, 9 New Square, Lincoln's Inn, London WC2A 3QN

Correspondent The Trustees

Trustees *N J Barker; C W H Welby; C N Robertson.*

CC Number 252973

Information available Full accounts were on file at the Charity Commission

The trust states that it considers supporting a range of charities, but has a preference for those of which the founder had special knowledge and for charities which have objects with which she was especially associated.

In 2007/08 it had assets of £1 million and an income of £42,000. Grants were made totalling £40,000.

There were 42 grants made during the year, beneficiaries included: Lincolnshire Agricultural Society (£7,500); Lincoln Cathedral (£5,000); Braceby Church (£1,500); Be Your Best Foundation, CAFOD, the Connection at St Martins, Hearing Dogs for Deaf People, the Lincolnshire Foundation, St John Ambulance, St Luke's Hospital for the Clergy, Stroxton Church and Usher Junior School (£1,000 each); and British Heart Foundation, British Red Cross, Community Care for the Elderly, Depaul Trust, Elizabeth Finn Trust, Great Ormond Street Hospital – Equipment Fund, the Royal British Legion, Samaritans – Grantham and University of Nottingham – scanner appeal (£500 each).

Exclusions Applications for individual assistance are not normally considered

unless made through an established charitable organisation.

Applications In writing at any time to the trustees, although they meet to consider grants in March and October.

The Wessex Youth Trust

Young people and general

£76,000 (2007/08)

Beneficial area Worldwide.

c/o Farrer and Co, 66 Lincoln's Inn Fields, London WC2A 3LH

Correspondent Jenny Cannon

Trustees *Mark Foster-Brown; Malcolm Cockren; Denise Poulton; Robert Clinton; Kate Cavelle.*

CC Number 1076003

Information available Accounts were on file at the Charity Commission.

The following information is taken from the trustees' annual report:

The charity's primary aim is to assist other registered charities and charitable causes and in particular those with which Their Royal Highnesses have personal connection or interests. The charity is particularly, although not exclusively, interested in supporting projects which provide opportunities to help, support and advance young people.

Most grants are one-off, although substantial grants may be made for up to five years.

In 2007/08 the trust had an income of £212,000 mainly from donations. Assets stood at £408,000. Grants to 21 organisations totalled £76,000.

Beneficiaries included: Blind in Business, the Brainwave Centre, Cardboard Citizens, Caring for Life, Children's Adventure Farm Trust, Classworks Theatre, the Country Trust, Demelza Hospice Care for Children, East Reading Explorer Scouts, Happy Days Children's Charity, Kidscape, Project Scotland, Tolerance International UK and the Wessex Autistic Society.

The accounts stated: 'The Charity Commission has been supplied with details of amounts given to each charity together with an explanation of the reasons for the non-disclosure of individual amounts in the financial statements.' Non-disclosure of grants information should only be made where the information being made public may be potentially harmful to the trust or its recipients; failing to disclose information without providing an explanation in the public sphere may prompt unjustified speculation about the nature of grants made.

Exclusions No grants are made to:

- non-registered charities or causes
- individuals, including to people who are undertaking fundraising activities on behalf of a charity
- organisations whose main objects are to fund or support other causes
- organisations whose accounts disclose substantial financial resources and that have well-established and ample fundraising capabilities
- fund research that can be supported by government funding or that is popular among trusts.

Applications In writing to the correspondent in the first instance. A response will be made within two weeks, in the form of an application form and guidelines to eligible applicants or a letter of rejection if more appropriate. Completed forms, which are not acknowledged upon receipt, need to be submitted by 1 May or 1 November, for consideration by the end of the month. Clarity of presentation and provision of financial details are among the qualities which impress the trustees. Successful applicants will receive a letter stating that the acceptance of the funding is conditional on an update being received before the next meeting. The trust's criteria state other correspondence cannot be entered into, and organisations cannot reveal the size of any grants they receive.

West London Synagogue Charitable Fund

Jewish and general

£42,000 (2008)
Beneficial area UK.

33 Seymour Place, London W1H 5AU
Correspondent The Fund Coordinator
Trustees *Elizabeth Shrager, Chair; Simon Raperport; Alan Bradley; Jane Cutter; Michael Cutter; Francine Epstein; Vivien Feather; Jacqui Green; Ruth Jacobs; Hermy Jankel; Monica Jankel; Phyllis*

Levy; Elaine Parry; Jean Regen; and four ex-officio trustees.

CC Number 209778

Information available Accounts on file at the Charity Commission.

The trust stated that it makes grants to both Jewish and non-Jewish organisations. It prefers to be involved with charities which synagogue members are involved with or helped by. In 2008 it had an income of £41,000, mostly from charity events and made 63 grants totalling £42,000. The sum of £4,100 was carried forward at year end.

Beneficiaries included: Motor Neurone Disease (£6,000); Hammerson House (£5,000); Karen Morris Memorial Trust (£4,000); Berkley Street Club and West London Synagogue (£2,000 each); Rabbi Freeman's Discretionary Fund (£800); Jewish Child's Day, Psoriasis Society and World Jewish Relief (£500 each); and Centrepoint Soho, City Escape, Dystonia Society, Headway, Oasis of Peace, Strongbones and World Union of Progressive Judaism (£250 each).

Exclusions No grants to individuals.

Applications In writing to the correspondent.

Mrs S K West's Charitable Trust

General

Nil (2007/08)
Beneficial area UK.

20 Beech Road, Garstang, Preston PR3 1FS
Correspondent P J Schoon, Trustee
Trustees *P Schoon; C Blakeborough; J Grandage.*
CC Number 294755

Information available Accounts were on file at the Charity Commission.

Established in 1986, the trust has come to distribute roughly half of its available funds between charities promoting the Christian faith and those charities 'having people as their main concern'. The majority of support given to organisations is recurrent from previous years.

In 2007/08 the trust had assets of £467,000 and an income of £35,000. No grants were made during the year.

The sum of £43,000 was distributed in the previous financial year when beneficiaries included Bible Society, BLESMA, Cancer Help – Preston, Christians Against Poverty, Go Africa, Holme Christian Care Centre, OMF International, Otley Meeting Room, Salvation Army, Shaftesbury Society, Spen Valley Faith In Schools Trust, Tear Fund and Turning Point.

Applications The trust states that it does not respond to unsolicited applications and would prefer not to receive any such applications asking for support.

The Westcroft Trust

International understanding, overseas aid, Quaker and Shropshire

£89,000 (2007/08)
Beneficial area Unrestricted, but with a special interest in Shropshire – causes of local interest outside Shropshire are rarely supported.

32 Hampton Road, Oswestry SY11 1SJ
Correspondent Mary Cadbury, Managing Trustee
Trustees *Mary C Cadbury; Richard G Cadbury; James E Cadbury; Erica R Cadbury.*
CC Number 212931

Information available Accounts were on file at the Charity Commission.

Currently the trustees have five main areas of interest:

- international understanding, including conflict resolution and the material needs of the developing world
- religious causes, particularly social outreach, usually of the Society of Friends (Quakers) but also for those originating in Shropshire
- development of the voluntary sector in Shropshire
- needs of people with disabilities, primarily in Shropshire
- development of community groups and reconciliation between different cultures in Northern Ireland.

Medical education is only helped by support for expeditions overseas that include pre-clinical students. Medical aid, education and relief work in developing countries is mainly supported through UK-registered organisations. International disasters may be helped in response to public appeals.

The trust favours charities with low administrative overheads and that pursue clear policies of equal opportunity in meeting need. Grants may be one-off or recurrent; recurrent grants are rarely made for endowment or capital projects.

In 2007/08 the trust had assets of £2.2 million, which generated an income of £106,000. Grants were made totalling £89,000, broken down as follows:

Category	Amount
International understanding, conflict resolution and material needs of the developing world:	
Relief work	£14,000
International understanding	£8,000
Education	£7,100
Medical aid	£6,100
Religious society of friends:	
Central Committees	£8,000
Meeting Houses	£1,600
Other funds, institutions and appeals	£14,000
Disabilities, health and special needs:	
National	£4,300
Shropshire	£3,900
Medical research	£3,900
Development of community groups:	
Social service – Shropshire	£10,000
Social services – England, Wales and Scotland	£5,600
Education – Shropshire	£500
Northern Ireland:	
Social service	£700

Exclusions Grants are given to charities only. No grants to individuals or for medical electives, sport, the arts (unless specifically for people with disabilities in Shropshire) or armed forces charities. Requests for sponsorship are not supported. Annual grants are withheld if recent accounts are not available or do not satisfy the trustees as to continuing need.

Applications In writing to the correspondent. There is no application form or set format but applications should be restricted to a maximum of three sheets of paper, stating purpose, overall financial needs and resources together with previous years' accounts if appropriate. Printed letters signed by 'the great and good' and glossy literature do not impress the trustees, who prefer lower-cost applications. Applications are dealt with about every two months. No acknowledgement will be given. Replies to relevant but unsuccessful applicants will be sent only if a stamped, addressed envelope is enclosed. As some annual grants are made by Bank Telepay, details of bank name, branch, sort code, and account name and number should be sent in order to save time and correspondence.

The Barbara Whatmore Charitable Trust

Arts, music and relief of poverty

£75,000 (2007/08)
Beneficial area UK.

Spring House, Priors Way, Aldeburgh IP15 5EW
Correspondent Mrs P M Cooke-Yarborough, Chair

Trustees *Patricia Cooke-Yarborough, Chair; David Eldridge; Denis Borrow; Gillian Lewis; Luke Gardiner; Sally Carter; Stephen Bate.*

CC Number 283336

Information available Accounts were on file at the Charity Commission.

This trust was registered with the Charity Commission in October 1981. In 2007/08 it had assets of £1.3 million. It had an income of £112,000 and made 44 grants totalling £75,000.

Beneficiaries included: Campaign for Drawing (£6,500); Foundation for Young Musicians (£6,000); Diocese of Norwich (£4,300); Pro Corda (£4,000); Kew Gardens – Marianne North Gallery, Leather Conservation Centre and Orange Tree Theatre (£3,000 each); National Youth Orchestra (£2,400); Aldeburgh Music, City and Guilds of London Art School, Edward Barnsley Educational Trust, Historic Royal Palaces, Hampton Court, Polka Theatre and Watts Gallery – Compton (£2,000 each); Aldeburgh Museum, Flag Fen, Ilketshall – St Andrews, St Botolph's – Cambridge, St Mary's – Troston and Wonderful Beast Theatre Company (£1,500 each); National Youth Strings Academy (£1,000); Southwell Minster (£800); Ashmolean Museum, Smaull Song, St Margaret's – Toppesfield, St Morwenna – Morwenstow and St Paul's Cathedral (£500 each); and New Lanark Conservation (£250).

Applications In writing to the correspondent.

The Whitaker Charitable Trust

Music, environment and countryside conservation

£122,000 (2007/08)
Beneficial area UK, but mostly East Midlands and Scotland.

c/o Currey and Co., 21 Buckingham Gate, London SW1E 6LS
Correspondent The Trustees

Trustees *E R H Perks; D W J Price; Lady Elizabeth Whitaker.*

CC Number 234491

Information available Accounts were on file at the Charity Commission.

The trust has general charitable objects, although with stated preferences in the following fields:

- local charities in Nottinghamshire and the East Midlands
- music
- agriculture and silviculture
- countryside conservation
- Scottish charities.

In 2007/08 the trust had assets of £7.5 million, which generated an income of £213,000. Grants to 47 organisations totalled £122,000.

A substantial grant of £36,000 was made to Atlantic College. Other beneficiaries included: Nottingham University – Faculty of Medicine and Royal Forestry Society (£10,000 each); Leith School of Art (£8,000); Opera North (£7,500); Bassetlaw Hospice and Game Conservancy Scottish Research Trust (£3,000 each); Lincoln Cathedral Fabric Fund (£2,500); Arkwright Scholarships (£2,000); VSO (£1,500); Drake Music Project, Music in Hospitals, Portland College and Tree Aid (£1,000 each); and Cambridge Arthritis Research Endeavour (£500).

Exclusions Support is given to registered charities only. No grants are given to individuals or for the repair or maintenance of individual churches.

Applications In writing to the correspondent. Applications should include clear details of the need the intended project is designed to meet plus a copy of the latest accounts available and an outline budget. If an acknowledgement of the application, or notification in the event of the application not being accepted, is required, a stamped, addressed envelope should be enclosed. Trustees meet on a regular basis.

The Simon Whitbread Charitable Trust

Education, family welfare, medicine and preservation

About £150,000 (2008/09)

Beneficial area UK, with a preference for Bedfordshire.

Hunters, 9 New Square, Lincoln's Inn, London WC2A 3QN

Correspondent E C A Martineau

Trustees *S C Whitbread; E C A Martineau; Mrs E A Bennett.*

CC Number 200412

Information available Accounts had been filed at the Charity Commission.

The trust supports general causes in Bedfordshire, and education, family welfare, medicine, medical research and preservation UK-wide.

In 2008/09 the trust had an income of £136,000 and a total expenditure of £172,000.

Previous beneficiaries have included All Saints Church, Army Benevolent Fund, Arthritis Care, Bedfordshire Historical Records Society, Bedfordshire Music Trust, Chillingham Wild Cattle, Countryside Foundation for Education, Gravenhurst Parish Council, Mencap, National Association of Widows, St Luke's Hospital for the Clergy, Spurgeons Child Care, Royal Green Jackets, Retirement Education Centre Bedfordshire, RSPB, St Mungo's and Scope.

Exclusions Generally no support for local projects outside Bedfordshire.

Applications In writing to the correspondent. Acknowledgements are not given. Please do not telephone.

The Colonel W H Whitbread Charitable Trust

Education and preservation of places of historic interest and natural beauty

£67,000 (2008)

Beneficial area UK, with an interest in Gloucestershire.

Fir Tree Cottage, World's End, Sinton Green WR2 6NN

Tel. 07812 454321

Email whwhitbread.trust@googlemail.com

Correspondent Mrs Susan M Smith

Trustees *H F Whitbread; J R Barkes; R T Foley.*

CC Number 210496

Information available Accounts were on file at the Charity Commission.

The following information is taken from the trust's annual report:

The trustees have resolved to support charitable organisations and general areas of charitable activity which were, or in the opinion of the trustees would have been, of interest to the trust's founder, the late Colonel William Henry Whitbread, which comprise the following:

1) The promotion of education and in particular: (a) the provision of financial assistance towards the maintenance and development of Aldenham School, and (b) the creation of Colonel W H Whitbread scholarships or bursaries or prizes to be awarded to pupils at Aldenham School.
2) Charitable organisations within Gloucestershire.
3) The preservation, protection and improvement for the public benefit of places of historic interest and natural beauty.

The trustees will only in exceptional circumstances consider grant applications for purposes which fall outside those described above. Within this framework the trustees will distribute a minimum of £500 per distribution.

The trustees make charitable distributions on an arbitrary basis, having reviewed all applications and considered other charities that they wish to benefit.

In 2008 the trust had assets of £5.6 million, an income of £161,000 and made 23 grants totalling £67,000.

Previous beneficiaries have included: 1st Queen's Dragon Guards Regimental Trust, Abbey School Tewkesbury, Army Benevolent Fund, CLIC Sargent, DEC Tsunami Earthquake Appeal, Friends of Alderman Knights School, Gloucestershire Historic Churches Trust, Great Ormond Street Hospital Children's Charity, Household Cavalry Museum Appeal, Hunt Servants' Fund, Queen Mary's Clothing Guild, Royal Hospital Chelsea and St Richard's Hospice.

Applications A brief summary (no more than one side of A4) in writing (by email if possible) to the correspondent. It is not necessary to send any accompanying paperwork at this stage. Should the trustees wish to consider any application further, then an application form will be sent out.

The Melanie White Foundation Limited

General

£271,000 (2007/08)

Beneficial area Unrestricted.

c/o 89 New Bond Street, London W1S 1DA

Correspondent The Trustees

Trustees *Mrs M White; A White.*

CC Number 1077150

Information available Accounts were on file at the Charity Commission.

Set up in 1999, the following was taken from the foundation's 2007/08 annual report:

The charity's principal activity during the year was the support of charities through the payments of donations. The objects of the charity are to promote any charitable purpose or support any charity selected by the directors. It is expressly contemplated that the Arbib Foundation [Charity Commission no. 296358] may be a beneficiary of the application of some or all funds or other benefits by the charity.

In 2007/08 the foundation had assets of £9.6 million and an income of £258,000.

Grants totalled £271,000, of which £245,000 went to the Arbib Foundation. Other beneficiaries included the Will Greenwood Testimonial Year (£25,000) and CLIC Sargent (£500).

Applications This trust does not accept unsolicited applications.

The Whitecourt Charitable Trust

Christian and general

£49,000 (2007/08)

Beneficial area UK and overseas, with a preference for Sheffield.

48 Canterbury Avenue, Fulwood, Sheffield S10 3RU

Correspondent Mrs G W Lee, Trustee

Trustees *P W Lee; Mrs G W Lee; M P W Lee.*

CC Number 1000012

Information available Accounts were on file at the Charity Commission.

Most of the grants given by the trust are recurrent and to Christian causes in the UK and overseas. Other grants are given to a few Christian and welfare causes in Sheffield.

In 2007/08 there were 141 grants made totalling £49,000, of which three totalling £10,500 were made to Christ Church Fulwood: General Fund (£5,500); Missionary Fund (£4,000); and the Vicar's Discretionary Fund (£1,000). This organisation has also received substantial support in previous years.

Other beneficiaries included: Monkton Combe School Bursary Fund (£3,000); SRSB Appeal (£2,000); Church Mission Society and South Yorkshire Community Foundation (£1,100 each); Children's Homes in India (£1,000); Careforce (£750); Frontier Youth Trust (£700); Extra Care Charitable Trust and London Institute for Contemporary Christianity (£300); Barnabas Fund, Daylight Christian Prison Trust, Leprosy Mission, Off the Fence and Yorkshire Cadet Trust (£100 each); Sheffield Botanical Gardens Trust (£50); and Muscular Disease Society and Royal Hallamshire Hospital (£25 each).

Exclusions No support for animal or conservation organisations or for campaigning on social issues.

Applications In writing to the correspondent, at any time. However, the trust states very little money is available for unsolicited applications, due to advance commitments.

A H and B C Whiteley Charitable Trust

Art, environment and general

£57,000 (2007/08)

Beneficial area England, Scotland and Wales, with a special interest in Nottinghamshire.

Marchants, Regent Chambers, Regent Street, Mansfield NG18 1SW

Correspondent E G Aspley, Trustee

Trustees *E G Aspley; K E B Clayton.*

CC Number 1002220

Information available Accounts were on file at the Charity Commission.

The trust was established in 1990 and derives most of its income from continuing donations. The trust deed requires the trustees to make donations to registered charities in England, Scotland and Wales but with particular emphasis on charities based in Nottinghamshire.

In 2007/08 the trust had assets of £1.3 million and an income of £51,000. Grants were made to eight organisations totalling £57,000.

Beneficiaries were: National Trust (£15,000); Southwell Minister (£12,000); St Peters Ravenshead PCC (£7,000); Lincolnshire and Nottinghamshire Air Ambulance, Macmillan Cancer Relief, Portland College and Queens Court Hospice (£5,000 each); and Friends of St Peter's and Paul's (£3,000).

Applications The trust does not seek applications.

The Norman Whiteley Trust

Evangelical Christianity, welfare and education

£104,000 (2007/08)

Beneficial area Worldwide, although in practice mainly Cumbria.

Lane Cove, Grassgarth Lane, Ings LA8 9QF

Correspondent The Trustees

Trustees *Mrs B M Whiteley; P Whiteley; D Dickson; J Ratcliff.*

CC Number 226445

Information available Accounts were on file at the Charity Commission.

This trust supports the furtherance of the Gospel, the relief of poverty and education. Grants can be made worldwide, but in practice are usually restricted to Cumbria and the surrounding areas.

In 2007/08 the trust had assets of £2.5 million and an income of £143,000. Grants were made totalling £104,000.

Beneficiaries included: Lakes Gospel Choir – All Who Thirst (£11,000); Osterreichische Evangelische Allianz (£10,000); Agape Osterreich and Alpha Osterreich (£6,900 each); Greenstones Christian Trust and Sports Reach (£5,000 each); Bibellesbund (£4,100); Before the Throne Ministries (£3,000); United Christian Broadcasters (£2,200); Assemblies of God and Lakes Christian Centre (£2,000 each); Christians Against Poverty and Washington Christian Centre (£1,000 each); and Bootle Evangelical Church and Millom Methodist Church (£500 each).

Exclusions Whilst certain overseas organisations are supported, applications from outside of Cumbria are not accepted.

Applications In writing to the correspondent. Trustees meet to consider applications twice a year.

The Whitley Animal Protection Trust

Protection and conservation of animals and their environments

£341,000 (2008)

Beneficial area UK and overseas, with a preference for Scotland.

Padmore House, Hall Court, Hall Park Way, Telford TF3 4LX

Correspondent M T Gwynne, Secretary

Trustees E Whitley, Chair; Mrs P A Whitley; E J Whitley; J Whitley.

CC Number 236746

Information available Full accounts were on file at the Charity Commission.

This trust supports the prevention of cruelty to animals and the promotion of their conservation and environment. Grants are made throughout the UK and the rest of world, with about 20% of funds given in Scotland.

In 2008 the trust had assets of £7.6 million and an income of £411,000. Grants to 15 organisations totalled £341,000.

Beneficiaries included: Whitley Fund for Nature (£162,000); Hawk and Owl Trust (£75,000); Rivers and Fisheries Trust of Scotland (£30,000); Wildlife Conservation Research Unit University of Oxford (£15,000); the Dee Fishery Association, Fauna and Flora International and Shropshire Wildlife Trust – The Hollies Appeal (£10,000 each); Murton Wildlife Trust (£7,500); RSPB Scotland (£5,000); The Wye and Usk Foundation (£3,000); Shropshire Wildlife Trust (£1,000); and Petsavers (£500).

Exclusions No grants to non-registered charities.

Applications The trust has previously stated that: 'The trust honours existing commitments and initiates new ones through its own contacts rather than responding to unsolicited applications.'

The Lionel Wigram Memorial Trust

General

£53,000 (2007/08)

Beneficial area UK, with a preference for Greater London.

Highfield House, 4 Woodfall Street, London SW3 4DJ

Correspondent A F Wigram, Chair

Trustees A F Wigram, Chair; Mrs S A Wigram.

CC Number 800533

Information available Accounts were on file at the Charity Commission.

The trustees 'have particular regard to projects which will commemorate the life of Major Lionel Wigram who was killed in action in Italy in 1944'. The trust makes grants to a wide range of organisations, especially in the areas of illness and disability.

In 2007/08 the trust's assets totalled £681,000 and it had an income of £91,000, including £58,000 from rental income. Grants totalled £53,000. The 43 donations made in the year were broken down as follows:

Coping with illness and disability – 26 grants totalling £42,000
Beneficiaries included: U Can Do IT (£32,000 in four grants); and Braille Chess Association, Compaid Trust, the Eyeless Trust, Music Alive, Spadework and Vitalise (£500 each).

Community projects/helping the disadvantaged – 13 grants totalling £6,250
Beneficiaries included: 9 Lives Furniture, Happy Days Children's Charity, Summer Adventure for Inner Londoners, the Vine Project and UK Youth (£500 each); and Community Links Trust Limited (£250).

Performing arts – 2 grants totalling £3,500
Beneficiaries were: Newbury Spring Festival Society Ltd (£3,000); and Hotham Arts Centre (£500).

Historical/restoration – 1 grant of £500
The sole beneficiary was the War Memorials Trust (£500).

Research and prevention of illness – 1 grant of £500
The sole beneficiary was Bath Institute of Medical Engineering.

Applications In writing to the correspondent.

The Richard Wilcox Welfare Charity

Health, medical research, welfare of patients, hospitals and animal welfare

£431,000 (2007/08)

Beneficial area UK.

Herschel House, 58 Herschel Street, Slough SL1 1PG

Correspondent Richard Oury, Administrator

Trustees John Ingram; Nick Sargent; Roger Danks.

CC Number 1082586

Information available Accounts were on file at the Charity Commission.

Registered with the Charity Commission in September 2000, the objects of the trust are to:

- prevent cruelty and to relieve the suffering and distress of animals of any species who are in need of care, attention and protection
- relieve sickness and protect and preserve good health
- promote the research and advancement of the causes and treatment of diseases
- relieve patients receiving treatment in hospital or on their discharge
- provide, maintain and improve hospitals and other institutions providing medical treatment
- assist or promote any charitable organisation or charitable purpose.

In 2007/08 the charity had assets of £2.1 million and an income of £154,000. Grants totalled £431,000.

Beneficiaries included: Ian Rennie Hospice (£210,000); DNA (£100,000); Chiltern Air Ambulance (£48,000); Nyumbarni (£41,000); Tiggywinkles (£20,000); Fairbridge Tyne and Wear (£5,000); Vision Aid Overseas (£3,000); and Hike for Hope (£500).

The charity stated in 2007/08 that it 'plans to increase its grant giving over the next twelve months by continuing to support, where appropriate, those charities it has supported in the past, and to look for further organisations that would benefit from the charity's financial support through one off or regular grants'.

Applications In writing to the correspondent. The trustees meet quarterly to assess grant applications.

The Felicity Wilde Charitable Trust

Children and medical research

£99,000 (2007/08)
Beneficial area UK.

Barclays Bank Trust Company Ltd, Estates and Trusts, Osborne Court, Gadbrook Park, Northwich CW9 7UE
Correspondent The Clerk
Trustee *Barclays Bank Trust Co Ltd.*
CC Number 264404
Information available Accounts were on file at the Charity Commission.

The trust supports children's charities and medical research, with particular emphasis on research into the causes or cures of asthma.

In 2007/08 it had assets of £1.8 million, an income of £82,000 and gave grants totalling £99,000.

Previous beneficiaries have included Action on Addiction, Asthma UK, Bobath – Glasgow, Breakthrough Breast Cancer, British Epilepsy Association, British Lung Foundation, ChildLine, Children's Liver Disease Foundation, Darlington Association on Disability, East Anglia Children's Hospices, Home-Start Leicester, Honeypot Charity, Kids Out, Meningitis Research Foundation, National Back Pain Association, National Eczema Society, Shooting Star Trust Children's Hospice, Southampton University Development Trust, Sparks, Starlight Children's Foundation, West Midlands Post Adoption Service and Who Cares? Trust.

Exclusions No grants to individuals or non-registered charities.

Applications In writing to the correspondent at any time. Applications are usually considered quarterly.

The Wilkinson Charitable Foundation

Scientific research

£63,000 (2007/08)
Beneficial area UK.

c/o Lawrence Graham LLP, 4 More London Riverside, London SE1 2AU
Correspondent B D S Lock, Trustee
Trustees *B D S Lock; G C Hurstfield.*
CC Number 276214
Information available Full accounts were on file at the Charity Commission.

The trust was set up for the advancement of scientific knowledge and education at Imperial College – University of London. Grants are only given to academic institutions.

The trustees have continued their policy of supporting research and initiatives commenced in the founder's lifetime and encouraging work in similar fields to those he was interested in.

In 2007/08 the foundation had assets of £1.5 million and an income of £62,000. Grants to nine organisations totalled £63,000.

Beneficiaries were: Wolfson College – Oxford (£31,000); Imperial College of Science, Technology and Medicine (£20,000); University College – London (£5,000); Lady Margaret Hall Development Fund (£2,500); British Heart Foundation (£2,000); and Foundation for the Prevention of Blindness, St Peter's Trust, Vassall Centre Trust and Wellbeing of Women (£500 each).

Exclusions No grants to individuals.

Applications In writing to the correspondent.

The Williams Charitable Trust

Education, medicine, theatre and general

£178,000 (2007/08)
Beneficial area UK.

85 Capital Wharf, 50 Wapping High Street, London E1W 1LY
Correspondent Stuart Williams, Trustee
Trustees *S K M Williams; Mrs H A Williams; J Riddick; A M Williams; M T M Williams.*
CC Number 1086668
Information available Accounts were on file at the Charity Commission.

The objects of the trust are to support education and training, the advancement of medicine and general charitable purposes.

The 2007/08 trustees' report stated that: 'During the year, the trustees have allocated funds to financially support the theatre, medical research and various local community initiatives.'

In 2007/08 the trust had assets of £2.8 million, an income of £181,000 and made 14 grants totalling £178,000.

Beneficiaries included: Donmar Warehouse (£107,000); Asthma UK (£28,000); Unicorn Theatre (£11,000); Prostate Scotland (£10,000); Almeida Theatre (£6,200); Gate Theatre and Theatre 503 Limited (£5,000 each); Mercury Music Developments (£2,000); Mousetrap Theatre Project (£1,000); Bliss (£500); and Kidbrooke Primary School (£300).

Applications In writing to the correspondent.

The Williams Family Charitable Trust

Jewish

£48,000 (2007/08)
Beneficial area Worldwide.

192 Gilbert Road, Cambridge CB4 3PB
Correspondent Barry Landy, Trustee
Trustees *Shimon Benison; Arnon Levy; Barry Landy.*
CC Number 255452
Information available Information was on file at the Charity Commission, without a list of grants.

In 2007/08 this trust had an income of £52,000 and made grants totalling £48,000. No further information regarding grantgiving was available for this year.

Previous beneficiaries have included But Chabad, Friends of Mifalhtorah for Shiloh, Holon Association for

Absorption of Immigrants, Ingun Yedidut, Israel Concern Society, Karen Denny Pincus, Mogdal Un, Yedidut Maabeh Eliahu and Yesodrey Hetorah Schools.

Applications In writing to the correspondent.

Dame Violet Wills Charitable Trust

Evangelical Christianity

£70,000 (2008)

Beneficial area UK and overseas, but there may be a preference for Bristol.

Ricketts Cooper & Co., 1 Deerhurst, Kingswood, Bristol BS15 1XH

Correspondent The Secretary

Trustees D G Cleave, Chair; S Burton; H E Cooper; Miss R Daws; J R Dean; G J T Landreth; Mrs M J Lewis; Revd Dr E C Lucas; Mrs J Persson; Mrs R E Peskett; Revd A J G Cooper; D R Caporn; Revd R W Lockhart; J P Marsh; Mrs E Street.

CC Number 219485

Information available Accounts were obtained from the Charity Commission website.

The trust continues to operate within the original terms of reference, supporting evangelical Christian activities both within the UK and overseas. It is not the practice of the trustees to guarantee long-term support to any work, however worthy. The trust does not make a practice of supplying funds to non-registered charities.

In 2008 the trust had assets of £1.4 million and an income of £97,000. Grants were made to 95 organisations totalling £70,000.

Beneficiaries included: WC and SWET – Evangelists Fund (£13,000); Echoes of Service – Bristol Missionaries (£2,400); Bristol International Student Centre (£2,000); FEBA Radio, International Fellowship of Evangelical Students and SAT-7 Trust (£1,500 each); Brass Tacks (£800); Medical Missionary News (£750); Cutting Edge Ministries (£500); SU Int Ukraine (£300); Open Air Mission and True Freedom Trust (£250 each); and Prison Fellowship – England and Wales (£200).

Exclusions Grants are not given to individuals.

Applications In writing to the correspondent. Trustees meet in March and in September.

Sumner Wilson Charitable Trust

General

£52,000 (2007/08)

Beneficial area UK.

Munslows, Mansfield House, 2nd Floor, 1 Southampton Street, London WC2R 0LR

Tel. 020 7845 7500

Correspondent N A Steinberg

Trustees Lord Joffe; Mrs A W S Christie; M S Wilson.

CC Number 1018852

Information available Accounts were on file at the Charity Commission.

This trust had general charitable purposes, with no preferences or exclusions. In 2007/08 it had assets of £2.6 million, an income of £107,000 and made grants totalling £52,000.

There were 17 grants of £1,000 or more listed in the accounts. Beneficiaries included: St James's Place Foundation (£20,000); Prostate Cancer Charitable Trust and Wheelpower (£5,000 each); Langalanga Scholarship Fund (£3,000); and Army Benevolent Fund, the Born Free Foundation, Breast Cancer Haven, Head and Neck Cancer Research Trust, Mission for Vision, Prospect Hospice, RAFT, Relate Winchester and Special Boat Service Association (£1,000 each).

Applications In writing to the correspondent, or to the trustees.

The Benjamin Winegarten Charitable Trust

Jewish

£55,000 to organisations (2007/08)

Beneficial area UK.

25 St Andrew's Grove, Stoke Newington, London N16 5NF

Correspondent B A Winegarten, Trustee

Trustees B A Winegarten; Mrs E Winegarten.

CC Number 271442

Information available Accounts were on file at the Charity Commission, but without a list of grants.

This trust makes grants for the advancement of the Jewish religion and religious education. In 2007/08 it had assets of £688,000 and an income of £153,000, including £100,000 from donations and grants. Grants to organisations totalled £55,000, with £4,000 going to individuals.

Previous beneficiaries have included Hechal Hatovah Institute, the Jewish Educational Trust, the Mechinah School, Merkaz Lechinuch Torani Zichron Ya'akov, Ohr Someach Friends, Or Akiva Community Centre, Yeshivo Hovomo Talmudical College and ZSVT.

Applications In writing to the correspondent.

The Francis Winham Foundation

Welfare of older people

£1.5 million (2007/08)

Beneficial area England.

41 Langton Street, London SW10 0JL

Tel. 020 7795 1261

Email francinetrust@btopenworld.com

Correspondent Mrs J Winham, Trustee

Trustees Francine Winham; Dr John Norcliffe Roberts; Josephine Winham; Elsa Peters.

CC Number 278092

Information available Accounts on file at the Charity Commission.

Grants are given to both national organisations (including their local branches) and local charities. Many organisations are regular recipients, although not necessarily on an annual basis.

In 2007/08 the trust had assets of £3.2 million and an income of £1.1 million. There were 676 grants made totalling £1.5 million.

Beneficiaries included: Cotswold Care Hospice (£100,000); Royal British Legion (£83,000 in 122 grants); SSAFA (£74,000 in 159 grants); Ashgate Hospice, East Cheshire Hospice, Eden Valley Hospice and St Michael's Hospice (£50,000 each); Ellenor Lions Hospice (£45,000); Rotherham Hospice (£32,000); Heart of Kent Hospice (£29,000); Care and Repair – Rhondda Cynon Taf (£27,000 in 35 grants); Prospect Hospice and Universal Beneficent Society (£20,000 each); Independence at Home (£10,000); Brendon Care Foundation (£6,000); Abbeyfield Bromley Society, the Ghurkha Welfare Trust, Henshaws Society for Blind People and Luton Community Housing (£5,000 each); Brighton and Hove Jewish Centre (£3,000); Age Concern – Solihull (£2,500); Chiltern MS Centre (£2,000); Newcastle Society for Blind People (£1,500); and Community Relief Project and Wiltshire Blind Association (£1,000 each).

Applications In writing to the correspondent. The trust regrets it cannot send replies to applications outside its specific field of help for older people. Applications should be made through registered charities or social services departments only.

Anona Winn Charitable Trust

Health, medical and welfare

£100,000 (2008)
Beneficial area UK.

New Inn Cottage, Croft Lane, Winstone, Cirencester GL7 7LN
Correspondent The Trustees
Trustee *Trefoil Trustees Ltd.*
CC Number 1044101
Information available Accounts were on file at the Charity Commission.

Registered with the Charity Commission in February 1995, the trustees maintain a list of charitable organisations which it supports. This list is reviewed periodically.

In 2008 the trust had assets of £867,000 and an income of £55,000. Grants to 34 organisations totalled £100,000.

Beneficiaries included: CAF (£40,000); British Heart Foundation (£10,000); RNLI (£5,000); Help for Heroes (£4,000); the Playhouse – Cheltenham

and the Smile Train (£3,000 each); St John of Jerusalem Eye Hospital (£2,000); St Wilfrid's Hospice (£2,000); the Sustainable Trust (£1,500); Motor Neurone Disease Association (£1,000); and Eyeless Trust, Rainbow Centre for Children and Trinity Hospice (£500 each).

Exclusions No applications are considered from individuals.

Applications Applications will only be considered if received in writing and accompanied by the organisation's latest report and full accounts.

The Witzenfeld Foundation

General

£76,000 (2007/08)
Beneficial area UK and Israel.

9 Chadwick Road, Westcliff on Sea SS0 8LS
Correspondent Alan Witzenfeld, Trustee
Trustees *Alan Witzenfeld; Lyetta Witzenfeld; Emma Witzenfeld; Mark Witzenfeld.*
CC Number 1115034
Information available Accounts are on file at the Charity Commission, without a list of donations or any details of its activities.

Set up in 2006, in 2007/08 the foundation had an income of £79,000 and made grants totalling £76,000.

Applications In writing to the correspondent.

The Michael and Anna Wix Charitable Trust

Older people, disability, education, medicine, health, poverty, welfare and Jewish

£56,000 (2007/08)
Beneficial area UK.

Portrait Solicitors, 1 Chancery Lane, London WC2A 1LF
Correspondent The Trustees
Trustees *Mrs J B Bloch; D B Flynn; Miss Judith Portrait.*
CC Number 207863
Information available Full accounts were on file at the Charity Commission.

In 2007/08 the trust had assets of £1.8 million and an income of £82,000. Grant management and administration costs were high at £20,000. Grants were made to 248 organisations totalling £56,000.

The largest grants went to: Nightingale House (£5,000); British Technion Society, Jewish Care and Weizmann Institute Foundation (£2,000 each); British Friends of the Hebrew University (£1,500); and British ORT, Norwood and World Jewish Relief (£1,000 each).

Remaining grants were in the range of £100 and £500 and included those to: Jewish Museum (£500); Action on Addiction, British Fiends of Ohel Sarah, Carers UK, Cosgrove Care, Eyeless Trust, Lupus UK, Motability, Queen Elizabeth's Foundation, Shelter and Whizz Kidz (£200 each); and British Blind Sport, Centrepoint, Daneford Trust, Elizabeth Finn Care, Gurkha Welfare Trust, Jewish Marriage Council, Migraine Trust, Rehab UK, Strongbones Children's Charitable Trust and Vitalise (£100 each).

Exclusions Applications from individuals are not considered. Grants are to national bodies rather than local branches or local groups.

Applications In writing to the trustees. Applications are considered half-yearly. Only applications from registered charities are acknowledged. Frequent applications by a single charity are not appreciated.

Women's World Day of Prayer

Promotion of the Christian faith through education and literature and audio-visual material

£148,000 (2008)
Beneficial area UK and worldwide.

369

Commercial Road, Tunbridge Wells
TN1 2RR

Tel. 01892 541 411 **Fax** 01892 541745

Email office@wwdp-natcomm.org

Website www.wwdp-natcomm.org

Correspondent Mrs Mary Judd,
Administrator

Trustees *Mrs J Hackett; Mrs Emma
Wilcock; Mrs M M Barton.*

CC Number 233242

Information available Full accounts
were available from the Charity
Commission website.

The trust makes grants to charitable
Christian educational projects and
Christian organisations publishing
literature and audio-visual material
designed to advance the Christian faith.

The main object of the trust is to unite
Christians in prayer, focused in
particular on a day of prayer in March
each year. The trust's income is mainly
from donations collected at this event.
After the trust's expenses, including the
costs of running the day of prayer, the
income can be used for grantmaking.

In 2008 the trust had assets of £290,000
and an income of £487,000. Grants were
made totalling £148,000 and were
broken down as follows:

Annual grants (£98,000 in 18 grants)
Beneficiaries included: Bible Society,
Feed the Minds and United Society for
Christian Literature (£15,000 each);
Lifewords and Wycliffe UK Ltd (£8,000
each); Bible Reading Fellowship and
International Reading Association
(£6,000 each); The Salvation Army –
Missionary Literature Fund (£3,000);
St John's Guild for the Blind, the
Leprosy Mission and United Christian
Broadcasters (£1,700 each); Mission to
Deep Sea Fishermen (£850); and
Churches Together in England – Women
(£65).

One-off grants (£15,000 in 7 grants)
Beneficiaries included: Operation
Mobilisation (£3,000); Connections
Trust and Fellowship of Women
Christians (£2,500 each); Sat 7 Trust
(£1,500); and Kafforwoda (£1,200).

**International donations (£31,000 in
4 grants)**
The beneficiaries were: World Day of
Prayer International Committee
(£21,000); World Day of Prayer National
Committee of Guyana (£10,000); World
Day of Prayer European Committee
(£200); and World Day of Prayer
International Committee – Seychelles
(£150).

**Grants to Welsh speaking churches
(£4,000 in 10 grants)**
Beneficiaries included: Bible Times –
Wales, The Word Publications and
Wales Sunday Schools Council (£500
each); Christians Against Torture –
Wales and Society for the Blind – Wales
(£400 each); and CAFOD and Christian
Aid – Wales (£300 each).

Exclusions No grants to individuals.

Applications In writing to the
correspondent, before the end of June.
Grants are made in November.

The Woodcock Charitable Trust

General and children

£315,000 (2007/08)

Beneficial area UK.

Harcus Sinclair, 40 Victoria
Embankment, London EC4Y 0BA

Correspondent The Trustees

Trustees *M N Woodcock; S M Woodcock.*

CC Number 1110896

Information available Accounts were
on file at the Charity Commission.

Set up in 2005, in 2007/08 the trust had
an income of £261,000, mostly from
donations, and made grants totalling
£315,000. The sum of £137,000 was
carried forward at year end.

Grants included those to: Egmont Trust
(£140,000); Kids Company (£127,000);
the Cambridge Foundation (£25,000);
Forever Angels (£11,000); and
Magdalene College Cambridge (£10,000).

Applications In writing to the
correspondent.

Woodlands Green Ltd

Jewish

£179,000 (2006/07)

Beneficial area Worldwide.

19 Green Walk, London NW4 2AL

Correspondent J A Ost, Secretary

Trustees *A Ost; E Ost; D J A Ost;
J A Ost; A Hepner.*

CC Number 277299

Information available Accounts for
year ending 2007/08 were overdue at the
Charity Commission. Those filed for
2006/07 did not include a list of grants.

The trust's objectives are the
advancement of the orthodox Jewish
faith and the relief of poverty. It mostly
gives large grants to major educational
projects being carried out by orthodox
Jewish charities.

In 2006/07 the trust had assets of
£1.3 million, an income of £248,000 and
made grants totalling £179,000.

Previous beneficiaries have included
Achisomoch Aid Co, Beis Soro
Schneirer, Friends of Beis Yisroel Trust,
Friends of Mir, Friends of Seret Wiznitz,
Friends of Toldos Avrohom Yitzchok,
JET, Kahal Imrei Chaim, Oizer Dalim
Trust, NWLCM, TYY Square and UTA.

Exclusions No grants to individuals,
or for expeditions or scholarships.

Applications In writing to the
correspondent.

The Woodroffe Benton Foundation

General

£257,000 (2007/08)

Beneficial area UK.

16 Fernleigh Court, Harrow, London
HA2 6NA

Tel. 020 8421 4120

Email alan.king3@which.net

Correspondent Alan King, Secretary

Trustees *J J Hope, Chair: Mrs
S E M Dickson; Mrs R A P G Foster;
P M Miles; C G Russell.*

CC Number 1075272

Information available Accounts were
on file at the Charity Commission.

This trust makes grants towards:

- people in need, primary care of people
  who are sick, older people or those
  effected by the results of a local or
  national disaster
- promotion of education
- conservation and improvement of the
  environment.

The trust rarely donates more than
£2,000 and does not normally make
more than one grant to the same charity
in a 12 month period.

In 2007/08 it had assets of £4.8 million and an income of £247,000. Grants totalled £257,000.

Ongoing support was given to 24 organisations totalling £77,000. Beneficiaries included: Queen Elizabeth's Grammar School (£17,000 in four grants); Ifield Park Care Home (£15,000 in two grants); Community Links (£10,000); Friends United Network, Prisoners' Families and Friends Service, Soundaround, St Jude's Community Association and Young People's Trust for the Environment (£5,000 each); Charity Search (£4,000); and Disability Aid Fund (£1,000 in two grants).

There were 138 grants made in response to 313 unsolicited applications. These grants totalled £102,000 (19 were for £1,500, 28 were for £1,000 and the remainder for less than £1,000 each).

A further £16,000 was given in grants made at the discretion of individual trustees, retired trustees and the foundation secretary.

Exclusions Grants are not made outside the UK and are only made to registered charities. No grants to individuals. Branches of UK charities should not apply as grants, if made, would go to the charity's headquarters.

Applications On a form available from the correspondent. Full guidance notes on completing the form and procedures for processing applications are sent with the form. Trustees meet quarterly.

The Geoffrey Woods Charitable Foundation

Young people, education, disability and health

£131,000 (2007/08)
Beneficial area UK and overseas.

The Girdlers Company, Girdlers Hall, Basinghall Avenue, London EC2V 5DD
Correspondent Brig. Ian Rees, Clerk to the Company
Trustees *The Girdlers Company; N K Maitland; A J R Fairclough.*
CC Number 248205

Information available Accounts were on file at the Charity Commission.

The foundation is administered by the Girdlers Company and its objects are the advancement of education and religion and the relief of poverty. It is responsible for three funds as shown below:

The Masters Fund is allocated an amount each year for the master of the company to donate to charities of his or her own choice.

Christmas Court Donations allow members to nominate charities at Christmas time.

The Jock French Charitable Fund encourages charitable donations from members of the livery of the company. The fund is allocated a sum that is four times the amount covenanted or donated to the foundation by the livery. The subscribing members are invited to nominate charities to receive donations. The total sum allocated is distributed in May and November each year, following ratification by the livery.

In 2007/08 the foundation had assets of £825,000 and an income of £77,000. Grants were made from the three funds totalling £131,000.

Applications 'Beneficiaries are nominated by members of the company and outside applications are no longer considered.'

The A and R Woolf Charitable Trust

General

£38,000 (2007/08)
Beneficial area Worldwide; UK, mainly in Hertfordshire.

Aldbury House, Dower Mews, 108 High Street, Berkhamsted HP4 2BL
Correspondent The Trustees
Trustees *Mrs J D H Rose; C Rose; Dr G L Edmonds; S Rose; A Rose.*
CC Number 273079

Information available Accounts were on file at the Charity Commission.

The trust supports a range of causes, including Jewish organisations, animal welfare and conservation causes, children and health and welfare charities. Both UK and overseas charities (through a British-based office) receive support,

together with local charities. Most of the grants are recurrent.

In 2007/08 the trust had assets of £2.4 million and an income of £69,000. Grants totalled £38,000.

There were 51 grants made in the year of which 20 were for £100 or more and were listed in the accounts.

Beneficiaries included: the Central British Fund for World Jewish Relief (£10,000); the Peace Hospice (£8,500); United Nations International Children's Emergency Fund and University of Hertfordshire Charitable Trust (£5,000 each); Northwood and Pinner Liberal Synagogue (£1,300); RSPCA and WWF UK (£1,000 each); the Multiple Sclerosis Society (£500); Jewish Child's Day and Wellbeing for Women (£250 each); National Schizophrenia Fellowship (£200); International Primate Protection League UK (£150); the Hertfordshire and Middlesex Wildlife Trust (£130); and Senahasa Trust (£100).

Exclusions No grants to individuals or non-registered charities unless schools, hospices and so on.

Applications Support is only given to projects/organisations/causes personally known to the trustees. The trust does not respond to unsolicited applications.

The Fred and Della Worms Charitable Trust

Jewish, social welfare, health, education, arts and young people

£87,000 (2007/08)
Beneficial area UK.

23 Highpoint, North Hill, London N6 4BA
Correspondent The Trustees
Trustees *Mrs D Worms; M D Paisner; F S Worms; A D Harverd.*
CC Number 200036

Information available Full accounts were on file at the Charity Commission.

In 2007/08 the trust had assets of £2.1 million, which generated an income of £95,000. Grants were made totalling £87,000.

Category	Value
Social and healthcare	£41,000
Young people	£24,000
The arts	£11,000
Education	£8,000
Religion	£3,000

Beneficiaries included: Joint Jewish Charitable Trust (£25,000); Maccabi Union (£18,000); Emunah (£6,100); Brai Birth Hillel Foundation and Jewish Care (£5,000 each); British Friends of the Art Museum of Israel (£3,100); Jewish Museum (£3,000); Jerusalem Foundation (£2,500); JNF Botanical Gardens (£1,500); Royal National Theatre (£1,300); English National Opera Company (£1,200); and Aleph Society and Ben Uri Art Gallery (£1,000 each).

Exclusions No grants to individuals.

Applications The trust has previously stated that its funds were fully committed.

The Diana Edgson Wright Charitable Trust

Animal conservation, social welfare and general

About £90,000 (2008)

Beneficial area UK with some preference for Kent.

c/o 2 Stade Street, Hythe, Kent CT21 6BD

Correspondent R H V Moorhead, Trustee

Trustees *R H V Moorhead; P Edgson Wright; H C D Moorhead.*

CC Number 327737

Information available Information was on file at the Charity Commission.

The trust has general charitable purposes. The policy is to support a small number of charities. In 2008 the trust had an income of £73,000 and a total expenditure of £97,000.

Previous beneficiaries have included Age Concern – Hythe, British Red Cross, Caldecott Foundation, Campaign to Protect Rural England, Paula Carr Charitable Trust, Chernobyl Children's Project, Combat Stress, Dragon School Trust, Folkstone Rainbow Trust, Kent Air Ambulance, Marine Conservation Society, the National Trust, Royal British Legion, Sellinge Parish Church, St James'

Church – Egerton, Sightsavers International, Sustain and Wildfowl and Wetlands Trust.

Applications In writing to the correspondent.

The Matthews Wrightson Charity Trust

General, smaller charities

£88,000 to organisations (2008)

Beneficial area UK and some overseas.

The Old School House, Church Lane, Easton S021 1EH

Correspondent Jon Mills, Secretary and Administrator

Trustees *Priscilla W Wrightson; Anthony H Isaacs; Guy D G Wrightson; Isabelle S White; Maria de Broe Ferguson.*

CC Number 262109

Information available Accounts were on file at the Charity Commission.

'The trustees favour smaller charities or projects, for example those seeking to raise under £25,000 and usually exclude large national charities and those with turnover in excess of £250,000.' In addition to donations to charitable bodies, the trust also gives to trainee doctors for medical elective expenses and to individuals taking 'gaps' abroad for personal development.

In 2008 it had assets of £1.3 million and an income of £75,000. There were 193 grants made totalling £97,000, including £9,300 to 23 individuals. Donations were broken down as follows:

Category	Value	No.
Young people	£43,000	52
Developing world	£13,000	19
Disability	£12,000	23
Individuals	£9,300	23
Christian	£8,300	15
Rehabilitation	£5,000	10
Arts	£4,100	6
Poor and homeless	£4,000	9
Medical	£2,700	7
Older people	£1,800	4
Miscellaneous	£3,300	5

During 2008, the standard grant was increased from £400 to £500. The largest donation was to The Royal College of Art towards student hardship grants and for awards to students to further ideas for UK industrial production (£18,000). During the year an additional donation

of £3,000 was made to support a pilot programme in training students in business financial management.

Other beneficiaries of larger grants included: Tools for Self-Reliance (£2,400); and the Butler Trust, Childhood First, the Daneford Trust, DEMAND, Help Tibet, Live Music Now! New Bridge and Practical Action (£1,200 each). Most other donations, with a few exceptions, were for £400 or £500 each.

Exclusions 'The trustees would not normally support the maintenance of the fabric of churches, schools and village halls, and do not make donations to animal charities.'

Applications In writing to the correspondent including a set of accounts. Applications received are considered by the trustees on a monthly basis. Applicants who wish to be advised of the outcome of their application must include a stamped, addressed envelope. Successful applicants are advised of the trustees' decision at the earliest opportunity.

Wychdale Ltd

Jewish

£145,000 (2007/08)

Beneficial area UK and abroad.

89 Darenth Road, London N16 6EB

Correspondent The Secretary

Trustees *C D Schlaff; J Schlaff; Mrs Z Schlaff.*

CC Number 267447

Information available Accounts were on file at the Charity Commission.

The objects of this charity are the advancement of the Orthodox Jewish religion and the relief of poverty in the UK and abroad. The charity stated in its 2007/08 accounts that it 'invites applications from religious and educational institutions as well as organisations providing services for the relief of poverty both in the UK and abroad'.

In 2007/08 the trust had assets of £956,000 and an income of £149,000. Grants were made totalling £145,000 and were broken down into the following categories:

Category	Value
General purpose charities	£61,000
Advancement of religion	£43,000
Religious education	£22,000
Relief of poverty	£19,000

Beneficiaries included: Dajtrain Ltd (£28,000); United Ttalmudical Associates (£24,000); the Society of Friends of the Torah (£18,000); Chevras Mo'oz Ladol (£16,000); and Tomchei Sharei Zion (£10,000).

Exclusions Non-Jewish organisations are not supported.

Applications In writing to the correspondent.

Wychville Ltd

Jewish, education and general

£358,000 (2007/08)

Beneficial area UK.

44 Leweston Place, London N16 6RH

Correspondent Mrs S Englander, Secretary

Trustees *B Englander, Chair; Mrs S Englander; E Englander; Mrs B R Englander.*

CC Number 267584

Information available Accounts were on file at the Charity Commission, but without a list of grants.

This trust supports educational, Jewish and other charitable organisations. In 2007/08 the trust had assets of £78,000, an income of £371,000 mostly from donations and made grants totalling £358,000. No further information was available.

Applications In writing to the correspondent.

The Wyseliot Charitable Trust

Medical, welfare and arts

£105,000 (2007/08)

Beneficial area UK.

17 Chelsea Square, London SW3 6LF

Correspondent J H Rose, Trustee

Trustees *Jonathan Rose; Emma Rose; Adam Raphael.*

CC Number 257219

Information available Accounts were on file at the Charity Commission.

This trust gives grants in the following areas: medical, especially cancer research and care; welfare; and arts, including music, visual arts and literature.

In 2007/08 the trust had assets of £1.9 million, which generated an income of £113,000. Grants were made to 29 organisations totalling £105,000.

Beneficiaries included: Alzheimer's Trust, Cystic Fibrosis Trust, New Avenues Youth Project, Oxford Foundation, Royal Marsden Cancer Fund, St Mungo's Trust and Time and Talents Association (£5,000 each); Enham Trust, Cancer Relief Macmillan Fund, St John's Hospice and Trinity Hospice (£4,000 each); Brain Research Trust and Notting Hill Foundation (£3,500 each); Defeating Deafness, Musicians Benevolent Fund, Vitalise and Vitiligo Society (£3,000 each); and Home Start and Runnymede Trust (£2,000 each).

Exclusions Local charities are not supported. No support for individuals; grants are only made to registered charities.

Applications In writing to the correspondent; however, please note that the trust states that the same charities are supported each year, with perhaps one or two changes. It is unlikely new charities sending circular appeals will be supported and large UK charities are generally not supported.

Yankov Charitable Trust

Jewish

£160,000 (2007/08)

Beneficial area Worldwide.

40 Wellington Avenue, London N15 6AS

Correspondent The Trustees

Trustees *J Schonberg; Mrs B S Schonberg.*

CC Number 1106703

Information available Accounts were on file at the Charity Commission.

The trust was established for the advancement of the Jewish religion and culture among the Jewish community throughout the world.

Set up in 2004, in 2007/08 the trust had an income of £196,000 including £143,000 from donations. Grants totalled £160,000, Assets at year end totalled £150,000.

Beneficiaries included: European Yarchei Kalloh (£53,000); Keren Machzikei Torah (£23,000); Kollel Tiferes Chaim (£21,000); Agudas Israel Housing Association (£12,000); Ponovez Hachnosos Kalloh (£7,600); Freiman Appeal (£7,200); Beth Jacob Grammar School (£4,000); British Friends of Tiferes Chaim (£3,000); Yeshiva Tzemach Yisroel (£2,000); British Friends of Rinat Ahsron (£1,500); and Yeshivat Givat Shaul (£1,000).

Applications In writing to the correspondent.

The Yapp Charitable Trust

Social welfare

£501,000 (2007/08)

Beneficial area England and Wales.

47a Paris Road, Scholes, Holmfirth HD9 1SY

Tel. 01484 683403

Email info@yappcharitabletrust.org.uk

Website www.yappcharitabletrust.org.uk

Correspondent Mrs Margaret Thompson, Administrator

Trustees *David Aeron-Thomas; Revd Timothy C Brooke; Annette Figueiredo; Peter G Murray; Stephanie Willats.*

CC Number 1076803

Information available Accounts were on file at the Charity Commission. The trust has a clear and helpful website.

The Yapp Charitable Trust was formed in 1999 from the Yapp Welfare Trust (two-thirds share) and Yapp Education and Research Trust (one-third share). However, rather than combining the criteria for the two trusts, the trustees decided to focus on small charities, usually local rather than UK-wide. The trust now accepts applications only from small charities and organisations with a turnover of less than £60,000 in the year of application. The objects are restricted to registered charities in England or Wales.

The following information is taken from the trust's website.

What we fund

We make grants to small registered charities to sustain their existing work with:

- older people
- children and young people aged 5 to 25

- people with disabilities or mental health problems
- people trying to overcome life-limiting problems of a social, rather than medical, origin – such as addiction, relationship difficulties, abuse, a history of offending.

We also make grants to sustain small registered charities' existing work in the fields of:

- education and learning (with a particular interest in people who are educationally disadvantaged, whether adults or children).

We are not able to fund work which does not come into one of the above categories.

Size and type of grant

We give grants for running costs and salaries for up to three years. Grants are normally for a maximum of £3,000 per year. Most of our grants are for more than one year because we give priority to ongoing needs.

Like most other funders we have many more applications than we can fund. We find we are able to give a grant to only about one in eight of the applications we receive. At present we give £300,000 each year in about 50 grants.

Criteria

Within our charitable objects, the trustees focus on making grants to small charities registered and working in England and Wales.

Applicants must have a total expenditure budget of less than £60,000 a year for the whole charity.

We concentrate on sustaining existing work rather than funding new work because many funders prefer new projects. We make a grant when other funding is coming to an end.

If you are looking for money to start a new project, to create a new paid post or to introduce extra services you should look elsewhere. Many other funders prefer to fund new developments.

We are happy to fund the core costs of small charities whose work falls totally within our objects.

The trustees give priority to charities:

- tackling work that is unattractive to the general public or unpopular with other funders
- helping to improve the lives of marginalised, disadvantaged or isolated people
- able to demonstrate effective use of volunteers.

In practice only charities whose work meets at least one of the above priorities are likely to receive a grant.

Medical and Scientific Research

At present the trust is not inviting research proposals. This is because our funding capacity is relatively small, and research projects are usually expensive. The trustees therefore accumulate funds to enable us to offer a larger grant to one project.

Our funds are currently committed to research into supporting young people with depression.

In 2007/08 the trust had assets of £5 million and an income of £330,000. Grants totalled £501,000.

Exclusions We do not accept applications from:

- Scotland and Northern Ireland – your charity must work in England or Wales
- charities whose total annual expenditure is more than £60,000
- charities that are not registered with the Charity Commission in England and Wales. You must have your own charity number or be excepted from registration. Industrial and Provident Societies and Community Interest Companies are not eligible to apply
- branches of National Charities. You must have your own charity number, not a shared national registration
- new organisations – you must have been operating as a fully constituted charity for at least 3 years, even though you may have registered as a charity more recently.

We do not make grants for:

- new work – we provide continuation funding to sustain existing work that has been happening for at least a year. We do not offer grants to launch new or additional activities nor to put on special events
- we do not offer funding to create new paid posts even if the work is now being done by volunteers
- capital-type expenditure – equipment, buildings, renovations, furnishings, minibuses
- work with under-fives
- childcare
- holidays and holiday centres
- core funding of general community organisations such as community associations, community centres and general advice services, because some of their work is outside our charitable objects
- bereavement support
- debt advice
- community safety initiatives
- charities raising money to give to another organisation, such as schools, hospitals or other voluntary groups
- individuals – including charities raising funds to purchase equipment for or make grants to individuals.

Applications We have a simple application form which we ask you to send in by post, together with a copy of your most recent annual report and accounts and any other information you wish to send.

Applications are processed continuously. When we receive your application we will be in touch, usually within two weeks:

- to ask for more information
- or to tell you the application will be going forward to the next stage of assessment and give an idea of when you can expect a decision
- or to let you know we can't help.

The time it takes to process an application and make a grant is usually between two months and six months. We always write to let you know the decision.

Previous Applicants

We will accept an application only once each year and you can have only one grant at a time from us. Current grant-holders may make a new application when their grant is coming to an end. If we refused your last application you must wait a year before applying again.

The application form and guidelines can be downloaded in Word or pdf format from the trust's website. Alternatively they can be obtained from the trust's administrator.

The Dennis Alan Yardy Charitable Trust

General

£33,000 (2007/08)

Beneficial area Overseas and UK with a preference for the East Midlands.

PO Box 5039, Spratton, Northampton NN6 8YH

Correspondent The Secretary

Trustees *Dennis Alan Yardy, Chair; Mrs Christine Anne Yardy; Jeffrey Creek; Mrs Joanne Stoney.*

CC Number 1039719

Information available Accounts were on file at the Charity Commission, but without a list of grants.

This trust was established in 1993. It supports major UK and international charities and those within the East Midlands area.

In 2007/08 the trust had assets of £567,000, an income of £36,000 and made grants totalling £33,000.

Exclusions No grants to individuals or non-registered charities.

Applications In writing to the correspondent.

The John Young Charitable Settlement

General

£43,000 (2007/08)

Beneficial area UK and overseas.

c/o Lee Associates, 5 Southampton Place, London WC1A 2DA

Correspondent The Trustees

Trustees *J M Young; D P H Burgess.*

CC Number 283254

Information available Accounts were on file at the Charity Commission.

In 2007/08 the trust had assets of £1.1 million, an income of £454,000 including £403,000 from donations and gifts. Grants to nine organisations totalled £43,000.

Beneficiaries were: Caius House (£13,000); the Boulase Smart, Médecins du Monde, Pancreatic Cancer Research Fund, RSBP and St Barnabas Hospice Trust (£5,000 each); Chichester Harbour Trust (£2,000); and Action Aid (£250).

Applications In writing to the correspondent.

The William Allen Young Charitable Trust

General, health and social welfare

£416,000 (2007/08)

Beneficial area UK, with a preference for south London.

Young & Co.'s Brewery PLC, Riverside House, 26 Osiers Road, London SW18 1NH

Correspondent Torquil Sligo-Young, Trustee

Trustees *T F B Young; J G A Young; T Sligo-Young.*

CC Number 283102

Information available Accounts were available from the Charity Commission.

The trust supports humanitarian causes, with a large number of health organisations supported each year. Grants are made to local and national organisations throughout the UK, although there appears to be a preference for south London.

In 2007/08 the trust had assets of £16.2 million with an income of £364,000 and made 181 grants totalling £416,000.

Beneficiaries included: Fly Navy Heritage Trust (£40,000); British Benevolent Fund of Madrid (£15,000); Southwark Cathedral (£11,000); Queen Alexandra Home (£7,000); Anti-Slavery International, the Ness Foundation, the Organ Appeal Fund and St Margaret's Yeovil Hospice (£5,000 each); the Ebbisham Association (£3,500); Fight for Sight, Leonard Cheshire Foundation and Shaftesbury Young People (£2,000 each); Association of Children's Hospices, Battersea Dogs and Cats Home, Chertsey Agricultural Project and Lowe Syndrome Trust (£1,000 each); and Diabetes UK, Keech Cottage Children's Charity, Strongbones Children's Charitable Trust and Wessex Heavy Horse Show (£500 each).

Applications The trust has stressed that all funds are committed and consequently unsolicited applications will not be supported.

Zephyr Charitable Trust

Community, environment and social welfare

£62,000 (2007/08)

Beneficial area UK and worldwide.

Luminary Finance LLP, PO Box 135, Longfield DA3 8WF

Correspondent The Trust Administrator

Trustees *Elizabeth Breeze; Roger Harriman; David Baldock; Donald I Watson.*

CC Number 1003234

Information available Accounts were on file at the Charity Commission.

The trust's grants are particularly targeted towards three areas:

- enabling lower income communities to be self-sustaining
- the protection and improvement of the environment
- providing relief and support for those in need, particularly from medical conditions or social or financial disadvantage.

In 2007/08 the trust had assets of £1.5 million and an income of £87,000. There were 23 grants made totalling £62,000. These were listed in the accounts as 21 'subscriptions' totalling £50,000 and 2 donations totalling £12,000.

Beneficiaries during the year included: Paddington Farm Trust (£10,000); UNICEF (£4,600); Friends of the Earth Trust (£3,000); Crisis and Survival International (£2,500 each); Womankind (£2,100); Karuna Trust, Organic Research Centre – Elm Farm and Tools for Self Reliance (£2,000 each); Quaker Social Action Group (£1,700); and MIND Brent and Missing People (£1,500 each).

Exclusions No grants to individuals, expeditions or scholarships.

Applications In writing to the correspondent. The trustees usually meet to consider grants in July each year. Unsolicited applications are unlikely to be successful, since the trust makes annual donations to a list of beneficiaries. However, the trust stated that unsolicited applications are considered on a quarterly basis by the trustees and very occasional support is given. Telephone applications are not accepted.

The Marjorie and Arnold Ziff Charitable Foundation

General, education, Jewish, arts, young people, older people and medicine

£664,000 (2007/08)

Beneficial area UK, with a preference for Yorkshire, especially Leeds and Harrogate.

Town Centre House, The Merrion Centre, Leeds LS2 8LY

Tel. 0113 222 1234

Correspondent Bryan Rouse, Secretary

Trustees *Mrs Marjorie E Ziff; Michael A Ziff; Edward M Ziff; Mrs Ann L Manning.*

CC Number 249368

Information available Full accounts were on file at the Charity Commission.

This foundation likes to support causes that will provide good value for the money donated by benefiting a large number of people, as well as encouraging others to make contributions to the work. This includes a wide variety of schemes that involve the community at many levels, including education, public places, the arts and helping people who are disadvantaged. Capital costs and building work are particularly favoured by the trustees, as they feel projects such as these are not given the support they deserve from statutory sources.

In 2007/08 the trust had assets of £9.5 million and an income of £1.8 million. There were 137 grants made totalling £644,000.

The beneficiaries of the largest grants were: the University of Leeds (£350,000); United Jewish Israel Appeal (£90,000); United Synagogue Youth Charity (£60,000); Leeds Jewish Welfare Board (£36,000); and the Chief Rabbinate Charitable Trust, Shabbaton Choir and Wellington College (£10,000 each).

Other beneficiaries included: Jewish Care Scotland and World Jewish Relief (£5,000 each); Manchester Jewish Federation (£3,000); Footwear Benevolent Society (£2,500); British Friends of Hatzolah Israel (£2,000); Benji Hillman Foundation, Jewish Care and Jewish Leadership Council (£1,000 each); Great Ormond Street Hospital (£500); Royal British Legion (£200); Cancer Research UK (£75); Au Israel (£30); and Foundation for the Study of Infant Deaths (£25).

Exclusions No grants to individuals.

Applications In writing to the correspondent. Replies will only be given to a request accompanied by a stamped, addressed envelope. Please note that funds available from the trust are limited and requests not previously supported are unlikely to be successful. Initial telephone calls are welcome but please note the foregoing comments.

Subject index

The following subject index begins with a list of categories used. The categories are very wide-ranging to keep the index as simple as possible. DSC's subscription website (www.trustfunding.org.uk)has a much more detailed search facility on the categories. There may be considerable overlap between the categories – for example, children and education, or older people and social welfare.

The list of categories is followed by the index itself. Before using the index, please note the following:

How the index was compiled

1) The index aims to reflect the most recent grant-making practice. It is therefore based on our interpretation of what each trust has actually given to, rather than what its policy statement says or its charitable objects allow it to do in principle. For example, where a trust states that it has general charitable purposes, but its grants list shows a strong preference for welfare, we index it under welfare.

2) We have tried to ensure that each trust has given significantly in the areas where it is indexed (usually at least £15,000). Thus small, apparently untypical grants have been ignored for index purposes.

3) The index has been complied from the latest information available to us.

Limitations

1) Policies may change; some more frequently than others.

2) Sometimes there will be a geographical restriction on a trust's grantgiving which is not shown in this index, or the trust may not give for the specific purposes you require under that heading. It is important to read each entry carefully.

You will need to check:

(a) The trust gives in your geographical area of operation.

(b) The trust gives for the specific purposes you require.

(c) There is no other reason to prevent you making an application to this trust.

3) It is worth noting that one or two of the categories list almost half the trusts included in this guide.

Under no circumstances should the index be used as a simple mailing list. Remember: each trust is different. Often the policies or interests of a particular trust do not fit easily into the given categories. Each entry must be read individually before you send off an application. Indiscriminate applications are usually unsuccessful. They waste time and money and greatly annoy trusts.

The categories are as follows:

Arts, culture, sport and recreation *page 378*

A very wide category including performing, written and visual arts, crafts, theatres, museums and galleries, heritage, architecture and archaeology, sports.

Children and young people *page 379*

Mainly for welfare and welfare-related activities.

Development, housing and employment *page 380*

This includes specific industries such as leather making or textiles.

Disability *page 381*

Disadvantaged people *page 382*

This includes people who are:

- Socially excluded
- socially and economically disadvantaged
- unemployed
- homeless
- offenders
- educationally disadvantaged

- victims of social/natural occurrences, including refugees and asylum seekers.

Education and training *page 383*

Environment and animals *page 384*

This includes:

- agriculture and fishing
- conservation
- animal care
- environment and education
- transport
- sustainable environment.

General charitable purposes *page 385*

This is a very broad category, and includes trusts that often have numerous specific strands to their programmes as a well as those that will consider any application (subject to other eligibility criteria).

Illness *page 389*

This includes people who are suffering from specific conditions.

Medicine and health *page 389*

Older people *page 391*

Religion – general *page 392*

This includes inter-faith work and religious understanding.

Christianity page 393

Islam page 394

Judaism page 394

Philanthropy and the voluntary sector
page 396

Rights, law and conflict
page 396

This includes:

- citizen participation
- conflict resolution
- legal and advice services
- rights
- equity and justice.

Science and technology
page 396

Social sciences, policy and research *page 396*

Social welfare *page 396*

This is another very broad category, and includes:

- community care and services
- counselling and advice
- social preventative schemes
- community centres and activities.

Arts, culture, sport and recreation

The A B Charitable Trust
The Victor Adda Foundation
Andor Charitable Trust
The Armourers' and Brasiers' Gauntlet Trust
The Ove Arup Foundation
A J H Ashby Will Trust
The Laura Ashley Foundation
The Astor Foundation
The Astor of Hever Trust
The Aurelius Charitable Trust
The Barcapel Foundation
The John Beckwith Charitable Trust
The Bedfordshire and Hertfordshire Historic Churches Trust
The Boshier-Hinton Foundation
The Bowerman Charitable Trust
T B H Brunner's Charitable Settlement
The Arnold Burton 1998 Charitable Trust
P H G Cadbury Charitable Trust
The Edward and Dorothy Cadbury Trust
The Carr-Gregory Trust
Elizabeth Cayzer Charitable Trust
The Cemlyn-Jones Trust
J A Clark Charitable Trust
Miss V L Clore's 1967 Charitable Trust
The Robert Clutterbuck Charitable Trust
The Francis Coales Charitable Foundation
The John Coates Charitable Trust
The Denise Cohen Charitable Trust
Country Houses Foundation
The Craignish Trust
The Crescent Trust
The Helen and Geoffrey De Freitas Charitable Trust
The De Laszlo Foundation
The Leopold De Rothschild Charitable Trust
Dischma Charitable Trust
The Houghton Dunn Charitable Trust
The Dyers' Company Charitable Trust
The Gilbert and Eileen Edgar Foundation
The Edinburgh Trust, No. 2 Account
The Elephant Trust
The Elmgrant Trust
The English Schools' Football Association
The Equity Trust Fund
The Ericson Trust
The Alan Evans Memorial Trust
The Fairway Trust
The Lord Faringdon Charitable Trust

Samuel William Farmer's Trust
The John Feeney Charitable Bequest
Gerald Finzi Charitable Trust
Marc Fitch Fund
The Joyce Fletcher Charitable Trust
The Follett Trust
The Football Association National Sports Centre Trust
Ford Britain Trust
The Jill Franklin Trust
The Gordon Fraser Charitable Trust
The Frognal Trust
The Galanthus Trust
Garrick Charitable Trust
Jacqueline and Michael Gee Charitable Trust
The Gibbs Charitable Trust
Golden Charitable Trust
The Jack Goldhill Charitable Trust
The Golsoncott Foundation
Golubovich Foundation
Nicholas and Judith Goodison's Charitable Settlement
The Grand Order of Water Rats' Charities Fund
The Greys Charitable Trust
Grimmitt Trust
The Harding Trust
Haskel Family Foundation
The Dorothy Hay-Bolton Charitable Trust
The Hellenic Foundation
The Derek Hill Foundation
The Hinrichsen Foundation
The Holst Foundation
The Homestead Charitable Trust
The Reta Lila Howard Foundation
The Geoffrey C Hughes Charitable Trust
The Idlewild Trust
The Iliffe Family Charitable Trust
The Inland Waterways Association
The Inlight Trust
The Ireland Fund of Great Britain
The Irish Youth Foundation (UK) Ltd (incorporating The Lawlor Foundation)
Jacobs Charitable Trust
The John Jarrold Trust
The JMK Charitable Trust
Jusaca Charitable Trust
The Stanley Kalms Foundation
The Boris Karloff Charitable Foundation
The Kathleen Trust
The Michael and Ilse Katz Foundation
The Marina Kleinwort Charitable Trust
The Kobler Trust
The Kohn Foundation
The Christopher Laing Foundation
The David Laing Foundation
Lancashire Environmental Fund
The R J Larg Family Charitable Trust

Children and young people

Development, housing and employment

Disadvantaged people

The Shanley Charitable Trust

The Charles Shorto Charitable Trust

The E C Sosnow Charitable Trust

R H Southern Trust

Spears-Stutz Charitable Trust

Tegham Limited

The Thornton Trust

The Tinsley Foundation

The Tresillian Trust

The Scurrah Wainwright Charity

Wakeham Trust

The Weavers' Company Benevolent Fund

The Barbara Whatmore Charitable Trust

The Michael and Anna Wix Charitable Trust

The Woodroffe Benton Foundation

The Yapp Charitable Trust

Education and training

The Acacia Charitable Trust

AF Trust Company

All Saints Educational Trust

The Pat Allsop Charitable Trust

Ambika Paul Foundation

Viscount Amory's Charitable Trust

The Armourers' and Brasiers' Gauntlet Trust

A J H Ashby Will Trust

The Association of Colleges Charitable Trust

The Astor of Hever Trust

The Balint Family Charitable Trusts

The Beaufort House Trust Limited

The Bestway Foundation

Blatchington Court Trust

The Boltons Trust

The Boshier-Hinton Foundation

The Harry Bottom Charitable Trust

The Arnold Burton 1998 Charitable Trust

The Edward and Dorothy Cadbury Trust

The Carlton House Charitable Trust

The Carr-Gregory Trust

The Carron Charitable Trust

The Cemlyn-Jones Trust

The Worshipful Company of Chartered Accountants General Charitable Trust (also known as CALC)

The Cheruby Trust

J A Clark Charitable Trust

Coats Foundation Trust

The Denise Cohen Charitable Trust

The Vivienne and Samuel Cohen Charitable Trust

The John and Freda Coleman Charitable Trust

The Coltstaple Trust

Gordon Cook Foundation

The Lord Cozens-Hardy Trust

The Craignish Trust

The Ronald Cruickshanks' Foundation

The Demigryphon Trust

Dischma Charitable Trust

The Dorcas Trust

The Dorema Charitable Trust

Double 'O' Charity Ltd

Dromintee Trust

The Dyers' Company Charitable Trust

East Kent Provincial Charities

The Gilbert and Eileen Edgar Foundation

The Edinburgh Trust, No. 2 Account

Educational Foundation of Alderman John Norman

The Ellinson Foundation Ltd

The Edith Maud Ellis 1985 Charitable Trust

The Elmgrant Trust

EMI Music Sound Foundation

The Emilienne Charitable Trust

The Emmandjay Charitable Trust

The Essex Youth Trust

The Fairway Trust

The Lord Faringdon Charitable Trust

Samuel William Farmer's Trust

Farthing Trust

The Ian Fleming Charitable Trust

The Joyce Fletcher Charitable Trust

Florence's Charitable Trust

The Flow Foundation

The Follett Trust

The Football Association National Sports Centre Trust

Forbesville Limited

Ford Britain Trust

Lord Forte Foundation

Foundation for Management Education

The Louis and Valerie Freedman Charitable Settlement

The Friarsgate Trust

Friends of Wiznitz Limited

Mejer and Gertrude Miriam Frydman Foundation

The Angela Gallagher Memorial Fund

Jacqueline and Michael Gee Charitable Trust

The Golsoncott Foundation

Nicholas and Judith Goodison's Charitable Settlement

The Everard and Mina Goodman Charitable Foundation

Grimmitt Trust

The H and M Charitable Trust

Sue Hammerson's Charitable Trust

Harbo Charities Limited

The Harbour Charitable Trust

The Harbour Foundation

The Harebell Centenary Fund

Haskel Family Foundation

The Dorothy Hay-Bolton Charitable Trust

The Haymills Charitable Trust

May Hearnshaw's Charity

The Heathcoat Trust

The Michael and Morven Heller Charitable Foundation

The Simon Heller Charitable Settlement

Philip Henman Trust

The Charles Littlewood Hill Trust

Hockerill Educational Foundation

The Sir Julian Hodge Charitable Trust

The Hope Trust

The Reta Lila Howard Foundation

The Humanitarian Trust

The Hyde Charitable Trust – Youth Plus

The Iliffe Family Charitable Trust

The International Bankers Charitable Trust (The Worshipful Compnay of Interntional Bankers)

The Ireland Fund of Great Britain

The Irish Youth Foundation (UK) Ltd (incorporating The Lawlor Foundation)

J A R Charitable Trust

The Ruth and Lionel Jacobson Trust (Second Fund) No. 2

The Johnson Foundation

The Ian Karten Charitable Trust

The Kass Charitable Trust

The Soli and Leah Kelaty Trust Fund

E and E Kernkraut Charities Limited

The Peter Kershaw Trust

The Kohn Foundation

The Kreditor Charitable Trust

John Laing Charitable Trust

The David Laing Foundation

The Lambert Charitable Trust

The Lanvern Foundation

The Lawson Beckman Charitable Trust

The Carole and Geoffrey Lawson Foundation

The Leche Trust

The Arnold Lee Charitable Trust

The Leigh Trust

The P Leigh-Bramwell Trust 'E'

The Leverhulme Trade Charities Trust

Lewis Family Charitable Trust

Localtrent Ltd

The Loftus Charitable Trust

The C L Loyd Charitable Trust

Henry Lumley Charitable Trust

The Ruth and Jack Lunzer Charitable Trust

Lord and Lady Lurgan Trust

The Sir Jack Lyons Charitable Trust

Malcolm Lyons Foundation

Ian Mactaggart Trust

The Magen Charitable Trust

Environment and animals

General charitable purposes

Older people

Religion – general

The Lolev Charitable Trust
The Ruth and Jack Lunzer Charitable
    Trust
The Sir Jack Lyons Charitable Trust
Malcolm Lyons Foundation
The M and C Trust
Macdonald-Buchanan Charitable Trust
The Magen Charitable Trust
Malbin Trust
Marbeh Torah Trust
The Stella and Alexander Margulies
    Charitable Trust
The Ann and David Marks Foundation
The Hilda and Samuel Marks
    Foundation
The Mason Porter Charitable Trust
The Violet Mauray Charitable Trust
Melodor Ltd
Melow Charitable Trust
Menuchar Ltd
The Minos Trust
The Mishcon Family Charitable Trust
The Mitchell Charitable Trust
Keren Mitzvah Trust
The Modiano Charitable Trust
The Moette Charitable Trust
The Mole Charitable Trust
The Morgan Charitable Foundation
The Oliver Morland Charitable Trust
S C and M E Morland's Charitable Trust
The Peter Morrison Charitable
    Foundation
Moshal Charitable Trust
Brian and Jill Moss Charitable Trust
The Mutual Trust Group
MYA Charitable Trust
MYR Charitable Trust
The Nadezhda Charitable Trust
The Naggar Charitable Trust
Nathan Charitable Trust
Ner Foundation
Nesswall Ltd
NJD Charitable Trust
The Norwood and Newton Settlement
The Ogle Christian Trust
The Owen Family Trust
The Doris Pacey Charitable Foundation
The David Pearlman Charitable
    Foundation
The Persson Charitable Trust (formerly
    Highmoore Hall Charitable Trust)
The Phillips Family Charitable Trust
The David Pickford Charitable
    Foundation
The J E Posnansky Charitable Trust
Premishlaner Charitable Trust
R S Charitable Trust
The Bishop Radford Trust
The Fanny Rapaport Charitable
    Settlement
The Rayden Charitable Trust

The Rayne Trust
The Albert Reckitt Charitable Trust
The Rest Harrow Trust
The Clive Richards Charity
The Sir John Ritblat Family Foundation
The Rock Solid Trust
Joshua and Michelle Rowe Charitable
    Trust
The Ruzin Sadagora Trust
Saint Luke's College Foundation
The Hon. M J Samuel Charitable Trust
The Annie Schiff Charitable Trust
The Schmidt-Bodner Charitable Trust
The Schreiber Charitable Trust
Sellata Ltd
The Cyril Shack Trust
The Leslie Silver Charitable Trust
The Simpson Foundation
The Moss Spiro Will Charitable
    Foundation
The Strawberry Charitable Trust
The A B Strom and R Strom Charitable
    Trust
T and S Trust Fund
Tadlus Limited
The Lili Tapper Charitable Foundation
C B and H H Taylor 1984 Trust
The Torah Temimah Trust
Toras Chesed (London) Trust
Truemart Limited
The Union of Orthodox Hebrew
    Congregation
Vivdale Ltd
The Weinstein Foundation
The Benjamin Winegarten Charitable
    Trust
Wychville Ltd
Yankov Charitable Trust
The Marjorie and Arnold Ziff Charitable
    Foundation

Christianity

The Alabaster Trust
The Alexis Trust
The Almond Trust
Alvor Charitable Trust
Viscount Amory's Charitable Trust
The Anchor Foundation
The Andrew Anderson Trust
The André Christian Trust
The Archbishop of Canterbury's
    Charitable Trust
The Armourers' and Brasiers' Gauntlet
    Trust
The AS Charitable Trust
Ashburnham Thanksgiving Trust
The Balney Charitable Trust
William P Bancroft (No. 2) Charitable
    Trust and Jenepher Gillett Trust

Barleycorn Trust
The Barnabas Trust
The Beacon Trust
The Beaufort House Trust Limited
The Bisgood Charitable Trust (registered
    as Miss Jeanne Bisgood's Charitable
    Trust)
The Sydney Black Charitable Trust
The Harry Bottom Charitable Trust
P G and N J Boulton Trust
The A H and E Boulton Trust
T B H Brunner's Charitable Settlement
Buckingham Trust
The Burden Trust
Henry T and Lucy B Cadbury Charitable
    Trust
The Carpenter Charitable Trust
The Catholic Charitable Trust
The Catholic Trust for England and
    Wales
The Roger and Sarah Bancroft Clark
    Charitable Trust
John Coldman Charitable Trust
The Costa Family Charitable Trust
    (formerly the Morgan Williams
    Charitable Trust)
Criffel Charitable Trust
The Daily Prayer Union Charitable Trust
    Ltd
The Dorcas Trust
The Dugdale Charitable Trust
The Houghton Dunn Charitable Trust
The Dyers' Company Charitable Trust
The Ebenezer Trust
The Edith Maud Ellis 1985 Charitable
    Trust
The Vernon N Ely Charitable Trust
The Emmandjay Charitable Trust
The Evangelical Covenants Trust
The Fairway Trust
Farthing Trust
The Forest Hill Charitable Trust
The Forte Charitable Trust
The Fowler, Smith and Jones Charitable
    Trust
The Fulmer Charitable Trust
The Gale Family Charitable Trust
The Angela Gallagher Memorial Fund
The Gibbs Charitable Trust
Golden Charitable Trust
The Gough Charitable Trust
The Grace Charitable Trust
Philip and Judith Green Trust
The Greys Charitable Trust
Beatrice Hankey Foundation Ltd
May Hearnshaw's Charity
The Joanna Herbert-Stepney Charitable
    Settlement (also known as The Paget
    Charitable Trust)
The Hesed Trust

Islam

Judaism

Philanthropy and the voluntary sector

Rights, law and conflict

Science and technology

Social sciences, policy and research

Social welfare

Geographical index

The following geographical index aims to highlight when a trust gives preference for, or has a special interest in, a particular area: county, region, city, town or London borough. Please note the following:

1) Before using this index please read the following information, as well as the introduction to the subject index on page 377. We must emphasise that this index:

(a) should not be used as a simple mailing list, and

(b) is not a substitute for detailed research.

When you have used this index to identify relevant trusts, please read each entry carefully before making an application. Simply because a trust gives grants in your geographical area does not mean that it gives to your type of work.

2) Most trusts in this list are not restricted to one area; usually the geographical index indicates that the trust gives some priority for the area(s).

3) Trusts which give throughout England or the UK have been excluded from this index, unless they have a particular interest in one or more locality.

4) Each section is ordered alphabetically according to the name of the trust. The categories for the overseas and UK indices are as follows:

England

We have divided England into the following nine categories:

North East *page 399*

North West *page 399*

Yorkshire and the Humber *page 399*

East Midlands *page 400*

West Midlands *page 400*

Eastern England *page 400*

South East *page 400*

South West *page 400*

Greater London *page 400*

Some trusts may be found in more than one category due to them providing grants in more than one area e.g. those with a preference for northern England.

Wales *page 400*

Scotland *page 401*

Northern Ireland *page 401*

Republic of Ireland *page 401*

Europe *page 401*

Overseas categories

Developing world *page 401*

This includes trusts which support missionary organisations when they are also interested in social and economic development.

Individual continents *page 401*

The Middle East has been listed separately. Please note that most of the trusts listed are primarily for the benefit of Jewish people and the advancement of the Jewish religion.

England

North East

The Barbour Trust
The Catherine Cookson Charitable Trust
The Dickon Trust
The Ellinson Foundation Ltd
The GNC Trust
The Millfield House Foundation
The P and D Shepherd Charitable Trust
T and S Trust Fund

North West

The Harold and Alice Bridges Charity
EAGA Partnership Charitable Trust
The Ellerdale Trust
The Eventhall Family Charitable Trust
The Fairway Trust
Famos Foundation Trust
The GNC Trust
The Johnson Foundation
The J E Joseph Charitable Fund
The Peter Kershaw Trust
The Ann and David Marks Foundation
Matliwala Family Charitable Trust
The Mushroom Fund
The Fanny Rapaport Charitable Settlement
The Rowan Charitable Trust
The P and D Shepherd Charitable Trust
T and S Trust Fund
The Norman Whiteley Trust

Yorkshire and the Humber

The Joseph and Annie Cattle Trust
The Marjorie Coote Animal Charity Trust
The A M Fenton Trust

The GNC Trust
The Constance Green Foundation
The Mayfield Valley Arts Trust
The P and D Shepherd Charitable Trust
The Scurrah Wainwright Charity

East Midlands

The Michael Bishop Foundation
Dromintee Trust
Ford Britain Trust
The GNC Trust
The Joanna Herbert-Stepney Charitable
Settlement (also known as The Paget
Charitable Trust)
The Hesed Trust

West Midlands

The Michael Bishop Foundation
The Bransford Trust
The Dumbreck Charity
The John Feeney Charitable Bequest
Ford Britain Trust
The GNC Trust
Grimmitt Trust
John Martin's Charity
The Bernard Piggott Trust
The Sheldon Trust
C B and H H Taylor 1984 Trust

Eastern

The Adnams Charity
The Bedfordshire and Hertfordshire
Historic Churches Trust
The Chapman Charitable Trust
The Ebenezer Trust
Educational Foundation of Alderman
John Norman
The Essex Youth Trust
Farthing Trust
Ford Britain Trust
The GNC Trust
Hinchley Charitable Trust
The John Jarrold Trust
The D C Moncrieff Charitable Trust
The Music Sales Charitable Trust
The A and R Woolf Charitable Trust

South East

The Chapman Charitable Trust
The John and Freda Coleman Charitable
Trust
The Dugdale Charitable Trust

The Gilbert and Eileen Edgar
Foundation
Ford Britain Trust
T F C Frost Charitable Trust
The GNC Trust
The Walter Guinness Charitable Trust
The Dorothy Hay-Bolton Charitable
Trust
R G Hills Charitable Trust
Stuart Hine Trust
The Michael and Shirley Hunt
Charitable Trust
The Iliffe Family Charitable Trust
The Ingram Trust
The James Trust
The JMK Charitable Trust
The Emmanuel Kaye Foundation
The Leach Fourteenth Trust
The Leonard Trust
Gerald Micklem Charitable Trust
The Moss Charitable Trust
The Earl of Northampton's Charity
The David Pickford Charitable
Foundation
The Rothermere Foundation
St Michael's and All Saints' Charities

South West

The Joyce Fletcher Charitable Trust
The Fulmer Charitable Trust
The GNC Trust
The Walter Guinness Charitable Trust
The Heathcoat Trust
The Michael and Ilse Katz Foundation
The Leach Fourteenth Trust
The Moss Charitable Trust
The Norman Family Charitable Trust
The Rock Solid Trust
Saint Luke's College Foundation
St Monica Trust Community Fund
The Starfish Trust
The Talbot Village Trust

Greater London

The Avenue Charitable Trust
Barleycorn Trust
The Bintaub Charitable Trust
The Sir Victor Blank Charitable
Settlement
The British Council for Prevention of
Blindness
The Chapman Charitable Trust
Coutts Charitable Trust
Dischma Charitable Trust
The Edinburgh Trust, No. 2 Account
Elshore Ltd
The Vernon N Ely Charitable Trust

Finnart House School Trust
Forbesville Limited
Ford Britain Trust
Friends of Wiznitz Limited
The B and P Glasser Charitable Trust
The Grahame Charitable Foundation
Limited
Grand Charitable Trust of the Order of
Women Freemasons
The Gur Trust
The Harbour Foundation
The Simon Heller Charitable Settlement
The Bernhard Heuberger Charitable
Trust
Highcroft Charitable Trust
The P Y N and B Hyams Trust
J A R Charitable Trust
Jacobs Charitable Trust
The Harold Joels Charitable Trust
The Nicholas Joels Charitable Trust
The J E Joseph Charitable Fund
The Stanley Kalms Foundation
The Boris Karloff Charitable Foundation
The Geoffrey John Kaye Charitable
Foundation
The Ruth and Stuart Lipton Charitable
Trust
The Peter Minet Trust
The Modiano Charitable Trust
The Music Sales Charitable Trust
MYA Charitable Trust
The Earl of Northampton's Charity
The David Pickford Charitable
Foundation
T and S Trust Fund
The Cyril Taylor Charitable Trust
The Geoffrey Woods Charitable
Foundation

Wales

Archbishop of Wales' Fund for Children
The Laura Ashley Foundation
Barchester Healthcare Foundation
Birthday House Trust
The Catholic Trust for England and
Wales
The Cemlyn-Jones Trust
The Chapman Charitable Trust
CLA Charitable Trust
Ford Britain Trust
The GNC Trust
The Goodman Foundation
Leonard Gordon Charitable Trust
J I Charitable Trust
Dezna Robins Jones Charitable
Foundation
The Ian Karten Charitable Trust
Llysdinam Charitable Trust
The McKenna Charitable Trust

Millennium Stadium Charitable Trust
Monmouthshire County Council Welsh Church Act Fund
The Noon Foundation
The Norwood and Newton Settlement
The Ouseley Trust
The Bernard Piggott Trust
St Teilo's Trust
TJH Foundation
Vale of Glamorgan – Welsh Church Fund
The Barbara Ward Children's Foundation
A H and B C Whiteley Charitable Trust
The Yapp Charitable Trust

Scotland

Barchester Healthcare Foundation
The Craignish Trust
The Dickon Trust
The GNC Trust
The Christina Mary Hendrie Trust for Scottish and Canadian Charities
The Ian Karten Charitable Trust
The Late Sir Pierce Lacy Charity Trust
The Merchants' House of Glasgow
Miss M E Swinton Paterson's Charitable Trust
The P and D Shepherd Charitable Trust
A H and B C Whiteley Charitable Trust

Northern Ireland

The GNC Trust
The Goodman Foundation

Republic of Ireland

The Edith Maud Ellis 1985 Charitable Trust
The Hospital Saturday Fund
The Reta Lila Howard Foundation
The Inland Waterways Association
The Ireland Fund of Great Britain
The Irish Youth Foundation (UK) Ltd (incorporating The Lawlor Foundation)
Mr and Mrs F E F Newman Charitable Trust
The Ouseley Trust

The Peggy Ramsay Foundation
C B and H H Taylor 1984 Trust

Europe

Armenian General Benevolent Union London Trust
C B and H H Taylor 1984 Trust
Marr-Munning Trust
Mr and Mrs F E F Newman Charitable Trust
Nazareth Trust Fund
Saint Sarkis Charity Trust
The Catholic Charitable Trust
The Edith Maud Ellis 1985 Charitable Trust
The Eleni Nakou Foundation
The Ericson Trust
The Hospital Saturday Fund
The Huxham Charitable Trust
The Inland Waterways Association
The Ireland Fund of Great Britain
The Irish Youth Foundation (UK) Ltd (incorporating The Lawlor Foundation)
The Old Broad Street Charity Trust
The Ouseley Trust
The Peggy Ramsay Foundation
The Reta Lila Howard Foundation
The Scott Bader Commonwealth Ltd
The Sylvanus Charitable Trust
Webb Memorial Trust
William Arthur Rudd Memorial Trust

Developing world

The A B Charitable Trust
The Ardwick Trust
The AS Charitable Trust
Buckland Charitable Trust
Burdens Charitable Foundation
Henry T and Lucy B Cadbury Charitable Trust
The Casey Trust
The Gershon Coren Charitable Foundation
The Evan Cornish Foundation
The Cumber Family Charitable Trust
The Eagle Charity Trust
The Gilbert and Eileen Edgar Foundation
The Ellerdale Trust
The Ericson Trust
The Anna Rosa Forster Charitable Trust
Sydney E Franklin Deceased's New Second Charity

The Jill Franklin Trust
The Fulmer Charitable Trust
The Fuserna Foundation
The Galanthus Trust
The Angela Gallagher Memorial Fund
The Constance Green Foundation
Hasluck Charitable Trust
Philip Henman Trust
The Joanna Herbert-Stepney Charitable Settlement (also known as The Paget Charitable Trust)
The Langley Charitable Trust
The Leonard Trust
Paul Lunn-Rockliffe Charitable Trust
The Lyndhurst Trust
Mahavir Trust (also known as the K S Mehta Charitable Trust)
The Marchday Charitable Fund
Mariapolis Limited
The Mirianog Trust
Mr and Mrs F E F Newman Charitable Trust
The Col W W Pilkington Will Trusts The General Charity Fund
Prairie Trust
The W L Pratt Charitable Trust
Ranworth Trust
The Eleanor Rathbone Charitable Trust
The Rhododendron Trust
The River Farm Foundation
Robyn Charitable Trust
The Rock Foundation
The Sir James Roll Charitable Trust
The Rowan Charitable Trust
The RRAF Charitable Trust
Ryklow Charitable Trust 1992 (also known as A B Williamson Charitable Trust)
The Shanti Charitable Trust
Rita and David Slowe Charitable Trust
The W F Southall Trust
The Peter Stebbings Memorial Charity
The Gay and Keith Talbot Trust
C B and H H Taylor 1984 Trust
The Loke Wan Tho Memorial Foundation
The Tinsley Foundation
The Tisbury Telegraph Trust
The Tresillian Trust
Ulting Overseas Trust
The Van Neste Foundation
Zephyr Charitable Trust

Africa

The Dugdale Charitable Trust
The Estelle Trust
Philip and Judith Green Trust
The Kiawah Charitable Trust

The Lauffer Family Charitable
    Foundation
Marr-Munning Trust
Nazareth Trust Fund
The Noel Buxton Trust
The Pestalozzi Overseas Children's Trust
The Scotshill Trust
The Scott Bader Commonwealth Ltd
SEM Charitable Trust
The Archie Sherman Cardiff Foundation
The Scurrah Wainwright Charity

Americas and the West Indies

The Beaverbrook Foundation
The Catholic Charitable Trust
The Christina Mary Hendrie Trust for
    Scottish and Canadian Charities
The Lauffer Family Charitable
    Foundation
Marr-Munning Trust
MYR Charitable Trust
Nazareth Trust Fund
The Scott Bader Commonwealth Ltd
The Helene Sebba Charitable Trust
The Archie Sherman Cardiff Foundation
St James' Trust Settlement
The Sylvanus Charitable Trust
G R Waters Charitable Trust 2000

Asia

The Acacia Charitable Trust
The Altajir Trust
Ambika Paul Foundation
The Ardwick Trust
The Bertie Black Foundation
The CH (1980) Charitable Trust
The Vivienne and Samuel Cohen
    Charitable Trust
Col-Reno Ltd
The Craps Charitable Trust
The Wilfrid Bruce Davis Charitable
    Trust
The Doughty Charity Trust
Mejer and Gertrude Miriam Frydman
    Foundation
The Everard and Mina Goodman
    Charitable Foundation
The Daniel Howard Trust
The Humanitarian Trust
The Norman Joels Charitable Trust
The J E Joseph Charitable Fund
The Bernard Kahn Charitable Trust

The Ian Karten Charitable Trust
The Kasner Charitable Trust
The Kiawah Charitable Trust
Kupath Gemach Chaim Bechesed Viznitz
    Trust
The Lambert Charitable Trust
The Lauffer Family Charitable
    Foundation
Lewis Family Charitable Trust
Jack Livingstone Charitable Trust
The Locker Foundation
The Sir Jack Lyons Charitable Trust
Marbeh Torah Trust
The Hilda and Samuel Marks
    Foundation
Marr-Munning Trust
Melodor Ltd
Melow Charitable Trust
MYR Charitable Trust
Nazareth Trust Fund
Ner Foundation
NJD Charitable Trust
Peltz Trust
The Pestalozzi Overseas Children's Trust
The Porter Foundation
The Rayne Trust
The Ruzin Sadagora Trust
The Scotshill Trust
The Scott Bader Commonwealth Ltd
The Helene Sebba Charitable Trust
SEM Charitable Trust
The Archie Sherman Cardiff Foundation
Sino-British Fellowship Trust
The Solo Charitable Settlement
Songdale Ltd
The Cyril and Betty Stein Charitable
    Trust
Tadlus Limited
The Witzenfeld Foundation

Middle East

The Acacia Charitable Trust
The Altajir Trust
The Ardwick Trust
The Bertie Black Foundation
The CH (1980) Charitable Trust
The Vivienne and Samuel Cohen
    Charitable Trust
Col-Reno Ltd
The Craps Charitable Trust
The Doughty Charity Trust
Mejer and Gertrude Miriam Frydman
    Foundation
The Everard and Mina Goodman
    Charitable Foundation
The Daniel Howard Trust
The Humanitarian Trust
The Norman Joels Charitable Trust
The J E Joseph Charitable Fund

The Bernard Kahn Charitable Trust
The Ian Karten Charitable Trust
The Kasner Charitable Trust
Kupath Gemach Chaim Bechesed Viznitz
    Trust
The Lambert Charitable Trust
The Lauffer Family Charitable
    Foundation
Lewis Family Charitable Trust
Jack Livingstone Charitable Trust
The Locker Foundation
The Sir Jack Lyons Charitable Trust
Marbeh Torah Trust
The Hilda and Samuel Marks
    Foundation
Marr-Munning Trust
Melodor Ltd
Melow Charitable Trust
MYR Charitable Trust
Nazareth Trust Fund
Ner Foundation
NJD Charitable Trust
Peltz Trust
The Porter Foundation
The Rayne Trust
The Ruzin Sadagora Trust
The Helene Sebba Charitable Trust
SEM Charitable Trust
The Archie Sherman Cardiff Foundation
The Solo Charitable Settlement
Songdale Ltd
The Cyril and Betty Stein Charitable
    Trust
Tadlus Limited
The Witzenfeld Foundation

Alphabetical index

409